THE DIARY OF
SAMUEL PEPYS

Pepys's library in the house in York Buildings, King Street, where he lived from 1679. This drawing by Nichols (c. 1693) is one of a pair of frontispieces to Pepys's catalogue. The book presses, made of oak with glazed doors, survive in the Pepys Library at Magdalene College, Cambridge.

Pepys Library, Magdalene

THE DIARY
OF
SAMUEL PEPYS

A new and complete
transcription edited by

ROBERT LATHAM
AND
WILLIAM MATTHEWS

VOLUME X · COMPANION

Compiled and edited by
ROBERT LATHAM

UNIVERSITY OF CALIFORNIA PRESS
BERKELEY AND LOS ANGELES
1983

First published in Great Britain by Bell & Hyman Limited

ISBN 0–520–02097–9

Library of Congress Catalogue No. 70–96950

Set in Monotype Bembo by
Richard Clay (The Chaucer Press) Ltd, Bungay, Suffolk
Printed in Great Britain by Fletcher & Son Ltd, Norwich
Bound by Hunter & Foulis Ltd, Edinburgh

CONTRIBUTORS

PROFESSOR A. RUPERT HALL
formerly Professor of the History of Science and Technology, Imperial
College, London
(*Royal Society; Science; Scientific Instruments*)

DR PETER HOLLAND
Fellow of Trinity Hall, Cambridge and Assistant-Lecturer in English
in the University
(*Theatre*)

PROFESSOR CHRISTOPHER LLOYD
formerly Professor of History, Royal Naval College, Greenwich
(*Tangier*)

DR RICHARD LUCKETT
Fellow and Pepys Librarian of Magdalene College, Cambridge, and
Lecturer in English in the University
(*Language; Music; Plays; Large Glossary* and biographies of musicians)

CHRISTOPHER MORRIS
Fellow of King's College, Cambridge and formerly Lecturer in History
in the University
(*The Plague*)

J. L. NEVINSON
formerly of the Department of Textiles, Victoria and Albert Museum
(*Dress and Personal Appearance*)

RICHARD OLLARD
(*Dutch Wars; Navy*)

THE LATE PROFESSOR T. F. REDDAWAY
Late Professor of the History of London, University College, London
(Articles on London topography)

DR HENRY ROSEVEARE
Reader in History, King's College, London
(*Exchequer; Finances*)

DR D. J. SCHOVE
(*Weather*)

DR MARTIN HOWARD STEIN
(*Health – a psychoanalyst's view*)

DR ANDREW TURNBULL
(*Dockyards; Navy Board*)

CONTENTS

LIST OF ILLUSTRATIONS

No plan survives of the first floor, which contained
the principal rooms of the palace. This is based on the
ground floor plan of 1669–70 (reproduced in H. M.
Colvin, ed., *History of the King's Works*, v.), with
additional information provided by the Ancient
Monuments branch of the Department of the Environment.
The locations and shapes of the rooms are in
many cases approximate.

SELECT LIST OF ARTICLES

PREFACE

The aim of the *Companion* is to equip the diary with a more detailed and extensive commentary than could be accommodated in the volumes of text (cf. vol. i, p. cxliv). At certain points – in some of the biographical articles and much of the Large Glossary, for instance – it is an expansion, or, where necessary, an authentication of material in the footnotes to the text. At other points it moves on to new ground, as in the articles on general topics. It is hoped that some of these may be of interest to readers who are not primarily concerned with the diary itself.

A prospectus of the contents was given in vol. i, pp. ix–x, cli–clii. Where changes have been made in the title, contents or authorship of articles referred to there the reader is informed in the main body of this volume.

The material provided here relates to (I) Persons, (II) Places, (III) General Topics, and (IV) Words and Phrases.

I. Persons. There is no attempt to deal with everyone Pepys mentions. Those I have not identified are omitted, and also those adequately dealt with in footnotes to the text. So too are persons who are insignificant in the diary, though often significant in their own right (peers, bishops, lawyers etc.). These are given brief identifications in the Index. Here treatment varies principally with the importance of the person in the context of the diary. A ship's carpenter, if the evidence about him allows it, will be awarded more space than an ambassador. It is also part of the purpose of these articles to make clear the connections between the persons mentioned in the diary and Pepys himself. In the case of well-known figures, therefore, such as the King and the Duke of York, the articles are not abbreviated biographies so much as essays on their relations with Pepys.

It will be noticed that certain naval officers are described as being 'dead by 1688'. The phrase derives from Pepys's Register of Sea-Officers in the Pepys Library (PL 2941), which runs to 1688 and in which the word 'dead' is occasionally entered by a name.

With many of the more obscure Londoners – small tradesmen and the like – an attempt is made not only to identify them (e.g. from parish registers) but to give some indication of their standing and material circumstances. Wills, where they exist, are an obvious source: but for this period there are others. Hearth-tax returns give the number of their hearths and hence roughly the size of their houses; poll-tax returns give their occupations, the number of their servants and an approximate indication of their wealth; while the rate-books give the relative locations of their houses, since they were compiled by collectors who never varied their routes.

II. Places. Almost all the topographical articles concern London and its environs. Important public buildings are described, special attention being paid to those which have now disappeared and to those most used by Pepys himself – royal palaces, government offices, the taverns and his parish church. Most churches have been omitted since they are well described by modern authorities such as Pevsner, and even when re-built after the Fire and the Blitz still remain for the most part on the same sites as those they occupied in Pepys's time. They rarely received any architectural comment from Pepys. Most streets etc. are included and where their 17th-century names have been altered the modern name is added in brackets. Their location is defined wherever their position is not clear from the maps printed in this volume and the text volumes, and in a few other cases too. Here complications arise from the changes made by reconstruction after the Fire. But the changes in the line and width of the streets were usually slight: where they were not, the fact is recorded in the article. The lengths of the streets and their reputations – as it were, their guide-book standing – are taken from Edward Hatton's *New View of London*, which, though published in 1708, is a good authority for the immediate post-Fire period.

III. General topics. For the most part these fall into five categories:
(1) *Historical events* (The Dutch Wars; The Great Fire; The Plague)
(2) *The Public Service* (The Admiralty; Chatham Chest; Dockyards; The Exchequer; The Navy; The Navy Board; The Privy Seal Office; The Royal Fishery; Tangier; Trinity House; The Wardrobe)
(3) *Personal Life* (The Diary and Related Manuscripts; Dress and Personal Appearance; Drink; Finances; Food; Health; Health – a psychoanalyst's view; Household: Domestic Servants; Language; Religion; Sabbath Observance)
(4) *Cultural Interests* (Art and Architecture; Books; Music; Plays; Royal Society; Science; Scientific Instruments; Theatre)
(5) *Social life* (Christenings; Christmas and Twelfth Night; Coffee-Houses; Funerals; Gunpowder Plot Day; St Valentine's Day; Taverns, Inns and Eating houses; Travel; Weddings)

The focus adopted varies with the topics and the evidence available for their discussion. In some, attention is paid to general conditions as well as to the diarist (e.g. Music); in others, only to Pepys himself (e.g. Health). In some the time range is confined to the diary period (e.g. Theatre); in others (e.g. Religion) it corresponds roughly with his lifetime.

IV. Words and phrases. These are listed and glossed in the Large Glossary, in accordance with a policy which is explained in its prefatory note.

Certain editorial practices call for elucidation:

(1) *References to the diary text.* These are given only where it is impossible or difficult to find the passages by using the Index. Otherwise their number would be overwhelming. They are given usually in the notes by citing volume and page, but where appropriate (e.g. in the article on the Plague) by date within the body of the article.

(2) *Cross-references within the volume.* These also could easily have bulked too large. They have been reduced to a minimum, the most important being added in square brackets at the end of certain articles.

(3) *Attributions.* The articles by the late Professor Reddaway and the biographical articles by Dr Luckett are signed with abbreviations – R or Lu; those in which I share authorship bear the signature La as well as the name of the co-author. For the rest, articles by contributors bear their names; those without attribution are my own.

ACKNOWLEDGEMENTS

I am deeply grateful for the considerable help I have received from others in the composition of this volume. First and foremost, from the contributors. I have been fortunate in being able to secure the collaboration of scholars distinguished in their various fields, without whose help it would have been impossible for the *Companion* to offer commentaries on the wide range of subjects touched on in Pepys's pages. The value of their contributions will be apparent to the reader: only I am in a position to know also the extent of the patience with which they have borne my editorial intrusions into their work.

Sadly, I lost through death the co-operation of my colleague in the edition, Professor Matthews, while volumes x and xi were being prepared. He had completed his main work – on the diary text – but had he lived would have compiled the Large Glossary and written the article on Language for this volume. Dr Luckett has kindly stepped into the breach and supplied both.

Professor T. F. Reddaway died in 1967, but not before he had written, or drafted, most of the articles on London topography contained here. In addition, he left for my use his notes on a small host of London householders – tavernkeepers, small tradesmen and the like – which have been of the greatest value to me. He was also generous with advice and help on a number of other problems.

I must express particular thanks to the History of Parliament Trust, who have allowed me to consult the typescript biographies of M.P.s which will shortly be published under the editorship of Professor Basil Henning (*History of Parliament: House of Commons 1660–90: Members*). John Ferris, one of the authors of that volume, has been a mine of information on biographical matters.

I am grateful also to the Society of Genealogists who have allowed me access to Percival Boyd's manuscript lists – 'Citizens of London' and 'Index to Marriages, 1538–1837' – which are housed in their Library.

The debts I owe to individuals for help on specific points are acknowledged in the Notes. Their names are listed in volume xi.

Other debts of a more general nature call for recognition here. One is to Peter Cochrane who smoothed the passage of the book through the press. Another is to Mary Coleman who typed and retyped my manuscript with unfailing accuracy and good-humour. A third debt is to my wife Linnet. She prepared the genealogical tables and the maps of the Thames and Pepys's journeys, and, to the book's immeasurable benefit, has acted not only as my research assistant but also as a critic on the hearth.

Robert Latham

COMPANION

Ableson, Capt. [James]. He served in the Commonwealth navy, held three commands 1664–5 and was killed in the *Guinea* in the Battle of Lowestoft (1665).[1]

Abrahall, [Thomas] (d. 1672). Ship's chandler and navy contractor, of All Hallows, Barking; Common Councilman for Tower Ward 1671–2.[1]

Acworth, [William] (d. 1671). Storekeeper at Woolwich from 1637; reappointed in 1660. His (third) wife Elizabeth was a sister-in-law of Commissioner Pett. A Sir Jacob Acworth was Surveyor of the Navy 1715–49.[1]

Adams, Mr. Edward Shipley's friend; of Axe Yard. Possibly Henry Adams, whose son Edward (? named after Shipley) was baptised at St Margaret's on 27 March 1661.[1] [*See also* Greenleaf]

Addis, ——. Wholesale fishmonger. Probably John Addis of London; possibly William Addis of Plymouth. Both supplied the navy.[1]

THE ADMIRALTY

Organisation. The degree to which the ruler and the Privy Council exercised authority over the Admiralty varied, and in practice since the late 15th century the crown had appointed an officer of state, the Lord Admiral (known as the Lord High Admiral from the 1620s) or (exceptionally) a commission to act on his behalf. A Vice-Admiral of the kingdom might also from time to time be appointed, as in 1660 when Sandwich was given the post. Under these authorities two subordinate bodies operated – one administrative (the Navy Board, with the Navy Treasurer), and the other judicial (the Court of Admiralty, staffed by judges, advocates and proctors). During the Civil War and Interregnum this machinery was almost totally dismantled, except for the court, whose work was necessary for the conduct of trade and war. For a few years (1643–5 and 1648–9) Parliament appointed its own Lord

High Admiral, the Earl of Warwick, but many of his powers were exercised by committees of the House of Commons, and, during the Commonwealth, government by navy and admiralty committees became the normal method. They were nominated by the Council of State which itself, like the Privy Council of old, often intervened in admiralty affairs. These committees proved to be among the busiest and most effective bodies at work during the Revolution. Their members, unlike those of the admiralty commissions of the old régime, were not politicians or courtiers, but mostly men of naval and mercantile experience, and their officials, paid by salary instead of by fee, were in some cases – like that of Robert Blackborne, Will Hewer's uncle – more akin in some respects to modern civil servants than to 17th-century placemen. These revolutionary committees doubled the size of the navy, handled unprecedentedly large sums of money, conducted almost continuous war and mounted expeditions to the W. Indies, the Mediterranean and the Baltic. They left behind, as the diary makes clear, a formidable reputation. At the Restoration the last of them – the Admiralty and Navy Committee appointed by the Rump in Feb. 1660 – was still at work. They then disappeared from public life, though occasionally an individual commissioner, such as 'Thomson with the wooden leg', was recalled for special duty by the Restoration government.

The return of the King brought with it the restoration of the historic structure of the Admiralty. Charles had already appointed the Duke of York as his Lord High Admiral and James had already appointed William Coventry as his secretary. Together these two, aided by a handful of clerks, now ran the Admiralty under the aegis of the King and Privy Council. James was a vigorous though spasmodic administrator. From 1662, he required the Navy Board to report to him weekly, and in the same year had Coventry made a Navy Commissioner to act as his voice on the Board itself. At the same time the King's own interest in naval affairs was an assurance that his supervision and that of the Privy Council would be no formality. He continually made his views known to James, especially on appointments, and liked nothing better than visiting a dockyard or taking part in the planning of a campaign. As for the Privy Council, an Admiralty committee was at work from Nov. 1660, among other things negotiating a bargain with the Victualler. With the approach of war the Duke of York was often at sea and in Nov. 1664 a council committee of 15 members – 'a great many troublesome Lords', as Pepys called them (vi.58) – was set up to act in his absence. Pepys welcomed their replacement by the Captain-General of the kingdom, Albemarle, who from March 1665 acted in their stead as the Duke's *locum tenens*. Throughout the war the King and Council kept a watchful control over admiralty business – summoned the Navy Board to their presence, set up prize courts, legalised impressment, and endlessly and fruitlessly discussed the difficulty of raising money. In Oct. 1668 the Admiralty Committee had so well established itself that it was made one of the four standing committees of Council.

In 1673 it acquired a new rôle. The Duke of York was in that year forced to quit office as Admiral in face of the 'test' – or declaration against Catholicism – imposed on officeholders by parliament. He remained, however, as a Privy Councillor advising the King, and retaining his admiralty office in Scotland, Ireland and the Plantations – to which the Test Act did not apply. The King for his part fell in with a plan said to have been suggested by Pepys.[1] The 15 members of the Council's Admiralty Committee were given patents of appointment as Lord Commissioners of the Admiralty which left the King himself virtually in control. He was to receive all the profits of the Court of Admiralty, was to preside over meetings of the commission and was free to issue orders at will to the navy and to the Navy Board. The new secretary of the commission – the key figure in the arrangements – was Pepys himself. Working immediately under the King and no longer hampered, as he had been at the Navy Board, by rigid procedures and by independent colleagues, he set about his new task with zest. He had come to think at the Navy Board that the best way of running a government department was to give general responsibility to a single departmental head;[2] he now had something like that position and in a much more important department. He and the King were able where necessary to bypass the commissioners, and did so continually between 1677 and 1679.[3] Pepys employed only a small staff of clerks – no larger in fact than that of his predecessors – but the results he achieved at the Admiralty between 1673 and 1679 were epoch-making – the foundation of a professional officer class, the construction of a larger navy, and everywhere a new air of discipline and purpose. These were however the effects of one man's energy and organising genius, and once he had gone the impetus slackened.

In 1679 the King, bowing to the Whigs' demands during the scare of the Popish Plot, dismissed his commissioners – their secretary with them – and replaced them with a board composed of opposition politicians whom he knew to be unversed in naval business – 'sporting himself', as Pepys later wrote, 'with their ignorance'.[4] Their secretary, until 1680, was Pepys's reliable old clerk Tom Hayter. Charles got rid of them as soon as it was politically safe to do so. In May 1684 the commission was revoked and for a few weeks the Duke of York acted as Lord High Admiral, the King himself signing orders and warrants so as to avoid conflicting with the Test Act. But in June Charles set on foot an experiment which was to last until the end of James's reign. He resumed all powers to himself and appointed Pepys as his 'Secretary for the affairs of the Admiralty' – a third secretary of state, as it were, and the equivalent of the French Secretary of the Marine. No-one had held such an office before; no-one has held it since. The arrangement was made doubly novel during most of James's reign by the virtual replacement of the Navy Board by Pepys's Special Commission.

The system fell with James in the Revolution of 1688, since when the Admiralty has normally been in the hands of commissions or boards. A century or so later, in response to the pressures of the Napoleonic wars, the Board in 1805 adopted the practice, which was to last as long as the Board itself, of assigning specific duties to the civil and professional members. It is a tribute to Pepys's part in the history of the Admiralty that in the course of the investigations eighteen volumes of his naval papers were borrowed from his library in Cambridge to be consulted by the reformers.[5]

The Admiralty had in his time developed into a department of state. From 1664 the Secretary, its administrative head, was paid by salary instead of by fees, and from the time of Pepys's first appointment in 1673 he ceased to be a personal aide to the Lord High Admiral and became a public official. The number of clerks in his office remained small – there were only four (with underclerks), and although their numbers were doubled in the French wars of the '90s they were again reduced with the coming of peace in 1697. But they too had by then changed in status. They had ceased to be personal assistants to the Secretary; they made their careers in the office and after 1694 were salaried public servants.[6]

Buildings. The growth of the Admiralty from a household office into a department of state is reflected in the history of its premises. Until the outbreak of the Civil War it was accommodated in the Lord Admiral's residence. In the '40s and '50s it was housed at various times in Westminster Palace and Whitehall Palace and, after 1655, in Derby House, Westminster, which also housed other government committees. When the Duke of York became Admiral the office was removed to his apartments in Whitehall and (in summer) St James's. After the appointment of the commissioners of 1673 the office returned to Derby House, where Pepys also had his official residence. With Pepys's appointment as Secretary for Admiralty Affairs the staff of clerks and a few other servants moved into his house in York Buildings, which became the Admiralty and declared its status by an anchor displayed on the outside of the wall fronting on to the river. An attempt was made to persuade Pepys to move elsewhere when he laid down office in Feb. 1689, but he refused. The new Board in 1690 was given the lease of a private house (that of the former Lord Chancellor Jeffreys in

Duke St), but in 1695 the government acquired the freehold of Wallingford House at the top of the modern Whitehall and erected a new building there. For the first time the Admiralty had a building of its own. By then the staff had roughly doubled, and continued to grow. The 1695 building was replaced in 1722–6 by another built on the same site and adjoining ground to the design of Thomas Ripley, who designed Houghton for Sir Robert Walpole. It still stands, with the screen built across the front of its yard by Robert Adam. To this was added in 1796 Admiralty House, as a residence for the First Lord, whose architect, as it happens, was Samuel Pepys Cockerell, a direct descendant of Pepys's sister Paulina.[7]

The Court of Admiralty. Dating in its 17th-century form from the late 15th century, this court exercised civil and criminal jurisdiction over marine causes, using a procedure based on Roman law. The judge was appointed by the Lord High Admiral who also maintained in the court his advocate (barrister) and proctor (solicitor). In wartime it was principally occupied in adjudicating on prize, in which it was assisted by prize commissioners acting as its executive officers. It became part of the High Court by the Judicature Acts of 1873 and 1875 and since 1970 has been part of the Queen's Bench division.

In the 1660s it met on St Margaret's Hill, Southwark on a site previously occupied by the church. It was removed after the great fire in Southwark to the hall of Doctors' Commons c. 1676, and since the 1870s has met in the Strand Law Courts.[1]

The naval courts martial (given statutory powers in 1661) were a separate organisation under the Judge Advocate-General.

The African House. Headquarters of the Royal Africa (Guinea) Company in Warnford Court, off Broad St, north out of Throgmorton St. Founded during Elizabeth's reign, the company had had a chequered existence. It received new charters in 1662 and 1672, and later transferred its headquarters to the s. side of Leadenhall St, east of Billiter St. Pepys usually refers to its house in Warnford Court as being in Broad St, the nearest large street to it, but its location in Throgmorton St is clearly shown on Ogilby and Morgan's map of 1677 and in the hearth-tax returns of the 1660s. It had 23 hearths.[1] (R)

Agar, [Thomas] (d. 1673). Chancery official. He had succeeded Edward Phillips in his post in the Crown Office after Phillips's death in 1631: shortly afterwards he married Phillips's widow, Anne, sister of John Milton. In 1660 he was appointed Clerk of Appeals.[1]

Albemarle, Duke and Duchess of: *see* Monck

Albrici (or Alberici), Vicenzo (1631–96). Italian composer and keyboard virtuoso; studied as a *putto soprano* under Carissimi at the German

College in Rome; entered service of Christina of Sweden 1652, subsequently holding appointments in her court in exile in Rome, and in the court of Dresden; came to London 1665 as Master of the King's Italian Musick (which was fully established by 1 March 1666); returned to Dresden with parting gift from the King, May 1668.[1] (Lu)

Alcock, Harry. Pepys's 'cousin'; presumably grandson of Elizabeth Pepys of Cottenham who married Henry Alcock of Rampton, Cambs., in 1593. A Grisel Alcock, widow, was living in Brampton, Hunts., in 1666.[1]

Alcock, [Stephen] (d. 1674). Merchant, of Rochester; long employed in the navy victualling; Mayor of the town 1663-4. His daughter Margaret married Sir William Batten's son William.[1]

Alcock, Tom. Pepys refers to him as a schoolfellow (at Huntingdon); he may also have been a relative. In 1675 Pepys recommended his 'cousin Thomas Alcocke' (? the same) as a ship's carpenter. In 1686 on hearing that his protégé (now carpenter of the *Elizabeth*) was suspected (unjustly as it turned out) of embezzling the King's goods, he wrote: 'By God's grace . . . he shall soon make a vacancy instead of filling one'.[1]

Aldersgate. One of the principal gates in the city wall, at the n. end of St Martin-le-Grand; the exit for the northern roads. Rebuilt in 1617 to a design by Gerard Christmas, it was repaired after the Fire, and not taken down until 1761. The mutilated remains of regicides were displayed on spikes there.

Aldersgate St. A handsome street, running north from Aldersgate to Goswell St and the Barbican. It was said to resemble 'an *Italian* street, more then any other in *London*, by reason of the spaciousness and uniformity of Buildings, and streightness thereof, with the convenient distance of the Houses'.[1] Several nobles had their town houses there: Dorchester, Lauderdale and, after 1676, Shaftesbury (in a house designed by Inigo Jones). Sutton Nicholls, publisher, artist and friend of Pepys in later life, also lived there. By the early 18th century it was no longer fashionable.[2]

Aldgate (gate and street). The gate was the easternmost of the city's gates and the exit and entry for traffic between London and Essex. From within the city it was reached by a short wide street of the same name, which ran from the junction of Leadenhall St and Fenchurch St. From outside, it was approached by Whitechapel (now Aldgate High St). Coming through it from Bow one evening by coach Pepys and the Bateliers were stopped by the watch and asked whether they were 'husbands and wifes'. The gate itself, an elaborate structure erected under James I, was taken down in 1761.[1] (R)

Aldridge, ——. Possibly Henry Aldrich (1648-1710), later Dean of Christ Church, Oxford 1689-1710 (matriculated 1662, B.A. 1666);

mathematician, composer, architect, logician, catch singer and *bon viveur*. He came from a Westminster family and attended Westminster School. That he was musically active in London comparatively early appears from his catch in *The Musical Companion* (1672).[1] (Lu)

Aldworth, [Richard]. Auditor of the Receipt in the Exchequer from Oct. 1661, having been granted a reversion to the office in 1643. A Richard Aldworth was an underclerk to the Privy Council in 1639.[1]

Aleyn, Sir Thomas, 1st Bt (d. 1690). Alderman 1653–83, 1688–90; Sheriff 1654–5; Lord Mayor 1659–60. To be distinguished from Sir Thomas Allen of Finchley (1603–81), M.P. for Middlesex 1661–2.[1]

Alington, William, 3rd Baron Alington of Killard (d. 1685). An Irish peer, of Horseheath, Cambs.; granted an English barony 1682. A soldier who fought against the Turks; Colonel of a foot regiment 1667, Major-General 1678; Constable of the Tower 1679–85. In 1680 he was nominated to command the Tangier garrison. He was M.P. for Cambridge borough 1664–81; in the spring elections of 1679 defeating Roger Pepys, whom he succeeded as Recorder. His (second) wife, whom he married in July 1664, was Juliana, daughter of Baptist Noel, 3rd Viscount Campden, who died in Sept. 1667 at the age of 21.[1]

Allen, Maj. [Edward]. Cashier to the Victualling Office; re-appointed 1660.[1]

Allen, Capt. [John]. Clerk of the Ropeyard, Chatham 1660–3.[1]

Allen, Dr [Thomas] (d. 1684). Physician; Fellow of Caius College, Cambridge 1651–60; F.R.C.P. 1671; physician to Bethlehem Hospital.[1]

Allen, Sir Thomas: *see* Aleyn

Allestry, [James] (d. 1670). One of the most important booksellers and publishers of his day. His shop was in Paul's Churchyard 1652–66 and 1669–70, and in Duck Lane 1667–9. He was bookseller to the Royal Society and stationer to the King.[1]

Allin, Sir Thomas, 1st Bt (1612–85). One of the most active and successful naval commanders of the Second Dutch War. A merchant-shipowner of Lowestoft, he turned to privateering on the King's side in 1644 and served as captain of a frigate under Rupert. It was his unprovoked attack on the Dutch Smyrna fleet off Cadiz in Dec. 1664 which sparked off the war, during which he served with distinction as a flag officer. His service afloat ended with two expeditions to the Mediterranean, 1668–9, in which he imposed terms on the Barbary states. He had been at sea almost continuously for ten years, and had held eleven commissions as captain since 1660. On Mennes's death he was made Comptroller of the Navy (1671–80). In that capacity he came in for some criticism from Pepys for 'very unsteady measures' in paying wages. But he was an experienced colleague and took part in the special conference which led in 1677 to one of Pepys's most important reforms – the establishment of examinations for lieutenants.

He was Master of Trinity House 1671–2 and was briefly Commander-in-Chief in the Channel in 1678. In 1680 he retired to his native Suffolk. The love of money which Pepys remarks on is witnessed by his will which shows him possessed of considerable landed wealth. The baronetcy died out with his son in 1696.[1] His journals have been published.[2]

Alsop, [Josias]. Rector of Norton Fitzwarren, Som. 1638–?49; Rector of St Clement Eastcheap 1660–6 (and illegal preacher there, 1649–60).[1]

Alsop, [Timothy]. Brewer to the royal household; dead by 1666.[1]

Anderson. Two Anderson brothers, sons of Edmund Anderson of Broughton, Lincs., were at Magdalene in Pepys's time. The elder, Edmund, matriculated in 1648. The younger, Charles, was at Magdalene 1653–7 and for a while shared a room with Pepys. Like Pepys he was admonished for drunkenness (though not on the same occasion). He was a physician but never became a licentiate or fellow of the Royal College. Lord Belasyse gave him a testimonial in Jan. 1665 presumably with a view to his serving in Tangier.[1]

Andrews, John. Steward to Lord Crew; not alive at Crew's death.[1]

Andrews, John. Timber-merchant and navy contractor, of Bow.[1]

Andrews, Matthew. Coachman to Lord Crew; alive at Crew's death, when he received (in common with other servants) a year's wages and £10.[1]

Andrews, [Thomas] (1632–84). Merchant and victualler for Tangier; Warden of the Drapers' Company 1677–8. A neighbour of Pepys, he lived on the n. side of Crutched Friars and had a country house (Denton Court) in Kent. He was a friend and business associate of Pepys's friend Thomas Hill. He married Hester Young in 1656; two sons were alive in 1669. In 1661 he stood godfather to a daughter of Daniel Milles.[1]

Angel, [Edward] (d. 1673). Actor in the Duke's Company Nov. 1662–73, specialising in low comedy parts.[1]

Angier (Aungier). Percival Angier married Elizabeth Pepys (daughter of Thomas 'the Red', Pepys's great-uncle) at St Sepulchre's, Cambridge, in 1633. He became a prosperous London business man, with investments in Irish land and E. India stock. He died in 1665, leaving two children, Thomas and Elizabeth, the former of whom married Anne Cope at St Paul's, Covent Garden, in 1654.[1] His brother John was a tailor and woollen-draper in Cambridge, but went bankrupt, and was appointed parish clerk of Great St Mary's in 1666. It was for John's son Jack, previously apprenticed to his father, that Pepys apparently obtained a place at sea in 1663. His death at Lisbon in the following year is reported at v.291. A John Angier was a house carpenter in the Admiralty in 1663 and a timber merchant in 1668. A 'T. Aungier' was in the navy in 1700 and wrote to Pepys as his 'humble servant and kinsman'.[2]

Annesley, Arthur, 1st Earl of Anglesey (1614–86). He first enters Pepys's world as a political associate of Mountagu and Crew – one of the moderate Puritans who by 1658 were anxious for restoration of the monarchy. He served as President of the Council of State from Feb. 1660, in the vital months immediately before the King's return. He was made a Privy Councillor by Charles, and was one of its most hardworking members, serving on the Council's Admiralty Committee, the Council for Foreign Plantations and the Royal Fishery. He became Treasurer of the Navy in 1667, exchanging offices with Carteret who became Vice-Treasurer of Ireland in his place. His tenure of the office was short and troubled. He had to face the investigations of the Commissioners of Public Accounts as well as the problems that arose through a chronic shortage of money, and all in the face of parliamentary criticism from the Buckingham and Arlington factions who posed as reformers in order to bring down the influence of the Duke of York. At the same time he was without powerful friends within the administration – the Duke himself had not been consulted about his appointment and suggested a reduction in the powers of his office in order to bring it into subordination to the Board. Pepys, for his part, complained of his failure to present estimates and accounts and to keep an adequate check on payments. He seems to have taken refuge by absenting himself from the Board. He was suspended in 1668, and replaced by Littleton and Osborne as joint-Treasurers. Later he became Lord Privy Seal (1672–82), and as Admiralty Commissioner and Tangier Commissioner (1673–9) was again associated with Pepys. A strange looking man – 'his face long and emaciated, his complexion between purple and green, his eyes frightening'[1] – he was never popular, but Pepys, though critical of his work as an administrator, admired his seriousness and solid abilities. He was a learned constitutional lawyer, published several books and amassed a great library. He remained a Presbyterian in private life after the Restoration, and was a friend of Milton.[2] His grandson, the 7th Earl (d. 1737), once a Fellow of Magdalene, gave the college £200 to cover the cost of the transport of Pepys's library from Clapham to Cambridge in 1724.[3]

Ansley, Capt. [Abraham]. Commissioned captain in 1664, he was Master-Attendant at Sheerness when it was captured by the Dutch in 1667. Later that year he became Deputy Master-Attendant at Deptford, and Master-Attendant in 1669. He was commissioned to the *True Dealing* in 1685 and had died by 1688.[1]

Appleyard, ——. Of Brampton or Huntingdon. The heirs of Thomas Appleyard are mentioned in the will of William Stankes (1676).[1]

Apsley, Sir Alan, kt 1646 (1616–83). A friend of the Duke of York, holding several offices, among them those of Master of the Hawks 1660–75, and Treasurer to the Duke's Household 1662–83. He sat for Thetford in the Cavalier Parliament.[1] The Sir 'Anthony' Apsley mentioned at vii.73 has not been traced and may be a mistake for Sir Alan.

Apsley, Col. [John]. Royalist soldier turned forger.[1]

Archer. A family from Bourn near Cambridge. 'The fair Betty' Archer was admired by Pepys in his undergraduate days. Her sister Mary (said to be worth £1000) married Clement Sankey, ex-Fellow of Magdalene, in 1669. Their uncle who lived in the Old Jewry was possibly Robert Archer, citizen and grocer, of that street, who occurs in a will of 1659.[1]

Arlington, Earl of: *see* Bennet, Sir H.

Arlington House: *see* Goring House

Armiger, [William]. A Norfolk connection ('cousin') of Pepys, who lodged with Pepys's brother Tom, the tailor. Richard Mansuer, his maternal uncle, had marred Alice, widow of Thomas Pepys of South Creake, Norf., who was great-grandfather of Jane Turner and great-great-uncle of Pepys. William Armiger and one of his sons owed money to Tom Pepys at his death. He had ten sons and nine daughters.[1]

Armourer, ——. Either Sir William, Equerry of the Great Horse to both Charles I and Charles II (d. c. 1676) or (more likely, because younger) his relative Sir Nicholas (d. 1686), also an equerry to Charles II.[1]

ART AND ARCHITECTURE

The best memorial to Pepys's interest in the visual arts is the remarkable collection of prints he left to Magdalene College as part of his library. He had assembled, mostly in the last ten or twenty years of his life, one of the largest and most orderly collections of the period. He was not a connoisseur in the same sense as he was a musician or an amateur of the theatre, and he did not respond to the visual and plastic arts with the same passion. His correspondence often suggests that in gathering prints he was concerned primarily to make the collection as complete and representative as he could – rather in the same way as he collected books. He never made any study, either by reading or practice, of the visual arts – as he did of music – and was content to lean on the advice of better informed friends, such as Evelyn. Nevertheless his interest was real. That sharp and roving eye of his – so appreciative of beauty – was not infrequently employed on observing the works of artists and of builders. He was in the habit of coming to judgement on what he saw, and the very fact that his vision was limited enhances in a way the value of his judgements. For it is that which makes them probably representative of the taste of the educated middle-class Londoner of his day.

In the '60s he was not collecting for collecting's sake. His interest had practical roots: he was setting up house and was buying at first pictures and prints and, later, tapestries for that purpose. The middle-class home was in these respects a modest replica of the grander houses of the gentry and aristocracy. Its walls were hung with pictures and textiles that were chosen to proclaim, in a general sense, the status of the owner, and in a particular sense, his family and social associations. Therefore portraits, as in the larger houses, would predominate. They formed the great majority of the pictures Pepys collected both in the '60s and in later life. The first he bought in the diary period (in Oct. 1660) was an engraving of Lely's portrait of Sandwich. Then, beginning in Nov. 1661, he commissioned three portraits of himself, three of his wife and one of his father. After 1669 he acquired other large and interesting canvases, including copies or replicas in oil of portraits of Sandwich and of the Duke of York. This last (Kneller, 1688) had pride of place over the fireplace in the library of his house in York Buildings.[1]

Next after portraits, in Pepys's order of priority, came sea pictures – tokens of his profession. He hung them both in his house and in his office – prints and, to a less extent paintings, of ships, dockyards and marine scenes, together with maps and charts.

Prints were quickly and easily enough acquired. Printsellers abounded in London – Cade's shop was close by in Fenchurch St – and their wares could be bought for a few shillings. Portrait painters abounded too. The more fashionable (mostly foreigners) were expensive, but Pepys had no difficulty in finding (exactly how he does not say) more modest native-born portraitists. Hayls charged £14 each for the portraits of Pepys and his wife, Savill £3.

The painting of other genres – landscapes and still-lifes etc. – was still mostly in the hands of foreign, especially Dutch, artists. In 1666 Pepys had one landscape – a Dutch snow-scene – and one religious piece, a head of Santa Clara (by an unknown artist). He did not possess, by the end of the diary, any still-lifes or illusionist pictures, though they were in many ways his favourite pictures. The boldest investment he made was to commission four paintings of royal palaces from the modish Dutchman, Hendrick Danckerts. These he hung in his dining-room, set, as was the fashion, into the panels of the wainscotting, where they would form a proud background to his dinner parties.

At the end of his life Pepys had some 61 pictures of which 33 were portraits.[2] There is no means of knowing with any certainty how many he had acquired by 1669. But they amounted to a fair number it seems, if we may judge from his habit of hanging and rehanging. He once spent the whole evening till almost midnight rearranging with 'extraordinary content' the pictures in his closet. Most would be prints. It is likely that in the course of the '60s he had become quite knowledgeable about them – buying them for their own sake, and often choosing books by virtue of their 'brave cuts'. His taste for topographical prints, which bulk large in his collection in its final form, was already marked. His knowledge of painting also made some advances. Apart from pronouncing that he liked or disliked a work, he was capable of comparing painters, and occasionally of commenting on matters of technique – Savill lacked skill in shadows; Samuel Cooper the miniaturist made the colour of Elizabeth's skin 'a little forced'; Lely, in painting the Duchess of York, failed to reproduce the proportions of the face. His education had come, no doubt, from his contacts with the painters he employed. He gave Hayls seven sittings – the diary's account of them is the fullest extant record of a 17th-century portraitist at work. Pepys watched the work as it progressed, insisting on alterations here and there, and in the process learnt much. He marvelled at the way a painting was transformed under the brush – how deftly Hayls put in clouds, and how likenesses might sometimes be achieved better in the first or second working than in the finished picture, but at other times contrariwise.

In all types of painting and sculpture it was verisimilitude that most impressed him, and it is rare to find him commenting on any other value. Writing of the tomb of Van Tromp in The Hague, he says the 'sea-fight [is] the best cut in Marble, with the Smoake the best expressed that ever I saw in my life'. In portraits verisimilitude was the one essential. 'Mighty fine', he writes when Cooper has caught Elizabeth's likeness. On the other hand, 'Good, but not like' – of Lely's treatment of the court beauties.

Verisimilitude was the particular virtue of the Dutch school, not only in their portraits but in their representations of everyday life – interiors, still-lifes etc. Its most extreme expression was the *trompe l'œil*. On his visit to The Hague in 1660 Pepys found and almost bought – but it was too expensive – a painting 'done upon woollen cloth, drawn as if there were a curtain over it'. Later in the year he admired in the King's Closet a picture of a book upon a desk 'which I durst have sworn was a reall book'. Most remarkable of all, in the closet of his elegant acquaintance Povey, he found a large illusionist painting by Hoogstraten which persuaded him by its sheer virtuosity into imagining that he was looking down a corridor into other rooms.[3] In Verelst's studio in 1669 he found a flower picture in which the leaves had dew-drops on them so realistic that he was 'forced again and again to put my finger to it to feel whether my eyes were deceived or no'. That sort of effect, he added, was 'worth going miles to see'.

It was typical of Pepys's enthusiastic temper that if he liked a picture there was nothing tepid in his approval. 'The painting so extraordinary,' he writes of one of Cooper's miniatures, 'as I do never expect to see the like again.' Or, of Lely's Lady Castlemaine, in a strikingly unexpected phrase – 'a most blessed portrait'. There is charm in this frank and unsophisticated approach to art. Pepys was never inhibited from saying what he thought by any knowledge of what he ought to think. In fact there were in 17th-century London very few means of establishing rules of taste – no academy, no public galleries, no published art criticism, no illustrated histories of the subject. Much the same was also true of architecture. The profession itself was only just beginning to emerge. Very few architects – if any – worked full-time throughout the whole of their working lives in the profession. (Wren, Hooke and Vanbrugh are famous examples.) Most buildings were designed anonymously by master-builders. The styles of architecture had not yet been named and dated. Pepys is not exceptional, therefore, in that he is not in the habit of looking critically at buildings as artefacts – as belonging to the work of a particular designer or to the culture of a particular period. He uses only two concepts – buildings are either old-fashioned or modern. If they were on the one hand medieval or Tudor he disliked them; if they were Palladian he liked them. He visits Hampton Court and the whole of Oxford and Cambridge without making a single comment on the actual buildings. The Great Fire is described without a word of regret for the destruction of so many medieval churches. Wanstead House was old-fashioned and 'looks desolately'. Hinchingbrooke had been improved, but 'there being nothing done to make the outside more regular and moderne, I am not satisfied with it'. On the other hand, Gauden's new house at Clapham is 'very regular and finely contrived', Clarendon's new house in Piccadilly is 'the finest pile I ever did see in my life', Southampton's buildings in Bloomsbury 'very fine and noble'.

It was rare for Pepys to spend time on describing a building's exterior, unless it had something of peculiarity to attract him, such as the bas-reliefs at Nonsuch. It was rather the interiors which interested him. At Audley End he remarks on the 'stateliness' of the ceilings and the defects of the staircase; at Swakeleys on the screens and the excessive use of marble. Or he would ignore the building and simply remark the furniture and *objets d'art*. These were matters on which he could pronounce. Moreover, given his strong interest in his fellow humans he tended to look on houses as habitations rather than as works of art. In his tour of the Franciscan friary at St James's Palace it is the friars and their way of life that concern him; hence the detailed description of the rooms and furniture with not a word about the structure. Similarly, with churches it is the monuments of the dead that attract him, not the architecture. Even churches were to him habitations.

But, to judge from his comments, there was one aspect of architecture to which he was sensitive, and this was the relation of a building to its surrounding gardens and landscape. He uses the word 'seat' to indicate both house and site – 'a fine seat but an old-fashioned house' (Wanstead); 'a very stately seat for situation and brave plantations' (Wricklemarsh). And of Windsor Castle, with its ranges of battlements and its wide views across the Thames – 'the most Romantique castle that is in the world'. Pepys knew little about architecture, but he knew how to use his eyes.[4]

Arthur, ——. Of Ashtead, Surrey. Pepys writes of him as 'Goodman' Arthur; he was therefore probably the Robert Arthur who occurs in the hearth-tax records as exempted from tax after 1664.[1]

Arundel House. The property of the Earls of Arundel, housing the notable collection of statues, busts and marbles made by Thomas Howard, 2nd Earl (d. 1646), who had toured Italy with Inigo Jones. A miscellany of buildings of various periods, it lay on the s. side of the Strand, west of Milford Lane and St Clement Danes Church, with fine gardens running down to the Thames. Arundel Stairs served it. After the Fire the Royal Society met there, moving from Gresham College to make way for the latter's use as a temporary Royal Exchange. Arundel, Norfolk and Surrey Sts now cover the site.[1] (R)

Ascue (Ayscue), Sir George (c. 1615–72). A Commonwealth admiral who went on to serve in the Restoration navy. He came of a Lincolnshire family with court connections and was himself knighted by Charles I. In 1648 he stayed with that part of the navy which chose to serve Parliament, and rose quickly to flag rank, but after 1652, possibly because the government was unsure of his loyalty, held no further command, though in 1658 Cromwell sent him to Sweden to mediate in the Swedish–Danish war. He was given command of the *Henry* in 1664 and served as a flag officer in the Second Dutch War. In the Four Days Fight (June 1666) his ship the *Royal Prince* – considered the finest in the navy – ran aground, and he and most of his company were carried off prisoners to Holland. He returned in Nov. 1667 and in 1672 was made Vice-Admiral of the Red at the start of the Third War, but died before he could take up his command.[1]

Ashburnham. The brothers, John and William, represented to Pepys an impressive type of courtier – rich and worldly-minded, but also touchingly faithful to their royal masters. John, the elder (c. 1603–71) – 'the great man' – was originally a protégé of the 1st Duke of Buckingham, and spent most of his life, during two reigns, as a Groom of the Bedchamber. During the Civil War he was also paymaster of the royal army. His part in Charles's escape to the Isle of Wight in 1648 led to the unjustified suspicion that he had led the King into a trap. The Cromwellian government had no doubt of his loyalty to the King and kept him for years in prison. In the diary he often appears as a friend of Carteret. His brother William (c. 1604–79) was Cofferer of the Household to both Kings, and Commissioner of Monmouth's household from 1665. His house in Westminster is now part of Westminster School.[1]

Ashfield, [Sutton]. Of Brampton; the only 'Esquire' in the parish in the hearth-tax return of 1666. His house is there rated on 15 hearths. If he and his wife Lucy left Brampton shortly afterwards, as Pepys was told, they nevertheless had a son John baptised there in Dec. 1668.[1]

Ashley, Lord: *see* Cooper, A. A.

Atkins, Col. [Samuel] (d. 1670). Merchant, of Stepney; appointed collector of the coal tax in 1670 for services to the King during the Interregnum.[1]

Atkinson, [Thomas]. Goldsmith, of St Mary Woolnoth.[1]

Austin Friars. North out of (Old) Broad St. At the Dissolution much of the house and grounds of the Augustine friary was granted to the 1st Marquess of Winchester: he and his successors had developed it by 1602 (when the 4th Marquess sold it) into a well-to-do residential area. Carteret, the Navy Treasurer, had his office and official residence there, in Broad St. Great Winchester St and Winchester House, (Old) Broad St, preserve the memory of the former owners. [*See also* Dutch Church] (R)

Axe Yard. A street of some 25 houses, forming a cul-de-sac off the w. side of King St, a few yards south of the modern Downing St. The yard and its houses have now disappeared, being absorbed, like King St itself, in the making of Whitehall, Parliament St and the blocks of government offices built in 1864–5 on the w. side of those two streets. In Pepys's day, the yard, opposite the s. end of the Privy Garden of Whitehall Palace and reaching almost to the wall of St James's Park, was excellently sited for those with no official residence but anxious to keep in touch with court and government. Like the other yards, lanes and rows in this part of Westminster it also had a sprinkling of well-to-do people who lived or lodged there during parliamentary sessions or law terms. In 1657–8 Downing, Pepys's employer at the Exchequer, who later gave his name to Downing St, was the largest ratepayer in the yard (as distinct from the well-to-do lodgers whose names have seldom survived); in Feb. 1660 Adm. John Lawson was lodging there. Strype described it in 1720 as 'a Place of no great Beauty for *Buildings*, having a very narrow and ill Entrance', adding: 'the Part towards

St James's Park is the best, as enjoying something of a Prospect into the Park'. Strype wrote after the burning down and abandonment of the palace as a residence and the making of Downing and Charles Sts whose greater width and new houses gave them an advantage over the previously more important Axe Yard.[1] (R; La)

Axe Yard: Pepys's house. Pepys lived here from c. Aug. 1658[1] to July 1660. The house was probably on the n. side, and the fourth from King St. It had eight hearths – about the average for a street which included one of 36 (probably a lodging house), one of three and others ranging from four to 15. It appears from the rate books of 1657–8 to have been divided, the Pepyses occupying two-thirds (assessed on five hearths). By the time the diary opens, the Beales, who had occupied the rest of the house, had moved along the street to the Axe tavern, and Pepys, now presumably in sole occupancy, was paying rent both to Beale and to the owner of the freehold, Valentine Wanley of Lambeth. On moving to Seething Lane, Pepys assigned the remainder of his lease to Richard Dalton, Serjeant of the King's wine cellars.[2] (R)

Baber, Sir John, kt 1660 (1625–1704). Physician in ordinary to Charles II and James II; Gentleman of the Privy Chamber from 1679; at this period living in Covent Garden. He was an ally of the Presbyterians, and acted as an intermediary in most of the negotiations between them and the court 1660–88. In the spring elections of 1679 Pepys resigned his interest at Castle Rising to him and Sir Robert Howard (his 'honoured friends') though both had recently revived the charge against him of being a papist. (Howard was elected.)[1]

Backwell, Ald. Edward (?1618–83). The most important goldsmith–banker of his day, and (with the Vyners) one of the founders of the modern banking system in England; M.P. for Wendover 1673–March 81. Pepys always refers to him as an alderman, although he held office only for about a year (1660–1). He had acted as the government's principal financial agent under the Commonwealth, and performed a similar function under Charles II. He arranged foreign exchange transactions (such as the sale of Dunkirk, the payment of war subsidies and after 1670 the transfer of Louis XIV's loans to Charles); managed the disposal of secret service money; above all advanced cash and credit. During the war the government relied largely on him.[1] At the time of the Stop of the Exchequer in 1672 his loans to the government amounted to over £250,000. Apart from his considerable property in Lombard St (greatly extended after the Fire),[2] he had, at different times, country houses in Middlesex, Huntingdonshire and Buckinghamshire.

Pepys dealt with him as a goldsmith, but principally in arranging his noticeably reluctant loans for the Tangier garrison. Backwell's assistant Robin Shaw was an old friend of his. Some of the Backwell ledgers survive in the archives of Messrs Williams & Glyn, successors to the business.

His (second) wife was Mary (b. Leigh) who died in 1669.[3]

Bacon, Capt. [Philemon]. Naval officer, holding eight commissions from 1661 until his death in action in 1666.[1]

Badiley, Capt. [William]. Master-Attendant, Deptford 1654; re-appointed 1660. Probably brother of Richard, the naval commander (d. 1657).[1]

Bagwell, [William]. Of Deptford; ship's carpenter and the complaisant husband of one of Pepys's mistresses. He came of a family of carpenters and shipwrights, and can be identified as William since two of the ships in which he served as carpenter are named in the diary.[1] His letters show that he was not very literate,[2] but he was clearly an able craftsman. In 1677, as carpenter of the *Resolution*, he was appointed by the Navy Board to oversee the construction of the *Northumberland* at Bristol. Thereafter until at least 1689 Pepys was much importuned for appointments both by him and his wife.[3] His father (still alive in 1681) was Owen Bagwell, foreman of the yard at Deptford: he was excused service as a parish constable in 1664 on account of his employment and his age.[4] The Christian and maiden names of his wife have not been discovered.

Baines, [Jeremy]. A contemporary of Pepys at St Paul's, and a graduate (1663) of Cambridge. Pepys refers to him as 'a great non-conformist'. His father (also Jeremy, a brewer at Horsleydown) had been a commissioner for sequestrations and an active committee man during the Interregnum.[1]

Baker, Capt. [Richard]. Commissioner of militia, London (app. July 1659); Commissioner of Customs and Excise (app. Sept. 1659).[1]

Ball, [John]. Treasurer to the Excise Commissioners, London 1660-8. A Cavalier, and awarded a pension in 1668 for 'special service'.[1]

Ball, Sir Peter (d. 1680). Attorney-General to the Queen Mother 1643-67; referred to by Pepys in 1700 as an 'old friend'.[1]

Ball, Richard (d. 1684). Master of the Temple 1661-84; Canon of Ely from 1661 and chaplain to the King from 1663. Several of his sermons were published.[1]

Ball, Capt. ——. Naphthali and Andrew Ball both commanded fireships in the action referred to at vii.288. Pepys gives the name clearly in longhand, as 'Bell', but there was no naval officer of that name at that time. Coventry thought Naphthali 'stout and ingenious'.[1]

[Ballow, Stephen]. Citizen and leatherseller. He had married Jane, daughter of Edward Whitwell, citizen and salter. She was alive when he made his will in 1674.[1]

Banes, ——. The well-bred gentleman arrested for shouting '*Vive le Roy*' is identifiable as Robert Banes, of Hampshire, on the strength of a reference in Clarendon's papers.[1] But there were several royalists of this name in Lancashire too.

Banister, John (c. 1625–79). Son of a London wait; composer, violinist, harpsichordist, and virtuoso flageolet player. Played violin in *The siege of Rhodes* 1656, subsequently ran 'music-rooms' in London taverns; entered the King's Musick 1660, 'Special Service' in France 1661–2; appointed Violin in Ordinary and Director of the 'Select Band' of 12 of the 24 Royal Violins, 3 May 1663; accused of malversation by his colleagues 29 March 1667; superseded by Luis Grabu, 4 August 1667; established public concerts at 'The Musick School, over against the George Tavern in White Fryers' 1672.[1] (Lu)

Banister, ——. The neighbours who appear at a party (vii.246) may well be William Banister and his wife Margaret, of St Olave's parish.[1]

Banks, Sir John (1627–99). Merchant and friend. 'Of small beginnings',[1] he rose to become one of the greatest merchants of the day, M.P. in 11 parliaments (1654–99), baronet (1661), F.R.S. (1668) and Governor of the E. India Company (1673–4). During the diary period he lived in Leadenhall St, and had a country house at Aylesford, Kent, bought in 1657; later, in 1672, he acquired a fashionable town house in Lincoln's Inn Fields. Pepys first met him in 1664 and greatly admired him. At that time he was better known to Gauden, to whom he supplied hops and grain from his estate. But after the diary period Pepys became a close friend of Banks and his family, and often visited them in London and in Kent. He was godfather to Caleb, the eldest son, for whom in 1677 he arranged a Grand Tour of the continent in the charge of John Locke.[2] He was also consulted about a daughter's marriage.[3] Banks came to Pepys's rescue in 1674 when his enemies tried to deprive him of his parliamentary seat by accusing him of Popery, and several times Pepys was the means of lending the Admiralty's support to Banks in his own electoral campaigns.[4] In 1677 they joined with others to finance an attempt to find the North-East passage.[5]

Baptista: *see* Draghi, G. B.

Barber, [John]. Purser of the *Kent* (May 1655) and of the *Assurance* (Oct. 1655) etc.[1]

Barber-Surgeons' Hall. In Monkwell St (w. side); rebuilt after the Fire by 1678. Altered 1752 and 1863–4, and rebuilt after being destroyed in the Second World War.[1]

Barbon, Praisegod (?1596–1679). Of Fleet St; a leading Anabaptist preacher and republican politician; a leatherseller by trade. He became nationally famous when the Little Parliament of 1653, for which he sat as member for the city, was called in ridicule 'Barebone's Parliament' (although he never spoke in it). He was imprisoned after the Venner rising of 1661. His son Nicholas, a physician and property developer, is credited with the introduction of fire insurance.[1]

Barbour, [William]. Clerk in the Navy Office from 1660; employed by Evelyn in the business of Sick and Wounded Seamen 1666; clerk in the Ticket Office 1666–7 and 1681–5; Chief Clerk to the Comptroller 1672–80; Clerk of the Cheque, Sheerness 1685.[1]

Barckmann, Johan, cr. Baron Leijonbergh (Swed.) 1658 (1625–91). A career diplomat in the Swedish embassy in London from 1653, becoming Commissary 1655, Resident 1661 and Envoy 1672; knighted and made baronet 1661. He married Batten's widow. The quarrel with Pepys over prize goods, which almost led to a duel in 1667, was not long lasting. In 1687 he presented Pepys with a copy of Pufendorf's *Commentariorum de rebus Suecicis Libri XXVI* (1686; PL 2836) with an inscription 'Dno. Samueli Pips' commemorating their 26 years of friendship.[1]

Barcroft [John]. Serjeant-at-Arms to the King from Nov. 1660. The serjeants, four of whom were in waiting each quarter, had powers of arrest and were used by the King, Privy Council or Secretaries of State for that purpose, especially in cases where the delinquent was of high rank. They were of higher social standing than the 'messengers' used in other cases.[1]

Barker, [William]. Leading Baltic merchant and navy contractor; assistant of the Eastland Company (app. 1654); Master of the Mercers' Company 1656–7. Son of Sir Robert, K.B.; and father of Sir William, Bt. Pepys refers to him as an alderman although he had avoided the office by fining on the day of his election in 1651.[1]

Barlow, [Thomas]. Pepys's predecessor as Clerk of the Acts. Originally in the service of the 10th Earl of Northumberland, he was a muster-master in 1627 and 1636, and became joint-Clerk of the Acts in 1639. He appears from the diary to have been a friend of the statistician Graunt, and was probably the Mr Barlow mentioned as a mathematician in a letter of William Petty in 1644.[1] A John Barlow was in Petty's service.[2]

Barnardiston, Sir Samuel, 1st Bt (1620–1707). Deputy-Governor of the E. India Company 1668, and Whig politician.[1]

Barnardiston, ——. 'Cosen Barmston' of Cottenham was probably George Barnardiston, whose mother was Anne, stepdaughter of Pepys's uncle Robert Pepys of Brampton. He was also godson of Robert Pepys.[1]

Barnard's (Bernard's) Inn Gate. The inn was one of the smaller inns of court – a Chancery inn attached to Gray's Inn. The building lay south off Holborn, between Castle (now Furnival) St and Fetter Lane, opposite Furnival's Inn (now replaced by the head office of the Prudential Assurance Company). It was bought in 1892 by the Mercers' Company and rebuilt for their school.[1] (R)

Barn Elms. A mansion with a few smaller houses on the Surrey bank of the Thames between Barnes and Putney. Its considerable grounds and lawns were a regular resort for well-to-do Londoners making an excursion upriver. Pepys's visits started in 1665, a sidelight on his increasing wealth. The property belonged to the canons of St Paul's, and had been leased to Elizabeth's Secretary Walsingham. In the '60s the lessees were John Cartwright and his family. The village of Barnes – a collection of some 108 houses in 1664[1] – lay upstream from it. (R)

Barnes, [William]. A relative of Pepys, proposed in 1667 as a match for Paulina. He was presumably the William Barnes, gent., of Cottenham who married Kate Phillips in 1668.[1]

Barnwell, [Robert] (d. 1662). Sandwich's steward at Hinchingbrooke from at least 1655.[1]

Baron, [Benjamin]. Merchant, and lieut.-colonel in the city militia.[1]

Baron, [Hartgill]. A relative of Secretary Nicholas and an important royalist agent in the '50s. He was granted a clerkship in the Privy Seal, with other posts, in 1660, and c. 1673–7 was secretary to Prince Rupert.[1]

Barr, Peter. Merchant, trading chiefly with France and Tangier; agent at Dieppe for James Houblon.[1]

Barrow, [Philip]. Storekeeper, Chatham, Sept. 1661–March 1666. He resigned, against Pepys's wishes, after differences with his colleagues.[1]

Barton, [Thomas]. He owned a house and land in Brampton which he sold to Robert Pepys, the diarist's uncle, and which Pepys and his father, having acquired it under Robert's will, sold in 1662. There was some difficulty in establishing title which was partially cleared up in 1664 when he signed a surrender.[1] But disputes about 'Barton's business' continued into the '70s.[2]

Barwell, [John]. An officer of the Wardrobe: Squire Saddler to the King.[1] He lived on the s. side of Fleet St in a house taxed on seven hearths.[2]

Basinghall St. This ran north out of Cateaton (Gresham) St to London Wall, and was often known as Bassishaw St. It contained several mansions and company halls. (R)

Bassett, Sir Arthur. Soldier; he commanded a company in the Governor's regiment at Tangier. He came from the West country and was possibly related to the Capt. R. Basset who in 1681 commanded a company of Cornish miners sent out to carry out engineering works there.[1]

Bassum, John. Servant to John Pepys, sen. A John Barrum (possibly a mistaken spelling) occurs in the parish register of St Bride's in 1643 as father of a child.[1]

Batelier. The Bateliers, friends and neighbours of Pepys, were a family of wine merchants who lived opposite him[1] on the n. side of Crutched Friars, next to Thomas Andrews. The father, Joseph (d.

1667), held a clerkship in the customs service to which his son Will (b. 1642) succeeded. Joseph, jun. (b. 1643) was until c. 1671 the tenant of a linendraper's shop in the Royal Exchange – presumably where Pepys met his pretty sister Mary.[2]

Bateman, Sir Anthony, kt 1660 (1616–87). Chosen Aldermen in 1657, Sheriff in 1658 and Lord Mayor in 1663, he was ruined by his losses in the Fire, and was removed from the Court of Aldermen in 1667. By 1675 he was in receipt of a pension from the city.[1]

Baths and Bathing: *see* Dress and Personal Appearance

Batten, Sir William, kt 1648 (?1601–67), Surveyor of the Navy 1660–7; Master of Trinity House 1663–4. Son of a Somerset mariner, Andrew Batten, he made the sea his career, serving for a while in merchant ships and as a sailing master in the King's ships. In 1638 he was made Surveyor of the Navy, holding the post until 1648. He became second-in-command of the parliamentary navy in 1642 and was responsible for the well-known incident in February 1643 in which his ships fired on Scarborough when the Queen was there. Despite Presbyterian sympathies, he was not a strong partisan and attempted to keep the fleet out of active participation in the Civil War. In 1647 he resigned his commission and in May 1648 took a squadron over to Holland to join the King, but was back with the parliamentary fleet by the end of the year. During the Interregnum he retired into private life. In 1660 he was reappointed Surveyor and in 1661 was elected M.P. for Rochester in the face of opposition from the cathedral interest. He and Pepys were soon on bad terms, quarrelling over the right to draft contracts and competing for the favours of suppliers. Pepys early formed an alliance with Warren the timber merchant, and Batten with William Wood, Warren's closest rival. Relations between them remained hostile or at best uneasy throughout the diary period, despite some efforts – always on Batten's part – to improve them. Pepys believed Batten to be corrupt, and no doubt (like Pepys himself) he feathered his nest, but whether he was seriously corrupt is impossible to determine. The charge of incompetence which Pepys also makes is easier to sustain, though it should be added that his job was one of great complexity.[1] He was a poor speaker and not at his best with ledgers and memoranda. According to Pepys's notes in his 'Navy White Book' he chose his clerks badly (*see* Gilsthorpe), and undermined the efficiency of the Navy Office by seconding them to the Ticket Office or Navy Treasury in order to earn extra pay.[2] Coventry criticised his slowness; Middleton, his successor, complained of the state of his papers at his death; and the Chatham Chest under his direction remained as badly run as ever. In 1665 and 1666 Batten spent a lot of time in the yards, where he was probably more at home than at an office desk.

He married twice – first, in 1625, Margaret, daughter of William Browne, cordwainer, of London (through whom he acquired his house at Walthamstow), and secondly, in 1659, Elizabeth (b. Turner), widow of William Woodstocke of Westminster, who later married Baron Leijonbergh, the Swedish Resident. Of his children (all of the first marriage) the eldest, William, was a barrister (admitted to Lincoln's Inn 1646) and married Margaret Alcock of Rochester in 1658; Benjamin was a naval lieutenant; Martha married William Castle the shipbuilder, and Mary married one Leming of Colchester. (A widow Mary Leming of St Mary's Colchester died in 1671; her husband James, who died in 1668, may possibly have been Batten's son-in-law if the date of his death can be reconciled with Pepys's statement that he was dying as early as 1662.)[3] The executors of Batten's will were all navy contractors – Sir R. Ford ('my loving friend'), William Wood and John Young.[4]

Batters, Christopher (d. 1666). A gunner serving in three ships 1661–5, captain of the *Joseph* fireship in 1666 and accidentally drowned shortly afterwards.[1]

Battersby, [John] (d. 1681). A prosperous apothecary, at the Great Helmet, on the n. side of Fenchurch St; Master of the Society of Apothecaries of London 1674–5. His wife Ann died in 1678.[1]

Battersby, ——. A minister who lent Pepys money. Possibly Nicholas Battersby, graduate of Oxford and of Leyden, who was preaching in London in 1664. It was not unknown for parsons to act as money-lenders.[1]

Batts, Capt. [George]. Served in the royalist navy and held five commands 1660–5 before being deprived of his commission by Albemarle in 1666 because of his conduct in the Four Days Fight. Both the Duke of York and Coventry thought him ill-used.[1]

Baxter, [Nicholas]. Equerry of the Great Horse to the Duke of York; previously Gentleman of the Horse to Oliver Cromwell. The stables were in the Haymarket.[1]

Bayles, Tom. Barrister; admitted to the Middle Temple 1654.[1]

Baylie, [Francis] (d. 1678). Shipbuilder, of Bristol. He built two 3rd-rates, the *Edgar* (1668) and the *Northumberland* (1679). He also built three 4th-rates between 1654 and 1674. Pepys in his *Naval Minutes* remarks on his ability to build 'good sailers' without making preliminary drawings.[1]

Baylie, Maj. [Matthew]. Secretary to the Master-General/Commissioners of the Ordnance 1660–8, and Storekeeper at Upnor 1668–70.[1]

Baynard's Castle. On the Thames, stretching up the hill to (Upper) Thames St, opposite Addle Hill; the second castle of that name, built by Humphrey, Duke of Gloucester c. 1428 downstream of the first. Since Elizabeth's time it had been leased to the Earls of Pembroke.

Burnt in the Fire and the remains converted into buildings and wharves.[1] (R)

Beach, Sir Richard, kt 1675 (d. 1692). An officer in the royalist navy; held five commissions in the '60s; Rear-Admiral and C.-in-C. Mediterranean 1670, Navy Commissioner at Chatham 1671–9, and at Portsmouth 1679–92. There were complaints about his treatment of his seamen in 1669,[1] but he was much valued by Pepys and was a member of the Special Commission, 1686–8. In 1679 he helped to defend Pepys against the charge of introducing papists into the navy.[2]

Beale, [Bartholomew]. 'Auditor Beale'; Auditor of the Imprests in the Exchequer, with special responsibility for the navy accounts, c. 1660–89.[1] He produced, with Creed, a report on the cost of the Tangier mole, 1669.[2] He was related to Pepys: a Robert Beale of Whittlesey, Cambs., married in 1601 Susannah, daughter of John Pepys of Cottenham. His house in the parish of St Andrew, Holborn, was a large one, taxed on ten hearths.[3]

Beale, [Charles]. Deputy-Clerk of the Patents 1660–5, with an official residence in Hind Court; husband of Mary Beale the portrait painter (d. 1697). An expert in chemistry, he made up colours for his wife and Lely as well as other painters.[1]

Beale, [Francis]. Pepys's landlord (1658–60) in Axe Yard. Beale had lived there since at least 1627–8, in a house whose freehold was owned by Valentine Wanley. Sometime before the diary opens, Beale moved to the Axe tavern. He died in 1662, and his widow Alice (b. Whittney), lived on till 1666.[1]

Beale, [Simon]. Shipbuilder: he built the brigantine designed to carry the King ashore at Dover in May 1660. He also rigged out the pleasure boat used by Oliver Cromwell. He does not appear to have been a government shipwright.[1]

Beale, Symon (fl. 1653–80). Trumpeter, of Westminster; played at Middle Temple entertainment, 1653, when described as 'State Trumpeter', and at Lord Protector's funeral 1658; appointed trumpeter in ordinary 11 June 1660. His silver trumpet was stolen at the Horse Guard 'and cannot be heard of', 1676.[1] (Lu)

Beane, ——. Merchant and neighbour: either Thomas, of Crutched Friars, or Humphrey, of Tower Hill.[1]

Beard (Bird),——. The Huntingdon carrier. The name, spelt Beard, occurs in the registers of St Mary's and of All Saints, Huntingdon. Possibly the carrier was Thomas, who was married at All Saints in 1627.

Bear Garden and Stairs. The Garden was an amphitheatre in which bears and bulls were baited and fencing matches held. The building Pepys saw – he went to four prizefights and one bull-baiting – was erected in 1613. Baiting, though proscribed in 1642, had continued illegally, and was officially revived at the Restoration under royal licence. The site was south off Bankside, Southwark, east of Paris Garden and west of the end of Clink St. It can now be traced, east of Southwark Bridge, by the narrow alley bearing its name. Bear Garden Stairs gave easy access to it by water. (R)

Bear's Quay. Between Sabb's Dock and Porter's Quay, west of the then Custom House. A market for corn was held there: Pepys has a reference to the granaries. (R)

Beauchamp, [James] (d. 1688). Goldsmith, of Foster Lane, off Cheapside.[1]

Becke, Betty. Sandwich's mistress. Her mother (whose first husband was a merchant) may have been the 'Mrs Becke' who was assessed for the Royal Aid of 1666 on two houses in Chapel St, Chelsea, neither of which she occupied.[1] Her father may have been the Joseph Beck who occupied a house of five hearths in Little Chelsea at this time. It was at Mrs Becke's house that Paulina, Sandwich's daughter, died in 1669.[2]

Becke, ——. Pepys's 'cousin'. There were several Beckes connected with the Norfolk branch of the Pepys family, but this was probably one of the two sons (John and George) of George Becke of Lolworth, Cambs. He had married in 1617 a first cousin of Pepys's father, Eleanora Pepys of Cottenham. A William Beck was uncle by marriage to Talbot Pepys.[1]

Beckford. 'Captain' Beckford was Sir Thomas (kt 1677, d. 1685); appointed slopseller to the navy in Feb. 1666. Son of a Maidenhead tailor, he became Sheriff (1677–8) and Alderman (1679–85), and served as Master of the Clothworkers' Company (1679–80). He was one of the group of Pepys's friends who stood bail for him in 1679.[1]

It has been plausibly suggested that the unnamed friend of Tom Fuller, the author, who was about to go to Jamaica (ii.6) was Peter Beckford (brother of Sir Thomas). He founded a line of rich planters, and among his descendants was William Beckford, author of *Vathek* and builder of Fonthill.[2]

Beckman, Sir Martin (d. 1702). With de Gomme, the principal military engineer in England. Originally a Swedish artillery officer, he became a captain in the royalist navy. As Engineer-General at Tangier from 1662, he supervised (with de Gomme) the construction of its fortifications, and in 1683–4 had sole charge of the demolition of the place. He also designed the fortifications of Portsmouth in 1678, and as a hydrographer carried out, with Thomas Phillipps, a survey of the English Channel. He was knighted in 1685, when he became Chief Engineer and Master-Gunner of England. Pepys kept in his library two examples of his work in another though related genre – his designs for firework displays.[1]

Bedell, [Gabriel] (d. 1668). Bookseller and publisher, at Middle Temple Gate; fl. from 1646.[1]

Bedlam. The name given both to the Bethlehem Hospital and to the area around it. The hospital in 1660 occupied a site immediately north of the modern Liverpool St. The land originally granted to it lay on the w. side of Bishopsgate St, north of the church of St Botolph, where Liverpool St Station and New Broad St now stand, and was by 1660 built over, forming a populous precinct. Founded in 1247 as a priory, by the end of the next century it had become a hospital for the insane. Down to the late 18th century it was common for the public to visit it to gape at the inmates. The buildings were by the 1660s so much decayed that they were taken down and a new hospital built in 1675–6 by the city corporation to the design of Robert Hooke. This stood immediately north of London Wall between the modern Blomfield St and Finsbury Pavement.[1] (R)

Beeston, Will (c. 1606–82). Actor-manager; he inherited his father's company 1639; managed a troupe at Salisbury Court theatre 1660, and by 1668 was a member of the King's Company.[1]

Belasyse. A prominent Catholic family with estates in Yorkshire and Lincolnshire. John Belasyse, 1st Baron Belasyse (1614–89) was the second son of Thomas Belasyse, 1st Viscount Fauconberg. A royalist commander in the Civil War – Governor in succession of York and of Newark – he was raised to the peerage in 1645 as a reward. At the Restoration he became Captain of the Gentlemen Pensioners, Lord-Lieutenant of the E. Riding, and Governor of Hull. Having resigned his command of the Pensioners because of a private quarrel, he served as Governor of Tangier, 1665–7. He accepted the post (according to Pepys) only for the profit it brought, which would not be surprising. During the Popish Plot scare suspicion fastened on him as allegedly the Commander-in-Chief of a projected Popish army and he spent several years in the Tower without being brought to trial. In 1686–8 he was First Commissioner of the Treasury – an appointment he owed almost entirely to the lack of competition for it. He proved to be one of the King's moderate advisers. His (third) wife (d. 1694) was Anne, daughter of John Paulet, 5th Marquess of Winchester. It is impossible to identify the daughter at vii.171: he left three unmarried daughters at his death.

Two of his sons appear in the diary, principally as duellists – Sir Henry, his eldest, and John. Sir Henry, an Anglican convert and briefly an M.P. (Grimsby 1666–7) served on the committee in charge of a bill to stop duelling. He was killed in a drunken quarrel in 1667.

Lord Belasyse's nephew Thomas Belasyse (1627–1700) succeeded as the 2nd Viscount Fauconberg in 1653. A Protestant, and a parliament-arian in the Civil War, he married Mary, daughter of Oliver Cromwell in 1657. He succeeded his uncle as Captain of the Gentlemen Pensioners. In 1689 he was made an earl.[1]

Bell, Edith (1599–1665). 'Aunt Bell', of St Bartholomew-the-Less. A sister of Pepys's father, she had in 1646 married John Bell of St James's Clerkenwell, a widower of 60, receiving a portion from her brother Robert. Her husband was alive in 1657, but predeceased her.[1]

[Bell, William]. Rector of St Sepulchre, Holborn, 1662–d. 83; also Canon of St Paul's from 1666, chaplain to the King from 1668, and Archdeacon of St Albans from 1671.[1]

Bell, Capt.: *see* Ball

Bell Alley. 'Over against the Palace-gate': possibly a slip for Bell Court, which lay off King St close by the Whitehall Palace gate. There was a Bell Alley lower down King St, opposite the road through to New Palace Yard and Westminster Stairs. (R)

Bellamy, [Robert and Thomas]. Connections by marriage. Thomas was a brewer at Rochester; Robert was purser of the *Dover* in 1660; both supplied harbour victuals to the navy. Margaret, step-daughter of Pepys's uncle Robert Pepys of Brampton, had married a Bellamy. A Mr Bellamy received a ring at Pepys's funeral as a relative.[1]

Bell Yard. North from Temple Bar to Lincoln's Inn Fields: 'a filthy old place' (Pope).[1]

Bence, Ald. [John] (d. 1688). Merchant; appointed Navy Commissioner 1646; M.P. for Aldeburgh Jan.–Apr. 1659, 1669–87; Alderman 1664 (discharged 1665). His (second) wife was Joan (b. Cotton).[1]

Bendish, Sir Thomas, 2nd Bt (d. 1674). A connection by marriage. He was a very successful ambassador to Turkey, 1647–60, and insisted on calling himself 'His Majesty's ambassador' throughout the Interregnum. Cromwell tried but failed to get rid of him.[1]

Benier, Tom. Barber. Since he shaved Pepys on his visits to Salisbury Court, he is probably the Tom Beniere who appears in a list of householders there in 1666.[1]

Bennet, Sir Henry, cr. Baron Arlington 1665, Earl 1672 (1618–85). Diplomatist and politician; Keeper of the Privy Purse 1661–2; Secretary of State 1662–74; also (*inter alia*) Commissioner of Prizes 1664–7, Admiralty Commissioner 1673–9, Tangier Commissioner 1680–4. His association with Ned Mountagu did nothing to endear him to Pepys, but, that apart, he was to Pepys – as to most of his contemporaries – pompous, over-ambitious and lacking in solid ability. He rose to power by court intrigue and the favour of royal mistresses, and used it to promote the catholicising policies of the King. His career was at its height during the Cabal ministry when the Secret Treaty of Dover (1670) was made with Louis XIV, but after his attempted impeachment in 1674 he ceased to exercise any real influence. He was received into the church of Rome on his deathbed. In his biographer's words, his conscience 'could have accommodated itself easily to the necessity of bowing in the house of Rimmon, though for a lifetime'.[1] His London house was Goring (later Arlington) House, on the site of Buckingham Palace. He spent lavishly both on that and on his great country house at Euston, Norf.[2]

His wife (b. Isabella van Beverweerd, m. 1666) lived until 1718.

Bennet, [?John]. Mercer; with a large establishment (of eight hearths) on the n. side of Paternoster Row.[1]

Bennet, [Thomas]. Secretary to the Ordnance Commissioners 1668–70; Storekeeper at Portsmouth 1670–4, and at Tangier c. 1675–c. 80.[1]

Bennet, 'Lady'. A well-known bawd: Dryden mentions her in *Sir Martin Mar-all* (1667; IV, i) along with 'mother Temple' and 'mother Gifford'. Wycherley ironically dedicated *The Plain Dealer* (1677) to her.

Benson, ——. A Dutchman: possibly the Benjamin Benson who appears in the records of the Dutch church.[1]

Bentley, ——. John Bentley, draper, married in May 1663 Anne, daughter of Anne, widow of John Wight of Braboeuf, Guildford, and (?) niece of Pepys's Uncle Wight. He was a bachelor of 27, she a spinster of 22.[1]

Berkeley. The main (Gloucestershire) branch of this ancient West-country family has rarely in modern times played a prominent part in national politics. Its head was now George, 9th Baron Berkeley of Berkeley, (1628–98), who was raised to an earldom in 1679. Pepys usually calls him by the incorrect title of Lord George Berkeley to distinguish him from Lord Berkeley of Stratton. He appears only occasionally in the diary and seems to have lived a largely unpolitical life. One of the original fellows of the Royal Society, he was interested in mechanical invention and overseas trade. He served on the Council for Foreign Plantations and its successors from 1661, on the Committee of the E. India Company 1660–99, and as Governor of the Levant Company 1673–96, as well as being a subscriber to the R. Africa Company in 1663. He had married Elizabeth Massingberd, daughter of the Treasurer of the E. India Company in 1646. His son Sir Charles (K.B. 1661; d. 1710) succeeded him in 1698.[1]

The Somerset branch of the family produced several men of national importance at this time. Sir John (d. 1678) was made Baron Berkeley of Stratton in 1658. In the Civil War he had been a prominent royalist commander in the west, and in exile served in both the French and Spanish armies. From 1660–5 he was a colleague of Pepys as an extra Navy Commissioner, having been brought in, as Pepys later wrote, 'for want of other ways of gratification'.[2] Possibly Clarendon's hostility may have been a bar to his progress, but, thanks to the support of the Duke of York and his kinsman St Albans, he was sufficiently (perhaps excessively) successful in gaining advancement. He was an absentee President of Connaught 1662–6, an Ordnance Commissioner 1664–70, Lord-Lieutenant of Ireland 1670–2, and ambassador to the

Nimeguen peace conference 1675–7. He was also a member of the Council of Trade, and the Fishery and Tangier Committees, Steward of the Duke of York's Household from 1660 and a Commissioner for the repair of St Paul's (1664). Pepys knew him well. The diary has references to his hot, fiery discourse (e.g. v.336) and some indications of his interest in finance. His wife was Christiana, daughter of Sir Andrew Riccard, Pepys's neighbour.[3]

His nephew Sir Charles Berkeley (1630–65) was a favourite of both the Duke of York and the King. He was made Viscount Fitzhardinge in 1663 and Earl of Falmouth in 1664. He held several court and army appointments and was Keeper of the Privy Purse from 1662. Pepys, who met him on the Tangier Committee, had a low opinion of him. So had Clarendon.[4] But he was a courageous soldier (serving with the Duke at the Battle of the Dunes in 1658, when he was wounded), and for all his success in accumulating offices did not enrich himself unduly. Coventry, Gramont and Bishop Burnet all found good things to say of him.[5] He was about to be made a duke, it was said, when he fell in action at the Battle of Lowestoft. He died leaving no estate.[6] He had married Mary Bagot (d. 1679), a Maid of Honour who 'blushed at everything but never did anything to raise a blush herself' (Gramont).[7]

Falmouth's younger brother Sir William Berkeley (1639–66, kt 1664) was, like him, one of the Duke of York's favourites. A flag-officer in the war, though only in his twenties, he was killed in action.[8]

Berkeley House. Along with Clarendon and Burlington Houses, one of the great new houses on the n. side of Piccadilly. It was built c. 1665–6 for the 1st Baron Berkeley of Stratton immediately west of Clarendon's house, to the design of Hugh May, and was then the westernmost in Piccadilly and on the very edge of the built-up area. Evelyn (25 Sept. 1672) describes it as a 'Palace' – 'all are roomes of state' – and says that it cost £30,000. In 1674 it had 57 hearths.[1] It was sold in 1697 to the 1st Duke of Devonshire and destroyed by fire in 1733. Stratton and Berkeley Sts, Berkeley Sq. and Devonshire House now cover the site of the house and its grounds.[2] (R)

Berkshire, Earl of: *see* Howard, Thomas

Berkshire House. Later Cleveland House. Built by Thomas Howard, 1st Earl of Berkshire c. 1628, it stood at the s.-w. corner of St James's St, fronting the palace. (Bridgewater House now covers some of the site.) It had extensive grounds, including a walled garden in the Dutch style. Clarendon lived there after the Fire, when his house in the Strand was destroyed, until he moved into his new house in Piccadilly. In 1668 it was sold to the King, who gave it to Lady Castlemaine. Her name (as Duchess) is preserved in Cleveland Row near by.[1]

Bernard. An influential family in Huntingdon and Brampton,

hailing originally from Northamptonshire. Sir Robert (1601–66; cr. bt
1662) was Recorder of Huntingdon until Sandwich had him removed
and himself appointed in 1662. He had sat for the borough in the Short
Parliament of 1640.[1]

His son Sir John (1630–79) went, like Pepys, to Huntingdon School
and Cambridge. A prosperous lawyer, like his father, he bought
Brampton manor in 1653. He was connected by marriage to the families
of Oliver St John and Cromwell (he married St John's daughter in
1656), and sat for the borough in the three Protectorate parliaments
and in the Convention (1660). In the election of 1660, in alliance with
his brother-in-law Nicholas Pedley, he defeated the Mountagu interest.
His relations with Pepys were friendly – in 1677 he gave him advice
about his Brampton property and was helped to a royal yacht for a
voyage to France.[2]

Another son of Sir Robert was William, of St James's, Piccadilly; a
member of the Grocers' Company. He died c. 1667.[3]

Bethel, Capt. A connection of Slingsby, Comptroller of the Navy.
Probably Hugh Bethel, whose father Sir Walter, of Alne, Yorks., had
married the Comptroller's cousin Mary, daughter of Sir Henry
Slingsby of Scriven, nr Knaresborough. He had served in the parliamentary army. His brother was Slingsby Bethel, leader of the city
republicans, who as Sheriff in 1680–1 was to become nationally famous.[1]

Bethnal (Bednal) Green. A hamlet of Stepney, containing in 1664
some 216 houses,[1] on the Epping road beyond Whitechapel, about a
mile from the Standard on Cornhill. In the '60s still rural, and a
favourite retreat for well-to-do Londoners. (R)

Betterton, Thomas and Mary. Thomas (1635–1710) was perhaps the
greatest figure in the contemporary theatre. In a career spanning fifty
years he played a remarkable variety of parts and earned the reputation,
with most of his contemporaries as well as with Pepys, of being far and
away the finest actor of his time. In addition he was a manager and
trainer of actors, and himself wrote plays (mostly adaptations). He was
a member and shareholder of the Duke's Company from 1661,
becoming its joint-manager with Harris on Davenant's death in 1668,
and had a controlling interest in the United Company formed by the
merger of the Duke's and King's Companies in 1682. From 1695 he
ran a troupe of actors who had left the United Company. After 1685
he was increasingly concerned with the production of opera, and put on
the first performances of Purcell's *King Arthur* and *Fairy Queen*.

His wife Mary (b. Saunderson, ?1637–1712, m. 1662) was also a
member of the Duke's Company from 1661. Pepys calls her 'Ianthe'
after her part in Davenant's *Siege of Rhodes*. She had an important
share in her husband's work of training young performers. Among
their pupils Anne Bracegirdle (d. 1748) was the most eminent.[1]

Bettons, Mrs. Probably the wife of Thomas Betton, merchant, who lived on the n. side of Fenchurch St.[1]

Beversham, [Robert] (d. 1665). Grocer, of Fenchurch St; his first wife had died in 1662.[1]

Bickerstaffe, [Sir Charles]. Clerk in the Privy Seal. Displaced in 1660 by the appointment of Hartgill Baron (a relative by marriage), he was admitted in 1662 to another clerkship there only to lose it in 1669 on the resignation of Lord Robartes, the Lord Privy Seal.[1]

Biddle, ——. Possibly Richard Biddle, a court sumpter-man, of Brewer's Yard, or Samuel Bedwell, of King St.[1]

Biddulph, Ald. Sir Theophilus, 1st Bt (?1610–83). Merchant (Master of the Drapers' Company 1657–8), with a country house at Westcombe, Kent; Alderman 1651, Common Councilman 1654–81; elected M.P. for London 1656, 1659; and for Lichfield 1661.[1]

Bill, Lady [Diana]. Daughter of the 2nd Earl of Westmorland, and widow of John Bill, the King's printer (d. 1630). Her husband built Kenwood in Highgate.[1]

Billing, [Edward] (c. 1623–86). A prominent Quaker. Once a cornet in Cromwell's Scottish army; a brewer living on Mill Bank, Westminster; later (c. 1674) a co-proprietor of New Jersey.[1]

Billingsgate. The busy quay and fish-market at the inlet on the n. bank of the Thames below London Bridge. The inlet was filled in in the mid-19th century. Its public landing stairs were a convenient landing place for those coming upriver to the city. (R)

Billingsly, ——. Possibly Richard Billingsly, citizen and vintner of St Bride's parish.[1]

Billiter Lane. Now Billiter St, this ran north from Fenchurch St to Leadenhall St, and consisted 'of poor and ordinary Houses' (Strype, 1720).[1] (R)

Billop, [Thomas]. Clerk to Matthew Wren in 1668; still an Admiralty clerk in 1679.[1]

Birch, Jane: *see* Edwards

Birch, Col. John (1616–91). Politician. A self-made Mancunian, originally a carrier. His interest in naval affairs brought him into frequent contact and occasional conflict with Pepys. He had fought for Parliament in the Civil War, and sat for Leominster 1646–60, for Penryn 1661–Jan. 79, and for Weobley March 1679–91, serving as a commissioner for paying off the forces 1660–1, as chairman of the Commons' Navy Committee in 1661, and as a member of the Committee on Miscarriages in 1667–8, as well as on numerous committees on financial and commercial matters. He supported the Navy Board against its critics in 1668. In the '60s he accepted office as an Admiralty Commissioner March–July 1660, as Auditor of the Excise 1661–91, and as a member of the Committee for Trade 1668–72. But in the

'70s he was more distrustful of the court, becoming a Whig and exclusionist, and led the outcry in the Commons in 1677–8 against the cost of Pepys's ship-building programme. A moderate Presbyterian, he supported attempts at union with the Church of England in 1668–9, and himself became an Anglican in 1673. He lived to welcome the Revolution of 1688. Most of his contemporaries, though they might suffer like Pepys from his rough tongue and abrasive manner, could not, any more than Pepys, withhold their admiration of his ability.[1]

Birchensha, [John] (d. 1681). Composer, musical theorist, and viol player. No copy of his 'Plaine Rules and Directions for composing Musick in Parts', alluded to by Wood, is known to survive. A proposed theoretical treatise, *Syntagma Musicum*, never materialised.[1] (Lu)

Birchin Lane. A short lane leading out of Cornhill (east of the e. end of the Royal Exchange) to Lombard St, and a centre of the ready-made tailoring trade.[1] (R)

Bird, [Theophilus] (1608–63). Actor (of minor rôles) in the King's Company 1645–42, 1660–3. He married Anne, daughter of Will Beeston, the actor; their son Theophilus was also an actor.[1]

Birkenhead, Sir John (1617–79). The most prolific and effective of the royalist journalists during the Civil War. Editor of the government newspapers 1660–3.[1]

Bishop, Sir 'Edward' [*recte* Richard]. Serjeant-at-Arms to the King.[1]

Bishopsgate. One of the city's gates, and the exit for traffic going on the w. side of the Lea towards Edmonton and Cambridge. At the n. end of the street of that name; pulled down 1731. Pepys often refers to Bishopsgate St and Bishopsgate St Without simply as Bishopsgate.[1] (R)

Bishopsgate St. A spacious and busy street running north-east from the junction of Cornhill, Leadenhall St and Gracechurch St to the city wall at Bishopsgate. The continuation outside the gate and wall was known as Bishopsgate St Without. (Both sections are now known as Bishopsgate.) Pepys bought musical instruments there, as well as cutlery and glasses, and took coach for Cambridge at the Bull. (R)

Blackborne, [Robert] (d. 1701). The leading naval official under the Commonwealth. After an apprenticeship as a clerk working with the parliamentary Commissioners of the Navy from 1643, he was made secretary of the Admiralty and Navy Commissioners in 1652, and held the post concurrently with that of secretary to the Customs Commissioners until the Restoration. His strong Puritan views seem to have prevented his continuing in office, though Pepys often consulted him. His most valuable service to Pepys perhaps was to introduce his nephew Will Hewer (q.v.) to him in 1660. By then he was living in the parish of St Bartholomew-the-Less, by the Exchange, and was, possibly, still employed in the customs service. In 1663 he acted as spokesman for a group of aggrieved pursers. But in Dec. 1666 he re-established himself, being appointed secretary to the E. India Company. The appointment was renewed in 1678. In 1690 he stood bail for Pepys when he was released from the Gatehouse prison.[1]

His brother has not been identified.

Blackbury, [Peter]. Timber merchant, Wapping.[1]

Blackfriars. Pepys normally uses the word to mean Blackfriars Stairs, a well-frequented river jetty. Strictly, it was a precinct occupying the site of a former Dominican friary. Its ground had stretched from the Thames northwards nearly to Ludgate, westwards to the city wall and eastwards to Puddle Dock. By the Restoration it was largely built over and the famous Blackfriars theatre had been pulled down (in 1655) and replaced by tenements. Its inhabitants then included rich and poor, and still claimed the immunities from the city's jurisdiction enjoyed by the monastery. The whole area was burnt in the Fire and subsequently rebuilt. (R)

Blackman, Capt. [James]. Ropemaker, Woolwich.[1]

Blackwall. On the Middlesex bank of the Thames just above its junction with the R. Lea. In 1660 prospering and growing fast, as the shipping and dock facilities below the Pool increased. Especially connected with the E. India Company whose ships, by finishing their voyages there, avoided the slow passage round the Isle of Dogs, and whose warehouses and dock were all-important to it. With Poplar it had some 680 houses in 1664.[1] (R)

Blagge, [Margaret] (1652–78). Maid of Honour to the Duchess of York; after 1672 to the Queen. Her charms and piety were celebrated in a memoir by John Evelyn, her close friend from 1672. She married Sidney Godolphin in 1675 and retired from the court in the following year. She died in childbed in 1678.[1]

Blagrave, Thomas (c. 1615–88). Violinist and composer, of Westminster; appointed to the King's 'Sagbutts and hautboyes' 1638; one of Cromwell's domestic music 1658; violinist ('but his patent is for the flutes')[1] in the King's Musick 1660; Clerk of the Cheque in the Chapel Royal 1662; Master of the Choristers, Westminster Abbey, 1664.[2] (Lu)

Blake, Capt. Robert (d. 1661). Of the *Worcester*. He is to be distinguished from the famous Cromwellian general of that name. Pepys probably got to know him as commander of the *Newbury* in the Baltic, 1659.[1]

Bland. John Bland, of St Olave's parish, was an unusually gifted and enterprising business man, who prospered in the Mediterranean trade, published a book on commerce, and became the first Mayor of Tangier (1668–9, 1670–1), later serving from 1676 as Comptroller of H.M. Revenues there. He died in St Olave's in 1680. His wife Sarah (daughter

of Giles Green; d. 1712) had shared in the management of his business
and was in Virginia at his death. Thomas Povey, whom Bland in his
will refers to as his 'choycest friend', was associated with them in some
of their enterprises (the Tangier victualling among them); and took
legal action against the widow and executors in 1691.[1]

Giles, their son, who was also employed in Tangier, had married
Povey's daughter Frances. He was executed in 1677 for his part in the
Virginian rebellion of 1676: his mother shocked the Navy Board by
writing in vindication of his innocence 'comparing thereof to that of
his sacred Majesty'.[2]

Blayney, [Robert]. Secretary to Lord Ashley (Shaftesbury) in the
'60s, he was employed as a shorthand writer at the trials of Danby in
1679 and the Seven Bishops in 1688. Pepys kept in his library Blayney's
notes of the trial of Samuel Atkins, Pepys's butler, in 1679. A man of
the same names was secretary to the Customs Commissioners in the
'70s.[1]

Blayton, [Thomas]. Brother-in-law of Dick Vines, whose sister
Elizabeth he had married in 1656. The purser mentioned at vi.190–1
may be this or another brother-in-law. No purser of his name has been
traced.[1]

Blinkhorne, ——. Miller, of Wisbech, Cambs. Possibly the Thomas
'Blinke' who paid tax on a house in Wisbech rated on one hearth in
1666.[1]

Blount, Col. [Thomas]. Of Wricklemarsh, south of Blackheath,
Kent. One of the most vigorous and important supporters of parliament and the Commonwealth in the county. After a brief spell in
prison in 1660 he retired into private life, devoting himself to mechanical inventions – a new chariot, a waywiser etc. – some of which
Pepys describes. He was elected F.R.S. in 1665, but withdrew from the
Society in 1668.[1]

Blow, John (c. 1648–1708). Composer. By 1664 he had already
written three anthems (the words only survive). Appointed organist
of Westminster Abbey, on probation, Michaelmas 1668.[1] (Lu)

Blowbladder St. This joined the w. end of Cheapside with Newgate
St. It is now absorbed into the latter. Before it was widened after the
Fire it was a notorious bottle-neck for traffic. (R)

Blurton, ——. A friend of Peter Llewellyn (q.v.), and mentioned in
his will.

Boate, Mrs. An Edward Boate was Master-Shipwright at Portsmouth
until 1650. Other Boates were in the navy's service in the '60s at
Deptford and Chatham.[1]

Bodham, [William]. Clerk to Penn 1660–4, and to the commission
of enquiry into the Chatham Chest 1662; appointed Clerk of the
Ropeyard, Woolwich July 1664.[1]

Boeve, [James]. A Dutch-born merchant and lawyer, of Chancery Lane. In 1672 he complained he had been in a debtors' prison for three years and had lost a fortune of £20,000.[1]

Bond, [Henry] (c. 1600–78). Teacher of mathematics, and author of many works on the subject; editor of *The Seamans Kalendar* 1631–51. For some time after c. 1633 he was employed as 'Reader of Navigation to the Mariners' at Chatham yard. After the Restoration he made important investigations into the variations of the compass and methods of determining longitude. When Pepys speaks of his living 'at our end of town', he was living in Tower Bulwark. He later moved to Ratcliff.[1]

Boone, [Christopher]. E. India merchant.[1]

Boone, Col. Probably Thomas Boone, Admiralty Commissioner in 1659 and (with Mountagu) one of the plenipotentiaries sent in that year to Sweden.[1]

BOOKS

Pepys as collector. In the diary period Pepys acquired by purchase or gift books, maps and prints which proved to be the foundation of a notable collection. By the end of his life it amounted to 3000 volumes and was the admiration of his learned friends. In a memorandum of 1695 he summed up the principles that had guided him in its construction. His design, he wrote, had been to make it different in character from the more 'Extensive, Pompous, and Stationary Libraries of Princes, Universities, Colleges and other Publick-Societies', and equally from the 'Voluminous Collections . . . of the Professors of Particular Faculties: as being calculated for the Self-Entertainment onely of a solitary, unconfined Enquirer into Books'. It was to comprise 'in fewest Books and least Room the greatest diversity of Subjects, Stiles, and Languages its Owner's Reading [would] bear'. In their binding he had aimed at 'Decency and Uniformity'; in the catalogue, at 'Clearness, Comprehensivenesse, and Order'.[1] In fact the library came to reflect almost as clearly as the diary itself the mind and personality of its owner.

The young Pepys of the '60s had not yet begun some of the collections that were to be important features of his later library. There were by 1669 no medieval manuscripts, no *incunabula*, no broadside ballads, no calligraphy and no great gatherings of naval papers. But nevertheless the library of the diary period had many of the characteristics of that of 1703. His small collection of prints already showed a strong interest in topographical items. In buying books, he was covering a broad range of interests – history, science, music, and contemporary affairs as well as plays and literature in several languages, ancient and modern. He had begun to experiment in the choice of bindings (buying most of his books in loose quires), though he was not to remain faithful to the intention (declared at 18 Jan. 1665) of having his books 'within a very few' bound in a single style – by the end of his life he was using six or seven.[1] Occasionally he had added a few opulent volumes such as the Ogilbys he acquired at auction in 1666, and he had already adopted the policy of discarding earlier or inferior copies for later or better ones[3] – a policy which led him to get rid of a Third Folio Shakespeare.

All told, by 1669 he must have had about 500 volumes or thereabouts. The two presses he acquired in 1666 each held about 250 and with the purchase of Fournier's *Hydrographie* and Kircher's book on China in Jan. 1668 they were both more or less full. On acquiring the presses he had made an 'alphabet' in Dec. 1666 (revised in 1668–9) and a 'catalogue' (or shelf-list) in May 1669. Other lists were made later, until, after his retirement in 1689, he was able to settle down to the task of perfecting everything – collections, lists and all – with the help of his nephew Jackson and a clerk. Purchases were then made at an unprecedented rate, and bookcases added to match their fellows. By 1693 there were seven, by 1698 eight and eventually twelve.[4] Meantime the work of shelving, marking and cataloguing the books had continued *pari passu* with their growth in number, culminating in the two great lists of 1693 and 1700 drawn up in tripartite form as a 'Catalogue', an 'Alphabet' and an 'Index Classica' or subject-index. Inserted in his catalogue volumes are two drawings by Sutton Nicholls (c. 1693) which show the room in which the bookcases stood in his house in York Buildings. Portraits hang over the presses and over the mantelpiece, and, near to the two long windows which give on to the river, is a study table, later to be replaced by a pedestal desk.

In 1699 Pepys sent Jackson on a two-year tour of the continent to make purchases, especially of prints (and incidentally to educate himself). From time to time Pepys had commissioned other friends, such as Creed, Batelier and Roger Gale to buy abroad for him.[5] He himself had bought a handful of books (ready bound) in Holland in 1660 and others in Seville in 1684,[6] and no doubt made similar purchases on his continental holiday of 1669. But for the most part he bought in London, occasionally at auctions and through book-agents such as Bagford,[7] but mostly in the shops. Booksellers and printsellers were thick on the ground in London. In Paul's Churchyard alone there were 23 booksellers in 1666.[8] Others congregated in the Temple district, in Little Britain and Duck Lane in the city, while in Westminster Hall there were stallkeepers who sold ephemera such as parliamentary speeches and newsbooks. Pepys's regular booksellers in the diary period were

Joshua Kirton of Paul's Churchyard (until the Fire), John Starkey and John Martin of the Temple, Henry Herringman of the New Exchange, William Shrewsbury of Duck Lane (for foreign books), and the Mitchells of Westminster Hall (for newsbooks). In the '80s Robert Scott of Little Britain had become an important supplier,[9] and at the end of his life Samuel Lowndes by the Savoy.[10] In those last years the work of binding his books and laying down his prints into a score of great albums had so fully occupied his bookbinder John Berresford of Mark Lane that he was included (with his sewer Mrs Wetton) among the 'retainers generall' who received rings at his funeral, in company with his physicians, surgeon and apothecary.[11]

Pepys as reader. It was the fashion among the more studious of Pepys's contemporaries to keep 'commonplace books' in which they gathered extracts from their reading. For all his love of memoranda books, Pepys never kept one, nor did he make notes in the books themselves, so that the only evidence we have about his reading in the '60s is that of the diary. There his comments, though brief – the book is 'well writ', 'excellent', 'pretty' and so on – are sufficient to indicate his tastes. He usually read for sheer enjoyment. At the same time there were few books he failed to finish. Robert Boyle's book on colours he found impenetrable, but persevered – 'I can understand but little of it' (this is five weeks or so after starting on it) 'but understand enough to see that he is a most excellent man'. Butler's *Hudibras* (the first part) he disliked, and sold on the same day as he had bought it, but a few weeks later, hearing it was much cried up, bought another copy determined to try again. What is remarkable, and typical, is the variety of his appetite, and the zest with which he satisfied it. He read early and late, over a meal,[12] in a bookshop, in his coach, or his river boat, and even 'by light of link' while walking in the dark.[13] Altogether he recorded having read, in whole or in part, some 125 books in the diary period.

Some books he read for their sheer usefulness. As a navy official (not to say also a property owner and occasional litigant) he had to con his law books – his Coke, Selden, Herne and Ridley. And in his general reading, although he was capable of enjoying an excursion into abstract thought – Hobbes on *Liberty and necessity*, for instance: 'a little but very shrewd piece' – his preferences were markedly for the practical and immediately useful. In its extreme form this bent shows itself in his rather youthful admiration for manuals of conduct – *Letters to a son* by Francis Osborne (whom he called 'father Osborne'), and Bacon's essay *Faber Fortunae* (every man the architect of his own fortune) 'which the oftener I read the more I admire'. When looking briefly at Erasmus's *De conscribendis epistolis* he picked out for praise – almost tore out for reference in fact (it was not his copy) – the letter of advice to a courtier. In history he read widely – Fuller on the Crusades,

Speed on the Lancastrian kings (a by-product of his interest in history plays), Cavendish on Wolsey, Davila on the French civil wars – but it was on his own times and their immediate antecedents that his interest was focused. He kept up to date with his reading of newsbooks and pamphlets about contemporary events. For recent history he read Weldon on James I, the *Workes* of Charles I, Heylyn on Laud, Bate and Lloyd on the Civil War and Fletcher's life of Cromwell. But, true to his cast of mind, he turned most often to historical sources – to the *Cabala or Mysteries of state and government in . . . the reigns of King Henry the Eighth, Queen Elizabeth, King James and King Charles* (1663) which he was still dipping into at the end of his life,[14] and to the first volume of Rushworth's *Historical Collections*, which covered events in England from 1618 to 1629. It is not fanciful to see in his admiration for Rushworth (which by 1701 comprised eight volumes of documents down to 1649) a presage of his own 'Miscellany of Matters Historical Political and Naval'.[15] His study of his own times was crowned in the last year of his life by his reading the first folio of Clarendon's *History of the Great Rebellion*, which had just appeared. After the third reading he was still left with an appetite for a fourth.[16]

In the '60s the sciences were being made accessible for the first time to the general reader. Some were of particular interest to Pepys. He welcomed, for instance, Graunt's exercise in the new science of statistics in his *Natural and political observations*, and the *Essay towards . . . a philosophical language* by Wilkins, on whose treatment of naval words he was able later to make critical comment.[17] But he was fascinated by the new world of science in general. Having acquired a microscope in 1664 he bought Henry Power's *Experimental Philosophy* – the first book in English on the subject – and later, in 1665, Robert Hooke's *Micrographia*, whose plates delighted him. It was 'the most ingenious book that ever I read in my life'. Other scientific books gave him some difficulty: Boyle's book on colour, as we have seen, he could not understand; his *Origins of formes and qualities* he struggled with for months on end and by Jan. 1669 'was glad to have over'. But nevertheless he greatly admired Boyle and eventually made so considerable a collection of his works that they occupy an entire 'chapter' in the subject index of his final catalogue.

His theological reading included a few sermons (Jeremy Taylor's he thought 'most excellent'), Henry More's *Antidote against atheism* ('a pretty book') and two of Stillingfleet's large defences of the rationality of the Christian faith. On his *Origines Sacrae* Pepys's verdict was: 'many things in it are very good, and some frivolous'. Much worse, of course – in fact 'ridiculous' – were some of the theological effusions of the young William Penn. But again, in religious matters as elsewhere, Pepys's taste was for the less speculative parts of the subject. He read more church history than theology – Fuller's *Church-history of Britain* being a special favourite.

In literature he had several languages at his command, though if the diary evidence is taken at its face value he made rather slight use of them. He had learnt Greek at St Paul's School, but read none in the diary period and then and later added only a meagre number of Greek books to his library. He knew French well, and already had enough French books by 1660 to make them an item in his first will, but (again if we are to take the diary's evidence as complete) read it mostly in translation in the '60s – a little Scarron, Corneille's *Pompée* and *Le Cid*, and (with his wife) parts of the novels of the *précieuses*. He had heard of Montaigne (probably of the Florio translation) and meant to read him. He speaks in the diary of reading or consulting only four books in French: Sorbière's *Relation d'un voyage en Angleterre*, Furetière's *Nouvelle Allégorique*, Besongne's *L'Etat de France* and (to his shame) Millot's *L'Escholle des filles*. Similarly with his Spanish. He had the language and had heard of Don Quixote and was capable of reading a Spanish guide book to Rome,[18] but he seems to have read hardly any Spanish literature and that only in translation. In 1667 he greatly enjoyed L'Estrange's version of Quevedo's *Sueños y discursos*. Perhaps his acquaintance with Spanish literature developed later: certainly by 1703 his library contained 185 books in the language, including 26 plays.[19] Latin however he read fairly frequently. He got up at 4.30 to read his Cicero, and seems to have had no difficulty in enjoying the later Renaissance Latin of Erasmus, Barclay, Bacon and Comenius and the language employed by the university wits who composed plays in Latin in honour of royal visitors.

In English literature Pepys's tastes were simple. He enjoyed light verse, such as Charles Cotton's parody of Virgil, and topical verse, such as the satires by Marvell and others on the conduct of the war. He read plays both for recreation and by way of preparation for a theatrical performance, and had a collection of them as early as 1666. Davenant's *Siege of Rhodes* he thought 'the best poem that ever was wrote', and he paid it the tribute of setting one of its songs to music.[20] He was capable of responding in this way to poetry, but seems to have read little or no poetry for its own sake. His favourite poet was Chaucer, whom he may well have valued for his dramatic qualities – his characterisation and story telling. As for Milton, poetry of that order was not for him. The publication of *Paradise Lost* in 1667 passes without mention in the diary (though he did acquire at least one later edition – that of 1688).[21]

For light reading he particularly enjoyed the occult and the marvellous, provided it were presented in respectable English. John Spencer's book on prodigies, for instance: 'most ingeniously writ, both for matter and style'; Francis Potter's book of prophecies for the year 1666

(based on the fact that 666 was the number of the Beast in the Book of
Revelation): 'well writ in good stile [and] whether . . . right or wrong
. . . mighty ingenious'; and the history of an apparition in Wiltshire –
good reading for Christmas Day 1668 though not to be taken seriously.
The comments do credit both to Pepys's taste and to his good sense.
[*See also* Jackson, John; Magdalene College]

Boreman, George (d. by 1683). Appointed Keeper of the Privy
Lodgings and Standing Wardrobe, Greenwich 1663; probably also the
ballast merchant at vii.4; possibly a relative of Sir William, but not
mentioned in his will.[1]
Boreman, Robert (d. 1675). Brother of Sir William; Fellow of
Trinity College, Cambridge 1633; Rector of St Giles-in-the-Fields
1663–75; Prebendary of Westminster 1667–75.[1]
Boreman, Sir William, kt 1661 (c. 1612–86). Clerk of the Kitchen
under Charles I; Chief Clerk 1660; younger Clerk Comptroller of the
Household 1661; elder Clerk 1664; junior clerk of the Green Cloth
1680. He had a house and property in Greenwich, and founded the
Green Coat School there in 1672.[1]
Boreman, ——. The Boreman who stood on the scaffold at Vane's
execution may be George, or (more probably) the Boreman who was
Clerk of the Kitchen to Sandwich.[1]
Borfett, [Samuel] (d. 1700). Chaplain to Sandwich 1660; a North-
amptonshire man; Fellow of King's, Cambridge 1653–60, and Rector
of High Laver, Essex 1659–62. He was ejected from his living for non-
conformity, and thereafter became an unbeneficed preacher.[1]
Boscawen, [Edward]. A rich Turkey merchant and a Presbyterian;
M.P. for Tregony Jan.–Apr. 1659, and for Truro 1660–81. He was
active in financial affairs and it was probably he rather than his brother
Hugh (M.P. for Tregony in the Cavalier Parliament) who was the
Boscawen who challenged Pepys in 1675 about the cost of the shipbuilding programme.[1]
Bostock, ——. Possibly Richard Bostock, clerk in the Post Office
1663.[1]
Boteler: *see* Butler
Bow. A hamlet of Stepney, Middlesex, on the w. bank of the Lea,
some 3 miles from the Standard in Cornhill, to which Pepys and his
wife often went by coach to take the air. It was important as a source
of market garden produce for the city. In 1664, with Old Ford, it had
about 170 houses.[1] (R)
Bowes, Sir Jerome (d. 1616). Envoy to Muscovy 1583–4.[1]
Bowles. Bowles the grocer is probably John, of New Palace Yard. It
may be his widow who is referred to at vii.394: he had recently died.[1]

The John Bowles who escorted Pepys and his money from Brampton in Oct. 1667, and taught him the 'terms of hunting' en route, was a servant of Sandwich's. In 1666 a John Bowles occupied a house of four hearths in Brampton; this is probably the same John Bowles who in 1680 made a will leaving property there. He signed with a cross. A year later Pepys let a meadow at Ellington to one John Bowles.[2]

Bowman, ——. Edward and Francis Bowman were made Gentlemen-Ushers to the King in June 1660. Shortly afterwards, c. 1663, Francis Bowman (? the same) was an officer of the King's Wardrobe.[1]

Bow St. The reference at ix.62 is to the well-known street of this name running north-west from Russell St, Covent Garden. (It then ended as a cul-de-sac short of Long Acre.) The Bow St at vi.1 was sometimes called Thieving Lane and ran west out of King St, Westminster. Its site is now obliterated by the government offices on the w. side of Parliament St. (R)

Bowyer. A Westminster family; friends of Pepys and his wife in their early married life. Elizabeth stayed with them in their country house (acquired in 1629) at Huntsmoor, nr Iver, Bucks., when Pepys was away on the Dutch voyage. The head of the family, Robert (1594–1664), younger son of Sir Henry, of Denham, Bucks., was 'father Bowyer' to Pepys in that he was the senior officer under whom Pepys and his brother clerks worked in the Exchequer. He held the post of Usher of the Receipt from 1654 until his accidental death by drowning. He also held a reversion to a post in Star Chamber which fell vacant on the very day the court was abolished. In Nov. 1663 he was appointed a Gentleman of the Privy Chamber in extraordinary at the nomination of the Earl of Manchester. His wife Mary (b. Buggins) died in 1667. They had 13 children, five daughters and three sons being alive at her death. The eldest son William (1624–94) was a doorkeeper in the Exchequer from c. 1655. He died a bachelor. The family country house was sold in 1696 and pulled down c. 1850.[1]

Bowyer, [William]. Tar merchant, of St Botolph's, Billingsgate.[1]

Boyle. An Anglo-Irish family which produced several men of talent at this time – sons of Richard Boyle, 1st Earl of Cork (d. 1643).

The most famous was the seventh son, Robert Boyle (1627–91), one of the greatest of English scientists and a founder of the Royal Society. He lived in Oxford until 1668, but Pepys met him at meetings of the Society. His published works came to be a proud feature of Pepys's library, in whose classified catalogue they occupy an entire 'chapter'.[1]

The eldest son was 'Richard the Rich' (1612–98), the 2nd Earl (from 1664 also Earl of Burlington), Lord Treasurer of Ireland 1660–95. He had acquired vast estates in the north of England by his marriage in 1634 to Elizabeth, *suo jure* Baroness Clifford (1613–91), daughter and heiress of the 5th Earl of Cumberland. Their daughters Anne and

Henrietta married respectively Sandwich's son Hinchingbrooke, and Laurence Hyde, son of the Lord Chancellor.[2]

The third son was Roger (1621–79), cr. Baron Broghill 1627 and Earl of Orrery 1661, a soldier, politician and dramatist. He was a brilliant commander of the royalist forces in Ireland, and in 1677 published a *Treatise on the art of war*. He went over to Cromwell's side to fight against their common enemy, the Catholic interest, in Ireland, and became an intimate and admirer of the Protector. With Monck he made a remarkable success of the Cromwellian government of Scotland. It was probably he who was responsible for the proposal that Charles II should marry Cromwell's daughter Frances (cf. v.296–7 & n.), and he constantly threw his weight behind attempts to produce a moderate settlement of the revolution – principally by making Cromwell King. After Oliver's death he abandoned support of the Commonwealth and returned to Ireland, where, like Monck in Scotland and England, he took command of the situation and invited Charles to his kingdom. His plays were popular with Pepys and his contemporaries. He also wrote political pamphlets and an unfinished romance in six volumes.[3]

Boynton, [Katherine] (d. 1678). Maid of Honour to the Queen from 1660. She was the daughter of Col. Matthew Boynton and in 1669 married Richard Talbot, later Earl of Tyrconnel. Gramont writes of her 'big, motionless eyes' which 'gave, at a distance, a certain air of beauty, that faded away as one approached. She affected to be languishing, to speak husky and low, and to be capable of feeling faint two or three times every day'.[1] At her only appearance in the diary she was seasick.

Boys, Sir John, kt 1644 (1607–64). Of Bonnington, Kent; a leading royalist; Gentleman of the Privy Chamber to the King 1663.[1]

Boys, [John]. Wholesaler at the Three Crowns, Cheapside; in Aug. 1662 he married Elizabeth, daughter of John Bligh, citizen and salter, later an Irish M.P. Her mother was Catherine, sister of Pepys's friend, Dean Fuller.[1]

Bradford, [Martha]. Housekeeper, Hill House, Chatham dockyard.[1]

Braems, Sir A[rnold], kt 1660 (1602–81). Of Bridge, Kent; a Dover merchant of Flemish descent. As a royalist agent he claimed to have secured the fleet for the King in 1659–60 through his friendship with Lawson. He also claimed in Apr. 1660 to have made sure of Mountagu. He supported Mountagu's candidature at Dover in the elections to the Convention and himself sat for the borough. In 1662 he was a member of the commission of enquiry into the Chatham Chest. His surname was variously spelt: the version given here is that used in his signature.[1]

Brampton, Hunts. A village 2 miles south-west of Huntingdon, close to Hinchingbrooke (Sandwich's residence) and home of Robert Pepys, elder brother of the diarist's father.

His house, a yeoman's farmhouse on the edge of the village, now known as Pepys House, had been built in the late 16th century, to judge by its structure and the mural paintings in the hall and w. bedroom.[1] On Robert Pepys's death in 1661 it passed, along with the greater part of his landed property (including some 74 acres in Brampton parish),[2] into the possession of Pepys's father for life, after which it was to be inherited by Pepys. John Pepys lived there with his wife and daughter Paulina from Aug. 1661, and made some alterations in the house and garden. There were outbuildings and at least one pasture field attached to the house, but old John, at Pepys's suggestion, kept no animals except a horse.[3] From time to time Pepys sent his wife with her maid for extended visits, and made shorter visits himself, usually on business connected with the landed property. In Oct. 1667 he made the memorable visit in which he searched the garden for the gold sent from London and buried there during the invasion scare of the summer – sieving the soil for his coins 'just as they do for Dyamonds in other parts of the world' (viii.474). He grew increasingly fond of the place and planned improvements; in moments of depression he cheered himself by the thought of retiring there with his books. The death of his mother in 1667 and Paulina's marriage to John Jackson in the following year led to the break-up of the household. John Pepys went to live with his daughter and son-in-law in Ellington near by, and the house was let for almost ten years. The name of one tenant (Merritt) is known; he may have been the only one, and may be identical or connected with the George Merritt who appears in 1703 in the Jackson family papers.[4] In 1677 the Jacksons and old John moved back to Brampton, and under their management the house was neglected. Both Jackson and Pepys's father died in 1680, and Pepys paid a month's visit in the autumn to make new arrangements, and to set repairs in train. Paulina, now in poor health, was brought to London for treatment and Pepys thought of letting the house to his cousin Roger Pepys, but his visit had renewed his affection for the place and he was soon dreaming once more of retiring there.[5] Instead, he introduced yet another dependant, Esther St Michel, wife of his brother-in-law Balty who was away on naval service. She and her children shared the house from April to Aug. 1682 with Paulina and her two sons.[6] Paulina stayed there until her death in 1689, after which the house was let once more to tenants. By virtue of being its owner, and the owner of the land inherited with it, Pepys was made a deputy-lieutenant of Huntingdonshire in May 1685 and reappointed in March 1688.[7] At Pepys's death the house passed, with most of his estate, to Paulina's younger son John Jackson, who lived in Clapham. He had some repairs carried out, and let the house on a yearly tenancy, leaving its management to a local agent, John Matthews, the schoolmaster of Huntingdon who had also acted for Pepys. One

tenant was Thomas Cook, 'a labouring man' 'of no condition suitable
to the place'; another (in early 1709) was Abigail Dickons, a widow
(and a bluestocking, to judge by her letters).[8]

In 1721–2 the tenant (Holmes, in possession since 1709) paid £7 p.a.
It was still in the hands of Jackson's heir, John Pepys Jackson, in 1743,[9]
but some time later in the 18th century (perhaps after his death in
1780 – he died unmarried) was absorbed into the Sandwich estate. The
house was enlarged by the addition of a wing to the south and became
a farmhouse. Since 1926 it has been leased to the Samuel Pepys Club.
[*See also* Jackson, John and Paulina; Pepys, Robert]

Bread St. This ran south from the middle of Cheapside to Bread St
Hill (now to Queen Victoria St). 'A good open Street, well built and
inhabited by great Dealers' (Strype, 1720).[1] (R)

Brereton, William, 3rd Baron Brereton (1631–80). Chairman of
the Brooke House Committee 1668–9. The strong criticisms he made
of Pepys when its report was presented to Council found no favour with
the King and were (according to Pepys's account) easily enough re-
butted by Pepys himself.[1] He was an original F.R.S. and a patron of
mathematical science.

Brett, Sir Edward (1605–82). A professional soldier, related to Capt.
Isham. He had served in the Swedish army under Gustavus Adolphus,
and was knighted by Charles I on the battlefield in 1644. At the
Restoration he was made a Gentleman Pensioner and given a commission in the Horse Guards. He held a command under William of
Orange in the Third Dutch War. At his death he was Groom Porter to
the King.[1]

Bretton, Robert (d. 1672). Vicar of Deptford and Rector of St
Martin Ludgate and chaplain to the King from 1662; D.D. (Cambridge)
1663; Prebendary of St Paul's 1663–72. Pepys found him conceited
and wordy; Evelyn thought better of him.[1]

Brewer, Capt. [William] (d. by 1668). A liveryman of the Painter
Stainers' Company; living in the parish of St Matthew, Friday St at
the time of his marriage (1635). His bills for 'divers painted works' in
the Navy Office buildings appear in the Treasurer's ledgers under
'Extra Service on the Seas'.[1]

Brewer's Yard. It is clear from Pepys's two references that he is
referring to a yard or yards in Westminster, but there were two, and
it is impossible to be sure which he meant. One ran south-east from the
Strand to the river (upstream from Hungerford Stairs); the other was
situated east off King St. (R)

Bride Lane. South out of Fleet St along the e. end of St Bride's
church and then, turning east, to the Fleet river. This section of the
river is now covered by New Bridge St. No detailed pre-Fire map of
the area has survived, but the tax returns suggest that a fork of the lane

may then have reached back west towards the line of Salisbury Court.[1]
(R)

Bridewell. A precinct and a house of correction on the w. bank of the
Fleet (now New Bridge St) opposite Blackfriars, to which it was
connected by a gallery over the river. The precinct, running south
from Bride Lane to the Thames and west from the Fleet to (approximately) Water Lane, was extra-parochial and densely inhabited. The
house built there by Henry VIII was presented by Edward VI in 1555
to the corporation of London as a workhouse for the poor and a house
of correction for the idle, and was still used as such in the 1660s. It was
burnt in the Fire and rebuilt, later (in 1863) being sold – Bridewell
Place, Tudor St and other streets now covering the site. (R)

Bridgeman, Sir Orlando, 1st Bt (?1606–74). Lawyer and politician.
Briefly a Fellow of Magdalene, he was called to the bar, becoming
Solicitor-General to the Prince of Wales in 1640. He made his peace
with the victors of the Civil War, and practised privately as a con-
veyancer during the Commonwealth. He was made Chief Baron of
the Exchequer in 1660 and presided at the trial of the regicides, afterwards being transferred to Common Pleas where he earned a high
reputation. He was less successful as a Chancery judge when made
Lord Keeper on Clarendon's fall in 1667. As a member of the government (1667–72) he supported attempts to reconcile the moderate
Puritans with the Anglican establishment, but found himself unable to
support the King's high prerogative claims. He resigned rather than
seal the Declaration of Indulgence of 1672.[1]

Bridges, [Richard]. Linen draper, of Cornhill. He supplied calico
and canvas to the navy.[1]

Brigden, Richard. Cutler, of Fleet St (which was noted for its
cutlers), and freeman of the Haberdashers' Company. A man of
substance, with three servants, and a captain in the trainbands. Possibly
'my cutler' (viii.136)[1]

Briggs, [Timothy]. A scrivener who also acted as a 'solicitor' or
shipping agent. In *The Newes*, 17 Dec. 1663, he advertised his services
as a notary public 'who daily attends the Duke of York's secretary for
the speedy despatch' of ships' passes.[1]

Brigham, [Thomas]. Coachmaker to the King and Duke of York
from 1660.[1]

Brisbane, [John] (d. 1684). An Edinburgh graduate 'brought into the
Navy', Pepys later wrote, 'for want of other ways of gratification',[1]
but in fact a man of some achievement. He was successively Deputy-
Treasurer of the fleet 1665, Judge Advocate-General 1672–80, and
Secretary to the Admiralty 1680–4. He went to Paris as secretary to the
embassy in 1675 and 1679 (in the latter year helping Pepys to gather
evidence against Col. Scott). He was about to go to Lisbon as envoy-

extraordinary in 1684 when he died. He is said to have suggested to
Burnet the writing of his history. The diary points to some connection
with Carteret.[2]

Bristol, 2nd Earl of: *see* Digby, G.

Broad St. Now known as Old Broad St; a spacious thoroughfare
running south-west out of London Wall and Wormwood St to
Throgmorton and Threadneedle Sts. Most of it escaped the Fire. It was
often frequented by Pepys since it contained the town house of Capt.
Cocke the hemp merchant, the Excise Office, African House and, after
Michaelmas 1664, the office and official residence of the Navy Treasurer.
(R)

Brodrick, Sir Alan (1623–80). A protégé of Clarendon and a leading
member of the royalist underground movement in the 1650s; M.P. for
Orford, Suff., 1660, 1661–Jan. 79. His drunkenness was notorious but
according to Burnet, he underwent 'an eminent conversion'.[1]

Bromfield, [William]. Father of Mary Harman, and uncle of
Anthony Joyce. He married Martha, sister of William Joyce, sen., and
had three children: Richard, Thomas and Mary.[1]

Brooke, Sir Robert (c. 1637–69). An active M.P. (for Aldeburgh,
Suff., 1660, 1661–9) and chairman of the committee for enquiry into
the miscarriages of the war, in which capacity he won Pepys's admiration. He was educated privately, his tutor being Daniel Milles, later
Rector of St Olave's. He married Ann, daughter of Sir Henry Mildmay,
the regicide (through whom he acquired Old Wanstead House). When
he died (in a bathing accident in the Rhone in 1669) Pepys tried unsuccessfully to persuade the burgesses of Aldeburgh to nominate him
as their candidate in the bye-election which followed.[1]

Brooke House, Holborn. Formerly Bath House, and mostly built by
the 4th Earl of Bath (d. 1623); bought by Fulke Greville, 1st Baron
Brooke (d. 1628); headquarters of the Brooke House Committee 1668–
9. Brooke St, (north out of Holborn between Leather Lane and Gray's
Inn Rd) now occupies its site. The family also owned Brooke House,
Hackney. (R)

Brookes, Capt. [John]. Master-Attendant, Chatham, from 1660. He
was suspended in 1668 and had vacated office by 1673.[1]

Brouncker, Henry (?1627–88). Brother of Pepys's colleague Lord
Brouncker; Groom of the Bedchamber to the Duke of York 1656–67;
M.P. for New Romney 1665–8. In Pepys's words 'a pestilent rogue, an
Atheist, that would have sold his King and country for 6d almost'.[1]
He was reputed to keep 'a little country-house . . . always well stocked
with several working girls'.[2] The only good thing said of him by
contemporaries was that he played a good game of chess. His action in
giving an unauthorised order to slacken sail after the Battle of Lowestoft
led to his impeachment and flight to France. He was then expelled

from the House; shortly before he had lost his post in the Duke of York's household because he had taken part in the attacks on Clarendon. In Charles's last years he was restored to favour, as Cofferer to the Household (1679–85). He succeeded to the viscountcy in 1684, and died in 1688, having made a will in which he directed that he should be buried by day 'without Torches or Escutchions or more ceremony then is absolutely necessary'.[3] His brother had virtually cut him out of his will, leaving him only £10, 'for reasons I thinke not fit to mencion'.

Brouncker, William, 1st Viscount (1585–1645). Son of Sir Henry, Lord President of Munster; created an Irish peer in 1645. He had served as a Gentleman of the Privy Chamber to the King and Vice-Chamberlain to the Prince of Wales, and at the outbreak of war with the Scots in 1639 had been made Commissary-General of Musters.[1]

Brouncker, William, 2nd Viscount (1620–84). Navy Commissioner 1664–79; Admiralty Commissioner 1681–4; Commissioner for the management of the Duke of York's Household to 1667; Chancellor to the Queen 1662–84. He had spent the years of the Commonwealth in private life in Oxford, where he gained a reputation as a mathematician, and was one of the circle of virtuosi from which the Royal Society sprang. He was nominated as its first President in 1662. In Nov. 1664 he was made a Navy Commissioner, perhaps by virtue of his interest in mathematics and shipbuilding. But his closeness to the King – whom he had helped to design a yacht in 1662 and with whom he was associated in the Royal Society – was no doubt another qualification. As an administrator he was active in all branches of the Board's work, but took a special interest in finance and accounts, being made assistant to Mennes the Comptroller in 1667. His relations with Pepys fluctuated, but were at bottom good. They had common interests in music and science, and despite occasional quarrels over competition for contractors' favours, came to respect each other's ability. 'The truth is,' Pepys wrote (25 Aug. 1668), 'he is the best man of them all.' This was at the time when reorganisation of the Board was in the air, and Brouncker seems to have been the only member apart from Pepys himself to contribute suggestions. (He asked, *inter alia*, for attendances to be recorded in the minutes.) As a peer, Brouncker seems to have taken the chair at meetings, in the Treasurer's absence. He remained on the Board until 1679, by which time he had five clerks.[1] About his work on the Admiralty Board (1681–4) little is known.

In mathematics his best work was done before the diary period, though Pepys has a complaint in the diary that he was spending too much time on it. His contributions to the subject – mostly in the numerical field – are said to have been the work of an 'ingenious' rather than a 'great' mathematician.[2] He clung on to office as President of the Royal Society a few years too long, and departed in a huff, but in the

'60s he was a useful Fellow and promoted a variety of experiments in ballistics and navigation. He was also a learned musician, interested in harmonic theory, devised a scale consisting of 17 semitones, and translated Descartes' *De Musica* (1653). He died in 1684, appointing Pepys one of the overseers of his will, and asking (like his brother) to be buried 'with as little expense as necessity and decency will permit'.[3] He was, as Pepys observed, no churchgoer.[4]

His mistress was Abigail Williams (q.v.). The 'little kinswoman' at ix.146 has not been identified; she is possibly the Mrs Owen who appears at vi.317.

Brouncker's house (assessed on 20 hearths) was one of the biggest in the Piazza, Covent Garden.[5] He also had official lodgings in the Navy Office.

Browne, [Abraham and Frances]: *see* Taverns etc: The White Horse, Lombard St

Browne, Sir Anthony (d. 1699). Of Weald Hall, South Weald, nr Brentwood, Essex; a descendant of the Elizabethan Sir Anthony Browne who founded Brentwood School. A royalist in the Civil War. His brother cannot be identified: there were four alive in 1666.[1]

Browne, Capt. [Arnold] (d. by 1688). Naval officer. It must be he who is the Capt. Browne Pepys met in the company of the Earl of Marlborough in 1664 – as captain of the *Dunkirk* he had commanded the squadron which took Marlborough to Bombay, 1662–3. He appears to have quarrelled with the E. India Company over his private trading. After 1664 he held no further commission in the royal navy.[1]

Browne, John (d. 1691). Clerk of the Parliaments. A connection of Sandwich by marriage, his first wife being Temperance Crew, aunt of Sandwich's wife Jemima, who came of a family distinguished in the service of the House of Commons, both her father (Sir Thomas) and her uncle (Sir Ranulph) having been Speakers. She had died in 1634; the wife who appears in the diary was his second, Elizabeth Packer, whom he had married in 1636, daughter of John Packer, Clerk of the Privy Seal 1604–40. He was then 27 and she 19. Browne served as Clerk from his appointment in 1638 until his death in 1691, except during the Interregnum when the House of Lords was abolished.[1]

Browne, Capt. [John] (d. 1663). Naval officer. He served under the Commonwealth, and afterwards held only one command (that of the *Rosebush*). He married a sister of Sir William Batten and like him had a house at Walthamstow.[1]

Browne, Capt. [John]. Ordnance officer. Son of Capt. George Browne, and Deputy-Storekeeper of the Ordnance, Chatham.[1]

Browne, [John]. Storekeeper at Harwich; reappointed 1660.[1]

Browne, Ald. Sir Richard, 1st Bt (d. 1669). One of the most influential figures in the city at the Restoration: Lord Mayor 1660-1 and M.P. for the city in 1656, Jan.–Apr. 1659 and 1660 (also for Wycombe 1645-8 and Ludgershall 1661-9). He had made a great reputation as leader of the London trainbands in the Civil War, but had broken with the war party and the political extremists in 1648, after which he spent some five years in prison. He supported Booth's royalist rising of 1659 and had to go into hiding after its failure. He was one of the city's deputies sent to the King at Breda, and headed the procession which brought the King into the capital in May 1660. In that year he became first a knight then a baronet. In 1661 he had to turn out the militia against Venner's Fifth-Monarchist rebels. To the end of his life he remained a favourite with the London apprentices.[1]

Browne, Sir Richard, 1st Bt (1605-83). Of Sayes Court, nr Deptford. An influential royalist: diplomatic agent, later Resident, at Paris for Charles I and Charles II 1641-52 (making his embassy chapel an important centre of Anglicanism); Clerk of the Privy Council 1641-72 (with, after 1660, an official residence in Whitehall); and Master of Trinity House 1672-3. John Evelyn married his daughter Mary.[1]

Brownlow, [William]. Schoolfellow of Pepys.[1]

Bryan, Jacob. Purser of the *Prudent Mary* (1665), the *Princess* (1667) and the *Royal Sovereign* (1670).[1]

Buck, [James]. Rector of St James, Garlickhithe, Dec. 1661–d. 86; Rector of St Peter, Cornhill at his death; chaplain to the Earl of Lincoln. He had suffered sequestration from his Suffolk living during the Interregnum.[1]

Buckingham, 2nd Duke of: *see* Villiers, G.

Bucklersbury. A street leading south-east from the junction of Cheapside and the Poultry to Walbrook. About 150 yards long in 1660,[1] it is now cut into two sections by the making of Queen Victoria St. (R)

Bucknell, Ald. Sir [William], kt 1670 (d. 1676). A rich brewer and shipper; M.P. for Liverpool 1670-6. He was a farmer of both the English and the Irish customs and excise, and often lent money to the government.[1]

Buckworth, [Sir John], kt 1681 (1623-87). A neighbour, living in a large house (taxed on 12 hearths) on the n. side of Crutched Friars.[1] He was a prosperous Turkey merchant, and served as Alderman 1683-?6. Pepys had dealings with him in the '70s about Mediterranean convoys.[2] In 1662 he married as his second wife Hester Goodyear (d. 1702). The daughters mentioned at ix.533 were Margaret (b. 1655), Elizabeth (b. 1657) and Mary (b. 1665). The son (vii.273 etc.) was probably John (b. 1662), who was created a baronet in 1697.[3]

Budd, [David] (d. c. 1676). From 1660 Proctor in the Court of Admiralty and advocate in the Court of Arches; also a commissary of the Archdeacon's Court, Huntingdon.[1]

[Bull, Nathaniel] (d. ?1672). Educated at Oxford; Surmaster of St Paul's School 1658–67; Headmaster of Leicester School 1667–70.[1]

Bulteel, [John] (d. 1669). Secretary to Clarendon from c. 1658; M.P. for Lostwithiel 1661–9; a relative of the Houblons.[1]

Bunce, Sir James, 1st Bt (d. 1670). Merchant and leatherseller. He was Sheriff in 1643–4 but was discharged from the corporation for his royalism in 1649. He was made a Gentleman of the Privy Chamber in 1667. He had a house at Greenwich.[1]

Bunn, Capt. [Thomas]. Naval officer. He served under the Commonwealth and held two commands 1660–1. In 1662 he helped to design the jetty at Tangier. He may have been the Thomas Bunn who was an alderman at Tangier from 1668. A John Bunn was Comptroller there at the same time.[1]

Burgess, [William]. Clerk to Sir Robert Long, Auditor of the Receipt in the Exchequer.[1]

Burlington, Earl of: *see* Boyle (Richard)

Burlington House. The smallest of the three great houses built in the '60s in the fields on the n. side of Piccadilly. (The others, neighbouring it to the west, were Clarendon House and Berkeley House.) The site had been granted in 1664 to Clarendon and his elder son and sold by them to Sir John Denham, Surveyor-General of the King's Works. The house (whose design is attributed to one of Denham's assistants, probably Hugh May) was completed by 1668 for the 1st Earl of Burlington. Pepys retained an engraving of it in his collection. It survives, much altered, and is now occupied by the Royal Academy and a variety of learned societies.[1] (R)

Burnet, [Alexander] (d. 1665). Pepys's physician, and a friend of his Uncle Wight. He appears also to have attended on Sandwich. M.D. (Cantab.) 1648; hon. F.R.C.P. 1664. He lived on the s. side of Fenchurch St in a large house (taxed on nine hearths). He died in the Plague, after performing a post-mortem on a plague victim.[1]

Burroughes, [William]. Clerk to Penn 1664–7; clerk (Victualling Accounts) 1667–8.[1]

Burrows, [Elizabeth]. The pretty widow of a naval lieutenant, Anthony Burrows, who was killed in action in 1665. Her mother Mrs Crofts kept a shop in Westminster where Elizabeth seems to have worked.[1] An entry in Pepys's private accounts for 1667–8 ('Burroughs . . . gloves') may refer to a purchase that was innocent.[2] Most of his dealings with her were not.

Burrows, [John]. Appointed slopseller to the navy in 1660, to provide 'wastecoats and drawers and . . . other commodities'. Probably of All Hallows, Honey Lane.[1]

Burston, [John] (fl. 1628–65). Chart maker of Ratcliff; one of the Thames school. 'The ablest man in Towne' (Sandwich). He had been apprenticed to Nicholas Comberford, one of the leading practitioners of the day.[1]

Burt, [Nicholas] (fl. 1635–90). Actor in the King's Company 1660–c. 82; originally playing leading rôles, but not so frequently as Hart and Mohun. As a boy, before the Civil War, he had played women's parts.[1]

Burton, [Hezekiah] (d. 1681). Fellow of Magdalene College 1651–60, 1660–7; Canon of Norwich from 1667 and Rector of St George's, Southwark from 1668. He also held other livings. His advancement was due to the patronage of Lord Keeper Bridgeman, to whom he was chaplain, and with whom he shared liberal views on church union with Presbyterians. It was he who wrote to Pepys in 1677 asking for a subscription towards the cost of the new building in which the Pepys Library is now housed.[1] The college possesses his portrait by Mary Beale.

Burton, [Richard]. Locksmith, Chatham yard.[1]

Butler, James, 12th Earl and 1st Duke of Ormond (1610–88). Politician and soldier. The richest and most powerful of the Anglo-Irish magnates of his day and at the same time a man of simple loyalties and the highest principles. For his services as royalist leader in Ireland during the rebellion, he was at the Restoration made a Duke and Lord Steward of the Household. In 1661 he was appointed Lord-Lieutenant and was responsible for the Restoration settlement in Ireland. He fell victim to Buckingham's enmity in 1669. In a second term of duty as Lord-Lieutenant (1677–85), he kept Ireland quiet during the turmoil of the Popish Plot. Contemporaries and historians agree in regarding him as one of the most admirable figures in 17th-century public life.[1]

Butler, Lord John (1643–76). Ormond's youngest surviving son; a profligate and the black sheep of the family. He was created Earl of Gowran in 1676 and married Anne, daughter of the 1st Earl of Donegal in the same year.[1]

Butler, Thomas, styled Earl of Ossory (1634–80). Ormond's eldest son. A courtier (Gentleman of the Bedchamber to the King); soldier (Lieut.-General of the Irish army 1665; commander of the English troops in Holland 1678); politician (twice deputy to his father as Lord-Lieutenant); and sailor (volunteer 1665; officer and Rear-Admiral 1672–4). He was an Admiralty Commissioner 1677–9 and was made Governor of Tangier just before his death. A remarkably talented and popular man – 'the Bayard of the English court'. A friend of Evelyn.[1]

Butler, Mr. A friend, living in Westminster; nicknamed 'Mons. L'Impertinent' because, presumably, of his garrulity. He disappears from the diary after Dec. 1660 when he goes with his parents and sisters to Ireland. It is clear from the diary that he was a brother of Frances Boteler (one of Pepys's favourite beauties), and a cousin of Pepys's friend Will Bowyer, and that he was still in Ireland at the end of 1662. Beyond that, almost everything is uncertain, except that he was an active Anglican churchman and (probably) high-born. There were several Botelers or Butlers in Westminster in 1660 (some in government service, like Pepys); and several Butlers among Pepys's contemporaries at Cambridge, and of course a whole clan of them in Ireland. The entry at i.209 suggests that Mons. L'Impertinent with his 'high discourse in praise of Ireland' was in fact Irish – possibly the nickname is proof enough too. He may have been a relative of the Duke of Ormond, head of the Butler clan, who had many places to bestow in Ireland as the newly appointed Lord-Lieutenant. A John Boteler took his B.A. at Dublin in 1655 and a man of the same names was appointed a prebendary of Cork in 1661. The identification suggested at i.22, n. 1 is based on the fact that a Daniel Butler was at St Paul's School with Pepys: he took his B.A. at Oxford in 1658, and held a living in Kent in 1663. However, the entry at i.178, which could be interpreted as implying that Mons. L'Impertinent was not a parson, might be held to disqualify both John and Daniel.[1]

Butt(s), [William]. Deb Willet's uncle; a Bristol broker; aged about 48 in 1656.[1]

Cadbury, [Humphrey]. Mastmaker, Deptford and Woolwich yards.[1]

Cade, [John]. 'My stationer'. Pepys bought prints and maps from him, and possibly – after he moved into the city – the notebooks in which the diary was written. Cade supplied the Navy Office with stationery – there are several of his bills, recorded in the Navy Treasurer's accounts, for paper, pens, ink, wax, wafers and 'books'.[1] He was a Presbyterian and conducted a prosperous business. His shop (the Globe) and house (taxed on seven hearths) were, before the Fire, immediately to the west of the Royal Exchange, where he owned the lease of four houses, one of them with stables. There was also a warehouse there.[2] One of the houses was a tavern – the Three Golden Lions. The buildings were destroyed in the Fire, when his landlords (the Mercers' Company) provided him with temporary accommodation in Gresham College. In 1671 his business was moved to a shop on the s. side of the rebuilt Royal Exchange, his £70 p.a. being one of the highest rents there.[3]

Cade, [Thomas]. Chaplain to the King in exile; ? Rector of Trimley St Mary, Suff., 1665.[1]

Calamy, Edmund (1600–66). A leader of the moderate Presbyterians; perpetual curate of St Mary Aldermanbury 1639–62. At his church doors there were said to be seldom fewer than 60 coaches for his weekday sermons during the Civil War. He retired into private life after the King's execution and at the Restoration played a leading part in the negotiations which aimed at including the Presbyterians in the Church of England. He went as far as accepting a royal chaplaincy but, after much hesitation, refused a bishopric. He continued to attend his church after being ejected from the living in Aug. 1662. His eldest son, Edmund Calamy jun. (also a Presbyterian parson), was an almost exact contemporary of Pepys at school and Cambridge. His grandson Edmund Calamy the younger (d. 1732) was the biographical historian of the nonconformists.[1]

Calthorpe. Sir Lestrange Calthorpe (1624–78) was a lawyer: Bencher of the Middle Temple 1667; and knighted 1675. He acted as man of business to his cousin Sir James Calthorpe. His kinsman in the city was Edward Calthorpe, member of the Grocers' Company and a Turkey merchant. They were family friends of the Pepyses – Pepys himself consulted Sir Lestrange about Robert Pepys's estate, and Roger Pepys witnessed his will. In 1637 Sir Henry Calthorpe had made a will in which his 'loving friend' Talbot Pepys had been appointed overseer.[1]

Cambridge: *see* Magdalene College

Campden, Viscount: *see* Hickes, B.

Cannon (Channel) Row. A particularly fashionable and aristocratic street, giving access to Derby House and Manchester House, and ending in a door which led into the orchard (later the Bowling Green) of Whitehall Palace. It ran north from New Palace Yard towards the s. limits of Whitehall Palace, between and parallel to King St and the river. At least one of the Rhenish wine-houses which Pepys frequented was there in the '60s. (R)

Cannon (Canning) St. A large and busy street running west from the end of Great Eastcheap to Walbrook; famous for its linen shops. It has been altered out of recognition since the 1660s, and runs from King William St to St Paul's Churchyard. (R)

Capel, Sir Henry cr. Baron Capel 1692 (d. 1696). M.P. for Tewkesbury 1660–87, 1690–2; Cockermouth 1689; Admiralty Commissioner 1679–81, Treasury Commissioner 1689–90, Lord Deputy of Ireland 1695. Brother of the Earl of Essex (who was implicated in the Rye House plot), and like him a Whig and an exclusionist. He was active in the attack on Pepys and Deane in 1679, and took a leading part in the impeachment of Danby in the same year. A friend of the architect Hugh May: later an executor of his will. His garden at Kew became the basis of the Royal Horticultural Society's garden there.[1]

Carew, [John] (d. 1660). Regicide, twice imprisoned under the Commonwealth and at the Restoration tried and executed at Charing Cross.[1]

Carkesse, [James]. Navy Office clerk. He began his career as a household official of the 1st Marquess of Dorchester (an original F.R.S.), and first appears in the Navy Office as a clerk to Brouncker, who was probably responsible for bringing him into the service. Possibly by the same influence, or Dorchester's, he was elected F.R.S. in 1664. In 1666 he was in the Ticket Office, but was dismissed in 1667 for corruption, only to be reinstated a few months later through the intervention of friends in the House of Commons. (Sir Edward Turnor, the Speaker, was godfather to his son William born in that year.)[1] He last appears in the office as a clerk to Edward Seymour, Extra-Commissioner, in 1672–3. Thereafter he disappears into Bedlam. His behaviour had been odd and he had caused embarrassment by posing as a clergyman. But his powerful connections were sufficient to secure his release in 1678 – in order (it was said) that he should publish a book of verse, *Lucida Intervalla*, in which Pepys and Hewer were satirised as part of the attack on the Duke of York. Pepys's dislike of him is echoed in the diary of Robert Hooke the scientist. He lived in St Olave's parish in a house taxed on five hearths.[2]

Carlingford, Earl of: *see* Taaffe, T.

Carlisle, Earl of: *see* Howard, Charles

Carnegie. Robert Carnegie, 3rd Earl of Southesk (d. 1688), styled Lord Carnegie 1658–69, had married Lady Anne Hamilton, daughter of the 2nd Duke of Hamilton c. 1660. Her infidelity was notorious, and led to their separation in 1671. From 1675 she lived abroad, mostly in Paris and Brussels, until her death in Holland in 1695. She was a Catholic and a friend of Lady Castlemaine.[1]

Carr, Sir Robert (c. 1637–82). M.P. for Lincolnshire in four parliaments 1665–81; Chancellor of the Duchy of Lancaster 1672–82; Tangier Commissioner 1673–80. A brother-in-law and ally of Arlington.[1]

Carter, Charles. A near-contemporary of Pepys at Magdalene, taking his B.A. in 1652; Rector of Irthlingborough, Northants. 1664–75. His living or curacy in Huntingdonshire (i.321) has not been traced. He was a native of Earith, Hunts.[1]

Carteret, Sir Edward. Gentleman-Usher to the King; great-uncle of Sir George.[1]

Carteret, Sir George, 1st Bt (c. 1610–80). Navy Treasurer 1660–7. He had served in the royal navy from 1632, rising to the rank of vice-admiral in 1637, and becoming Comptroller of the Navy in 1638. On the outbreak of civil war he escaped first to France, and then to his native Jersey where he was appointed Governor and waged a privateering war against the Parliament until the island fell in 1651. In 1660 he returned to England from exile in France and Italy, was appointed Vice-Chamberlain and established himself as one of the most powerful figures at court in Clarendon's entourage. He was made one of the proprietors of the Carolinas (1663, 1665) and in 1664 was granted by the Duke of York a share in the land between the Hudson and Delaware rivers which was named New Jersey in his honour. He was a not very active M.P. for Portsmouth 1661–Jan. 79. Pepys met him not only as an officer of the Navy but also as a member of the Tangier and Fishery Committees, and as Master of Trinity House (1664–5).

As Treasurer he was, according to Clarendon, 'most dextrous', 'a punctual officer and a good accountant'.[1] Pepys at first held him in high regard, and was careful to gain his favour – for he was a friend of Sandwich as well as of Clarendon – but came to be more critical as he grew closer to Carteret's rival, Coventry. Certainly Carteret was both incorrupt and industrious. His attendance at the Board (where he took the chair) and at pays of ships was intermittent, but that was hardly surprising in view of his other commitments, and the principal criticism his colleagues made of him was that he kept the Board in ignorance of his operations. His accounts were usually presented twice a year, but in such a way that the Board could not easily examine them. The same difficulty was experienced by his successor and the Lord Treasurer, and by the Brooke House Committee appointed to investigate the navy's accounts. In their report they expressed dissatisfaction over his explanation of amounts totalling £326,000, but the Privy Council in 1670 came to the conclusion that only £1,873 could be regarded as outstanding.[2] Meantime in 1667 Carteret had exchanged his Navy post for that of Vice-Treasurer of Ireland, which was less demanding and more lucrative. He also served as an Admiralty Commissioner 1673–9.[3]

In 1640 he had married his cousin Elizabeth Carteret. Philip, their eldest son (1643–c.78; kt 1667) in July 1665 married Lady Jemima Mountagu, Sandwich's daughter, and after 1667 settled at Hawnes, Beds., to the life of a country gentleman. He was an F.R.S. and an amateur of painting and watchmaking. He was made a Gentleman of the Chamber in 1670.[4] Philip's son George (1667–95) was created a baron in 1681 and was father of the Viscount Carteret who became George II's prime minister. Another son of Sir George mentioned in the diary was Benjamin, a naval lieutenant: he held five other commissions before being dismissed by the Duke of York in 1673.[5] Of his daughters, Anne married Sir Nicholas Slaning, 1st Bt, of Maristow, Devon, in 1663; Caroline married Thomas Scott of Scot's Hall, Kent, also in 1663; Louisa-Margueretta married Sir Robert Atkins, the topographer of Gloucestershire, in 1669.[6]

Sir George had a private house on the s. side of Pall Mall. His official residences were lodgings in Whitehall as Vice-Chamberlain (on the n. side of the Great Court), a house at Deptford as Navy Treasurer, and Cranbourne Lodge nr Windsor, as Keeper of the Lodge.[7]

Carteret, Philip. Son of Sir Philip of Jersey and second cousin of Sir George Carteret; commissioned lieutenant to four ships 1660–5; drowned in the Battle of Sole Bay 1672.[1] [*See also* foregoing entry]

Cartwright, [William] (c. 1606–86). Actor in the King's Company

1660–82 and in the United Company 1682–5; retired at the age of 80. An experienced player from pre-Civil War days. During the Commonwealth he had been a bookseller.[1]

Cary, [John] (1612–86). Master of the King's Buckhounds 1660–86. The reference at i.157 may be to his second wife, about whom little appears to be known.[1]

Cary House. A large building on the s. side of the Strand, near to the Savoy. Here Pepys attended Anglican services in the '50s: in 1667 he found it 'a house now of entertainment'. The house was in fact divided into five tenements sometime in the '60s and all five in June 1669 were destroyed by fire. It may have derived its name from the Cary family.[1]

Case, Thomas (1598–1682). A leading Presbyterian divine; in 1662 ejected from his living (St Giles-in-the-Fields) for nonconformity. In politics a strong royalist, he had been arrested in 1653 on suspicion of taking part in a plot. His sermons, punctuated by gasps and winks, were easy meat for the mimics.[1]

Castell, [John]. Rector of Great Greenford, Mdx 1661–86.[1]

Castle, Dr [John] (d. 1664). Admitted to Gray's Inn 1616, and Clerk of the Privy Seal from at least 1643, when he compounded for delinquency, having joined the court at Oxford. He is possibly the John Castle who was awarded a doctorate in medicine at Oxford in 1644. In 1663 he lived in Great Sanctuary, Westminster.[1]

Castle, [William]. One of the largest private shipbuilders on the Thames: besides supplying timber to the navy (and occasionally workmen) he built several royal ships – one 3rd-rate and a yacht in the diary period, and three 3rd-rates in 1677. Both Pepys and Commissioner Pett were critical of his ability: something of Pepys's distrust no doubt derived from the fact that he had married Batten's stepdaughter. At his marriage to Martha Batten in 1663 he was a widower of 34 and she (daughter of Batten's first wife) a spinster of 26.[1] Robert Castle, presumably their son, had succeeded to the business by 1686.[2]

Castlemaine, Lady: *see* Palmer, Barbara

Catherine of Braganza (1638–1705). Daughter of Juan IV, King of Portugal 1640–56, and, from 1662, wife of Charles II. Unequipped by nature or upbringing to play any part in public affairs, she remained to the end a very private person. She had to suffer exile and the neglect and infidelities of her husband. In the end Charles came to respect her and stoutly defended her against the attacks made on her during the Popish Plot. She amused herself with her cards and music, and consoled herself with her religion.

She took over Somerset House when Henrietta-Maria left England in 1665 and as a widow lived both there and at the nunnery she had founded at Hammersmith. She left England in 1692 to spend her last years in Portugal, where she acted as Regent to her brother Pedro in 1704–5.[1]

Cave, John (d. 1664). Gentleman of the Chapel Royal; his setting of Lovelace's 'Now Whitehall's in a Grave' survives.[1] (Lu)

Cervington, [Charles]. Tally-cutter in the Exchequer from at least 1655.[1]

Chamberlayne, Sir Thomas, 1st Bt (1635–82). Deputy-Governor of the E. India Company 1661–2; Governor 1662–4.[1]

Chandler, ——. Presumably a tenant of Robert Pepys; possibly William Chandler of Ellington.[1]

Channell, Luke. In 1660 a well-known master of a dancing school at the Glasshouse, Broad St; in Nov. 1664 sworn in as dancing master to the Duke of York's theatre company. A contemporary pamphleteer has a slighting reference to him (1660), and calls him (in a cant phrase which lasted into the 19th century) a 'hop-merchant'.[1]

Chaplin, [Sir Francis], 1st Bt (d. 1680). A provision merchant; once Denis Gauden's assistant, later his associate, in victualling the navy. Alderman 1668; Sheriff 1668–9; Lord Mayor 1677–8; Master of the Clothworkers' Company 1668–9. Described in 1672 as 'a person truly loyall . . . active in businesse, but too quick and open sometimes in declaring his opinion'.[1] At his death he had over £14,000 in personalty and £1000 of Royal Africa stock, as well as land in Suffolk, Wiltshire and Jamaica.[2]

Chard, Adam. Shopkeeper, Pope's Head Alley. He owed Tom Pepys over £3 at Tom's death.[1]

Charett: *see* Cherrett

Charing Cross. One of the most important public places in Pepys's London; on the main route between Westminster and the city, at the junction of the then Strand, Haymarket and Whitehall, and taking its name from one of the stone crosses built at the staging places of the funeral procession of Eleanor, Queen of Edward I. The cross itself was destroyed – with that at Cheapside – in 1647, by order of Parliament, but its site, marked by rails, was chosen as the place of execution of Maj.-Gen. Harrison and other regicides in 1660. The area which passed by the name of Charing Cross was ill-defined – a house might be at the s. end of St Martin's Lane or the n. end of what is now Whitehall, but in common parlance it would be described (as Pepys describes the house of Unthanke, his wife's tailor) as at Charing Cross. (R; La)

Charing Cross Stairs. Not marked on contemporary maps. Possibly another name for Hungerford Stairs. (R)

Charles II (1630–85). The King is one of the principal *dramatis personae* of the diary, and the extent and detail of Pepys's information about him one of the most valuable features of his record. Their first meetings – one formal interview apart – were on board ship in May 1660, during the voyage that brought the King back from exile, and it was their common concern with the navy that formed the basis of their association throughout the reign. Both came to identify themselves with the conviction that control of the seas was the principal part of national greatness.

'Rebellion and necessity',[1] Pepys wrote, had made Charles a sailor. As an exile he had learnt to sail a pinnace around the Jersey coasts and in 1648 had taken part in one of the operations of Rupert's squadron of royalist warships. He grew up to have a taste for navigation and ship design, and as King became, in Pepys's phrase, one of the most 'mathematic' of 'Admirals',[2] encouraging the study of navigation in the Royal Society, the Royal Observatory and the Royal Mathematical School in Christ's Hospital (this last being the first English school of navigation and founded largely by Pepys's own enterprise). He had a hand in the design of royal yachts and, when disputes arose, pronounced on the final form of the 30 new warships of 1677.[3] He attended ships' launches not only for ceremony's sake but also to appraise them with the other experts. His duties as monarch were never so delightful as when they required him to journey downstream in the royal barge to inspect his ships at anchor in the Medway, or, better still, to sail the royal yacht – at which he was expert – on a visit to his fleet riding in Portsmouth or Plymouth harbour. In the day-to-day government of the navy he also played a part. Although he was too lazy to become an administrator of the calibre of Louis XIV, he never allowed admiralty affairs to slip altogether from his control even when they were delegated to others. When the Duke of York was Lord High Admiral, Charles expected to be consulted on the appointment of commanders – and occasionally overrode him. He presided over the deliberations of his Privy Council on navy strategy and on the enquiries that followed from the war's disasters in 1668–70. When in 1673–9 a commission replaced the Duke of York he came closer to being a king on the French model. Under the terms of the commission he retained sole power over the appointment of commanders and commissioned officers, and reserved to himself the power to issue orders on any aspect of naval affairs independently of the commission. Things were different again in 1679–84, when the navy was governed by a new commission composed of opposition politicians ignorant of the sea whom Charles had appointed (in cynical disregard of naval and national interests) purely for political reasons. He deliberately allowed them greater powers than the commission of 1673, distanced himself from their work, laughed at their incompetence,[4] but again was careful to assert his right to make appointments to high command.

Through all these phases Pepys was one of the King's indispensable men of business – by 1673 the most indispensable of them all. During the Dutch war of the '60s the administrative work of the Clerk of the Acts and the other Principal Officers of the Navy was of first-rate political importance and not infrequently demanded attention at the highest level. The King several times heard Pepys explain Navy Office business to the Privy Council and its committees, but it was in 1673–9, when the navy was ruled by a commission of which Pepys was secretary, that he and the King came to work together closely. In the last two years of its life, 1677–9, he and Charles virtually controlled everything without reference to the members of the commission.[5] Pepys found nothing to complain of in this, except that Charles's informal habits gave gentlemen-captains (those enemies to good discipline) too easy an access to the King's favour.[6] The King had by now developed the habit of consulting Pepys, and this was not allowed to end when he was forced for political reasons to dismiss him. Pepys was more than once, even when out of office in 1679–84, called upon to advise on appointments or on those matters of precedent and regulation which no-one but he knew so well. It was therefore natural that in 1683 the King should appoint him to the expedition sent to evacuate Tangier. In May 1684, shortly after Pepys's return, the King found it safe to dismiss his Admiralty Commissioners and in June he embarked on a new experiment, issuing letters patent appointing Pepys as his Secretary for the affairs of the Admiralty. At whose instance the arrangement was devised is not known, but Charles had in effect made Pepys his Colbert. He now had a secretary of state for the marine. This was the climax of their relationship, and this above all others was the moment at which Pepys, now virtually a secretary of state, might most fittingly have been rewarded with the knighthood which so mysteriously never came his way. But within a few months, in Feb. 1685, Charles had died.

Pepys was under no illusions about the weaknesses of his master – his laziness, his self-indulgence, his extravagance, his irresponsibility. But writing after Charles's death he gave his final verdict in terms of praise: 'It . . . had . . . pleased God to give us a King . . . that understood the sea.'[7]

Charleton, Walter (1619–1707). Physician to the King (1641). Educated at Oxford; a pupil of Wilkins and an original F.R.S. (1662). An author rather than a practising physician. According to Wood 'a learned and an unhappy man'.[1]

Charnock, [Roger]. An able Treasury official; first clerk before 1665; appointed serjeant to the Chancellor of the Exchequer in 1669; dismissed in 1671 when Downing left the office, but made serjeant to Shaftesbury in 1672.[1]

Charterhouse Yard (or Sq.). A large enclosed space on the south of the Charterhouse and midway between Goswell St and St John St; containing some notable houses. (R)

[Chase, John]. The King's apothecary from June 1660; Master of the Society of Apothecaries of London 1664–5.[1]

Chatham. Its dockyard, originally an advance base, was developed under Elizabeth and James I so that it became and for long remained the greatest of the royal yards. It was sufficiently near to London; its position on the Medway gave it easy access to the timber supplies of the Weald; and it was equipped by the 1620s with docks and storehouses (one of them 660 ft long). Its labour force amounted to c. 300 in 1661, and rose to over 1000 during the war years. Expansion brought with it problems of discipline, and in 1668 Commissioner Middleton complained that his workers at Portsmouth (whom he had sometimes governed with a cudgel) were saints compared with those he found at Chatham. Under the Special Commission of 1686–8 further building development took place and some 21 new storehouses were erected.[1]

The yard lost its pre-eminence in the course of the 18th century when the French wars made the Channel yards tactically more useful, and warships became too large for the Medway.

Hill House, an Elizabethan building close by the yard and north of the church, was leased to serve as a payhouse and to accommodate official visitors such as Pepys. It was pulled down 1803–5.[2]

THE CHATHAM CHEST

A fund established in 1590 for the relief and support of disabled seamen, its income derived mainly from compulsory contributions. It was managed by a board which was supposed to meet monthly and which consisted of five officers of the Chatham yard (its clerk being usually the Clerk of the Survey), under the presidency of a Principal Officer. It had no medical adviser, and beneficiaries were required to travel to Chatham where the chest itself (now in the National Maritime Museum) was kept. Its administration was lax despite occasional attempts at reform, and its income often used for other purposes. Payments, not surprisingly, were intermittent throughout the 17th century. Nothing seems to have come of an order for an investigation issued by the Admiral in Oct. 1660, but a commission of enquiry was set up in Nov. 1662, and of the 19 members Pepys proved the most active. Their letter book[1] shows that after a slow start they pursued their enquiries with vigour in the spring of 1664, fastening their criticisms particularly on Batten (who was Master) and Commissioner Pett. The Chest's functions were largely transferred in wartime to the Commissioners of the

Sick and Wounded. Pepys had a plan in the '80s for bringing merchant seamen into the scheme,[2] but it was never effected and the Chest remained a byword for inefficiency and corruption until its absorption into Greenwich Hospital in 1803.[3]

Cheapside. One of London's most important shopping streets. A busy and unusually wide thoroughfare, running west from the Poultry for 450 yards to St Paul's Churchyard. Traditionally famous for its fashionable shops – especially goldsmiths and mercers – it had by 1660 a more mixed character, though rents there remained very high. Its great food market was held in the street at its western end.[1]

Chelsea. A village on the Middlesex bank of the Thames, 2 miles upstream from London. A stretch of marshland effectively divided it from Westminster, but its proximity and the ease of access by road and river ensured that it was well-tenanted. Its gardens and its reputation for good air added to its popularity. According to one estimate, it had under 40 houses in 1664,[1] but the hearth-tax of that year shows 126 with another 36 too small to be taxed.[2]

Little Chelsea was a hamlet upstream from the main village and in the parish of Kensington. (R)

Cherrett (Charett), Madame. Milliner, at 'The French house', in Covent Garden. The establishment (in James St, off the Piazza) was a large one, Abel Cherrett, a registered alien, paying on 15 hearths in 1666. John Cherrett appears as a taxpayer on a smaller house in the same street in 1668 and 1669; thereafter Madame Cherrett occupied one of the lowest-rated houses in the Piazza itself.[1]

Chetwind, [James] (d. 1663). Chancery clerk; a member of Pepys's 'old club' of government clerks in the '50s; related to two other members in that he his sister Margaret was the wife of Thomas Lea and his wife Margaret the sister of Will Symons. He lodged with Richard Hargrave of St Martin's Lane. At his death in 1663 he had over £2000 on deposit with his bankers. Lea, Symons and Hargrave were appointed executors under his will.[1]

Chicheley. A Cambridgeshire family settled at Wimpole since Henry VI's reign. Henry Chichele, the 15th-century Archbishop of Canterbury, was a member. Its head in the diary period was Sir Thomas (1614–99), whom Pepys first met as an officer of the Ordnance where he was an industrious Commissioner (1664–70) and Master-General (1670–9). Knighted and made a Privy Councillor in 1670, he held several other national and local offices (including that of Admiralty Commissioner 1677–9) and was, in Pepys's phrase, a 'high-flying' M.P. for the county (1640–2, 1661–Jan. 79) and for Cambridge borough (March 1679–90). Pepys remarks on his extravagance: it led in fact to his having to sell Wimpole in 1684. He had a town house (taxed on nine hearths) in Great Queen St.[1]

His second son Sir John (c. 1640–91) – no friend of Sandwich – was counted 'the best of the young seamen' by Coventry.[2] He served with distinction in the war of 1665–7 and was knighted after his first campaign. He was Vice-Admiral of the squadron sent to the Mediterranean in 1670, and flew his flag as Rear-Admiral throughout most of the war of 1672–4. He was briefly a prisoner of war after the Battle of Sole Bay 1672. He later served as a Commissioner on the Navy Board 1675–80, the Admiralty 1682–4 and 1689–90, and the Ordnance 1682–90. He was M.P. for Newton, March 1679–91, voted against exclusion, and accepted the Glorious Revolution unwillingly.[3]

Sir Thomas's brother, Sir Henry, Pepys met only once, on his way to Holland in 1660. He had lived in Virginia since c. 1656 and later (1670–83) became a Councillor of State and Deputy-Governor of the colony.[4]

Chiffinch. The brothers Tom and Will Chiffinch made their careers as court officials of Charles I and Charles II, and after the Restoration became associated with the worst aspects of court life – its libertinage, corruption and subservience to the French connection. Tom, the elder (1600–66), was Keeper of the Closet and Keeper of the Jewels to Charles II and often acted as the King's agent in the purchase of pictures. Will (1602–88) succeeded to most of his brother's offices at his death, and it is he who is primarily responsible (with Walter Scott in *Peveril of the Peak*) for the brothers' reputation. He handled the pension paid by Louis XIV to Charles and acted as Charles's pimp. His biographer in the *Dictionary of National Biography* remarks that he carried 'the abuse of backstairs influence to scientific perfection'.[1]

Child, Sir Josiah, 1st Bt (1630–99). One of the greatest merchants of the day (Director of the E. India Company from 1677; later Deputy-Governor and Governor) and as author of *A new discourse on trade* (1668) an important theorist of mercantilism. A man of these names was Deputy-Treasurer of the fleet in 1655. In the '60s Child supplied victuals to the fleet and in 1668 was considered for the post of official victualler. From humble beginnings he ended as one of the richest men in London and as grandfather of a duke (Beaufort) and of a duchess (Bedford). His alterations to the grounds of Wanstead manor (bought in 1673) were, according to Evelyn, both vast and tasteless. He was generally unpopular, but Pepys found him 'mighty understanding'. He was made a baronet in 1678.[1]

Child(e), William (c. 1606–97). Lay clerk, St George's Chapel, Windsor 1630, organist 1632; appointed to the King's Private Musick and an organist of the Chapel Royal 1660; D.Mus. Oxon. 1663. A composer of anthems, catches and ayres whose works were studied by Blow and Henry Purcell.[1] (Lu)

Chillenden, Capt. [Edmund]. A prominent sectary; lieutenant in Whalley's regiment 1647–8; captain 1650. In the quarrels between Parliament and the New Model army (1647–8) he took the side of the radicals, helping to present their case in the Putney debates in the General Council of the army. Later, in 1653, he became a preacher. In 1668 he appears to have been used in Coventry's moves to defend himself against charges of corruption.[1] In 1677 a warrant for his arrest was issued on charges of publishing and disseminating false news in a coffee-house he kept in Leadenhall St.[2]

Chiverton, Ald. [Sir Richard] (1606–79). Merchant; Governor of the Eastland Company 1654–5; knighted 1658 and 1663; Sheriff 1650–1; Lord Mayor 1657–8. He ceased to live in London after the Fire.[1]

Cholmley, Sir Hugh, 4th Bt (1632–89). Engineer; son of Sir Hugh Cholmley of Whitby, Yorks. Having established his reputation in the construction of Whitby pier, he was given charge in 1663 of the building of the mole at Tangier. He and his wife (Lady Anne Compton, daughter of the 2nd Earl of Northampton) lived there at intervals until he was replaced by Sheeres as Surveyor-General of the project in 1676. Pepys had a high regard for him[1] but preferred Sheeres's method of constructing the mole. From c. 1662 he was First Gentleman-Usher to the Queen – hence his flow of information about the court – and in parliament in 1679 and 1685 proved to be a loyal but not uncritical opponent of exclusion. His personal papers are impressively tidy and well-ordered,[2] and his account of his Tangier career (published in 1787) very readable.[3] [*See also* Tangier: the mole]

CHRISTENINGS

Pepys gives the impression, no doubt correctly, that these were predominantly social occasions. Of the 16 he describes only one (a Huguenot ceremony) took place in church,[1] and rather more than half were held on weekdays. The habit of holding the ceremony privately in the home was allowable as a means of ensuring baptism for infants who were in danger of dying, as many were, and during the Interregnum it had had the additional advantage of enabling the Prayer-Book service to be used in safety. But used generally, as the practice now was (even Milles, Pepys's parish priest, had his child baptised privately in 1667) it negated or obscured one of the purposes of baptism – the public admission of the child into the church. Evelyn thought that the practice was rooted in 'the pride of Women',[2] who came to regard it as a mark of social success to have the ceremony held at home, and in circumstances which allowed them to choose sponsors

for their social importance. The number of titled sponsors mentioned
by Pepys is in fact striking. The practice persisted, especially among the
middle and upper classes, despite the protests of bishops and reforming
clergy, until the late 19th century.[3]

Christmas, ——. Schoolfellow of Pepys. The records of St Paul's
School before the Fire are defective and he has not been traced. The
diary suggests that he came of a landed family in Essex, and there were
several of that name in the south and south-east of the county. Whitear's
guess that he was probably a son of Thomas Christmas, a tailor, seems
to have no basis except the coincidence that the father was admitted a
freeman of the Merchant Taylors' Company at the same time as Pepys's
father.[1]

CHRISTMAS AND TWELFTH NIGHT

There were other styles of Christmas than Pepys's. One is the Christmas
of the country gentleman who took it as a duty that followed from his
station in life to dispense hospitality at this season to his tenants and
poor neighbours. Evelyn's Christmases were a series of dinners between
Christmas Day and Epiphany at which he was the host to gatherings of
this sort. Pepys gives a glimpse of that same variety in his marvellous
vignette of the Scrooge-like Christmas of the Downings in their
country house, with Downing and his old mother congratulating themselves on the broth with which they treat their neighbours (viii.85).
Pepys's own Christmas may be taken as typical of the celebrations of
the middle-class Londoner. His celebrations, too, express social obliga-
tions – in his case to family, neighbourhood and colleagues. All join in
provided they live within easy reach. Even with old enemies like the
Penns there was 'much correspondence' at Christmas time.

The Christmas fare Pepys ate was much the same as ours – turkey,
beef, mince pies and plum porridge. There were evergreen decorations
(at any rate in public places); wassailers sang carols; the household
played games until the small hours; theatres put on plays (though no
recognisably modern pantomimes until 1717).[1] The biggest difference
was perhaps that the season had a shape – a beginning, a middle and an
end. It began with a holy day; it had at its centre a festive day, New
Year's Day, and it ended with a carnival, Twelfth Night. During the
twelve days work did not entirely stop – Boxing Day was often a busy
day for the Navy Board – but for most of the season it took second
place to entertainment. For Pepys – with guests even for breakfast – it
was a season of almost unending sociability.

Christmas Day itself was a quiet day for him. He usually spent it alone with his wife and always went to church. Once, in 1662, he almost went to communion. On Boxing Day (which he never refers to by that name – it did not then exist) he would distribute his 'boxes' to tradesmen, porters and the like. The last days of the year were the time for paying bills, making up the old year's accounts and writing out the new year's vows. Placeholders at court exchanged presents and were in duty bound to give them to the King, but there was very little present-giving between private individuals. Pepys once gave a New Year's gift of gloves to his mistress, Doll Lane, and at New Year 1669 gave his wife a valuable walnut cabinet – probably a peace offering after his affair with Deb. New Year's Day was the great day for feasting, but the climax came on Twelfth Night when guests were bidden to supper. Sometimes there was music and dancing; always there was the eating of the Twelfth Night cake in which (according to immemorial custom) a bean and a pea were concealed. The cake was divided so that one of the men got the bean and one of the women the pea. They then became king and queen for the evening and ruled the revels until midnight, when the company dispersed and Christmas was over.

Christmas had been frowned on by the Puritans, but Cromwell's London was not Calvin's Geneva and little had been changed except for the abolition (itself never completely enforced) of the Prayer-Book service for Christmas Day. In describing his Christmases in the '60s Pepys never remarks on their being novel or different from those of the '50s.[2]

Christ's Hospital. The Bluecoat school for orphans and other poor children – mostly boys – founded in 1552 under the authority of the city corporation and occupying the site of the dissolved Greyfriars monastery in Newgate St. Its buildings were badly damaged in the Fire and the children dispersed to Ware and Hertford. By 1680 the school was rebuilt, and by 1687 housed close on 800 pupils.[1] In 1892 it was transferred to Horsham in Sussex.

From the 1670s Pepys was to have a close connection with it. He took a leading part in the establishment in 1673 of the Royal Mathematical School in which 40 boys were trained in the science of navigation for the royal and mercantile navies. After his appointment as a Governor of the foundation in 1675 he produced two masterly memoranda – one on the administration of the Mathematical School (1677), the other on the grammar school (1682) – but then ceased to attend meetings for about ten years in protest against the appointment of a master of the former who besides knowing nothing of navigation had never seen the sea. In 1692 he began a remarkable single-handed campaign to reform the financial administration of the Hospital and to improve the standard of teaching in the Mathematical School. Faced by obstruction on the governing body, he presented a report which set out his charges in crushing detail to the Lord Mayor and Aldermen. When, in turn, the Lord Mayor blocked discussion, Pepys forced his hand by publishing pamphlets. He won: by 1699 his critics were flattened and the two principal offenders (the treasurer and the mathematics master) replaced. Pepys was made Vice-President; but by then was too ill to do more. There remains in his library, besides a charming coloured drawing of a boy and girl of the Hospital, a vast manuscript of 800-odd pages in which are collected his papers on the disputes. It is as impressive a memorial as any other to the qualities that made him so efficient and so formidable a public servant.[2]

Churchyard Stairs. The landing-stairs at the foot of Churchyard Alley, Upper Thames St, immediately upstream of old London Bridge; now absorbed in the approaches to the present London Bridge. (R)

Clapham, [John]. Clerk in the Navy Office to Sir T. Hervey 1667–8.[1]

Clapham, Surrey. A village of 92 houses in 1664,[1] some 4½ miles from the Standard on Cornhill, on the road to Richmond. A number of well-to-do Londoners lived or had country villas there, including Gauden, the Navy Victualler, who lived in a large house which after 1688 became Pepys's country retreat. He spent many happy months in his 'Paradisian Clapham' as Evelyn called it,[2] and it was there that he died. (R)

Clare (New) Market. To the south-west of Lincoln's Inn Fields, between them and the Strand. Established by the 1st Earl of Clare when the district was growing in the second quarter of the 17th century, it was at first known both as the 'New Market' and as 'Clare Market' (its later name). It specialised in meat and fish. (R)

Clarendon, Earl of: *see* Hyde, E.

Clarendon House. A palatial house on the n. side of Piccadilly built for Clarendon in 1664–8 to Roger Pratt's design. It stood on eight acres (now bisected by Albemarle St) in open country, save for the great houses of Lord Berkeley and Lord Burlington on either side, and was assessed on 101 hearths. It looked down onto the modest Tudor of St James's Palace – a conspicuous symbol of Clarendon's power and an obvious target when he fell into disrepute in the Second Dutch War. Scandalmongers put it about that he had built it from the proceeds of bribery, using stone meant for the repair of St Paul's and timber meant for the navy. Pepys reports its unpopularity in a famous passage at 14 June 1667, but there is no evidence that it became unpopular before that disastrous summer. Clarendon himself later regretted his folly in undertaking such a 'rash enterprise, that proved so fatal and mischievous . . . not only in the accumulation of envy and prejudice

... but in the entanglement of a great debt . . .'. The house proved too much for his heirs. Let to the Duke of Ormond in 1670, it was sold in 1675 to the 2nd Duke of Albemarle who got rid of it to speculators in 1683. The house was then demolished and its grounds converted into streets.[1]

Clarges, Sir Thomas (c. 1618–95). Son of a London blacksmith and trained as an apothecary, he served in the parliamentary army as a doctor. His association with Monck, who married his sister, gave him his chance to enter politics: in 1656 he was elected to Parliament and by 1658–60 was acting as Monck's political agent in London. He was made Commissary-General of Musters when Monck arrived with his army in London in Feb. 1660 and was sent as the army's envoy to Breda to invite the King over. In Parliament (where he sat for various constituencies in 1660 and 1666–95) he proved to be a frequent and effective speaker. He was critical of the Navy Board, and especially of Batten and Penn, in the debates of 1668, and remained an independent-minded member under James and William.[1]

Clarke, [Julian]. Pepys's 'Aunt Kite'; widow of Elias Clarke. Her first husband, whom she married in 1638, was William Kite, butcher, of Whitechapel (d. c. 1652), brother of Margaret Kite, Pepys's mother. She was living in Wentworth St, Stepney, when she made her will on 7 Sept. 1661. She died on the 12th, leaving most of her property (which included houses and money) to Margaret, her only child, a daughter by her first marriage, and small legacies to her second husband's three sons. Her 'cousin' Pepys and her brother-in-law Thomas Fenner were executors.[1]

Clarke, Capt. Robert (d. by 1688). A friend of Pepys who had risen to captain's rank in the Commonwealth navy. He held ten commands during the diary period, and was rated 'very good' by Coventry.[1] In May 1666, leading a squadron in the *Gloucester*, he captured seven Dutch ships off Texel. He was criticised in 1667 for his conduct during the raid on the Medway in allowing the *Monmouth* to be towed away from the scene of action.[2]

Clarke, Dr [Timothy]. Friend and royal physician. He took his M.D. at Oxford in 1652, and in 1660 (after sailing in the *Naseby* with Pepys to bring home the King) was made physician to the royal household, becoming physician-in-ordinary to the King's person in 1667. He was an original F.R.S. and in 1662–4 served on the Council of the Society. In the war he was employed by the Commissioners for Sick and Wounded. A man of wide culture, he was fond of the theatre, and wrote a play. His wife Frances was alive at his death in 1672. Her wit and good looks, Pepys found, did not compensate for her conceit and her sluttish housekeeping. Besides, she painted her face.[1]

Clarke, Sir William (?1623–66). One of the new men who rose in the public service – apparently from nothing – during the Civil War: he was Assistant-Secretary to the General Council of the Army 1646, Secretary 1647; joint-Secretary to General Fairfax 1648-9; Secretary to the Scottish command 1650, and to Monck and the army H.Q. in Scotland 1651-60. He came back to England with Monck at the Restoration and was knighted and made Secretary at War in 1661. He remained Monck's right-hand man, and was killed on board his ship in 1666. John Rushworth, his senior in the service of the army council, was possibly his most important ally before he was attached to Monck. Like Pepys, he was a man of method: the diary he kept on board ship in the campaign of 1666 has much useful information.[1] Many of his papers now survive at Worcester College, Oxford, and include his well-known reports of the debates in the army council which reveal the political state of the army in the period leading up to the execution of the King. In taking his notes he used a shorthand similar to that used by Pepys.[2]

Claxton, ——. Hammond Claxton, of Booton, Norf.; possibly the Hammond Claxton who was admitted to Caius College, Cambridge, in 1637. He married Pepys's cousin Paulina, daughter of Talbot Pepys of Impington, in Dec. 1647, she being then 24. She kept house at Impington for her brother Roger when he was a widower 1662-3.[1]

Cleggat, Col. Of St Alfege's parish, Greenwich. A Capt. Thomas Clygate occurs in the parish register for 1648.[1]

Clements, ——. Bo'sun of the *Royal Charles* in 1662. He appears to be the John Clements who was recommended as a ship's master by Phineas Pett in 1665, and from 1667 onwards (until at least 1688) served as captain of several royal yachts. In 1688 he was captain of the *Cambridge*, a 3rd-rate.[1]

Clerke, Sir Francis, kt 1660 (c. 1624-86). Gentleman of the Privy Chamber to the King 1660; elected M.P. for Rochester 1661, 1681, 1685. A member of the committee of enquiry into the Chatham Chest 1662, and a sub-commissioner for prizes 1665. Charges of peculation were brought against him in the latter capacity in 1670. His (second) wife was Elizabeth, widow of John Hastings of Woodlands, Dorset.[1]

Clerke, Mrs. Pepys's landlady at Greenwich, Oct. 1665-Jan. 1666. Possibly Sara, daughter of Thomas Clarke; baptised May 1624.[1]

Clerke, ——. Milliner, Fenchurch St. Probably Andrew Clerke, who in 1666 had an establishment taxed on five hearths on the corner of Fenchurch St and Philpot Lane.[1]

Clerkenwell. A rapidly developing suburb immediately north of the city, within walking distance for Pepys over the fields. Formed into a separate parish at the Dissolution, it contained some of the great houses which have always ringed central London. In the '60s the Bishop of London, the Duke of Newcastle, the Earls of Essex and of Elgin, Lord

Berkeley and a number of other notables had houses there. It contained schools too – Peg Penn went to boarding school there – and prisons. The New Bridewell (vi.66, n.1) was a workhouse established under an act of 1662 maintained by the parishes of Middlesex. Later in the 17th century it became a 'House of Industry' for pauper children and then a Quaker workhouse and charity school. The 'new prison' (ix.130), north of Clerkenwell Green, was established in 1615 and demolished c. 1804. (R)

Clifford, Sir Thomas, 1st Baron Clifford (1630–73). One of the ablest and boldest politicians of his day; a strong supporter of royal power and the Catholic interest and a violent enemy of the Dutch. M.P. for Totnes 1660, 1661–72; a Privy Councillor from 1666; cr. baron 1672. The principal offices he held were those of Comptroller, then Treasurer of the Household 1666–72; Treasury Commissioner 1667–72 and Lord Treasurer 1672–3; he was also a Gentleman of the Privy Chamber 1660–73, a Fishery Commissioner from 1664, a sub-commissioner of the Sick and Wounded and a Commissioner for Prizes 1664–7. He served in the fleet in the Second Dutch War and had a large part in precipitating the war of 1672–4. Pepys remarks more than once on his ability and his astonishing rise to power. He resigned after the Test Act in 1673, being received into the Catholic church at about that time. His death shortly after was said (probably wrongly) to have been suicide.[1]

Clodius (Clod), [Frederick]. Physician and 'mystical chemist', probably of German extraction. He lived in a sizeable house (taxed on eight hearths) in Axe Yard, next door to the Hartlibs, whose daughter Mary he married in 1660. A minor figure in scientific circles and a friend of Robert Boyle.[1]

Clothes: *see* Dress and Personal Appearance

Clothier, [John] (d. by 1670). Rope merchant, Woolwich.[1]

Clothworkers' Hall. 'A brave hall' (i.187). The building (set back from Mincing Lane, just south of Fenchurch St) was put up in the mid-16th century; the dining hall itself (to which Pepys probably refers) was rebuilt in 1633–4. It was all destroyed in the Fire and rebuilt by 1668. This Hall was replaced in 1856–7 by a building which was itself destroyed on 10 May 1941. It has since been rebuilt.

Pepys was elected Master of the Company in 1677 (though having no previous connection with it); the Company still possesses the cup, rose-water dish and ewer he gave to mark his term of office.[1]

Clun, Walter. Actor in the King's Company from 1660; murdered 1664. One of Pepys's favourite actors. He had taken women's parts as a boy before the Civil War.[1]

Clutterbuck. The member of the Mercers' Company (v.37) was Richard Clutterbuck (Master 1650–1; d. 1670).[1] The consul at Leghorn (ix.346) was Thomas (kt 1669), contractor for the Mediterranean victualling 1674–8.[2]

Cocke, Col. Charles George. Civil lawyer; a member of the Hale commission for the reform of the law (1652), a judge of Admiralty and Probate and of the High Court (app. 1653). Author of *England's compleat law-judge and lawyer* (1656) which argued for the retention of the civil law in the administration of probate. He was Steward of the city of Norwich and an active committee man in Norfolk during the Interregnum.[1]

Cocke, Capt. [George] (c. 1617–79). Baltic merchant and navy contractor, of London and Greenwich; a native of Newcastle upon Tyne (which played an important part in trade to Scandinavia). He was an influential member of the Eastland Company, dealt extensively in hemp and owned a tannery in Limerick. He had served in the Marquess of Newcastle's royalist army and had been taken prisoner 1643–4. His claim to have been in the confidence of Charles I (v.335) may, if true, have related to the King's stay in Newcastle. Pepys found him a lively companion, though inclined to talk and drink too much. He had a wide range of interests and was elected F.R.S. in 1666. He had a sinecure post in the Newcastle customs service, was a farmer of the hearth-tax and served on the commission of enquiry into the Chatham Chest.[1] As Treasurer of the Commission for Sick and Wounded Seamen (1665–7) he ran into trouble with his accounts and had to face trial in 1670.[2] There are several indications in the diary of his being regarded as untrustworthy. He was never employed on any of the Council committees for trade.

His house in London was in the parish of St Peter-le-Poer and was taxed on ten hearths. His (first) wife was Anna Maria Solomons of Danzig (where he lived in 1656 as an agent of the Eastland Company). He had five sons at his death. Brouncker was given a ring at his funeral.[3]

Cocke, [Robert]. Merchant at Lisbon; navy victualler in the Mediterranean from 1661. Brother of George.[1]

Cocker, [Edward] (1631–76). The best-known English writing master of the period; unique in the charm as well as the sheer volume of his published work. He was both a calligrapher and an engraver, and his books gave practical advice (as he himself did to Pepys) as well as examples of his work. He is said to have died of drinking brandy. Pepys retained four of his books in his 'Calligraphical Collection': they bear titles like *Penna Volans, or The young man's accomplishment*. The proverbial phrase 'according to Cocker' (meaning exact) refers to the popular and long-lived arithmetic text-books attributed to him.[1]

Cockpit Playhouse. Set back to the east of the e. side of Drury Lane, Pit (formerly Cockpit) Court possibly indicating its site. Built as a cockpit c. 1610 but converted into a playhouse by Christopher Beeston in 1616. Used as a theatre until 1642 and again, in 1648–58, when government regulations could be interpreted to allow it. In 1658 and after, John Rhodes reassembled a company there which was acting at the Restoration. In Oct. 1660 companies under Davenant and Killigrew acted there until, in November, Davenant and his company moved to Salisbury Court Playhouse and Killigrew to the King's Playhouse. Save for George Jolly's performances in 1662 and 1665 and various unauthorised productions this seems to have been the end of the Cockpit Theatre as such. References to it often omit the word 'theatre'. It is to be distinguished from the Cockpit in Whitehall Palace where plays were also given. [*See also* Theatre] (R)

COFFEE-HOUSES

Coffee and coffee-houses were innovations in London. They were introduced to the capital from Oxford where the first coffee-house had been set up by Jacob, a Jew, in 1650.[1] Two years later he moved to London and established himself in Holborn. By May 1663 there were 82 similar traders in the city, most of them near the Exchange, paying 1s. annually for their licences and giving sureties for good behaviour.[2] They provided simple accommodation (usually stools and tables in a single room) and the simplest of refreshment – coffee at 1d. a dish, and in some cases tea or chocolate. But their success was immediate. Coffee-houses proved to be useful resorts at which friends could gather, business could be transacted and (above all) news retailed. The landlords responded to demand and to competition by providing newsbooks and newsletters, selling pamphlets and displaying notices and advertisements. Their number rapidly increased with the development of the London season. At the same time the number of taverns did not decrease; there was plenty of business for both. By Anne's reign the coffee-houses whose names are known totalled about 500.[3]

Early in their history they were used by coteries in need of regular meeting places. In 1655 at Oxford the premises of Arthur Tillyard over against All Souls became a centre for the meetings of a group of virtuosi some of whom were later to form the nucleus of the Royal Society of London. Similarly fellows of the Royal Society from about 1664 often met at the Grecian in Threadneedle St after official meetings of the Society.[4] Miles's coffee-house in Westminster (the first mentioned in the diary) was the venue of the Rota Club which met for a few weeks just before the Restoration for discussion of James Harrington's model for a republican constitution. But once the monarchy was restored political discussion of this sort was inappropriate and, in the view of officialdom, dangerous. Clubs for political debate were closed or went underground; coffee-houses in a sense replaced them, becoming centres for the political malcontents in Restoration London. They often provided customers with opposition newsletters written specially for their clients. In 1666 Clarendon for a while favoured a proposal to close them all down because of the danger in time of war of false news, and in Dec. 1675 a proclamation was issued to that effect – probably in order to terrify the coffee-house keepers into good behaviour – only to be withdrawn after a few weeks.[5] It always remained possible to take action in particular cases. In 1677 Edmund Chillenden, who appears in the diary as a Cromwellian army captain and a sectary, and in the '70s had become keeper of a coffee-house in the city, was arrested for 'publishing and dispersing' false news.[6] At the same time the coffee-houses could be to some extent used by the government for its own purposes. Clarendon in 1666 came to prefer this to a policy of suppression. Pepys himself was in 1665 asked by Batten to use the coffee-houses to put about stories of Dutch maltreatment of our seamen. They would there 'spread like the leprosy'.[7]

Coffee-houses throughout their history have usually been known by the names of their proprietors – Lloyd's (which became the insurance exchange), and two which became clubs (Boodle's and White's) being among the best-known surviving examples. Pepys made some 80 visits but rarely gives the house a name. Miles's, or the Turk's Head, where Pepys went to meetings of the Rota Club, was by the waterside at Westminster. John Aubrey, also a member, describes how the members sat round a large oval table 'with a passage in the middle for Miles to deliver his coffee'.[8] Grant's has not been identified. The coffee-houses Pepys went to near the Royal Exchange are difficult to disentangle from one another. There are references, which cease with the Fire, to 'the great house' by the Exchange. This was almost certainly the house in Exchange Alley (taxed on four hearths)[9] kept by Walter Elford, one of the most active of the first generation of coffee-house keepers, who is reputed to have invented a mechanical turning jack to operate his coffee roaster. His house was sometimes known as the Great Turk, or Morat's Head. Another house near by, in Sweeting's Rents, taxed on six hearths, was kept by Thomas Garraway. Thomas Grant appears to have been selling coffee there since c. 1658. The house was sometimes known as the Sultaness's Head and was much used by merchants from the Exchange. After the Fire Garraway moved eventually (c. 1670) to Exchange Alley to larger premises (taxed on 16 hearths, 1675), built on the site of Elford's house.[10] There Garraway's became famous for its auctions and enjoyed a long and prosperous history. It figures in Dickens and ceased business as a coffee-house only in 1866.

In a famous passage (v.37) Pepys describes a visit to the 'great coffee house' in Covent Garden, at which Dryden and the wits met. This was almost certainly Will's, at the corner of Bow St and Russell St, so-called (it is usually held) because kept by William Urwin. (A difficulty is that Urwin does not occur in the rate books of St Paul's parish until 1671.) Pepys however does not give it that name. When he refers to 'Will's' he is referring to a tavern in Old Palace Yard.[11] [*See also* Drink]

Coke, Sir John (1563–1644). Navy Commissioner 1618–25; Secretary of State 1625–38.[1]

Coke, Sir Robert (d. 1653). Son of Chief Justice Coke (d. 1634), and a neighbour of John Pepys of Ashtead. His wife was Theophila, daughter of Elizabeth Lady Berkeley, through whom he acquired his house, the Durdans, nr Epsom. He bequeathed it to his nephew George Lord Berkeley, afterwards Earl of Berkeley.[1]

Colborne, Nicholas, vintner: see Taverns etc.: Sun, Threadneedle St

Cole, ——. Lawyer, of Gray's Inn. Probably either William, admitted 1634, or William, admitted 1644.[1]

Coleman, [Catherine]. Actress and singer, wife of Edward Coleman. It has been claimed that she was, as Ianthe in *The siege of Rhodes*, the first woman to appear on the English stage (Davenant's patent specifically permitted this).[1] (Lu)

Coleman, [Edward] (d. 1669). Composer and singer, appointed to the King's Private Musick, and to the Chapel Royal, 1660. Set James Shirley's masque *The contention of Ajax and Ulysses* (1653), sang Alphonso in *The siege of Rhodes* (1656), represented in *Select musicall ayres and dialogues* (1653) and *The musical companion* (1672).[1] (Lu)

Coleman, [Edward]. Gentleman-pensioner of the King's Band of Pensioners.[1]

Coleman, young. Not identifiable for certain. Dr Charles Coleman (d. 1664) composer and violist, who was a member of the King's Musick by 1625, had two sons, Edward (q.v.), and Charles (d. 1694), violist and member of the Private Musick from 1660. Charles, who appears to have been the younger brother, could therefore have been known as 'young Coleman'; so, equally, could Edward.[1] (Lu)

Co(o)ling, [Richard] (d. 1697). Public servant and friend. His unashamed delight in bribes is reported at viii.369. He came of a family that produced several public servants, among them William Coling who was Thomas Turner's assistant in the Navy Office just before the Restoration.[1] He himself was secretary to the Lord Chamberlain from 1660 until his death, combining it with other offices such as Commissioner for licensing hackney coaches (app. 1670), Clerk of the Robes in the Great Wardrobe (app. 1670), and Clerk-in-extraordinary to the

Privy Council (app. 1679).[2] His brother (i.206) seems to have been the Benjamin Coling who when he died in 1700 was Usher to the House of Lords, Chief Crier to the King's Bench, Keeper of the Chamber to the Privy Council and a customs official.[3] Richard also had a well-placed cousin as Keeper of the Marshalsea to whom he appealed on Pepys's behalf in 1679 when Pepys was a prisoner there. In 1687, he sent Pepys 12 bundles of 'state letters' to peruse. (Pepys in his turn had in 1678 used his influence to find a place on board the *Bristol* for his son.)[4]

Colladon, Sir John, kt 1664. Physician to the Queen; a naturalised Frenchman, living in St Martin's-in-the-Fields, not far from Alexander St Michel with whom he shared a patent for curing smoky chimneys.[1]

Colleton, Sir John, bt 1661 (d. 1666). Merchant; a Devonshire kinsman of Albemarle and an ex-royalist who had large plantations in Barbados. He served on several committees on trade 1660–6, and was one of the proprietors of the New Carolinas (1663).[1]

Collins, ——. Employed by the Brooke House Committee: possibly John Collins, until c. 1668 in the excise service.[1]

Colvill, [John]. Goldsmith-banker of Lombard St 1655–66, and of Lime St 1666–d. 70; Prime Warden of the Goldsmiths' Company 1669–70. Pepys dealt with him on both private and Tangier business. It was reported that he died £400,000 in debt but with 'an estate to satisfie his creditors to a penny, and a very great estate over-plus'.[1]

Colwall, [Daniel] (d. 1690). A wealthy citizen; an original F.R.S. and Treasurer of the Society 1665–79. He lived on Tower Hill in 1666 in a large house taxed on 12 hearths.[1]

Comberford, [Nicholas] (fl. 1646–66). Chart-maker at the sign of the Platt in the w. end of the School House, Ratcliffe. Like his pupil Burston, a leading member of the Thames school of chart-makers.[1]

Commander, [Henry]. Scrivener: he lived in a house taxed on seven hearths in Round Court off the e. side of Warwick Lane in St Faith's parish.[1]

Compton, Sir William (c. 1625–63). Master-General of the Ordnance 1660–3; M.P. for Cambridge borough 1661–3; Tangier commissioner 1662–3. The ablest of six remarkable sons of the 2nd Earl of Northampton, he had given distinguished service to the royalists both in the Civil War and in the underground resistance movement of the '50s, being briefly imprisoned in Sept. 1659. His sobriety and godliness won him the respect and admiration of Cromwell.[1]

Conny (Coney), [John]. Surgeon to the extraordinaries, Chatham, (app. June 1660); still in post 1679; Master of the Barber-Surgeons' Company 1689.[1]

Cooke, [Edward]. Underclerk in the Council of State; dismissed May 1660.[1]

Cooke, Capt. Henry (c. 1615–72). Composer, chiefly of verse anthems, but there are catches in *Catch that catch can* (1667); singer (bass); and lutenist. Appointed Master of the Boys in the Private Musick, and of the Children of the Chapel Royal, 1660. Served in royalist forces in Civil War; took part in Davenant's operatic enterprises during the Interregnum, both contributing music to, and singing in, *The siege of Rhodes*. According to Evelyn (28 Oct. 1654) 'esteem'd the best singer after the Italian manner of any in England'. John Blow, Pelham Humfrey and Henry Purcell were among his pupils. On his death the Treasury owed him over £1000.[1] (Lu)

Cooke, [John] (d. 1691). Elected Fellow of Trinity College, Cambridge 1637; (possibly) employed by the Prize Commissioners in the First Dutch War; secretary to Lockhart, Governor of Dunkirk 1658–60; under-secretary in the Secretary of State's office 1660–88; Secretary for the Latin Tongue 1682–91.[1]

Cooke, Capt. [Thomas] (d. by 1698). Master of the Tennis Court, Whitehall c. 1660–c. 98; possibly the Thomas Cooke who c. 1666 was an assistant groom of the Privy Chamber. He was responsible for the construction of the new tennis court in 1662–3.[1]

Cooke, ——. Bookbinder. Probably Samuel Cook, made free of the Stationers' Company Dec. 1660. From 1668–77 in White Lion Court, Bell Alley.[1]

Cooper, Sir Anthony Ashley, cr. Baron Ashley 1661, Earl of Shaftesbury 1672 (1621–83). Pepys knew him in the diary period as a financial administrator – as Chancellor of the Exchequer (1661–72), Treasury Commissioner (1667–72), Treasurer of the Commission for Prizes (1665–7), and as an active member of the Tangier and Fishery Committees. He was, as Pepys recognised, one of the ablest men in public life. Later, his attacks in the '70s on the Duke of York inevitably made him Pepys's enemy, and it is clear that he was behind the attempt to unseat Pepys as an M.P. in Feb. 1674, though not so clear that he was responsible for the attempt to implicate him in treason in 1679.

His reputation has always stood low – and for two reasons. One is that he changed sides so often in the Civil War and Interregnum. But this was typical of the behaviour of many of his contemporaries whose concern, like his, was to keep government on an even keel; and it is clear that through all the changes he was faithful to a lifelong belief in limited government and religious toleration. The other reason for his low reputation is that he is blamed for bringing the country to the edge of civil war in the Popish Plot crisis by exploiting stories of a Catholic rising, stirring up the London rabble, riding armed with armed followers to the Oxford parliament of 1681 – and all in order to force his puppet Monmouth onto the throne. The likelihood is however that he was never committed to Monmouth's cause and never seriously plotted violence: his aim was to force a change of policy and ministry on the King, and he was using the only methods (admittedly extreme ones) open to him. He failed, and died in exile. All told, his contributions to political and religious liberty, to legal and financial reform, and (in his work for Carolina) to the establishment of new English societies across the Atlantic, are those of a creative statesman. It is not inappropriate that John Locke was his devoted secretary.

His (third) wife was Margaret, daughter of the 2nd Baron Spencer and niece of the Earl of Southampton; she married him in 1655 and died in 1693.

In 1660–3 his London house was in Great Queen St; in 1663–76 he lived at Little Exeter House in the Strand.[1]

Cooper, [Henry] (d. 1687). Clerk of the Works, Hampton Court and Bushey Park 1661–87.[1]

Cooper, [Richard]. The one-eyed sailing master (iv.133). Pepys had known him in the *Royal Charles* in 1660, and in July 1662 met him again when paying off the *Royal James*, on which he had served as master's mate. Then unemployed, he was taken on by Pepys to teach him mathematics and other lore of his trade. His payment, it seems, took the form of promotion: in Aug. 1662 he was made, at Pepys's request, master of the *Reserve* in which Robert Holmes flew his flag on a voyage to the Mediterranean. They quarrelled – Holmes was not invariably an easy man and Cooper was not invariably sober – and their dispute came before the Navy Board. Pepys at first resisted Holmes's demand for Cooper's discharge, but gave way to dark threats of a duel. But almost immediately afterwards – it is easy to guess at whose suggestion – Cooper was made master of Sandwich's flagship the *Prince*. Sandwich's journal records his observations of two meteors.[1]

Cooper, Samuel (1609–72). Miniaturist. He lived in Henrietta St, Covent Garden c. 1650–72. His cousin Jack was the son of John Hoskins, the uncle from whom Cooper seems to have learnt painting. Cooper was said to be one of the best lutenists of his day.[1]

Cooper, [William] (d. by 1666). Timber purveyor to the Navy Board in Epping Forest and Alice Holt.[1]

Coppin, Capt. [John]. Held commands in both the First and the Second Dutch Wars; killed in action in 1666.[1]

Corbetta, [Francesco] (c. 1615–81). Italian composer and virtuoso guitarist, who taught his instrument both to the young Louis XIV and to Charles II. In England by 22 Feb. 1661 when he petitioned for a monopoly on the gambling game *L'acca di Catalonia*; on 29 May 1665 Charles II sent pieces by 'francisco' which pleased him to his sister, the Duchess of Orleans. Corbetta subsequently returned to France, perhaps frustrated in his attempt to exchange his place as groom of the privy chamber to the Queen to that of page of the backstairs to the King, but dedicated his *La guitarre royalle* (Paris, 1671) 'a roy de la Grande Bretagne', and was in England in 1674.[1] (Lu)

Corey, [Katherine] (b. Mitchell, c. 1635). Actress in the King's Company from c. 1660, after 1682 in the United Company; played her last recorded part 1692. Achieved popularity mainly as a comic actress.[1]

Cornhill. One of the principal streets of the city – 'extraordinary publick, pleasant and spacious . . . [and] inhabited mostly by rich Traders'.[1] The standard, near its junction with Leadenhall St, was the mark from which distances to and from London were measured.

Cornwallis, [Henrietta-Maria]. Of the Queen Mother's Household; sister of the 3rd Baron Cornwallis (1655–98).[1]

Cotterell, Sir Charles (1615–1701). Son of Sir Clement (Groom Porter to James I); Assistant-Master of Ceremonies 1641–6, Master 1660–86; M.P. for Cardigan 1663–Jan. 79. His son Clement (born c. 1650) became a close friend of Sandwich – accompanied his son Sidney on the Grand Tour, served in the Madrid embassy and lost his life, like Sandwich, in the Battle of Sole Bay. Sir Charles was one of the six bannerol bearers at Sandwich's funeral.[1]

Cottle, [Mark] (d. 1682). Of Greenwich; Registrar of the Prerogative Court of Canterbury from at least 1655.[1]

The Counter (Compter). The name given to the two prisons owned by the city corporation and used for the punishment of civil offences. They were in Great Wood St (on the e. side), and the Poultry (on the n. side, well back from the street at the end of a passage), each being administered by one of the sheriffs. Both were destroyed in the Fire and rebuilt. There was a third Counter, which does not appear in the diary. It was for debtors, and situated in Southwark. (R)

Country, Capt. [Richard]. 'My little Captain that I loved' (ii.185). He had carried Pepys to the Baltic in 1659 on board the *Hind*. Wounded in the First Dutch War, he served under Sandwich's command in the Mediterranean voyage of 1661–2 and in the campaign of 1665. Together with his brother John, he gave evidence on Coventry's behalf when he was charged with corruption. He held two other commands 1673–4.[1]

Covent Garden. Once the garden of Westminster Abbey, it was granted in 1552 to the Bedford family. In the 1630s they developed it, largely to the designs of Inigo Jones, as a residential square in the fashionable red brick, with a piazza and approach streets. In 1660 it was well-tenanted and newly risen to the dignity of a separate parish (St Paul's). Sorbière thought it more attractive and better built than the Place Royale in Paris.[1] Pepys more than once expresses admiration for the houses. Several of his acquaintances lived there – Brouncker, the Swedish Resident Leijonbergh, and Pearse, the surgeon. There were some ugly streets close by, such as Long Acre where the St Michels lived 'among all the bawdy-houses'. Pepys never mentions the market, which was just beginning to develop. He once refers to the district as 'Common-Garden'.[2] [Illust. in ix, facing p. 421] (R; La)

Coventry, Henry (c. 1618–86). Diplomatist; younger brother of Sir William and a close friend of Clarendon; M.P. for Droitwich in three parliaments 1661–81. An able and attractive figure, admired even by his enemies, who 'in thirty years of public life . . . kept his unclouded reputation, his empty pocket, his Rabelaisian speech, his taste for hunting, and his gouty frame'.[1] After serving as envoy to Sweden 1664–6, and ambassador 1671–2, and as a plenipotentiary to the peace conference at Breda 1667–8, he became Secretary of State 1672–80, and Admiralty Commissioner 1673–9.[2]

Coventry, Sir William (1627–86). Youngest son of Charles I's Lord Keeper, and Pepys's most valued mentor and colleague. He was Secretary to the Lord High Admiral 1660–7, Navy Commissioner 1662–7, and a member of the Tangier and Fishery Committees and of the commission of enquiry into the Chatham Chest.

Pepys, who came to know him well, greatly admired his industry, his regard for detail and his reforming zeal. On the Navy Board he took a smaller part in routine matters than his colleagues, because of his Admiralty work, but he was active in financial business and a constant supporter of Pepys's efforts to regularise the administrative work of the office. Equally, as Admiral's Secretary, he enforced high standards of efficiency as far as he could and dreaded the approach of a war which would be bound to create chaos and bankruptcy. When it came, he favoured the appointment to command of professionals ('tarpaulins') rather than gentlemen-captains, and like many of his predecessors undertook active service himself. He was accused of feathering his his nest – a charge much relished by his enemies Sandwich and Carteret. It is true that he accepted money for places, as was usual, but he never sold officers' commissions, and after 1664 he commuted his income from fees into a salary of £500 p.a.[1] Another criticism he came under was that of having been responsible for the failure to prevent the Dutch invasion of the Medway in July 1667. The lack of preparedness however was a fault for which the King and the Duke of York, together with the rest of the Privy Council, as well as Coventry, must share the blame. By May 1667 he had been transferred to the Treasury where his gift for orderly administration was seen at its best. It is typified in his famous desk-cum-filing-cabinet. It had a hole in the middle in which he sat, turning now to one business, now to another.

He had been knighted and made a Privy Councillor in 1665 and was ambitious of climbing still higher. As an M.P. (for an Admiralty borough, Great Yarmouth 1661–July 79) he led a small group of court members, but held himself aloof from Clarendon and from the main body of Clarendon's supporters. He led the attack on Clarendon in 1667, demanding his dismissal (though not his impeachment) in the conviction that Clarendon stood in the way of efficient government. But he in his turn fell victim to Clarendon's enemies (Buckingham and Arlington) and was relieved of his posts. In the '70s he proved a vigorous critic of Charles's pro-French policy and of the Danby ministry, though never supporting the proposal to exclude the Duke of York from the succession. He refused to stand again after the spring elections of 1679.

Clarendon in his memoirs has a hostile portrait of him. He grants him ability but writes him down as 'sullen, ill-natured, proud'.[2] The picture is overdrawn, and there are other accounts of him (from Whigs like Burnet as well as Tories like Roger North) which more nearly agree with the impressions left by Pepys.[3] But Clarendon was stating an important aspect of the truth. Splendid as Coventry was as an administrator, he lacked the politician's art of pleasing.

Cowes, Capt. [Richard] (d. by 1688). A captain in the Commonwealth navy, he was commissioned to the *Paradox* in 1660.[1]

Cow Lane. Now known as King St, this ran north-east out of Holborn or Snow Hill to West Smithfield, and was famous for its coachmakers. (R)

Cowley, Thomas (d. 1669). Clerk of the Cheque at Deptford 1660–5 and brother of Abraham the poet. At his death he left bequests to Moses and Aaron, sons of Thomas Turner of the Navy Office. The 'kinsman' who served him as clerk may have been the Thomas Waldron who appears in his will as a servant. The name was pronounced and often spelt 'Cooley'.[1]

Cox, Capt. Sir John. 'An understanding stout seaman', according to Coventry. Originally commissioned in the Commonwealth navy, he was appointed Master-Attendant at Chatham in 1660 and at Deptford in 1666. He served as master of the Duke of York's flagship the *Royal Charles* in the Battle of Lowestoft – hence his evidence (viii.489–90) about the ship's failure to pursue the enemy. He succeeded Pett as Commissioner at Chatham in 1669, and fell in action in the *Prince* at the Battle of Sole Bay in May 1672, having been knighted shortly before.[1]

Capt. George Cocke, the hard-drinking navy contractor, is probably the drunken Capt. Cox at ii.232, and also the Capt. Cox at iv.212, where Pepys clearly enough implies that he is referring to the merchant.

Cox, Col. [Thomas]. Appointed militia commissioner for Berkshire, 1657, 1659; and for London, March 1660. He was Lieut.-Colonel of the Blue regiment of the city trainbands in 1660.[1]

Cragg, Mrs. Possibly Alice, wife of Francis Crake, or Susanna, wife of Thomas Crake. Both lived in the parish of St Margaret, Westminster.[1]

Craven, Sir William, 1st Lord Craven (1608–97). Soldier and courtier. He served abroad with the Dutch in the 1620s, and became the champion of James I's daughter, Elizabeth, 'Winter Queen' of Bohemia, fighting in her cause under Gustavus Adolphus. He established himself as her principal adviser and spent much of his large fortune on her cause. He was knighted in 1627 and made a baron in 1645. After the Restoration he brought her to London where she died in 1662. He himself was loaded with honours, being made a colonel in the Coldstream Guards (1662; commanding the Anglo-Dutch brigade in Holland 1662–4), an earl (1665), a Privy Councillor (1666) and Lieut.-General of the kingdom (1667). His military experience led to his becoming Albemarle's principal associate. Pepys got to know him at the Fishery Committee (where he often presided) and as Albemarle's deputy. In 1670, when examined by the Privy Council about the wartime administration of the navy, Pepys asserted that Craven could bear witness to his diligence. He later knew him as a member of the Tangier Committee (from 1673) and of the Admiralty Commission (1677–9). He died unmarried: later rumours that he had been secretly married to the Winter Queen were baseless.[1]

Creed. John Creed (d. 1701) was Pepys's principal rival for Sandwich's favour. Born in or near Oundle, by (?) Apr. 1656 he was in London conducting financial business at the orders of the Council of State, possibly through attachment to Mountagu's service in the Treasury. Certainly by March 1659 he was established in the Mountagu household as a secretary. In that summer he accompanied his master on the Baltic voyage as Admiral's secretary and Deputy-Treasurer of the fleet.[1] But for the Dutch voyage of 1660 Mountagu preferred to employ Pepys, and thereafter Pepys overhauled him in the race for advancement, although Creed remained on Mountagu's household staff and held three more appointments as muster-master and Deputy-Treasurer to the fleet in 1660–3.[2] One reason for his falling back in Mountagu's favour was his puritanism. His letters to Mountagu before the Restoration drip with sanctimonious jargon.[3] The diary has several indications of his puritanism, and in 1664 he was examined by the Privy Council on suspicion of being associated with sectaries.[4] He had to content himself (from 1662) with the secretaryship of the Tangier Committee, in which he had no such opportunities for profit as Pepys enjoyed in the treasurership. He had some private wealth, and (if Pepys is to be believed) was thoroughly mean with it – refusing loans to Sandwich, and moving his bachelor apartments from time to time in order to avoid the poll-tax. Pepys has however to admit to his being accomplished – his letters to Pepys are often written in Latin and French for fun, and in 1663 he was elected F.R.S.[5] In 1668 he had his revenge over his rival. After setting his cap at the daughter of the wealthy navy victualler, Sir Denis Gauden, he married – 'devilish presumption'

Pepys called it – Sandwich's niece, Elizabeth Pickering – a 'comely' bride, in Pepys's words, 'but very fat'. He thereafter lived in the country, mostly in Oundle where he became a magistrate.[6] He had 11 children, five of whom died in infancy. His wife (who lived on into her eighties) clearly had literary and artistic gifts. In the church of her native Tichmarsh in Northamptonshire she composed and erected a series of eloquent tablets: to her husband ('A Wise Learned Pious Man'), to her two soldier sons (the younger of whom, Richard, was killed at Blenheim, his body being carried from the field by his brother John); and to her Dryden relations (John Dryden was a cousin). At Barnwell, where she lived in later life, is a tablet to her daughter Jemima, and two of her paintings of members of the Dryden family.

Richard Creed, brother of her husband, was, like John, a fervent Puritan (once servant to the Fifth-Monarchist Maj.-Gen. Harrison) and a naval official under the Commonwealth. He was a clerk to the Admiralty Committee from c. 1653 and served as Admiral's secretary and Deputy-Treasurer to the fleet 1657–60.[7]

Creighton, Robert (1593–1672). Dean of Wells 1660–70; Bishop of Wells 1670–2; chaplain to the King; and former Regius Professor of Greek at Cambridge (1625–39). A Scotsman whose lively sermons made him much in demand as a preacher – e.g. to the houses of Parliament. Preaching before the King at The Hague in 1660 he summarised responsibility for the execution of Charles I in the words: 'the Presbyterians held [him] by the hair and the Independents cut off his head'. His sermon before Charles II on adultery was a 'strange bold' one (viii.362–3).[1]

Cresset, ——. Francis Cresset(t), Groom of the Privy Chamber extraordinary since Aug. 1660, became Groom-in-ordinary in Dec. 1667. A John Cresset(t) was Groom-in-ordinary from March 1669.[1]

Crew. A leading parliamentarian and Presbyterian family, of Stene (now Steane Park), Northants.: 'the best family in the world for goodness and sobriety' (vii.356).

John Crew (1598–1679), cr. Baron Crew of Stene 1661, was the father of Sandwich's wife, Jemima. Son of Sir Thomas Crew (Speaker 1623–5), he was a prominent M.P. 1624–48 – critical of the King's administration but opposed to extreme measures such as the execution of Strafford, and finally arrested and secluded in 1648 in Pride's Purge. Elected to the Protectorate parliament of 1654, he was excluded by the government, and finally resumed his seat in the Rump in Feb. 1660, when the secluded members were re-admitted. He moved the resolution condemning the execution of the King. He was a Councillor of State Feb.–May 1660, and went on the deputation to invite Charles II back, but retired from politics at the Restoration with a peerage, and is said to have twice refused the Chancellorship of the Exchequer.[1]

The diary reveals him as a man of principle, but also prudent and worldly wise. He came from a Puritan family, with sisters named Patience, Temperance, Prudence and Silence, and the well-known Presbyterian minister Thomas Case was his close friend. He married (1648) Jemima Waldegrave of Lawford Green, Essex, who died in 1675. He was rich, and c. 1656 took a large house (taxed on 20 hearths) in Lincoln's Inn Fields, moving to the house next door in 1661. His daughters Jemima and Anne married Sandwich and Sir Henry Wright respectively.[2]

His brother Nathaniel briefly appears in the diary. He died unmarried at Feltham, Mdx, in 1693, leaving most of his wealth to his nephew Thomas.[3]

This same Thomas (c. 1624–97), eldest son of the baron, was knighted in 1660, and succeeded to the barony in 1679. He was a strict Puritan, to judge by the wording of his will. He sat as M.P. for Northamptonshire 1656–8, and for Brackley in 1659 and 1679, but was not an active member. He had six daughters by his two marriages. Jack, a son by his first wife, died young.[4]

Thomas's youngest brother Nathaniel (1633–1721) succeeded him as the 3rd Baron. He was a smooth and successful clergyman – Fellow, then (1668) Rector of Lincoln College, Oxford, made Bishop of Oxford in 1671 and of Durham in 1674. He was a royal chaplain from 1666 and Clerk of the Closet 1669–88. It is said that he bought the Durham appointment by a bribe to Nell Gwyn. His subservience to the ecclesiastical policy of James II was an inglorious episode in the family history.[5]

The other sons of the 1st Baron mentioned in the diary are John, his second son, who died in France in 1681 at the age of 53;[6] Samuel, a clergyman (M.A. Oxf. 1658), who died unmarried in 1661;[7] and Waldegrave (whom Pepys calls 'Mr Waldegrave'), of Hinton, Northants., who married Susanna Mellor in 1670 and died in 1673.[8]

Cripplegate. One of the city's gates in the n. wall at the n. end of Little Wood St (now Wood St), leading into Fore St. Commanding no road to the north or east comparable to that through Bishopsgate, it had less traffic and fewer inns and stables in its vicinity. Pepys's mother, however, seems to have arrived there by carrier on one of her journeys from Brampton. The gate was repaired in 1663 and taken down in 1760. (R)

Crisp (Cripps). There were several families of this name established in Westminster in 1660. Pepys's friend and neighbour, Mrs Crisp, lived in a roomy house (taxed on eight hearths) near the s.-w. corner of Axe Yard, next door to the Hartlibs. Her daughter Diana attracted Pepys's attention. Her son Laud was by 1663 an officer of the King's Wardrobe. He then petitioned for a place as gentleman of the Chapel Royal –

Pepys admired his voice – but his name does not appear in the establishment lists of the period. He was still in the Wardrobe in 1667.[1]

Crisp, Capt. [Edward]. Elder Brother, Trinity House Jan. 1665; Master, Nov. 1665–July 66; appointed commissioner for the relief of widows and orphans of officers and seamen, Jan. 1673.[1]

Crisp, Sir Nicholas, kt 1641, bt 1665 (?1599–1666). A wealthy merchant, who pioneered the W. African trade in the 1630s; a customs farmer (1640 and c. 1661–6); M.P. for Winchelsea Nov. 1640–1 (being expelled as a monopolist); member of the Council of Trade (from 1660) and for Foreign Plantations (from 1661); and a Gentleman of the Privy Chamber from 1664. He was interested in inventions – Pepys mentions his proposals for a wet-dock. The superb mansion he built at Hammersmith was later the home of George IV's Queen Caroline. In his will he directed that his heart should be buried in the chapel at Hammersmith and his body in St Mildred's, Bread St, and that his monument should record that he had lost 'out of purse about a Hundred Thousand pounds' by his pioneering efforts in the Guinea trade.[1]

Crispin, [Arthur]. Appointed waterman to the King 1660.[1]

Crofts, ——. Clerk in the Signet Office; probably the Dr Thomas Crofts who in 1667 petitioned for the place of master in Chancery.[1]

Crofts, [William], 1st Baron (?1611–77). Of Little Saxham, Suff.; an influential courtier (first app. c. 1635); after 1660 Master of the Horse to the Duke of York; Captain of the Guards to the Queen Mother and Gentleman of the Bedchamber to the King. He was also from 1658 Governor of the Duke of Monmouth, who for some time went by the name of James Crofts.[1]

Cromleholme (Crumlum), [Samuel] (1618–72). Schoolmaster; graduate of Oxford (B.A. 1639); Surmaster, St Paul's School 1647–51; Master of the grammar school, Dorchester, Dorset, 1651–7; High Master of St Paul's 1657–72. His library, reputedly the best private collection in London, was destroyed in the Fire.[1]

Croone, [William] (1633–84). Anatomist; an original F.R.S. and first secretary of the Society; Gresham Professor of Rhetoric 1659–70.[1]

Crow, Ald. [William] (1617–68). Upholsterer, in St Bartholomew's the Great (in large premises, taxed on 18 hearths); after the Fire in Blackfriars. Master of the Skinners' Company 1662–3.[1]

Crow, Capt. Possibly George Crow, second lieutenant in the *Royal Catherine* 1665, and captain of the *Sarah and Elizabeth* in 1667.[1]

Crown Office. A branch of Chancery presided over by the Clerk of the Crown and situated in King's Bench Walk, Temple. Pepys visited it in 1669 when he was drawing up an account of the recent history of the Navy Office for the Duke of York. Among other records it retained the dockets which registered the issue of patents appointing naval commissions and commissioners. It gave its name to Crown Office Row.

[Crowther, Joseph] (d. 1689). Chaplain to the Duke of York; Principal of St Mary Hall, Oxford 1664–89.[1]

Croxton, [?Jane]. Mercer; of Salisbury Court.[1]

Crutched Friars. Earlier known as Hart St. Hatton (1708) calls it a 'very considerable (tho' crooked) str.', '380 yards long'.[1] In the diary period, as now, it ran out of Hart St, Mark Lane, towards Aldgate. (R)

Cuckold's Point. Also known as Cuckold's Haven; on the Surrey bank of the Thames at the n. end of Limehouse Reach; said to derive its name from the story of a miller of Charlton, Kent, who was cuckolded there by King John.[1]

Cumberland, [Henry]. Tailor, of Salisbury Court; brother of Pepys's friend Dick. He was the eldest son and had inherited his father's estate.[1]

Cumberland, Richard (1631–1718). Clergyman and friend – 'a man of breeding and parts' (ix.56) whom Pepys badly wanted as a husband for Pall. His father, like Pepys's, was a tailor in Salisbury Court (a Select Vestryman in 1662),[1] and he himself was at St Paul's and Magdalene with Pepys, leaving school in 1650 and taking his B.A. in 1653. He stayed on as a Fellow from 1653 until 1658 when he accepted a living as Rector of Brampton, Northants. He retained it after the Restoration, taking the new tests and like Pepys making his peace with the new régime. He married Anne Quinsey, a spinster of 24, at St Paul's, Covent Garden, in 1664.[2] In 1670 he became Rector of All Hallows, Stamford, a Crown living to which he was presented by Lord Keeper Bridgeman, who had made him his chaplain and who was in sympathy with his liberal churchmanship. In 1691 he was made Bishop of Peterborough. His later years were very different from Pepys's. He lived on in the see (since bishops could not retire) until his death in his 87th year, and if we are to believe the hostile evidence of his successor White Kennett, he did little but 'eat and drink and . . . sleep and . . . amuse himself, without preaching once in . . . 20 years, or reading anything but a diverting short pamphlet'.[3] He had been a serious scholar. Pepys retained in his library copies of his refutation of Hobbes (*De legibus naturae*, 1672), and his *Essay towards the recovery of Jewish measures & weights* (1686). The latter was dedicated to Pepys and referred to the 'constant love' between them begun at Magdalene. The college has two portraits.[4]

The brother Pepys mentions is probably either William (b. 1636) or John (b. 1638).[5]

Curle, [Edmund] (d. by 1688). A captain under the Commonwealth, he held only one commission (to the *Little Mary*) after 1660.[1]

Currency: *see* Large Glossary under names of coins

Cursitors' Alley. East off Chancery Lane, almost opposite the gate of Lincoln's Inn. (R)

Curtis, Capt. [Edmund] (d. by 1688). A captain under the Commonwealth; commissioned to the *Newcastle* in 1660.[1]

Custis, [Edmund]. Merchant, of St Dionis Backchurch; he lived for some time in the '60s and '70s in Bruges. In 1679–80, when Pepys was accused of treason, he supplied useful information against Scott, his accuser.[1]

Custom House. In 1660 this stood on the s. side of what is now Lower Thames St, a little to the west of the Tower and opposite the s. ends of Water and Bear Lanes, its wharf separating it from the river bank. An Elizabethan building, it was burnt in the Fire and, with the help of a loan of £1000 from the Farmers of the Customs, rebuilt immediately below the old site by Wren. His work was completed by 1671. In the interim, customs business was transferred to the town house of the former Viscounts Bayning in the unburnt part of Mark Lane. The delay in rebuilding referred to at 7 Sept. 1666 was largely due to the mixture of interests in the site and the buildings: Sir Anthony Cope, the freeholder, his lessees, the Crown, and the Customs Farmers all being concerned and none wishing to yield either their rights or their chances of compensation. Wren's building was damaged by fire in 1715 and rebuilt and enlarged in stages. Its successor was burnt in 1814. A new Custom House, seriously damaged in the Second World War, was then built a short distance upstream.[1] (R)

Cutler, Ald. Sir John (1609–93). Merchant; knighted June 1660, cr. bt Nov. 1660; four times Master of the Grocers' Company; elected M.P. for Taunton Oct. 1679, 1690.[1]

Cutler, [William] (d. 1670). Merchant, of Austin Friars and Hackney; Warden of the Drapers' Company 1660, 1664; appointed 'garbler of spices' to the city 1661. He supplied the navy with victuals and with Baltic goods, often in association with Sir W. Rider. His wife Elizabeth died c. 1678; her mother Frances Freeman (cf. iv.398) was one of her executors.[1]

Cuttance. Sir Roger Cuttance (d. 1669) was a naval commander well thought of by both Sandwich and Coventry. Under the Commonwealth, he took a leading part in the Dutch war and in Blake's Tunis expedition of 1655. Between 1660 and 1665 he was Sandwich's flag-captain in the *Royal Charles*, the *Royal James* and the *Prince*, and had to share with his superior officer the blame for the prize goods scandal. (Pepys in fact puts the greater part of the blame on him.) After that he held no further command. He was a member of the Fishery and Tangier Committees, and was knighted in 1665.

His son Henry served in the Commonwealth navy and held three commissions 1660–5. He had died by 1688.[1]

Cuttle, Capt. [John]. A captain in the Commonwealth navy, in May 1660 he wrote to Sandwich that it was 'the height of his ambition to serve and wait upon his lordship'; but he was not commissioned to any ship until given command of the *Hector* in 1664. He was killed in action in 1665.[1]

Daking, Capt. [George]. A Commonwealth naval officer (captain since at least 1653) dismissed in 1660 as an irreconcilable Anabaptist. He then took command of a merchantman trading with the Mediterranean, and may well be the 'Capt. Dekins' of iii.50. The name is spelt variously: the Anabaptist spelt it Daking or Dakinge.[1]

Dalmahoy, [Thomas] (d. 1682). Of the Friary, Guildford, Surrey. He came of an old Scottish family, and had been Master of the Horse to the 2nd Duke of Hamilton, whose widow he had married in 1655. It was through her that he acquired his Surrey property. He was a friend of Ormond and Lauderdale and sat as M.P. for Guildford 1664–July 79.[1]

Dalton, [Richard]. Serjeant of the wine cellar to the King.[1]

[Dalziel (Dalyell), Thomas of the Binns] (c. 1599–c. 1685). Scottish soldier; Maj.-General at Worcester fight; thereafter served in the Russian army; Lieut.-General and Privy Councillor 1666; active in crushing the Covenanters' rising 1679. A tough and picturesque figure who never wore boots on campaign. His beard reached to his middle as a result of a vow never to shave after the execution of Charles I.[1]

Danby, 1st Earl of: *see* Osborne, Sir T.

Dances: *see* Large Glossary under names.

Daniel, [Richard]. Clerk in the Victualling Office from 1655.[1]

Daniel, [Samuel]. Lieutenant on the *Royal Charles* in 1665; commissioned captain to a Dutch prize 1665, and to a frigate in 1666. His pretty and complaisant wife was a daughter of Pepys's Greenwich landlady, Mrs Clerke. A Mr Daniel was storekeeper at Sheerness in 1676.[1]

Darcy, [Marmaduke] (d. 1687). Yorkshire royalist, fifth son of Conyers Darcy, 6th Baron Darcy (cr. Earl of Holdernesse 1682); Gentleman-Usher of the Privy Chamber from at least 1663.[1]

Darcy, Sir William, kt 1639. Of Witton Castle, Co. Durham; appointed to the Royal Fishery, Aug. 1661.[1]

[Darling, Thomas and Edward]. Landlords of the Three Tuns tavern, Charing Cross. In 1660 Thomas had been landlord for at least 20 years. He was Warden of the Vintners' Company 1649–50, 1658–60, and an active churchwarden and vestryman of St Martin-in-the-Fields. According to the ratebooks he was succeeded c. 1661 by his son Edward (d. c. 1675). The landlord's 'fayre Sister' (1 Nov. 1661) is therefore the same person as 'the pretty maid the daughter of the house' (6 Dec. 1661).[1]

Darnell, ——. 'The fidler'. Conceivably Richard Dorney, jun.

(variously Darney, Dornye, Dorlin), one of the royal violins, who died in 1681.[1] (Lu)

Dartmouth, Lord: see Legge, W. and G.

Dashwood, Ald. [Francis] (d. 1683). Turkey merchant; of St Botolph-without-Bishopsgate.[1]

Da Silva, Don Duarte. Portuguese merchant: 'a Jew of great wealth and full credit at Amsterdam' (Clarendon).[1]

Davenant, Sir William (1606–68). Poet and dramatist; manager of the King's Company of Players 1660–8. During the Commonwealth he was responsible for at least two productions of 'entertainments of music' in private premises in London (Rutland House) which evaded the official ban on plays. It was from one of these – *The siege of Rhodes* – that Pepys took the words of the song 'Beauty Retire' that he composed in 1665, though there is no evidence that he had attended any of the productions themselves.

The history of this work has been the subject of some misunderstanding. It seems likely that the best account is in Dryden's preface to *The conquest of Granada*, published in 1672 when the facts would have been within the recent recollection of his readers. It would appear that Part I, performed in 1656, was set to music throughout, and that when it was restaged, along with Part II, in 1659 at the Cockpit theatre (by which time the ban on plays was no longer effective) it was presented as a spoken drama. Neither the 1659 reprint of Part I nor the 1663 quarto containing both parts has any list of composers or musical performers. Pepys indeed might not have valued his setting of 'Beauty Retire' had another setting already existed. The strongest evidence against this interpretation is Evelyn's statement (9 Jan. 1662) that he then heard Part II in '*Recitativa* Musique'. But it is almost certain that this passage was a later addition to his diary text and that he was mistaken.[1] (Lu)

Davenport, [Frances]. Actress in the King's Company c. 1664–8; probably Buckingham's mistress. Possibly related to Jane and Elizabeth Davenport, also actresses.[1]

Davenport, [Hester]. (?1641–1717). Actress in the Duke's Company 1660–2, playing leading parts. Known as 'Roxalana' from her part in Davenant's *Siege of Rhodes*; not related to Frances Davenport. She became the mistress of the Earl of Oxford in 1662, and after his death in 1703 married Peter Moet.[1]

Davenport, ——. Of Brampton, Hunts.; probably John Davenport, who held land in Brampton manor in 1653.[1]

Davies, [John]. Storekeeper, Deptford 1649–63.[1]

Davies, [Sir Thomas] (1631–80). Bookseller ('the little fellow'); a contemporary of Pepys at St Paul's School. Master of the Stationers' Company 1668–70, and of the Drapers' 1677–8; Sheriff 1667–8; Lord

Mayor 1676–7. He inherited a large fortune, consisting mainly of the Ebury estate in Westminster which later passed to the Grosvenors, Dukes of Westminster.[1]

Davis, [John], sen. and jun. Navy Office clerks. The father was clerk to Berkeley of Stratton 1660–4, and spent some time in Ireland, 1661–c. 63, Berkeley being also Governor of Galway.[1] The son was appointed to a clerkship c. 1661.[2]

Davis, Mary (Mall). Actress in the Duke's Company ?1660–8; an accomplished dancer and singer. She left the stage in 1668 to become the King's mistress and bore him a daughter in 1673 (Lady Mary Tudor, later married to the 2nd Earl of Derwentwater). In 1686 she married the French-born musician James Paisible; they followed James II into exile, returning to England in 1698. There are portraits by Lely and Kneller.[1]

Davis, [Thomas]. Messenger, Admiralty office.[1]

Day, [John]. 'Uncle Day'; of Leverington, Cambs. His sister Mary had married in 1596 Thomas Pepys of Eaton, Pepys's grandfather. After his death (c. 1649) she married Rice Wight, father of Pepys's 'Uncle Wight'. Day's widow Beatrice died c. 1650.[1]

Day, [John]. Fishmonger (freeman of the Company 1621); probably related to 'Uncle Day'; William Wight was apprenticed to him.[1]

Deane, Sir Anthony (?1638–1721). Shipwright and friend. Charles II and James II, as well as Pepys, looked on him as the most skilful designer of his day. (Even Louis XIV engaged him to design two of his yachts.) Pepys's admiration, clear from the diary, is even clearer in their correspondence (virtually continuous from the '60s until Pepys's death) and in Pepys's 'Naval Minutes'.[1] Appointed the assistant at Woolwich in 1660, he became Master-Shipwright at Harwich (his native town) in 1664, and at Portsmouth in 1668. He was Navy Commissioner at Portsmouth 1672–5, and a member of the Navy Board 1675–80, and was Pepys's principal ally both in the shipbuilding programme of 1677–8 and in the work of the Special Commission of 1686–8. Like Pepys, he fell under the unjust suspicion during the Popish Plot scare of selling naval secrets to France, and was briefly imprisoned with him in 1679. In June 1680 both were discharged before being brought to trial. In two parliaments – those of 1679 and 1685–7 – he shared the representation of Harwich with Pepys. He was a pall-bearer at Pepys's funeral.

Pepys kept in his library a portrait drawing of Deane,[2] as well as several volumes of his manuscript calculations and drawings, including the 'Doctrine of Naval Architecture' written at Pepys's request in 1670.[3]

Debusty, [Laurence]. Merchant; born in Bayonne (letters of denization granted Apr. 1665). He dealt in provisions for the royal household.[1]

Delaune, [George] (d. 1662). Eastland merchant; of St Margaret,

Lothbury. His wife was Dorothea, daughter of Sir Thomas Allen of Finchley, M.P. for Middlesex 1661–2.[1]

Denham, Sir John (1615–69). Poet (author of 'Cooper's Hill') and Wren's predecessor as Surveyor-General of the King's Works, 1660–9. In Evelyn's words 'A better *Poet* than *Architect*'.[1] Among the buildings sometimes attributed to him are Greenwich Palace and Burlington House, but Mr H. M. Colvin believes there is no evidence that he designed either. This seems to be true also of the alterations at Hinching-brooke, about which Sandwich consulted him. He married his second wife Margaret Brooke in 1665, she being then about 18. Very soon afterwards she became mistress to the Duke of York, and her early death in 1667 gave rise to the (unfounded) suspicion that the jealous Duchess had poisoned her.[2]

Deptford. The principal centre for naval stores and unique in that (in association with Woolwich, its sister yard) it was directly supervised by the Navy Office. A busy yard in the 15th century, and the first of the Thames yards to be developed under Henry VIII. In spite of the shallowness of its water it prospered because of its nearness to London, and during the Dutch wars it was, with Chatham, the busiest of all the yards. By 1688 it had a double dry dock, a two-acre wet dock, a mast house and a number of storehouses (12 of them built in 1686–8). Pepys in 1698 remarked that it had doubled in size since Elizabeth's reign.[1] From the mid-18th century it housed the principal victualling yard of the navy.[2] [*See also* Bagwell, [William]; Dockyards; Trinity House; Woolwich]

Dering, Sir Edward. There were two half-brothers of these names; sons of Sir Edward, 1st Bt, M.P. for Hythe, Kent, by his second and third marriages. The elder (1625–84) succeeded to the baronetcy in 1644; the timber he supplied to the navy (vi.77) was probably from his own estate at Pluckley, Kent. He was a Commissioner for executing the act of settlement in Ireland 1662–9, a Commissioner of the Privy Seal 1669–73 and of the Treasury 1679–84. He sat in Parliament in 1660 and 1670–March 81.

The younger Sir Edward, kt 1680 (1633–1703), known as Red Ned, was an Eastland merchant, and Governor of the Hamburg Company 1683–4. From Aug. 1660 he had occupied the post of 'King's Merchant', charged with the duty of keeping the government informed of the prices of Baltic and Eastland products. The office had been made virtually redundant by the growth of trading.[1]

De Vic [Anne Charlotte] (d. 1717). For many years Lady of the Bedchamber to Princess (later Queen) Anne. Her father Sir Harry (1st Bt) was Comptroller of the Household to the Duke of York from 1662 until his death in 1671. She married John Frescheville, 1st Baron Frescheville (d. 1682) in 1666.[1]

Devonshire House. Town house of the Earls of Devonshire, on the
e. side of Bishopsgate St, where Devonshire Sq. now stands. The
hearth-tax returns suggest that it was split into several dwellings.[1] (R)
Diamond, Capt. [Thomas]. During the Commonwealth, captain of
a privateer and twice imprisoned, on the first occasion for piracy and
on the second for sheep stealing. He held one commission after 1660.[1]
The Diary: for the manuscript and its history, *see* vol. i, pp.xli +

THE DIARY AND RELATED MANUSCRIPTS

The diary was only one of a mass of manuscripts which Pepys preserved
from the diary period. Some he mentions have now disappeared – his
book of anecdotes, for instance, and his 'Brampton book'.[1] Those that
survive are to be found in four repositories – the Pepys Library at
Magdalene, the Bodleian, the National Maritime Museum and the
Public Record Office.
The Pepys Library. Here there is a wealth of miscellaneous office
papers – some original, others copies made in Pepys's later life by
clerks and included in his great folio series of 'Naval Papers', 'Navy and
Admiralty Precedents' and 'Miscellanies'.[2] They were kept not as
records of his career, for the Library was not a personal archive, but as
material for his projected history of the navy. A rather more personal
relic is the book of memoranda (1663–72) which he called his 'Navy
White Book' and in which he kept a record of office matters for his
own purposes.[3] Like his copy of the Admiralty journal and his collections of Admiralty letters from the '70s, it does not appear in the body
of his Catalogue of 1700, but in the 'Additamenta' written in by
Jackson after his death. All these volumes were until then presumably
kept separate from the Library proper. Of purely personal papers the
Library has very few apart from the diary itself. There are no letters
for this period from Pepys himself, and only one from a correspondent
– the long letter from Evelyn of 21 Aug. 1669 giving Pepys advice on
what to see and do on his continental holiday.[4]
The Bodleian Library. Some 80 volumes of Pepys's papers found
their way to the Bodleian in 1755 as part of a bequest from the antiquary Richard Rawlinson. They include practically all the personal
papers of the diary period – accounts and letters (some of which were
published in 1933 by R. G. Howarth and in 1955 by H. T. Heath),[5]
together with many others concerning most aspects of his official life
in the '60s. They also include a number of items from a later period
which one would have expected Pepys to have had bound and put
into the Pepys Library itself – his parliamentary diary of 1677,[6] for

instance, his Tangier papers[7] and a large number concerning the history of the navy. It may be that he lacked time, or room, to incorporate them. Their history is difficult to trace. It is possible that they were never transported to Clapham with the rest of his collections at the end of his life, or that, if transported, they were left at Clapham when the library was sent to Cambridge in 1724. There is a mysterious reference to papers belonging to Pepys in a compilation of the Duke of York's letters as Admiral published in 1729 – *Memoirs of the English affairs, chiefly naval, from . . . 1660 to 1673*. Both the publisher and the compiler – who may have been the same person – were anonymous. The compiler announced (p. 280) that if his book were well received he would continue it to 1688 'from the *Original Manuscripts* of Samuel Pepys, Esq.; now in our Possession'. He thanked Lord Frederick Howard for making the manuscripts available, and dedicated the book to him. He never published a sequel and we have no knowledge of what the manuscripts were. We know that some time before Apr. 1749 Rawlinson had acquired his collection of Pepys papers from a bookseller.[8] These may be the same manuscripts as those referred to by the compiler of the 1729 book. But there is another possibility. Not long before 1749 the Jackson household at Clapham was broken up. John Jackson's daughter Frances was married in 1747 and soon was living in Somerset; the Clapham house was abandoned (and in 1754 demolished to make room for building development).[9] The papers which became Rawlinson's may therefore have been put on to the market in about 1747 as a result of these changes. But this is conjecture. Whatever their origin, Rawlinson, having bought them, had the loose papers bound (only a few were already bound), sent a few volumes to friends to peruse (George Vertue and Thomas Carte among them),[10] and then bequeathed them, with the rest of his vast collections, to the Bodleian.[11]

The National Maritime Museum. The library of the museum possesses the most important book of Pepys's letters surviving from the '60s. It has an 18th-century binding and is rather misleadingly entitled on the spine 'S. Pepys's Official Correspondence 1662–79'.[12] It consists of three gatherings of letters, not all of them official, covering 1662–5; 1665; and 1665–79. It is clearly a collection of letters which Pepys regarded as confidential. They are written mostly in his own hand and sometimes in shorthand. The greater part belongs to the diary period and concerns official business. That part of it is referred to in the diary. After his move to the Admiralty in 1673 it changes in character and becomes a record of private and semi-official matters. The book must originally have been a part of Pepys's library because it has two shelf-marks, the second belonging to the series of marks which are known to have been written in his library books immediately after his death. The likelihood is that Jackson incorporated it in his own library at Clapham when he made up his own collection of Pepys's papers c. 1703–5, at the same time as he was making the final additions to Pepys's library authorised by Pepys's will. This volume would complete the series. The rest of his collection of Pepys papers, which are bound and lettered in the same style as the Greenwich volume, consisted of four volumes entitled 'Private Correspondence and Miscellaneous Papers of S. Pepys 1679–1703'. This was material closely connected with Jackson himself – letters to and from him, and dating mostly from the last years of Pepys's life when Jackson was his amanuensis. All five volumes passed to Jackson's descendants, the Pepys Cockerells. At the sale by auction of their Pepys papers in 1931 the four volumes of 'Private Correspondence' etc. passed into private possession, where they still remain.[13] They were published (except for a handful of items) by J. R. Tanner in 1926 in two volumes which bear the title of the original MSS. The volume of 'Official Correspondence' was acquired by the National Maritime Museum. Of the 940 items in it just over one third have been published. (In 1929 Tanner brought out a selection of the longhand letters which was followed in 1933 by E. Chappell's version of those in shorthand.)[14]

The Public Record Office. Here, kept nowadays in the series of State Papers Domestic, are the Navy Office papers which Pepys as Clerk of the Acts had the duty of preserving. They are now incomplete – the out-letters, contract-books, bill-books and certain other papers which are known to have survived in the office until 1688[15] having since then disappeared. Even so, what remains – mainly the letters addressed to the Office – forms the most voluminous single source of information about Pepys's work in the '60s. They are both a guide to the business he transacted and a means of identifying the people he dealt with. Despite their bulk they are easy to consult since summaries, with indexes, have been published in the *Calendars of State Papers Domestic*[16] – a shelf-full of large and well-organised volumes of which Pepys himself would have approved. To some extent the diary and Pepys's related papers fill in the gaps they leave. [*See also* Jackson, John; Magdalene College]

Dickons. John Dekins, or Dickons (as he spelt the name),[1] was a hemp merchant whose daughter, Elizabeth, Pepys called his 'Morena'. Father and daughter died within a few days of each other in Oct. 1662. An Elizabeth 'Dickins' (? the widow) was a ratepayer in St Olave's parish in 1663.[2]

Digby, Capt. [Francis]. Son of the 2nd Earl of Bristol, he held four naval commissions 1666–8, served as captain in the Duke of York's Regiment at Sea, and was killed in action in 1672.[1]

Digby, George, Baron Digby 1641, succ. as 2nd Earl of Bristol 1653 (1612–77). Politician, soldier, and playwright – a man of brilliant gifts, but almost no achievements, having, in Burnet's words, 'no judgment nor steadiness'. He had served Charles I, briefly and disastrously, as a Secretary of State in 1643 and was appointed to the same office by Charles II in 1657, but was made to resign on becoming a Roman Catholic. His religion excluded him from high office thereafter and he played a spoiling game in the politics of the diary period, making himself unpopular and mistrusted on all sides. The diary has several revealing references to his vendetta against Clarendon. The only play he published was *Elvira* (1667).[1]

Dillon, Cary, succ. as 5th Earl of Roscommon 1685 (d. 1689). Soldier and Irish politician; M.P. for Banagher 1661–6, Privy Councillor (Ireland) from 1674 and Master of the Irish Mint from c. 1675. In 1689 he fought in the English army under James II and was attainted as a rebel.[1]

Dobbins, Capt. [Joseph]. In 1653, captain of a merchantman, the *Peter of London*; Elder Brother of Trinity House 1665; recommended as sailing master of the *Royal Sovereign* 1666; appointed commissioner for relief of widows and orphans of officers and seamen 1673.[1]

DOCKYARDS

The royal dockyards constituted, even in peacetime, the most considerable industrial unit in the country.[1] Their administration lay in the hands of the Navy Board, whose control was effected in two ways: by visits from members of the Board, and by delegation of the Board's powers to resident Commissioners. The Thames yards at Deptford and Woolwich were supervised directly from the Navy Office; Chatham had a resident Commissioner for most of the diary period, and Portsmouth a resident Commissioner in wartime. In addition to these main yards it was also considered desirable in wartime to have an advanced base; in the Second Dutch War it was Harwich, and, to a lesser extent, Sheerness. (Plymouth was not used in this way until the French war of William III.) The Thames and Medway yards were particularly important not only because of their strategic location, but also because of their extensive facilities and equipment, and their proximity to London, the major market of stores and a valuable source of labour. These considerations explain their continued use at a time when the silting of their rivers, and the increased size of ships, made the approaches very hazardous.

In peacetime the yards were employed in maintaining and repairing ships, and in preparing them for the summer and winter guards or for convoy duty. In wartime the extra volume of work tended to be seasonal, especially in the Thames yards where activity slackened off during the campaigning season. All the yards except Harwich were staffed by full-time standing officers. Their number depended on the size of the yard, and included clerical officers – the Clerk of the Cheque, the Storekeeper and the Clerk of the Survey – as well as the executive officers, the Master-Shipwright and the Master-Attendant. These last two were assisted by subordinate officers: the Master-Caulker, the Master-Carpenter, the Master-Boatmaker, the Master-Mastmaker and the Boatswain of the yard. In addition, at Chatham, Woolwich and Portsmouth, there were ropeyards, each with its Clerk and Master-Ropemaker. The ropeyard was usually considered a separate unit even though it was situated inside the yard or close by. In most of the yards the permanent staff would include a number of assistants to the standing officers – clerks, watchmen, porters, and sometimes a surgeon and a minister. The workmen consisted mostly of shipwrights, joiners, sawyers, caulkers, sailmakers, coopers and labourers.

Of the three clerical officers, the Clerk of the Cheque was the chief. He was required to keep a record of the men employed in the yard, their work, length of service and absences. To do this he had to take musters of the yard and of any ships laid up at least once, if not more often, each day. From this information he prepared the pay books. He also had to act as a check on other officers, particularly the Store-keeper. The Clerk's duties were probably the most difficult of all, and they were wide open to abuse and neglect. Those of the Storekeeper were simpler: he received and inspected all materials delivered to the yard, provided that he had first received a warrant from the Board empowering him to accept them. He was also supplied with copies of contracts to enable him to certify that the goods conformed to specification. He kept accounts of all goods delivered to the stores and of their subsequent issue to other officers; and presented them quarterly or annually to the Board, after they had been checked by the Clerk of the Cheque and the Clerk of the Survey. This latter officer was the third clerical officer of the yard. His principal duty was to survey the stores with the other clerical officers and to certify with them the requirements of the yard. It was also his responsibility to take a survey of the ships' equipment when they came into the yard.

The most senior of the executive officers was the Master-Shipwright. As well as supervising all building and repair work, he authorised the issue of stores and checked the Storekeeper's accounts. The Master-Attendant, next in seniority, was responsible for the ships after they had been built or repaired – for their docking and cleaning, and for their movement within the yards and anchorages. He also supervised the preparations for setting the ships out and for laying them up.

The salaries paid to these officers (which remained static for the most part until the end of the century) are indicators both of their importance within the yard and of the relative importance of the yards themselves. For example, from 1661 to 1665 the Clerk of the Cheque at Chatham was paid £120 p.a., at Deptford £80, at Woolwich £70 and at Portsmouth £68 13s. 10d. The Storekeeper at Chatham received £100, at Deptford more (£144 18s. 4d.) since Deptford served other yards from its stores, at Woolwich £70 and at Portsmouth £50.[2] With the salaries went allowances for clerks, stationery and travel. But there were few of them who did not also feather their nests. Pepys often remarks wryly on the luxury of their houses and style of living (though it must be added that he himself in 1666 had his handsome bookcases made free of charge by the Deptford carpenters). But much as he and his colleagues tried to eradicate the worst abuses, dockyard officers retained a reputation for corruption until the early 19th century. Equally, the workforce was undisciplined. The men were expected to work long hours – 5.30 a.m. to 6.30 p.m. in the summer, with half an hour off for breakfast and one-and-a-half for dinner – for wages that were never generous and often in arrear. They stole, grumbled, cheated and slacked; they occasionally went on strike and they frequently absented themselves at harvest time to earn a little ready money.

Supervision of the yards was best tackled by the appointment of resident Navy Commissioners, but it was not until the First Dutch War (1652–4) that they were introduced – at Chatham, Portsmouth and Harwich. After the war only Peter Pett (at Chatham) remained. No further appointments were made until 1664, when Thomas Middleton was appointed to Portsmouth and John Taylor to Harwich. The resident commissioners were regarded as being of lowlier status than the other commissioners. The inferior position of Pett (reflected in his salary) lay in the fact that he 'was not obliged to a continual personal attendance' on the Board.[3] He exercised his right only rarely and in practice was its least influential member. Middleton and Taylor were specifically excluded from the Board, and required to obey the Board's orders. Their subordinate position was emphasised during the war when members of the Board were sent to the yards to hasten out the fleet and to lend authority to orders. Moreover, the local commissioners – seamen and shipbuilders to a man – were of inferior social status to the members of the Board. The resident commissionership was normally in fact the peak of a career in the dockyards.

The yards were at all times supervised by visits, or inspections, by members of the Board – in the more distant yards three or four times a year, in the case of the Thames and Medway yards, much more frequently. The extent of this supervision can be seen in 1662; by the beginning of that year the Board had settled into their duties and had been given their Instructions.[4] The Duke of York, in his letter accompanying the Instructions (28 Jan. 1662) ordered the Board to take an 'exact accompt of the behaviour of the several officers in the yards . . .' and to dismiss unnecessary or unfit workmen.[5] In the following April Batten went to Chatham, and Carteret, Penn and Pepys to Portsmouth. After his return to London Pepys composed a letter to Portsmouth pointing out the number of unnecessary workmen.[6] Similarly at Chatham, Pepys on 4 Aug. 1662 found 'great disorder by multitude of servants and old decrepitt men'. The Board as a result sent a strong letter to all yards complaining about the 'remissness' of their officers and calling for strict observance of the Instructions.[7] More visits, and more reprimands, followed. During 1662 at least 10 visits were made to Woolwich and 17 to Deptford, one of the Deptford inspections being a surprise muster carried out on 8 August by Pepys which uncovered an alarming number of abuses. The result of all this activity was the introduction by Pepys of specially designed call-books for use in the yards, by means of which the clerks of the cheque could keep a full and accurate record of the work done.[8] Control by the Board was thereafter in theory easier.

A similar pattern of supervision can be seen in 1663 when members of the Board made 5 visits to Chatham, 4 to Portsmouth, about 14 to Woolwich and 23 to Deptford. The situation changed with the advent of war; Portsmouth and Harwich then had their resident commissioners and members of the Board were sent for longer periods to assist them. During 1665 Batten was at Harwich and Portsmouth; Mennes, Penn and Brouncker at Chatham, and occasionally at Portsmouth. The Thames and Medway yards received less attention because they were less important once the fleet was at sea, and in the summers of the war years they had little work, apart from the receipt and distribution of stores. After the war the visits became even less frequent because no money was available to pay the yards or buy stores; thus two of the main reasons for visits ceased to exist. Pepys, a regular visitor to Deptford, remarks on 4 March 1669 that he had not been there for twelve months.

Apart from personal visits, the main form of communication between the Board and the yards was by correspondence and the issue of regulations. But however frequent the letters and however stringent the regulations, the yards escaped detailed invigilation. When challenged on this subject by the Brooke House Committee in 1668, Pepys replied that the Board could hardly be expected to exercise more than a general control over the more distant yards and had to rely on the local supervision of the resident commissioners.[9] He was in fact acknowledging the justice of the criticism.[10] [*See also* Chatham; Deptford; Harwich; Portsmouth; Woolwich]

(Andrew Turnbull)

Doctors' Commons. A 'college' of doctors of civil and canon law, principally the judges and advocates of the Court of Admiralty and the Prerogative Court of Canterbury. Situated on St Benet's Hill, below St Paul's Churchyard, destroyed in the Fire, and pending re-building (on the same site), accommodated in Exeter House, Strand. The court, memorably described in *Pickwick Papers*, was abolished in 1857. The buildings were demolished ten years later and Queen Victoria St now passes over its gardens. The name still attaches to the remains of the area between Knightrider and Queen Victoria Sts. (R)

Doling, Thomas. Messenger to the Council of State, 1660.[1]

Dorset House. A large house, with extensive outbuildings and gardens, in Salisbury Court off the Strand; its site now marked by Dorset Rise. Once the London house of the bishops of Salisbury, it was sold before 1571 to the Sackvilles, later Earls of Dorset, who in the 17th century let on lease some of the buildings and gardens. The main house was occupied in May and June 1660 by Lord Chancellor Hyde; in July he moved to Worcester House near by. After the Fire (in which the house was destroyed) the site was again built on, one of the buildings being used (from 1671) as the theatre of the Duke's Players. (R)

Douglas, James, 2nd Marquess of Douglas (1646–1700). Major in Lord George Douglas's foot regiment 1666; colonel of his own foot regiment 1678. He became 'morose and peevish' in later life and had to hand over management of his estates to a commission.[1]

Dover Castle, clerk of: *see* Raven, J.

Doves, Capt. Possibly Capt. Douce (of the *Pembroke* 1665). The name (written in longhand) might be read as 'Dows': in which case he might be Henry Dawes, who commanded the *John and Thomas* in 1665–6 and was killed in the *Princess* in 1667.[1]

Dowgate. Dowgate Hill ran up from the river to Walbrook. The inlet or dock there was known as Dowgate. Commercially important in the 1660s, it is now relatively insignificant, but its position can be found immediately upstream of the approaches to Cannon St station. (R)

Downes, [Elkanah]. Vicar of Ashtead, Surrey 1662–d. 83; also Rector of St Leonard's, Eastcheap 1661–6.[1]

Downing, Sir George, kt 1660, bt 1663 (?1623–84). Pepys's employer at the Exchequer 1656–60. A vain, ruthless and extremely able man whom Pepys both admired and disliked, and whose passion to establish England's commercial power chimed in well with Pepys's concern for her navy. He had lived in New England (where he was the second man to graduate from Harvard), but had returned in 1645 and, after a period as a regimental preacher, became Scoutmaster-General to Cromwell's army in Scotland. He rose quickly to political influence, thanks to Cromwell's favour and to a shrewd marriage to the sister of Col. Charles Howard, later Earl of Carlisle and one of Cromwell's major-generals. As an M.P. in 1654 and 1656 he was associated with the group (to which Pepys's patron Mountagu also belonged) which urged Cromwell to take the title of king. At the Restoration he was knighted and retained his post (held since 1657) of envoy to the United Provinces, having given valuable information to the royalists. He admired the economic and financial enterprise of the Dutch and was convinced that it was vital to English interests to break their naval power and their virtual monopoly of the European carrying trade. As envoy he blocked all attempts at compromise with them and did all that could be done by his native arrogance and aggressiveness to promote the war of 1665.

As an Exchequer official (Teller of the Receipt 1656–84) and M.P. (sitting for all the parliaments of Charles II's reign) he made his reputation as a well-informed and outspoken expert on finance and trade. He vigorously promoted the Navigation Acts of 1660 and 1661 and was almost entirely responsible for the appropriation clause in the Additional Aid Act of 1665 which removed some of the government's difficulties in raising loans. His most remarkable achievements were as secretary to the Treasury Commission 1667–71, where with colleagues such as Duncombe, enterprising and energetic like himself, he re-organised office methods and in 1667 introduced the Treasury orders which were to be the basis of government finance until the establishment in the '90s of the Bank of England.

In 1671 he was sent once more to The Hague as envoy. War broke out in the following year and he fled home in fear of his life. In 1677 he was one of the M.P.s who strongly supported Pepys's proposal for the building of 30 new ships.

The niggardliness Pepys remarks on was a complaint his own mother made of him.[1]

His name is preserved in Downing St, Westminster (site of a building development he undertook in 1682); that of his family in Downing College, Cambridge, founded by his grandson.[2] [*See also* Exchequer]
Downing, [John]. An anchorsmith in private business at Deptford, the navy being amongst his customers. In 1666 he applied for the post of official anchorsmith in the yard, but withdrew his application.[1]
Downing, Capt. ——. Probably John Downing of the 1st Footguards; commissioned ensign in 1661 and captain in 1668.[1]
Doyly, Sir William, bt 1663 (?1614–77). Of Shottesham, Norf. He sat in every parliament from 1654 until his death. He first came into contact with Pepys as chairman of the parliamentary commission for paying off the army in 1660. In both the Second and Third Dutch Wars he was an active Commissioner for the Sick and Wounded.[1]
[Draghi, Giovanni Battista] ('**Seignor Baptista**') (c. 1640–1708). Keyboard player, composer and librettist. Came to England in 1666 as 'poet' of the King's Italian Musick, remained as organist to Queen

Catherine, and continued in the royal service under James II and William III until crippled by gout and finally pensioned in 1698.[1] (Lu)
Drawwater, Mr and Mrs. Guests of the Strudwicks at a Twelfth Night party. James Drawwater had married Jane Strudwick in 1654.[1]

DRESS AND PERSONAL APPEARANCE

Introduction. Throughout the opening years of Charles II's reign fashions for both men and women were changing from Dutch to French models. The changes, however, cannot be dated with any precision. Few suits and dresses of the period have survived apart from those in the Verney collection at Claydon House and the Isham collection in the Victoria and Albert; portraits are not very helpful since the sitters were rarely painted in the clothes they habitually wore, and evidence such as exists for France in Jean Donneau de Vizé's illustrated articles[1] is not to be found. The diary does something to fill this gap. Having an observant eye for the world he lived in, Pepys often writes in detail about dress. He was extremely interested in his own clothes, perhaps because he was a tailor's son, or (more probably) out of pride or vanity – the style to which he aspired being that of the successful public servant. His dress in fact tended to typify the upper middle class of London.

Men's Dress. At the Restoration, as before the Civil War, men still wore short doublets, often unbuttoned at the waist, full breeches open at the knee, cloaks or coats with turn-down collars, and high-crowned felt hats with feathers or silver cords about the brim. Cloaks were becoming less fashionable except for riding, and coats were becoming shorter.[2] The doublet, sometimes slashed for easier fit, was discarded indoors, and an undress gown of rich material – a 'morning gown' or 'Indian gown' – was worn for reading or writing. Pepys hired a gown of figured silk when sitting to Hayls for his portrait.

Dress swords, often with silver hilts, replaced rapiers at the Restoration as part of the everyday outdoor wear of the gentleman.[3] He was improperly dressed if he were without sword or cloak,[4] and his footboy would wear a small sword as part of his livery,[5] thus emphasising the fact that the weapon was for decoration rather than utility. The sword could, of course, be useful in an awkward corner even to middle-class men not in the habit of drawing their blades to defend their honour. But in the only fracas in which Pepys was involved, according to the diary – on 11 May 1663 when he was attacked and almost 'worried' by a great dog – he was in such a 'maze' that he quite forgot to unsheath his sword.

Breeches, as Hollar's engravings show, were of different types; the grandest, edged with ribbon, might well measure more than a yard about at each knee, like Edmund Verney's pair still kept at Claydon House.[6] (These were 'Rhinegraves' or petticoat breeches, so wide that on 6 Apr. 1661 Mr Townsend by mistake put both his legs through one of the legs of his breeches 'and went so all day'.) They were kept up not by braces or gallowses running over the shoulders, but by large metal hooks fastening through eyes in the lining of the doublet, and were lined sometimes with baize for warmth or with white linen which showed at the knees when the wearer sat down. In 1662 Pepys had close-kneed breeches to go with his riding coat and feared that they might be too hot for summer wear.

For formal dress the best evidence is Hollar's engravings published in John Ogilby's *Entertainment of Charles II in his passage through the city of London to his coronation* (1661). For the coronation Pepys wore the long velvet coat made for him in the previous August.

As he became more affluent, he laid out more money on clothes. In 1661 he had worn a white coat made from one of his wife's old petticoats, but by 1661 he was having his new bands edged with deep lace, and his cloaks made stylishly – one in 1664 matching his suit and lined with plush. In Oct. 1666, when the King, declaring independence of French fashions in wartime,[7] decreed a change in men's fashions at court, Pepys immediately obeyed. The new fashion consisted of a vest (a 'long Cassocke close to the body', which Pepys was wearing by 4 November) with a coat over it; and short, low-hung, ruffled breeches just showing at the knees or below the coat. The vest replaced the doublet for good and became the buttoned waistcoat or 'justaucorps' worn under a coat or 'surcoat'. Despite the King's intention the new fashion came in the end to be not so far removed from the French style. In 1668 in fact Pepys was wearing a French fashion – a new 'stuff' suit with a shoulder-belt for the sword; and with the cuffs of his long vest and waistcoat ('tunic') laced with silver lace. The waistcoat sleeves no doubt showed inside the broad cuffs of the coat. He had worn a sword from 1661 ('as the manner now among gentlemen is')[8] and occasionally carried a varnished walking-staff or a silver-headed Japan cane. He may be said to have dressed carefully – even proudly; he had an awareness of the importance of neat clothes to a young man on the make. But with all his prosperity he drew the line at appearing too courtier-like in appearance. When the gold lace on his sleeves drew comments from Mr Povey, he resolved 'never to appear in Court with it, but presently to have it taken off, as it is fit I should'.[9]

During the diary period more Flemish and Venetian lace came to be worn, especially in men's bands and trimmings. When Pepys was wearing a plain band on a Sunday in 1667 he was mistaken for a servant.

The fashion in hats was changing. The felt hat of the Commonwealth period, resembling an inverted flower-pot, was replaced by one of velvet – cocked up behind – or a low-crowned beaver. It would normally be worn at meals, as well as outdoors. For riding, the close fitting velvet 'montero' was the usual wear.

Gentlemen usually carried gloves, and often wore them, especially for riding. To Pepys it was a sign of the 'working goldsmith' that he went 'without gloves to his hands'.[10] Men could in addition wear muffs (hung on a string around the neck) without any derogation from dignity. (The fashion continued into the 18th century.) Boots might be bought ready-made[11] but presumably those which Pepys bought from his shoemaker Wotton were made to measure. Square-toed shoes continued in fashion in the '60s, but Pepys in 1660 mentions the new fashion of silver buckles, which replaced the shoe strings of an earlier generation.

Underwear consisted of linen drawers, and (in cold weather) flannel waistcoats (the modern vest). Occasionally an extra shirt would be worn for warmth. Nightwear consisted of a nightshirt worn with or without underwear. The old habit of wearing no nightclothes (of going to one's 'naked bed') seems to have been no longer so common.
Men's Hair. Pepys wore his hair long and curled in the early years of the diary – difficult though he found it to keep clean – but in 1663 adopted the new fashion of the periwig. Wigs had been worn in Tudor England only if needed: the practice of wearing them for fashion's sake is said to have originated in France in the 1630s at the court of Louis XIII when the King went bald. It spread to England rapidly after the Restoration (the word wig in this sense seems to have entered the language in the '70s) and lasted for over one-and-a-half centuries. (Dr Routh, President of Magdalen College, Oxford, who died in 1854, is said to have been the last person to have worn a wig habitually for fashion's sake.) By 1663 Charles II's hair was already turning grey and when he and the Duke of York began wearing wigs, Pepys had two made for himself and wore them from Nov. 1663. While both long hair and wigs could and did become infested with nits, wigs were more easily cleaned. In 1665 there was a risk that wigs might have been made from the hair of plague victims, but Pepys resolved to continue wearing one over his hair (cut short for the purpose). His successive wigs illustrate the movement of fashion towards artificiality. That worn in the early portrait by Hayls (1666) resembles a full head of hair. In the Kneller portrait of 1686 the wig is a quite different object – large, portentous, and bearing little relation to the natural hair. It was meant to proclaim the owner's importance. Whatever its size the wig was a valuable means of keeping the head warm. The fashion in fact led in the '80s or thereabouts to the abandonment of the indoor use of the hat.

Twice Pepys mentions having a 'beard' (i.e. moustache).[12] But it was shaved off in Jan. 1664, and in all his portraits he appears clean-shaven. He normally shaved – or was shaved – at home, and rarely went to a barber's shop. He once remarks that he does not feel awake or ready to face the day's business without a morning shave.[13] It was common enough for townsmen to shave every other day as Swift did;[14] but to Pepys it was one of the horrors of the Fire that it forced him to go a whole week without shaving. He was in the habit of allowing himself the luxury on Sundays of having a barber come to his house and shave him before morning service. The practice was perhaps particularly necessary in 1660–2 when he was shaving for the rest of the week with a pumice-stone. This he abandoned in Jan. 1664 in favour of a razor, which would have been an instrument similar to the 'cut-throat' razor of modern times. It is noticeable that the barber's Sunday visits were less frequent afterwards.

Women's Dress. Women, as early as the Civil War, were abandoning the high-waisted gowns and short jackets with over-lapping tabs familiar from Van Dyck's portraits. Instead, they began to adopt long stiff bodices pointed in front and reaching below the waist. Skirts were draped so as to show a lace-trimmed petticoat at the front. The horizontal neck-opening with a kerchief edged with lace, fashionable in the early 17th century, was still retained. Women's fashions to some extent changed annually at Easter. Pepys's cousin Mrs Turner once told him it was 'in vain to make new clothes till Easter, that they might see the fashions as they are like to be this summer'.[15]

Elizabeth Pepys's own style is not very well described in the diary, but it is virtually certain that her best gowns, throughout the '60s, were of the new low-waisted variety and worn open from the waist to show the petticoat. In June 1661 Pepys was satisfied that her black silk taffeta gown with gimp lace was fashionable enough, but in the following year he was reminded that she needed a winter gown, and was ashamed to appear in taffeta 'when all the world wears Moyre'.[16] Lace, often stiffened with silver- or gold-wire thread, played a great part in women's dress. Pepys bought lace for the kerchief Elizabeth wore about her neck and point lace for the trimming of her gown. It was normally re-used. When the stiffened whisk collar was going out of fashion, she gave hers to her brother or her maid. Hats were worn in 1663 with large plumes of feathers curled about the brim. For outdoor wear the hair was protected by a hood, usually black – white hoods being associated with servants.

Gentlewomen had increased liberty after the Restoration, but when walking in parks and places of resort, and especially in theatres, they often wore masks to conceal their identity. Elizabeth wore a small vizard in the theatre. Masks – first shown on Englishwomen in Hollar's engravings c. 1640 – were also used to protect the complexion when travelling. For riding, fashionable ladies wore clothes which made them look like men. Pepys was shocked: he found it 'an odde sight' to come across the maids of honour in the galleries of Whitehall accoutred in coats and doublets, with deep skirts and petticoats dragging under their men's coats.[17] This appears to be the first mention of what in the 18th century became an accepted fashion.

Underwear consisted of smocks and drawers. The supposition that drawers were a recent French innovation copied from the dress of ballet dancers appears to be without substance. The fact that they are rarely mentioned in inventories merely reflects the fact that they were usually home-made. Both Elizabeth Pepys and Peg Lowther wore them, and there is plenty of literary evidence for their use.[18]

Women's Hair Styles. Lady hairdressers were at this period beginning to establish themselves in London – the mother of the Duchess of Albemarle is said to have been the first – but none are mentioned in the diary, and Elizabeth, we assume, did her own hair, with the help of her companion. The new fashion in the early '60s was the use of 'locks' inserted into the hair. They were plaited and curled, and secured by pins. She wore a 'pair of peruques' of this sort made of her own hair as early as March 1662. When however she began to wear blanched locks not her own Pepys objected, pretty though they looked.

Cosmetics. Fashion demanded – whatever the moralists might say – the employment of aids to beauty, and the use both of native and imported products greatly increased in this period. (They consistuted the entire cargo of one ship which arrived at London in 1684.)[19] The most widespread novelty was the use of patches made of velvet, silk, thin leather or paper, variously shaped – as stars, hearts and so on. These were a French fashion (referred to in 1653 as recently introduced into England)[20] and for a while not quite respectable. Pepys was reluctant to allow his wife to wear them, but perhaps his hesitation was overcome by the example of the ladies of the Sandwich family.[21] Their popularity at court, Pepys noticed, was not unconnected with their usefulness in covering blemishes.[22] Rather more controversial, as always, was the use of paint. For actresses (now playing women's parts previously played by boys) it was necessary; but Pepys disliked Nell Gwyn's using it offstage, and he positively hated its use by other lady friends.[23] It may be assumed that Elizabeth did not paint. She used rouge and powder and perfumes, no doubt, and certainly wore scented gloves. Her toilet preparations included May Dew, gathered at dawn, and puppy-dog water.[24]

Women Servants. The dress of the ladies' companions seems to have been indistinguishable from that of their mistresses.[25] In fact, they often wore their mistresses' cast-offs. White hoods made of linen were the usual mark of the lower servant. In Hollar's engravings of maidservants

doing the shopping, they wear white hoods, long aprons, and pattens.
Ceremony. Pepys and his contemporaries were punctilious about the
proper management of the hat – a matter all the more important because it was often worn indoors as well as out. It was removed, for
instance, during the drinking of healths. They also paid careful attention to the dress appropriate to the various periods of mourning. For
royalty and the aristocracy there were three periods, each lasting several
months.[26] When the Duke of Gloucester died in 1660, Pepys, though
only a young civil servant, gave his wife £15 to buy full mourning for
the two of them, a few days later buying a new hat band and short
black stockings for himself. How long they wore it is not clear. Deaths
in the family were the occasion for plunging the entire household into
black. In July 1661 they went into full mourning for the death of Uncle
Robert, and after three months into second mourning. For Pepys this
was the excuse for buying 'a handsome belt'.[27] At funerals black was
applied with special thoroughness; at that of his brother Tom, Pepys
had the soles of his boots blacked, perhaps because they would be
visible when he knelt.
Washing and Bathing. It is no doubt generally true that standards of
personal cleanliness were lower in the 17th century than nowadays.
London had good supplies of fresh water, from the New River and the
Thames and other sources, which were piped into the more substantial
houses, but the houses themselves usually lacked internal plumbing and
had no means of heating the water except on a fire. On the other hand,
there was soap enough. The price of English soap was reduced by the
excise act of 1661; scented varieties were imported from France and the
popular Castile soap, made from olive oil, from Spain. No doubt it is
dangerous to generalise about cleanliness. Members of the same household, enjoying the same lack of facilities, could adopt different standards.
Pepys makes it plain that he thought Elizabeth's were lower than his
own. She once went to a public hothouse (a Turkish bath), but his
comment was – 'How long it will hold, I can guess'.[28] As for his own
habits, he himself abhorred slovenliness and dirt. He implies at one
point (v.320) that he normally washed each morning, but whether that
involved anything beyond washing hands and face is doubtful. Clearly
enough when he 'washed' on 2 May 1662, after a hot journey, it meant
something more. On other occasions he mentions using a footbath, but
with some reluctance, fearing he would catch cold. According to the
evidence of the diary he never immersed himself except at Bath, in the
spa waters.
　　Bathrooms were in his time rarities in England, and it was long
before the middle-class home or the gentleman's country house had
them. Thomas Povey, whose possessions and life-style Pepys so much
admired, had a bathroom at the top of his house. But Pepys never

thought of emulating him in that respect, many though the alterations
were that he made to his lodgings in Seething Lane.

(J. L. Nevinson; La)

DRINK

Introduction. The alternatives to alcohol were few in the London of
the '60s. Water was not always piped into houses and was regarded as
dangerous if not fresh and in any case too cold and heavy to be good
for the health. Pepys distrusted it in particular for its effect on his
kidney-stones.[1] Tea and coffee were only just beginning to be imported
and were still expensive. Total abstinence therefore was rare – the only
person mentioned in the diary who is known to have practised it was
the traveller Sir Henry Blount, who had acquired the Moslem habit of
abstinence (and a taste for coffee) on his journeys in the Near East.[2]
Even the strictest moralists during the Puritan Revolution themselves
drank in moderation and did no more than denounce drunkenness and
the dangers of tavern life. It is doubtful if the Puritan Revolution
reduced the *per capita* consumption of alcohol, and in fact the establishment of large standing armies and navies may well have increased it.
As for the '60s, later generations, judging general standards of behaviour
from that of the royal court, have often assumed that at the Restoration
drunkenness increased, along with other forms of immorality.[3] Certainly Pepys and his friends drank freely, but the only statistical
evidence we so far have on the problem concerns a later period – the
decade beginning in 1684.[4] The excise revenue from ale and beer shows
a marked increase during the reign of James II that cannot be accounted
for by a rise in population or by any other cause than a rise in consumption. Equally there was a marked decrease of the same revenue in
the 1690s. Some have suggested that this was due to the work of the
societies for the improvement of manners which were founded after
the Glorious Revolution.[5] Others may wonder whether the explanation may not lie in the emergence of a new factor – the availability of
cheap gin.

For Pepys's own drinking habits in the diary period, see vol.xi,
Index: Drink. They were those of a young man prone to pleasure but
at the same time, from about 1662, increasingly concerned to discipline
himself, and in particular to protect himself from the harmful effects
of over-indulgence in wine. (Ale and beer of course hardly counted.)
The diary shows his steady, or occasionally unsteady, progress. He made
monthly vows against wine drinking and towards the end of the
diary it is clear that the habit had been broken. In 1677 he wrote a

memorandum on his health in which he recorded his success. He was by then in the habit of confining his drinking almost always to meal times. He then drank 'liberally' but 'with a temperance still', and avoided the thin French wines which flew too easily to his head.[6] **Ale and beer.** These were still the national drinks. Beer was cheap, in London costing 2*d*. or 3*d*. a quart in the taverns and 4*s*.–8*s*. a barrel (i.e. 36 gallons). Ale was a little cheaper, but less stable. Cheapest of all was small beer: a light brew, popular with children and as a summer drink. Porter or stout was unknown in London until the 1720s: its 17th-century equivalent was mum, a heavy ale made from wheat and matured for two years. Beer and ale might be brewed by households, taverns and elsewhere (Pepys mentions the domestic brews at Eton and Magdalene), but for the most part the market was supplied by brewers' products. Among the best-known mentioned in the diary were Alderman Byde's ale, made at Mile End Green; Lambeth ale; Northdown (or Margate) ale, often carried aboard ships in the Downs; and Hull ale (the name given to the products of the Trent valley shipped from Hull). Andrew Marvell, as M.P. for Hull, received a barrel each session. Bottled beer was not uncommon, but was distrusted by writers on health as 'windy and muddy'.[7] Beer was sometimes drunk mixed with wine or sugar or water. Rather more frequently, ale was sophisticated to give it flavour or medicinal virtue. Served hot, and possibly buttered, it was a favourite winter drink and a specific against colds.[8] At Christmas it would appear as lamb's wool – hot and garnished with roasted apples. A tavern might specialise in a particular variety – as a 'cock-ale tavern', or a 'china-root house' etc.

Wine. Londoners of Pepys's class drank wine almost as freely as ale or beer, both in taverns and at home. They took pride in their domestic stores. Pepys only once found there was no wine in his cellar: he normally kept several varieties and on one occasion reflected that never had any Pepys possessed so much at one time. English wine could be obtained but only by the curious and the adventurous. Wine growing in England outside the monasteries had never been extensive, and from the 14th century had declined with the growth of trade in French wines and had virtually ceased with the Dissolution. France was still the main supplier of red wine – principally clarets. Even the Graves imported at this time was a red. The only château-bottled wine well-known in England at this time – Pepys mentions it – was a claret: Haut Brion, marketed in London by a family of restaurateurs, the Pontaques, who owned the vineyard.[9] The trade in Burgundies did not develop until the 19th century when the difficulties of land transport within France had been overcome. French whites were hard to come by, and champagne as yet a rare novelty. (Pepys was accused during the Popish Plot of being bribed by hogsheads of it.)[10] German whites became very popular in the '60s and there were several Rhenish winehouses in London and Westminster which served little else. They were often known by their names of origin – Hock, Mosel etc. – but the only one named in the diary was 'Bleakard' (Bleichert). The supplies of Rhenish wine at source were so small and the demand so great that the Dutch and other merchants handling the trade were commonly suspected of producing it by doctoring French reds. Another source of white wines was, of course, Spain and the Canaries whose dry white or sack (*secco*) was the most popular of all tavern wines in 16th- and 17th-century England. Sherry, still unfortified at this date, was one of the varieties; Malaga another (more expensive: hence Pepys's mixing it with his sherry). Oxford, according to Wood, was turning from sack to claret in the '60s.[11] If so it was a fashion that went unobserved in the capital. Spanish red (or 'tent': *tinto*) was not consumed in such large quantities as sack. Other sources of supply were Italy, Greece and the Levant, from which were imported fruity dessert wines such as Florence wine and Muscadine.

All wines were drunk young. They had not been clarified or matured before sale, and the cork stopper, which allowed them to be stored in bottles, was not introduced until the end of the century. They were normally stored in casks, and bottles (of the squat upright variety) were used for serving at table. (The cylindrical bottle did not come in until the 1770s.) Being young, wine was treated without respect. A dry wine would be sweetened with sugar, a sweet wine embellished with fruits and herbs. Either might be infused with ginger and a variety of spices to make 'hippocras', which, like 'burnt' or mulled wine, was often drunk in winter.[12]

Spirits. Spirit drinking is said to have been brought into England in Elizabeth's reign by soldiers returning from the wars in the Low Countries. The habit spread rapidly; spirits were easy and cheap to make and though distilling was confined to members of the Distillers' Company, no licence was required for selling them, and by 1621 there were 200 strong-water houses in London.[13] They sold mostly a spirit known generically as *aqua vitae* made from fermented grain, or occasionally from wine lees and other unwholesome ingredients. At the same time Dutch gin, French brandy and Irish whiskey were imported in increasing quantities, and to a less extent rum.[14] But Pepys and his friends in the '60s drank spirits only infrequently.

Non-alcoholic drinks. The first mention of lemonade is said to be in a play of 1663, and Pepys drank orange juice for the first time in his life in 1669.[15] Water of course was often drunk (Pepys mentions taking it with meals), but the significant non-alcoholic drinks were the new-comers that were to become standard items of the English diet – coffee and tea. They, together with chocolate, were coming into use in the diary period, though at different rates. They were all mild stimulants – chocolate being reinforced with sack for the purpose – so that they served as social lubricants. Their growing consumption, however, does not seem to have reduced the consumption of alcohol.

Coffee had already been known for a generation or so on the Continent where it had been introduced from Greece and the Near East. In England it was first drunk by a Greek at Oxford in 1637, and it was at Oxford that the first English coffee-house was established in 1650. London had the second in 1652 and by the time of Pepys's death coffee-houses were so numerous in the capital that it must have been difficult to imagine town-life without them. Coffee drinking in the home spread much more slowly, and opinion was divided about the merits of the drink. 'Useless,' was one verdict, 'since it serveth neither for Nourishment nor Debauchery.'[16] But its flavour was irresistible and so was its price. Coffee beans were advertised in 1662 at 1s.–6s. 8d. a lb,[17] and in the coffee-houses a dish or bowl could be bought for a penny.

Tea on the other hand was dear. Supplies had first come into England from China via Holland in about 1658, and the price was high: 16s.–50s. a lb in 1660.[18] In the '60s the E. India Company began to import it from Malaya and the price slowly dropped to £1 a lb by the end of the century. It was served weak, without milk, in the Chinese fashion. Pepys mentions it three times: once he drinks it with Sir Richard Ford, an E. India merchant, and on the other two occasions it seems to have been taken medicinally. But the taste grew; Queen Anne liked it and the first tea garden was opened in 1732 at Vauxhall – a sign that the middle classes were taking to it. But the heroic, Johnsonian, days of tea drinking were still to come, and it was not until new sources of supply were opened up in India and Ceylon in the 19th century that it became the national drink.

Chocolate was cheaper than tea but dearer than coffee. Originally imported into England from the Spanish America via Spain, after 1655 it came mostly from the newly conquered colony of Jamaica. The first advertisement appeared in 1657[19] and soon afterwards it was on sale in the London coffee-houses. It was a rich drink, containing at this period the cocoa-butter which in the 19th century was extracted to make eating chocolate. Even so, eggs, sack and spices were often added to make it richer still. Sandwich, when in Madrid, was greatly taken with its popularity and entered several recipes in his journal. Pepys, who drank it occasionally as a morning draught in the '60s, seems to have become very fond of it when visiting Spain in 1684, and acquired a pot to boil it in.[20]

Milk, often drunk hot at bedtime, was held to be dangerous when taken cold. Francis Osborne, one of Pepys's favourite authors, thought that 'in a heat' it was 'not seldom deadly'.²¹ But Pepys drank it often, and there was a milk house at the lodge gates to Hyde Park which drove a thriving trade in tankards of cold milk. To some, buttermilk, with its wholesome tang and purgative virtues, was preferable. Pepys not only drank it casually at the 'wheyhouse', but kept supplies at home and once took a 'course' of it in the summer.²² [*See also* Coffee-houses; Taverns etc.]

Drumbleby, ——. Maker of wind instruments; son of Thomas, spectacle-maker; made freeman of the Turners' Company, 1655.¹ (Lu)

Drury Lane. Great Drury (now Drury) Lane ran south-east from St Giles's High St (now High Holborn) to Wych St, continuing as Little Drury Lane to the Strand just west of the Maypole. Pepys makes no distinction between the two. The former was a spacious and well-inhabited street, and from May 1663 the King's Playhouse was situated there. Some of the lanes near by had an unsavoury reputation. Wych St and Little Drury Lane disappeared in the clearances (1901–5) which ended in the making of Aldwych. (R)

Dryden, John (1631–1700). A contemporary and acquaintance of Pepys at Cambridge (Trinity 1650–4), and distantly related to him, being a cousin of Sir Gilbert Pickering, Mountagu's brother-in-law. Pickering is said to have employed him as his clerk under the Commonwealth – in much the same way as Mountagu employed Pepys. And just as Pepys also served at that time in the Exchequer, Dryden was employed by Thurloe as a secretary for the French and Latin tongues.¹ His *Sir Martin Mar-all* was one of Pepys's favourite plays, though he did not preserve a copy in his library. In 1699 Dryden accepted a suggestion from Pepys that he include Chaucer's Parson's Tale among the pieces he translated for his *Fables*.² [*See also* Plays; Theatre[

Duck Lane. Largely inhabited by booksellers, it ran from Little Britain to West Smithfield and Long Lane. By 1799 its name had become Duke St, and since 1885 it has been renamed Little Britain, of which earlier it had been an extension. (R)

Dudley, Mr. Probably William Dudley of Clopton, Northants. (1597–1670); bt Aug. 1660; Sheriff of Northamptonshire 1660–1, and M.P. for Northampton 1663–70. He was put into the commission of peace for Huntingdonshire at Sandwich's request in July 1661.¹

[Duell, Fleetwood]. Sexton, St Olave, Hart St: appointed 1645, re-appointed 1661.¹

Duke, [George]. Secretary to the Committee of Trade 1660–3, 1667–?; to the Fishery Corporation 1664–?7; and possibly to Sir George Downing at The Hague 1664. Perhaps the Mr Duke who opposed Pepys's candidature in the bye-election at Aldeburgh in 1669.¹

The Duke's (Lincoln's Inn Fields) Theatre. Managed by Sir William Davenant and often referred to as 'the Opera'. A theatre made out of Lisle's tennis court (built 1656–7) south of the gardens of the houses in Portugal Row on the s. side of Lincoln's Inn Fields. Its s. front faced on to the new Portugal St opposite the turn into Carey St. It remained in use until 9 Nov. 1671 when the company moved to its newly built theatre in Dorset Gardens, Dorset St (now Rise), Fleet St. [*See also* Theatre] (R)

Duncombe, Sir John, kt ?1646 (1622–87). M.P. for Bury St Edmunds 1660, 1661–Jan. 79; Ordnance Commissioner 1664–70; Treasury Commissioner 1667–72; Chancellor of the Exchequer 1672–6; Privy Councillor from 1667. 'A very proper man for business' (viii.178). Pepys's words, used of his work in the Ordnance, apply equally to his more important career in the Treasury which was never better administered in the whole century than under him and his colleagues. The 'lodgings' Pepys mentions were a large house in Pall Mall, where he lived from 1666; previously he had lived in Drury Lane.[1]

Dunn, ——. Possibly Thomas Dunn, of Ratcliff, a ship's master in 1666; or Thomas Danes, an Admiralty messenger.[1]

Dunster, [Giles]. Merchant; brother of Sir Henry Dunster, M.P. for Ilchester. Member (? secretary) of the Brooke House Committee; appointed in 1671 to the new post of Surveyor-General of the Customs.[1]

Dupuy, [Lawrence]. Yeoman of the Robes to the Duke of York from at least 1662; French by birth, and granted denization in 1664. A Henry Dupuy was Keeper of Pall Mall and a Mrs Dupuy sempstress and laundress to the Duke.[1]

Durham Yard. A street with landing stairs at its foot which ran from the Strand down to the river just east of the New Exchange. It was formerly part of the town residence of the bishops of Durham, its full name being Durham House Yard. Much transformed since the 17th century by the building of the Adelphi and other changes, it was at the time of the diary a well-to-do and fashionable street, much developed in the 1650s.[1] (R)

Dury, Madam. Probably Elizabeth Drury, widow, a ratepayer living at the Axe in Axe Yard c. 1660–6.[1]

The Dutch Church. The Dutch Reformed congregation of London had since 1550 used the nave of the church of the dissolved Augustinians in Old Broad St, known as Austin Friars, where it was served by a minister and his assistant. Its numbers had long been dwindling as members became naturalised. The building, destroyed in the Second World War, was rebuilt by 1954.[1]

THE DUTCH WARS

There is an intimate intensity about the Anglo-Dutch wars of the third quarter of the 17th century that brings to mind the observation that there are no rows like family rows. Less than a century earlier both countries had helped each other as far as they dared against the Catholic colossus that bestrode Europe and the New World. Both had been narrowly but triumphantly victorious, to emerge as the champions of Protestantism and representative government. With the accession of the house of Stuart two generations intermarried with the house of Orange. Even the constitutional struggles between the Dutch Regent party and the descendants of William the Silent have certain similarities to those which plunged England into civil war and culminated in Cromwell's dictatorship. By the end of the 17th century they were once again allied against the domination of France as at its opening they had been against Spain. Why should two second-class powers with so much in common fight at all, let alone three of the hardest-fought wars in our naval history?

The classic answer given by contemporaries was most succinctly expressed by Pepys's friend, Captain Cocke: 'that the trade of the world is too little for us two, therefore one must down'.[1] Variations of this view can be found everywhere in the diary. Carteret, for instance, without necessarily accepting Cocke's fashionable assumption that the volume of trade in the world was limited, 'doth now [in 1664] confess that the trade [to W. Africa] brought all these troubles upon us between the Dutch and us'.[2] Downing, Pepys's old employer, who as ambassador at The Hague under both Cromwell and Charles II exerted as much influence on English policy towards Holland as any man, insisted on the unreasonableness of Dutch attempts to engross the lucrative ocean trades to themselves: 'These people doe arrogate to themselves St Peter's powers upon the seas. It is *mare liberum* in the British Seas but *mare clausum* on ye Coast of Africa and in ye East Indies.'[3] Downing's use of the Latin phrases alludes to another bitter cause of contention between the two countries: the English claim to sovereignty of the Narrow Seas. This was denied by the great Dutch lawyer Grotius who in his *Mare Liberum* asserted as his title makes plain the doctrine of the freedom of the seas. Grotius was answered by an English lawyer of no less learning, John Selden, in his *Mare clausum seu dominium maris* published in the time of Charles I.[4] How seriously the Stuarts took these pretensions may be inferred from the naming of the greatest warship built in the 17th century, the pride of the Royal Navy, the *Sovereign of the Seas*. Their successors under the Commonwealth took an equally high line. The actual outbreak of the First Dutch War in 1652 was occasioned by the refusal of the Vice-Admiral of a Dutch squadron to strike his sails to a pair of English warships on their way down Channel.[5] It was hardly possible for Charles II, had he been so disposed, to take a less aggressive attitude. In fact he found a pretext for the Third Dutch War (1672-4) by stretching the doctrine to breaking point.[6] Bound up with the doctrine of the sovereignty of the seas was the question of fishing rights. The Dutch were not at all willing to accept exclusion from the rich herring grounds off the coasts of Scotland and the Orkneys and Shetlands.

Besides these real or factitious causes of conflict there were tributary irritations of resentment and jealousy. The Amboina massacre of 1623, when the English merchants resident on the island had been condemned and executed by their more powerful rivals of the Dutch E. India Company for an alleged conspiracy, was a ready resource for any Englishman who wanted to stir up hatred for the Dutch. Less inflammatory but still a long-standing grievance was the dispute over the sovereignty of the island of Pulo Run, which the English claimed and the Dutch held. Most obvious of all was the simple jealousy of Dutch success, Dutch wealth, Dutch efficiency. The period of England's most humiliating failures, the expeditions against Cadiz and the Ile de Rhé, was the period of such glittering Dutch successes as Piet Heyn's capture of the Spanish treasure fleet. Dutch merchant ships were better designed, cheaper to build and more economical to operate. Nothing except the Dutch involvement in the Thirty Years War which drove up costs and dried up the supply of cheap capital could have prevented them from undercutting the English in the carrying trade of Europe, even on the home ground of our own import and export trade. When in 1648 the Thirty Years War at last came to an end the truth of this proposition was quickly demonstrated. Something had to be done. That something was the Navigation Act of 1651.[7]

The proponents of this policy were well aware that though it could be justified on protectionist arguments it nonetheless struck at the vitals of the Dutch economy. The Dutch miracle was especially miraculous in that the United Provinces were almost entirely devoid of any of the raw materials needed in shipbuilding. Any threat to the free movement of Dutch shipping, any constriction of maritime activity, was thus a threat to undermine the whole enormous structure of their commerce and finance, of empire and industry. War was the probable, perhaps the inevitable, response. Yet here lay the paradox of the Dutch predicament. Though the country had won life and health and strength by war, war was in fact fatal to it, since war not only interfered with the free movement of ships but exposed them to capture or destruction. As Professor Charles Wilson has so well argued,[8] the Dutch miracle could only be sustained in a general peace while the 17th century from first to last rang with the clash of arms. The Dutch reaction to the Navigation Act was therefore ambivalent. War was the obvious answer and in war they could call on some of the greatest fighting leaders in the history of sea warfare, the elder Tromp and Michiel de Ruyter prominent among them. On the other hand the English had all the geographical advantages. They were astride the sea approaches, whether from north or south: and in the Channel, then as now the great artery of trade, they had not only bases but the only safe anchorages in the prevailing south-westerly gales. And because their own seaborne trade was so far inferior to the Dutch they had much less to lose. As the Grand Pensionary of Holland, Pauw, put it in June 1652 after the failure of his best efforts to avoid war: 'the English are about to attack a mountain of gold; we are about to attack a mountain of iron'.[9]

The First Dutch War (1652–4) vindicated Pauw's gloomy prediction. In Robert Blake the English had found an admiral to match the great Dutchmen, and he was ably seconded by Deane, Monck, Ascue, Penn and Lawson, of whom the last four survived to fight in the Second War. The superior weight of the English broadsides, the heavier build of their capital ships, their pioneering of formal tactics as against scrambling into action and grappling the nearest enemy, won some notable victories. Both at Portland and the Gabbard the Dutch were driven into headlong flight, leaving the English undisputed masters of the Narrow Seas whose sovereignty they had somewhat presumptuously claimed. The death of Tromp in the last battle of the war off Scheveningen was the final blow. Of the whole series of Dutch Wars the first was the only one which the English won outright. Fortunately for the Dutch they were let off very lightly at the peace settlement. Cromwell who had seized power at the end of 1653 had strong religious and ideological objections to making war against Protestants. He would much have preferred to ally himself with Holland against the Catholic empire of Spain, thus reviving the glorious memory of Queen Elizabeth. The Dutch had to accept the Navigation Act and the right to the salute in the Narrow Seas but even this was no more sharply defined than it had been. After so complete and so hard-won a victory the terms were anything but harsh.

But if there had been no extortion of cash or colonies from the beaten side there had yet been enormous gains. Huge numbers of Dutch merchant ships – estimated at 1000–1700 – had been captured. The result may well have doubled the size of the English merchant fleet and certainly increased its profitability by a larger factor.[10] Two ideas thus lodged themselves firmly in the consciousness of the city men and shipowners and sea captains – often the same people at different stages in their careers: first, that we could beat the Dutch any day; second, that this was likely to prove a profitable operation.

Cromwell's preoccupation with fighting the Spaniards obstructed any such opportunity. But Charles II's restoration re-opened the possibility. Monck, the chief contriver of the Restoration and himself a distinguished commander in the earlier war, favoured the resumption of hostilities, partly because he thought war abroad the best remedy for divisions at home and partly because, in his own characteristically blunt words 'What we want is more of the trade the Dutch now have.' As Pepys records in the diary, the King himself was not so ready to risk an encounter with the Dutch Republic whose naval power he knew well from personal inspection. His principal ministers, the elder statesmen of royalism – Clarendon, Southampton and Ormond – were also reluctant to engage in such an adventure, made the more rash by the conclusion of a Franco-Dutch alliance in 1662. But the war party had powerful friends both among the courtiers and in the circle that surrounded James, Duke of York. It gained strength from high-handed treatment of English mercantile interests oversea by the Dutch E. India Company. Among these were the ships and trading posts of the Royal Africa Company, a speculative enterprise in which the King, the Duke of York, Prince Rupert and several courtiers had a large financial stake. In 1663 a small naval squadron under the command of Robert Holmes, a notably daring and combative officer, was sent out to W. Africa to show the flag and demand compensation. Holmes carried out his instructions with some exuberance, capturing a number of ships and all but one of the Dutch forts. Downing urged the government in London to treat the outraged Dutch reaction as bluff. But for once Downing had been overreached. Without his knowledge the Dutch squadron in the Mediterranean under the command of de Ruyter was ordered to restore the *status quo* in W. Africa. De Ruyter's movements remained unsuspected until the news reached Pepys and others of 'our being beaten to dirt at Guiny'.[11] Public opinion in both countries demanded war. Even the House of Commons voted the unheard-of sum of £2,500,000 without hesitation.

War was declared on 22 Feb. 1665, though actual hostilities had already broken out in different parts of the world. A squadron under Sir Thomas Allin had attacked the homeward bound Dutch Smyrna convoy in Dec. 1664, three months before the official declarations of war. Even taken at such an unfair disadvantage the Dutch had given as good as they got. Those who, like Pepys, felt far from confident of an easy victory soon began to find their view confirmed by events. An important early success was the Dutch capture of the English Hamburg convoy in May 1665, a severe blow since the cargo consisted largely of naval stores. The English like the Dutch depended on the Baltic and North European trade to supply them with the means of keeping their ships at sea.

The first set-piece battle of the war, the battle of Lowestoft, that took place a month later, did much to revive English optimism. After a long and hard fight, in the course of which the Dutch flagship blew up, the English won a clear victory. It might and should have been as crushing and decisive as either Portland or the Gabbard, had not a courtier, tired of the noise and disturbance of fighting, usurped the authority of the Lord High Admiral to call off the pursuit. This incident, hardly credible even by the 17th-century standards of aristocratic irresponsibility, took place in the middle of the night. It was so successfully covered up that three years were to pass before the truth was exposed and the culprit named.[12] The courtier was the brother of Pepys's colleague, Lord Brouncker, and claimed that he was actuated by concern for the safety of the King's brother and heir. It stands as the supreme example of what Pepys on shore and the sea officers afloat had to contend with in attempting to create a disciplined, efficient, professional fighting service.

Nonetheless the English were left in the immediate aftermath with the command of the sea approaches to Holland. The two principal objectives thus brought within their reach were the capture of the homeward bound Dutch E. India convoy, a prize of enormous value, and the interception of de Ruyter's squadron returning from its long and distinguished service in the Mediterranean and the Atlantic. It was thought imprudent to expose the Duke of York to the further risk of battle with so tenacious an enemy, the more so as James had shown himself a fearless and resourceful commander. Sandwich was given command of the fleet and was at sea again early in July.[13] While he was cruising off the Dogger Bank de Ruyter slipped past him. Even under such a commander a small squadron that had been at sea for so long, its crews depleted by disease and weakened by an inadequate diet, would not have stood a chance against a fleet fresh out from its base, victualled, watered and with plenty of ammunition. Meanwhile part of the returning E. Indies fleet had taken refuge in the neutral harbour of Bergen, hoping to creep down the Norwegian coast when the English fleet was no longer at sea. Sandwich rashly accepted the opinion of the English ambassador at Copenhagen that the Danish King would be glad to denounce his treaty with the Dutch and share the prizes with the English. Twenty-two ships were detached under Sir Thomas Teddeman to enter the fiord and attack the ships. But the Governor of Bergen had received no clear instructions. After unsuccessful negotiations Teddeman sent his force in, to be severely mauled by the combined fire of the Danish forts and the Dutch ships. The defeat was unmitigated and costly. Immediately afterwards de Ruyter put to sea with a fresh fleet to escort the Indiamen home. In this he was largely successful though Sandwich at the end of August fell in with part of the convoy that had been separated by bad weather and took four warships and two great E. Indiamen. Unhappily he allowed the captors to break bulk, that is to rifle the cargo under hatches, and helped himself to some of the loot. His enemies moved to impeach him but the King forestalled them by sending him as ambassador to Madrid.

In the following year, 1666, the command was divided between Rupert and Monck. It was intended that they should act wholly in conjunction but unfortunately the French declaration of war in support of their Dutch ally led to a literal division of the fleet at the beginning of the campaigning season. A French fleet was reported to have been sighted coming out of the Mediterranean, presumably to attempt a junction with the Hollanders. Rupert was detached to the westward to intercept them with about 20 ships while Monck with the remaining 60 covered the mouth of the Thames. Here early in the morning of 1 June his scouts made contact with the van of the Dutch fleet of some 90 sail that de Ruyter was bringing against him. There was still time to take the fleet within the shelter of the Gunfleet shoal, to decline action and to defend the navigable channels of the Thames estuary. Monck summoned a Council of War aboard the flagship at eight o' clock in the morning at which the momentous, much criticised but magnificent decision was taken to go out and fight. Thus began one of the greatest battles in the history of maritime war, the Four Days Fight. For the first two days the English suffered terrible punishment. By the third day there were only 28 ships at Monck's disposal but nonetheless he again went out to fight. It became known early in the battle that the intelligence of the French being out was false and urgent messages were sent to recall Rupert. On the afternoon of 3 June when Monck was at last conducting a fighting withdrawal, ranging the 16 best ships he had left into a protective barrier behind which the worst damaged could struggle home, the topmasts of Rupert's squadron were sighted coming up the channel. Monck at once altered course to join them so that the battle could be renewed, a manoeuvre which led to the flagship of the White squadron under Sir George Ascue running aground on the Galloper sand. The Dutch captured her but, unable to get her off, burnt her. The whole ship's company including the Admiral were taken prisoner to Holland. This is the only instance of a flag officer of the Royal Navy surrendering in battle. It was a decision that must have taken great courage.

On the fourth and last day terms were more nearly equal. The rough weather that had prevented the English from running out the lowest tier of their guns had eased and a fierce and bloody action ensued. Fog, exhaustion and the difficulty of keeping their battered ships afloat eventually separated the combatants.

The noise of the guns had been clearly audible in London. The excitement, the tension, in the capital are memorably described in the diary. Although the battle was indisputably a considerable victory for the Dutch, London responded more enthusiastically to the heroism of this great fight against odds than it had to the English victory off Lowestoft a year earlier. Wonders were achieved in refitting the shattered fleet.[14] The one problem that remained intractable was manning. The Plague, the war and the heightened demand of both King's ships and merchantmen had drained the reservoir of seamen. 'The want of men is very great and everyone bestirs himself to get what he can. We have sent enclosed a list of the men wanting in the ships that are here [2780 men for six ships at the Nore], by which you will guess what will be wanting those in the River and so of the whole. But ships and guns without men will signify little,' wrote the Commanders-in-Chief on 28 June. On 4 July they asked that the Deputy-Lieutenant of Essex might raise a troop of militia horse to beat the woods in which runaway seamen were thought to be hiding.[15] When the fleet put to sea on 18 July, just six weeks after the fiercest and most destructive engagement of the war, they took the seamen out of 15 of the smaller warships so that the most powerful vessels should have a full complement.

Pepys had quickly recognised that the Four Days Fight was a defeat. He listened attentively to reports and opinions that laid the responsibility at the doors of the Commanders-in-Chief. 'Pierce the surgeon – who is lately come from the fleet, and tells me that all the commanders, officers, and even the common seamen, do condemn every part of the late conduct of the Duke of Albemarle.' Sir George Carteret 'tells me, as I hear from everybody else, that the management in the late fight was bad from top to bottom'.[16] When Pepys was recording these judgements and emphasising his own agreement with them the fleet had fought two major actions almost exactly a year apart: one had been an English victory that had been so ineptly handled as to have little discernible effect on the course of the war; the other had been a damaging defeat. Pepys and his colleagues were deeply conscious that the results achieved did not bear comparison with those of the first war. It was a sensitive point.

Within three days of the fleet's going out again the English and the Dutch were in sight of each other and battle followed on 25 July, St James's Day, which gave its name to the action. Strict instructions had been issued by the Commanders-in-Chief that the fleet was to fight in line 'and upon pain of death that they fire not over any of our own ships'.[17] The result was as clear an English victory as any of the first war. Pearse, the surgeon, who was present, has left a remarkably clear diagram of the development and course of the battle.[18] The Dutch were routed. But once again there was murmuring against the conduct of the pursuit. Such criticism gained credence from the fierce recriminations between two of the English flag officers, Sir Robert Holmes and Sir Jeremy Smith, the first the particular protégé of Rupert, the second of Monck. A challenge was issued and a duel only avoided by the intervention of the King. Pepys's criticism 'This is all; only, we keep the sea; which denotes a victory, or at least that we are not beaten. But no great matters to brag on, God knows' [19] sums up the grudging, disenchanted reception of the victory in well-informed circles.

On the Dutch side the prophetic pessimism of Grand Pensionary Pauw received new force when, a fortnight later in early August, Sir Robert Holmes took a few fireships and other light vessels into the anchorage of the Vlie and burnt almost the whole of the returned E. India fleet with a great part of its cargo still aboard. Estimates of the number of merchantmen destroyed range from 114 to 165. Holmes followed up this brilliant stroke by landing on the island of Terschelling and burning the town, an act of somewhat dubious military value and propriety since it was inhabited by pacifist Mennonites. The whole episode, known as Holmes's Bonfire, concludes the campaign of 1666. The Fire of London, held by the Dutch to be an act of divine retribution for Holmes's misconduct, occupied the energies and resources of government and even required the presence of Monck to sustain the morale of the capital.

The closing year of the war witnessed the greatest humiliation ever suffered by English arms. The Dutch raid on the Medway, a spectacular retaliation for Holmes's Bonfire, stands as one of the most daringly conceived and brilliantly executed exploits in naval history.[20] It would scarcely have been possible if Pepys and Coventry had paid more attention to the warnings of men they had agreed to deride such as Monck and Holmes.[21] Although negotiations for peace had already opened there was ample intelligence of large-scale and continuous activity in the Dutch arsenals and naval bases. To meet this threat Coventry, with Pepys's approval, advised against fitting out a fleet and even continued to pay off such ships as were manned. When danger was imminent with a Dutch fleet under de Ruyter (of all commanders) actually at sea off the approaches to the Thames Pepys apparently saw no reason to alter his long round of habitual Sunday pleasures. His freedom in accusing others of frivolity and irresponsibility by no means exempts him from similar charges. The shock of the Medway disaster, the ignominy and the impotence that it exposed, removed the last vestiges of the complacency engendered by English successes in the first war. In the peace treaty that followed little was altered. Judged by national interest the Second Dutch War had been a waste of blood and money.

The peace treaty signed at Breda in 1667 was followed in 1668 by the Triple Alliance of England, Holland and Sweden intended as a counterweight to Louis XIV's France. This reversal of alliances was popular both in Parliament and the city: money was regularly voted to continue the naval building programme. Charles II however had embarked on the personal diplomacy, ratified by the secret Treaty of Dover (1670), by which England was to join France in a treacherous attack on her Dutch ally. It was thus by no means the case in the Third War as in the first two that the government was borne along on a tide of anti-Dutch feeling. The King had to find his pretext for declaring war and fight and win before the overwhelmingly strong anti-French, anti-papist opinion in the country had time to stop him. Accordingly after Parliament had been prorogued in the spring of 1671 an excuse was found in the failure of the Dutch fleet to strike topsails to a yacht that was bringing home the English ambassador's wife. This was in August. In spite of Dutch readiness to let this absurd complaint be decided by the precedents agreed by treaty, the King and his ministers pressed on their preparations for a naval campaign and a landing in Holland to be synchronised with a French invasion. As on the last occasion the English dishonourably opened hostilities before declaring war, and once again Sir Robert Holmes 'the cursed beginner of the two Dutch wars' was chosen to do the dirty work. In spite of his eminent qualification of unscrupulous courage the business was badly bungled.[22] The Dutch Smyrna convoy which had been selected for attack as it came up Channel in March 1672 gave an excellent account of itself. One big merchantman was taken and another sunk but the attacking force was very badly mauled. Not all the ships taking part were fit to rejoin the fleet in time for the first great action of the war, the battle of Sole Bay, which took place on 28 May.

The English began this battle with an advantage that had been denied them in the two earlier wars, namely the active alliance of the French. In the Second War indeed the Dutch had had them on their side. Although they did not actually put in an appearance it will be remembered how reports of their movements forced the English into dividing the fleet on the eve of the Four Days Fight. This time a French squadron under the Comte d'Estrées formed one of the three divisions of the fleet whose commander once again was James, Duke of York. The Admiral of the other English squadron was Sandwich. The Dutch commanded by de Ruyter were inferior in numbers, 62 against 72, and in guns (the proportion was about 5 to 6).[23] Their ships were neither so stout nor so new as those of their opponents. On the other hand they had long been expecting a French attack and had kept their fleet on a war footing for some time past. The ships were better worked up than those of the allies and all accounts agree that in this war, unlike the other two, their gunnery was decidedly superior to the English in spite of their lighter weight of metal. Finally they were fighting for the life of their country under the greatest admiral of his time, indeed one of the greatest in history.

It was not the least of de Ruyter's achievements that though the fleets had made contact with each other at least ten days earlier he yet managed to take his enemy by surprise. It was luck that the Duke of York and the French commander had not understood each other's assumptions or agreed on a clear tactical plan. The consequence was that the French went off on the port tack and the English squadrons on the starboard, thus at once robbing them of their numerical advantage. In a hot, hard-fought battle Sandwich's flagship was burnt to the water-line and he himself was drowned. Damage and casualties were heavy on both sides, though few ships were sunk and none taken. But the Dutch were the moral victors. They had gained their strategic objective of preventing an English landing and, though weaker, they had more than held their own. They crowned their naval success by bringing home their rich E. India convoy almost intact, another severe blow to Charles II's plans for a quick smash-and-grab operation. The English fleet cruised in the North Sea until early autumn but took nothing of value. 1672 was a poor year.

1673 was, if anything, worse. Prince Rupert had succeeded his cousin as Commander-in-Chief, probably because it was by now clear that the war was not going to be won easily and the life of the heir presumptive was an unnecessary additional stake. This, the last campaign of the Dutch Wars, was fought entirely in Dutch coastal waters where the English and French were not altogether confident of their pilotage. The two battles of the Schooneveld on 28 May and 14 June shared the characteristics of Sole Bay. The Dutch, inferior in strength, got rather the better of two hard-fought battles in which no ship of the line was lost and in so doing achieved their strategic objective. The third and final battle off Texel on 11 August repeated the pattern in a yet more emphatic form. The fight between Spragge, the Admiral of the Blue or rear squadron, and the younger Tromp was so fierce that hardly a mast or a piece of rigging was left on the English flagship yet still no vessel, however torn or shattered, was actually lost. The carnage was, as in the two previous battles, terrible. But once again the Dutch were unbeaten and this time the allied fleet retired to leave them masters of their own sea approaches. Charles II and the promoters of the secret entente with Louis XIV were faced with total failure. A peace treaty was accordingly signed at Westminster in Feb. 1674.

The heroism of the English as of the Dutch sailors shines in a naughty world of greed and trickery. These vices extended unhappily to the way in which they were paid and fed and cared for while serving in the Royal Navy. 'We did heretofore fight for tickets; now we fight for Dollers.'[24] The jeers of the English deserters aboard the Dutch ships in the Medway recorded by Pepys were in his judgement 'that of worst consequence' of all that he heard about that day of unredeemed disaster. That he recognised the significance of that anger and despair and, as the diary everywhere reveals, set himself to mend matters as far as he could is one of the many reasons for endorsing Professor Lloyd's description of the Dutch Wars as the 'crucible' of the Royal Navy.[25] [*See also* Royal Fishery]

(Richard Ollard)

Dyke, [Elizabeth]. A relative; daughter of John Pepys of Ashtead and sister of Jane Turner. Her husband (? dead by the time of the diary) was Thomas Dyke.[1]

Dymoke, [Sir Edward], kt 1661 (d. 1664). King's champion at the the coronation 1661. The office – held since the 14th century by the Dymokes – was hereditary in the family owning the manor of Scrivelsby, Lincs. The champion's function was to ride fully armed into Westminster Hall during the coronation feast, and to challenge to combat anyone denying the sovereign's right to the throne. The ceremony fell into disuse, with the feast, after the coronation of George IV in 1821.[1]

Eagle Court. North out of the Strand between Catherine St and Little Drury Lane – an area since transformed by the construction of Kingsway and Aldwych. (R)

East India House. Originally the town house of Lord Craven, on the s. side of Leadenhall St. An Elizabethan building, it escaped the Fire, and was much extended after 1670. Defoe described it as 'very convenient, though not beautiful'. It was replaced by a classical building 1726–9. The paintings of ships mentioned by Pepys (ii.77) were executed on a wooden superstructure built over the top windows.[1]

Edisbury, [Kenrick]. Surveyor of the Navy 1632–d.38; much criticised for nepotism. His name was originally Wilkinson. One of his descendants, also Kenrick Edisbury, had a clerkship in the Ticket Office in 1702.[1]

Edlin, ——. Identifiable as Samuel Edlin, of Watford, clergyman (d. 1698) who graduated from Magdalene in 1657 (cf. his association with Hertfordshire: i.59; ii.139, and with Clement Sankey of Magdalene: iii.58). He took orders in 1662, becoming Rector of Silchester, Hants., in 1667. But there were several families of this name in Westminster around 1660.[1]

Edwards, Tom and Jane. Pepys's servants. Tom came into Pepys's service in Aug. 1664 from the Chapel Royal where he had been a singing boy until his voice broke. He served both in the Pepys household and in the Navy Office where he was paid as one of Pepys's clerks from Oct. 1664. In March 1669, much to the Pepyses' delight, he married Jane Birch, their beloved servant, who had been with them, except for a few months, since Aug. 1658.[1] He was then 24 and she 25. He stayed until 1678 when he was made Deputy Muster-Master and Navy Agent at Deal.[2] After his death in 1681 Jane re-entered Pepys's service but does not appear in the lists of his servants (given in his receipts for the poll-tax) after July 1689. Around 1688 or a little earlier she seems to have acted as Will Hewer's housekeeper. It is possible that the Jane Penny, widow of George Penny, to whom Pepys gave an annuity in 1690 was the same person. She was still alive when Pepys died, and her annuity was continued under his will.[3]

The elder of her two surviving children by Tom Edwards, Samuel (Pepys's godson), was sent at Pepys's request to Christ's Hospital and put to the Mathematical School there. He was a naval lieutenant by 1695, and received a ring at Pepys's funeral.[4]

Elborough, [Robert]. Born at Hamburg and a contemporary of Pepys at St Paul's School, where he was awarded a leaving exhibition. He took his B.A. from Emmanuel College, Cambridge, in 1655 and in 1664 was appointed curate of St Lawrence Poultney.[1]

Elliott, Capt. The Capt. Elliott incorrectly referred to at vii.142, 143 as captain of the *Portland* (which was in fact commanded by Richard Haddock) must have been Thomas Elliott of the *Revenge*, who was well known to both Coventry and Pepys. In 1669 his interest (as a bailiff of Aldeburgh) was engaged on Pepys's behalf in a parliamentary bye-election – to no avail.[1] He served in the Third Dutch War, and had died by 1688. 'Very stout but given to plunder' (Coventry).[2]

Ellis, 'Solicitor'. Sir William Ellis of Gray's Inn, kt 1671 (d. 1680); Solicitor-General 1654; King's Serjeant 1671; Justice of Common Pleas 1673–6, 1679–80.[1]

Ensum, [Robert]. Of Ellington, Hunts.; nephew of Lewis Phillips the lawyer; son of Matthew Ensum. An unsuccessful suitor for Pall's hand, and 'brother-in-law' (? step-brother) of the successful suitor John Jackson. Jackson succeeded him in the lease of Ellington parsonage. He died possessed of substantial property, but to Pepys he was a 'clowne'. His will was signed in March 1666 and proved in June 1667.[1]

Ent, Sir George, kt 1665 (1604–89). Anatomist, F.R.C.P. 1639 (and President seven times); an original F.R.S. A friend of William Harvey, he published on respiration and the circulation of the blood.[1]

Erith (Eriffe). A village in Kent on the s. bank of the Thames below Woolwich and some 14 miles downstream from London. Pepys's references are usually to the roadstead in the river.

Erwin, Capt. [George]. River agent to the Navy Board from 1664. In 1677 a George Erwin was master of the *London*, an E. Indiaman; he was conceivably the same man or a relative since Pepys's Erwin had a store of traveller's tales about Siam.[1]

Esquier, Mons. Servant to Edward Mountagu of Boughton. A 'Peter Eschar' was appointed 'sewer of the Chamber extraordinary' in Jan. 1664 on the recommendation of William Mountagu; a 'John Escharr' was a footman in the Queen's service and went in Ralph Mountagu's ambassadorial suite to Paris in 1669.[1]

Essex House. Situated south of the Strand, near St Clement Danes church. Once the Outer Temple, it had been rebuilt in the early years of Elizabeth's reign by the Earl of Leicester, who left it to the 2nd Earl of Essex. Pepys had no fondness for Tudor Gothic, and thought it 'large but ugly' (ix.425). By 1683 it had been pulled down and its site, outbuildings and gardens covered by Essex St and Devereux Court. (R)

Ethell, Robert. Of Huntingdon. He occurs as a witness to a legal document in 1653.[1] His relationship to Harry Ethell has not been established.

Evans, [Lewis] (d. 1666). Musician-in-ordinary for the lutes and violins, appointed in 1633. Another Evans, Charles, was made harper for the Italian harp in the King's Musick in 1660 and was drawing an annual £5 for strings until 1684. It was Lewis whose death Hingston reported to Pepys, but there is no evidence that Lewis played the harp. Pepys may have confused the two.[1] (Lu)

Evelyn, John (1620–1706). The diary years see the beginning of an association between Pepys and Evelyn which matured into a close and affectionate friendship. They were men of different temperaments and belonged, in a sense, to different worlds – the professional middle classes in the one case, and the cultivated gentry in the other. But they were united by a common interest in public affairs and private culture. In the former, Pepys was an expert, Evelyn an amateur. In the latter the rôles were reversed – Pepys was the pupil, while Evelyn, brought up from earliest youth among the leading virtuosi of England and France, was the master. To Pepys, culture was an acquirement, to Evelyn almost an inheritance. Yet despite these and other differences – or because of them – the two men came to value each other increasingly. Their correspondence, which begins in 1665, continues unbroken to the end of Pepys's life.

Born the younger son of a Surrey squire, Evelyn had spent the years of the Civil War in France and Italy, but had returned in 1652 to settle at Sayes Court, nr Deptford, owned by his father-in-law Sir Richard Browne, the royalists' diplomatic representative at the French court. Evelyn himself was a royalist and a pious Anglican, and, like Pepys, attended the illegal Prayer-Book services held in London in the 1650s. He was then living a secluded life, busying himself with his books and prints at Sayes Court, and practising as well as studying the

art and science of gardening. At the Restoration (which he had anticipated and welcomed in two pamphlets in 1659–60) he accepted posts
on government commissions – for the Mint, for the rebuilding of St
Paul's and, on the outbreak of war, for the Sick and Wounded. It
was in this last post that he met Pepys, who not only thought him a
'very fine gentleman' but also found him an alert and business-like
administrator. By 1666 they were planning the project (later carried
out under William III) for the establishment of a naval hospital at
Greenwich. In 1666 Pepys thought that his new friend would make an
admirable member of the Navy Board (as Hervey's successor).[1] In 1680
the same idea was mooted,[2] but Evelyn never rose higher in the service
of the navy than as a Commissioner of the Sick and Wounded (1665–7,
1672–4) and as Treasurer of the Greenwich Hospital. He served briefly
as a Commissioner of the Privy Seal at the beginning of James II's
reign, but resigned rather than cooperate with the King's policy of
appointing Catholics to office.

At an early age a leading virtuoso, he was one of the original fellows
of the Royal Society and was probably responsible for giving it that
title. He served on its council fifteen times, secured for it the Norfolcian
Library, and was one of its most valued advisers on business matters.
It was to Evelyn the virtuoso that Pepys addressed most of the letters he
wrote to him – usually requests for advice and information about books
and prints. Evelyn's replies, particularly on the subject of prints, were
both informative and prolix.[3] It seems to have been at Evelyn's suggestion that Pepys made his collection of engraved portraits. There is
also a long letter of 21 Aug. 1669 about what Pepys is to see and buy in
Paris: one of the very few personal letters Pepys preserved in his
library.[4] Appropriately Pepys had Kneller paint a portrait of his friend
for his library in York Buildings.[5] After Pepys's first dismissal from
office in 1679 Evelyn urged him to write the history of the navy Pepys
had long had in mind. He both lent and gave him manuscripts and
flooded him with arcane information.[6] He himself had been commissioned by the King to write a history of the Dutch Wars, but had
produced only a fragment – *Navigation and commerce, their original and
progress* (1674). Pepys was to complete it, but never did.

Evelyn was a prolific author and translator, and was responsible for
the publication of thirty books. In *Sculptura* (1662) he gave the first
published account of mezzotint engraving, and his *Sylva* (first pub.
1664) proved to be the most influential book on tree-planting ever
published in England. Pepys had copies of both in his library, along with
six others. Today Evelyn's best-known work is his diary, which was
first published in 1818. Compared with Pepys's it is stilted, impersonal
and unevocative. Evelyn lived and wrote less spontaneously than Pepys,
designing his diary to be read by his descendants and rewriting most

of it for that purpose. But it has considerable virtues. It is a unique and faithful record spanning more than fifty years of the political, intellectual and religious life of England.[7]

Evett, Capt. Possibly Philip Evett, a naval captain.[1]

Ewens, Capt. [Thomas]. Captain of the *Kent* 1664, 1665; Elder Brother, Trinity House 1662–7.[1]

The Exchange: *see* New Exchange; Royal Exchange

Exchange ('Change') Alley. A short, much traversed alley south out of Cornhill to Lombard St, opposite the Royal Exchange. After the Fire it was enlarged out of Backwell's property, and then, or at any rate by 1708, a branch running east was added to it.[1] (R)

THE EXCHEQUER

The 17th-century Exchequer – occupying a series of buildings within the palace of Westminster, on the e. side of New Palace Yard[1] – was one of the largest and most complex departments of English government. It was not simply a depository in which royal treasure might be counted, stored and disbursed. It was also a court of common law and, on occasions, a court of equity. It was above all an elaborate auditing department, the supreme court of record for the kingdom's finances. Presided over customarily by a Lord Treasurer and the Chancellor of the Exchequer, the Court of Exchequer or Upper Exchequer numbered well over 100 officials, such as the King's Remembrancer, the Clerk of the Pipe, the Auditors of Imprests and the Receivers General, who between them exercised a mixture of judicial and administrative responsibilities.[2] In the Lower Exchequer or Exchequer of Receipt, numbering some 20 officials, the functions were more humbly executive. This was where the money actually came in, was counted by one of the Tellers of the Exchequer, receipted by the Auditor of the Receipt and recorded, in duplicate, by the Clerk of the Pells. It was here that the wooden tally sticks were used – long hazel-wood laths – with carefully graded cuts for thousands, hundreds and tens of pounds, down to the merest scratch for a penny. Split down the middle and half given to the person who had paid in the money, they constituted a fool-proof receipt but in an archaic and cumbersome form which typified so much of the Exchequer's procedures. Indeed, for generations the Exchequer had cried out for reform. Medieval sovereigns had sometimes by-passed it altogether; Elizabeth's ministers had tried, and failed, to change its ways. In the Civil War its demolition seemed overdue, for it was moribund and redundant. But in 1654, after careful deliberation, Cromwell had revived the 'ancient course' of the Exchequer, reformed only to the extent that its proceedings would be recorded in English instead of the traditional dog-Latin.[3]

Among those to benefit from the reconstruction was George Downing, a rising young army officer. In 1656 he acquired one of the four posts of Teller of the Exchequer, which was not exactly a sinecure, although much could be done by a deputy and his clerks. A Teller was responsible for the receipt of money: it came to him first. It was also issued by him, and of receipts and issues he had to keep a daily, a weekly and a half-yearly account. As a contemporary handbook says of the Tellers – 'they attend constantly every morning throughout the yeare (except on Sundayes and the great festivalls) & in the afternoones when neede requires for the Receiving & paying of his Majesties Treasure there'.[4] It could therefore be demanding work and for a busy man like Downing, who was an M.P. and England's representative at The Hague both before and after the Restoration, help was regularly required. Pepys – the date of whose appointment is unknown – was only one of the clerks Downing employed to do the routine work of his department. It was hardly a prestigious position. Although lucrative, the Teller's office was not one of the most important and the duties of Pepys were almost wholly menial. As Downing's personal employee he scarcely counted as an Exchequer official, and in a department so rigidly and exclusively bound by hereditary life appointments and reversionary interests there could be little question of his rising through mere merit. He did well, in June 1660, to leave Downing's service.

In 1665, following his appointment as Treasurer for Tangier, Pepys returned to Exchequer business, but this time as a spending official, obliged to extract money from the Lower Exchequer and liable to render account for it in the Upper Exchequer. He was now faced with the sharp edge of Exchequer procedures, which were formidably equipped with powers to make him come to heel. But, as he soon appreciated, the Exchequer's bark was worse than its bite. A writ of distraint, calling him to account or face the seizure of his goods, was disturbing, but it was a formality,[5] and what Pepys increasingly observed about the Exchequer was its inefficiency and incompetence. Former colleagues, clerks with whom he may have dined on the Exchequer's all-too-frequent holidays, were now 'drowsy', 'lazy rogues', of boring conversation and mindful only of their fees.[6] Pepys now viewed with exasperation the dilatory rituals of the 'ancient course' of the Exchequer, which made it so slow and expensive for the King to receive, issue, or get accounts for his revenue.

Yet Pepys was also the beneficiary of a system which allowed spending officials to profit privately from the handling of public money, at small risk to themselves. The opportunity arose from the considerable delay which invariably occurred between the authorisation for a payment of money from the Exchequer and its actual availability for issue. The traditional manner of bridging this gap was to allow the spending official to go directly to the source of the money, to the revenue collectors themselves. Alternatively, he might be encouraged to go out into the London money market and borrow the money as best he could. In either case, he would be carrying with him those wooden tally sticks which purported to record the receipt of specific sums in the Exchequer. That is why Pepys, on 19 May 1665, received 'payment' of £17,500 at the Exchequer not in cash but in tally sticks – cumbersome, embarrassing, easily lost. It was now his task to raise money on them, and in subsequent days he is to be found following a well-beaten track to the principal goldsmith-bankers, Vyner, Backwell and Colvill, persuading them to advance cash in exchange for the Exchequer's fictitious receipt. The profit for them was certain to be the statutory maximum of 6% interest,[7] plus the 4% gratuity which Charles habitually conceded to the privileged bankers. Since they more often than not waited up to two years for their money from the Exchequer the cost to the King could easily be the 20% which Pepys calculated it to be.[8] But if the loss was wholly to the King, the profit was not always exclusively the bankers'. Departmental Treasurers like Pepys could take their cut, particularly if they were willing to put up their own money as collateral, and this is evidently what Pepys did. Operating on a much bigger scale, his contemporary Sir Stephen Fox was to make a huge fortune in this way as Paymaster of the Forces.[9]

It says much for Pepys as a public servant that he could applaud efforts to amend those Exchequer shortcomings from which he indubitably profited. Much as he disliked his former master, Downing, he had to commend his zeal and efficiency and he was grudgingly impressed by Downing's efforts during the war to attract easier, cheaper credit for the Exchequer by appealing to the general public for loans.[10] Offering 6% p.a. payable half-yearly on the security of the Additional Aid of 1665, Downing's scheme succeeded as well as it could in the difficult circumstances of 1666. As an attempt to make the Exchequer into something like a central bank, taking deposits against interest-bearing notes which could be easily transferred by endorsement, it was a visionary scheme very close to Downing's heart (and to his pocket) as a Teller of the Exchequer. But geography, and the Exchequer's reputation, were against him. As the merchant and financier Sir John Banks pointed out to Pepys,[11] no bank could succeed which lay at Westminster, as the Exchequer did, some 2 miles from the financial centre of the City round Lombard St and Threadneedle St. The future of English banking lay there.

For the present, however, Pepys was reluctantly caught up in Downing's other schemes to rationalise and improve the King's finances. As secretary to the Commission of May 1667, which marks the birth of the modern Treasury department, Downing pressed forward his simpler alternative to the Exchequer tally as a credit instrument. This was the Treasury Order, a foolscap paper document signed by the Treasury Lords, authorising payment (sometimes with interest) from a specified fund of the King's revenue, and numbered and registered in chronological sequence to guarantee orderly encashment. Introduced on a small scale in 1665 it was extended to the revenue as a whole in 1667 to the satisfaction of Pepys and the delight of his former colleagues at the Exchequer.[12] But as Sir William Coventry and Downing had predicted to Pepys, their reforms had come too late to save Charles II from the extravagance of earlier years[13] and in Jan. 1672 Downing's system of Treasury Orders collapsed with the declaration of royal bankruptcy known as the 'Stop of the Exchequer'. Yet the Exchequer and its tally sticks survived into the 19th century in a form which Pepys would still have recognised and when finally abolished in 1834 the bonfire of old tallies occasioned by the reform destroyed much of the palace of Westminster, including both Houses of Parliament.[14] [*See also* Finances]

(Henry Roseveare)

Excise Office. The first office, after the tax was introduced in 1643, was in Smithfield and was pulled down in 1647. By 1653 it was established in Broad St but in 1661 moved to a house on the w. side of Bartholomew Lane (opposite the church of St Bartholomew, Exchange) previously occupied by Ald. John Kendrick (a Commissioner of Excise 1643–58). Pepys refers to it as 'behind the Exchange'. It was a sizeable house assessed on 19 hearths, and was destroyed in the Fire. The office was then transferred to a house on the n. side of Bloomsbury Sq. After another move to Aldersgate St (in 1668) it found quarters in Sir John Frederick's house in Old Jewry.[1] (R)

Exeter House. On the n. side of the Strand opposite the Savoy Palace. A Tudor turreted building, begun under Edward VI and completed in Elizabeth's reign by William Cecil, Lord Burleigh. At first known as Burleigh House; later renamed after his son the 1st Earl of Exeter. After Exeter's death in 1622 it was let to various tenants, among them the 8th Earl of Rutland, under whose tenancy during the Commonwealth its chapel became a centre of illegal Anglican worship, most of the services being conducted by Peter Gunning. Pepys attended one on the first day of the diary; on a famous occasion on Christmas Day 1657 Evelyn and the rest of the congregation had been arrested for attending communion there. After the Fire, it temporarily housed Doctors' Commons and the Admiralty court and other courts. From

1667 (or possibly earlier: see vi.15) Ashley (later Shaftesbury), who had married a daughter of the 3rd Earl of Exeter, lived there. When his lease expired in 1676 and he moved to the city, the building was pulled down, Burleigh and Exeter Sts and the Exeter Exchange being then built on the site of the house and garden.[1] (R; La)

Exton, [John] (?1600–?65). Civil lawyer; LL.D. (Cantab.) 1634; Judge of the Admiralty Court 1648 (reappointed 1660); appointed one of the Duke of York's advocates in Admiralty 1660; Dean of the Court of Arches 1664; author of *The maritime dicaeologie* (1664). Father of Sir Thomas Exton, Master of Trinity Hall, Cambridge 1676–88.[1]

Eyres, Col. [William]. Succeeded to the command of Lambert's foot regiment Jan. 1660; not to be confused with the Leveller of the same name.[1]

Fage (Fyge), [Valentine]. Apothecary; Common Councilman from 1660; a leading Presbyterian.[1]

Fairbrother, William (d. 1681). Civil lawyer; Fellow of King's College, Cambridge 1633–81. He served with the royalists and in 1660 was awarded his LL.D. by royal mandate. His association with Pepys was close – he seems to have been a friend or relative of Pepys's cousins the Angiers, and when in London he lodged near to the Pepys family home in Salisbury Court. His father was a Londoner, but there were several of that name living in the region of Wisbech and Parson Drove, where Pepys's relatives the Perkins lived.[1]

Fairfax, Thomas, 3rd Baron (1612–71). With Cromwell, the most important of the parliamentary generals in the Civil War; but, unlike Cromwell, a Presbyterian. He abandoned public life after the execution of the King, of which he disapproved, and settled at Nun Appleton, his Yorkshire home. His activities from Nov. 1659 onwards, in urging upon Monck the necessity of free parliamentary elections and in occupying York with an armed force, were among the most decisive moves leading to the Restoration. In March 1660, as M.P. for Yorkshire and a Councillor of State, he led the deputation sent by the Houses to the King at The Hague. After the dissolution of the Convention he took little or no part in public affairs.[1]

Faithorne, William, sen. (1616–91). Engraver, of St Clement Danes. He was trained as a painter and engraver in England and France, and his shop was at the sign of the Drake on the n. side of the Strand (on the site of the present-day Law Courts). By Apr. 1679 he had moved to Printing House Yard, Blackfriars.[1]

Falconer, [John] (d. 1664). Clerk of the ropeyard, Woolwich ?1660–4. His widow Elizabeth claimed compensation at his death.[1] A John Falkener was a clerk in the Ordnance in the Tower during the Commonwealth.[2]

Falcon Inn and Wharf. On Bankside, Southwark, a little to the east of the Surrey end of Blackfriars Bridge. (R)

Fanshawe, Sir Richard, 1st Bt (1603–66). Diplomatist and author; a friend of Evelyn. A gifted linguist, he went on diplomatic missions to Spain in 1635 and in the 1650s; was appointed Secretary of the Latin Tongue in 1659; and was sent as ambassador to Portugal twice – in 1661–2 (to complete the marriage negotiations and bring over Charles's queen) and in 1662–3. He was ambassador to Spain from 1664 to 1666, when he was superseded (by Sandwich) for committing his home government to the terms of a trade treaty without authority. He died in Madrid a few weeks after Sandwich's arrival. His wife, whom he married in 1644, was Anne Harrison (1625–80); a devoted and able woman, who wrote a charming memoir of her husband, first published in 1829.[1]

The 2nd Viscount Fanshawe (d. 1674) and Thomas Fanshawe were his nephews; Lyonel Fanshawe his cousin. The last applied to Arlington for a post in the customs in 1667.[2]

[Farriner, Thomas, sen.]. Conduct of the King's Bakehouse; citizen and baker. It was in his bakehouse that the Fire is said to have started. The house was in Pudding Lane in the parish of St Margaret, New Fish St, and had five hearths and one oven.[1]

Fauconberg, [Edward]. Exchequer official from c. 1655; Deputy-Chamberlain of the Receipt 1661–c. 75.[1]

Fauntleroy, ——. An old acquaintance. There is a Thomas Fauntleroy who appears in the overseers' accounts of the parish of St Margaret's Westminster from 1656 onwards, but not in those for 1661.[1]

Fazeby, Capt. [William]. Naval officer; he held 11 commissions 1661–85, mostly to royal yachts.[1]

Fenchurch (Fanchurch) St. A spacious street, 600 yards long[1] running from Aldgate St to Gracechurch St. The church of St Gabriel, Fenchurch, stood in the middle of the roadway and seriously limited passage through the street. On the occasion of his only visit Pepys found few people 'of any rank' in the congregation. It was burnt in the Fire and not rebuilt. The well-known tavern, the Mitre, was near by. (R)

Fenn, John. Paymaster to the Navy Treasurer 1660–8. A friend of Capt. Cocke. His son may be the Nicholas Fenn who was appointed a Victualling Commissioner in 1683.[1]

Fenner. Thomas Fenner (d. 1664), of St Sepulchre's parish, freeman of the Blacksmiths' Company, was Pepys's uncle, having in 1633 married as his first wife Katharine Kite, sister of Pepys's mother. His will shows him as living as a lodger in the Old Bailey. By his first wife (d. 1661) he had two daughters, who married William and Anthony Joyce. His second wife, whom he married after a short widowhood, was, according to Pepys, an old and ugly midwife: Hester, widow of William Ayres, citizen and cordwainer who had died c. 1649, leaving her with four children. She received a legacy of £300 from Thomas Fenner and lived until 1674. The executor of her estate was her 'cousin' Philip Harman, who leased a house in Cornhill from her.[1]

Ferrabosco, Mrs. The Ferraboscos were a family of Bolognese origins active as court musicians in England between 1560 and 1682. The 'Mrs Ferrabosco' mentioned by Pepys was presumably one of the nieces of Alfonso Ferrabosco III. Alfonso is not known to have had issue male or female, but his brother Capt. Henry (d. 1658), court musician and royalist soldier, had two daughters, Elizabeth (b. 1640) and Jane (bapt. 1647) besides other children. Elizabeth seems the natural candidate.[1] (Lu)

Ferrer(s), Capt. [Robert]. A dashing and volatile soldier – cornet in Sandwich's regiment from c. 1656; lieutenant by 1660, and captain from Aug. 1660. By 1663 he appears to have a commission in Sir C. Berkeley's regiment. He was a member of Sandwich's household, accompanied him to sea in 1661-2 and was his Master of Horse in the Spanish embassy. His accounts and letters (normally signed without a final 's') are in the Sandwich papers. In Dec. 1668 he was given the place as yeoman tailor in the Great Wardrobe which Pepys had once hoped to obtain for his father. He had died by July 1673.[1] His wife Jane, sister of a Scottish earl, was thought by her family to have married beneath her.[2]

Nan Ferrer is also mentioned in the diary. A William Ferrer was chamberlain to Sandwich in Madrid, and a secretary to him by 1672.[3]

Fetters, [Henry, jun.]. Watchmaker; admitted 'brother' of the Clockmakers' Company 1654.[1]

FINANCES

The late 17th-century statistician Gregory King reckoned that (of a total population of 5½ m.) 5000 'persons in office' earned an average of £240 p.a. and another 5000 lesser officials about £120 p.a.[1] This placed them lower in the scale of average earnings than country gentlemen and better-off merchants, but well above the 10,000 clergy and the 9000 naval and military officers. These in turn stood well clear of the mass of the agricultural community – farmers, labourers, cottagers. Indeed, King estimated that over 60% of working heads of families earned less than they and their families consumed and were therefore dependent on that minority whom he saw as 'increasing the wealth of the kingdom'. The average expense for the purposes of subsistence he seems to have put at just over £7 10s. p.a. per head.[2] A modern

inquiry into the county of Herefordshire, c. 1663, has found that the
mean annual income per household was £7 2s.[3]

Thus, even at the outset of his career, when he may have been earning
little more than £50 p.a. as a servant to Edward Mountagu and as
clerk in the Exchequer, Pepys was comfortably placed on the fringes
of the 'middling sort' of 17th-century English society. Wealth, however, is a relative concept, not to be confused with well-being or
reputation. In the opening entry of his diary, Pepys neatly differentiates
between these several criteria of prosperity. Objectively, he admits, he
was 'very poor'. Indeed, he was in debt and had to borrow to pay his
rent. Subjectively, however, he felt his condition to be 'very handsome',
and in public estimation he was thought to be rich,[4] which was a useful
asset in a society where credit-worthiness mattered quite as much as it
does today. The basis of Pepys's reputation was that he had a powerful
patron in his kinsman Mountagu, and it was this, as much as hard work
or merit, which set him on his path to prosperity.

The diary is virtually our only source for the history of his finances,
his accounts having disappeared apart from a few memoranda relating
to 1667–9 preserved among his private papers.[5] It is perhaps fortunate
that the diary begins before he grew rich. It allows one to appreciate
his pleasure in those small gains which carried him upwards from an
estate which he valued at a mere £25 in Jan. 1660. One shares his
dismay at losing 6d. at cards, and his satisfaction in the wisdom of a
man keeping only 3d. in his pocket lest he be tempted to spend more.[6]
But the days of penny-pinching were to end in July with his appointment to the office of Clerk of the Acts at an enhanced salary of £350
p.a. True, he had to surrender £100 p.a. of this to Thomas Barlow,
who had prior claim to the office, but this itself was a guarantee of the
security which Pepys now enjoyed, for a public official appointed under
a royal patent acquired a legal tenure for life and was customarily
immune from dismissal for anything short of a criminal conviction.
At best he could only be bought out, and notwithstanding legislation
against the sale of offices even senior government appointments often
changed hands for a handsome consideration. Thus Pepys bought out
Barlow and within a few weeks was being offered £1000 to be bought
out himself, 'which made my mouth water'.[7] But he was wise to
refuse. Even at £250 p.a. net his salary was a substantial one, and it
represented only a portion of his prospective gains. For, like most
public officers, Pepys could look forward to a whole range of windfalls –
fees, perquisites, gratuities and downright bribes, and it was these
rather than any official stipend which were to make Pepys a wealthy
man. He hardly needed to be told by his patron that 'it was not the
salary of any place that did make a man rich, but the opportunities of
getting money while he is in the place'.[8] As Downing's clerk in the

Exchequer he had lived off fees related to the business he had handled, and as Mountagu's protégé he had pocketed small bribes to put in a good word with 'my Lord'. Already on 7 July, before he had been officially appointed, he was demanding £100 for the favour of a clerical post in his new department. Thereafter, Pepys's cash balances climbed steadily, to £200 in Sept. 1660, £300 in Jan. 1661 and £500 by the end of May. £600 was reached in Sept. 1661 and there could have been more but for the expense of keeping up appearances. Furnishings and new clothes for himself and his wife absorbed worryingly large amounts and by the beginning of March 1662 Pepys reckoned he had spent £250 in six months. Even a year later his savings had risen very little and his ambition, to be worth £2000, be a knight and keep his own coach,[9] seemed as remote as ever. There is a surprising note of desperation in his resolution of 31 Oct. 1663 that 'I must look about me to get something more then just my salary, or else I may resolve to live well and die a beggar'. Living well, spending £690 during a year in which he earned £444, delayed the moment at which he attained four figures, but on 28 July 1664 he was 'over-Joyed in hopes that upon this month's account I shall find myself worth 1000*l* . . .', as indeed he was.

It is significant to find that, having reached this target, Pepys began to take an interest in investment. Although he had talked of buying land as early as June 1661 it had been empty boasting; in July 1664 he considered it more seriously.[10] He was also encouraged to think about depositing money with Backwell, the goldsmith-banker, at 6% interest, but in the end did nothing 'being doubtful of trusting any of these great dealers because of their mortality'.[11]

This may strike the reader as natural prudence in a primitive economy, but in fact the money-market of Restoration London was more sophisticated than is often appreciated and this is not the only occasion on which Pepys displays a slightly exaggerated caution in his monetary dealings. Hundreds of his contemporaries were content to trust the goldsmiths who, acting as safe-deposits for money and valuables during the Civil War, had developed many of the essential functions of banking. They issued notes against receipts, they cashed cheques against deposits, they accepted loans at interest and re-invested in a wide range of securities offered by the Exchequer, government departments, revenue farmers, trading companies and merchant houses. Backwell, doing profitable business with the King and revenue farmers, had over £½m. on deposit from 1000 customers in Sept. 1664, offering them 4½%, 5% or up to the statutory maximum of 6% interest on terms for withdrawal which were very sensitively adjusted to his expectations of profit.[12] The scriveners Morris and Clayton, whose re-investments were more cautiously placed in the land-market, held

deposits approaching £1½m. during the '60s,[13] and the E. India
Company, with its impeccable credit, regularly offered an interest-
bearing security on its short-term borrowing from the general
public.

Pepys was not fully drawn into this world until 1666 by which time
his financial prospects had been transformed by several concurrent
strokes of good fortune. In Feb. 1665 Barlow died, releasing £100 of
his salary as Clerk of the Acts. Then in March Thomas Povey surrendered to Pepys the lucrative position of Treasurer to the Tangier
Committee. Once again, office-holding convention entitled Povey to
claim a half-share of Pepys's profits, but these profits were now likely
to be large, for the crowning stroke of fortune for Pepys was the onset
of the Second Dutch War. The conflict, which commenced in Nov.
1664, was inevitably a naval war, and few public officials were better
placed than Pepys to profit from the huge sums which now began to
flood through the navy's hands. The greed of contractors and the
necessities of government quickly inflated prices: there were business
fortunes to be made, and throughout 1665 Pepys was receiving a
golden shower of bribes and gratuities for deals involving flags,
hammocks, masts, freight-charges, convoy-protection, victualling
contracts and misappropriated prize-goods. A close relationship with
Warren, the navy's principal supplier of timber, promised handsome
rewards. Friendship with Gauden, the Navy Victualler, brought still
more. By 28 Aug. 1665 Pepys's iron chest held £1800 and at the close
of the year he was worth £4400. Indeed, the multiplicity of his
financial dealings was beginning to create confusion in his accounts and
it was more and more difficult to tell where his private fortune ended
and the public funds, of which he was a trustee, began. If a distinction
had to be drawn it was drawn in his own favour and throughout 1666
he profited increasingly from the handling of government money. He
acquired £3560 in 1665, £2986 in 1666, and by the end of that year
was worth £6200.

Yet he remained very reluctant to trust his growing treasure in other
hands, rebuffing the importunities of Downing to lend directly to the
King on the Additional Aid of 1665. He was still nervous about lending
to the bankers and withdrew £2200 from Vyner within a few weeks
of its deposit. But in the course of 1666 he brought himself briefly to
the point of speculating in a government security. Merchants who in
1665 had been happy to bribe their way into contracts were by 1666
desperate to bribe their way out. Holding nothing but Exchequer
orders – paper promises to pay in due course – they were eager to
discount them for ready cash, and it was just such an opportunity
which Warren offered him in April.[14] In return for £1900, cash down,
Warren assigned to Pepys an Exchequer order promising payment for

naval goods priced at £2602. Four months later Pepys was able to transfer the order to the banker, Colvill, for £2432. £300 of this profit he regarded as a reward for services rendered; £232 was his speculative gain – equal to a rate of about 36%. This is some measure of Warren's necessities, but Warren was probably not the loser and the transaction gives some credence to allegations that the government was paying up to 40% premiums on its purchases of naval supplies. And on its cash borrowings it was paying the bankers a premium of 4% above the legal limit, a premium in which Pepys the private citizen was able to share by lending money to the bankers to lend to Pepys the public official. For all his lamentations about the King's finances he was not averse to reaping 10% at His Majesty's expense.

Yet on 30 June 1666 his profound anxieties about the security of his fortune come to the surface again and he records his decision 'to get as much money into my hands as I can, at least out of the public hands, that so, if a turn (which I fear) do come, I may have a little to trust to'. He turned towards gold, as men always do, and by 12 November had nearly £2800 in gold coins purchased with increasing difficulty at steadily rising premiums. Gold coins of recent origin, with their milled edges, were a sounder, more convenient store of value than silver ones of which a high proportion were worn or clipped. He was determined to have £3000-worth, but viewing his hoard of coin and plate one November midnight was 'in great pain to think how to dispose of my money, it being wholly unsafe to keep it all in coin in one place.'[15] It had narrowly escaped the Great Fire two months before; seven months later it faced the perils of a Dutch invasion. Thus in June 1667, with the enemy fleet in the Thames, Pepys despatched to the country as much gold as his wife and servants could carry – £2300-worth. Another £300 hung awkwardly in a girdle round his waist. As for his silver, he could think of nothing better than to consider flinging it into the privy. What threatened to be tragedy ends in comedy – at least for posterity. The spectacle of Pepys burrowing anxiously in a country garden to repossess his buried treasure is irresistibly comic. In the end he scrabbled up most of it from its ill-chosen hiding place and could take rueful satisfaction in a useful lesson learned – 'how painful it is sometimes to keep money, as well as to get it'.[16]

The episode is indeed a memorable comment on the precariousness of wealth in the form Pepys chose to hold it. Still reluctant to buy land which could yield little more than 3% p.a., he had no alternative to the iron chest under his bed. His distrust of the goldsmiths seemed to be amply confirmed. Backwell, who narrowly survived a run on his bank in 1665, suffered with the rest of Lombard St in the panic of June 1667. Five years later, he and his fellow bankers were to be paralysed by the 'Stop of the Exchequer', an act of bad faith by the King in suspending payment of his debts, which justified all that Sir Richard Ford had told Pepys about 'the unsafe condition of a bank under a monarch'.[17] Although actual bankruptcy was slow to overtake the major financiers of Restoration England, their credit was fatally impaired and it required another generation to build up the system which revolved round the Bank of England of 1694. Though Pepys was worried by having large sums bound up in loans to the King he was probably lucky to be the creditor of a Treasury which, after May 1667, was run with considerable probity and thrift by a group of young, tough-minded men. Loans and liabilities on the public revenue were efficiently registered for payment 'in course' and their date of maturity was advertised weekly in the *London Gazette*. Underwritten by parliamentary guarantees and assured of the legal transferability of their new 'Treasury orders', the investing public was assiduously wooed by Downing, now Secretary to the new Treasury Board. Pepys and the navy were the indirect beneficiaries of the more orderly flow of funds.

But the new brooms at the Treasury were only one symptom of a marked change in the management of public finance. The disasters of the war had sharpened public demand for a searching inquisition into mismanagement and peculation in high places. The navy, impotent and unpaid in 1667, had much to answer for. What had happened to the £5¼m. which Parliament had voted for defence since 1664? The inquiry launched at Parliament's insistence in 1666–7 cast a lengthening shadow over Pepys's public and private life. Although he felt he had covered his tracks adequately he could not be entirely sure that his profiteering would escape public exposure: even a false accusation could be damaging.[18]

It may be this danger which brought about a distinct change in the diary's record of Pepys's financial dealings. After May 1667 the proud record of accumulated savings ceases. We learn little more about gifts, bribes and profits, and although peace brought an end to the richer pickings the opportunities for gain had not entirely disappeared even if Pepys's appetite for them was almost glutted.[19] Indeed, by 1668 he was confident that he had enough to retire on.[20] But the likeliest explanation must lie in the increasing complexity of his accounts and the deterioration of his eyesight. On 31 Dec. 1668 he admitted that his accounts were nearly two years in arrears, and despite a New Year's resolution 'to look into my accounts and see how they stand' he was forced to admit in late March that he was no longer able to examine 'what my state is of my accounts and being in the world; which troubles me mightily'.

By this stage Pepys was evidently running his finances on a simple hand-to-mouth basis, relying on the visible evidence of his cash hoard for reassurance about his solvency. It was a normal procedure in his day.[21] Substantial merchants with assets and liabilities running into thousands rarely struck balances of their capital account, and there was no external compulsion, such as income tax or Companies Acts, to enforce 'annuality' in accounts, public or private. Indeed, Pepys was almost certainly exceptional in the meticulous accounting which keeps us so well-informed, month by month, until May 1667.

In other respects he is more typical of his age. Money chests, heavy with locks, were a normal feature in any prosperous household, and contemporary wills amply testify to hoards of coins safely stowed in wainscots and closets. There were some legendary hoarders in 17th-century England, such as the philanthropist Thomas Sutton (d. 1619), founder of the Charterhouse, who 'had so many great Chests full of money that his chamber was ready to groane under it'.[22] Value stored in silver and gold utensils was also a conventional and convenient way of combining investment with social ostentation. Pepys already had £250-worth of plate by Aug. 1665 and by 1667 felt he had a little too much.[23] But most of this had come as gifts. Pepys's own expenditure was distributed normally across the humdrum range of domestic requirements, only growing more lavish and imaginative as his resources grew. In 1662 he thought that the £7 per month which he spent on housekeeping was 'a great deal' – as indeed it was, relative to most people's expenditure – but by the close of 1666 he found he had been spending nearly £100 a month. 1668 saw a further surge of conspicuous consumption – on clothes, paintings, tapestries, refurbishment of all kinds, culminating in October in the purchase of a coach and horses. This gratified a long-held ambition and gave Mrs Pepys profound satisfaction. There was no more potent symbol of wealth and status than the private coach. But to some of Pepys's jealous colleagues it all seemed a little too much. By May 1669 Pepys was left in no doubt that he had overstepped an invisible mark and was guilty of imprudence, if not bad taste.[24] The gold lace on his sleeves would have to go; the coach and horses would have to be more discreetly aired.

Indulgent to himself, he was generous to his kin. He relieved his brothers, supported his father and endowed his sister. He made loans, very reluctantly, to the Mountagus and advanced a £1000 mortgage to his cousin Roger. Only his wife seems to have lacked a full share in this bounty. There were a few pearls in 1660, and a diamond ring in 1665, worth £10 but acquired for nothing. A little later, Pepys was promising her a pearl necklace worth £60 – in two years' time! Surprisingly, by 1668 Elizabeth Pepys thought her jewels were worth £150 'and I am glad of it, for it is fit the wretch should have something to content herself with'.[25] But after the great drama of 25 Oct. 1668 the tables were turned. £300–400 would be her price of silence, and in the end the condescending husband made her an allowance of £30 p.a. for all expenses, 'clothes and everything; which she was mightily pleased with, it being more then ever she asked or expected.' [26]

Clearly Pepys would have hated to be thought 'a stingy fellow' like Downing just as much as he feared to be known as a corrupt one. By modern standards he was both, and even by 17th-century standards his dealings would not bear scrutiny. Yet Pepys, in his passion for efficiency and his zeal for the public interest, amply offset the gains which came his way by considerable savings to the King. It was no empty boast that in settling the victualling contract for Tangier 'I can with a safe conscience say that I have therein saved the King 5000*l* per annum, and yet got myself a hope of 300*l* per annum without the least wrong to the King'.[27] On numerous occasions he put his interests second to those of the public, and if his professions of virtue were sometimes hypocritical there is no mistaking the pricking conscience which enabled him to draw a wavering line between legitimate profit and rank plunder. He could look with unfeigned distaste at a man like Richard Coling, 'made up of bribes' and there were others around him in the navy – Creed, Batten, Penn – whose rapacity far outstripped his own.

By the time the diary closes, Pepys was probably worth £10,000 – an estate which his colleague Creed had attained some years before. His later career, as Secretary to the Admiralty (1673–9), must have multiplied this fortune, for not only did the post carry a higher salary, of £500 p.a., but it offered a greatly enlarged entitlement to fees and perquisites, worth at least £1250 p.a.[28] As Secretary for Admiralty Affairs (1684–9), his salary was £2000 p.a. which ranked him among the higher officers of state. In a comparable position, his old master Downing had made himself one of the richest commoners in England. Unlike Downing, Pepys never sought to become a territorial magnate. Bereft of wife and denied children, he lacked the usual incentive for acquiring lands. Indeed, he appears never to have overcome his reluctance to venture his capital and does not figure among that growing investing public which underwrote the commercial growth of late-17th century England. Nor did he ever buy a house. Perhaps it was enough that the government actually owed *him* money – £28,007 2s. 1¼d. in 1679 deriving from his services at the Navy Board and as Treasurer for Tangier and still unpaid at his death.[29] Many will feel that this was the least of the debts which the nation owed for his services. [*See also* Brampton; Exchequer]

(Henry Roseveare)

Finch, [Francis] (c. 1602–77). Landowner and ironmaster, of Rushock, Worcs.; kinsman of the 2nd Earl of Winchilsea and a friend of Clarendon. Excise Commissioner 1660–8, 1674–7; M.P. for Winchelsea 1661–77.[1]

Finch, Sir Heneage, cr. Baron Finch 1674, Earl of Nottingham 1681 (1621–82). Of Ravenstone, Bucks.; a cousin of the following. A distinguished constitutional lawyer and judge: Solicitor-General 1660–70, Attorney-General 1670–3; Lord Keeper 1673–5; Lord Chancellor 1675–82. He was M.P. for Canterbury in 1660, and for Oxford University 1661–73, and served on the Admiralty Commission 1674–9. He held strong Anglican and conservative views, but was respected on all sides for his ability, eloquence and probity.[1]

Finch, Sir Heneage, 2nd Earl of Winchilsea (1628–89). Of Eastwell, Kent; a friend of Monck. Ambassador to Turkey 1660–9. There, it was said, he 'had many women. He built little houses for them'. On his return to England the King greeted him with the words: 'My Lord, you have not only built a town, but peopled it too'. 'Oh Sir', was the reply, 'I was your Majesties representative'.[1]

Finch, ——. Mercer in the Minories, whose wife was admired by Pepys. Possibly William Finch, mercer, of the Minories, who had married Hester Flesher (d. 1673).[1]

THE GREAT FIRE

The Great Fire which engulfed the city for four days and nights in Sept. 1666 has become – partly because of Pepys's remarkable day-by-day account – one of the best-known events of the century. Its disastrous effects were unparalleled in England until the Second World War.[1] But, as was the common experience then, life somehow went on. Pepys's own daily round was not seriously affected – the Navy Office in Seething Lane, the Navy Treasurer's Office in Broad St, the Victualling Office on Tower Hill, all were untouched. The Royal Exchange, which was vital to him, was given temporary quarters in Gresham College and there the merchant community met much as before. Those with whom Pepys had official or private dealings on the Exchange found accommodation near the College,[2] and there was no real break in their transactions. Westminster, Pepys's political headquarters, was not affected.

For the rest, the speed with which London recovered was remarkable. Shops reopened in makeshift wooden shacks; some moved temporarily, others more permanently, westward to Westminster. Most of the new dwelling-houses were erected and inhabited within four or five years; even the larger buildings, such as the parish churches, were replaced by the 1680s. The inhabitants were normally leaseholders bound by their leases to meet the cost of any rebuilding themselves. This in the circumstances would have been both inequitable and unenforceable. A special court of justice was set up by statute which, adopting informal methods of procedure, settled any disputes and varied the terms of the leases by lengthening their terms and reducing the rents, so as to enable the leaseholders to meet the expense.[3] At the same time special commissioners acting under the authority of the city corporation enforced new building regulations which required the use of brick and slate so as to minimise the risk of future fires. Many houses were replaced within a year. This speed has been condemned by some modern critics who bemoan the loss of a unique opportunity to design anew the entire street plan and make a stylish baroque capital out of the ruins. This however is to ignore the fact that the Fire had destroyed buildings but not the ground on which they stood. The authorities had insufficient powers over property rights to do much beyond making slight alterations in the alignment and levels of the streets. In any case the city's first duty was to get houses built and trade restored as quickly as possible.

In other towns than London there were fires just as destructive proportionately as that which devastated the capital. In 1675 one half of Northampton was laid waste; in the following year most of Southwark, and in 1694 the centre of Warwick.[4] In all these cases, as in London, the civic authorities regulated the rebuilding in order, *inter alia*, to make fires less likely.

In London itself, the danger of fire had always been an everyday peril, and Pepys records 15 fires in the diary apart from the Great Fire itself. The first he mentions, at 17 Jan. 1662, broke out in the newly-built quarter of Covent Garden where the houses were of brick. In the greater part of London, however, they were of timber-frame construction, often high and closely huddled together. There was constant risk from household fires and candles – Pepys was made nervous by his maids' carelessness with both [5] – and in addition there were large stocks of combustible material outside the houses – hay in the stables, pitch and tar in the marine storehouses near the river, wood in the timber yards, kindling in the bakeries. (It was in a bakery that the Great Fire began.) In some outlying places – e.g. Southwark – there were thatched roofs, wooden chimneys and even scattered hayricks in the manner of country towns. The provision made for fire-fighting was hopelessly inadequate – an inefficient watch and ward system, an uncertain water supply, and no equipment beyond a few buckets, ladders and grab-hooks kept in the larger public buildings and in the porches of the parish churches. There were no efficient water pumps so that half the buildings on London Bridge were burnt down in 1633 for lack of means to raise jets to the required height.[6] Rich as well as poor were at risk, and in fact Whitehall Palace, that royal rabbit-warren, was

particularly vulnerable. The problem there was not a whit reduced
by the Lord Steward's repeated orders for the provision of pumps,
buckets and ladders. Pepys reports two of the five major fires which
occurred there in the '60s. On a single night, 17–18 Feb. 1662 when
there was a high wind, four separate fires broke out.[7] In the end the
palace perished in flames in Jan. 1698. A Dutch servant had put clothes
to dry over a fire and very soon the greater part of the palace was
ablaze.[8]

The Navy Office's escape in 1666 was due to the destruction of
buildings in the neighbourhood by gunpowder. In Jan. 1673 Pepys was
to have no such good fortune. A fire which started in the closet of
Brouncker's mistress in the middle of the night spread through the
entire building and ended by engulfing both that and several neighbouring buildings. Fortunately only a few records were destroyed.[9] The
brick-built houses in Westminster to which Pepys then moved were
not fireproof. There were fires in his neighbourhood in 1680 and 1684.
On the latter occasion 12 houses were burnt down, that occupied by
Pepys and Hewer being saved by the blowing up of the house next
door. The worst they suffered, apart from the fright, was the loss of
some of Hewer's goods by looting.[10]

One important result of these fires was the introduction of fire
insurance. In London it was available from about 1680, at first for
property and later for goods. The insurance companies thereupon,
after about 1722, made it their business to establish fire brigades. It
was not until much later – in the metropolitan area of London in
1865 – that the provision of fire brigades was made a function of public
authorities. Other improvements followed from technical developments. Water supplies were redesigned – this was often part of the
rebuilding process – and suction pumps, using reservoirs and leather
hoses and worked by teams of men, replaced the old hand pumps or
syringes operated by a single fire-fighter. Pepys has in his collection of
London prints an engraving of one of the new pumps symbolically
casting its jet over the Monument erected in 1671–7 to commemorate
the disaster of 1666.[11]

Fisher, Capt. Pepys appears to refer to two Capt. Fishers. The customs
officer was Thomas Fisher; the shipowner was possibly Robert Fisher,
a captain in the city trainbands.[1]
Fisher, Mrs. Pepys's 'Cosen Nan Pepys'. The exact relationship has
not been established. The diary has the information that she lived in
Worcestershire and had married a Mr Hall, and on his death in 1662 a
Mr Fisher. From a note among Pepys's papers for 1688 it appears that
he owed her a letter of thanks, probably for a visit he had paid her in

the late summer of 1687 when he was in Worcester with James II on his western progress. She was presumably the daughter of John and Anne Pepys of Littleton, Worcs.; letters of administration were granted to John for the administration of the estate of his late wife on 18 Apr. 1660. Pepys refers to Fisher as an 'old Cavalier'; it is therefore possible that he was Robert Fisher of Carmarthen, who was in 1663 given a grant from the fund for royalist veterans.[1]

Fishery: *see* Royal Fishery

Fishmongers' Hall. A notable building on the Middlesex bank of the Thames about 100 yards upstream of old London Bridge and approached from Thames St by a short alley. Burnt in the Fire and rebuilt. (Pepys kept in his library an engraving of 1667.)[1] Pulled down in George IV's reign for the making of new London Bridge and rebuilt slightly further upstream. (R)

Fish St and Fish St Hill. There were two Fish Streets: Pepys does not always distinguish between them but it is usually clear which is meant. The one to the west, often known as 'Old Fish St', was a very narrow street, now curtailed by the making of Queen Victoria St and absorbed into Knightrider St. It served as the fishmarket for west London before Billingsgate supplanted it. It is referred to three times – twice when Pepys visits the Swan, and once (vii.237) when he visits 'the very house and room' where he had kept his wedding dinner. He had never been there since. The easterly Fish St running north, was wider, and served as a main thoroughfare to London Bridge. It figures more prominently in the diary. Pepys would buy fish there (it was the main fish market for the city) and dine at the Sun. It was at the Sun on 15 March 1660 that after a salmon dinner he promised to leave Elizabeth all he had in the world (except his books) if he were to die at sea. Until the reconstruction which followed the Fire the street sloped very steeply from the Sun down to the river (hence 'Fish St Hill'). Pepys tells of the street-boys whipping the horses up the slope and of the drivers leading their horses up and down to 'warm their legs' before attempting the ascent. (R; La)

Fishyard, the. Eastwards off St Margaret's Lane, stretching towards the s.-w. end of Westminster Hall. (R)

Fist, [Anthony]. Clerk to the Surveyor of the Navy c. 1664–7; after Batten's death Clerk to the Comptroller and Clerk (Victualling Accounts). He disappears from Navy Office records c. 1670. It is possible that he was the Mr Fist who was a clerk on the Tangier expedition 1683–4.[1]

Fitch, Col. [Thomas]. Republican; Governor of Inverness and a Scottish M.P. under the Protectorate; Governor of the Tower June–Dec. 1659; suspected of plotting against the government 1661–2.[1]

Fitzgerald, Col. [John]. Catholic soldier; Deputy-Governor of

Tangier 1662–5 and Colonel of the Irish regiment there. By 1672 he was in England, made Governor of Yarmouth and given a regiment of foot to serve at sea. 'Hee owed his ende to his modesty which would not suffer him to discover a clapp till a gangreen made it publick to the world and mortal to himselfe' (Rochester).[1]

Fleet Alley. Its exact location is uncertain, though it seems to have been one of the many alleys on the e. side of the Fleet Valley between Fleet and Holborn Bridges. Presumably it was in St Sepulchre's parish but it is not mentioned by name in the unusually full list given in the hearth-tax returns. (R)

Fleet Bridge. Spanning the River Fleet from the foot of Ludgate Hill to the e. end of Fleet St. Damaged in the Fire and rebuilt, the ground level having been raised several feet with rubble from St Paul's. Ludgate Circus now covers the site. (R)

Fleet Lane. West out of Old Bailey to the River Fleet (now, after the covering of the river, to the street made above it, Farringdon St). Much altered by the making of the railway to Holborn Viaduct Station. (R)

Fleet Prison. Off Fleet Lane; by 1660 used mainly for debtors, bankrupts and persons charged with contempt by the courts of Chancery, Exchequer and Common Pleas. Its Warden had the rents and profits of the shops and stalls in Westminster Hall. The building was destroyed in the Fire and rebuilt. 'Fleet marriages', solemnised in the prison chapel by a priest (imprisoned usually for debt), but without licences or other formalities, were becoming common in Pepys's time.[1]

Fleet St: the Conduit. Most great thoroughfares had their conduits. This (orig. 1478; rebuilt 1582) was in the centre of the street, west of Shoe Lane and Salisbury Court; supplied by water from Marylebone. It was 'a fair Tower of Stone', with a chime of bells and decorated with images of saints and angels.[1] Pepys mentions it as a landmark. It was destroyed in the Fire and not rebuilt.

Fletcher, Capt. [John]. Naval officer, holding four commissions 1660–72. In 1672 he fled to Holland to escape trial for the loss of his ship the *French Victory*.[1]

Fogarty ('Fogourdy'), ——. An Irish Catholic priest living in Paris; possibly a Fogarty of Fittemore, co. Tipperary. A younger member of the family (Malachi) took his doctorate at the Sorbonne c. 1700 and was Prefect of the Collège des Lombardes in Paris in 1705.[1]

Foley. The two leading ironmasters of the day were Thomas and Robert, sons of Richard Foley, who had founded a manufacturing dynasty in Worcestershire in the early part of the century. Thomas (1617–77) was said by the Puritan moralist Richard Baxter (also from Worcestershire) to have got £5000 p.a. by fair dealing. Robert (1626–76) was appointed ironmonger to the navy in July 1660; his son Robert succeeded him in the post at his death. Thomas's grandchildren moved

into a different world, his grandson Thomas becoming the 1st Baron
Foley in 1712, and two of his granddaughters marrying the politicians
Robert and Edward Harley.[1]

The Folly: *see* Taverns etc.

FOOD

Supplies.[1] Food shops in London were rare except for bakers and
grocers. It was still normal for perishables to be sold not in shops but in
markets where their quality and the conditions of sale could be controlled by municipal authorities. In the suburbs, which had fewer
markets, shops developed earlier. The city itself contained about a
dozen markets, mostly in the streets, serving both wholesale and retail
trades. They were open six days a week, usually from 6 a.m. to 4.30
p.m. in summer and from sunrise to dusk in winter. On each day the
first two hours were reserved for housewives – hence Elizabeth's early
rising on 13 Jan. 1663 to shop for her dinner party. Apart from the
meat markets at Smithfield and the Shambles in St Nicholas St, the
most important specialised markets were Leadenhall for poultry, New
Fish St for fish and the Stocks for meat and fish. At the Gracechurch St
and Cheapside markets virtually anything edible could be bought,
Cheapside being the busiest of all. Westminster had a market in King
St; elsewhere new ones were set up as new areas were developed –
Clare Market near Lincoln's Inn Fields in 1650, Covent Garden in 1661,
and Southampton Market in Bloomsbury in 1662. Another new
development, which came as a result of the Fire, was the construction
of four market halls to replace the street markets, the largest of them –
Leadenhall – being reputedly the biggest in Europe. Street vendors also
played their part in the distribution of supplies. Laroon's *Cryes . . . of
London* (c. 1688)[2] depicts milkmaids, sellers of poultry ('fat chickens'),
game (rabbits), fish (crab, mackerel, oysters, flounders and eels), fruit
(lemons, oranges, cherries, strawberries, pears, baked apples), vegetables (asparagus, onions, cucumbers), biscuits and vinegar.

Diet. The most striking feature of the diet of the better-off was its lack
of balance – its heavy reliance on proteins, particularly meat, and its
comparatively low content of vegetables and fruit. Pepys's everyday
dinners often included two varieties of meat, and his party dinners
half-a-dozen. Vegetables and salads, brought in from the market
gardens of Middlesex and Essex, were plentifully available in season to
Londoners, and contemporary cookery books make much use of them.
The fact that they appear only rarely in the diary – cabbage three times
and salads twice, for example – may mean that Pepys took them for
granted, like bread. (Similarly Parson Woodforde in his diary men-

tions vegetables of several sorts as crops in his garden, but hardly ever as dishes on his table.) At the same time, it is true that medical experts often distrusted vegetables and fruit, and that visiting foreigners often remarked on the Englishman's excessive appetite for meat.[3] A diet sheet for St Bartholomew's Hospital in 1687 provides beef or mutton on four days a week, cheese on three, and sugar sops on one, and though bread is mentioned fruit and vegetables are not.[4]

Meals. Habits differed between classes, and between country and town, but generally speaking Londoners of Pepys's sort had two meals a day – dinner and supper. The former was the main meal and was taken about noon; supper was less substantial, and was eaten at no fixed time. In the '70s Pepys found that late suppers made him dizzy and he gave up eating them for a few years.[5] Breakfast, which had been common enough in the 16th century, was not taken regularly by townsmen and did not become universal in England until the 18th century when the dinner hour had moved forward beyond noon, and tea and coffee had become cheaper. Pepys may well have had a drink and a bite of bread on rising which pass unnoticed in the diary. But not a meal. He was advised to take breakfast medicinally, as it were, against the 'fenny ague' when visiting Brampton in 1680.[6] But in the diary he mentions taking breakfast only five times, and then in exceptional circumstances, such as before a journey. On the other hand he normally took a 'morning draught', often with a snack, at mid-morning.

At meals all or most of the food would be put on the table at once. Pepys's descriptions of party dinners suggest that normally two courses would be served, that both would consist primarily of meat, and that the second (and less frequently the first) would also include a sweet or pudding. This was still the case in the countryside in Woodforde's time. The French habit of serving a succession of courses was coming in during the diary period but was adopted by Pepys's household only for grand occasions. There would then be a meal which began with soup, continued through a series of substantial dishes served singly, and ended with a course consisting of several sweets. *The gentlewoman's delight in cookery* (1685) advised that boiled meats be presented first, then the roasted and after them the baked meats, and finally 'Pyes, Tarts and Dishes of Fruit or Sweetmeats'. Plates had by this time displaced wooden trenchers, and forks (still the two-pronged variety introduced from Italy in James I's time) were gradually coming into use. Pepys is known to have possessed them; but he mentions several occasions, including a Lord Mayor's banquet, when they were not provided,[7] and in the shops they were sold separately from knives. French visitors did not enjoy being asked to eat meat with their fingers,[8] though the barbarism might be made less inelegant by the use of napkins and finger bowls.

Dishes. Pepys did not despise minced meat and offal, but the meat he
bought was mainly in the form of joints. The first occasion on which he
was able to buy a sirloin was on 21 Nov. 1661: thereafter, with his
growing prosperity, beef appeared more often on his table, and he took
delight in providing 'rare chines' for his guests. Fresh meat is said to
have been difficult to obtain in the winter, because cattle, for lack of
winter feed, were killed off in the autumn, so that housewives had to
preserve their meat in brine or by powdering it with salt. The cookery-
books right through the century recommend methods of removing the
salinity. But Pepys mentions eating salted or powdered beef only very
occasionally – possibly city butchers had greater supplies than other
butchers of freshly killed beasts. The quality of the meat however was
not high. Improved strains of beef-cattle and sheep were not developed
until the 18th century, and butchers, lacking means of refrigeration, did
not allow the carcases to hang long enough to make them tender. Of
other meats mentioned in the diary, mutton comes a poor second to
beef, but venison figures prominently, being a party dish. For middle-
class Londoners it was available only to those, like Pepys, who had
friends with deerparks. Pork, rabbits and pigeons were the more
common alternatives to beef and mutton. A few wild birds, such as
larks, were eaten, and poulterers drove a thriving trade – Pepys notes
the death of one who left a fortune[9] – buying on contract from breeders
in the home counties and fattening the birds in their yards. Turkeys
were becoming increasingly popular and were driven to London from
Norfolk and Suffolk in droves of a thousand or more. Geese, hens and
rabbits were usually sold by farmers' wives who set up in the markets
where 'foreigners' operated, such as the Stocks and Leadenhall.

Fish. The Friday and Lenten fasts were no longer strictly observed, but
nevertheless Londoners spent a lot of money on fish. Fishmongers, such
as Pepys's Uncle Wight, were often wealthy men, and their livery
company was an important city company. Some fish came from
abroad – herrings from Holland, oysters from France, anchovies from
Italy – but most were supplied by the English and Scottish North Sea
fishing fleets. Catches of herring, cod, haddock and ling were sent to
London, often already dried and salted, from the East coast ports, where
the industry was to some extent financed by London fishmongers. Fresh-
water fish (e.g. salmon) was available but more expensive because of
the cost of keeping it in watercarts and tanks. The shellfish that are
regarded as luxuries today were plentiful and cheap. Oysters, as in
Dickens's London, were a popular dish with all classes, and it is no
mere reflection on Pepys's taste that (with lobsters) they are the most
frequently-mentioned seafood in the diary.

Vegetables and salads. The commonest of modern vegetables, the
Virginian potato, though cultivated in Ireland, was unknown in

England, which until the mid-18th century knew only the sweet variety. New and better strains of what were the standard English vegetables – cabbages, carrots, peas, beans and onions – had been introduced from Holland in the early and middle parts of the century. Pepys occasionally made a treat of them, and enjoyed a dish of new peas or a plate of buttered asparagus. The poor used root vegetables, with cereals and minced meat, to make pottages, of which Pepys's nettle porridge was probably a variant. As for salads, the gardeners produced a wide range of suitable plants, and cookery books suggested a great variety of constituents – flowers, herbs and fruit as well as lettuces and radishes.

Fruit. Fruit growing was greatly improved in the course of the century so as to produce more varieties and larger and sweeter crops. The native apples, pears and cherries benefited, but strawberries and goose-berries remained small and unimproved. In country-house gardens and royal parks it was fashionable to cultivate the more exotic fruits under glass or on sheltered walls. Oranges, peaches, apricots, grapes, melons and figs were all grown in this way, but did not reach the general market. Some fruit, as always, was imported, especially sweet oranges from Spain and Portugal (known as China oranges because they had been introduced from the Far East), and dried fruit (raisins, dates, prunes and figs) which was brought from Greece and the Levant. All told, Londoners were well supplied. Nevertheless, since the growing season for native fruit was short, prices remained high for the most part, and fruit played a smaller rôle in the English diet than in the French. There was some distrust, on medical grounds, of fresh fruit, and Pepys himself habitually ate it cooked.

Puddings etc. It is said that the first cookery book to mention a pud-ding-cloth was published in 1617,[10] and certainly it was in the course of the century that the boiled puddings for which the English cuisine be-came famous established themselves as part of the national diet. But according to the evidence of the diary Pepys never ate them. The 'plum-porridge' he had at Christmas was a thick broth of beef and plums. At the end of a meal he normally ate fruit tarts or, less frequently, syllabubs and tansies.

Other foods. Bread and cheese was a staple food for those who could not afford meat, and the most popular form of snack or supper dish for those who could. They were usually eaten without butter, which was highly salted in order to preserve it. The bread of southern England was mostly white, made from wheaten flour, and was sold in loaves that cost something between $\frac{1}{2}d$. and $2d$. Rougher bread made from rye and beans was not unknown in the north country, and Pepys himself had a liking for brown bread (eaten with cream). Cheese was available in many varieties and came not only from Essex and E. Anglia, but also from Cheshire and other distant counties, as well as from Holland and Italy. Eggs were cheap and used in great quantities in cooking. It is common enough to find 17th-century recipes beginning 'Take a dozen eggs', and not unknown for them to say 'Take thirty'.

Sugar was costly, and sugar-loaves were often given as presents. So, too, were cakes. Presentation cakes (such as those Elizabeth Pepys received from navy contractors as *douceurs*) were monumental structures and quite costly. Pepys spent £1 on the ingredients of the cake he provided for his Twelfth Night party in 1668.[11]

Recipes (select). A venison pasty is often mentioned by Pepys as the main course of a dinner party. Sometimes he simply records that he was 'invited to' or 'attended' a venison pasty. Cookery books of the period have many recipes: the following is taken from a small book in the Pepys Library:[12]

To make a Venison-Pasty, the best way

Take a Haunch of Venison, powder it well with Salt and Pepper: take out the bone, and remove the skinny part, and with your Rowler beat it in proportion to the Pasty, which must be made with fine Flower, Butter and Eggs, proportionably: lay in the Venison and cover it, then fix your borders and garnish, then vent it on the top, and let it bake four or five hours, after that pour in melted Butter.

Beef was sometimes substituted for venison, as at the Twelfth Night dinner at his cousin Thomas Pepys's in 1660 when 'the venison pasty was palpable beef, which was not handsome'. Robert May's famous *Accomplish't Cook* (1685 ed.)[13] has a recipe *To bake Beef, red deer fashion in Pies or Pasties, either Sirloin, Brisket, Buttock or Fillet*:

Take the sirloin, bone it, and take off the great sinew that lies on the back, lard on the leanest parts of it with great lard, being seasoned with nutmegs, pepper, and lard three pounds; then have for the seasoning four ounces of ginger, and a pound of salt, season it and put it into the Pie; but first lay a bed of good sweet butter, and a bay leaf or two, half an ounce of whole cloves, lay on the venison, then put on all the rest of the seasoning, with a few more cloves, good store of butter, and a bay leaf or two, close it up and bake it, it will ask eight hours baking. Being baked and cold, fill it up with clarified butter, serve it, and a very good judgement shall not know it from red Deer. Make the paste either fine or coarse to bake it hot or cold; if for hot, half the seasoning, and bake it in fine paste. To this quantity of flesh you may have three gallons of fine flower heapt measure, and three pound of butter; but the best way to bake red deer, is to bake it in coarse paste either pie or pastry, and make it in rye meal to keep long.

Venison must often have been several days old by the time it was cooked, since the deer were not slaughtered by the butcher. Pepys was once given half a buck by Lord Sandwich which smelt 'a little strong', and at the Penns' was served 'a damned Venison pasty that stunk like a devil'.[14] The authors of cookery books made a point of providing remedies: Robert May has two suggestions to offer;[15] one is:

To make meer sauce, or a Pickle, to keep Venison in that is tainted

Take strong ale and as much vinegar as will make it sharp, boil it with some bay-salt, and make a strong brine, scum it, and let it stand till it be cold, then put in your venison twelve hours, press it, parboil it, and season it, then bake it as before is shown.

Alternatively 'Bury it in the ground in a clean cloth a whole night, and it will take away the corruption, savour, or stink'.

Sack possets and tansies were both popular sweet dishes, in which eggs, cream and sugar were the main ingredients. Both were provided for Pepys's guests on festive occasions such as the stone feast of 1662 and his great dinner party in Jan. 1663. Recipes run much as follows:

A Sack Possett

Take three pints of cream; boil in it a little cinnamon, a Nutmeg quartered, and two spoonfuls of grated bread; then beat the yolks of twelve eggs very well with a little cold Cream, and a spoonful of Sack. When your Cream hath boiled about a quarter of an hour, thicken it up with the Eggs, and sweeten it with Sugar; and take half a pint of Sack and six spoonfuls of Ale, and put into the basin or dish you intend to make it in, with a little Ambergreece, if you please. Then pour your Cream and Eggs into it, holding your hand as high as conveniently you can, gently stirring in the basin with a spoon as you pour it; so serve it up. If you please you may strew Sugar upon it.[16]

To make a Tansie

Take fifteen Yelks of Eggs, and Six whites, beat them very well, then put in some Sugar, and a little Sack, and about a pint of Cream, then beat them again, then put in Tansie, Spinnage, and Primrose-leaves, or the like, chopt as small as possible may be, and beat them all well together, then put it in a Skillet, and set it over the fire, stirring it continually till it be pritty stiff, then put it into a Pan & fry it with sweet Butter, and make Sauce for it with Rose water, Butter and Sugar.[17]

The most remarkable dish referred to in the diary is the triune pie made for the Battens' third wedding anniversary – made up of three separate pies.[18] The following recipe given by May suggests that joke pies such as these were part of a good cook's repertoire:

To make an extraordinary Pie, or a Bride Pye of several Compound, being several distinct Pies on one bottom

You may bake the middle one full of flour, it being baked and cold, take out the flour in the bottom, and put in live birds, or a snake, which will seem strange to the beholders, which cut up the pie at the Table. This is only for a Wedding, to pass away the time.[19]

Ford, Sir Richard, kt 1660 (1613–78). Merchant, of Seething Lane; Alderman from 1661; Sheriff 1663–4, Lord Mayor 1670–1; Master of the Mercers' Company 1661–2, 1674–5; M.P. for Southampton 1661–78; member of the Council of Trade 1660–8. He had been educated at Oxford, and had spent some time in Holland during the Civil War. As a Common Councillor 1659–61 he was active in promoting the Restoration. He was responsible for securing the publication in 1664 of Thomas Mun's *England's treasure by foreign trade,* which argued the need for war against the Dutch, and in 1664 himself wrote a memorandum on the subject.[1] As an M.P. he served on several committees concerned with trade. A man of wide interests, he was elected F.R.S. in 1673. His connection with Pepys and the Navy Board was close – as a neighbour (his house abutted on the Navy Office to the south), as a contractor, a partner in privateering and as a member of the commission of enquiry into the Chatham Chest and of the Tangier Committee. He was an overseer of Batten's will. He himself died intestate and left no great fortune.[2]

His house, a large one, taxed on 18 hearths,[3] was destroyed in the Navy Office fire of 1673. Of his children, two sons, John and Samuel, and two daughters (Grace, wife of Peter Proby, a partner, and Mary, wife of Thomas Ducke) were alive when his widow Grace died (at Bexley, Kent) in 1681.[4]

Fossan, [Thomas]. Pepys's contemporary at Magdalene 1651–4; Rector of Little Gaddesden, Herts. 1660–82; Master, Berkhamsted School 1662–70.[1]

Foster, Mrs. A friend of Mrs Knepp. Possibly the Mrs Foster who was for a while one of Rochester's mistresses.[1]

Foulkes, ——. A friend of William Chiffinch: probably Thomas Foulkes, Groom of the Buckhounds, who appears to have lent Chiffinch money to buy a house at Newmarket.[1]

Fountaine, [John] (1600–71). A distinguished lawyer and a distant connection of Pepys by marriage, his first wife being Susan, daughter of William Armiger. Serjeant in 1658 (reappointed 1660); Commissioner of the Great Seal in 1660.[1]

Fowke, Ald. [John] (d. 1662). A rich haberdasher; Alderman 1642–62; Sheriff 1643–4; Lord Mayor 1652–3. In the Civil War a prominent parliamentarian; one of the four Puritan M.P.s elected for the city in 1661. Trustee of bishops' lands 1648.[1]

Fowler, [John]. Judge-Advocate to the fleet c. 1653–60; Clerk to the

Chatham Chest 1660–?4; and Judge Advocate-General 1663–72. A friend of Hewer.[1]

Fowler, [Robert]. Timber merchant; Mayor of Rochester 1665–6.[1]

Fowler, ——. Ludwig Fowler was made a freeman of the Society of the Apothecaries of London 1657.[1]

Fownes, [William]. Clerk to the Storekeeper, Deptford 1662–6; Clerk of the Cheque from 1666.[1]

Fox, Sir Stephen, kt 1665 (1627–1716). Paymaster-General of the army 1661–76, 1679; Treasury Commissioner 1679–1702. In many ways the most successful of all public servants in Pepys's time. Originally a household officer employed by the Percy family, he was brought by Clarendon into the King's service as a steward in 1654, becoming Clerk of the Green Cloth in 1660. In 1661 he was given charge of the army finances, first as paymaster of the Guards then as Paymaster-General. He had an extraordinary flair for finance, and also for making the public interest and his own coincide, as he once explained to Pepys.[1] By the 1680s he was said to be the richest commoner in England, with an income of over £14,000, larger than that of even the greatest merchant princes. At the same time his office was a model of efficiency and he himself quite incorrupt, and so modest and affable that he attracted no envy. The foundation of the Royal Chelsea Hospital was due to his initiative. In Parliament (he sat for nine between 1661 and 1714) he was, despite his official status, a thoroughly independent member. He opposed, for instance, the impeachment of Clarendon.

His wife (admired of old by Pepys) was Elizabeth, daughter of William Whittle. She died in 1696, having borne him seven sons and three daughters. In 1703, in his late seventies, he married a young woman of 25 and had four children. One of them, Henry (later 1st Baron Holland) was the father of Charles James Fox.[2]

Foxe, Dr [Thomas] (d. 1652). A rich physician of Waltham Abbey, Essex, whose daughter Alice married Sir Richard Willys. He was the grandson of John Foxe the Elizabethan martyrologist.[1]

Foxhall: *see* Vauxhall

Fraiser, Sir Alexander, kt c. 1667, bt 1673 (c. 1610–81). Physician-in-ordinary to the King in exile and after; royalist agent during the Interregnum. F.R.C.P. 1641; F.R.S. 1663. According to Clarendon, 'good at his business, otherwise the maddest fool alive'.[1]

Frank(e), [Edward]. Citizen and Merchant-Taylor. In his will (proved July 1661) he left to his wife three freehold houses he had bought from Mr Fisher in St Bride's parish. One was at that time let to 'Mr John Peapes', Pepys's father. This was the house in which Pepys was born.[1]

Frank(e), [Francis]. Mayor of Worcester 1651–2.[1]

Franklin, Mrs. Probably wife of Richard Franklin (d. 1672), physician to the Tower.[1]

Frederick, Ald. Sir John, kt 1660 (d. 1685). E. India merchant;
Sheriff 1655–6; Lord Mayor 1661–2; M.P. for Dartmouth 1660; for
London 1663–Jan. 79.[1]
Freeman, Sir Ralph (d. 1667). Appointed Joint-Master of the Mint in
1635; Master 1660–2; Joint-Master 1662–7.[1]
Freemantle, ——. A John Freemantle was a servant of the 2nd Lord
Crew.[1]
The French Church. There were two French congregations in
London at this time (their number had by 1700 grown to 28 after Louis
XIV's persecution of the Huguenots) – one in the city in Fenchurch St,
which had been there since 1550 and was strictly Calvinist, and a more
recent one in Westminster in the Savoy (founded 1642, refounded 1661)
which held Anglican services conducted in French. Both were exempted
from the Act of Uniformity (though accepting the authority of the
Bishop of London), and both attracted wealthy and fashionable
congregations.
    Pepys attended the Westminster church only once in the diary period.
It was the church used by his wife's parents, the St Michels, and from
c. 1667 her father received a pension from it.[1] On moving to York
Buildings, Pepys subscribed regularly to its funds from c. 1688, and in
1699 he appealed to Archbishop Tenison to relieve the poverty of its
minister.[2] From July 1661 it met in the 'little chapel' of the Savoy
hospital in the Strand. In 1817 it moved to Bloomsbury and is now the
French episcopal church of St John, Bloomsbury St.
    Pepys went to services at the city church several times in the '60s,
almost always in the Christmas season. It was served by two ministers –
Louis Hérault (1643, 1660–75) and David Primerose (1660–?1713). The
building was on the n. side of Threadneedle St. It was burnt in the Fire
and rebuilt by 1669. In the 1840s it moved to St Martin-le-Grand,
and in the late 1880s to Soho Sq. where it remains.[3]
Frost, [Gaulter, jun.]. Treasurer for the Council's Contingencies
1652–60.[1]
Frowde, Sir Philip, kt 1665 (d. 1674). Secretary to the Committee for
Foreign Plantations and to the Duchess of York from 1660; farmer of
the Post Office; Commissioner of Prizes during the Second Dutch
War. A man of slow wits and dim understanding, according to
Marvell. But the grandfather of Philip Frowde, dramatist and poet (d.
1738).[1]
Fuller, [Richard] (d. 1669). A neighbour of Pepys living in Mark
Lane; wine merchant and freeman of the Drapers' Company.[1]
Fuller, Thomas (1608–61). The author and wit – 'the great Tom
Fuller' (ii.6) – now best remembered for his history of English families,
The history of the worthies of England (first pub. 1662). In his day he was
popular as a preacher, and influential (especially with moderates like

Pepys) as a proponent and exemplar of a pragmatical style of church-manship which put its emphasis on the value of a national church to national unity. A royalist, he spent most of the Civil War years in Oxford, but from c. 1647 was active as an Anglican preacher in London, where Pepys heard him. He preached mainly at the Savoy, but also elsewhere, including St Bride's (1647, 1655–6). A Northamptonshire man by origin, he was patronised by the Mountagus of Boughton. He later became chaplain to the 8th and 9th Barons Berkeley. Of his books, Pepys was especially fond of reading (on Sundays) his *Church-history of Britain* (1655). This he retained in his library, along with the *Worthies*, *The historie of the holy warre* (i.e. the Crusades), and *The holy state*. Aubrey (who like Pepys remarks on his phenomenal memory) adds that he had a 'very working head' which often led him to forget dinner.[1]

Fuller, William (1608–75). Clergyman and friend. A royalist, he lost his studentship at Christ Church, Oxford, and spent most of the Interregnum teaching at Twickenham, where Mountagu's son Edward was among his pupils. It was perhaps through this connection that Pepys got to know him. At the Restoration he was rewarded in 1660 with the deanery of St Patrick's, Dublin, and in 1664 with the bishopric of Limerick. In 1667 he was translated to Lincoln, where he did much to repair the damage done to the buildings during the Interregnum. He composed anthems and left a chest of viols and a chamber organ to Christ Church.[1]

Fulwood, [Gervase]. Chaplain to Sandwich; born at Huntingdon in 1635, son of Gervase; Fellow of St Catharine's College, Cambridge 1655–72; Rector of Coton, Cambs. 1662–?72. He was a candidate for the High Mastership of St Paul's School in 1672 when Thomas Gale (Pepys's cousin by marriage) was appointed. He was then described as a 'Latitude man' who would make the boys 'as errant . . . Enthusiasts as himselfe'.[1]

FUNERALS

The importance of paying due honour to the deceased is clear enough in the diary. The first and apparently the easiest duty of the bereaved was to ensure that as many relatives and friends as possible would attend. Tickets would be issued, but do not seem to have succeeded in limiting the numbers – to gatecrash might be a mark of respect. Public assembly rooms might be hired for the gathering – two city halls were required at the funeral of the goldsmith Sir Thomas Vyner – but even so, they were often, in Pepys's experience, uncomfortably crowded. According to his estimates, four or five hundred people attended the funeral of Anthony Joyce, and roughly two hundred coaches were required to carry Sir William Batten's mourners from London to his burial at Walthamstow. The numbers in the funeral procession might, in the case of an important person, be swollen by the hiring of professional mourners – old men or women (according to the sex of the deceased) who walked in couples ahead of the hearse, their number corresponding to his or her age.[1]

The second duty of the deceased's family was to provide the proper habiliments of mourning. Black cloth would be given beforehand to near relatives and servants. At the funeral, scarves and hatbands would be distributed, together with mourning rings that were graded to the rank and degree of relationship of the recipients. The rings, of gold and black enamel, would often be provided for in the will of the deceased. The house and church would be draped in black for days on end, and mourning coaches would be hired for the funeral and for the customary month's mourning afterwards.[2] At Pepys's own funeral in 1703 mourning was presented to 40 people and 123 rings (of three grades costing 20s., 15s. and 10s.) were distributed.[3] In the case of men of gentle birth (Edward Pepys of Broomsthorpe for example), hatchments displaying their arms would be hung from the windows of the house and placed on the hearse. Afternoon was the usual time for the ceremony,[4] but the upper classes preferred to be buried at night. Pepys himself was buried at 9 p.m.[5] The rich spent lavishly on these occasions – there are records of funerals at about this time costing over £1000, and a state funeral (like Albemarle's) cost £6000[6] – and humbler folk probably overspent. The wine and biscuits, the hire of a hall and undertaker, the charges for parson, sexton and ringers were all expenses that could hardly be avoided. [*See also* Dress etc.]

Furniture: *see* Large Glossary under names
Furzer, [Daniel]. Private shipbuilder at Lydney and Conpill, Glos.; employed also as a timber purveyor to the navy. His son Daniel, shipwright and Surveyor of the Navy 1699–1714, received a ring at Pepys's funeral.[1]
Fyge: *see* Fage

Gale, ——. Possibly Henry Gale, who graduated from Magdalene in 1658 and took deacon's orders in 1663.[1]
Gallop, ——. Clergyman. The context suggests that he may have been John Gallop, chaplain on board the *Hector* in 1659.[1]
Games, sports and pastimes: *see* Large Glossary and footnotes to diary text. For mock-weddings, *see* Weddings
Gardener's Lane. In Westminster, approximately on the line of the

modern King Charles St, running west off Parliament St to St James's
Park. (R)

Garraway, William (1617–1701). M.P. for Chichester 1661–Jan. 79,
Arundel March 1679–90. A captain in the royalist army, he became one
of the leading critics of the court (having a particular interest in finance),
and, while retaining his independence, often acted with the Buckingham and Shaftesbury factions. He appears from the diary to have been
a friend or acquaintance of Capt. Cocke. One of the best speakers in
the House, he proved to be a formidable enemy of Pepys in the '70s:
he challenged the validity of his election (1674), questioned the need
for his shipbuilding proposals (1675 and 1677), and pressed the charges
of treason (1679). He was a strong Protestant (but in favour of toleration) and supported the attempts to exclude the Duke of York from the
succession. He welcomed the Revolution of 1688, but continued to be
a watchful critic of government policy.[1]

The Gatehouse, Westminster. A prison at the e. end of Tothill St,
near the w. end of the Abbey. It contained two sections, each with a
gate – one entered from College Court or Great Dean's Yard which
contained the Bishop of London's prison for convicted parsons; the
other, on the w. side, which housed offenders from Westminster. In the
latter Pepys's clerk Tom Hayter was imprisoned in 1665 for trading in
gunpowder, and Pepys himself in June 1690, for just under a week, on
suspicion of Jacobitism. The building was pulled down, together with
the adjoining houses, in 1776.[1] The gatehouse where the 'pretty
Madam' Frances Butler and her family lodged (i.208) was probably
the gatehouse which commanded the entry into New Palace Yard from
King St. (R; La)

Gauden, Ald. Sir Denis, kt 1667 (1600–88). Navy Victualler 1660–77;
employed in the victualling from c. 1650 and made Surveyor-General
Sept. 1660. He had sole responsibility for supplies 1660–9 and joint
responsibility with partners in the contracts of 1669, 1672 and 1673. He
was also victualler for Tangier 1663–77. The government's inability to
pay his bills ruined him; by the end of the Third Dutch War he was
unable any longer to advance credit, and was omitted from the 1677
contract for the navy, and at the same time withdrew from the Tangier
business. He was in that year briefly arrested as a debtor.[1] He had been
an Alderman 1667–76, Sheriff 1667–8 and Master of the Clothworkers'
Company 1667–8, but c. 1677 he retired to his country house at Clapham, built for his brother John, Bishop of Worcester (d. 1663)[2] and
which later was acquired by Will Hewer. His London house until 1671
was by the Victualling Office in E. Smithfield; in that year he built a
house and victualler's yard at Deptford which later became the principal
victualling centre for the navy. The diary of John Luke of Tangier
speaks of him as 'very devout'.[3]

His (second) wife was Elizabeth Clarke of Clapham whom he married in 1653. The children mentioned in the diary are Samuel, his eldest son (alive in 1688 but never apparently employed in the family business), and Sarah (by 1688 married to Creshell Draper of Crayford, Kent). Two of his sons, Benjamin and Jonathan, were at various times partners with him in the navy victualling.[4] His sister-in-law (the bishop's widow), whose conversation so delighted Pepys, was Elizabeth (d. 1671), daughter of Sir William Russell, Navy Treasurer under Charles I. She wrote c. 1662 a long memorandum claiming for her late husband authorship of the *Eikon Basilike* attributed to Charles.[5]

Gualtier (Gotier), ――. Probably Jacques Gaultier, a lutenist and singer, son of the French lutenist Ennémond Gaultier (1575–1651). He came to England in 1617 and joined the King's Musick, but was replaced in his post in 1660. He is not, however, then described as 'deceased', and thus could quite possibly have been still alive in 1663. He had two brothers – both musicians – in Paris and Rome.[1] (Lu)

Geere, ――. A neighbour of Pepys's father in Salisbury Court. He was John Geere, possibly the John Geere who married Christian, daughter of Sir Andrew Riccard.[1]

[Gens, Jan de]. Captain of the royal yacht *Mary*.[1]

Gentleman, ――. A cook: he served in Sandwich's household in the Madrid embassy.[1]

[Gery, Mr ――]. A 'Mr Gary' was a servant of Sandwich and is possibly the John Gering who took part in Sandwich's funeral. Ann Gery was a poor relative of Sandwich: in 1660 she wrote asking him for a place for her son. Now a widow, she had been hard put to it for 17 years to keep her husband out of a debtor's prison.[1]

Gibbons, Christopher (1615–76). Composer and keyboard player; second son of Orlando Gibbons. Organist, Westminster Abbey, 1636; served in royalist forces;[1] with Matthew Locke composed *Cupid and Death* 1652;[2] heard by Evelyn, Oxford 12 July 1654; played in *The siege of Rhodes*; 'musician upon the Virginalls', King's Musick, 1660; D.Mus.Oxon. 1664; alleged a 'grand debauchee' by Anthony Wood;[3] organist of the Chapel Royal by 1668. (Lu)

Gibbs, ――. A Navy Office clerk, but employed privately by one of the higher officers since his name does not appear in official lists. A 'Mr Gibbs' was on Sandwich's staff in Madrid 1665–8, and a Thomas Gibbs was an Admiralty clerk 1694–5.[1]

Gibson, Richard. One of the ablest and most experienced of Pepys's assistants; more than once commended by Pepys for his diligence, sobriety and honesty.[1] Originally a purser (1652, 1655–65), he was given charge of the wartime victualling at Great Yarmouth 1665–7. From Aug. 1667–Aug. 1670 he was clerk to Pepys in the Navy Office and after a spell as Purser-General to the Straits fleet (1670–2) served as chief

clerk to three successive Clerks of the Acts 1672–7, as Clerk of the
Cheque at Deptford 1677–80, as chief clerk to the Comptroller 1680–6,
and as chief clerk of the Victualling Accounts 1686–8. He then moved
to the Admiralty and appears to have gone out of office after 1693 with
the resignation of Lord Cornwallis, the First Commissioner, whom he
had also served as chief clerk. In that year he wrote (somewhat in
Pepys's manner) a comprehensive memorandum to the King on the
state of the Navy and sent a copy to Pepys.[2] In the '90s he contributed
largely to the notes Pepys made for his projected history of the navy.[3]
He had made a collection of naval MSS – now in the British Library[4] –
again in Pepys's manner. His handwriting is curiously (perhaps
significantly) very similar to Pepys's. He was alive in 1703 when he
received a ring at Pepys's funeral as a former servant and dependant.[5]

Gifford, [George]. Rector of St Dunstan-in-the-East 1656–d. 86;
Professor of Divinity, Gresham College 1661; President Sion College
1677–8. Pepys admired his sermons; several were published. In his
Naval Minutes Pepys notes that Gifford has informed him that the
Ancient Britons were unaware that Britain was an island. He was a
witness to Daniel Milles's will.[1]

Gifford, ——. Probably Henry, assistant to Gaulter Frost, Treasurer
to the Council of State.[1]

Gifford, ——. Merchant: probably Thomas Gifford, of St Giles,
Cripplegate.[1]

Giles, Thomas and Sarah. Cousins of Pepys. Thomas Giles, of St
Giles, Cripplegate, had married Sarah, ?daughter of Lettice Haines, later
Howlett (b. Kite), sister of Pepys's mother. He predeceased his wife,
whose will was made in July and proved in Sept. 1670. The will was
signed with a mark and dated, in the Quaker style, on the 4th day of the
5th month. She left bequests to a son-in-law John Price and his daughter
Sarah.[1]

Gilsthorpe, —— (d. 1667). Clerk to Batten in the Navy Office: a
personal servant not included in official lists. The subject of a complaint
in Pepys's 'Navy White Book' to the effect that he had been trained as
a justices' clerk and had no knowledge of the navy.[1]

Glanville, [William] (c. 1618–1702). Of Greenwich; Evelyn's
brother-in-law; barrister 1642; Commissioner of the Alienation Office
1689–1702. He and Pepys served together from 1696 on the Grand
Committee for Greenwich Hospital. Evelyn has a kindly notice of him
at his death referring to their 'long & greate' friendship and to the
'displeasure' Glanville took at Evelyn's 'not concurring with him, as
to his opinion of the Trinity'.[1]

Glascock, Charles and John. Relatives of Pepys; sons of Francis
Glascock, of Stoke-by-Clare, Suff., who had married Mary, sister of
Judith, first wife of Sir Richard Pepys (Lord Chief Justice of Ireland,

1654–9).[1] Charles (d. 1665) was a grocer, of Fleet St,[2] John was Rector of Little Canfield, Essex, from 1649 until his death in 1661. He had been a Fellow of Magdalene, where he had taken his B.A. in 1643 and his M.A. in 1646.[3]

Glemham, [Henry]. Dean of Bristol 1660–7; Bishop of St Asaph 1667–d. 70. Lady Castlemaine's great-uncle and 'a drunken swearing rascal' (viii.364). He was already well-beneficed before the Civil War.[1]

Goddard, [Jonathan] (c. 1617–75). Physician to Oliver Cromwell, and inventor of Goddard's drops (for fainting). Warden of Merton College, Oxford 1651–60; M.P. 1653; Councillor of State 1653 and an original F.R.S. He lived at Gresham College where he was Professor of Physic from 1653.[1]

Godfrey. Richard Godfrey, gentleman, of Broughton, Hunts. – or rather his estate – was involved in the disputes which arose from the will of Pepys's uncle Robert Pepys. He had died by Nov. 1661, but it was he who had held the bond for £200 which led Pepys deep into Chancery with the Trice family. Godfrey's son Henry (who had witnessed the bond) had married Mercy, sister of the Trice brothers. A smaller matter was that Robert Pepys died owing Godfrey £40. His son Henry secured the money after threatening a lawsuit. Henry later lived at Burford, Oxfs., and was an executor of Tom Trice's will (1672)[1].

Godolphin, Sir William (c. 1635–96). Diplomat; secretary to Sandwich's Spanish embassy 1667–8, and knighted for his services.[1] He had been an under-secretary to the Secretary of State from 1662, and was later envoy-extraordinary and then ambassador to Spain (1669–80). In his later years he fell into disgrace by his conversion to Rome. Pepys thought highly of his ability and there is a note in his *Naval Minutes* of an ingenious deduction he had made from a passage in Herodotus. He was second cousin to Sidney Godolphin the politician, Queen Anne's minister.[2]

Goffe (Gough), Stephen. An Oxford graduate who became a chaplain to Charles I, was converted to Rome and by 1652 was an Oratorian living in Paris as friend and confidant of Henry Jermyn, later 1st Earl of St Albans. To Clarendon he was one who 'could comply with all men in all the acts of good-fellowship' (which agrees well enough with Pepys's story at vii.290). By 1665 (probably earlier) he was a chaplain to the Queen Mother.[1]

Gold (Gould), Sir Nicholas, bt 1660. Merchant and politician; an active M.P. (for Fowey 1648–53, 1659–60). His wife was Elizabeth, daughter of Sir John Garrard, 2nd Bt. Less than five months after his death she married Thomas Neale. She died in 1683. Her brother has not been identified: she had four.[1]

Gold, ——. Hemp merchant and navy contractor. The Mr Gould, merchant, who spoke 'very well and very sharply' against the city's levying a tax for water baillage may have been the same man, or possibly Edward Gould. Both were involved.[1]

Golding, Capt. [John]. Naval officer; he held three commissions 1661–4, and was killed in action in 1665.[1]

Goldsmiths' Hall. On the e. side of Foster Lane; dating from c. 1407: according to Stow 'a proper House but not large'. Burnt in the Fire, it was rebuilt, and in its new form was 'a Stately Structure of Brick and Stone' with 'a spacious Hall'. It was again rebuilt 1829–35.[1]

Gomme, Sir Bernard de (1620–85). Military engineer, Dutch by birth. He came to England with Rupert, and in the Civil War was made Engineer and Quartermaster-General to the King's forces. After the Restoration he was Chief Engineer to the Ordnance 1661–85, and Surveyor-General 1682–5. Pepys mentions his works on the Medway: others were at Dover, Tilbury, Portsmouth, Plymouth, Harwich and Dublin, as well as at Dunkirk and Tangier. He died rich.[1]

Goodenough, ———. Edward Goodenough was paid for plasterer's work in the Navy Office 1662–3. He was buried in the chancel of St Olave, Hart St in 1671.[1]

Goodgroome, [John] (c. 1625–1704). Royal musician in ordinary; counter-tenor; viol, violin and lute player; singing-master and composer.[1] Two of his songs are printed in *Musica Britannica* 39/items cxii, cxiii. The 'Theodore' Goodgroome who appears in previous editions [2] seems to be a ghost. (Lu)

Goods, John. Servant to Sandwich; Groom of the Bedchamber in his embassy to Spain.[1]

Goodson, [William]. He served with distinction in the Commonwealth navy, and was second in command to Penn on the W. Indies expedition in 1654–5, and Vice-Admiral under Sandwich in the Baltic in 1659. He retired at the Restoration into private life. The date of his death is unknown.[1]

Goodyear. Aaron and Hester, children of Moses Goodyear, merchant, a neighbour of Pepys, and his wife Hester.[1]

Gordon, Eleanor, Lady Byron (1633–64). 'The King's seventeenth whore abroad' (viii.182). She was the daughter of Viscount Kilmorey, an Irish peer, and at the age of 11 had been married off to the 1st Baron Byron, who later became governor to the young Duke of York. After his death in 1652 she married Peter Warburton.[1]

Gorham, Goody. Alehouse keeper, Brampton. Her house was inherited by Pepys's father from his brother Robert. Her will survives: signed Nov. 1670, proved Oct. 1676. She was Margaret, a widow, and signed by making a mark. Her son Henry was cut off with a shilling; the rest of the goods went to Thomas Kent, a grandson. Will Stankes signed as a witness.[1] Keepers of alehouses were often widows: at Bideford in 1660 they numbered about one quarter of the total.[2]

Goring House. On the site of the present-day Buckingham Palace: a Jacobean house bought in 1633 by Lord Goring (later Earl of Norwich, d. 1663) who extended both house and grounds. His absence from London on the King's service from 1642, together with legal disputes about the title, led to its being taken over by the government, and in 1647 it was used as the French ambassador's residence. In 1660 rooms were let out for entertainments, but later that year Daniel O'Neill took over the tenancy. Bennet (Arlington) was the tenant in 1665, and possibly earlier; on his buying the property in 1677 it became known as Arlington House. (He had it reconstructed after a fire in 1674.) Pepys admired it (and kept two etchings of it); Evelyn thought it 'ill-built'. After 1702 it was named after the new owner, the Duke of Buckingham. It was acquired by the Crown in George III's reign, and was completely rebuilt by Nash and Blore, 1825–37.[1]

Gosnell, [?Winifred]. Actress and singer in the Duke's Company from 1663; briefly in Pepys's service as a companion to his wife, Dec. 1662. There is an unflattering reference to her looks and morals in Scroope's *In defence of satire*.[1]

Gotier, Monsieur: *see* Gaultier

Gouge, [Thomas] (d. 1681). Nonconformist divine. Fellow of King's College, Cambridge 1628–39; Vicar of St Sepulchre-without-Newgate from 1638 until his extrusion in 1662. A reluctant Dissenter, he devoted himself after his extrusion to charitable works in London and evangelism in Wales, distributing Welsh versions not only of the Bible but of the Anglican prayer-book.[1]

Grabu, [Luis] (d. 1694). French composer of Catalan origin, who worked in England (except for the years 1679–83) from 1665, when he was appointed a composer to the King's Musick; he became the Master in March 1666, and was dismissed 1674, though he still continued to make a career in England, collaborating with Dryden on *Albion and Albanius* in 1685. He directed the twenty-four violins from 1666 and the *Petits violons du roy* (the select band of twelve) from 1667. He died in Paris. Pepys owned copies of his *Albion and Albanius* and *Pastoralle*.[1] (Lu)

Gracechurch St. Pepys's spelling ('Gracious') was common. Stow, writing in Elizabeth's reign, used the medieval version 'Grasse Street' – so-called from the grass (herb) market held by the church of St Benet. In 1660 it was a spacious street, running south from the junction of Cornhill, Bishopsgate St and Leadenhall St to Fish St Hill. It was destroyed in the Fire and rebuilt. The conduit Pepys mentions was a castellated structure given by the Lord Mayor in 1491.[1]

Gramont. Antoine, 3rd Duc de Gramont (1604–78) was a distinguished soldier and politician who supported the court in the wars of the Fronde. He married a niece of Richelieu. His eldest son Armand, Comte de Guiche (1638–73), was a soldier who was disgraced in 1663 for paying too much attention to Henriette d'Orléans (Charles II's sister), and for his intrigues against Mme de la Vallière. He travelled Europe fighting in turn for the Poles, the Turks, the Dutch and (in 1666) the English. He returned to France in 1671 and accompanied Louis XIV on his Dutch campaign. His memoirs were published in 1713.[1] [*See* Hamilton]

Graunt, Capt. John (1620–74). A draper and pioneer demographer (author of *Natural and political observations . . . upon the bills of mortality*, 1662); F.R.S. 1662. Captain, later Major, in the trainbands; Common Councilman 1669–71. His house and shop were on the w. side of Birchin Lane.[1] Aubrey wrote of him that 'he had an excellent working head, and was very facetious and fluent in conversation . . . a very ingeniose and studious person, and generally beloved, and rose early in the morning to his study before shop-time'. Pepys does not mention (as Aubrey does) his great expertness in shorthand, but he does mention his collection of prints, about which little or nothing is known. (He was a friend of Samuel Cooper the miniaturist.) Sometime before the Fire, he was converted to Roman Catholicism, and the story was put about that, in his capacity as trustee for one of the managers of the New River Company, he had turned off the water supply on the night before the Papists had arranged for the conflagration to break out. He was an intimate friend of Sir William Petty and Thomas Barlow – both skilled mathematicians.[2]

Gray's Inn. One of the four principal inns of court; on the w. side of Gray's Inn Lane (now Gray's Inn Rd) in grounds that stretched north as far as Theobalds Rd. The tree-lined walks in these grounds, reputedly designed and planted by Francis Bacon when Treasurer,[1] provided a pleasant and fashionable promenade, with a view over Gray's Inn Fields of the countryside to the north as far as Highgate and Hampstead.

Greatorex, [Ralph] (1625–?1712). Scientific instrument-maker, at the Adam and Eve on the s. side of the Strand; particularly accomplished in the design of diving bells and waterpumps. One of his bells was meant for use in the construction of the Tangier mole. He attended early meetings of the Royal Society before its incorporation, but never became a Fellow.[1]

Greene, [John]. Of Brampton. There were two of these names, father and son, who are referred to in the will of Robert Pepys (1657) as his 'cousin' and godson respectively. John Greene the elder also occurs in the will of Thomas Trice (1672) as a 'cousin' of the testator. In 1673 he was sued by Pepys and his father in Chancery for the recovery of a loan allegedly made by Robert Pepys to Mary Greene, his deceased wife.[1]

Green(e), Maj. [John]. Fishmonger (freeman of the company 1637); Common Councilman 1654–6, 1658–60, 1664–d. 67.[1]

Green(e), Capt. [Levi]. Naval officer: twice commissioned as lieutenant, and four times as captain 1666–71; discharged for embezzling powder in 1672. Both Pepys and Coventry wrote of him as drunken.[1]

Greene, [William]. Hemp and tar merchant.[1]

Greenleaf, Mrs. Widow of Maj. John Greenleaf. He died in March 1659; she remarried in the following year.[1]

Greeting, [Thomas] (d. 1682). Flageolet player and teacher, also violinist in the King's Musick, sackbut in ordinary in the Chapel Royal, composer, and, in Christopher Welch's words, 'provider of quadrille bands'. He was appointed musician in ordinary without fee in the King's Private Musick 1662.[1] The earliest extant copy of his *Pleasant companion . . . for the flageolet* is of the 2nd edition (1673). (Lu)

Gregory, [Edward, sen.] (d. 1682). Clerk of the Cheque, Chatham 1661–5.[1]

Gregory, [Sir Edward]. Son of the foregoing. A clerk in the yard at Chatham (employed 1663–4 by the committee enquiring into the Chest), he succeeded his father in 1665, and was later knighted and made Navy Commissioner at Chatham (1689–1703). Pepys has in his papers an account of his 'Comicall froward manner' of speech.[1]

Gregory, [John]. An old colleague of Pepys in the Exchequer. He moved in 1660 to the office of Secretary Nicholas, and in 1668 was in the service of the Brooke House Committee.[1]

Gregory. Musicians. Two Gregorys are traceable in 1666: Henry, a violinist and flautist, son of William Gregory (d. 1663), and another William, also a wind player. Both men were still active in the 1680s and both were in royal employ.[1] (Lu)

Grenville, Sir John, 1st Earl of Bath (1628–1701). A Cornish royalist (Governor of the Scillies 1649–51) who in the late '50s helped to persuade his kinsman Monck to espouse royalism. Though never in favour with Hyde, he acted as an intermediary between the Council of State and the exiled court in the days immediately before the King's return. At the Restoration he was loaded with honours and grants (including an earldom, 1661), and held high court office as Groom of the Stole and First Gentleman of the Bedchamber. But the general view of him was Burnet's: 'a mean minded man, who thought of nothing but getting and spending money'.[1]

Gresham College. Founded under Sir Thomas Gresham's will in 1596 as an academy of learning for the city, and governed by the city corporation. Its buildings until 1768 occupied his former mansion between (Old) Broad St and Bishopsgate St; they are now at the corner of Basingstoke St at its junction with Gresham St. Its emphasis was on the practical uses of knowledge, and it provided (as it still does) lectures on Divinity, Civil Law, Physic, Astronomy, Geometry, Rhetoric and Music. In the '60s a group of able men held these posts, but Pepys does not seem to have attended any of their lectures. According to John Wallis, the first meetings held in England for scientific discussion were at the College in 1645. It is certain that such meetings were organised there before the Restoration, and it was after a Gresham College lecture on 28 Nov. 1660 that the first steps towards the inauguration of what became the Royal Society were taken. The Society met in its building for most of the period 1660–1710, and in Pepys's usage in the diary 'Gresham College' and 'Royal Society' are usually synonymous. The building was used for a short time after the Fire as a substitute for the Royal Exchange and for meetings of the city corporation, and the Royal Society met elsewhere.[1] [*See also* Royal Society]

Grey (Gray), [Thomas] (c. 1625–72). Eldest son of the parliamentarian Lord Grey of Warke (d. 1674); Deputy-Governor of the R. Africa Company 1665, 1667–8; Sub-Governor 1666, 1670; member of the Fishery Corporation, of the Committee for Trade 1668–72, and of the Committee for Foreign Plantations 1670–2. As an M.P. (for Ludgershall, 1669–72) he was an ally of Buckingham and a critic of the established church.[1]

Griffin, Col. Probably Sir Edward Griffin, Treasurer of the Chamber (d. 1710). He was a Lieut-Colonel in the Duke of York's regiment of foot; later (1688) cr. Baron Griffin of Braybrooke, and an active Jacobite.[1] But possibly Col. John Griffin, his younger brother.[2]

Griffith, Sir John, (kt 1665). Lieut-Colonel in Sir W. Killigrew's Foot regiment 1662; Captain in the Admiral's Sea Regiment 1664 (Maj. 1667, Lt-Col. 1668); Governor of Gravesend blockhouses from 1667.[1]

Griffith, William (d. 1683). Doorkeeper/housekeeper to the Navy Office 1660–83. His widow Alice succeeded him. She received a ring at Pepys's funeral.[1]

Griffith(s), [William]. Batten's ward; he appears in his will (1665) as a witness, but was given no legacy.[1] Possibly the foregoing.

Griffith, ——, courtier. He could be one of three: Rowland, gentleman-harbinger to the Duke of York; Hugh, page in the King's bedchamber; or William, groom of the Great Chamber.[1]

Grocers' Hall. Built in the 15th century, it stood north of the Poultry at the end of Grocers' Alley (now Grocers' Hall Court). Destroyed in the Fire and rebuilt; again rebuilt 1802 and altered 1827. The topography of this area has been wholly altered by the construction, after the Fire, of Princes St and by its subsequent widening, straightening and conversion into a major traffic route between the Bank crossroads and Moorgate. The Hall thereby connects with Princes St instead of the great mart of Cheapside. (R)

Grove, Capt. [Edward] (d. by 1688). River agent for the Navy Board and Tangier committee. He had served in the Commonwealth navy and held three commands 1661–5. He was in disgrace after 1665 when he failed to take his ship the *Success* out of port during the Battle of Lowestoft, and was not employed again. Described in 1660 as 'of Lynn', by 1664 he was living in Wapping.[1]

Guildhall. A mostly 12th-century building, rebuilt in 1441, set back from the n. side of Cateaton (now Gresham) St, and approached by a large court flanked by offices and other buildings concerned with the governance of the city. It struck a French visitor at this time as 'an inconsiderable Building and in a narrow Street'.[1] It was burnt in the Fire, but afterwards (1667–71) restored and re-edified and the approach to it much enhanced by the making of King St.[2] (R)

Gunning, Peter (1614–84). One of the most influential conservative churchmen of his day. He defied the Commonwealth government by holding Anglican services at Exeter House chapel in the '50s. It was there that, in a famous incident on Christmas Day 1657, soldiers were sent to arrest the communicants.[1] Pepys at the beginning of the diary period was often a member of this same congregation. At the Restoration Gunning was given a royal chaplaincy and a canonry, and at Cambridge (as professor of divinity and as Master successively of Clare Hall and St John's) rooted out the puritans. In 1661 at the Savoy Conference he was chief spokesman of the party which refused concessions to the moderate Presbyterians. He became Bishop of Chichester in 1669 and of Ely in 1675.[2]

GUNPOWDER PLOT DAY

The fifth of November was well established as a public holiday by 1660. In London on that day shops were shut and congregations gathered for a service added to the Prayer Book in 1606 – the year after the Plot – in which they heard sermons on the subject of God's deliverance of the kingdom from Fawkes and his fellow conspirators. Afterwards the bells were rung and the day reached its climax with an evening festival of fireworks and bonfires. Pepys, for his part, never went in the diary period to the church service, but his comments, made more than once, about the strictness with which the day was observed[1] are a witness to the popularity of the holiday. In only one year during the '60s were the celebrations notably reduced, when in Nov. 1666, barely two months after the Great Fire, they did not, understandably enough, include bonfires.

In the '70s the holiday acquired an additional significance. In Sept. 1673 the Duke of York, heir to the throne, was married by proxy to a Catholic bride, and in consequence on the Fifth of November of that year there were more bonfires in London, it was said, than had been seen for thirty years.[2] It was in this same year that Josselin, keeping his diary in his Essex parsonage, began to enter a record of his Gunpowder sermons.[3] With the Popish Plot scare, from Oct. 1678, the demonstrations in London became more aggressive. They now took the form of mass demonstrations organised by the anti-Catholic politicians – Shaftesbury's Whigs – and included processions in which the guy was dressed as the Pope and stuffed with cats which were burnt alive on the bonfire. These processions took place on the Fifth, and also, for good measure, on the 17th of the month, Queen Elizabeth's birthday.[4] The Whigs had so closely associated Gunpowder Plot Day with their own party policy (of excluding the Duke of York from the succession) that with the collapse of their cause the government discouraged street celebrations of any sort. On 7 Apr. 1680 a proclamation was issued forbidding bonfires without permission from the local authorities. That the proclamation was reissued in 1682 and 1683 was probably a sign of its ineffectiveness.[5] On the other hand, its reissue on 6 Nov. 1685[6] – in the first November of James's reign – was rather a sign of the embarrassment of the new régime in the face of popular expressions of anti-Catholic feeling. In 1686–8 James almost succeeded in suppressing the bonfires, but the sermons took on an even sharper anti-Catholic tone, and on 5 Nov. 1688, when his régime was about to fall, there was unprecedented excitement in London.[7]

Though the London crowds did not know it at the time, it was precisely on Gunpowder Plot Day in 1688 that William of Orange's fleet, blown by a 'Protestant' wind which immobilised James's ships in the Thames estuary, had sailed into Torbay to deliver the kingdom from papist rule. To contemporaries these events were, literally, providential. Thereafter there were two deliverances to celebrate on the Fifth, and the fact that the second was followed by a long and successful series of wars against the most powerful of the Catholic monarchies, France, gave the day a still deeper meaning. The preachers of what became known as the Revolution sermons now had a new version of the old theme. The history of the nation, the history of its established religion and the history of its historic constitution, all seemed to hinge on events that had happened, under God, on 5 November.

With the original events of 1605 Pepys had a slight and accidental connection in that his relative John Pepys of Ashtead, whom he knew as a boy, had been one of the lawyers employed to hunt out and convict the plotters.[8]

Guy, Capt. Thomas. Soldier; a member of the Dunkirk garrison 1659–60; probably Pepys had got to know him on his visits to the Exchequer in 1659 for the garrison's pay. A Capt. Thomas Guy served in Kirke's regiment in Tangier c. 1680–3, and was wounded in 1680.[1]

Guy, Capt. ——. Naval officer. The Capt. Guy who talked on 28 Oct. 1666 about the year's campaign must be Thomas Guy, who commanded the *Assurance* throughout 1666 and had taken part in all the actions referred to. He had come ashore on 9 October. Leonard Guy's ship the *Paradox* was still at sea.[1]

Guyat (Gayet), Susan. Probably the daughter of John Baptista Guyat (d. 1665) and his wife Bridget (d. 1674), of St Olave's parish. In 1666 the widow was living in a large house (taxed on 10 hearths) on the n. side of Crutched Friars.[1]

Gwyn, Nell (?1650–87). Actress in the King's Company c. 1664–Feb. 1671. 'Brought up', according to her own story, 'in a bawdy-house',[1] she entered the theatre as an orange-girl employed at the Bridges St Theatre in 1663. Charles Hart, of the King's Company, made her his mistress and introduced her to the stage. She soon became one of the most popular comic and character actresses of the period. She was mistress to Charles Sackville, Lord Buckhurst from 1667 until about 1669 when Buckingham, for political reasons, arranged for her to replace Lady Castlemaine in the King's favour. She was, in Burnet's words, 'the indiscreetest and wildest creature that ever was in a court, yet continued to the end of the king's life in great favour . . . She acted all persons in so lively a manner, and was such a constant diversion to the king, that even a new mistress could not drive her away. But after all, he never treated her with the decencies of a mistress, but rather with the lewdness of a prostitute, as she had been indeed to a great many: and therefore she called the king her Charles the third, since she had been formerly kept by two of that name.'[2] She bore him two sons, Charles, 1st Duke of St Albans (1670–1726) and James Beauclerk (1671–80).

In the diary period she lodged, according to legend, in a house on the w. side of Drury Lane opposite Wych St. At least by 1670 she had moved to a newly-built house in Pall Mall previously occupied by the fashionable physician Thomas Sydenham. Later she moved to what is now 79 Pall Mall, the freehold of which was given to her by the King.[3]

Haberdashers' Hall. A late 15th-century building on the e. side of Staining Lane and the north of Maiden Lane (now Gresham St). Burnt in the Fire and rebuilt (to Wren's design), it was destroyed in the Second World War and has since been rebuilt. (R)

Hackney. A pleasant and healthy village in Middlesex on the Epping Road. It lay to the north-east of the city, under 3 miles from the Standard on Cornhill, and had a high proportion of well-to-do residents whose businesses lay in the city or who had moved to Hackney on retirement. Excluding Clapton, Dalston, Kingsland, Shacklewell and Newington, it had some 260 houses in 1664.[1] Pepys's favourite summer jaunt by coach was to go to Islington and home by Hackney. Until it was engulfed by the 19th-century spread of London it contained several girls' boarding schools: and on the one occasion on which Pepys went to church there it was to see the young ladies. He makes one reference to having boarded there as a child; whether this was in addition to his being put to nurse at Kingsland is uncertain. (R; La)

Hadley, [James] (d. 1698). Parish clerk, St Olave, Hart St, from 1664; Master of the Parish Clerks' Company 1676–7.[1]

Hailes, ——. Exchequer official. If the 'old Mr Hales' whose death is mentioned at iii.174 is the same as the Mr Hales of the Exchequer (i.320), he was Thomas Hailes (buried Aug. 1662 at St Margaret's, Westminster). There was also an Edward Hailes, Teller of the Exchequer June 1660.[1]

Haines (Haynes,) [Joseph] (d. 1701). Actor and dancer in the King's Company from 1668; an Oxford graduate. Said to have been 'more remarkable for the witty, tho' wicked Pranks he play'd, and for his Prologues and Epilogues, than for his acting'.[1]

Halfway Tree. Pepys's two references are far from clear, but it appears to be a landmark between Deptford and Rotherhithe.

Halifax, 1st Earl of: *see under* Savile, G. and H.

Hall, Betty. Actress in the King's Company. On first seeing her on 23 Jan. 1667 Pepys mistakenly calls her 'Mrs. Ball'.[1]

Hall, Jacob (fl. 1668–80). Acrobat and rope dancer; c. 1671 he petitioned the King for permission to erect a booth for his company in Lincoln's Inn Fields. Lady Castlemaine was said to have had an affair with him.[1]

Hall, Capt. ——. The officer court-martialled for cowardice must be Robert Hall, who had commanded the *Princess* under Sandwich 1661–2. Sandwich's journal has no information about the trial. He had died by 1688.[1]

The Hall: *see* Westminster Palace

Halsall (Halsey), [James]. A royalist agent in the 1650s; Gentleman-cupbearer in ordinary 1663; Scoutmaster-General 1665–89.[1]

Hamilton. The six sons of the Irish Catholic Sir George Hamilton of Dunalong and his wife (Ormond's sister) were all servants of Charles II and his brother. The most famous was Anthony (?1646–1720), a soldier (Governor of Limerick 1685) and writer. He was the author of the *Mémoires* of the Comte de Gramont (q.v.), a lively account in remarkably natural French of Charles II's court, based on material supplied by the Comte, and first published anonymously in 1713. He died in exile at St Germain. His eldest brother James (d. 1679) was a soldier and a convert to Anglicanism. He was a Groom of the Bedchamber to Charles. The second brother George was a page to Charles during the exile.[1]

Hammersmith. A village on the Middlesex bank of the Thames, some 4 miles west of London, and containing in 1664 some 370 houses.[1] (R)

Hammon(d), Mrs. Mary, sister of Sir John Mennes; a widow, living with the Mennes family. She died in Apr. 1668, leaving one son (Francis) and two daughters, and was buried at Sandwich, Kent.[1]

Hampstead. A hill-village in Middlesex some 5 miles north-west of London, already a pleasant resort containing in 1664 about 160 houses.[1] (R)

Hampton Court. Largely built by Wolsey, and rebuilt by Henry VIII. Charles II made alterations to both the building and the park but used it only for occasional visits (as during the Plague). In William III's time the royal apartments were completely reconstructed to Wren's plans, and the gardens and park redesigned.[1]

Hanbury, Mrs. Of Brampton. Lucy Hanbury (? a widow) occupied a large house of 15 hearths in the village. After 1664 it was occupied by Sutton Ashfield, possibly her second husband (certainly his wife was named Lucy). A Lucy Hanbury who died in 1674 at the age of 18 is buried in the chancel of the church: she may have been a daughter of the first marriage.[1]

Hannam, Capt. [Willoughby]. 'A very stout able seaman' (Coventry). He had served under the Commonwealth and held seven commissions after 1660; in 1668 he was Master-Attendant at Woolwich. He was killed in action in 1672.[1]

Hanson, [Edward]. In July 1660 he was forced to surrender a 'bullet clock' which had formerly belonged to Charles I and which he had bought at auction in Dec. 1649. He does not appear in the lists of the Clockmakers' Company and may have been a dealer. By an order of 12 May 1660 all purchasers of those goods not disposed of to pay Charles I's debts had to restore either the property or its value to the Crown. Evelyn on 11 Feb. 1655 saw and admired a similar clock belonging to Cromwell. It was worked by 'a Chrystall ball, sliding on parallel Wyers'.[1]

Harbord, Sir Charles, jun., kt 1665 (1637–72). A protégé of Sandwich, distrusted (probably unfairly) by Pepys; third son of Sir Charles, sen. (d. 1679), Surveyor of Crown Lands, a friend of Sandwich. The young Harbord accompanied Sandwich to Tangier in 1661 and by 1662 was commanding a company of foot in the garrison, looking after Sandwich's property there and doing a little trading on his own account.[1] After serving under Sandwich in the 1665 campaign, he went with him to Madrid as a private secretary, afterwards visiting Tangier and executing the very skilled drawings which Sandwich later had engraved. In 1668-9 Sandwich proposed to have him made paymaster at Tangier (much to Pepys's annoyance), but the post was never established. At the outbreak of war in 1672 he joined Sandwich as a volunteer on board his flagship and perished with him at the battle of Sole Bay.[2] His elder brother William was to prove one of the fiercest of Pepys's parliamentary critics during the Popish Plot crisis.[3]

Harding, [John] (d. 1684). Viol player in the King's Private Musick, Gentleman of the Chapel Royal, formerly Westminster chorister. Other members of the family were also royal musicians.[1] (Lu)

Hardy, Nathaniel (1618–70). A popular Anglican preacher who conducted Prayer-Book services in London during the Commonwealth. He even held services in memory of Charles I. At the Restoration he was rewarded with a royal chaplaincy, the rectory of St Dionis Backchurch, the deanery of Rochester and the vicarage of St Martin-in-the-Fields. When Pepys met him at The Hague in 1660 he was in attendance on the commissioners sent to the King by the city.[1]

Hargrave, ——. A cornchandler of Duke's Yard, off St Martin's Lane, at whose house Chetwind lived. Either Richard Hargrave (d. 1666) or his son Richard (d. 1668). He was executor of Chetwind's estate.[1]

Harley, Col. Sir Edward (1624–1700). Son of Sir Robert, of Brampton Bryan, Heref.; and like his father a Presbyterian and (in the Civil War) a parliamentarian. M.P. seven times for the county, and twice for New Radnor; Councillor of State Feb.–March 1660; Governor of Dunkirk 1660–1; K.B. 1661 and F.R.S. 1663–85. Later a Whig and Exclusionist. Edward Harley, Earl of Oxford, Queen Anne's minister, was his nephew.[1]

Harley, Maj. Sir [Robert], kt 1660 (1626–73). Sir Edward's younger brother, and like him a Presbyterian and a parliamentarian officer who became a royalist in the '50s. He served under his brother in the Dunkirk garrison. M.P. 1647 and 1660 for New Radnor; F.R.S. 1661; in Barbados as Chancellor of the Caribee Islands 1662–4.[1]

Harman, Sir John, kt 1665 (d. 1673). One of the most experienced of contemporary seamen, he served in all three Dutch wars; in the last two as a flag-officer. A parliamentary enquiry exonerated him for his failure to pursue the enemy after the Battle of Lowestoft (1665). A John Harman lived in New Palace Yard in 1658 and 1661.[1]

Harman, [Philip] (1637–97). Upholsterer, of Cornhill; 'cousin' of Pepys by virtue of marrying in 1663 Mary, daughter of Thomas Bromfield, who was related to the Joyces. According to the marriage licence he was a bachelor of 27 and she a spinster of 20. (They were probably related: a Philip Bromfield, painter-stainer, had married Elizabeth Harman in 1626.)[1] She died in childbirth in July 1665. Pepys thought well of him, though he found his house 'mean', and would gladly have had him marry Pall after his wife's death. In 1668 he was a suitor to Anthony Joyce's widow, but was rejected as too 'poor'. However poor he may have been he rebuilt his house after the Fire. He leased it from Hester Fenner, who appointed him her executor in 1674.[2]

Harper, [Thomas]. Storekeeper, Deptford; appointed Oct. 1663.[1]

Harrington, William (d. 1671). Eastland merchant, navy contractor and member of the Mercers' Company; younger brother of James Harrington, author of *Oceana*. He lived in Mark Lane (St Olave's parish) in a house taxed on 11 hearths.[1]

Harris, [Henry]. Actor in the Duke's Company from 1661, and later in the United Company. A friend of Pepys. An accomplished and versatile performer, his last performance was in 1681.[1]

Harris, [John]. Sailmaker to the Navy at Deptford, Woolwich and Portsmouth; appointed June 1660.[1]

Harrison, Capt. [Brian]. Deputy-Master, Trinity House 1662-3.[1]

Harrison, [James]. Keeper of the Privy Lodgings, Whitehall.[1]

Hart, [Charles] (d. 1683). The leading actor of the King's Company. A great-nephew of Shakespeare, he is said to have introduced Nell Gwyn to the stage.[1]

Hart, Capt. [John, sen.] (d. by 1688). Naval officer. He held eight commissions 1664-72, and was well thought of by Coventry.[1]

Hart, Maj. [Theo]. Major in Mountagu's regiment 1657-60. He had distinguished himself in the Scottish campaign 1653-4. He later claimed that he had refused to fight against Booth's royalist rising and had supported Monck in 1659-60. In 1667 he was temporarily commissioned during the scare of invasion from France.[1]

Hartlib. Samuel Hartlib, sen. (d. 1662) was a refugee from Polish Prussia who lived from c. 1658 in Axe Yard. He was a friend of Petty and Comenius, and responded to the revolutionary spirit of the '40s and '50s by publishing schemes of social, political and economic reform for the consideration of the authorities – 'disseminating useful knowledge interfused with messianic speculations'.[1] His son Samuel was a friend of Pepys and one of his 'old club' of government clerks. At first an underclerk to the Council of State and later to the Privy Council, he had moved by 1666 to a post at the Hearth Office. In 1672 he was briefly imprisoned in the Tower, presumably on a political charge. The elder Hartlib's daughters married members of his own circle of foreign-born virtuosi – Clodius and Rothe.[2]

Harvey, Sir Daniel, kt 1661 (1631-72). Rich Turkey merchant; of Coombe Nevil, Kingston, Surrey. A connection of Sandwich, his wife being Elizabeth Mountagu, daughter of the 2nd Lord Mountagu of Boughton. His connection with Lady Castlemaine (who took herself off to his house at Covent Garden after a quarrel with the King) was presumably through his wife, who was reputedly mistress for a while to the Duke of York. He was made Ranger of Richmond Park in 1661, and ambassador to Constantinople in 1668. His uncle was the William Harvey who discovered the circulation of the blood.[1]

Harwich. A small dockyard used mainly for storage and repairs. Though strategically well placed during the Dutch wars, it was too far from supplies to develop into a major dockyard. A small yard was built in the '50s and fortifications erected, but the yard was leased to a private individual in 1662. With the approach of war the Crown took it over again in 1664; a Commissioner (John Taylor) was appointed and Anthony Deane was made Master-Shipwright. Harwich then played an important part as a forward base in the Second Dutch War, and ships were built there, including one 3rd-rate. After the war, the commissionership lapsed and was never revived. Sheerness replaced it as the most active forward base in the Third War.

Pepys served as one of its two M.P.s in the First Exclusion parliament and in that of 1685, but was defeated there in the elections to the Convention in 1689.[1]

Hatton, Christopher, cr. Baron Hatton 1643 (1605–70). A distant relative of Sandwich (having married Elizabeth, daughter of Sir Charles Mountagu of Boughton). At the Restoration he appealed for his support in an attempt to be made Treasurer of the Household (he had been Comptroller 1643–6), but had to content himself with the governorship of Guernsey and a place on the Privy Council.[1] His son Christopher (the 2nd Baron) was responsible for bringing Sandwich into direct correspondence with the King Feb.–March 1660.[2] His younger son Charles belonged to Pepys's circle of virtuosi in the '80s and '90s and was a pall-bearer at his funeral.[3]

Hatton, Sir Thomas, 2nd Bt (1637–82). Of Long Stanton, Cambs.; nephew of the 1st Baron Hatton. A royalist; in early 1660 in some disfavour with Hyde for having fought a duel at Calais. M.P. for Cambridgeshire 1674–9.[1]

Hatton Garden. Between Holborn (now Holborn Circus) and Clerkenwell Rd, in 1660 it was a pleasant well-to-do street 460 yards long near the edge of the town. In 1664 it had 56 houses.[1] (R)

Hawkyns, [William]. Fellow of Magdalen College, Oxford 1653–69; Canon of Winchester 1662–7; Canon of Norwich 1667–91.[1]

Hawles (Hollis), [Anthony]. Chaplain to the King in exile, and 1660–d. 64; appointed Archdeacon of Salisbury 1658 and Canon of Windsor 1660.[1]

Hawley, [John]. A colleague of Pepys in the Exchequer, where like Pepys he was clerk to Downing c. 1658–60. In March 1658 Downing refers to him as 'my servant at my house'; by the following September he was living at Maj. Greenleaf's in Axe Yard.[1] According to the diary, he was clerk to the merchant Sir Thomas Ingram 1660–1, entered the service of the Bishop of London 1661–6, and ended as under-clerk to the parish of St Giles [-in-the-Fields].

Hayes, [James]. Secretary to Prince Rupert.[1]

[Hayes, Walter] fl. 1651–92. Mathematical instrument-maker, Moor-fields. Reputedly the best of his day; many of his instruments survive.[1]

Hayls, John (d. 1679). Portrait painter. There are several of this surname (variously spelt) associated with the Painter-Stainers' Company. During the Civil War and Interregnum he built up a sound and fashionable practice. He was employed by, in particular, the Russell, Bertie, Harley, Poulett and Greville families.[1] In 1664 he was living in a house taxed on ten hearths in Southampton St, Bloomsbury, next to the new Market House, but by June 1668 had moved to Long Acre.[2] He was buried at St Martin-in-the-Fields on 27 Nov. 1679.[3] He died intestate and letters of administration were granted to his widow Katherine.[4] Little is known of his *œuvre*.

Haynes: *see* Haines

Hayter, Thomas (d. c. 1689). He was already established as a clerk in the Navy Office when Pepys became Clerk of the Acts and made him one of his clerks. In the diary Pepys usually gives him the prefix 'Mr', in distinction from his other clerks who are referred to by name only. This may indicate his age, or Pepys's respect for him, or both. His arrest for conventicling in 1663 was not allowed to injure his career: in the following year he became chief clerk and in 1668 Purveyor of Petty Emptions, proving himself a valuable ally of Pepys in his campaign against sharp practices.[1] He succeeded Pepys as Clerk of the Acts in 1673, serving jointly with John, Pepys's brother, until 1677. Later he was Secretary to the Admiralty 1679–80, Comptroller of the Navy 1680–3, assistant to the Comptroller 1682–6, assistant to the Commissioners for old accounts 1686–8, and again assistant to the Comptroller Oct.–Dec. 1688. His character seems to declare itself in his neat and regular handwriting.[2]

Ha[y]ward, [Charles] (c.1640–c.1687). Virginals-maker, Aldgate St. There are twelve spinets surviving, one (oblong) virginals, and a harpsichord.[1] (Lu)

Hayward, [Edward]. Clerk and Treasurer of the Chatham Chest in the First Dutch War; Clerk of the Survey, Chatham, from c. 1652.[1]

Hayward, Capt. [John]. A naval associate of Sandwich and one of the most experienced officers never to reach flag rank. A captain from 1651, he commanded the *Essex* in the Baltic in 1659, and held 11 commissions between 1660 and his death in action in 1673.[1]

Haywood, ——. Probably Thomas Heywood, described in 1669 as the Duke of York's servant;[1] possibly Edward Hayward (above).

Hazard, ——. Musician. Probably Thomas (?1608–67), Gentleman of the Chapel Royal and singing man of Westminster Abbey. In 1665 he was living in Stable Yard, Westminster. The Henry Hazard apprenticed to Robert Strong, citizen and musician, on 14 Oct. 1657, though presumably a relation, is too young to be the subject of Pepys's allusion.[1] (Lu)

HEALTH

General.[1] It is clear from the diary that Pepys was a physically energetic and reasonably healthy young man, capable of hard work and hard exercise, and able to withstand the strains of a busy and competitive professional life. During the diary period he never had a day in bed from illness, never suffered from an ague, was bled only twice, and seems to have caught only an Englishman's normal quota of colds. He took physic, or a glister, as everyone did, at fairly regular intervals, as a purge and to get rid of what were known in the Galenic jargon of the day as 'peccant humours'. But according to a memorandum on his health he wrote on 7 Nov. 1677[2] he had never had to take a long 'course' or 'season' of physic. Two fears, however, cloud parts of the diary and give a false impression of his health: fear in the earlier years of a recurrence of the trouble from stone for which he had been operated on in 1658, and fear, in the later years, that he was going blind. It is these fears which explain why the diary has so much information about his health. He was no hypochondriac, but felt that his well-being – and even his life – were in jeopardy. His concern is expressed in frequent notes about pains and about the movements of his bowels and kidneys. He was, so far as one can judge, a grateful and undemanding patient both of his surgeon, Thomas Hollier, and of his physician, Alexander Burnet. He accepted, as a matter of course, the orthodox medical beliefs of his day. If for a while he carried a hare's foot as a charm against colic, he took care at the same time to swallow his pills. When on another occasion he wrote down a series of therapeutic charms it was only to record them as curiosities.

The stone. Stones in the bladder were much commoner than now, especially in children. In the memorandum of 1677, Pepys recalled that he had had symptoms from his cradle onwards. He went on to say that when he was 20 years old 'upon drinking an extraordinary quantity of conduit-water out of Aristotle's well near Cambridge . . . the weight of the said water carried after some days' pain the stone out of the kidneys more sensibly through the urater into my bladder, from which moment I lived under a constant succession of fits of stone in the bladder till I was about 26 years of age when the pain growing insupportable I was delivered both of it and the stone by cutting'.[3] The pain must have been intense if a major operation – without anaesthetics, and at considerable risk of death – were preferable. It was performed in the house of Pepys's cousin Jane Turner, on 26 March 1658, and a 'very great stone' was removed.[4] The surgeon, Thomas Hollier of St Thomas's Hospital, is likely to have used some form of the formidable 'Marian' method. This – devised in the mid-16th century by Mariano Santo – made lithotomy more practicable in adults, but was one of the most terrible operations in surgery. It involved the making of an incision between the scrotum and the anus about three inches long, just to the left of the mid-line, down to the neck of the bladder, which was then opened. It seems that in the process both the ducts from Pepys's testicles were so cut or damaged that the patient became sterile without being impotent.[5] The operation was successful, but had been risky in the extreme. It is known that in one year Hollier had cut thirty patients for the stone who all lived, but afterwards cut four who all died. That is, Pepys had been lucky enough to be operated on with new instruments before they had become infected. He kept an annual stone-feast to celebrate his recovery. (At least one other patient is known to have done the same.)[6]

The cause of stone in the urinary tract is still obscure; and since we have no knowledge of the composition of Pepys's stone, speculation is idle. All we can say with certainty is that the Pepyses had a family history of it: his mother, his aunt Anne and his brother John all had it. Pepys kept his stone in a case and Evelyn, to whom he showed it in 1669, wrote that it was the size of a tennis ball – i.e. it must have weighed c. 2 oz.[7] Pepys passed two small stones on 7 March 1665 after an attack of renal colic on the previous day. The colic would be caused by passage of the stones from the kidney to the bladder. He had another attack suggestive of renal colic on 7–8 July 1666, but probably no others, because although he had attacks of pain in the testicles (and renal colic radiates to the testicles on the same side) the pain was on the right side, and his bladder stones were on the left. These pains in the testicles were accompanied by swelling, and were almost certainly inflammations in the ducts near the testicles. He thought they were due to minor injury, but they were probably due to the operation, and as time passed they became less frequent; there were none in 1668 and 1669.

He also had attacks of pain in the back on passing water, occasionally accompanied by pus in the urine and fever. Their frequency also decreased: he had none after 1664. He attributed these pains, as he did most ills, to cold (e.g. 'staying too long bare-legged to pare my cornes', or to drinking water).[8] In fact they were probably caused by inflammation of the bladder, which sometimes spread to the kidneys, and was possibly a result of the operation. He also had pain in the back after shaking in a coach,[9] which may have been due to stones in the kidney, or to an injury to his back. Equally, some of the attacks may have been due to inflammation of the kidneys caused by alcohol.

'Wind cholique'. It has usually been supposed that this was renal colic.

Pepys himself always associated it with what he called 'cold'. He used the concept of 'taking cold' not in the modern sense, but in the Galenic sense of ingesting a lump of coldness, as it were. This notion became an obsession of doctors and laymen alike. 'Taking cold' might cause the patient to feel cold, or, by his reaction to it, might make him feel hot. Pepys thought he 'took cold' in various ways – principally by getting his legs and feet cold or wet,[10] or by drinking too much cold water or other weak drinks, such as milk or small beer. It was not so much that he had observed that cold caused colic; but rather that he took the fact he had colic to mean that he had taken cold, even if he had no idea when or how. He believed that the 'cold' acted by causing wind, either in the bowels, his usual trouble, or in some other part of the body. He also believed that wind rose to whatever part of the body was uppermost: for instance, he attributed Sandwich's illness at Alicante, which was probably dysentery, to 'Wind got into the Muscles of his right side'.[11] The cure was to break wind – hence his enemas and purges. His descriptions of symptoms are in no instance complete: it was only the more serious aspects of an attack, e.g. constipation, or stoppage of urine, which he found worth recording. But all the symptoms would disappear at once when he passed wind. He recognized that his attacks were associated with anxiety, with press of business, with going too long without food, or with irritation. They occurred most frequently, in fact, in the middle years of the diary period, when work was making its greatest demands on him. But the trouble did not disappear with his professional success – he was still complaining of it when he drew up his memorandum on the state of his health in 1677.

Eye trouble. He had a trivial accident to his eyes on 22 May 1660, but this had no influence on his subsequent troubles. He first recorded that something was wrong on 25 Apr. 1662: 'I was much troubled in my eyes, by reason of the healths I have this day been forced to drink'. This may have been an attack of conjunctivitis partly caused by an excess of alcohol, but similar attacks later were sometimes clearly enough caused by common cold. On 4 May 1664, when he was under some stress in his work, his eyes failed him by candlelight, and next day even by daylight. Later attacks, in July 1665 and May and June 1666, he attributed to drinking beer or strong waters. He first complains of what must undoubtedly have been a refractive defect on 19 Feb. 1663: '. . . and to bed, being weary, sleepy, and my eyes begin to to fail me, looking so long by candlelight upon white paper'. On the evening of 1 Apr. 1664, reading a manuscript on shipbuilding 'writ long ago', he 'durst not stay long at it,' 'being come to have great pain and water in my eyes after candle-light'. He attributed the trouble at first, and probably correctly, to candlelight, but later came to think it was excess of light which irritated his eyes. He did, however, continue

to observe that they were worse after working at night, and there is
little doubt that it was in a poor light that he suffered most. The
deterioration of his vision is shown by the enlargement of his handwriting in the diary from 1668, and by the remarkable increase in the
number of references to his eyestrain – eight between 1660 and 1666,
but 110 between 1667 and May 1669. The trouble however was not in
the end progressive: it continued, but did not get worse.

It is generally agreed that the nature of Pepys's eye trouble was a
combination of long sight with astigmatism.[12] Both were probably of
minor degree, because serious defects make reading impossible. The
effects are painful, watering eyes, soreness and headache. Pepys had
them all, with the added fear of going blind. Astigmatism is easily
enough dealt with nowadays by cylindrical lenses turned to the correct
angle, but this remedy was not discovered until 1825.[13] Pepys tried a
glass globe to intensify the light, but found little improvement.
Equally, green spectacles were no better. John Turlington, the great
spectacle-maker, gave him the disastrous advice to use 'young' (concave) rather than 'old' (convex) spectacles, and told him that reading
glasses were the worst thing he could use. On the advice of Robert
Boyle, he then consulted Dr Daubeny Turberville, the most famous
ophthalmologist of his time: an expert, according to the lights of his
day, but, as Pepys observed, one who had never until 1668 seen an eye
dissected by an anatomist. Turberville treated him first with eye-drops
and purges, later with pills and venesection. On 11 Aug. 1668 Pepys
found much relief from 'a Tube-spectacall' made of paper. Looking
through a narrow tube in a strong light can in these cases be most
efficient: but candlelight is not strong enough. However, Pepys preferred his paper tubes to any other aid and finally had a vizard made to
hold them, and the result 'did content' him 'mightily'. On 8 May 1669
he had glasses made to put in and out of the vizard, which was even
better. But these were poor alleviants, and did not prevent the abandonment of the diary soon after.

Later life. His letters, from 1669 to the eve of his death, contain recurrent complaints of the agony caused to his eyes by any close work –
especially by reading or writing in a bright light. He was convinced
that he had worn out his eyes by overwork; his only recourse was to
employ clerks whenever he could. Yet his handwriting remained firm
and clear to the end of his life, and did not grow greatly in size. He no
longer put his eyes to the strain of keeping an elaborate diary in shorthand, but he used shorthand fairly freely into the 1690s. He used it in
his office work from early 1670[14] – shortly after he had abandoned the
diary in the conviction that he was going blind – in the parliamentary
diary of 1677, the Boscobel manuscript of 1680 and in the Tangier
diary of 1683–4.

He continued to suffer from what he feared was the stone. In Dec. 1686 he was in such pain night and day that he thought he might have to resign his office. An ulcer was diagnosed. In 1690, when he was in prison as a suspected Jacobite, Dr Richard Lower obtained his release on the grounds that the ulcer endangered his life.He suffered serious illnesses in 1694, 1697 and the winter of 1699–1700, before retiring to a largely indoor life at Hewer's house at Clapham. He himself spoke of the last of these illnesses as 'a most severe ague and feaver';[15] they were all probably fevers caused by renal suppuration. In March 1700 the lithotomy wound of 1658 broke down and produced a painless and, except for the leaking of urine, a symptomless fistula.[16] This was laid open and successfully treated by rest. At any rate it healed well enough to hold urine: it was found to be open at the post-mortem examination. Unless it was due to a slow-growing cancer (which was not noted post-mortem), it is difficult to guess its cause.

He fell ill finally in Feb. 1703, and died emaciated and in convulsions and coma at 3.47 a.m. on 26 May,[17] probably of brain damage caused by high blood-pressure, the latter being due to the destruction of his left kidney. A post-mortem was ordered by his nephew Jackson because of what he called the 'uncommonness' of the case. A nest of seven irregularly shaped stones, weighing about $4\frac{1}{2}$ oz all told, was found in the left kidney.[18] They were firmly impacted in the kidney, which explains why he had felt none of the ordinary pains of the stone in his last years. His doctors concluded that 'his stamina in general were marvellously strong'.

HEALTH – A PSYCHOANALYST'S VIEW

The unrivalled candour and detail of the diary offer the psychoanalyst the opportunity of using it as though it were a series of notes taken by a consultant. I have here set down some conclusions (necessarily speculative in some respects) which I have reached on certain aspects of Pepys's behaviour and on the function which the diary seems to have performed in helping Pepys to preserve his psychological balance.

Clearly the diary is not the work of an introspective: when Pepys writes about his thoughts, feelings and dreams he writes objectively, at no greater length than he writes about the world outside himself. And equally clearly, the diary is the work of a man who had to an unusual degree the capacity to live happily and effectively. He was disciplined and well organised, yet at the same time never lost his zest and flexibility. He loved order and neatness (it was the basis of his success in all sorts of ways – as a diarist, a civil servant and a collector) yet he never allowed this love to become an obsession. He may have been a physical coward – most of us are, and Pepys is only exceptional in confessing to it – but he had considerable moral courage (e.g. in writing his letter of reproof to Sandwich), and the resilience with which to withstand stress – in his work: constant competition from rivals and criticism from enemies; and in his private life: the sorrows of bereavement (perhaps more easily borne in those days of high mortality) and the tensions of marriage.

Pepys's philandering offers a more difficult problem in evaluation. Beginning with relatively casual sexual encounters during the first two or three years of the diary period, generally with women of a lower social class, by the last years of the decade he found himself driven to seek sexual relief with many different women. This was to culminate in his seduction of his wife's companion, Deb Willet.

The diary entries in which he mentions extramarital sexual activity were before 1664 usually written in clear English, in his normal short-hand. After that they were written in his polyglottal private language, and eventually in garbled shorthand as well. During the first two-three years of the diary these adventures were relatively infrequent and did not extend to intercourse. Indeed he records being tempted to 'have a bout' with various maidservants only at times when Elizabeth was away (28 July–27 Sept. 1662). In May–June 1663 he became irrationally jealous of Pembleton, the man whom he had engaged to teach his wife to dance. Although he was clearly critical of himself for being such a fool about it, he found it difficult to rid himself of his obsessive concern (15 May–15 June 1663). On 29 June he encountered Betty Lane, a shopgirl with whom he was to have many more meetings, and 'towsed' her. On 9 July he arranged to meet Mrs Bagwell, who was to be his mistress for many years. In spite of enjoying his wife 'with great content' on her return from the country (12 August) his interest in these two women did not become less urgent. By 1664, however, we find him using his private language to describe sexual thoughts and intentions as well as actual adventures. All of these had become far more frequent and began to take on a driven quality, particularly during the latter half of the year, which includes ten references to extra-marital sexuality.

In 1665, the year of the Plague, we observe a marked increase in the frequency of sexual references during the last half of the year, after he became fearful of the contagion. He would not be the first or the last man to have responded to the fear of death by urgent sexuality. 1666 reveals a similar pattern. In the months immediately after the Fire he reports a marked increase in promiscuity. This continued into 1667, being especially marked during the first three months. He was still troubled by dreams of the Fire. Later in the year his sexual activities became less frequent and less driven in quality. But this was not to last. In Sept. 1667 Deb Willet, then aged about 15, joined the household as Elizabeth's companion. Pepys was immediately attracted to her, and, aware of her fascination, struggled to avoid the danger of embarking on a sexual adventure within his own household. During the months of May and September of the following year he was especially active with a variety of other women, unusually so even for him. Inevitably, however, he succumbed, and was caught by his wife *in flagrante*. Perhaps his fear of blindness was making him careless of consequences.

Elizabeth's rôle in this contretemps was probably not purely passive or accidental. She seems to have made a point of exhibiting this charming young girl to him even though she knew him to be highly susceptible. Whether she was aware of it or not, the effect of her action was to set a trap for him. Having detected him fondling Deb, and having forced him to dismiss (and humiliate) her, Elizabeth had achieved at least a temporary victory and some sense of control over him. Was there an element of unconscious planning in her behaviour? The fact that she teased him in March 1669 (five months or so after Deb's departure) about the dangerous attractions of a new maid suggests that there may have been. Certainly after the Deb affair he paid rather more attention to his wife. He may now for the first time have taken more trouble to arouse her sexually since he uses a few words of his private language to describe his pleasure with Elizabeth, referring to her as his 'moher', a term formerly reserved for women with whom he had illicit relations:

> 'I must here remember that I have lain with my moher as a husband more times since this falling-out then in I believe twelve months before – and with more pleasure to her then I think in all the time of our marriage before' (14 Nov. 1668).

All this was written during a period when he was still trying to meet Deb – even talking of her in his sleep. His longing for her continued into May 1669, when he wrote in the last entry of the diary: '. . . now my amours to Deb are past and my eyes hindering me in almost all other pleasures'.

We know almost nothing about his later sexual life. After Elizabeth's death in 1669 he acquired a housekeeper of middle-class background and accomplishments, Mary Skynner, who may well have been his mistress as well. She remained with him until his death, being treated more as a wife than a concubine, and was left a bequest in his will.

Some of his later attitudes toward sex are revealed by his references in the Tangier diary of 1683–4 to Col. Percy Kirke, the acting Governor. His contempt for the man seems altogether justified, but his entries describing Kirke's gross and brutal sensuality do reveal more than a little fascination, combined with a certain self-righteousness. Pepys should not, however, be accused of hypocrisy: he detested brutality and scandalous behaviour, especially when it did, as in this case, threaten the discipline of the armed forces and the functioning of society. His own behaviour may have been often inconsiderate but it was generally distinctly humane – and private.

There were many factors which must have contributed to the urgency of his sexual desires. He may well have been a lusty young man since early puberty. He married for love, which was not usual for ambitious young men of his time. Not long afterwards, his life was threatened by a large stone in his bladder which was removed by surgery which in itself carried a high degree of risk. Such an assault on the body, especially on the genital organs, has profound psychological consequences, and in many individuals increases the need for reassurance about one's potency. Still another factor may have been his disappointment at his failure to have a child. This may have contributed to his drive to seek sexual satisfaction elsewhere, which, however, only served to confirm his fears that he was indeed sterile. A further factor in the later years of the diary may have been his fear of going blind. Whatever the symbolic and unconscious links between the eyes and sexuality, there was no question of the devastating effect that blindness would have had on him; and he could not possibly have known that he would not in fact lose all his useful vision within a few years.

What is remarkable is not so much the symptomatic nature of so much of his sexual behaviour during the years 1664–9, as how well he employed other means, especially to deal with the memories of his brush with death in 1658, the year of his operation. He conducted yearly celebrations on the anniversary of his recovery, he talked freely to other sufferers from the disease and he wrote extensively of it in his diary, most often after his recurrent attacks of pain and urinary difficulty.

Circumstances which turn some men against sexual activity, impel others towards it. Pepys was clearly one of the latter. The waxing and waning of his sexual needs are therefore readily understandable as the outcome of a complex interplay of forces within a man to whom sex was a particularly important mode of reassurance as well as being at the same time a great source of pleasure. In the simplest terms, it was through sex that he achieved a psychological victory over death and managed to enjoy himself at the same time.

For the most part he was not deeply guilty about his sexual adventures. He did think them improper and he recorded them usually in his private language, as if to disguise or conceal the meaning of such entries. He could not, however, have seriously considered that this would have been an effective shield from prying eyes. Anyone who could go to the trouble of deciphering his shorthand could readily get the sense of the simple mixture of foreign words he employed. It would seem more probable that he was in this way attempting to separate those thoughts from himself, to make them less immediately part of his own consciousness and yet at the same time more titillating. Perhaps the remnant of the Puritan in him had to be deceived.

And so, of course, had Elizabeth. He was often insensitive to his wife's feelings. It was not that he did not care for her, for he did love her and was not only jealous but even faithful in his fashion. But it took the Deb Willet catastrophe to teach him that his philandering and neglect of Elizabeth were responsible for so much of her unhappiness. Here indeed he demonstrates a capacity for self-deception which impairs but need not negate our view of him as a reasonably healthy person.

(Martin Howard Stein)

Heath, [John], kt 1664 (1614–91). Lawyer; son of Sir Robert Heath, C.J. (d. 1649); Auditor of the Court of Wards 1643–6; Attorney-General of the Duchy of Lancaster 1653–83; and M.P. for Clitheroe 1661–Jan. 79. He served on the commission of enquiry into the Chatham Chest 1662, and was Recorder of Gravesend 1686–8. In 1664 he married at St Olave's a niece of Sir John Mennes – Margaret, daughter of Sir Matthew Mennes of Sandwich, and widow of John Pretyman.[1]

Hebdon, Sir John, kt 1663 (d. 1670). Muscovy Company merchant, of Peckham. A navy contractor; agent (sometimes referred to as Resident) of the Tsar in Holland and England; envoy to Russia 1667. A John Hebdon (? his son) in 1681 appealed for help to Pepys from the Fleet prison.[1]

Heemskerck, Laurens van. Dutch traitor. In 1666 he was employed by Rupert to reconnoitre the Dutch coast. His information led to Sir Robert Holmes's raid on the Vlie ('Holmes's Bonfire'), and he received £200 and a captain's commission. In 1669 he was knighted for his design of the *Nonsuch* frigate. He later entered the service of France. His Christian name is sometimes given as Louis.[1]

Hely, Mrs. Pepys's first sweetheart. Unidentified; possibly a servant employed by John Pepys of Ashtead. There were several families of this name (variously spelt) in London and environs: none, however, are known to have had associations with John Pepys or Ashtead.[1]

Hempson, [William]. Clerk of the Survey, Chatham. He was granted a moiety of the clerkship of the market in the King's Household in 1670.[1]

Henrietta, Princess (1644–70). Charles II's youngest, and favourite, sister; 'the most brilliant of Stuart women'.[1] She was brought up from childhood in France and as a Catholic, and was married in March 1661 to Philippe Duc d'Orléans, brother of Louis XIV. The marriage was miserably unhappy but she used her charm and the friendship of the King to promote an entente between France and England. Her efforts culminated in the disastrous Secret Treaty of Dover (1670) in which Charles undertook to impose Catholicism on his kingdom. She seems to have played an important part in its negotiation but died shortly afterwards.[2]

Herbert, Philip, 5th Earl of Pembroke (1621–69). Both he and his father (whom he succeeded in 1650) were parliamentarians in the Civil War. (Other members of the family took the precaution of supporting the royalists.) He sat for Wiltshire 1640, Glamorgan 1640–9, and Berkshire 1649–50; and was a Councillor of State 1651–2. After the Restoration he was active in the affairs of the Council for Trade, the Fishery Corporation and the Royal Africa Company. He was a convert to Quakerism, and, according to Pepys, held original views on original sin.[1] His son William (1640–74) succeeded him in the title and died unmarried.

Herbert, Capt. ——. The naval officer at vi.237, 238 is likely to have been Charles Herbert of the *Revenge*. The better-known Arthur Herbert (later First Lord of the Admiralty and 1st Earl of Torrington) was then a lieutenant.[1]

Hercules' Pillars Alley. Off Fleet St; opposite St Dunstan's church.

Hermitage, the. A river stairs and dock in Wapping, much used by ships plying to and from Scotland and Ireland.[1]

Herring, [John] (d. ?1672). Presbyterian Vicar of St Bride, Fleet St c. 1656–62; extruded for nonconformity. Possibly a minister in Coventry c. 1648–50.[1]

Herring, [Michael]. Goldsmith, Coleman St; Treasurer of the fund for the Scottish army 1643 and 1645; and Treasurer of the Goldsmiths' Hall committee for delinquents' money from 1647.[1]

Herringman, [Henry] (d. 1704). One of the greatest London booksellers of the period; Master of the Stationers' Company 1685–6. His shop, at the Blue Anchor, in the Lower Walk of the New Exchange (used by Pepys after the Fire) was a resort of the literary world. He later gave up bookselling and became 'the first London wholesale publisher in the modern sense'.[1]

Hervey, Sir Thomas, kt ?1660 (1625–94). Of Ickworth, Suff.; Vice-Chamberlain of the Household 1658; Extra Commissioner of the Navy 1665–8; M.P. for Bury St Edmunds March 1679–90. His appointment to the Navy Board was a political one and he earns no praise from Pepys. On the other hand his memorial in Ickworth church – and memorials do not always lie – records that he and his wife were 'most eminent examples of piety, charity and conjugal affection'. Lord Hervey the memoir-writer was his grandson.[1]

Hesilrige, Sir Arthur, 1st Bt (d. 1661). M.P. for Leicestershire 1640, 1640–53; for Leicester 1654, 1656, 1659–60. A forceful but clumsy politician, written off by Clarendon (quite rightly) as 'an absurd, bold man'. But his devotion to the cause of parliament is impressive. He fought Charles I both in the Commons and on the battlefield, because the King in his view was a danger to the public liberty, and in the same cause he opposed, after 1653, the military rule of Cromwell. By the spring of 1659 the Protectorate was in ruins. Hesilrige – 'one of the most powerful men in England' [1] – now had his chance to establish a parliamentary republic. The task was probably impossible and in any case Hesilrige lacked the tact and wisdom required for party leadership. He failed to retain the support of Lambert and the army officers, and though he welcomed Monck's intervention, he completely misread its meaning. At the Restoration his life was spared, partly by Monck's help and partly because he had refused to be one of the regicides. He died a prisoner in the Tower.[2]

Hetley, [William] (d. 1661). Of Brampton; son of Sir Thomas Hetley, serjeant-at-law (d. 1637), and until 1653 owner of Brampton Park. After c. 1656 he was an associate (?servant) of Mountagu (Sandwich) and in June 1660 offered him £1000 in return for a place.[1] His wife was Carina, daughter of Henry Cromwell, a cousin of the Protector.[2]

Hewer, [Thomas and Anne]. Parents of Will. Thomas was a printer and stationer in St Sepulchre's Holborn who supplied pay tickets, surgeons' bills etc. to the Navy Office.[1] He died in the Plague. His widow (sister of Robert Blackborne whom he had married in 1639) carried on the business after his death. In 1670 she was living in St Olave's parish; she later moved to her son's house in York Buildings and by 1690 to a 'little house' he provided for her in Clapham. She died at Clapham in July 1693.[2]

Hewer, Will (1642–1715). Naval official and merchant; Pepys's lifelong friend and the executor of his will.

He entered Pepys's service on the recommendation of his uncle Robert Blackborne and until Nov. 1663 when he went into lodgings he combined the duties of office clerk with those of manservant. He moved with Pepys to the Admiralty in 1673–9, becoming chief clerk in 1674 and Judge Advocate-General in 1677. In 1675 he accompanied Sir Anthony Deane to Paris, and in 1683–4 went with Pepys to Tangier and Spain. He was a leading member of the Special Commission which replaced the Navy Board in 1686–8 and with Deane defended its work on ship repairs before a parliamentary committee of enquiry in 1691–2.[1] Like Pepys he was briefly imprisoned in 1689 by the new régime but no charge was brought against him. He was also – the parallel with Pepys's career is again close – a member of the Royal Fishery (1677), Treasurer of Tangier (1680–4), Master of the Clothworkers' Company (1686–7) and an M.P. (for Yarmouth, I. of W., 1685–7). He used the same shorthand as Pepys and kept a diary in it, of which only a few sermon notes (Feb. 1665) survive.[2] His handwriting was ungainly and as a clerk he was not always an impeccable copyist,[3] but clearly he was able and diligent. More, he came to be a friend on whose affection and loyalty Pepys could always rely.

His most remarkable achievement was to become extremely rich. Evelyn (25 July 1692) wrote of his having gained his 'very considerable Estate in the Navy'. No doubt profits came his way, as they did to most officials (and we know from the diary that on one occasion he came under suspicion of making illicit profits), but he never held any lucrative office except that of Treasurer for Tangier and that for only four years. He may have inherited money from his father, who died in 1665: certainly there are signs in the diary after that date of a certain affluence – a banking account, stylish lodgings and in Jan. 1668 the gift of a diamond necklace to Elizabeth Pepys which cost £40 (at a time when his salary as clerk was £30 p.a.). But he made most of his wealth from trade. In 1667 his uncle Blackborne became secretary to the E. India Company, and Hewer soon began trading, possibly under his guidance. By 1674 he was rich enough to provide ready money for the building of three warships whose construction was contracted out to private builders. After 1689 his ventures were on a large scale, at their peak reaching £24,000 in 1701–2. He became a director of the old E. India Company (1698–1703) and was twice deputy-chairman before ceasing to hold office in 1712.[4]

In 1677 he acquired one of the new houses known as York Buildings in Buckingham St off the Strand (now no. 12), and from c. Oct. 1679 shared it with Pepys. From 1684 it served also as the Admiralty office. In 1686, as a Navy Commissioner, he moved to official lodgings in the Navy Office. Pepys – and the Admiralty – moved in the spring of 1688 to the house which is now no. 14, also owned by Hewer, while he in turn either then or earlier took a house in Villiers St near by where Jane Edwards – 'little Jane' Birch, the Pepyses' first servant – joined him as housekeeper.[5] Meantime, c. 1683, he had also acquired a country villa in Clapham from which he moved to Sir Denis Gauden's house there on Gauden's death in 1688. Hewer had purchased a mortgage on the property in 1683 when Gauden was in financial difficulties. It was a large mansion on the n. side of the common – the exact site is difficult to establish – its rooms built alongside both sides of a long gallery, with a formal garden behind.[6] He filled it with 'Indian and

Chinese curiosities'.[7] Pepys used it as his own country retreat and died there, in Hewer's presence, in 1703. Hewer lived there until his death in Dec. 1715.[8] Like Pepys he refused the oaths to William and Mary and in consequence paid double taxes. (He complained that he paid more tax on personal property than anyone in the whole country.)[9] A monument was erected to him in the parish church in the gallery which he had built. His books were sold by auction in 1730.[10]

The greater part of his property (mostly houses and land in Clapham, London, Westminster and Norfolk) passed to his godson Hewer Edgley, then a student of the Inner Temple, who was the son of Hewer's cousin Ann (wife of Samuel Edgley, Rector of Wandsworth), and who in consequence changed his surname to Edgley-Hewer. He married the daughter of Sir Simeon Stuart and died in 1728 without children.[11] To seal, as it were, the long connection with Pepys, Edgley-Hewer's sister Ann married Pepys's nephew John Jackson, jun. The house was pulled down in 1754 to make room for building development.[12] From 1703–1724 it housed Pepys's library.

Hewet (?Howet), Tom. Clerk to Sir W. Penn; from 1660–1 clerk to the Comptroller.[1]

Hewitt, Capt. [Simon]. Merchant; one of a committee of five appointed in 1664 to examine the papers of Teviot, the late Governor of Tangier.[1]

Hickes, Baptist, 3rd Viscount Campden (1612–82). His London house (Campden House; taxed on 32 hearths in 1664) was on what is now Campden Hill, Kensington. Burnt down in 1862, it was rebuilt soon afterwards and has since been demolished.[1] (R)

Hickes, Sir William, 2nd Bt (1596–1680). Keeper of Waltham Forest; M.P. for Marlow 1626 and 1640, and for Tewkesbury 1628–9. His father Sir Michael Hickes (d. 1612) had been secretary to Elizabeth's Cecil and had built the house at Ruckholts, Essex, which Pepys visited.[1]

Hickman, [Henry] (d. 1692). Fellow of Magdalen College, Oxford 1648–60; a Puritan controversialist and a friend of the Crews.[1] After he was ejected from his fellowship he lived mostly in Leyden, as minister of the English church. His publications (1658–74) were mostly in defence of nonconformity. According to John Durell, one of his adversaries, he was 'twelve times in a year troubled with deliriums, and therefore his writings [were] not to be regarded'.[2]

Hickman, Sir William, 2nd Bt (1629–82). M.P. for E. Retford in five parliaments 1660–82; Ordnance Commissioner 1679. He was a member of the Commons' committee of enquiry into the miscarriages of the war, and on 3 Dec. 1667 was teller for the (unsuccessful) motion declaring Carteret guilty of negligence over the slopseller's accounts.[1]

Highgate. A hill-village in Middlesex on the Great North and Holyhead roads some 5 miles from the Standard in Cornhill. Among its

residents was the Earl of Lauderdale. Some of its sizeable 17th-century
houses survive to show its growing popularity. In 1664 it had rather
over 160 houses.[1] (R)

Hill, [George]. Maker of musical instruments. A George Hill, instrument maker, was living on the s. side of the Strand, east of Spur Alley.
There is no evidence for or against a connection with the Hill family
of violin-makers, the first recorded member of which was Joseph
Hill (1715–84).[1] (Lu)

Hill, [John]. Tar merchant, of Thames St.[1]

Hill, [John]. Employed from 1664 as victualling agent by John
Lanyon.[1]

Hill, Joseph (1625–1707). A biblical scholar 'very knowing in the
affairs of state' (ii.141); elected a Fellow of Magdalene in Nov. 1649,
and one of the dons whom Pepys came to know well. It was in Hill's
chamber that Pepys in Oct. 1653 was reproved by the fellows for
drunkenness.[1] He ceased to be a fellow c. Dec. 1660, and after a period
as a freelance preacher in London emigrated to Holland, entering the
university of Leyden in 1664. In 1667 he was elected pastor of the
Scottish Presbyterian church at Middelburg, but came back to England
in 1673 on the outbreak of war. In Feb. 1673 the Secretary of State sent
him £50, probably for providing news.[2] In 1678 he returned to Holland
to become second minister of the English Presbyterian church at
Rotterdam, where he remained until he died.[3] Several of his letters to
Pepys survive (1682–97): they give political and naval news, and offer
help in the acquisition of books and prints.[4] Pepys retained in his library
two of his works of biblical scholarship (*Historical Dissertations*, 1698)
together with his anti-French pamphlet *The interest of these United
Provinces* (1673).

Hill, [Roger] (d. 1674). Singer and composer; appointed Gentleman
of the Chapel Royal 1661. There are songs by him in *Catch that
catch can* (1667), *Select ayres and dialogues* (the second book, 1669), and
Choice Ayres (the second edition 1675); one is reprinted in *Musica
Britannica* 33/item cxviii.[1] (Lu)

Hill, Thomas (?1630–75). Merchant and close friend. His father was
Ald. Richard Hill, of Lime St (d. 1660), who was Treasurer of Sequestrations 1642–9 and a Prize Commissioner 1652–9. The eldest of Thomas's
five brothers was Abraham, who, inheriting a fortune from his father,
became one of the original fellows of the Royal Society and its
Treasurer 1663–5 and 1679–1700. Thomas himself had a minor post in
the prize commission during the First Dutch War but went into
business and was in Italy in 1657, after which he spent most of his
working life in Lisbon as an agent of the Houblons. He occasionally
supplied victuals etc. to Tangier.[1] He died at Lisbon in 1675 and James
Houblon jun. – with Pepys, his closest friend – was one of his executors.

It was Hill who introduced Morelli the musician into Pepys's household in 1673.[2]

Hill, Capt. [William] (d. by 1688). He had served in the Commonwealth navy, and commanded the *Augustine* in Sandwich's Tangier expedition 1661–2. He was not employed after the loss of the *Coventry* in 1667.[1]

Hill, ——. Of Axe Yard (i.100): possibly John Hill, who appears in the rate books of 1661 as living there. His marriage (i.215) has not been traced: the registers of St Margaret's are defective for the period.[1]

Hill, ——. Clearly (i.276) a different man from the foregoing (though also living in St Margaret's parish). Possibly Thomas Hill, in 1663 a messenger of the chamber. He may be the Thomas Hill of Gray's Inn who married Elinor Webb on 18 Sept. 1655 at St Margaret's. She was a widow by 1665.[1]

Hilton, [Edward]: *see* Taverns etc.: Hilton's

Hinchingbrooke, Viscount: *see* under Mountagu, Edward, 1st Earl of Sandwich

Hinchingbrooke, Hunts. Half-a-mile west of Huntingdon; seat of the Earls of Sandwich until 1956. Originally a nunnery; acquired by Sir Richard Cromwell at the Dissolution, and lavishly rebuilt and extended by his son Sir Henry. The latter's son Sir Oliver (uncle of his namesake the Protector) was forced, largely by Sir Henry's extravagance, to sell both house and estate. They were offered to James I, who had stayed there several times, but in the end were sold separately in 1627, the estate to Sir Henry Mountagu, 1st Earl of Manchester, and the house and manor to Sir Sidney Mountagu (father of the 1st Earl of Sandwich). The latter paid £3000. Sandwich made some alterations in the '60s; other alterations were made c. 1760, and much of it was reconstructed later, particularly in 1830–2 and 1894–6. Some vestiges of the nunnery still remain. Horace Walpole described it as 'old, spacious, irregular, yet not vast or forlorn'.[1]

Hind Court. North out of Fleet St between Fetter and Shoe Lanes. (R)

Hingston, [John] (c. 1612–83). Organ and virginal player, tuner and repairer. Pupil of Nicholas Lanier, musician-in-ordinary to Charles I,[1] state organist to Oliver Cromwell, musician-in-ordinary and keeper of the instruments to Charles II. Composer, chiefly of fancies for strings.[2] (Lu)

Hinton. Edmund (d. 1680) was a goldsmith of Lombard St. Sir John, his 'cousin', was a physician-in-ordinary to both Charles I and Charles II, who served in the royalist army and was appointed Gentleman of the Privy Chamber in 1663. He is said to have earned his knighthood by persuading Edmund to lend £10,000 or more to the King. He was alive in 1679.[1]

Hoare, [James], sen. and jun. Both served in the Mint under the

Commonwealth. The father (d. 1679) became Comptroller in 1660, holding office jointly with his son (d. 1685) after 1662. Hoare's Bank (originally at the Golden Bottle, Cheapside) was founded by the son in 1673 in partnership with his cousin Richard Hoare, goldsmith. Pepys had an account there c. 1680–c. 98.[1]

Hoare, [Richard]. Calligrapher; once librarian to John Evelyn, who praised him as 'an incomparable writer of severall hands', and obtained a post for him in the Prerogative Office at the Restoration. Pepys retained an example of his work in his library. He had only one eye.[1]

Hoare, [William] (d. 1666). Physician and musician; of Westminster and Isleworth. He had taken his M.B. and M.D. at Cambridge in 1655 and 1660 and was an original F.R.S. He lived in Great Sanctuary in 1659–60, and in St Martin-in-the-Fields in 1666.[1]

Hodges, [Thomas]. Vicar of Kensington and Dean of Hereford 1661–d. 72. At his death he owned two houses in Kensington.[1]

Hodges, ——. Of Lincoln's Inn Fields. Possibly Edmond Hodges, of Princes St, east from Drury Lane towards Lincoln's Inn Fields.[1] (R)

Hogg, Capt. [Edward]. Master's mate of the *Royal Charles* 1666; captain of Pepys's privateer the *Flying Greyhound* 1666–7. A Mr Hogg was sailing master of one of Sir W. Warren's timber ships in 1664.[1]

Holborn. The main 'extraordinary spacious highway' running west for almost a mile from Holborn Bridge to St Giles's High St.[1] The bridge, which spanned the Fleet, disappeared when the river was piped. The opening of Holborn Viaduct in 1864 has not substantially altered the general line of the highway, but the cutting of New Oxford St has eliminated the awkward bend south through St Giles. In the 1660s the name was sometimes given to the whole district traversed by the highway. The section west of the city's boundary, Holborn Bars, just east of the end of Gray's Inn Lane (Road) was, and still is, termed High Holborn. (R)

Holborn Conduit. Half-way up the hill east from the Fleet, at the junction of Snow Hill, Cock Lane and Cow Lane; an important and much used conduit, often known as Lamb's Conduit. Destroyed in the Fire and rebuilt; taken down 1746. The London conduits were simpler structures than the public fountains commonly to be found in the great continental cities. They were described by a visiting Frenchman in 1663 as nasty square towers with two little doors admitting the public.[1]

Holborn Conduit Hill. The steep hill from Holborn Bridge eastwards out of the Fleet valley to the conduit and beyond it by one of the three roads which there forked, to Newgate via Snow Hill and to Smithfield by Cock Lane or by Cow Lane. The hill has since been much modified but remained sufficiently steep for horse traffic to cause the city corporation to build Holborn Viaduct. (R)

Holborn: the King's Gate. At the s.-w. end of the King's private road from Holborn to Enfield Chase and Theobalds Palace. Theobalds Rd, Holborn, now marks the line of the road, and Kingsgate St (now destroyed) parallel to and east of the s. end of Southampton Rd, preserved the memory of the gate. Cockpit Yard in Great James St, off Theobalds Rd, is said to mark the site of the cockpit Pepys visited in 1668. (R)

Holcroft, John. Cousin; son of Robert Holcroft of Balderton, Notts., who in 1620 had married Mary, sister of Pepys's father. He and his brother Thomas received legacies from Robert Pepys of Brampton and witnessed his will. A Samuel Holcroft received a ring at Pepys's funeral as a 'former servant and dependant'.[1]

Holden, [Joseph] (d. 1680). Citizen and haberdasher, of Bride Lane (a street noted for its haberdashers); living in a large establishment taxed on nine hearths. He had married as his second wife Priscilla Watt; after his death she married Thomas Parkhurst, bookseller, in 1689. One of his sons (Joseph) became a haberdasher; another (Samuel) Governor of the Bank of England.[1]

Holder, Mr and Mrs. Possibly identical with the Holdens. But there were several families of Holders in the parish of St Margaret, Westminster.

Holder, [Thomas]. Treasurer of the Royal Adventurers trading with Africa (precursor of the R. Africa Company); Auditor-General of the Duke of York's revenues; employed by the Prize Commissioners 1664–7. He resigned his office in the Duke's household in 1673 in favour of his son Tobias.[1]

Holinshed, ——. The tobacconist who married the widowed Kate Joyce in 1668. In 1682 they were living at the sign of the Black Swan in Wood St, nr Cheapside.[1]

Holland, Gilbert. Possibly the man of these names who was a naval lieutenant in 1665–6. But the entry at i.95 suggests that he may have been a cutler or a cutler's servant. A William Holland was a member of the Cutlers' Company in 1703.[1]

Holland, Capt. Philip. With his wife, a friend of the Pepyses in the early diary period. A veteran of the First Dutch War, he had commanded the *Assurance* in the Baltic (1659). In 1665 he was commissioned to a fireship, the *Loyal Merchant*, but deserted to the Dutch and took part in the Medway raid. He was arrested in 1672 but released on undertaking to act as a spy.[1]

Holles, Denzil, 1st Baron Holles (1598–1680). M.P. for St Michael 1624–5, Dorchester 1628–9, 1640, 1640–8 and 1660; cr. baron 1661. A leading parliamentary opponent of Charles I (and one of the five members whom the King attempted to impeach in 1642), he tried throughout the Civil War to end the fighting and find terms of accommodation which would secure the constitutional liberties which

the King had put at risk. In 1647–9 he opposed the army in the name of
the same liberties and was driven out of politics. After Monck's intervention in Jan. 1660, he resumed his parliamentary seat and as a
Councillor of State went as one of the official deputation to the King
at The Hague. At that point he accepted – no doubt as a *pis aller* – the
unconditional return of monarchy. In the diary period he was ambassador in Paris (1663–6) and one of the plenipotentiaries who negotiated
the Treaty of Breda with the Dutch (1668). In the '70s he opposed the
French alliance and the arbitrary policies of the government, and in the
parliaments of 1679–81 (typically) was against the extreme policy of
excluding the Catholic heir from the succession and in favour of
imposing limitations on any Catholic monarch.[1]

Holles, Sir Frescheville (1642–72). A gentleman-captain: son of
Gervase Holles the antiquary, he held several commissions in foot
regiments before being commissioned in the navy during the Second
Dutch War. He lost an arm in the Four Days Fight. As an M.P. (for
Grimsby from 1667) he was a follower of Buckingham and usually
therefore a violent critic of Coventry and the Navy Board. He carried
the articles of Penn's impeachment up to the Lords. Out of friendship
however he defended Brouncker in the debates on pay-tickets. He was
killed in action at Sole Bay.[1]

Hollier, [Thomas] (1609–90). Pepys's surgeon: he operated on him
for the stone in March 1658, and attended him and Elizabeth throughout the diary period and almost certainly after. In 1677 Pepys consulted
him about his father's condition.[1] He had been apprenticed to James
Molins the elder, surgeon to St Thomas's Hospital and lithotomist to
St Thomas's and Bartholomew's, and was appointed to St Thomas's as
barber-surgeon ('surgeon for scald heads') in 1638. When Edward
Molins (James's son and successor in his hospital posts) went away to
serve with the royalist army, Hollier (a staunch Puritan) took over his
work. In the First Dutch War he was employed to treat seamen. In
1660 he was replaced by Molins at St Bartholomew's and alternated
with him at St Thomas's. After 1664 he alternated with Edward's son
James as lithotomist at St Bartholomew's and earned the reputation of
being in his day the most skilful and successful lithotomist in London.
He was Master of the Barber-Surgeons' Company in 1673–4, and
though retiring from St Bartholomew's in 1680 seems according to his
monumental inscription in Christ Church Newgate to have continued
practising at St Thomas's until his death. He lived for most of the diary
period in Warwick Lane, where he owned several properties, one of
which he sold in 1669 to the Royal College of Physicians as the site for
its new college. Two of his sons, Thomas and James, were surgeons.
There is a portrait (by an unknown artist) in the Royal College of
Surgeons.[2]

Hollins, [John] (d. 1712). Physician and Fellow of Magdalene 1656–c. 65. He entered Magdalene in 1651, and took his B.A. in 1655 and his M.A. in 1658. He proceeded M.D. in 1665 and later practised medicine in Shrewsbury. His son John (also of Magdalene) became a royal physician and physician-general to the army under George II.[1]

Hollond, [John]. Originally a dockyard clerk at Chatham (c. 1624), he became Paymaster of the Navy 1635–42; Navy Commissioner 1642–9, 1649–53, and Surveyor of the Navy 1649–53. He was the author of two important discourses on the navy (1638 and 1659).[1]

Hollworthy, Mr and Mrs. Neighbours living on the n. side of Crutched Friars in a house taxed on 12 hearths. Richard Hollworthy was a citizen and draper, and left ten children at his death in 1665. He had married Mary, daughter of Sir George Strode, in 1652. She was still a widow when she made her will in 1676.[1]

Holmes, Sir John, kt 1672 (?1640–83). Naval commander; younger brother of Sir Robert. He served in Robert's expedition to W. Africa in 1663–4 and in several of the actions of 1665–6, including his brother's raid on Terschelling, after which he was advanced to the command of a 2nd-rate, the *Triumph*. His career thereafter was steadier and more continuous than his brother's. He obtained a peace-time commission in 1670–1 under Spragge in the expedition against Algiers and returned to take part in the attack on the Dutch Smyrna fleet and the war that followed. He achieved flag rank in 1673 and in 1677–9 was Commander-in-Chief of the Channel. By his brother's influence he was made Governor of Hurst Castle in 1675 and was four times elected M.P. for Newtown (I. of W.) 1677–83.

In 1668 he married Peg Lowther, sister of Peg Penn's husband.[1]

Holmes, Sir Robert, kt 1666 (1622–92). Naval commander. Son of an English settler in Ireland, he had fought under Rupert in the royalist army and navy (Pepys often refers to him as Major), and had much of Rupert's dash and flair in action. In 1660–1 and 1663–4 he commanded two expeditions to W. Africa, the second of which did much to provoke the outbreak of the Dutch War in 1665. In that war he was one of the most successful of English admirals, his most spectacular achievement being his brilliantly executed raid on Dutch shipping sheltering behind the island of Vlieland ('Holmes's Bonfire,' Aug. 1666). Later, in March 1672, it was his action in attacking, on government orders, the Dutch Smyrna fleet in the Channel which led to the Third Dutch War. He was not however given flag command in the campaign of 1672 and by the next year his active naval career was over. Since 1660 he had been Deputy-Governor and since 1668 Governor of the Isle of Wight, which he now turned into a lucrative satrapy. He served in parliament, mostly for Isle of Wight constituencies, from 1669–79 and 1685–92.

The diary's references give several evidences of his courage in action, as well as of his rough manners and explosive temper. It was probably these faults which explain why he was not employed in the highest posts after 1667. Pepys had a particular animus against him in the early diary years because of the 'old business' – whatever that was – he had attempted on his wife. But the two men drew together in later life. Pepys consulted him about the design of the 30 new ships of 1677, though he disagreed with him about the size of the 1st-rates, and was twice involved in negotiation with him (in Feb. 1679 and Feb. 1690) to secure a parliamentary seat.[1] After the Revolution they both remained faithful to James II without becoming active Jacobites.

Holmes had in him more than a touch of the buccaneer, and lost no chance of amassing wealth. He was not politically ambitious and his only attempt at playing a political rôle, when in 1682 he suddenly and inexplicably adopted Monmouth's cause, almost led to dismissal from all his posts. But as Richard Ollard's delightful biography shows, he was a superb 'man of war' – a thoroughly professional serving officer.

Pepys kept in his diary the journals, and other papers, of his two voyages to W. Africa.[2]

Holt, ——. Probably Francis Holt, navy agent at Portsmouth since 1660. There was another Holt (W——), navy victualler there.[1]

Homewood, ——. Edward Homewood was a privately employed clerk in the Navy Office in 1663. One 'Homewood' was clerk of the survey at Harwich (dates unknown) and at Chatham in 1675 and 1676.[1]

Honywood. The sons of Robert Honywood, of Marks Hall, Essex, used the Pepys house in Salisbury Court as their town lodgings. The family is often mentioned in the diary of Pepys's contemporary, Ralph Josselin, Vicar of Earl's Colne, Essex.[1] The eldest (a particular friend of Josselin) was Sir Thomas (1586–1666), a leading parliamentarian in his day (M.P. for the county in 1654 and 1656 and a member of Cromwell's Upper House) but distrusted by hard-line Puritans as a 'knight of the old Stamp . . .' 'rather soft in his spirit'.[2] He retired from public life in 1660. His daughter mentioned by Pepys was Elizabeth (d. 1702) who in 1658 had married Sir John Cotton, grandson of the antiquary Sir Robert Bruce Cotton. Sir Thomas's half-brother Sir Robert (1601–86), of Charing, Kent, was also a prominent parliamentarian and served on the Council of State in 1659. Henry Vane the younger was his brother-in-law.[3] Of Sir Thomas's other brothers the best-known was the youngest, Michael (1597–1681), Fellow of Christ's College, Cambridge 1618–43, who lived in the Low Countries during the Interregnum, and became first a canon and afterwards Dean of Lincoln in 1660. A generous benefactor to the cathedral, he rebuilt much of the close and constructed the library now named after him which houses most of his collection of books and MSS.[4] Philip, another brother, was knighted at the Restoration for his services as a courier for the secret royalist organisations in the '50s. He became in 1662 Deputy-Governor and in 1665 Governor of Portsmouth.[5] The other two brothers were Peter (d. 1685, aged 96) who spent more time at the Pepys house than the others (the Elizabeth Wyld who went with him to Pepys's stone feast was his niece);[6] and Col. Henry (1593–1663).[7]

Hooke, Robert (1635–1703). Operator to the Royal Society from 1662, Fellow from 1663 and Secretary 1677–82. A strange and unattractive character, but extraordinarily gifted. There are few scientific investigations of his time – in astronomy, physics, chemistry, geology, meteorology, physiology and linguistics – to which he did not make a significant contribution. As an experimentalist and inventor he was remarkably resourceful, and contrived new telescopes, barometers, carriages and spring watches. He was employed in the survey of London undertaken after the Fire, and designed, among other buildings, Montagu House and Bethlehem Hospital in London, and (possibly) the building in Cambridge in which Pepys's library was eventually housed. (He appears to have been asked to submit a design in 1677.)[1] Pepys retained several of his published works in his library, including the famous *Micrographia*.[2] He kept a diary which was published (incompletely) in 1935.[3]

Hooke, [Theophilus]. A near-contemporary of Pepys at Cambridge; entered at Clare Hall in 1653, he graduated B.A. in 1657. He was Rector of Garboldisham, Norf., 1663–89, and of Sudborne, Suff., 1666–1700.[1]

Hooker, Ald. Sir William, kt 1666 (1612–97). Merchant, of Birchin Lane; Alderman 1664–89; Sheriff 1665–6; Lord Mayor 1673–4; Master of the Grocers' Company 1679–80. His daughter Anne married John Lethieullier.[1]

Hooper, [William]. (1610 or 1611–63). Minor canon of Westminster Abbey; grandson of the late 16th-century composer Edmund Hooper.[1] (Lu)

[Horneck, Anthony]. Preacher and author of devotional works; curate of the Savoy 1671–d.97; later chaplain to William III. Of German origin.[1]

Horse Guards House. On w. side of Whitehall to the north of the Holbein Gate; built 1663–4; burnt Nov. 1666 and rebuilt; replaced in the 1750s by the present building.[1]

Horsleydown. An area on the Surrey bank of the Thames in the parish of St Olave, Southwark, approximately opposite the e. end of the Tower. Originally a grazing ground, but gradually built over during the 17th century, it contained the landing stairs, lane and square as well as the street of that name. (R)

Hosier, Frank. Clerk of the Cheque and Muster-Master, Gravesend

1665; victualling agent, Dover 1665; Clerk of Control, Deptford 1669–79.[1]

Houblon. A remarkable family of merchants – father and five sons – notable for their success, liberality and mutual affection. They traded with France, Portugal, Spain and the Mediterranean. James Houblon, sen. (1592–1682) was the son of a refugee Huguenot from Lille. He lived in Bearbinder Lane in a house which was rebuilt after the Fire. Bishop Burnet preached his funeral sermon and Pepys is said to have composed his epitaph.[1] His son Sir James (?1629–1700) became Pepys's closest friend. He stood surety for him on the two occasions in 1679 and 1690 when he was imprisoned, gave him invaluable help in gathering evidence against his enemies during the Popish Plot, and was his chief informant and adviser on trade and shipping – and often enough on naval matters too. He lived in some state – '*en Prince*' was Evelyn's phrase[2] – in Great Winchester St, and conducted his business from there. He was a Whig – knighted and made an alderman in 1691, a director of the Bank of England from 1694, and M.P. for the city from 1698. He and Pepys exchanged portraits, and in his library Pepys kept a drawing of Sir James's, grouped with those of Deane, Evelyn, Thomas Gale and Hewer – the intimates of his old age.[3]

His family, too, became Pepys's intimate friends. His wife (b. Sarah Wynne, m. 1658) and her daughter-in-law planned to accompany him on a trip to France and Flanders in 1674, which never came off, and the whole household in 1680 shared a country cottage with him at Parson's Green.[4] The daughter-in-law – whom Pepys sometimes refers to as 'cousin' – was Sarah, wife of Wynne Houblon. She and her children were particular favourites of Pepys.

Of the other brothers two are named in the diary – Peter, the eldest (1623–91), and Isaac (1638–1700). The latter was a director of the E. India Company from 1695. Sir John, the third eldest son (1632–1712), knighted in 1689, was Lord Mayor 1695–6, and the first Governor of the Bank of England (1694–7). He was an Admiralty Commissioner 1694–9. Abraham (1640–1722) was also a Governor of the Bank (1703–4) and became a Commissioner of Victualling in 1702.[5]

HOUSEHOLD: DOMESTIC SERVANTS[1]

Numbers. In the Pepyses' first home, a turret room in Mountagu's lodgings in Whitehall Palace, there was no servant and Pepys later recalled how Elizabeth herself would 'make coal fires and wash my foul clothes with her own hand . . ., poor wretch'.[2] The first servant they employed was Jane Birch who came to them in Aug. 1658 when they moved to Axe Yard. On their removing to Seething Lane in July 1660 their immediate need apparently – or Pepys's – was a footboy, appointed before the move, whose attendance on Pepys in public would mark the new importance of the master of the household. In the following November a second maid was engaged, in Aug. 1663 a third, and in Sept. 1664 a waiting-woman for Elizabeth, appointed at her request and just as significant of her new status as the arrival of the footboy had been of her husband's. This complement – a waiting-woman for Elizabeth, three maids (one of them a 'little girl') and a footboy – remained the normal establishment throughout the diary period, though from time to time numbers were temporarily depleted as servants left or were dismissed. Just before the diary ends, Pepys acquired a coach, and, in Dec. 1668, a coachman. All lived in.

The little that is known of the history of Pepys's household after 1669 reflects Pepys's growing wealth and importance. In the '70s his household, now presided over by his companion, Mary Skynner, included both a housekeeper and a butler. The butler (John James), who had come highly recommended, was dismissed for having an affair with the housekeeper, and took his revenge by giving false testimony to implicate Pepys in the Popish Plot. Defending himself in the House of Commons, Pepys said: 'All know that I am unfortunate in my Servants, but I hope that it is no crime to be so'.[3] From the '80s when he was living in some style in York Buildings, he employed a large staff (including for a while a black boy)[4] typical of the household of an upper middle-class Londoner. From at any rate 1689 he had eight servants – a housekeeper, a cook, a laundrymaid, a housemaid, two footmen, a coachman and a porter – and joined with his neighbours in employing a gardener.[5] One of the menservants lived in a small house near by which Pepys rented for him. Six of the servants were present at his deathbed.[6]

The pioneer statistician, Gregory King, making his calculations in the '90s, concluded that in 1688 the average number of people in the household of a lower official (such as Pepys in the '60s) including parents and children as well as servants, was around six, and in that of a higher official (such as Pepys in the '90s) around eight. As we have seen, in Pepys's case the servants alone amounted to these numbers. It would be wrong, however, to accuse him, on this basis, of living above his station. It is much more likely that King's figures are misleading, particularly since they have been shown to be faulty in other parts of his calculations.[7]

Wages. The only precise information given in the diary concerns cook-maids, perhaps because their wages varied. Jane Birch, appointed in 1662, was given £3 p.a. (the going rate – 'she would not serve under'); another had £4 (given unwillingly, but she was said to be good and had cooked for a duke); and a third asked for £5 and was given £3 10s.[8]

The footboys would receive less, and the chambermaids more. The waiting woman was paid around £8–10 if we may judge from the fact that Deb Willet on her departure received £10 for a year-and-a-quarter. Wages slowly increased during Pepys's lifetime. In 1697 he was paying his laundrymaid, housemaid and cookmaid a level £6. The porter received £12, the first footman £10, the housekeeper and coachman £8, and the second footman £6.⁹ In addition to wages, servants received free lodging (or board-wages in lieu of it), food and clothes. They could expect also a few extras. Visitors might leave tips – Pepys himself gave 2s. to a maid after a dinner party, and 14s. to his father's servants after Elizabeth had stayed at Brampton for several weeks.¹⁰ And on special occasions there would be gifts from their employers. When Jane Birch and Tom Edwards married they received £40 from the Pepyses. On a similar occasion the Battens gave a dinner at which friends and neighbours contributed gifts of money. Good servants who had given long service might be pensioned off: in 1690 Pepys gave an annuity of £15 to Jane Penny, a widow (who may well have been the beloved Jane Birch of the diary).¹¹ They might also expect to be remembered in their employers' wills: Pepys for his part left a year's wages to each servant remaining with him at his death, gave £20 to one of them for his help 'in several matters relating to my books' and ordered Jane Penny's annuity to be continued.¹²

Status and duties. The most junior in years and status was the footboy who ran errands and accompanied his master abroad, wearing sword and livery and, it might be, carrying a link to light the way. Wayneman was taught how to put Pepys to bed, and Jack who came when Pepys's eyesight was failing was required to read to him. The lowliest of the women servants was the cookmaid, who might also double as scullery maid. Men cooks, in middle-class households, were engaged only for special occasions – even in the '90s Pepys had none. Next in rank above the cookmaid was the chambermaid, whose superiority arose from the fact that as well as cleaning the house she looked after the clothes and persons of her employers. The most important of the female servants was the waiting woman, who sat at table with her employers. It was often the case that she came of a respectable family down on its luck. Gosnell, though 'humble and poor' was the niece of a magistrate, Ashwell the daughter and Barker a poor relative of an Exchequer official, and Mercer the daughter of 'a decayed merchant'. The waiting woman dressed her lady's hair, looked after her clothes and provided her with companionship whenever required. Elizabeth, for instance, would rarely go to the theatre in her husband's absence without taking her companion with her. Since, like all women servants, she wore no uniform, she was easily mistaken for a lady.¹³

The duties of each servant were sufficiently clear, though not so strictly defined as in a large household. Pepys called on 'the little girl' Susan to comb his hair, or Nan the cookmaid to cut it. Mercer the waiting woman was once required to wash his ears. The whole family cooperated when required – the mistress herself not excluded – in the household wash, or to clear up after a domestic disaster, such as the Fire or a visit from the painters and decorators.

In the absence of a housekeeper it was Elizabeth's duty to supervise the household. It was she who appointed and dismissed most of the servants, planned purchases, did much of the shopping, and made up the housekeeping accounts. She also, especially in the early years, cooked, baked and made the conserves. With her maids she worked at her needles, making not only nightcaps, shirts and smocks, but also cushion covers and hangings. A whole week was once devoted to fitting hangings in the bedroom and in Pepys's dressing room.[14]

Hiring and firing. At 10 May 1663 Pepys remarks with approval on the French habit of requiring testimonials. His own method of appointing servants was not much different from the French except that he did not insist that the recommendations should be in writing.[15] Of the 38 servants mentioned (excluding Pall), 24 had been personally recommended in one form or another. Once, in desperation, he engaged a girl from the workhouse, but she ran away the day after and he never tried the experiment again.[16] It seems more than probable that in London there were agencies through which employers and servants could get in touch with each other. Otherwise it is unlikely that Elizabeth would have been able to summon several applicants for interview on a single morning.[17] There may well have been a few employment bureaux, such as are known to have existed in the '90s (and which usually had an unsavoury reputation),[18] but it is more likely that the local tavernkeepers and shopkeepers were the usual sources of information.

As for the conditions of employment, the first of Pepys's footboys entered into indentures, like an apprentice.[19] Maids were normally employed on a monthly basis, though one of Pepys's maids insisted on six months' tenure.[20] It is noticeable, if we may trust Pepys's evidence about the departure of servants, that the servants themselves were rarely upset by the prospect. On the contrary, several maids gave notice on what seem to be trivial grounds. In two cases we are told what happened to them after leaving. Sarah, dismissed in Dec. 1662, was established next door at the Penns' by the end of the month; and Mary, dismissed in Oct. 1665, was by December working for Pepys's friends the Pearses. The diary's evidence in fact supports the view that with the growth in the number of middle-class households there was a shortage of trained servants in London.

Discipline. Servants at this time and for long after were looked on as part of the master's 'family'. He was responsible for their welfare – physical, moral, and spiritual. He clothed them and fed them; he saw that they attended church and family prayers; he also saw that they had their share in family jaunts and festivities. The aim was in Pepys's words 'a family living . . . in most perfect content and quiet',[21] and there were moments when Pepys could congratulate himself that he had achieved it. But of course there were other moments – crises caused by a naughty footboy or a drunken cookmaid, and the constant bother of dealing with servants who were insubordinate or gossipy or just plain idle. The punishment in such cases was often dismissal – and the Pepyses in the diary period got rid of approximately 12 servants. (The number is difficult to calculate.) The younger servants were, like children, kept in order by physical punishment. Not even her sex saved Jane Birch from a basting with a broom, and her scallywag brother Wayneman the footboy was beaten eight times in two years. The belief that young people should be corrected by the rod – challenged by John Locke – was a belief that died hard.[22]

Black servants, of whom there were increasing numbers with the growth of the W. Indian trade, were a special case.[23] Pepys had one (Doll the cookmaid) in the diary years and at least two others later. They were slaves and if the law were strictly applied, could be bought and sold like chattels. Pepys sold a black boy in 1680, and in 1688 another, whose misbehaviour had upset the household, was sent back to be sold into service in the plantations.[24] Batten's Mingo, on the other hand, whose good-humoured tricks Pepys had enjoyed, must have become a family favourite, for he was left a legacy of £10 and an annuity of £15 in his master's will.[25] There is no hint in the diary of how Doll the Pepyses' blackamoor cookmaid was treated.[26]

Houses (Pepys's): *see* Axe Yard; Brampton; Hewer, W.; Navy Office

Howard, Bernard (d. 1717). Eighth son of Henry Frederick, 15th Earl of Arundel, and brother of Cardinal Howard; a noted breeder of race-horses. He had a colonelcy in James II's army, and was twice arrested after 1689 on suspicion of Jacobitism.[1]

Howard, Charles, 1st Earl of Carlisle (?1629–1703). Soldier and diplomatist. Though by inclination royalist, he had accepted office under the Commonwealth, served in the army (at Worcester and in Oliver Cromwell's bodyguard) and in three parliaments. In 1659 his support for Booth's rising had led to his imprisonment. At the Restoration he was made a Privy Councillor (1660) and created earl (1661). He went on diplomatic missions to Russia, Sweden and Denmark between 1663 and 1668, was made Lieut-General of the kingdom in 1667, and was Governor of Jamaica 1677–81. He was elected F.R.S. in 1665. His wife, whom he married c. 1645, was Anne, daughter of Lord Howard of Escrick.[1]

Howard, [Dorothy]. Maid of Honour to the Duchess of York; after 1671 to the Queen. Daughter of William Howard, fourth son of Thomas Howard, 1st Earl of Berkshire; in 1675 she married Col. James Graham, Keeper of the Privy Purse to the Duke of York.[1]

Howard, [Elizabeth]. Housekeeper to the Duke of York at the Navy Treasurer's house at Deptford; mother of Dorothy. She and her daughters were friends of Evelyn.[1]

Howard, Lady Essex. Daughter of James Howard, 15th Earl of Suffolk and his first wife Susan. In 1667 she married Sir Edward Griffin of Braybrooke, Northants. (cr. Baron Griffin 1688), a Jacobite who died in the Tower in 1710. It was through this marriage that Audley End House passed into the possession of the Braybrooke family.[1]

Howard, Henry, cr. Earl of Norwich 1672, succ. as 6th Duke of Norfolk 1677 (1628–84). A leading Catholic and a generous patron of the Royal Society. In 1673 at the instance of the King and the Duke of York he procured Pepys's election at a parliamentary bye-election for Castle Rising, Norf. Both in the election and afterwards, when the result was challenged by the Duke of York's enemies in the Commons, Pepys had to rebut the charge that he himself was a papist.[1]

Howard, James, 13th Earl of Suffolk (1620–89). Earl Marshal. In May 1669 he sold Audley End House, Essex, to the King, but since only £30,000 of the £50,000 due was ever paid, it was reconveyed to the 15th Earl in 1701.[1]

Howard, Sir Philip, kt 1660 (1631–86). Brother of the 1st Earl of Carlisle; Captain of the King's Lifeguard 1660–78; Governor of Jamaica 1685–6; M.P. for Malton 1659–60, 1660, Carlisle 1661–81. 'He discourses as well as ever I heard man' (vii.378). None of his speeches in parliament is recorded. He took a leading part in the hostile questioning of Pepys's servant Atkins in the Popish Plot scare.[1]

Howard, Cardinal Philip Thomas (1629–94). Elder brother of Bernard; appointed chaplain to Queen Catherine 1661, and Lord Almoner 1665. A friend of the King, and influential in promoting the Portuguese match. He was forced to go abroad by the strength of anti-Catholic feeling in 1674, and settled at the priory he had founded in 1657 at Bornhem in Flanders. He was made Cardinal in 1675, and Cardinal Protector of England in 1679. His relations with English Protestants – even with Bishop Burnet – were always excellent. Titus Oates of course accused him of planning to take over England as papal legate; in the event, like Innocent XI, he strongly disapproved of James II's headlong policies.[1]

Howard, Sir Robert (1626–98). Dramatist and politician; a younger son of Charles Howard, 1st Earl of Berkshire, and brother-in-law of

Dryden. Caricatured as the boastful Sir Positive At-all in Shadwell's *The Impertinents*. M.P. 1661–98 (except 1685–7); Secretary to the Treasury 1671–3; Auditor of the Receipt in the Exchequer 1673–7. A troublesome critic of Clarendon's ministry (in Dec. 1666 he is said to have proposed the formation of the parliamentary committee of accounts) and of the Navy Board (e.g. in Penn's impeachment). After 1668 an unreliable supporter of the court. In 1679 he replaced Pepys as M.P. for Castle Rising, Norf., and did not hesitate to improve his chances by traducing Pepys as a papist.[1] Pepys had six of his plays in his library.[2]

Howard, Thomas, 2nd Earl of Berkshire (c. 1590–1669). In the royal service from 1614; Gentleman of the Bedchamber to the King from 1661. Clarendon scornfully writes of him that 'his interest and reputation were less than anything but his understanding'. Parliament did not trouble to keep him under constraint during the Civil War since he was 'a man that could do them no harm anywhere'.[1]

Howard, Thomas (d. 1678). Fourth son of Sir William of Naworth, and younger brother of Charles Howard, 1st Earl of Carlisle; Lieutenant of the Yeomen of the Guard. Sometime before Nov. 1664 he married (as her third husband) Mary, Duchess of Richmond (d. 1685).[1]

Howe, Will. A junior colleague of Pepys in Sandwich's service, living in 1660 in Sandwich's Whitehall lodgings and later at the Wardrobe. He was Sandwich's clerk on his voyages to the Baltic, Holland and the Mediterranean, 1659–62, before succeeding Creed as Secretary and Deputy-Treasurer to the fleet in 1664–5. In Oct. 1666 he was admitted to Gray's Inn, and by 1668 was attempting to buy a place in the Patent Office, where his younger brother John already had employment. By 1680 he was married (to a god-daughter of Pepys whose name has not been traced),[1] with two children, and living in Barbados, where he became a judge. He is described in the admission register of Gray's Inn as a son of William Howe of Windsor. He may have been related to the Susan How, widow, who was a legatee in the will of the 2nd Lord Mountagu of Boughton.[2]

Howell, [Richard]. Appointed turner to the Navy, July 1660. Pepys preserved a note that he had allegedly overcharged for *lignum vitae*. His widow Sarah married Dr Edward Hickes, Rector of St Margaret Pattens in 1668.[1]

Howell, [William] (?1638–83). Lawyer and historian; 'my old acquaintance of Magdalen' (iv.274). He was a Fellow 1652–c. 56.[1] He took his LL.D. in 1665, was admitted an advocate in Doctors' Commons 1678, and became Chancellor of Lincoln diocese 1678–83. He wrote among other works an *Institution of general history* (first pub. 1661, reissued 1662) which proved useful to Gibbon. Pepys retained the 1685 edition.[2]

Howet: *see* Hewet

Howlett, Lettice (Lissett). Sister of Pepys's mother. She married firstly, —— Haines, and secondly —— Howlett.[1]

Howlett, ——. Shopkeeper in Westminster Hall: father of Betty Mitchell. Possibly John Howlett of the Sanctuary, Westminster, assessed for the subsidy of 1663. The tax he was collecting at viii.121 was probably the hearth-tax.[1]

Hoxton (Hogsden). A hamlet in the n. part of the parish of St Leonard Shoreditch, just over a mile from the Standard on Cornhill and on the main road through Tottenham to Waltham Cross. Sometimes spelt as Hoddesden, which is on the same road but in Hertfordshire. In 1660 still distinct from the built-up area of London and comparatively rural, though its population was probably increasing fast. By 1664 it had about 160 houses assessable to the hearth-tax and over 200 too small to be assessed.[1] (R)

Hubbard, Capt. Of the two naval officers named John Hubbard alive at this time (? father and son: their commissions run from 1662 and 1665 respectively), this is the junior, who is known to have commanded the Admiral's ship, the *Royal Charles*, (cf. vii.333). Coventry thought him 'very able and stout'. His independence of spirit is clear from the diary. His death in action against the Algerines 1668 was attributed to his 'over much courage'.[1]

Hudson, [James]. Wine cooper, Seething Lane; taxed on seven hearths 1666.[1]

Hudson, [Michael]. Appointed chaplain, Chatham dockyard, July 1660; probably the Rector of Witchling, Kent 1653–6.[1]

Hudson, [Nathaniel]. Scrivener, of St Olave's parish.[1]

Hudson, ——. Of Westminster. Probably John Hudson of Brewer's Yard.[1]

Hughes, Peg. Actress in the King's Company 1667–9 and the Duke's Company 1675–7, playing mostly minor rôles; after c. 1670 mistress of Prince Rupert to whom she bore a daughter Ruperta in 1673.[1]

Hughes, [William]. Appointed ropemaker, Deptford and Woolwich, July 1660.[1]

Hughes, ——. Housekeeper of Parliament: described in 1671 as Keeper of the Speaker's Chambers.[1]

Humfrey, Pelham (1647–74). Composer and singer (tenor): Child of the Chapel Royal under Captain Cooke whose daughter Katherina he married (1672); in France, and perhaps Italy, at royal expense early 1665–7; often said to have studied with Lully (but there is stylistic evidence only); appointed composer in ordinary for the band of violins 1672. His compositions, mainly anthems, are powerful and original.[1] A friend of Blow's, to whom he left 20*s*. for a mourning ring.[2] (Lu)

Hunt, [John and Elizabeth]. Friends and neighbours in Axe Yard.

Their house, taxed on eight hearths, lay a few doors from Pepys's. John (a Cambridgeshire man) seems to have been sympathetic to the political and ecclesiastical extremists: in Feb. 1660 he disapproved of the return of the secluded M.P.s, and in 1665 stood bail for the sectary Hayter. His wife was a relative of Cromwell. His employment was in the Excise; after some doubt about his future after the Restoration, he was serving in the excise commission for Oxfordshire and Buckinghamshire in 1661, and for Cambridgeshire in 1666.[1]

Hunt, ——. Musical instrument-maker: probably George Hunt, on the n. side of Paul's Churchyard; though there was also Richard Hunt who lived in Paul's Alley.[1] (R)

Hutchinson, [Richard] (1597–1670). One of the leading naval officials of the Civil War and Commonwealth period. A merchant and a protégé of the younger Vane in both Massachusetts and England, he was Treasurer for the relief of maimed soldiers 1643–50; Deputy-Treasurer of the Navy 1645–50, Treasurer 1650–60; M.P. for Rochester 1659; and joint Paymaster of the Navy 1668–70. In the 1690s Pepys wrote of his régime: 'never was . . . [the Navy Treasury] better managed, or with more credit or satisfaction to the service'.[1]

Hyde, Edward, cr. Earl of Clarendon 1661 (1609–74). Charles II's principal adviser in exile, and Lord Chancellor 1658–67. Perhaps the wisest minister the Stuarts ever had. His firm belief in a balanced monarchy led him, before the Civil War, to criticise both Charles I's interpretation of the prerogative and the extreme claims of his parliamentary enemies. He did his utmost to avoid war (by drafting conciliatory royal declarations in 1642), and in 1643–4 to find terms for a settlement. In exile with Charles II he held the King to the policy of waiting until the Revolution should blow itself out and the country restore itself peacefully to its historic allegiance to King and Church. When this became possible in early 1660 it was the statement he made on the King's behalf (in the Declaration of Breda) of the principles of a healing settlement, including some form of religious toleration, that provided the understanding on which Charles came back. The settlement in fact proved to be more illiberal, particularly in religion, than Clarendon had intended or wanted, and it is ironic that the legislation against Dissent of the early '60s (inspired mainly by the fervour of the Anglican House of Commons) lives in the history books by the title given it in the early 19th century of the 'Clarendon Code'.

The diary is a first-rate source for the history of Clarendon's ministry. It gives a vivid impression of the man himself – of the majesty and charm of his bearing, of his air of effortless superiority, of his easy and fluent speech. It gives also the material for judging the inherent weakness of his position – his insecure hold on the King, the hostility of Lady Castlemaine and the younger courtiers and politicians, the jealousies caused by his daughter's marriage to the Duke of York, and his failure to organise support in the Commons. Of his fall in 1667 the diary's account is the fullest to survive.

In the sad years of exile in France that followed his fall Clarendon wrote the history of his own times. He had begun it in Jersey after the first Civil War when he composed a draft of what became his master-piece, *The history of the Great Rebellion*, as a manual of instruction for the young Prince of Wales, of whom he was Governor. It was finished in his second exile and eventually published by his son Laurence in 1702–4. Pepys read with avidity the first volume – the only one to appear in his lifetime. Clarendon's autobiography – a by-product of the *History* – is less satisfactory. The section dealing with the '60s was written with the help of very few notes and with the restricted purpose of answering the charges against him in the attempted impeachment of 1667. It is a much thinner and less reliable account of the history of his ministry than Pepys gives in the diary.[1] [*See also* Clarendon House]

Hyde, Henry, styled Viscount Cornbury, succ. as 2nd Earl of Clarendon 1674 (1638–1709). Politician; elder brother of Laurence. M.P. for Wiltshire 1661–74; Lord-Lieutenant of Ireland 1685–7. In his youth he acted as his father's amanuensis and was devotedly loyal to him at the time of his impeachment, and a leading critic of the Bucking-ham and Arlington factions which overthrew him. Like his brother a strong Anglican and loyalist, he refused the oaths to William. A friend and correspondent of Pepys, and a pall-bearer at his funeral.[1]

Hyde, Laurence, cr. Earl of Rochester 1681 (1641–1711). Politician; Clarendon's second son. M.P. for Oxford University 1661–Jan. 79, Wootton Bassett 1679. In the latter part of Charles's reign he was the leading member of the Tory ministries 1679–85, and his dismissal from the Lord Treasurership by James II in Dec. 1687 marked the King's break with Anglican support. Leader of the High Church Tories under William and Anne.[1]

Hyde, Sir Robert (1595–1665). Lawyer; a cousin of the Lord Chancellor. Serjeant-at-law 1640; Recorder of Salisbury 1638–46, 1660–5; Justice of Common Pleas 1660–3; Chief Justice of King's Bench 1663–5. 'An authority upon pleas of the crown, but . . . not learned otherwise'.[1]

Hyde Park. Acquired from Westminster Abbey by Henry VIII and used for hunting until the 1620s when it was opened to the public. Under the Commonwealth it was sold in three lots to private owners and a charge made for admission. Used principally by coaches, especi-ally on May Day when there was a parade of fashion round a 'Ring' marked out for the purpose. Footraces, coach races and musters were also held there. The deer fences were replaced in Charles II's time by a brick wall which in turn was replaced by iron fences under George IV.[1]

Ibbot, [Edmund]. Rector of Deal 1662–d.77. Apparently a protégé of Sandwich: at Huntingdon school before going to Cambridge; a naval chaplain from 1656; chaplain 1660–1 in two of Sandwich's ships, the *Naseby* and the *Royal James*. He was chaplain to Sandwich's embassy in Lisbon 1667–8.[1]

Impington, Cambs. Two-and-a-half miles north of Cambridge. The manor was acquired by John Pepys (d. 1589), the diarist's great-grandfather. The manor house which stood close by the church, to the south, was built in the 1580s and '90s, and in the 1660s (when it was the home of Talbot Pepys and of his son Roger) was taxed on 17 hearths. It was modernised in 1725, and stayed in the hands of the family until 1805. It was pulled down in 1948. There is a description of it (1774) by William Cole.[1]

Inchiquin, 1st Earl of: *see* O'Brien, M.

Ingoldsby, Col. [Richard] (d. 1685). A regicide and Oliver Cromwell's cousin. He worked his passage at the Restoration by suppressing Lambert's rising in Apr. 1660. He was M.P. for Aylesbury in the Convention and in four of Charles II's parliaments, and was made K.B. in 1661.[1]

Ingram, Sir Arthur, kt 1664 (1617–81). Son of Robert, a city merchant; himself a prosperous merchant trading with Spain, mostly in wine. He was a Common Councilman 1662–7, Master of the Haberdashers' Company 1665–6, and held office in the Canary, E. India and R. Africa Companies.[1]

Ingram, Sir Thomas, kt 1639 (d. 1671). Son of the Sir Arthur (d. 1642) who was Secretary to the Council of the North. Gentleman of the Privy Chamber 1660; Privy Councillor and Chancellor of the Duchy of Lancaster 1664; made a member of the Tangier Committee in 1665 when his brother-in-law Lord Belasyse was Governor.[1]

Ingram, Mrs. Possibly Ann, wife of Rowland Ingram, of St Olave's, nephew of Sir Arthur. But Rowland's brother Ralph and his family also lived in the same parish.[1]

Inns: *see* Taverns etc.

Ireton. The Ireton who appears at ix.464 in the company of Will Howe, a member of Gray's Inn, could well be Jerman Ireton, admitted to the Inn in Dec. 1664.[1]

Irongate Stairs. The gate guarded access from the Thames to the s.-e. end of Tower Wharf and so to the approach to the Tower. It lay at the downstream end of the Crown's property with St Katharine's below it. The stairs were the landing stairs for the foot of Little Tower Hill. (R)

Ironmongers' Hall, Fenchurch St. On the n. side of the street; a mainly Elizabethan building which escaped the Fire; rebuilt 1748. Again rebuilt after the Second World War.[1]

Isham, Capt. [Henry] (c. 1593–1668). Brother of Sandwich's stepmother, Ann, who married Sir Sidney Mountagu in 1644. He lived in the Canaries and Portugal for most of his life and claimed to have assisted the royalist ambassador to Portugal in 1646–8.[1] By 1657 he was serving under Mountagu (Sandwich), probably as a volunteer in the navy.[2] After petitioning for a number of places in 1660–1 (including that of Navy Victualler) he was appointed Groom of the Privy Chamber to the Queen in 1664.[3]

Isle of Dogs. The peninsula jutting out from the Middlesex bank of the Thames, bounded west by Limehouse Reach, south by Greenwich Reach and east by Blackwall Reach. In the '60s it was marshland valuable mainly for its summer grazing; since then it has included some of the principal London docks. (R)

Islington. A thriving Middlesex village on the road north from the city – the Great North Road – and a favourite resort of Londoners. The bulk of its houses lay between 2 and 3 miles from the Standard on Cornhill, but the parish included straggling clumps of dwellings all the way to its end of the slope of Highgate Hill, and included Newington Green, Kingsland (where Pepys had been put out to nurse as a baby), Stroud Green and Tollington – altogether, in 1664, some 460 houses.[1] Traversed by the New River, it was famous for its pastures, dairies and refreshment houses, as well as for the ponds on which Londoners shot duck. Pepys knew the district well as a boy, when he played with his bow and arrows in the fields and had cakes and ale with his father at the King's Head. Towards the end of the diary period he was in the habit of taking his wife there for an evening airing by coach – 'our Grand Tour' (vii.126). [*See also* Kingsland; Taverns: Katherine Wheel, King's Head, White Lion]

Ivy Lane. This ran from the Strand to the Thames side. Its original line ran approximately under the middle of the modern Shell Mex House.[1] (R)

Jackson, John and Paulina. Pepys's brother-in-law and sister. Paulina (Pall) was born on 18 Oct. 1640 and entered Pepys's household as a servant in Jan. 1661. Pepys writes of her at this time as both ill-natured and ill-favoured. She was not thought worthy of being Elizabeth's waiting-woman and was made to stand in her presence. In the following August when her parents moved to Brampton she was sent there to look after them. By 1664 Pepys was trying to marry her off. Seven potential husbands are named in the diary, including (perhaps surprisingly) Will Hewer, a younger son of Sir Denis Gauden, and Richard Cumberland, a future bishop, but in the end it was a Huntingdonshire farmer who in Feb. 1668 won her hand and the dowry of £600 which Pepys provided. He was John Jackson, of Ellington, close by Brampton – a man 'of no education nor discourse' (ix.56) who had since his father's death in 1652 been farming the land at Parsonage Farm,[1] together with some fields he had inherited in copyhold. He had also inherited from his stepbrother (?brother-in-law) Robert Ensum the 'Tiled House' in Ellington and between 20 and 30 scattered acres of pasture in the parish – all in the hands of tenants.[2] But he was a poor manager and soon after his marriage was in trouble with his landlord, Peterhouse, Cambridge. Pall had virtually to take over his affairs, from time to time consulting her brother John and after John's death, Pepys himself. At the same time she was bringing up her two sons and looking after her father, who lived with her after his wife's death in 1667. In 1677 they all left Ellington and went to live at the Pepys family house at Brampton. Pepys, believing that Jackson was 'not made . . . of stuff capable of any amendment'[3], thought of buying some of the Ellington land from Peterhouse and settling it on Pall and her sons, leaving Jackson with a small annuity. But in Sept. 1680, before the arrangements could be made, Jackson died, leaving debts and chaos. A few weeks later old John Pepys died, and Pepys had no choice but to go to Brampton and spend several unhappy weeks sorting out the affairs of both the Ellington and Brampton estates. In the end he provided Pall with an allowance from the Brampton revenues.[4] By this time she was in poor health and in 1681–2 was in London receiving treatment. She died on 17 Nov. 1689 and was buried at Brampton.

She left two sons: Samuel, Pepys's godchild, born in 1669, and John, born in 1673, who after their father's death had been boarded with the master of Huntingdon School, John Matthews. Samuel was described by Pepys in 1684 as 'healthy, strong but not so forward and pregnant at his books as I could wish'.[5] He was taken from Mr Matthews's care and put to school in London to learn writing and casting up accounts. In 1684 Pepys arranged for him to be sent as a cabin-boy on board an E. Indiaman. He is next heard of in July 1688 as a powder monkey on His Majesty's ship the *Foresight*, just home with Narbrough's squadron from the W. Indies. By 1694, and probably earlier, he was settled ashore, living at the Brampton house and managing Pepys's property there. As godson and next of kin he was made heir to all Pepys's Huntingdonshire property in his will of 2 Aug. 1701. He then thought fit to marry against his uncle's 'positive advice and injunctions'. Nothing is known of the circumstances but in the final will of 12 May 1703 he was cut off with an annuity of £40.[6] He married again, as a widower, in Feb. 1714, Elizabeth Wiggson of Steeple Gidding, Hunts., and was described in the marriage bond as a 'gentleman, of Ellington'.[7]

His younger brother John was more to Pepys's liking. He took to his books and music at an early age, and was sent to Pepys's old college, Magdalene. After taking his bachelor's degree in 1690 he joined his uncle's household in York Buildings and acted as his clerk and amanuensis. It was at this period that Pepys was busy adding to his library, and the young Jackson was sent off abroad in 1699 with a manservant, partly for his own education and partly to make acquisitions for the collection. The tour occupied two years and took in France, Italy, Spain and Portugal. Jackson learnt Italian and Spanish at Pepys's particular behest, saw the Jubilee ceremonies of 1700 in Rome and a bullfight in Madrid, wrote regularly to his patron and dutifully kept a journal. On his return Pepys, being ill, was ready to abandon Westminster for Clapham – all the more readily perhaps because he could leave young Jackson in charge of his household and library in York Buildings. In his final will and its codicil he made him heir to the greater part of his wealth and gave him charge, for his lifetime, of the library. Jackson, acting under the instructions in Pepys's codicil, made purchases to complete the collection, drew up the final recension of the catalogue and chose the room in the new building at Magdalene where it was to be housed after his death. After Pepys's death he moved, with the library (at some date unknown) to the Hewer household at Clapham and in 1712 married Ann Edgley, first cousin once removed of Will Hewer – a union which would have pleased his uncle as much as his brother's mésalliance displeased him.[8] He died intestate in 1723: letters of administration were granted to his widow and his son John in March of that year.[9] [*See also* Brampton; The Diary etc.; Pepys, Robert]

Jackson, ——. The Jackson at vi.164 is clearly a merchant, trading to Tangier – probably Stephen Jackson (d. 1678), who had a connection with Tangier in that his wife was the daughter of John Bland.[1]

Jacombe, [Thomas] (1622–87). A leading Presbyterian divine; Rector of St Martin, Ludgate from 1650 until his extrusion in 1662; thereafter active as an unofficial preacher or lecturer. Known to Cromwell as 'Long Tom of Ludgate'.[1]

Jaggard, [Abraham] (1634–94). Merchant, of Thames St; one of the victualling contractors 1673. He married Sarah Day in 1653. At his death he owned property in Thames St, Love Lane (nr Billingsgate) and Rickmansworth, Herts. Described in 1682 as 'a good Tory'.[1]

James, Duke of York, James II 1685–8 (1633–1701). The only known representations of a room inhabited by Pepys – two drawings of his library in 1693[1] – have a three-quarter length portrait in pride of place over the fireplace. It is, appropriately, the Kneller portrait of James as a naval commander, painted at Pepys's request in 1688. James had occupied a central place in Pepys's official life: they entered and left the service of the navy in the same years, and he was Pepys's master for longer than anyone else.

James's naval career had hardly begun at the Restoration. He had been nominally Lord High Admiral from the age of five, and from 1649 or 1650 had assumed office and received the Admiral's share of prize-money. But Prince Rupert – older by 14 years – had taken command of the royalist flotillas which operated during the period of exile. James had become a soldier and fought with distinction for the Spaniards against the French in the campaign of 1658. But in days when naval commanders were as often as not – as in Rupert's own case – soldiers by training, this was no bad preparation for a naval career. James was made Lord High Admiral by letters patent in June 1660 and stayed in office until forced out in 1673 after his conversion to Catholicism.

Pepys's comments in the diary on his régime amount in all to a favourable verdict. James knew very little about ships in 1660, but he took happily to the sport of yachting, and soon acquired a respectable knowledge of sailing, navigation and, to a lesser degree, of shipbuilding. In addition he already knew something of guns and fortification from his military service abroad. He was not badly equipped therefore to be Lord High Admiral. As a royal Admiral he had the authority to impose discipline, though his habit of appointing to commands gentlemen-captains too haughty to be ordered about often weakened it. As an administrator he proved capable of applying himself to business, as Pepys several times remarks, and –what was really far more important – of giving support to subordinates who were more expert than himself, such as Penn, his adviser on naval warfare, and Coventry and Pepys, his advisers on naval administration. The achievements of his régime in 1660–73, not all of which appear in the diary, were made by these means – the introduction of the rank of volunteer (later the midshipman) in 1661, the wartime victualling arrangements of 1665, and the enquiries into the working of the Navy Office in 1668. That he occasionally or often neglected business is of little consequence. Business was carried on without him, though he might miss a few of the regular Monday morning meetings with the Navy Board. He was by nature not an administrator at all, but a fighting man. He belonged in the tradition of sea-going admirals, and his record for bravery as a soldier was more than sustained by his conduct as a naval commander in the two campaigns he fought in 1665 and 1672.

Pepys's association with James, which was close during his period as Lord High Admiral, did not cease when he withdrew from the admiralty in 1673. James remained Admiral of Scotland, Ireland and the Plantations, and was also allowed, behind the curtain, an informal part in English naval affairs. For that association Pepys was to suffer imprisonment when the political storm broke on James and his friends during the Popish Plot. When Pepys was released in July 1679 James was in the Low Countries where the King had sent him while the worst of the storm should blow itself out, and from there he wrote to Charles urging him to appoint Pepys to the new admiralty commission (composed of politicians) so that at least one expert should be on it.[2] But in vain: Charles was playing a political game and was determined to keep James and his friends out of sight for a while. On his return James was sent off to Scotland as High Commissioner and Pepys accompanied him there on a visit in May 1682. It began disastrously when the Duke's ship was wrecked with great loss of life on a shoal off the Humber, James himself being miraculously preserved. Pepys, travelling in another vessel, was safe, but it was one of the most frightening experiences of his life. Later, attending two council meetings in Edinburgh, Pepys observed the mixture of firmness and clemency with which James (faced by disloyal nobles and rebellious Presbyterians) was governing, though only briefly, that almost ungovernable country.[3]

When James became King in 1685 he retained Pepys in his newly-created post of Secretary for the affairs of the Admiralty, and gave him a virtually free hand. In the interventions James made in everyday administration and his occasional inspections of forts and dockyards he showed all his old interest in the navy and more than his old knowledge of detail. What Pepys thought of the catholicising policies that led to his downfall there is no means of knowing. He was close to the King, often at court and in 1686 accompanied him on his famous western progress,[4] but he was not likely to be in the King's confidence on matters of high policy, and in any case was absorbed in the affairs of his own department. In the diary period he had been disquieted by James's Catholic associations, and there is no reason to believe that his attitude had changed: on the contrary, he now knew from personal experience the force of anti-Catholic prejudice.

The last and fatal crisis of the reign was a naval one, when William of Orange's fleet sailed unchallenged down Channel to land an invading force at Torbay. Throughout it all Pepys was at his post. That James's fleet failed to intercept the invader was no fault of Pepys: all necessary preparations for the fleet had been made: the blame lay with the weather and the bad tactics of Dartmouth the commander. During the final days of the reign Pepys was much in James's company. The King was in fact sitting to Kneller for a portrait commissioned by Pepys – presumably the one that later hung in his library – when he heard news of William's landing on 5 November. On the 17th Pepys was one of the witnesses to James's will, and seizing his opportunity, obtained in return the King's signature to a certificate pledging the government to pay Pepys the debt of £27,000 which Pepys claimed he was owed.[5] On the 31st Pepys arranged for a yacht to carry the baby Prince of Wales over to France.[6] He does not however appear to have been made privy to James's plans to escape to France himself in December.

After James's departure Pepys put himself under the orders first of the provisional government and then of the Prince of Orange. But a

week after William and Mary assumed the throne he resigned. Apart
from two attempts to enter parliament in 1689 and 1690 he was now
content to retire into private life. He never took the oaths to the new
monarchs and paid the penalty in double taxation.[7] His loyalty to
James was simply a matter of his private conscience and much as he
might have liked to see the new régime fall – he particularly disliked
the new admiralty commission which was composed mostly of his old
enemies[8] – he did not conspire against it. After 1690 James lived out his
days at St Germain as a guest and pensioner of Louis XIV, finding
solace in an unending round of religious exercises. Pepys found more
worldly means of solace in a life of learned leisure, and above all, in his
library. That collection came to contain several tokens of his Jacobitism
– besides Kneller's portrait, an engraving of James at prayer;[9] a shorthand note (1695) of evidence confuting the fashionable lie that the
Prince of Wales was supposititious; and a manuscript copy of James's
declaration of 1697 that if restored he would respect the liberties of the
kingdom.[10] In the following year Pepys took advantage of the peace
to send his nephew Jackson (who had also not taken the oaths) to the
continent to buy books, but undertook to his friend Secretary Vernon
not to attempt to put him in touch with St Germain.[11] [For his residences, *see* St James's Palace; Whitehall Palace: Prince's Lodgings]

James, —— (d. 1666). 'Aunt James'; probably a married sister of
Thomas Fenner. Pepys usually met her in his company or that of his
children, and at her death she left bequests to the Joyces and to Sarah
Giles.[1] There are some indications in the diary that she may have lived
in Wales.[2]

Jefferies, ——. A distant relative: Edith Pepys (b. 1591), first cousin
of Pepys's father, had married John Williams of Cottenham and their
daughter had married one Jeffrey: possibly the Westminster
apothecary 'Jefferies' whom Pepys refers to as a 'kinsman'. He was
Thomas Jefferies, made free of the Society of Apothecaries of London
in 1652 and married at St Olave's Jewry in 1665.[1]

Jefferys, Capt. Naval officer. Probably John Jefferies or Geffery who
had held commissions as captain since 1653. He is possibly the man of
these names who held commissions as lieutenant and captain in the
Second Dutch War.[1]

Jegon, [Robert]. A J.P. of Westminster. He was one of the justices to
whom the King gave plate in recognition of their services during the
Plague.[1]

Jenifer, Capt. [James] (d. 1677). A protégé of Sandwich; he held
three commands 1664–6 and was made captain of the Queen's yacht in
1671. His spirited journal of a voyage to Lisbon 1672–3 is in the Pepys
Library.[1]

Jenkins, [Eliezer]. Of Westminster; Pepys's footboy 1660. His father was possibly Nicholas Jenkins, Bailiff of Westminster 1657–60, but there were other families of that name living there at the time.[1]

Jennens (Jennings), Sir William, kt 1665 (d. 1690). A naval commander in almost continuous employment 1661–88. 'A proud, idle fellow' (ix.430), he was in trouble in 1665 for ill-treating his sailing-master, in 1670 was imprisoned for having his wife aboard, and in 1688 was fined for brawling. He then fled to France and fought in the French navy against the English in the Battle of Beachy Head, 1690.[1]

Jermyn, Henry, cr. Baron Jermyn 1643, Earl of St Albans 1660 (?1604–84). A courtier and diplomat 'of only middling accomplishments, who [rose] from nothing to the possession of considerable means which, by losing heavily at cards and keeping open house, he made to appear even greater than they actually were' (Gramont). He was attached to the service of Queen Henrietta-Maria from 1628, and was rumoured (wrongly) to have secretly married her in her widowhood. Ambassador to France 1644, 1660, 1667–9; Lord Chamberlain 1671–4.[1] [*See also* St James's Fields]

Jermyn, Henry, cr. Baron Dover 1685, Earl of Dover 1689 (c. 1636–1708). Nephew and heir of St Albans. Courtier and debauchee; 'the favoured of Venus and the desperate duellist' (Gramont) – counting among his conquests Anne Hyde and Lady Castlemaine. He was Master of Horse to the Duke of York; and when the Duke became King was made Gentleman of his Bedchamber, Lieut-General of his bodyguard, Privy Councillor and Treasury Commissioner. He accompanied him into exile but made his peace with William in 1692. His wife was the daughter of Sir Edmund Pooley.[1]

Jervas, [Richard]. Barber, of New Palace Yard; his shop was between the Bull Head and Leg taverns, and his assessment (5s. 4d.) for the Royal Aid (1664–5) suggests a certain prosperity. He gave evidence in King's Bench in 1660 against another barber accused of helping regicides to escape to Holland.[1] His name disappears from the parish ratebooks in 1668–9.[2]

Jessop, [William] (c. 1603–75). One of the most important public officials of the Commonwealth. Throughout virtually the whole of his career he acted also as man of business to members of the Rich and Devereux families. He entered the public service as clerk, later secretary, to the Providence Island Company. After the outbreak of the Civil War he became an Admiralty official (secretary to Warwick 1642–5 and to the Admiralty Committee 1645–53), after which he moved to the Council of State (as Assistant-Clerk in 1653, and Clerk 1654–9, 1659–60). He was also, from 1648 until his death, Deputy-Clerk of the Duchy of Lancaster and from c. 1650 Registrar of the Duchy Court. In the Convention he was Assistant-Clerk of the Parliaments (i.e. Clerk of the House of Commons). After the Restoration, apart from

a spell as Secretary to the Brooke House Committee in 1668, he concerned himself with Duchy business. Like Pepys and other public
officials, he used shorthand.[1]

Johnson, Sir Henry, kt 1680 (1623–83). Shipbuilder. After an
apprenticeship to his cousin Phineas Pett he moved c. 1652 from Deptford to Blackwall, and there in 1656 purchased the E. India Company's
dockyard, where he built both E. Indiamen and men-of-war. (He built
five 3rd-rates 1660–88.)[1] According to Pepys's comment in his *Naval
Minutes* he was 'never famous for building the best or biggest ships'.[2] He
sat in the First Exclusion Parliament (1679) for his native town, Aldeburgh. Pepys composed the letter from the King and Duke of York
recommending him to the electors.[3]

Jolliffe (Jolly), [George]. Physician, of Garlick Hill, London; M.D.
(Cantab.) 1652. He attended Pepys after his operation in March 1658
and died in the following November.[1]

Jolliffe, [John] (1613–80). A prominent merchant in the E. India,
Levant and Muscovy trades; a member of the Council of Trade 1660;
elected M.P. for Heytesbury, 1660, 1661; Master of the Skinners'
Company 1661–2. Some of his correspondence with Sandwich
survives.[1]

Jones, Anne. Of St Olave's parish; possibly Anne, wife of John.[1]

Jones, Col. [Philip] (?1618–74). Leader of the parliamentary cause in
S. Wales; Councillor of State 1653; Controller of the Household to
both Oliver and Richard Cromwell; and one of Cromwell's peers in
1657. He made his peace with Charles II and was appointed Sheriff of
Glamorgan in 1671.[1]

Jordan, Sir Joseph, kt 1665 (1603–85). He served in the parliamentary
navy 1642–8, and after a short period abroad, resumed his naval career
in 1650. He was a flag-officer in the First Dutch War and in Blake's
expedition (1655) against Tunis and Algiers. In 1664 he was brought
into service again and served as a flag-officer in the Second and Third
Dutch Wars. He took a prominent, and controversial, part in the Battle
of Sole Bay (1672) in which Sandwich was killed. It was alleged that he
had deliberately chosen to expose Sandwich to danger in order to
protect the Duke of York. He was granted a pension after the war and
lived in retirement to a ripe old age.[1]

Jowles, [Henry]. Of Chatham; naval lieutenant; husband of Rebecca,
daughter of John Allen, Clerk of the Ropeyard, Chatham.[1]

Jowles, Capt. [Valentine]. A master's mate in 1658, commissioned
captain to the *Wexford* 1659 and the *Dolphin* 1660. He had been recommended to Mountagu in 1660 by one T. Bayles, also a master's mate,
who went on to ask for a lieutenant's place for his wife's aunt's half-
brother.[1]

Joyce, William and Anthony. Tallow chandlers. They were

brothers who had married sisters: Mary and Kate Fenner respectively (cousins of Pepys). The whole 'crew' were among Pepys's least congenial relatives. Their father William Joyce, of St Sepulchre's parish (d. 1658), was a citizen and freeman of the Leathersellers' Company, though probably also a tallow chandler by trade.[1] The sons were made free of the Leathersellers' by patrimony in 1654, and inherited their father's business. William, the elder, conducted his trade from the Eagle and Child on Snow Hill, near the Holborn conduit, probably his father's premises (rated on seven hearths). He seems to have prospered; in 1665 he had a house in Russell St, Covent Garden, and in the poll-tax of 1667 paid tax on three servants. His landlords on Snow Hill, the Saddlers' Company, had to force him by legal action to rebuild after the Fire.[2]

His brother Anthony was less successful and according to Pepys was fit for no employment. He owned several houses (presumably by inheritance); some were destroyed in the Fire but seven survived. In 1664 he took up innkeeping (at the Three Stags, Holborn conduit), but failed to prosper and in 1668 died after attempting to drown himself. He was then living in St Giles's-without-Cripplegate.[3]

Joyce: *see* Norton, Joyce

Keene, ——. Possibly Edward Keane, who with his wife Margaret had been living in St Olave's parish since at least 1648.[1]

Kelsey, Capt. [John] (d. by 1688). Naval officer; he held eight commissions 1665–72.[1]

Kelyng, Sir John, kt 1662 (c. 1607–71). Lord Chief Justice, King's Bench 1665–71. An able and learned judge but a stranger to judicious moderation, and well known for his conservative opinions and rough manners. The diary has several examples of his brusque conduct in court. As a King's Serjeant he had taken part with relish in the prosecution of the regicides. Clarendon (who engaged him to draft the bill of uniformity) admired his learning and excused his manners on the grounds of his sufferings as a royalist.[1] When he died – of a 'lethargy' – a newsletter wondered that 'a man of so bilious a complexion should have so phlegmatic a conveyance to the other world'.[2]

Kembe, Harry. Navy Office messenger; of Boar's Head Yard, Westminster.[1]

Kempthorne, Sir John, kt 1670 (1620–79). He was bred to sea in an E. Indiaman and held 12 commissions 1664–79, serving as flag-officer in 1666 and 1672–3. He became Navy Commissioner at Portsmouth in 1675, and at Chatham in 1679.[1]

Kensington. A village in Middlesex on the Bristol road some 1½ miles due west of Piccadilly. It was then on the outer edge of the built-up area of London and a place of resort for Londoners. (The tavern Pepys visited was probably the Talbot, in the gravel-pits.) With the increase of coaches as opposed to river travel, it came to house a growing number of the well-to-do, either in the main village or in the hamlets or big houses lying within the parish, such as Knightsbridge, Little Chelsea, Earl's Court and Holland House. In 1664 it had some 200 houses.[1] (R)

Kent St. Now Tabard St, Southwark, running south-east from St George's church to the Canterbury and Dover high road (now the Old Kent Road): 'a miserable, wretched, poor place' (vi.279). Before the formation of Great Dover St it was the highway to Deptford and Greenwich. The hearth-tax returns for 1664 show that of the 376 houses assessed in the street and its alléys and other offshoots, 324 were too small or poor to be taxed.[1] It remained a notably poverty-stricken neighbourhood until far into the 19th century. (R)

Kentish Knock. Shoal off the North Foreland.

Killigrew, Henry (1613–1700). Brother of Thomas the dramatist. From 1660 chaplain to Charles II and Almoner to the Duke of York; appointed Canon of Westminster 1660 and Master of the Savoy 1663.[1]

Killigrew, Henry (1637–1705). 'Young Killigrew'; son of Thomas the dramatist. Page to the King 1661; Groom of the Bedchamber to the Duke of York 1662, and to the King 1674; 1694 Jester to the King. One of the most disreputable of the court sparks. 'A most notorious lyer', according to the King; twice banished from the court.[1]

Killigrew, Sir Peter (d. 1668). King's messenger during the Interregnum; Gentleman of the Privy Chamber in 1663.[1]

Killigrew, Thomas (1612–83). Dramatist, theatrical manager, rake and wit. Employed as a diplomatic agent 1651–2; Groom of the Bedchamber to the King 1660; Master of the Revels 1673. Very free in his mockery of the King. For his work for the theatre *see* Theatre. Pepys kept a copy of his *Comedies and tragedies* (1664).[1]

Killigrew, Sir William (d. 1695). Elder brother of Thomas the dramatist, and himself a dramatist and courtier.[1]

Kinaston, [Edward]. Merchant dealing in victuals for Tangier.[1]

King, Col. [Edward]. Commissioner for paying off the armed forces, 1660–1.[1]

King, [Thomas] (d. 1688). M.P. for Harwich Jan.–Apr. 1659, 1661–Jan. 79. Notorious for his corruption – in the Fishery business, as hearth-tax assessor and as M.P.[1]

King, [William]. Clerk (?) to the Treasurers at War, 1660.[1]

King, [William] (1624–80). ('one Smith' in error in text.) Composer and organist of New College, Oxford.[1] (Lu)

King, [William] (c. 1602–c. 71). Vicar of Chobham, Surrey, from 1626; Rector of Ashtead from 1643 until his ejection for nonconformity in 1662. He continued to live at Ashtead and in 1669 was preaching at Ewell and Pirbright.[1]

King St, Westminster. The most spacious and busy street in Westminster – thronged with traffic and full of the inns and taverns needed by those coming to Whitehall, the law courts or parliament. It had once extended from Charing Cross southward to Westminster Palace, past York House, the London house of the Archbishops of York. Henry VIII, on Wolsey's downfall, obtained possession of York House, and added to it lands and buildings on both sides of King St. Since it was impossible to close or divert the common highway of the street, covered access from one side of the palace to the other was provided by building the Holbein and King St Gates, whose gatehouses bridged the street at first floor level. York House was renamed Whitehall, and the street to the north of the King St Gate gradually acquired the name of Whitehall. The remainder is now known as Parliament St, the name given during the 18th century to a street then opened parallel to and east of King St. Subsequent street widenings have removed the houses which once separated the two thoroughfares. King St Gate was pulled down in 1723 and the Holbein Gate in 1760. [Map: below, pp. 480–1] (R)

Kingdon, Capt. [Richard]. A financial expert, and a colleague of Ashley (Shaftesbury) at the Prize Office, where he was a Commissioner 1665–7. (He had had a similar post in 1656.) After service in the parliamentary army he had done well out of speculation in confiscated Irish land, and had also gathered to himself several lucrative posts – in 1659 as auditor for the army accounts, in 1666 as Comptroller of the Excise and in 1669 as farmer of the Irish revenue.[1]

Kingsland. A Middlesex hamlet on the road from Bishopsgate to Ware, about 2½ miles from the Standard on Cornhill, where Pepys had been put out to nurse at Goody Lawrence's and where later he and his brother Tom were boarded out. An area of grazing land and market gardens.

The King's Theatre. Adapted from Charles Gibbons's Tennis Court (built in 1634) in Vere St, Clare Market, close to the s.-w. corner of Lincoln's Inn Fields. (Vere St ceased to exist as such following the making of Kingsway and Aldwych.) In 1663 the company moved to a theatre it had built on land leased in Bridges St (now Catherine St) just west of Drury Lane, giving their first performance on 7 May. There it was often termed the 'Drury Lane Theatre', since the old Cockpit Theatre had been near the Lane, or the 'Covent Garden Theatre', as the Garden was hard by. It was burnt down on 25 Jan. 1672, and the Company moved to Lisle's Tennis Court, Portugal Row, which had housed the Duke's Company until its move on 9 Nov. 1671 to Dorset Gardens. The theatre in Bridges St was rebuilt and opened again on 26 March 1674, when the King's Company returned to it. [*See also* Theatre] (R)

Kinnersley, young. Probably a son of Clement, who was Keeper of the Protector's Wardrobe in 1656 and Yeoman of the King's Wardrobe in 1661.[1]

Kinward, [Thomas]. Master-Joiner, Whitehall, Sept. 1660–d.82; he carried out a great deal of the work done there and in other royal buildings in Charles's reign.[1]

Kipps, ——. Thomas, Seal-bearer to the Lord Chancellor.[1]

Kirby, Capt. [Robert]. Commissioned captain in the Commonwealth navy; held three commands after 1660; killed in action 1665.[1]

Kirton, [Joshua], (d. 1667). Pepys's principal bookseller before the Fire when he lost everything – shop, stock and home. His shop (on the n. side of Paul's Churchyard) was assessed on five hearths. His 'kinsman' was William Kirton (freeman of the Stationers' Company by patrimony, 1664).[1] The apprentice mentioned by Pepys was Richard Randall.[2]

Kite. Pepys's maternal family, of whom little is known. His mother was Margaret Kite, who married John Pepys in 1626. She is known to have had three sisters and one brother. Of the sisters, Katherine (d. 1661) married Thomas Fenner; Lettice married, first —— Haines, and secondly —— Howlett; and Ellen (alive in 1664) appears to have been unmarried. The brother was William, a Whitechapel butcher, who died in 1652. His widow Julian married Elias or Ellis Clarke, and died in 1661, Pepys and Thomas Fenner acting as her executors. Her daughter Peg Kite (who had received a legacy of £80 from her father) was married in 1661 to a weaver, whom Pepys does not name, but calls 'a beggarly rogue' (ii.209).

Pepys states (v.360) that his parents were married at Newington, Surrey. No trace of their marriage has however been found in the registers of the parish church, St Mary's. All available facts about the Kites, in fact, suggest that their associations were with Newington Green, Mdx, north of the river – Pepys's mother had a sister there in 1664; she recalled 'old stories' of Islington, sent Pepys as a baby to Kingsland, worked for Lady Vere of Clapton and had a brother (the butcher) in Whitechapel. But no trace of the marriage has been found at Newington Green or Islington.[1]

Knapp, [John]. Self-styled physician. There were many so-called quacks in practice in London – some of them medically qualified and only lacking membership of the Royal College of Physicians. Knapp however had no qualifications and falsely claimed to have been at Cambridge.[1]

Knepp (Knip), [Elizabeth]. Actress, singer and dancer in the King's Company 1664–?78; a friend of Elizabeth Pearse and of Pepys (who dubbed her Bab Allen after one of her songs). She was born Elizabeth Carpenter and married Christopher Knepp (whom Pepys calls a 'jockey' i.e. horse-dealer) at Knightsbridge in 1659. In 1668 she was twice arrested at the Lord Chamberlain's charge for misdemeanours at the Theatre Royal.[1]

Knight, [John]. Appointed Serjeant-Surgeon to the King 1660; and to the fleet in the Second and Third Dutch Wars; Master of the Barber-Surgeons' Company 1663–4.[1]

Knight, Sir John, kt 1663 (d. 1684). Of Bristol; alderman, merchant and navy agent; M.P. for Bristol 1660–81. To be distinguished from Sir John Knight, also of Bristol (M.P. 1689–95, d. 1718), his first cousin once removed. He lived in Temple parish.[1]

Knightley, [Richard] (d. 1695). Rector of Charwelton, Northants. 1663–95; Canon of Durham 1675–95; Rector of Byfield, Northants. 1688–95.[1]

Knightley, [Robert], kt 1677 (d. 1699). A merchant long resident in Seething Lane; also of Ashtead, Surrey; churchwarden of St Olave's in 1667; and a Common Councilman in 1675. Pepys consulted him about the history of customs dues when gathering material for his history of the navy.[1]

Knightsbridge: *see* Kensington

Kynaston, [Edward] (?1640–1712). In his day perhaps the best-known boy actor playing female parts; a member of Rhodes's company at the Cockpit Theatre 1659–60 and of the King's Company and its successors 1662–99.[1]

Lacy, [John] (d. 1681). A leading actor and dancer and a shareholder in the King's Company from 1662; originally trained as a dancer. He specialised in comic and dialect rôles, and also wrote plays. A favourite both of Pepys and of Charles II.[1]

Lamb, [James] (1599–1664). Canon of Westminster 1660–4; Rector of St Andrew's, Holborn 1663–4; a distinguished orientalist.[1]

Lambert, [David]. Lieutenant of the *Naseby* 1660; commissioned captain to the *Norwich* 1661 and the *Hopeful* 1664.[1]

Lambert, [James]. Served in the Commonwealth navy; captain of the Duke of York's yacht *Anne* 1662; killed in action 1665.[1]

Lambert, John (1619–83). One of the ablest of Cromwell's generals. In 1657 he broke with the Protector when Cromwell showed signs of assuming the title of king, and was disgraced. With the collapse of Richard Cromwell's régime and the return of the Rump in the spring of 1659, he was restored to his commands and became the leading member of the Committee of Safety, the executive organ of government. He crushed Booth's royalist rising in August, but in October he and his fellow officers in the Council of the Army destroyed the only hope left to the revolutionary cause by quarrelling with the Rump and preventing it from sitting. Support in the army and navy as well as among civilians fell away from him when Monck intervened to bring back the

Rump (Jan. 1660), and he was arrested in March. His last fling was to escape from the Tower and attempt a rebellion. His troops refused to fight and he was taken prisoner at Daventry (22 April). He was tried on a charge of high treason for his part in the original rebellion against Charles I, and found guilty, but the death sentence was commuted to one of life imprisonment. He lived on Guernsey (1662–7) and then on St Nicholas Island in Plymouth Sound until his death. Pepys visited him there briefly in Aug. 1683 on his way to Tangier.[1] The Lady Lambert at ix.215 is perhaps unlikely to be his wife since she died in 1676.[2]

Lambeth. A large straggling village on the Surrey bank of the Thames opposite Westminster and communicating with it by ferry. Pepys set off from Lambeth when making coach journeys to Portsmouth, and during the Plague travelled to Whitehall via London Bridge and Lambeth ferry in order to avoid the streets of the city and Westminster. Lambeth marsh separated it from Southwark and, the whole area being low-lying, concentrated building was confined to a small strip round the Palace and the parish church of St Mary, with a scattering further upstream in the manor of Fox Hall (Vauxhall). Elizabeth occasionally sent the household linen to be dried in the fields there. [For the Palace, *see* vi.164, n.2][1]

Lane, Betty and Doll: *see* Martin, Betty; Powell, Rowland

Langford, [William]. Pepys's tailor after 1664, when he took over Tom Pepys's house and business. He paid tax on five hearths as against Tom's four. A Henry Langford made the inventory of Tom's goods on his death and was listed as the householder in 1666.[1]

Langley,——. Government clerk 1661, 1664; possibly related to Julian Langley, in 1663 a messenger of the Chamber.[1]

LANGUAGE [1]

Hobbes, the most eminent English philosopher in Pepys's day, held that 'The first author of *speech* was God himself, that instructed Adam how to name such creatures as he presented to his sight'. He maintained that speech was 'the most noble and profitable invention of all'; and considered it as essential for any process of self-discovery, as the means by which mankind achieved self-consciousness, and as an index of wisdom or folly: 'as men abound in copiousness of language, so they become more wise, or more mad than ordinary'.[2] Many of the early endeavours of the Royal Society were directed towards the creation of a universal language; these found their fullest, though ultimately unfulfilled, expression in John Wilkins's *Essay towards a real character, and a philosophical language* (1668).[3] Pepys himself is our witness that, with Hobbes, Wilkins maintained that 'were it not for speech, man would be a very mean creature', and the impingement of Wilkins's concerns on Pepys's cast of mind is implicit in his notion of the relation asserted in the title of his book, between language and orthography: Wilkins believed that a universal language would naturally be expressed in a universal shorthand, the two having as their common foundation the Deity's immutable ordering of Nature, philosophically elucidated. Wilkins's aspiration was towards the ideal; a more empirical approach was adopted by his contemporary, the naturalist John Ray, who collected proverbs and dialect usages in the hope that he might adduce from them general principles of human behaviour.

Such concerns were naturally congenial to Pepys. The cognisance of terms of art – such as the 'seamen's manner of singing when they sound the depths' – was a necessary part of his business. In 1660 we find him studying a *Seaman's grammar and dictionary*, and consulting Capt. Cuttance to the same end. But it was pleasure and curiosity that impelled him to 'satisfy' himself from John Bowles 'in some terms of Hunting', and to record his delight in hearing, at his coachmaker's, some 'poor people . . . call their fat child "punch"; which pleased me mightily, that word being become a word of common use for all that is thick and short'. In setting down his reactions to plays and poems he frequently singles out the language for particular comment, distinguishing between the 'conceit, wit, design and language' of a play, concurring with Mennes in his opinion of the 'many fine expressions' in Chaucer, approving Jonson's *Every man in his humour* for its 'propriety of speech', and his *Catiline* for its 'much good sense and language', but finding in Fletcher's *A wife for a month* 'no great wit or language' and displaying evident exasperation at 'a little book . . . concerning English Gentry' which, though written in 'good words', did not contain, from beginning to end, 'one entire and regular sentence'.

This sensitivity went with an acute awareness of the day-to-day importance of an adequate command of language. He took an evident pleasure in commending a letter as 'a very well writ one', and in noting that a woman used 'the best language that ever I heard in my life'. He urged the necessity of good expression on his relatives. In the diary he gave vent to his impatience at 'poor discourse and frothy' and recorded how Mr Bland, the mayor of Tangier, 'spoiled his business' before the Committee for the colony because of his ineptitude 'in the use of grammar and knowledge how to tell a man's tale'. Pepys himself owed his triumphant defence of the Navy Office in 1668 in large measure to the excellence of his language, being told that 'the Sollicitor generall did protest that he thought I spoke the best of any man in England'. Ben Jonson, whom Pepys held in high regard, had asserted that 'Language most shows a man: Speak, that I may see thee. It springs out of the most retired and inmost parts of us, and is the image of the

parent of it, the mind. No glass renders a man's form or likeness so true
as his speech'.⁴ Just such an assumption underlies Pepys's praise of Sir
William Petty, 'who in discourse is methinks one of the most rational
men that ever I heard speak with a tongue, having all his notions the
most distinct and clear'.

Pepys's exercise of language was not restricted to the vernacular. In
the diary he displays no false modesty about his ability as a linguist,
and as a linguist his natural aptitude had benefited from local advantages,
deriving from his education, his family circumstances and his environment. At St Paul's the teaching of Latin was, as in all grammar schools
of the period, the basis of the curriculum; he would also have learned
some Greek there (he gave a copy of Stephens's *Thesaurus Graecae
Linguae* to the school in 1662); and his residence in Cambridge coincided
with a resurgence of interest in the language in the university, exemplified by the scholarship of Henry More of Christ's and Joseph Duport of
Trinity and intimately bound up with the influential achievements of
the Cambridge Platonists. It is also noteworthy that one of his closest
Cambridge friends, Richard Cumberland, subsequently Bishop of
Peterborough, was a redoubtable student both of Greek and Hebrew –
the latter a subject in which Pepys was sufficiently interested to buy a
grammar in 1660. Pepys's Latin was convenient as a vehicle for communication with Admiral Opdam and other foreigners whose native
tongue he did not know; it was also the medium for some of the reading that he most relished, above all Bacon's *Faber Fortunae*. His brother
John wrote to him in Latin, to Pepys's satisfaction, but his cousin
Thomas Pepys, of Hatcham, in his work as a Justice of the Peace,
experienced the disadvantages of not knowing the language. Pepys
also took an evident pleasure in teaching Latin, and commented tartly
on those who attempted more in that language than they could
adequately accomplish. He could be equally critical of 'False Greek' in
a sermon.

Nevertheless it is probable that Pepys took more pride in his accomplishments in the modern than in the classical languages. In 1669 he
dined at the Spanish Embassy and reflected that the Oxford scholar in
a Doctor of Law's gown also present, 'though a gentle sort of scholar,
yet sat like a fool for want of French or Spanish' and, moreover, spoke
Latin 'like an Englishman'; Pepys, by contrast, was able to make much
use of his French and Spanish, 'to my great content'. Having a French
wife, who evidently continued to use her native language a good deal,
must have helped; but it is also significant that his brother Thomas's
deathbed ravings were in French. When Sandwich wished to discuss
court gossip with Pepys in front of the servants, French was the natural
recourse, and Pepys was sufficiently adept at writing French to conduct
a correspondence in the language with Lady Wright. His Spanish may

seem a more surprising accomplishment; it was undoubtedly one in which he took some pride. He would most certainly not have acquiesced in Samuel Butler's opinion that the study of Greek and Latin affords a man 'a very pitiful Returne of Knowledge in comparison of the intollerable Paines and Industry that is spent upon It . . .' and that this 'slavery . . . does but render him the more unready at his owne language';[5] but he no less certainly believed in the value of the 'modern languages', an accomplishment which, according to Anthony Wood, had played a substantial part in the advancement of the early Caroline courtier, Endymion Porter, and which greatly signified in the career of a diplomat who successfully served both Charles I and II, Sir Richard Fanshawe. Pepys was not unusual in his possession of Spanish books; several English collectors and libraries had comparatively large holdings of these, and Spanish literature was also well represented in English translation. Pepys's Spanish gave him at least some understanding of Portuguese. He lacked Italian, but in the 17th century, although Italian was of obvious importance in the world of connoisseurship and the arts, Spanish, supported by the gold, silver and spices of Spain's still vast empire, occupied a commanding position in the mercantile and commercial world. Spain, moreover, retained her Italian possessions, and it is appropriate that, at the very beginning of the diary, we should find Pepys reading a Spanish book on Rome.

Pepys's language in the diary is the immediate and ultimate testimony to the liveliness of his linguistic concerns. Diaries are not always such reliable guides to usage, or indeed habit of mind, as they might at first seem. The degree of self-consciousness implied in the writing of a readable diary carries with it an evident ambivalence. Colonel Byng, in 1789, illustrates the difficulty: 'As I proceed in Tour Writing . . . I get Bold and Vain, Believing that all Diaries become Valuable from Age; tho' I often Revert to some sad Diaries I have read, or heard of, on one of a punctual woman, who wrote:

> Friday. Buried my poor dead Husband.
> Saturday. Turned my *Ass* to Grass.

and tho' this is ludicrous, yet with over Study, and devoid of Nature, what does Tour Writing or any other Writing become?'[6] In his awareness of 'naturalness' as the virtue proper to diary writing Byng unavoidably qualifies the sense of 'natural'. He is extremely conscious of how 'sadly do Recollection and Invention Clash' – a point that will ring true for any reader of Dr de Beer's edition of John Evelyn, where Evelyn's dependence on aids to recollection is repeatedly demonstrated. Evelyn's whole intention in his diary – at least in its final, revised form – that it might contribute to his descendants' knowledge of the world, suggests the preclusion of certain kinds of naturalness.

Ralph Thoresby, in 1708, 'read in my dear and pious father's diary in
secret' but such discretion in succeeding generations was scarcely to be
presumed by any diarist.[7] Pepys's own notion that his diary might
come to his aid in the event of an arraignment in Parliament provides
an obvious demonstration of the restricted 'naturalness' of the form.
Yet his regrets after he had revealed its existence to an acquaintance
argue the other way, and some such oscillation is apparent in the text
itself. At 19 Oct. 1663 he permits himself a reflection on death which in
its literariness recalls Evelyn's set pieces; it is at a far cry from the
conversational idiom with its characteristic use of 'well' as a resumptive,
of 'Well, by and by the child is brought, and christened Katherine'. Yet
it is a fact of death that, reflected upon, it tends to present itself in a
literary mode, and such passages in Pepys are comparatively uncommon.

In general the evidence for Pepys's style in the diary, so clearly
distinct from his official style and from even the most familiar of his
letters, as an echo of his speaking voice, is persuasive. There are features
to be associated primarily with the pressures imposed by the actual
keeping of a diary, above all the frequent ellipses: 'this night my boy
Wainman, as I was in my chamber, overheard him let off some Gunpowder'; 'talking and eating and drinking a good ham of English
bacon'; 'eat and drank a Jole of salmon at the Rose and Crown'; Knipp
'sings as well and is the best company, in the world' ('as anybody',
understood); 'down with' (for 'goes down well with'); 'then home,
between vexed and joyed' ('being' understood); 'though the Swedish
Agent was there with all the vehemence he could to save the goods . . . ';
'where upon a fine couple of pigeon, a good supper'; 'who is it that the
weight of the war depends'; 'but the interest which I wholly lost while
in my trunk' (where the inherent absurdity is a demonstration of the
lack of self-consciousness). Such ellipses can occur in phrases and even
words: 'so' for 'so long as'; 'refrain it' for 'refrain from it'; 'stay' for
'stay for'; 'which' for 'about which'; 'faintness' for 'faintheartedness'.
But they do not predominate, and indeed it is their absence that can
so often authenticate the ring of the spoken word, the convincing
casualness of: 'I protest it is very strange to observe' or 'I never could
have thought there had been upon earth a man so little curious in the
world as he is'. But it is not the case that redundancy is a defining feature
of Pepys's speaking voice: there is the directness of 'I see what he
means', the immediacy of 'wrapping myself up warm', the tautological
and idiomatic naturalness of 'miserable hot weather all night it was', the
frequent and revelatory apostrophes such as 'But Lord', and the un-
intentional admission of a habit of thought in 'with horrour I speak it',
'I protest it is very strange to observe', or (of a watch) 'and am apt to
think with myself: how could I be so long without one?'. When

Pepys commended his own performance in speaking in the House of Commons in defence of the Navy Office in 1668 he noted that he had developed his argument 'with full scope and all my reason free about me, as if it had been at my own table', and the excellencies and intimacies of table-talk are never far removed from his most compelling writing in the diary, whether in the ironical observation of others (Balty 'as fine as hands could make him') or himself ('practising to sing which is now my great trade'), the delighted discovery of the apposite word (Mr Milles's 'nibbling' at the Book of Common Prayer), or even an inelegant but effective superfluity of phrase ('a most horrid malicious bloody flame').

The faults of Pepys's style are those of haste and informality. Confusing concatenations of negatives are liable to occur: 'This day my wife killed her turkey that Mr [Sheply] gave her, that came out of Zeeland with my Lord; and could not get her maid Jane by no means at any time to kill anything'; Mr Chetwind who had 'not dined no more than myself'; 'so that I could not sleep hardly all night'; 'The Duke of York gone down to the fleet; but, all suppose, not with intent to stay there – as it is not fit, all men conceive, he should'; and, perhaps a reflection of the extremity of the occasion (and also an illustration of his habit of ellipsis), 'I lacked a pot but there was none, and bitter cold, so was forced to rise and piss in the chimny, and to bed again'. The positive aspect of this tendency is to be detected in Pepys's inventive use of 'un'-forms; in the 17th century 'un' confusingly interchanged with modern 'in', so we find 'uncapable', 'unsufferable', but 'inmethodical'; however, 'unbespeak' and 'uninvite' strongly suggest Pepys's own coinage, and tally with his innovative compounds using over: 'overworking', 'over-wrought', 'over-handsome'. The sequence of tenses sometimes fails to follow truly; the same is true of number, as in: 'And so we dined and was very merry. At 5 a-clock we set out again . . . and were very merry all the way'. Adjectives, adverbs and phrases are on occasion left floating: in 1666 business (and the need to be seen to be minding it) 'is now so great a burden upon my mind night and day, that I do not enjoy myself in the world almost'; during the Fire, 'the poor pigeons I perceive were loath to leave their houses, but hovered about the windows till they were some of them burned, their wings, and fell down'. But redundancy, in general, did not concern Pepys, who was apparently unabashed by 'beautifullest', 'activest' (recorded as nonce by the *Oxford English Dictionary*), or 'the justice himself very hardly escaped'.

Pepys's linguistic criteria, and his linguistic agility, are nowhere better demonstrated than in his epithets for the sermons that he enjoyed or endured. He could admire 'a good plain sermon', a 'most excellent and eloquent sermon', a 'ready, learned, and good sermon', 'the best

sermon for goodness – oratory without affectation or study – that ever
I heard in my life', 'a very pretty, neat, sober, honest sermon', 'a very
good and seraphick kind of sermon', 'a very excellent and persuasive,
good and moral sermon'. He could equally be abruptly dismissive of
'a cold sermon', 'a poor dry sermon', 'a dull drowzy sermon', 'a lazy
poor sermon', 'a mean sorry sermon', 'a long and sad sermon', a 'flat
dead sermon, both from matter and manner of delivery'. These are the
comments of a man for whom the linguistic dress of thought was a
matter of constant concern, and whose report of Mrs Turner's tirade on
21 May 1667 reveals an unerring ear for the tenor of the spoken word.

It seems probable that, in the course of the last three hundred years,
the literary language has been far more variable than the spoken
language. Pepys uses a succession of past participles which are instantly
recognisable as archaic: 'ris' for 'rose', 'durst' for 'dared', 'lien' for
'layed', 'ketched' for 'caught', 'drow' for 'drew', 'drownded' for
'drowned'. These we can associate with his innumerable spelling
variants, which illustrate the arbitrariness of the relation between
orthography and pronunciation: 'e' for 'i' in 'engenious', 'enveigh',
'entend', 'endeed', but 'i' for 'e' in 'imbroidery', in 'sense' for 'since',
and 'i' for 'a' in 'imbassador'. A similar pattern emerges with 'c', 't'
and 's': thus we have 'arbitracion', 'corrupcion', 'objeccions', 'particion',
'stacioner', but 'lissen' for 'listen', 'pention' for 'pension', 'iching' for
'itching' and 'centry' for 'sentry'. Sometimes the spelling indicates a
change in pronunciation as in the open vowels of 'guarden' for 'garden'
and 'guarrison' for 'garrison', or the three syllables implied in
'Colonell'/'Coll'. Many of the forms suggested by Pepys's spelling
still survive in dialect usage, notably 'th' for 'd', as in 'blather' for
'bladder', 'lather' for 'ladder', and its inversion, as in 'farding' for
'farthing'. Other examples are 'fallow' for 'follow', 'perticular' for
'particular', 'fur' for 'far', and 'spile' for 'spoil'. Occasionally the
orthography can be etymologically revealing, as in 'Akehorne' which,
if some way from the Anglo-Saxon *æcern*, is much further away from
the modern form, with its logically attractive but false association with
corn, though 'sparrowgrass' for 'asparagus' achieves just the opposite
effect. Again a phonetic spelling such as 'piattza' can take us nearer to
the actual sound of a foreign word than its correct representation in the
conventional orthography of its language of origin, whilst the fact
that a word is an importation, though we now would be unlikely to
notice it as such, is often signalled orthographically, as in 'attaque' for
'attack', 'choque' for 'shock', or 'banquiers' for 'bankers'. Pepys still on
occasion spells out the old form of the genitive, as in 'Mr Philips his
chamber' or 'Mr Pepys his meaning', and can prove disconcerting in
his use of prepositions, as when he 'dined together with a good pig',
or is to be found 'at a haunch of venison' or 'at oysters', or preserves the

ancient 'fear of him' for 'fear for him' (that is, 'on his behalf'). Other usages are less archaic than racy, most of all the contraction of 'ily' forms to 'y', that is, of the use of adjective for adverb, as in 'extra-ordinary' for 'extraordinarily', 'mighty' for 'mightily', 'perfect' for 'perfectly', 'infinite' for 'infinitely'. But Pepys is perfectly capable, on occasion, of using the uncontracted form, as in 'I am mightily taken with them'. Here a linguistic affectation of the Commonwealth and Restoration is at war with Pepys's natural tendency to intensify as much as he is able, the habit exemplified by 'the justice himself very hardly escaped' where 'very' has to be read in relation to 'hardly', which does not now seem natural, and spelled out (the contracted form triumph-antly winning the day) when Pepys records how the captain of the *Naseby* 'treated me huge nobly'; nevertheless the way in which this simply reflects fashionable usage is demonstrated by the occurrence of 'huge gentlemanlike' in a Verney letter of 1653.[8]

Pepys's phrasal inversions are equally a period feature, but he uses them with a frequency that suggests a personal predilection. In part they are due to the redundancy that, for reasons that may superficially appear paradoxical but are in fact perfectly straightforward, is as characteristic an aspect of diary-writing as the ellipsis. It is often in effect a short cut to repeat a phrase, or to neglect its natural place in the sequence of sense. When Pepys writes of calling on 'Mitchell and his wife, which in her night linen appeared as pretty almost as ever to my thinking I saw woman' we come up against just such a failure to anticipate the full run of what he is endeavouring to write. But, as always, its disjunctions are dampened by those natural cadences of a speaking voice that it still contrives to convey. This habit in Pepys (and in his contemporaries) may have been accentuated by the way in which Latin was taught in the period, and, beyond that, by the construction of Latin itself, which is so frequently at odds with the principles governing English usage. The standard Latin dictionary of the day (Philemon Holland's edition of Thomas Thomas's *Dictionarium*, published by the Cambridge University Press)[9] was constructed on a method which offered to the student a repertory of phrases, and these could be put together like building blocks in order to convey a required sense by any student with a sufficiently retentive memory. The inculcation of such an arbitrary habit of phrasal organisation at an early age was not con-ducive to the spontaneous creation of smooth sequences in English sentences, and the interaction, in educated writing, of Latin and English, can too easily be overlooked. In 1680 John Aubrey, having just completed his life of Hobbes, sent it off to his friend Dr Richard Blackbourne, a Fellow of Trinity College, Cambridge, and in his covering note wrote: 'Pray be my Aristarchus. . . . First draughts ought to be rude as those of paynters, for he that in his first essay will be

curious in refining will certainly be unhappy in inventing . . . Should
mine be in Latin or English? . . . Is my English style well enough?'[10] In
the preceding year John Dryden, urging on the Earl of Sunderland the
foundation of a British Academy, had raised the same questions,
though with an altered emphasis: 'how barbarously we yet write and
speak, your Lordship knows, and I am sufficiently sensible in my own
English. For I am often put to a stand, in considering whether what I
write be the Idiom of the Tongue, or false Grammar, and nonsense
couch'd beneath that specious name of *Anglicisme*. And have no other
way to clear my Doubts, but by translating my English into Latine, and
thereby trying what sense the words will bear in a more stable Language'.[11] Both Aubrey and Dryden habitually wrote a fine, flowing
and natural English, yet neither of them was wholly convinced that
this was in fact the case, and both (though not in the same way) had
the alternative of Latin running in their minds. The privacy of Pepys's
diary obviously protected him from comparable anxieties, but that
two such able writers should have such doubts is illuminating, and the
readiness of their recourse to Latin significant. Something of the same
habit of mind as Aubrey and Dryden evince is arguably a factor
contributing to Pepys's stylistic oddities, albeit in an indirect way. This
process is more familiar to us in the realm of high and deliberated
literary art, notably in the syntactical complexities of Milton. But there
is, in any case, more of a connection between the selfconsciously poetic
and the unselfconsciously colloquial than might at first be imagined:
Milton is Pepys's rival virtuoso (in a competitive field) in the employment of forms with 'un':

> Among innumerable false, unmov'd,
> Unshak'n, unseduc't, unterrifi'd
> His Loyaltie he kept . . .
>
> (*Paradise Lost*, bk v, ll. 897+)

But the differences between Pepys's idiom and our own are less
significant than the resemblances. When we hear his speaking voice it
is because we recognise the way in which every individual establishes
that individuality by slight departures from a norm, and an apprehension of such a norm underlies our sense of Pepys's individuality. He
does not search for the sonorous, in the way that Evelyn on occasion
does; he does not take Aubrey's evident delight in the pungency of the
vocabulary available to him; he does not experience, as Anthony
Wood so notably did, pleasure at his own sarcasms. His language is
above all a reflection of its objects, not, to Pepys, an object in itself. Its
naturalness, its truth to common speech, strikes home because the
fundamentals of that speech have changed comparatively little in
three hundred years, though in recent years the influence of radio and

television has accelerated the process, and in modern England the accents of Pepys are most likely to find their echo amongst the indigenous inhabitants of rural areas and of the few remaining urban districts which have preserved a relatively uniform class structure and avoided redevelopment. In comparable areas of the eastern United States it is probable that the connection is even more immediate.

Pepys's vocabulary may be less exploratory than Aubrey's, but it remains exceptionally vivid in effect. Though Pepys had a liking for apparently novel constructions with 'un-' or 'over-' he was not a neologiser, though neologising has been a habit of mind by no means uncongenial to many private memoirists – the Duc de Saint-Simon, whose high hand with his French vocabulary is notorious, providing the most remarkable example. The *Oxford English Dictionary* records many more first uses from Evelyn than from Pepys, despite Pepys's much greater length, and this is indicative of Pepys's inwardness with the language; Evelyn, whose manner is stiffer, and play of mind within the language more restricted, frequently resorts to foreign terms where Pepys would have had a native word or phrase to hand. Nevertheless the Restoration was a period of linguistic expansion, as it was a period of mercantile and imperial expansion, and there are frequent demonstrations of this in Pepys, and in the words of which he provides our first record. The sea terms, upon a command of which he was professionally dependent, are frequently Dutch in origin; the accounts of meals eaten (which illustrate a different dependence) as frequently involve words deriving from the French. The years after 1660 were, in any case, particularly productive so far as French borrowings were concerned and, given the close connections between the courts and intellectual circles of the two countries, this was scarcely surprising. The utility and availability of French as a second language for Englishmen in the period is demonstrated by the English sojourns of French exiles such as Gramont and St Evremond, who appear never to have needed to learn English, whilst a French newsletter (the *Nouvelles Ordinaires*) appeared in London under the Commonwealth and had a successor (the *Gazette de Londres*) after the Restoration.[12] Huguenot refugees must also have played their part in the anglicising of French vocabulary. It was a tendency that was resisted, frequently by those most fluent in French: Etherege, in *The man of mode* (1676), got great fun out of Sir Fopling Flutter's malapropos excursions into the language, and was merely one amongst the many dramatists who exploited the gag. Yet at the end of the century Aubrey, reflecting on the number of English words used by even so lively a writer as Philemon Holland at its beginning which had by then become archaic, recorded Dryden's opinion that some thirty or forty French words had been naturalised into English in the thirty odd years since the Restoration.[13] It was a subject about which Dryden had been thinking for a long time: as early as 1664 he had expressed the wish that 'we might at length leave to borrow words from other nations, which is now a wantonness in us, not a necessity', though he had gone on to admit that 'so long as some affect to speak them, there will not want others, who will have the boldness to write them'.[14] In 1673 he had again returned to the attack, with a pregnant anticipation of the figure of Sir Fopling, disapproving those 'who corrupt our English idiom by mixing it too much with French: that is a sophistication of language, not an improvement of it: a turning English into French, rather than a refining of English by French. We meet daily with those fops, who value themselves on their travelling, and pretend they cannot express their meaning in English, because they would put off to us some French phrase of the last edition; without considering that, for aught they know, we have a better of our own'.[15]

Pepys would almost certainly have agreed with these sentiments. In 1667 he praised Sir Roger L'Estrange's rendering of Quevedo's *Sueños y discursos* because it did not read like a translation; he evidently regarded English as having a spirit of its own, which good writing should preserve, and his words of French derivation appear to stem less from any proclivity to exploit the resources of that language than from a natural turning to customary usage. When he writes 'volary' (Fr. *volière*), notwithstanding the pre-existence in English of the wholly adequate 'aviary', he is merely following accepted practice. Perfectly good native terms can die out, despite their sufficiency, and be replaced by alien intruders; even so unsophisticated a writer as Edmund Coxere could call on the phrase 'where we lay perdu' without appearing affected.[16] Pepys is equally innocent, and his French borrowings are almost all in essence functional and conventional. They are employed because they are current, and because they serve his purpose: he had no ambition to be an 'absolute Monsieur'. But he can on occasion turn to French to achieve a witty or pleasing effect, as in his account of his journey to Portsmouth in 1661, where the remark that he had had 'this day no other extraordinary rancontre but my hat falling off of my head into the water, by which it was spoiled and I ashamed of it' not only provides an example of a usage ('off of') still to be encountered in N. America though almost extinct in Britain, but also provides an example of a French word deliberately used to suggest the atmosphere of the romances which derived from France and were the staple form of light reading in the mid-17th century; Pepys riding southwards saw himself as a knight errant.

Given the colloquial tenor of the diary, and Pepys's evident liking for classical apophthegms, the relative poverty of proverbial material is revealing. Pepys could not have shared Jane Austen's opinion that proverbs were 'gross and illiberal': he uses them, on occasion, with great effect: 'Though I love the treason I hate the traitor', 'You have brought your hogs to a fair market', 'Sometimes all honey and then all turd', are instances of his feeling for proverbs that were striking and apt. But he employs them sparingly; his natural habit of mind is too individual to incline him to acquiesce in a proverb unless he feels that it really strikes home. He makes, by contrast, considerable play with proverbial phrases, which have an evident appeal both for their economy and their pithiness: there are those that are alliterative (to have 'a back broad enough to bear it', 'mince the matter', 'as supple as a spaniel', 'as drunk as a dog', 'beat one's brains', 'Bridewell birds', 'hang in the hedge'), and the vivid ('take eggs for . . . money', 'be at dagger-drawing', 'worth a fart', 'calm as a lamb', 'pull a crow'); some have passed out of circulation ('take in snuff' – but we still say 'snuffy', 'to keep a quarter', 'have snaps at', have 'a month's mind', to go to one's 'naked bed'), but others remain alive and kicking ('stick at nothing', 'get into the saddle', 'shift for myself', 'take it very well', 'work like a horse', 'cheek by jowl', 'make no bones of it', 'eyes ready to fall out of my head', 'out of play', 'make the pot boyle', to put someone's 'nose out of joint', 'the main chance'). Once again we can perceive a use of language, rather than a subjection to it.

Francis Atterbury, the future Bishop of Rochester, wrote in 1690 a preface to an edition of Edmund Waller's posthumous poems in which he asked what might seem to us the surprising question as to whether it was not the case that 'in Charles the second's reign, English did not come to its full perfection; and whether it has not had its Augustan Age, as well as the Latin. It seems to be already mixed with foreign languages as far as its purity will bear; and as Chymists say of their Moenstruums, to be quite sated with the infusion. But posterity will best judge of this'. Atterbury's estimate of the state of the language under Charles II may be extravagant, and there were many writers during that reign who would have disputed it. But Pepys in the diary provides one good reason for supposing it to be a judgement not far off the mark; it was an instrument supremely able to 'show' both the complexities and simplicities of the man.[17]

(Richard Luckett)

Lanier, [Nicholas] (1588–1666). Composer, lutenist and singer, active in the King's Musick from 1616; appointed Master 1626, which post he resumed at the Restoration. Keeper of the King's Miniatures, and painter (notably of scenery for masques), he travelled extensively in Italy collecting pictures for Charles I. Propagandist for the *stilo recitativo* (*see below*, Music, p. 269). He maintained contacts with the court in exile during the Interregnum and bought many of the royal pictures when these were auctioned. Songs in *Musica Britannica*, 33/items i–ii.[1] (Lu)

Lanyon, [John]. Of Plymouth. Victualling contractor (with Yeabsley) for Tangier; from Sept. 1661 navy agent at Plymouth. His correspondence with Pepys suggests that they were on friendly terms.[1]

Lashmore, ——. Navy Office servant; possibly the Will Lashmore who appears in the Navy Treasurer's ledgers in 1662 as a labourer, and elsewhere as a messenger.[1]

Lauderdale, 1st Earl and Duke of: *see* Maitland, J.

Lawes, Henry (1595–1662). Regarded by contemporaries as the greatest composer of his time. Epistoler and Gentleman of the Chapel Royal from 1626; appointed to the King's Musick 1631; at the Restoration appointed composer to the King's Private Musick. A friend of Milton (for whose *Comus* he provided the music), and of Herrick (who lodged in Lawes's house when ejected from his living). He was involved in the setting of *The siege of Rhodes*, and wrote numerous songs, many of which were published by Playford and ultimately made up the greater part of *The treasury of musick* (1669; PL 2223). (Lu)

Lawrence, Ald. Sir John, kt 1660 (d. 1692). Merchant, of Great St Helen's, Bishopsgate; Lord Mayor 1658–9, 1664–5, 1677–8, and a prominent Whig. His father was Abraham, of the same parish, also a merchant.[1]

Lawson, Sir John. A leading naval officer in the parliamentary and Commonwealth navy, dismissed in 1656 as a republican and Anabaptist. He returned to favour in Dec. 1659 when he was made Commander-in-Chief of the fleet. He then cooperated with Monck to re-establish government by the civil authority by bringing his ships into the Thames and declaring for the Rump. In the spring of 1660 he was Vice-Admiral of the fleet in which the King returned home, and was knighted for his services. In 1663–4 he led two important expeditions against the Barbary corsairs. He was particularly concerned with Tangier as one of the contractors for the mole. At the beginning of the Second Dutch War he was made Vice-Admiral, and died from wounds received at the Battle of Lowestoft. His wife was Isabella Jefferson of Whitby, Yorks. Of his daughters, the eldest married Daniel Norton; Elizabeth and Anna were minors and unmarried at his death. He died far from wealthy but not penniless (cf. vi.145). His pension (£500 p.a.) was continued (since he had died in service), he had two houses, and an interest in a ballast quay and the Tangier mole. He was able to bequeath £100 to the poor of his native parish in Scarborough.

The Mr Lawson who was involved in the settling of his affairs after his death was either his cousin John Lawson, grocer, or the grocer's son James. Both were overseers of his will. The father received under the will a velvet coat and a 'flea-bitten gelding'.[1]

Laxton, ——. Apothecary; probably John Layton, Upper Warden of the Society of Apothecaries of London 1664–5.[1]

Lea. The brothers Matthias and Thomas Lea (Leigh) were the only underclerks to the Commonwealth Council of State to retain their posts in Jan. 1660, according to the diary. Thomas later appears on the Irish establishment of 1661–2 as Keeper of the Council Chamber in Dublin. He was brother-in-law of another of Pepys's old 'club' of government servants, James Chetwind.[1]

Leadenhall Market. The principal market for provisions, especially meat and poultry, in 17th-century London. The hall and market houses stood to the south of the s. side of Leadenhall St. They were destroyed in the Fire, after which the corporation acquired additional ground, built a new market hall, and issued new regulations. [*See also* Food]

Le Brun, ——. Probably Christian Lebrun who married Rebecca Lemmon in 1654. They lived in St Olave's parish.[1]

Lee, Sir Thomas, bt 1660 (1635–91). M.P. for Aylesbury in six parliaments 1660–91, and for Buckinghamshire 1689–90. Usually active in opposition: he was among the members who pressed charges against Carteret in 1669. He was an Admiralty Commissioner 1679–81 and 1689–91, but did not attend regularly. According to Burnet: 'a man that valued himself upon artifice and cunning . . . without being out of countenance when it was discovered'.[1]

Leeson, [Robert]. Barber-surgeon; Warden of the Company 1684–5; Master 1686.[1]

Legge, William and George. William (?1609–70) was appointed Master of the Armouries and Lieut-General and Treasurer of the Ordnance in 1660. He learnt his soldiering in the Dutch and Swedish armies as a young man; became Lieutenant of the Ordnance during the Scots war 1639–40, and in the Civil War was an officer under Rupert and Governor of Oxford 1645–6.

His eldest son George (1648–91), cr. Baron Dartmouth in 1682, succeeded him at the Ordnance (but not in the treasurership which became a separate office). He was one of the Duke of York's household officers and on his accession was made Master of the Horse and Governor of the Tower. He had also proved himself as a seaman in the Second and Third Dutch Wars, and it was a cruel disappointment to James that, as commander of the fleet in 1688, he failed to intercept the Dutch invading force. To Pepys his failure was perhaps less of a surprise. He had known him well when he commanded the Tangier expedition (1683–4), and though he found him a fine sailor and an admirable man, he thought him an indecisive leader. He died in the Tower under the unjust suspicion of Jacobitism.[1]

Leicester House. This stood on the n.-e. side of Leicester Fields (now

Sq.), its gardens taking the rest of the northern frontage of the fields. A residence of the first rank throughout the 17th and 18th centuries, it was occupied in 1668 by the French ambassador. (R)

Leigh Road. The roadstead opposite Leigh-on-sea, Essex.

Leighton, Sir Ellis, kt 1659 (d. 1685). A civil lawyer and Catholic convert, and, according to Roger North, 'the most corrupt Man . . . living'.[1] Pepys found him a lightweight character but an entertaining table companion. He was in turn secretary to Buckingham and the Duke of York before 1660 and later secretary to the Royal Adventurers to Africa, to the Prize Commission (1664), to Berkeley of Stratton as Lord Lieutenant of Ireland (1670) and to his embassy in France (1675). In 1677 he was imprisoned for taking bribes in Paris, and was expelled from the Royal Society. In the Popish Plot he acted as one of Buckingham's agents and seems to have been involved in procuring evidence against Pepys from Col. Scott.[2]

Lely (Lilly), Sir Peter, kt 1679 (1618–80). The most fashionable and accomplished portrait painter at work in London at this time. Born in Holland, he had lived in England since the early or mid-1640s. His name was commonly spelt and pronounced Lilly. By 1650 he was living in a house in the Piazza, Covent Garden, possibly the one in which he died. In the hearth-tax returns of 1666 a Mr Lilly is shown as occupying premises on the n. side of Long Acre, which contained a number of painters' studios (those e.g. of Hayls, Gibson and Streeter).[1] The best-known of his works in the diary period are the series of court beauties (now at Hampton Court) and of the admirals who fought the Battle of Lowestoft (now in the National Maritime Museum). Pepys was himself painted by Lely, or in his studio, in 1673, probably on his appointment to the Admiralty. This picture now hangs in the Hall of Magdalene College. Pepys possessed at least two other portraits by him – those of Sandwich and Morland[2] – and preserved in his library a number of engravings of Lely's portraits.[3]

Le Neve, [Richard]. Naval officer: he held seven commissions between 1666 and his death in action in Aug. 1673.[1]

Lenthall. William Lenthall (1591–1662), Speaker of the House of Commons 1640–53 and of Parliament 1654–5, 1659–60, was the best-known of 17th-century Speakers. He is generally reckoned a weak man. His absenting himself from the chair in Jan. 1660 (i.25) on the excuse of ill-health was not untypical: he had behaved similarly in the summer of 1647 rather than brave the pressure from the Westminster mob. He never forgave himself for failing to resist the decision to try the King in 1648. *Vermis sum* was the inscription he ordered for his gravestone. His moment of glory was in Jan. 1642 when he boldly defended the rights of the House in face of the King's attempt to arrest the five members.[1]

His brother Sir John (d. 1668) was an active J.P., with a reputation for corruption and extortion as Keeper of the Marshalsea prison in Southwark.[2]

His son Sir John (c. 1625–81) was elected M.P. for Gloucester in 1645, and for Abingdon in 1659 and 1660. He had the reputation of being a timeserver. Wood calls him 'the grand braggadocio and liar'.[3]

Leonard, [John]. Underclerk to the Council of State 1660.[1]

Le Squire, [Scipio]. Vice-Chamberlain of the Receipt in the Exchequer from c. 1642; buried in Westminster Abbey Sept. 1659.[1]

L'Estrange, Sir Roger, kt 1685 (1616–1704). One of the most prolific pamphleteers of the age. He wrote with unsparing vehemence in defence of church and king, and achieved fame by his newspapers (*The Intelligencer* and *The News* 1663–6, and *The Observator* 1681–7), and by his denunciation of the Popish Plot, when he was widely suspected of being a crypto-papist. He was Surveyor of the press and one of the licensers 1663–88, and M.P. for Winchester 1685–7. In 1695–6 he was imprisoned for allegedly supporting Fenwick's conspiracy. In private as charming as in public he could be savage. A musician, and an able translator from several languages. Pepys retained in his library a run of the *Observator*, and two of his books, including his famous *History of the plot* (1679).[1]

Lethieullier, Sir [John], kt 1674 (1632–1719). Merchant, of St Olave, Hart St and Lewisham, Kent; Sheriff 1674–5; Lord Mayor 1676–7. He married Anne (d. 1703) daughter of Sir W. Hooker in 1658.[1]

Lever, [William]. Purser-General to Sandwich's fleet 1661–2.[1]

Levitt, [William] (d. 1679). A cook who kept the Ship, an eating house in Bartholomew Lane behind the Royal Exchange. He died in office as second master of the Cooks' Company. A George Levitt was 'caterer' at Clare Hall, Cambridge 1665–c. 92.[1]

Lewin, ——. Of the King's Lifeguard. Possibly John Lewin, adjutant in Sir W. Lockhart's regiment of foot 1672; lieutenant in Earl Craven's regiment 1678.[1]

Lewis, Ald. Sir John, kt and bt 1660 (d. 1671). E. India merchant; Master of the Ironmongers' Company 1657–8; member of the Council of Trade 1660, and the Council for Foreign Plantations 1661.[1]

Lewis, [Thomas]. Clerk in the Victualling Office under the Commonwealth; accountant and Clerk of the Issues in March 1660; Manager, Ticket Office 1673–4.[1]

Lewis, Ald. [Thomas]. Merchant trading to Aleppo; partner of and possibly related to Ald. Sir John, though not his brother. Chosen alderman 1661 but fined for discharge.[1]

Lewis, ——. A cook. Possibly John Lewis, freeman of the Cooks' Company.[1]

Ley, James, 3rd Earl of Marlborough (1618–65). An officer in the royalist army and navy and active in colonial ventures. He attempted to settle the Caribbean islands; served on the Council for Trade from 1660 and the Council for Foreign Plantations from 1661; and led the expedition to take over Bombay 1661–2. In 1664 he was nominated Governor of Jamaica but was killed in action (as captain of the *Old James*) in 1665. His thoughts before battle were published in Henry Smith, *Fair warnings to a careless world* (1665), pp. 1–3.[1]

Lidcott, Capt. [Robert]. Identified as Robert because his brother Leonard had been commissioned colonel in Nov. 1659.[1]

Liddell, Sir Thomas, 2nd Bt (d. 1697). A member of the Northumberland family; in 1662 described as of Chelsea. He took no part in politics and lived abroad for extended periods in the '60s with his wife and daughter.[1]

Lilly, William (1602–81). The most prolific writer of his day on astrology. A supporter of the popular party, he forecast victories for parliament in every campaign during the Civil War, and prophesied on behalf of every successive régime from the outbreak of the troubles to the Restoration. In 1670 he turned to the practice of astrological medicine.[1]

Limehouse. A vast village (technically a hamlet of the great parish of Stepney) of some 1200 houses;[1] important for its shipbuilding and all things maritime. On the n. bank of the Thames between Ratcliffe and Poplar, some 2 miles downstream of the city, to which, by the time of the diary, it was joined by a continuous line of buildings. (R)

Lincoln's Inn. On the w. side of Chancery Lane, its gardens and walks reaching to Lincoln's Inn Fields. The walks, like those of the other Inns of Court, were used as a pleasant and fashionable strolling ground. Pepys refers to them at 4 Sept. 1663 as recently improved and 'very fine'. The Hall and other 19th-century buildings have much diminished the former gardens, and have virtually swallowed up the walks. (R)

Lincoln's Inn Fields. One of the most splendid additions made to 17th-century London – much admired by foreign visitors. The fields (immediately to the west of Lincoln's Inn) had been laid out as public walks in James I's reign under the supervision of Inigo Jones, and later (1638–70) partially built over, the greater part being enclosed within an impressive square of houses, each with a small court in front guarded by a low wall. From the outset a fashionable quarter. Several of Pepys's grand acquaintances lived there – Lord Crew; Thomas Povey whose domestic luxuries Pepys so much admired; and Sandwich, who leased a house there in 1664 – 'a fine house, but' [at £250 p.a.] 'deadly dear'.[1] (R)

Lincoln's Inn Theatre: *see* Duke's Theatre

Lion Quay. Off Lower Thames St.

[Lisle, Thomas]. Surgeon; Master of the Barber-Surgeons' Company 1662–3; appointed King's Barber 1662.[1]

Lisson (Lyssen) Green. A small village, its green being about half-a-mile east of Paddington on the opposite side of the Edgware Rd, north of the eastern end of the modern Chapel St where it joins the Marylebone Rd. Building in its neighbourhood began at the end of the 18th century and was completed early in the 19th. Lisson Grove, to the east of the green, preserves the name. (R)

Littleton, [James]. Merchant; a younger brother of Sir Thomas: cashier to the Navy Treasurer 1668–?71, and employed in pressing seamen 1672.[1]

Littleton, Sir Thomas, 2nd Bt (1621–81). Joint-Treasurer of the Navy, with Sir T. Osborne, 1668–71 – in Pepys's words 'brought into the Navy for want of other ways of gratification'.[1] As an M.P. (in the Cavalier Parliament, for Much Wenlock) he was one of Arlington's faction. He rather than his colleague appears to have taken responsibility for the receipt and payment of money. Both had been, and remained, critical of the Navy Office, and regarded themselves more as overseers than colleagues of the Principal Officers. Littleton was later victualler to the navy in 1671–3 and an Admiralty Commissioner in 1681. His son, also Sir Thomas, was Navy Treasurer 1699–1710, and acted as a pall bearer at Pepys's funeral.[2]

Little Turnstile: *see* Turnstile

Llewellyn, [Peter] (1636–65). Son of David Llewellyn, underkeeper of the Privy Lodgings, Windsor; appointed underclerk of the Council of State in Feb. 1660. After service in Ireland with Anglesey he became clerk to Edward Dering, timber merchant. He died unmarried.

His brother (about to go to Constantinople in 1660) was David. He was still alive when Peter made his will, and still 'far distant'.[1]

Lloyd, Sir Godfrey, kt 1657. Chief engineer of ports, castles and fortifications 1661–7. Pepys later wrote that his work at Sheerness was so badly executed that it had to be done again. It was alleged that he had been appointed only because he was English.[1]

Lloyd, Sir [Philip], kt 1674. A not very successful clerk to Sir W. Coventry, dismissed for idleness in 1667, he entered the Treasury as a clerk and rose to become First Clerk (1673), Clerk of the Privy Council (1674) and Commissioner of the Hearth Tax (1685).[1]

Lloyd, Sir Richard, kt 1642 (1606–76). M.P. 1628–9 for Montgomery boroughs, Apr.–May 1640 for Newcastle-under-Lyme, and 1661–76 for Radnorshire. He and his drinking companions (iv.77) were all old Cavaliers: he had been a leading royalist in N. Wales.[1]

Lloyd, [Thomas]. Secretary to the Prize Commissioners 1665–7.[1]

Lock, [Matthew]. Secretary at War 1666–83. A protégé of Monck, he had been a clerk in the office of the Council of State from 1650, and was Clerk-Assistant to the Army Council in Scotland 1655–9.[1]

Locke, Matthew (1622–77). Composer and keyboard virtuoso.

Exeter chorister, in the Low Countries 1648, composer in the Private Musick (1660), organist to Queen Catherine at Somerset House (by 1671; a prolific composer of chamber music (mainly for viols), sacred and theatrical vocal music and keyboard music. According to Roger North 'much the best master in his time; for by the service & the society of forreiners he was not a little Italianised'.[1] (Lu)

London Bridge. A stone structure of 19 arches and a wooden drawbridge built 1176–1209 in place of an earlier wooden bridge. The only bridge across the Thames below Kingston, it ran from Fish St Hill immediately west of St Magnus church to the Surrey shore between St Olave's church and St Mary Overies (now Southwark Cathedral). The road across it carried a line of houses on each side with shops at the road level: they suffered badly in the Fire. The bulky starlings, of timber enclosing chalk and rubble, which protected the stone piers so narrowed the waterway that, except at high and low tide, shooting the bridge was a dangerous business. Many passengers disembarked and either walked the rest of their journey or re-embarked on the other side. As the proverb had it, 'London Bridge was made for wise men to go over and fools to go under'. Pepys retained an early 17th-century drawing of it in his library.[1] Its defects led to the building of a new bridge (opened in 1831) some 180 ft upstream from the old, which was then demolished. This 19th-century bridge was in turn replaced in 1973.

The diary's occasional references to other 'bridges' on the London banks of the Thames – e.g. to Westminster Bridge – are to wooden piers projecting into the river and carrying landing stairs. There was no bridge across the river at Westminster until 1750. (R)

London Wall. A street running approximately along the inside of the city's wall from (Old) Broad St to Cripplegate. Pepys's reference at viii.6 is not to the street but to the actual wall of the city which survived the Fire and parts of which survive to this day. (R)

Long, Sir Robert, 1st Bt. A friend and servant of the Queen Mother, and an able public servant: Auditor of the Receipt in the Exchequer 1662–d. 73; Privy Councillor 1672–3. He lived at Worcester Park, Surrey, and had an official residence in New Palace Yard, Westminster.[1]

Long, ——. Lawyer: possibly Israel Long, admitted to the Middle Temple 1656.[1]

Long Acre. A long and spacious street running south-west from Drury Lane to St Martin's Lane. Largely built up in the reign of Charles I and then well-inhabited, by 1660 it was slipping in the social scale, and contained brothels and coachmakers.[1] (R)

Long Lane. A 'pleasant spacious lane'[1] running westwards out of Aldersgate St, at the carfax with Goswell St and Barbican, to W. Smithfield. (R)

Longrack, [John]. Purveyor of timber to the navy.[1]

Loriners' Hall. The Loriners or Lorimers (bit-makers) are one of the smaller city companies and were not incorporated until 1711. Pepys had never heard of their hall before 15 May 1668 when he went there to attend the burial of Sir Thomas Teddeman. It was situated at the corner of Basinghall St and London Wall, and was pulled down in the mid-18th century. Today the company has no hall.

Loud. Sandwich's page in 1660–1. A 'Mr Loud' was a member of his household in Madrid 1665–8. Lowd Cordell was his steward in 1672.[1]

Love, Ald. [William] (d. 1689). A rich Turkey merchant and a leading London Independent, suspected of Levelling and republican sympathies. Councillor of State in 1660; M.P. for London 1661–89. He probably never took the sacramental test for M.P.s.[1]

Lovelace, Col. [Francis]. Collector of the tax for loyal and indigent officers (1662). There were two of his name. The Francis Lovelace who was appointed Governor of New York in 1668 is perhaps the more likely to be the collector, since he was in the Duke of York's service; but his namesake, brother of Richard Lovelace the poet, is also possible. Both had seen service in the royalist army.[1]

Lovell, ——. Lawyer: probably Charles Lovell, admitted to Lincoln's Inn 1650.[1]

Lower, Richard (1631–91). 'The prime physician of his time' (R. North).[1] M.D. (Oxon.) 1665; F.R.S. 1667; F.R.C.P. 1675. A pioneer experimenter in blood transfusion, he often advised the navy on medical matters. It was he who in 1690 certified Pepys as dangerously ill and thus secured his release from the Gatehouse prison.[2]

Lowther. Anthony Lowther, of London and Marske, Yorks., was the son of Ald. Robert Lowther (d. 1655) by his second wife, Elizabeth (b. Holcroft). An original F.R.S., and M.P. for Appleby in both Exclusion parliaments. He married Peg Penn, daughter of Sir William, in 1667. He had a half-sister Peg, who married Capt. John Holmes in 1668.

The brothers mentioned at viii.234–5 are impossible to identify: he had six.

Sir John Lowther, 2nd Bt (1642–1706), was his cousin. He was of Lowther, Westmorland; and was returned as M.P. for Cumberland at a bye-election in 1665, and for eight subsequent parliaments. He served as an Admiralty Commissioner 1689–96.[1]

Loxton, ——. Possibly a musician; conceivably, but unlikely to have been, the Francis Loyscoean (Loiscan) appointed trumpeter in ordinary 5 Oct. 1687.[1] (Lu)

Lucy, ——. Merchant: probably Jacob Lucy, merchant and ship-owner, of Fenchurch St; Alderman 1683–5. The Navy Board owed him £1000 in 1670.[1]

Lucy, ——. Soldier: possibly Thomas, son of Richard Lucy of

Charlecote, Warwicks. (d. 1684); commissioned captain 1666, 1678–9, 1679. He succeeded to Charlecote in 1677.[1]

Ludgate. One of the principal gates in the city wall on the w. side commanding the way up from the Fleet river and the access to Westminster via Fleet St and the Strand. The hill below the gate was in 1660 known as Ludgate Hill, the section above the gate being termed Ludgate St (both are now Ludgate Hill). Burnt in the Fire but restored with a postern gate on each side. The prison for debtors adjoined its s.-e. side. The gate was demolished in 1760.[1] (R)

Luffe, William. His will (signed Nov. 1668) described him as a yeoman, of Stirtloe in the parish of Buckden, and shows him possessed of barns, stables, outhouses, an orchard and 15 acres. He signed it with his mark. A John Luffe lived in Brampton in 1642. Sandwich had a footman of this surname.[1]

Luke, Sir Samuel (1603–70). M.P. for Bedford 1660. A prominent Presbyterian; Scoutmaster-General of the parliamentary army; and usually identified as the original of Butler's Hudibras.[1]

Lurkin, Mrs. A neighbour of Will Joyce (a leatherseller); possibly therefore the wife of William Larking, cordwainer, of St Martin-in-the-Fields.[1]

Lynes, ——. Surgeon: possibly Matthew Line, a naval surgeon in 1660.[1]

Mabbot, [Gilbert]. Radical journalist and newsletter writer; with Rushworth joint-censor of the press 1644–7; chief censor 1647–8; licenser of military news to the Council of State 1653–6. In 1650 living in Axe Yard. At the Restoration, thanks to Monck's protection, he was granted a lucrative patent to sell wine and strong waters in Ireland. He was always a journalist rather than a censor.[1]

Mackworth, ——. Possibly a son of Col. George Mackworth, a colleague of Sandwich on Cromwell's Council of State and Treasury Commission.[1]

Madden, [John]. Surveyor of the Woods south of Trent. He held the office jointly with Thomas Agar.[1]

Maddox, Robert. Clerk in the Navy Office from 1660; first attached to the Surveyor, then appointed clerk of control in 1669 and paymaster to the Navy Treasurer in 1671.[1]

Ma(d)ge, [Humphrey] (d. 1679). Violinist and wind player, member of the King's Musick from the Restoration, but known as a violin virtuoso as early as 1653, when he is referred to in a poem by Nicholas Hookes.[1] (Lu)

Magdalene College, Cambridge. Founded in the second quarter of the 15th century as a monastic house of study; known as Buckingham College in the early 16th from the benefactions of the 2nd and 3rd

Dukes; refounded 1542. Pepys was an undergraduate from 1651–4, and sent his nephew John Jackson there in 1686.

The buildings were mostly grouped around the four sides of a single court. To this had been added (as far as may be judged) a second court with a small Elizabethan building on its e. side and, after 1629, a brewhouse alongside.[1] Small groups of students usually shared accommodation, having a living room-bedroom in common, and off it studies for private use. The course for the B.A. degree, still based on the medieval curriculum, included some Aristotelian physics and a little cosmography and mathematics, but consisted mainly of classical literature (mostly Latin) and Aristotelian logic. The students were encouraged to take systematic notes. After chapel at 6 a.m., they usually attended classes in logic and philosophy until dinner time and afterwards played their games and worked on their classical texts until bedtime.[2] The degree was normally taken after ten terms of residence, the examination consisting of disputations performed in the second and third years. Teaching was mainly by college officers: Magdalene had three lectureships in Pepys's time, held by the fellows in rotation.[3]

In the 1620s the college enjoyed a high academic reputation[4] and by the time Pepys went up was, in common with the rest of the university, recovering from the effects of the Civil War when student numbers had dropped and nine of its eleven fellows had been deprived for political reasons. In 1650 another fellow and the Master (Edward Rainbowe) were deprived for refusing the declaration of loyalty to the Commonwealth. In 1651, when Pepys matriculated, the college contained just over 30 undergraduates (11 in his year) and six fellows, four of whom had been elected in 1649–50.[5] The new Master was a government nominee – John Sadler, lawyer and Hebraic scholar, and also Town Clerk of London and M.P. for Cambridge borough in 1653 and for Great Yarmouth in 1659. His periods of residence were brief, and it was said of him that 'he was not always right in his head, especially towards the latter end of his being master of the college'.[6] Pepys, at first a sizar, was elected to scholarships in Apr. 1651 and Oct. 1653. His tutor was Samuel Morland, the mathematician (q.v.).[7] Among his contemporaries at Magdalene were a few who became illustrious – his friend Richard Cumberland as a scholar and ecclesiastic, and his chamber-fellow Robert Sawyer as an Attorney-General.

The college was not greatly disturbed at the Restoration. Rainbowe replaced Sadler as Master until his appointment as Bishop of Carlisle in 1664. In 1662 only two fellows refused the oaths imposed by the Act of Uniformity.[8] The mastership of Dr James Duport (1668–79) brought to the college one of the most distinguished of contemporary Greek scholars. In 1687 occurred the famous brush with royal authority when the Master, Dr John Peachell (known in Pepys's time for his red nose),[9]

defied the orders of James II's Ecclesiastical Commission to confer a
degree on a Benedictine monk. He was dismissed as Vice-Chancellor
and suspended as Master. College numbers remained steady in 1660–
1700 but in the early 18th century began to decline. In 1703, the year
of Pepys's death, only three undergraduates matriculated.[10]

After taking his degree Pepys never lost touch with Magdalene,
largely because his journeys to look after his inheritance at Brampton
took him often enough to Cambridge. There was a move in 1681 to
make him Provost of King's College, but he withdrew in favour of a
local candidate.[11] To his old college he had shortly before subscribed
£60 towards the cost of a new building which was to occupy the site
of the Elizabethan building in the second court. Planned as early as
1640, its construction was delayed first by the Civil War and later by
financial difficulties. Robert Hooke submitted plans in 1677 and by the
1690s it seems to have been finished.[12] Pepys chose it to house his
library when in his will of May 1703 he decided to leave it to Magdalene.

Maitland, John, 2nd Earl of Lauderdale, cr. Duke 1672 (1616–82).
Originally a Covenanter, he developed extreme views on royal
authority. Secretary for Scottish Affairs 1660–80; appointed to the
Fishery Corporation 1664; Admiralty Commissioner 1673–9. His
(first) wife (m. 1632, d. 1671) was Anne, sister of the 2nd Earl of
Home.[1]

Mallard (Maylord), [Thomas] (d. 1665). Viol player and composer;
once musician to Oliver Cromwell; in service with Sandwich on his
Spanish embassy.[1]

Man, [William]. City Swordbearer.[1]

Manchester, 2nd Earl of: *see* Mountagu, E.

Manley, Maj. [John] (c. 1622–99). Puritan politician: Postmaster
1653–5; M.P. for Denbigh boroughs 1659. He withdrew into private
life for some years at the Restoration and was Master of the Skinners'
Company 1673–4; but sat for Bridport in the Convention of 1689. His
(first) wife (d. 1675) was Mary, daughter of Isaac Dorislaus, the Commonwealth diplomat. Possibly related to Thomas Manley, Storekeeper at Deptford under James I.[1]

[Manning, Edward]. City Remembrancer 1665–6.[1]

Mansell, [Francis]. A Chichester merchant trading with France who
in 1651 helped in the King's escape after Worcester fight by arranging
for the provision of the ship from Shoreham in which he got away. At
the Restoration he was awarded a pension and a place in the customs.
It seems virtually certain that he was the Mr Mansell to whom
Mountagu paid great respect when he came on board the *Naseby* on the
way over to Holland in Apr. 1660. There was a royalist agent named
Mansell in 1659 who may have been the same man.[1] A Rowland

Mansell was a relative of Mountagu and was later a lieutenant at Tangier.[2]

Marescoe, [Charles] (d. 1672). Eastland merchant and Common Councilman. In the early '60s he had a virtual monopoly of the importation of tar.[1]

Marget(t)s, [George]. Rope merchant, Limehouse. Margetts, the 'young merchant' (ix.518) was probably his son, if we may argue from the fact that Stapely the rope merchant was present on the same occasion.[1]

Markham. A kinsman of Sir William Penn (vii.235) who in 1666 married Lady Penn's maid, or companion, Nan Wright. Probably William Markham, Penn's nephew, who witnessed his will in 1670. He was later (by 1682) Deputy-Governor of Pennsylvania.[1]

Marlborough, 3rd Earl of: *see* Ley, J.

Marlow, [Thomas]. Messenger in the Navy Office 1665–1711.[1]

Marriott. Richard Marriott (d. 1664), Keeper of the Standing Wardrobe and of the Privy Lodgings at Hampton Court under the Commonwealth; reappointed 1660. His son James succeeded him at his death.[1]

Marsh, [Alphonso]. (1626 or 27–81). Lutenist, keyboard player, singer (bass) and composer. He took part in Davenant's *Siege of Rhodes* and at the Restoration was appointed to the King's Private Musick and the Chapel Royal. The son and father of royal musicians, his songs appear in a number of contemporary anthologies. There is a specimen of his work in *Musica Britannica*, 33/item *xix*.[1] (Lu)

Marsh, [Sir George]. Son of Capt. Richard. Assistant-Storekeeper in the Ordnance 1667–72; Storekeeper 1672–3.[1]

Marsh, [James]. A cook in the service of the Commonwealth government. Pepys's references to 'Marsh's' appear to be to a tavern; they are in fact to Marsh's rooms in Whitehall where in the early months of 1660 Pepys and his friends gathered for drinks and food.[1]

Marsh, Capt. [Richard]. Of a prominent Limehouse family; aged 83 at death. Storekeeper of the Ordnance before the Civil War and 1660–72. Both his father Francis and his son Sir George held the same office. Possibly the 'Esquire Marsh' who owed money to Tom Pepys the tailor at Tom's death.[1]

Marsh, Tom (d. 1673). Underclerk in Parliament/House of Commons 1660–?63; Clerk-Assistant to the House of Commons 1663–73. Son of Col. John Marsh, a royalist.[1]

Marshall, Anne and Rebecca. Sisters; actresses in the King's Company. Anne, the elder, joined the Duke's Company in 1676. Pepys's mistake about their parentage is corrected at viii.503, n.1.[1]

Marshall, ——. Timber merchant: either Richard or Samuel Marshall, of East Ham.[1]

Martin, Betty (b. Lane). Pepys's mistress, together with her sister
Doll Powell, though for a longer period. Neither found marriage any
impediment to her association with Pepys. Betty was presumably the
elder since she is usually referred to as 'Mrs' Lane. Both were linen-
drapers in Westminster Hall. (The tax returns which show them as
paying tax suggests that they were not mere assistants.)[1] Professor
J. H. Wilson has found that the career of Betty's husband Samuel
Martin is sufficiently documented to yield further information.[2] They
were daughters of John Lane of East Retford, Notts., and had a brother
James (alive in 1686) whose address was Clement's Inn and who was
presumably therefore connected with the Chancery bar, as a lawyer or
clerk. Moreover he finds that Martin's career was very different from
what might be expected from Pepys's account of him ('a sorry simple
fellow', 'without discourse', 'not worth a farthing'). When he married
Betty in 1664 he was working in the Ordnance Office in the Tower.
He then became a purser (James Lane standing as one of his sureties) in
at least five ships before 1672, when he was appointed to the important
post of consul at Algiers. His correspondence with Pepys in that
capacity, pitched in tones of great respect, shows him as a man of some
ability. In 1674 he sent Pepys a tame lion which Pepys found 'good
company'.[3] In 1677 he found himself in a debtors' prison through having
engaged in some unhappy trading ventures, and in 1678 he died. Betty
was granted a pension of £100 p.a. in July 1680 and herself died six
years later. She had had several children (to the first of whom Pepys
had stood godfather)[4] but none are mentioned in her will.

Martin, [John]. Bookseller, at the Castle, Fleet St, later at the Bell,
Temple Bar (fl. 1649–80). In 1670 he returned to his shop in Paul's
Churchyard (also the Bell) which had been destroyed in the Fire. He
entered into partnership with James Allestry and with him was in
1663 appointed printer to the Royal Society. Pepys bought mainly
foreign books from him.[1]

Martin, [Capt. William]. Naval officer: he held two commissions
between 1665 and his death in action in 1666.[1]

Marylebone (Marrowbone). A small semi-rural village of some 70
houses[1] in the fields north of the modern Oxford St, the present
Marylebone High St roughly coinciding with its village street. The
tide of building was already making northwards, but had much ground
to cover before it reached the Oxford Road (now Oxford St). Golden
Sq. and Soho Sq. were still projects for the future. A century later it
could still be termed a village. (R)

Marylebone Gardens. In the fields behind Marylebone manor house,
Beaumont St and part of Devonshire St now covering the site. In the
1660s, and for more than a century thereafter, a notable place of
entertainment with a fine bowling green. (R)

Mason, [John] (d. ?1680). Timber-merchant, Maidstone; the principal supplier to Chatham yard; originally a carpenter.[1]

Matthews, [John]. Clerk in the Privy Seal office.[1]

Matthews, Capt. Richard. Soldier; he occurs as Sandwich's servant in 1659–60 and 1664.[1]

Mauleverer, Sir Richard, 2nd Bt (d. 1675). Royalist; twice imprisoned in the Interregnum; released in Sept. 1659 and in 1660 made Gentleman of the Privy Chamber and Captain of Horse. M.P. for Boroughbridge 1661–75; Sheriff of Yorkshire 1667–8.[1]

May, Adrian. Groom of the Privy Chamber in ordinary to the King.[1]

May, Baptist (Bab) (1628–97). Courtier; servant to the Duke of York by 1648; Registrar of Chancery 1660–97; Keeper of the Privy Purse 1665–85; M.P. for Midhurst 1670. According to Burnet his power at court came from his 'serving the King in his vices' rather than from sharing his absolutist views.[1]

May, Hugh (1622–84). Architect. Paymaster of the King's Works 1660–8; promoted Comptroller 1668; responsible for work at White-hall and Windsor. One of the three surveyors appointed by the King to supervise the rebuilding of London after the Fire. A cousin of Bab May.[1]

Mayer(s), [Robert]. Purveyor of timber to the navy, Woolwich; appointed 1660.[1]

Maynard, Sir John (1602–90). Lawyer; unpopular at the Restoration because he had held judicial office in the Interregnum. He was, and remained, a Presbyterian and was 'to his last breath . . . true as steel to the principles of the late times' (R. North). Nevertheless he conscientiously performed his duties as government counsel in treason trials. He was knighted and made a King's Serjeant by Charles II, but not advanced to the bench until 1689 when he became a Commissioner of the Great Seal. His wife was b. Jane Selhurst.[1]

Mayne, [Jasper] (1604–72). The Canon of Christ Church who in preaching before the King dragged in references to adultery (iii.60). 'A quaint preacher' and 'a witty and facetious companion' (Wood). He wrote plays, one of which – *The city match* – Pepys saw in 1668.[1]

The Maypole in the Strand. The pole stood near the junction of Drury Lane and the Strand, roughly where the church of St Mary-le-Strand now stands. Taken down in the Interregnum, it was re-erected in 1661 but eventually removed in 1718. Pepys's references are not to the pole, or to the tavern named after it, but to the location. It was much used by hackney coaches as a stand and stopping place.[1]

Medicine: *see* Health

Meggot, [Richard] (d. 1692). Pepys's contemporary at St Paul's and Cambridge. Appointed Rector of St Olave, Southwark in 1662, Vicar of Twickenham in 1668, chaplain to the King in 1672, Canon of

Windsor in 1677 and Dean of Winchester in 1679. Evelyn, like Pepys, enjoyed his sermons. Sherlock, Dean of St Paul's, spoke of him at his funeral as 'an admirable preacher, not of noise and lungs, but for well digested, useful, pious discourse'.[1]

Meggs, Mall. A widow who became well-known as the orange-woman at the Theatre Royal. The Company granted her the right to sell oranges to theatre-goers in Feb. 1663; she was still there in 1667.[1]

Mennes (Minnes), Sir John (1599–71). Comptroller of the Navy 1660–71. He entered the navy as a youth, saw service in the W. Indies, was a captain by 1626 and was chosen in 1629 to command the ship which brought Rubens to Charles I's court. During 1635–9 he was continuously at sea, attaining the rank of Vice-Admiral, and later (1642) Rear-Admiral. He served in the army in the Scottish war and commanded a troop of horse for the King in the Civil War, becoming Governor of N. Wales in 1644. He resumed his naval career as the King's fortunes declined on land and in 1645 commanded his navy. In 1648–50 he was flying his flag as Rear-Admiral under Rupert, and during the '50s acted as a royalist agent abroad. At the Restoration he was commissioned to the *Henry* in 1660, becoming Commander-in-Chief in the Downs and Narrow Seas 1661–2. He had by this time won a reputation as a man of action, a witty conversationalist, a learned chemist who dabbled in medicine and a writer of amusing, if usually coarse, verse. But in Nov. 1661 he was made Comptroller and moved into a world of government finance and book-keeping in which he was a stranger and ill at ease. That he was no administrator is indisputable, but it is also true that the comptrollership, involving scrutiny and control of all expenditure by all the Principal Officers, made impossible demands on its holder, especially as business grew with the approach of war. Like all his colleagues, Pepys found him unequal to the task, and in the end, despite his protests, he was forced in Jan. 1667 to delegate work to Brouncker and to Penn. He would have been dismissed had it not been that his dismissal would have looked like a surrender to his parliamentary critics. In the diary and elsewhere Pepys often expresses the despair to which he and his colleagues were reduced by Mennes's incompetence. In addressing the King and Privy Council in Jan. 1670 on the occasion of presenting the Board's reply to the report of the Brooke House Committee, Pepys expressed a gentler verdict. After asserting quite plainly that the greatest of the Board's failures of management had been due 'to the Age and weakness' of Mennes, he went on to say that Mennes had served in three reigns and that he was 'a gentleman of the strictest Integrity, and that his weaknesses both of mind and body had been hastened upon him by his labors in his Majesty's Service'.[1]

Mennes was also Governor of Dover and Gentleman of the Privy Chamber from 1660, member of the Council for Foreign Plantations from 1661, of the Tangier Committee from 1662, the Fishery Corporation from 1664, and Master of Trinity House 1662–3.[2]

His wife died in July 1662, without leaving children, and does not appear in the diary. Pepys mentions his sister, Mary Hammon(d), and her daughters. One of her daughters, Elizabeth, was Mennes's executrix and inherited most of his personal property.[3]

Mercer. Mary (b. 1647) was Elizabeth Pepys's companion 1664–6; the daughter of William and Nichola Mercer of St Olave's parish. Her mother (probably a widow by 1664) lived on the n. side of Crutched Friars (? in French Ordinary Court), where Will Hewer lodged with her. She died in 1673. Mary had two brothers: James (b. 1649) and William (1651–71), the latter of whom is mentioned by name in the diary. Her sister Nan or Anne also appears in the diary. The parish registers record only her sisters Sarah and Elizabeth.[1]

Mercers' Hall and Chapel. On the n. side of Cheapside, just west of its junction with the Poultry, between Ironmonger Lane and Old Jewry. On the site of the college or hospital of St Thomas of Acon, bought by the Company, which ran a school there. All the buildings were destroyed in the Fire, rebuilt, and again largely rebuilt in 1879, but much damaged in 1939–45 and now restored. Pepys retained in his library an engraving of c. 1690.[1] (R)

Meres, Sir Thomas, kt 1660 (1635–1715). M.P. for Lincoln in ten parliaments 1659–1710; a strong Anglican, a leading though wayward member of the country party, and an enemy of Pepys. He opposed Pepys's admission to the Commons in 1674 on the ground that he was a papist, and later opposed his shipbuilding programmes. In 1679 he was a member of the parliamentary committee which condemned Pepys, with Deane, for alleged treason. He was an incompetent member of the incompetent Admiralty Commission of 1679–84.[1]

Meriton. Pepys's 'old acquaintance' – 'the old dunce' – was presumably his contemporary at Magdalene, Thomas Meriton (B.A. 1652), Rector of St Nicholas Cole Abbey 1662–1705. The 'known' Meriton was John (1636–1704) who graduated from St John's College, Cambridge in 1652; he became Rector of St Michael, Cornhill 1664–1704, and President of Sion College 1676–7. He was a popular preacher and published several sermons.[1]

Merrett, [Christopher] (1614–95). Physician; M.D. (Oxon.) 1643, F.R.C.P. 1651; Librarian R.C.P. 1654–66. He was expelled from the college in 1681 for non-attendance.[1]

Mervin, [John]. Merchant supplying provisions to the Tangier garrison.[1]

Meynell, Ald. Francis (d. 1666). Goldsmith, of Lombard St; one of the principal Government bankers. His personal estate is said to have taken ten years to settle.[1]

Middleton, Col. Thomas (d. 1672). Navy Commissioner, Portsmouth 1664–7; Surveyor of the Navy 1667–72; Navy Commissioner, Chatham 1672. Little is known of his background except that he had risen to colonel's rank in the parliamentary army, had traded with the W. Indies and New England, and had travelled both in the New World and the Mediterranean, becoming a member of the Council for Foreign Plantations in 1660. His wartime letters from Portsmouth show him as a vigorous officer and stern disciplinarian. His remedy for desertion (and he expected that seamen would be bound to desert when their ships came in) was to recommend that gallows be set up in every town between Portsmouth and London and that every tenth deserter be hanged. He broke up a mutiny in Nov. 1665 by the use of a 'good cudgel', and reported to the Board that he had not been troubled since. Both Pepys and Coventry thought highly of his work in the dockyard.[1] As a Surveyor, however, he proved incapable in Pepys's view of paying attention to detail.[2] In fact after his appointment to the Board in 1667 he spent most of his time at Chatham, and was obviously at his happiest at the workface.[3]

His (first) wife was Elizabeth, who died in 1669. John Buckworth, a merchant, was an overseer of his will.[4]

Mile End. A hamlet of the parish of Stepney, containing in 1664 some 240 houses,[1] and situated a mile from Aldgate on the road to Bow, Colchester and Harwich. A favourite country resort for Londoners. (R)

Miller, Lt-Col. [John]. Adjutant-General of the foot under Monck; he commanded the guard put on Parliament on 21 Feb. 1660 when the secluded members were admitted. Given a commission in Albemarle's regiment of foot 1661; retired 1673.[1]

Milles, Daniel (1626–89). Pepys's parish priest; Rector of St Olave, Hart St 1657–89. Also minister of the yard, Deptford, from 1660, Rector of Wanstead 1667–89, chaplain to the Duke of York 1667–85; President of Sion College 1670–2; Commissioner for the relief of widows and orphans in the Third Dutch War. At Cambridge he had been a Fellow of St Catharine's College, and Junior Proctor 1653–4. Pepys gives him the title of Doctor, but he did not take his D.D. until 1679.[1] Pepys was critical of him, as of all parsons – and his absence from his parish during the Plague appears to deserve criticism – but he was clearly a man of ability, though his performances in the pulpit were, according to Pepys, variable. Relations between them in the '60s were friendly without being close – it was not until June 1668 that Pepys paid his first visit to the rectory.[2] More than once in later life he certified Pepys's attendance at communion in order to scotch rumours of his being a papist.[3] In his turn he asked Pepys (in 1681) to place a son-in-law in the Navy Office, and himself (in 1687) in a prebend.[4]

His (first) wife Mary came of a Brampton family, and it was through her that he died possessed of land in Huntingdonshire (she having predeceased him).[5] Their son David was one of the clerks to the Clerk of Acts 1697–1722.[6] Their daughter Anna married Thomas Coppin in 1683.[7] [*See also* Religion]

Millet, Capt. [Henry] (d. by 1688). He held six commissions 1660–9 and was awarded a prize-ship in 1667 for his 'former sufferings and late reverses'.[1]

Minnes: *see* Mennes

Minors, Capt. [Richard]. He held three commissions 1661–72 and commanded the *Leopard* in the expedition of 1661–2 sent to take over Bombay.[1]

Mitchell. Miles and Ann Mitchell were booksellers in Westminster Hall from whom Pepys often bought newsbooks, political pamphlets and the like. They also advertised the sale of lozenges. They kept the first shop in the Hall from c. 1656, and were old friends of Pepys, he and Elizabeth often using their stall as a rendezvous. Their house, in St Margaret's parish, appears to have been a substantial one.[1] Their son Michael married Betty Howlett (whom Pepys called his 'wife') and kept a strong-water house on the w. side of Old Swan Lane. He was living there in 1680.[2]

Mohun, [Michael] (1620–?91). An actor before the Civil War; manager of the company at the Red Bull Theatre, Clerkenwell in 1660. Leading actor, director and shareholder in the King's Company and United Company.[1]

Mohun, Capt. [Robert] (d. by 1688). He held six commissions 1662–6, and was possibly the Capt. Moon who in 1679 gave evidence against Sir A. Deane alleging that (with Balty St Michel and others) he had improperly used the sloop *Hunter* as a privateer in 1673.[1]

Molins. Members of three successive generations of this family became leading surgeons for the stone. The first (not mentioned in the diary) was James (d. 1638), who was probably the practitioner to whom Pepys's surgeon, Thomas Hollier, was apprenticed. His son Edward (d. 1663) – 'the famous Ned Mullins' (iv.340) – succeeded to his father's posts as surgeon at St Thomas's Hospital and lithotomist at both St Thomas's and St Bartholomew's. After serving as a surgeon with the royalist forces, he went into private practice and was called in to treat Oliver Cromwell for the stone. (As a good royalist, he is said to have refused payment.)[1] He resumed his hospital posts in 1660, alternating annually with Hollier as lithotomist at Thomas's. Pepys reports his death from the effects of an amputation of a leg. His son James (d. 1687) succeeded him at Thomas's and was appointed surgeon to the royal household in 1680.[2]

Monck, George, cr. Duke of Albemarle 1660 (1608–70). Younger

son of a Devon squire, Monck devoted himself to the profession of
arms as both soldier and sailor. In 1625–7 he took part in the expeditions to Cadiz and La Rochelle. He then served a succession of masters:
in the 1630s the Dutch republic, in the Civil War first the King, then
after his defeat the Parliament; later the régimes that in turn followed
the execution of the King. In 1653 he fought alongside Blake and
Deane as a general-at-sea, taking part in the battles of Portland and the
Gabbard, and with his colleagues pioneering the use of the line-ahead
formation in action. But in Oct. 1659, as Commander-in-Chief in
Scotland, he refused to serve under the army officers who had displaced the Rump, and declared himself against them. He had from the
earliest days of his service firmly believed in the subordination of the
military to the civil power. The height of his career up to this point had
been his rule as Cromwell's proconsul in Scotland. From the moment
he had pacified that country in 1654 he had governed it with moderation and good sense, and had built up under his command the most
considerable force in the Commonwealth. From Oct. 1659 he was set
on a course which led to even more memorable achievements. He
decided to march south at the end of the year to restore parliamentary
and (probably) royal government. Pepys's diary begins on the same
day on which he crossed his Rubicon, the Tweed. Thereafter the diary
is the principal authority for the story of Monck's decisive part in the
power struggle which led first to the re-admission of the moderate
(secluded) M.P.s to the Rump, and then to the recall of the King. He
had been in touch with the royalists since the time of Booth's rising
in Aug. 1659, and now made his moves with great deliberation, mask-
ing his intentions by a soldierly taciturnity. He and his army had made
a peaceful restoration possible. Monck was a popular hero. The King
rewarded him with the Garter and a dukedom. He was made Captain-
General of the kingdom, a privy councillor and a member of most of
its important committees.

Pepys's references to him, once the Restoration is achieved, are mostly
hostile. It is true that his account of Monck's activities in 1665 when he
acted as the Duke of York's deputy as Admiral of the Kingdom has
few if any criticisms, and witnesses to his energy and care for detail.
But in committee work Pepys found him a 'blockhead'; and as a naval
commander (he had charge of a fleet in the campaign of 1666) thought
him much inferior to Sandwich whom he displaced. For his part
Monck had hard words for the Navy Office's inefficient victualling
system, which, he claimed, had cramped his tactical mobility. His
health having deteriorated, he retired to his country house (New Hall,
Essex) for the last two years of his life.

Fate has been unkind to him. As a military and naval commander he
had the makings of greatness – courage, technical knowledge (especially

of gunnery) and an unfailing regard for his men's welfare. But no famous victories on either land or sea are associated with his name. His greatest achievement – his share in bringing about the Restoration – has never quite sufficed to establish a reputation: it is a complex matter because so many influences were running the same way. His belief in the subordination of the military arm to the civil authority, however admirable, limited his impact on events. Together with his personal modesty, and the heaviness of temperament to which Pepys draws such frequent attention, it explains his lack of political drive. In crises – the Plague or the Fire – he could still be useful because of his capacity to rally the support of his soldiers and of the London public. But after his few months of eminence in 1659–60 he failed to hold the stage. If there had been popular disturbances in the '60s as there were after Waterloo, he could have become another Wellington. As it was, he played only a minor rôle in the politics of the diary period.[1]

His wife, whom he married in 1653, was Anne Clarges, whose brother Thomas became Monck's most influential aide. She was a farrier's daughter and was said to have been still married to her first husband when she became Monck's mistress and later wife. Her sluttishness and rapacity are well attested by other witnesses than Pepys. She died three weeks after Monck.[2]

Their only son Christopher, the 2nd Duke, died in 1688, after which the line became extinct. Albemarle St, off Piccadilly, is named after him.[3]

Montouth, ——. Possibly Patrick Monteith, army captain.[1]

Moore, Frank. Elizabeth's cousin of these names has not been identified. His namesake, Lambert's 'man', was made a cornet in Lambert's regiment in July 1659.[1]

Moore, Henry. Lawyer; Sandwich's man of business. He is said to have been a connection of Sandwich and was in his service from at least 1657.[1] After the Restoration he virtually took over Pepys's responsibilities in the Sandwich household. He lived mainly at the Wardrobe and seems to have had responsibilities there as well as in Sandwich's household affairs. He was reputed 'very honest' but too slow.[2] Sandwich when in Spain conducted a close correspondence with him.[3] Although he once had chambers at Gray's Inn he does not appear to have been a member of that or any other inn. That he was intelligent and well-informed is clear from Pepys's love of his conversation and trust in his legal judgement. He does not appear in Pepys's correspondence after the diary ends.

Moore, Sir Jonas, kt 1663 (1617–79). Of humble birth (originally a clerk in the service of the Chancellor of Durham) he was one of the most gifted mathematicians and surveyors of his day; F.R.S. 1674. Like most 17th-century practitioners of mathematics he owed nothing to university teaching, but learnt from apprenticeship to a master – in his case Oughtred. He was appointed to teach the Duke of York in 1647, and in 1649 was made surveyor to the Fen Drainage scheme. In 1669 he became Surveyor-General to the Ordnance and served until his death, being one of the last ordnance officials to go on active service (in 1673). He was one of Pepys's learned acquaintance: their interests coincided at several points – in the theory of number, the problems of surveying, in navigation and in engineering. He was consulted, along with Wren, on Cholmley's design for the Tangier mole, and he made for John Seller a survey of the s.-e. coasts of England. He was influential in the foundation both of the Royal Mathematical School of Christ's Hospital in 1673 (established at Pepys's suggestion) and of the Royal Observatory at Greenwich in 1674. Tompion the clockmaker was among his protégés. Pepys retained several of his books in his library. No correspondence between the two appears to survive.[1]

Moorfields. A large marshy area north of the city wall, built over in the 18th and early 19th centuries, and today covered by Finsbury Sq., Finsbury Circus and adjacent streets. Part of it was drained early in the 16th century, and by 1598 three windmills had been built. In 1605 the southern section was laid out by the city in pleasant walks, set with trees. It was much used for recreation.[1]

Moorgate. A comparatively unimportant gate in the city's wall commanding the exit to Moorfields but approached by no major road. Not damaged in the Fire but rebuilt in 1672 and demolished a hundred years later. The street of that name, which passes over its site, was made c. 1846. (R)

Moray, Sir Robert kt 1643 (?1608–73). Chemist and politician; a founder of the Royal Society and its first pre-charter President. 'The most universally beloved and esteemed by men of all sides and sorts of any man I have ever known in my whole life' (Burnet).[1]

Mordaunt, Elizabeth, Lady Mordaunt (1645–87). After Elizabeth Pepys's death, she and her sister Mrs Stewart ('the ladies in Portugal Row')[1] – both widows – became Pepys's close friends. Affectionate and witty, they conducted a delightful correspondence with him in which they employed 'all the sighings and teasings of an *amitié amoureuse*' (Ollard).[2] In 1674 they planned an expedition to France with him which never came off.[3] Evelyn and Thomas Hill also valued their friendship. Both were musical. Lady Mordaunt died in 1687; her sister was still alive in 1692 when with Pepys she was a godparent at the christening of a granddaughter of Evelyn. Their father was Sir Nicholas Johnson, of St Gregory's, London, who had married a sister of Sir William, husband of Jane Turner: they were therefore Pepys's cousins by marriage. Lady Mordaunt had married Sir Charles Mordaunt (4th Bt) in 1663; he had died in 1665 and she had then married Francis

Godolphin of Colston, Wilts. After the death of her second husband she reverted, as was customary, to the name of her previous husband since he was superior in rank.[4]

Mordaunt, Henry, 2nd Earl of Peterborough (1623–97). Governor of Tangier 1661–2; living 1665–74 in Long Acre. A close associate of the Duke of York; a commissioner of his household (from 1667) who negotiated his marriage with Mary of Modena in 1673. In James's reign he was made Groom of the Stole, First Gentleman of the Bedchamber, and Privy Councillor, but was mistrusted by colleagues because of his fiery temperament. He became a Roman Catholic in 1687. After William of Orange's invasion he was caught trying to escape abroad, and was impeached but never tried. He had a strong interest in genealogy and antiquities and published a largely mythical history of his family under the *nom-de-plume* of Robert Halstead.

His wife Penelope (m. 1645, d. 1702) was the daughter of the 5th Earl of Thomond. She was Groom of the Stole to Queen Mary of Modena.[1]

Mordaunt, John, 1st Viscount Mordaunt (1627–75). Younger brother of the foregoing. One of the most important leaders of the royalist underground faction which in 1658–60 aimed at restoration by allying with the Presbyterians and the city. He was captured and tried in June 1658 and escaped death only by the casting vote of the president of the court. In the following July and August he took a prominent part in the organisation of a nation-wide rising. Its failure led to much recrimination among the royalists (*see* Willys, Sir Richard). Mordaunt's quarrelsome nature – evident from the diary – did nothing to help the cause. The King rewarded him with a viscountcy in the spring of 1659 but only with consolation prizes at the Restoration – principally the governorship of Windsor castle. This he had to resign in 1668 after his persecution of a subordinate led to his being impeached. The later years of his life were spent in litigation against his brother Peterborough about family property.[1]

Morden (Morton), [William]. Bookseller, Cambridge (fl. 1652–79). Among the books he published was John Ray's *Collection of English proverbs* (1st ed. 1670). He was living in the parish of St Mary-the-Great in 1653, and was buried in St Michael's church in 1679.[1]

Morice, Sir William, kt 1660 (?1602–76). Secretary of State (Northern Department) 1660–8; M.P. for Plymouth 1660, 1661–76. He had little or no political experience in 1660 and reached high office only because of his part in the royalist negotiations of the spring. It was he who put his kinsman Monck into touch with the royalist agent Sir John Grenville. All three were Devonians. He was learned, pious, and a good parliamentary speaker though politically unambitious. He retired to his books and country pursuits in 1668, selling his office to Trevor.[1]

Morland, Sir Samuel (1625–95). Mathematician, inventor, and
Pepys's tutor at Magdalene, where he was a Fellow from 1649–54. He
left Cambridge for the public service and held a post under Secretary
Thurloe. By the summer of 1659 he was passing information to the
royalists abroad. His reward at the Restoration was a knighthood, a
baronetcy, a pension and a place in the Privy Chamber. But nothing
went right with him: he passed the rest of his life 'in a state of perpetual
and clamorous impecuniosity' (Bryant).[1] He sold his English pension;
for a while after 1668 he acquired a French one. He lived in the '60s in
Pall Mall; moved to Bloomsbury, later to Vauxhall, and by 1687
was living in what he called a 'hut' by Hyde Park gate.[2] He produced
inventions by the dozen, but could not invent a means of staying
solvent. The most interesting of his inventions, technically, was his
calculating machine. The most important, politically, was a device for
opening and resealing letters – much used by the Post Office until the
instruments were destroyed, with the Post Office building, in the Fire.
He pressed on Pepys and the Admiralty several varieties of water pump,
each better than the last, and a design for naval gun carriages. For his
own delight he contrived indoor fountains, a portable cooking stove
and a mechanical glyster with which he could administer an enema to
himself without getting out of bed. To pay his debts he fell back in
1687 on the oldest contrivance of all: he married, as he thought, an
heiress – but she turned out to be an adventuress who was scheming to
saddle him with her debts and her bastard. He managed to get rid of her
after a few years by divorce, since she had set herself up as the mistress of
Sir Gilbert Gerard, feeling cheated of her expectations. He told the
whole tragi-comedy in a series of letters to Pepys, in the hope that his
old pupil would be able, through his influence with the Chancellor
and the King, to expedite the legal proceedings.[3]

Morrice. 'Madam' or Mrs Morrice and her husband were clearly
friends (or relatives) of John and Jane Turner of St Bride's parish. The
wife was possibly the 'Mrs Morris' of St Bride's parish who died of the
plague in Aug. 1665.[1] The husband may have been an Exchequer
official (cf. iv.272). A Humphrey Morris was appointed Auditor of the
Land Revenue there in 1667.[2] The Morrice who sang bass (i.19) may
have been William Morris, vicar choral of St Paul's in 1661.[3]

Morris, [John]. Landlord of the Ship, Fenchurch St; he was possibly
also the John Morris who issued an undated token from the Exchange
tavern in the same street. His wife was the daughter of his predecessor
at the Ship, Richard Brome.[1]

Morris, Capt. [Robert] (1619–75). Appointed upholsterer-extra-
ordinary to the royal Household in 1661; a captain in the city trainbands.[1]

Morris, [Roger] (1607–90). Wine cooper; Common Councilman
1665–77; still owed money by the Navy Board at his death.[1]

Mossom, [Robert] (d. 1679). Clergyman: he conducted the illegal Anglican services at Cary House in the Strand which Pepys was attending in the early months of 1660. He had also conducted them at St Peter, Paul's Wharf since c. 1650 when he was ejected from his curacy at Teddington. He had published two tracts in defence of the royal power in 1642–3. At the Restoration he was rewarded by a prebend at York (1660), the deanery of Christ Church, Dublin (1661) and the bishopric of Derry (1666).[1]

Motham (Mootham), Capt.[Peter]. Naval officer; he held captain's commissions from 1652 until his death in action in 1666.[1]

Mount, [Jeremiah]. Apparently a clerk or servant of the Council of State in 1660; in 1661 a Gentleman-Usher to the Duchess of Albemarle. A friend of Peter Llewellyn who was also employed by the Council of State in 1660 – he received a ring at his funeral. Possibly the Jeremy Mount, gentleman, of Bridewell, who died c. 1699.[1]

Mountagu, Edward, 2nd Earl of Manchester (1602–71). First cousin of Sandwich; Lord Chamberlain 1660–71. A leading opponent of Charles I in the early years of the Long Parliament, he had proved unwilling to fight the King to a finish in the Civil War, and had been displaced as Major-General of the Eastern Association by Cromwell in 1644–5. He had opposed the King's trial and execution and during the Interregnum retired into private life. From Apr. 1659 he was in touch with the royalists and engaged in plans for a restoration, hoping, for his own part, to become Lord Treasurer.[1] As a leader of the moderate Presbyterians he presided over the House of Lords in the Convention. At the Restoration he was made Privy Councillor, Lord Chamberlain and Knight of the Garter. A strong Puritan, he was willing to accept a modified episcopacy as the price of national unity in church matters. He was of a mild and generous temper, and widely esteemed.[2]

Mountagu, Edward, cr. Earl of Sandwich 1660 (1625–72). Sandwich belonged to that generation of country gentlemen who in most cases, had it not been for the Civil War, would have been content to live out their days as local notabilities. Throughout his life, Sandwich had the affability and fairmindedness that characterised the best sort of squire. But he and his family had to play their parts on a larger stage. His father, who held court office as a Master of Requests, was a royalist, but Sandwich, in common with his Mountagu relatives at Boughton and Kimbolton and his wife's family the Crews, joined the parliamentary cause. In 1643 he raised a regiment of foot in the army of the Eastern Association commanded by his cousin the 2nd Earl of Manchester. He saw action in 1644–5 at Marston Moor and Naseby and in the last assault on Bristol, and won a reputation for bravery. He showed courage too in joining his friend and neighbour Oliver Cromwell in the movement to replace Manchester, who was loath to conduct the war *à outrance*. However he took no part in the Second Civil War, retiring to his family home at Hinchingbrooke, near Huntingdon, where, after his father's death in Sept. 1644, family affairs called for his attention. There he stayed during the confused and harrowing years that led to the King's execution and did not re-emerge until Apr. 1653 when he was chosen to serve in Barebone's Parliament. By now the course of revolution had carried events so far that Sandwich counted as a moderate, and it was as one of the most active of the moderates in that parliament and one likely to have the support of Cromwell and the army leaders that he was made President of the Council of State in November. With the establishment of the Protectorate in Dec. 1653 he rose to a certain political eminence as an M.P., Councillor of State, Treasury Commissioner and after 1657 member of the Upper House. He was one of the conservative group of Cromwell's advisers who came close to success in urging him to assume the title of king as a guarantee of order. Cromwell introduced him to a naval career in Jan. 1656 by making him joint General-at-Sea with Blake in the fleet which sailed to the Mediterranean against Spain. But Blake's campaign in the previous year had established virtual control there and events in 1656 proved an anti-climax. Sandwich and Blake were meant to capture a Spanish treasure fleet but arrived too late, and Sandwich had to be content with bringing back the treasure captured by another admiral, Stayner. In 1657–8 he was in the Channel covering operations against Dunkirk, and in 1659 he commanded a squadron sent to the Baltic to mediate in the Danish-Swedish war and to check the advance of Dutch power there which threatened our sources of naval supplies. It was in the Baltic that he was first approached by royalist agents. As a Cromwellian who had no love for a republic and as one of the many who were tired of revolutionary instability, he was, after the death of Oliver and the fall of Richard, ripe for conversion to royalism. He and Monck, by arrangement with the King, accepted appointment from the Rump as generals-at-sea and Councillors of State. The diary tells the story of his bringing the King home from exile, after which he was rewarded with an earldom, the Garter, and court office as Master of the Great Wardrobe, and was marked out for further naval command by his appointment as Vice-Admiral of the kingdom and Admiral of the Narrow Seas.

His greatest achievement as commander was his part in the first great battle of the Second Dutch War off Lowestoft in June 1665, when he was responsible for the breaking of the Dutch line. The remainder of the year brought disappointment, and worse. He failed (through no fault of his) to take the Dutch E. India fleet in Bergen harbour; he failed to intercept de Ruyter's squadron on its way home from the Mediterranean, and, having captured two richly laden E. Indiamen from the enemy, he brought scandal on himself by allowing the cargo to be rifled before being declared prize. Finally in October he gave a handle to his critics by refusing to take his fleet out in the autumn storms. He was thereupon sent off to Spain as ambassador (1666–8) where he did much to retrieve his reputation. He proved a shrewd and tactful negotiator – mediating between Spain and Portugal to end their long war, and concluding with Spain a commercial treaty which was the foundation of a prosperous trade for over a century. But he came back an impoverished man, his pay and allowances badly in arrears. Finance so often proved his undoing. It was his carelessness over money that had led to the prize-goods scandal, and it was his incapacity to tackle the difficult problems of the Wardrobe finances which bedevilled his régime as Master there.

On his return from Spain he was active in the House of Lords as an ally of Ormond and an opponent of the Cabal. It is doubtful if he made any serious attempt to rise to high office, though office of the right sort might well have been the answer to his financial problems. But he did not find politics greatly to his taste, and in any case Clarendon, his patron and ally, was now in exile. The best of his public work in his later years was done in 1669–71 for the Council for Foreign Plantations, of which he became President. He was interested in colonial and commercial affairs, and the task of presiding over debates was one to which he was temperamentally well suited. He did not welcome the Dutch War in 1672 and in particular disapproved of the attack on the Dutch Smyrna fleet which provoked it, but he resumed his command and perished on his flagship the *Royal James* in the opening battle in Sole Bay.

Like Pepys, Sandwich was a man of varied gifts and tastes – interested in mathematics and astronomy, a good linguist, though not bookish, a musician capable of composing in three parts, and a gifted pen-and-ink artist. He kept a journal, but unlike Pepys's, it was a memorial of his public life – a vast miscellany in ten large volumes (some in the hands of his clerks, but never in Pepys's) running from 1652 and containing admirals' logs (the only parts yet published), scraps of correspondence, copies of official documents, Lords' debates and (best of all) a diary of his Spanish embassy.[1] This last is a record of the topography and curiosities of the country, illustrated with sketches of whatever he found remarkable – from harbours and fountains to earrings and doorknockers. In it he shows something of Pepys's own powers of observation and zest for novelty.

By the time the diary ends, relations between Sandwich and Pepys were no longer close, and in the summer of 1669 Pepys was not called in to help him face the parliamentary enquiry into the prize-goods scandal. Sandwich now had other advisers; and Pepys for his part had an assured position and other powerful friends. The old quarrel over Betty Becke may have left its scars, and Pepys had compounded his offence by neglecting to write during the Spanish embassy. In Sandwich's will (signed in Aug. 1669) Pepys, who might have expected to be an executor if not a trustee, was not even mentioned. Yet there is evidence that Pepys continued to hold Sandwich in high regard; in the '80s he was thinking of writing a life of that 'noble and yet (I fear) unparalleled Lord'.[2]

Besides his house at Hinchingbrooke he had an official residence in Whitehall Palace, from 1653 until his death, which included part (or probably all) of the gatehouse of the King St gate, and rooms adjacent to it on both sides of the street. He also had official lodgings (1660–8) at the Wardrobe, and from 1664 rented houses in Lincoln's Inn Fields and Hampstead.

Family. In 1642 Sandwich married Jemima, the 17-year old daughter of John Crew of Stene, a leading parliamentarian of Northamptonshire. The sweetness of her disposition and her unfailing kindness to Pepys make her one of the most attractive figures in the diary – 'so good and discreet a woman I know not in the world'.[3] She died in 1674.[4]

They had seven sons and four daughters, most of whom are identified in footnotes to the text. The two eldest sons, Edward (1648–88) and Sidney (1650–1727), were sent to be schooled in France in 1661. Edward, who succeeded to the title, took little part in public life, because of ill-health (except for a short service as M.P. for Dover 1670–2 and later two inactive turns of local duty as Lord-Lieutenant), and died in France at Saintes (Charente-Inférieure) where he had lived in retirement for some years. His wife (b. Lady Anne Boyle, daughter of the 1st Earl of Burlington) had died in 1671 only three years after their marriage. Sidney, the second (and favourite) son, was given what his father called 'a liberal breeding'[5] – his schooling in Paris 1661–4, a Grand Tour of the Continent 1669–71, and in between a spell in Madrid at the embassy. He served in the army as an ensign and sat for Huntingdon in the first Exclusion Parliament. He took the name Wortley-Montagu on marrying a Yorkshire heiress, and lived on her estates for most of his life. His daughter-in-law Lady Mary Wortley-Montagu has a description of him wearing 'a huge flapped hat, seated majestically in his elbow chair, talking very loud and swearing boisterously at the servants'.[6]

A few members of later generations of the family have become well known: Lady Mary Wortley-Montagu (d. 1762), the letter-writer; the 4th Earl (d. 1792), who is said to have invented the sandwich; and Mrs Montagu (d. 1800), the republican bluestocking who so enraged Dr Johnson, who was the wife of the 1st Earl's grandson Charles.[7]

Mountagu, Edward (Ned) (1635–65). Eldest son of the 2nd Baron

Mountagu of Boughton (d. 1684) and Sandwich's first cousin twice removed. M.P. for Sandwich from 1661, and Master of the Horse to the Queen Mother. He acted as go-between when the royalist agent Whetstone first made contact with Sandwich on the Baltic voyage in the summer of 1659, and in 1661–2 helped to manage Sandwich's affairs during his absence in the Mediterranean. But he was foolish and vain, quarrelled with Clarendon and his own family by attaching himself to Arlington's interest (like Arlington he was said to be a crypto-papist), and ended by being dismissed from court for making improper advances to the Queen. He was killed in the attack on Bergen.[1]

Mountagu, George (1622–81). Fifth son of the 1st Earl of Manchester; first cousin, once removed, of Sandwich. M.P. for Huntingdon Nov. 1640–8, Dover 1660, 1661–Jan. 79; also *Custos Rotulorum* for Westminster, Master of St Katharine's Hospital near the Tower, and, after 1666, Gentleman of the Privy Chamber. He looked after Sandwich's affairs during his absence on the Spanish embassy, and acted as an executor and trustee under his will. He had accompanied him on both the Baltic and Dutch voyages.

His wife (m. 1645) was Elizabeth, daughter of Sir Anthony Irby of Whaplade, Lincs., who had seven sons and four daughters by him. Their house in London was in Cannon Row, Westminster (taxed on 23 hearths)[1] and in the country at Horton, Northants.[2]

Mountagu, Ralph, succ. as 3rd Baron Mountagu of Boughton 1684, cr. Duke of Montagu 1705 (?1638–1709). Pepys refers to 'scurvy stories' of him.[1] His career consisted of nothing else. He was several times ambassador to Paris between 1666 and 1678, and used his embassies to become Louis XIV's paid agent in English politics, his principal achievement being to bring down the anti-French Danby by impeachment in 1678. He scored several successes in matrimony. He married first the daughter of the Earl of Southampton, the Lord Treasurer, who was the widow of the Earl of Northumberland. His second wife was the daughter of the Duke of Newcastle, and was so mad that he had to court her by pretending to be the Emperor of China. And he obtained his own dukedom by marrying off a son to Marlborough's daughter. He built two remarkable houses – Boughton House, Northants., and Montagu House (later enlarged as the British Museum) in Bloomsbury.[2]

Mountagu, Abbé Walter (?1603–77). Second son of the 1st Earl of Manchester, and cousin of Sandwich. A Catholic convert, he was one of the circle of Catholic intellectuals around Queen Henrietta-Maria in the 1630s. During the Civil War he was in France organising supplies for the royalist armies. He then took Holy Orders and was given the rich abbey of Pontoise by Marie de Medici. He lived for the most part in Paris and became the spiritual director and political adviser of

Henrietta-Maria and later of her daughter Henrietta. He was used to attempt the conversion of Charles II's brother, the Duke of Gloucester, in 1654, and to help in the negotiations of the Treaty of Dover in 1670. He published a play and books of verse as well as works of devotion and of Catholic propaganda.[1]

Mountagu, Sir William, kt 1676 (?1619–1707). Second son of the 1st Baron Mountagu of Boughton; Sandwich's cousin and principal legal adviser. M.P. for Huntingdon Apr.–May 1640, Cambridge University 1660, and Stamford 1661–Jan. 79; Attorney-General to the Queen 1662 and L.C. Baron of the Exchequer 1676–86. He was dismissed from the bench for refusing to give unqualified approval to James II's use of the prerogative of suspension. He lived in Lincoln's Inn Fields in the diary period. His (second) wife (m. 1651, d. 1700) was Mary, daughter of Sir John Aubrey.[1]

Mountney, [Richard]. Officer of the Customs House; appointed Joint Comptroller 1669.[1]

Moxon, [Joseph] (1627–?1700). Pioneer globe-maker (using Dutch models), printer, type-founder and mathematical instrument-maker. In Cornhill in the 1660s. He supplied the Navy Office with globes and printed stationery.[1] Hydrographer to the King 1662; F.R.S. 1678. Pepys retained nine of his publications in his library.[2]

Moyer, Samuel (d. c. 1683). Republican merchant: a member (from 1647) and chairman (from 1650) of the Committee for Compounding, and a member of the High Court of Justice set up in 1650. Along with Ireton and other republicans he was imprisoned after Venner's rising in 1661. His brother Laurence secured his release in 1667. Laurence himself narrowly escaped arrest in 1661, arms having been discovered in his house, by virtue of having taken the oaths as a member of Trinity House.[1]

Moyses, Capt. [?Richard]. Cromwellian army officer, and a farmer of recusants' estates.[1]

Muddiman, [Henry] (1629–92). Journalist; he wrote most of the contents of the government newspapers Apr. 1660–Aug. 1663, the earlier numbers of the *Oxford/London Gazette* 1665–6, and a remarkable run of newsletters 1660–88, in which he gave correspondents both domestic and foreign news. He worked under successive secretaries of state, and in close association (until 1666) with Joseph Williamson, the Under-Secretary. Together they built up a system of news gathering and news distribution far superior to any previously known in England.[1]

The Mulberry Garden. Established by James I in 1609 to encourage the making of English silks, it occupied the site of the present Buckingham Palace and gardens. A house was later built on one part which became Goring House, the remainder of the original garden degenerating by Cromwell's day into a place of public entertainment. Pepys never went to it until 20 May 1668, when he found it full of 'a rascally, whoring, roguing sort of people'. It closed down as a public resort sometime in the 1670s, possibly about the time when, in 1674, Goring House was burnt down. (R)

Mumford, Mrs. Shopkeeper, Westminster Hall. There are several of this name in the parish registers of St Margaret's, but none listed among the shopkeepers in the Hall who paid tax. Possibly a mistake for Murford (q.v.).[1]

Murford, Will. Navy Office messenger. Pepys's personal accounts 1667–8 refer to 'young Murford'.[1]

Murford, Capt. [William]. Timber merchant; of Cannon St. He died in 1666 leaving a widow, Bridget.[1]

Murford, Mrs. Shopkeeper, Westminster Hall. The assessments for the Royal Aid (1666) record a Mrs Mugford/Muckford as a shopkeeper there.[1]

MUSIC

The diary is an extraordinary record of what was, in a perfectly precise sense, a passion for music. Pepys felt for music with an intensity that he could compare only to his love of women.[1] It was the 'thing of the world' that he loved most,[2] and though he from time to time reflected that his enslavement to it threatened to encroach on business he never bound himself to resist music in the way that he periodically, and unavailingly, bound himself to resist the pleasures of the playhouse or women. Rather, he allowed music to exercise a considerable influence on his friendships, on the composition of his household, on his weekly routine, and on the physical arrangement of his house; it was his great consolation in plague time and it was to be a source both of tribulation and of reconciliation in his dealings with his wife.

Yet, for all that the animating emotion is so immediate and direct, its circumstances are often complex, even paradoxical. The diary is an unparalleled account of music-making, of response to music, of the material and social factors conditioning musical activity. But its context is necessarily implicit, and it is in the relation of detail to context that problems arise. There is, first of all, the question of Pepys's own musical competence. He steps before us armed with a wealth of skills. He was a bass (we would think of him as a bass-baritone) sufficiently accomplished to take his part, 'and with much ease', in the choir of the Chapel Royal,[3] and acceptable, as a singer, at the private gatherings of professional musicians. He was a player of the viols, of the violin, of the lute and its close cousin the theorbo, and of the flageolet. During the diary period he learned the recorder and contemplated taking whistling lessons; he also became the owner of the King's whistling starling. He was ambitious to compose, devoted much time to composition, and formed the conviction that he had a contribution to make to musical theory. Against this must be set his need to ask professional musicians to provide the basses for the songs of which he had written the treble lines, his apparent inability to master the principles underlying the essential discipline of thorough-bass, and his lack of any competence as a keyboard player (when he bought a spinet it was not so that he might play it, but in order to use it as a means of exploring the mysteries of concords and discords). Nevertheless, he was perfectly able to put a keyboard instrument in tune. The picture as a whole suggests a man of great natural aptitude, gifted with an excellent ear and possessed of a determined curiosity in musical matters, but deficient in formal training, immediately appreciative of melody but less responsive to or understanding of harmony.

If we pursue the metaphor of a picture we find the foreground clear, the background obscure, or at least shaded. In 17th-century England it was still possible to receive a first-rate musical education as a matter of course. Such an education, which in no way presumed a subsequent musical career, was enjoyed by Pepys's acquaintance Elias Ashmole, the herald, antiquary, and astrologer with whom he sang on 24 Oct. 1660. Ashmole's schooling at Lichfield took place partly in the Grammar School, partly at the 'Music School' or 'Song School' in the Cathedral Close, where he was 'competently grounded' in the art.[4] This was made possible by the survival of late medieval and early renaissance educational theory, which had treated music as a necessary branch of philosophy and mathematics rather than as primarily an affective phenomenon. It was a theory that died in England during the course of the century; it lasted a little (though not much) longer in Scotland. It is notable that Pepys himself was to recommend at the end of his life that an element of music be preserved in the Oxford curriculum, maintaining that it was a social and psychological good, 'a science peculiarly productive of a pleasure that no state of life, publick or private, secular or sacred; no difference of age or season; no temper of mind or condition of health exempt from present anguish; nor, lastly, distinction of quality, renders either improper, untimely, or unentertaining . . .', and that in so recommending music he assumed it to be a 'part of mathematick knowledge'.[5] It was a suggestion that went unheeded; the Augustan temper did not favour a view of music as other than a luxury, a matter of sound rather than sense.

We know nothing of Pepys's musical upbringing. There was evidently a tradition of musicality in his family; his father played the bass viol, and there was a virginals amongst the chattels at his death.[6] His brother was an adequate performer on the bass viol, his cousin

Frank Perkin a sufficiently accomplished (or, at least, determined)
fiddler to earn his living with a violin cadged from Samuel after his
mill, the instrument of his original avocation, had been blown down.
But there is no indication that attention was paid to music teaching at
St Paul's or at Magdalene, though there was a good deal of music-
making in Cambridge during the Interregnum, and Pepys's entry for
26 June 1662 suggests that he had formed musical friendships there. In
Mountagu's household there was evidently much musical activity
when circumstances permitted; Mountagu himself played the viol, the
keyboard, the guitar and the lute, as well as singing and composing.
Indeed Pepys's musicianship may well have been one of the things that
recommended him to Sandwich; it is noteworthy that several 17th-
century composers occupied positions in households which required of
them duties not primarily musical; John Wilbye, John Ward and
Christopher Simpson are examples, and no doubt a musicianly steward
was as valuable as a stewardly musician. Ashmole was directed towards
his 'Music School' by a patron who intended to take him into his
household. The desirability and difficulty of attaining an adequately
musical 'family' was something that would later much preoccupy
Pepys. As it is, the absence of evidence appears to confirm the implication of the diary record, that Pepys was dependent, in musical matters,
upon a natural gift developed without early formal training. He was by
no means unaware that his chief virtue as a performer lay in his 'judgment and goodness of eare'.

He had, in any case, grown up in a period during which the musical
profession laboured under extraordinary difficulties. There was no
puritan objection to secular music. Cromwell had an organ in the
Great Gallery at Hampton Court, employed John Hingston as his
organist, maintained other musicians besides, and attended 'music-
meetings'. He used music to entertain ambassadors, and his ambassadors
likewise used music to entertain the courts to which they were sent.
The occasion of his daughter's marriage was marked by the performance of a masque. Eight masters of music walked in the Lord Protector's
funeral procession.[7] In *The Pilgrim's Progress* Bunyan imagined 'a pair
of excellent virginals' in the House Beautiful, where, as Mercy said,
there was 'Music in the house, music in the heart, and music also in
heaven', for joy that the pilgrims had arrived. Wood recorded, as a
characteristic of the Presbyterians and Independents at Oxford in the
period of their ascendancy, that 'they encouraged instrumental musick
and some there were that had musick meetings every week in their
chambers; but vocall music the heads of these parties did not care for
and the juniors were afraid to entertaine it because used by the prelatical
party in their devotions'. Roger North writing a half-century later but
on the evidence of those impeccable if informal authorities, his own

intensely musical kinsmen, considered that the Civil War and its after-math had actually served as an incentive to domestic music making, 'for many chose rather to fidle at home, than to goe out, and be knockt on the head abroad'.[8]

But none of this can soften the fact that, during the Interregnum, of the three principal musical establishments of the realm, the court was in exile, the Church of England and the theatre proscribed. There was no longer a King's Musick; the cathedral and collegiate choirs were disbanded; organs in cathedrals, churches and college chapels destroyed, removed (Cromwell's organ at Hampton Court was from Magdalen College, Oxford), or silenced. The playhouses, and thus the music that had prospered in them, were similarly slighted. Many of the King's musicians had followed him to the wars ('Captain' Cooke's title acknowledges such service); of them William Lawes, perhaps the most original composer of the 1630s and '40s, was killed at the siege of Chester, whilst others were forced to go abroad or to live circumspectly in the country. Parliamentary committees were not wholly unsym-pathetic to musicians caused hardships by the flight of the court and the disestablishment of the cathedrals; they occasionally paid debts left outstanding by the King, or pensions out of forfeited cathedral revenues, but nothing was done to replace these vanished sources of musical employment. It was up to musicians to make a living as best they could, whether as teachers of music, as musicians in private house-holds, or in some employment unconnected with their original profession. Domestic musicians apart, only the humbler practitioners, the town waits and civic or military trumpeters (whose tasks were primarily functional and belonged to the domain of ceremony rather than of art) and, lowlier still, street and tavern musicians, remained unaffected. In 1657 five members of the Lord Protector's music petitioned the Council of State 'on behalfe of themselves and others the Professors of Musick . . . That there bee a Corporacion or Colledge of Musicians erected in London. . . '. John Hingston's name heads the list of signatories; that the petition was made demonstrates that the official attitude to music was not hostile; that it had to be made and that nothing came of it demonstrates the extent to which conditions under the Interregnum were inimical to a flourishing musical pro-fession.[9]

The Interregnum, then, was marked by the destruction of former centres of musical activity and prestige. It was equally distinguished by the cultivation of domestic music, particularly in the form of the consort for viols, of which John Jenkins and Matthew Locke were the major composers. At Worcester Thomas Tomkins, debarred from the practice of his profession either at court or in the cathedral (he held posts in both) solaced himself by the composition of keyboard pieces of great complexity and originality. In Lincolnshire Christopher Simpson elaborated his no less remarkable pieces for the division viol. The art of music was far from dead, but it had become predominantly private, and was necessarily modified by its changed circumstances. Much of the best music composed in the Interregnum, whether it tended to technical difficulty (as with Tomkins and Simpson) or to relative simplicity, was characterised by gravity, reflectiveness and a degree of introversion. The comparative political isolation of these years (together with the lack of a court and of the more ostentatious kinds of aristocratic patronage) reduced musical contacts with the continent. This had consequences for styles of composition and for performing technique: when the violinist Thomas Baltzar of Lübeck visited Oxford in 1658 his use of high positions astonished the other players present at a weekly music meeting and Dr John Wilson, the Professor of Music, in his 'humoursome way' stooped down to see if he had a cloven hoof: 'that is to say, to see whether he was a Devil or not'.[10] The cultivation of the fantasy aside, music was positively aided by the exile of the King in one respect only – the effective disappearance of the monopoly for music printing allowed John Playford, an enterprising publisher and bookseller, to concentrate on music, and the dispersion of the musical profession and to a lesser extent of its public, which made the transmission of pieces in manuscript less convenient than it had been, furthered him in his new line of business. Pepys was to be a frequent customer at Playford's music shop 'near the Church door' of the Temple, and the possessor of copies of many of his publications.

The Restoration had the abrupt effect of putting the clock both back and forwards. The King's Musick was re-embodied; old members returned to their places, new ones were taken on. As servants of the King under the discipline of the Lord Chamberlain they enjoyed a privileged status; they were, for instance, ordinarily free from the risk of arrest for debt, a fortunate circumstance since the invariable tardiness of their pay left many of them chronically indebted. The Chapel Royal was re-established. This institution was not, any more than the court itself, an entity restricted to a particular building; wherever the King based himself, at Whitehall, Windsor, or elsewhere, his household chapel would be set up and the Gentlemen and boys of the choir expected to fulfill their duties. In cathedral and collegiate establishments the remnants of the choirs gathered. When Charles was proclaimed at Winchester the mayor mounted a platform which had been draped with a red cloth; after he had read the document and a file of musketeers had fired a 'gallant volley' silence was commanded and, from a room specially built over the platform, 'the remaining part of the Cathedral Singing-men (whereof Mr Burt, a gentleman of 80 years

old was one), with the Master of the Choristers and other Musical
Gentlemen, sung a Solemn antheme'.[11] But though there was a titular
Master of the Choristers there were no trained boys, and it was to be
a long time before the tradition of cathedral treble singing, and consequently of the full four or six part choral anthem, was wholly recovered.
Captain Cooke, the Master of the Musick in the Chapel Royal, did not
endear himself to the Deans and organists of provincial cathedrals by on
occasion poaching their most promising choristers.

Professional English musical life thus reverted to its traditional
pattern: predominantly centred on the court and predominantly
metropolitan - in both respects more so than it had been before the
Interregnum. In Elizabethan and Jacobean times the provincial cathedrals had provided livelihoods for a number of composers (Weelkes
at Chichester, Tomkins at Worcester are important examples) and,
in part through their associated song-schools, nurtured much musical
talent besides. After the Restoration they never fully recovered their
old vitality as musical institutions. A further, if less significant metropolitan concentration, followed the reopening of the theatres. For
reasons amongst which the need for political censorship was of obvious
importance, there was close court control over theatrical affairs:
consequently Sir William Davenant, Thomas Killigrew and their
troupes were able to achieve a virtual monopoly of dramatic activity
and to suppress unauthorised acting. In this they were never wholly
successful, but they were altogether more effective than the Westminster
musicians, who tried to achieve the same thing through their 'Corporation of the Art and Science of Musick.'[12] The actors succeeded because
their liberty to act was directly dependent on royal patents issued to
Davenant and Killigrew. The musicians failed because they inherited a
state of affairs in which music had been practised widely and continuously in a way that acting had not been, and because historically they
had enjoyed far greater liberty than actors. Nor did musicians require,
as actors did, to be protected from a potentially hostile element of
public opinion. But the effect of the successful operation of a monopoly
in the theatre meant that there were only two playhouses, and that
playhouse music became far more an appendage of the royal household
than it had been before the closure of the theatres.

The return to old conditions had, therefore, the effect of making
English music all the more susceptible to fresh influences, since it left it,
at least in theory, so very much an instrument of the royal taste or
whim. The tradition of court music had been broken, necessary procedures and skills lost: Charles could not mount a masque, a form
dependent on the participation of his courtiers, since, as he reported to
his sister the Duchesse d'Orléans on 9 Feb. 1663, there was not one man
in the court 'that could make a tolerable entry'.[13] Moreover Charles

and his followers in exile had been able to experience at first hand those new musical fashions which England had largely been denied. One of the King's first acts was to reform his Musick in accordance with the most significant of these fashions. Roger North, rather contemptuously, noted that Charles liked music to which he could beat time, 'a mode among the *Monseurs*'; this habit is attested to by Pepys.[14] In exile Charles had spent much of his very considerable leisure dancing, and constantly sought out the latest dance music. He was perfectly aware of his own predilections; in a letter to his aunt written from Cologne on 27 July 1654, he looks forward to the arrival of 'fideldedies', violinists who were to be brought by his friend Lord Taaffe, and observes phlegmatically that 'in the meantime we must content ourselves with those that makes no difference between a hymn and a coranto . . .'.[15] Nor, when he was restored, did he disguise his reactions to what he encountered; Pepys noted how at Whitehall chapel on 14 Oct. 1660 there was 'an anthemne, ill sung, which made the King laugh'. The reconstruction of the King's Musick was designed to create, as its nucleus, a string band on the lines of that which served Louis XIV, the *vingt-quatre violons du roy*. That this was Charles's urgent wish is demonstrated by the great speed with which it was accomplished. The band was in being by 5 July 1660, and the symmetry of the former disposition of the royal music into consorts of related instruments (viols; violins; recorders; flutes; shawms) was forever destroyed.[16] Players of instruments other than the violin family continued in royal employment, as indeed they had done (and, in a richer court, to a greater extent) in France, but a string orchestra had now become the chief vehicle of court music. It played when the King dined in state, and at court balls; in Dec. 1662 it made its appearance in the Chapel Royal and by early 1664 it was to be found in the playhouses, 12 players being assigned to each house.[17] In practice a band of 24 proved too unwieldy and difficult to muster to be worth summoning for the comparatively modest day-to-day requirements of the court itself, and a select 12 players were designated for all but major occasions.[18]

Charles was a far from passive patron. Dr Thomas Tudway, whose knowledge was acquired at first hand as a Child of the Chapel Royal in the 1660s, recollected how 'some of the forwardest & brightest Children of the Chapel, as Mr Humfreys, Mr Blow, &c., began to be Masters of a faculty in Composing. This, his Majesty greatly encourag'd, by indulging their youthfull fancys, so that ev'ry Month at least, & afterwards oft'ner, they produc'd something New, of this Kind; In a few years more severall others, Educated in the Chapell, produc'd their Compositions in this style, for otherwise, it was in vain to hope to pleas his Majesty'.[19] The preferred style was French, and in encouraging it Charles, although he gratified his own taste, by no means ran against that of many of his subjects. Even before the Restoration, in 1658, the then Lord North, in a letter to the composer and organist Henry Loosemore, was complaining that 'Our Frenchified Age requires rather a recollection and settling towards sobriety and gravity, than to be bubbled up to an over-Airy humour and lightness'.[20] It was to further knowledge of the style that Charles sent John Banister, the 'master of the twenty-four', over to France in the winter of 1661–2; the young Pelham Humfrey, whose metamorphosis as 'an absolute Monsieur' Pepys experienced on 15 Nov. 1667, studied in France (and perhaps Italy also, but he returned with predominantly French allegiances) at the royal expense from 1665 to 1667.[21]

At this time French music had succumbed to a régime as authoritarian as that of Louis himself, though its monarch was no Bourbon, but Jean Baptiste Lully, a former Florentine page of unattractive personal characteristics. Lully's clarity of artistic purpose, together with his brilliant command of the politics of patronage, gave the forms that he developed, the overture and the dance suite, a popularity that soon extended far beyond France. Within France his musical hegemony was most notably operatic, and was to exercise a decisive influence on the French lyric drama for the next century; but Lullian opera was not a successful export, since it depended to a great extent on Lully's individual manner of musical declamation, and this in turn depended upon, and was deliberately subservient to, the accentuation of the French language. What was at issue here was a problem of which, in its English context, Pepys was particularly aware, and which was to exercise him a great deal.

For Pepys lived at a time of abrupt musical change, and the proof of his innate sensitivity is that he was able to identify the main features of this process, when most of his contemporaries apparently did not. He did not necessarily recount this with great clarity, but it is absurd to demand that he should have done so. Music, of all the arts, was the most immediate, transient, temporal in every sense, and hence the least classical, if we take the meaning of 'classical' to presume the existence of an accepted canon of 'classical' works. This is not now the case, since an abrupt distinction between 'popular' and (the nomenclature itself makes the point) 'classical' music, abetted by the continuity of institutions such as the symphony orchestra and the opera house, is embedded in our culture. The catalyst in this has been the concept of the public concert, but the public concert did not exist in the period during which Pepys kept his diary, though it was to come into being very shortly afterwards, in 1672. It was the creation of John Banister, whose arrogance, shiftiness in money matters, and failure to achieve the French manner as convincingly as his rival Luis Grabu (a Catalan by birth) had led, in 1666, to his effective supersession as leader of the twenty-four, and to his dismissal from that post, though not from his office as a member of the King's Musick, in 1667. There is no indication that Banister's motives in establishing concerts were other than opportunistic, or that he was aware of the importance of his innovation, but the circumstances demonstrate aptly enough the transition from a world in which music was predominantly institutional, affiliated to court, church, city or household, to one in which it became, in a sense, an article of commerce. The 'music meetings' of the earlier half of the century were private affairs at which professionals and amateurs would foregather and play together; they might be overheard by an audience, but always on a basis of personal association, even though money must sometimes have changed hands. The concert was a radical departure from this club-like arrangement, since it supposed exclusively professional performers receiving formal and predetermined subventions from their listeners. One phase of the musical revolution through which Pepys lived, the destruction of the old ordering of instruments by consorts, was confirmed, as we have seen, by the reorganisation of the King's Musick at the Restoration. The other crucial phase, the destruction of an umbilical relationship between a country's musical idiom and national character – a relationship that assumed that every country's musical idiom was as naturally distinct as its language – would not be completed for a long time; it is arguable that it has never been fully completed. Nevertheless, it was vastly accelerated during Pepys's lifetime, and in the diary period.

Charles possessed as marked a taste in music as in women, but was no more inclined to single loyalties in the one field than the other, though he favoured lightness in both. On his return from exile, as well as reforming the King's Musick along French lines, he also established a King's French Musick; it consisted of a chamber group of French musicians, directed by Ferdinand de Florence, and including the notable bass Claude Desgranges. By 1666 Charles was bored with this, and, cynically alleging a necessity for retrenchment, broke it up; though Desgranges was retained in the royal service, the other musicians were obliged to return to France, their removal expenses only part paid, and their salaries in arrears.[22] At just the same time Charles had taken on a company of Italian musicians, each member of which commanded a stipend equivalent to that of the Master of the King's Musick (£200 p.a.). The Italians insisted on special methods of payment to ensure that they would receive money regularly; Charles sold four gondolas, which had been presented to him by the Venetian republic to mark his restoration, in order to float the enterprise. This he did at a time when the emoluments of the majority of his English musicians were almost four years in arrears. The financial detail may seem trivial (it did not to the musicians, and here, too, Pepys is a witness), yet it eloquently testifies to the dramatic way in which Charles's active but inconstant musical tastes, connived at and influenced by courtiers such as Arlington and Killigrew (who both urged on the Italian venture), both led to musical eclecticism and hastened the end of the whole conception and ordering of the world of music that made such eclecticism possible. The King's Italian Musick, which at full strength comprised two women singers, two castrati (Pepys's 'Eunuches'), a tenor, a bass, the Master (Vicenzo Albrici) and his brother as composers, and a 'poet' (whose presence establishes that an ultimate intention was to mount operas), was eventually dissolved in 1679, ostensibly for political reasons, but largely because Charles had long since lost interest; several of the musicians associated with it, however, stayed on in England, and its influence was thus more permanent than the bare record suggests. There were, besides, French musicians in the Queen Mother's household, and Italian musicians in the Queen's household; the Portuguese musicians, all in orders, who came over with her, had been sent home as a result of parliamentary disquiet at the size of her ecclesiastical establishment.

It was the presence of so many foreign musicians in London, and the conflict of styles this involved, that provoked Pepys to reflect so frequently and so extensively on the nature of the relationship between words and music. He sets down his thoughts on the subject with a copiousness that he does not otherwise manifest when touching on matters of a theoretical or an abstract nature; indeed the reader may feel that this is almost the only subject about which Pepys becomes tedious or repetitive. But he deserves sympathy, because the matter was both topical and inherently perplexing, and made the more so by the nature of Pepys's musical inheritance – the repertoire of English music, above all vocal music, with which he was familiar.

When Pepys went aboard the *Naseby* on the expedition to bring back the restored Charles he appears to have taken with him two song-books, Henry Lawes's *Third book of ayres* and one of John Playford's compilations, published in 1659, *Select ayres and dialogues* 'Composed by John Wilson, Charles Colman, Doctors in Musick; Henry Lawes, William Lawes, Nicholas Laneare, William Webb, Gentlemen and Servants to his late Majesty in his Publick and Private Musick; And other Excellent Masters of Musick'. If he had had an eye on posterity he could hardly have taken anything more representative of what was to become a largely forgotten and much misunderstood epoch of English song: the period that separates the age of Dowland from the age of Purcell. The intervening years are properly, if we adopt such a principle of nomenclature, the age of Henry Lawes; Pepys's volume of songs by Lawes alone, set alongside the anthology, in which Lawes and his brother William are prominent, neatly makes the point. Henry Lawes was universally admired by his contemporaries, celebrated by

Milton in a famous sonnet, yet almost wholly forgotten, except by a handful of literary and musical scholars, after the 1680s. He devoted hi talents almost exclusively to the song; his preoccupation with one chosen form, and prolific output within that form, is comparable only to Domenico Scarlatti's cultivation of the keyboard sonata. As with Scarlatti, the preoccupation is in part attributable to the circumstance of patronage. Lawes's most productive period was that of the last year of the Caroline court, and the essence of his art was the musica presentation, in the most lucid and transparent way possible, of the lyric poetry which the writers of the period, and the writers within the court circle in particular, furnished in such abundance. Jonson Herrick, Carew, Suckling, Lovelace and Waller are the representative poets; they had a host of imitators. That a poet's verses had been set by Lawes conferred sufficient prestige to merit mention on several title-pages, even though the music remained unprinted; many poets beside Milton addressed encomiums or wrote in praise of Lawes, amongs them Waller, Herrick, Harrington and Katherine Philips.[23]

Lawes customarily composed his songs in one or the other of two clearly distinct forms. The less individual is metrical and ballad-like yielding short tuneful pieces, often in three time, and having an obviou relation to the contemporary dance tune. It is a mode appropriate to the simple strophic poem, commonly in quatrains. Though these songs do not lack musical subtlety they never obtrude it. Such subtlety is mos apparent when the song is cast as a canon or 'catch' for two or more voices, often so contrived as to produce an ingenious (frequently - though not in Lawes – indecent) reordering of the words of the text Catch singing became a popular tavern pastime during the Interregnun and thereafter, a convivial recreation in which Pepys took part, though he did not rate catches in general as more than 'fooleries'. Yet catche could be, and often were, sober and serious; Orlando Gibbons's *The Silver Swan* survived as a catch after it had been forgotten as a madrigal Lawes's more distinctive and personal form is the declamatory ayre born in late 16th-century Italy as a twin to the new art of opera. It wa the culmination of a series of experiments which had as their object the establishment of a just relation between words and music. Such a relation, it was believed, had existed in ancient Greece, and was at the root of the Greek dramatic achievement; Greek tragedy had used word and music, so united, as its medium, and the recovery of that unity wa vital if the drama was to be restored to its Grecian dignity. The mod that came into being as a consequence of this line of thought was no the invention of any one man, though it largely owes its popularisation and the particular shape it assumed, to the Florentine compose (probably Roman by birth) Giulio Caccini, who published his propa gandist *Le nuove musiche* in 1602. The idiom was introduced into

England by immigrant Italian musicians and by English musicians who had visited Italy; the most notable of its early English exponents was Nicholas Lanier, one of the composers represented in the anthology which Pepys took aboard the *Naseby*, and still alive, though not apparently writing music, in the diary period. In 1617 Lanier set *Lovers made men*, a masque by Ben Jonson, wholly in the *stilo recitativo* which had become the *lingua franca* of the Caccinian movement. It was a bold innovation, though Lanier does not seem to have achieved popular success in the declamatory vein until his return from a visit to Italy in 1625–7. It was then, according to Roger North, that 'he composed a *recitativo*, which was a poem being the tragedy of Hero and Leander . . . The King was exceedingly pleased with this pathetick song, and caused Lanneare often to sing it to a consort attendance, while he stood next, with his hand upon his shoulder'. Another admirer of 'Hero and Leander' was Pepys, who had it transcribed c. 1680 by Cesare Morelli, his domestic musician, and is likely to have known it earlier.[24] North goes on to call 'Hero and Leander' a *non-pareil*, and to remark that it 'hath bin little followed', but this is true only in the sense that such very elaborate ventures in the *recitativo* manner were seldom attempted.[25] What is clear and what North neglects to say, is that it furnished an idiom which Henry Lawes made peculiarly his own, half melody, half recitative strictly conceived, not unakin in concept, if not in actuality, to modern *arioso*. It is significant that, in his 'Story of Theseus and Ariadne', alluded to by Milton in his sonnet, Lawes had created a *scena* on the same scale as 'Hero and Leander', and on a comparable subject. This we know to have been a favourite with Pepys during the diary period.

This idiom had its influence on all serious English song, however loosely or strictly it adhered to a *recitativo* manner, and the consequence was the declamatory ayre. The distinctive features of the declamatory ayre were the restriction of the vocal line to one or two parts only, attention to the 'humouring' of the text, a comparatively simple accompaniment on theorbo or bass viol (the latter, if the accompanist was sufficiently accomplished, being played 'lyra way', that is, chord-ally), and the provision of adequate opportunity for the performer to display his skill in ornamentation, or 'gracing'. It was an essential premise of the idiom that such gracing should not be excessive; ideally it would seem an extension of the natural 'humouring' of the words, the term used by Milton in his commendation of Lawes, and by Pepys in his discommendation of some songs by Captain Cooke, to describe the faithfulness with which the music adhered to the signification and syllabification of the text. A principal and difficult ornament was the trill: not the modern alternation between two notes, but the rapid rhythmic breaking of a single note. This was an accomplishment the mastery of which Pepys laboured to acquire and of which it gave him great pleasure to discover his wife the mistress. In 1664 Playford introduced into a new edition of his elementary compendium *An introduction to the skill of musick* an anonymous and unacknowledged translation of Caccini's preface to *Le nuove musiche*, entitled 'A Brief Discourse of the *Italian* manner of Singing'. This tract, as Playford is at pains to point out in an afterword, represents 'the way and manner of the excellent Compositions of Mr. *Henry Lawes* and other excellent Masters in this Art, and was by them Taught for above this forty years past, and is daily used and taught by several eminent Professors at this day'. Its eventual appearance in an English guise 62 years after the original Italian publication demonstrates the dislocations and discontinuities of English musical life that have already been remarked; its frequent misrepresentations of Caccini illustrate the insular inflection of the Italian declamatory ideal. But it expresses the general principle happily enough: 'I have framed my last *Ayres* for one Voice to the Theorbo, not following that old way of *Composition*, whose Musick not suffering the Words to be understood by the Hearers, for the multitude of Divisions made upon short and long syllables . . . But I have endeavoured in those my late *Compositions*, to bring in a kind of Musick, by which men might as it were talk in Harmony, using in that kind of singing a certain noble neglect of the Song (as I have often heard at *Florence* by the Actors in their singing *Opera's*) in which I endeavoured the Imitation of the Conceit of the Words . . .'.

Declamatory ayres were composed with less frequency after the court of Charles I, that had nurtured the form, had disintegrated. But, through the entrepreneurial activities of John Playford, the style was publicised, as it had not been whilst that court was in being. The style was aberrant in that it insisted on the peculiarly vocal nature of vocal music; it resisted the temptation to treat the voice as just another musical instrument, and it depended on a respect for the sense and accent of the words. *Prima le parole, dopo la musica*: for a composer it is a self-abnegating ordinance, uncommon in the history of music. But it prevailed in England in the mid-17th century and, to differing extents, the same principle prevailed in France and Italy also. It implied a sharper distinction between vocal and instrumental music than any to which the 20th century is accustomed; it closely bound the literary and the musical sensitivity, and it accentuated (quite literally, since the stress accent of syllables was crucial to the issue) national divisions, for it assumed music to be governed by language. The premises of this aesthetic may now be alien to us, but they deserve our serious attention. We have other premises, which most of us take for granted. Pepys was a natural and instinctive adherent of the declamatory aesthetic, and this makes his capacity to analyse it the more remarkable; his disappoint-

ment in the fashionable French and Italian music, a disappointment
made the sharper by the fact that in other matters he was seldom
disinclined to follow fashion, caused him to reflect, painstakingly and
even painfully, on the assumptions which he took for granted, and
which formed the foundations of his musical culture. Consequently we
find ourselves eavesdropping on a wise, not a foolish, *bourgeois gentilhomme*. Molière's Monsieur Jourdain had to be told that he was speaking in prose, though he was delighted by the discovery; Pepys learned,
through his habit of self-analysis, something of which most of his
contemporaries who shared his tastes but lacked his reflective cast of
mind were entirely oblivious: that because as a matter of course he
demanded that sound should be allied to sense, sense constituted a major
part of the pleasure to be had from song. One reason why this aesthetic
is likely to seem distant from us is that the work that might have been
the keystone of this movement failed to establish itself in its own time
and is now lost without trace. In 1656 Sir William Davenant staged
The siege of Rhodes, the first true English opera, though described by
Davenant himself as 'a Representation by the Art of Prospective in
Scenes, And the Story sung in *Recitative Musick*'. The music was
provided by a consortium of composers, the 'Vocal Musick' by Henry
Lawes, Matthew Locke and Captain Cooke, the 'Instrumental Musick'
by Charles Coleman and George Hudson. *The siege of Rhodes* was a
commercial and social success since, as an 'entertainment in music' it
evaded the parliamentary prohibition of stage plays, and a literary
success since, with the addition of a continuation which Davenant had
completed by 1659, it became the model for the Restoration heroic
play and continued to excite interest for the next quarter century. Yet
it was a musical failure since, so far as is known, in its post-1660 revivals
it was presented as a 'just' (i.e. spoken) drama, with only incidental
music.[26] The memory of the music did not die: Pepys heard Mrs
Coleman singing one of Lawes's contributions on 31 Oct. 1665, and we
encounter Captain Cooke holding forth about his part in the work on
13 Feb. 1667 in terms that make it clear that, at least amongst the
cognoscenti, 'The Opera' had been a memorable event; they also make
it clear that it had been *sui generis*. Pepys's experience of it must have
prompted his impulse to set 'Beauty retire' himself, Davenant's words
inspiring him to what he evidently regarded as his most profound
composition. But *The siege of Rhodes* did not survive as an opera on the
Restoration stage and though plays, such as Davenant's version of
Macbeth, attended by Pepys, incorporated musical scenes, there was no
attempt to perpetuate the form. There were indeed, as Pepys reports,
endeavours to establish 'an Opera', but it was to be Italian, not English;
the King's Italian Musick had been enlisted with such an end in view.
An active English opera could have served as a regenerative agent for

and justification of the Lawesian declamatory manner, but the richness of the resources of the 'just' drama made it superfluous and when eventually a native form, 'dramatick opera', did emerge, its defining characteristic, the use of spoken dialogue rather than recitative, testified to the way in which English dramatic diction and delivery was sufficiently heightened and 'musical' in itself, and its tonal embellishment failed, therefore, to fulfill any very evident need. Furthermore, royal patronage and the interest of fashionable court circles was directed at establishing originally an Italian, subsequently (just after the diary period) a French opera.

If Pepys's first great musical perplexity was the outcome of his need to define the critical basis of his musical inheritance, his second, which caused him much trouble and expense, was the product of his desire to remedy his lack of formal musical training, a desire complicated by his possession of a mind sufficiently analytical to be dissatisfied with the solutions most readily to hand – a state of affairs again made more acute because he was living through a time of accelerated musical change.

Something of this emerges from a consideration of the modifications taking place in the world of musical instruments. A few of these modifications were cosmetic. In England the commonest domestic keyboard instrument, the rectangular virginals, was being superseded by the spinet, triangular in form and incorporating, as did the harpsichord, a bentside. Though Italian and French examples exist, the spinet enjoyed its greatest popularity in England, where it remained standard for over a century. The Italian Girolamo Zenti, employed by Charles II as 'King's virginal maker', has a good claim to have invented this new shape for a plectral keyboard instrument. Pepys bought his spinet from an English maker, Charles Hayward of Aldgate St, in 1668; in plain walnut or oak it would have assorted much more elegantly with recent fashions in furniture than the coffer-shaped virginals.[27]

A change altogether more radical, since it altered the whole tone-colour and range of the instruments concerned, took place in the woodwinds. In the 1650s a group of Parisian wind-makers and players, prominent amongst them the Hotteterres, redesigned the recorder, oboe, bassoon (known in England as the 'curtal') and the transverse flute. Their modifications to all of these instruments involved constructing them in several parts, rather than out of a single piece of wood, narrowing the bore, and giving this a pronouncedly conical form. The effect was so greatly to increase the range and the expressive capacity of the instruments as to create what was virtually a new type.[28] Pepys'. reactions are revealed by his account of the music in *The Virgin Marty* and his subsequent visit to Drumbleby to order a recorder. The earlier single-piece cylindrically bored recorder had fallen into disuse, except amongst town waits and rustic musicians. Its substitute in fashionable circles was the French *flageolet*, of which Pepys, until enticed by the recorder, had long been enamoured, but this was an instrument of limited resources, and of no attraction to serious composers. The three-piece recorder in due course ousted the flageolet. (The old single-piece transverse flute had suffered the fate of the single-piece recorder, and the new model gained ground so slowly that it scarcely signified in Pepys's lifetime.) Pepys's enthusiasm for the recorder was eventually shared by the majority of musicians, though as late as 1679 John Hudgebut, in his *A vade mecum . . . shewing the excellencies of the rechorder*, was still concerned to 'allow the Flagilet all its just attributes, and see if the Rechorder do not equall or excel them . . . The Flagilet is a good Companion being easily carried in the Pocket, so is the recorder: The Flagilet is always in Tune so is the Rechorder: Besides the sweetness of the Sound, which is much more Smoother and Charming, and the Extent and Variety of the Notes, in which it much excells the Flagilet'. The remodelling of the woodwind hastened the demise of the old familial ordering by instrumental consorts, since these new and more expressive instruments were heard to best advantage when used singly or in pairs with continuo, or as obbligato instruments in compositions where the principal force was a string band.

Amongst the strings we find revolution rather than modification. In England, until 1660, viols were the principal bowed instruments of serious music, though violins had been used at court since Queen Elizabeth's day; Pepys played both viol and violin. What took place at the Restoration was an abrupt reversal of priorities. Viols and violins formed two quite distinct families. The former were flat-backed, fretted, and six stringed; the latter round-backed, unfretted, and four stringed. Viols were particularly well suited for intricately contrapuntal pieces, where their slightly nasal clarity of tone gave to the independent parts the separateness that the construction of the fantasy presumed, whilst at the same time blending in a total sonority of a delicate and peculiarly satisfying kind. The chief limitation of the viol was the restrained nature of the articulatory process, in part a consequence of the fact that all the viols, treble, tenor and bass, were played *a gamba*, between the knees, with the bow held in an underhand position that restricted the degree of pressure that could be put upon the strings. The violin was an altogether more robust instrument and, because it was played on the shoulder, naturally tended to a pronounced articulation with a marked initial emphasis, which it was not possible to attain on the viols. The violin was therefore well suited to the dance music that Charles loved, the viol to that kind of consort music which he stigmatised for its gravity. Pepys tends to use 'fiddling' pejoratively, and in 1667 realised that he had left his violin untouched for 'three years or more'.[29] In his own circle violins appear chiefly when dancing or some other levity is on foot, but the trend of the times was to neglect the viols and, even in those musical contexts where the viols had once held sway, increasingly to favour the violins.

A more tangled fate, involving both modification and supersession, befell the lute. In Elizabethan and Jacobean times the lute had been the principal accompaniment for serious vocal music and was required, besides, for much instrumental music; it also possessed a rich solo literature of its own. During the 17th century the range of the instrument was increased by the addition of extra bass strings carried on an extension of the neck. A lute with such additional strings was known as a 'theorbo'; a theorbo could either be built as such or, as commonly happened, be constructed by adapting an existing lute. This was what Pepys had done, and it is why he sometimes refers to his 'lute', sometimes his 'theorbo'. It was one and the same instrument; his references do not fully explicate themselves, but before 30 Oct. 1661 it was probably, in the strict sense, a lute, and thereafter a theorbo. Already, however, the spinet and harpsichord were beginning to be used where once lute and theorbo had seemed the natural choice; between 1650 and 1700 wire strings plucked by quills controlled from a keyboard took over from gut strings plucked by the fingers.

The vogue for the guitar, fostered by Charles, who was an ardent admirer of the playing and compositions of the Italian virtuoso Francesco Corbetta, played its part in this process. The guitar was easier than the lute; though it lacked the lute's richness of musical resource, it was more incisive and better suited to music with dance-like rhythms; it distracted attention from the cultivation of the lute, but when its vogue ended left nothing in its place.

The decline of the lute was related to the decline of the viol, and this in turn was related to those perplexities experienced by Pepys in his forays into the field of musical theory. Because lute and viol were fretted instruments, and tuned on the same principle, a player might readily attain to a command of both, just as, within the family of viols a mastery of, say, the bass, implied some ability on tenor and treble. Again, because they were fretted they were suited to notation in tablature – a system by which the printed or written sigla designated not which note or notes the player was required to play, but where he should place his fingers on the fingerboard (aided in this by the frets) to produce such sounds as the composer desired. The system may appear cumbersome, but had many practical points in its favour. The player had no need to be concerned with a key-signature, and the remoter keys could be made as accessible as the most common simply by an instruction to alter the tuning of the instrument; that done, the player had only to place his fingers as the tablature instructed him. Chords could be expressed as they lay under the hand. In theory at least one phase of the mental operation required by the reading of staff notation was eliminated. But there were disadvantages. Tablature only applied to the specific instrument for which it had been written.[30] The indication of time was awkwardly separated from the instructions for the placing of the fingers. Tablature was complicated by the proliferation of strings on the theorbo. It was not an appropriate system for the unfretted instruments of the violin family. It had no relevance for a keyboard player. Above all it was incompatible with the principles of thorough-bass.

Thorough-bass, or *basso continuo*, originated in Italy in the late 16th century. It was a system for the harmonisation of bass lines. It bound the performer to a series of fundamental harmonic rules, yet at the same time allowed him (it could be said imposed on him) considerable freedom of interpretation. In practice it assumed two forms – unfigured or figured. An unfigured bass was a naked bass line, demanding of the performer that he clothe or 'realise' it according to the understood conventions of thorough-bass. This effectually presumed an acquaintance with the principles of composition. The other form, figured bass, provided an indication, expressed in numbers, modified where necessary by sharps and flats, of the harmony that the composer required, though it still assumed a great deal to be understood. The first published English treatise on thorough-bass was Matthew Locke's *Melothesia* (1673). Before then knowledge of the technique depended either directly on music masters, or upon acquaintance with manuscripts such as, for unfigured bass, Giovanni Coperario's *Rules how to compose*. In England in the mid-17th century unfigured basses were commonplace; Henry Lawes's songs were all printed with a skeletal bass line to which the accompanist was expected to give flesh. No doubt they were often performed with a treble and bass line only. But Lawes himself would have presumed an harmonic infilling, a musicianly ear demanded it, and Pepys was naturally determined to achieve it. Unfortunately its provision was beyond his powers of musicianship; it was in order to acquire an adequate harmonic scaffolding that he was compelled on 24 Nov. 1660, and other occasions, to get 'Mr Childe to set the base to the Theorbo',[31] in other words, to provide in tablature an interpretation of the figuring that the bass line implied. Nor, had Pepys commanded the principles of thorough-bass, would he have been compelled to seek assistance from professionals in the composition of the bass lines of his own songs.

Why was he unable to attain this skill, given his inherent musicality, and his intense desire to learn? Once more the explanation is to be found in a major transition, in this instance in the matter of musical theory, a transition intimately bound up with the evolution of the *basso continuo.* The traditional notion of music in 17th-century England (as elsewhere in Europe) was hexachordal: that is to say, it was based not on the octave (eight tone) system, in which every octave, whatever its pitch, is considered as identical and begins and ends with the note C, but on a pattern of six tones, unrelated to the note C, that might begin and end at any of three points within our modern C scale, and that, unlike the octave pattern, overlapped. As in the case of tablature, it sounds a more cumbersome system than it actually was. It had many practical advantages when applied to the composition and performance of the music written during the later Middle Ages and the Renaissance. It was particularly well suited for singers, and shared some of the features of modern tonic solfa. Its main disadvantages were the mental gymnastics required when a piece involved frequent mutation (not a feature of the music in conjunction with which the system had become established), and its association with a method of composition founded on the polyphonic elaboration of a middle part. The 'new music' proceeded from one or other of the two outer parts, treble or bass, these being harmonically, not polyphonically, related. The hexachordal system was thus inappropriate to the type of composition premised by the emergence of the thorough-bass. When composers began to work predominantly in terms of a chromatic C scale, they were at odds with performers who thought in terms of the hexachordal system. An author writing as late as 1686 described the symptoms of this conflict in a way with which Pepys would have thoroughly sympathised: 'That so few persons (out of Cathedrals) understand *Prick-Song* [i.e. staff notation], a main reason is, the Obscurity and Confusion in the Method commonly taught, wherein the following Particulars make it a long Drudgery to attain Proficiency . . . (1) a long Bead-roll of hard and useless Names, to be conn'd backward and forward in the *Gam-ut* . . . (2) When this Drudgery is over, follows a worse, to learn the differing Names of the Notes, according to the several places of *Mi*, which in each Cliff [i.e. clef] hath three several Stations . . . (4) the many Cliffs, which no less than seven ways change the places of the Notes upon the Lines and Spaces'.[32]

Pepys could read a single line of music well enough, but he did not know 'the scale of Musique' and we find him on 11 Apr. 1668 'Conning my gamut' and much baffled. The works to which he might have turned for enlightenment would not have helped him. He possessed Thomas Morley's *A plain & easy introduction to practical music* but found it good but 'inmethodical'. Published in 1597, it was wedded to the hexachordal system. The editions of Playford's *Introduction to the skill of musick* published between 1655 and 1683 contained Thomas Campion's *A new way of making fowre parts in counterpoint*, first published in 1613, and annotated for Playford by Christopher Simpson.

This succinct treatise in fact elucidates the principles necessary for the understanding of thorough-bass, but it does this incidentally, and in Playford's compendium it comes as the final item of a manual which begins with a laborious exposition of the gamut along the traditional lines.

Matters were brought to a head for Pepys by his purchase of the recorder. Woodwind instruments, like the fretted strings, could be written for in tablature, but in the case of the woodwind the method had no advantages except for a complete novice, unacquainted with any other instrument, and Pepys was not at all in this category. What he desired to do was to pick up an instrument, look at a passage of 'prick song', and translate it into sound. His first encounter with the recorder revealed to him the extent to which he was inhibited from achieving this because he did not know 'the scale of Musique' [i.e. the gamut with all its complexities] by heart; and it was of no help to him that he had a natural command of the hexachord in practice, a positive hindrance that he had no command of the keyboard, which might be thought of as the simplest practical exemplification of the new octave-based chromaticism. The experience enabled him to see that the gamut was something that it was 'necessary for a man that would understand music as it is now taught, to understand, though it be a ridiculous and troublesome way and I know I shall be able thereafter to show the world a simpler way'. But though he could gesture towards this ideal, he seems never to have found it fully within his grasp.

This simpler way would surely have been the modern chromatic system conceived of in octave patterns based on C. It is a system independent of instrumentation, and it facilitates the chordal (or vertical) harmonic under-pinning required by compositions in which the main interest is in a single melody. It lends itself to a fairly straightforward exposition, which relates the rules of harmony to certain mensurable principles of acoustics. In these principles Pepys – together with several of his contemporaries, notably Lord Brouncker, Robert Hooke, Lord Keeper North and Dr John Wallis – took a lively interest, although he was unconvinced when Brouncker and Hooke suggested to him the proposition (in fact perfectly sustainable) that 'the reason of Concords and Discords in music . . . is from the aequality of the vibrations'. Brouncker, besides being an early President of the Royal Society, was an enthusiastic amateur musician with whom Pepys on several occasions played, and also the translator of Descartes' *De Musica*, a work almost exclusively mathematical in its emphasis, a copy of which Pepys bought after his frustrations with recorder tablature and with the gamut had caused him to reconsider the state of musical theory. Pepys's appetite for theoretical works was voracious: he was prepared to spend £1 15s. 0d. on Athanasius Kircher's *Musurgia Universalis*, and £3 2s. 0d.

on Marin Mersenne's *Harmonie Universelle* (an exceptionally rare and hence costly book, since it was originally published in parts, and seldom to be found complete). To comprehend what this outlay represented it is pertinent to recall that in the same year his spinet had cost him no more than £5.

Several years earlier (though with less awareness as to what was at stake) Pepys had already engaged with exactly the same problems which would so preoccupy him in 1668. Seeking to learn how to compose, he had taken lessons from John Birchensha, whose claim to have, as Evelyn put it, 'invented a mathematical way of composure very extraordinary', attracted Pepys. Birchensha later became involved, with Thomas Salmon, in an endeavour to create a musical 'Universal Character', a system of notation which did away with the gamut, and was in some ways even simpler (for its purposes) than modern staff notation.[35] Birchensha's 'Great card of the body of musique' anticipated the functions of the 'musical machine', now preserved in the Pepys Library, which Pepys was to purchase after the diary period, a kind of calculator indicating the possible consonances (within the permitted range of harmonic progressions) for any given sequence of notes. But Pepys's efforts, whether sooner or later, were to no avail. From 1673 Pepys employed, as his domestic musician, Cesare Morelli, who eventually proved to be the answer to the problem which Pepys, unable to educate his wife to a sufficient musical competence, or to keep those of his servants who possessed musical ability, had repeatedly failed to solve in the diary period. One of Morelli's principal labours was to produce tablatures so that Pepys might accompany himself in his favourite songs. Had the current system for learning to sight-read been in kilter with the system for learning thorough-bass and composition it is probable that Pepys would have been spared his difficulties; but it was not, and the obstacle posed by the incompatibility of the two set a limit to the extent of his musical attainments.

It is only fair to insist that those of Pepys's contemporaries who had reflected on the topic were equally baffled by a problem that was at once practical, physical (in the scientific sense) and aesthetic. Some, like Birchensha, were able to apprehend the principles underlying the modern key system, but unable to express them adequately; Pepys's observation on Birchensha's translation of Alstedius's *Templum Musicum*, 'the most ridiculous book as he has translated it, that ever I saw in my life', was perfectly just, although Alstedius and Birchensha had a theoretical understanding of what was involved. It is indicative of the state of affairs that when, after the diary period, Lord Keeper North published his *A philosophical essay of musick* (1677), of which Pepys would duly buy a copy, this admirably clear exposition of the physical basis of music, of the working of the modern key system, and of musical aesthetics should have had very little impact on contemporary thought or practice.[34] The old myths and muddles persisted, because music is in the end an art not a science, something practised and passed on, a thing done, not a system which the practitioner is apt coolly to consider from a viewpoint outside.

Pepys's frustrations will be shared by the reader of the diary only to a limited extent. He lived so intently inside his world of musical experience that its boundaries do not seem a constriction. North, in his essay, stopped short at a crucial point: 'I will not go about to describe Excellent *Musick*, which would require a *Poet* as well as a *Musician*; I am only in the part of a *Philosopher*, to show what is allowable *Musick*, in order to make the Reasons upon which these Rules are founded understood . . .'. Pepys did not understand the reasons, but he was consummately the poet, albeit in informal prose, of musical effect. He responded to that whole world of sound which he inhabited, a world of sound in many ways alien to the latter part of the 20th century. There was less noise, though we must not assume any idyllic state of calm; iron-rimmed wheels and iron-shod horsehooves on cobbled setts in narrow streets must have been deafening; Boileau in his VIth Satire chronicled the shattering sounds of Paris in 1660, and London would have been no different. But when the traffic ceased the silences had a profundity not now recoverable; they allowed Pepys to sing on the leads or to play his flageolet at his window and draw his neighbours to theirs, to delight at 'Fox hall' in the intermingling of nightingales' song and buskers' tunes, to discover the 'brave echo' on the stairs at Somerset House, to relish sound for its own sake in conditions lost to us. His gusto was extraordinary; he loved to see others take pleasure in music, he could enjoy the 'innocence' of the Marlborough waits, he courted the company of musicians of any class and was happy to drink with 'the music of a booth at Sothworke-Fair', he approved a good ring of bells, he was always willing, encountering a 'snapp of musique' to take into account 'the circumstances of the time and place'; he felt, and recorded, a deprivation when he had anticipated or had been promised music that did not materialise; he thought a bridal morning unadorned by music a slatternly affair. The puzzlements consequent upon living through a period of musical change in no way blunted his appetite; indeed, the circumstances of the period in several ways conspired to satisfy it, as those of other periods might not have done.

It would be misleading to represent it as, musically, a golden age. Music was not universally accepted as a social good: Pepys reports Lauderdale's distaste; Dean Bathurst of Trinity College Oxford 'amidst his love of the polite arts . . . had a strong aversion to music' – the art, as Pepys's later remedial recommendations indicate, was falling into academic disrepute.[35] Pepys's difficulties in finding sufficiently accomplished 'music friends' more than give the lie to the notion that every gentleman could sing or play. Yet, as he witnesses, instruments were to hand in barbers' shops, in the expectation that waiting customers might pass the time and entertain the company by playing on them, and a barber could prove an able fiddler. Music was still a thing of utility, interweaving daily life through the dances played before the troupes of milkmaids returning from the fields, the hawkers' cries in the streets, the tunes of the perambulating waits, who offered both the solace of sound and (at least in theory) the security of a night watch. It was worth 10s. to Pepys, and dignified a special day, to be woken by the King's trumpets; if there is anything surprising about this it is that they were willing to perform the service for a personage of his modest social standing.

In 1667, according to a survey of royal expenditure conducted by means of an analysis of the warrants drawn by the Lord Chamberlain on the Treasury Chamber account, the King spent in all some £9931 12s. 8d. on music. It was a vast sum of money, but to be seen in perspective it has to be realised that this amounted to no more than 2% of the total cost of running the royal household for that year – though this, of course, included many expenses that we might regard as pertaining to the conduct of government business rather than to domestic matters. The function of the royal music cannot neatly be defined as falling within either category; it was a condition of the culture in which it played its part.

Pepys, so far as we know, never analysed his musical expenditure. But it was certainly very considerable, as he admitted to himself when he reflected on his good fortune in that 'God Almighty hath put me into condition to bear the charge of all this', and, even randomly considered, it tellingly reveals the circumstances and contradictions of the times. Playford's publications were relatively inexpensive, though the price of any book now appears inordinate when compared to the cost of instruments; manuscript music, still needed by any serious amateur, whose demands (particularly in the instrumental field) could not have been met by the printed supply, commanded a high price, and the hunt for it involved the expense of time and the cultivation (by no means cheap in terms of tavern hospitality) of 'the musicians of the town'. 'Musique and the musicians of the town' were not, in any case, readily separated. The social function of music might create an obligation to meet expenses, unhappily unapproved by the ear; Pepys had occasion to regret, as well as to delight in, the visitations of the waits, and to overreach himself in the pursuit of manuscript music, realising too late that the wares available (sound unheard) might not be worth the money; he could also be perturbed that an evening with a professional musician might make it difficult to avoid buying his songs. Musical tuition too, was a costly and hazardous business; Mrs Pepys's limited repertoire of songs learned by rote scarcely represented a satisfactory return on the sums involved. But there was, of course, no charge for attendance at the Chapel Royal, or at the Queen's and the Queen Mother's chapels, where the most fashionable, exotic, and (in absolute terms) the most expensive music was to be heard, and at court there were numerous opportunities, eagerly seized upon by Pepys, for listening at royal expense. In an epoch which saw the crucial transition from music as mandatory social activity to music as vendible social commodity Pepys's disbursements did not at all conform to the pattern to which subsequent developments have accustomed us.

In this transitional age he emerges as a conservative of a characteristically English cast, swimming steadily against a current which nevertheless proved the preponderant force, but not, seemingly, unhappy to find himself in those new waters to which it brought him. At the beginning of the diary period he reproaches himself for stringing a lute on the Sabbath; by the end of it Sunday has become a suitable day for regular music-meetings. His suspicion of Italian music gradually evaporates; by 1669 he is commending the singing at the Queen's Chapel and is ravished by the voice of an Italian-trained *castrato* at the King's Playhouse. He speaks well of the music offered by the twenty-four (though he is still unable to resist calling them 'the King's fiddling concert') and one of his last entries approves an anthem by Pelham Humfrey, of whose merits he had previously been unconvinced. Shortly after the diary closes he will turn to the cultivation of the instrument that he at first found a 'bauble', the guitar. By 1680, to judge from the 'Systeme and Tablature to the Guitarr' (PL 2805) with its 'Prelude for every Key and a Table of Transposition' which Morelli prepared for him, he was thinking chromatically, rather than hexachordally, since, although the hexachordal names are retained, the 'Systeme' is in essence conceived in terms of the new approach, though there is no indication (the record points the other way) that he mastered thorough-bass. In later life we find more traces of Pepys as patron of music than as practitioner, and as patron he seems to have taken a delight in what was both the newest and the best. There is evidence of his pleasure in Purcell, who was so brilliantly to resolve the problem that had beset Pepys, as to the way in which an Italianate melodic style might express 'the proper energy of *English* words', whilst John Evelyn records how in 19 Apr. 1687 he heard the *castrato* Siface, being one of 'a select number of some particular persons whom Mr Pepys (Secretary of the Admiralty & a greate lover of Musick) invited to his house, where the meeting was, & this obtained by peculiar favour & much difficulty of the Singer, who much disdained to shew his talent to any but Princes'. The comment is more telling than Evelyn knew; not the least of the revolutions through which Pepys lived took place in the realm of music; its effect was to put gentlemen in the position once occupied by kings; by the end of the century the taste of the public, not of a monarch, shaped what was composed and how it was performed; this, in turn, tended to make music increasingly less of an activity, and more of a commodity. It is a process that Pepys participated in, which he fought against, furthered, and in its earlier stages, uniquely observed.[36]

(Richard Luckett)

Myddelton, [Elizabeth]. Daughter of Sir W. Rider and wife of Richard, son of Sir Thomas Myddelton.[1]

Myngs, Sir Christopher (1625–66). A 'tarpaulin', born of poor parents in London: no friend of Sandwich, but admired by Pepys for his ready speech and remarkable powers of command. He had fought in the parliamentary and republican navies, earning a special renown in the W. Indies (1655–7). At the Restoration he held seven commissions 1662–6, attaining flag rank 1664–6. He was knighted after the Battle of Lowestoft and fell in action in the Four Days Fight. The scene at his funeral when his men offered to avenge his death (vii.165–6) is one of the most moving passages of the diary.[1]

THE NAVY

Pepys's life work was the administration of the navy. Of all the great figures who have laboured in that field he has the clearest and strongest claim to have professionalised the service. The navy of Drake and Hawkins, even of Charles I and Cromwell, was not a recognisable, permanent, continuous force. Its ships might, or might not, have been built for the single purpose of war; they might, or might not, belong to the Crown or, in the terminology of the Commonwealth, to the State. Neither the officers nor the seamen were employed on a regular and permanent basis. They wore no uniform. No central record was kept of their service. Appointment and promotion were thus necessarily somewhat arbitrary. Rates of pay had early been standardised but were, in the case of the seamen, only capriciously honoured. Victualling and medical care ranged from the inadequate to the miserable. Small wonder that the problem of manning could only be resolved by the press gang, that barbarously inequitable form of conscription.

Much of this was still true when Pepys in Evelyn's words 'layed

down his Office & would serve no more'.[1] But even where there was
no large or obvious change, Pepys had generally taken an inconspicuous
but decisive step in the direction of the rational, the systematic, the
orderly and the efficient. As Michael Lewis has well written:
'Apparently he did nothing really drastic: only a number of seemingly
small things. And yet, in each case, that small thing led on inexorably
to another small thing: and that to another: and so on until, somehow –
long after he was dead and gone – the whole conception of the Naval
Officer as he had found it had given place to an entirely different one.'[2]
Professor Lewis is here writing about his reformation of the officer
structure but the same principle applies *mutatis mutandis* to every other
department of the service: to the construction and fitting out of ships,
to the dockyards that serviced and repaired them, to their armament,
to their stores both military and marine; to the standards of diet and
health, to the promotion of discipline and professional knowledge;
above all to the discountenancing of favouritism and corruption and
to the establishment of financial and administrative control through
proper methods of accountancy and the regular keeping of records.

What was the navy on which Pepys had such a transforming effect?
Why and how did he become the agent of such far-reaching changes?
What does the diary tell us about these matters? The term 'navy' in
Pepys's time did not always bear the sense we put on it today. 'Chance
without merit brought me in' wrote Pepys (vi.285), by which he
meant that he owed his start in the Navy Office to his kinship with
Sandwich, not to any professional qualification. The navy might mean,
as here, the permanent administrative body charged with the maintenance or provision of ships and men and officers to fight the country's
battles at sea. Or it might mean, as it originally did, the totality of
English ships and English seafarers without the distinction, implicit in
our eyes, between military and civilian. It could not mean a permanently embodied, salaried, uniformed and ultimately pensionable force
such as we know because it did not then exist. Pepys was to help to
create it. What he meant when he used the word navy was something
larger and less strictly defined. Essentially he meant the maritime
interests and resources of the country viewed in relation to their defence.
In its immediate application this narrowed itself down to the Navy
Board, the permanent governmental body whose job it was to look
after these matters.

The confusion of what we should now call the merchant marine with
the fighting service was not muddle-headed: it reflected the facts. As
Professor Ralph Davis has pointed out in his *The rise of the English
shipping industry* (1962), a number of the most important and lucrative
trades such as the Levant or the E. India Companies engaged in could
only be carried on by vessels that could give a good account of them-

selves when the guns were run out.[3] By an act of 1662 all Mediter-
ranean-going ships over 200 tons were to carry at least 16 guns and
to have a crew of at least 32 men. East Indiamen, mostly of 500 tons or
upwards, were even more formidably armed and manned. There was
nothing absurd in such ships appearing in the hugely expanded fleets
of Cromwell and Charles II though Pepys's patron, Sandwich, one
of the pioneers of the tactics of fighting in line, urged that they should
be left out of the line of battle.[4] Long before Pepys had severed his
connection with the navy this had been accomplished. The ships had,
so to speak, been professionalised. Their officers, thanks almost entirely
to his efforts, were in a fair way to being so.

   Nonetheless, to understand Pepys's life work in its proper context the
mixed character of English maritime endeavour must be kept in mind.
From the beginning trade and war were complementary, not, as we
think of them, antithetical. Even in the next century Pitt's monument
in Guildhall commemorated the fact that under his administration
commerce had been 'united and made to flourish by war'.[5] It was to
this that England owed her supplanting of the Dutch as the leading
European seapower. Pepys's lifetime exactly coincided with this
process. When he was born in 1633 the Dutch were our superiors in
every branch of maritime activity: fishing, the European carrying
trade, the Mediterranean trade, the oceanic trades to Africa, the Far
East, the Americas and the E. Indies. When he died in 1703 the position
had been almost entirely reversed. As Professor Charles Wilson has
pointed out Dutch prosperity depended to a degree unique in the 17th
century on peace.[6] Her neighbours, France and England, on the other
hand, had, or thought they had, much to gain by war. In the Dutch
Wars of Pepys's youth and manhood the United Provinces might hold
their own, or rather more than hold their own, in the fighting and yet
be bound to lose. England was astride their trade routes; England
afforded the only safe riding for ships bound up Channel in which to
shelter from the prevailing south-westerly gales; England did not have
an expensive and vulnerable land frontier to garrison and reinforce
against the first military power of Europe.

   This forcible take-over of the Dutch interest was the foundation on
which the English shipping industry rose to prominence, if not to
primacy, in the nation's economy. And this rise was both cause and
effect of the rise of English seapower. Foreign seaborne trade was what
seapower was about. Readers of the diary and of Pepys's correspondence
are left in no doubt that merchants and shipowners were his chief
sources of naval intelligence and his preferred advisers on naval policy.
The activities of these men provided the *raison d'être* of the Royal Navy:
the seamen they employed were its source of manpower. Even their
ships still continued to supply a considerable part of the force needed in

time of war. Above all the splendid officer corps that the Restoration navy inherited from the Commonwealth came very largely from the same stable. The professional sea officer like the professional seaman learned his trade and earned his livelihood in merchant ships when the Royal Navy had no employment to offer him. In peacetime this was the general condition. Pepys wished to build up and maintain a cadre of officers in continuous service as the French navy had already begun to do.

The transformation of the officer structure lay at the heart of Pepys's aims and achievements. The navy he was introduced to in the early months of the diary was the force that Warwick had shaped into the instrument of victory in the Civil War and that Blake had led to victory against the Dutch and the Spaniards. Apart from a sprinkling of Cromwellian army officers such as Monck and Pepys's own cousin and patron, Sandwich, the officers were what he called 'bred seamen' or as they were disparagingly nicknamed after the Restoration 'tarpaulins'. Charles II as King and his brother the Duke of York as Lord High Admiral lost no time in bringing in a number of new officers of a very different type, courtiers, favourites, noblemen, collectively known as 'gentlemen'. Thus from the moment that he became Clerk of the Acts Pepys was faced with a serious and sharp division between the rival groups. The 'gentlemen' were almost by definition ardent royalists: the 'tarpaulins' were, like Monck and Sandwich themselves, men who had served the usurping governments of the Commonwealth. Much more to the point the tarpaulins were in general thorough masters of their business both as practical seamen and as fighting commanders. They shared a tradition of winning battles and enjoyed the confidence in themselves and in each other that Nelson so eagerly fostered in his captains. The gentlemen usually had courage enough; some of them had experience of military command; a few such as Prince Rupert, Sir Robert Holmes and Sir Thomas Allin had put in a considerable amount of sea time. But their real strength lay in the fact of their political or court or family connections.

The diary is full of references to this alarming fissure. Pepys and his friend and mentor Sir William Coventry were on the side of the tarpaulins. They knew their job. They obeyed orders themselves and imposed discipline on their subordinates. But as Pepys found in his own professional life it was not enough to be right or to be on top of one's job. It was often more important to have the ear of the monarch or the backing of some powerful group. This the gentlemen were much better placed to obtain than the tarpaulins. Hence from quite early on, even in the diary years, Pepys's irritation at the indiscipline and incompetence of the gentlemen is balanced by an unwilling recognition that they could do things for the service that no one else could. What was wanted was an officer corps that combined the prestige and power of the gentlemen with the professional skills of the tarpaulins. The decisive step towards this was taken in 1677 with the introduction of an examination for the rank of lieutenant, for which candidates had to produce certificates of three years sea service in the rank of midshipman.[7] No single measure did more to establish the Royal Navy as a profession.

The appointment of commissioned officers normally belonged to the King or to the Lord High Admiral. The Navy Board of which Pepys was a member up to 1673 was charged with looking after ships, dockyards, stores and pay, and, through the Victualler and the Ordnance Board, with food and guns and ammunition. The only ships' officers who traditionally came within its competence were the so-called standing officers who belonged to a particular ship and who, unlike the commissioned officers, were continuously employed: the carpenter, the gunner, the cook, the master and the boatswain. None of these officers would have been described as sea officers, a term that bears an essentially military connotation. The master was responsible to the captain for the navigation and handling of the ship; the boatswain was similarly responsible for the boats, anchors, rigging and cables. Other officers who might be carried on the larger ships in time of war were the surgeon and his mates, few of whom were as capable and high-minded as Pepys's friend James Pearse. The muster-masters were an administrative invention of Pepys's to check the collusive frauds of the captain and the purser.[8] (Pepys's erratic brother-in-law, Balty, appears to have been surprisingly successful in this capacity.) The purser was in charge of the men's food and drink (supplied by the victualler) and sold them clothing and other necessities. The pursership of a 1st-rate was a lucrative and much sought after position. Sometimes purely administrative officials accompanied their masters to sea as Pepys and Creed did in 1660 as Secretary to the Commander-in-Chief and Deputy Treasurer of the fleet respectively, or as Sir William Coventry did in 1665 as Secretary to the Lord High Admiral. Chaplains though appointed by warrant from the Navy Office like the master and the rest were not standing officers and disappeared into civilian life when their ship paid off.

It is perfectly clear that from the beginning the Navy Board of the Restoration collectively and Pepys individually had considerable say in the appointment and promotion of commissioned officers. Partly this was because the Board was of an exceptionally high calibre. In Sir George Carteret, Sir William Penn and Sir William Batten it had three members, all experts, in whom both the King and the Duke of York had long trusted, so far as the cynicism of the one and the narrowness of the other permitted them to trust anyone. The presence of Sir William Coventry, secretary to the Lord High Admiral, at meetings of the Navy Board as an additional Commissioner further obscured the old boundaries. The affairs of the navy and of the admiralty were more and more seen as a totality.

In all this Pepys and his royal masters were following more closely than they would have cared to admit the precedents set by the naval administration of the Interregnum. Perhaps the chief reason for this is that the Cromwellian period was unique in our history in that a relatively vast army and a huge fleet had been kept in permanent commission. The economic burden of such an establishment had previously been unthinkable. But revolutionary times are revolutionary just because the unthinkable is thought and even put into effect. In the case of the navy it could be argued that the immense expenditure had yielded proportionable gains. The prizes taken in the First Dutch War (1652–4) virtually reconstituted the English merchant fleet and may even have doubled its size.[9] In the war against Spain (1655–60) the results had not been so happy because the Spaniards were better placed to prey on our seaborne commerce than we were on theirs. But this provided a complementary argument for a strong navy. Defence if only negatively could be as profitable as attack. Shipping and seaborne trade dominated the economic thinking of the age of Pepys. As Professor Ralph Davis has written: 'The latter part of the seventeenth century was . . . the period in which economic problems relating to the shipping industry bulked largest in men's eyes and were most rapidly increasing in importance. The extensive literature on its problems, dying away from about 1680 and ceasing abruptly soon after 1700, was not merely a response to Dutch competition and the problems it posed; it also reflected the growing significance of the shipping industry to the whole English economy.'[10] The policy enunciated in the Navigation Act of 1651 and restated in the more comprehensive measure of 1660 necessarily implied a stronger navy and a larger peacetime establishment than Elizabeth or the first two Stuarts had maintained. The central principle of these acts was that goods imported into England should be carried either in English ships or in those of the country from which the product came. This was the logical and systematic extension of a protectionism first discernible in the 14th century and most conspicuously exemplified in the Tudor acts confining the great wine trade with Bordeaux to English ships. The growth of colonies, notably in North America, widened the scope and importance of this monopoly. A larger navy in its turn could only be manned if there were more seamen in an expanded merchant marine.

The Restoration navy was fortunate in inheriting a body of officers second to none. It also inherited, in spite of Pepys's frequent assertions to the contrary, a very formidable fleet, most of it of recent construction. The fleet that sailed over to bring Charles II back in May 1660 consisted of 32 ships out of a total of 156.[11] They included three 1st-rates, 11 2nd-rates and 16 3rd-rates. All of these were a match in size, firepower and stoutness for anything the Dutch could bring against them. Indeed the 1st-rates and the larger 2nd-rates were bigger and stronger than any Dutch man-of-war. With the adoption of an aggressive foreign policy, new building became essential. In 1663 one 1st-rate was added, in 1664 two 2nd-rates. In 1666 to replace the losses of the war the heroic total of a dozen new warships was reached, including one 2nd- and four 3rd-rates. A 1st-rate carried 90 to 100 guns, a 2nd-rate 80 to 90, a 3rd-rate 60 to 70. These gradations were not entirely logical or consistent. Some 3rd-rates were more powerful than some 2nds and guns were not standardised until Anson's time at the Admiralty in the 1750s. Pepys's efforts had taken matters a long way in this direction. But the contribution to naval strength of which he was most justly proud was the building programme of the 30 new ships initiated by the act of 1677, the same year that saw the introduction of the lieutenants' examination. The fleet that he handed over to his successors in Feb. 1689 was even stronger and better found than the powerful force inherited from the Commonwealth in May 1660: 59 ships of the first three rates as against 30: total tonnage and total of guns both increased by over 50%.[12]

Size and gunpower gave the fighting ships of the Royal Navy their decisive superiority over the Dutch, whose warships had to be built with a shallower draft to give them the necessary freedom of movement in their own coastal waters. Because their keels were not so deep they could not carry the heavy cannon of their English opponents. This again dictated the battle tactics of the two navies. The Dutch, like the Spaniards before them, sought to deny the English advantage in gunnery by boarding and hand-to-hand fighting. The English could only exploit their weight of metal by bringing their broadsides to bear, which, if one ship were not to mask another, must mean fighting in line ahead on a course parallel to the enemy. To form these huge fleets of sailing ships into one long continuous line was a heroic undertaking. The fleet that sailed out to meet the Dutch in June 1665 consisted of 84 men-of-war besides merchantmen and fireships.[13] This would, as Dr R. C. Anderson points out, have stretched over several miles of sea. To maintain any degree of control some devolution of command was essential. The fleet was therefore divided into three squadrons, the Red or Centre, the White or Van and the Blue or Rear. Each squadron was itself similarly divided into Centre, Van and Rear commanded by an Admiral, a Vice-Admiral and a Rear-Admiral respectively. The vessels in which these officers sailed were distinguished by flags; hence the still familiar term 'flagship' and the now obsolete

title habitually used by Pepys, 'flagmen'. The famous series of Lely
portraits known as the Flagmen of Lowestoft now in the National
Maritime Museum brings us face to face with some of the most
eminent commanders, both tarpaulins and gentlemen, of the navy
Pepys knew.

The extent of that service has repeatedly been emphasised. Even in
peacetime the building and maintenance of ships, the management of
dockyards, the purchase of stores, timber, cordage, canvas and a
hundred other commodities made the navy by far the biggest spending
department of government. In war, with huge numbers of men to feed
and (in theory) pay, its financial demands could only have been met by
a modern system of taxation and debt-funding far beyond the antiquated machinery of Charles II's Treasury. Hence two aspects of naval
administration that no reader of the diary can have helped noticing:
first, the reiteration of the theme that all is lost for want of money and
second, Pepys's vigilance against fraud and corruption, or perhaps more
accurately against corruption which he had not sanctioned as reasonable
in itself or as valuable to him personally. In the 17th century and long
after, a post in the public service was generally regarded as the property,
often a very valuable property, of its occupant. He could sell it,
exchange it, transfer it to a relation or protégé. Pepys himself certainly
took this view. Implicit, obviously, was the idea that 'places' as they
were called should be exploited for profit. Very few carried a high
salary. The money mostly came from bribes, tips, presents, rake-offs:
how difficult sometimes it is to draw a clear line between these terms.
Or it might come from cheating pure and simple, such as claiming
wages and allowances for men who did not exist, or, as was particularly
common in the dockyards, from barefaced theft. It was against these
last two, deeply engrained in traditional practices, that Pepys set his
face. 'A purser without professed cheating is a professed loser' Pepys
had early observed.[14] The counter-measure he devised against this type
of swindle was the appointment of muster-masters who would return
their muster books direct to the Navy Office. This provided an independent check on the figures supplied by pursers and captains who were
often in collusion. To prevent the purser swindling a vigilant and
efficient bureaucracy was comparatively simple. What was much harder
was to stop him swindling the wretched seamen by accepting from the
victualler food and drink too cheap and nasty for human consumption.
Pepys was fully alive to the importance of the issue:

> Englishmen, and more especially seamen, love their bellies above
> anything else, and therefore it must always be remembered in the
> management of the victualling of the Navy that to make any abate-
> ment from them in the quantity or agreeableness of the victuals is

to discourage and provoke them in the tenderest point, and will sooner render them disgusted with the King's service than any one other hardship that can be put upon them.[15]

In spite of this pithy diagnosis, the cure escaped him. He himself occupied the post of Surveyor-General of the Victualling during the second half of the Second Dutch War and subsequently drew up the terms of the contract under which the navy was victualled. These appear to have been little more than pious aspirations. As in every department of naval life the government did not pay up. The Victualler eventually went bankrupt and the seamen were, as they always had been, generally half-starved.

The matter of pay itself was obviously bedevilled by the same fundamental failure. The money was never there. Even the Commonwealth government which had raised the pay of the seaman by 25 % had not managed to honour its commitments. The Restoration navy inherited a huge debt in respect of unpaid seamen's wages and resorted to the time-dishonoured evasions of keeping ships in commission to avoid paying the men off and of paying wages not in cash but by tickets theoretically redeemable at the Navy Office. Such tickets were often bought up at a cruel discount by brokers who were better placed than the poor seaman to thread the maze of public finance. Pepys himself constantly inveighs against both these practices in the diary and elsewhere. From time to time he put forward schemes of reform but improvements in administrative technique were beside the point. For at least a century the government had been getting away with theft and exploitation on an enormous scale and it was not going to mend its ways until it was forced to. The mutinies at the end of the 18th century and the reforming spirit of the Victorian age at last achieved this.

The navy that Pepys knew was thus in a stage of transition complementary to so much else, to science and social life to take but two examples to which its concerns bear some relation. In the field of science the connection with the Royal Society was early and strong. Pepys himself was a Fellow, and the first President, Lord Brouncker, was one of his colleagues at the Navy Board. Scientific principles were applied to the design of ships by Sir Anthony Deane and Sir William Petty, the latter of whom also attempted to supply a statistical basis to the solution of the manning problem. The navy in its turn made useful contributions to geography, hydrography and navigation. In social life the gradual evolution of the professional naval officer and of the professional administrator such as Pepys himself typified the wider changes of the period. The character of the transition in the service itself has been well summed up by Professor Christopher Lloyd:

The naval profession and the administrative basis of the service during the age of sail was forged in the crucible of the three Dutch Wars, 1652–4, 1665–7, 1672–4. The 'new model' navy formed during the Commonwealth was institutionalized during the reigns of Charles II and William III so successfully that its administrative structure, the build of its ships, the method by which it was officered, manned and supplied, continued without fundamental change until half way through the nineteenth century.[16] [*See also* Dockyards; Dutch Wars; Navy Board]

(Richard Ollard)

THE NAVY BOARD

Introduction. The Navy Board was the body of officials which under the authority of the Lord High Admiral and ultimately of the King had charge of the civilian administration of the navy – i.e. the building and repair of ships and the management of the dockyards. In medieval times the navy, besides being small, had been in effect a transport force used only occasionally for fighting, and most of what later became the Navy Board's functions were then performed by a single official, the Clerk of the Ships, whose office is traceable to John's reign. With the exploitation of overseas trade and the growth of the state's power in the 16th century a great expansion of maritime and naval activity took place. The number of royal ships was increased (from 5 to 70 in Henry VIII's reign); the distinction between warships and armed merchantmen was developed; and dockyards were built or extended. In the process a new administrative body, the Navy Board of 1546 (consisting of five, later four, officials) was created. It consisted normally of a Treasurer, Comptroller, Surveyor and Clerk of the Navy – the last often being given the title of Clerk of the Acts.

During the Civil War and Interregnum the Board was replaced by a series of commissions staffed by up to eight or ten members, mostly experienced seamen and merchants armed with general and flexible powers and deliberately made free of the constrictions attaching to the traditional officers of the Board. Some of these bodies presided over the remarkable increase in the size of the navy under the Commonwealth. After the return of the King the Board was replaced, the former Commissioners continuing to act for a short period while the members of the Board were chosen and empowered to act. The new Board set up on 4 July 1660 consisted of four Principal Officers – the historic officers of the Board: the Treasurer (Sir George Carteret), the Comptroller (Sir Robert Slingsby), the Surveyor (Sir William Batten) and the Clerk of the Acts (Pepys), together with three Commissioners –

similar to those who had governed the navy during most of the Inter-regnum – Sir William Penn and Lord Berkeley of Stratton as full Commissioners and Peter Pett as a local Commissioner supervising the dockyard at Chatham. There was a staff of clerks who were required to attend on the Board for eight hours a day,[1] of whom the senior was a Chief Clerk to the Board. He had an assistant. Each member of the Board had two clerks who were paid by their masters (from an allowance given them for the purpose) and had the status of personal servants, like Pepys's Will Hewer. In addition there were other clerks at the Navy Treasury and the Ticket Office. During the war at least seven clerks were added to the strength of the main office in Seething Lane and more to the other offices.[2] Besides the clerks, there was a subordinate staff of messengers (usually two), a porter, a doorkeeper, a labourer and two watchmen.

In its work the Board was guided partly by tradition and precedent, and more explicitly by instructions issued by the Lord High Admiral. In 1660 those of 1640 were still in force. They were not replaced until Jan. 1662 when the Duke of York issued them in a slightly amended and expanded form.[3] In theory these controlled the work of the Board and its members. But it was one thing to issue instructions and another to see that they were properly observed. Later enquiries were to reveal that subordinate officials and the Principal Officers alike were negligent in observing them and in some cases ignorant of their contents. Moreover, it can now be seen that the Instructions of 1662 were an inadequate guide to the government of the greatly enlarged navy of the 1660s.

General powers. The Board was to make most of its decisions jointly. It was required to meet twice a week, the hours and days being varied during parliamentary sessions for the benefit of members who were M.P.s or peers. In 1660, when it was getting into its stride, and in crises, during the war and after, it met more frequently. Two members constituted a quorum. Clerks were present except when the Board resolved to meet 'close'. The duties of the Board were set out in detail in 20 articles of the Instructions. They were to see to the repair, build-ing and setting out of ships, and to the pay, clothing and victualling of the seamen. A principal part of their duties was to make contracts at their meetings with the merchants who supplied naval stores. Three articles, added in the 1662 version, required the Board to familiarise itself with current market prices, to avoid restricting itself to a single supplier, and to make certain that the goods were delivered according to the terms of the contracts. The officers of the Board were required to live as close together as possible and 'to trace one another in their distinct duties'. In 1662 there was one significant omission from the Instructions – that of the article concerning the power to 'press and take up all seamen, ships, hoyes and provisions whatsoever . . .', a power always unpopular and of doubtful legality. In practice, however, the strain of war led to the use of the press both with regard to men and ships, an order in council being issued for the purpose.

The Treasurer. Of the four Principal Officers the most important in status was the Treasurer (Sir George Carteret until June 1667, the Earl of Anglesey until Nov. 1668 and after 1668 Sir Thomas Littleton and Sir Thomas Osborne jointly). Since the navy was the largest of all spending departments, accounting for roughly a quarter of the government's expenditure during the diary years,[4] he was a figure of national importance, often unable, like Carteret, because of his duties elsewhere, to attend meetings of the Board. The post had considerable financial attractions because in addition to a salary of £2000 the Treasurer enjoyed the proceeds of poundage, i.e. 3*d.* in every pound sterling he handled. (In contrast, his colleagues the Comptroller, Surveyor and Clerk of the Acts received salaries of £500, £490 and £350 respectively – and no poundage.) The poundage system was regarded as extravagant by the (national) Treasury Commissioners in 1667 and consequently when Anglesey was appointed to the post certain payments, especially those to the Victualler, were made direct from the Exchequer instead of from the navy Treasury. At about the same time the feeling that the Navy Treasurer was too powerful gave rise to the suggestion that the post should be abolished and replaced by a chief cashier who would be subordinate to the rest of the Board.[5] Changes effected in 1671 went some way in this direction – the Treasurer was reduced in status and required to submit weekly accounts to the Board.

His duties, according to the Instructions of 1662, were to receive and pay monies, to see that sums allocated to the navy were made available by the national treasury, to prepare estimates for the Board and the Lord High Admiral, and check payments authorised by the Board. He was also to attend most 'pays' (the occasions when ships were paid off) and ensure that the correct rates and allowances were observed. Finally, he was to prepare ledgers which were to be audited annually and presented to the full Board. These were substantially the same duties as those defined in 1640. Despite the growth in the size and cost of the navy since 1640 nothing was now done to make appropriate changes in the management of naval finances. Some of the financial problems of the navy in the '60s were due in part to this administrative inadequacy, though the main reason was of course a chronic shortage of money.

The Comptroller. The office of Comptroller was originally envisaged as a check on the actions of the Board as a whole and as a means of preventing waste and extravagance. This was always difficult, particularly in view of the large number and variety of ledgers used, and the lack of an efficient system of cross-reference. With the expansion of the navy since the early part of the century the Comptroller's task had become virtually impossible, even in peacetime. War, and the incompetence of Sir John Mennes (Comptroller 1661–71) made things even worse.

The Comptroller's duties were set out in 11 articles of the Instructions. He was to ensure that the correct rates of seamen's pay were observed and that the Board was informed of current market prices when negotiating contracts. He was also responsible – and this constituted the greater part of his work – for auditing the accounts of the Treasurer, the Victualler and the storekeepers, and had to present an annual audit of these accounts to the Board and the Lord High Admiral. The Comptroller was thus in function primarily an accountant, but neither of the Comptrollers in the diary period – Slingsby and Mennes – had the slightest experience in accountancy. In 1663 and 1664 proposals were made to make Penn an assistant to Mennes, but were dropped in face of Mennes's resistance. In Jan. 1667 however (in response to pressure from Coventry and Pepys) an order in council was issued imposing two assistants on him, so that the office was effectively divided into three. Brouncker was to audit the Treasurer's accounts, Penn the Victualler's, and Mennes (given after 1669 five extra clerks) was to do the rest. The practice of appointing subsidiary officers continued: in 1671 a fourth was added to examine storekeepers' accounts, and during the Third Dutch War a fifth to deal with the Ticket Office.

The Surveyor. The Surveyor had responsibility for the design, building and repair of ships. This involved supervising work at the dockyards (through the local Clerks of Survey) and ensuring that an adequate supply of materials was obtained. But the expansion of the service had meant that he had to devote more time to administration and less to supervision, for which he was forced to rely on subordinate officials in the yards and in some cases on the dockyard commissioners. According to the Instructions he was to take an annual survey of the stores and to estimate what was required for the following year. Together with his subordinates, he was to ensure that all materials and stores delivered for the use of the navy were according to contract in quantity, quality and dimensions. He was also to make an annual survey of the ships, dockyards, storehouses, and other buildings, and provide an estimate of any necessary repairs. Finally, he was to supervise the issue of stores to the ships and to compare the storekeepers' accounts with those of the carpenters and boatswains which related to the use of stores while the ships were at sea. It was on him that the Board relied for an accurate account of the condition of the ships, yards and stores and for advice on what materials to purchase. As a result it was to be expected that he would have a major rôle in the making of contracts.

The Clerk of the Acts. It would be incorrect to see the Clerk of the Acts as a direct descendant of the medieval Clerk of the Ships, who was often the only permanent administrative official and had responsibility for most of the duties later undertaken by the Comptroller and Surveyor. With the expansion of the navy and its administrative framework the Clerk was increasingly restricted to the functions of a secretary. Such was the situation in 1660 when Pepys obtained the post. He was able to arrest the decline of the office and to make it the lynch-pin of naval administration. The Instructions required the Clerk to attend all meetings of the Board, to present correspondence, record decisions and prepare letters for signature and despatch. An unambitious Clerk could have exercised his duties almost entirely from the London office. Pepys decided differently. He mastered the office routines quickly and then set himself to learn the trades of his colleagues – especially that of the Surveyor. Very soon he was not only composing the letters of the office, but visiting dockyards and negotiating contracts. In addition, by virtue of his energy and ability, he became the natural spokesman for the office in its relations with Admiralty, Privy Council and Parliament. He introduced reforms in office methods – particularly in dockyard procedures and wartime victualling arrangements – and after the war conducted an investigation (supposedly the work of the Duke of York as Admiral) into the conduct of the entire office. His conclusion – accepted by the Duke – was that there were no deficiencies in the Board's structure, but only a failure by the officers (except himself) to carry out the duties defined in their Instructions.[6] Similarly in 1688 at the end of his career, when the Special Commission he had set up in 1686 had done its work (which had involved superseding the Navy Board for current business) he recommended that the Board should be restored in its old form. Other able men have held the office of clerk – e.g. Charles Sergison (Clerk 1690–1719) – but none have succeeded in making it so important as it was in Pepys's hands.

The Commissioners. During the diary period ten commissioners were appointed, two of whom (Berkeley of Stratton and Hervey) contributed little to the work of the Board. Their functions were various. Sir William Penn (1660–9), most versatile of them all, not only played a part in everyday work, at meetings, pays and in the yards, but also – in addition to serving in the battlefleet in 1665 – took on special assignments: hastening out the fleet in 1665 and 1666, and after 1667 taking over the inspection of the Treasurer's accounts from the Comptroller. Brouncker (1664–79) was also used to assist the Comptroller. Sir William Coventry (1662–7), despite his absences from London with the court or the navy, was in many ways the most important of the commissioners by virtue of being secretary to the Lord High Admiral. He acted as the link between the Duke and the Navy Board. Of the other commissioners, five were dockyard officers: Pett and Cox at Chatham, Taylor at Harwich, Middleton and Tippets at Portsmouth.

Collective duties. The work for which the Board was collectively responsible was: (1) the building and repairing of ships (according to the Admiral's directions), and the supply of materials for this purpose; (2) the payment of officers and seamen; (3) the supervision of victualling; and (4) the control of the dockyards.

(1) *Shipbuilding and repair.* The Board's function was to provide supplies and pay the workmen. The commonest method of obtaining supplies was by contract, made after tenders had been received, which specified the price and quantity of the goods, and sometimes the time and place of their delivery. They could be concluded only in a formal meeting of the Board. The principal materials were timber, masts, iron, canvas, hemp and tar. All or nearly all were imported, which meant that not only were supplies at risk in wartime but the Board was forced to conduct business with a relatively small group of merchants. The merchants did not limit their trade to any one commodity, and the larger and more important the merchant, the greater the range of naval goods he offered. Sir William Warren offered virtually everything the navy used in bulk. The smaller merchants usually restricted themselves to one product and were likely to specialise in English materials. It was these small suppliers who were hit most severely when the Board could not pay with ready money. Other methods than contract were occasionally employed. For timber there were the resources of oak in the royal forests – obtainable only after lengthy administrative delays. There were navy 'purveyors' who dealt (on commission) in a variety of materials, and the 'purveyor of petty emptions' (usually the Chief Clerk of the Navy Office) who supplied small quantities or specialised goods. In wartime there was also the possibility of using goods taken as prize, but since these had to be bought at auction for ready money no great quantity found its way to the navy. There were a few occasions – the diary has mention of only one – when because of pressure of work the Board had to have ships built in private yards. In these cases the Board's function was to conclude a contract and inspect the shipbuilder's work before authorising payment.

(2) *Pays.* The Board conducted pays principally through the Treasurer who was assisted by members of the Board. The Board as a whole was responsible for calculating the rates of pay,[7] checking that the officers and seamen were correctly rated and seeing that the ships' books corresponded with the muster books. In the case of officers the scale of pay depended on the rate of the ship. The captain of a 1st-rate received £21 per month; the captain of a 6th-rate only £7. The discrepancy

was less marked for standing officers: the carpenter on a 1st-rate received £4 per month and on a 6th-rate £2. The seamen's pay was not affected by the rate of the ship; scales ranged from 24s. per month for an able seaman to 19s. for an ordinary seaman and 9s. 6d. for boys. All these rates applied when the ships were on active service: a lower rate (about half) applied when they were in harbour.

During 1660–2 the seamen were being paid for their service under the Commonwealth – in some cases for arrears of two or three years. The Board was not involved here except in the calculation of the amount due to the men, the pays being handled by parliamentary commissioners appointed by statute to pay off the armed forces. In the period leading up to the war, with a small number of ships in service and a reasonable supply of money, the Board was usually able to ensure fairly prompt payments. Even during this time there were occasional problems such as finding £3000 to pay off the *Guernsey* in March 1662. These difficulties became acute during the war. They posed a problem which the Navy Board of itself was incapable of solving.

(3) *Victualling.* Under the Commonwealth victualling had been managed by a board of commissioners appointed for the purpose. This system was abandoned along with other innovations at the Restoration and the duties farmed out to a single contractor as before the Civil War. Denis Gauden, who had been associated with victualling during the '50s, was appointed in Sept. 1660. His contract (Apr. 1661) required him to provide victuals at the rate of 6d. per man while the ships were in harbour and 8d. per man at sea. He was to keep a reserve stock sufficient for 4,000 men for two months and to deliver these and, given notice, any additional supplies to any port on the English, Scottish or Irish coasts. He had his headquarters in a complex of storehouses, slaughter-houses etc. on Tower Hill, with subsidiary establishments at certain ports. It was left to him to contract with suppliers and to hire the small vessels which carried the supplies to the navy. The victuals themselves consisted mainly of beef, pork, biscuit, peas and beer. The 1661 contract was drawn up by the Lord Treasurer and the Privy Council with little reference to the Navy Board. The Board's duty consisted simply in examining the victualler's accounts and of doing what they could – which was little – to see that he was paid. But the difficulties of the war years, which caused a virtual breakdown in the system, forced them into active intervention. The commanders complained that the victuals were brought too slowly to the fleet and were insufficient to keep the ships at sea. The seamen complained about the quality – stinking beer and mouldy biscuit – and of short allowances. For his part Gauden complained of shortages, rising prices and above all of slow and late payments from the navy Treasury. After the campaign of 1665 it was clear that something had to be done. A new contract was

ruled out by the provision in the old one for a year's notice before any major change could be introduced. To provide Gauden with partners would improve his credit and prevent confusion in the event of his death, but no suitable merchants were available. It was therefore left to Pepys to examine the situation and to make recommendations to the Lord High Admiral. During Oct. 1665 he was at work on a variety of propositions; at the same time as searching around for reforms he was looking for a way of making 'lawful profit' for himself. His recommendation was that a number of surveyors should be appointed at the main victualling ports; they were to report to a central officer in London who would co-ordinate the reports and from time to time present an accurate account of the state of supplies to the Board and the Lord High Admiral. His suggestion was accepted by the King and the Duke 'with complete applause and satisfaction', and in Nov. 1665 he was appointed Surveyor-General of Victualling at a salary of £300. However, during 1666 the joint commanders, Rupert and Albemarle, renewed their complaints. They claimed in August that they were forced to bring back the fleet from the Dutch coast for lack of victuals. The only noticeable change, they claimed, was in the number of estimates and accounts they had to cope with. Pepys was able to demonstrate, to those ashore at least, that the situation was better than in the previous year. After the war, in 1668, tenders were invited for a new contract, and this time, in contrast to what had happened in 1661, the Board was invited by the Admiralty Committee of the Privy Council to adjudge between the contestants. At the same time it was also asked to comment on the relative merits of the two methods of victualling – by contract and by direct management. Their report (largely the work of Pepys) decided in favour of the contract system as being the cheaper, and recommended the acceptance of Gauden's tender. In its final form, as approved by the Treasury in March 1669, it nominated two partners to act with him – his son Benjamin and Sir W. Penn. Three other similar contracts were negotiated in Charles's reign but in 1683 the victualling was handed over to a board of commissioners. There is no doubt that this arrangement made control by the state easier. But the ineradicable difficulties of feeding the men at sea remained.[8] [*See also* Dockyards; Victualling Office]

(Andrew Turnbull)

THE NAVY OFFICE

From 1630–49 the Board had occupied a house in Mincing Lane and from 1649–54 part of the Victualling Office on Tower Hill. In 1654 the government acquired for £2400 from Sir John

Wolstenholme the building in which the office was housed until 1673. It was the northern section of a large house on the e. side of Seething Lane, a few doors south of its junction with Crutched Friars, with a courtyard opening onto the Lane and a garden stretching from the Lane to the n.-w. corner of Tower Hill. The site is now occupied, approximately, by the offices of the London Port Authority. It was a rambling building lit by over 180 windows,[1] taxed on 48 hearths in 1666,[2] with lodgings for four Principal Officers and a clerk, as well as office accommodation and a porter's lodge. During the diary period the government spent close on £950 on repairs, alterations and decorations, carried out for the most part by workmen from the Deptford yard.[3] From time to time the Navy Board made unsuccessful efforts to obtain the southern section of the house, leased to Sir Richard Ford. No representation of the house is known to survive. The building, which had narrowly escaped destruction in the Great Fire of 1666, was burnt down (without fatalities) in the night of 29 Jan. 1673 by a fire which spread to 30 neighbouring houses.[4] The office records did not escape unscathed, nor did Pepys's collection. He is known to have lost his engraved portraits by Nanteuil.[5] For a few days the office was lodged in Trinity House, after which the Mark Lane mansion of the Blayning family was acquired for their use. By 1683 a new building erected on the old site and adjoining ground was ready for occupation. It was designed by Wren and was re-oriented to open on to Crutched Friars.[6] There the office remained until it moved to the new Somerset House in 1786. In 1869 it moved again to Spring Gardens close by the Admiralty.[7] (R; La)

Navy Treasury. In 1654 in Leadenhall St; from Michaelmas 1664 onwards in Broad St in the former house (taxed on 24 hearths) of Sir Thomas Allen. It escaped the Fire and was enlarged in 1686.[1] (R)

Naylor, [Oliver] (1628–1705). Clergyman and relative by marriage – he married Jane Pepys of Mileham, Norf., in 1661. Fellow of Caius College, Cambridge, 1651–9; Rector of Tavistock, Devon, c. 1652–66; Prebendary of Exeter 1661–1701; Rector of Clovelly 1666–81.[1]

Naylor, [William]. A relative by marriage: probably son of Richard Naylor of Offord Darcy, Hunts., and brother of Jasper Trice's third wife.[1]

Neale, [Thomas] (1641–99). Courtier and projector. Pepys describes the brisk tactics which won him a rich widow in 1664. After her death he almost won an heiress.[1] He made and spent two fortunes, engaged in the E. Indian and Guinea trades, prospered (and broke) as a brewer, undertook building developments in the Seven Dials, and founded a penny post in the American colonies. He was elected F.R.S. in 1664 and sat in all parliaments (except that of 1681) from 1668. In 1678 he became Groom Porter at court, and in 1679 a Groom of the Bedchamber. From 1684 he had a place at the Mint, becoming an absentee Master in 1686 (to be succeeded by Isaac Newton in 1699). He managed the state lottery of 1694.[2]

Neat Houses, Chelsea. A number of market-gardeners' houses on the fertile heavily-manured low ground by the Thames west of the present position of Vauxhall Bridge. Since Elizabethan times celebrated also as places of entertainment. In the 1830s the area was laid out in streets and St Gabriel's, Pimlico, built. (R)

Neile, Sir Paul, kt 1633 (1613–86). Son of Richard Neile, Archbishop of York; an original F.R.S.; Gentleman-Usher of the Privy Chamber 1662–84; M.P. for Ripon Apr.–May 1640 and Newark 1673–Jan. 79. He owned a notable collection of telescopes, and is said to have been the original of Sidrophel the astrologer in Butler's *Hudibras*.[1]

Nevill, [Thomas]. Draper, of Paul's Churchyard.[1]

Newbery, [Capt. Richard]. A veteran who had served since c. 1644 and was in command of the *Portland* when put out of his commission in Apr. 1660. Blake and Monck had recommended him for the command of a frigate in 1653.[1]

New Bridewell: *see* Clerkenwell

Newell, ——. 'An old fellow-student' of Cromleholme's (iii.199). There were two Newells at Oxford in Cromleholme's time (1635–9): Joseph (an undergraduate at New Hall 1637–41 and by 1662 Vicar of Leckhampstead, Northants.), and John (a Fellow of Corpus Christi 1634–48 – Cromleholme's college – and by 1662 Rector of Combe Martin, Devon).[1]

The New Exchange, Strand. Pepys often calls it simply 'the Exchange'; but usually makes its location clear enough to avoid confusion with the Royal Exchange in the city. It was situated on the s. side of the street, opposite Half Moon (now Bedford) St and was built in 1608–9 by the Earl of Salisbury (on the site of the stables of Durham House) in imitation of the Royal Exchange. It was designed to be, like its model, both a bourse for merchants and a shopping precinct specialising in luxury goods. Its central walks were flanked by double galleries containing eight rows of shops, many of them little more than booths. The bourse failed but the shops prospered, especially after the residential development of the Covent Garden area in the 1630s. The destruction of the Royal Exchange in the Fire gave it a further fillip, and it was by then well-established as a resort of fashionable society, and figures as such in many Restoration plays. The building was taken down in 1737.

The river and stairs which took their name from the building lay at the end of Durham Yard.[1] (R)

Newgate/Newgate Prison. The gate was in the city wall on the w.

side, north of Ludgate and at the w. end of Newgate St. In Pepys's time the building on each side of it still served as the common gaol for the malefactors of the city and of the county of Middlesex. The gate itself was closed at night. Burnt in the Fire, it was rebuilt, improved and used as before. The open space west of it was used for executions. (R)

Newgate Market. Before the Fire Newgate St was encumbered with a middle row of stalls and houses which ran from St Martin-le-Grand to Ivy Lane and an open market west of that. Part was used for butchers' stalls and was known as the Shambles: the whole being referred to as 'Newgate Market'. After the Fire, which destroyed this whole quarter, the middle row was thrown into the street and a covered market made south of the street. It ceased to be a market in 1869. [*See also* Food] (R)

Newington Green. A separate part of Stoke Newington, Middlesex, less than 4 miles north of the city and to the west of the road through Stoke Newington village to Edmonton and Ware and so to Cambridge. Pepys's maternal aunt, Ellen Kite, lived there, and he knew it well as a child. (R)

Newman, Col. [George]. Committee-man in Kent during the Civil War and Interregnum.[1]

New Palace Yard: *see* Westminster Palace

Newport, Andrew (1623–99). Second son of the 1st Baron Newport. A royalist agent in the '50s, he was rewarded at the Restoration with an equerry's place at court (1660) and a company of foot at Portsmouth (1662). He had business interests, and served on the customs commissions (of 1662 and 1681) and on the Royal Fishery (1664). The comptrollership of the Wardrobe to which he was appointed in 1668 was a new post: he held it until 1681. He was an M.P. for Montgomeryshire 1661–Jan. 79, Preston 1685–7 and Shrewsbury 1689–99.[1] He died unmarried: Pepys's 'young Newport' was his brother, Richard, a well-known rakehell.[2]

Newport St, Westminster. This fashionable street ran to the west from St Martin's Lane opposite the end of Long Acre. Pepys's rich cousin Thomas Pepys lived there until 1663, and the ambitious John Creed moved there in 1669. It still survives (as Great Newport St), its length much reduced by the cutting through of Charing Cross Road. (R)

New Spring Garden: *see* Vauxhall

Nicholas, Sir Edward, kt 1641, bt 1653 (1593–1669). Secretary of State to Charles I (1641–9) and to Charles II (1654–62). A protégé of the 1st Duke of Buckingham and secretary to the Admiralty Commissioners 1628–38. A strong Anglican and a man of high principles, his replacement in 1662 by Arlington was a blow to the Clarendonian old guard. His younger brother Matthew was Dean of St Paul's, 1660–61.[1]

Nicholas, Sir John, kt 1661 (c. 1623–1705). Eldest son of Sir Edward; nephew of Thomas Povey. One of the clerks in ordinary to the Privy Council 1660–1705.

Nicholson, [John]. A Cambridge contemporary of Pepys (at Magdalene 1651–5), son of Christopher, a prominent Presbyterian merchant of Newcastle upon Tyne. A John Nicholson was a clerk in the Post Office 1661.[1]

Nixon, Capt. [Edward] (d. by 1688). A captain in the Commonwealth navy, he held three commands 1661–4.[1]

Noble, Jack. Servant to Pepys's brother, Tom. Tom died owing him £6.[1]

Noell, Sir Martin (c. 1600–65). The most prominent of the merchants and financiers operating in the Interregnum; much involved in government finance; brother-in-law of Cromwell's Secretary of State, Thurloe. At the Restoration he escaped financial disaster and both he and his eldest son were knighted. At his death he left seven sons unprovided for. His wife was Elizabeth (b. Blake). Thomas Povey's brothers, Richard and William, were employed as his agents in the W. Indies.[1]

Nokes, ——. Probably Nathaniel Nokes, silkman. A Nathaniel Nokes lived 'over against Bow Church', and his late master, Ald. Francis Dashwood, dealt in silk.[1]

Nonsuch House, Surrey. A royal palace near Ewell begun by Henry VIII and completed by the 12th Earl of Arundel (d. 1580). It had not remained continuously in the possession of the royal family, but had since 1625 belonged to Henrietta-Maria, now Queen Mother. It was built in the showiest Tudor-Gothic style, with high corner towers and an inner court whose upper storey was decorated with bas-reliefs and painted panels. Pepys visited it several times in 1665 when the Receipt of the Exchequer was moved there during the Plague. In 1670 it was granted by the King to the Duchess of Cleveland who pulled down the house, sold the contents and divided the park into farms. There are now only a few traces of the foundations left.[1]

Norbury. Relatives: in 1665 living in Islington.[1] George Norbury had married Sarah Sutton, sister of Mary, wife of William Wight. His wife had a house and land in Brampton, and sold some land there in 1664 – possibly the property offered to Pepys in 1662 (iii.13). Mary Wight in her will (1696) forgave him a debt of £500 used for the purchase of land at Brampton. He may be the George Norbury (son of John) admitted to Gray's Inn 1639. In 1665 his daughter Katherine (of Islington) married Robert Woolley.[2]

Norman, [James] (d. 1668). Clerk to the Surveyor of the Navy 1660–4; Clerk of the Survey, Chatham 1664–8. In a letter of 1668 Pepys wrote of him that he was 'as honest, active and improving an officer as any . . . in the Navy'. Two years later his widow was petitioning for his arrears of pay.[1]

Norris, ——. Frame maker of Long Acre; possibly the John Norris who lived on the n. side.[1] Henry Norris (fl. 1647–84) was frame maker to the King.[2]

North. A Cambridgeshire family related to the Mountagus through Sir Dudley North (1602–77; succ. as 4th Baron North 1666) who in 1632 married Anne Mountagu, niece of the 1st Earl of Manchester. He was a parliamentarian in the Civil War and sat as M.P. for Cambridgeshire in the Short and Long Parliaments until excluded in 1648. In the elections to the Convention in 1660 he was defeated for the county because he would not commit himself to an unconditional restoration, and sat for the borough. After the dissolution he retired to his books at Kirtling.

He had a progeny of gifted sons, all virtuosi – musical, learned, and patrons of the arts. The eldest, Charles (1635–91), knighted sometime before 1667, was summoned to the Lords in 1673 as Lord Grey, and succeeded as 5th Baron North in 1677. He was a prominent Exclusionist, and married the daughter of the Exclusionist Lord Grey of Warke. Francis (1637–85) became a distinguished lawyer – Solicitor-General and knight in 1671, Attorney-General in 1673, Chief Justice of Common Pleas in 1675 and Lord Keeper in 1682. He was created Baron Guilford in 1683. Two other brothers who do not appear in the diary were Roger (1653–1734), author of *The lives of the Norths*, and other works, and the youngest, Sir Dudley (1641–91), merchant, financier and economist – whom Macaulay judged to be 'one of the ablest men of his time'.[1]

Norton, [Daniel] (d. 1666). Son of Col. Richard Norton and husband of Isabella, daughter of Sir John Lawson. His widow later married Sir John Chicheley.[1]

Norton, Joyce. Often referred to simply as 'Joyce'; a member of the Norfolk branch of the Pepyses; daughter of Barbara Pepys (b. 1575) who had married Richard Norton of South Creake, Norf., in 1601. She appears to have lived with her cousin Jane Turner.[1]

Norton, [Mary]. Actress in the Duke's Company.[1]

Norton, Col. [Richard] (1615–91). A leading Presbyterian and parliamentarian in Hampshire and a friend of Oliver Cromwell. M.P. under the Commonwealth and 1661–91.[1]

Norwood, [Henry] (c. 1614–89). Royalist soldier and conspirator; imprisoned 1655–9 and employed in the negotiations between Mountagu and the King in late 1659. After the Restoration he was rewarded with a post at court as equerry (1660) and with the deputy-governorship of Dunkirk (1662) and of Tangier (1665–9). He was a Gloucestershire man and after his return from Tangier served Gloucester

as Mayor (1672–3) and M.P. (1675–Jan. 79). He was also Treasurer of
Virginia 1661–73; Tangier Commissioner 1673–80; and member of the
Royal Fishery Company (1677). Pepys rented from him the little house
at Parson's Green which he used as a week-end retreat in 1679 and 1681.
His letters to Pepys are full of life and humour. He gave the name
Parson's Green to part of Tangier.[1]

Nott, [William]. Bookbinder and bookseller; in Ivy Lane and at the
White Horse, Paul's Churchyard before the Fire; afterwards at the
King's Arms, Pall Mall until at least 1696. He bound much of Claren-
don's library. Pepys still dealt with him in 1681.[1]

Nun, Madame. Of the Queen's household; probably Elizabeth Nunn,
laundress. Pepys refers to her as Will Chiffinch's sister (i.e. sister-in-
law); his wife was Barbara Nunn.[1]

The Nursery Theatre. On 24 Dec. 1660 the King granted to George
Jolly the right to set up a third theatre in London in addition to those
of Killigrew and Davenant. This grant after a devious history led to
Killigrew and Davenant obtaining the right to set up a nursery for
training actors for the two authorised theatres. By 1667 there were
probably two nurseries, one in Fig Tree Court (to the west of the later
Play House Yard and south from the middle of the Barbican) for the
Duke's Company under Davenant, the other in Hatton Garden for the
King's Company under Killigrew. The latter was opened in that year
under Capt. Edward Bedford, and moved in 1668 or early 1669 to
the former theatre of the King's Company in Vere St, Lincoln's Inn
Fields. [*See also* Theatre] (R)

Oakeshott, Capt. [Benjamin]. Captain in Sandwich's troop, and an
inventor of a variety of machines (fire-engines, waterpumps etc.). His
letters show him as a man of deep piety.[1]

O'Brien, Capt. [Charles]. A gentleman-captain, he held five commissions 1665–8. In 1668 the King made him a gift of a fireship. In
the same year much to Pepys's annoyance he made fat profits from
private trading on a voyage to Constantinople in one of the King's
ships.[1]

O'Brien, Murrough, 1st Earl of Inchiquin (c. 1614–74). An Irish
soldier and adventurer, known as 'the Incendiary'. He had joined the
French army in the 1650s, and had governed Catalonia for the French.
When Pepys met him in 1660 he had just returned from Algiers, where
he had been held captive after being taken on his way to 'a great
command' in Portugal.[1]

Offley, [Robert] (1634–78). Lawyer; admitted Middle Temple 1652;
Bencher 1675. He was the parliamentary candidate whom Pepys
defeated at Castle Rising, Norf., in 1673 and who then unsuccessfully
petitioned the House to have Pepys unseated on the grounds that he

was a papist and that the election had been improperly influenced by a Catholic peer (Lord Howard, later Earl of Norwich and Duke of Norfolk). Offley had tried but failed to get Howard's support.[1]

Ogle, [Anne] (d. 1682). Maid of Honour to the Duchess of York. In 1673 she married Craven Howard. An Edward Ogle was gentleman-waiter to the Duke of York. They came of a Lincolnshire family.[1]

Ogilby, John (1600–76). Originally a dancing master, he became an impresario, versifier, translator, publisher and cartographer, and, according to Aubrey, learnt Latin at the age of 40. He published several illustrated folios, the best-known of them being his account of the coronation procession of Charles II (with engravings by Hollar): *The entertainment of . . . Charles II, in his passage through London.* He also composed the verses declaimed on that occasion. Pepys describes one of the lotteries which he organised for the sale of his publications. As Master of the Revels in Ireland (from 1662) he built and ran a theatre in Dublin; as one of the surveyors appointed by the city after the Fire he plotted out disputed property; as 'Cosmographer and geographic printer' to the King (after c. 1671) he brought out an important series of maps and atlases. His maps of English roads (*Britannia*, 1675) were the first detailed maps produced for travellers and the first to give distances in measured miles instead of by estimates. Pepys retained several of his books and maps in his library.[1]

Okey, [John]. Republican and regicide. A parliamentary colonel, he opposed the Protectorate both of Oliver and of Richard Cromwell. After taking part in Lambert's attempted rising in the spring of 1660, he fled to Germany. In 1662 he was arrested at Delft and executed at Tyburn.[1]

Old Bailey. A spacious street south for 250 yards from Newgate St, outside the city wall, to Ludgate Hill.[1] The Sessions House there was a justice hall on the e. side of the street approximately opposite Fleet Lane, where assizes, as well as quarter-sessions for Middlesex, were held. The building was destroyed in the Fire, and rebuilt with Sessions House Yard flanking it along the wall to the north and its garden to the south.[2] The Central Criminal Court which has now replaced it is on the site of Newgate prison, at the corner of Old Bailey and Newgate St. (R)

Oldenburg, Henry (c. 1620–77). German-born savant; protégé and friend of Robert Boyle; first Secretary of the Royal Society 1662–77 and editor of its *Philosophical Transactions*. In 1663 he was living in Pall Mall, on the s. side.[1]

Old Ford. A Middlesex village on the w. bank of the Lea, in the parish of Stepney, and less than 4 miles from the Standard on Cornhill and half a mile north of the village of Bow. (R)

Old Palace Yard: *see* Westminster Palace

The Old Swan. Pepys used the name loosely (as a modern Londoner might refer to the Angel at Islington or the Nag's Head) to refer to the area and traffic point round Thames St served by the Old Swan landing stairs. This included a lane and a notable tavern of the same name. He was often in the district after the Fire, when Betty Mitchell had moved there to a strong-water house kept by her husband. There is only one entry (viii.412) which may refer to his using the tavern. (R)

The Old Swan Stairs. The first public landing place on the n. bank above London Bridge, at the s. end of Old Swan Lane. As it was only 30 yards above the Bridge, Pepys, travelling by boat from Whitehall to the Navy Office, would normally disembark there and walk the rest of the way unless high or low tide made passage through London Bridge safe. He usually refers to it simply as The Old Swan. The modern stairs are at the end of the next lane upstream, Ebgate (now Swan) Lane. (R)

Ordnance, Board of. Established in its modern form under Henry VIII at about the same time as the Navy Board, it was responsible until 1855 for the manufacture and supply of munitions to both army and navy. It consisted of a Master (the equivalent of the Navy Treasurer) and a board of officers similar to the Principal Officers of the Navy and similarly charged with the duty of mutual supervision – the Lieutenant, Surveyor, Clerk, Storekeeper, Clerk of deliveries and (after 1670) Treasurer. In 1664–70 and 1679–82 their work was performed by commissioners. The offices and principal storehouses were in the Tower where many of the officers had official lodgings. By this time much of the *matériel* was manufactured elsewhere than in the Tower, in gunpowder factories and gun foundries.

In common with other departments in the late 17th century – such as the Treasury and Pepys's Navy Office and Admiralty – the Ordnance was to a significant extent, though not completely, reformed under the pressure of increased business. It grew in size – from 9 clerks in 1660 to 38 in 1703, and from 175 technical officers in 1675 to around 450 under Anne – and at the same time improved in efficiency. Pepys greatly admired its methods. The Commissioners of 1664–70 began a process whereby contractors were paid 'in course', salaries were substituted for fees and life-tenures were abolished. From 1667 the office assumed responsibility for all fortifications in the kingdom. The Instructions of 1683 issued by Lord Dartmouth, the Master, codified new and old practices.[1] [*See also* Tower]

Ormond, Duke of: *see* Butler, James

Osborne, [Henry], kt 1673. Member of the Brooke House Committee (1667–9) on war expenditure; in the Third Dutch War a Commissioner of the Sick and Wounded. A brother of Dorothy Osborne, the letter-writer. Francis Osborne (d. 1659), author of *Advice to a son*, one of Pepys's favourite books, was their uncle.[1]

Osborne, [Nicholas]. Of St Botolph, Aldgate; clerk to Sir D. Gauden; by 1669 his cashier. He married Eleanor Brent in Feb. 1660.[1]

Osborne, Sir Thomas, 2nd Bt, cr. Earl of Danby 1674 (1631–1712). Joint-Treasurer of the Navy (with Littleton) 1668–71, Treasurer 1671–3; Admiralty Commissioner 1673–9. 'Brought into the Navy for want of other ways of gratification', was Pepys's comment.[1] He was the nominee of Buckingham, and Littleton that of Arlington. Both treated the Navy Board *de haut en bas*.[2] But Osborne proved a good ally of Pepys in the cause of efficiency. He became virtually prime minister, as Lord Treasurer 1673–8, but fell victim to Whig clamour in the Popish Plot, and was impeached in 1678, being rescued by the King's pardon. In 1689–99 he was Lord President. Pepys remarks on his poverty in 1669, but he died rich.[3]

Ossory, Earl of: *see* Butler, Thomas

Oviatt, [John]. Eastland merchant; of St Olave's, Hart St; son-in-law of Sir Richard Ford.[1]

Owen, [George] (d. 1665). York Herald.[1]

Owen, [John]. Clerk of the Ropeyard, Chatham; appointed 1663.[1]

Packer, Philip (c. 1618–86). Son of John Packer (d. 1649) of Groombridge, Kent, secretary to the 1st Duke of Buckingham. Deputy-Paymaster of the King's Works 1660–8; Paymaster 1668–86; Usher of the Exchequer 1682–6; an original F.R.S. A friend of Evelyn and a connection by marriage of Sandwich, his sister Elizabeth having married John Browne, Clerk of the Parliaments, whose first wife Temperance Crew was a sister of Sandwich's wife. He advised Sandwich about the alterations at Hinchingbrooke. He married Isabel, daughter of Sir Robert Berkeley.[1]

Page, Damaris. The 'madame' of a seamen's brothel; 'the most Famous Bawd in the Towne'.[1] Sir Edward Spragge – and probably other commanders – used her to furnish him with seamen. At a Trinity House dinner on 7 June 1669, according to a scandalised note by Pepys in his Navy White Book,[2] Spragge told Pepys that as long as she lived 'hee was sure hee should not lack Men. This among others Mr Evelin heard & tooke notice of it to mee with great affliction'.

Page, Farmer. Of Ashtead, Surrey: presumably the William Page whose house was rated on six hearths in 1664.[1]

Page, Capt. [Thomas] (d. by 1688). Given his first command in 1661, he held nine commissions thereafter until 1673. He commanded the *Breda* when she ran aground off Texel in 1667.[1]

Pall Mall. A fashionable street running from the s. end of the Haymarket to the s. end of St James's St, and taking its name from the game which became fashionable in London in the early 17th century. The Mall of Charles I's reign, in which the game was then played, was on

the s. side of St James's Field and north of the old highway from
Charing Cross to Hyde Park, which was, in turn, north of the wall of
St James's Park. In 1661 this Mall was abandoned and the old highway
replaced by a new one made over the Mall of Charles I's reign and on
the line of the present Pall Mall. It soon contained several large town
houses – Pepys's grand acquaintances Sir William Coventry, Sir Hugh
Cholmley and Sir John Duncombe all lived there. Meantime the game
moved inside St James's Park to a new Mall.[1]

Palmer, Barbara, Countess of Castlemaine (1641–1709). Daughter
of the 2nd Viscount Grandison and cousin of the 2nd Duke of Buckingham; married Apr. 1659 to Roger Palmer, later Earl of Castlemaine
Mistress at 15 to the Earl of Chesterfield and c. 1659–70 to the King
Tall and fair, with blue eyes, she was to Pepys the loveliest of all the
court ladies. She exercised considerable political influence as the ally
of Arlington and the enemy of Clarendon. Her greed and bad temper
were notorious: so too was her promiscuity. Among her lovers were
John Churchill, later Duke of Marlborough, Wycherley the dramatist
and Jacob Hall the rope-dancer. Her hold over the King (at its greatest
when she made him force her on the Queen as a Lady of the Bedchamber in 1663) was almost gone when she had herself created
Duchess of Cleveland in 1670. She was soon afterwards displaced by
Louise de Keroualles (Duchess of Portsmouth). Between 1661 and 1665
she had borne five children acknowledged by the King and surnamed
Fitzroy. A pension of £4700 paid to one of them, the Duke of Grafton,
was continued to his descendants until 1856 when it was commuted
for £91,000.[1]

In 1660 she was living in a house belonging to her husband on the e.
side of King St, Westminster, backing on to the palace orchard, later a
bowling green, and next to the e. end of Sandwich's lodgings. In the
spring of 1663 she moved into the palace, over the Holbein Gate with
further rooms to the east of it. In Apr. 1668 she was given Berkshire
House (q.v.) but still kept her apartments in the palace.[2]

Palmer, Ben. Of Westminster; probably the son of Edmond and
Anne Palmer, baptised at St-Martin-in-the-Fields in 1629. It is possibly
his parents who were known to Pepys at the time of his 'differences' with
his wife (iv. 277).

Palmer, [James] (1585–1660). Pepys's parish priest in childhood. A
graduate of Magdalene, he was Vicar of St Bride, Fleet St, from 1616
until his resignation because of ill-health in 1645. In 1637 he was charged
with failure to wear a surplice and to read the prayers for bishops
During the Civil War he often preached before parliament.[1]

Palmer, Roger, cr. Earl of Castlemaine (Irel.) 1661 (1643–1705)
Husband of the King's mistress; separated from her 1666. A fervent
Catholic; author of *The Catholique apology* (defending Catholics against

the charge of having caused the Fire) which Pepys thought well of. Twice imprisoned in the Popish Plot; rewarded by being sent as James II's ambassador to Rome (1686–7), where his tactless attempts to have the Jesuit Petre made a cardinal caused offence.[1]

Pannier Alley. North out of Paternoster Row to the junction of Blowbladder St and the middle row in Newgate St (now to Newgate St). (R)

Papillon, [Thomas] (1623–1702). Merchant, of Huguenot origin; four times Master of the Mercers' Company; Deputy-Governor of the E. India Company 1680–2; victualling contractor 1671–3; Victualling Commissioner 1689–1701. A leading city Whig (M.P. for Dover 1674–March 81, 1689–95, for London 1695–1701; Alderman 1689); prominent in the hostile examination of Pepys 1679.[1]

Pargiter. The goldsmith was John Pargiter the elder, who was made free of the Goldsmiths' Company in 1630. He thrice served as Warden but was never chosen Prime Warden,[1] presumably because of the scandals Pepys mentions. The merchant was Francis Pargiter of the Muscovy Company.[2]

Parham, [Richard]. Citizen and fishmonger; freeman of the Fishmongers' Company by patrimony 1645; appointed to the Council for Foreign Plantations 1660, and to the Council for Fishery 1662; will signed 1676.[1]

Parish Clerks' Hall. A 16th-century building in Brode Lane (now Upper Thames St); destroyed in the Fire and replaced by a building in Silver St.[1]

Parker, Capt. [John]. Naval officer. A captain under the Commonwealth; held three commands 1661–6; killed in action in 1666.[1]

Parker, ——. Merchant, of Mark Lane. Probably John Parker, who in 1660 was lodging there with John Bland. He was appointed to the Council of Trade in 1660.[1]

Parkhurst. Sir Robert Parkhurst of Pyrford, Surrey (kt 1660, d. 1674), son of Sir Robert (Lord Mayor 1635–6). Silence, sister of John Crew, 1st Baron Crew, was his second wife. According to Evelyn 'he spent a fair estate'. His son John (c. 1643–1731) (first son by his second marriage) married Catherine Dormer in 1667 and sat in Parliament for several constituencies March 1679–1701.[1]

Parliament, buildings of: *see* Westminster Palace

Parliament Stairs. The public landing stairs for Old Palace Yard; upstream of Westminster Hall and New Palace Yard, some 3400 yards by water from London Bridge.[1] (R)

Parry, ——. Probably Thomas Parry, assistant to the Treasurer for the Council's contingencies in 1659 and 1660.[1]

Parson's Green. In Fulham parish. Here Pepys rented a villa for summer weekends in 1677–9 and 1681.[1]

Paternoster Row. A 'very considerable' street,[1] famous for its mercers. When Pepys bought 'things' there (iii.65, v.145) he would be buying at the silk and lace shops.

Payler, [George]. Navy Commissioner 1654–60.[1]

Peachell, [John] (1630–90). Elected Fellow of Magdalene College in 1656; appointed Master in 1679; Rector of Childerley, Cambs. 1663–81 and Prebendary of Carlisle 1667–9. Pepys remarks on the red nose which gave him his local reputation. He achieved national fame in 1687 when as Vice-Chancellor he defied James II's order to admit a Benedictine monk to a master's degree (Magdalene was originally a Benedictine house of study). He was dismissed from the vice-chancellorship and suspended as Master. In Oct. 1688 he was restored to his mastership. A few weeks before, he had declined Pepys's offer of the chaplaincy to the commander of the fleet, Lord Dartmouth.[1]

Pearse, [Andrew]. Purser: a friend or relative of James Pearse, the naval surgeon. His association with Mountagu dated back to at least 1656. He was purser of the *Naseby* 1657–60 and the *Royal Charles* 1666. In 1667 he (or a namesake) was purser and captain of the fireship *William and Susan*.[1]

Pearse, James. The most distinguished naval surgeon of the period. He and his beautiful wife Elizabeth were friends of Pepys close enough to be invited to the stone feast and, in the case of Elizabeth, close enough to make Elizabeth Pepys jealous. He served first as an army surgeon, but his career lay in the navy. From being surgeon on the *Naseby* (c. 1658–60) he rose to become Surgeon-General of the Fleet in both the Second and Third Dutch Wars, and was responsible for the introduction of hospital ships and other reforms, such as the use of medical records which ensured that the wounded received appropriate treatment ashore.[1] After the Second War he went into private practice – among his patients was Lady Catherine, Sandwich's daughter, whom he treated for 'sore eies'[2] – but after the Third was given a retainer and stayed in office until 1689. The report he wrote in 1687 on the treatment of the sick and wounded is the most important 17th-century statement about the organisation of the naval medical service. (Pepys kept a copy in his library.)[3] He was made surgeon to the Duke of York in 1660 and to the King's Household in 1672, and held a sinecure post in the Queen's household.[4] Much of Pepys's news of the court, especially of the court ladies, came from him. He was chosen Master of the Barber-Surgeons' Company in 1676 and Governor of St Thomas's Hospital in 1686.[5] Living at first by St Margaret's churchyard, Westminster, he moved in 1664 to the fashionable area of Covent Garden where he occupied a house taxed on 13 hearths in Bedford St, and later to Pall Mall.[6] He died c. 1693, leaving Pepys to act as a trustee of his property on behalf of his widow.[7] Her beauty had been extraordinary and was remarked on by others than Pepys. In 1678 she had her 19th child and was said still to look only 20. She was alive in 1696.[8]

Their eldest son James – 'the best company in the world' (vii.100) – became a clerk in the Navy Board (and later a purser). He was married at the time of his father's death.[9]

The connection with Abraham Cowley (vii.400) was through the poet's mother, who was Pearse's aunt.[10]

Pedley, Sir [Nicholas], kt 1672 (1615–85). Lawyer; of Abbot's Leigh, Hunts.; brother-in-law of Sir John Bernard and father-in-law of Bishop Stillingfleet. Bencher, Lincoln's Inn 1663; Treasurer 1669–70; Recorder of Huntingdon 1672–85. M.P. for the county 1656, 1659, 1673; and for the borough 1660 and March–July 1679. His victory in the 1660 elections was a blow to the Mountagus, but, like Mountagu himself, he stood for the government interest, having served on several local committees during the Commonwealth. The inscription on his monument speaks of his having been returned several times to Parliament 'by free and unbought votes'. He acted for Pepys in the settlement of his father's estate in 1680.[1]

Pedro: *see* Reggio

[Pelling, John], (d. 1621). Rector of Bath from 1590, Canon of Wells from 1613; chaplain to the King.[1]

Pelling, ——. Apothecary: an amateur of music and a frequent visitor at Pepys's house from 1667. The best-known London apothecary of this name was Walter Pelling, Master of the Society of Apothecaries of London 1671–2. However, the musician is more likely to have been John Pelling, son of Thomas Pelling of Trowbridge, who was apprenticed to his kinsman Walter in 1650 and was therefore a contemporary of Pepys. He supplied medicines to the navy. He was a Common Councilman 1682–3 for the Tower ward, and died in 1689.[1]

Pembroke, 5th Earl of: *see* Herbert, P.

Penington, Judith. Daughter of Sir Isaac Penington, parliamentarian Lord Mayor 1642–3, and sister of Isaac, the Quaker leader. Her behaviour with Pepys gives point to the plea addressed to her by her brother Isaac: 'Is thy soul in amity with God or art thou separated from Him? Whither art thou travelling? Oh, whither art thou travelling?'[1]

Penn, Capt. [George] (c. 1601–64). Merchant; Sir William's elder brother. He lived for many years in Spain. In 1643 he was arrested by the Inquisition in Seville and kept for three years in close confinement. According to a petition he addressed to the English government in 1659 he had been tortured, his property to the value of over £10,000 confiscated, and his wife, a native of Antwerp, divorced from him and married off to a Spaniard. His nephew William, the Quaker, was still hoping to obtain compensation from the Spanish authorities at the time of the negotiations for the Treaty of Utrecht in 1712–13.[1]

Penn, Sir William, kt 1660 (1621–70). Navy Commissioner 1660–9. Bristol sea-captain and bred to the sea from an early age, Penn was (with Batten, to whom he had once been apprenticed) the most experienced seaman among Pepys's colleagues. In the Civil War he had risen to the rank of Rear-Admiral (1648) and Vice-Admiral (1649), his service being in squadrons guarding the Irish Sea. Under the Commonwealth he had made an important voyage to the Mediterranean (1651) and in the Dutch War as Vice-Admiral under Blake had seen action in both major campaigns. With Blake he was one of the pioneers of fighting in line ahead in order to bring maximum fire-power on the ships of the enemy.[1] Several of his letters to Cromwell survive, in which he proffers advice – on the need to increase the number of lieutenants on board ship, and the unwisdom of allowing hired merchantmen to be commanded by their own captains, who cannot help but be nervous of running their ships into danger.[2] From Dec. 1653 he was briefly a member of the admiralty and navy commission.[3] With the conclusion of peace he made his famous voyage to the W. Indies (1654–5) in the course of which Jamaica was captured. On returning, both he and Venables (in command of the soldiers) were disgraced and imprisoned, primarily, it seems, for having returned too precipitately. In 1654 both are said to have made approaches to the King, and on his release Penn was content to retire to the estate in Munster which he had been granted from confiscated royalist property, and where he now waited on events. Meantime he accepted a knighthood from Henry Cromwell in 1658. In the following year he went to England hoping for a naval appointment from the Rump. Monck gave him charge of the preparation of the fleet which sailed to bring home the King from exile. He was on board Sandwich's ship, and soon had made himself known to the Duke of York. Probably at the Duke's request he presented a memorandum in June 1660 to the King about the government of the navy, which shows a considerable knowledge of administrative detail.[4] In it he expounded the advantages of government in the Commonwealth manner by commissioners acting collectively and without rigidly defined duties. The reconstituted Navy Board set up shortly afterwards showed several traces of this advice, and he was himself made a Commissioner. At about the same time he drew up for the Duke a new version of the Admiral's Instructions, issued later, in Jan. 1662. Pepys, who probably resented Penn's superior knowledge and his intimacy with the Duke,[5] has hardly a good word to say for him either as a colleague or as a person. But he clearly played an active part in the work of the Board, undertaking a wide range of duties and in particular throwing himself with energy into the task of preparing the fleets for action in 1665–6. In that work he earned the praise of Rupert and Albemarle.[6] Much of 1665 he spent at sea, as flag-captain to the Duke on board the *Royal Charles* in the Battle of Lowestoft and later in the summer as commander of one of the fleets that attempted, without success, to intercept de Ruyter. In Jan. 1667, in the reorganisation of the Comptroller's work which was long overdue and which he had urged in his original memorandum of June 1660, Penn was made responsible for the victualler's accounts. But in March 1669 he resigned to join the victualler, Gauden, as a victualling contractor to the navy. He was by this time in poor health and had found himself, as a friend of the Duke of York, the butt of parliamentary criticism of the war's miscarriages, particularly of the prize-goods scandal in which he was, with Sandwich and others, badly at fault. Articles of impeachment were brought against him in Apr. 1668 and passed unanimously, but not proceeded with. He died in Sept. 1670 at his house in Walthamstow and was buried at St Mary Redcliffe, Bristol.

His wife, whom he married in June 1643, was Margaret, daughter of John and Marie Jasper of Ballycase, co. Clare and widow of Nicasius 'Vanderscure' (van der Schuren), of Kilconry, co. Clare. Both her father and her first husband were Dutch. She died in 1682 and was buried at Walthamstow.[7]

His elder son William, the Quaker leader, is noticed separately. The younger son Richard died in Apr. 1673 and was buried at Walthamstow. He was under 21 when his father made his will in 1670. In that year Richard was on board his cousin Capt. William Poole's ship the *Jersey* at Leghorn.[8]

Penn's house at Walthamstow was next door to Batten's, in Marsh (now High) St. His widow was still the ratepayer in 1676. Close by in the same street were, in the rate book of that year, —— Gauden Esq., and Dr Daniel Whistler.[9]

Penn, William (1644–1718). The Quaker leader; elder son of Sir William. Pepys's comments on him in the diary are hostile – first mocked as a Frenchified dandy, and later condemned as an unhinged theologian. Just before the diary ends, he had begun his remarkable career as preacher and author, much to his father's distress. But by Aug. 1669 the two were reconciled and Sir William obtained the Duke of York's help in securing his son's release from the Tower for publishing an attack on Trinitarianism. At his death in 1670 he left him a generous bequest which enabled him to pursue his vocation.[1] Later in 1682 part of the cost of setting up the colony later known as Pennsylvania was met by the government in settlement of a debt of £16,000 owed to Sir William – after whom the colony, by his son's decision, was named. Pepys and Penn came closer together in the reign of James II when Penn had great hopes of securing a régime of tolerance for Quakers and all dissident Protestants. One of his works – *Some fruits of solitude*

(1693) – is to be found in Pepys's library. He received a ring at Pepys's funeral.[2]

Penny, [Nicholas]. Tailor, of Fleet St. There are some of his bills and receipts among Pepys's papers.[1]

Penrose, Capt. [Thomas]. A captain in the Commonwealth navy, he held two commands 1665–7. He was arrested for debt in 1660, and Coventry's comment on him c. 1667 was: 'grows debauched'.[1]

Pepper, [Robert] (1636–1700). John Pepys's tutor at Christ's College, Cambridge. A civil lawyer; Fellow of Christ's c. 1658–67, and nephew of Ralph Widdrington, whose pupils he took over in 1661. Chancellor of Norwich diocese 1673; advocate in Doctors' Commons 1678.[1]

THE PEPYS FAMILY

Pepys, the complete townsman, came from a family which until his father's generation had been deeply and almost immovably rooted in the countryside. They lived at Cottenham in Cambridgeshire, and the line stretched back through Tudor yeomen to a succession of medieval farmers who had been settled there since at least the late 13th century. Apart from a few who had entered the church, none, so far as is known, had until the early 17th century moved into the professions, and none had achieved county office. On the other hand they had often held posts at the parochial and manorial level, and some before the Dissolution had been employed as agents by the Benedictine monastery at Crowland in the management of their local estates. The Elizabethan head of the family, John (d. 1589), had opened up new prospects for the Pepyses. By a shrewd marriage to an heiress he had vastly enlarged his estate and had built himself a manor house at Impington, one of his newly acquired manors, suitable to his newly acquired status.[1] His daughter Paulina married into the upper gentry in the person of Sir Sidney Mountagu, father of Pepys's patron, and his son Talbot became a fashionable lawyer and M.P., and in London rubbed shoulders with the future Lord Chancellor Clarendon. It was in Talbot's generation and the succeeding one – that of Pepys's father – that the Pepyses' talent for professional success – especially at the law – suddenly flowered. Pepys's father, a working tailor, was an exception. But his cousins, of various degrees of consanguinity, included Roger, son of Talbot and like him a Recorder and M.P., Sir Richard, Lord Chief Justice of Ireland under the Protectorate, John, a civil lawyer and Fellow of Trinity Hall, and John of Ashtead, secretary to the great Sir Edward Coke. This background is perhaps the explanation of why Pepys himself, before he went to Magdalene, was entered for a lawyers' college, Trinity Hall.

John of Ashtead belonged to a line which in the early 16th century had established itself at South Creake, Norfolk. Its founder, John (d. 1542), was an uncle of the Elizabethan John of Cottenham, and like his nephew greatly enriched his branch of the family. He is described in his will as a merchant and left land in nine parishes to his son Thomas. The son was granted arms in 1563, and several of his descendants married into the Norfolk gentry. John Pepys of Ashtead (whose wife was a Walpole of Houghton) was his great-grandson, and much of the family wealth passed through him to his daughter Jane Turner (Pepys's cousin) and from her to her daughter Theophila ('The' of the diary). With Theophila's marriage to Sir Arthur Harris of Hayne, Devon, the Norfolk inheritance passed out of the Pepyses' hands.[2]

'It is a sad consideration', Pepys wrote, 'how the pepys's decay'.[3] The genealogist of the family, writing in 1887, found no Pepys after 1604 described as 'of Cottenham'.[4] Nor was there a single Pepys rated under the hearth-tax in Cottenham in 1666,[5] though according to Roger Pepys there had been 26 male householders bearing the family name there in Elizabeth's reign.[6]

Of later members of the family the most notable have been Sir Lucas Pepys, physician to George III; the 1st Earl of Cottenham, Lord Chancellor 1836–41, 1846–50; and Henry Pepys, Bishop of Worcester 1841–60 (all descendants of the Cromwellian judge); and the architects Samuel Pepys Cockerell (d. 1827) and his son Charles Robert (d. 1863), descendants of Pepys's sister Paulina.

Pepys, Anne. Of Littleton, Worcs.; daughter of John and Anne Pepys, a 'cousin' by marriage. Her mother died c. 1660. She married first —— Hall, and second, in 1662, —— Fisher, 'an old Cavalier'. In 1687 Pepys stayed with her in Worcester when accompanying James II on his western progress.[1]

Pepys, Barbara (Bab) and Betty. Daughters of Roger Pepys by his second wife Barbara Bacon. In 1674 Bab (1649–89) married Thomas Gale, High Master of St Paul's School 1672–97, and Dean of York from 1697 until his death in 1702. He was a distinguished scholar, and Pepys frequently consulted both him and his son Roger on antiquarian matters. Betty (1651–1716) married Charles Long, Rector of Risby, Suff., in 1680. He had been a Fellow of Caius College 1670–9.[1]

Pepys, Charles (c. 1632–c. 1701). Pepys's first cousin; second son of Thomas Pepys, elder brother of Pepys's father. In Feb. 1662 he married Joan Smith, a widow.[1] He was a joiner and was then and for some years later living in a small house (rated on two hearths) in Creed Lane, St Gregory's parish, Stepney,[2] but later moved to Chatham where he became Master-Joiner in the yard in 1689. Several of his letters to Pepys survive: they are humble, grateful and very badly spelt.[3] He seems to have prospered in a modest way and in his will was able to leave bequests to his two apprentices, to the poor of his parish, and to several of his relatives, including Pepys himself who received £100.[4] For his part Pepys made highly provisional bequests to him and his children. In his first will (1701) Charles was to inherit all of Pepys's Huntingdonshire properties, but only in the unlikely event of Pepys's two Jackson nephews predeceasing him. Under his second will of 1703, by which time Charles had died, Pepys left £1000 to each of Charles's two sons, though only if the government paid the debt of £27,000 odd they showed no signs of honouring.[5]

Pepys, Edward (1617–63). Son of John Pepys of Ashtead, Surrey, and brother of Jane Turner; admitted to the Middle Temple 1636. His wife (1632–68) was Elizabeth, daughter of John Walpole of Broomsthorpe, Norf.[1]

Pepys, Elizabeth (1640–69). Pepys's wife; daughter of Alexander and Dorothea St Michel. She was born on 23 Oct. 1640 at or near Bideford where her mother had inherited a property and where it is possible that she spent her early childhood. At the age of about 12 she went briefly to Paris with her parents and her brother Balty, and, according to Balty's later account, was for a few days abducted by relatives of her father – he was a Huguenot – in an attempt to force her into an Ursuline convent.[1] Three years later she was married to Pepys. He was just starting his career and this 15-year old girl, without money or connections, was on any calculation of worldly advantage highly unsuitable. But her charm and good looks were too much for him. He fell passionately in love – so passionately, as he later recalled, that he felt ill.[2] The marriage was a civil ceremony conducted by a magistrate according to the form laid down in the ordinance of 1653, and was solemnised on 1 Dec. 1655 in St Margaret's Westminster, Pepys's parish church, the banns having been promulgated on three successive Sundays from 15 October. The parish register describes the bride as living in St Martin-in-the-Fields; and it is perhaps a little odd that she was not married in her own parish, as would have been usual. The magistrate conducting the ceremony was Richard Sherwyn, a J.P. for the city and liberties of Westminster, who may have been related to or identical with the Richard Sherwyn who at this time was Secretary to the Treasury Commissioners of whom Pepys's patron, Mountagu, was one. The wedding feast was held in a city tavern in Old Fish St. Although the ceremony was on 1 December, Pepys and his wife, according to the diary, celebrated the anniversary of their 'wedding night' on 10 October. It is possible that having been married in December they waited until the following October before living together, a practice common enough when the bride was young. But in such case one would expect the bride to be under the age of consent – 14 – and Elizabeth was already 15 in Dec. 1655. Moreover, Pepys was violentl in love and would not willingly have postponed cohabitation for ten months. The more likely alternative is that the October anniversary was a celebration of a religious service which had preceded the December ceremony.[4] Such services were not unknown among Anglicans despite their illegality, and it is clear from the diary that Pepys was in the habit of attending illegal Anglican services during the Commonwealth. The diary's evidence on the mystery is unhelpful. Pepys and Elizabeth, though agreed that their wedding had been on 10 October, disagreed about the year. Elizabeth thought it was 1656, Pepys thought it was 1655. On general grounds any historian would prefer the wife's evidence on a point of this sort, and it is noticeable that Pepys as it happens was curiously unsure in his calculation of years. He was not even sure of the year of Charles I's execution or of his own operation for the stone.[5] But he had the final word on his wedding. On the monument which he erected to Elizabeth after her death on 10 Nov. 1669 she is said to have died in the fifteenth year of her marriage. That would seem to settle the argument in favour of 1655, especially if we may assume that Pepys consulted his marriage certificate (which we know he possessed) before giving orders to the sculptor.

They had not lived together for more than a few months before they separated because of 'differences', Elizabeth going to live with her 'friends' (possibly her family) at Charing Cross.[6] Perhaps the trouble was caused by what Pepys called his 'old disease'[7] of jealousy. They were reunited by Dec. 1657, and in the following May were established in Axe Yard.[8]

The story of the marriage that is told in the diary cannot unfortunately be supplemented or corrected from other sources. No letters between the two survive. But it is clear enough that Pepys, though genuinely affectionate, was unfaithful, insensitive and overbearing. It is a comment on his quality as a husband that in a diary which only once (in 1668) fails to record his own birthdays, those of his wife are not mentioned. Nor does he ever refer to her by name. However, they were tolerably happy together, though she was made nervous by his susceptibility to other women and hurt beyond bearing by his affair with Deb Willet. He for his part was made miserable from time to time by jealousy and by a nagging fear that she would turn Catholic – a prospect with which when provoked she would deliberately torment him.

Her health was never robust. She suffered a good deal from dysmennorrhoea as well as from toothache and gastro-enteritis. In the period of strain which followed the Fire her hair fell out.[9] Her most serious affliction was a recurring abscess (nowadays known as Bartholin's cyst) of the labia. This clearly made it difficult for her to enjoy physical relations with her husband and may, to some extent, explain his infidelities.

In late Aug. 1669 she went with Pepys and Balty on a tour of the Low Countries and Northern France which lasted for two months and which, though 'full of health and content' for Pepys, was to prove fatal for Elizabeth. On 10 November, three weeks after her return, she died of a fever, probably typhoid. She received communion on her deathbed from Milles, the Rector of St Olave's, and was buried in the chancel of the church on the 13th.[10] Pepys did not attend the Navy Board until 2 December.[11] When Pepys died in 1703 his body was by his direction brought from Clapham to be laid beside hers.[12]

High on the chancel wall her monument, in the manner of the times, makes the most of her claim to a distinguished lineage: *Patrem e praeclara Familia de St Michel Andegavia; Matrem e nobili Stirpe Cliffordorum Cumbria*. Little is known about her father's Angevin forebears – though his father has been identified as holding court office in 1612;[13] and the exact connection (if any) of her mother's family with the Cliffords who were Earls of Cumberland has not been established. Elizabeth's maternal grandmother was Dorothea, daughter of Sir Conyers Clifford (d. 1599) Governor of Connaught, whose family had been settled in Kent since at least the reign of Richard II.[14]

Apart from the memorial bust in St Olave's by John Bushnell, the only likeness to survive is an engraving of the Hayls portrait of 1666.[15] [*See also* Dress etc.]

Pepys, John and Margaret. The diarist's parents. John was the third son of Thomas Pepys 'the Black', and was born at Impington in 1601. As a boy of about 14 he went to London to serve his apprenticeship to a tailor in St Bride's parish, off Fleet St, and never moved from the parish until he surrendered his house and business to his son Tom in 1661. It seems virtually certain therefore that he succeeded his own master there, eventually being made free of the Merchant Taylors' Company as a 'foreign' tailor (i.e. living outside the city boundaries) in 1653. The house had three storeys and abutted onto St Bride's churchyard. On 15 Oct. 1626 he married Margaret Kite of Newington Green,[1] a girl of simple birth who had been a washmaid in her youth. The baptisms of eleven of their children and burials of seven are recorded in the church registers. In 1649 he paid a fine rather than become parish 'scavenger', but in 1658 accepted church office as sidesman.[2] He is known to have had some 'Irish business' (probably investments in soldiers' debentures) and to have made at least one journey to Holland – in 1656.[3] On inheriting the Brampton property from his brother Robert in 1661 he moved there with his wife. A list of the possessions he left behind in London includes virginals, a sea-chest, a chronicle and a history of Britain.[4] The letters he wrote to the diarist from Brampton reveal however an unsophisticated and rather dependent character. He gladly allowed first the diarist and then, in the '70s, his other surviving son

John to look after his affairs. His wife – tetchy, improvident and invalidish – seems to have been less likeable. She was apparently a sectarian,[5] and it may be significant that before marriage she worked in the household of Lady Vere, a prominent Puritan, and that some of her relatives (the Gileses) were Quakers. She died in 1667 and thereafter John lived with his daughter Paulina, first at Ellington and later at Brampton. He died at the age of 79 and was buried at Brampton on 4 Oct. 1680. There is evidence that Pepys, who was at Newmarket with the King at the time, broke off his engagements to attend the funeral. (His shorthand account of the King's escape after Worcester fight taken down at Charles's dictation has a note that it was written at Newmarket on 3 and 5 October.[6] The 4th is not mentioned.) By his will John divided his small estate mostly between his children, leaving the diarist in charge of its administration.[7]

Pepys, John (1576–1652). Of Ashtead, Surrey; Pepys's third cousin once removed; father of Jane Turner. The much-loved man of business and executor to Chief Justice Coke. He married Anne, daughter of Terry Walpole of Houghton, Norf., in 1610. They had a son Edward (named after Coke) and two daughters, Elizabeth (Dyke) and Jane (Turner), and lived for some time in Salisbury Court, possibly in the house the Turners occupied in the diary period. Their Ashtead house was taxed on ten hearths.[1]

Pepys, Dr John (1618–92). Second son of Talbot Pepys of Impington; a civil lawyer. He was called to the Bar (Middle Temple) in 1640, became a Fellow of Trinity Hall, Cambridge, in 1641, and was admitted to Doctors' Commons and proceeded LL.D in 1647. He was later licensed as an advocate in the Court of Arches and appointed Commissary of the archdeaconry of Norwich. He married Catherine (d. 1703), widow of Thomas Hobson of Cottenham, and died without children. He was buried at Cottenham.[1]

Pepys, John, jun. (1641–77). A younger brother of Pepys. He went to St Paul's School and Cambridge, being entered first at Magdalene in May 1659, and then transferred as a sizar to Christ's in the following February. He took his B.A. in 1663 and his M.A. in 1666,[1] when he entered Holy Orders, without, it appears, having any vocation for them. He failed to obtain preferment, and in 1670 Pepys had him nominated by the Duke of York as Clerk of Trinity House. On this occasion Pepys recommended him for his 'sobriety, diligence and education',[2] a description which hardly tallies with the impression given in the diary. He thereupon took up residence in the Trinity House buildings on Tower Hill. In 1673, on Pepys's promotion to the Admiralty, he was made a joint-Clerk of the Acts – a surprising appointment, made workable perhaps by the fact that his partner was the experienced Tom Hayter. In the '70s his letters show him taking an active and responsible part, with Pepys, in the management of family affairs,[3] but he seems to have neglected his duties at Trinity House, whose accounts at his death in 1677 were found to be in some disarray. Pepys had to advance £300 to the corporation before they were settled, and the court thereupon ruled that in future their clerk should not be allowed to hold another post.[4] John remained unmarried and was buried in St Olave's churchyard.[5]

Pepys, Richard (d. 1664). Of Ashen, Essex, eldest son of Sir Richard Pepys, Lord Chief Justice of Ireland 1654–9, who was a first cousin of Pepys's father. Admitted to the Middle Temple 1642 and administrator of his father's estate July 1660.[1]

Pepys, Richard (d. c. 1677). Citizen and upholder (upholsterer), of St Bartholomew by the Exchange; son of William Pepys of Norwich, draper, and grandson of Richard Pepys of Cottenham, later of Norwich. A governor of Christ's Hospital.[1]

Pepys, Robert (d. July 1661). Of Brampton; eldest son of Thomas Pepys 'the Black' and brother of Pepys's father; often known as Captain Pepys from his service in the militia. He is described in a bond of 1630 as 'of Hinchingbrooke'[1] and it is likely that he was a bailiff employed by the Mountagus after they acquired the property in 1627. (Sir Sidney Mountagu was a witness to the bond.) In Aug. 1630 he married Anne, widow of Richard Trice, at All Saints, Huntingdon,[2] and then or soon after moved to the house at Brampton which Pepys was ultimately to inherit and where it is likely that he lived when attending Huntingdon school c. 1642–c. 1644. Robert Pepys became a man of substance, owning property in Brampton and three neighbouring parishes and holding several local offices, as a receiver of assessments (1647), and as a commissioner of assessments (1657) and of militia (March 1660).[3] When appointed to the two last posts he was described as an esquire.

He left no children of his own, but two stepsons (Jasper and Tom Trice), both lawyers. Perhaps foreseeing trouble he expressed the wish in his will that 'all occasions of differences and suites of law [be] avoided amongst my bretheren and kindred about my estate'.[4] But disputes quickly arose. The stepsons were concerned that their mother (and they themselves) were bequeathed nothing. She was even deprived of the £200 which their stepfather had on their marriage undertaken to leave her. In his will he justified himself by saying that not only had he been deceived about the size of her jointure and about her income from her first husband's estate, but he had also been involved in expenses connected with Richard Trice's will that in themselves amounted to almost £200. His widow died soon after him, in Oct. 1661,[5] but her aggrieved sons set Chancery in motion to get their £200. By an out-of-court agreement reached in Nov. 1663 they settled for half.[6]

A more complicated series of disputes arose about the real estate, which consisted of the Brampton house and its land, together with other property in Offord, Graveley and Stirtloe. The greater part of the land was willed to Pepys and his father, who were to act as executors. John was to have possession for life and Pepys an annuity of £30 (rising to half the annual value after the death of Thomas Pepys, the testator's brother) and a reversionary interest in the whole estate after the death of his father. The gross annual value (apart from the Brampton house) was £128, which was reduced by debts, legacies and annuities to £29.[7] Most of the land was held in copyhold – i.e. on terms based on the custom of the manor. Difficulties now arose from the fact that some of the surrenders (documents by which the copyhold land was transmitted) were missing. In those cases the property would be inherited by the testator's brother Thomas Pepys (of St Alphage's parish, London) as heir-at-law. Apart from half-an-acre at Buckden which he had received by manorial custom as heir-at-law, he had been bequeathed only an annuity of £20, and his two sons legacies of £35 each. All three were therefore determined to press every possible claim the law would allow. The executors had no trouble about the Stirtloe land, which was sold immediately in 1661 to the tenant to pay debts.[8] The Graveley property however (worth £24 p.a. gross) was adjudged by the manorial court in Sept. 1661 to pass to the heir-at-law in the absence of the surrenders.[9] The Brampton property – much the largest (74 acres, let in 14 parcels)[10] – was awarded a year later, in Oct. 1662, to the executors, although the surrenders were also missing in that case. Thomas Pepys, after an attempt at arbitration, appealed on the ground that this offended manorial custom, and also on the ground that the settlement had been made conditional on the payment of annuities and legacies which had not yet been paid – his own among them. He threatened to prosecute any Brampton tenants who paid their rents to the executors.[11] Negotiations for an out-of-court settlement which would apply to the whole estate were resumed and agreement was reached in Feb. 1663. The heir-at-law abandoned his claims in Brampton, Buckden and Offord, and the executors their claims in Graveley. The executors were to be free to sell more land to pay debts (provided the proposals were approved by three named arbitrators), and the heirs-at-law were given half of the personal estate in excess of the probate value of £372. This done, the executors were to pay all annuities and legacies and the remainder was to be settled on the heirs' family in the event of a failure of male heirs in the executors' family.[12] Even after Thomas Pepys's death in 1676 Pepys was still fearing litigation from his son.[13]

The estate was managed at first by Will Stankes, a Brampton neighbour, and later (much less satisfactorily) by John Jackson, sen.,

Pepys's brother-in-law. Pepys inherited the whole estate on his father's death in 1680 and at first planned to settle the Brampton and Buckden lands on Jackson's two sons, but the difficulty of devising the copyhold defeated him and he ended by settling an annuity on their mother, and providing for the nephews from his own income. The elder nephew until c. 1695 acted as his agent.[14] From time to time Pepys also employed other agents – the Huntingdon schoolmaster John Matthews (a connection by marriage), and the Rector of Eynesbury, John Turner. At his death the Brampton estate – slightly larger than in 1661 – consisted of 84 acres held in copyhold and let in nine parcels. Together with the Brampton house and the Offord land it brought in an income of £77 11s. 6d.[15] It was bequeathed to his heir, John Jackson jun., and some time after the death of Jackson's unmarried son, John Pepys Jackson (1716–80), was absorbed into the Sandwich estate. [*See also* Brampton; Jackson, John and Paulina]

Pepys, Roger (1617–88). Of Impington; eldest son of Talbot Pepys, Pepys's great-uncle. A lawyer, educated at Christ's College, Cambridge; Recorder of Cambridge 1660–79; Bencher of the Middle Temple from 1664; M.P. for Cambridge borough 1661–Jan. 79. Although Pepys speaks slightingly of his ability he was consulted by Pepys on legal matters and was an executor of Sandwich's will and a trustee of his estate. There are several signs in the diary of his puritanism, and as an M.P., although active mostly in local business, he was usually critical of the court and a friend of the Presbyterians. But he never failed to defend Pepys against parliamentary attacks and was reckoned by the organisers of the court party as an opponent who might be 'prevailed' on by Pepys.[1] He lost his seat in the spring elections of 1679 as a result of differences with the Tory corporation.

He married (1) Anne Banks (d. before 1641); (2) Barbara Bacon c. 1646 (d. 1657); (3) Parnell Duke (d. before 1663); and (4) in 1669 the 'good-humoured fat' widow Pepys so much liked, Esther Dickenson (d. 1684) who had already buried two husbands: Richard Conyers (Rector of Cawston, Norf.) and Bernard Dickenson of Westminster.

Of his children, three appear in the diary: Barbara and Betty (qq.v.), and Talbot, his eldest son (1647–81), called to the Bar in 1670. Another son John was M.P. for Cambridge borough 1695–d. 96.[2] [*See also* Impington]

Pepys, Samuel. The diarist. For his biography, *see* vol. i, pp. xvii–xl; for his houses, *see above* Houses (Pepys's). *See also* Select List of Articles, above, p. ix.

Pepys, Talbot (1583–1666). Of Impington; Pepys's great-uncle and the patriarch of the family. Like so many Pepyses in his generation and the next, he made his career in the law. He graduated at Cambridge from Trinity Hall, was a member of the Middle Temple and became its

Treasurer in 1640. He was an M.P. briefly in 1625 for Cambridge borough which he served as Recorder from 1624 until succeeded by his son Roger in 1660. Between 1643 and 1660 he was appointed to a large number of the committees which ran government business in the borough and county.

He married four times; his fourth wife had died in 1653. Roger was a son of the first marriage to Beatrice, daughter of John Castell of Raveningham, Norf.[1]

A portrait (dated 1614, by an unknown artist, reproduced in Whitear, facing p. 50) is now in the Pepys Library. [*See also* Impington] **Pepys, Thomas** (1595–1676). Pepys's uncle; elder brother of Pepys's father; described in his will as of St Alphage's parish.[1] Possibly the Thomas Pepis who was admitted to the freedom of the Mercers' Company in 1615 after apprenticeship to Richard Craicrofte.[2] He quarrelled with Pepys over his brother Robert's will and was by then clearly a poor man. In 1660 he had enquired about a place in the order of Poor Knights of Windsor, and at his death was living as an almsman in Sion College. His wife was Mary Syvret or Chiveret of Jersey. They had three children: Tom the Turner, Charles the joiner and Mary, who married a weaver, Samuel de Santhune.[3]

Pepys, Thomas ('the Executor'). Pepys's cousin; variously referred to as 'cousin', 'the Executor' and 'Hatcham Pepys'. His biography is difficult to establish at several points. He cannot have been (as Chappell suggests) the Thomas Pepys born in 1640 to Fermor Pepys of the Norfolk branch, who was far too young a man, and he cannot have been (as Manning and Bray suggest) a Keeper of the Jewel House under Charles II and James II, because he was very far from being a courtier.[1] It seems likely that he was the Thomas Pepys who was born in 1611 at Sutton to Thomas Pepys 'the Red', cousin of Pepys's father, and who was married at St Paul's, Covent Garden in 1654 to Anne, daughter of Sir John Cope, a witness to the marriage being Percival Angier, son-in-law of Thomas the Red.[2] The diary makes it clear that he was a puritan (probably a Presbyterian), and it is therefore virtually certain that he was the Thomas Pepys who served as a magistrate for Middlesex and as a commissioner for the assessment and the militia in the late '50s.[3] In Dec. 1660 he took out a pardon.[4] The facts clear from the diary – that he was rich, that he had a partner, and that he was ignorant of Latin – suggest that he was a business man rather than a member of a profession. He lent money to Mountagu in 1658.[5] His nickname 'the Executor' may refer to his usefulness to the family in that function.

He was living in 1661 in St-Martin-in-the-Fields, later in Newport St, Covent Garden, whence in 1663 he moved to Hatcham, Surrey. He died in 1675 at Merton Priory, Surrey, which he had acquired in 1668.[6] Pepys was appointed a trustee of his estate for the benefit of his widow.

She was his second wife (b. Ursula Stapelton of Myton, Yorks) whom he had married at Kensington in March 1660 and by whom he had a son and daughter. She died c. 1693.[7]

Pepys, Thomas (Tom) (1634–64). Tailor; a younger brother of Pepys. What schooling he had is not known – nothing very thorough, to judge by his only surviving letter[1] – though he had a smattering of French. He was apprenticed to his father, succeeding him in the business in 1661, and employing two men and a maid. The hearth-tax returns of 1664 show him as taxed on a house of four hearths in Bride Lane.[2] It seems likely therefore that he used only the back part of the house occupied by his father. He rebuilt the upper storey of his house, but did not prosper and left debts of over £300.[3] He died a bachelor, despite Pepys's attempts to find him a bride, and left an illegitimate daughter by his maid who was put out to foster parents.

Pepys, Dr Thomas (1621–c. 65). Pepys's cousin; physician; third son of Talbot. Educated at Westminster and Trinity, Cambridge (M.A. 1648, Fellow 1649), he went on to study medicine at Leyden and Padua, and was admitted a candidate of the Royal College of Physicians in 1661. He was an executor of the will of Pepys's brother Tom, and the angry, coarse and badly spelt letter he wrote to old John Pepys in that connection supports Pepys's view that he was 'a shame to his family and profession'.[1] He died at Impington unmarried.[2]

Pepys, Thomas ('the turner'). Pepys's cousin; elder son of Thomas Pepys of St Alphage's parish. Until the Fire he had a house and shop (shared with Richard Bullock) in Paul's Churchyard, taxed on six hearths.[1] Afterwards he moved to Smithfield, and seems to have prospered as a trader with the W. Indies, making several voyages there. The last trace of him is of his returning from Jamaica some time after Pepys's funeral. He was given a funeral ring.[2] Pepys refers to him as a fanatic, and judging by his letters, he was ill-educated.[3] He married Elizabeth Howes at St Botolph, Aldgate in 1664.[4]

Perkin. The Perkins, of Parson Drove, Cambs., were relatives of Pepys. The father (John) had married Jane, sister of Pepys's father. She died c. 1666. They had a son Frank, a miller (who after 1661 took up the fiddle for a livelihood) and who in 1666 was living in a house taxed on one hearth in Parson Drove.[1] There were also three daughters – Jane (who was brought up by her uncle Robert Pepys of Brampton), Mary and Elizabeth. The mother and children received small legacies from Robert Pepys. Mary (m. James May), and Elizabeth (m. Thomas Bray) were alive in 1678.[2]

Perkins, ——. Witness in the Carkesse case. Possibly George Perkins, third lieutenant on the *Sovereign*, 1665.[1]

Perriman, Capt. [John]. River agent to the Navy Board.[1]

Petit, Monsieur [Henry]. He married Kate ('Catau') Sterpin, maid to Elizabeth Pye of Axe Yard, on 16 Oct. 1660. Letters of denization were issued to both in July 1664.[1]

Peterborough, 2nd Earl of: see Mordaunt, H.

Petre, Lady (d. 1665). Lady Elizabeth Savage, daughter of the 2nd Earl Rivers, and first wife of the 4th Baron Petre (d. 1684), of the well-known Catholic family of Ingatestone, Essex. She was separated from her husband. Her drunkenness, to which Pepys alludes, is presumably also the explanation of her arrest by the parish constable in Covent Garden in 1655. In the Popish Plot scare, her husband was allegedly nominated as Commander-in-Chief of the Catholic army that was to overrun the kingdom. He was imprisoned without trial and died in the Tower.[1]

Pett, Christopher (1620–68). Eleventh son of Commissioner Phineas Pett, and himself father of 11 children. Assistant Master-Shipwright, Deptford and Woolwich 1647–52; Master-Shipwright 1652–60, 1660–8. An able shipbuilder who worked by hand and eye alone.[1] Badly and irregularly paid, he died in debt. His wife Ann (b. Brace) died in 1679. The daughter who occurs in the diary cannot be identified: at his death he had three.[2]

Pett, Commissioner Peter (1610–72). Fifth son of Commissioner Phineas Pett whom he succeeded as Navy Commissioner at Chatham 1648–60, 1660–7. He was also Master-Shipwright at Chatham 1664–7. The Pett family almost monopolised offices in the Thames yards under the Commonwealth and came under attack in 1651 for alleged large-scale corruption and embezzlement. The charges were dropped on the outbreak of the war in 1652. In 1667 Commissioner Peter's career ended when he was made scapegoat for the Medway disaster. He was dismissed, arrested, and threatened with impeachment, but in the end allowed to retire into private life. Pepys and Coventry had little good to say of his management of the yard, but whether he deserved all the obloquy he met in his career is doubtful. There is evidence, even in the diary, of his being an active administrator and efficient shipbuilder. That he and others of the clan lined their pockets only too well is very likely: Pett himself certainly lived in luxury and died rich, owning landed property in Kent and Suffolk.[1] He was elected M.P. for Rochester (1659, 1660), and Fellow of the Royal Society (1662). He married three times: the wife mentioned in the diary is his second, Mary (b. Smith), who died in 1664. The daughter mentioned is probably Ann (or Agnes) who married Rowland Crisp of Chatham in 1660. The stepdaughter has not been identified.[2]

Pett, [Peter] (d. 1709). Eldest son of Commissioner Peter; lawyer, of the Middle Temple; admitted 1656, called 1664. To be distinguished

from the lawyer Sir Peter Pett (1640–99), already knighted in 1660, who later became a friend of Pepys. He was the son of Commissioner Pett's half-cousin Peter Pett, Master-Shipwright of Deptford (d. 1652).[1]
Pett, Commissioner Phineas (1570–1647). Master-Shipwright, Chatham 1605–29, Navy Commissioner, Chatham 1630–47. One of the greatest of English shipbuilders. He built the *Royal Sovereign* (launched in 1637), first of the three-deckers, and many other large ships for both the royal and merchant navies. He wrote an unfinished autobiography of which Pepys's MS. copy is the best surviving version.[1]
Pett, Phineas (1628–?78). Of Limehouse; son of John, eldest son of Commissioner Phineas. Master-Caulker Chatham 1671; Assistant-Shipwright Woolwich 1672; Master-Shipwright Woolwich 1675.[1]
Pett, Capt. Phineas, kt 1680 (1635–94). Appointed Assistant Master-Shipwright, Deptford 1652, Chatham 1660–1, Master-Shipwright Chatham 1660–80. He was the second son of Peter Pett of Deptford, who was a half-cousin of Commissioner Peter. He became Comptroller of Store Accounts 1680–6 and Navy Commissioner, Chatham 1686–8.[1]
Petty, Sir William, kt 1661 (1623–87). A founder of the Royal Society, a friend of Hobbes, and one of the most ingenious and productive thinkers of the age. The diary has important information about his work on ship design – his 'double-bottomed' vessel – some indications of his versatility, and frequent expressions of Pepys's admiration. A self-educated man, he became Professor of Anatomy at Oxford in 1651, and then, after serving as physician-general to Cromwell's army in Ireland, made his name (and a considerable fortune) by undertaking a great survey of Irish landholding (the 'Down Survey') and completing it within a year. In all his activities – as scientist, economist and chemist – his aim was usually to find a mathematical means of expressing his findings. He even hoped for a system of notation that could express 'the mixture of relishes and tastes' (vi.63). By virtue of his statistical investigations into taxation and the economy he was a founder of the science of political arithmetic. He combined a gift for wide-ranging speculation on practical affairs (a decimal coinage and a National Health Service were among his proposals) with a flair for mechanical invention. He was more inventive than studious and told Aubrey that he 'was of Mr Hobbes his mind, that had he read much, as some men have, he had not known so much'. Pepys often marvelled at his conversational powers.

Pepys retained in his library eleven of Petty's published works, and manuscript copies of a number of his writings on ship design. Among his papers in the Bodleian is a copy of Petty's 'Dialogue on Liberty of Conscience' written in 1687 at Pepys's request.[1] [*See also* Science]
Phelps, ——. Probably John Phelps or Phillips, Auditor of the Receipt at the Exchequer.[1]

Philips, ——. Cook; probably John Phillips, who by his will (1674) was a benefactor of the Cooks' Company.[1]

Phillips, [Henry]. Messenger to the Privy Council.[1]

Phillips, Lewis (d. 1670). Lawyer, of Brampton; uncle of John Jackson, sen; Under-sheriff of Huntingdonshire 1642. He arranged a purchase of land for Sandwich in 1654, and acted for Pepys in several law businesses in the '60s. His wife Judith was buried at Brampton in Dec. 1665.[1]

Phillips, ——. Servant of Christopher Pett. Probably Philip Phillips, labourer, of Woolwich.[1]

Philpot Lane. North out of Eastcheap into Fenchurch St. (R)

Phipps, ——. Presumably Thomas Phipps, of Rochester. The nature of his connection with Chatham yard has not been discovered.[1]

Pickering. A family of Northamptonshire landowners (owning the manor of Tichmarsh 1553–1778), related to Sandwich. Sir Gilbert, 1st Bt (1613–68), was a prominent Cromwellian and had married Sandwich's sister Elizabeth in or before 1640. He served in all the Councils of State appointed under the Commonwealth, 1649–53, and – 'so finical, spruce and like an old courtier'[1] – was put in charge of both Oliver and Richard Cromwell's households as Lord Chamberlain. John Dryden, a cousin, is said to have been a clerk in his service. At the Restoration, Sandwich's influence, together with the fact that he had sat on the regicide tribunal for only two days, saved him from heavy punishment, and he was allowed to retire into private life.[2] He had 12 children, of whom Betty, who married John Creed, is the most prominent in the diary. His eldest son John (d. 1703) had a place in the Exchequer until the Restoration.[3] Another son, Gilbert, went to sea as a volunteer in the late '60s and was commissioned first lieutenant in 1678.[4]

Sir Gilbert's younger brother Edward (Ned) (1618–98) was attached to the service of the 2nd Lord Mountagu of Boughton[5] and like him obtained a place in the Queen's Household, from which he was soon dismissed in disgrace.[6] He appears to have been disliked by almost everyone, not only by Pepys. Roger North wrote him down as a sanctimonious 'money-hunter' and has a story of his altering a will to his own benefit.[7] His wife was Dorothy (d. 1707) daughter of Sir John Weld of Arnolds, Mdx, a great benefactor of her parish.[8]

Piggot, ——. Francis Piggot, citizen, an amateur musician, of the 'Musick Society and Meeting in the Old-Jury', whose name, with that of George Piggot, gentleman, appears in a contemporary list of members. To be distinguished from the Francis Piggot (d. 1704), who was organist of Magdalen College, Oxford and subsequently of the Inner Temple, composer of songs and keyboard music, and was active chiefly in the 1690s.[1] (Lu)

Piggot, [Richard]. Of Brampton. In his will (Jan. 1666) he is described as a yeoman.[1]

Pinchbeck, [John]. An army officer under Charles I and Charles II: by 1673 Lieut-Colonel of the Duke of Albemarle's Regiment of Foot.[1]

Pinkney. The parish clerk was George (d. 1681), elected to that office (of St Benet, Paul's Wharf) in 1644, and Warden of the Parish Clerks' Company in 1662. He was also an embroiderer and was granted a moiety of the office of King's embroiderer in 1663. The goldsmith was either Henry or his less prominent brother William, of Fleet St. Henry was Warden of the Goldsmiths' Company in 1669, 1676 and 1677. Their firm became Gosling and Sharpe's Bank, later Barclay's.[1]

Pitt(s), [John]. Secretary and Deputy-Treasurer of the fleet 1660; Clerk of Control, Portsmouth, 1670–7.[1]

THE PLAGUE

There are several reasons why the plague of 1665 is called the Great Plague of London. Although it may not have killed as high a proportion of Londoners as some of its predecessors (the outbreak of 1563 has good claims to have scored the highest percentage),[1] that of 1665 undoubtedly can claim the biggest aggregate. Furthermore, it is thought of as the 'Great' Plague because it was the last of numerous and grievous visitations. But above all, it is the Plague which has been etched for ever on the minds of later generations by the pens of Daniel Defoe and of Samuel Pepys. In 1665, however, Defoe was a child of five or six, an impressionable age no doubt; and doubtless also he heard all the folklore and reminiscences that his elders could provide – though it is more than possible that his family left London during the outbreak.[2] His memoir (published in 1722) is, admittedly, what would now be called 'well-researched' and even quotes from one manuscript source (William Boghurst's *Loimographia*) which was not printed till 1894.[3] Yet parts of Defoe's account are self-evidently fiction or, at best, hearsay; and, unlike Pepys, he was not present as an adult throughout all the horrors.

John Evelyn was indeed present; but on the Plague his diary is strangely perfunctory and disappointing. He does little but reproduce, inaccurately, some of the weekly mortality bills, although on occasion he confirms Pepys's account when, for example, he notes 'the streete thin of people, the shops shut up, and all in mournefull silence, as not knowing whose turne might be next' (7 September); or when he finds himself 'invironed with multitudes of poore pestiferous creatures, begging almes' (10 November). What he does not give us, as Pepys so marvellously does, are his own inner feelings and reactions in all their fluctuations. There is, then, a case for calling the Plague of 1665 'Pepys's Plague' just as we might call the Black Death Boccaccio's.

Pepys and his contemporaries, though very justifiably frightened, were frightened of the wrong things; for plague is not, as they thought, carried by a miasma through the air. Nor is it quite as contagious as they supposed. They can in no way be blamed, for the full facts about plague were not understood until early in this century.[4] Plague is basically a disease of rodents, especially of rats. But it can and does infect man through the bite of a rat's flea. Not all rat fleas will bite men but *Xenopsylla Cheopis* will do so readily; and, once an epidemic has started, the common human flea *Pulex Irritans* can become a carrier. The flea itself does not get the plague, but it injects the causative bacillus *Pasteurella Pestis*, producing a painful bubo or swelling in the lymph glands which drain the affected limb – in most cases the groin glands since most bites are in the leg. Thence various destructive symptoms can arise, including internal haemorrhages; and in these bubonic cases the mortality rate, unless modern drugs are available, ranges between 60% and 85%, death on the average occurring after five days. But plague in its bubonic form is not seriously contagious so long as flea-bites are avoided, which of course in 17th-century slums they seldom could be.[5]

In some epidemics the bacillus goes directly or indirectly to the lungs producing a pneumonia that is invariably fatal and kills in three days or even less. Pneumonic plague is spread by droplet infection from the patient's coughing or sneezing and is therefore extremely dangerous to nurse. It is commoner when the disease is invading virgin territory; and, for this or other reasons, a high proportion of plague cases in the Black Death of 1348–9 had been pneumonic, thus accounting for that outbreak's immense destructiveness. But in 1665 in London pneumonic plague was not very prevalent; so, even if Pepys is truthful in reporting (12 Feb. 1666) that plague victims were deliberately breathing through ground floor windows on passers-by, 'in spite to well people', they were not likely to be spreading the disease. A pneumonic patient would very quickly become far too ill to be capable of any such behaviour.[6]

Nevertheless, the Plague of 1665 was, so to speak, a direct descendant of the Black Death. Western Europe during the Christian era had experienced two great pandemics of plague. The first, recorded in Procopius, in Gregory of Tours and in the Venerable Bede, began in the reign of Justinian in 542 A.D. and persisted for just over a century. The second, after a long lull, began with the Black Death in 1348 and lasted rather more than 300 years. Britain suffered repeated visitations which, for over a century, kept down population growth; and London had devastating periodic outbreaks in the 15th and early 16th centuries, culminating in the terrible Plagues of 1563, 1593, 1603 and 1625. The

Plague of 1665 was part of the pandemic's last effort before it burnt itself out, leaving north-western Europe and receding gradually into Russia, the Balkans and the Middle East, where by the 18th century it had become domiciled – apart from two severe but territorially limited raids on Marseilles in 1720 and Messina in 1743.[7]

There are reasons for thinking that, throughout the pandemic, in some parts of the country, including London, plague had assumed a smouldering endemic form between epidemic flare-ups.[8] For the 64 years preceding 1666 the annual mortality bills record only 16 years in which London's plague deaths were fewer than ten; and they show 20 years in which the plague deaths were some one thousand or over.[9] Moreover, in 1665 the epidemic began in the west end – in Westminster and St Giles-in-the-Fields – and groped its way along Holborn into the City and beyond.[10] This does not suggest reimportation through the dockland from abroad. On the other hand, London's plague deaths in the five years preceding 1665 were officially 13, 20, 12, 9 and 5; while only once since 1649 had the figure risen to over 23 and then only as far as 36.[11] It might well have been thought that the plague was dying out.

So the storm, when it broke, must have seemed to Pepys and his generation to have come upon them from an almost cloudless sky. 'This day', he wrote on 7 June, 'much against my Will, I did in Drury-lane see two or three houses marked with a red cross upon the doors, and "Lord have mercy on us" writ there – which was a sad sight to me, being the first of that kind that to my remembrance I ever saw. It put me into an ill conception of myself and my smell, so that I was forced to buy some roll-tobacco to smell to and chaw – which took away the apprehension'. Tobacco was believed to be a prophylactic against plague. Indeed plague pits can often be identified by the fragments of clay pipes found among the coffinless skeletons, since the sextons smoked furiously while at work. A boy who was at Eton recalled later that he was never flogged so hard as he was for not smoking in that year.[12]

With Pepys of course cheerfulness was always breaking in, as it did the very next day when he could rejoice over the naval victory off Lowestoft. But soon he was gloomily recording the progress of the plague on its march eastward to the City, and he quotes regularly and correctly from the weekly mortality bills, although he is aware of some at least of the reasons for mistrusting them. 'In the City', he writes at the end of August, 'died this week 7496; and of them, 6102 of the plague. But it is feared that the true number of the dead this week is near 10,000 – partly from the poor that cannot be taken notice of through the greatness of the number, and partly from the Quakers and others that will not have any bell ring for them'. There was, too, the parish clerk of St Olave's who had told Pepys only the day before' "there died nine this week, though I have returned but six;" ' 'which', says Pepys, 'is a very ill practice, and makes me think it is so in other places, and therefore the plague much greater then people take it to be'.

In temperate climates bubonic plague almost invariably 'peaks' in the late summer and then dies down in the cold weather when fleas tend to hibernate. By September 1665 London's mortality had become so overwhelming that the keeping of proper records was virtually impossible. Besides, there was much faulty diagnosis and much deliberate concealment – to evade the 40-day shutting up of the inmates in houses where cases had occurred. Some parishes were self-evidently dishonest. St Giles's, Cripplegate, is a case in point; for its records, compared with those of other parishes, show an absurdly low proportion of plague deaths to deaths from other causes. It is improbable that the parish clerk and his wife both died of 'dropsy' on the same day in the worst plague week of September.[13] London's official death-roll from all causes for the year is 97,306, of whom 28,710 people died supposedly of something other than plague, a figure which is over twice London's average annual mortality for the previous five years. Significantly the only figure to have fallen, compared with previous years, is 'executed 21'.[14] Modern authorities estimate that the true death-roll from plague was over 100,000 – perhaps a quarter of London's total population and probably amounting to a third of those living in the worst-hit areas.

It must be remembered that the well-to-do, with rare exceptions, ran away. Not for nothing was the Great Plague known as the Poor's Plague.[15] The court moved to Hampton Court, then to Salisbury and finally to Oxford.[16] The Royal Society suspended its meetings and left London almost as a body. Milton and Dryden left for the country and devoted six lines between them to the Plague.[17] The Dean of St Paul's, who as Archbishop Sancroft was later to lead the Seven Bishops, displayed less nerve on this occasion and spent most of the year at Tunbridge Wells.[18] Many dissenting ministers took the place of absent Anglicans, thus acquiring a popularity which made it impossible fully to enforce in London the so-called Clarendon Code forbidding any nonconformist presence within a corporate town.[19]

Those who stayed in London could expect little help from the medical profession. Plague victims were not taken to hospitals; and even when the official 'pest houses', for isolating patients, grew in number from one to five, the largest of them (in what is now Golden Sq., Soho) could at most hold 90 and the others fewer than 60 each.[20] In practice almost all suspected cases were locked up with their families, and armed guards set at their doors. Cases were reported by wholly unqualified 'ancient women' known as 'searchers'. Having no other means of subsistence, they were compelled to undertake this unsavoury employment. Pepys sometimes met them on their rounds.

The doctors could only prescribe bizarre remedies such as 'Dragon Water', 'Mithridatum', or the popular 'Venice Treacle' which Pepys once imbibed (11 July). There was also the 'Plague Water' sent him (on 20 July) by Lady Carteret.[21] But the doctors, for all their ignorance, were often heroic – including Dr George Thomson who performed an autopsy on a plague victim, wrote a treatise on it, caught the disease and survived in spite of putting a dried toad on his chest when he felt the first symptoms.[22] Pepys's own doctor, Alexander Burnet, assisted at the autopsy but was less fortunate when he too caught the plague.[23]

The City Fathers stayed on and did all they could to keep prices and unemployment down and food supplies in motion, led by the Lord Mayor Sir John Lawrence, whom it would be unfair to blame for giving audience, as the Venetians reported, standing in a glass case[24] – or even for ordering the destruction of those excellent rat-catchers, dogs. He was acting in accordance with received medical opinion, as he was when he ordered bonfires in all the streets for three successive days in September.[25] How, in view of those projecting upper storeys, he failed to start the Great Fire a year early is not very clear. Pepys on one of his river journeys saw the fires 'all the way on each side the Thames' (6 September).

There were, too, those who stayed to keep the fleet in fighting trim against the Dutchmen – the Duke of Albemarle, Lords Brouncker and Craven, and their juniors Pepys and Evelyn. As Pepys wrote to Sir William Coventry on 25 August, 'You, Sir, took your turn at the sword; I must not therefore grudge to take mine at the pestilence'. By the beginning of July he had sent his wife away to Woolwich, whence she later moved to Greenwich; and in August he induced the Navy Board itself to move to Greenwich. Early in September he moved his own sleeping quarters to Woolwich, though he still commuted daily, usually by water, to his house and office in Seething Lane. He had stayed, he told Lady Carteret on 4 September, till over 6,000 in the City had died of plague in one week, 'and little noise heard day nor night but tolling of bells'; till fewer than 20 persons could be met with in Lombard St; till his own doctor, 'who undertook to secure me against any infection . . . died himself of the plague; till the nights are grown too short to conceal the burials of those that died the day before; . . . lastly, till I could find neither meat nor drink safe, the butcheries being everywhere visited, my brewer's house shut up, and my baker with his whole family dead of the plague'.[26]

As he went about his business Pepys kept an ear to the ground and duly records all the plague gossip that he heard. He kept, too, a wide open eye and, above all, an eye that looked inward, noting every oscillation in his own moods and feelings. He observed the grass growing in the now-deserted streets around Whitehall (20 September) and the churchyards rising higher with new burials; and he tells how the sight of this in his own parish of St Olave's had 'frighted' him long after he had supposed himself de-sensitised to horrors (30 Jan. 1666). He recounts the sentimental story of the one surviving child rescued naked through the window of a stricken house (3 September); and the macabre story of the gallant who, wishing to accost a lady in a curtained coach, 'thrust his head . . . into her coach to look, and there saw somebody look very ill, and in a sick dress and stunk mightily' (3 August).

On 15 August Pepys meets in a narrow alley, 'to my great trouble', his first 'dead Corps, of the plague' but he thanks God he 'was not much disturbed at it'. On the night of 20 August he is 'in great fear of meeting of dead corses carrying to be buried; but blessed be God, met none, but did see now and then a Linke (which is the mark of them) at a distance'. Yet ten days later he succumbs to a morbid itch to visit the plague pit in Moorfields (it may have been the one where Liverpool St Station stands now) and 'see (God forgive my presumption) whether I could see any dead Corps going to the grave; but as God would have it, did not'. By 7 October when he comes close to the bearers of a corpse Pepys can exclaim 'but Lord, to see what custom is, that I am come almost to think nothing of it'; and, by the 16th, on realising that he has just been in an infected place, he can say 'we now make no bones of it'.

But this steeling of the nerves was no steady progression. Pepys had recurrent ups and downs. His first real shock had come on 17 June when he hired a coach to take him 'down Holborne' and 'the coachman I found to drive easily and easily; at last stood still, and came down hardly able to stand; and told me that he was suddenly stroke very sick and almost blind, he could not see. So I light and went into another coach, with a sad heart for the poor man and trouble for myself, lest he should have been stroke with the plague – being at the end of the town that I took him up. But God have mercy upon us all'. Six weeks later (26 July) Pepys confides to his journal that he has just enjoyed 'four days of as great content and honour and pleasure to me as ever I hope to live or desire'; and yet, within a few lines, he says that the plague has reached his parish, 'so that I begin to think of setting things in order, which I pray God enable me to put, both as to soul and body'.

Soon there were other worries and alarms, especially when his servant Will Hewer had come in 'ill of the head-ake' and 'is laid down upon my bed . . . which put me into extraordinary fear, and I studied all I could to get him out of the house, and set my people to work to do it without discouraging him'. Having spent the day persuading friends to leave London and reflecting 'that it is great odds that we ever all see one another again', Pepys returns home and, after working late, 'then to bed – in some ease of mind that Will is gone to his lodgings and that he is likely to do well, it being only the head-ake' (29 July).

By mid-August Pepys's fears had increased but his subconscious was providing compensations. He recalls his 'last night's dream . . . which I think is the best that ever was dreamed – which was, that I had my Lady Castlemayne in my armes and was admitted to use all the dalliance I desired with her' (15 August). Nor was this the last time that, for Pepys, lust overmastered fear. On 5 October he went by water to Deptford to visit his 'Valentine' Mistress Bagwell, observing that 'round about and next door on every side is the plague, but I did not value it but there did what I would con ella'.

In late November, when the plague had somewhat abated, it was a different appetite that vanquished Pepys's fears. 'I to London; and there in my way, at my old Oyster-shop in Gracious-streete, bought two barrels of my fine woman at the shop, who is alive after all the plague'. And the same evening, at an impromptu dinner with Sir George Smith, one barrel was duly opened and found to be 'good, though come from Colchester, where the plague hath been so much' (24 November).

Yet even in Pepys's more ebullient moments the Plague could bring about a sudden chill. 'Up', he writes on 3 September, 'and put on my colour silk suit, very fine, and my new periwigg, bought a good while since, but darst not wear it because the plague was in Westminster when I bought it. And it is a wonder what will be the fashion after the plague is done as to periwigs, for nobody will dare to buy any haire for fear of the infection – that it had been cut off the heads of people dead of the plague'. Nor does Pepys fail to notice how the plague has brought out the worst in human nature, 'making us more cruel to one another then we are to dogs' (22 August). It is indeed much to Pepys's credit that he sensed the cruelty of shutting up whole families in houses where one case had occurred – although he could not be aware of its futility. On the other hand, when, by mid-September, the shutting-up had ceased to be enforceable, Pepys had renewed worries. 'I did endeavour all I could to talk with as few as I could', for 'to be sure we do converse and meet with people that have the plague upon them'.

That same day (14 September) Pepys drew up a kind of balance sheet. On the credit side, he had found his plate and money safe in his abandoned London house, and the day had been profitable financially. Moreover, the week's mortality bill for all London had dropped by nearly 500 although the total for the 'City within the walls is increased and likely to continue so and is close to our house there'; and during the day Pepys has experienced an inordinate accumulation of depressing incidents. 'My meeting dead corps's of the plague, carried to be buried close to me at noonday through the City in Fanchurch-street – to see person sick of the sores carried close by me by Grace-church in hackney-coach – my finding the Angell tavern at the lower end of Tower-hill shut up; and more then that, the alehouse at the Tower stairs; and more then that, that the person was then dying of the plague when I was last there, . . . and I overheard the mistress of the house sadly saying to her husband somebody was very ill, but did not think it was of the plague – to hear that poor Payne my waterman hath buried a child and is dying himself – to hear that a labourer I sent but the other day to Dagenhams to know how they did there is dead of the plague; and that one of my own watermen, that carried me daily, fell sick as soon as he had landed me on Friday morning last, when I had been all night upon the water (and I believed he did get his infection that day at Brainford) is now dead of the plague . . . to hear that Mr Lewes hath another daughter sick – and lastly, that both my servants, W Hewers and Tom Edwards, have lost their fathers, both in St. Sepulcher's parish, of the plague this week – doth put me into great apprehensions of melancholy, and with good reason. But I put off the thoughts of sadness as much as I can; and the rather to keep my wife in good heart, and family also. After supper (having eat nothing all this day) upon a fine Tench of Mr Sheldens taking, we to bed'.

Pepys could and did put a brave face on things, and he possessed an indubitably brave heart. But even so and even if we recall that the plague had abated by the end of the year, it is still hard, remembering that September day, to believe our eyes when we read Pepys's entry for the last day of 1665. 'I have never lived so merrily (besides that I never got so much) as I have done this plague-time'.

Without knowing it Pepys had perhaps been safer in the City than he might have been elsewhere, for the City proper came off relatively lightly – at any rate in aggregate of deaths. This was not because the bacillus was less virulent or toxic inside the walls than in the liberties or out-parishes but simply because in the City people were thinner on the ground. The City buildings consisted largely of noblemen's big houses surrounded by quite spacious gardens, or else of business premises only partially occupied at night. People slept, and died, for the most part, in appalling crowded tenements outside the walls – in Holborn or Clerkenwell, in Cripplegate or Bishopsgate, or alongside the Fleet River, or along the Whitechapel Road and the Ratcliffe Highway. Further dense populations with corresponding high mortality were to be found along the river in Wapping and Rotherhithe, or across it in Southwark or Bermondsey, or yet again in the then almost isolated villages of Stepney or Shoreditch. In the official mortality bills all 97 parishes of the City suffered some 10,000 plague deaths whereas the suburb of Stepney alone had 7,000.[27] Incidentally London as a whole was, relatively speaking, fortunate, since in the same century Venice, Milan, Rome, Naples and Vienna suffered visitations that were very considerably worse.

Nor, again, was Pepys running undue risks in bringing back his family to Seething Lane on 7 Jan. 1666. The plague had died down, as was its wont in the cold weather; and, although some 2,000 more Londoners were to die of plague in 1666, as well as others in Colchester, Cambridge and elsewhere in Eastern England, the disease was in fact withdrawing not only from England but from North-west Europe. It had already left Scotland, Ireland, Wales, Denmark and Sweden, and by 1669 it had also left South Italy, the Netherlands, Switzerland and France.[28] The last recorded case in Britain occurred in 1679 in Rotherhithe. It was the last at any rate until 1900–01 when Glasgow and Liverpool were touched lightly by the new pandemic which since 1896 had engulfed so much of India and China.[29] The plague was then en route for Brazil and the south-western United States where cases still occur.

In the last years of the 17th century no Englishman could know that the pestilence had left his country. In 1682 therefore the great pioneer of statistics Sir William Petty was predicting that the plague would come back on the average once every 20 years and, by killing one Londoner in five on each occasion, would keep the population stationary once it had reached two million, since 400,000 plague deaths would be more than the rest of the country could 're-furnish' in the next 20 years.[30]

Petty was quite wrong, but exactly why is still an unsettled and slightly controversial matter. Almost certainly the departure of plague was not due to the Great Fire, which destroyed relatively little outside the City and thus spared the worst hotbeds of the plague.[31] Personal habits and living quarters were, it is true, very slowly becoming a little more hygienic, which may have reduced the presence of rats and the incidence of flea-bite. But there is no reason to think that Ireland, Scotland, Wales and the North-west – undoubtedly the poorest regions of the British Isles – had become more hygienic than South-Eastern England. Again, the newer buildings were usually of brick or stone and therefore less hospitable to rats and less easy than lath and plaster for a rat to gnaw. Yet it is doubtful whether many Londoners were much cleaner or much better housed in 1680 than they had been a hundred years before. Nor is it by any means certain that the plague bacillus undergoes any periodic or spontaneous decline in virulence or infectivity.[32]

Some authorities have argued that the replacement in England of the black rat by the brown was the decisive factor. Both rats are susceptible to plague but the black one lives much nearer to human habitations – never in fact more than 200 metres distant [33] – and is therefore much more dangerous. But the brown or Hanover rat, as his name implies, did not reach the British Isles in any force until about 1730 and had not fully supplanted the black rat before the mid-18th century, long after the disappearance of the plague from Britain.[34]

What is much more likely is that either the rodent or the human population, or perhaps both, had in some sense begun to 'breed immune'. This would mean that the more susceptible stocks had virtually died out, or at least radically thinned out, leaving only those with some natural or acquired resistance. Experts are uncertain as to how far, if at all, resistance to the actual disease can be either inherited or acquired.[35] Quite a number of people have had plague twice. But there could well be an immunity of a different kind, since there appears to be a certain correlation between susceptibility to plague and the possession of blood group 'A', a group which happens even now, after much mingling of populations, to be commoner in South-East England than elsewhere in the British Isles;[36] and it was in the South-East that plague lingered longest. It is almost certain that some men have blood which is less than normally attractive to fleas; and there is some evidence that this uninviting quality in the blood can be inherited.[37] It would follow that the stocks least liable to flea-bite would be those tending to survive.

If this is the missing clue, the first man to lay his hand on it, however unwittingly, was Samuel Pepys. On the night of 23 Apr. 1662 he had to share a bed in his Portsmouth lodging with his friend Dr Timothy Clarke F.R.S.; and during the night Pepys noted 'that all the fleas came to him and not to me'. Perhaps it was no mere accident that Pepys survived the Plague.[38]

(Christopher Morris)

Playford, John, the elder (1623–?86). The most productive music publisher of his day in England. His shop was in the Inner Temple. His *English Dancing Master* (1650) and his collections of songs and catches stayed in print for many years. His son Henry inherited his business.[1]

PLAYS

Neither as playgoer nor as reader of plays was Pepys an easy man to please. That he should experience pleasure was his principal desire when he went to see or sat down to read a play; he repeatedly alludes to his 'expectation' on going to the playhouse; once there he awaited the satisfaction of his appetite. The extent to which this was accomplished depended upon a number of factors: his mood, the quality of the performance, the qualities of the play itself. He was displeased by *Henry IV Part I* on 31 Dec. 1660, pleased by it on 4 June 1661, only partially pleased (by Cartwright's speaking of 'Falstaffe's speech about *What is Honour*') on 2 Nov. 1667. *Henry VIII* caused him to be 'mightily dissatisfied' on 1 Jan. 1664, but he was 'mightily pleased, better than I ever expected, with the history and shows of it' on 30 Dec. 1668. He was aware that seeing a play too frequently might well make him tire of it, noting of *The Tempest* on 12 Dec. 1667 that 'as often as I have seen it, I do like very well'; if a play survived recurrent viewing over a long period he was apt to be surprised, though his habit of ruthless self-exposure to what he liked (in part enforced on him by the workings of the Restoration repertory system) make this more explicable; he saw Dryden's *Secret Love* seven times, and attended three out of four performances of Dryden and Newcastle's *Sir Martin Mar-all* within five days, eventually seeing it at least ten times. Shirley's *The Traitor*, which he commended on 22 Nov. 1660, he found that 'still I like as a very good play' on 2 Oct. 1667; Jonson's *The Alchemist*, 'a most incomparable play' on 22 June 1661, was 'still a good play' on 17 Apr. 1669. But Jonson's *Epicoene* (*The silent woman*), which he had seen for the first time and judged 'an excellent play' on 7 Jan. 1661, he thought much less well of on 1 June 1664, though by 19 Sept. 1668 he had come round to the view that it was 'the best comedy, I think, that was ever wrote', an opinion apparently shared, in part at least, by his neighbour on the playhouse benches, that ardent imitator of Jonson, Thomas Shadwell. Webster's *The Duchess of Malfi*, which had seemed 'a good play' when read on 2 Nov. 1666, proved but a 'sorry play' when seen on stage on 25 Nov. 1668, and Davenant's *The Wits*, which Pepys had admired on 15 Aug. 1661, he disliked on 18 Apr. 1667. Pepys was ardent for plays, but fickle in his admirations.

He made a clear distinction between the effectiveness of plays read and plays seen. Jonson's *Catiline* pleased in the closet but not in the playhouse: 'a play of much good sense and words to read, but that doth appear the worst upon the stage, I mean the least divertising, that ever I saw any, though most fine in clothes and a fine Scene of the Senate and of a fight, that ever I saw in my life – but the play is only to be read'.[1] Its actual production provided him with 'no pleasure at all'. Some plays improved exceptionally in the reading, notably Massinger's *The Bondman*, which Pepys perused on 2 Nov. 1666, and Davenant's *The siege of Rhodes*, read and reread, which on 1 Oct. 1665 he considered 'certainly (the more I read it the more I think so) the best poem that ever was wrote' – the word 'poem' being significant here as to his view of the play's character, and his approach to it.

Pepys's criteria are clear enough, even if his employment of them at times seems erratic. He expected to be better pleased by plays that were new rather than 'old' ('old' plays being those written before Parliament closed the theatres in 1642), though in practice he was often surprised by the excellence of 'old' plays (notably in the case of *The Tempest*) and disappointed in the new. He required an excellence both of 'plot' or

'design', and of 'language'; he greatly approved 'variety', though he
recognised that this compromised the 'depth' – elsewhere characterised
as the 'eminence' – of, for instance, a tragedy.[2] He commended
'humours' in a play, discerning these, for instance, in Shakespeare's *The
merry wives of Windsor*, in Heywood's *Love's Mistress*, and Shadwell's
The sullen lovers where he was recognising the very quality on which
the playwright, as a disciple of Jonson, most prided himself. But 'good
humours' did not necessarily make for lively theatre; Pepys could
recognise the quality but still feel the play vitiated by lack of design, and
find Polchinello 'three times more sport' – above all Polchinello offered
the elusive quality of variety, and became in consequence 'extraordinary
good entertainment'.[3] Nevertheless, in different circumstances, puppets
were not things to conjure with; Heywood's *If you know not me you
know nobody* was roundly damned as 'merely a puppet play acted by
living puppets. Neither the design nor language better'. When Pepys
was recording what he felt as critic or wit, rather than straightforwardly
sensual spectator, the puppet Punch became a truncheon with which to
beset the Judys of the legitimate drama. If post-Restoration plays by
and large had more of 'design' in them than 'old plays', thus avoiding
the short shrift accorded to *The Midsummer Night's dream* ('the most
insipid ridiculous play that ever I saw in my life'), they were, however,
more prone to contain smut – an element by which Pepys, unlike (if we
are to go by the evidence of the fare provided for them) the majority of
his fellow playgoers, was unamused. Dryden's *An evening's love* fell
down on this score, though Pepys esteemed the same writer's *The rival
ladies* as 'very innocent', and praised Richard Brome's *The jovial crew*
for the same reason. Other qualities admired by Pepys were 'wit', good
similes, and 'good sense'.[4]

It emerges from this that Pepys was not a roistering rake in the playhouse, but a considering, though inconsistent, critic; if in this he does
not fit one modern image of the age, he nevertheless conforms to an
important aspect of the age's image of itself. In 1674 Thomas Rymer, in
his preface to his translation of Rapin's *Réflexions sur la poétique
d'Aristote*, contrasted the recent progress of the drama in France and in
England. In France '*Malherb* reform'd their ancient licentious *Poetry*;
and *Corneille's Cid* rais'd many Factions amongst them. At this time
with us many great Wits flourished, but *Ben Jonson*, I think, had all the
Critical learning to himself; and till of late years *England* was as free
from Criticks as it is from *Wolves*, that a harmless well-meaning Book
might pass without any danger'.[5] In terms of Rymer's metaphor Pepys
was a critical wolf, though his howl was of no literary significance and
his bite erratic. He perfectly exemplifies the state of affairs that Rymer
describes. He had read *The Cid* 'with great delight', but when he saw it
(as *The valiant Cidd* on 1 Dec. 1662) he thought it 'a most dull thing

acted' and, reverting to his instinctive rather than his intellectual criteria, pronounced that there was 'no pleasure in it', despite the excellence of the cast. The other plays by Corneille which he saw evoked equally mixed responses: *Heraclius* he found 'excellent' and was able to be enthusiastic about on three separate occasions; *The mistaken beauty* (*Le Menteur*) was at least good in parts; but *Horace* and *Pompey the Great* all notably failed to please him.[6] However in all these instances he was subjected to translations and adaptations that endeavoured to assimilate Corneille to the English taste. Ben Jonson, by contrast (and also by contrast with Shakespeare, whose plays were being adapted, at just the same time as those of Corneille, though not with the same intentions), was played unadapted, and gave Pepys unalloyed pleasure, though he found, as we have seen, that both *Catiline* and *The Cid* were good when read and poor on the stage. This admiration for Jonson is unsurprising, since it was, as Rymer implies, Jonson who had established the terms of 'Critical learning' ('plot', 'design', 'wit', 'humour', 'language') which Pepys customarily deployed. The terms had been taken up by those exceedingly influential 'sons of Ben', Sir William Davenant and Thomas Hobbes, in the disquisitions prefatory to Davenant's poem *Gondibert* (1650), which initiated, for England, an entirely new style of critical discourse. 'Discourse' is the word which, in his *An essay of dramatic poesy* (1668) John Dryden applies to the reconstructed conversation of Eugenius, Crites, Lisideius and Neander, who, on 3 June 1665, 'when our navy engaged the Dutch' and Pepys was preoccupied with law business, though also 'full of concernment for the Duke, and . . . perticularly for my Lord Sandwich and Mr Coventry after his Royal Highness', moved from reflection on the dire literary harvest of Panegyrics and Elegies that the battle would inevitably produce to consideration of the construction and the poetry of plays. Dryden's *Essay* is in a classical tradition of deliberated dialogues, but this is no reason to suppose it untrue to the concerns and conversational likelihoods of the times. Pepys would not have wholly agreed with any of the debaters, though he would presumably have endorsed the opinion of Crites (Sir Robert Howard) that rhyme did not really suit the constraints of dramatic composition.[7] But Pepys certainly thought in the terms presupposed by Dryden, and many of his waverings of opinion come directly out of the conflict between a theoretical notion of what the drama ought to be, and a lively apprehension of what it actually was. The same conflict can be discerned in Pepys's sensitivity to audience reaction – his feeling on 5 May 1668, for instance, that Shadwell's *The sullen lovers* might be better than he had thought it because it was generally approved, or the confirmation of his own opinion which he deduced from their Majesties' coldness when confronted by *The Cid*: 'nor did the King or Queene once smile all the whole play, nor any of the company seem to take any pleasure but was in the greatness and gallantry of the company'. We are reminded, as the texts of the plays do not remind us (nor did they Pepys), that the theatre is necessarily a social event, and as such impinged on Pepys in a way that qualified, if it did not restrict, his critical stance.

Perhaps the greatest insight that Pepys allows us in his response to plays is that afforded by his reaction to Sir Samuel Tuke's *The adventures of five hours*. It was a work that he preferred to *Othello, Moore of Venice*, considering the latter, which he had 'heretofore esteemed a mighty good play', a 'mean thing' by comparison.[8] It seems probable that, in common with most of his contemporaries, for whom Shakespeare's works were a staple of the stage, he took their excellences for granted, and did not give a great deal of thought to them. To those features that he perceived as constituting their weaknesses he was altogether more alive and, again in common with most of his contemporaries, he was not afflicted by bardolatry. His low opinion of *Othello*, for example, was shared by Thomas Rymer, who found it, though diverting, in its 'tragical part . . . plainly none other than a Bloody Farce, without salt or savour'. What *The adventures of five hours* offered was above all, in Gerard Langbaine's words, 'Oeconomy and Contrivance'; it had a perspicuous and clear design which conformed to the unities of time and place demanded by neo-classical criticism and much valued by Pepys. It was also, as Tuke observed in his 'Preface' to the third impression (1671), an '*Innocent Piece*, not guilty of so much as that Current Wit, *Obscenity* and *Profaneness*'; in this it again precisely met Pepys's requirements. The diction was consistently lofty; indeed the play was criticised by Evelyn on these grounds: 'the plot was incomparable but the language stiffe & formall'.[9] In its high and serious sentiment it compared with *The siege of Rhodes*. Its Spanish origin (Tuke erroneously supposed his model to be by Calderón; the true author is probably Antonio Coello y Ochoa) makes it typical of many of the most successful Restoration plays in that it is an adaptation, and would in any case have had an appeal for Pepys; Tuke thought the Spanish 'the Nation of the World who are the happiest in the force and delicacy of their *Inventions*', and in so doing attributed to them two of the main qualities that Pepys valued in plays.

Pepys's taste in the drama is certainly more explicable when seen in the context of contemporary criticism, but in the end remains something of a random phenomenon. Rymer, pondering why so wretched a play as Beaumont and Fletcher's *The maid's tragedy* could succeed, decided that it was because of the way in which it was acted: 'whatever defect may be in *Amintor* and *Melanthius*, Mr. *Hart* and Mr. *Mohun* are wanting in nothing'. The rules might be a constant subject of debate amongst the *cognoscenti*, and a matter for close consideration by any aspiring dramatist, but in practice excellence of performance could well prove the decisive factor. Pepys had real feeling for the 'design' and 'wit' of plays (to the point of postulating, on 26 Dec. 1668, a rewriting of Beaumont and Fletcher's *Women Pleased*), but was equally responsive to singing, dancing, or a well-spoken scene. He was not critically prescient: his cool notices of Etherege suggest that the direction taken by the English drama in the 1670s and '80s, which *Love in a tub* and *She would if she could* so clearly presage, was not something that he would readily understand. His reactions, partially shaped by and generally couched in the language of an evolving school of dramatic criticism, were at root eclectic and personal, though they often conformed to those of his contemporaries. What is never in question is the avidity of his appetite for the drama, even though 'expectation' was so often unfulfilled.[10] [*See also* Theatre]

(Richard Luckett)

Pointer, [Thomas]. Clerk in the Navy Office. He worked under Pepys in the victualling business in 1665; after which he was clerk and from 1668 chief clerk to the Comptroller until 1672.[1]

Poole, Jonas and William. Jonas was flag-captain to Penn (his brother-in-law) on the Jamaica voyage 1654–5; held six commands 1660–5 and died in 1666. William, his son (kt 1672) held 13 commands 1660–85. Pepys sometimes adds a descriptive phrase to distinguish them, but until the father's death it is not always clear to whom he refers. He retained in his library the journal of Sir William's voyage in 1677–8 to Newfoundland and the Straits.[1]

Poole's tavern, Deal. Used for the reception of sick and wounded seamen. The licensee was John Poole.[1]

Pooley, Sir Edmund, kt 1646 (1619–71). Of Badley, Suff. A royalist; M.P. for Bury St Edmunds 1661–71 (one of Arlington's followers); sub-commissioner of prizes 1665–7; clerk-extraordinary in the Privy Council by 1667: envoy to Brandenburg-Prussia. He was disappointed of the hope of becoming secretary to the Treasury in 1668 and was compensated by the grant of several revenue posts. His wife was a daughter of Sir Henry Crofts, of Little Saxham, Suff.[1]

Poortmans (Portman), [John]. A Fifth-Monarchist and a friend of Richard Creed. In the service of the Commonwealth navy (e.g. as Secretary and Deputy-Treasurer to the fleet 1654) until arrested in July 1656.[1]

Pope's Head Alley. A centre for the sale of cutlery, turnery and toys. It ran north out of Lombard St to Cornhill, opposite the Royal Exchange. It was demolished during the rebuilding of Lloyd's Bank c. 1927–9, and a new alley made to the west of it. (R)

Popinjay Alley. Now Poppin's Court, on the n. side of Fleet St next to Ludgate Circus. (R)

Porter, Sir Charles, kt 1686 (1631–96). Solicitor-General to the Duke of York 1660; Lord Chancellor of Ireland 1686–7, 1690–6. He was dissipated and drunken and 'had the good fortune to be loved by everybody' (North).[1]

Portsmouth. The oldest of the royal dockyards. Already important in the later Middle Ages, with a dry dock (1496) which was the first to be built in England, it was deliberately run down by Henry VIII in favour of the Thames yards. Its revival was marked by the appointment of a commissioner in the First Dutch War. In the '50s almost as many warships were built there as at Chatham, but in the Second War it acted mainly as a repair base and victualling station. In 1686–8, 20 storehouses were constructed and with the French wars, from 1689 onwards, it became a dockyard of the first importance.[1]

POSTAL SERVICES

These centred on the Post Office in the city (q.v.), and were under the management of a Postmaster-General (from 1666 Secretary Arlington). Inland letters were despatched in the early hours of Tuesdays, Thursdays and Saturdays and had to be handed in by midnight. There were a number of subsidiary letter offices, mostly shops, at which letters could be left for carriage to the main offices in the city. The shopkeepers were employed by the Post Office and made no charge to the customer. Occasionally the government issued a list of authorised agents to prevent the public from being imposed on.[1] Letters consisted of folded and sealed sheets – envelopes were not introduced until 1840 – with the address written on the exposed fold. A 'stamp' (imprinted by machine, giving the day and month numbers) was added by the Post Office. The postal charges under an act of 1660[2] (modelled on an act of 1657) were fixed according to the number of sheets and the distance. Pepys could send a single sheet to Brampton for 2d. – by paying extra he could have it sent express. His official correspondence was of course franked in the office and went free.

There were six post roads out of London, with a certain number of 'by-posts' serving market towns which lay off the main routes. Letters were carried by mounted messengers (equipped with bag and horn) based on the posthouses which were situated every 15 miles or so along the road. Where common carriers offered a more direct service, letters might be sent in their waggons, though they were not allowed to carry letters as a regular part of their service. Pepys used them occasionally;

Dorothy Osborne used them regularly in the 1650s to escape the risk – not quite so great in the '60s – of having her letters opened by the Post Office.

Inland letters arrived in London during the nights of Mondays, Wednesdays and Fridays and were collected for delivery by the subsidiary letter offices.

Letters within London were often carried direct, and it was one of the main functions of Pepys's domestic servants and office messengers to perform this service. In 1680 a penny post was introduced which provided four or five deliveries a day. It proved such a resounding success that two years later it was taken over by the Post Office, though kept as a separate organisation.[3]

Post Office. Headquarters of the government postal service, often known as the General or Grand Letter Office; a large building taxed on 33 hearths,[1] situated at the bottom of Threadneedle St, on the n. side of its junction with Cornhill, roughly where the Bank of England now stands. The staff consisted of a few administrative officers, three 'window-men', who received the mail, and about 50 sorters. The building was destroyed in the Fire, after which the office moved to Bridges St, Covent Garden. In Aug. 1667 it moved to Bishopsgate and in 1678 to Lombard St where it remained until it was transferred in 1829 to St Martin's-le-Grand. There was a separate letter office for Kent and Sussex in Love Lane, Billingsgate, also destroyed in the Fire, after which it was included in the main office in Aug. 1667.[2]

Poundy, ——. Waterman: possibly the James Powndey who in 1701 was in receipt of a pension from Trinity House.[1]

Povey, Thomas (1615–c.1702). Pepys's colleague on the Tangier Committee. Son of Justinian, Auditor of the Exchequer under James I, accountant-general to Anne of Denmark and a commissioner of the Caribbees. A close friend of Sir Martin Noell, Cromwell's principal financier, he was active in the Interregnum in the promotion of colonial and trading ventures. He is said to have proposed the establishment of the Committee of Trade in Nov. 1655, and to have been the most effective member of the Council for America (1657). In 1660 he was made Treasurer of the Duke of York's Household, a member of the Council of Trade, and in 1661 secretary and receiver-general of the Committee for Foreign Plantations. He also held other posts and when he was appointed Treasurer of Tangier in 1663 Pepys came to know him well, and found him incapable (perhaps because of his other commitments) of keeping his accounts in order. In 1665 he resigned his duties to Pepys, making an arrangement whereby they shared the profits equally. In 1686 he tried, without success, to apply the same rule to

Pepys's successor, Will Hewer (1680–4). At the same time he complained that Pepys had not always paid him his share.[1]

He was an original F.R.S., skilled in mechanics, a man of taste, and well known for the elaborate formality of his speech and manners.[2] His London house, which Pepys greatly admired, was one of the smaller ones in Lincoln's Inn Fields built in 1657, and was taxed on 14 hearths.[3] At Hounslow he had a country house, the Priory, inherited from his father, which he sold in 1671.[4]

A number of his relatives were in the public service, the best-known (also a colleague of Pepys) being his nephew William Blathwayt, Secretary at War 1683–1704. (Blathwayt's bookcases were copied from Pepys's.)[5] Two of his brothers, Richard and William, had colonial posts, and his half-brother John was a clerk to the Privy Council and a Commissioner for the Sick and Wounded under William III.[6]

Powell, John. Messenger to the Admiralty office. He had served under the Commonwealth.[1]

Powell, [John]. Steward to the diplomatic mission to Sweden, 1659. Possibly identical with the Admiralty messenger.[1]

Powell, [John]. Pepys's contemporary at school and Cambridge: he left St Paul's School with an exhibition in 1648 and graduated from Emmanuel College in 1652. In 1664 he was curate of Much Hadham, Herts.[1]

Powell, [Rowland]. Clerk to Brouncker, Navy Office, 1667.[1]

Powell, [Rowland]. Clerk to Sir W. Coventry in the Navy Office or Admiralty 1667. Possibly identical with the foregoing. In 1676 Coventry appealed to Pepys for a place for him. A man of these names was purser of the *Loyal London* in 1670.[1]

Powell, Rowland and Doll (b. Lane). Doll was Betty Lane's younger sister. Like her she had a stall in Westminster Hall, and like her, though not for so long, she was Pepys's mistress. She claimed to be the widow of Rowland Powell, a seaman.[1] [*See also* Martin, Samuel]

Poynton, Col. ——. Possibly one of the Yorkshire Boyntons: of Barmston and Burton Agnes.[1] His reported marriage to Doll Stacey (the pretty New Exchange woman) has not been traced.

Poyntz, [Francis]. Yeoman arras- and tapestry-maker to the King in the office of the Robes from ?1660; Master of the New Bridewell, Clerkenwell c. 1665–7. During the war he supplied the navy with canvas made in Bridewell.[1] In ?1667 he made proposals for the reorganisation of tapestry making in England.[2]

Poyntz, [John]. Clerk-Comptroller of the office of the Master of the Revels.[1]

Prat, Monsieur du. Lord Hinchingbrooke's tutor in Paris. A Spaniard ('Monsr. da Prata'; 'Maestro del Prata') occurs in the Sandwich family papers from 1656 onwards.[1]

Price, [Gervase] (d. 1689). Serjeant trumpeter and yeoman keeper of the bows, crossbows, and guns. (The existence of a James and a John Price, also trumpeters, suggests that this was a family business.) In Sept. 1664 he was ordered by the Duke of York to press trumpeters for sea service.[1] (Lu)

Price, Jack. Underclerk to the Council of State 1660. His name is spelt Brice in the council records.[1]

Primate, [Josiah]. Projector and leatherseller, of Fleet St.[1]

Prin, Monsieur. Huguenot bookseller and player of the trumpet-marine. Father of the virtuoso player of that instrument, Jean-Baptiste Prin (c. 1669–c. 1742).[1] (Lu)

Pri(t)chard, [Sir William], kt 1672. Of Woolwich; ropemaker to the Ordnance Office.[1]

PRIVY SEAL OFFICE

The Lord Privy Seal was one of the historic officers of state, but by this time usually greater in dignity than importance. The Court of Requests over which he had presided did not sit after 1642, and the four Masters of Requests who were its judges now did nothing more than handle petitions to the Crown. For the rest, the minister's administrative duties consisted in running an office whose functions were entirely formal, and consisted in preparing the Privy Seal instruments (warrants or writs) which authorised the issue of letters patent under the Great Seal, or in some cases, the payment of money.[1] The post was occupied from 1661–73 by Lord Robartes, whom Pepys found to be lazy and obstructive – and it was particularly easy for any Lord Privy Seal to be both.

His office was headed by four clerks usually appointed for life and performing their duties by deputy. Sandwich had a family connection with the office – his father had been a Master of Requests – and he himself had in 1637 been granted a reversion to a clerkship and to the post of Registrar of the Court of Requests.[2] On assuming the clerkship in 1660 (the post of registrar being now obsolete) he nominated Pepys as his deputy, with Moore as Pepys's assistant. Their first month 'in waiting' was Aug. 1660. Payment was entirely by fees, which were shared between the clerk and his deputies. Business was always brisk at the beginning of a reign – and never more so than at the Restoration – because of the number of new appointments that had to be made under the Great Seal, each stage in the process of preparing a grant being paid for by a fee. The work was undemanding and called for Pepys's attendance for only one month in each quarter, and then only at sealing days and for a few hours during the working week. He was often able

to do all that was required of him after his work as Clerk of the Acts
was finished. The office building of the Privy Seal, in the Great Court
of Whitehall Palace,[3] was within easy reach of his normal haunts. His
only complaint was that pardons, of which there were many after the
Interregnum, were by virtue of statute mostly issued without fee.
'Signed deadly number of pardons' was his summary of an afternoon's
work on 7 Dec. 1660.

In Aug. 1662 on his appointment to the Tangier Committee, he
resigned. Moore then succeeded him.

Proctor, [William]. Landlord of the Mitre, Wood St, c. 1641–d. 65;
'the greatest vintener . . . for great entertainments' (vi.176). The story
that he died insolvent (ib., n.1) is a canard. He left a considerable
estate administered by four executors.[1]

Proger(s). A Monmouthshire family of Catholic royalists. Several
held court office after the Restoration. Pepys's references are usually to
Edward (1617–1714), Groom of the Bedchamber (and pimp) to the
King. At viii.67 Pepys seems to refer to his elder brother Henry. Their
father, Col. Philip, had held court office in the two previous reigns.[1]

Prowd, Capt.[John]. River agent for the Navy Board; Elder Brother,
Trinity House 1660; Deputy-Master 1667–8; Master 1677–8.[1]

Prujean, Sir Francis, kt 1661 (1593–1666). One of the leading medical
practitioners of his day; F.R.C.P. 1626; President 1650–4.[1]

Puddle Wharf/Dock. Near the Wardrobe; a sizeable inlet and wharf,
with a landing stair, at the foot of Puddle Dock Hill (now St Andrew's
Hill). (R)

Pulford, ——. Employed by Nathaniel Waterhouse, Steward to the
Lord Protector. Possibly the John Pulford who was man of business to
the widowed Countess of Dirleton (d. 1659).[1]

Pumpfield, [Edward]. Ropemaker.[1]

Punnett, [Augustine]. River pilot: referred to in 1673 as 'old
Punnett'.[1]

Punt, ——. Probably one of the Ponts who served on several county
commissions in Huntingdonshire.[1]

Purcell. Thomas Purcell (d. 1682) was a tenor in the Chapel Royal, a
member of the Private Musick, and groom of the robes and under-
housekeeper at Somerset House.[1] His brother Henry (d. 1664) was
musician-in-ordinary for the violins and the lutes and voices, master of
the choristers at Westminster Abbey, and father of the composer Henry
Purcell (1659–95). A catch by the elder Henry appears in *Catch that
catch can* (1667).[2] (Lu)

Putney, Surrey. In 1664 a small village of some 196 houses, 6 miles
by water from the city.[1] The church (St Mary and All Saints) stood (and

stands) on the river bank a few yards downstream of the present bridge. Until 1729, when the first (wooden) bridge was completed, communication with Fulham was by ferry.[2] (R)

Pym, [William]. A fashionable tailor; he lived in the Strand in a house of 13 hearths 'over against Salisbury House'.[1] He was patronised by Sandwich, as well as by Pepys, and two of his assistants were tailors on Sandwich's staff in Madrid. Clarendon, when he took flight to France, owed him £350. He died c. 1672, possessed of a considerable fortune, and with many debts still outstanding.[2]

Pye. Sir Robert Pye, jun. (c. 1622–1701) was the son of Sir Robert, an Exchequer official. He was a parliamentarian in the Civil War (as befitted the son-in-law of John Hampden), and a moderate Presbyterian who was imprisoned in Feb. 1660 for petitioning for the admission of the secluded members. He sat for Berkshire in 1654 and in the Convention of 1660. Charles II made him an equerry. Elizabeth Pye (d. 1660), Kate Petit's mistress, was his sister.[1]

Pyne, Capt. [Valentine]. Originally a ship's gunner; Master-Gunner (Ordnance Board) 1668–77. He had long been deputy to his predecessor, Col. James Wemyss, and had executed the office since about 1665 in Wemyss's absence. In July 1668 he was granted £71 p.a. in recognition of his distinguished service in the war.[1]

Quartermain, William (c. 1618–67). Physician in ordinary to the King from July 1660; F.R.S. and F.R.C.P. 1661; M.P. for New Shoreham 1662–7. Clarendon was one of his patients.[1]

Queenhithe. A waterside quay, south of St Paul's, halfway between the Steelyard and Blackfriars. Once the principal wharf for the city.

Radcliffe, [Jonathan]. Clergyman and schoolfellow of Pepys at St Paul's. Admitted to Christ's College, Cambridge in 1652 (at 17); B.A. 1656; Vicar of Walthamstow 1660–2.[1]

Rainbowe, Edward (1608–84). Fellow of Magdalene College 1633–42; Master 1642–50, 1660–4; Vice-Chancellor 1662–3; Dean of Peterborough 1661–4; Bishop of Carlisle 1664–84. A famous preacher and, at Magdalene, a noted tutor. As a country parson in the 1650s he based his services on the forbidden Prayer Book. Shelton's *Tachygraphy* (1647), from which Pepys learnt his shorthand, has a verse addressed to Shelton by E[dward] R[ainbowe] 'his Friend'. There is a portrait of him in Magdalene.[1]

Ram Alley. On the s. side of Fleet St, opposite Fetter Lane; a privileged place for debtors, it bore a bad reputation. (R)

Ratcliff. The riverside area between St Katharine's (east of the Tower of London) and Wapping. The Ratcliff Highway (now The Highway) ran along its n. edge, connecting E. Smithfield and Shadwell and formng the straight base of the bend in which lay Ratcliff, Wapping and Shadwell. In 1664, technically a hamlet of the parish of Stepney, but having (counting those on the Ratcliff Highway) perhaps 2000 houses.[1] (R)

Raven, John. Clerk of Dover Castle 1660.[1]

Rawlins, Col. Giles. Gentleman of the Privy Purse to the Duke of York.[1]

Rawlinson, Daniel (1614–79). Landlord of the Mitre, Fenchurch St, one of the busiest and most elegant of London taverns. A royalist, he draped his sign in black when Charles I was executed.[1] The diary shows that Pepys's Uncle Wight was a friend or relative of his, and that Pepys more than once consulted him about private investments. One of his acquaintances anxious for a deputy-purser's place first made application to Rawlinson, begging him to 'move squire Pepys' to use his influence with Coventry.[2] His house was burnt in the Fire; he rebuilt it in some splendour. He became Master of the Vintners' Company in 1678 and died possessed of a considerable estate, with landed property in several counties, including his native Lancashire. His son Sir Thomas (also a vintner) was Lord Mayor 1705–6; Sir Thomas's sons Thomas and Richard were the well-known antiquaries. It was through the latter's enterprise and generosity that a large body of Pepys's papers found their way to the Bodleian Library.[3] [*See also* Taverns]

Raworth, [Francis]. Lawyer; admitted Gray's Inn 1653.[1]

Rayner, [Edmund]. Appointed boatmaker to Deptford and Woolwich yards July 1660.[1]

Reade, Dr [Thomas] (d. 1669). A civil lawyer; D.C.L. (Oxon.) 1638. 'A most noted royalist' (Wood), he served in the force raised by the university. The King made him Principal of Magdalen Hall 1643–6. He became a Roman Catholic during the Interregnum and after the Restoration was surrogate for Sir William Merrick in the Prerogative Court of Canterbury.[1]

Red Bull Theatre. At the upper end of St John St, Clerkenwell, on the site later, and perhaps earlier, known as Red Bull Yard. Built by Aaron Holland, yeoman, in or shortly before 1605, it suffered the vicissitudes of most of its kind. During the Interregnum clandestine or semi-clandestine performances were staged there. Soon after the Restoration it was re-opened, and the King's players under Killigrew performed there for a few days in the autumn of 1660. It could not survive against the monopoly given by Charles's grant to the King's and the Duke's players and was converted to other uses. [*See also* Theatre] (R)

Reeve(s), [Richard], fl. 1641–79. Of Long Acre; perspective-glass maker to the King; the leading maker of optical instruments. His son John (fl. 1679–?1710) succeeded to the business.[1]

Reeve(s), Ald. [Samuel] (d. c. 1683). Upholsterer, of Long Lane; Alderman 1668–9; Sheriff of Hertfordshire 1671–2.[1]

[Reggio, Piero] ('Pedro') (1632–85). Genovese composer, singer and lutenist. Employed in Stockholm (along with G. B. Draghi, q.v.) by Queen Christina, 1652. In France 1657, in England by 1664. Heard by Evelyn, 23 Sept. 1680. Published a treatise on singing and a volume of *Songs set by Signior Pietro Reggio* (1680).[1] Lute tutor to the dramatist Thomas Shadwell. (Lu)

RELIGION

When the diary opens, Pepys was attending the illegal Anglican services which survived, with only occasional interruption from the authorities, in the London of the Commonwealth. He was not a regular member of any congregation, but in the manner of the time attended several, his favourites being those which met under Peter Gunning and Robert Mossom (both made bishops after the Restoration), Timothy Thurscrosse and Thomas Warmestry.[1] These were all accomplished preachers, and Pepys found Presbyterian sermons dry and prolix by comparison. But it is also clear that he attended their services because he was devoted to the liturgy of the Prayer Book. On the voyage to Holland on 8 Apr. 1660 he was provoked to 'very hot' dispute by the ship's chaplain's defence of extemporary prayer. He welcomed the restoration of the Prayer Book service to the churches after the King's return and began to use it himself in the family prayers he instituted in his new and expanded household in July 1660.[2] No doubt there had been a time when, with Anglicanism proscribed after the first Civil War, he had attended the official puritan services. But those days, like the Puritan Revolution itself, were over. His mother (and possibly his father) apparently regretted them. Pepys did not, and was happy to return to 'the Religion I was born in'.[3] He was probably speaking the truth though with a certain pardonable exaggeration when he told the Commons in 1674 on being accused of being a papist, that he had always been a 'good Protestant and good churchman'.[4]

His churchmanship was of the moderate and pragmatic sort – neither 'enthusiastic' on the one hand nor high-flying on the other. He set store by orthodoxy in doctrine, being prepared to accept the tradition of the church in matters where Scripture was not clear,[5] and had a particular dislike of sermons in which points of doctrine were incompetently handled, just as he had of preachers guilty of false quantities in their Greek or Latin.[6] He approved of a decent ceremonial – of the use of the ring in marriage, of kneeling at communion and of the sign of the cross in baptism[7] – all of which were objected to by the

Puritans. He disliked what he called 'silly devotions'[8] – but what they
were he does not disclose. In matters of church government he believed
that a national establishment was necessary for the sake of national
unity and well-being. 'Fanatics' – the extreme Puritan sects – he
abhorred as holding beliefs that were dangerous to civil peace as well
as offensive to common sense. At the same time he distrusted those of
the established clergy who made absurdly high claims for their
authority. Londoners were often strongly anti-clerical and Pepys was
no exception. He repeatedly remarks on the dangerous pretensions of
the bishops of the early '60s and criticises his own parish priest, Milles,
for setting too high a value on his order. (At one point he appeared to
be threatening to introduce the confessional.)[9]

Pepys never sets out his views on the church as clearly as he makes
known his views on the state, but his sympathies and prejudices and
some of his beliefs can be gathered easily enough from the diary. The
church, he thought, was only a human institution,[10] and the established
church in England should for the sake of national unity and peace make
concessions in liturgy and church government to those of its critics –
the moderate Presbyterians – who had no quarrel with it over doctrine.
This was the point of the campaign waged unsuccessfully, throughout
the '60s, for church 'comprehension' by friends of Pepys such as Bishop
Wilkins of Chester. Beyond the limits of that union, he favoured
toleration for all dissidents, provided they were peaceful. The Quakers
whom he saw carted off for worshipping illegally should have the
sense, he thought, either to conform or 'not be ketched'. He more than
once expressed the view that ecclesiastical disputes were futile. Religion
might turn out to be but a 'humour'; he himself was 'wholly
Scepticall'.[11] But he fell in easily with most of the observances required
of a practising Anglican. He attended his parish church with a moderate
regularity, sometimes twice on a Sunday, though there were times, as
in 1664, when he absented himself for no good reason for weeks on
end.[12] It may be significant (as has been observed)[13] that he went to
church more regularly after the Fire than before – such is often the
result of danger and disaster. At home he said grace before and after
meals,[14] and conducted prayers on most Sunday evenings, reading from
a silver-embossed Bible for the purpose. He kept his Sabbaths, on the
whole, with a quiet decency, working perhaps if business pressed hard,
but denying himself (in the early years of the diary) the pleasure of
secular music and often choosing for his reading Fuller's church history
or a chapter of the Bible. But he made little effort to observe Lent and
no effort at all to attend communion.[15]

If there were traces of a sort of Puritanism in him it was of a moralism
common enough among Anglicans of the period, and by no means
typical in itself of left-wing Protestantism. He disliked swearing, for

instance, disapproved of women who painted their faces or wore skirts above the ankle, and condemned card-playing on Sundays.[16] Most Puritan beliefs he abhorred or derided, insofar as he ever thought of them at all – surgeon Hollier's belief that the Pope was anti-Christ, or Aunt James's conviction that it was to the prayers of a fanatic preacher that Pepys owed his recovery from his operation.[17] For Pepys was first and last a worldling. At 23 July 1666 he reports a prayer wrung from him at the dinner table. 'Reflecting', he writes, 'upon the ease and plenty that I live in, of money, goods, servants, honour, everything, I could not but with hearty thanks to Almighty God ejaculate my thanks to him while I was at dinner, to myself'. If he lived 'pleasing to God', he thought on another occasion, he would be eased of 'much care, as well as much expense'.[18] He approved of the preacher who told him to cleave to righteousness as a 'surer moral way of being rich then sin and villainy'.[19] Similarly the vows he imposed on himself and enforced by fines for the poor-box were all designed to produce worldly success. They were usually to avoid wine, to cut down on theatres, to do more and more work. He read omnivorously, but never works of devotion. If he was bored by a sermon he might read the Bible but it would be the Book of Tobit. When he writes, after an admission that he has committed sin, 'God forgive me', he seems to mean little more than when, on reporting the arrival of a new camlet cloak, he adds 'I pray God to make me able to pay for it'.[20] He records scores of sermons, but no occasion in which they touched him. They were performances to be judged as he judged performances in the theatre. As for church services in general, the height of his experience is: 'A good sermon, a fine church, and a great company of handsome women'.[21] Even a personal crisis which he felt profoundly, like the death of his brother Tom, did not evoke a much deeper response. Pepys gave the dying man what confort he could, but it did not amount to more than asking him 'whither he thought he should go'.[22]

The Tangier diary of 1683–4 reveals much the same man as that of the '60s. He is constantly in the company of the saintly Ken, chaplain to the expedition, but has no words of admiration for him except when he preaches on political obedience.[23] It is true that he joined Ken in expressing horror at the indiscipline and immorality of the Tangier garrison. Dining with him on 23 Oct. 1683, 'a great deal of discourse we had upon the viciousness of this place and its being time for God Almighty to destroy it'.[24] Did Pepys really believe this? There is no more in this strain, and it may be that he is merely expressing Ken's views and a general agreement with them.

The evidence becomes a little clearer in the later years. There is a memorandum – undated but certainly from the '90s – in which Pepys in the manner of an old man shaking his head over the state of the world lists the signs he sees of the growth of 'publique depravity' – among them neglected religion and 'profane plays'[25] (like Jeremy Collier, whose books he bought). Even more expressive are the letters he exchanged with his friend Evelyn in 1700–1 in which the two old men speak to each other of the need to 'sit loose' to the concerns of this world and to prepare themselves for those of the next.[26]

The time came when Pepys had to make his specific preparations. From 1701 his health had been failing and he had moved from London to the country air of Clapham. On 23 Feb. 1703 he celebrated his 70th birthday – the fulfilment of his three score years and ten – and about that time and possibly in consequence of it, he wrote a letter to Robert Nelson, a leading layman in the nonjuring community of London. As a nonjuror himself (unwilling to take the oaths to William and Mary) Pepys's connections since 1689 had been increasingly, though by no means exclusively, with nonjuring churchmen, both lay and clerical. His letter to Nelson does not survive, but Nelson's reply (of 2 March) implies that Pepys had asked to be put in touch with a nonjuring clergyman within reach of Clapham. There were none of 'our clergy', Nelson wrote, nearer than the excellent Mr Higden of Mitcham. 'Our friend, Dean Hickes, is at present at Oxford; but if you will be pleased, whenever your occasions require it, to send to Mr Spinckes, who has the honour of being known to you, he will be sure to wait upon you, and take such measures that you may alwaies be supplied, whenever you stand in need of such assistance'.[27] Nathaniel Spinckes was a nonjuring clergyman of great learning and piety whose book on visiting the sick[28] became well-known. Spinckes however was not called on. Two months or so later, in Pepys's last illness, it was Dr Hickes who was sent for. George Hickes, one of the most remarkable historians and philologists in Europe, was the nonjuring Dean of Worcester and in 1695 was illegally consecrated Bishop of Thetford. Pepys had known him for many years and in 1685 had chosen him as preacher of the Trinity Monday service when he took office as Master of Trinity House.[29] They had corresponded on historical and other learned topics but never (to judge from the surviving letters) on religion. On Monday 24 May he arrived at Clapham. Jackson describes the events of the last two days of Pepys's life.[30] 'Monday afternoon came Dr Hickes, and prayed by him, he then lying on the couch; which done, the Doctor, taking him by the hand and finding his pulse very low, told him he had nothing to do but say "Come Lord Jesus, Come quickly". Upon which U[ncle] desired his prayers to God to shorten his misery . . .'. The next morning Pepys said farewell to Mary Skynner and Jackson and, on hearing that Dr Hickes had arrived again, 'ordred himselfe to be raised up in his bed, and the Doctor coming in performed the Office for the Sick, and gave him the Absolution, laying his hand upon his head.

The Service done, U[ncle] said, "God be gracious to me"; blessed the Dean and all of us, and prayed to God to reward us all.' By four on the following morning he had died.[31]

Reymes, Col. Bullen (1613–72). Pepys's colleague on the Fishery Corporation and the Tangier Committee. A Dorset landowner active in the trade of importing sailcloth from France; M.P. for Weymouth and Melcombe Regis 1660, 1661–72: responsible for obtaining money for the improvement of the harbour there. A friend of Penn, Coventry, Clifford and Ashley; a Commissioner for the Sick and Wounded in the Second and Third Dutch Wars; appointed Surveyor of the Wardrobe 1668. Elected F.R.S. 1667 on Evelyn's nomination.[1]

Reynolds, Capt. [Jacob] (d. by 1688). Naval officer; he served in the Commonwealth navy and held two commands 1664–6.[1]

Riccard, Ald. Sir Andrew, kt 1660 (d. 1672). Merchant, of St Olave's parish; patron of the living 1650–5; occupying a large house (17 hearths) on the w. side of Mark Lane;[1] a leading member of the Levant and E. India Companies; Master of the Drapers' 1652–3; Alderman 1651–3; M.P. for London 1654; appointed to the Council of Trade (1660), the Council for Foreign Plantations (1661) and the Committee of Trade (1669). He died very wealthy, leaving one child, a daughter married to Lord Berkeley of Stratton. Among his bequests was £50 to Daniel Milles, the Rector. There is a monument to him in the church.[2]

Richardson, [William]. Bookbinder; made free of the Stationers' Company in 1652. It is possible that he worked for John Cade and that he bound the diary. His son Edmond was made free by patrimony in 1687.[1]

Richmond, 3rd Duke and Duchess of: *see* Stuart, F. T.

Rider, Sir William, kt 1661 (d. 1669). Baltic merchant and navy contractor; member of the Tangier Committee and the committee of enquiry into the Chatham Chest from 1662, and of the Royal Fishery from 1664. He was considered for appointment as Commissioner at Harwich in 1664; Pepys preferred Capt. John Taylor. He had an imposing Elizabethan country house at Bethnal Green and was allowed by licence to drive his coach across the green to church.[1] At the time of the Fire, Pepys sent his valuables there (including his journal) for safekeeping. His wife was Priscilla, daughter of Roger Tweedy.[2]

Robartes, Sir John, 2nd Baron Robartes, cr. Earl of Radnor 1679 (1606–85). Pepys's chief as Lord Privy Seal, an office he held from 1661–73. A wealthy and influential West-country figure, he had fought on the parliamentary side as a Presbyterian in the Civil War but had withdrawn from politics in the 1650s, and like Sandwich and Crew formed one of the group of moderates who supported the cause of restoration in 1659–60. He was rewarded by a place on the Treasury commission and the post of Lord-Deputy of Ireland, but resigned the latter out of pique at not being made Lord-Lieutenant. At the Privy Seal, to which he was appointed in compensation, he was slow and obstructive. In 1669–70 he had a disastrous year as Ormond's successor as Lord-Lieutenant, and later served as Lord President of the Council 1679–84 and on the Tangier Committee. He was a morose and unsociable man, unpopular not only with Pepys but with almost everyone who knew him. He ceased to be a Presbyterian after 1660, but supported the cause of toleration of nonconformists. His London house was in Chelsea, opposite Crosby Hall.[1]

His eldest son, Robert, styled Viscount Bodmin from 1679, whose marriage to Sara Bodville drew Pepys's attention, died before his father, in 1682. He had been appointed ambassador to Denmark in 1681.[2]

[Robert, Anthony] (1593–1677). The anonymous Frenchman referred to at ix.507. Music and dancing master to Queen Henrietta-Maria 'for the space of forty years'[1] and owed £175 in wages at her death.[2] Retained his contacts with the French court; buried in Somerset House chapel.[3] (Lu)

Robins, Anthony. Messenger to the Council of State during the Commonwealth. He lived in Round Woolstaple, Westminster.[1]

Robins, Mrs. Possibly the Judy Robbins of Chatham who came as a housekeeper to Pepys for a few weeks in 1688.[1]

Robinson, [Henry] (1605–?73). Merchant and publicist; chiefly remarkable as the author of a large and interesting corpus of pamphlets produced during the revolution (many of them on his own printing press imported from Holland) in which he championed religious liberty and economic and social reform. One of his many schemes was for the creation of a national bank.[1]

Robinson, Ald. Sir John (1625–80). Lieutenant of the Tower 1660–79; a prominent merchant; Master of the Clothworkers' Company 1656–7. A relative of Laud and a strong royalist (a colonel in the Civil War), he is said to have had some part in bringing about the Restoration and in 1660 was given the key post of Lieutenant of the Tower, as well as a knighthood and baronetcy. He was Sheriff 1657–8 and Lord Mayor 1662–3, and sat as M.P. for the city in 1660 and for Rye in 1661–July 79. His wife, whom he married in 1634, was Anne, daughter of Sir G. Whitmore (Lord Mayor 1631–2). Their son John (1660–93) succeeded as 2nd Baronet.[1]

Robinson, Luke (1610–69). M.P. for N. Yorkshire constituencies in four parliaments 1645–60; Councillor of State 1649–51, 1659–60. After his dramatic conversion to the cause of monarchy (i.122) he was disabled from sitting in Parliament, but spared further punishment.[1]

Robinson, Sir Robert, kt 1675. Naval officer, holding 17 commands

1653–c. 82 and accounted 'stout and understanding' by Coventry. But never achieved flag rank. Pepys retained in his library Robinson's journals of two voyages in the *Assistance*, 1680–2. He is said to have been the son of a schoolmaster named Roberts but to have changed his name so that he could claim kinship with the Lieutenant of the Tower, and to have held dances on board ship when in harbour to prove his claim to be a gentleman-captain.[1]

Robson, [Thomas]. Clerk to Coventry for his Navy Office business (c. 1665–6); clerk in the Ticket Office (c. 1668). 'Cozen' of Edward Gregory, jun. Pepys once (ix.169) refers to him as Robinson.[1]

Roche, [Peter] de la. An 'operator for the teeth' to the King, practising near Fleet Bridge.[1] An elder of the French church in the city 1652–6.

Rochester, Earl of: *see* Wilmot, J.

Roettier(s), John (1631–1703). One of a talented family of medallists active in France, Spain and England in the 16th and 17th centuries. He left the Antwerp Mint in 1661 for London where he became chief engraver to the Mint until 1698. He was responsible for the new coinage of 1662, the new Great Seal of 1667, and the coronation medals of 1685 and 1689.[1]

Rogers, ——. A neighbour of Pepys in 1660; probably Matthew Rogers, who died in Oct. 1665.[1]

Rolls, Court of. On the e. side of Chancery Lane, where the Public Record Office now stands. The Rolls were the record rolls of the Court of Chancery, in the custody of the Master of the Rolls, who during the Commonwealth was replaced by the commissioners of the Great Seal. The buildings on the site included his official house, the Rolls Chapel and the court itself. The construction of the Public Record Office (1856–70) and the removal of the Rolls Court to the Law Courts in the Strand ended some 500 years of association between office and site. The Chapel was demolished when the Record Office was extended 1896–1900 but its chancel arch was re-erected in the courtyard. (R)

Rolt, Capt. [Edward]. Originally of Brampton; member of a family well known to Pepys and Mountagu,[1] and related to Cromwell (his mother being Mary, daughter of Sir Oliver Cromwell, the Protector's first cousin).[2] He had served in the army of the Eastern Association and became a prominent member of Cromwell's court as Gentleman of the Bedchamber. In 1655–6 he was sent as envoy to the King of Sweden.[3] The diary shows him as a friend of Harris the actor and as a lively and musically accomplished companion. The Ingoldsby in whose regiment he accepted a cornetcy in 1667 was his uncle by marriage.[4]

Rooth, Capt. [Richard] (d. by 1688). A 'stout' seaman, according to Coventry. He served under the Commonwealth and held 13 commissions 1661–80. The Mrs Rooth whom Pepys met at Penn's may have been his wife.[1]

Rothe, Sir John (1628–1702). The son of a rich Amsterdam merchant; knighted in Aug. 1660 for his services to the King in exile. He came to London in 1660 and married Nan, daughter of Samuel Hartlib, sen. He spent most of the rest of his life as a Millenarian evangelist in the United Provinces, preaching the Second Coming and hoping to unite the Protestant churches of Europe in preparation for it. The peak of his career came in 1672 when Holland was invaded by the French – an event he mistook for the end of the world. His denunciations of established authority were so uncompromising that even the tolerant Dutch were provoked into imprisoning him, from 1676–91. His wife died in 1679.[1]

Rotherhithe. Between Bermondsey and Deptford. The expansion of London eastwards had in 1660 long reached it and it had been regularly included in the Bills of Mortality since 1636. The buildings were mainly riparian and the village of nearly 400 houses (1664)[1] depended for its living on the river and the river industries.

The stairs of that name, 2290 yards below London Bridge,[2] were the first down-stream of the parish boundary, at the foot of Love Lane (approximately the modern Cathay St). (R)

Rouse, ——. Of Ashtead, Surrey; said to be the Queen's tailor. A 'Mr Rous' occupied a house there taxed on ten hearths in 1664. He is possibly the Lewis Roch, tailor to the Queen, who took out letters of denization in 1663 and still held the office in 1671–2.[1]

[Rowley, John]. Vicar of Brampton from 1664 and of Hemingford Abbots, Hunts. 1669–d. 88.[1]

THE ROYAL EXCHANGE

The first bourse in England and one of the principal buildings in the city. A quadrangular structure, situated in the angle formed by Threadneedle St and Cornhill, it had been built by Sir Thomas Gresham, and opened by the Queen in 1571. It was owned jointly by the city corporation and the Mercers' Company as trustees under Gresham's will. Its central courtyard, open to the sky and surrounded by a covered walk, was the place of business of the merchant community. The ground floor and the first storey (or 'pawn') were divided into shops selling mainly high quality and luxury wares. The whole property included 11 houses and some 135 shops.[1] Burnt in the Fire, it was rebuilt on an enlarged site to the design of Edward Jerman, the merchants returning in Sept. 1669 and the shopkeepers in March 1671. In the interval a temporary Exchange had been set up in Gresham College and the shopkeepers transferred there. By Anne's reign much of the merchants' business had

moved to the taverns and coffee-houses nearby, and many of the shop
stood empty. The second Exchange was destroyed by fire in 1838 and
the present one built shortly after.[2]

Pepys did a little shopping there and a great deal of newsgathering
It was usually his best source of information about shipping, nava
engagements, and foreign affairs. But his visits were primarily or
business for the Navy Board or the Tangier Committee – more ofter
than not (though he rarely gives details) concerned with shipping. He
went alone, without clerks or colleagues, and at noon, shortly before
dinner, when the morning exchange was at its height and the merchants
and shipowners he dealt with were likely to be there. He went only
twice to the evening exchange.[3] He once drafted a contract in a nearby
coffee-house,[4] but for the most part used his visits to gather information
and start negotiations. He reports at 24 June 1662 that he was becoming
known; in 1664 and thereafter, during the war, he must have become a
familiar figure.

The Royal Exchange is to be distinguished from the New Exchange
(q.v.) in the Strand which contained only shops. Pepys occasionally
refers to the Royal Exchange as the 'old' one (this during the Interregnum) or as the 'great' one.

(T. F. Reddaway; La)

THE ROYAL FISHERY

The English, though forward in the development of the Atlantic cod
fisheries, were slow to exploit the herring fishery of the North Sea,
which since the 15th century had been dominated by the Dutch. In the
17th century there was sent out annually from Holland and Zeeland
a great fleet of herring boats (or 'busses'), a thousand or more strong, to
fish the North Sea grounds from the north of Scotland to the Channel.
The whole operation was closely controlled by the College of the
Great Fishery with its headquarters at Delft. No nets were cast until
24 June when the fleet began to work off the Shetlands. Thereafter it
moved by fixed stages southwards, reaching the grounds off Yarmouth
by 25 September and the mouth of the Thames by December. No
fishing was allowed after January. At certain Scottish ports and at
Yarmouth facilities were provided locally for the drying and mending
of the nets. No fish could be sold by the fishermen themselves, the
entire catch being sent at intervals by transport vessels to the ports from
which the fleet had set out. There it was pickled by methods far
superior to those used in other countries, packed in barrels, and
registered, before being exported all over Europe. The Mediterranean

countries were, thanks to the Catholic fast days, a ready market. Even the Scandinavian countries bought Dutch herrings, thereby providing the Dutch with the currency with which to buy their naval stores.

Under Elizabeth publicists had urged the creation of a national fishery organisation to loosen the grip of the Dutch on the industry, and under James I the government began to take steps to that end. James had a special interest in the matter as King of Scotland, whose islands and small ports depended almost entirely on fishing for a livelihood. Moreover he was much given to defining and asserting his regalian rights. He claimed that the waters fished by the Dutch were part of his territory, and encouraged schemes for the development of the Scottish industry. At the same time, in England, writers on trade began to point out the necessity of breaking the Dutch monopoly if mercantile prosperity were to grow. But the task was beyond the resources of the fishing industry itself. The fishing boats alone (usually of about 100 tons) cost in the region of £1000 to build. Attempts were made in 1611 and 1613 to start national enterprises, but the first effective steps were taken in 1632 when an 'association', or joint-stock company, was formed. Money was to be raised to build the busses and to provide the large quantities of nets, salt and barrels that the operation demanded. The headquarters of the association were to be in the Isle of Lewis and the supply base at Deptford. But the association got off to a faltering start, failed to attract capital, and was virtually extinct by 1638. Fewer than 20 busses were built. Rather more successful was the other part of the enterprise – the attempt to enforce the claim that the Dutch were trespassing in British waters. There was no international agreement on the extent of territorial waters at this time, though sailors had often in practice adopted the convention that any waters in which land could be seen from their main-tops was territorial. But the lawyers, now brought into the debate by the competing governments, and having to address their arguments to the question of freedom of passage as well as freedom to fish, could not accept any such rule of thumb. Grotius, the Dutchman, argued in his *Mare Liberum* (1609) for complete freedom of the seas, while the Englishman Selden in his *Mare Clausum* (1635) claimed territoriality for all bordering waters up to the opposite foreign shore. Both James I and Charles I required the Dutch to buy licences to fish in the North Sea – Charles with some success since in the 1630s (thanks to the unpopular ship money) he had a fleet with which to enforce his claims.

During the disturbed years 1640–60 no English government had the opportunity to pursue a national fishery policy, and in the negotiations which followed the First Dutch War (1652–4) the Dutch successfully fought off Cromwell's claim that they should agree to pay for

licences. After the Restoration the attempts to set on foot an English
venture were renewed in the face of clear indications from the United
Provinces that they would resist any invasion of their interests. Advisers
such as Downing, English ambassador at The Hague, prompted the
government to action and in Aug. 1661 a Council of the Royal Fishery
was established by royal commission. It consisted mostly of courtiers
and was to arrange for the construction of a fleet of boats which were
to be paid for by a national lottery. By an act of 1663 Dutch methods of
pickling were made compulsory. The scheme however soon drooped
for lack of money, and a committee, on which Sandwich served, was
appointed by the Privy Council to make recommendations. As a
result in 1664 the Council of the Royal Fishery was converted by
charter into a corporation, or joint-stock company, which would raise
capital from subscribers. The Duke of York was appointed its governor,
and the Lord Mayor and Chamberlain of London its treasurers, while
the 36 assistants who comprised its governing body were chosen so as
to include representatives of the court, the navy and the mercantile
community of London. Among them were Sandwich and, at Sandwich's instance, Pepys. The diary in fact gives the best available account
of its not very exhilarating history. Pepys found that its meetings were
ill-attended and almost entirely concerned with the difficulty of raising
money. Like its predecessors the scheme failed to attract capital from
the city, which was nervous of flouting the Dutch, who since 1662 had
an agreement with the French to assist each other in defence of their
fishing rights. The Fishery Corporation was thrown back on expedients,
such as collections from the public, and proceeds from the issue of
licences authorising lotteries and the manufacture of farthings. Without
the backing of the city it was bound to fail. Moreover it had been
founded at an unfortunate moment. The outbreak of war with the
Dutch in 1665 quickly put an end to deep-sea fishing in the North Sea
by both nations. In the peace negotiations which followed, England
was in no position to enforce exclusive claims. Again, in 1674, after the
Third Dutch War, the Dutch were able to refuse to make any concessions.

Similar attempts were made in 1677 and 1692 to launch national
companies, only to meet similar fates. The last of the series was 'The
Society of Free British Fishing' founded by act of parliament in 1750
under the patronage of the Prince of Wales. It had its headquarters in
Southwold, Suff., and managed to build or buy 30 busses, but by 1772
was in liquidation. By that time the Dutch North Sea fishing was itself
in decline, in the face of competition from Denmark, Prussia and elsewhere. Britain's own share (no longer based on extravagant claims to
maritime sovereignty) was to be greatly increased by the development
in the 19th century of the large fishing boats of Scotland.[1]

The Royal Mews. A large area between Whitcomb St (then continued south as Hedge Lane) and St Martin's Lane at their junction at Charing Cross; now the site of the National Gallery and Trafalgar Sq. Much was occupied by the royal stables, which were as unworthy of royalty as Whitehall Palace itself. After their rebuilding in 1732 they still looked 'like a common inn yard'.[1] They were pulled down in 1830. There were also grace-and-favour lodgings in the area.[2]

The Royal Mint. In the Tower of London, in the eastern part, between the Beauchamp Tower and the Bell Tower. It was moved in 1810 to the e. side of Tower Hill, where it remained until 1969 when it was transferred to S. Wales.

THE ROYAL SOCIETY

It is clear that the scientific club which came into existence at the end of 1660 was the coalescence of several groups:[1] there were members of an Oxford circle dating back to about 1650, of which John Wilkins had been the prime organiser, such as John Wallis the mathematician, Robert Boyle the chemist and physicist, Christopher Wren (mathematician, astronomer, physiologist, microscopist and later architect) and Thomas Willis the medical scientist; there were men associated with Gresham College, among them the astronomer Lawrence Rooke, as well as a considerable number of physicians and mathematicians living in London, and there were also the royalists (some of whom had been in exile with Charles, while many more had simply lived quietly out of sight) of whom Sir Robert Moray and Viscount Brouncker proved the most influential. Virtually all the founders of the Royal Society were connected with mathematics, medicine or science either by profession or by strong inclination; of the latter many were also connected with the court, and it was they who enlisted the King's patronage of the new Society.

For if the first intent was simply to institute an organised club (each member paying a weekly shilling towards its expenses) more ambitious designs soon took shape. The establishment of an accurate natural history, the reformation of natural philosophy, were costly objectives seeming to require correspondence, rewards, expeditions, instruments and apparatus, buildings, a museum and library and so on. If state aid were secured an ample programme of collection and research could be begun, possibly somewhat on the lines of 'Salomon's House' in Bacon's *New Atlantis*. The philosophers set out to woo the King, and also to secure their position. They asked for few positive privileges (the right to dissect human bodies, for example) but the advantage of a legal and corporate standing was obvious enough. Hence the club of virtuosi became on 15 July 1662, with the sealing of their charter, The Royal Society; a name amplified in the second, revised Charter of 22 Apr. 1663 to The Royal Society of London for the Promotion of Natural Knowledge (*Regalis Societas Londini pro Scientia naturali promovenda*). This second charter increased the Society's privileges and brought its governing Council into existence. It was to be in turn revised in 1669. Thus, although the club went back to 1660, the true Fellowship of the Royal Society is normally taken to date from the creation of the original Council (22 Apr. 1663) and the constitution of the original list of fellows (20 May 1663). As a permanent memorial the charters were inscribed in a Charter-book in Jan. 1665 'nobly writ', said Pepys when he inspected it on the 9th, 'to be signed by the Duke [of York] as a Fellow; and all the Fellows' hands were to be entered there, and lie as a monument; and the King hath put his with the word Founder'. (This still exists, and is still signed.) There were 115 original councillors and fellows, increased by 24 further elections in 1663, 25 in 1664, and seven in 1665 before Pepys himself signed the Charter-book on 15 February (among the signatories being the King and the Duke). In this Society of under 200 members – which included some highly distinguished foreign fellows such as Christiaan Huygens and Johannes Hevelius – Pepys's acquaintance was already wide. Besides those already mentioned, he would notice in the Charter-book the names of John Dryden 'the poet I knew at Cambridge', John Wilkins, Henry Oldenburg the secretary with whom he had already had fine discourse at the coffee-house, Peter Pett the shipwright, Dr Alexander Fraizer (to whom Pepys gave an ill repute), Lord (George) Berkeley, Sir Ellis Leighton and Clarendon, the Lord Chancellor, all of whom were very familiar to him. So that when Pepys was proposed as a candidate for the Fellowship by Povey on 8 Feb. 1665 his name was not unknown, and a week later he was unanimously elected and admitted.

Why did Pepys become a virtuoso? Partly because fashion and the taste of the time that he shared drew him towards such things. He was now closely associated in business with the Society's President, Brouncker, whom he had begun to respect, and with others like Creed or Povey who (seemingly) at least wished to see the Society prosper. Pepys was clever, suggestible, and obviously rather bored by his home life and family friends when not plunged in navy business. But he had a strong natural appetite for knowledge. The diary shows how he took to serious scientific books to fill his mind and how much he delighted in good scientific conversation.

Why was Pepys elected to the Royal Society? The answer is obvious enough. Few of the fellows, even at its foundation, were profoundly learned in mathematics, medicine or science, though a good number no doubt had more proficiency than Pepys. There were many other

Creeds and Poveys, while virtually all the members of the nobility did nothing for the Society at all. As Pepys had already seen (on 1 Feb. 1664), even the Royal Founder mightily laughed at Gresham College 'for spending time only in weighing of ayre, and doing nothing else since they sat'. While there was something serious in Charles's attitude to his Royal Society beneath this frivolous incomprehension, he conspicuously failed to give it such slight practical support as would have been within his powers.

It would be a mistake, then, to suppose that on any grounds of intellectual seriousness Pepys might have been found wanting; certainly he was more serious than most, and it must also have been obvious to those more learned in the sciences than he, that Pepys was no fool at business, that he was not a rogue, and that he was not without influence. The Society was eager to grasp all support, and Pepys was a promising recruit – it must be remembered too that Pepys's official position was one of potential value to the Society. The navy could provide information about the sea, ships, tides, and navigation; the navy could provide transport; and perhaps maritime affairs would prove the field wherein the Society might display some utilitarian triumph of scientific knowledge.[2] Pepys was a rising and useful man – and his purely human qualities must also have had their effect.

Certainly Pepys's association with the virtuosi grew closer in the course of 1664. After sympathising with Petty in face of the royal ridicule in February, by April (14th) he listened with interest to Creed's account of Hooke's experiments on the expansion and contraction of glass by heat and cold. On 16 May he witnessed some seemingly mismanaged experiments by Timothy Clarke and the surgeon James Pearse to determine the effects of opium on dogs (making also himself some physiological experiments on dogs that were equally fruitless). On 10 Aug. 1664 he accompanied his learned naval colleague Silas Taylor to the Post Office to hear the music-teacher and viol player Birchensha perform in the presence of two leaders of the Royal Society, Lord Brouncker and Sir Robert Moray, and later in the summer he took up microscopy. On 5 October, after meeting Oldenburg at the coffeehouse, he went again to the 'Musique-meeting at the post office' where two of Pepys's pleasures united, for 'thither anon come all the Gresham College [the Royal Society], and a great deal of noble company' to hear the 'Arched Viall' (an unsuccessful attempt to sound strings by a keyboard). Towards Christmas he was out like the virtuosi (and indeed most other men) looking for the comet of 1664–5. Early in January, having some time previously instructed Viscount Brouncker in the duties of his new post as a Commissioner ('so he is become my disciple'), he not only had occasion to admire Peter Pett's knowledge of shipwrightry ('a man of an extraordinary ability in any thing') but saw that

Brouncker was 'a very able person also himself . . . as owning himself to be a master in the business of all lines and Conicall Sections'.[3]

After his admission to the Royal Society on 15 Feb. 1665, when he saw some experiments on combustion made with the air-pump and participated in 'a club supper' at the Crown Tavern, Pepys was assiduous in attendance at Gresham College for some weeks, not missing a single Wednesday until 29 March. He heard Robert Hooke's second lecture on the recent comet, suggesting that it was the same as that of 1618,[4] and enjoyed other 'fine discourses – and experiments' of which he lamented, however, 'I do lack philosophy enough to understand them'.[5] He also saw some experiments on the action of poisons, and on respiration. But his involvement in the Dutch War (and the profits to be made from it), followed by the Plague and the disruption of the Royal Society's meetings (the largest group of its members assembled with the court at Oxford), banished philosophy from his thoughts. The diary only records an examination of new single-horse chariots devised by Thomas Blount and by Hooke, but Pepys further improved his acquaintance with Brouncker (who one day entertained Pepys in slightly odd fashion by taking his watch to pieces and re-assembling it) and with John Evelyn. If Pepys found the latter a little conceited, conceit was allowable in so excellent a man, whose conversation about botany and painting he much enjoyed, though his version of Naudé's *Instructions* for building a library Pepys (who was to create one) found above his reach.

A pleasing picture of the Royal Society in session during these early days is given by Samuel Sorbière, who visited London in 1663:

The Room where the Society meets [at Gresham College] is large, and Wainscotted; there is a large Table before the chimney, with Seven or Eight Chairs covered with Green-cloth about it, and Two Rows of Wooden and Naked Benches to lean on, the First being higher than the other, in form like an Amphitheatre. The President . . . sits at the middle of the Table in an Elbow Chair, with his back to the Chimney. The Secretary sits at the End of the Table on his left Hand, and they have each of them Pen, Ink and Paper before them. I saw nobody sit on the Chairs . . . All the other Members take their Places as they think fit, and without any Ceremony; and if any one comes in after the Society is fixed, no Body stirs but he takes a Place presently where he can find it, that no Interruption may be given to him that speaks. The President has a little Wooden Mace in his Hand, with which he strikes the Table when he would command Silence; They address their Discourse to him bare-headed, till he makes a Sign for them to put on their Hats; and there is a Relation given in few Words of what is thought proper to be said concerning the Experiments proposed by the Secretary. There is no body here eager to speak, that makes a long Harangue, or intent upon saying all he knows: He is never interrupted that speaks, and Differences of Opinion cause no manner of Resentment, nor as much as a disobliging Way of Speech: There is nothing seemed to me to be more civil, respectful, and better managed than this Meeting.[6]

The interval in the Royal Society's meetings caused by the Plague and the consequent abandonment of the capital by polite society lasted almost eight months. Pepys missed the Society's first ordinary meeting after the Plague, not held until 14 March 1666. Much earlier, however, on 22 January, he had been present at the virtuosi's first 'club supper' following their reassembly in town, again at the Crown, where he seems to have thought little of Dr Jonathan Goddard's attempted defence of the physicians' flight from the stricken city after their well-to-do patients, but to have been much impressed by Sir George Ent's conversation about respiration. Ent evidently felt that the subject was a very dark one, and indeed the Royal Society was to devote many experiments and discourses to its elucidation. The chief dispute was between those who held that the air inspired only refrigerated the blood, and those who held that some interaction between air and blood took place. Lower was the first to demonstrate clearly (1669) that it is the air in the lungs that causes venous blood to change into arterial blood. On this festive occasion Dr Christopher Merrett, a learned physician and chemist, got quite drunk. Further, on 21 February Pepys went to Gresham College itself to hear another Cutlerian lecture by Hooke (his second, apparently, on the subject of felt-making) and enjoyed a private conversation with him. There are no more significant references to the Society, or to the reading of scientific books, during the next busy months – only records of a call from Hooke to collect materials on shipbuilding for use in John Wilkins's universal language, and of a conversation with Brouncker on optics after they had dined in company with Dr Walter Charleton, who had talked of the correlation between an animal's diet and the form of its teeth. Soon afterwards, however, Pepys's curiosity was stirred anew by the optical instrument-maker Richard Reeve. But the moment was not propitious. Continued pressure of business and a series of attacks upon the Navy Office, and to crown all the destruction of London by fire, rendered the summer of 1666 almost as desperate for Pepys as for many other citizens of London. He had no time for the Royal Society, which was itself put into difficulties by the commandeering of Gresham College to serve as an Exchange instead of Gresham's destroyed Royal Exchange. The Society was not settled again until it moved to Arundel House in Jan. 1667 by courtesy of the Hon. Henry Howard ('of Norfolk' as he always signed himself that there might be no mistake of his ducal descent) whose admission to the Royal Society Pepys witnessed on 28 November. This, the election meeting, was the only one

Pepys attended during this period. He was impressed by Howard's generosity in presenting his grandfather's library to the Society, and 'undertaking to make his house the seat for this College'. Indeed, Howard proposed to give land for a permanent building of the Society's own, of which Wren was to be the architect, but this project (to the infinite impoverishment of the Strand) was never realised.

Still, Pepys heard a little of the Society's doings. At supper on 14 Nov. 1666 he learned from Dr William Croone of the Society's early experiments on transfusing blood between dogs – experiments begun long before by Wren and Richard Lower, which led finally to the earliest experiments of the kind on a man. The first Englishman to undergo the experiment, in Nov. 1667, was one Arthur Coga, a 'poor and a debauched man' as Pepys was told, even if he had been 'a kind of minister'; or as Pepys thought himself 'cracked a little in his head, though he speaks very reasonably and very well'.[7] Despite some ill effects he survived the ordeal, as indeed the dogs on which the first experiments were made are said to have done. The idea behind transfusion at this time was that sickness originates in 'bad blood'; replace this by healthy blood and the patient will make a fresh start. No one then imagined that there are important differences between the blood of different individuals of the same species, not to say individuals of different species. As there are quite a number of reports of transfusion experiments about this time – they were tried extensively at Paris, and at Rome and in Germany too – with little evidence of the occurrence of shock and severe after-effects, it seems likely that the difficulty of the technique generally impeded the passage of blood from one individual to another. In one instance, however, a transfused human patient *did* die (c. 30 Jan. 1668) – though it is not at all certain that transfusion was the cause, he had certainly suffered severe damage from it – and after this the practice fell into ill repute. It is unfortunate that Pepys only gives secondhand accounts of the actual experiments in England, but nevertheless his reports constitute an important part of the evidence.

As the Dutch War continued, Pepys had little leisure for intellectual pleasure though frequently tempted by fleshly ones. Accordingly five months passed before the change in the day of the Society's meeting at Arundel House from Wednesday to Thursday (on 25 Jan. 1667) became known to him; he gives the reason (not stated in the Society's minutes) as the clash with the King's Council, also meeting on Wednesday. Forewarned, at any rate on this occasion, he did present himself after this long absence to the assembly on 30 May 1667 at which the Royal Society entertained the 'antic' (i.e. crazy) Duchess of Newcastle regarded by herself alone as the intellectual marvel of the age, whom he had seen a few days earlier attended by hooting street urchins. Though forming no high opinion of the lady, Pepys seems to have enjoyed the experimental demonstrations, particularly one of Boyle's in which a piece of roasted mutton was dissolved into 'pure blood'. A month later on 25 June he was distressed to learn that the Society's Secretary, Henry Oldenburg, had been carried off to the Tower [upon Lord Arlington's warrant], 'which makes it very unsafe at this time to write, or almost do anything'. Pepys was told that Oldenburg had been imprisoned for writing news to a virtuoso in France, but the evidence now available suggests rather that he had been guilty of expressing with some imprudence – as Pepys himself did in his diary – his belief that the nation's disasters were caused by her ministers' negligence. Having apologised in due form, he was released on 26 August and gained even greater privileges than before. However, he did cease to write about politics.

During that stormy summer of national disgrace in 1667 when the Dutch fleet invaded the Medway, there was only leisure for quiet reading of scientific books, often during evening excursions upon the river. The Royal Society was in any case usually in recess from July until October or November, when once again Pepys presented himself at Arundel House. This lack of activity was not, it seems, wholly voluntary: on 14 November he wished he could accompany Creed to a meeting, just as, on the 30th, he would have welcomed election to the Council, if he had enjoyed leisure to attend it. Between these two dates, arriving too late for the meeting at Arundel House, he joined the 'club supper' (where there was more talk of politics than science, except for some on transfusion). He was there again after the anniversary meeting, having a good talk with Wilkins.

During the next many months the Society was rather a cause of loss to Pepys than profit. On 12 March 1668 he did indeed 'show himself' again there, and was congratulated on his recent great defence of the Navy Office before Parliament and saw some experiments with burning-glasses made by the optician Francis Smethwick 'which was mighty pretty'. A few weeks later he went again to try the ear-trumpet or otacousticon ('only a great glass bottle, broke at the bottom'), but – more important – was forced to write his name down for a gift of £40 towards the Society's new buildings. (Others gave less, some more, and others hung back altogether, so Pepys feared the collection would be a source of ill-will.) At this time, having been ousted from the convenient hospitality of Gresham College, the Royal Society pressed particularly hard for an endowment to enable it to build on the land which Henry Howard had offered at Arundel House, in the Strand. When Chelsea College, an ancient but decayed church foundation, was begged from the King the claims of sitting tenants were found to make it valueless. Hence the whip-round among the Society's own members. Much was promised, but as the sum seemed insufficient to begin building, none was ever called in. In any case, it seems that Henry Howard was unable to secure the breach of entail that would have enabled him to alienate land to the Royal Society.

Before the next anniversary meeting of the Society on 30 Nov. 1668 (upon which he has no comment) Pepys only attended one further session, that of 16 July at which trial was made of an experiment devised by the Danish anatomist Steno (then living at Florence under the patronage of the Grand Duke of Tuscany): an artery near the spine was ligated so as to render a dog insensible. The Society had had great difficulty with this experiment, carried out on the present occasion by Dr King, to the point of even doubting Steno's account of it. However, at Brouncker's request Pepys did on 21 October endeavour to be one of a group paying a courtesy call on the French ambassador; that Pepys arrived too late mattered the less as the ambassador was not at home.

After the election of November 1668 Pepys had during the remainder of the diary period no more direct contact with the Royal Society, though fairly often in touch with the virtuosi. In 1672 he was elected to the Council for the first time, and two years later was a member of a small committee appointed to invest a legacy from John Wilkins. His administrative gifts and his wealth were often at the Society's service both before and after his two years as President (1684–6). And in the later years of his retirement he continued to enjoy visits at York Buildings and Clapham from his scientific friends, among them Isaac Newton.[8] [*See also* Gresham College; Science; Scientific Instruments]

(A. Rupert Hall)

Ruddiard, [Thomas]. Teller to the Excise Commissioners.[1]

Rumbold. Most of Pepys's references are to William (d. 1667), who had served in the Wardrobe from 1629. He was a royalist agent in the Interregnum and became joint-Clerk of the Wardrobe in 1660 (with his 'cousin' Thomas Townshend), and Comptroller in 1662. His widow Mary died shortly after him. The 'Rumball' at vii.23 may be the same man, but the fact that he visits Pepys with Col. Norwood of Tangier suggests that he may be William's nephew Henry, Storekeeper at Tangier and, with Norwood, one of the prize commissioners there.[1]

Rundell(s), [Edward] (d. 1667). Appointed house carpenter at Deptford and Woolwich yards in 1660.[1]

Rupert (Robert), Prince (1619–82). Son of Frederick Elector Palatine and Elizabeth, daughter of James I; cousin of Charles II. He lives in popular memory as the dashing and quarrelsome cavalry leader of the Civil War; in fact he was also a dashing and quarrelsome seaman and spent the greater part of his career in naval service – as commander of the royalist navy (1648–52), as a fighting admiral in the two Dutch

Wars of Charles's reign, and as First Commissioner of the Admiralty 1673–9. His achievements in the first phase of his naval career were considerable and out of all proportion to the size of his forces, which amounted to little more than a squadron. He lacked a proper base and had to improvise his organisation and supplies. Although some successes eluded him – he was unable to prevent Cromwell's invasion of Ireland in 1649 and sailed to the W. Indies in 1652–3 too late to save Barbados for the royalists – he conducted an effective running campaign against the republic's merchantmen in the Atlantic, the Mediterranean and the Caribbean and supported himself largely by taking prizes. After the Restoration, he held admiral's rank and was unlucky not to be preferred to Sandwich as Commander-in-Chief in the later part of the 1665 campaign against the Dutch. He fought with both skill and courage throughout most of the campaigns of the two Dutch Wars, without achieving any spectacular victory for which he could claim the credit. His complaint at the close of the fighting season of 1666, when he had served as joint-commander with Albemarle, that the navy had been hamstrung by the inefficiency of the civilian administration ashore brought him into head-on collision with Pepys. No doubt the fault lay at bottom with lack of money, but Pepys was wrong to impute so much of the blame for the condition of the fleet to the commanders. Pepys's low opinion of Rupert – which is expressed as early as 1660, before the days of his rivalry with Sandwich – was probably unjust. Rupert was an able organiser as well as a superb fighter, and in other respects a not inconsiderable figure. He took an active part in the affairs of Tangier, as Pepys himself makes clear in the diary, and, in the '70s, in those of the Hudson's Bay Company and the Council for Trade and Plantations. He was well known for his interest in science and drawing.[1]

Rushworth, John (?1612–90). Historian and public servant; a kinsman of Fairfax, the parliamentary general. In the diary period he held the posts of clerk to the Council of State (March–May 1660), and Treasury solicitor (1661–5); previously he had been clerk-assistant to the House of Commons (1640–8), and secretary to Fairfax and the Council of War (1645–50). M.P. for Berwick in six parliaments 1657–83. His Yorkshire birth and connections explain his interest in the Derwentdale Plot (iv.377). Nowadays best known for his *Historical Collections* (7 vols, 1659–1701), in which he assembled materials relating to the political history of the period 1618–49. He died miserably, suffering from total amnesia.[1]

Russell, Henry. Waterman to the Navy Office; alive in 1688.[1]

Russell, Col. [John] (d. 1687). Third son of Francis Russell, 4th Earl of Bedford. From Nov. 1660 in command of the 1st Regiment of Foot (the Grenadiers). Pepys mentions his presence at a court ball. According to Gramont he was 'one of the most desperate dancers in all England for country dances . . . He had a printed list of three or four hundred varieties, which he danced with the open book before him . . . His way of dancing resembled the fashion of his clothes; both were twenty years out of date'.[1]

Russell, Robert the elder (1600–63). Of St Dunstan's-in-the-East; appointed ship's chandler to the Navy, July 1660. In his will he asked that his funeral sermon be preached by his dear friend George Gifford, Rector of St Dunstan's, and failing him, by Daniel Milles of St Olave's. After his death his widow Elizabeth carried on the business. She later married Ald. Sir G. Waterman.[1]

Russell, Maj. [Robert]. Of Bride Lane, Salisbury Court; he lived in a house taxed on eight hearths next door to the Pepyses.[1]

Russell, Sir William, 1st Bt (d. 1654). Treasurer of the Navy under Charles I.[1]

Russell, ——. The donor of the 'great cake' (viii.19) was probably Peter Russell, master ropemaker at Woolwich yard. But John Russell, timber purveyor to the Navy, is a possibility.[1]

Rutherford, Andrew, cr. Baron Rutherford 1661, Earl of Teviot 1663 (d. 1664). A Roman Catholic and a professional soldier, of Scottish birth; Colonel of the Gardes Ecossaises in the French army in the 1650s; Governor of Dunkirk 1660–2 and of Tangier 1663–4. His heir was a relative, Sir Thomas Rutherford of Hunthill, who succeeded to the barony by nomination, the earldom becoming extinct.[1]

SABBATH OBSERVANCE

Pepys's early life, before 1660, coincided with a period when the laws and conventions on this subject in England were becoming stricter. In Elizabethan times, although inns and taverns were closed during service hours, it had been common for Sundays to be used for parish games (bull- and bear-baiting among them) or performances by strolling players. By Charles I's reign a reaction had set in. A statute of 1625 forbade interludes, common plays, and bull- and bear-baiting on Sundays and made it illegal to attend assemblies outside one's own parish for any games or pastimes.[1] Another act of 1627 laid penalties on carriers and butchers who plied their trades on Sundays.[2] In 1633 – the year of Pepys's birth – the government had to reissue James I's Book of Sports which permitted parishioners to play lawful games outside service hours (archery, for instance, which was orderly and of military use, but not football which was neither). It was by this time clear that the official attempt to encourage approved Sunday sports (if only to keep men from talking politics in the tavern) was meeting increasingly strong resistance from Puritan opinion which equated Sunday with the Hebrew Sabbath and demanded that it should be entirely devoted to public and private devotions.

In the '40s and '50s the Puritans attempted to introduce their New Jerusalem. An ordinance of Jan. 1645 enjoined abstention not only from sports and pastimes but from 'all worldly words and thoughts', and urged heads of families to employ their Sunday leisure in catechising members of their households.[3] This was clearly unenforceable, but although the laws could not be completely put into effect, there is no doubt that they achieved much of their aim. They imposed a series of prohibitions, not all of them novel, on Sunday work, travel, sports and public entertainments. Inns and taverns were to be closed during service hours, and shops and markets for the whole day. Of the street vendors only milkmaids were allowed to cry their wares, and they only in the early morning and late afternoon. The most comprehensive of the acts was that of 1657, which included a clause forbidding secular music in private houses[4] – yet another unenforceable rule, of course, but one which probably coincided with the views of many private citizens.

Pepys himself had clearly been brought up to a strict observance of the Sabbath. In the early years of the diary he expresses guilt if on a Sunday he strings his lute or composes a secular tune, or reads a French romance. Although he could now, as a government official, escape the general prohibition against the hire of boats, horses and coaches on Sundays, it was rare that he did so. (The trip to Epsom on 14 July 1667 was one such exception and he was punctilious in going to church there before taking his dinner.) He felt guilty on 7 Apr. 1661 about working on Sunday, even though the work did not prevent him from 'putting in' at St Paul's to hear part of a sermon. This particular inhibition weakened from about 1664 onwards when he found it necessary and not shameful to use some part of Sunday, or even the whole of it, for work. At first it was on his private accounts, then his Tangier accounts and finally, with the war, the defences were down and he allowed work of all sorts to invade his day of rest whenever necessary, without feeling any need to justify himself. In 1668 his great speech to parliament and his great letter on the reorganisation of the office were both prepared on Sundays. After all, the Privy Council and Cabinet often met on the Sabbath.

The old Sabbatarian laws of pre-Civil War days had automatically come back into effect with the Restoration and were reinforced by a proclamation of 1663.[5] But with a difference. No attempt was now made by authority to defend Sunday sports. In this respect churchmen – even high churchmen – might have said 'We are all Puritans now'. Calling in several churches on 9 Nov. 1662, Pepys observed that Sunday was kept as well as ever. He was also to find that it was not only his clerk the Anabaptist Tom Hayter who objected to work on Sundays but also the ex-Cavalier Sir Philip Warwick, secretary to the Lord Treasurer. His friend in later life, the nonjuring Dean Hickes of Worcester, was among those Anglican moralists who took the puritan line that the whole of Sunday – not just the hours of service – should be kept holy.[6] The House of Commons at intervals pressed for more stringent regulations and in 1677 an act was passed tightening up the prohibitions on Sunday work which remained the basis of the statutory law on the subject until well on in the 19th century.[7]

St Albans, 1st Earl of: *see* Jermyn, H.

St Botolph's Wharf. An important wharf with a lane serving it south out of (Lower) Thames St opposite the end of Botolph's Lane and on the e. side of St Botolph's, Billingsgate. The church was not rebuilt after its destruction in the Fire. (R)

St James's Fields. The open space west of the Haymarket and north of Pall Mall covered now by St James's Sq and adjacent streets. Also known in the '60s as Pall Mall Field. Regarded in the '50s as ripe for development, hitherto forbidden by the Crown. In 1651 Hugh Woodward bought the fields from the trustees for the sale of Charles I's lands, and building began. In March 1661 the 1st Earl of St Albans, a trustee on behalf of Henrietta-Maria, the Queen Mother, was granted a lease of it, followed in Apr. 1665 by a grant of the freehold of about half the fields including the site of St James's Sq. Development was comparatively rapid.[1] [*See also* St James's Sq.; Pall Mall] (R)

St James's Palace. Acquired by Henry VIII from the Hospital of St James 'for leper maidens', and, with St James's Park, ringed by a brick wall uniting it to Whitehall Palace. The lack of a contemporary plan and the destruction of a large part by fire in 1809 make it impossible to locate the galleries mentioned by Pepys. Used by the army in the last years of the Commonwealth, it was fitted up as the Duke of York's principal residence at the Restoration. He and his Duchess occupied the garden front where they were said to be more handsomely lodged than the King and Queen. A new range of buildings and a stable block were added in the '60s. It became the Queen's residence in the reign of James II and after Whitehall was destroyed by fire in 1698 the principal royal residence until George III acquired what became Buckingham Palace.[1]

The Chapel (now known as Marlborough House Chapel), designed by Inigo Jones, was fitted out for Catholic worship and used by Henrietta-Maria and after 1662 by Catherine of Braganza. It lay at the end of an easterly wing of the palace, now destroyed. During the Commonwealth it was used as a library.[2] Queen Catherine carried out extensive repairs and greatly embellished it, largely at her own expense, adding an altarpiece by Huysmans and carvings by Grinling Gibbons. After 1700 it was used by congregations of foreign Protestants.[3]

The friary which Pepys visited was built at the Queen's charge to house the Portuguese Observant Franciscans who served the Chapel. It was built as a single quadrangle to the east of the Chapel, and to some extent rebuilt after a fire in 1682. It was later demolished to make room for the house built by the 1st Duke of Marlborough.[4]

St James's Park. Formed and walled in by Henry VIII, transformed by Charles II and much modified by George IV. The diary has many references to its use by the King and his circle, to the degree of semi-privacy preserved there, and to the great alterations in its lay-out made in the '60s, but no set of plans of those alterations has yet appeared. It contained at this time a lake and canal, a physic garden and several deer-houses.[1] (R)

St James's Sq. A large and fashionable square whose development began in earnest when, in 1662, the 1st Earl of St Albans received from the Queen Mother an extension until 1720 of his existing lease of St James's or Pall Mall Fields. In Apr. 1665, despite strong opposition (especially from the Lord Treasurer Southampton, who was a rival developer) St Albans obtained a grant of the freehold of over 11 acres on which and on his adjacent leaseholds he proposed a piazza, or square, of 13 or 14 houses, with subsidiary streets and a large covered market, a plan similar to that of the Earl of Southampton's estate in Bloomsbury. Building the square itself met with opposition and difficulties but St Albans in 1665 began his own house there. It was rated in 1667, and others followed during the next ten years.[1]

Of the remainder of St Albans's development plan, the market has now gone, but Jermyn St and St Albans St survive the alterations made by the construction of Nash's Regent St. (R)

St John, Oliver (?1597–1673). Lawyer and politician; related by marriage to Oliver Cromwell; 'my Lord' by virtue of his judicial office and membership of the Council of State in 1659–60. He had been a leading protagonist of the parliamentary cause against Charles I, but on becoming Chief Justice of Common Pleas in 1648 ceased to be closely involved in politics, using his judicial position and his ill health to distance himself from them. He refused to sit on the tribunal which tried the King and although accepting office from Cromwell as Councillor of State and Treasury Commissioner took little part in their proceedings. He was reputedly a 'Protectorian' in 1659–60 but was secretly in favour of a restoration of monarchy. He was declared incapable of office in 1661, and retired into private life. In Nov. 1662 – shortly after Pepys saw him at church – he went into exile in Germany.[1]

St Katharine's. A precinct immediately east of the Tower, belonging to St Katharine's Hospital (founded in the 12th century), it contained some 24 acres, over 1000 inhabitants and an important river frontage, the whole forming a privileged community ruled by the Master of the Hospital and exempt by reason of its charters and its royal patronage from control by most of the normal authorities. The Masters in 1661–85 were, successively, George Mountagu and Lord Brouncker. When the hospital was removed in 1825 to Regent's Park to allow the construction of St Katharine's Dock, the precinct ceased to exist.[1] (R)

St Martin's Lane, Westminster. A 'very spacious' lane[1] running north out of the Strand, east of Charing Cross past the church of St Martin-in-the-Fields towards that of St Giles. The section south of St Martin's church is now absorbed in Trafalgar Sq. By the '60s the fields were things of the past, the Lane being built on both sides. (R)

St Martin's [le Grand]. A 'considerable street'[1] running north from the end of Blowbladder St (now merged in Cheapside and Newgate St) to Aldersgate. Pepys refers to it by the current abbreviation 'St Martins'; it was also known as St Martin's Lane.

St Michel, Alexander and Dorothea. Parents of Elizabeth Pepys. The father, born Alexandre le Marchant de St Michel, was the son and heir of a gentleman or minor nobleman of Anjou. As a young man he had been converted to Protestantism while fighting in the German wars and was disinherited in consequence. He thereupon crossed to England on being appointed to the household of Queen Henrietta-Maria as a gentleman carver. But he was dismissed for having assaulted one of the Queen's friars in the course of a religious argument, and is next heard of in Ireland where he met and married, in about 1639, Dorothea (b. 1609) widow of Thomas Fleetwood of co. Cork and daughter of Sir Francis Kingsmill, a Devonshire landowner who had served in Ireland under Sir George Carew and had acquired Ballybeg Abbey, co. Cork. From her mother she claimed relationship with the Cliffords, Earls of Cumberland; from her father she inherited property near Bideford, where her children, Elizabeth and Balty, are said to have been born. Alexander's movements in the '40s and '50s are difficult to trace. He is said to have fought in France and Flanders in 1648–9, and later under Cromwell in Ireland. His wife and children were in Paris in 1652 when an attempt was made to convert them to Catholicism, but by 1655 were back in London where Pepys married Elizabeth, who was then living in the parish of St Martin-in-the-Fields with her family, possibly at Charing Cross.[1] In 1662 they moved to new lodgings in Covent Garden and by 1664 to an 'ill-looked' place in Long Acre 'among all the bawdy-houses' (v.50). Alexander was restless – he planned to join the Imperial army to fight the Turks, and in 1667–8 visited Paris with his wife, presumably in search of his lost inheritance. Meantime, having in Balty's phrase a head 'Full of wheemesis',[2] he occupied himself with delusions of the wealth that would come from his inventions. He designed a machine for perpetual motion and took out patents for curing smoky chimneys, for keeping pond water clean and fit for horses to drink, and for manufacturing ornamental bricks in moulds.[3] In reality he had to content himself with occasional jobs (such as ruling office paper for Pepys), a small pension from the French church in the Savoy and an allowance from his son. Pepys prudently tried to keep clear of him. He never visited the St Michels nor they him.

According to Balty, his father was a tall man of striking presence and courtly ways. He died in 1672; his widow was still alive in 1674.[4]

St Michel, Balthasar and Esther. Balty, son of Alexander; Pepys's brother-in-law. An 'absurd, posturing, melodramatic egotist' in Richard Ollard's words,[1] he yet managed under Pepys's guidance to make a success in the naval service by virtue of sheer brashness and energy. He expected to be put on the way to becoming a gentleman-captain when Pepys was made Clerk of the Acts. Instead he had to serve in the Dutch army for a year or so, after which Pepys found him a place in the Guards. The outbreak of war gave him his chance. Pepys was prepared to risk having him made a muster-master on board the fleet (1666–8) and he proved a successful one. In the Third Dutch War he was made muster-master again, this time ashore, at Deal, and a sub-commissioner of the Sick and Wounded. His next appointment, as Muster-Master and Surveyor of the Victualling at Tangier, with some responsibility for stores at Gibraltar, was less happy. He regarded it as being 'sent to the Divill',[2] postponed his departure until 1680 and came home two years later without leave. Things then took a turn for the better. He was made Commissioner at Deptford and Woolwich in 1686 and served to Pepys's complete satisfaction on the Special Commission of 1686–8, losing office, like Pepys, at the Revolution. Pepys had always distrusted him, but for his sister's sake forgave him much. Ever ready for a jaunt, Balty had accompanied them on their continental holiday in 1669. When Pepys was faced with charges of treason in 1679 he spent several happy months in Paris at Pepys's expense gathering evidence to discredit Pepys's accuser Col. Scott. He had visited Paris the year before, probably in the hope of recovering his father's lost inheritance.

In Dec. 1662 he married Esther, daughter of John Watts, a Northamptonshire yeoman who failed to provide her with the portion Balty had expected.[3] Balty proved an impossible husband – improvident, overbearing and secretive, and keeping her, as she later told Pepys, 'in a worse condition then the meanest servant'.[4] Pepys found her 'discreet' and 'humble'[5] and gave her his Brampton house to live in with her children during Balty's absence in Tangier. She had had eight children by him when she died in Feb. 1687. In Jan. 1689 Balty made a second marriage to a widow, Margaret Darling, who compounded his troubles by bringing into the household two children of her own. Balty now had no employment, no pension, no savings, and ten children. His appeals to the Admiralty for a place continue into Anne's reign. Pepys wrote to the Admiralty in his support, and came to his rescue with money and old clothes. The last trace we have of him is of his petitioning the Cabinet in 1710.[6]

His letters to Pepys, with their comic extravagance of language and feeling, perfectly reflect the man. 'If Balthasar St Michel had not existed', writes Richard Ollard, 'only Dickens could have invented him'. [7]

St Olave's Church, Hart St. On the s. side of Hart St, at the n.-w. corner of Seething Lane. The advowson was bought by Sir Andrew Riccard, E. India merchant, in 1650 but devised to trustees in 1655. One of the smallest city churches, it dates mostly from the 15th century. A gallery for the Navy Office was added in 1660, a vestry in 1661, and in 1674 a porch on the n. side. It escaped the Fire, but was extensively damaged in 1939–45. Both Pepys and his wife were buried here, and the bust Pepys erected to his wife's memory is still to be seen in the chancel. There are contemporary monuments to Sir J. Mennes and Sir A. Riccard, and a Victorian monument (1883) to Pepys. A memorial service to Pepys is held there annually.[1]

St Pancras. A village in Middlesex, its centre over a mile north of Holborn at Gray's Inn. In the '60s it was remote and agricultural with no major road passing through it, and lacked the noted pleasure gardens which brought so many Londoners to Islington, Marylebone or Vauxhall. (R)

St Paul's Cathedral. The old cathedral (built after the fire of 1087) was seriously damaged by lightning in 1561 when it lost its steeple. Inigo Jones's rebuilding (1633–42) resulted in a remodelled exterior and a new portico. During the Commonwealth the eastern end was used for the meetings of a congregation of Independents, the rest as a cavalry barracks. The plans for rebuilding were revived at the Restoration and a commission was appointed in 1663 for which Wren produced a design. After the building was gutted in the Great Fire, it was pulled down 1668–87, and replaced by Wren's cathedral. The foundation stone was laid in 1675, the dome finished in 1710, and the whole building completed in 1711. In the early '60s the nave seems no longer to have been a public meeting place as in the 16th and early 17th centuries.[1]

St Paul's Churchyard. Before the Fire, the centre of the book trade, and much frequented by Pepys, especially in 1660–3. In the '60s it was not a narrow courtyard, as it later became, but an extensive area surrounding the cathedral, still containing the Bishop's Palace and various buildings connected with the cathedral. Shops, taverns and tenements had been added in the 16th and early 17th century. The area was badly burnt in the Fire. The name has gradually become limited to the s. section from Cannon St to the top of Ludgate Hill. The book-shops have gone, but it remains as in the '60s a centre for textiles. (R)

St. Paul's School. Both Pepys and his brother John were pupils. It was a medieval school refounded and endowed by John Colet, Dean of St Paul's (d. 1519) and governed by the Mercers' Company. It was the largest of the fee-paying schools in London in Pepys's day, though supposedly limited to 153 boys (the number of the fishes caught in the miraculous draught), all of them day boys except for a few boarders in the High Master's house. The building, fronting the street on the e. side of the Cathedral, was not large (taxed on 12 hearths in 1666),[1] and after its destruction in the Fire was rebuilt (by 1670–1) on a more spacious scale on an enlarged site.[2]

The school had a distinguished reputation and included among its 16th-century High Masters two of the greatest of English pedagogues – William Lily and Richard Mulcaster. In the 17th century it numbered among its pupils Milton, Pepys and Marlborough.

The curriculum was weak on mathematics (Pepys had trouble with his multiplication table long after school and university) and consisted almost entirely of Greek and Latin, with a little Hebrew in the top form (of which Pepys betrays no knowledge). The teachers were three in number – a Surmaster and a chaplain, or usher, as well as the High Master himself – who taught in a single great classroom. (There is a drawing of it in Pepys's collection.)[3]

Pepys was a pupil from c. 1646 to 1650 when he was awarded a leaving exhibition to Cambridge. The High Master in his time was John Langley (d. 1651) a Hebrew scholar who was said to have 'had a very awful Presence and Speech, that . . . struck a mighty Respect and Fear into his Scholars, which however wore off after they were a little used to him.'[4] A later High Master (1672–97) was the antiquarian Thomas Gale who married Barbara Pepys, daughter of Pepys's cousin Roger.

The school moved in 1884 to Hammersmith and more recently to Barnes.[5] [*See also* Cromleholme, S.]

St Thomas's Hospital. In 1660 in Southwark a short distance beyond the s. end of London Bridge on the e. side of the Borough High St north of St Thomas's St. London Bridge Station and its approaches now cover much of the site. Rebuilt 1868–71 in Lambeth on the Albert Embankment opposite the Houses of Parliament. Much damaged in the war of 1939–45 and now rebuilt. (R)

St Valentine's Day. St Valentine's Day customs echo the belief that birds begin to mate on that day. The ritual in its modern form is in essence a form of mock-betrothal between young people in which the girl is allowed, for this once, to take the initiative. This is the sense in which Dorothy Osborne, in love with William Temple, treated the matter on St Valentine's Day 1654.[1] She wrote his name on a slip of paper along with friends who wrote on other slips; the papers were folded and when her turn came – wonder of wonders! – she picked out the slip inscribed with the name of her beloved. Pepys and his circle played other varieties of the game. The man could take his wife or a married cousin as a valentine; equally, he could have several valentines at once. Children were allowed to join in and choose adults as their valentines. The methods of choice were various. Drawing names by lot, as Dorothy Osborne did, was perhaps the commonest. The paper could then be worn as a 'favour'. Another method was to choose the first person of the opposite sex you saw – Elizabeth had once to close her eyes in order to avoid seeing the painters at work in the house[2] – or the first to cross your threshold. The one fixed rule was that the woman (or child) should receive a present. Pepys usually gave gloves or a money present to his girl friends; and once £5 to his wife, in the form of a ring. At court the game was played for high stakes: Frances Stuart was given a jewel worth £800 by the Duke of York in 1668.[3]

Some hints appear in the diary of the way in which the conventions were later to develop. On 14 Feb. 1667 little Will Mercer called on Elizabeth with 'her name writ upon blue paper in gold letters, done by himself, very pretty'. Two days later Pepys visited Mrs Pearse and found that her little girl had drawn him as her valentine. 'But here I do first observe', he adds, 'the fashion of drawing of Motto's as well as names; so that Pierce, who drew my wife, did draw also a motto, and this girl drew another for me. What mine was I have forgot; but my wife's was (*Most virtuous and most fair*)'. No 17th-century examples of valentine cards survive – as far as is known the earliest written card dates from 1750 and the earliest printed card from 1761.[4] By then, with the development of postal services, the card had become the most important element in the ritual, and present-giving had died out.[5]

Sal(i)sbury, ——. Painter. Identity uncertain; cf. ii. 23, n. 2.

Salisbury Court. A thoroughfare of some importance running from Fleet St by the west of the w. end of St Bride's Church down to the landing place at Dorset Stairs. Now much altered, all south of Salisbury Sq. being renamed.

Salisbury Court Theatre. On the s. side of the Court immediately below the great garden of Dorset House (now probably below and parallel to Hutton St); built in 1629, by lessees of the Earl of Dorset who converted the barn of Salisbury House (140 × 42 ft) for the purpose.[1] Plays were acted there until forbidden in 1642 by Parliament. Wrecked by soldiers in 1649, it was first repaired, then largely rebuilt and, in 1660, reopened as a playhouse by William Beeston, son of Christopher Beeston who in 1616 had converted the cockpit in Drury Lane into the Cockpit Theatre. From Nov. 1660 the Duke's Company under Davenant played there and also at Apothecaries' Hall until in June 1661 Lisle's Tennis Court had been adapted for them. That autumn, George Jolly's company used it. Thereafter, thanks to Charles II's limiting the number of playhouses to two, it ceased to be an authorised playhouse and was let, as private residences, to the Dowager Countess of Exeter and Sir Heneage Finch. Pepys in early 1661 sometimes uses the term 'Whitefriars' when noting visits to it (1, 16 and 19 March). Destroyed in the Fire and not rebuilt as such, though the new Duke's Theatre, built nearby in Dorset Gardens after the Fire, preserved the theatrical traditions of the area. [*See also* Theatre] (R)

Saltonstall, Lady. Widow of Sir Richard (d. 1658), Lieut-Governor of Massachusetts 1630–1. At the time of her death she was living in York St, Covent Garden. Pepys mistakenly calls her Lady Sanderson.[1]

Samford, ——. One of Pepys's friends in government service in the 1650s. Probably Samuel Sandford, Surveyor-General of the Excise. 'Samford' was a common variant.[1]

Sanderson, Sir William, kt 1625 (?1586–1676). An historian and distant relative of Pepys: the connection may have been through Anne Sanderson, second wife of Richard Pepys of the parish of Great St Bartholomew's, or/and through Mary Pepys, sister of the same Richard, wife of Robert Sanderson. He wrote two historical works, *A compleat history of the lives and reigns of Mary Queen of Scotland, and of her son and successor, James* (1656); and *A compleat history of the life and raigne of King Charles from his cradle to the grave* (1658), the latter an exercise in hagiography. Evelyn thought them 'large but meane'. Neither is preserved in the Pepys Library. He was made a Gentleman of the Privy Chamber to the King c. 1660.

His wife Bridget (c. 1592–1682) was the daughter of Sir Edward Tyrrell, Bt; she served at court as laundress to Henrietta-Maria and from 1669 as Mother of the Queen's Maids of Honour. Her brother Sir Timothy Tyrrell (d. 1633) was Master of the Buckhounds; his son (also Sir Timothy) was one of the acquaintances Pepys pressed into service in defending himself against the accusation of treason in 1679.[1]

Sandwich, 1st Earl of: *see* Mountagu, E.

Sandys. The Mr Sandys who congratulated Pepys on his parliamentary speech was William Sandys, member for Evesham 1640–1 and 1661–9, who lived in Axe Yard during parliamentary sessions. He was known, from his interest in drainage schemes, as Waterworks Sandys. He died in Dec. 1669.[1] The Col. Sandys mentioned in another connection was Samuel Sandys of Ombersley, Worcs., member for Worcestershire in the Cavalier Parliament, and Governor of Evesham during the Civil War. He was now a Gentleman of the Privy Chamber.[2]

Sankey, [Clement] (?1633–1707). A Magdalene graduate (B.A. 1652); elected Fellow 1652, re-elected 1660; Rector of St Clement

Eastcheap 1666–1707, and Canon of York 1669–1707. He married Mary Archer of Bourn, Cambs. in 1669. In 1666 he paid tax on a small cottage (assessed on one hearth) at Bourn.[1]

Sansum, Rear-Adm. [Robert]. Naval commander. A veteran of the Commonwealth navy (serving from 1650) he held two flag commands 1664–5, and was killed in action at the Battle of Lowestoft.[1]

[Santhune, Samuel de]. A weaver, of Huguenot origin, born in Canterbury, who on 12 Nov. 1662 married Mary Pepys, daughter of Pepys's uncle Thomas Pepys of St Alphage's parish, he being then a widower and she a spinster of 25. She died in 1667, having had three children. His first wife (m. 1651) was Anne Duquesne, whose sister married Christopher Cisner, minister of the French church in Thread-needle St. He himself was an elder of the church 1667–70. He married for the third time in Canterbury, 1687, Jeanne Cornuel of Jersey.[1]

Saunders, Capt. [Francis] (d. by 1688). Of the *Sweepstake*: held two commands in 1665.[1]

Saunders, Capt. [Joseph]. Held three commands 1665–6; killed in action 1666.[1]

Saunders, Capt. ——. Gabriel or Robert; both Commonwealth veterans.

Savage, Sir Edward, kt 1639. Courtier under both Charles I and Charles II; appointed Gentleman of the Privy Chamber 1660; granted pension 1666. He lost his right hand in the Civil War.[1]

Savile, Sir George and Henry. Nephews of Sir W. Coventry. Sir George (4th Bt, 1633–95), Marquess of Halifax (1681), appears in the diary as a member of the Brooke House Committee. One of the most important and interesting statesmen of his generation: the 'trimmer', as he called himself, or moderate, who in the Exclusion crisis and the Revolution of 1688–9 was the leading proponent of limited monarchy. His pamphlets (particularly *The character of a trimmer* and *A letter to a dissenter*) are among the most eloquent and influential of their time.[1]

His brother Henry (1642–87) was a wit, rake and diplomatist. He was a crony of Henry Sidney and served as a Groom of the Bedchamber to the Duke of York 1665–72. Like many of his kind he fought valiantly as a volunteer in the Dutch wars of the '60s and '70s. In 1682–4 he was a Commissioner of the Admiralty, put there as Pepys wrote 'for want of other ways of gratification'. But as envoy to Paris in 1679 he had helped Pepys to hunt out evidence against his enemy Col. Scott.[2]

Savoy, The. A great town house or palace, on the s. side of the Strand, with grounds stretching down to the river, only its chapel existing today. Built c. 1350 and rebuilt early in Henry VIII's reign, it was in the 1660s a royal 'hospital' or almshouse under a master and chaplains, who occupied parts, leasing out the remainder, so that its buildings and

purlieus housed *inter alia* a French church, the King's printing press,
two gaols and a number of shops and private lodgings. It was used
occasionally for parliamentary committees and in 1661 for the Savoy
Conference between the episcopalian and presbyterian parties within
the Church. From 1642–60 most of it had served as a military hospital,
and again in 1664 it was made available for sick and wounded seamen
and soldiers. It was rebuilt after being seriously damaged by fire in June
1669. The bulk of it, other than the chapel, was removed in 1816 to
make room for the approaches to Waterloo Bridge.[1] (R)

Sawyer, Sir Robert, kt 1677 (1633–92). Fellow of Magdalene College
1652–?55; M.P. for High Wycombe 1673–9; for Cambridge University
1689–90, 1690–2; Attorney-General 1681–7. Once Pepys's 'Chamber-
fellow' at Magdalene (vii.386). An able lawyer with a reputation for
subservience to the court (redeemed by his defence of the Seven
Bishops 1688), and for pedantry. His wife (m. 1665) was Margaret,
daughter of Ralph Suckley of Islington.[1]

Sayer(s), [John]. Master-Cook, King's privy kitchen.[1]

Scarburgh, Sir Charles, kt 1669 (1616–94). Anatomist and friend of
William Harvey; Lumleian lecturer at the Royal College of Physicians
1656; an original F.R.S.; M.P. for Camelford 1685–7. He attended
Charles II in his last illness and was present at the birth of James II's son.
He had a library which Evelyn considered 'the very best collection
especially of Mathematical books . . . in all Europe'. Accident brought
him and Pepys together in May 1682 when the ship in which he was
sailing to Scotland with the Duke of York foundered on a reef. Pepys,
also on the same voyage but in a different vessel, welcomed him
aboard. He had survived by fighting off the Duke's dog Mumper from
a plank.[1]

Scawen, [Robert] (1602–70). One of the ablest financial experts
thrown up by the Civil War. From being an attorney and man of
business to the Earl of Northumberland, he became M.P. for Berwick
in the Long Parliament, chairman of the army committee in 1645
and one of the architects of parliamentary victory. In Jan. 1659 he sat
for Grampound and was made a commissioner for the management of
the revenue. When Pepys met him he was one of the commissioners for
the disbanding of the armed forces (1660–1). He was a commissioner of
appeals in the excise service from Oct. 1660 until his death.[1]

SCIENCE

Introduction. The most celebrated book in the history of English
science bears Pepys's name on its title-page. True, its author was Isaac
Newton and Samuel Pepys could not have understood a word of it, but

the fact remains that the immortal *Philosophiae naturalis principia mathe matica* was in press while he was President of the Royal Society and bear under its title the words: 'Imprimatur. S. Pepys, *Reg. Soc.* Praese: Julii 5. 1686'. Later Pepys and Newton became well acquainted, but th diary was closed before the outside world had heard of the Cambridg mathematician. The conjunction of the names of two men both s singular in intellect and character – yet how different from each other was at one level a mere historical accident (for another man might hav been elected President on 30 Nov. 1684) but at another level it was a appropriate consequence of the condition of science in England then When the *Principia* was written Newton was supremely representativ of the highest level of academic science, down to the formal geometr and textbook Latinity of his greatest work. Pepys similarly wa supremely representative of the virtuosi, the amateurs, whom circum stances sometimes promoted to positions of patronage. Of professional there were very few; of the virtuosi a fair number, though not all s earnest or so humble as Pepys. And while the true distinction o English science in Pepys's day was the creation of 'professionals' – word to be taken widely, for not all to be classed as 'professionals' live by science or medicine – the strength and size of the scientific move ment came from the virtuosi who composed the mass (often an iner mass) of the Royal Society.

This state of affairs was new. 'Science' is a modern word; its rang of knowledge had been in the Middle Ages and to a lesser extent wa still in Pepys's day assigned to three provinces: mathematics (including mechanics and astronomy), medicine (including much of botany chemistry and so on) and natural philosophy. All of these were, and hac long been, university subjects. Until the Renaissance, in fact, no on outside the universities paid any attention to them, apart from th qualified physicians who had been university trained. The growth o science had rested with a very limited group of academics scattered through a score of universities. A learned European public that woul buy books on scientific, mathematical and medical topics first appeared at the end of the 15th century. Printing supplied its curiosity. Books i the vernacular on such topics began to circulate in some numbers. B the mid-17th century men in various countries, some academic, som not, were beginning to group themselves into clubs and societies, som of them specialising in the sciences. These formed an environment int which the Pepyses of England, France, Italy and Germany could ente with pleasure.

These societies usually flourished in capital cities, often with a strong court interest. And while science was thus spreading beyond th lecture-hall, its nature was changing swiftly. What had begun with Vesalius and Copernicus (c. 1540) passed through the dynamic mind:

of Harvey, Kepler and Galileo (c. 1630) to the no less vigorous and challenging generation among whom the young Pepys grew up – for he was born into the world of Descartes, Gassendi, Pascal, Mersenne, Fermat, Hobbes and Kenelm Digby. By the time the diary opens, educated, lively young men all over England had heard of wonderful new instruments like the telescope, accepted the earth's motion without difficulty as a fact, thought Aristotle very much old hat in comparison with the truer guide to the basic nature of things furnished by Descartes, and commonly were fired by ambitions for the progress of knowledge learned from Francis Bacon. They were accustomed to the idea, though it was a novel one, that knowledge changes year by year, that it advances; and that one may (to the limits of one's natural capacity) follow this advance by reading appropriate books in which it is recorded. Pepys, like his generation, had a profound admiration for 'sound learning' of the old sort (as did many of the most active scientists too), but he was far from feeling that all the truths were locked up in ancient authors.

The foundations of modern science, with the Renaissance itself, had been laid in Italy, resort alike of Copernicus (a Pole) and Vesalius (a Fleming), not to say of many hundreds of the English. The early 17th century saw glorious names everywhere (in Britain, those of Gilbert, Bacon, Napier and Harvey) but by about 1640 the centre of gravity was undoubtedly in Paris, while Germany and Britain were distressed by civil wars. This French influence on scientific thought (particularly that of Descartes) was very great; but it was intellectual rather than practical or, to use pejorative terms, speculative rather than factual. It was the English genius to strengthen the factual content of science and to improve its mathematical rigour. It would be a mistake to over-emphasise the empiricism of the Royal Society (of which Pepys was an early Fellow), for its membership was very much influenced by theoretical notions, indeed by a whole metaphysic of nature stemming from France. One may see in Pepys himself that while he delights in an ingenious experiment, he was no less satisfied by the discussion of wide-ranging hypotheses. Yet – as befitted a virtuoso – what pleased him most was a device that he could take home and use himself.

Pepys's diary, it must be said, gives only a very slight glimpse of the richness of developing English science at this time. It wholly omits pure and applied mathematics in which the English, for once, shone. Although Pepys heard much of chemistry (which signified chiefly, at this period, the preparation of medical remedies by pyrotechnic art), and read some of Boyle's philosophic discourses, he admired the experiments without comprehending the thought. He knew something of spherical astronomy (part of the 'use of the globes') since he endeavoured to teach his wife, but this subject did not interest him. The telescope was now making qualitative observation of the planet possible, but Pepys seems hardly to have apprehended this. He had no eye for natural history, cultivated contemporaneously by Ray and Willughby, Morison and Lister. It is very likely that more general questions of natural philosophy – the problems of motion associated with the 'mechanical philosophy', of the reality of atoms and the void (denied by Descartes), of perception and the nature of the soul – must surely have been raised when Pepys recorded only a 'fine discourse'. We cannot tell. We know only that Pepys's associates were exercised by these issues. What Pepys did find in himself were a sharp, but short-lived, interest in microscopy, a continuing interest in matters of anatomy and physiology, and the capacity to listen with attention to most new topics. In the diary period Pepys only attended meetings of the Royal Society about a score of times, so that it is hardly surprising that if its activities had to be reconstructed from this document alone the historian would be sure of the Society's vigour and catholic interest but little more.

The making of a virtuoso. Although the transformation of scientific thought was going on about him in youth and manhood, Pepys can have known little of it. In the 1650s, when Pepys was at Magdalene as for that matter when Newton was at Trinity a decade later, the new science and the 'mechanical philosophy' were outside the university curriculum. Old subjects, Latin and Greek, rhetoric, logic, certain writings of Aristotle, held the field still. There was some teaching of geometry, but no science. There were as yet, of course, no laboratories in the universities, nor any apparatus of science. The undergraduate was trained through a series of college 'disputations' and tested by maintaining two 'Acts' and two 'Opponencies' on, usually, trivial and time-worn themes. Style and language counted more than matter. There was Puritan pressure for reform of the universities, and some reform was indeed effected, but the impact on teaching and examining was small enough.

Thus the virtuoso like Pepys and the 'professional' scientist like Isaac Newton, or Pepys's near-contemporary the naturalist John Ray, were alike self-made men. Each had to raise himself from an almost medieval level of learning to the level of the contemporary masters – Descartes, Hevelius, Pecquet. Newton was as much a self-taught professional as Pepys a self-taught amateur. Of course there were in each generation men of the front rank or near it willing to give special help to the best student – Henry More at Christ's, for example, or Isaac Barrow at Trinity. Possibly Pepys did not seem to wish for such help, or perhaps it was not readily available; at least we have no evidence of anyone's inspiring him to tread new ways. In consequence, Pepys always lacked a firm grounding in modern science. He was almost comically an arts man – bewildered by mathematics (except when rendered mechanical), hopeless at chemistry, and seemingly with no very deep roots in natural philosophy (at least, he seems to have closed Boyle's *Origine of Forms* with relief). This was absolutely typical of his time. The distinction of the virtuoso from other men was that he was interested in natural phenomena, especially curiosities, and made an effort to understand. The distinction between the virtuoso and the professional lay in the latter's penetrating to the roots of understanding in mathematical analysis, dissection, systematic observation, or experiment. Pepys was never trained for these, and had no leisure for them. But if in science he fell far below a Brouncker or a Moray, not to say Ray and Newton, in the conventional knowledge of books for which school and university prepared a man he came much closer; while in modern literature and history, or music, he was far more skilled. What one can see in the diary as in the history of the Royal Society at large, is the result of a mixture of opposites: seriousness and frivolity, philosophy and plays, telescopes and virginals which in all degrees was typical of Pepys's age, and of the man. The early portion of the diary, written before Pepys himself was enrolled among the virtuosi, shows how scientific proclivities – mingled, of course, with hopes for self-promotion and perhaps even the profit of a workable invention – were diffused about the court of Charles II. If it was the mode to keep a mistress and talk bawdy, it was also the mode to keep an elaboratory and talk chemistry. Charles himself made the mode. And he made the world talk of his philosophers, even if only by laughing at them.

When Pepys's own career began to rise with that of his master, Mountagu, Pepys soon entered into acquaintance with other virtuosi and future colleagues in the Royal Society – Elias Ashmole, whom he encountered at the astrologer Lilly's; Dr Timothy Clarke, the royal physician, who proved a genial acquaintance on the voyage to Holland and later through the years; Sir Jonas Moore, the mathematician; Sir Samual Morland, once Pepys's tutor, now the King's master of mechanicks; Dr Charles Scarburgh; Sir Paul Neile and Henry Slingsby, later Master of the Mint. Pepys was emerging, with the Restoration, from the world of petty clerks and great men's servants, as he noted with naive satisfaction from the respect paid to him by the naval officers when he went to sea.[1] In a few years he would be ashamed of such former jovial companions, now considered low.[2] Some men of a deeper intellectual cast than himself Pepys had long known. One of his neighbours was Samuel Hartlib the elder – that tireless schemer for the public good whose house in Axe Yard was a refuge and clearing-station for religious and philosophical men. Sam Hartlib the younger was one of Pepys's 'old club' and among his familiar acquaintances were the daughter Nan, and the chemical son-in-law, Clod. Possibly at

Hartlib's Pepys may have met the inventor Kuffeler, son-in-law of Cornelius Drebbel, whose terrible 'engine' for destroying ships was considered by the Navy Board on 14 March 1662. A more intimate friend was Ralph Greatorex, an instrument-maker with a shop in the Strand, whose first armillary sphere Pepys saw on 10 Jan. 1660. It was his device for raising water (probably an archimedean screw) that Pepys admired in St James's Park, and it was Greatorex also who first took Pepys to Gresham College on 23 Jan. 1661 to see 'the manner of the house' and the 'great company of persons of Honour there'.

However, Pepys showed no sign of aspiring to virtuosity at this stage; he was too much occupied with his new work, new house, and new wealth. As a curiosity he bought a small perspective glass from an optical instrument-maker, Richard Reeve, on 11 Feb. 1661, and learned with interest of the so-called Prince Rupert's drops; Greatorex attempted to explain to him the law of the lever, without great success – but the fault may not have been Pepys's. He reported Jonas Moore's views on the separation of Britain from the Continent, and Ashmole's (less sensible) views on rains of frogs and insects from the sky. But these are the only records of such conversations. On their journey in company to Portsmouth Pepys evidently reinforced his good impression upon the genial Dr Clarke, since after a philosophical 'discourse exceeding pleasant' (their earlier conversations had been merry ones) Clarke 'offered' on 28 Apr. 1662 'to bring me into the college of the Virtuosoes and my Lord Brunkard's acquaintance. And to show me some anatomy . . .'.

Although Dr Clarke remained affable to Pepys he seems to have done nothing for him, since Pepys's election to the Royal Society was to be long deferred, while his introduction to anatomy took place at Surgeons' Hall under the able direction of Dr Scarburgh. (However, Pepys's interest was rather in his own disease of the stone and the operation that had relieved him from it, than in anatomical science, though he called the lecture he had heard 'very fine'.[3]) Such glimpses of Pepys's widening intellectual horizons are all related to his profession – for his visit to Surgeons' Hall with Commissioner Pett was a semi-official one, as was another some months later, with Sir John Mennes, to the Mint at the Tower, about which he made notes almost adequate for the 'History of a Trade'.[4] For purely practical ends again, not for love of mathematics, Pepys set himself in 1662 to master arithmetic under the tuition of Cooper, then mate of the *Royal Charles*, with whom he went on to study the hull and rigging of a ship guided by a model at the Navy Office. Did Pepys previously do his figuring in accounts and so on with the aid of an abacus or some such device, since he was ignorant of the multiplication table until he learned it from Cooper? At any rate, he enjoyed arithmetic enough to teach his wife addition, subtraction and multiplication in 1663, after which he proposed 'not to trouble her yet with Division, but to begin with the globes to her now'.[5] As for nautical technology it was best learned, as Pepys learned it, from shipwrights and working seamen, though books were beginning to appear.

Slightly later, in 1664, Pepys was initiated into the mysteries of ship-building by an able instructor, Anthony Deane, who presented him with a model of his own, and convinced Pepys that though conceited and ignorant of chemistry, still he had taken much pains in shipbuilding. Perhaps fortunately there was as yet no theoretical science of naval architecture for the King's servants to master, and as for navigation, it was outside Pepys's sphere. But at least he tried to introduce quantitative accuracy into the business of timber procurement with the aid of his various 'rules', and he was much impressed by Dr Daniel Whistler's 'extraordinary good discourse . . . upon my Question concerning the keeping of Masts, he arguing against keeping them dry . . .', because Whistler was able to derive this recommendation from 'the nature of Corrupcion in bodies, and the several ways thereof'. Perhaps naively, Pepys was readily willing to believe that the philosophical knowledge of men more learned than himself must be of value in dealing with such practical issues. Whistler was another F.R.S. – as indeed were Pepys's own great patron, Sandwich, and John Creed (Pepys's disliked but respected rival in Sandwich's service), and many more with whom Pepys had to do.

Pepys's increasing importance in the affairs of the navy and at court continually widened his acquaintance among the virtuosi, such as Thomas Povey, the Treasurer of the Tangier Committee, whose life-like *trompe-l'œil* painting and neat cellar Pepys so much admired. Even Mennes, though no administrator, could talk to him of chemistry in a way that Pepys, at least, could not improve, and he learned more of this subject from Dr Thomas Allen, better known as a physician and anatomist. Pepys also met on 6 Feb. 1663 Arlington's creature, Joseph Williamson, soon to be Secretary of State and like himself a future President of the Royal Society; indeed, business was soon to bring Pepys into intimate acquaintance with the founding and present President, Lord Brouncker, who became a Navy Commissioner in Dec. 1664. (It would seem likely that Pepys encountered him first at Gresham College on 23 Jan. 1661, but was not really acquainted with him before his own election to the Royal Society.)

Another F.R.S. closely concerned with navigation was Sir William Petty, whom Pepys must have met long before in his Axe Yard days, for Petty had as a young man been a protégé of Samuel Hartlib. Pepys's first references to him are familiar. Petty – like his associate John Graunt, author of the *Observations on the bills of mortality* – looked after the interests of old Barlow, the ousted Clerk of the Acts to whom Pepys allowed a pension. Petty had distinguished himself at Oxford as an anatomist and in Ireland as a surveyor. He was one of those who entertained Pepys in intellectual conversation, being (Pepys thought) 'one of the most rational men that ever I heard speak with a tongue, having all his notions the most distinct and clear'.[6] During 1663 Petty was long in Ireland, where he made trials of small boats built on his 'double-bottomed' or catamaran principle, with good success. The second of these, after performing well in the Irish Sea, was sailed over to the Thames where Pepys visited her on 22 Jan. 1664. He found her appearance strange, but not so bad as people made out, feeling confident that Petty would not have praised his invention so highly unless it had proved good. Most people, including the King, either laughed at Petty or feared his innovation. Among the latter was Commissioner Pett, who called it 'the most dangerous thing in the world'[7] because it might fall into the hands of enemies. The King was hardly more logical than his shipwright, though Pepys admired Petty's endurance of his raillery, since the King refused either to argue seriously about Petty's boat or to compete with it. Charles sympathised with the rival efforts of Brouncker 'and the virtuosos of the towne' in constructing a pleasure-boat which, from Pepys's reports, behaved poorly.[8]

A third and larger vessel, *The Experiment*, was built on the Thames and launched by the King on 22 Dec. 1664. 'It swims and looks finely' wrote Pepys who was present at the launching, 'and I believe will do well'. On 13 Feb. 1665, having been on board, he called it a 'brave roomy vessel'. Unfortunately Pepys's faith in his friend's works was belied to the extent that after a successful voyage to Portugal *The Experiment* was lost with all hands on its return – though indeed in a great storm, and not without some suspicion of negligence in her crew. Petty then abandoned his shipbuilding ventures for some 20 years. Consequently Pepys was never in a position to be of service to his friend; indeed the Royal Society quite denied itself any further concern with shipbuilding. In the world of the Restoration his position was far more secure than that of Petty, the old Commonwealth's man, and despite his intellectual inferiority it was Pepys who was to have the greater influence in the later affairs of the Royal Society.

His attitude to superstition. Pepys was a level-headed, realistic man, a natural Aristotelian who never showed any resentment against the conventional philosophy which was the chief intellectual food Cambridge had given him. To Pepys, since he was no mathematician, entrance into Plato's Academy was forever barred, nor is there any sign that the 'hermetic' variety of science then fashionable in some circles held the least appeal for him. The diary makes no mention of Hermes Trismegistus, the Cabbala, or Robert Fludd. If some realm of experience

and knowledge existed other than that of ordinary human affairs, he
saw it in commonplace or popular terms as a strange farrago of
astrology, ghosts, witchcraft, palmistry, talismans and portents. The
only point of distinction seems to be that though like the common
people Pepys loved to chatter about these nebulous and frightening
mysteries, he was highly incredulous about their reality. A man who
listens to and tells after-dinner ghost stories, and is amused at his own
momentary midnight panic on waking to see a white figure seated on
his bedroom chair (his pillow)[9] is not a serious believer in the appearance of spirit visitants. Pepys endorsed Sandwich's scepticism concerning the Mompesson manifestations of the 'Wiltshire drummer' and
shows no sign of falling into Glanvill's credulity, though he thought
Glanvill had made a good story of the events.[10]

Like many other Londoners, Pepys bought the popular astrological
almanacs, clearly without taking them seriously. When the Second
Dutch War made Lilly's predictions of Dutch dissension and dis-
comfiture in 1667 absurdly wrong, Pepys joked with others about them,
just as he had accepted a rival astrologer's assurance that Lilly thought
more of pleasing friends than of following the principles of art. He
more than once refers to the Duke of Buckingham's involvement with
the 'conjuror' John Heydon; among the charges that led to Buckingham's imprisonment in the Tower was the accusation that he had
ordered Heydon to calculate the King's nativity, that is, foretell the
hour of his downfall or death. There is a suggestion in Pepys's comments that he finds such a conception of crime superstitious, and a clear
implication that what interested him in the tale was Buckingham's
political folly in consorting with such creatures and building aspirations on their nonsense. In fact, most of the diary allusions to the
'occult' seem to be reports of others' foolish thoughts or reactions –
including his wife's – rather than of his own beliefs. So, a shooting-star
provokes talk of another burning of the city and a possible rising of
'the papists to cut our throats',[11] but clearly this is to Pepys just idle
talk; God forbid these things should happen, he says, but without any
real supposition that the visit of the meteor makes them more likely.

As a traveller might today, Pepys notes without comment old
beliefs and practices he encountered -- the sowing of sage in graveyards,
or the laying of iron bars on casks of ale to prevent its spoiling by
thunder. But one does not sense, as in reading Ashmole, that a sensitive
chord in his own psyche responded to such tales. What he valued above
all was a good story. So, sitting a great while on 21 Aug. 1666 talking of
witches and spirits, what he actually wrote down in his diary was the
tale of a fraudulent trick played on some wine-merchants. Of course
Pepys was in a commonplace way superstitious. He would wear a
hare's foot against the colic, and would impress Elizabeth by telling her

that a great storm of wind might presage the death of the Queen.[12] But (like most of us) he probably thought the occult world of which others talked, though he himself had no knowledge of it, harmless enough, so long as one avoided a foolish plunge into its doubtful mysteries.[*See also* Royal Society; Scientific Instruments]

(A. Rupert Hall)

SCIENTIFIC INSTRUMENTS

Since remote antiquity astronomers had made use of simple divided scales for making measurements, otherwise one might say that the whole history of devices for rendering man's senses more subtle and discerning began with the 17th century. Both telescope and microscope were known before Pepys was born, the perfection and application of the former proceeding the more rapidly, while at the time of the diary the scientific application of the microscope was just beginning in the hands of Henry Power, Robert Hooke and others. The air was measured as to heat by the thermometer (weatherglass) and as to pressure by the barometer (baroscope), of which several quite complex forms were devised. The mathematical-instrument makers manufactured a large variety of scales (in box-wood, brass and silver) for facilitating operations in arithmetic and geometry, especially those encountered in the practical arts, like navigation. After purchasing quite early a weatherglass from his friend Greatorex, and a double-horizontal dial (maker unknown), Pepys was much interested in these mathematical 'rules', of which he himself devised a special form to aid in the computation of timber-volumes.[1] The double-horizontal dial shows the time by means of two gnomons, one throwing its shadow on the ordinary hour-circle, the other on a stereographic projection of the sphere. When the two gnomons show the same time the dial is properly set (needing no compass), since it works by both the altitude and azimuth of the sun. The projection can also be used to determine some questions about the sun's motion – the times of sunrise and sunset, for example. 'Rules' usually signified at this period (beside ordinary rulers) what is also called the sector, an instrument of two hinged pieces, carrying various scales (mathematical, gunnery, trigonometric, architectural etc.); problems were solved by using a pair of dividers upon these engraved scales, employing the theory of proportions and (later) logarithms.

The maker of Pepys's rule was John Browne (d. c. 1695) whose shop was near Aldgate, and Pepys got the writing-master Edward Cocker to engrave 'tables' (?scales) upon it which (seemingly) he could not read himself, so their usefulness is obscure. He got another from Anthony

Thomson of Hosier Lane, a man of great skill who died in the Plague. Browne also furnished Pepys with a spiral calculator for arithmetic, presumably a version of the logarithmic calculator invented by William Oughtred (d. 1660) which was the direct ancestor of the modern engineer's slide-rule. Not surprisingly Pepys was much taken by 'Napier's bones' – multiplication tables set out on rods so that they can be manipulated and the multiples read off – when he heard about them from Jonas Moore.[2] Devised by John Napier, the inventor of logarithms, in 1617, they have always been more ingenious than practical.

A still more direct aid was the monetary adding-machine (which Pepys thought 'very pretty, but not very useful'), made by the King's master-mechanic, Sir Samuel Morland.[3] (The first of this kind had been devised by Blaise Pascal.) Then there were various types of instruments for surveying, and those devoted specifically to navigation which must have been familiar enough to Pepys even if he fails to mention them. Maps, charts and plans always delighted him, however, and from the well-known and learned maker Joseph Moxon of Cornhill he bought a pair of globes at £3 10s. 0d., and later another pair for the Navy Office. These no doubt facilitated the lessons Pepys gave his wife. In July 1664 Pepys was tempted into his greatest extravagance of this sort so far (at £5 10s. 0d., the price of a 'fair state-cup' in silver), the purchase of a microscope. We can imagine what it was like: a short tripod base, into which the whole body of the instrument screwed, so that the object placed on the base could be brought into focus, and in the body (probably) three convex lenses. The body would consist of sliding pasteboard tubes covered with ornamental vellum or leather, with turned pearwood mounts holding the lenses. It was a crude instrument, magnifying perhaps 25 or 50 diameters at most, with much distortion of the image, but impressive to the uninitiated. No wonder the Pepyses were delighted, and at a later date glad to seek instruction from the maker himself, Richard Reeve.[4] As an optical instrument-maker Reeve (whose shop-and-home was in Long Acre) was now at the head of his craft, perhaps a little boastful and conceited. His telescope lenses were highly esteemed, so that in the summer of 1666 Pepys was pleased to entertain him in his own house, in order to enjoy the sight of Jupiter 'and his Girdle and satellites', as well as the moon through Reeve's 6-ft and 12-ft glasses. These were quite simple astronomical telescopes, having uncorrected object-lenses of the focal length stated, with a single convex eye-lens to give a magnified, inverted image. They would of course have needed some kind of support, which presumably Reeve brought with him. Seventeenth-century telescopes were made of very long focal length for their aperture – those shown to Pepys on this occasion would have had an aperture of only $1\frac{1}{2}$–$2\frac{1}{2}$ ins – in order to minimise the distortions caused by uncorrected lenses.

On the same occasion and in conjunction with John Spong, a mathematical practitioner living in Bloomsbury Market (and perhaps an associate of Greatorex) of whom Pepys was to write a little later 'a man that I mightily love for his plainness and ingenuity', Reeve demonstrated some simple optical experiments – the passage of light-rays through smoke-laden air and a magic-lantern – but Pepys was asking too much in expecting this practical artisan to explain the theory of optical instruments; 'he understanding . . . not one bit the theory, nor can make anybody understand it – which is a strange dullness, methinks'.5 Precisely for this reason, that the instrument-makers however skilled went by rule-of-thumb alone, astronomers often preferred to learn how to grind their own lenses. Pepys himself – and Spong – proved themselves no less ignorant of the elements of spherical astronomy, for they found that neither could explain why the stars do not always rise and set at the same hours. Reeve's visits ended with Pepys's purchase of a telescope and magic-lantern.

The next instrument to take Pepys's fancy was what he calls a 'parallelogram', that is, a pantograph, an instrument permitting a drawing to be copied with or without change of scale. Spong first described it to him and then demonstrated it by reducing a map of England – to Pepys's great delight. Spong also gave him a hydrometer. A pantograph was soon ordered and was received as 'the instrument that I have longed for', but on seeing another in the shop of the instrument-maker Henry Wynne in Chancery Lane Pepys could not resist buying that too. Finally he was much taken by a related device, the perspective instrument, which permitted position to be plotted on paper or objects to be outlined as they were seen by the eye through a fixed rectangular screen. A well-known form was invented by Christopher Wren. The French traveller Balthasar de Monconys saw it in London in 1664 (and asked Henry Oldenburg for an exact description of it) but no account was printed until the *Philosophical Transactions* for March 1669 (no. 45). However, Hooke did mention it to Pepys in conversation on 21 Feb. 1666 while indicating his own preference for the *camera obscura* as a sketching aid. Perhaps Pepys was not so very interested at this stage; at any rate it must have been the *Philosophical Transactions* that spurred him to inspect one at the shop of the well-known engraver and printseller William Faithorne, without success, and so go on to see it at Oldenburg's instead. In the end he ordered one from Browne and received it on 8 May 1669.

Of course, to Pepys and many others scientific instruments were instructive toys, just as they are for children today. He made no serious use of any of them, except perhaps his timber-rules. As a virtuoso he was properly fascinated by the practical marvels that instruments seemed to yield; and some, he could see, possessed potential utility if only he could find time to employ them, and overcome the sad defect of his vision. Drawing and the art of perspective, for example, were of long and deep interest to him. His interests were direct, rather than subtle, and ocular demonstration counted for much with him. But again he realised that practice is not everything, and that knowledge is not the same as deftness with gadgets; he admired above all the philosopher who could give the reasons for appearances – even if these took Pepys into deep waters.[6] [*See also* Royal Society]

(A. Rupert Hall)

Scobell. Henry Scobell (d. 1660) was a Chancery official (Deputy-Register 1635–45) who rose to be Clerk of the Parliament 1649–58 and of the House of Lords 1659–60. He wrote several tracts on parliamentary procedure and privilege, and compiled a standard collection of statutes and ordinances. He also held the lucrative post of registrar for the sale of lands of deans and chapters from 1649. He died childless, leaving gifts to his brother Richard (father of Pepys's friend Dick Scobell), and to his nephew Will Symons (also a friend of Pepys).[1]

The Scot. The young man who for about a year from Oct. 1662 sometimes preached, and always disastrously, at St Olave's. It is possible that he was the Alexander Mill, M.A., who received a preacher's licence in Aug. 1662. An Alexander Milne took his M.A. at Aberdeen in 1658.[1]

Scotland Yard. On the e. side of Whitehall with its entrance some 100 paces south of Charing Cross and stretching, behind the grounds of Northumberland House, to the Thames. Divided into Great and Little Scotland Yard, the name of the former still surviving. Once the property of the Kings of Scotland it had, in Pepys's day, been virtually absorbed into Whitehall Palace, the Surveyor of Works living in part of it. Not to be confused with Norman Shaw's New Scotland Yard, which is further upstream. (R)

Scott, [Benjamin]. A relative, his wife being Judith, daughter of Sir Richard Pepys (Lord Chief Justice of Ireland 1655–9), and a member of a branch of the family with strong Essex connections. He was a citizen and pewterer of St Sepulchre, Holborn; to judge by the names in his will, he himself came of an Essex family. His wife died in Apr. 1664, he in the following December.[1]

Scott, Sir Edward (d. c. 1688). Soldier; a member of the family of Scotts of Scot's Hall. In 1668 captain in Col. John Russell's regiment and granted a pension; in 1672 lieut-colonel in Buckingham's regiment of foot. In 1672 it was expected that he would be made Governor of Portsmouth by the Duke of York.[1]

Scott, ——. Surgeon. He attended Jemima Mountagu from c. 1659 for a malformation of the neck. He also attended Evelyn's son John for a crooked leg. Possibly Blundell Scott, of London, who died abroad c. 1669.[1]

Scott, Mrs ——. Shopkeeper, Westminster Hall. Her stall neighboured on one side Betty Martin's, on the other, Doll Powell's.[1]

[Seabrook, ——]. Rector of St Andrew-by-the-Wardrobe until his death c. 1663; probably the John Seabrook who graduated B.A. at Oxford in 1626.[1]

Seale, Capt. [Thomas]. Lieutenant 1664, captain 1664–5; killed in action at Bergen 1665.[1]

Seddon, [John]. Clerk to Lord Brouncker.[1]

Sedgwick, [Joseph]. Lawyer, of Cambridge: son of Joseph Sedgwick of Cambridge; admitted Gray's Inn 1647; Steward of Graveley manorial court.[1]

Sedley, Sir Charles, 2nd Bt (1639–1701). Wit, libertine and dramatist; M.P. for New Romney 1668–1700 (except 1685–7 and 1689–90). Author of the song 'Phillis is my only joy' and father of James II's mistress, the Countess of Dorchester. Pepys retained a copy of his play, the *Mulberry Garden*.[1]

Seely, Capt. [William]. He held three commands of fireships 1665–7 and was shot on board his own ship for cowardice in 1667.[1]

Seething Lane. This ran north out of Great Tower St for 220 yards to Crutched Friars.[1] [For Pepys's house *see* Navy Office; *also* Household]

Servants: *see* Household

Seymour, Sir Edward, 4th Bt, succ. 1685 (1633–1708). He appears in the diary as a commissioner of prizes (in fact, a sub-commissioner for London, dismissed March 1666)[1] and as 'a most conceited fellow' ('ambitious and proud in the highest degree' was Roger North's phrase). He later became Speaker 1673–8; and was also a Navy Commissioner 1672–3, Navy Treasurer 1673–81 and Admiralty Commissioner 1673–9. He had control of several constituencies in the West country and it was to him that Pepys applied in Feb. 1690 for nomination at Maiden Bradley, Wilts.[2]

Seymour, Capt. [Hugh]. Held five commissions 1663–6; in 1665 accused of embezzling prize goods. He was, according to Sir T. Clifford, a brave officer.[1]

Seymour, [John]. With Henry Seymour (probably his father, Groom of the Bedchamber to the King) he received the grant in March 1663 of the office of Comptroller of Customs in the port of London, previously held by Henry alone.[1]

Seymour, [John]. Brother[-in-law] of Sir Thomas Crew; he assisted George Mountagu in looking after Sandwich's affairs during his absence in Madrid and joined him there in June 1668. Possibly the John Seymour admitted to the Middle Temple 11 Apr. 1654.[1]

Shadwell, [Thomas] (d. 1683). Clerk to Sir Robert Pye, sen., Auditor of the Receipt in the Exchequer; one of Pepys's 'club' of government clerks in the 1650s and still in post at the Exchequer in 1670.[1]

Shadwell, Thomas (1641–92). Dramatist and wit; friend of Sedley. A better conversationalist than writer, if we may believe Rochester. ('If Shadwell had burnt all he wrote, and printed all he spoke, he would have had more wit and humour than any other poet'.)[1]

Shadwell. On the Middlesex bank of the Thames between Wapping and Limehouse, with which, in the 1660s, it formed a continuous line of buildings. Technically a hamlet of Stepney until 1670 when it was constituted the parish of St Paul, Shadwell. (R)

Shaftesbury, Earl of: *see* Cooper, A. A.

Shafto, [Robert], kt 1670 (1634–1705). Of Gray's Inn; Recorder of Newcastle upon Tyne 1660–85; appointed Serjeant-at-law 1675.[1]

Shalcross (Shelcrosse), ——. Supplied goods to the Tangier garrison. Probably Thomas Shalcross, haberdasher (b. 1641), buried All Hallows, Bread St, 1673.[1]

Shales, Capt. [John]. Victualling agent at Portsmouth 1660–8 (also surveyor of victualling and sub-commissioner for prizes there during the war); clerk to Brouncker in the Navy Office from 1668; ? a purser in 1670; by 1677 a clerk in the Lord Treasurer's office with special responsibility for naval accounts, and afterwards Auditor of Land Revenues. At the parliamentary elections of Spring 1679 he was proposed by Rupert to the electors of Hull (as Marvell's successor), but defeated.[1] In 1686 he declined to serve in the Special Commission of the Navy though strongly recommended by Pepys.[2]

Shatterell (Shotrell), [Robert]. A leading actor in the King's Company 1660–80; previously at the Red Bull and the Cockpit, Drury Lane. He was living in Playhouse Yard, Drury Lane, 1681–4.[1]

Shaw, Sir John, kt 1660, bt 1665 (c. 1615–80). Merchant and financier. He lived in London Wall in a large house (taxed on 22 hearths) next door to James Houblon, sen.[1] He had provided money for the King when he was in exile and was a confidant of Clarendon, to whom he acted (with Sir G. Carteret) as business adviser. Among the many offices he held were those of Commissioner of the Customs 1660–2, farmer of the customs 1662–71, collector of customs in London from 1669, and Treasurer of the Dunkirk garrison 1660–2. He served on the Council for Trade 1660–8 and that for Foreign Plantations 1661–70; and was M.P. for Lyme Regis 1661–Jan. 79.[2]

Shaw, Robin (d. 1665). Pepys's colleague in the Exchequer; after 1660 managing clerk to Backwell the goldsmith-banker. Possibly a relative of Sir John Shaw, who was an associate of Backwell. He was awarded £1000 for special (i.e. secret) services in 1662. He was about 30 when he died.[1]

Sheeres, Henry, kt 1685 (d. 1710). Military engineer and surveyor;

F.R.S. 1675; with Sandwich in Madrid c. 1666–7; in charge of the construction of the mole at Tangier from 1675; and of its demolition 1683–4. Surveyor-General of the Ordnance 1685–9; present at Sedgemoor as artillery expert; imprisoned on suspicion of Jacobitism 1690, 1696. Pepys found that he 'doth talk a little too much of his travels' (viii.444); he also distrusted his attentions to Elizabeth. Similarly John Luke, his colleague in Tangier, found him vain and flirtatious. But Pepys greatly admired his ability and versatility, often consulted him, and warmly recommended him for his ordnance post.[1] He wrote on Tangier and on navigational problems – works which Pepys retained in his library; he translated works from the classics and composed original verses. He received a ring at Pepys's funeral.[2]

Sheldon, Sir Joseph, kt 1666 (d. 1681). Nephew of Gilbert Sheldon, Archbishop of Canterbury, and brother-in-law of John Dolben, Bishop of Rochester. Sheriff 1666–7, Lord Mayor 1675–6; Master of the Tallow Chandlers' Company 1667–8, and of the Drapers' 1676–7.[1]

Sheldon, William. Appointed Clerk of the Cheque at Woolwich 1660. Elizabeth Pepys lodged at his house during the Plague and after the Fire.[1]

Shelston, ——. Possibly Robert Shelston, a grocer of Leadenhall St, who married Judith Ealy, widow, at Stepney in 1650.[1]

Shepley: *see* Shipley

Sheppard, [Robert] (d. by 1688). Captain of the Duke of York's yachts *Anne* (1664, 1668) and *Falcon* (1666).[1]

Shergoll, [Henry]. Doorkeeper to the Navy Office.[1]

Sherwyn, [Richard] (d. 1675). A wealthy and senior colleague of Pepys in the Exchequer; M.P. for Ludgershall Jan.–Apr. 1659. He was a clerk from the early 1640s to Sir R. Pye; auditor in 1650 to the Commissioners for Composition and Sequestration and from 1653–5 co-Treasurer; Secretary to the Treasury Commissioners 1654–60. He may well have been the Westminster magistrate of those names who conducted Pepys's marriage ceremony in Jan. 1655.[1] In 1660 he lost all his posts except that of deputy to Pye but became secretary to the Chancellor of the Exchequer in 1661, and to the Customs Commissioners in 1671. Later in the year he retired because of ill health.[2]

Shipley (Shepley), [Edward]. Sandwich's steward. His main charge after 1662 was the Hinchingbrooke household, but from 1659 until 1662 he helped Pepys with the management of the Whitehall lodgings. He accompanied Sandwich on the Dutch and Mediterranean voyages in 1660 and 1661–2. The diary has many complaints of his inefficiency and in 1668 he was dismissed because of 'age and good-fellowship' (ix.475). He usually signed his name Shipley. The Pepys Library has a book given by him to Pepys.[1]

Shipman, Sir Abraham (d. 1664). Royalist soldier; Gentleman of the

Privy Chamber to the King from 1660; Governor of Bombay from 1662.[1]

Shipman, Mrs. Of Walthamstow; possibly Dorothy Shipman, whose husband Robert had bought the great tithes of the parish in 1663.[1]

Ships: *see* Navy; for types, *see* Large Glossary; for named ships, *see* Index (vol. xi): Ships

Shish, Jonas, sen. (d. 1680). Assistant-Shipwright, Deptford and Woolwich, under the Commonwealth and 1660–8; Master-Shipwright 1668–80.[1] A skilful shipbuilder, though illiterate and working by eye alone.[2] It was he who built Petty's double-bottomed ships. He died of drink, according to Pepys.[3]

Shoe Lane. A 'considerable lane'[1] running north out of Fleet St near St Bride's Church to the e. end of St Andrew's Church, Holborn Hill. Now extended under Holborn Viaduct to Charterhouse St. The cockpit there is commemorated by an undated token issued by Samuel Clever.[2]

Shoreditch. A manor and formerly a separate village immediately north of Norton Folgate on the road north through Bishopsgate to Edmonton and Ware. By the '60s joined by a continuous line of buildings to the city of London. (R)

Shortgrave, [Richard]. Instrument-maker and surveyor, of Moorfields; operator to the Royal Society 1663–d. 76. Engaged by the city in the survey of London after the Fire, and by Ogilby for his maps in his *Britannia*.[1]

Shorthand: for Pepys's use of shorthand, *see* vol. i, pp. lvii–lxi

Shotrell: *see* Shatterell

Sidley: *see* Sedley

Shrewsbury, [William] (d. ?1703). Bookseller at the Bible, Duck Lane.[1] John Dunton, also a bookseller, wrote of him that he kept 'his stock in excellent order' and would 'find any book as ready as I can find a word in the dictionary'.[2]

Sidney. Three sons of the 2nd Earl of Leicester, of Penshurst (d. 1677) appear briefly in the diary. Algernon (1622–83), the most distinguished, was a leading republican and chief of the commissioners sent with Mountagu's fleet to mediate between Sweden and Denmark in the summer of 1659. He there (quite rightly) suspected Mountagu of collusion with royalist agents, and violently opposed his plan to bring the fleet home.[1] He went abroad from 1660 until 1677 when he returned to take part in the Whig opposition to Charles. He was executed after the Monmouth rising in which he had taken no part: he had however been guilty of writing a justification of resistance – his famous *Discourse concerning government*. (The fact that he never put it into print was of no avail to save him.) Henry, his brother, was a courtier and said to be the handsomest man in the kingdom. Pepys has stories of his amorous exploits. At first a servant of the Duke of York, he attached himself to the interest of William of Orange after 1679, and commanded the English regiment in the Dutch army 1681–5. He was one of the seven who in 1688 signed the invitation to William to invade England. After the Revolution he was rewarded with a viscountcy, an earldom and high office.[2] The third brother Col. Robert was a professional soldier who served in the English regiment in Holland and died in 1668.[3]

Signet Office. In Whitehall Palace in the range of buildings (now part of the site of the Old War Office on the e. side of Whitehall) on the n. side of the 'great' (entry) court of the palace with rooms facing also on to the court beyond. [*See also* Privy Seal Office]

Simcotes, [John] (?1592–1662). Physician, of Huntingdon; M.D. (Cantab.) 1636. He had a fashionable practice and attended Oliver Cromwell.[1]

Simpson, [John], kt 1678 (d. 1681). Barrister, of the Inner Temple; one of the four Common Pleaders of the city of London; Recorder of St Albans 1661–81; Judge of the Sheriffs' Court, London 1671–81; Bencher Inner Temple 1673; King's Serjeant 1678.[1]

Simpson, [Thomas]. Master-Joiner at Deptford and Woolwich yards, appointed (or re-appointed) June 1660.[1] Probably the Thomas Simpson who was apprenticed to his father (also Thomas) c. 1618, and who became a liveryman of the Joiners' Company.[2] He built Pepys's first two bookpresses in 1666 and did other work for him in his official lodgings. He was also responsible for work on the Duke of York's yacht *Anne*.[3]

Singleton, [John]. (d.?1679). Musician-in-Ordinary for the lutes and voices, and, in the private consort, for the violin; appointed 1660.[1] (Lu)

The Six Clerks' Office. An office of Chancery on the w. side of Chancery Lane, south of the modern Carey St, and opposite the Rolls. Rebuilt 1774–8 on a new site in the garden of Lincoln's Inn.[1] The offices of the Law Society now cover the site. (R)

Skinners' Hall. On the w. side of Dowgate Hill. Burnt in the Fire and rebuilt; damaged in 1939–45. (R)

Slater, [John]. Appointed messenger to the Navy Office in July 1660; it was he who usually collected the travelling charges of the Principal Officers from the Navy Treasury.[1]

Slingsby, Sir Arthur, bt 1657 (1623–66). Younger brother of Sir Robert. Active as royalist agent in Interregnum.[1]

Slingsby, Henry (c. 1621–c. 90). Master of the Mint from 1662. Third son of Sir William, of Kippax, W. Riding; cousin of the foregoing. Suspended from office in 1680 for falling into arrears with his accounts, he resigned in 1685. Active in the early days of the Royal Society, but expelled in 1675 for not paying his dues. A friend of Evelyn.[1]

Slingsby, Sir Robert, bt 1661 (1611–61). Comptroller of the Navy 1660–1. Second son of Sir Guilford (himself Comptroller 1611–d. 31);

entered naval service 1633; secretary to Strafford and protégé of Digby. He refused in 1642 to serve under the parliamentary admiral and after a brief imprisonment became a colonel in the royalist army, and later an active royalist agent, well thought of by Clarendon. Author of a 'discourse' on the state of the navy, written in 1660 and first published in 1801. Pepys did not regard it highly, but kept copies in his library.[1]

His sister has not been identified: he had four.[2]

Smallwood, [William]. Barrister, of the Middle Temple; admitted 1654.[1]

Smegergill, [alias Caesar], William. Composer, lutenist and angler. A chorister at Ely in 1615 (and presumably, from his alias, adopted by the then Dean, who had strong musical interests). His songs, dialogues and catches are extensively represented in Playford's publications. Alive in 1667. Alleged by Wood to have been a Roman Catholic. There are three songs in *Musica Britannica*, 33/items xciii–v.[1] (Lu)

[Smethwick, Francis] (fl. 1667–85). Amateur optical instrument-maker; F.R.S. 1667. He invented a method of grinding non-spherical glass.[1]

Smith, Sir George, kt 1660 (1615–67). Merchant and Common Councilman. A friend of Cocke, and a 'croney' of Lady Robinson. He lived in Throgmorton St in a house taxed on 11 hearths. His wife was Martha, daughter of John Swift, merchant.[1]

Smith, Sir Jeremy, kt 1665 (d. 1675). Served in the Commonwealth navy; held five commands 1660–8, a flag-officer 1665–8 and a Navy Commissioner 1669–75.[1]

Smith, [John] (d. 1673). Herald painter, of Fleet St, 'provider of all Tinsells and other necessaries' to the King. Son of Antonia Maria Smith, herald painter.[1]

Smith, [Richard]. Appointed boatswain at Woolwich yard 1660.[1]

Smith, [Robert]. Navy Office messenger; appointed 1660; also a messenger of the King's Chamber, and authorised thereby to conduct prosecutions on the Office's behalf.[1]

Smith, Thomas (d. 1658). Secretary to the Earl of Northumberland as admiral of the fleet 1636 and as acting Lord High Admiral 1638–42; appointed secretary to the Admiralty by parliament, 1642; Navy Commissioner 1646, re-appointed 1649. His widow (supported by her kinsman Speaker Grimston) appealed to the government in 1660 for payment of debts due to her late husband.[1]

Smith, [Walter]. Scrivener, of Ludgate Hill; brother of Richard Smyth the obituarist.[1]

Smith, [William]. (d. 1695). A leading actor in the Duke's Company from 1662; co-manager of the United Company 1682. Originally a barrister.[1]

Smith, ——. Clerk to Auditor Wood of the Exchequer.[1]
Smith, ——. Mercer. Possibly Theophilus, of the White Lion, Paul's Churchyard.[1]
Smith, ——. Musician; *see* King, William
Smithfield. An irregularly shaped area of 5¾ acres on the north-west of the city, adjoining the churches and hospital of St Bartholomew. Famous for its great cattle, horse and fodder market, the pens occupying the w. side of the site, leaving the remainder as an open space used, after the Fire, for temporary shops. Famous also for its Bartholomew Fair (q.v. ii.166, n. 2). The market for live cattle survived until 1855. The central market for meat then succeeded, occupying the northern parts of the site. (R)
Smythes, [Simon]. A graduate (1650) of Trinity College, Cambridge; chaplain in the service of the E. India Company 1663–8. Smyth's *Obituary* records a funeral sermon in London by 'Mr Smithies' in 1674.[1]
Snow, [John]. Relative; of Blackwall (in 1666 occupying a house taxed on six hearths).[1] The connection has not been established with certainty, but may be through the Glascocks. (A John Snow married Sarah Glascock at Romford, Essex, in 1628, and a Joseph Snow married Susan Glascock at Chigwell, Essex, in 1631.) A John Snow was one of the under-officers of the House of Lords in 1665.[2] A Ralph Snow received a ring as a friend at Pepys's funeral.[3]
Somerset, ——. Son of Lord John Somerset, whose father was the 1st Marquess of Worcester (d. 1646). Lord John had three sons of whom Thomas, the eldest, was unmarried at this time.[1]
Somerset House. Built by Protector Somerset in Edward VI's reign, under James I and Charles I it had become the official residence of the Queen Consort. Henrietta-Maria had added a chapel (designed by Inigo Jones) in 1623–5. She took possession again 1660–6, after which it passed to Queen Catherine who used it to house her domestic officers, both lay and clerical. She moved there on the King's death and occupied it until her departure for Portugal in 1692. After her death it reverted to the Crown, but was never again used as a royal residence. In 1776–86 it was replaced by the present building designed, mostly for Government offices, by Sir William Chambers. Pepys mentions some of the work done on the building in the early '60s. More was done later in the reign – in particular the building of a new stable block (probably by Hooke) in 1669, and the renovation of the chapel in 1674–5.[1]
Somerset Stairs. The landing stairs for Somerset House.
Soulemont, [Solomon]. Clerk to Sir G. Carteret in the '60s, and to the Comptroller 1673–5, 1678–80. (A Thomas Soulemont was clerk and later secretary to Thomas Cromwell in the 1530s.)[1]
Southampton, 4th Earl of: *see* Wriothesley, T.
Southampton Market. On the s. side of Hart St (now Bloomsbury

Way) between Bloomsbury Sq. and the future St George's church. Established by the Earl of Southampton c. 1662 to serve this growing area, it disappeared in the formation of New Oxford St c. 1847. Often referred to as Bloomsbury Market. (R)

Southerne, James. Clerk to Blackborne in the Navy Office in 1660; to Coventry in the Navy Office 1660–7; clerk in the Admiralty in the 1670s; Clerk of the Acts 1677–86, 1688–90; Navy Commissioner (Old Accounts) 1686–8; Secretary to the Admiralty 1690–4; Extra Navy Commissioner 1695–1702 (retired).[1] Pepys took a low view of his ability as Secretary to the Admiralty and found him an ungrateful protégé.[2]

Southesk, Earl of: *see* Carnegie, R.

Southwark. A town at the s. end of London Bridge, in Surrey. In 1660 connected by a continuous line of buildings with Bermondsey to the east, but developing only slowly along Bankside over the marshes to the west. Famous for its inns and gaols. The area next to the Bridge head and known as the 'Borough' was within the city of London's jurisdiction, the remainder was not. (R)

Southwell, Sir Robert, kt 1665 (1635–1702). Diplomatist; ambassador to Portugal 1665–9; Secretary of State for Ireland 1690–1702; President of the Royal Society 1690–4. A relative and friend of Petty. His quarrel with Sandwich did not prevent him from becoming an 'honoured friend' of Pepys.[1] They sat together in three parliaments between 1673 and 1687, and conducted a delightful and affectionate correspondence. In one letter Pepys, indulging himself with the company of Southwell's 14-year old son, complains that 'hee makes mee sweat with one confounding Quaestion or other'.[2]

Sparke, ——. Clergyman: probably Edward Sparke (d. 1693), who conducted Anglican services at Clerkenwell during the Commonwealth. In 1652 he published *Scintillula Altaris*, a defence of the church's feasts and fasts, a work which went through eight editions by 1700. At the Restoration he became a royal chaplain, Vicar of Clerkenwell 1660–5, of Walthamstow 1662–6 and of Tottenham 1666–93.[1]

Sparling, Capt. [Thomas] (d. by 1688). A captain in the Commonwealth navy, but after commanding the *Assistance* in the Dutch voyage (1660) held no further commission.[1]

Spicer, Jack. One of Pepys's colleagues in the Exchequer: in 1660 a messenger of the Receipt; in 1669 clerk to Loving, Teller of the Receipt; still in post in 1683.[1]

Spong, [John]. The Spong who is a clerk in the Six Clerks' Office of Chancery in 1660 is apparently the same man who after 1662 is a maker of optical instruments, living in 1668 in Bloomsbury market. His arrest on suspicion of treason in 1662 would explain his disappearance from government service. He was born in 1623; a 'John Spoung' (? his father) died in St Bride's parish in 1644.[1]

Spragge, Sir Edward, kt 1665. Naval commander; nephew of William Legge; M.P. for Dover 1673. A favourite of the Duke of York, he held 12 commands 1660–73, and was advanced to flag rank from 1666. His greatest exploit was the destruction of the Algerian fleet at Bougie Bay in 1671. He was drowned in the Battle of Sole Bay 1673.[1]

Spry, [Arthur] (1612–85). M.P. for St Mawes 1660, 1661–Jan. 79; appointed additional commissioner for paying off the Navy, Dec. 1660.[1]

Squibb, [Arthur, jun.] (d. 1680). Lawyer, republican and Fifth-Monarchist. He had sat in Barebone's Parliament in 1653 and was associated with its extremists. In 1656 he was involved in a Fifth-Monarchist rising. He had been a Commissioner for Compounding 1650–4 and 1659–60, and in early 1660 unsuccessfully claimed Downing's tellership in the Exchequer, together with the house that went with it, by virtue of a reversion granted him in 1640. In 1671 he was briefly imprisoned for a Fifth-Monarchist sermon but thereafter lived quietly in Chertsey, Surrey.[1] His royalist brother Laurence (d. 1674) held a tellership in the '60s.[2]

Stacey, Doll: *see* Poynton

Stacey, [John]. Tar merchant; probably the Common Councilman for Billingsgate 1669–83, 1689–d. 96 who appears to have lived in Thames St.[1]

Sta(i)nes, [Thomas]. Appointed glazier and plater, Chatham 1664. He appears to have earned the place by giving information about abuses in the work of government glaziers.[1]

Stangate. An area on the Surrey bank of the Thames in Lambeth round the foot of the modern Westminster Bridge. (R)

Stankes, Will. Described in his will (1676) as a yeoman, of Brampton. He looked after Pepys's property there. He died owning copyhold and freehold lands in Brampton, as well as cottages and cash. He left a widow Mary whom he had married after the death of his wife Joan in 1668.[1]

Stanley, [William]. Vicar of Walmer and Rector of Ripple, Kent 1648–d. 80.[1]

Stapely, [Joseph]. Ropemaker: his ropeground was at Wapping dock.[1]

Star Chamber: *see* Westminster Palace

Starkey, [John]. Bookseller in Paul's Churchyard from 1658; after the Fire on the s. side of Fleet St by Middle Temple Gate next to the Devil Tavern, in a house taxed on six hearths.[1] Usually referred to by Pepys in 1667 as 'my new bookseller'. His identity is established by the entry at viii.156. From 1668 he brought out trade catalogues of books published in London which later became the term catalogues of the Stationers' Company. He was an Anabaptist, and later a prominent critic of the court in the newsletters[2] he wrote for the Whigs. He was imprisoned in 1674, and in 1683 was outlawed for his support of Monmouth. By 1690 he was once more serving as an assistant of the Stationers' Company.[3]

Starkey, [Philip]. Cook, of London Wall; employed as master-cook in Oliver Cromwell's household; Master of the Company of Cooks 1668–9; Captain of the Red Company of trainbands 1679. When he officiated at the entertainments given by Cromwell to foreign ambassadors his fee was £20.[1]

Starkey, ——. A friend of Will Howe; presumably therefore Samuel Starkey, of Gray's Inn, of which Howe was a member. Son of George Starkey of Windsor, he was admitted in 1664.[1]

Starling, Ald. [Samuel] (d. 1674). Brewer, of Seething Lane.[1]

Stationers' Hall. On Ludgate Hill; once the town house of the Earls of Pembroke and Abergavenny. Destroyed in the Fire; rebuilt on the same site 1670.[1]

Stayner, Sir Richard. Naval commander, knighted by both Cromwell and Charles II; friend of Sandwich. He played a distinguished part in the First Dutch War, and served as Rear-Admiral in the fleet that brought the King home in 1660. Died at Lisbon 1662.[1]

The Steelyard. On the s. side of (Upper) Thames St, now covered by Cannon St Station. Once the London house of the Hanse merchants. The property extended to the river, its four acres including the merchants' hall, wharves, warehouses, and private dwelling houses, and in earlier centuries had been an important factor in the life of the city. Burnt in the Fire and rebuilt by the merchants. (R)

Stefkins, [Dietrich, angl. **Theodore]** (d. 1673). Viol player and composer; of German birth, resident in England by 1634, musician-in-ordinary 1636, a particular friend of John Jenkins, and known to Constantijn Huyghens, he maintained his continental contacts and died at Cologne.[1] (Lu)

Stephens, [Roger]. Silversmith, of Foster Lane. He was apprenticed in 1616, and made free of the Goldsmiths' Company in 1625.[1]

Stepney. A village in Middlesex, its vast parish covering most of the riverside area between St Katharine's (downstream of the Tower) and the R. Lea and including the riverside hamlets of Shadwell, Wapping, Ratcliffe, Limehouse and Poplar and the inland hamlets of Bethnal Green, Mile End, Stratford-le-Bow and Spitalfields. The riverside hamlets were linked to the city by an unbroken line of buildings along the river front as far east as the Isle of Dogs, and the next hundred years was to see several of them made into independent parishes. The church of the mother parish, St Dunstan, Stepney, though itself both large and notable, was surrounded by a mere handful of houses. (R)

Sterry, [Nathaniel] (d. 1698). Secretary to the mission sent with

Mountagu's fleet in the summer of 1659 to mediate in the Swedish-Dutch war. Brother of Peter Sterry, chaplain to Oliver Cromwell. Probably the 'Mr Sterry' appointed in Sept. 1657 to assist Milton as Latin Secretary.[1]

Stevens, [Anthony]. Clerk, later cashier, in the Navy Treasury; c. 1671 serving under the Treasury Commissioners and afterwards Assistant-Auditor, later Auditor, of the Land Revenues.[1]

Steventon/Stevenson. St John Stephenton was appointed Clerk of the Cheque at Portsmouth in 1660; and served as Mayor in 1664–5 and 1675–6.[1] His wife, according to Pepys a 'very debauched woman',[2] was accidentally burnt to death in 1665 when in a drunken stupor. The Stevenson/Steventon who was Hewer's uncle may have been John Stephenson, traceable as a purser in 1655, 1664 and 1676.[3]

Steward, Capt. [Francis]. Served in the Commonwealth navy; held three commands 1665–6; thereafter none. Written off by Coventry as 'naught'.[1]

Stoakes, Capt. [John] (d. 1665). A leading Cromwellian naval commander; held four commands after the Restoration.[1]

Stockdale, [Robert]. Appointed 1665 to administer the seamen's share of prize; by 1673 a customs officer.[1]

The Stocks. North of the church of St Mary Woolchurch and south of the junction of Cornhill, Threadneedle St and The Poultry. Once the site of the city's stocks, but, since Edward I's time, a market building with stalls mostly for butchers and fishmongers. Burnt in the Fire and rebuilt further back from the cross roads, taking in the site of the church. Often thereafter known as Woolchurch market, its dealings were then altered to fruit, roots and herbs. Removed c. 1739 to make room for the Mansion House (R)

Stokes, [Humphrey]. Goldsmith, at the Black Horse, Lombard St (rebuilt after the Fire). He provided plate given by the Navy Board to shipbuilders. Alive in 1677.[1]

Stone, Capt. [John] (d. 1678). One of the Tellers of the Exchequer 1654–60. Elected M.P. for London 1653, and for Cirencester 1654 and 1656, and holder of various offices under the Commonwealth in the customs, excise and prize commissions, he was also briefly in 1653 a Councillor of State and a Commissioner for the Admiralty and Navy.[1]

Story, Capt. [Thomas]. Of Guilden Morden, Cambs.; receiver of assessments and farmer of excise for the county.[1]

Stowell, ——. Robert Stowell, receiver of clerical tenths, Rochester 1667. A Robert Stowell (? his father) was diocesan registrar under Charles I.[1] But possibly Pepys meant to refer to Robert Sewell, Storekeeper at Chatham under the Commonwealth and reappointed in 1660.[2]

Strachan, Capt. [John]. Navy agent at Leith since before the Civil War; reappointed in 1660 and given charge of navy business in Orkney in 1665.[1] An old and faithful royalist – 'Honest John' – he received several gifts of money from the King: in Nov. 1660 half the proceeds of the sale of two ships (over £1000) and in 1665 £200 'for service by him done and to be done'.[2]

Strand Bridge and Stairs. A name still given in 1660 to the place in the Strand where, until 1549, there had been a stone bridge carrying the roadway over a lane and a small stream running into the Thames. The bridge was then demolished and a large section of the road levelled for the building of Somerset House, the lane apparently being diverted round the e. end of the grounds of the new house. The lane thereupon became known as Strand Bridge, the landing stairs at its foot often being also so called. The present Strand Lane preserves its memory. (R)

Strand, the Maypole in: *see* Maypole

Strange, Maj. [Edward]. Solicitor to the commissioners of excise.[1]

Strangeways, Col. [Giles] (1615–75). Royalist and enemy of Dissenters; M.P. for Weymouth and Melcombe Regis 1640, Bridport 1640–4, Dorset 1661–75; a critic of government finance during the Second Dutch War. A great drinker and smoker and a friend of Sir John Robinson.[1]

Stratford. The road from London to Colchester passed through two small Middlesex villages with this name, one, short of Bow by some 2½ miles, and the other beyond Bow, some 4 miles from the Standard in Cornhill. Strictly, the latter was Stratford Langthorn, or Stratford at Bow, the former Stratford by or le Bow, but either might simply be referred to as Stratford. (R)

Streeter, Robert (1621–79). The principal English decoration painter of the time; Serjeant-painter to the King 1663–79. At the time of Pepys's visit to his studio (1 Feb. 1669) he was living in Long Acre.[1]

Strode, [John] (d. 1686). Governor of Dover Castle 1660–86. A volunteer in the King's guards 1658; captain 1st Foot Guards at Dunkirk 1661; Major 1678; Lt-Col. 1682, 1684. Pepys consulted him in the '80s about the history of the Cinque Ports and the question of territorial waters in the Channel.[1]

Strudwick, [Thomas and Elizabeth]. Elizabeth, daughter of Sir Richard Pepys (Lord Chief Justice of Ireland 1654–9) was a cousin of the diarist. She married Thomas Strudwick, confectioner, who in 1666 occupied a house taxed on eight hearths in Turnagain Lane, west of Snow Hill, Holborn.[1] After the Fire the area was rebuilt and by the late '70s he was living on Snow Hill itself at the sign of the Three Sugar Loaves.[2] In 1664 he acted as executor of the estate of Benjamin Scott, his brother-in-law. He was still alive in 1686. The John Strudwick, grocer, at the Star, in whose house Bunyan died in 1688, may have been a relative.[3]

Strutt, [Thomas]. Purser of the *Resolution* 1662.[1]

Stuart, Frances Teresa, Duchess of Richmond (1647–1702). 'La belle Stuart'; daughter of Dr Walter Stuart, a physician in Henrietta-Maria's household, and educated in France. 'Slender, straightly built and taller than the generality of women' (Gramont). Her beauty attracted the attention of Louis XIV. Charles II, equally attracted, was unable to persuade her to become his mistress. She was Maid of Honour to the Queen in 1663, and after her marriage in 1667 to Charles Stuart, 3rd Duke of Richmond, was made Lady of the Bedchamber. She lived at court for the rest of her life after the death of her husband in 1672. She died a Catholic.[1]

Stuckey, [Valentine]. Linen draper to the Wardrobe.[1]

Suffolk, 13th Earl of: *see* Howard, J.

Suffolk St. Parallel to and east of the Haymarket.

Sutton, [Abraham]. Brother of Pepys's Aunt Wight. He died in his 55th year at Ghent in 1675, having spent 30 years there as a merchant. He was buried at his own request in St Andrew Undershaft. By his will his cousin Robert Woolley (q.v.) was appointed his executor.[1]

Swaddell, [John]. Clerk to Arlington 1663–c. 73; Clerk of the Ordnance 1689–90.[1]

Swan, [Humphrey]. Broom and reed merchant.[1]

Swan, Will. Possibly the Treasury solicitor of that name, active under the Commonwealth.[1]

Swynfen. 'The great Swynfen' was John (1613–94), a leading Presbyterian M.P. who sat in most parliaments 1640–94 and was M.P. for Tamworth during the diary period. Later a prominent Exclusionist. His grandson Samuel Swynfen was a godfather of Dr Johnson; his great-grandson was the 1st Earl St Vincent, the admiral.[1] The other Swynfen mentioned was his son Richard (b. 1634), an Oxford graduate, admitted to Gray's Inn 1660 and shortly afterwards made secretary, with Richard Coling, to Manchester, the Lord Chamberlain.[2]

Symons, [Thomas]. Surgeon to Alured's regiment (formerly Mountagu's); Warden of the Barber-Surgeons' Company 1678–9.[1]

Symons, Will. A contemporary of Pepys in the service of the Commonwealth (as an underclerk to the Council of State), and married shortly after Pepys, on 9 July 1656, at St Margaret's, Westminster, to Margaret Sherring in a civil ceremony conducted by his uncle Henry Scobell, a Middlesex J.P. (and clerk to the Commonwealth parliaments). He lost his place at the Restoration and by 1669 – no longer such 'a very brave fellow' as Pepys once thought him – was a clerk employed by the Brooke House Committee. No doubt the fact that he was the nephew of his uncle was of less than no advantage to him in 1660. Under Scobell's will he inherited the remainder of the lease of a house in Westminster and, subject to certain charges, the manor of Luffnall and Cromer in Norfolk.[1]

Symons, ——. Dancing master. Possibly the 'Simons' who was a dancing master in Cambridge in 1655.[1]

Taaffe, Theobald, 2nd Viscount Taaffe, cr. Earl of Carlingford 1661 (d. 1677). Irish Catholic; a royalist commander in Ireland during the Civil War, and a close friend and confidant of the King in exile. In 1666 envoy-extraordinary to the Emperor and the Prince-Bishop of Münster – a post in which his capacity for drink was said to be his best qualification.[1]

Talbot, [Charles] (d. by 1688). Naval officer; held nine commissions 1661–85.[1]

Talbot, Peter (1620–80). Almoner to the Queen; brother of Col. Richard, and a protégé of Arlington. He was said to have secretly received the King into the Catholic church before the Restoration. According to Clarendon, as Almoner he 'walked with the same or more freedom in the King's house (and in clergy habit) than any of his majesty's chaplains'. He was later (1669–80) Archbishop of Dublin, and died in prison under a false accusation of treason.[1]

Talbot, Col. [Richard], cr. Earl of Tyrconnel 1685 (1630–91). Groom of the Bedchamber to the Duke of York from 1660; gentleman-volunteer at the Battle of Lowestoft 1665. Leader of the Catholic interest in Ireland; and from 1685 commander of the army and James II's chief agent there.[1]

Tallents, [Philip]. Clergyman. He took his B.A. from Magdalene in 1651, and was a Fellow in 1652; he was intruded as (Presbyterian) minister of Lilford-cum-Wigsthorpe, Northants. 1654–62; after which he conformed and became Vicar of Moulton, Lincs. 1678–1705. He was Sheriff's chaplain to Sir D. Gauden.[1] His elder brother Francis (Fellow of Magdalene 1645–8 and Presbyterian Vicar of Chesterton, Cambs. 1650) was in 1662 ejected for nonconformity from the curacy of St Mary's, Shrewsbury.[2]

TANGIER

General. During the first part of the 17th century English and Dutch shipping in the Mediterranean suffered much from the depredations of the Barbary corsairs – the pirates from the Regencies of Algiers, Tunis and Tripoli. By that time the Deys of these city states were virtually independent of the Sultan and the real power lay in the hands of pirate captains. Algiers was a pirate state flourishing on the proceeds of captured prizes and the ransoms extorted from their crews. The ships were put into the service of the corsairs, and their seamen were housed in huge *bagnios* to await ransom, or (if they were not so fortunate) a life of slavery in a Moorish city. When the English began to trade extensively in the Mediterranean and the Levant in the reigns of James I and Charles I many adventurous seamen, with their Dutch counterparts, joined the corsairs by 'turning Turk' and becoming renegades, in which capacity they often achieved great wealth and a high position in Moorish society. These renegades proved useful as experts in the sailing of the vessels taken as prize. In this way the square-rigged northern type of round ship gradually superseded the war galley with which the corsairs had preyed upon Spanish and Venetian shipping in the preceding century. They were stouter and more commodious than the long galleys and mounted more guns. The galley was a weapon of limited endurance: these northern ships carried larger crews and more provisions, thus greatly extending the range of the corsairs and adding to the number of pirate states by making Salli on the Moroccan coast (which was unsuitable for galleys) an additional corsair base. By the middle of the century Algerine or Saletin corsairs were able not only to cruise about the Straits of Gibraltar but to venture far afield to the banks of Newfoundland, the southern coasts of Ireland and Cornwall, even the mouth of the Thames. For a brief season a crew occupied Lundy Island in the Bristol Channel and one renegade was reputed to have reached Iceland.

The acquisition of Tangier by the marriage treaty with Portugal signed on 23 Jan. 1661 was therefore hailed as of great importance for the safeguarding of trade using the Straits of Gibraltar. Robert Blake, on a cruise off those coasts during the Commonwealth in 1655, had remarked on the strategic importance of the place.[1] After its acquisition, his successor in those seas, Sir John Lawson, declared that once a mole had been constructed 'ships would ride securely in all weather, and they would keep the place against all the world, and give the law to all that trade in the Mediterranean'.[2]

As soon as the marriage treaty was signed, Pepys's patron, Sandwich (who had earlier accompanied Blake on his cruise off Salli) was sent to take possession of the place and to escort Catherine to England for the wedding ceremony. The first Governor, the Earl of Peterborough (1662–4), was sent to meet him with troops for the garrison; but Sandwich arrived first to find the place besieged by Moorish troops under 'Abd Allāh al-Ghailān (known to the English as Guyland or Gayland) who had rebelled against the Emperor of Morocco and was in control of the region around Tangier. With commendable promptitude Sandwich landed seamen to man the derelict defences. Among them was the ordinary seaman Edward Barlow, the author of the most interesting diary written in the 17th century, apart from that of Pepys: 'We kept guard and stood sentry about the town, and upon the walls night and day. And sometimes in the daytime, we all of us, being about

400 men, upon the walls which lay open to the country, gave volleys of small shot, when we saw any of the Moors, to put them in fear and let them know that the town was well manned'.[3] Such was to be the situation in Tangier for the next twenty years.

Peterborough fortunately arrived shortly afterwards with 500 horse and 2000 foot. His commission defined the national aim in securing the town: 'Our main design in putting ourself to this great charge for making this Addition to our Dominions being to gaine our Subjects the Trade of Barbary and to enlarge our Dominion of that Sea'. Within a few weeks, however, Peterborough was back in London to report that the town was 'in none of the best condition', and that attacks by Guyland in command of 17,000 Berber rebels must be expected for some time to come.

On 12 Aug. 1662 Pepys was appointed to the Privy Council's Committee for Tangier. He was co-opted 'to bring in some Laws for the Civill government of it', though the town was not incorporated as a municipality until 1668. The Committee was a distinguished body headed by the Duke of York because, Pepys wrote, Tangier 'is likely to be the most considerable place the King of England hath in the world'.[4] Its members included such men as Peterborough, Sandwich, Albemarle, Carteret and William Coventry. Pepys considered his own appointment 'a very great Honour to me and may be of good concernment to me'.[5] It proved also a fruitful source of income. He found that the merchants and contractors dealing with the colony found it to their advantage to press *douceurs* on him – so that Tangier became 'one of the best flowers'[6] in his garden. And in 1665 when he succeeded the incompetent Povey as Treasurer even brighter horticultural prospects opened up. Even though, by arrangement, half of the proceeds went to his predecessor, the profits of the office from 'poundage' over and above his modest income of £300 p.a. were considerable.

Pepys however had all the misgivings of a good civil servant about the management of affairs in Tangier. Not only was he shocked at the mounting costs of the mole (see below), but he was astounded at the casual way successive governors presented their accounts and the equally casual manner in which they were accepted by the Commissioners. No one dared to question the figures: 'Lord, how I was troubled to see my lord Tiviotts accounts of 10000*l* passed in that manner and wish 1000 times I had not been there'.[7] According to him the Earl of Teviot (Lord Rutherford), the second Governor of Tangier (1663–4), was 'a cunning fellow'.[8] On the other hand, the inhabitants of the town regarded him as their best governor and certainly he died a gallant death riding into an ambush at the head of his troops. He was a professional soldier, chiefly responsible for the evacuation of Dunkirk, from which town he brought the soldiers who formed the Tangier

Regiment. These were mostly Irishmen and Pepys was not alone in his apprehension that so many Catholic soldiers should be commanded by a Roman Catholic, Col. Fitzgerald, a friend of the Duke of York. Lord Belasyse, the next Governor who was appointed at the beginning of the Second Dutch War, was also a Catholic.

In his day the power of Guyland began to decline, only to be replaced by that of the Emperor of Morocco, al-Rashīd (Taffiletta) and the infamous Mawlāy Ismāʿīl, who succeeded him in 1672. Guyland himself fled to the protection of the English, but was killed in battle in 1673. Ismael extended imperial rule throughout Morocco by means of a formidable *corps d'élite* composed of negro slaves from the Sudan, aided by European renegades responsible for the artillery and a magnificent force of cavalry. A remarkable feature of his army was the use of stink pots as big as 'a large hand Granado'. 'They have found a way of Stinck Pots,' wrote the English commander, 'which upon its breaking makes a suddaine flame and from them proceeds such a stinck that men are sufficated with itt.'[9]

In 1680 the civilian population of Tangier was reckoned at 600; the two regiments composing the garrison numbered about 1400, and there were 300 slaves in 'His Majesty's Bagnio'. This was really a prisoner-of-war camp, the slaves or prisoners being employed in building the mole, or ransomed according to the practice of the Barbary corsairs.

In 1667 Belasyse was succeeded as Governor by the Earl of Middleton, the first civil Governor. Pepys's view of him, shared by Clarendon and Burnet, was that he was 'a man of moderate understanding, not covetous, but a soldier-of-fortune and poor'.[10] He continued in office until his death at Tangier in 1674. He was followed by the 2nd Earl of Inchiquin (Governor 1675–80), whose deputy was Sir Palmes Fairborne, the only attractive personality in a succession of idle and often corrupt administrators.

Fairborne was a professional soldier and no courtier. He lived at Tangier for 18 years and never sought advancement beyond that of commanding the garrison. He was responsible for erecting new forts on the perimeter and for strengthening the town walls in order to withstand attacks by Ismael's army. It was fortunate that he was in command at the time of the most serious assault in 1680, but he himself was killed in the moment of victory leading his troops in a sortie.

Fairborne was succeeded as Commander-in-Chief and Lieut-Governor by the notorious Col. Percy Kirke, another professional soldier commanding the regiment of foot known as the Tangier Regiment (or Kirke's Lambs, so called from their regimental crest of a Paschal Lamb). During the truce which followed the great siege of 1680–1 Kirke made friends with the tyrant Ismael. They seem to have

been birds of a feather. Kirke was the most foul-mouthed man Pepys
ever met and a letter which he wrote after visiting Ismael's capital
suggests that he was almost illiterate. After his stay at the court of the
Emperor he wrote; 'I am among the most sevilisde pepell in the worlde
and iff ever I have a sone I will rather choose to send him hether for
breading than to the Corte of France'.[11] On the other hand, an officer
who accompanied him described the Emperor as one who 'excels all
mankind in barbarous and bloody actions, massacre and murder being
his Royal game and divertisement'.[12] This was the man who ruled
Morocco for 55 years. In the negotiations for the release of prisoners
from his *bagnio* at Meknes, which was reputed to hold 30,000 slaves,
including 2500 Christians and 70 prisoners of war, he demanded too
high a price, so that only a few were redeemed.

Nevertheless, Ismael was gracious enough to send an embassy to
London in 1682 with gifts including two lions and 20 ostriches. Pepys
may well have met his ambassador when the latter visited the Royal
Society, but the unfortunate man was arrested on his return and the
treaty which he had negotiated was repudiated. The repudiation was
accompanied by letters which even Kirke described as 'the highest
piece of impudence which could be imagined'.[13] Charles II was called
'an old woman, a slave to his Parliament. As to the peace by sea which
thou desirest of us, we have no need of it, for we do not concern ourselves in shipping'.[14] Whereupon the Emperor set about preparing a
fresh attack on Tangier.

As the attacks by the Moors proved unrelenting and the cost of the
construction of the mole mounted, so did doubts about the value of
retaining the place increase at home. Similar doubts were first expressed
by Pepys and Sandwich as far back as 1667. Clarendon was blamed for
its acquisition, as he had been blamed for the evacuation of Dunkirk.
There was continual dissatisfaction about the financial burden, which
many assumed to be due as much to lax administration as to the difficulties of constructing the mole. In Pepys's words 'there is nothing in
the world done with true integrity but there is design along with it'.[15]

What had been intended as a supply base and a harbour of refuge for
shipping of all kinds had proved an illusion. Ships of the Levant
Company continued to be harassed by the Barbary corsairs and the
many expeditions sent to sign treaties with the Regencies never
succeeded in achieving more than temporary respite. There were
faults committed on both sides – by unprincipled English captains as
well as by ambitious pirates who took little heed of what their Deys had
promised. Sandwich's fleet of 1661 was followed by those of Lawson,
Allin and Narbrough, but every treaty entered into foundered on the
right of search clause on which the corsairs insisted. Passes were issued
to ships in order to enable them to escape the humiliation of such

visitations (Pepys obtained some for his friends the Houblons who traded in the Mediterranean), but inevitably there were arguments about their validity, and governments whose subjects lived by seizures and ransoms never kept faith over promises extorted by foreign fleets. As a base for such fleets, Tangier had proved unsatisfactory because supplies were still drawn from Lisbon or Cadiz and until the mole was completed the port remained an open roadstead.

The House of Commons was therefore increasingly unwilling to meet the colony's mounting debts. As early as 1680 the King, who never showed any interest in the place, threatened to give it up unless more supplies were voted. The matter was postponed for the time being because of the disturbances of the Popish Plot period, but in 1683 Lord Dartmouth was given a secret commission to abandon Tangier. Pepys, now in retirement, was summoned at the shortest possible notice to accompany him as his adviser on matters affecting the civilian population, and made his way to Portsmouth in total ignorance of the real object of the voyage. The Admiralty sent as chaplain Dr Ken, the future Nonjuror and the author of the most beautiful evening hymn in the language.

Dartmouth's fleet of 21 ships sailed ostensibly to succour Tangier. Writing to Evelyn on 7 Aug. 1683, Pepys told him of 'the King's command (without any account for the reason of it), requiring my repair hither, at less than eight-and-forty hours warning: not but that I, now not only know, but am well pleased with the errand; it being to accompany my Lord of Dartmouth in his present expedition . . ., with a very fair squadron of ships to Tangier. What our work nevertheless is, I am not solicitous to learn nor forward to make griefs at, it being handled by our masters as a secret. This only I am sure of, that over and above the satisfaction of being thought fit for some use or other ('tis no matter what) I shall go in a good ship, under a very worthy leader, in a conversation as delightful, as companions in the first form . . . in divinity, law, physic and the usefullest parts of mathematics can render it, namely Dr Ken, Dr Trumbull, Dr Laurence and Mr Shere'.[16]

The events of the following months are described in Pepys's Tangier journal,[17] a worthy appendage to the great diary though far less well known. It differs from the diary in being less concerned with personal activities because it deals almost exclusively with the matter in hand, but it is written with all the old vitality and abounds in incisive character sketches, as well as being an appalling revelation of how the town and its inhabitants struck a man who was himself by no means straitlaced.

It was not until the fleet had been at sea for some days (Pepys being dreadfully seasick all the time) that Dartmouth summoned him to his cabin in order to inform him of the true aim of the voyage: 'my Lord in his cabin first broke to us the truth of our voyage for the destroying and deserting of Tangier'.[18] One look at the place on their arrival inspired this comment: 'But Lord! how could anybody ever think this place fit to be kept at this charge, that by its being overlooked by so many hills can never be secured against an enemy!'[19] Not only that, but the main water supply was now controlled by the Moors.

As Pepys soon found out, the place was a sink of iniquity and corruption – 'nothing but vice in the whole place of all sorts, for swearing, cursing, drinking and whoring'.[20] The man who was soon to become the President of the Royal Society was revolted by the barbarism of this frontier town, which had all the shortcomings of such a place and was governed by men who reflected its worst aspects. Col. Kirke, now acting Governor, Pepys dismisses as 'a very brute' with a temper as foul as his tongue. As for Admiral Herbert, who had resided there for many years, 'Of all the worst men living, Herbert is the only man I do not know to have any virtue to compound for all his vices'.[21] The comment is somewhat unfair because Herbert had been the first commander to sign a lasting treaty with Algiers and on more than one occasion had proved himself a resolute commander. But it was on his considered advice that Tangier was evacuated, he having declared 'the total incapacity of the Mole and the port of Tangier and this after all the expense of more than £400,000 thereon'.[22]

While the mole was being demolished, Pepys and the lawyers spent their time on the complicated business of clearing the town of its European inhabitants and compensating the residents for the loss of their properties. Invalids had to be shipped home in two hospital ships, Portuguese merchants had to be repatriated, the families of residents had to be compensated and conflicting property claims reconciled. Disabled soldiers were sent home to the new Royal Hospital at Chelsea and all the forts and walls were mined for destruction at the last minute. A typical entry in Pepys's journal is that for 26 September: 'Busy till 8 or 9 at night without an interval but only to dinner and then presently again to receive the claims of people to propriety [property]. But [they were] so silly and supine all of them, even the people of most understanding among them, that it is plain there was a habit of disorder and forgetfulness of all method and discipline in [all] they did, even in their own private concernments'.[23]

He himself was able to get away for a short holiday in Seville, where it rained all the time. When his part in the evacuation was finally wound up, he congratulates himself that he 'slept mighty well, and the better that the business of my being employed in a foolish treaty is over'.[24] Royal gratitude for the part he had played was shown on his return by his appointment for a second time to the Admiralty, now that the Popish Plot scare was over.

Dartmouth officially evacuated Tangier on 5 Feb. 1684, leaving the town in ruins. The besieging Moors entered the place while the last soldiers were being embarked and the flag hauled down.

Tangier had proved a failure as a base for fleets engaged in the unending task of protecting trade against the Barbary corsairs. None the less, the naval pressure brought to bear against them, whether by English, Dutch or French fleets, did succeed to the extent that the treaty with Algiers signed by Herbert in 1682 lasted in essentials for 150 years. By its terms corsairs were permitted to board English ships in order to examine their passes, but they were to offer no violence and they were to redeem their captives at a reasonable price. The terms of the treaty were so often renewed and adopted by so many other nations that it must be regarded as the beginning of the decline of piracy on the part of the Barbary states, though their depredations were not finally extinguished until the French occupation of Algeria in 1830.

As naval strategy took a new turn with the commencement of a century of wars with France, the existence of a base in those parts continued to be essential. Cadiz was only useful as long as we were at peace with Spain. It was William III who brought the nation into conflict with France, so that it was in his reign that the first battle fleet entered the Mediterranean with the object of fighting the French rather than carrying out punitive expeditions against the Algerines or the Tunisians. It was in 1704, when Sir George Rooke took the fleet into the Mediterranean in order to support Marlborough's grand design which culminated in the battle of Blenheim, that the final solution of the problem of a base was found at last.

After an inglorious summer cruise, it occurred to Rooke almost as an afterthought that he might as well attack Gibraltar, which was so manifestly ill defended. The place had hitherto been little regarded because it was not much better than Tangier as a harbour of refuge. Its acquisition in the war of Spanish Succession, according to Burnet, was 'much questioned by men who understand these matters well, whether our possessing ourselves of Gibraltar and our maintaining it so long, was to our advantage or not'.[25] The lesson of Tangier on the opposite side of the straits was evidently still deeply felt; but when Minorca, with its magnificent harbour of Port Mahon, was added by the peace treaty of 1763 Britain was admirably placed to pursue the long-deferred Mediterranean strategy.

(Christopher Lloyd)

The Mole. The town had lacked a defensible harbour when it was in the hands of the Portuguese. On taking possession in his first voyage there, Sandwich had arranged for the bay to be surveyed in July 1662 by Martin Beckman, the military engineer, who produced a proposal to

build a mole across the n. side of the bay for protection against the
Atlantic seas, with a shorter return at its e. end. The longer arm was to
be 400 yards in length (it proved eventually to be longer), and the whole
was to be wide enough to carry guns and their emplacements so that it
could be defended from both land and sea. It was a formidable task to
undertake so far from the home base, and in fact no engineering
project of such a size had ever been attempted before by Englishmen.
Hugh Cholmley, who had carried out harbour works at Whitby, was
appointed engineer, and a contract was concluded in March 1663
with him and two partners, the Governor (Teviot) and the commander
of the Mediterranean squadron (Lawson). Work began in the following
August. Cholmley brought in Yorkshire quarrymen who were settled
in a village (which they named Whitby) built for them three miles or
so from the site of the harbour. From the cliffs nearby they blasted and
hewed stone which was then carried to the site by cart and boat. There
the workforce came more and more to consist of soldiers from the
garrison, though there were some labourers from home, including a
few 'stout and laborious Irishmen',[26] and a handful of Italians, Dutchmen and galley slaves.

Until 1670 Cholmley employed traditional methods of pier building.
Blocks of masonry, held together by cement and iron cramps, were
built up on a foundation of loose rocks thrown on to the sand of the
seabed, and the whole structure protected by a breakwater of iron-shod
wooden piles and pillars of rock disposed in echelon formation on the
seaward side. Despite setbacks from heavy storms the work was pushed
forward so well that as early as 1665, after the outbreak of the Dutch
war, it was possible to mount a battery on the mole. But in 1670
Cholmley was persuaded against his better judgement to adopt a
different technique, using caissons (i.e. wooden chests packed with
masonry and rubble) instead of stone blocks. This was the method
favoured by his assistant Henry Sheeres, who had seen it used in the
construction of the new harbour at Genoa. But the lowering of
caissons into rough tidal water posed problems which had not existed
at Genoa, and the change of method slowed down progress.

Meantime control of the project had in 1669 passed out of the hands
of the original contractors, two of whom had died, and was assumed by
the Tangier Committee itself, which set up a mole office with Cholmley
at its head as Surveyor-General. By the time of the war of 1672-4 the
harbour could accommodate smaller ships of the Mediterranean
squadron, and several had been careened there for cleaning. But
criticism was mounting, both at home and in Tangier, over the delay
in finishing the work. In 1676 Cholmley was replaced by Sheeres, who
set about his task with vigour. In that year the mole was described by a
visitor as 'in its design the greatest and most noble Undertaking in the

World . . . a very pleasant thing to look on . . . with several pretty Houses upon it and many Families; on the inner side 24 Arched Cellars and before them a curious Walk, with Pillars for the Mooring of Ships. Upon [it] . . . a vast number of Great Guns, which are almost continually kept warm during fair weather, in giving and paying salutes to ships which come in and out'.[27] Shortly after this description was penned a series of storms wrecked part of the works, and further delays and expenses followed. Sheeres, like Cholmley before him, was kept short of money. The committee's grants, inadequate in the first place, were slow to arrive, and paid in tallies and Treasury bills that were convertible only at a discount. Finally work was brought to a halt for months on end in 1680 by the Moors' siege of the town, in the course of which the quarries were captured. By now the main limb was incomplete and the return not started. On the abandonment of the colony the mole was – with the greatest difficulty – destroyed. Two thousand men were hard at work for months blowing it up to prevent its use by an enemy. To this day its remains can be seen at low water.

Pepys kept in his library a number of representations of the town and harbour, among them a set of engravings by Hollar and some vivid water-colour sketches of the demolition of the mole by Thomas Phillips, a gunnery officer.[28]

Tasborough, [John]. Clerk to Thomas Povey.[1]
Tatnell, Capt. [Valentine] (d. by 1688). First commissioned in 1653, he held only one command (the *Adventure*) after the Restoration.[1]

TAVERNS, INNS AND EATING-HOUSES

The number of drinking- and eating-houses visited by Pepys – well over 100 in London and Westminster alone – is a sign of their general popularity as well as of Pepys's convivial habits. There were more than 1000 alehouses within the square mile of the city in 1614, and in 1638 over 400 taverns.[1] Both had increased in numbers by 1660. In addition there were inns, strong-water houses and a variety of eating-houses. No Londoner as he walked his streets was more than a few yards from refreshment, and the only limit on opening hours for the sale of alcoholic drinks (in law at any rate) was that it was prohibited during service times on Sundays.[2] More than once Pepys was able to get a drink after midnight.[3]

Establishments were of several types. The largest and most elaborate were inns – the equivalent of modern hotels, with accommodation for guests and their horses as well as bars. Some of them – especially those in

Holborn and Bishopsgate St near the city boundaries – catered for the coaching and carrier services which ran between the capital and the provinces, and had extensive stabling. Landlords of inns were among the most prosperous of traders: the greatest, such as Colborne of the Sun in Threadneedle St or Rawlinson of the Mitre in Fenchurch St, were rich city notables who died possessed of country properties. At the other end of the scale were alehouses, usually small, sometimes squalid, with only one or two rooms, and enjoying at best a steady and modest trade. They might serve snacks to accompany a morning draught and might specialise in a particular ale such as mum or china-ale etc. Strong-water houses were a 17th-century innovation growing in number since they required no licence.

But the most important house of refreshment to Pepys and to the middle-class Londoner in general was the tavern, whose trade was based on the sale of wine. It was found only in large towns, and in London its numbers and importance had never been greater than in the Restoration period.[4] Members of the Vintners' Company (established in 1614) could open a tavern without any formality, and all that the law required of non-members was a licence from the wine commissioners which they were only too anxious to bestow. The tavern was to Londoners of Pepys's time what the coffee-house, club and restaurant have been to later generations. It rarely occupied an entire building and might consist of the upper floor of a city house or houses with shops on the ground floor (the Pope's Head off Lombard St had 15) and cellars in the basement. Close by the entrance would be a bar, where the landlord would sit ready to receive guests or (if they were in a hurry) to have them served in their coaches. Beyond that would be a series of small rooms, with fireplaces, furnished with table and chairs.[5] in which the customers could be assured of privacy. The drawer or potboy would bring their drink; food could be brought in from a cookshop or the market;[6] they could write letters and do business with tradesmen;[7] or (as Pepys did so often) enjoy a little feminine company, or meet in a 'club' with friends. The larger taverns had ordinaries, or restaurants, which could cater for wedding parties or parish feasts,[8] and might provide music, ninepins or other entertainment.[9]

The habit of eating out in the middle of the day seems to have been common. Keepers of eating-houses could make fortunes.[10] On a number of occasions Pepys complains of crowds, and once of having to wait for two hours to be served.[11] Prices on the whole were reasonable. A smart French eating-house like Chatelin's in Covent Garden might charge as much as 8s. 6d. for an indifferent meal, but dinner at the King's Head, Charing Cross, one of the most fashionable taverns, would cost 2s. 6d. at the host's table, and only 1s. at the second table. In addition there were the modest eating-houses known as ordinaries,

where a fixed-price meal (of two courses, often with beef) would cost
1s. There were also the cookshops which served their own pies and
other simple dishes.[12] It was not until the 18th century that these became
the resort of the poor. Pepys found them useful – he would eat there, or
take their dishes home, or hire the cook himself for a party.[13] [*See
also* Drink; Food]

Taverns etc. (named)

[The list which follows is not complete. It omits those houses of entertainment for which no information or no significant information has been
discovered, and those outside London and its immediate neighbourhood. The
latter are dealt with in footnotes to the text. The very few houses described
in the footnotes are also omitted here.]

Anchor. Probably the Golden Anchor tavern, Paul's Churchyard,
traceable from c. 1648.[1]

Angel, King St, Westminster. Tavern or eating house on w. side
near s. end kept by William Wells (d. 1663). 9 hearths, 1664.[2] (R)

Angel, Tower Hill. Tavern at lower end of hill. Token, 1649.[3]

Axe, Axe Yard. Tavern on w. side kept by Elizabeth Drury, widow
(1660–6). 14 hearths, 1665.[4]

Bear at the Bridge Foot. Well-known tavern on s. end of Bridge on
w. side of Borough High St, kept by Abraham Browne, vintner (1667;
in 1650 by Cornelius Cooke, vintner). Pulled down 1761 when houses
on Bridge demolished.[5] (R)

Bear, Drury Lane. Probably the Bear and Harrow in Bear Yard (off
Butcher Row, a continuation of the Lane towards the Strand). 'A
noted Eating House' (Strype, 1720).[6]

Bear, nr Salisbury Court. Probably the Bear tavern commonly
described as 'at Fleet Bridge' (actually on s. side of Fleet St by Bride
Lane). 8 hearths, 1664.[7] (R)

Bell, King St, Westminster. Old tavern, kept by Samuel Walker,
vintner (1655–64), after him by his widow; on w. side opposite gatehouse of New Palace Yard. 20 hearths, 1664. Its low rates (2s.), compared with its neighbour's the Sun (20s.), suggest that it was of second
rank at this time. Later, under Anne, famous as meeting place of High
Tory October Club.[8] (R)

Bell, Strand. Large inn, known as 'the Bell at the Maypole'; to the
north of what was then the Strand near the present church of St Mary-
le-Strand. Kept by Thomas Lisle (1664). 'A Place of great Resort for
Horse, Coaches and Waggons' (Strype, 1720). 26 hearths, 1664.[9] (R)

Black Swan, Holborn. Coaching inn, with services especially to the
West country; on s. side between Fetter Lane and Barnard's Inn.[10] (R)

Blue Balls, Lincoln's Inn Fields. Ordinary; untraced; possibly a mistake for the Blue Bell, Duke St, nr Clare Market, at which von Uffenbach, a German visitor, had dinner in 1710 and watched a Scotsman breaking glasses with his voice.[11]

Bottle of Hay, St John's St, Clerkenwell. Traceable to ?1760s.[12]

Bull (Black Bull), Bishopsgate. Large coaching inn, on w. side immediately north of Gresham College. 33 hearths, 1666. 'Of a considerable Trade, and resort for Waggons and Stage Coaches that go Northwards' (Strype 1720), among them, in the early 17th century, those of the legendary Cambridge carrier Hobson (of 'Hobson's choice'). It fell off in repute and in Roach's *London pocket pilot* (1796) was recommended 'to the lovers of frugality'.[13] Demolished 1866.[14]

Bull, nr Southampton Market. Traceable from c. 1648.[15]

Bull Head. Possibly the Bull Head in New Palace Yard kept in the 1650s by Hugh Steadman, half-way down the n. side of the yard and assessed on 6 hearths in 1664. On the other hand, the Bull Head at Charing Cross fits the context better on those occasions when Pepys was accompanied by his father or travelling to his father's house in Salisbury Court.[16]

Cardinal's Cap. Well-known tavern in Cardinal's Cap Alley, westernmost of the alleys linking Lombard St and Cornhill; kept by John Steele, vintner (d. 1679). 10 hearths, 1666.[17] (R)

Chatelin's, Covent Garden. Fashionable French eating-house often mentioned in plays of the period. Henry Cateline supplied provisions to the royal household in 1660 and 1661.[18]

Chequer (Exchequer), Charing Cross. Large coaching inn on s.-w. corner of St Martin's Lane at its junction with Charing Cross and about a dozen doors east of the Royal Mews, its site being nearly at what is now the s.-e. corner of Trafalgar Sq. Kept by Paul Rogers (c. 1660–c. 67). 22 hearths, 1664.[19] (R)

Chequer (Exchequer), Holborn. Coaching inn on n. side, east of Furnivall's Inn, its yard being the first turn west off Leather Lane. The site is now included in the head office of the Prudential Assurance Company.[20] (R)

Clerke's: *see* Leg, King St.

Coach and Horses, Aldgate. Kept since at least 1651 by John Game.[21]

Cock, Bow St (Oxford Kate's). Well-known licensed victualling house, on e. side.[22]

Cock, Strand. Well-frequented alehouse, on s. side, just outside Temple Bar and in the parish of St Clement Danes; still in the 1720s a 'noted' house. Often wrongly identified with a later Cock inside Temple Bar (on n. side of Fleet St, opposite Middle Temple Gate) which was pulled down in 1882 to make room for the Law Courts branch of the Bank of England. Some of its fittings were removed to 22 Fleet St (s. side) where another Cock was opened in 1888.[23] (R)

Cross Keys, Cripplegate. Possibly the inn on the e. side of White-cross St. But there was another house of that name on the w. side of Little Wood (now Wood) St, close to the gate.[24]

Crown, Hercules' Pillars Alley. Ordinary, in alley south of Fleet St; kept by William King. He made a fortune and had moved from the district or died by 1670. 5 hearths, 1664; 13 hearths, 1666 (an adjoining house to which he had moved).[25] (R)

Crown, King St, Westminster. Cookshop on w. side, between Sea Alley and Axe Yard; kept by William Wilkinson since at least 1637. Pepys mentions his death in 1668: his widow Alice, who died shortly afterwards, ordered the house to be sold. 14 hearths, 1664.[26] (R)

Crown, Leadenhall St. A large and important tavern, on n. side, a few yards west of Bartholomew Lane, kept from 1663 by Thomas Blagrave, vintner, a commissioner under the Wine Act 1668. 'Behind the Exchange', in Pepys's words, because the Exchange's main entrance was in Cornhill. Used for suppers by fellows of the Royal Society after their meetings, and once (20 Jan. 1666) for an informal meeting of the Society itself. Also used by the parish (St Christopher-le-Stocks) for its audit-day and Ascension day dinners. 19 hearths, 1664; 28 hearths, 1666 (as rebuilt after the Fire).[27] (R)

Devil, Fleet St. A large and prosperous tavern, on s. side, between Temple Bar and Middle Temple Gate, almost opposite St Dunstan's church; now the site of no. 1, Fleet St. Kept 1646–60 by John Wadlow, 1660–8 by Ald. Jonathan Barford and 1668–81 Richard Taylor (all vintners). Earlier made famous by Ben Jonson's patronage and by a notable landlord, Simon Wadlow (John's father). 19 hearths, 1664.[28] (R)

Dog, New Palace Yard. Notable tavern on n. side, one door from junction with King St, kept since at least 1656–7 by William Hargrave, vintner, one of the wine commissioners appointed under the Wine Act 1668. One of the largest taverns in town; 30 hearths, 1664. Renamed the Horn and Feathers by 1727.[29] (R)

Dolphin, Bishopsgate. Coaching inn with services to E. Anglia; on e. side outside city wall, between Houndsditch and Devonshire St. 'Old . . . very large, and of a good Receipt' (Strype, 1720).[30] (R)

Dolphin, Tower St. Tavern, on n. side, near s.-e. end of Mark Lane with an entry into each street, kept by Richard Weedon. Much frequented by officers of the Navy Board. Destroyed in the Fire; rebuilt and reopened in spring 1668. 15 hearths, 1666.[31] (R)

Feathers, Fish St. Probably the tavern in Old Fish St; but there was also another of that name in Great Trinity Lane off Old Fish St.[32]

Five Bells. Mentioned only once, when Pepys went there from Greatorex's shop (on the s. side of the Strand). Therefore probably the tavern in Hungerford Market rather than one of the other two of that name near by in Fleet St and in Shoe Lane off Fleet St.[33]

Fleece (Golden Fleece), Cornhill. Tavern, in a passage off s. side just west of Birchin Lane, to which also it had a passage. Cowper's Court now marks the site. Kept by William Hinton, vintner, in 1660; after the Fire by Nicholas Colborne. 'A very large House and of a great Resort' (Strype, 1720). 16 hearths, 1664.[34] (R)

Fleece, Covent Garden. Large tavern; on w. side of Bridges (now Catherine) St, just south of Russell St, kept by William Clifton, vintner (overseer for the poor 1644), and after his death in 1672 by his widow Martha. It had an unfortunate reputation for violence and by 1692 had become a private house. 24 hearths, 1664.[35] (R)

Folly. Wooden house of (expensive) entertainment built on barges anchored in river off Somerset House. Described 1661 as a floating playhouse measuring 400 × 100 ft. Much used in summer. In the '90s rebuilt and renamed The Royal Diversion (print in Pepys Library).[36]

Fountain, Old Bailey. Tavern; on w. side of Little Old Bailey (now Old Bailey), kept by Nathaniel Holhead and Thomas Manning. 17 hearths, 1664.[37] (R)

Fountain, [Strand]. Pepys gives no location, but on both occasions on which he visited it he walked there from houses in the Strand (Clarendon's and Mr Pim's the tailor). Probably the tavern on s. side, east of Worcester House and some dozen doors west of the Savoy, roughly where Savoy Buildings now stands. Strype's map of the parish (1720) shows a Fountaine Court. There was however another Fountain in this area kept by Roger Hart.[38]

Fox, King St, Westminster. Small tavern with garden, on w. side, on either side of Sea (Says) Alley. 4 hearths, 1664.[39] (R)

George, Holborn. Coaching inn on s. side, by a yard named after it, north of Snow Hill, and approximately half-way between Holborn Conduit and Holborn Bridge. 'Very large, and of a considerable Trade' (Strype, 1720).[40] Probably the unnamed inn from which Elizabeth Pepys took coach to Buckden on 15 June 1663.

Globe, Eastcheap. Tavern, in Little Eastcheap; traceable 1636–63.[41]

Globe, Fleet St. Fashionable tavern on n. side, just west of Shoe Lane, by Peterborough Court, in the angle made by the junction. 18 hearths, 1664. Burnt in the Fire and rebuilt, and later a favourite resort of Goldsmith and Macklin. [42] (R)

Goat, Charing Cross. Tavern between the Chequer Inn at the s.-w. corner of St Martin's Lane and the Royal Mews further west. The block of which it formed part is now absorbed into Trafalgar Sq.[43] (R)

Golden Lion. At i.19 probably the tavern on the river side of the street at Charing Cross; at vii.424 apparently a tavern in the Strand near the Savoy.[44] (R)

Green Dragon, Lambeth Hill. The street was in the city and ran south into Thames St. Token, 1651.[45]

Green Man. Fashionable tavern on Strand Green, nr Islington; beside Crouch Hill, north of its junction with what is now Stapleton Hall Rd; traceable c. 1625–c. 1760s. A Jacobean house belonging to the Stapletons converted in Charles I's reign into a tavern.[46] (R)

Greyhound, Fleet St. Tavern, probably that on s. side close to Salisbury Court. Burnt in the Fire.[47] (R)

Half Moon, Strand. Large tavern, on n. side opposite the New Exchange and on the s.-w. corner of Bedford (later Half Moon) St; kept 1642–62 by John Doe, vintner and churchwarden; in 1664 by Henry Henderson. Doe in 1662 employed five male and three female servants. 17 hearths, 1664.[48] (R)

Halfway House. Riverside eating-house halfway between London Bridge and Deptford, c. 1660–c. 1800.[49]

Hare's: *see* Trumpet

Harp and Ball, nr Charing Cross (Roberts's). Large tavern on river side of the street which led from Whitehall Palace to Charing Cross, standing approximately on the site of the present no. 25 Whitehall, kept in 1660 and for many years past by Hugh Roberts, described in his will (1671) as 'gent'. 20 hearths, 1666.[50]

Harper's, King St, Westminster. Tavern on e. side immediately outside King St gate of Whitehall Palace, almost opposite Axe Yard. Kept until 1638 by Henry Hayer, after his death by his widow Mary (d. 1669) and from 1664 by their son James. 13 hearths, 1664.[51] (R)

Harvey's. Tavern in Salisbury Court. 4 hearths, 1664.[52] (R)

Heaven, Old Palace Yard, Westminster. Tavern or eating-house by the s.-w. end of Westminster Hall in the angle made by the Court of Requests and the Court of Wards; like Hell possibly once used as part of the offices of the Exchequer. Presumably so-called from its position on an upper storey. Much used by M.P.s and government clerks. Smaller than Hell.[53] (R)

Hell, Old Palace Yard, Westminster. Small but prosperous eating-house on the corner of St Margaret's Lane and the range of buildings fronting on New Palace Yard and running westwards from the Court of the Exchequer. It was partly under and partly alongside the Exchequer and had possibly once been used as its prison. (In 1648 the M.P.s excluded by Pride's Purge were held there for the night.)[54] (R)

Herbert's: *see* Swan, New Palace Yard

Hercules' Pillars, Fleet St. Ordinary on s. side, nr Temple, probably in Hercules' Pillars Alley opposite St Dunstan's, its site now occupied by no. 27, Fleet St; probably kept by Edward Oldham. In 1666–7 he kept one apprentice, and two male and two female servants. John Locke (1679) commended its mixed ales. 5 hearths, 1664; 17 hearths, 1666.[55] (R)

Hilton's, Axe Yard. Probably a tavern; Edward Hilton appears in the ratebooks as living next door but one to Pepys in 1658 and 1661. [56] (R)

Hoop (Golden Hoop), Thames St/Fish St Hill. Busy tavern standing back from e. side of Fish St Hill just north of Thames St, entered from Thames St. After the Fire when Fish St Hill was widened and the house rebuilt, an entry was made from that street as well. Kept by Richard Spire who rebuilt it at a cost of some £1200. 13 hearths, 1664.[57] (R)

Horn, Fleet St. Well-known tavern on n. side just outside parish of St Dunstan's.[58] (R)

Horseshoe, nr Navy Office. There was a tavern of this name in Hart St, another in St Dunstan's-in-the-East, and a third on Tower Hill. It was at the last that a coroner's jury returned a verdict of wilful murder against Col. Scott, Pepys's enemy in the Popish Plot. (He took flight and was never brought to trial.)[59]

Jacob's. Probably the Salutation tavern, Charing Cross. There is an undated token issued by Christopher Jacob from this house. There was also a tavern kept by George Jacob in 1664 in Rhenish Wine Court.[60]

Jamaica House, Bermondsey. Tavern, with pleasure gardens, probably at s. end of what is now Cherry Garden St, Bermondsey. Later a Tea Garden.[61] (R)

Kent's: *see* Three Tuns, Crutched Friars.

King's Head, Bow. Token issued by John Hanscombe, 1666.[62]

King's Head, Chancery Lane. Old and notable tavern on e. side almost at the junction with Fleet St, set back and connected to each street by passages; its signboard a picture of Henry VIII. Kept by Thomas Kent in 1660, after 1666 by William Marte, vintner. Famous as the meeting place of Shaftesbury's Green Ribbon Club at the time of the Popish Plot. 20 hearths, 1666.[63] (R)

King's Head, Charing Cross. Large and prosperous inn, on n. side of Strand, east of its junction with St Martin's Lane and opposite Hartshorn Lane; kept by Peter Griffith, a wealthy and charitable bachelor, executor of the will of Hugh Roberts of the Harp and Ball. 22 hearths, 1664; 25 hearths, 1666.[64] (R)

King's Head, Fish St Hill. Old and famous tavern on e. side, north of Thames St, with a back entrance in Pudding Lane, kept by Thomas or Robert Craddock. 14 hearths, 1666.[65] (R)

King's Head, Islington. In Upper St opposite w. end of parish church; kept in Pepys's youth by Pitts 'the old man'.[66] (R)

King's Head, nr Royal Exchange. Probably an eating house behind the Exchange kept by Thomas Browning, citizen and cook.[67]

King's Head, Tower St. Ordinary, on s. side, traceable c. 1648–66; kept by Thomas Mills, 1666. 10 hearths, 1666.[68]

Lamb's. Alehouse kept by Patricia Lambe, widow, in Gardiner's Lane, Westminster.[69]

Leg, King St, Westminster (Clerke's). Tavern or eating-house, on w. side, between George Yard and Boar's Head Yard; kept by Thomas Clerk(e).[70]

Leg, New Palace Yard. Tavern, kept from at least 1654–5 and possibly throughout the diary period by Thomas Stone (overseer for poor 1665). 14 hearths, 1664 (with a payment for ovens).[71] (R)

[Lockett's]. Large and fashionable ordinary, established c. 1668 on w. side of Charing Cross, by Adam Lockett, next door to the Earl of Mulgrave's house (Kirke House). Traceable until c. 1722.[72]

Mitre, Cheapside. Tavern, on n. side, four shops occupying the ground floor, kept from 1659 by Francis Pochin, vintner. 10 hearths, 1664. Not rebuilt after the Fire, its site probably being absorbed into the rebuilt Mercers' Hall.[73] (R)

Mitre, Fenchurch St (Rawlinson's). Important tavern, on n. side, the third house east of the s.-e. corner of Lime St; kept by Daniel Rawlinson. 19 hearths, 1666. Rebuilt after the Fire on an enlarged site so that it had a street frontage of 40 ft.[74] (R)

Mitre, Fleet St. Tavern on s. side, nr Mitre Court, later made famous by Dr Johnson. 16 hearths, 1664. Rebuilt after the Fire; ceased to be a tavern after 1788, and, as no. 39 Fleet St, was demolished in 1829 for the enlargement westwards of Hoare's Bank.[75] (R)

Mitre, Mitre Court, off Fleet St (Paget's). Tavern off s. side of street, kept by William Paget who in 1660 moved to the Mitre, Fleet St, a few yards away. In 1662 he moved to the Mitre nr St Paul's. At all three taverns he provided music: possibly he was related to the William Paget of the King's Musick.[76] (R)

Mitre, Wood St. 'A house of the greatest note in London' (i.248); on w. side of Great Wood St (north out of Cheapside), roughly opposite the Compter; kept by William Proctor. 29 hearths, 1664; 30 hearths, 1666. After the Fire the name was transferred to a tavern on the other side of the street.[77] (R)

Nag's Head, Cheapside. Probably the tavern of that name on s. side next door to and east of the Star. It lay behind the street frontage and was approached by a long passage. 17 hearths, 1664.[78] (R)

New Exchange. Tavern 'over against the Change' and close by the Stocks, kept by Ralph King, vintner (1659) and by Ben Stanley, Pepys's old schoolfellow (1663). There was a New Exchange tavern in Exchange Alley, off Lombard St, kept by Arthur Stanley.[79]

Old/Great James, Bishopsgate St. Tavern, probably that on the e. side, one door from the boundary of St Helen's parish with the parish of St Ethelburga; kept by Edward Drayton who died a rich man in 1677. 18 hearths, 1666.[80] (R)

Old Swan, Fish St Hill. Noted and ancient tavern, on w. side, just above (Upper) Thames St, hard by Old Swan Lane; kept by Gilbert Brandon, vintner, 1646–62, then by Cornelius Cage, vintner and in 1665 by Benjamin Rushton, haberdasher. Rebuilt after the Fire. 14 hearths, 1666.[81] (R)

Paget's: *see* Mitre, Mitre Court.

Penell's, Fleet St. Tavern, kept by Robert Penell. 10 hearths, 1666.[82]

Pope's Head, Chancery Lane. Large tavern standing back from n. side of Fleet St, and w. side of Chancery Lane, by Bell Yard, in the angle between the Lane and Fleet St. 22 hearths, 1666.[83] (R)

Pope's Head, Pope's Head Alley. Large and ancient tavern off Lombard St, consisting of an upper storey and cellars, the ground floor being occupied by 13 shops. Kept (at least 1660–74) by John Sawyer. Destroyed in the Fire and moved to temporary premises in St Helen's Bishopsgate before returning to its original site. 20 hearths, 1664; 25 hearths, 1675. Usually referred to by Pepys by name alone.[84] (R)

Prior's Rhenish Winehouse: *see* Rhenish Winehouses

Rawlinson's: *see* Mitre, Fenchurch St

Red Lion, Aldersgate St. Small coaching inn, on w. side just north of Long Lane, Barbican, its site now obliterated by Aldersgate St Station and the railway lines. Kept by Thomas Newberry. 14 hearths, 1666 (post Fire).[85] (R)

(Red) Lion, King St, Westminster. Tavern on w. side, a door or two south of the turning into Boar's Head Yard. 5 hearths, 1664.[86]

Reindeer, Westminster. Possibly the tavern of that name in Tothill St, 1682.[87]

Rhenish Winehouses. There were several in London (including one at the entrance to the Steelyard) and two (possibly three) in Westminster. The largest in Westminster, often used by Pepys (and probably the one he refers to as the 'old' one at 1.221) was in Wise's Alley off the e. side of King St, kept since at least 1638 by members of the Genew family and in 1664 taxed on 12 hearths.[88] 'Prior's' lay on the w. side of Cannon Row, Westminster (the fourth house south of its junction with Brewer's Yard) and was taxed on 11 hearths in 1664. This was probably the 'further' one of iv.203. It was kept by Arthur Prior (churchwarden, St Margaret's in 1674 and 1675). He made a reasonable fortune, leaving dowries of £500 apiece to his two daughters and £100 to his cousin Matthew Prior, the poet.[89] (R)

Ringstead's: *see* Star, Cheapside

Roberts's: *see* Harp and Ball

Rose, Covent Garden. Tavern in Russell St on e. corner of Bridges (now Catherine) St, kept throughout the diary years by one of the Long family. Often mentioned by contemporary playwrights, being adjacent to the theatre in Drury Lane. 19 hearths, 1666.[90] (R)

Rose, King St, Westminster. Tavern close to Westminster Hall, probably the one on the e. side of King St some seven doors north of the turning into New Palace Yard, kept (at least 1661–8) by Thomas Martin.[91] (R)

Rose, nr Navy Office. Possibly the well-known tavern on s. side of (Great) Tower St opposite the s. front of All Hallows Barking and the entry to Seething Lane. The landlord in 1655 was Thomas Mitchell, vintner. Robert Parker issued an undated token from it. Rose Court still exists there.[92] (R)

Royal Oak, Lombard St. Probably on n. side between Cock Alley and George Alley, kept (1666) by William Smith, vintner. 9 hearths, 1666.[93]

Salutation, Billingsgate. Ancient and important tavern in Salutation Court, north out of (Lower) Thames St, between Love (Lovat) Lane and St Mary-at-Hill. Monument St now covers its site. 16 hearths, 1666.[94] (R)

Sampson, Paul's Churchyard. Possibly the house kept by William Clarke between Petty Canons and Pissing Alley. 5 hearths, 1666.[95] (R)

Ship 'behind the Exchange'. Old and large tavern on n. side of Threadneedle St, just west of Bartholomew Lane and two doors east of the Crown; its site now a part of the Bank of England. Kept by Charles Young, vintner (d. 1663), after him by his widow. Burnt in the Fire and rebuilt. 20 hearths, 1664.[96] (R)

Ship, Fenchurch St. Tavern on n. side, one house west of junction with Billiter Lane. 9 hearths, 1666.[97] [*See also* Morris, John]. (R)

Ship, nr Vere St. Probably the tavern of that name in Ship Yard, outside Temple Bar, c. 1660–72.[98]

Ship, nr Whitehall. Possibly the tavern of that name in Westminster Market 1665–6.[99] But there were several others in that district.

Star, Cheapside (Ringstead's). Tavern on s. side just east of the Royal Exchange, lying back from the street, like many city taverns, and approached by a narrow passage; kept (1660) by Francis Ringstead, vintner. After the Fire moved further east, its former site having become a court. 10 hearths, 1666.[100] (R)

Star, 'hard by' the Navy Office. Probably the tavern in Tower St from which an undated token was issued by Thomas Taylor.[101]

Sugar Loaf, by Temple Bar. A licensed victualler's just inside Temple Bar on the s. side of Fleet St, its site now part of Child's branch of Williams & Glyn's Bank. Owned by Thomas Postan. It escaped the Fire. 10 hearths, 1664.[102] (R)

Sun, Chancery Lane. Tavern, on w. side south of Crown Court, kept by William Johnson, vintner, in 1660 and after 1663 by Henry Redman. 16 hearths, 1666.[103] (R)

Sun, Fish St Hill. Old and notable tavern, on e. side immediately south of the church of St Margaret, kept c. 1636–69 by Thomas

Padnoll, Warden of the Vintners' 1660–1. 13 hearths, 1666. After the Fire the church was not rebuilt (its site being used for the Monument) and the rebuilt Sun occupied the s.-w. corner of Monument Yard or Sq.[104] (R)

Sun, King St, Westminster. Large tavern, on w. side, between Bell Alley and George Yard, kept by Edmund Waters c. 1637–c. 70 (Warden of the Vintners' 1655–6, 1662–3; parish overseer 1638, churchwarden 1644, 1645, 1660). Pepys usually refers to it by name only. 22 hearths, 1664.[105] (R)

Sun, Threadneedle St. A large and notable tavern, on n. side a few yards east of Bartholomew Lane, behind the Exchange. Kept by Nicholas Colborne, vintner 1648–64 (who retired to a considerable estate in Esher and Walton, Surrey), and then by John Wadlow (late of the Devil, Fleet St). After the Fire he moved to temporary premises in Bishopsgate (14 hearths), which, judging from Pepys's mention of Buckingham's dining there, attracted a fashionable trade. He rebuilt the original house magnificently: 22 hearths (1664), 31 (1675).[106] (R)

Swan, Dowgate. Tavern on w. side of Dowgate Hill, south out of Cannon St to (Upper) Thames St, a few doors south of the church of St John. Kept (at least 1641–66) by Thomas Cox, vintner. 12 hearths, 1666. Burnt in the Fire; still unbuilt in 1671 when a rebuilding lease was obtained.[107] (R)

Swan, New Palace Yard (Herbert's). Tavern or eating-house kept by William Herbert from 1654–5. 9 hearths, 1664.[108] (R)

Swan, Old Fish St. Tavern on n. side near Distaff Lane. Rebuilt after the Fire. (But possibly the Swan on the Hoop, at the s.-e. boundary of the Fish Market.)[109] (R)

Three Cranes, Old Bailey. Small tavern on e. side, near the Sessions House.[110]

Three Cranes 'at the Stocks'. Tavern on s. side of Poultry opposite St Mildred's church, its site now part of Queen Victoria St. Later famous as the King's Head.[111] (R)

Three Tuns, Charing Cross. On the river side of the main street continuing the Strand towards Whitehall Palace, some eight doors south of Angel Court and just north of Scotland Yard. Later known as the Rummer, a name it kept well into the 19th century, it appears in Hogarth's *Night*. It was then 14 Charing Cross but is now numbered in Whitehall. 16 hearths, 1664.[112] [*See also* Darling, [T. and E.]] (R)

Three Tuns, Crutched Friars (Kent's). 'The new tavern come by us' (vii.373); on n. side of Hart St (New London St now covering the site). Kept by John Kent until his death in Dec. 1689. He had previously kept the Cock in Gracechurch St and the Three Tuns in Lombard St. Both had been destroyed in the Fire and presumably Kent had been allowed to re-establish the Three Tuns in an unburnt section.[113] (R)

Three Tuns, nr Guildhall. Tavern by the gate in Guildhall Yard, destroyed in the Fire, its site being taken for street improvements. Token issued by Thomas Ailay, 1665.[114]

Triumph, Charing Cross. A tavern whose name commemorates one of the arches put up for the coronation in 1661. A similar sign (the Pageant) appears in Fleet St.[115]

Trumpet, King St, Westminster (Hare's). Licensed victualler's, on w. side, between Fountain Court and Bell Alley, at the s. end of the street almost opposite New Palace Yard. Kept by John and Alice Hare until 1663–4; afterwards by Arthur Ashton. Hare's will was proved in Oct. 1668.[116] (R)

[White Hind], Cripplegate. Coaching inn, outside the gate. Listed by John Taylor (1637) as having a service of coaches to E. Anglia.[117]

White Horse, Lombard St. An ancient and notable tavern, on s. side, with an entrance also on to the e. side of Sherborne Lane; kept by Abraham Browne, vintner, from at least 1660. After the Fire he was given the right to rebuild, his leases being renewed accordingly, but the site appears to have been sold to Sir Robert Vyner for his house. Browne moved to the Bear at Bridge Foot, where he died in 1672. Pepys reports at 24 Feb. 1667 the suicide of Frances, his (second) wife. 18 hearths, 1666.[118] (R)

White Lion, Islington. Tavern; traceable from 1630s, kept 1668–77 by Christopher Busbee.[119]

Wilkinson's: *see* Crown, King St

Will's. Sometimes mistakenly identified as the well-known coffee-house in Bow St made famous by the patronage of Dryden and the wits. It was in fact an alehouse in Old Palace Yard, the second house after the turn into the yard from St Margaret's Lane; kept by William Griffith (Griffin). Pepys records at 8 Aug. 1665 the death by plague (in a single day) of 'poor Will that used to sell us ale at the Hall-door' and his wife and three children. By 1691 it seems to have become a coffee-house.[120] (R)

Wood's, Pall Mall. Tavern, on s. side, kept by William Wood, vintner. Pepys's 'old house for clubbing' as a young government clerk.[121]

World's End, Knightsbridge. Tavern, by Hyde Park. It had an equivocal reputation.[122]

Taylor, Goodman. Matthew Taylor; from June 1660 a 'labourer' and messenger at the Navy Office.[1]

Taylor, Capt. John (d. 1670). One of the foremost shipbuilders of his day. He built the *London* in 1657 and her successor the *Loyal London* in 1666. Like many shipbuilders, he was unversed in the theory of naval architecture, and unable to 'give a good account of what he doth as an Artist' (vii.106). The accounts he made up for the *Loyal London* showed an unpractised hand, 'and yet plaguy wise sayings will come from the man sometimes' (viii.108). He served as Master-Shipwright at Chatham under the Commonwealth until he was replaced in 1660 at the instigation of the Duchess of Albemarle by Phineas Pett. He then resumed business as a private shipbuilder and timber merchant with a yard at Wapping. In 1663 Pepys in his Navy White Book records receiving money from him wrapped up in a handkerchief.[1] In the war he was Navy Commissioner at Harwich 1665–8, leaving Pepys to see to his own yard's business with the navy. His appointment in 1665 gave rise to opposition on the double ground that he was a merchant and a 'fanatic'. But he proved to be a vigorous administrator, and gave satisfaction in managing a yard which, because of the location of the naval campaigns, had to cope with a sudden and large access of business. His letters to the Board in 1667 urging the case of the starving workmen and seamen in his charge are strikingly eloquent.[2]

Taylor, Capt. [Silas] (1624–78). Parliamentarian soldier, Storekeeper of Harwich yard 1665–78, antiquary, and amateur composer of vocal and instrumental music. There are instrumental pieces in *Court Ayres* (1655) and a setting of Cowley in *Catch that catch can* (1667). Aubrey reports Taylor's great friendship with Matthew Locke, and notes 'I have heard anthems of his sung before his majestie . . . and the king told him he liked them'. Compiled a 'Collection of Rules in Musicke'.[1] (Lu)

Taylor, Thomas. Schoolmaster and clergyman; Master of the grammar school, Huntingdon 1641–d. 79. Pepys was a pupil there in his time.[1]

Taylour, [John]. Clerk to William Wardour, Clerk of the Pells in the Exchequer; still in office in 1689.[1]

Teddeman, Sir Thomas, kt 1665 (d. 1668). Naval commander; a close ally of Sandwich. He served in the Commonwealth navy and held seven commands 1660–8, attaining flag-officer's rank 1665–6. He led the inglorious attack on the Dutch fleet in Bergen harbour, 1665. In 1667 he retired from active service and became port admiral of Dover.[1]

'Old Teddeman' was his cousin, Henry Teddeman, sen. He served in the Commonwealth navy and held only one command afterwards, in 1664. Coventry had a low opinion of him.[2]

Teil, Capt. [Jean Baptiste] du. French by birth, he was one of the Duke of York's less successful protégés. He had had some naval experience with the royalists in Jersey in 1649, and at the Restoration was given a post in the Queen Mother's household.[1] After the Second Dutch War (in which he was deprived of his commission, his guns doing more damage to his own side than to the enemy) he was made cupbearer to the Duke of York and was employed on a series of minor diplomatic missions before being given another naval command (captain of a galley in the Mediterranean) in 1671.[2] He was knighted at some date unknown and had died by 1688.[3]

Tempest, [Thomas]. Amateur musician, member of 'the Musick Society in the Old-Jury', contributor to *Catch that catch can* (1667) and *The musical companion* (1672). (Lu)

Tempest, ——. Possibly Rowland Tempest, traceable as a clerk in the office of the Secretary of State in the 1680s.[1]

Temple, [James] (d. 1668). Sir Robert Vyner's chief assistant. Cocke, Fenn and Porter figure in the diary as Temple's friends and were beneficiaries in his will.[1] Not to be confused with John Temple, a goldsmith in partnership with John Seale at the Three Tuns, Lombard St 1670–84.

Temple, Sir Richard, 3rd Bt (1634–97). M.P. for Warwickshire 1654, and for Buckingham borough 1659, 1660, 1661–95 (except for the first Exclusion Parliament). A member of the Duke of Bucking-ham's faction in the '60s, he attempted in 1663 to gain office (and a badly-needed income) by a promise to manage the Commons. On the failure of the scheme he resumed his attacks and led the parliamentary critics of Coventry and Clarendon in 1667–8. He went over to the court interest in 1670 and was given a place on the Council for Foreign Plantations 1671, and the Customs commission 1672. He later became a Whig and an Exclusionist.[1]

Temple, Mrs. One of the ladies at a court ball in Nov. 1666. Probably Anne Temple, Maid of Honour to the Duchess of York, of whom there were many stories. Strictly speaking she was now Mrs Lyttelton, having been married in the previous May to Charles Lyttelton (later the 3rd baronet), a widower more than twice her age. She was 'flirta-tious and prudish' and 'as gluttonous of every kind of sweetmeats, as if she had been not more than nine or ten years old' (Gramont).[1]

The Temple. A walled and gated liberty or district stretching from the s. side of Fleet St to the Thames (now to the Victoria Embank-ment), the name being a relic of its ownership by the order of Knights Templars (dissolved 1313). Owned and governed by the Benchers of the Middle and Inner Temple and comprising those two Inns of Court and the Temple Church. It suffered extensive damage in the Fire and in 1939–45.[1] (R)

Temple Bar. The gate and gate-house at the city's s.-w. boundary marking the end of Fleet St and the beginning of the Strand, the end of the city's jurisdiction and the beginning of that of Westminster. Destroyed in the Fire it was rebuilt, remaining until 1878 when it was taken down as an obstruction to traffic and re-erected in Theobalds Park, Waltham Cross.[1] (R)

Temple Gardens and Walks. The extensive gardens and walks within the Temple between the various ranges of buildings. In the '60s the river front of the Inner and Middle Temple was open, several lines of buildings coming down to it at right angles to the river, leaving open spaces between them. Temple Stairs gave direct access by boat. (R)

Temple Gate. The gate on the s. side of Fleet St, opposite Bell Yard, giving entrance to the Middle Temple and, continuing south through the liberty, to the Temple landing stairs. A similar gate, with the same name, opened opposite Chancery Lane into the inner Temple. (R)

Templer, [Benjamin]. Fellow of Trinity College, Cambridge 1656–7; Rector of Ashley, Northants. 1657–d. 87.[1]

Temple Stairs. The landing stairs at the bottom of Middle Temple Lane.

Terne, [Christopher] (d. 1673). Physician, of Lime St; M.D. (Leyden) 1650; F.R.C.P. 1655; an original F.R.S.; assistant-physician to St Bartholomew's Hospital until 1669.[1]

Terne, Capt. [Henry]. Served in the Commonwealth navy and from 1661 held five commands before his death in action in 1666.[1]

Teviot, 1st Earl of: *see* Rutherford, A.

Thames St. One of the most spacious of London streets, it ran from Tower Hill west past the Custom House, Billingsgate, London Bridge and Queenhithe to Puddle Dock (the modern, w. end of Queen Victoria St). Parallel to the line of wharves and landing stairs and connected to them by frequent short, narrow lanes, it was a centre for the commodity importers and always thronged with carts and drays. After the Fire, rubble from the burnt houses was used to raise it above flood level and to reduce the steep ascent to the line of Eastcheap and Cannon St. It was still, despite its widening, too narrow for the traffic seeking to use it. Now divided above and below London Bridge into Upper and Lower Thames St respectively. (R)

Thatcher (Thacker), ——. Musician; untraced. A John Thatcher was a child of the Chapel Royal in 1679.[1] (Lu)

THEATRE

The re-opening of the theatres. On 9 July 1660 Charles II issued an order for a royal warrant giving Sir William Davenant and Thomas Killigrew the exclusive right to raise companies of actors to perform in London. Furthermore their monopoly over theatrical operation in the capital was made hereditary, to be passed on to their 'heirs and assigns'. The King's action on that day fixed the pattern of theatrical activity in London for the next 150 years.

Professional performances in London had officially been banned from 2 Sept. 1642 but in practice the acting companies had not come to a complete halt. Again and again, defying the ordinances, those actors left in London gave clandestine performances. Needless to say, the plays were frequently interrupted by the arrival of soldiers who would remove the costumes and arrest the players. There were also private performances in country houses – Pepys at 30 May 1668 mentions what may possibly have been one such performance – and actors who accompanied the King during the war often put on plays to entertain the court. But the London companies, for all the dogged perseverance with which they reopened every time they were closed down, found that Parliament was increasingly harsh in its treatment of offenders against the orders prohibiting public plays. By 1649 most of the playhouses had been dismantled or had had their interiors stripped completely. Attempts were still made to train actors or give secret performances, but the theatre had effectively been suppressed.

By the mid-1650s references to irregular performances begin to reappear. The actors at the Red Bull Theatre in Clerkenwell were raided whenever they tried to act in 1654 and 1655 but they still attempted to perform. At least as early as April 1656 Davenant had found a way round the prohibition on plays by performing music-dramas or operas with the speeches given in recitative – such as his *Siege of Rhodes* – and in May he was confident enough that he was not going to be closed down to open the performances to a paying public. But these experiments do not really amount to the re-establishment of professional theatres. Plays were continually being banned throughout the late 1650s and the early part of 1660 but the frequency of the orders in itself indicates their ineffectiveness. Faced with the emergence of a number of acting companies, Davenant and Killigrew saw their opportunity to use their friendship with the King to establish a monopoly over what promised to be an extremely lucrative activity. In the years before the Interregnum theatre companies had been licensed for performance by the Lord Chamberlain in his capacity as Master of the Revels. Davenant and Killigrew now represented to Charles – quite falsely – that they had the agreement of the Lord Chamberlain, Sir Henry Herbert. The two entrepreneurs were given considerable rights under the monopoly patents: they were allowed to build theatres wherever they chose, to have the exclusive right to present 'tragedies, comedies, plays, operas, music scenes and all other entertainments of the stage whatsoever', to charge whatever they thought 'reasonable', and to present actresses for the first time on the public stage. There were a few restrictions, including a requirement to ensure that their plays should not contain 'any passages offensive to piety and good manners', but by and large they were given a free hand, since all other companies were, in law at any rate, 'silenced and suppressed'.

The patentees did not find it quite as easy as they expected to eliminate their competitors. At the time of the grant of the patents there were three companies operating regularly in London. The indomitable Red Bull company, under the management of Michael Mohun, had coped with Parliament and was certainly not going to be intimidated by Davenant and Killigrew. It continued playing until 1 Oct. 1660 when Killigrew had Mohun imprisoned. In the meantime Killigrew had discovered that the King was not particularly concerned to enforce the monopoly – Charles had in fact attended a performance by this illegal company in Aug. 1660. In the end Mohun's actors and Mohun himself – most of whom had acted before the Civil War – became the nucleus of the troupe Killigrew now formed.

A second company, managed by John Rhodes, secured a licence to act from General Monck early in 1660, before the return of the King, and performed at the Cockpit Theatre in Drury Lane. It was this company that Pepys visited on 18 Aug. 1660, his first visit to the re-opened theatres. Rhodes's was not a particularly strong or experienced group of actors but it did include Kynaston and Betterton. This company provided the basis for Davenant's troupe.

The third company, under William Beeston, probably did not begin performing until June 1660 at the repaired theatre in Salisbury Court and did not survive many weeks.

In spite of support from Sir Henry Herbert, who had reached agreement to receive payment for each day's performances, the unlicensed companies were finally silenced by Oct. 1660 and on 8 October a United Company, made up of the best actors from all three companies, opened at the Cockpit Theatre. The union was only a temporary marriage of convenience and on 5 November Davenant moved his company, now known as the Duke's Company, to Salisbury Court. On the same day Killigrew transferred his troupe, the King's Company, to the Red Bull Theatre for three days until his new theatre in Vere Street was ready to open. From then on the pattern of theatrical activity that was to last throughout the period of the diary was established.

The only disturbance of the pattern arose from the sad case of George Jolly. Throughout the Interregnum, Jolly had led a group of travelling actors who toured in Germany, performing for the exiled Charles in Frankfurt in 1655. Returning to England, he petitioned the King to grant him a licence to act. On 24 Dec. 1660, in spite of having already granted a monopoly to Davenant and Killigrew, Charles licensed Jolly as well. Jolly had not waited for the licence; he had organised a company and was acting at the Cockpit Theatre by Nov. 1660, thereby causing Killigrew to move out to the Red Bull. Jolly's company continued to act in a number of London theatres for the next eighteen months: it was at the Cockpit Theatre late in 1661, at the Red

Bull in March 1661 when Pepys saw *All's lost by lust* there, at Salisbury Court in September (Pepys visited it on 9 September). The patentees found Jolly's activities a continual irritation, and in Jan. 1663 he was granted a new licence to perform in the provinces, after agreeing with the patentees to sell them a lease of his warrant for £4 a week. Davenant and Killigrew pretended to the King that Jolly had sold his licence outright to them and it was promptly revoked. Jolly was furious, returned to London and continued performances. Finally stopped in 1667 from giving even the irregular performances he had managed for the previous few years, Jolly reached agreement with the patentees to raise a nursery company – one of the training companies for young actors. It was small compensation for having been cheated of his licence.

The King's Company. On 8 Nov. 1660 the King's Company began playing at the Vere Street Theatre, their first permanent home. Though Pepys called it 'the finest play-house, I believe, that ever was in England' (20 Nov. 1660), the building, originally a tennis-court, cannot have had much to recommend it. It had been used in 1653 for a clandestine performance of *Claracilla* by Killigrew. (The production had had to be abandoned when the theatre was raided by soldiers tipped off by one of the actors.) The speed with which Killigrew was now able to begin acting there implies that he did little to the building. It probably measured about 70 × 25 feet and Killigrew constructed within it a theatre, seating at most 500 spectators, modelled closely on the private theatres, the roofed playhouses, that were in use before the Civil War. It is likely to have had a large platform stage with doors at the back. But it had no provision for scenery – a disadvantage that was to cost Killigrew dearly in competition with Davenant.

He had however substantial advantages over his rival. His company included a number of highly experienced actors who had worked before the Civil War as well as a brilliant new comic actor, John Lacy. But his trump card was that he had managed to assert exclusive rights to the performance of almost all well-known plays, on the grounds that they had belonged to the pre-Restoration acting companies, particularly the King's Men, from which his company claimed descent. As a result, Davenant was left without any plays to perform while the King's Company had the whole range of Elizabethan and Jacobean drama to call on. It was a brilliant coup on Killigrew's part, and one that he exploited to the full. Yet this initial advantage proved of limited value. Killigrew had no need to provide scenery since his plays did not require it, but he also had no need to encourage new writers or to find new plays. Though Dryden was contracted to the company, Killigrew failed to develop a modern repertory.

It was not until 7 May 1663 that he was able to open at his new theatre, the Theatre Royal in Bridges Street, and move out of the increasingly unsatisfactory Vere Street premises. The plans for a new theatre had been started in Dec. 1661 when agreement was reached with the Earl of Bedford, who owned the land, to lease the Riding Yard to William Hewett and Robert Clayton for 41 years. Hewett and Clayton in turn acted as trustees and made over the land to Sir Robert Howard, Thomas Killigrew and eight actors in the company, Hart, Burt, Lacy, Mohun, Robert Shatterell, Clun, Cartwright and Wintershall. The condition of the lease was that a theatre should be built on the site (which measured 112 × 58 or 59 feet), before Christmas 1662 at a cost of £1500, and that the ground rent should be £50 p.a. The interest in the land was divided between the 'building sharers' in 36 shares, of which Howard and Killigrew had nine shares each, Lacy four, and the others two each. In Jan. 1662, when the agreement between the building sharers was reached, the acting company, made up of the eight actors who held building shares and five more actors (Bird, Baxter, Kynaston, Blagden and Loveday), agreed with the building sharers to act in the projected theatre and pay £3 10s. rent to them for each acting day. The payments for the construction work were made by Robert Clayton to Richard Rider, the builder and quite possibly the designer of the new theatre. The cost – £2500 – far exceeded the estimates, with the result that the building sharers had to pay nearly £70 per share. Nevertheless the building shares proved to be a profitable investment: Clun sold his two shares in Nov. 1663 for £215 each.

The building shares represented investment in the building; the acting shares reflected the actors' relative worth to the company. There would seem to have been $12\frac{3}{4}$ acting shares initially. Killigrew had 2, the three leading actors, Mohun, Hart and Lacy, had $1\frac{1}{4}$ share each, and five other actors, Wintershall, Cartwright, Burt, Clun and Bird, had 1 each, leaving 2 shares for company poets and others. (Dryden, for instance, later owned $1\frac{1}{4}$ shares as part of his contract.) Before long, Killigrew had delegated the direction of the company to Mohun, Hart and Lacy and they had taken over one of the extra shares and raised their holding to $1\frac{1}{2}$ shares each. Following protests from the other actors, they were forced to give up the extra share. Killigrew tried to take over the share left after Bird's death; again there were protests. In little, the disputes over the distribution of the shares anticipate the wrangling and sharp practices which were ultimately to destroy the company. The sharing agreements gave the appearance of having established a finely-tuned balance of interests, but Killigrew's bad management and financial manoeuvrings were given too much scope.

These financial details are, inevitably, better documented than the appearance and equipment of the finished building. This – the first of a long line of theatres to be known as the Theatre Royal – suffered from the fact that its size was limited by the site. Pepys complained about the narrow passage-ways in and out of the pit, the distance from stage to boxes and the position of the music-room, which was placed under the stage so that the music was virtually inaudible (8 May 1663). Most of the praise of the theatre, from Pepys and others, is remarkably un-helpful to an understanding of its structure. It used to be thought that a description of the circular shape of the theatre visited by Cosimo III of Tuscany referred to the Theatre Royal, but in fact it referred to the Duke's Theatre in Lincoln's Inn Fields.[1] Contemporary prints show the cupola which surmounted it and through which the hail-storm leaked when Pepys visited the theatre on 1 June 1664, but there are no illustrations of the interior. The result is that any description of this, the first purpose-built theatre of the Restoration, is mostly guess-work. Almost certainly, it had a pit surrounded by boxes with a middle gallery of boxes above it and a further undivided gallery above that. Pepys saw the building work undertaken in 1666 to make the stage wider, and perhaps Killigrew took that opportunity to move the music-room to its more usual location over the stage. The stage was equipped with trap-doors, flying machinery and other pieces of theatrical trickery. The audience capacity was probably between 700 and 1000.

The true glory of the theatre was its scenery. In front of the pro-scenium arch, on either side of the stage, were two doors which provided entrances and exits onto the principal acting area. Upstage, behind the proscenium, the company displayed exciting and elaborate scenery. After the frustrations of playing in Vere Street without scenery, while Davenant attracted away the audience to see the scenes he could display, Killigrew must have been relieved to offer spectacular scenery at last. He was certainly prepared to pay for it. In 1669, for instance, the company commissioned a scene of Elysium for Dryden's *Tyrannic Love* from the painter Isaac Fuller. It took Fuller six weeks to produce, and, after much litigation, the company paid him £335 10s. The play ran for 14 consecutive days, according to Fuller[2] – an almost unheard-of run – and took £100 a day at the box office, compared with the usual receipts of £40 or £50. Restoration scenery consisted of flats running across the stage in grooves placed at varying depths behind the proscenium. The flats were divided in the middle and each half was drawn off to the side of the stage, where it stayed concealed by the wings. The different depths at which the flats or cut-out pieces were set allowed for different depths of acting area and for the discovery of elaborate tableau scenes as the flats were drawn back. Pepys found the scenery particularly effective when viewed from a box rather than from the pit.[3] Indeed it must have been difficult to keep the perspective true, particularly when actors had to be close to the scenery if discovered upstage and far away from it if acting on the forestage. But the result usually worked, especially with elaborate costumes and props. Evelyn, visiting the theatre to see *The Indian Queen* by Dryden and Sir Robert Howard on 5 Feb. 1664 noted that it was 'so beautified with rich Scenes as the like had never ben seene here as happly (except rarely any where else) on a mercenarie *Theater*'. Pepys praises the sets used in this production again and again. Foreign visitors were similarly impressed.

Yet the company did not base its repertory primarily on spectacular heroic tragedies. Even though plays like *The Indian Queen* were remarkably successful, the company may well have found the costs too high and Davenant's competition too successful. They could of course make use of their large repertory of pre-Restoration plays but they were still looking for a new and individual form of play to guarantee them success. On 5 June 1665 the Lord Chamberlain closed the theatres until further notice because of the Plague. It was not until Nov. 1666, and then only by dint of promising large donations to charity, that the theatres were able to reopen. But in the months before the closure the company had found exactly what it needed. In a series of plays, Charles Hart and Nell Gwyn had begun to map out a type of play, a witty battle between rakish hero and independently-minded heroine, that proved to be the perfect recipe. Tentatively in plays like James Howard's *The English mounsieur* and *All Mistaken* and more confidently with a revised version of Dryden's *The wild gallant*, his *Secret Love* and *An evening's love*, Hart and Gwyn achieved a new style of comedy and ensured the success of the company. The company's success was such that it could be claimed in 1678 – possibly with exaggeration – that an acting share was worth £280 a year.[4]

But on 25 Jan. 1672 disaster struck. At about 8 p.m. a fire started under stairs at the back of the theatre which destroyed not only the building but also the stock of scenery and costumes so assiduously built up over the years. By an appropriate irony, the Duke's Company had moved out of the Lincoln's Inn Fields Theatre into their new theatre in Dorset Garden only a few weeks previously, and the King's Company were able to move into the empty theatre, choosing to reopen with the aptly named *Wit without money*. They appealed to the King for help to rebuild and Charles sent out a letter to the parish churches throughout the country to collect subscriptions. The new theatre, the Theatre Royal in Drury Lane, cost nearly £4000. Significantly, none of the building sharers for this theatre were actors or in any other way connected with the theatre; investing in theatres had become a profitable commercial speculation. The money to build the scene-store and provide new scenery and costumes was raised from the actor-sharers. The new theatre, designed by Wren, opened in March 1674. Less elaborate than the Dorset Garden theatre – Dryden speaks of its 'mean ungilded Stage'[5] – it was far better acoustically and, in many ways, was the finest Restoration playhouse.

By this time however the company's fortunes were already on the wane. In 1673 Killigrew had transferred almost all his work as manager to Hart and Mohun. He had pawned his building shares, his interest in the acting shares and his patent itself in return for cash. In spite of such concern for the actors' welfare as the provision of a company prostitute,[6] his relations with his actors deteriorated. In 1676 a revolt by the senior players was only prevented by bribing Hart and Kynaston and by a new agreement with the actors, which required Killigrew to hand over his shares and interest to his son, Charles. The decline did not stop there. Charles proved as bad a manager as his father. Actors stole costumes and props. Charles and Shatterell were accused of mortgaging the company's stock. Some of the best younger actors ran off to Scotland. The Lord Chamberlain intervened time and again to settle arguments. Performances were given intermittently and to small audiences. New plays were almost entirely restricted to parodies of the rival company's successes. Profits were no longer sufficient to pay the rent to the building sharers, even when the sharers agreed to accept half-rents. Eventually, after Hart and Kynaston had agreed with the rival company to do everything they could to promote an agreement for a fee of 5s. for every day that they did not act for the King's Company, the Theatre Royal was closed. Charles Killigrew thereupon signed articles of union – more akin to a take-over than a merger – with the Duke's Company. On 16 Nov. 1682 the resulting 'United Company', the only company permitted to act in London, gave its first performance. For the next thirteen years it held a complete monopoly in the capital.

The Duke's Company. Though Davenant had taken his company to Salisbury Court and opened there in Nov. 1660, he had already begun work on the theatre that the company was to use for the next ten years. As early as March 1660, when plays were still banned, he leased from Thomas Lisle a tennis court in Lincoln's Inn Fields (built in 1656–7) with the purpose of converting it into a theatre.

In the meantime, however, the company performed intermittently at the Salisbury Court Theatre. Davenant used the time to train his comparatively inexperienced company. Most of his actors had come from Rhodes's company; only one, Betterton, was immediately recognised as a major talent, but there were others of ability like the comedians James Nokes and Cave Underhill and Mary Saunderson (who later married Betterton). Davenant's greatest problem was that he had nothing to act, since Killigrew had secured nearly the entire pre-Restoration repertory (including, ironically, Davenant's own early plays). Of the plays that Davenant's actors had performed in the months before he took control, only two, *The Changeling* and *The Bondman*, were now legally theirs. On 12 Dec. 1660 he obtained permission from the Lord Chamberlain to keep six plays from their old repertory for two months more, some of which the company continued to perform long after the time limit had expired. At the same time Davenant was granted the exclusive right to 11 other plays (nine by Shakespeare and one each by Denham and Webster) as well as his own early works. It was still, by comparison with the repertory of the King's Company, pitifully small. Davenant had to make the most of every new production; he had no room for failures. For that reason in particular he chose to present Shakespeare adapted and rewritten to suit contemporary tastes.

Unlike Killigrew, Davenant, at the earliest opportunity, established his company on a firm foundation which left him unequivocally in control and closely involved in its day-to-day running. The articles of agreement between him and the ten sharing actors were signed on 5 Nov. 1660. Davenant was required to provide a new theatre equipped with scenery. He was given two-thirds of the shares in the company, in return for which he would pay the house-rent, make the scenery, props and costumes, pay the actresses and find his own profit. He agreed to hire the staff required to sell tickets, and to work back-stage. He was to fix their salaries and also those of the hired actors (i.e. those actors who were not sharers in the profits of the company). He also gained the right to appoint successors to any actor-sharers who died. Finally, it was agreed 'that the said Sir William Davenant alone shall be Master and Superior and shall from time to time have the sole government' of the actor-sharers. The net result of the many clauses of the agreement was to leave him in complete control over the company – a control that he could, quite clearly, have exercised in a thoroughly dictatorial way. Yet he never did so, and the firm nature of the agreement allowed for the creation of remarkably congenial working conditions. Even such apparent oddities as the decision to have the actresses paid directly by Davenant proved advantageous: he had the actresses live in his own house adjoining the theatre, so that the Duke's Company was far less troubled by unwanted pregnancies and sudden departures than was the King's Company.

Using all his theatrical expertise, Davenant quickly made clear that his was to be the better of the two companies. When both mounted Heywood's *Love's Mistress* in March 1661, Pepys preferred Davenant's production. Davenant eked out his meagre repertory until he was able to play his master-card – the opening of the Lincoln's Inn Fields Theatre.

The company rehearsed at Apothecaries' Hall and on 28 June 1661 performed the First Part of Davenant's opera *The siege of Rhodes* in their new theatre, 'having new scenes and decorations, being the first that e'er were introduced in England' as John Downes, later prompter for the company, recorded.[7] Downes was not strictly accurate; there had been scenery earlier (in performances at court), but Davenant had recognised that any new public theatre after the Restoration had to have scenery and that it was guaranteed to draw the audience. As Pepys noted when he went to the rival theatre on 4 July, 'strange to see this house, that use to be so thronged, now empty since the opera begun'. The opera ran for 12 days – an unheard-of triumph at a time when a run of three days was normal.

The scenery became the key to Davenant's success. The company performed his play *The Wits* in August; Pepys comments on the 15th – 'never acted yet with Scenes'. Their production of *Hamlet* later in the same month impressed Pepys both because it was 'done with Scenes very well', and because Betterton 'did the Prince's part beyond imagination'. The productions became more and more elaborate, the costumes more opulent, the sets more startling. When, after a short break in performances, Davenant put on his *Love and honour* in Oct. 1661 the costumes included the coronation robes of the King, the Duke of York and the Earl of Oxford, all loaned for the purpose. The production of *Henry VIII* in Dec. 1663 had dozens of new costumes, rather than the stock ones used for most productions, and was such a success that its run was extended to 15 consecutive performances. *Hamlet* and *Henry VIII* were two of the plays assigned to Davenant in Dec. 1660. By the time *Henry VIII* was put on, the King's Company could compete on better than equal terms, now that they were installed in their new theatre in Bridges Street, and they replied with a spectacular production of *The Indian Queen* for which Killigrew had gained a special subsidy of £40 for new costumes for the musicians (Pepys noted the traffic congestion around the theatre on 27 Jan. 1664).

In exactly the same way as Davenant created a triumph out of a restricted list of available plays, he overcame the defects of the Lincoln's Inn Fields Theatre as a building. Like the Vere Street Theatre used by the King's Company, the Duke's playhouse suffered from being a conversion from an existing structure. It was probably about the same size and with roughly the same capacity. Davenant however had experience of working with the tiny stage at Rutland House used for his operas in 1656 and knew he could fit surprisingly elaborate scenery into a small theatre. The Lincoln's Inn Fields Theatre did not have much stage machinery, particularly during the period of the diary. But Davenant discovered, with Betterton's assistance, how to make the best use of the stage for his scenic effects.

Davenant could not rely on elaborate productions of the few plays Killigrew had left him. His search for new plays led him to concentrate on new forms of drama. In this he showed a remarkable sensitivity to what the audience wanted. The heroic play was ideally suited to the scenic spectacles his theatre could provide, in exactly the way that his own adaptations of earlier work emphasised the spectacular (his version of *The Tempest* written in collaboration with Dryden, for instance). The Duke's Company mounted a series of plays by Roger Boyle, Earl of Orrery, making an especial success of *Mustapha* in 1665 (though Pepys disliked it). Davenant also exploited the possibilities of farcical comedy. It was his company that performed the first successful new comedy of the Restoration, Etherege's *Love in a tub*, and they performed it over and over again. Davenant enticed Dryden away from the King's Company to write for him his most farcical comedy, *Sir Martin Mar-all*, with the title-rôle written with Nokes's talents specially in mind. Pepys could not get into the first performance but on the next day found it 'the most entire piece of Mirth, a complete Farce from one end to the other, that certainly was ever writ' (16 Aug. 1667) and went to see it twice more in the following week. With the King's Company having staked out their claim for the more intellectual comedy with Charles Hart and Nell Gwyn, Davenant showed that farce would draw the crowds. A third type of play that he made peculiarly successful – the Spanish romantic comedy – seems to mark out a middle ground in his repertory between the heroic and the farcical. Tuke's *The adventures of five hours*, the best example of the genre, was so successful that Dryden's first play, *The wild gallant*, was a complete flop at the rival theatre the next month, Feb. 1663.

Davenant's company deserved its brilliant and sustained success. Building on their early disadvantages they discovered how to attract their audience. Their style was so firmly established that it was not affected by Davenant's sudden death in Apr. 1668. His widow took over nominal control, leaving the artistic and financial details in the hands of Betterton and Henry Harris. They had been well trained by Davenant and continued where he had left off. The Duke's Company had none of the troubles of their rivals in succeeding years. Eventually, in 1671, they moved into the Dorset Garden Theatre, the grandest of the Restoration theatres. Appropriately enough, it proved far more suited to opera and spectacle – Davenant's own preferences – than to drama itself.

Actors and Acting. The Restoration repertory system made enormous demands on the actors, who were expected to play a new part every two or three nights on average and to learn ten or more new rôles in a season. The only way to cope with the rapid turnover of plays and the minimum allowance for rehearsal was to rely on a limited range of conventional gestures and movements. There was no room for the minutely detailed work undertaken by the modern actor. Performances could go hopelessly wrong. Pepys complains with genuine indignation about those days when the actors forgot their lines.[8] Such disasters were more likely to occur at the premieres of new plays when there had been too little time to prepare the production; Pepys notes Etherege's anger after the first performance of *She would if she could* (6 Feb. 1668), because the actors 'were out of humour, and had not their parts perfect'. There were other days when the actors had fits of the giggles or when they ad-libbed to a dangerous extent.[9] Yet the evidence suggests that these occasions were exceptional. The actors in both companies were professionals and used their skill to carry them through the season.

Reliance on technique however did not result in a style that was emptily or aridly conventionalised. On the contrary, it required the playwrights to respond to the particular talents of the actors and to suit their plays to the blend of types available in a particular company at a particular time. In this situation most actors developed a range of parts, a 'line', that best fitted their abilities. Samuel Sandford, for instance, became triumphantly successful playing villains, starting with Malignii in Porter's *The Villain* (Oct. 1662). Colley Cibber recorded in his autobiography an occasion when Sandford was cast as an honest statesman: the audience sat through the first four acts expecting Sandford's honesty to prove to be a disguise for his villainy 'when, at last, finding . . . that Sandford was really an honest man to the end of the play, they fairly damned it, as if the author had imposed upon them the most frontless or incredible absurdity'.[10]

Most actors found themselves playing one type of rôle in comedy and another in tragedy. The two forms required radically different techniques. Cibber tells of seeing Nokes 'giving an account of some table-talk to another actor behind the scenes, which a man of quality accidentally listening to, was so deceived by his manner that he asked him if that was a new play he was rehearsing'.[11] All the evidence points to the predominantly natural way in which the main parts in comedy were performed. The fools, of course, were caricatures but normally ease and naturalness were expected of the actor in comedy. Sir John Hill advises him 'to deliver what he has to say in the very same manner that he would have spoken it off the stage if he had been in the same circumstances in real life that the person he represents is placed in'.[12] 'Natural', is, of course, a relative term; movement and gesture in Restoration public life were subject to conventions completely alien to anything we might call natural and it was that rather more formal naturalness that the actors in comedy were expected to imitate.

The actor in tragedy had a different problem. Charles Gildon, in his *Life of Mr Thomas Betterton* (1710), prints a long treatise on acting, supposedly written by Betterton, with exact descriptions of the gestures needed to represent the various emotions on stage. In addition to this operatic style of gesture the Restoration tragedian appears to have intoned his lines, chanting them in a style that, according to the satirists, was partly derived from the delivery of canting preachers. There are anecdotes of actors rehearsing tragedies in the street and being arrested and tied up as madmen.

Given the lack of evidence, it is difficult to be precise about Restoration acting style; even Pepys is noticeably uninformative about such matters. Yet of one thing there is abundant evidence: at their best the Restoration actors were very great indeed. Betterton, Hart and others created standards for performance that established – or renewed – a tradition for English acting. Betterton's Hamlet, it appears, derived ultimately from Shakespeare; as Downes records, Davenant, 'having seen Mr Taylor of the Blackfriars company act it, who being instructed by the author, Mr Shakespeare, taught Mr Betterton in every particle of it, which, by his exact performance of it gained him esteem and reputation superlative to all other plays'.[13]

The Audience. It used to be easy to describe the Restoration audience. Allardyce Nicoll, writing in 1923, could sum up the spectators as 'courtiers and their satellites . . . noblemen in the pit and boxes, the fops and beaux and wits or would-be-wits who hung on to their society, the women of the court . . . [and] the courtesans with whom these women of quality moved and conversed as on equal terms'.[14] In recent years, however, critics have re-examined the traditional picture and found it grossly misleading. Pepys's comments in fact reveal a different and more probable audience than that assumed by Nicoll. Pepys himself is, after all, neither courtier nor mere 'satellite'. Of course he carefully noted the presence of famous people in the audience. The visits of the court to the theatre are in the nature of things likely to be more completely recorded than those of most other theatre-goers. But that is not the same thing as claiming, as Nicoll did, that this group represents four-fifths of the audience.

Nor does the diary suggest that Pepys was exceptional as a theatre-goer. On the contrary, it seems that his friends and colleagues went to the play as often as he did. Indeed the number and range of his friends and acquaintances mentioned in this context suggests that a large group of predominantly middle-class and professional people saw the theatre as a regular form of entertainment. The diary also belies the legend that all the women in the audience were whores or aristocrats or both. In the period between 1 January and 31 Aug. 1668 Pepys visited the theatres 73 times. Thirty-three of the visits were made while his wife was away between 1 April and 18 June. Of the remaining 40 performances, Pepys took his wife to 32, with Deb Willet usually in attendance. On other occasions Mrs Pepys quite happily attended the theatre without him. On 7 Jan. 1668, for instance, Pepys arranged to meet his wife to see the play at the Nursery Theatre but, since there was no performance there, he looked for her at the other two theatres. She had gone to the Theatre Royal and seen *Henry IV Part I* 'and saw me, but I could [not] see them'. On 19 June she went to the Theatre Royal 'thinking to spy me there' at Dryden's new play, *An evening's love*. At no time does Pepys give even the slightest hint that the theatre was a dangerously immoral place for his wife to attend. His own scruples over the frequency of his visits to the theatre arose from his fear of wasting money and of neglecting work. More than once he expresses fear of being seen at the theatre in wartime.[15]

Prices for theatre tickets were not expensive. They ranged from 4s. for a seat in a box to 1s. for admission to the upper gallery. That is considerably more than the penny charged to stand in the yard at Shakespeare's Globe (which attracted audiences of over 3000) but is closely in line with the admission prices for the indoor theatres of the pre-Restoration period.

Inevitably the different prices tended to separate the audience according to social class. The anonymous author of *The country gentleman's vade mecum* (1699) provides a satirical description of an audience similar to that familiar to Pepys: the upper gallery is full of servants; the middle gallery contains 'the citizens' wives and daughters, together with the Abigails, serving-men, journey-men, and apprentices' with 'some desponding mistresses and superannuated poets'; the pit is reserved for 'judges, wits and censurers . . . in common with these sit the squires, sharpers, beaus, bullies and whores and here and there an extravagant male and female cit'; the boxes are for the 'persons of quality' unless 'some fools crowd in among 'em'. Pepys is especially careful to remark on any disproportionate numbers of citizens in the pit. On 1 Jan. 1668, for instance, he recorded 'a mighty company of citizens, prentices and others; and it makes me observe that when I begin first to be able to bestow a play on myself, I do not remember that I saw so many by half of the ordinary prentices and mean people in the pit, at 2s.-6d. apiece, as now'. He voiced similar complaints on 27 Dec. 1662 and 1 Jan. 1663. Significantly all three occasions are at holiday time when one might reasonably expect the citizens to treat themselves to better seats. Equally significantly all the occasions refer to visits to the Duke's Company at the Lincoln's Inn Fields Theatre.

Davenant's spectacular scenery and farcical comedies seem to have attracted a merchant audience, less intellectually discriminating than the audience at the performances of the King's Company. Dryden's prologue to *Marriage à-la-mode* (1673), produced at the Theatre Royal, makes the same point:

Our City friends so far will hardly come;
They can take up with pleasures nearer home
And see gay shows and gaudy scenes elsewhere:
For we presume they seldom come to hear.

In 1702 John Dennis lamented the change in the audience of his day from that of the early years of the Restoration. He complained of the increased proportion of men of business so preoccupied 'that they merely come to unbend and are utterly incapable of duly attending', of the newly-rich merchants who are still 'in love with their old sports', like tumbling and vaulting and expect to see these activities in the theatres, and of tourists who cannot even understand the words.[16] Perhaps the audience Dennis found was less attentive; even though Pepys and his friends came to the theatre to unwind they seem to have been informed and interested spectators. Pepys communicates one thing above all in his references to the theatre – a genuine enthusiasm and affection. He alone, of all those who have left comments on the 17th-century theatre, makes us feel the special excitement that the theatre can generate.[17] [*See also* Plays]

(Peter Holland)

Thom(p)son, [Anthony]. A leading maker of mathematical instruments, of Hosier Lane, Smithfield; patronised by Hooke and Wren. Author of *The uses of a quadrant* (1652); died in the Plague.[1]

Thomson, [Col. George, Maj. Robert and Sir William]. Brothers: Presbyterian merchants prominent in the service of the Commonwealth. Col. George (with the wooden leg – he had been wounded in action in 1644), elected M.P. for Southwark 1645, was a Councillor of State 1651–3, 1659–60, an Admiralty Commissioner 1652, and an Admiralty and Navy Commissioner 1659, 1660. Under suspicion for disaffection in 1661, he made his peace with the government and was put on the Brooke House Committee in 1668.[1] Maj. Robert was a Navy Commissioner from 1649 throughout the Interregnum, serving in 1657–60 as victualling commissioner at Plymouth.[2] The youngest of the brothers, Sir William, was the most successful – an Alderman 1653–61, M.P. for the city 1659, 1661–Jan. 79, several times Governor of the E. India Company, and a Customs Commissioner from 1671.[3] There was a fourth brother, Maurice, also a merchant, who does not appear in the diary. With Robert he was accused in 1665 of spying on behalf of the Dutch.[4] All the brothers were alleged to have made large fortunes during the Interregnum, mainly from dealing in bishops' lands.

Thornborough, [Gilbert]. Yeoman of the wine cellar to the King.

His house (taxed on five hearths) was in Axe Yard, next door but one to the Hunts. There was also a family of this name in St Olave's parish, so that it is not certain that the ladies mentioned at ii.87 and ii.192 are the same.[1]

Thornton, [Isaac] (1615–69). Of Snailwell, Cambs.; M.P. for the county 1660; knighted 1661.[1]

The Three Cranes (Stairs). Before the Fire, public landing stairs at the end of Three Cranes Lane some 500 yards above London Bridge.[1] After the Fire, when King and Queen streets were formed to provide a direct route from Guildhall to the river, the stairs were apparently moved a few yards upstream to the end of Queen St, though the name persisted. At these new stairs the Lord Mayor embarked on his way to Westminster Hall to be sworn in before the Barons of the Exchequer. (R)

Throgmorton, Joseph, kt 1661. Merchant, trading to the Mediterranean.[1]

Ticket Office. Conveniently placed for seamen, between the river and the Navy Office – until the Fire in a rented house on Tower Hill; afterwards in a house built for the purpose in Colchester St close by. In 1683 it moved to a two-storey wing of the new Navy Office, with a separate entrance from Seething Lane.[1]

Tickets: *see* Dutch Wars; Navy; Navy Board

Tinker, Capt. [John] (d. by 1688). Held three commands 1663–70, Master-Attendant at Portsmouth 1665–70.[1]

Tippetts, John, kt 1675. Shipwright and naval official. He began his career in the Portsmouth yard where he served as Master-Shipwright 1660–8. In 1668 he was promoted to the post of Navy Commissioner, at first with general duties, but after July 1668 with responsibility for the Portsmouth yard only. In 1672 Pepys procured his appointment as Surveyor of the Navy, praising his 'vigour and method',[1] and he occupied that office until 1686, and again from 1688–92. The fact that he was chosen to be a member of the Special Commission of 1686–8 is significant of his merit and of Pepys's high opinion. Pepys's *Naval Minutes* has many references to him.[2] John and Robert Tippetts, presumably relatives, were Navy Office clerks from 1677.[3]

Tite, [Margaret and Hester]. Of St Olave's Hart St; daughters of Lewis and Margaret Tite, of Crutched Friars.[1]

Titus, [Silius] (c. 1623–1704). A Presbyterian royalist of Italian descent. He served in the parliamentary army but held court office from 1648 and acted as a royalist agent in the 1650s. After the Restoration he was active in the W. African trade and a member of several government committees on trade and the plantations. M.P. 1660 and in five parliaments thereafter.[1]

Toilet: *see* Dress and Personal Appearance

Tolhurst, Maj. [Jeremiah]. Presumably known to Pepys, in his days at the Exchequer, as excise farmer for Northumberland. A protégé of Hesilrige; major in his regiment 1649; M.P. for Dumfries Burghs 1654, Jan.–Apr. 1659, and Carlisle 1660. He was prominent in the Newcastle coal trade and served in the customs house there. In 1671 he emigrated to the W. Indies.[1]

Tomkins, Sir Thomas, kt 1662 (?1608–74). M.P. for Weobley, Heref. 1640–4, 1660, 1661–74. A discontented Cavalier, active in opposition to the court and especially to Clarendon, who called him 'a man of very contemptible parts and worse manners'.[1] His violent speeches (e.g. against a standing army in July 1667) often did more harm than good to the causes he championed.[2]

[Tompson, Joseph]. Vicar of St Dunstan-in-the-West 1662–78; Vicar of Mortlake, Surrey 1671–d. 78; Rector of Putney at his death. Possibly identical with the man of these names who matriculated from St John's College, Cambridge in 1636.[1]

[Tompson, Richard]. Of Bedfordbury St, north off the Strand; probably the unnamed printseller at viii.383 and the 'Mr Tomson of Westminster' of vi.339. A leading dealer in mezzotints.[1]

Tooker. John Tooker (d. 1667), excise officer under the Commonwealth, was messenger and river-agent to the Navy Board from 1664. Ann Tooker (widow), housekeeper at the payhouse, Chatham, in 1669, may well have been his widow.[1] The Mrs Tooker who with her daughter Frances was a neighbour of Pepys at Greenwich (neither of them any better than she should have been) was possibly the same person, but it does not seem likely.

[Topham, John]. City Remembrancer 1659–60.[1]

Tor(r)iano, ———. Probably George (d. 1685), merchant; in 1660 living in St Nicholas Acon's. Common Councilman 1666–7, 1675–80.[1]

Tothill (Tuttle) Fields. A large open space in Westminster, Vincent Sq. being now the only substantial remnant of it. South-west of the built-up part of that city, by the footpath to Chelsea, with fields and marshy ground beyond it. (R)

The Tower. As a fortress, it held a garrison, commanded by the Lieutenant (Sir John Robinson 1660–79) and was still, even after the Interregnum, of some political importance as a means of controlling the capital. When relations between the city corporation and the monarchy deteriorated in the early '80s, plans were made to improve its fortifications, and in Nov. 1688, at the height of the crisis which led to the fall of James II, mortars were mounted on two of the batteries overlooking the city.[1] Important political prisoners were kept there – among them in his turn Pepys himself in 1679. Within its walls were also the headquarters of the Ordnance Office and many of its stores. Additional storehouses were built in 1663–4, 1667 and 1688–92, of which the New Armouries are nowadays the principal relic. That the Tower escaped the Fire and that none of the gunpowder stores blew up was due to the King's prompt action in ordering the destruction of neighbouring properties.

It was also a royal palace where monarchs slept on the night before their pre-coronation procession from London to Westminster. Charles II was the last to do so.[2]

In addition it contained a Jewel House (which Col. Blood penetrated in his famous raid on the crown jewels in 1671), the Mint, a record repository (mostly of Chancery records) and a menagerie. The last was transferred to the Zoological Gardens in Regent's Park in 1828. In 1710 it housed four lions, one tiger, two wolves, two 'Indian cats' and two eagles.[3] [*See also* Ordnance, Board of]

Tower Dock. An inlet at the w. end of the river frontage of the Tower and Great Tower Hill. (R)

Tower Hill. The open space which forms an arc on the landward sides of the Tower; divided into Little and Great Tower Hill to the east and west respectively, with the houses and alleys of the 'precinct of Old Tower' in between. These latter reached almost to the n. boundary of the Tower, leaving a narrow route between. The two Tower Hills were commonly referred to simply as Tower Hill. (R)

Tower Wharf and Stairs. The river frontage of the Tower and Tower Hill were wharfed and there were public landing stairs both at the w. end, at the foot of Great Tower Hill, and at the e. end (Iron Gate Stairs). (R)

Townshend, Thomas (d. c. 1680) Joint-Clerk of the Great Wardrobe; and deputy to Sandwich. 'A fool and a knave' (ix.52). In 1667 he was accused of extortionate practices and suspended.[1] Two of his sons had places in the Wardrobe.[2]

TRAVEL

By road. The commonest complaint of travellers in England in Pepys's day, as it had been for a long time, was about the condition of the roads. Never very good, they had probably deteriorated with the increase in the volume of traffic which followed from the expansion of trade in the 17th century. Their maintenance was still the responsibility of the parishes. Every year the inhabitants were by statute required to provide six days' unpaid labour, using their own implements and carts. The work, if done at all, was done badly and amounted to little more than filling up holes. The surveyor in charge, himself unpaid, was elected by the parish and held office for only a year. It would be a happy accident if he had much knowledge of what he was about. The law required the work to be finished by midsummer – it was a few days before Midsummer's Day 1668 that Pepys found the roadmenders at work (or at any rate collecting tips) on his way to Bristol.[1] In 1662 an attempt was made by statute to reduce the damage caused by heavily laden waggons by imposing minimum widths of wheel rim. But to little purpose. Pepys thought the Low Countries had more chance of success by requiring waggon horses, like coach horses, to go abreast instead of in tandem.[2] The most effective improvements in fact were to come with the local turnpike acts of the 18th century, which transferred the duty of road maintenance from the parishes to trustees who were empowered to lay charges on the road users. The first of these acts was passed in 1663 but only a few turnpikes had been established by the end of the century.

The traveller had always to reckon on the likelihood of delays caused by broken road surfaces and quagmires of mud. Coaches were not infrequently damaged or upset. But the worst difficulties, according to Pepys's evidence and that of many contemporaries, arose from floods. Pepys has several references to 'dangerous waters'. Neither the roads nor the fields through which they ran were properly drained, and a stranger might be caught unawares by a flooded stream indistinguishable from the washes of water around it. Pepys's colleagues Batten and Mennes were almost drowned in this way when riding home from Portsmouth in Dec. 1662. The diary of Ralph Thoresby the antiquary has a passage made well-known by Macaulay in which he relates an incident at Ware in May 1695 when passengers were forced to get out of their coach and swim.[3]

Another difficulty was that of finding the way. Signposts (not required by law until 1697)[4] were rare, and there were no detailed route maps with measured mileages until Ogilby's *Itinerarium Angliae*, published in 1675. Many roads and fields were unenclosed and the traveller had not so much to follow a road as to choose between the several tracks made by others before him in their efforts to skirt the worst stretches. Pepys once mistook the way on a road he knew well, from Cambridge to Ware, and his coachman managed to get lost in broad daylight between Newbury and Reading. There was much to be said therefore, for this as well as other reasons, for travelling in company, as did the stage coaches setting out from Bath,[5] or for employing a guide. Even so, Pepys was once lost in Windsor Forest and had to navigate by the moon, although he had picked up a local guide at Staines.

The highwayman, contrary to popular belief, seems to have been one of the lesser perils.[6] Pepys often rode on lonely roads in the dark and he took it for granted that his womenfolk could go on long journeys by carrier or coach with only their fellow travellers for protection. In fact he was more alarmed than reassured when he heard that Elizabeth had a

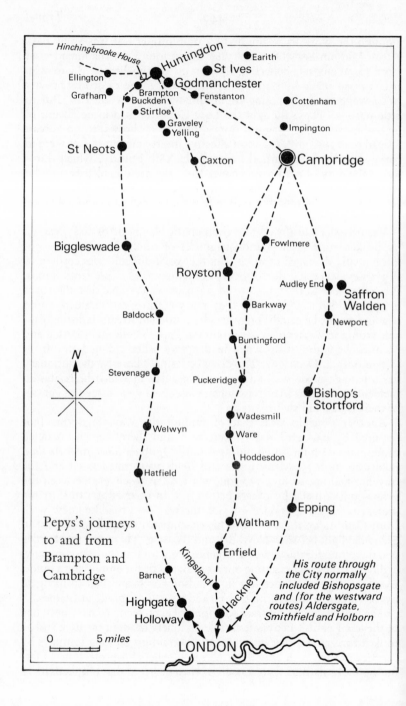

Hinchingbrooke House
Huntingdon
Earith
Ellington
St Ives
Grafham
Godmanchester
Brampton
Fenstanton
Cottenham
Buckden
Stirtloe
Impington
Graveley
Yelling
St Neots
Caxton
Cambridge
Biggleswade
Fowlmere
Royston
Audley End
Saffron Walden
Baldock
Barkway
Newport
N
Buntingford
Stevenage
Puckeridge
Bishop's Stortford
Welwyn
Wadesmill
Ware
Hatfield
Hoddesdon
Epping
Pepys's journeys
to and from
Brampton and
Cambridge
Waltham
Kingsland
Enfield
Barnet
His route through
the City normally
included Bishopsgate
and (for the westward
routes) Aldersgate,
Smithfield and Holborn
Highgate
Hackney
Holloway
0   5 miles
LONDON

dashing young soldier for company.[7] Yet he was aware of the risk of robbery. When he walked from Deptford with money left over from a pay he had three armed men from the yard accompany him. When in 1667 he carried a large part of his life savings in a coach from Brampton to London he took a guard of four horsemen and even so rode 'in great fear'.[8] He was later to be the victim of an attack when riding with his nephew Jackson in his coach near Chelsea in 1693. Finding a pistol clapped to his breast he 'very readily' gave the villain all he asked.[9]

But possibly we exaggerate in retrospect the difficulties and dangers of travel. Whatever they were, and however great, land carriage of both goods and people increased considerably throughout the 17th century.[10] Regular services of waggons and coaches operated from London. There were over 200 carrier services by 1637 and over 300 by 1690[11] – among them, in the diary periods Beard, the Huntingdon, carrier, who arrived every Wednesday at his Cripplegate inn, and left on the following day. The waggons carried goods for the most part, but also provided rough and ready accommodation for passengers. Pepys thought them good enough for his parents and sister and servants, but not for himself and Elizabeth.

Compared with carrier services, coach services were an innovation. The coaches themselves were heavy vehicles suspended on leather straps. They lacked windows and had leather flaps instead of doors. Doors and glass windows were introduced in the '60s.[11] In the same decade lighter and better-sprung vehicles became fashionable for the private owner. Pepys describes some of the experiments in carriage design conducted by members of the Royal Society. But the heavier coaches continued to be built, especially for the public coach services and for travelling over long distances. They occur frequently in contemporary engravings of street scenes. Pepys made several journeys by coach in the '60s and never suffered a single upset. Services of coaches running from London were well established by 1660 – in 1690 there were 118 operators with vehicles running to and from the capital, sometimes several times a week.[13] The London inns they used were large establishments, well equipped with coachhouses and in some cases with extensive underground stabling.[14] The coaches, drawn by four horses, usually held six passengers, all inside, and would cover perhaps 25 miles a day on average in S. England. In the '60s an express service of 'flying coaches' was just beginning which in summer enabled Oxford to be reached within a day from London.[15] For many cross-country journeys it was necessary, for those who had no coach of their own, to hire one, as Pepys did for his holiday in 1668.

On most of his long journeys Pepys rode, hiring a horse from an inn or livery stable. If he were in a hurry he would ride post, hiring fresh mounts from the posthouses that were to be found on the most important roads. He would then ride to the next post town, usually 10 to 15 miles on, accompanied by a postboy who acted as guide and took the horses back at the end of the stage. The method was expensive – 3*d* a mile for the horse and 4*d* a stage for the postboy was the statutory charge[16] (plus tips) – and Pepys used it only when the occasion warranted it, as on 6 July 1661 when he heard of the death of his Brampton uncle from whom he had expectations. He then did the 55 miles or so within a day. On 16 Jan. 1661 he rode from Southwark posthouse to Rochester (c. 29 miles) in four hours, 'having good horses and a good way', and next day spent only two hours on the return journey of 15 miles from Dartford.

The journeys Pepys most commonly made were to Brampton. He used three routes, separately or in combination. The most easterly, via Epping and Bishop's Stortford, meant going through the muddy lanes of Epping Forest. His favourite route – and that recommended by John Ogilby, the contemporary mapmaker – was via Enfield, Ware and Puckeridge, and was by a slight margin the most direct. It also had the advantage of running along comparatively high and dry ground north of Puckeridge. The third route was the most westerly – the Great North Road through Barnet, Hatfield and Baldock. By any of the three he was within reach of Cambridge. If he was travelling without Elizabeth he would normally hire or borrow a horse and spend a night at an inn on the way. To Cambridge (c. 52 miles according to Ogilby's 'measured miles') would take just over a day; from there it was 15 miles or so to Brampton. On one occasion Elizabeth, who was a good horsewoman, rode with him, but made the return journey a few days later by coach. His average speed was about four miles an hour in summer, rather less in winter. By dint of an early start (and 4 a.m. was not unusual), and by riding hard, he could make Cambridge within the day. If Elizabeth were to accompany him he would normally travel by coach, either hiring one and staying overnight en route, or using the public coach that left from Holborn and did the journey in a day. The fare he gives to Huntingdon is 17*s*. 6*d*.[17]

The inns at which the traveller stayed were in better repute than the roads along which he journeyed.[18] Many were old, even historic; and their landlords prosperous and important local figures. Towns lying on busy roads were well supplied with accommodation for both man and beast: they had numerous inns, and the largest (such as the Red Lion at Guildford, where Pepys slept in the room the King had been given on a recent visit) had 50 bedrooms and an equivalent amount of stabling. On all his journeys Pepys never failed to find a bed, though once in a Wiltshire village the landlord had to expel a drover in order to find room for him.[19] The fact that he usually has little or nothing to report

about his visits probably means that all went well. He might have to
share the bed with a friend and both might have to share it with fleas,
but he would be fed, even at three or four in the morning.[20]

Within London, Pepys, like most Londoners, would sometimes
travel by river, but for the most part he either walked or hired a
hackney. His reports are sometimes more laconic than informative. 'Up
betimes and to Whitehall', he writes on 1 Dec. 1664, leaving posterity
to guess which mode of travel he used. Often enough he would walk,
especially if he had calls to make. It was his practice also to walk on his
journeys to Deptford yard – over the bridge and through Southwark;
a fair distance, but through fields most of the way. He rarely complains
of weariness from walking, and was a brisk walker who could, like the
King himself, outwalk his companions.[21] He once timed himself by
his watch, but that was more out of pride in the watch than in his
walking.[22]

Normally it was easy to engage a hackney. They had grown greatly
in number with the development of the London 'season' during his
early lifetime. Their number was in law limited to 400.[23] They could
be found anywhere, according to Monconys, a French visitor writing
in 1663.[24] At the Maypole in the Strand and elsewhere there were
stands where they waited for custom. Pepys seems to have had no
difficulty in picking them up – except of course in bad weather or after
the theatre. They were, in Monconys' words, *'fort rudes et peu suspendus'*
and gave a rough ride over the cobbles. Pepys's reference at 10 July
1668 to a glass hackney suggests that few until then had windows. But
Pepys used a hackney almost daily, especially if he had his wife or other
company with him. (His lady friends more than once got to know what
sort of advantage Pepys was likely to take of the closeness and darkness
of a coach interior.) The hackney, drawn by a single horse, could hold
four passengers. Its minimum statutory charge was 1s. – a little more in
bad weather and at holiday time – beyond that the cost would depend
on the distance or duration of the ride, and the coachman would always
resist any attempt by passengers to share the fare. The highest charge
given in the diary is 6s. 6d. for a journey from Drury Lane to Kensington,[25] but the hackney-and-four paid for by the Navy Treasury which
during the Plague took him on official business to the Exchequer at
Nonsuch must have cost more. So too must the jaunts to the Easter Day
parade in Hyde Park – to his shame taken too often in a shabby public
hackney – and the evening tours to villages outside the city to which he
and Elizabeth treated themselves in the summer months. For longer
trips he would hire a coach-and-four. On 14 July 1667 for instance he
and his party set off at 5 a.m. on a Sunday outing to Epsom, the coach
having been hired the day before. The journey took three hours there
and four hours back.

The diary has occasional notes of grander equipages than Pepys could afford. Sandwich lent him a coach-and-six for a funeral; Carteret provided a similar vehicle for the journey to his son's wedding, and it was in Brouncker's coach-and-six that Pepys bowled up Highgate Hill to call on Lord Lauderdale. He was often taken to Whitehall or Westminster in a colleague's coach, the price being a tip to the coachman, for until 1668 he was the only Principal Officer of the Navy without a coach of his own. In that year, after enquiring from experts and dealers, he bought two coach horses and a new-style 'chariot' – a light variety of coach made of leather stretched over a wooden frame, with glass at both front and sides, and with a 'forepart' that opened up.[26] The May Day of 1669 on which he used it for the first time – when he and Elizabeth spanked through the town with 'the horses' manes and tails tied with red ribbon' – gave Pepys something more than the ordinary pleasure of a new toy. He had a few years earlier told Elizabeth that he would one day be knighted and have a coach of his own.[27] He had now achieved one of those ambitions; he had arrived. By 1679, if a hostile pamphleteer is to be believed, he owned an even more resplendent vehicle, fit for a Secretary to the Admiralty, with painted panels that depicted 'Tempestuous Waves, and wracks of ships'; 'Forts and great Guns' and 'a fair Harbor and Town, with Ships and Galleys . . . kindly saluting each other'.[28]

As for the condition of the streets, Pepys complains in wet weather of flooding at Westminster, and in dry weather of dust on the roads in Hyde Park and on those leading into the Middlesex countryside. They were badly lit and remained so until the mid-18th century. Until then pedestrians relied, as Pepys did, on link boys to guide them. Hurrying over London Bridge one dark night Pepys almost broke his leg by falling into a hole.[29] The street by Whitehall was so dark that the royal coach itself once overturned.[30] Elsewhere the darkness held a new menace after 1666 in the open cellars left unfenced after the Fire.

But the principal difficulties of travel within the capital were those created by the sheer volume of the traffic. The city's regulations prohibiting the entry of ironshod vehicles and requiring draymen to lead their forehorses were ignored. Congestion was worst in the narrow streets of the city itself, where at certain points, particularly in the steep streets leading up from the river, traffic blocks would form for half an hour and more.[31] Drays, coaches and carts jostled for position; pedestrians, in the absence of pavements, were driven to the wall; and the air was clamorous with drivers' shouts, the rattle of wheels and the clatter of hooves. Accidents were frequent – Tom Killigrew is said to have told Charles II that 'coaches in London streets destroyed him more subjects every year than ever he had lost in any Dutch fight'.[32] Pepys's visitor from Brampton, Will Stankes, pronounced a countryman's verdict on London and its traffic when he announced that he would go home – the 'noise and ado' were more than he could stand.

By river. Unlike the Seine at Paris, London's Thames was extensively used for passenger traffic as well as for the carriage of goods. Along both banks, in addition to large quays for the handling of goods, such as the Customs House Quay, there were small landing stairs and jetties for the use of passengers. In 1676 the river was said to carry some 2,000 watermen, plying for hire in a variety of boats.[33] One reason for the extent of this passenger traffic was that London, unlike Paris and Rome, was poorly provided with bridges. Until Westminster Bridge was built in 1750 there were no bridges between London Bridge and Kingston. The crossing from Westminster to Lambeth, much used by Pepys, was until then served by boats and by a horseferry whose memory is preserved by the modern Horseferry Rd. Another reason for the volume of river traffic was that for journeys along the line of the river, from the city to Westminster, it was often quicker to travel by water than to struggle through crowded streets in a hackney. 'By coach to the Temple', wrote Pepys on 27 Dec. 1667, 'and then, for speed, by water thence to Whitehall'. The larger river boats were equipped with tilts (canvas shelters), but naturally the winter brought a decrease in the watermen's trade. In Jan. 1665 Pepys went by river only once in the whole month. In the following July, when admittedly there were special reasons for using the river (the Plague; Elizabeth's lodging in Woolwich; and the Carteret wedding at Dagenhams) he used boats 29 times and hackneys only 16. A similar pattern can be discerned in other years.

But the river was the axis along which his business journeys normally ran: upstream to Westminster and Whitehall, downstream to the docks and waterfront industries of Deptford and beyond. He had at his disposal an official barge and an official waterman, but he more often hired boats himself, later charging the expense to the government. The most expensive boat he used was a galley, rowed by several oarsmen. He employed it only rarely, on the longer official journeys he made below bridge. Even so, he was afraid of being thought 'too profuse' when he used a galley to go to Woolwich.[34] For his journeys to Westminster, he normally went by a 'pair of oars' or a single sculler. He had a regular sculler on whose boat he allowed his arms to be painted, but he preferred a pair of oars if he was in a hurry or had to cope with an adverse tide. Even for very short distances the river could be useful, if it were quicker and more direct than the land journey. For that reason, he often covered the few hundred yards between Westminster and Whitehall by water.

To all this water traffic, London Bridge offered something of a hazard. Its stone piers so restricted the waterway that except at high and low tide the flow was dangerously fast downstream. The watermen would ship oars and shoot through; passengers had to have a stomach for adventure to stay on board. (The diary has several stories of what might follow.) More often they would disembark above the bridge and either finish the rest of their journey by other means or re-embark on the other side. Pepys often took boat at the Old Swan Stairs and walked from there to the Navy Office.

Occasionally the Thames was the scene of river pageants reminiscent of Venice. There were the annual processions of decorated barges on Lord Mayor's Day, which Pepys, as it happens, never witnesses. He describes a similar spectacle, however, on 23 Aug. 1662, when Charles II brought his bride to London by water. Surrounded by an attendant flotilla, they were rowed from Hampton Court in a barge canopied in cloth of gold, and wreathed with flowers. Off Whitehall they were greeted by a fleet of vessels belonging to the city and its livery companies, tricked out with all manner of symbolic tableaux.

The river had also more everyday delights. Upstream from the city were the pleasure gardens of Chelsea and Vauxhall; beyond them Pepys had the lawns of Barn Elms for a family picnic, and, further up, the riverside resorts of Mortlake and Richmond. More than once he took Elizabeth downstream for a blow on the river to see the great ships of the navy at their moorings or to watch a race between the royal yachts.[35]

Tresham, [Maurice]. Friend and tenant of Sandwich.[1]

Treswell, Col. [Daniel]. Surveyor-General of woods south of Trent 1660–70; an office previously held by his father. He surrendered it on being commissioned Captain of the Halberdier Guard, Ireland.[1]

Trevanion, Capt. [Richard]. Naval officer; held 16 commissions between 1665 and 1688.[1]

Trice, Jasper and Thomas. Sons of Richard Trice of Brampton, who died c. 1628 and whose widow married Pepys's uncle Robert Pepys in 1630. They brought an action in Chancery about the payments due to Robert's widow after his death, but accepted an out-of-court settlement in Nov. 1663. Thomas was a civil lawyer and public notary practising in Doctors' Commons: he took the lead in the litigation. Despite their differences, Pepys employed him in the settlement of his brother Tom's estate. Jasper, the elder brother (admitted to the Middle Temple in 1636) lived in the family house at Brampton – a roomy one taxed on nine hearths – until 1667 when he moved to Offord to board with a brother-in-law. He was married three times, and was buried at Brampton in 1675.[1]

TRINITY HOUSE

Dover, Hull and Newcastle had their Trinity Houses, but the most important was that of London, the principal port of the kingdom. Originally a seamen's guild at Deptford, charged primarily with religious and charitable duties, it became from 1514 onwards by virtue of a series of charters and statutes a public authority which provided the means of safe navigation, particularly in the Thames. Its main responsibilities in the river were for lights, beacons and buoys, for the licensing of pilots and watermen, and for the clearing of the navigable channels (the spoil being sold as ballast). This last duty was until 1663 shared with the city, and its licensing of watermen with the Watermen's Company. In 1566 its authority over lights was extended to the whole kingdom. In addition it acted as a minor maritime court under the aegis of the Admiralty. Its members, mostly Thames masters and pilots, had since 1604 been divided into Elder Brethren, the executive authority, and Younger Brethren, the elective authority: corresponding, respectively, to the court and liverymen of a city company. During the Commonwealth a parliamentary committee had replaced the Elder Brethren, but the status quo was restored in 1660 and sealed by the issue of a new charter in Nov. 1660.

In the early 17th century its relations with the Navy Board had become increasingly close, and its main headquarters had been moved to Water Lane in the city. At the Restoration Pepys and most of his colleagues and associates in the naval service were made members, Sandwich being elected Master in 1661, and Pepys a Younger Brother in 1662. In days when the mercantile marine and the royal navy were almost a single service, cooperation between the two was essential, especially in wartime. The Navy Board looked to Trinity House to examine and certify sailing masters, to provide pilots in the Thames, and to help in the recruitment of seamen, the hiring of merchant vessels and occasionally in the design of warships and their ordnance. Conversely Trinity House looked to the Board for the provision of convoys and the protection of its members from land service.

Pepys in 1672 was elected an Elder Brother and in 1676–7 and 1685–6 served as Master. The diary has perhaps a disproportionate amount of information about the weekly dinners which his status at that time allowed him to attend only as a guest, and about which his comments, for a guest, often have an unseemly frankness. In his business contacts too he occasionally had reason to complain. 'I can't but give you an account', he wrote to Coventry in Nov. 1665, 'how we have been dealt with by the Trinity House in the business of pilots . . . Fourteen days ago I was directed by the Duke of Albemarle and presently signified it to Captain Bodiley and two days after to Trinity House, and after that procured a letter from the Duke to the Master and Wardens thereof for the providing some pilots forthwith to go with his Majesty's fleet to Hamborough. All that with frequent message[s] and calling on them I could obtain from them was the naming 5 to me: one whereof had never taken charge of a ship, great or small, thither in all his life; a second, not within these 10 years; another taken out of a collier, where he serves as mate, and declared by the master to be insufficient; the fourth (as the party says) taken out of his bed, where he had been for some time sick. However, he and one more only were with great violence imprested to go.'[1] One personal advantage he reaped from his association with Trinity House – in 1670 he was able through his influence with the Duke of York to secure the appointment of his brother John as clerk to the corporation. In 1671 he acted as spokesman for the corporation before a committee of the Privy Council when it successfully asserted its right, founded on precedent, of appointing the consul at Leghorn. As Master in 1675–6 he carried out a typically Pepysian reorganisation of office records and office methods, and arranged for the corporation to undertake the examining in navigation of the boys in the mathematical school of Christ's Hospital which he had been instrumental in setting up. In 1677 he took the lead in the Commons in securing the defeat of a bill which threatened to remove Trinity House's rights in the licensing of Thames watermen. In the early '80s, when it was troubled like all corporations by the King's enquiries into its legal status, the Elder Brethren put their trust in Pepys's influence at court to steer them through. He supervised the surrender of the old charters and was nominated Master in the new one of 1685. The large collection of papers concerning the history of the corporation which he amassed in his library[2] is a witness to his interest in its affairs and his belief in its importance in the maritime history of the nation.

The corporation used three buildings in the diary period. Trinity House, Deptford, their original home, was used for the annual elections on Trinity Monday, which were followed by a service at the parish church of St Nicholas (and, of course, a dinner). Until 1670 they also used a house they leased in Trinity Lane, Ratcliff. But their main headquarters remained in Water Lane near the Tower. After Aug. 1661 the court meetings, held twice a week, took place there. The building was destroyed in the Fire but rebuilt in 1669–70.[3]

Troutbeck, [John] (d. 1684). Army surgeon; serving under Lambert and (principally) under Albemarle. Appointed surgeon to the King 1660, and physician-general to the fleet 1666.[1]

Trulocke, ——. Gunsmith. There were three of this name active as gunsmiths in the '60s – Edmund, George and William. The last lived in St Martin's Lane, Westminster.[1]

Trumbull, [William] (?1594–1668). Clerk to the Signet 1660–8. His son Sir William (Clerk to the Signet 1683–1716, envoy-extra-ordinary to France 1685 and Secretary of State 1695–7) accompanied Pepys on the Tangier expedition 1683–4 as a very ineffective Judge-Advocate.[1]

Turberville, [Daubigny] (1612–96). The leading oculist of his day; M.D. (Oxon.) 1660. Prince Rupert was among his patients.[1]

Turlington, [John] (d. 1669). Spectacle maker, of Cornhill. His daughter (viii.486) cannot be identified: at his death he had four, three of them unmarried.[1]

Turner, Frank. Son of Thomas Turner of the Navy Office. He held a captain's commission in 1666, and after the war sailed in an E. Indiaman to Madras. As a parting present he had received from Pepys a copy of *Lex Mercatoria*, and from Elizabeth Pepys her husband's 'old pair of tweezers'. In 1672–3 he was back in home waters commanding fireships.[1]

Turner, John (d. 1705). Chaplain to Sandwich. A Fellow of Mag-dalene 1645–c. 76; Rector of Eynesbury, Hunts. 1649–89, and of Wistow, Hunts. 1687–1705.[1] In Sandwich's will he was made a trustee of Sandwich's Eynesbury lands: his correspondence with Sandwich had often been about business matters.[2] So too was his correspondence with Pepys, for whom he sometimes acted in the management of his Brampton property.[3]

Turner, John and Jane. Relatives. Jane ('Madam Turner') was the daughter of Pepys's cousin John Pepys of London and Ashtead (a lawyer), and herself married a lawyer, John Turner (1613–89), whom she predeceased. He was born in Kirkleatham, Yorks., and educated at Sidney Sussex College, Cambridge. He entered the Middle Temple in 1634, was called to the bar in 1639, became a Bencher in 1661, Recorder of York in 1662 and King's Serjeant in 1669. In London they lived in style – kept a coach and had a large house in Salisbury Court (assessed on 10 hearths, 1666, pre-Fire).[1] In 1669 they went to live in Yorkshire. Four of their children appear in the diary. From the eldest son Charles (who married Margaret, daughter of Sir William Cholmley, Bt) descended a line of baronets which died out in 1810; William, the second son, married Mary, daughter of Sir David Foulis; Theophila (b. 1652) married Sir Arthur Harris of Hayne, Devon, in 1673, and Betty married William, son of Sir William Hooker.[2]

Turner, Thomas (d. 1681). Purser 1642; Clerk-General of the Navy Office c. 1646–60; Purveyor of Petty Provisions 1660–8; clerk to the Comptroller 1661–8; Storekeeper at Deptford 1668–?80.[1] Evelyn thought more highly than Pepys of him, and in 1680 appealed to Pepys on behalf of 'our disconsolate neighbour', threatened with the loss of his place.[2] In his will he is described as of Tower St, London, gentleman.[3] His wife Elizabeth (daughter and heiress of Sir John Holmden) was left £100 in the will of Sir J. Mennes. She died in 1685.[4] Their son Moses was an administrator of his father's will.

Turner, Thomas, jun. (1644–87). Naval chaplain; eldest son of Thomas Turner of the Navy Office; educated at Westminster and Trinity, Cambridge (B.A. 1665, M.A. 1668); chaplain of the *Sweepstake* 1680; ? Vicar of Boxted, Essex 1684–7.[1]

Turner, Sir William, kt 1664 (d. c. 1670). Civil lawyer; Fellow of Wadham College, Oxford 1628–37; advocate Doctors' Commons 1641; Judge of the Admiralty Court under the Commonwealth; M.P. for Bodmin Jan.–Apr. 1659; Attorney to the Duke of York; Chancellor of Winchester diocese 1660–70.[1]

Turner, Ald. Sir William, kt 1662 (1615–93). Younger brother of John, the lawyer. A draper (both Pepys and Tom Pepys had accounts with him), Master of the Merchant Taylors' Company 1661–2, 1684–5; prominent in the R. Africa and E. India Companies. Sheriff 1662–3; Lord Mayor 1668–9; M.P. for the city 1690–3. In 1668 he claimed and received £400 from the King – a gift traditionally made to bachelor Lord Mayors – and gave it towards the rebuilding of Guildhall. A Puritan, who headed each page of his accounts *Laus Deo*,[1] he founded a hospital and free school at Kirkleatham, Yorks., in 1676.[2]

Turner, Mrs. Mercer's neighbour. Possibly Martha (b. Pettiward) who had married John Turner, merchant, at St Olave's in 1655: but there were several others of this name in the parish.[1]

Turnham Green. A small hamlet in Middlesex, some 8 miles from the Standard on Cornhill, on the main Bristol road. In 1664, according to the hearth tax, it only had three houses.[1] (R)

Turnstile. Passages leading south out of the s. side of Holborn – Great Turnstile to the e. side of Lincoln's Inn Fields, and Little Turnstile to the w. side. Slightly further west the latter was paralleled by New Turnstile. All three are still so named. There was also a Turnstile at one of the s. exits from the Fields. They had been put up to allow pedestrians to pass, whilst excluding horses. (R)

Tweedy, [Roger] (d. 1653). Navy Commissioner 1642–9; godfather to Peg Penn; father-in-law of Sir W. Rider.[1]

Twelfth Night: *see* Christmas

Twysden, [John] (1607–88). Physician; uncle of Sir Hugh Cholmley, who gave him power of attorney in his business concerning the Tangier mole.[1]

Tyburn. A gallows and place of execution at the open space where the road to Edgware forked from the road to Oxford by the n.-e. corner of Hyde Park. The site of the gallows is now shown by a triangular stone in the roadway. The stream of the same name flowed a short distance to the east of it. (R)

Tyler. Tyler the purser (viii.272) is Richard, who cleared his accounts with the Navy Board in Feb. 1666. 'Mr Tyler a neighbour' (v.202) who spoke to Pepys about purser's business, may be the same man or his brother Francis, who in 1663 had obtained a purser's place for Richard.[1]

Tyrconnel, 1st Earl of: *see* Talbot, Col. [R.]

Udall, Frances and Sarah. Sisters; serving maids at the Swan, New Palace Yard. Sarah was married in 1666.[1]

Unthank, [John]. Elizabeth Pepys's tailor; his shop at Charing Cross (a large establishment taxed on nine hearths)[1] was used by Pepys and his wife as a convenient meeting place in Westminster, especially when Elizabeth was visiting her parents.

Utber(t). Riches Utber (d. 1669) was a naval commander who held five commissions as captain 1661–8, and was made Rear-Admiral in 1666. His wife was Mary, sister of Sir Thomas Allin. Their son John (captain, 1663–5) was killed in action in 1665. Thomas Fenner's sister 'Utbert' has not been identified.[1]

Uthwayt, [John]. Clerk of the Survey Deptford, 1660–d. 74. A John Uthwayte was King's waiter, London port in 1671.[1]

Vallière, Françoise-Louise de la (1644–1710). Mistress to Louis XIV; cr. duchess 1677. Her pregnancy (iv.189) ended in the birth in Dec. 1663 of a son Charles, who was put out to foster parents and not acknowledged as royal.[1]

Vandeput, [Peter] (d. 1669). Merchant, of St Olave's parish. His wife was Margaret, daughter of John Buckworth.[1]

Vaughan, [Edward] (d. 1684). Son of Sir John, he succeeded him as M.P. for Cardiganshire 1669–March 81, and inherited his ability and powers of speech. He was in 1669 a critic of Carteret's work at the Navy Treasury and in the '70s of Pepys's programme of shipbuilding. He married Ald. Sir W. Hooker's daughter, Laetitia, in 1665.[1]

Vaughan, Sir John (1603–74). Politician and judge; a friend of Selden. M.P. 1628, 1640, 1640–5; for Cardiganshire 1661–8. A moderate critic of Clarendon. His reputation for eloquence explains Pepys's delight at his praise of his parliamentary speech in March 1668. In May 1668 he was made Chief Justice of Common Pleas and knighted. It was he who delivered the famous judgement in Bushell's case (1670) limiting the power of judges to imprison juries.[1]

Vaughan, John, styled Lord Vaughan, succ. as 3rd Earl of Carberry 1686 (1639–1713). Irish peer; M.P. Carmarthen borough

1661–Jan. 79, Carmarthenshire March 1679–March 81, 1685–6; an ally of Buckingham. President of the Royal Society 1686–9.[1]

Vauxhall. Riverside gardens; a favourite place of resort for Londoners and visitors to London: consisting 'entirely of avenues and covered walks where people stroll up and down, and green huts in which one can get a glass of wine . . . although everything is very dear and bad. Generally vast crowds to be seen here, especially females of doubtful morals, who are dressed as finely as ladies of quality . . .' (von Uffenbach, 1710).[1] The 'New Spring Garden' there was formed about 1661 and lay a little east of the modern Vauxhall Bridge. 'Foxhall' was the common contemporary spelling.

Venner. The Bath doctor whose tomb Pepys admired was Tobias Venner. Pepys possessed his *Via recta ad vitam longam*, which was published in 1660, the year of the author's death. The Dr Venner whom Pepys's Aunt Wight doted on may have been his son John (M.D. Oxon., n.d.), or William Venner (B.Med., Oxon., 1634).[1]

Vere, Aubrey de, 20th Earl of Oxford (1632–1703). Soldier; in the Dutch army 1644–50; imprisoned under the Commonwealth. Chief Justice in Eyre of the Forest south of Trent 1660–73; Colonel of the Royal Regiment of Horse from 1661. He lived in a large house (taxed on 17 hearths) in the Piazza, Covent Garden.

With his death this line of the Earls of Oxford became extinct.[1]

Vere, Lady (1581–1671). Mary, wife of the soldier Baron Vere of Tilbury (d. 1635). She had a London house at Clapton. A strict Puritan, she had her servants sing psalms after supper. Pepys's mother in her youth had worked for her as a washmaid.[1]

Vernatty, [Philibert]. Secretary to Peterborough, Governor of Tangier; Muster-Master and Treasurer of the garrison 1661–5.[1] Possibly the Vernatti who applied to Secretary Thurloe for employment in 1654.[2]

Vernon, Col. [Edward]. Member of Ormond's entourage; Gentleman of the Privy Chamber to the King. As a landowner near Sheerness he made large profits from the development of the naval base.[1]

Vernon, [John]. Quarter-Master General, Apr.–July 1659.[1]

Victualling: *see* Navy Board

Victualling Office. Situated east of Little Tower Hill (now Tower Hill) and north of E. Smithfield; headquarters since the reign of Henry VIII of the navy victualling. The buildings included, besides the office itself, houses accommodating the Victualler and many of his staff, and a growing number of bakeries, brewhouses, cooperages, storehouses and so on, in which supplies were gathered, prepared and stored ready for despatch from the nearby wharves to the navy. Access to the river however was not easy and the site became increasingly crowded, so that after 1742 the yard was moved to Deptford.[1]

Villiers, Barbara: *see* Palmer, Barbara

Villiers, Col. Edward, kt 1680 (d. 1689). Master of the Robes and Groom of the Bedchamber to the Duke of York. Uncle of Lady Castlemaine; father of the 1st Earl of Jersey.[1]

Villiers, George, 2nd Duke of Buckingham (1628–87). One of the most brilliant and irresponsible politicians of the period. The son of the great Duke who had been first minister to both James I and Charles I; the greatest territorial magnate in the kingdom; a man of superb physical presence and dazzling intellectual gifts – a wit, versifier, chemist and musician – he allowed his talents and wealth to run to waste. Both during the Commonwealth and later he attached himself too closely to the Presbyterians and political radicals to be trusted by his friends. Though brought up in childhood with Charles II he never managed to secure the King's favour for long, and though a great courtier he never held high executive office. He was at his best in attracting popular support and in managing an opposition campaign – against Clarendon in 1666–7; against the Duke of York and the Navy Office in 1667–8; above all, in cooperation with Shaftesbury, against the Danby ministry and the Catholic interest in 1674–9. In 1678–9 he was the paymaster of the Col. Scott who provided the evidence for the accusations of treason brought against Pepys and Deane.[1] When a member of the Cabal ministry in 1667–74 he was not admitted fully to his colleagues' secrets and quickly lost ground to Arlington. He accepted a French pension in the late '70s, and managed to combine an admiration for Louis XIV with support of the cause of religious toleration in England (the only consistent line of policy he ever followed). After the collapse of the exclusionist cause in 1681 he played no further part in national politics.

He married Mary, daughter of Fairfax, the Presbyterian leader, in 1657 in order to recover his confiscated estates. She was discarded a little later in favour of his mistress the Countess of Shrewsbury, over whom he fought the famous duel of 1668 described by Pepys. He abandoned the Countess and lived with his wife again after 1674 when as an opposition leader appealing to city opinion he decided to go in for respectability. She died in 1704.

His London house in the '60s was Wallingford House, to the west of Whitehall Palace.[2]

Vincent, ——. Butcher: probably Edward Vincent, of Round Wool Staple, Westminster. He occurs as a purveyor to the royal household 1660–2.[1]

Vincentio: *see* Albrici

Vine(s). Members of this family were colleagues of Pepys in the Exchequer. The father Christopher, of New Palace Yard, was Chamberlain of the Receipt from at least 1623. He died in 1663, leaving property in London and Southwark.[1] His eldest son George (d. 1672) was in 1666 a tally clerk and in 1669 a messenger in the Receipt; by 1666 he owned the tavern known as Hell. Jack Spicer was one of the overseers of his will.[2] The sixth son Dick was also a messenger in the Receipt.[3] His daughter (mentioned i.10) had been buried on 16 Dec. 1659, the day after her birth.[4]

Vyner. A family of goldsmith-bankers; among the most important financiers of their day. Sir Thomas (1588–1665) established the firm, at the sign of the Vine, in Lombard St. He was knighted by both Cromwell and Charles II, and made a baronet in 1661. He was Sheriff 1648–9 and Lord Mayor 1653–4. His country house was at Hackney. His partner and successor was his nephew Robert (1631–88), knighted in 1665, made a baronet in 1666. He remade many of the regalia at the Restoration, and is said to have had £400,000 involved in the Stop of the Exchequer in 1672. He was Sheriff 1666–7 and Lord Mayor 1674–5. His wife was Mary (d. 1675), widow of Sir Thomas Hyde, who brought with her a great fortune. Their country house was Swakeleys, nr Ickenham, Mdx. Sir Thomas's son George, the 2nd baronet (c. 1639–73) was also a goldsmith-banker. His wife (m. 1663, d. 1673) was a daughter of Sir John Lawrence, Lord Mayor 1665–6.[1]

Wade, [Thomas]. The diary evidence makes it probable that the Mr Wade of the victualling, the Mr Wade of Axe Yard and the Mr Wade who attempted to discover treasure in the Tower were all the same person. He was Thomas, who occurs as an officer of the Commonwealth victualling commission, first appointed 'deputy-check' for Dover, Deal and Sandwich in Feb. 1653. He was also the Mr Wade, ratepayer, of Axe Yard (1658) and probably also the Thomas Wade who in July 1660 was engaged in discovering concealed royal lands.[1]

Wadlow, [John]. Landlord of the Devil Tavern, Fleet St 1646–65 – his father Simon (d. 1627) had kept it before him – and afterwards of the Sun, Threadneedle St. Both were large and fashionable houses. In 1665–6 he was Warden of the Vintners' Company, and from 1668 a commissioner under the Wine Act. Pepys refers to his overspending, but he retained most of his Yorkshire estate and was able to settle it on his son in 1671.[1]

Wager, Capt. [Charles] (d. by 1688). Father of Adm. Sir Charles (1666–1743). After service in the navy of the Commonwealth, he held two commissions 1660–6.[1]

Waith, [Robert]. Appointed Paymaster to the Navy Treasurer 1660, and possibly the 'Wayte' who was a royalist financial agent in Brussels in 1659. As paymaster he was much distrusted and, after investigation by the Brooke House Committee, was joined in the treasurership by the upright Richard Hutchinson. His office was in his official house in

Deptford. In 1661, as a widower of 36, he married Elizabeth, daughter of Timothy Lowe of Greenwich. He was living in Camberwell at his death in 1685.[1]

Waldegrave, Dr. William Waldegrave, a Roman Catholic physician (M.D., Padua, 1659); later physician to Queen Mary of Modena, and knighted in June 1688 after delivering her son. A 'rare *Lutinist*' (Evelyn).[1]

Walden, Sir Lionel, kt 1673 (1620–98). Son of the Lionel Walden who as Huntingdon's first mayor (1630–1) had been involved in the dispute with Oliver Cromwell which had led to Cromwell's leaving the town. Royalist soldier; M.P. for the borough 1661–Jan. 79 and for the county 1685–7; a strong supporter of James II's policies, often accused of being a 'church-papist'; Mayor 1686–7. Pepys refers to his slighting words about Sandwich. But in his first recorded speech in parliament he defended him against criticisms of his conduct at Bergen.[1]

Waldron, [Thomas] (d. 1677). Physician to the King and Household. M.D. (Oxon.) 1653; F.R.C.P. 1665.[1]

Wale, Ald. Sir William, kt 1660 (d. 1676). Wine merchant. An influential city figure on the eve of the Restoration. Monck lodged with him at his house near to Drapers' Hall in Feb. 1660; in April he went to Breda as one of the city's delegation to the King.[1]

Walker, Sir Edward, kt 1645 (1612–77). Garter King of Arms (appointed 1645 in exile); Clerk of the Privy Council (from 1644); busy, learned and quarrelsome. Well known to Secretary Nicholas and Clarendon, both of whom found him importunate and self-centred.[1]

Walker, Sir Walter, kt 1661 (d. 1674). Civil lawyer; LL.D. (Cantab.) 1640; in the 1650s an advocate in Doctors' Commons and Judge of the Admiralty Court and Prerogative Court; appointed Advocate-General to the Duke of York 1670. Noted for the 'indecorous warmth of his language'.[1]

Wallace, [James] (d. 1678). Leader of the Pentland Rising in Scotland, 1666, and author of a narrative of it. After its collapse he fled, first to Ireland and later to Holland. In 1676 the King demanded his return; the States of Holland agreed, but did nothing. The sentence of forfeiture of life and fortune passed against him in 1667 was rescinded after the Revolution.[1]

Waller, Edmund (1606–87). Poet and politician. M.P. for several constituencies between 1624 and 1687; by 1685 father of the House. A champion of religious toleration and an attractive though lightweight speaker. He supported the attack on Clarendon ('Touch a lawyer and all the lawyers will squeak') and helped to draw up Penn's impeachment.[1]

Waller, Sir Hardress. Regicide; prominent in the conquest and settlement of Ireland 1649–51. After Dec. 1659 he was suspected of favouring Lambert and the fanatic party, and was removed from the command of Dublin castle. He fled at the Restoration but returned to face his trial. He died in prison in Jersey under a suspended death sentence c. 1666.[1]

Wallington, [Benjamin]. Goldsmith and amateur composer: there are songs by him in Playford's *Musical Companion* (1673); Brome's *New ayres and dialogues* (1678); and Playford's *Choice Ayres* (1679).[1] (Lu)

Wallis, John (1616–1703). Scholar and divine; Savilian Professor of Geometry at Oxford 1649–1703; a founder of the Royal Society and one of the greatest mathematicians of the age.[1] Pepys came to know him well and to have the deepest admiration for his learning and character. In 1702 he presented Kneller's portrait of Wallis to the university of Oxford, and it was to Wallis that he addressed one of the last letters written in his own hand.[2] A connection of a different sort is that Wallis was once domestic chaplain to the Lady Vere to whom Pepys's mother was washmaid.[3] He received a ring at Pepys's funeral.[4]

Walter, Lucy (d. 1658). Charles II's Welsh-born mistress 1648–50 (in the Low Countries, France and Jersey); mother of James Scott, Duke of Monmouth. She was also the mistress of Robert Sidney and of Henry Bennet, later Arlington, and according to Aubrey 'could deny nobody'.[1] Her brother who was given a place at court was possibly David Walter, Groom of the Bedchamber.[2]

Walthamstow. A village in Essex some 6 miles from London, south of Epping forest and just east of the R. Lea. Prosperous in 1660 and within the radius for the country houses of well-to-do Londoners such as Batten and Penn. (R)

Walton, Valentine. Regicide; as a strict republican, he was hostile to Cromwell, though he was his brother-in-law. His most important achievement was to secure Portsmouth for the Rump in Dec. 1659 in defiance of Lambert and the army leaders. He was a Navy Commissioner and a commissioner for the government of the army Oct. 1659–Feb. 1660. At the Restoration he fled to Germany where he died shortly afterwards.[1]

Wandsworth. A large, straggling village of some 340 houses (1664)[1] in Surrey, on the R. Wandle, between Battersea and Putney and on the road to Kingston. Some 7 miles from the Standard on Cornhill. (R)

Wanley, [Valentine]. Owner of the freehold of Pepys's Axe Yard house, Francis Beale being the leaseholder. He was a foreign denizen (originally a tailor), in 1656 and 1658 paying rates for a house in St Margaret's Lane, Westminster, and by 1660 living in Lambeth.[1] His Westminster properties yielded £1,000 p.a. in rent. He died in 1666 leaving bequests to the Dutch church in Austin Friars and to the university of Basel.[2] A William Wanley was enabled by a private act of 1695 to build several messuages and tenements in Axe Yard.[3]

Wanstead. A village in Essex some 7 miles from the Standard on

Cornhill and north of the main road from London to Colchester. (R)

Wapping. A hamlet of St Mary Whitechapel on the Middlesex bank of the Thames separated from the Tower by the precinct of St Katharine. Concerned almost solely with the port and the trade of the river, it had five well-frequented public landing stairs. Its population of rough seamen was the source of Shaftesbury's mob of 'Wapping boys'. It was then growing fast, the continuous built-up area already extending past it to include Limehouse, but, inland from the river, development was slower and fields predominated for many years after the close of the diary. (R)

Warcupp, [Edmund] (1627–1712). Middlesex J.P.; from 1664 Bailiff of Southwark. A nephew of Speaker Lenthall and a kinsman of Albemarle, he was often employed in minor government posts: in 1648 as secretary to the parliamentary commissioners at the Treaty of Newport, in 1654 as secretary to Downing's mission to France, and after the Restoration as an aide to Albemarle (in 1660 in the parliamentary elections at the university of Oxford, in 1665–6 in prize business). After his disgrace in 1666 he was removed from the magistracy but within a year or so had obtained a post in the excise and in the commission for collection of wine licences. He became notorious as a government agent rigging the trials of the Whigs after the Popish Plot.[1]

Ward. The Muster-Master was Richard.[1] The Mr Ward of vi.235 appears to have been an Exchequer officer, but I have traced none of that name, and he may have been one of the two Richard Wards who were in the customs service in 1663.[2] The naval officer was James, a lieutenant who in 1665 served on Sandwich's flagship the *Royal Prince* and was in the same year commissioned lieutenant to the captured prize *Golden Phoenix*. He played a considerable part in distributing the prize-goods.[3] The Wards of ii.7 have not been identified.

Wardour, [William] (d. 1698). Appointed Clerk of the Pells in the Receipt of the Exchequer 1646; restored to the office in 1660.[1]

THE WARDROBE

The King's Great Wardrobe was the court department which provided the Household with robes, liveries, furnishings etc. There were also 'standing wardrobes' at each of the royal palaces and smaller 'removing wardrobes' in attendance on the persons of the King and Queen. The office consisted of a Master responsible for general management and finance and under him a chief clerk and his assistants. The staff in 1669 was composed of about 25 tailors, cutters, lacemen and so on, and a number of hands.[1]

Its headquarters were at Puddle Dock, Blackfriars, and included official lodgings for the Master on St Andrew's Hill and other living accommodation. The buildings were destroyed in the Fire and the Wardrobe then moved first to Hatton Garden and afterwards to Lord Lumley's house in the Strand before being accommodated after 1669 in the Savoy Palace.[2]

The office was reorganised in the course of the economy campaign of 1668, after which the Master was paid by salary (£2000 p.a.) instead of by fees and allowances, and two new officers were added as a means of financial control – the Comptroller and Surveyor. A limit of £20,000 was then set on annual expenditure and arrangements were made for the principal officers to meet at least once a week.[3]

Sandwich was made Master in 1660 and was disappointed not to make more profit in the early years of his administration when the process of refurnishing the palaces and providing for the coronation greatly increased business. It was difficult to get money from the Exchequer and he seems to have been badly served by his deputy Thomas Townshend. Pepys estimated his income at not more than £1000. He sold his office to his cousin Ralph Mountagu in 1671.[4]

Ware, ——. Owner of the house at which Creed was lodging in 1661. Possibly Thomas Ware, of King St, Westminster.[1]

Warren, Thomas. Merchant, of St Olave's parish; brother of Sir William. Consul at Salli 1654–6 and possibly later; in the '60s trading to Tangier and Madeira.[1] He was possibly also the Thomas Warren who traded to the Baltic, where in 1664 he represented the Eastland Company at Danzig.[2]

Warren, Sir William, kt 1661 (1624–?). Timber merchant, of Wapping and Rotherhithe; Master of the Drapers' Company 1668–9. The greatest of contemporary timber merchants, dealing in home supplies but principally with the Baltic and also (for masts) with New England. He was Pepys's mentor in the '60s in business matters generally as well as in the timber trade. The 'firm league'[1] they made over contracts was one of the main sources of Pepys's prosperity, though he claimed to have held Warren strictly to the public interest. Its effect was to give Warren a virtual monopoly in supplies to the Navy Board from about 1664. To that charge, made first by his rivals and later by the Brooke House Committee, Pepys's reply was that Warren gave the best bargain and that it was no part of the Board's duties to spread its favours.[2] His accounts with the Board for the war of 1665–7 were not settled for some years. In 1675 an official investigation under the auspices of the Lord Treasurer revealed that Warren owed the government over £44,000, mostly in unpaid freight charges, insurance premiums and uncleared imprests.[3] The account was discharged in

1679 when £6,500, the last instalment of his debt, was paid to the Duke of Monmouth and Viscount Latimer to whom the government had granted it.[4] He suffered some reverses in the later part of his career from trading losses and two fires in his timber yards, and in Aug. 1688 appealed to Pepys to have him made a Navy Commissioner. But he was still trading in 1689–90.[5]

He had married Joan Mortimer in 1652 in St Olave's parish, and his son William (d. 1699) married into the great trading dynasty of the Ingrams.[6] He had houses attached to his timber yards at Wapping and, after 1665, at Rotherhithe, and a country property at Abridge, Essex.[7] He appears to have been a prominent Anabaptist.[8]

Warwick, Sir Philip, kt 1660 (1609–83). Secretary to the Treasury Commissioners June–Aug. 1660, and to Lord Treasurer Southampton Aug. 1660–May 1667; Pepys's mentor on the subject of the national finances. He was an experienced official, and had been secretary to Lord Treasurer Juxon 1636–41 and to the King at Hampton Court and Carisbrooke 1647–8. He now carried the weight of the department under Southampton's régime, though leaving no lasting mark on it, and was active as its spokesman in the House of Commons. (He sat for Westminster 1661–Jan. 79.) His honesty was beyond reproach – 'honest but weak' was Burnet's verdict – but to his remark about his low profits (v.69) should be added the fact that he also enjoyed the proceeds of the lucrative post of Clerk of the Signet.

His (second) wife was Joan, daughter of Sir Henry Fanshawe and widow of Sir William Boteler. The new house Pepys mentions was a square three-storey building in the Outer Spring Garden taxed on 20 hearths. It was demolished in 1827; Warwick House St now preserves the name.[1]

Washing, shaving etc.: *see* Dress and Personal Appearance

Washington, [Henry]. Excise officer, Berkshire, from at least 1665.[1] His wife had had a shop or stall in Westminster Hall.[2]

Washington, [Henry] (1615–64). Soldier. Eldest son of Sir William (who was third son of Sir Laurence Washington of Sulgrave, ancestor of George Washington); and friend of Henry Norwood. An officer in the royalist army; in exile under the Commonwealth; in 1660 lieut-colonel of the regiment of the Duke of Buckingham (to whom he was related); major and captain of H.M.'s Own Regiment of Foot 1661.[1]

Washington, [Richard]. Purser of the *Nightingale* 1664.[1]

Washington, ——. Of the Exchequer (1660–1). Possibly Richard Washington, of the Navy Treasury (1666).[1]

Waterhouse, [Edward] (1619–71). 'The Doctor that is lately turned Divine' (ix.432). Waterhouse was in fact not a doctor but an author and an F.R.S. One of the seven books he published, *Gentleman's Monitor*

(1665), is a study of 'the rises and decay of men and families'. He took orders in 1668 and became a preacher in London.[1] Pepys confuses him with his kinsman of the same names who was made M.D. at Oxford in 1651 by mandate from Cromwell in recognition of his work as an army physician in Ireland.[2]

Waterhouse, [Nathaniel]. Joint-Steward of the Household 1654–7; Master of the Board of Green Cloth 1657–9.[1]

Waters, [Edmund]: *see* Taverns etc.: Sun, King St

Watkins, [William] (d. 1662). Clerk in the Privy Seal Office. His kinsman (i.207) who had hoped for the place Pepys was given in 1660 may be the 'Mr Watkins' who was Sandwich's deputy in the Privy Seal in 1671, and the Thomas Watkins who was one of the four clerks c. 1682–c. 1698.[1] There is an undated letter to Thomas Watkins of the Privy Seal Office in PL 2582, pp. 53–4.

Wealth: *see* Finances

WEATHER

Sources. The first statistical register of English weather was kept by John Locke at Oxford and London (June 1666–June 1683), and was printed in Boyle's *General history of the air* (1692). Locke recorded temperature, humidity, atmospheric pressure, wind-direction and wind-strength – though his 'hygroscope' was only 'the Beard of a wild Oat'[1] – and interspersed the daily notes of his readings with occasional descriptive comments. Unfortunately none of his London material is contemporaneous with Pepys's diary. Robert Hooke, his colleague in the Royal Society and a pioneer meteorologist, planned a 'Method for making a History of the Weather'[2] and invented several instruments for the purpose, but no results were published. His diary has some information for London, with thermometer and barometer readings, for 1672–80.[3] The weather registers which the Royal Society later published were for Oxford (1684) and Upminster, Essex (1697–1702).[4] Two London astrologers, John Goad and John Gadbury, published records of London weather in the '60s in order to demonstrate its relation to astral influences. Goad's *Astrometeorologica* appeared in 1686, and Gadbury's *Nauticum Astrologium* in 1710. Both are very brief: Goad has many gaps, and Gadbury, though giving a continuous daily calendar, does not begin until 11 Nov. 1668. There are some weather observations made in Raynham, Norfolk for 1657–86 which survive in a MS. preserved in the Norfolk Record Office.[5] In addition naval records provide a certain amount of information. Thanks to the Dutch War, the '60s are rich in reports of offshore weather – not only in ships' logs but also in captains' letters addressed to the Navy Board, often to Pepys himself. And, as always, phenomena such as storms are amply reported, if sufficiently disastrous, in pamphlets and newspapers.

But all in all the historian of the weather of the 1660s has to rely for the most part on personal diaries similar to Pepys's. John Evelyn, writing in or near London, and Wood, writing in Oxford, have a few useful notes, mostly about unusual weather. Rugge, in his 'Diurnal' (1659–72) has scraps of information about London and elsewhere, taken mostly from newspapers.[6] By far the best of the diaries, for this purpose, is that kept by Ralph Josselin, Vicar of Earl's Colne, Essex.[7] His work as a farmer gave him a special interest in the subject and he gives frequent summaries throughout his diary (1644–82). Since his weather in Essex was not likely to be very different from that in London, his evidence can be used to supplement and check that of Pepys.

Being a townsman, Pepys did not treat the weather with the same system and seriousness as did Josselin, except when on his voyage to and from Holland. He usually reported it intermittently, simply writing of what happened to affect or interest him, and his evidence is often indirect. It can for instance take the form of a note of when he changed his clothes with the seasons. Nevertheless, the facts he gives, though scattered and unsystematic, can often be useful because they are precisely dated and sometimes detailed.

Summary. The main abnormality of the '60s was the frequency of severe hailstorms and thunderstorms, to which Pepys has many references. Otherwise the weather in the diary period was not greatly different from that of our own day. One difference was that Pepys's London (like Dickens's and Conan Doyle's) suffered fairly regularly from the November fogs which, since the Clean Air Act of 1956, have become rare. The use of coal and wood for domestic fuel, together with the increase in population, led to extensive smoke pollution in the 17th century. Evelyn published a book on it (*Fumifugium*) in 1661. Another difference is that the Thames froze over in Pepys's day as it never does now – not because temperatures were lower (though in the 17th century they were in fact lower by about one degree), but because of the river conditions. The water flowed more sluggishly in the absence of embankments containing the stream and the current was blocked by London Bridge and the large number of river piers or jetties above the Bridge. In the diary period the river froze in the winters of 1660, 1663, 1665 and 1667. The most famous of the river frosts occurred in 1683–4. It lasted for several weeks; refreshment booths and entertainments were set up on the solid ice, and coaches crossed between Westminster and Lambeth. [*See also* vol. xi, *Index:* Weather]

(D. J. Schove)

Weaver, [Elizabeth]. Actress in the King's Company 1660–78, playing minor rôles. Born Farley, and briefly (c. 1660) mistress to the King.[1]

Weaver, [Richard]. Of Huntingdon; buried 5 Apr. 1667 in St Mary's church there.[1]

WEDDINGS

The putting of the bride and bridegroom to bed after the ceremony is described in several passages of the diary. The untying of ribbons and garters was a survival of the older custom of undressing the bridegroom. In the 'flinging of the stockings' the bridesmaids flung the bridegroom's stockings backwards over their shoulders, and the bridesmen's the bride's. If a stocking thrown by a man hit the bride or one thrown by a woman hit the bridegroom it was a sign that the thrower would soon be married. After the flinging, a sack posset was served to the bridegroom – the sack to make him lusty and the sugar to make him kind.[1] These games were sometimes played at wedding anniversaries, or at parties as sheer romps.[2] [For Pepys's wedding, *see* Pepys, Elizabeth]

Weld, George (c. 1635–1701). Son of Sir John Weld of Arnolds, nr Barnet; M.P. for Much Wenlock 1661–Jan. 79 and in five succeeding parliaments. A 'coxcombe' (iii.242). He took a leading part in Penn's impeachment. From 1662–7 he was deputy to the Governor of the Tower, Sir John Robinson, whose wife was his cousin. Weld's sister Dorothy married Ned Pickering.[1]

Wells, [John]. Storekeeper, Deptford c. 1618–49; resigned 1663. A mathematician: in his *Sciographia* (1635) and other writings he made an important contribution to the discussion of how to calculate ships' tonnage. Probably author, with Matthew Baker, of the MS. 'Fragments of Ancient English Shipwrightry' (PL 2820) usually attributed to Baker alone. This may be the MS. mentioned at v. 108.[1]

Wells, [William]. A Cambridge graduate; Vicar of Brampton 1650–d. 64.[1]

Wells, Winifred. Maid of Honour to the Queen from 1662; mistress to the King 1664–74. 'A big, splendidly handsome creature, who dressed finely [and] had the carriage of a Goddess . . . [but with] the physiognomy of a dreamy sheep' (Gramont). He adds: 'She put up a feebler resistance than would have been proper'. In 1675 she married Thomas Wyndham.[1]

Wendy, [Sir Thomas], kt 1661 (1614–73). Of Haslingfield, Cambs.; M.P. for the county 1660, 1661–73.[1]

Werden, Col. Robert (c. 1622–90). Courtier in the service of the Duke of York – Groom of the Bedchamber from ?1662, Commissioner for the regulation of the Household from 1667, and Comptroller 1675–85. Major-General 1685, Lieut-General 1688.[1]

WESTMINSTER PALACE

General.[1] The chief palace of English sovereigns from the time of its building by Edward the Confessor to its destruction by fire in 1512; then replaced by Whitehall as a royal residence and the centre of the household, but remaining the home of the principal courts of law, the houses of Parliament, and older administrative departments such as the Exchequer. Like Whitehall, a jumble of buildings of various dates, added to and rebuilt by many kings from William II onwards. The greater part of it was destroyed by fire in 1834, only Westminster Hall and the Jewel House remaining.

Court of Exchequer. A large chamber in a wing built out on the n.-w. side of the Hall and reached by a staircase starting inside the Hall's entrance. The present grand committee room of the House of Commons is approximately on its site.

Court of Wards and Liveries. The court had ceased to function after the Civil War and was abolished by statute in 1660, but the name remained as the title of its premises. These consisted of two courtrooms and various ancillary chambers in one of the ancient buildings of the palace running east and west across the s. end of the Hall. They were used as a depository for parliamentary records.

Hall. The great hall of the palace, built by William II and enlarged by Richard II, opening north into New Palace Yard. The early parliaments had often met in it and, in 1660, it was still the chief building in the palace, housing (in draughty wooden structures) the courts of Common Pleas, King's Bench, and Chancery, besides (in 1666) 46 shops and booksellers' stalls ranged along the walls.[2] Charles's restoration was followed by a notable repair and renovation, including the moving of the courts of King's Bench and of Chancery from the sides to the s. end of the hall, the repaving of much of it, and the opening out of a doorway at the s. end, followed by a thorough overhaul for the coronation.[3] For Pepys and his contemporaries it was one of the most important places of public resort in the capital. He frequently refers to it simply as 'the Hall' and describes it as very similar to that of the Dutch States-General, though larger and much less neat.[4]

Outside the Hall but abutting on to or leading out of it were, on the north, the offices and court of the Exchequer and, on the south, the two

Houses of Parliament and various courts and officials' rooms in buildings dating from the 13th century onwards. Other buildings, official and unofficial, were ranged along its w. side occupying the space between the Hall and St Margaret's Lane.

After the fire of 1834 the Hall became, in the rebuilding, the vestibule of the new palace. St Margaret's Lane and the intervening buildings have all disappeared, only St Margaret's Church remaining in the open space created as Parliament Sq.

House of Commons. The Commons met between 1547 and 1834 in St Stephen's Chapel, a remarkable two-storeyed structure (the lower section being what is now called the 'crypt' of the House) of the late 14th century. It ran west to east from the s. end of the Hall. A door at the s.-e. end of the Hall led to the Lobby of the house, originally the ante-chapel, to which Pepys, like other members of the public, had access. The chamber was furnished in the manner of a college chapel, with seats (by this time covered in green serge) facing each other on either side. It was small – its interior, after 1692, when Wren had lowered the ceiling, measuring 60 ft long, 28 wide and 30 high. Wren's alterations also included new wainscotting and a small internal gallery. In 1678-9 he built a wooden gallery connecting it to the Painted Chamber. The royal arms were once more put up over the Speaker's chair in 1663.

House of Lords. The Lords met (until 1801) in what had been one of the halls (the White Hall) of the original medieval palace, which had become known as the Parliament Chamber since it was there that the parliament strictly so-called (King, Lords and Commons) always met. Like St Stephen's Chapel it had a lower hall beneath it. It was in the s. section of the palace, running north and south from the s.-e. end of the Painted Chamber. Charles II was fond of attending debates there – he thought they were as good as a play – and would stand warming himself by the fireplace. The benches were (as they still are) red in contrast to the green of the Commons. The chamber was pulled down in 1823.

New/Old Palace Yard.[5] Pepys's references are sometimes confusing. He often refers to Palace Yard (though there were two), sometimes to Old Palace Yard, never to New Palace Yard. It is therefore almost certain that by Palace Yard he meant the new one. This seems also to tally with his likely routes. He occasionally called it simply the Palace. New Palace Yard was in fact very much his stamping ground. It was in origin the courtyard of the palace projected by William Rufus, and lay at the n. (downstream) end of Westminster Hall, with approaches from Westminster Stairs, St Margaret's Lane and King St. It was larger than Old Palace Yard – at the coronation of Charles II 4881 sq. yds of paving were relaid in the New Yard, as against 1461 in the Old.[6] Hollar's etching (vol. iii, facing p. 60) shows it as an enclosed rectangle, with a range of houses built on to either side of the Hall, coach-stands in the centre, a row of shops, taverns and eating-houses on the n. side, and an entry into King St under a large square gatehouse (pulled down in 1707).

Old Palace Yard, originally the courtyard of the palace of Edward the Confessor, lay at the s. (upstream) end of the Hall, and was approached via Parliament Stairs, St Margaret's Lane and Millbank.

Painted Chamber. A large chamber running eastwards at right angles from the end of the House of Lords, towards the river, with inside measurements of $82\frac{1}{2}$ ft long, 20 wide and 50 high. Its name came from the notable paintings on its walls executed for Henry III. In it were held the conferences between the two Houses of Parliament. The body of Charles II lay in state there. When the fire of 1834 destroyed much of the two Houses, it was fitted up as a temporary House of Lords.

Prince's Chamber. A small chamber at the s. end of the range of buildings which included the Hall, next to the House of Lords to the north. The sovereign passed through it on his way to the Lords. Often used as a robing room.

Speaker's Chamber. A suite of four rooms over the w. cloister walk in St Stephen's Court, used by committees. The Speaker also had a private chamber on the n. side of the House of Commons. He had no official residence in the palace until 1794.

Star Chamber. The building put up in the last years of Elizabeth's reign on the e. side of New Palace Yard close to the river. The Court of the Star Chamber had occupied a part of it and the name continued after the abolition of the court in 1641, Evelyn regularly using it when, after 1661, the former court's rooms were used for parliamentary committees. By the 1690s it was absorbed into the Exchequer offices.

Treasury. In early 1660, within the range of buildings which included the Hall. The Restoration caused the Treasurer to remove his own office to Whitehall, where it was near to the Council. The old Treasury offices were then taken over by the Auditor of the Receipt. How far the staff then moved to Whitehall is not clear, but it is probable that this was done in or before 1667. [*See also* Exchequer; Gatehouse; Privy Seal. Maps in vol. i, pp. xxv, xxvii.]

(T. F. Reddaway; La)

Westminster Stairs ('Bridge'). The public landing place at the e. end of New Palace Yard. Downstream of Parliament Stairs, and above the various landing places for Whitehall Palace. (R)

Wheatley, ——. Probably of St Bride's parish; but hardly likely to have been the Common Councilman William Wheatley of that parish since his daughter was proposed as a match for Tom Pepys. Tom's accounts at his death record payment of a bill for £2 14s. to 'Mr Wheatley'.[1]

Wheler, Sir William (c. 1601–66). Of Cannon Row, Westminster; kt 1657 and 1660; bt 1660. A rich friend of Sandwich, and his financial adviser from the '50s. By 1640 he held posts in the First Fruits Office, the Court of Exchequer, and the Mint, and during the Civil War and Commonwealth was nominated to a large number of local committees, especially on taxation. He also served in the Westminster Assembly as a lay member. As an M.P. (elected Nov. 1640, 1660) he was active in financial and fiscal business and belonged to the same moderate, Presbyterian group as the Crews. His wife (d. 1670) was Elizabeth Cole, once laundress to Charles I. They lived in a house taxed on 11 hearths.[1]

Whetstone(s) Park. A narrow road running between the n. side of Lincoln's Inn Fields and the s. side of Holborn, notorious for its prostitutes. Attacked in an apprentices' riot 1682; mostly pulled down and rebuilt as stables 1708.[1]

Whistler, Daniel (1619–84). Physician; author of the first book on rickets. M.D. (Leyden) 1645; Gresham Professor of Geometry 1648–57; an original F.R.S. He had been a naval doctor in the First Dutch War, and had accompanied Whitelocke on his embassy to Sweden 1653–4. He married a rich widow in 1657 (mother of Anthony Lowther) and according to Aubrey earned £1000 p.a. by his practice, but when he died (in the midst of his term as President of the Royal College) it was discovered that he was heavily in debt and had embezzled the College's funds. Evelyn thought him 'the most facetious [amusing] man in nature'.[1]

White, [Thomas]. Navy agent and Storekeeper at Dover since at least 1657. He had a salary of £100 p.a. and looked after the despatch, repair, cleaning and refitting of H.M. ships. In 1667 he applied for permission to surrender the post.[1]

Whitechapel. The name of a principal street and a district east of Aldgate. Increasingly built up under the Tudors and Stuarts, it was made a separate parish by the mid-17th century. Lying across the high road to Essex it was a centre for inns and for butchers dealing in the cattle coming to the city. In 1660 it was prosperous, with a number of sizeable houses, but already possessed a big poor quarter. (R)

Whitefriars. On the s. side of Fleet St between Water Lane and the Temple. A precinct or liberty formerly the site of a House of the Carmelites; in 1660 a maze of small courts and alleys notorious under the name of Alsatia. Pepys, visiting his father in Salisbury Court or the theatre nearby, often used either its landing stairs (at the foot of Waterman's Lane) or Dorset Stairs. (R)

WHITEHALL PALACE

General.[1] Originally York House, the town house of the archbishops of York; after 1528 a royal residence used by most rulers from Henry VIII to James II; almost totally destroyed by fire in Jan. 1698. In 1694 it was described by de Muralt as 'an old, large building, very ugly but very convenient. It contains nothing resembling a palace unless it be the building called the Banqueting House. The remainder is an accumulation of badly built houses not constructed to be joined together'.[2] The unspoken comparison with Versailles is clear. But the description is reasonably accurate. Henry VIII had acquired it from Wolsey and he and most of his successors had made additions and alterations. Reputed in the '60s to contain 2000 rooms, it straggled from the Thames to St James's Park. In Jan. 1660 it lay empty. It had not been used since the death of Oliver Cromwell and in May 1659 had been put up for sale – to no effect – in order to pay off the arrears due to the army. Charles II occupied it immediately on his return and both he and his successor carried out extensive works to refurbish the interiors and repair and extend the buildings. It included, besides the royal apartments, those of many of the great officers of state and of the Household, together with the rooms needed for the business of their departments. Tennis courts, a cockpit used for plays, various gardens and a bowling green provided amusements. Policy or gratitude rewarded men like Albemarle and Sandwich with substantial apartments, and generosity or weakness added others. The public road from Charing Cross to Westminster (the modern Whitehall and Parliament St) bisected it. Most lay to the east of this road, the Cockpit, Tilt-Yard and Horse-Guards (this last not being strictly within the palace) being on the west. Access from the Thames (or eastern) side of the palace to the western (or St James's Park) side lay at first floor level through the two gate houses, the King St Gatehouse to the south and the Holbein Gatehouse to the north, only the latter route being open to those who, like Pepys, had the right of entry. From Whitehall, important road traffic entered the palace by the main palace gate (the Great Gate) at the n. end of the Banqueting House; less important, or administrative traffic by the two gates into the two Scotland Yards (further north and nearer to Charing Cross). Fuel and provisions used the wharf and Scotland dock. The Privy Stairs gave access from the river to the area of the royal apartments, the public stairs lying at the end of the way through to the main palace gate. Inside the river side of the palace, access to the most important section, that between the Great Court to the north and the Bowling Green to the south, was given by three galleries: the Stone Gallery, with the Matted Gallery above it, and, at right angles to them, the Privy Gallery.

General jurisdiction over the palace above stairs was exercised by the Lord Chamberlain whose orders show the careful restriction on entry to the Privy Gallery which served the Council Chamber and the first floor route to the King's and Queen's private rooms.[3]

In the early months of 1660 Pepys was living in a turret room in Mountagu's apartments over the Holbein Gate; thereafter, as a government official he had the entrée to most parts of the building. He retained several views of it in his library.[4]

No complete room plan exists for this period. The plan of the first floor (pp. 480–1) is constructed from a plan of c. 1670 (probably drawn on Wren's instructions) which shows only the less important ground floor. So far as possible the list which follows includes all the parts of the palace mentioned by Pepys apart from the government offices and grace-and-favour residences. (For these *see* main series under names.)

Banqueting House. Built by Inigo Jones, 1619–22, on the site of a former banqueting house destroyed by fire. The only part of Jones's new palace to be erected, and nowadays the only part of the palace of 1660 to survive above ground. It now stands on the e. side of the modern Whitehall (i.e. the street); it then stood on the s. side of the entrance court and was used principally for the audience of ambassadors and great ceremonial occasions. Between 1698 and 1895 it was used as the Chapel Royal. The ceiling by Rubens, put into place in 1635, still survives as a remarkable image of early 17th-century conceptions of monarchy. Painted on a huge scale – with nine-foot cherubs – it has as it centrepiece the apotheosis of James I.

Boarded Gallery. A wooden gallery, location uncertain, but probably that from the Banqueting House, passing at right angles to it between the Great Court and the Pebble Court, eastwards to the block which included the Great Hall and the Chapel. If so, it was replaced in brick in 1669.

Bowling Green: see Garden

Chapel. Part of the original Tudor building, in the e. section of the palace near the river. Restored to use in the '60s after a period of neglect under the Commonwealth; extensively redecorated in the '70s. The organ was replaced and a new organ loft built in 1663. The King's Closet, which Pepys often visited, was in a gallery. Curtains separated the King from the ladies of the bedchamber who sat at either side.

Cockpit. A name used indiscriminately to denote (a) either one or all of the various buildings lying between the Holbein and King St Gates on the w. side of the street (now Whitehall) through the palace, or (b) the building once a cockpit in the n.w. corner of the park side of that range. In the '60s, as in the 1630s, the Cockpit proper was regularly used as a theatre, and also for any unofficial gathering requiring space for an audience, whilst the whole range of buildings included various lodgings or apartments (e.g. Albemarle's and Sandwich's), the tennis courts, and sundry courts and gardens. Some 70 years later the site of the actual cockpit (pulled down c. 1675) was included in William Kent's Treasury building. [*See also* Theatre]

Council Chamber. On the n. side of the first floor, over the council offices, facing the Pebble Court and in the middle of the line of buildings running east–west from the Holbein Gate to the n. end of the Stone Gallery. Reached either by the staircase from the court below known as the Council Chamber stairs or, for those exalted enough to use it, by the Privy Gallery.

Court. By this name Pepys usually refers to the first court inside the Great or Whitehall Gate. It was often known as the Great or Whitehall Court. To the south of it was Pebble Court.

Duke of York's side: see Prince's Lodgings

Garden (Privy Garden) and Bowling Green. Divided by a wall and trees. The Garden was a square of ground of some $3\frac{1}{4}$ acres behind the high wall running north and south from the Holbein to the King St Gates. Lying to the east of that wall, it was bounded in 1660 by the ranges of building (containing the Privy Gallery) which on the north separated it from the Pebble Court behind the Banqueting House, and on the east by the Stone Gallery. Despite its name, Pepys observes that it was 'now a through-passage, and common'. It has now all but disappeared under the new government offices built since the Second World War on the e. side of Whitehall. The Bowling Green, formed as such after the Restoration, lay south of it, bounded on the east by the Thames and on the west by the houses in King St. Over 2 acres in area, it had been acquired by Henry VIII separately from York House and used as an orchard. Richmond Terrace and its forecourt now occupy its site.

Gate and Gatehouse. By 'Gate' Pepys normally means the Great or Whitehall Gate, which was the main entrance. The Gatehouse was occasionally used as a place of confinement. Inigo Jones built the Banqueting House immediately south of it, and both buildings survived the fire of 1698. It was pulled down in 1765. *See also Holbein Gate.*

Great Hall. Built c. 1528; at the s.-e. end of the Great Court. Used from Elizabethan times for masques and other entertainments. In 1665 it was adapted for use as a theatre by the construction of a proscenium stage and tiring rooms.

Green Chamber. On the first floor in the e. half of the palace, off the gallery leading to the passage over the Holbein Gate and between that gate and the e. end of the Banqueting House.

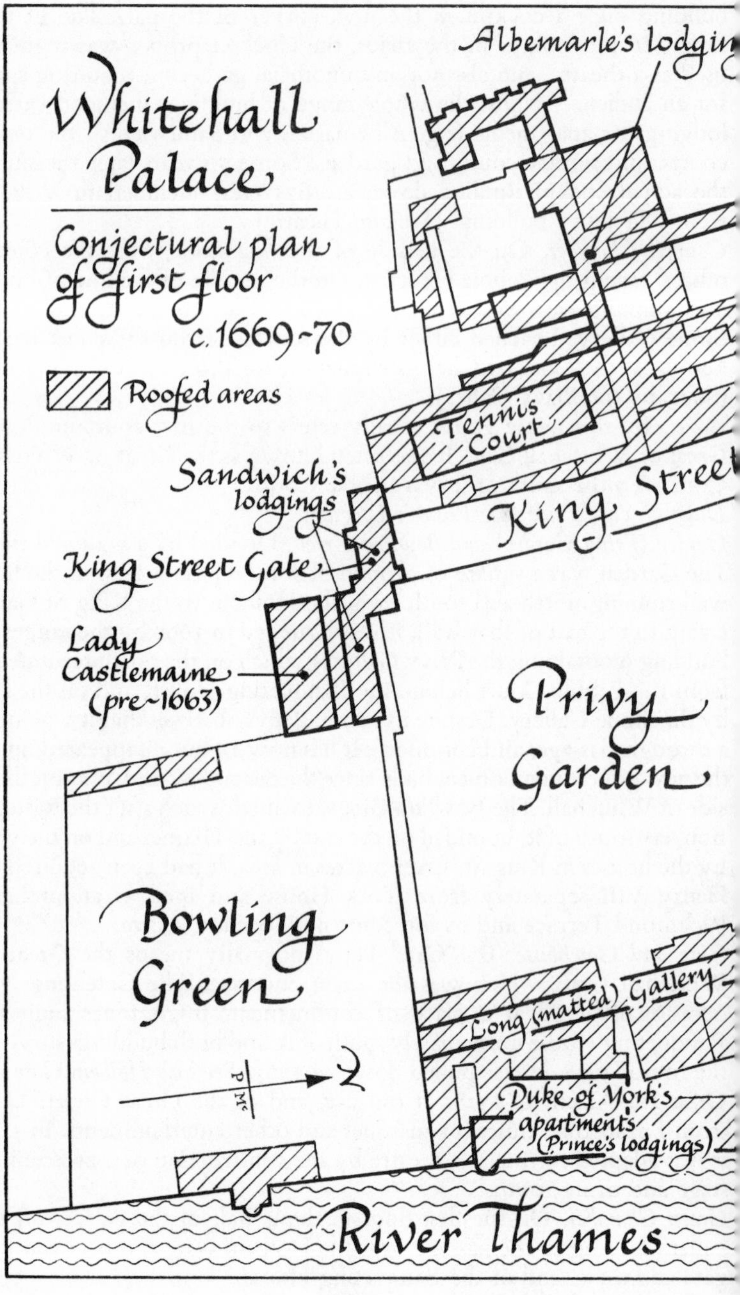

Whitehall Palace

Conjectural plan
of first floor
c. 1669~70

▨ Roofed areas

Albemarle's lodging

Tennis Court

Sandwich's lodgings

King Street Gate

Lady Castlemaine (pre~1663)

King Street

Privy Garden

Bowling Green

Long (matted) Gallery

Duke of York's apartments (Prince's lodgings)

River Thames

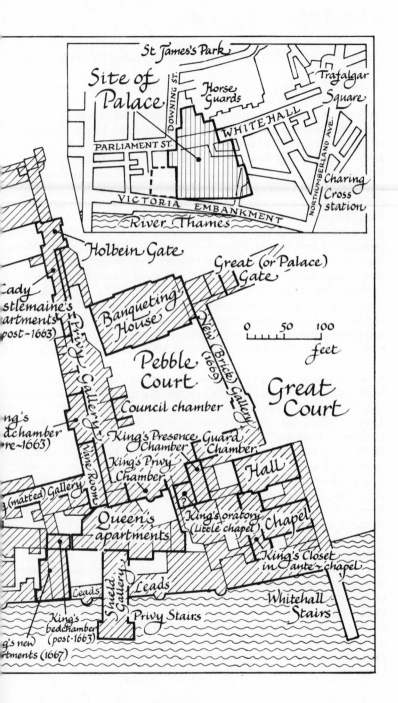

St James's Park

Site of Palace

DOWNING ST.

Horse Guards

Trafalgar Square

WHITEHALL

PARLIAMENT ST.

NORTHUMBERLAND AVE.

Charing Cross station

VICTORIA EMBANKMENT

River Thames

Holbein Gate

Great (or Palace) Gate

Lady Castlemaine's apartments (post~1663)

Banqueting House

Privy Gallery

New Brick Gallery (1669)

0   50   100

feet

Pebble Court

Great Court

Council chamber

King's bed chamber (pre~1663)

Vane Room

King's Presence Chamber

Guard Chamber

King's Privy Chamber

Hall

(matted) Gallery

?

King's oratory (little chapel)

Chapel

Queen's apartments

King's Closet in ante~chapel

Leads

Shield Gallery

Leads

Privy Stairs

Whitehall Stairs

King's bedchamber (post~1663)

King's new apartments (1667)

Guard Chamber. On the first floor of the main range which included the Chapel and the Hall; over the Wine Cellar. Staffed by the Yeomen of the Guard.

Henry VIII's Gallery. On the e. side of the palace, leading into the Boarded Gallery. Exact location uncertain.

Holbein Gate. The northernmost of the two gates straddling the Charing Cross–Westminster road. It lay immediately south of the Banqueting House. It was pulled down in 1760.

Horse Guards House: see under that name in main series

Jewel Office. On the ground floor in the range of buildings on the n. side of the Great Court. In 1660 it was the depot to which were brought the furniture and fittings that had been sold in the Interregnum, but bought by loyalists against the King's return.

King's apartments. In the buildings fronting the river on the southern (up-stream) side of the Privy Stairs and the Shield Gallery. More numerous and less compact than the Queen's apartments and including, after substantial building work in 1667–8, accommodation for bathing, for books, and possibly for scientific experiments. (By 1670 there were three laboratories here and elsewhere in the palace.) Mainly on the first floor and communicating with the rest of the palace via the Matted and Privy Galleries. Pepys at this period was not sufficiently important to go to more than a few of the individual rooms, though he was immensely impressed by the pictures in the closet (or cabinet) which could be seen by anyone of reasonable standing. This was on the first floor, leading out of the Privy Gallery, but its exact position is uncertain.

Long Gallery. Probably another name for the Matted Gallery.

Matted Gallery. On the first floor, roughly parallel to the river, immediately above the Stone Gallery, running from the e. end of the Privy Gallery to a staircase leading down to the Bowling Green. For those with business at the palace, it was a convenient semi-private walk. The Duke of York's closet and chief apartments were reached from it in the '60s, with subsidiary rooms belonging to him on the floor below.

Music Room. The 'King's Musick house' was in the range of buildings on the s. side of Scotland Yard.

New Banqueting House. So called by Pepys. Location uncertain; probably by the river.

New Gallery. So called by Pepys. A covered way, in brick, constructed in 1669 and running from the n. end of the Banqueting House to the main range containing the Great Hall, thus separating the Great and Pebble Courts.

Porter's Lodge. On the ground floor of the gatehouse at the main entry from the Charing Cross–Westminster road.

Presence Chamber. On the s. side of the interior court east of the Guard Chamber. Open only to those who had the entrée to court.

Prince's Lodgings. So called probably since the later years of Henry VIII, the Prince being the future Edward VI. A group of apartments and a chapel between the Stone and Matted Galleries and the river. Occupied in early 1660 by Monck and after the Restoration by the Duke of York.[5] Reconstructed 1664–5.

Privy Gallery. On the first floor at right angles to the Matted Gallery and the river front with doors into the Council Chamber and some of the chief rooms in the palace. Running along the n. side of the Privy Garden it gave access from the Matted Gallery and the Privy Lodgings via the passage over the Holbein Gate to the w. side of the palace and down the stairs there into the park. The Lord Chamberlain had strict instructions, enforced by a gallery keeper stationed at the Privy Gallery door next to the Council Chamber, to ensure that the gallery was not used as a walk or passage save by a carefully limited few.[6]

Privy Stairs. The covered landing stairs for the King's and Queen's apartments in the palace, approximately mid-way between the Garden Stairs (upstream) and Whitehall Stairs, used by the public (downstream). The privy watergate was at the head of the stairs.

Queen's apartments. In the buildings fronting the river on the northern (downstream) side of the Privy Stairs and the Shield Gallery. The principal rooms were on the first floor with 'leads' between them and the river – a favourite place from which to view river pageants. They included a presence chamber, great bedchamber, privy chamber, withdrawing room, eating room, guard chamber and chapel. In common with the rest of the palace they were altered from time to time, 1664 seeing a new closet and 1668 a new bathroom (supplied by a pump with Thames water).

Robe Chamber. Position uncertain; probably on the first floor and either near the Council Chamber or, possibly, above the Wardrobe in the range immediately north of the Great Gate.

Shield Gallery. This ran east and west on the first floor; at its river end looking out over the Privy Stairs. The Queen's apartments lay to the north of it, the King's to the south. The name originated in the custom of hanging there the shields won in the Tilt Yard tournaments.

Stone Gallery. A long ground floor gallery, running from Pebble Court to the Bowling Green along the e. side of the Privy Garden, between the garden and the river and roughly parallel to both. The most convenient route from the entrance court to the range of apartments along the river between the Privy Stairs and the garden stairs. Above it lay the Matted Gallery.

Tennis Courts. The palace still had, in 1640, three tennis courts – the little open tennis court next to the Tilt Yard gallery, the large close (covered) tennis court on the n. side of the Cockpit passage, and the great open tennis court (the Brake) on the s. side of the same passage.

The second of these was converted in 1663-4 to form part of Monmouth's lodgings, while the third (the Brake) was converted under the Commonwealth into a garden used in connection with the apartments occupied towards the end of that period by Edward Mountagu, later Earl of Sandwich. In 1662-3 much of this garden was taken to form the new tennis court, mentioned by Pepys at iii.147, which functioned as a court until 1809. [*See also* Cooke, Capt. Thomas].

Vane Room. On the first floor at the point of intersection of the Matted Gallery (above the Stone Gallery) and the Privy Gallery; so named because the principal weather-cock of the palace stood above it. In the '60s chapters of the Order of the Garter seem to have been held there, and Pepys records the King dining there in public. It ceased to be the King's withdrawing room and was converted into a waiting room at some date between 1670 and 1687.

Wine Cellar. Part of Wolsey's original palace; under the Guard Chamber. It was not wholly destroyed by the fire of 1698 and still survives. The King's or Privy Cellar was separate. [*See also* King St]

(T. F. Reddaway; La)

Whitehall Stairs (Bridge). The public pier and landing stairs for the palace. The approach to it from Charing Cross lay through the main gate of the palace, across the first court and past the chapel. Downstream of the Privy Stairs. (R)

Whitfield, [Nathaniel] (d. 1696). Clerk in the Navy Office. He was appointed in 1663, and served in the Ticket Office c. 1667-92, becoming chief clerk 1674-82 and 1689-92. In 1679 a man of these names was clerk to Sir R. Haddock in the Admiralty.[1]

Whittington, Capt. [Luke]. Royalist agent at Dunkirk 1649-51; appointed to a post in the customs as searcher at Hull 1660.[1]

Whitton, Tom (d. 1661). Clerk and accountant to the Chatham Chest 1656-60; afterwards clerk in the Navy Office, first to Commissioner Pett, later to the Comptroller.[1]

Whitty, Capt. [John]. Commissioned to the *Vanguard* 1665.[1]

[Wiborow, Thomas]. Vicar of Impington, Cambs. 1639-c. 56 and 1662-d.69. He kept a private school there when he was extruded from the living.[1]

Widdrington. Ralph Widdrington (d. 1688) was John Pepys's tutor at Christ's College, Cambridge; Public Orator 1650-73; Regius Professor of Greek 1654-60; Lady Margaret Professor of Divinity 1673-88. John was originally entered at Magdalene; it is not known why he was transferred to Christ's, but a relative of Ralph's, Sir Edward Widdrington, was a neighbour of the diarist in Axe Yard. Ralph's elder brother, Sir Thomas (d. 1664) appears in the diary as one

of the Commissioners of the Great Seal in 1660. He was a prominent
figure in the Commonwealth (Councillor of State 1651, 1659, 1660;
Speaker 1656; Lord Chief Baron of the Exchequer 1658–60), and a
colleague of Mountagu on the Treasury commission (1654–9).[1]

Wight. William Wight ('Uncle Wight') was a half-brother of Pepys's
father, being son of Mary, widow of Thomas Pepys 'the Black' by her
second marriage to Rice Wight, merchant. He was a prosperous fishmonger (elected liveryman of the Fishmongers' Company 1669), and
engaged in general trade as a merchant. He had a country house at St
Catherine's Hill, nr Guildford, Surrey, and in town lived in the parish
of St Andrew Undershaft, in a house taxed on nine hearths.[1] At his
death in 1672 he was buried in London, in his parish church. He had had
four children, but all had died by 1664. (Hence the remarkable proposal
he then made to Elizabeth Pepys in 1664 that they should have a child.)[2]
He died intestate worth c. £4000 leaving a widow Mary (b. Sutton,
d. 1696). Pepys's father successfully claimed one-sixth of the estate.

There is difficulty in identifying some of his relatives mentioned in
the diary. The Norburys are clear enough: Sarah Norbury was a sister
of Mary Wight. 'Mr Wight' was a man of property, and lived at
Braboeuf Manor in or near William Wight's Surrey home. He was
John Wight, great-grandson of John Wight of Wimbledon who had
acquired the manor in the mid-16th century. His father (also John) had
died in 1656. He had three sisters who appear in the diary – Anne (who
married John Bentley in 1663); Margaret (often admired by Pepys)
who married John Perryen of St Giles Cripplegate in 1668; and
Mary (called cousin by Pepys).[3] Three other relatives – Robert
Wight and Aunt Wight's sister Con and her husband – have not been
identified.

Wildman, Maj. John (?1621–93). A republican and Leveller who
survived into Restoration politics. He had, in Macaulay's words, 'a
wonderful skill in grazing the edge of treason'.[1] He surfaced briefly
in 1667–9 as an ally of Buckingham, but later devoted himself once
more to his game of conspiracy, and in 1679 was an accomplice of
Scott, Pepys's accuser.[2] After Monmouth's rising of 1685 (in which he
played an ambiguous part) he fled to Holland, returning in 1688 to
achieve respectability as an M.P. (1689–90), Postmaster-General
(1689–91), alderman and knight (1692–3).[3]

[Wilford, Francis] (d. 1667). Chaplain to the King from 1660;
Master of Corpus Christi College, Cambridge from 1661; Dean of
Ely from 1662.[1]

Wilgress, Capt. [John] (d. by 1688). Served in the First Dutch War
and held five commands 1660–71. Coventry did not trust him.[1]

Wilkes, [Luke]. There were two men of these names – one a yeoman
of the King's Wardrobe, and the other a clerk or steward in the service

of Sir Joseph Williamson. The latter died c. 1674. They may have been the same person, or related.[1]

Wilkins, John (1614–72). Mathematician and divine: Warden of Wadham College, Oxford 1648–59, Master of Trinity, Cambridge 1659–60; Vicar of St Lawrence Jewry from 1662, Dean of Ripon from 1663, Bishop of Chester 1668–72. One of the most original scholars of his day; a founder of the Royal Society (one of its two secretaries 1663–8), and a liberal churchman who strongly supported toleration of Nonconformists and church union with moderate Presbyterians. During the Commonwealth his personal influence as Cromwell's brother-in-law had done much to protect Oxford from political interference. His written works, composed in language notable for its simplicity and clarity, included forecasts of submarines and inter-planetary travel. His most ambitious work was his *Essay towards . . . a philosophical language* (first pub. 1668) in which he devised a universal language in the form of symbols. Pepys had some criticisms to make of its naval section.[1] There are six of his works, besides this, in the Pepys Library.

Wilkinson, Capt. [Robert]. He had served in the Commonwealth navy. After his surrender of his ship to the Dutch in the Battle of Lowestoft he held no further command, but was commissioned lieutenant to three ships 1672–8.[1]

Wilkinson, [William]: *see* Taverns etc: Crown, King St

Wilkinson, ——. Chancery attorney; possibly related to John Wilkinson, one of the Six Clerks 1663–8 and Comptroller of the Hanaper 1668–80.[1]

Willet, Deborah. Elizabeth Pepys's companion 1667–8. Daughter of Robert Willet, of St Stephen's parish, Bristol, she was baptised there on 12 Sept. 1650. The family lived in Marsh St, a poor quarter. The father was admitted as a burgess in Apr. 1652; his occupation is not known. The register of baptisms gives the name of the father only, and it is possible that her mother died at the birth. (But the registers of St Stephen's have no record of her burial, and it was common enough for the mother's name to be omitted in this register.) Both parents had died by 1668 when Deb visited Bristol with Pepys, and the fact that her old neighbours in Marsh St welcomed her as one they had not seen for a long time suggests that she may have been brought up by her aunt in London, Mrs Hunt of Jewen St, with whom she was living before she entered the service of the Pepyses.[1]

Williams, [Abigail]. Brouncker's mistress; usually referred to by Pepys as 'Madam Williams'. She was alive at Brouncker's death in 1684 and as his 'beloved friend' was the chief beneficiary and sole executrix of his will. She was the daughter of Sir Henry Clere, Bt, and the separated wife of John Cromwell *alias* Williams, third son of Sir

Oliver Cromwell. Her husband – a cousin of the Protector – had been
a soldier in the Dutch service and had parted company with her c. 1650.
(In common with other members of the royalist branch of the Crom-
wells, he had changed his name to Williams, the original name of the
family before it was changed to Cromwell in Henry VIII's reign in
deference to Thomas Cromwell.) An actress named Abigail Williams
was performing in the King's Company in 1663.[1]

Williams, Dr John. Physician; Elizabeth Pepys was his patient. His
Christian name is given once (ii.156). That he was the Dr Williams who
advised Pepys from time to time on Graveley business and the quarrel
with the Trices is made clear by the entry at iv.350. Presumably he had
local knowledge; there are several indications in the diary that he knew
the district. [*See also* Jefferies]

Williams, ——. Courtier. Probably Vincent Williams, Groom of the
Great Chamber in ordinary to the King.[1]

Williamson, Sir Joseph, kt 1672 (1633–1701). One of the ablest of
Pepys's colleagues in the public service. Under-Secretary of State 1660–
74; Keeper of State Papers and of the Royal Library 1661–1701;
Secretary of State and Admiralty Commissioner 1674–9. He sat in all
parliaments 1669–1701 except that of 1689. As Under-Secretary, he
was particularly active in control of the press.

In some ways his career parallels that of Pepys. Virtually contemporaries, they both rose from small beginnings; both were formidable administrators who created new standards of efficiency; and both
had learned tastes and served as Presidents of the Royal Society
(Williamson in 1677–80). They were both Masters of the Clothworkers'
Company (Williamson in 1676–7), and were instrumental in founding
Mathematical Schools (Pepys's in Christ Hospital, Williamson's in
Rochester, by bequest). Williamson kept a diary, but only of public
events and only for a short period (Dec. 1667–Jan. 1669).[1]

Williamson, Capt. [Robert] (d. by 1688). A captain in the Commonwealth navy 1658; commissioned to the *Harp* frigate 1660.[1]

Willoughby, Maj. [Francis]. Commonwealth official: Navy Commissioner 1653–7; Navy and Victualling Commissioner 1657–60.[1]

Willys, Sir Richard. Of Fen Ditton, Cambs. A cavalry officer under
Rupert, he had been Governor of Newark in 1644 until dismissed by
the King. After a spell in Italy he returned to England in 1652 where he
became a member of the royalist underground organisation known as
the Sealed Knot. He seems to have played a double game. Though
twice imprisoned by the government, he established contact with
Cromwell's secret service in 1656 or 1657, possibly for money – he
was very poor – or to secure his safety in case the royalist cause failed.
In 1659–60 he was denounced to the King by Samuel Morland,
Thurloe's assistant and Pepys's old tutor, who accused him of having

betrayed Booth's rising in Aug. 1659. He also charged him with having betrayed Ormond's whereabouts in 1658, and of having attempted to inveigle the King into England in the spring of 1659 in order to have him assassinated. Willys's fellow conspirators in the Sealed Knot disbelieved the charges, but Clarendon and the King were convinced by the evidence of the handwriting in the letters which Morland sent over. At the Restoration he was forbidden the court.[1] He was brother of Sir Thomas, the first baronet, elected M.P. for Cambridge borough in 1659 and 1660.[2]

Wilmot, John, 1st Earl of Rochester (1647–80). Groom of the Bedchamber to the King from 1666. Poet, wit and libertine, he was, with his friends Buckingham and Henry Savile, one of the aristocratic rakehells who gave Restoration courtiers their reputation for sexual immorality, duelling, and drunken pranks. His father was a royalist cavalry officer and he himself served with splendid courage as a gentleman-volunteer in the fleet – in 1665 under Sandwich at Bergen and in 1666 under Spragge. In 1667 he married Elizabeth Malet, the heiress whom he had tried to abduct two years before. He died at the age of 32 worn out by venereal disease (and its treatment) – in the words of his funeral oration, a martyr to sin.[1] At the end of his life he had turned to religion under the ministrations of Gilbert Burnet, who published an account of his repentance.

He wrote some of the coarsest and wittiest obscene verses in the language, as well as some of the most complex and delicately beautiful lyrics. The obscene verses attributed to him circulated in manuscript. Pepys had a collection and kept it in a drawer of his desk,[2] later having it bound up with a copy of Burnet's *Life*, so that only Burnet's title appears on the spine.[3]

Wilson, Tom. Naval official. He served under the Commonwealth; was clerk for victualling accounts 1660; briefly Clerk of the Cheque at Chatham 1661; clerk to Batten 1663; Surveyor of Victualling at London 1665–7; and Storekeeper at Chatham 1667–d. 76. His wife was Jane, daughter of Richard Beckford of London.[1]

Winchilsea, 2nd Earl of: see Finch, Sir H.

Wine, [Arthur]. Purveyor of sea fish to the King c. 1660–8. He lived on the e. side of Fish St Hill in a house taxed on seven hearths.[1] The surname is sometimes spelt Wind.

Wingate, [Edward]. Of Lockleys, Herts.; elected M.P. for St Albans Nov. 1640; active as a magistrate into the 1670s.[1]

Winter, Sir John (1600–c. 86). Grandson of the Elizabethan admiral Sir William Winter, and cousin of the 2nd Marquess of Worcester. Secretary to the Queen Mother 1638–42, 1660–9. He and his father were the principal developers of iron and timber in the Forest of Dean. He bought 18,000 acres in 1640, but was deprived of it as a papist in

1642. In 1662 he was granted an eleven-year lease, but by 1668 the contract had lapsed through his failure to deliver the agreed quantities of shiptimber. He had an interest in all sorts of technology. Pepys liked his 'good discourse' (though not his timber). But his Catholicism, combined with his expert knowledge of gunpowder, made him an object of mistrust.[1]

Wintershall (Wintersell), [William] (d. 1679). Actor at the Red Bull Theatre, Clerkenwell; later an original member of the King's Company. He played both comic and tragic rôles.[1]

Wise, [Lucy]. 'Mother' of the Maids of Honour to the Duchess of York; wife of Richard Wise.[1]

Wiseman, Sir Robert, kt 1661. Civil lawyer; Fellow of Trinity Hall, Cambridge 1631–53; appointed 'advocate for marine causes' 1660; Dean of the Arches and Vicar-General 1672–d. 84.[1]

Witherley, [Thomas] (d. 1694). Physician; M.D. (Cantab.) 1655; F.R.C.P. 1677; President R.C.P. 1684–8. Physician in ordinary to the King 1677. A friend of Sir Thomas Browne.[1]

Withers. Probably – since Pepys met him in Batten's company – the shipwright Robert Withers, who in 1665 was recommended by Jonas Shish to conduct a survey of a new ship. Possibly the man of the same names who was a shipbuilder in Bolton-le-Sands, Lancs.[1]

Wivell, [Edward]. Victualling agent, Dover.[1]

Wolfe, [William]. Fishmonger: freeman of the Company 1643. He lived on Fish St Hill in a house rated on four hearths (before the Fire). His will was proved in 1666.[1]

Wolstenholme, Sir John, kt 1639. Merchant, of Fenchurch St; son of the great Jacobean merchant Sir John; appointed Customs Commissioner 1660, reappointed 1667.[1]

Wood, Sir Henry, kt 1644, bt 1660 (1597–1671). Son and grandson of courtiers; himself in court office since 1623. Clerk-Comptroller of the Board of Green Cloth from 1644 (Clerk from 1662); Treasurer to Henrietta-Maria from 1644; member of Catherine of Braganza's council from 1662; M.P. for Hythe from 1661. An eccentric and unpopular official. His (second) wife (m. 1651) was Mary, daughter of Sir John Gardiner; Maid of Honour to Henrietta-Maria, dresser and woman of the bedchamber to Queen Catherine.[1]

[Wood, Thomas]. Appointed Dean of Lichfield in 1664 and Bishop of the see in 1671. It was said that he obtained the bishopric by marrying off his niece to a son of Lady Castlemaine. As Dean, he was excommunicated by his bishop in 1667, and as Bishop he was suspended by his archbishop for non-residence and scandalous living in 1685. He then retired to Astrop Wells in 1690 and died in 1692, aged 85.[1]

Wood, Capt. [Walter]. Served in the Commonwealth navy and held three commands between 1660 and his death in action in 1666.[1]

Wood, [William]. Timber merchant and mastmaker, Wapping. He worked in close association with Batten (and was a witness to his will) as well as in frequent partnership with Castle, Batten's son-in-law. Pepys profoundly distrusted them all, and in a letter of 1665 complained that Castle had cornered all the masts in the river.[1] When he made his will in 1676 he had a timber yard at Rotherhithe as well as at Wapping. He lived close by the Wapping yard.[2] His son William inherited both the house and the yards.[3] Pepys occasionally refers to him in error as an alderman,[4] possibly through confusion with Ald. Edward Wood.

Woodall, Thomas. Surgeon to the Household 1660; Surgeon-in-ordinary to the King 1663.[1]

Woodcock, [Thomas] (d. 1695). Presbyterian clergyman, and Senior Proctor at Cambridge 1651–2, in Pepys's time. He was a Fellow of Jesus College 1645–62, Rector of Graveley, Cambs. 1654–5 and of St Andrew Undershaft, London, from 1660 until his extrusion for non-conformity in 1662. At the time he went over to The Hague to the King in May 1660 he was a commissioner for the approbation of ministers.[1]

Woodeson, ——. Clerk to William Trumbull of the Signet Office, 1660. Possibly George Woodeson, Deputy-Clerk of the Signet c. 1682–1716.[1]

Woodfine, ——. Possibly Thomas Woodfine, who in Sept. 1660 was made sailing master of the *Plymouth* frigate.[1]

Woodroffe, [Edmund]. Chief clerk to Downing as Teller in the Exchequer; dismissed on Downing's death 1684 and made a tax agent. He married Margaret, daughter of Commissioner Pett.[1]

Woolley, [John]. Underkeeper, by 1669 Keeper, of Privy Council records.[1]

Woolley, [Robert] (1638–96). Broker, of Mincing Lane. A Tory Common Councilman in 1682. His wife (m. 1664) was Katherine, daughter of George and Sarah Norbury of Islington, and niece of William Wight. He is described in a legal document of 1679 as 'of Bishop's Stortford, gent'.[1]

Woolwich. Oldest of the Thames yards and especially valuable because of its deep water. Some of the greatest warships were built there – the *Harry Grace à Dieu* under Henry VIII and the *Sovereign of the Seas* under Charles I, both the largest British ships afloat in their time. In 1664 it employed 302 workmen, a larger number than any other yard except Chatham. In 1676 it was made administratively independent of Deptford.[1]

Worcester House. A mansion (taxed on 64 hearths, 1665) on the s. side of the Strand, west of the Savoy. Originally the town house of the Bishops of Carlisle, it now belonged to the Marquess of Worcester, who on 9 June 1660 offered it to Clarendon rent-free during the

Marquess's life. Clarendon later wrote that he paid £500 p.a. for it. It was here that his daughter Anne Hyde married the Duke of York on 3 Sept. 1660. Known after 1682 as Beaufort House; burnt down in 1695. Savoy Court now marks the site.[1]

Wotton, [William]. Shoemaker, on the n. side of Fleet St close to Fetter Lane. In 1666 he had two apprentices and paid tax on eight hearths. He was a liveryman of the Cordwainers' Company and a man of some breeding, to judge by the frequency with which he gave Pepys news of theatrical events.[1] The 'Wooton' who was Pepys's manservant in 1699 may have been a relative.[2]

Wren, Sir Christopher, kt 1673 (1632–1723). The architect; Professor of Astronomy at Gresham College 1657–61; Savilian Professor of Astronomy at Oxford 1661–73; Surveyor of the King's Works 1669–1718; President of the Royal Society 1680–2. Pepys collected for his library a number of engravings of Wren's buildings.[1]

Wren, Matthew (1629–72). Son of Matthew Wren, Bishop of Ely, and cousin of Sir Christopher. Secretary to Clarendon 1660–7, and to the Duke of York as Admiral 1667–72. M.P. for Mitchell, Cornwall 1661–72. To Pepys he was a poor exchange for Coventry. But he was a man of ability – he published two political tracts, and was a founder F.R.S. The diary indicates a close association with George Cocke, the Baltic merchant. Besides being both Fellows of the Royal Society, they were also both members of the Fishery Committee and of the Eastland Company. Cocke's son Matthew was named after him and in his will Wren left a cabinet to Cocke's wife, £300 to his godson and gifts to Cocke's servants.[1]

Wren, ——. Naval officer. Not identified with certainty: there was a James Wren who was a naval lieutenant in 1667, a Ralph Wren who was a captain in 1672, a John Wren who was a purser in 1669, and a 'tarpaulin' Capt. Wren who in 1683 earned Pepys's disapproval by doing as much private trading as any gentleman-captain.[1]

Wright, Sir Henry, cr. bt 1658, 1660 (c. 1637–64). Of Dagenhams, Essex; son of Dr Laurence Wright, one of Cromwell's physicians; Sandwich's brother-in-law, having in 1658 married Anne Crew, sister of Sandwich's wife. A Commissioner of Trade 1656–7, and in 1660 and 1661 elected M.P. for the admiralty borough of Harwich, but an inactive member, through ill health. His wife, a Presbyterian like him, was, to judge by Pepys's comments and by her letters, a lively character.[1] Their daughter, mentioned in the diary, was Anne, who inherited Dagenhams on her mother's death in 1708. The cousin mentioned by Pepys may have been Anne Wright, a beneficiary under Sir Henry's will.[2]

Wright, Dr ——. Physician; a friend of Charles Anderson. Probably Anderson's contemporary at Cambridge, Laurence Wright, who was admitted to Trinity College in 1652 and was a Fellow in 1660. He took his M.D. in 1666.[1]

Wriothesley, Thomas, 4th Earl of Southampton (1607–67). Lord Treasurer 1660–7. Son of Shakespeare's patron, and a friend of Clarendon, and like Clarendon, a man of the old régime who was soon out of favour with the young Cavaliers of the court. An incorrupt but ineffective administrator, he left most of the work to his assistants, Warwick and Ashley. The modern Southampton Row commemorates the building development he carried out in Bloomsbury in the '60s.[1]

Wyld, Elizabeth. A niece of the Honywood brothers. Roger Pepys thought of marrying her in 1667, despite her ugly looks. She was still unmarried in 1681, when Dean Honywood made his will.[1]

Wyndham. Col. Wyndham was Edmund (d. 1683), a member of a leading royalist family in Somerset. He had been Governor of Bridgwater during the Civil War, and after exile during the Commonwealth was made a Groom of the Bedchamber in 1660. He served as M.P. for Bridgwater in the Short, Long and Cavalier Parliaments. His wife Christabella (b. Pyne, d. c. 1662), a strikingly beautiful woman, had been Charles II's nurse, and retained a strong influence over him for several years – so strong that she almost succeeded in having her husband made Secretary of State.[1]

Mr Wyndham, killed in the attack on Bergen in 1665, was John, a younger son of Edmund.[2]

Wynn(e), [Rowland]. E. India merchant; elected committee of the Company 1665 etc.[1]

Yeabsley, [Thomas]. Victualler, of Plymouth: with his partners Allsop and Lanyon he supplied Tangier. James Yonge, the naval surgeon, also of Plymouth, refers to him in his journal as 'my intimate and ingenious friend'.[1]

Yelverton, Sir Henry, 2nd Bt (1633–70). A contemporary of Pepys at St Paul's; elected M.P. for Northamptonshire 1660 (with Manchester's support), and for Northampton borough 1664. Author of two works in defence of episcopacy. 'A very pretty little gentleman' (Dorothy Osborne).[1]

Yorke, ——. Huntingdon carrier; alive in 1674.[1]

York House. A mansion on the s. side of the Strand east of the modern Charing Cross Station, with grounds running down to the river. Granted to the archbishops of York by Mary Tudor in exchange for Suffolk House, Southwark, and later leased to a succession of Lord Keepers of the Great Seal. Obtained from James I by George Villiers, 1st Duke of Buckingham and sold by his son in 1672 to a syndicate which pulled it down and built streets on the site of the house and grounds. They were named Villiers St, Duke St, Of St and Buckingham St. Only the watergate remains of the original house. Pepys and Hewer lived in York Buildings from 1679. View by Hollar in PL 2972/237b.[1]

Young, [John]. Actor; in the Duke's Company from 1662; he played secondary rôles.[1]

Young, [John]. Of Cornhill; appointed flagmaker to the Navy (with Henry Whistler) in July 1660; overseer of Batten's will.[1]

Young,[John, sen.] (d. 1667). Yeoman tailor in the King's Wardrobe.[1]

EDITORIAL ABBREVIATIONS

[The place of publication is London unless otherwise stated.]

Aubrey: John Aubrey, *Brief Lives* (ed. A. Clark), 2 vols, Oxford 1898

Aylmer: Gerald E. Aylmer, *The state's servants: the civil service of the English republic, 1640–60*, 1973

Baxter: Stephen B. Baxter, *The development of the Treasury, 1660–1702*, 1957

Beaven: Alfred B. Beaven, *The aldermen of . . . London*, 2 vols, 1908–13

BL: British Library, Reference Division

Bodl.: Bodleian Library, Oxford

Boyd: Percival Boyd, 'Citizens of London': lists in Lib. Soc. Genealogists, London

Boyne: William Boyne, *Trade tokens issued in the seventeenth century* (ed. and rev. G. C. Williamson), 2 vols, 1889–91

Braybrooke (1825): *Memoirs of Samuel Pepys . . .* (ed. Richard, Lord Braybrooke), 2 vols [The various editions are indicated by date.]

Bryant, i, ii, iii: Sir Arthur Bryant, *Samuel Pepys*, Cambridge 1933–
    i *The man in the making*, 1948 ed.
    ii *The years of peril*, 1947 ed.
    iii *The saviour of the navy*, 1949 ed.

Bull. IHR: *Bulletin of the Institute of Historical Research*, London

Burnet: Gilbert Burnet, *History of my own time* (ed. O. Airy), 2 vols, Oxford 1890

Calamy Rev.: Arnold G. Matthews, *Calamy Revised*, Oxford 1934

Carte: Carte MSS, Bodleian Library

Cat.: James R. Tanner, *A descriptive catalogue of the naval manuscripts in the Pepysian Library at Magdalene College, Cambridge*, 4 vols, NRS, 1903–23

Chappell: Edwin Chappell, *Eight generations of the Pepys family, 1500–1800*, 1936

Chester-Foster: Joseph L. Chester, *London marriage licences, 1521–1869*, (ed. J. Foster), 1887

CJ: Journals of the House of Commons

Clarendon, *Hist.*: Edward, Earl of Clarendon, *The history of the rebellion* (ed. W. Dunn Macray), 6 vols, Oxford 1888

Clarendon, *Life*: *The life of Edward Earl of Clarendon . . . in which is included a continuation of his History of the Great Rebellion*, 3 vols, Oxford 1827

Clowes: Sir William L. Clowes, *The Royal Navy*, 7 vols, 1897–1903

Collinge: John M. Collinge, *Navy Board Officials, 1660–1832* [*Office-Holders in Modern Britain*, vol. vii], 1978

Colvin: Howard M. Colvin (ed.), *History of the King's Works*, 1963–

CSPClar.: *Calendar of the Clarendon State Papers . . .* (ed. O. Ogle et al.), 5 vols, Oxford 1869–1970

CSPD: *Calendar of State Papers, Domestic Series*

CSPVen.: *Calendar of State Papers . . . relating to English affairs . . . in the archives . . . of Venice*

CTB: *Calendar of Treasury Books . . . preserved in the Public Record Office*

D: the present edition

Dalton: Charles Dalton, *English army lists and commission registers, 1661–1714*, 6 vols, 1892–1904

DNB: *Dictionary of National Biography*

Duke of York, *Mem.* (*naval*): James, Duke of York, *Memoirs of the English affairs, chiefly naval, from . . . 1660 to 1673 . . .*, 1729

EHR: *English Historical Review*

Ehrman: John P. W. Ehrman, *The navy in the war of William III*, Cambridge 1958

Evelyn: *The diary of John Evelyn* (ed. E. S. de Beer), 6 vols, Oxford 1955

Family Letters: Helen T. Heath (ed.), *The letters of Samuel Pepys and his family circle*, Oxford 1955

Firth and Davies: Charles H. Firth and Godfrey Davies, *The regimental history of Cromwell's army*, 2 vols, Oxford 1936

Firth and Rait: Charles H. Firth and Robert S. Rait (eds), *Acts and ordinances of the Interregnum*, 3 vols, 1911

Foster: Joseph Foster, *Alumni Oxonienses . . . , 1500–1714*, 4 vols, Oxford 1891–2

Further Corr.: *Further Correspondence of Samuel Pepys, 1662–1679* (ed. J. R. Tanner), 1929

GEC: G. E. Cockayne, *The complete peerage . . .* (ed. V. Gibbs et al.), 13 vols, 1910–40

GL: Guildhall Library, London

GLRO: Greater London Council Record Office

Gramont: Anthony Hamilton, *Memoirs of the Comte de Gramont* (trans. P. Quennell, ed. C. H. Hartmann), 1930

Gray's Inn Reg.: Joseph Foster, *The registers of admission to Gray's Inn, 1521–1889*, 1889

Grove (6th ed.): *The new Grove dictionary of music and musicians* (ed. S. Sadie), 20 vols, 1980

Harl. Soc. Reg.: *Publications of the Harleian Society, Registers*
Harl. Sóc. Vis.: *Publications of the Harleian Society, Visitations*
Harris: Frank R. Harris, *The life of Edward Mountagu, K.G., first Earl of Sandwich*, 2 vols, 1912
Hatton: Edward Hatton, *A new view of London*, 2 vols, 1708
Highfill: Philip H. Highfill, Jr, K. A. Burnim and E. A. Langham, *A biographical dictionary of actors and actresses . . . in London, 1660–1800*, Carbondale and Edwardsville, Ill. 1973–
HMC: Historical Manuscripts Commission. [References where possible cite the name of the owner of the collection. Elsewhere they cite the number of the report, of the volume (and part, if necessary) and of the page in the following form: HMC, *Rep.*, 12/7/1/25.]
Howe: Ellic Howe, *A list of London bookbinders, 1648–1815*, Bibliog. Soc., Oxford 1950
HP: 'The History of Parliament: the House of Commons, 1660–90' (ed. Basil D. Henning); typescript of the forthcoming vol. in the History of Parliament series; in the possession of the History of Parliament Trust, London
La: Robert Latham (as co-author)
Lafontaine: Henry C. de Lafontaine, *The King's Musick . . ., 1460–1700*, 1909
LCC, *Survey*: *The Survey of London* (issued by the London County Council, afterwards the Greater London Council, in association with the Committee for the Survey of the Memorials of Greater London, afterwards the London Survey Committee), 1900–
Letters: Robert G. Howarth (ed.), *Letters and the second diary of Samuel Pepys*, 1933
Lillywhite: Bryant Lillywhite, *London Signs*, 1972
LJ: *Journals of the House of Lords*
LRO: Records Office of the Corporation of the city of London
Lu: article by Richard Luckett
McAfee: Helen McAfee, *Pepys on the Restoration stage*, New Haven, Conn. 1916
Marvell: Herschel M. Margoliouth (ed.), *The poems and letters of Andrew Marvell*, 2 vols, Oxford 1952
Middle Temple Reg.: Herbert A. C. Sturgess, *Register of admissions to . . . the Middle Temple from the fifteenth century to . . . 1944*, 3 vols, 1949
MM: *Mariner's Mirror*
Munk: William R. Munk, *The roll of the Royal College of Physicians of London*, 3 vols, 1878
N. & Q.: *Notes and Queries*
Naval Minutes: *Samuel Pepys's Naval Minutes* (ed. J. R. Tanner), NRS, 1926

NMM: National Maritime Museum, Greenwich

North (ed. Jessop): Roger North, *The lives of the Norths* (ed. A. Jessop), 3 vols, 1890

NRS: Navy Records Society

NWB: Pepys's MS. 'Navy White Book', PL 2581

Occ. Papers: *Occasional Papers read by members at meetings of the Samuel Pepys Club* [1903–23], 2 vols, 1917–25

OED: *Oxford English Dictionary*

Oppenheim: Martin Oppenheim, *A history of the administration of the Royal Navy . . ., 1509–1660*, 1896

Pepys, *Mem.*: Samuel Pepys, *Memoires relating to the state of the Royal Navy . . . 1679–88*, 1690 (ed. J. R. Tanner, Oxford 1906)

Pepysiana: Henry B. Wheatley, *Pepysiana: The diary of Samuel Pepys* (ed. Wheatley), vol. x, 1899

PL: Pepys Library, Magdalene College, Cambridge

Plomer: Henry R. Plomer, *A dictionary of printers and booksellers in England, Scotland and Ireland*, vol. i, *1640–67*; vol. ii (ed. A. Esdaile), *1668–1725*, Bibliog. Soc., Oxford 1907–22

Priv. Corr.: *Private correspondence and miscellaneous papers of Samuel Pepys, 1679–1703* . . . (ed. J. R. Tanner), 2 vols, 1926

PRO: Public Record Office, London

Pulver: Jeffrey Pulver, *A biographical dictionary of old English music*, 1927

R: article by or reference from the late Prof. Thomas F. Reddaway

Rawl.: Rawlinson MSS, Bodleian Library

Rimbault: Edward F. Rimbault (ed.), *The old cheque book or book of remembrance of the Chapel Royal, 1561–1744*, Camden Soc., 1872

Routh: Enid M. G. Routh, *Tangier: England's lost Atlantic outpost, 1661–84*, 1912

Sainsbury: Ethel B. Sainsbury (ed.), *A calendar of the court minutes . . . of the East India Company* [1635–79], 11 vols, Oxford 1927–38

Sainty: John C. Sainty, *Admiralty Officials, 1660–1870* [*Office-Holders in Modern Britain*, vol. iv], 1975

Sainty, *Sec. of State*: id., *Officials of the Secretaries of State 1660–1782* [*Office-Holders in Modern Britain*, vol. ii], 1973

Sandwich: *The journal of Edward Mountagu, first Earl of Sandwich . . . 1659–1665* (ed. R. C. Anderson), NRS 1929

Sherwood: Roy Sherwood, *The court of Oliver Cromwell*, 1977

Shorthand Letters: *Shorthand Letters of Samuel Pepys* (ed. E. Chappell), Cambridge 1933

Smyth: *The obituary of Richard Smyth, 1627–74* (ed. Sir Henry Ellis), Camden Soc., 1849

Steele: Robert R. Steele, *Bibliotheca Lindesiana. A bibliography of proclamations of the Tudor and Stuart sovereigns . . .*, 2 vols, Oxford 1910

Strype: John Stow, *The survey of London* (ed. John Strype), 2 vols, 1720
Tangier Papers: *The Tangier Papers of Samuel Pepys* (ed. E. Chappell), NRS, 1935
Tanner: James R. Tanner, *Mr Pepys*, 1925
Taylor: Eva G. R. Taylor, *The mathematical practitioners of Tudor and Stuart England*, Cambridge 1954
TLS: *Times Literary Supplement*
Tomlinson: Howard C. Tomlinson, *Guns and government: the Ordnance Office under the later Stuarts*, 1979
TRHS: *Transactions of the Royal Historical Society*
Van Lennep: *The London Stage 1660–1800*, pt i, *1600–1700* (ed. William Van Lennep), Carbondale, Ill. 1965
VCH: *The Victoria History of the Counties of England*
Venn: John Venn and John A. Venn, *Alumni Cantabrigienses*, pt i (*From the earliest times to 1751*), 4 vols, Cambridge 1922–7
Walker Rev.: Arnold G. Matthews, *Walker Revised*, Oxford 1948
Wheatley: *The diary of Samuel Pepys* . . . (ed. H. B. Wheatley), 10 vols, 1893–9
Wheatley and Cunningham: Henry B. Wheatley, *London Past and Present: based upon The Handbook of London by Peter Cunningham*, 3 vols, 1891
Whitear: Walter H. Whitear, *More Pepysiana* . . ., 1927
Wilson: John H. Wilson, *All the King's ladies*, Chicago 1958
Wood, *Ath. Oxon.*: Anthony à Wood, *Athenae Oxonienses* (ed. P. Bliss), 4 vols, 1813–20
Wood, *L. & T.*: *The life and times of Anthony Wood* . . . (ed. A. Clark), 5 vols, Oxf. Hist. Soc., 1891–1900
Woodhead: John R. Woodhead, *The rulers of London, 1660–89*, London and Middlesex Arch. Soc., 1966
WRO: Westminster City Records Office

NOTES

Ableson 1 Clowes, ii. 210; *Cat.*, i; Sandwich, pp. 174, 229
Abrahall 1 *CSPD*, e.g. *1664–5*, p. 136; Woodhead
Acworth 1 *Journ. R. Artillery*, 85/2+; *CSPD*, e.g. *1650*, p. 410 etc.; PRO, Adm 2/1725, f. 5; *N. & Q.*, March 1954, p. 132; Collinge
Adams 1 *Harl. Soc. Reg.*, 64/3
Addis 1 *CSPD 1660–1*, p. 199; Boyd 13153. cf. James Yonge, *Journal* (ed. Poynter, 1963), p. 139
Admiralty 1 N. A. M. Rodger, *The Admiralty* (1979), p. 23
2 ix. 151
3 PL 2879, pp. 222–3
4 PL 2866, p. 76
5 *First report of commissioners for revising and digesting the civil affairs of the Navy* (1806), i. 5
6 Further reading: G. F. James and J. J. Sutherland Shaw in *Bull. IHR*, 14/10+, 166+; 17/13+; Rodger, op. cit.
7 BL, Add. MSS 9303, f. 187r (R); PRO, LR 1/307, ff. 33–42 (R); *Bull. IHR*, 14/181–2
Adm. Court 1 Strype, iv. 28
African Ho. 1 PRO, E 179/147/617, p. 154; ib., 179/252/21 (R); K. G. Davies, *R. African Co.* (1957), p. 164
Agar 1 PRO, E 403/1760, f. 46v; BL, Add. MSS 33590, f. 172v; D. Masson, *Milton* (Camb. 1859–94), ii. 100–1; vi. 763, 770–4; Bodl., Clar dep. c 408, p. 11
Albrici 1 T. D. Culley, *Jesuits and music* (Rome 1970), i. 216–18;

PRO, SP 44/23, p. 29; ib., 29/66, nos 30, 66; Lafontaine, p. 203
Alcock, H. 1 Chappell, pp. 42, 103n.; PRO, E 179/249/1, Brampton
Alcock, S. 1 *CSPD 1660–1*, p. 297; Boyd 9013
Alcock, T. 1 *Further Corr.*, p. 277; Bryant, iii. 191
Aldersgate St 1 James Howell, *Londinopolis* (1657), p. 342
2 Strype, iii. 121; K. H. D. Haley, *Shaftesbury* (Oxf. 1968), p. 411; R. Seymour, *Survey of London* (1736), p. 771
Aldgate 1 Wheatley and Cunningham
Aldrige 1 'Additional Sheet' appended to copy in Bodl., Harding Coll. ~ W. G. Hiscock, *Henry Aldrich* (Oxf. 1960)
Aldworth 1 Baxter, p. 139; BL, Add. MSS 5657, f. 157
Aleyn 1 M. A. Wren and P. Hackett, *James Allen* (1968), esp. pp. 19–20
Alington 1 GEC; HP
Allen, E. 1 *CSPD*, e.g. *1659–60*, p. 450 etc.; PL 2873, p. 486
Allen, J. 1 PRO, Adm 2/1732, f. 28r
Allen, T. 1 iv. 362, n. 1; Venn; Munk
Allestry 1 Plomer, i; *Bull. IHR*, 19/20
Allin 1 *DNB; Cat.*, i. 12, 41; iv. 527, 543, 544; Collinge; PRO, PCC Cann 117
2 ed. Anderson (2 vols, NRS, 1939–40). There is an engraved portrait in PL 2979/232.
Alsop, J. 1 *Walker Rev.*
Alsop, T. 1 PRO, E 101/441, nos 3, 4; *CSPD 1665–6*, p. 371

Anderson 1 Venn; Magd. Coll., Reg., ii, f. 3a; *CSPD 1664–5*, p. 165

Andrews, J. (i) 1 *Letters*, p. 13

Andrews, J. (ii) 1 *CSPD*, e.g. *1664–5*, p. 370

Andrews, M. 1 PRO, PCC King 158

Andrews, T. 1 PRO, E 351/357; Boyd 16251; PRO, E 179/252/32(18), f. 27*v*; *Harl. Soc. Reg.*, 46/68

Angel 1 Highfill

Angier 1 Whitear, pp. 9–11; *CSP Ireland Adv.*, p. 354; Sainsbury, *1650–4*, pp. 116, 117; *1664–7*, pp. 121–2

2 Boyd 43541; E. A. B. Barnard, *A 17th-cent. country gent.* (Camb. 1948), pp. 14, 15; *Diary S. Newton* (ed. Foster, Camb. Antiq Soc.,. 1890), p. 17; PRO, Adm 20/4, p. 291; PRO, Works, 5/12; *Priv. Corr.*, ii. 44

Annesley 1 W. E. Knowles Middleton (ed.), *Lorenzo Magalotti* (Waterloo, Ont. 1980), p. 57

2 Venn; Magd. Coll., Reg., iii. 400

3 *DNB;* Sainty; PRO, SP 29/40, no. 75; Adm 2/1745, f. 163; Adm 49/54, f. 106; Rawl. A 478, ff. 77, 78; Burnet, i. 174

Ansley 1 *Cat.*, i; *CSPD Add. 1660–85*, pp. 231, 267, 268, 270

Appleyard 1 Hunts. Rec. Off., Wills, Brampton Peculiar

Apsley 1 HP; PRO, Adm 2/1745, f. 30

Apsley, Col. 1 *CSPD 1661–2*, p. 215

Archer 1 Venn, s.n. Sankey, C; Boyd 24724

Armiger 1 Whitear, pp. 12–13; Rawl. A 182, f. 302

Armourer 1 PRO, SP 29/26/78; LS 13/31 (1662), p. 37; Evelyn, iii. 487, n. 3, 488, n. 4

Art & Archit. 1 The drawings by Sutton Nicholls which form frontispieces to the two volumes of the MS. catalogue of his library show the portraits which hung over the book-presses in his study.

2 There is a list of the pictures he owned at his death in Harvard, Houghton Lib., b MS Eng 991.

3 Illust. vol. iv, facing p. 18

4 Further reading: M. Whinney and O. Millar, *Engl. Art 1625–1714* (Oxf. 1957)

Arthur 1 *Surrey hearth-tax returns 1664* (ed. C. A. F. Meekings, Surrey Rec. Soc., 1942), p. 3

Arundel Ho. 1 Views in PL 2972/94 a, b

Ascue 1 *DNB*; *Cat.*, i. 313, 320; Clowes, ii. 121, 157, 166, 274

Ashburnham 1 *DNB*

Ashfield 1 PRO, E 179/249/1; parish reg.

Atkins 1 *CSPD Add. 1660–70*, p. 292; Boyd 16310

Atkinson 1 Sir A. Heal, *London Goldsmiths 1200–1800* (Camb. 1935), p. 97; Boyd 93231

Axe Yd 1 WRO, E 172; E 176; *CSPD 1659–60*, p. 365; Strype, vi. 63

Axe Yd (P's ho.) 1 ii. 162; cf. vol. i, p. xxiii

2 WRO, E 172; E 176; E 1608 p. 32; E 1609

Baber 1 Munk; N. Carlisle, *Gent. of Privy Chamber* (1829), p. 193; G. F. Nuttall and O. Chadwick (eds), *From uniformity to unity 1662–1962* (1962), pp. 198 +; John Miller, *James II* (Hove 1978), pp. 77, 197; *Further Corr.*, pp. 340–1

Backwell 1 vii. 215 & n. 2

2 iv. 214 & n. 3; ix. 517 & n. 1

3 *DNB;* HP; Woodhead; *Ec. Hist. Rev.* (ser. 1), 9/48–9. Engraved portrait in PL 2979/121

Bacon 1 *Cat.*, i

Badiley 1 *CSPD 1654*, p. 504; PRO, Adm 2/1732, f. 8*v*

Bagwell 1 vii. 176; viii. 39 & n. 1; PRO, Adm 20/6/167, no. 961

2 Rawl. A 195a, f. 43

3 B. Pool, *Navy Board contracts 1660–1832* (1966), pp. 14–16; Bryant, ii. 372; iii. 166–7, 388

4 ib., loc. cit.; PRO, Adm 20/5, no. 137; NMM, LBK/8, p. 105

Baines 1 Sir M. McDonnell, *Registers St Paul's School 1509–1748* (1957); Venn; Firth and Rait, e.g. ii. 1082, 1116

Baker 1 ib., ii. 1294, 1349

Ball, J. 1 CTB, ii. 429; *CSPD 1667–8*, p. 566; PRO, E 403/1760, f. 25*v*

Ball, P. 1 Foster; *Priv. Corr.*, i. 332–3

Ball, R. 1 Venn; *Walker Rev.*

Ball, Capt. 1 *Cat.*, i; Longleat, Coventry MSS 99, f. 91*r*

Ballow 1 iv. 265, n. 1; Boyd 47603; PRO, PCC Bunce 54

Banes 1 *CSPClar.*, iv. 370

Banister, J. 1 Pulver, pp. 28–36; PRO, SP 29/195, no. 62; *London Gazette*, no. 742

Banister, —— 1 *Harl. Soc. Reg.*, 46/72

Banks 1 Evelyn, iv. 96 ~ see D. C. Coleman, *Sir J. Banks* (Oxf. 1963); HP

  2 Coleman, op. cit., pp. 43, 67–8; *D*, ix. 495–6 & n.; *Further Corr.*, p. 306 etc. Pepys possessed a portrait of Caleb: Harvard, Houghton Lib., b MS Eng 991

  3 *Further Corr.*, pp. 305–8

  4 *CJ*, ix. 306; Bryant, ii. 253, 277

  5 ib., ii. 174

Barber 1 *CSPD 1655*, pp. 498, 569

B-S Hall 1 Wheatley and Cunningham

Barbon 1 *DNB*

Barbour 1 PRO, Adm 20/1, no. 598; *Letters*, p. 27; Collinge

Barckmann 1 L. Bittner und L. Gross, *Repertorium des diplomatischen Vertreter*, vol. i (Berlin 1936); inf. from Prof. R. Hatton

Barcroft 1 G. E. Aylmer, *King's*

Servants (1961), p. 23; PRO, LC 3/73, pp. 75, 203

Barker 1 Beaven; *Further Corr.*, p. 19; R. W. K. Hinton, *Eastland Trade* (Camb. 1959) p. 220

Barlow 1 *CSPD 1636–7*, p. 428; *1637–8*, p. 195; BL, Add. MSS 9307, ff. 14–15; R. Vaughan, *Protectorate of O. Cromwell* (1839), ii. 360

  2 Bodl., MS Lyell empt. 32, f. 84

Barnardiston, S. 1 *DNB*; HP

Barnardiston, —— 1 viii. 466, n. 2; Chappell, pp. 53, 65; Whitear, pp. 15, 146

Barnard's Inn Gate 1 Wheatley and Cunningham

Barn Elms 1 Meekings (*see* Arthur, n. 1), p. xcii

Barnes 1 Chappell, pp. 44, 60; Whitear, p. 13

Barnwell 1 Carte 73, f. 60

Baron, B. 1 *CSPD 1665–6*, p. 122; *1670*, p. 659

Baron, H. 1 D. Underdown, *Royalist Conspiracy* (New Haven 1960), p. 210 etc.; *CSPD 1660–1*, p. 522; *1668–9*, p. 208; *CTB*, esp. i. 66, 380; *Cat.*, ii; iv

Barr 1 *CSPD*, e.g. *1666–7*, pp. 357–8, 380–1; Lady A. Archer Houblon, *Houblon Family* (1907), i. 205; N. Yorks. Rec. Off., Cholmley – Strickland MSS

Barrow 1 PRO, Adm 2/1732, f. 143*v*; *CSPD 1665–6*, p. 308; *Further Corr.*, pp. 14–15

Barton 1 Essex Rec. Off., D/DBy/Z 11, no. 1

  2 *Family Letters*, pp. 12, 42, 45; Whitear, pp. 13–14; *Trans. Cambs and Hunts. Antiq. Soc.*, 5/316; Hunts Rec. Off., dd M 43a/9; Carte 73, f. 170

Barwell 1 PRO, LC 5/40, p. 4 etc.

  2 PRO, E 179/252/32, St Dunstan-in-the-West (R)

Bassett 1 v. 176, n. 3; John Davis,

Hist. Queen's Royal Reg. (1887–1906), i. 71; Routh, pp. 320, 326; *CTB*, iii. 108, 192

Bassum 1 GL, MS. 1638; burials 3 Sept. 1643

Batelier 1 cf. vii. 110
2 Boyd 6565, 13357; GL, MS. 872; PRO, E 179/252/32, f. 27*v*; *CTB*, i. 193; ii. 107; Mercers' Co., Gresham Comm. Accts, passim; *Harl. Soc. Reg.*, 46/69

Bateman 1 Woodhead

Batten 1 NWB, p. 10
2 ib., pp. 184–6
3 Essex Rec. Off., D/ABR 9/87, 88; *Essex par. reg.* (ed. T. M. Blagg, 1914), iv. 7
4 PRO, PCC Carr 144 ~ *DNB*; HP

Batters 1 PRO, Adm 2/1732, f. 141*v*; *CSPD 1664–5*, p. 581; *Cat.*, i

Battersby, J. 1 Leslie G. Matthews, *Royal Apothecaries* (1967), pp. 123–4; Woodhead; PRO, E 179/252/32 (19), p. 4 (R); PRO, PCC North 116

Battersby, —— 1 Foster; GL, MS. 10116/2; A. Tindal Hart, *Country counting house* (1962), p. 96

Batts 1 *Cat.*, i; *Rupert and Monck letter book 1666* (ed. J. R. Powell and E. K. Timings, NRS, 1969), pp. 180, 197; Longleat, Coventry MSS 99, f. 91*r*

Baxter 1 HMC, *Rep.*, 8/1/281; Sherwood, pp. 57, 173; HMC, *Portland*, iii. 249

Bayles 1 *Middle Temple Reg.*

Baylie, F. 1 *Naval Minutes*, pp. 200–1 & n.; Pool (*see* Bagwell, n. 3), pp. 14–16

Baylie, M. 1 Tomlinson, p. 226; PRO, WO 51/9, p. 150; 51/12, p. 12 (refs from H. C. Tomlinson)

Baynard's Cas. 1 Wheatley and Cunningham

Beach 1 NWB, pp. 206–7; cf. *CSPD 1668–9*, p. 343
2 *Cat.*, i; iv; *Further Corr.*, p. 330

Beale, B. 1 *CTB*, i–ix, passim; Longleat, Coventry MSS 99, f. 195*r*
2 Rawl. A 341, ff. 99, 127
3 Chappell, p. 57; PRO, E 179/252/32, p. 38 (R)

Beale, C. 1 Sir H. C. Maxwell-Lyte, *Hist. notes on Great Seal* (1926), p. 95; inf. from J. Daniels

Beale, F. 1 WRO, Wills 5 June 1662; WRO, E 174; WRO, Act Bk 5, f. 87 ~ A. M. Burke, *Mem. St Margaret's* (1914), p. 328

Beale, Simon 1 *CSPD 1658–9*, p. 425; *1659–60*, p. 556

Beale, Symon 1 WRO, F 4541; J. B. Williamson, *Hist. Temple* (1924); Lafontaine

Beane 1 *CSPD 1665–6*, p. 311; PRO, E 179/252/32 (18), f. 24*v* (R)

Beauchamp 1 Heal (*see* Atkinson, n. 1), p. 104; Goldsmiths' Co., Survey of 1651, f. 30*v* (R)

Becke, B. 1 iv. 114; WRO, E 1610
2 GLRO, MR/TH/3, m.13d; ib. 12 (1670), p. 47; Harris, ii. 184

Becke, —— 1 Chappell, pp. 39, 51, 102

Beckford 1 *CSPD Add. 1660–85*, pp. 457–9; Woodhead; Rawl. A 173, ff. 69, 85, 87
2 Braybrooke (1854), i. 138, n. 2; John E. Bailey, *Fuller* (1874), p. 673

Beckman 1 iii. 37, n. 2; *DNB*; *Tangier Papers*, pp. xliv, 67–71; BL, Harl. MSS 6844, f. 104; Taylor, p. 252; PL 2972, p. 236; 2973, pp. 370–1; Tomlinson, pp. 237, 239

Bedell 1 Plomer, i

Bedlam 1 View in PL 2972, pp. 84–5

Beeston 1 Highfill

Belasyse 1 GEC; *DNB*. Engraved portrait in PL 2576(2)/10

Bell, E. 1 Chappell, p. 40; Whitear, pp. 136–7, 146

Bell, W. 1 Foster

Bellamy 1 iv. 374, n. 2; *CSPD 1661–*

2, p. 13; *1664–5*, p. 564; Chappell, p. 53; *Priv. Corr.*, ii. 314

Bell Yd 1 Pope, *Works* (ed. Roscoe, 1824–5), ix. 407

Bence 1 Woodhead

Bendish 1 Chappell, p. 29; P. Morant, *Hist. Essex* (1768), ii. 351–2; Alfred C. Wood, *Levant Co.* (1935), pp. 91–6

Benier 1 GL, MS. 14819, f. 18

Bennet, H. 1 V. Barbour, *Arlington* (Washington, D.C., 1914), p. 262 ~ *DNB*; GEC; K. Feiling, *Brit. for. pol. 1660–72* (1930). Engraved portraits in PL 2576(2)/78; 2979/36b
2 Views in PL 2972/102c, d

Bennet, J. 1 PRO, E 179/252/32, Mr Izod's acct (R)

Bennet, T. 1 PRO, WO 51/12, p. 98; ib. 16, p. 110; ib. 18, p. 36 (refs from H. C. Tomlinson)

Benson 1 *Reg. Dutch Reformed Church 1571–1874* (ed. W. J. C. Moens, priv. ptd Lymington 1884), p. 5

Bentley 1 Whitear, p. 68

Berkeley 1 GEC; *D*, viii. 338, n. 1. Engraved portrait in PL 2979/42b
2 *Naval Minutes*, p. 257
3 *DNB*; GEC
4 *Hist.*, ix. 294
5 Gramont, p. 99; Burnet, i. 137; Burnet, *Supplement* (ed. Foxcroft, Oxf. 1902), p. 65
6 GEC; *DNB*; HP; James S. Clarke (ed.), *James II* (1816), i. 397
7 p. 223
8 *Cat.*, i; Clowes, ii. 271. Engraved portrait in PL 2979/239

Berkeley Ho. 1 Basil H. Johnson, *Berkeley Sq.* etc. (1952), p. 51
2 Wheatley and Cunningham

Berkshire Ho. 1 LCC, *Survey*, 30/490–1

Bernard 1 HP
2 *Family Letters*, pp. 55, 56, 62 ~ HP
3 PRO, PCC Carr 90

Bethel 1 ii. 13; Firth and Davies, p.

263; *Pub. Surtees Soc.*, 36/228

Bethnal Green 1 GLRO, MR/TH/3, m.64

Betterton 1 Highfill; engraved portrait in PL 2980/219b

Bettons 1 PRO, E 179/252/32, St Gabriel (R)

Beversham 1 PRO, E 179/252/32 (19) (R); *Harl. Soc. Reg.*, 3/234, 236

Bickerstaffe 1 *CSPD 1661–2*, p. 409; *1668–9*, pp. 208, 435; *Harl. Soc. Vis.* 61/167

Biddle 1 PRO, LS 13/31, p. 37; WRO, E 174

Biddulph 1 Woodhead; HP

Bill 1 GEC; Sir J. Summerson, *Iveagh Bequest* (n.d.)

Billing 1 W. C. Braithwaite, *Second period of Quakerism* (1919), p. 402; WRO, E 1613

Billingsly 1 PRO, PCC Bruce 139

Billiter Lane 1 Strype, ii. 54

Billop 1 *CTB*, iii. 1001; Bodl., Tanner 38, f. 151

Birch 1 *DNB*; HP; Bryant, ii. 111, 164, 194, 196; Burnet, ii. 90

Birchensha 1 Bodl., MS. Wood 19 D (4); Grove (6th ed.)

Birchin Lane 1 Wheatley and Cunningham

Bird 1 Highfill

Birkenhead 1 iii. 283, n. 5; *CTB*, iii. 842; *DNB*

Bishop 1 *Bull. IHR*, 19/17; *CTB*, ii. 567. For his functions, *see* Barcroft

Bishopsgate 1 View in PL 2972/86a

Blackborne 1 Aylmer, pp. 266–7; *CSPD 1660–1*, p. 378; GL, MS. 4384/2; Sainsbury, *1664–7*, p. 268; *1677–9*, p. 176; *Priv. Corr.*, i. 36

Blackbury 1 *CSPD*, e.g. *1664–5*, p. 132

Blackman 1 ib., e.g. *1665–6*, p. 130

Blackwall 1 GLRO, MR/TH/4, mm.93d–99 (R)

Blagge 1 Evelyn, esp. iv. 148+; Evelyn, *Life of Mrs Godolphin* (1847)

Blagrave 1 PRO, LC 3/25, f. 58
2 Pulver; Lafontaine; Sherwood, p. 170; Rimbault; PRO, PCC Exton 160

Blake 1 Sandwich, p. xviii etc.; *CSPD 1652–3*, p. 223

Bland 1 PRO, C 5/179/67 ~ Boyd 35185; PRO, PCC Bath 76; Routh, pp. 120, 122, 123, App. II; V. A. Rowe, *Sir H. Vane yr* (1970), pp. 103, 136
2 *Cat.*, iv. 430–1

Blayney 1 *CSPD 1666–7*, p. 154 etc.; Haley (*see* Aldersgate St, n. 2), p. 440; Evelyn, iv. 615, n. 2; PL 2250 (1); *CTB*, e.g. iii. 299

Blayton 1 Burke (*see* Beale, F., n. 1), p. 369

Blinkhorne 1 PRO, E 179/244/22, p. 154

Blount 1 *DNB*; A. E. Everitt, *Community of Kent 1640–60* (Leic. 1966)

Blow 1 J. Clifford, *Divine services and anthems* (1664); Pulver. Engraved portrait in PL 2980/216b

Boate 1 *MM*, 14/33n.; *CTB*, ii. 551; PRO, Adm 2/1732, ff. 8, 11; Longleat, Coventry MSS 99, f. 195*v*

Bodham 1 Collinge; BL, Add. MSS 9317, f. 3*r*

Boeve 1 *CTB*, iii. 1263; *CSPD 1668–9*, p. 250

Bond 1 Taylor, pp. 207–8

Boone, C. 1 Sainsbury, *1668–70*, p. xix

Boone, Col. 1 Firth and Rait, ii. 1277; *CSPD 1659–60*, p. 1

Books 1 *Priv. Corr.*, ii. 247–8
2 Inf. from H. M. Nixon
3 ix. 144
4 PL, Pepys's Catalogue (frontispieces); *Priv. Corr.*, i. 167
5 i. 260; ix. 428; *Priv. Corr.*, i. 179–81, 262–3
6 i. 140; Rawl. A 190, f. 146*r*; *Tangier Papers*, pp. 251, 252

7 *Letters*, p. 267
8 Dorothy Davis, *Hist. Shopping* (1966), p. 166
9 *Letters*, p. 189
10 *Priv. Corr.*, i. 167; ii. 317
11 ib., ii. 315
12 viii. 10
13 vi. 340
14 *Naval Minutes*, e.g. p. 381
15 PL 2869–80
16 *Priv. Corr.*, ii. 266
17 *Naval Minutes*, p. 177
18 i. 49 & n. 4
19 S. Gaselee, *Span. books in library of Pepys* (Bibliog. Soc. Trans. no. 2, Oxf. 1921), p. 15
20 vi. 247, 320 & n. 4
21 PL 2699

Boreman, G. 1 PRO, LC 3/73, p. 120; *CSPD 1664–5*, p. 258; *1666–7*, p. 509; *CTB*, ii. 183

Boreman, R. 1 Venn; *DNB*

Boreman, W. 1 Evelyn, iii. 270, n. 3; E. Hasted, *Hist. Kent*, pt i (ed. Drake, 1886), pp. 44n., 80; PRO, PCC Lloyd 91

Boreman, —— 1 Mapperton, Sandwich MSS, App. f. 83

Borfett 1 Venn; *Calamy Rev.*

Boscawen 1 HP

Bostock 1 *CSPD 1663–4*, p. 59

Bow 1 MRO, MR/TH/4, mm. 155–6

Bowes 1 *DNB*

Bowles 1 WRO, E 292, p. 219; Westminster Abbey Muniments, St Margaret's Reg. (burial of John 'Boulds', 21 Aug. 1666)
2 PRO, E 179/249/1, Brampton; Hunts. Rec. Off., Wills (Brampton Peculiar); Rawl. A 171, f. 91*v*

Bowman 1 Bull. IHR, 19/16; PRO, LC 3/73, p. 49; ib. 5/39, pp. 180, 304

Bowyer 1 PRO, E 403/1756, pp. 104, 151, 163; *CTB*, i. 629; Carte 223, f. 333; PRO, LC 3/73, p. 36; W. H. Ward and K. S. Block, *Hist. Iver* (1933), pp. 166–7; G.

Lipscomb, *Hist. Bucks.* (1831–47), iv. 525; VCH, *Bucks.*, iii. 293

Bowyer, W. 1 *CSPD*, e.g. *1664–5*, p. 132; PRO, PCC Duke 44

Boyle 1 Life by R. E. W. Maddison (1969). Engraved portraits in PL 2979/124d, 125a
2 GEC: *see also* Burlington House
3 GEC; *DNB*

Boynton 1 p. 249 ~ *Pub. Surtees Soc.*, 36/126; *CTB*, i. 231

Boys, Sir J. 1 Everitt (*see* Blount, n. 1); *Bull. IHR*, 19/15

Boys, J. 1 R. M. Glencross, *London marriage licences* (1937–40), ii, *1660–1700*, p. 4; *DNB*, s.n. Fuller

Bradford 1 iv. 225, n. 3; PRO, Adm 20/2, p. 220. *See also* Tooker, Mrs

Braems 1 HP; *CSPClar.*, iv. 618, 646, 689; *CSPD 1660–1*, p. 152; BL, Add. MSS 9317, f. 1

Brampton 1 R. Comm. Hist. Mon., *Hunts.*, (1926), pp. 25–6
2 *Family Letters*, pp. 4–5
3 viii. 237, 471
4 *Family Letters*, pp. 43, 46; PL (unoff.), Jackson MSS 4
5 *Family Letters*, p. 43n., p. 178
6 ib., pp. 202, 204
7 Tanner, p. 264; *CSPD 1687–9*, p. 179
8 *Priv. Corr.*, ii. 322–3
9 PL (unoff.), Jackson MSS 17, 18, 19

Bread St 1 iii. 206

Brereton 1 PL 2874, pp. 387+ ~ GEC; Aubrey, i. 121–2

Brett 1 *Northants. Past and Present*, 2/266–7; J. Le Neve, *Mon. Anglicana 1680–99* (1718), pp. 50–1; inf. from late Sir G. Isham

Bretton 1 Venn; Evelyn, iii. 317 etc.

Brewer 1 Boyd 44645; PRO, Adm 20/1, no. 1179 etc.

Bride Lane 1 PRO, E 179/147/627, pp. 181–3, 194–7; E 179/252/32 (St Bride's), pp. 7–8, 35

Bridgeman 1 *DNB*; Burnet, i. 454; R. North, *Life of Guilford* (1742), pp. 88–9. Engraved portraits in PL 2552 (2)/116; 2980/162g

Bridges 1 v. 292 & n. 1; *CSPD Add. 1660–70*, p. 130; Boyd 2049

Brigden 1 GL, MS 2969/1, f. 112r; *CSPD 1678*, p. 318

Briggs 1 cf. also *CSPD Add. 1660–85*, p. 107

Brigham 1 i. 181, n. 4; PRO, Adm 2/1732, f. 56v

Brisbane 1 *Naval Minutes*, p. 257
2 Evelyn, iv. 416, n. 4; PRO, Adm 20/6, p. 440, Sainty; T. E. S. Clarke and H. C. Foxcroft, *Burnet* (Camb. 1907), p. 187; corresp. with Pepys in *Further Corr.*, p. 279; PL 2881, pp. 143+

Brodrick 1 HP; Burnet, *Supplement* (ed. Foxcroft, Oxf. 1902), pp. 138–9

Bromfield 1 PRO, PCC Wootton 245; ib. Hene 14

Brooke 1 HP; Ranft in *Journ. Mod. Hist.*, 24/369

Brookes 1 ix. 258, n. 3; PRO, Adm 2/1732, f. 12v; *CSPD Add. 1660–85*, pp. 369, 404

Brouncker, H. 1 viii. 406
2 Gramont, p. 262
3 PRO, PCC Exton 125; ib. Hare 39 ~ *DNB*; HP; Evelyn, v. 575

Brouncker, W., 1st Ld 1 GEC

Brouncker W., 2nd Ld 1 Bodl., Tanner 38, f. 151
2 *DNB*
3 PRO, PCC Hare 39
4 ix. 452 ~ *DNB*; Collinge; Sainty. Engraved portrait in PL 2979/124a
5 PRO, E 179/252/32, Cov. Gdn, p. 4 (R)

Browne, Sir A. 1 Essex Rec. Off., T/G37; D/DBg/9/1

Browne, A. 1 Sainsbury, *1660–3*, pp. 163, 170; *1664–7*, p. 70; *CSPD 1661–2*, p. 314; *Cat.*, i

Browne, J. 1 i. 177, n. 1; Chester-

Foster 199; M. F. Bond, H. of Lords Rec. Off. Memo. 18, p. 6

Browne, Capt. J. *CSPD 1653–4*, p. 471 etc.; *Cat.*, i

Browne, Capt. J. (ordnance) 1 *CSPD 1658–9*, p. 475; E. Straker, *Wealden Iron* (1931), p. 189

Browne, J. (storekeeper) 1 PRO, Adm 20/2, p. 283; *CSPD* e.g. *1664–5*, p. 12

Browne, Sir R. (alderman) 1 *DNB*; Woodhead

Browne, Sir R. 1 *DNB*; Evelyn, esp. iii. 247–8

Brownlow 1 ix. 153, n. 3: Venn; *Harl. Soc. Reg.*, 64/179

Bryan 1 *CSPD Add. 1660–70*, p. 522; *Add. 1660–85*, p. 133

Buck 1 ii. 192, n. 5; Venn; *Walker Rev.*

Bucklersbury 1 Hatton, vol. i, sect. i

Bucknell 1 ix. 507, n. 4; Woodhead; *CTB*, e.g. i. 664–5

Buckworth 1 PRO, E 179/252/32 (18), f. 27 (R)

2 Woodhead; *Cat.*, e.g. ii. 136

3 Woodhead; GEC

Budd 1 Venn; PRO, Adm 2/1725, f. 3

Bull 1 McDonnell (*see* Baines, n. 1)

Bulteel 1 *DNB*; HP; Bodl., Tanner 47, f. 7; *Priv. Corr.*, i. 328, 330, 331

Bunce 1 Woodhead; Carlisle (*see* Baber, n. 1), p. 179

Bunn 1 *CSPD 1659–60*, pp. 516, 553; *1660*, p. 315; *Cat.*, i; BL, Sloane MSS 3496, f. 1; 3509, f. 43; 3510, f. 40; Routh, pp. 86, 120

Burgess 1 PRO, E 407/128, n.d.; *CSPD 1665–6*, p. 105

Burlington Ho. 1 LCC, *Survey*, 32 pt ii, pp. 390+; PL 2972/108–9

Burnet 1 Venn; Munk; PRO, E 179/252/32, London 2 (R); *Family Letters*, p. 12

Burroughes 1 Collinge

Burrows, E. 1 *CSPD 1665–6*, p. 103; Sandwich, p. 273

2 Rawl. A 185, f. 23*v*

Burrows, J. 1 PRO, Adm 2/1725, ff. 28*v*–29*r*; *CSPD 1664–5*, p. 353; Boyd 15047

Burston 1 *Shorthand Letters*, p. 28; inf. from Thomas R. Smith and S. Tyacke

Burt 1 Highfill

Burton, H. 1 *Letters*, pp. 66–7, 89–90 ~ Venn; Magd. Coll., Reg., ii., f. 73a; Wood, *Ath. Oxon.*, iv. 513n.

Burton, R. 1 PRO, Adm 2/1725, f. 15*v*; *CSPD Add. 1660–70*, p. 39

Butler (Ormond) 1 GEC; *DNB*

Butler, Ld J. 1 GEC

Butler, T. 1 GEC; Sainty; Evelyn, iv. 210–11; Gramont, p. 100

Butler, 'Mons.' 1 Venn; H. Cotton, *Fasti eccles. Hibern.* (Dublin 1845–78), i. 272; Foster; McDonnell (*see* Baines, n. 1)

Butts 1 P. McGrath (ed.), *Merchants in 17th-cent. Bristol* (Bristol Rec. Soc., 1955), pp. 242, 245

Cadbury 1 *CSPD*, e.g. *1663–4*, p. 658; PRO, Adm 2/1732, f. 13*v*

Cade, J. 1, e.g. PRO, Adm 20/7 pt i. 324

2 PRO, E 179/252/27, f. 53*v* (R); D, iv. 434

3 Mercers' Co. MSS, Gresham Committee Accts; BL, Add. MSS 5075, nos 29–32 ~ Plomer, i; Howe

Cade, T. 1 R. S. Bosher, *Making of Restoration settlement* (1951), p. 286; Foster

Calamy 1 *DNB*; Venn. Engraved portrait in PL 2980/121b

Calthorpe 1 i. 6, n. 3; Venn; Whitear p. 74; Boyd 16634

Capel 1 *DNB*; HP; Bryant, ii. 312; PRO, PCC Hare 32; Evelyn, iv. 144 & n.

Carew 1 i. 266, n. 1; *DNB*

Carkesse 1 *Harl. Soc. Reg.*, 46/74

2 PRO, E 179/252/32 (18), f. 22*v*

(R) ~ Collinge; PL 2874, p. 471;
E. G. O'Donoghue, *Bethlehem
Hosp.* (1914), pp. 219–22; R.
Hooke, *Diary 1672–80* (ed. Robinson and Adams, 1935), pp. 318,
480

Carnegie 1 vi. 60 & n. 2; ix. 154–5
& n.; GEC; *Letters of Philip 2nd
Earl of Chesterfield* (1829), pp. 88–9

Carr 1 HP

Carter 1 i. 321, n. 4; viii. 51, n. 2;
Venn

Carteret, E. 1 A. Collins, *Hist. of
Carteret* (1756), pp. 34–6; *Bull.
IHR*, 19/16

Carteret, G. 1 *Hist.*, ii. 225, 458–9;
iii. 130

2 HMC, *Rep.*, 8/1/129+; PRO, PC
6/1, f. 415

3 See *DNB*; Sainty; HP; PRO, PCC
Bath 17

4 Harris, ii. 181–2; PRO, LC 5/12,
p. 258

5 *Cat.*, i. 332

6 Chester-Foster 1197

7 PRO, E 179/252/32, St Martin's-
in-Fields, f. 2v (R)

Carteret, P. 1 *Cal. Comm. Comp.
1643–60*, p. 2329; *Cat.*, i

Cartwright 1 Highfill

Cary 1 *CSPD* e.g. *1660–1*, p. 75;
Genealogist (n.s.) 23/202–3

Cary Ho. 1 Sir R. Somerville, *The
Savoy* (1960), pp. 83–4; W.
Knowler (ed.), *Strafford's Letters*
(1739), i. 177; Boyne, p. 760

Case 1 *DNB*; *Calamy Rev.*; Peter W.
Thomas, *Sir J. Berkenhead* (Oxf.
1969), p. 203

Castell 1 ii. 52, n. 2; Venn

Castle, J. 1 *Cal. Comm. Comp. 1643–
60*, pp. 91, 1615; Foster; *CSPD
1661–2*, p. 367; WRO, E 1621

Castle, W. 1 Chester-Foster 254 ~
CSPD 1664–5, pp. 403, 453; *Cat.*,
i. 224, 226; *Shorthand Letters*, pp.
36, 37; *Priv. Corr.*, i. 116

2 Pepys, *Mem.*, p. 30

Catherine of Braganza 1 *DNB*

Cave 1 *Musica Britannica*, 33/item 116

Cervington 1 PRO, E 403/1756,
1757; Sir R. Colt Hoare, *Hist.
mod. Wilts* (1830), iii. pt 5, p. 27

Chamberlayne 1 GEC; Sainsbury,
1660–3, pp. xx, xxx, xxxvii

Chandler 1 Whitear, pp. 75, 78

Channell 1 PRO, LC 3/73, p. 189;
Wheatley, 24 Sept. 1660, n.

Chaplin 1 Woodhead

2 qu. Beaven, ii. 190

Chard 1 Rawl. A 182, f. 302

Charles II 1 *Naval Minutes*, p. 62

2 ib., p. 418

3 *D*, iv. 123 & n. 1; *Naval Minutes*, p.
318

4 *Naval Minutes*, pp. 71–2

5 *See* Admiralty p. 3

6 *Naval Minutes*, p. 194

7 ib., p. 84. Further reading:
'characters' by Normanby (PL
2142); and Halifax (*Works*, ed.
W. Raleigh, Oxf. 1912, pp. 187+).
Engraved portraits in PL total 37.

Charleton 1 *DNB*; Munk; Wood,
Ath. Oxon., iv. 752. Engraved
portrait in PL 2980/187a

Charnock 1 Baxter, pp. 207, 216–20;
Sainty

Chase 1 PRO, LC 3/73, f. 77r;
C. R. B. Barrett, *Hist. Soc. Apoth.*
(1905), p. 76; Matthews (*see*
Battersby, J., n. 1), pp. 123–4

Chatham 1 VCH, *Kent*, ii. 336+;
Ehrman, ch. iii; D. C. Coleman in
Ec. Hist. Rev. (n.s.), 6/134+

2 Sketch and plan in BL, King's
MSS 43, f. 7; accounts in *Arch.
Cant.*, 6/67n.; J. Presnail, *Chatham*
(1952), pp. 75+; VCH, loc. cit.

Chatham Chest 1 BL, Add. MSS
9317

2 *Naval Minutes*, p. 6

3 *MM*, 8/176+, 41/332–3, 42/232–3,
and refs in Chatham, n. 2

Cheapside 1 Davis (*see* Books, n. 8),
pp. 107+

Chelsea 1 D. Lysons, *Environs of London* (1806–22), ii. 17

2 GLRO, MR/TH/3, mm. 13–14 (R)

Cherrett 1 WRO, E 1621, p. 85 (R); PRO, E 179/252/32, Cov. Gdn, p. 5 (R)

Chetwind 1 PRO, PCC Juxon 3

Chicheley 1 HP; Tomlinson, pp. 59, 223; Sainty; PRO, E 179/252/32, St Giles-in-Fields, Hart's Coll., p. 16 (R)

2 *Tangier Papers*, p. 171; Longleat, Coventry MSS 99, f. 91r

3 HP; *Cat.*, i; Collinge; Sainty; Tomlinson

4 C. M. Leonard, *Gen. Assembly Virginia: a bicentennial register* (Richmond, Va. 1978), p. xix

Chiffinch 1 DNB; North, (ed. Jessop), i. 274; iii. 171

Child, J. 1 DNB; *Cat.*, i. 155, 165; *CSPD 1655*, p. 431; PRO, Adm 20/3, p. 323; Evelyn, iv. 306

Child, W. 1 Grove (6th ed.)

Chillenden 1 Longleat, Coventry MSS 101, ff. 105+ ~ Firth and Davies pp. 214, 224, 226–7; A. S. P. Woodhouse (ed.), *Puritanism and liberty* (1938), esp. pp. 400–1

2 *CSPD 1677–8*, p. 338

Chiverton 1 Woodhead

Cholmley 1 *Naval Minutes*, p. 104

2 N. Yorks Rec. Off., ZCGV

3 *An account of Tangier* ~ HP; *CSPClar.*, v. 358; H. A. Kaufman (ed.), *Journal of J. Luke 1670–3* (Geneva and Paris 1958), p. 24

Christenings 1 iii. 296

2 iv. 634

3 M. Strong, *The indecency and unlawfulness of baptizing children in private* (1692); J. H. Overton, *Life in Engl. church* (1885), pp. 163+; Alan Macfarlane, *Family Life of R. Josselin* (Camb. 1970), p. 89; J. Obelkevich, *Religion and rural society 1825–75* (Oxf. 1976), pp. 127+

Christmas, —. 1 Whitear, p. 113; *Pepysiana*, pp. 16–17

Christmas 1 DNB, s.n. Rich, John

2 Further reading: C. A. Miles, *Christmas* (1912); T. G. Crippen, *Christmas* (1923)

Christ's Hosp. 1 Evelyn, iv. 542

2 PL 2973/406 (drawing); PL 2612 ~ R. Kirk, *Mr Pepys upon the state of Christ-Hospitall* (1935); E. H. Pearce, *Annals Christ's Hosp.* (1908)

Clapham, J. 1 Collinge; *CSPD 1667*, pp. 298, 516

Clapham 1 Meekings (see Arthur, n. 1), p. xci

2 *Priv. Corr.*, ii. 299

Clarendon Ho. 1 View in PL 2972/106–7 ~ Clarendon, *Life*, iii. 457; Johnson (see Berkeley Ho., n. 1), ch. xiii

Clarges 1 DNB; HP

Clarke, J. 1 Whitear, pp. 34+, 142+; Lib. Soc. Geneal., P. Boyd, Index to Marriages 1538–1837 (Mdx) (where her Christian name is given as Joan)

Clarke, R. 1 Clowes, ii. 428; *Cat.*, i. 335; Longleat, Coventry MSS 99, f. 91r

2 Carte 73, f. 104r; Philip G. Rogers, *Dutch in Medway* (1970), pp. 84, 97

Clarke, T. 1 Munk; PRO, LC 3/24; *CTB*, iii. 179; PRO, PCC Eure 26

Clarke, W. 1 BL, Add. MSS 14286

2 E. J. Sams and J. Moore in *TLS*, 4 March 1977, p. 253; C. H. Firth (ed.) *Selections from the papers of W. Clarke* (4 vols, Camden Soc, 1891–1901); Woodhouse (see Chillenden n. 1) ~ DNB; Aylmer

Claxton 1 Venn; Chappell, pp. 43–4, 102; W. P. W. Phillimore and E. Young, *Cambs. parish reg.* (1907–27), *Marriages*, v. 121

Cleggat 1 Inf. from J. Watson

Clements 1 *Cat.*, i; *CSPD 1664–5*, p. 361

Clerke, F. 1 HP
Clerke, Mrs 1 *Trans. Greenwich and Lewisham Antiq. Soc.*, 2/18
Clerke, —— 1 PRO, E 179/252/32 (19, p. 6) (R)
Clifford 1 *DNB*; life (1937) by C. H. Hartmann; Evelyn, iv. 18–23 & nn.
Clodius 1 R. and M. Hall (eds), *Corresp. of H. Oldenburg* (Madison 1965–), i. 103; GLRO, MR/TH/7, m.1d; (b); G. H. Turnbull, *Hartlib* etc. (Liverpool 1947), p. 44
Clothier 1 *CSPD*, e.g. *Add. 1660–85*, pp. 204, 420
Clothworkers' Hall 1 T. Girtin, *Golden Ram* (1958), pp. 23–4, 101, 142–3, 146+
Clun 1 Highfill
Clutterbuck 1 Beaven
   2 *Cat.*, i. 165, 177; PL 2867, pp. 455+
Cocke, C. G. 1 Firth and Rait, ii. 671, 702, 713, 781; *EHR*, 83/691 n. 6
Cocke, Capt. 1 *Pub. Surtees Soc.*, 93/135; 101/99; 111/158–9; BL, Add. MSS 9317/1; *CTB*, ii. 361; *CSPD 1664–5*, p. 365 etc.
   2 J. J. Keevil, *Medicine and the navy 1200–1900* (1957–8), ii. 109
   3 PRO, E 179/147/617, p. 156 (R); Chester-Foster 300; R. W. K. Hinton (*see* Barker, n. 1), pp. 118, 221; PRO, PCC King 45
Cocke, R. 1 PRO, Adm 2/1725, f. 55; Adm 20/3, p. 320; corresp. in HMC, *Heathcote*, pp. 33, 66, 70, 79
Cocker 1 J. I. Whalley, *Engl. Handwriting 1540–1853* (1969), p. xv; Sir F. Meynell in A. S. Ostley (ed.), *Calligraphy* (1966), pp. 169+; *DNB*; PL 2981. Engraved portraits in PL 2981/107; 2983/333b
Coffee-Houses 1 Wood, *L. & T.*, i. 168–9
   2 LRO, Alchin Coll., Box H/103
   3 Davis (*see* Books, n. 8), p. 164; J.

Ashton, *Social Life* (1882–1904), i. 216
   4 Wood, op. cit., i. 201; Edward F. Robinson, *Early hist. coffee-houses* (1893), pp. 73–9. There was only one in Cambridge in the '60s and none in Pepys's time: North (ed. Jessop), i. 197–8
   5 ib., loc. cit. & n. 5; Steele, no. 3622
   6 *CSPD 1677–8*, p. 338
   7 *CSPD 1664–5*, p. 365
   8 Aubrey, i. 289–90
   9 Robinson, op. cit., pp. 121+; B. Lillywhite, *London Coffee-Houses* (1963), nos 1390, 491; PRO, E 179/252/32 (3), p. 2 (R); BL, Add. MSS 5100 (55/2) (R)
   10 Lillywhite, op. cit., nos 433, 1284; Robinson, op. cit., p. 124; PRO, E 179/147/617, p. 136 (R); ib. 252/23 (R)
   11 v. 37, n. 2; Lillywhite, op. cit., no. 1548
Coke, J. 1 v. 177, n. 2; *DNB*
Coke, R. 1 ix. 218, n. 1; VCH, *Surrey*, iii. 276–7; GEC
Cole 1 *Gray's Inn Reg.*
Coleman, C. 1 L. Hotson, *Commonwealth and Restoration stage* (Camb. Mass. 1928), pp. 139+
Coleman, E. (musician) 1 Lafontaine; Rimbault; *Musica Britannica* 33/ items cx, cxi
Coleman, E. (soldier) 1 *CTB*, iii. 854
Coleman, —— (young) 1 Lafontaine; Pulver
Coling 1 PL 2873, p. 483
   2 E. S. de Beer (ed.), *Corr. J. Locke* (Oxf. 1976–), vi. 104, n. 3; *CSPD 1670*, p. 545; PRO, PC 2/68, p. 12; PRO, LC 5/12, p. 191; N. Luttrell, *Relation* (Oxf. 1857), iv. 240
   3 Luttrell, op. cit., iv. 714; cf. also PRO, SP 29/140 no. 96
   4 *Further Corr.*, pp. 322–3; Bryant, ii. 274; Rawl. A 189, f. 123.

Engraved portrait in PL 2979/112a

Colladon 1 iv. 315, n. 1; Munk; *CSPD 1663–4*, pp. 244, 263

Colleton 1 GEC; Haley (*see* Aldersgate St, n. 2), pp. 237+; *Merc. Pub.*, 6 Dec. 1660, pp. 781–3; Rawl. A 478, f. 78

Collins 1 *CSPD 1668–9*, p. 447

Colvill 1 Woodhead; Smyth, p. 88

Colwall 1 *DNB*; PRO, E 179/252/32, London 18, p. 1 (R)

Comberford 1 Taylor, pp. 228–9

Commander 1 PRO, E 179/252/32 (R)

Compton 1 HP

Conny 1 PRO, Adm 2/1725, f. 5*v*; *Further Corr.*, pp. 354–5; Sidney M. Young, *Hist. Barber-Surgeons* (1890), p. 10

Cooke, E. 1 *CSPD 1659–60*, p. 599

Cooke, H. 1 PRO LC 9/258; Pulver; Lafontaine; Rimbault

Cooke, J. 1 Venn; *CSPD 1654*, p. 482; *1658–9*, p. 362; Sainty, *Sec. of State*

Cooke, T. 1 iii. 147; *CTB*, i. 512; *CSPD 1666–7*, p. 397; Julian Marshall, *Annals Tennis* (1878), pp. 88, 91, 92–3 & nn.

Cooke, ——. 1 Howe

Cooper, A. 1 Evelyn, iii. 624, n. 1 ~ Life by K. H. D. Haley (1968) on which this account is based

Cooper, H. 1 PRO, SP 29/58, no. 114; Colvin, v. 475

Cooper, R. 1 *CSPD 1661–2*, p. 468; *1663–4*, p. 77; *1665–6*, p. 266; R. Ollard, *Man of war: Sir R. Holmes* (1969), pp. 78–80 & nn.; Sandwich, pp. 159, 163, 171, 179, 210–11

Cooper, S. 1 D. Foskett, *Samuel Cooper* (1974), pp. 33, 36

Cooper, W. 1 *CSPD 1662–3*, p. 497; *1664–5*, p. 181; *1665–6*, p. 191; PRO, SP 46/136, no. 62

Coppin 1 *CSPD 1654*, p. 28; *1659–60*, p. 557; *Cat.*, i

Corbetta 1 PRO, SP 29/29, f. 79; *CSPD 1665–6*, p. 143; C. H. Hartmann, *The King my brother* (1954), p. 158; Lafontaine

Corey 1 Highfill

Cornhill 1 Hatton, vol. i, sect. i

Cornwallis 1 Braybrooke (1854), iii. 349, n. 3

Cotterell 1 *DNB*; HP; Evelyn, iii. 616–17 & n.; Harris, ii. 185 etc.; Mapperton, Sandwich MSS, Journal, ii. 6, vi. 146; *Pepysiana*, p. 286

Cottle 1 Evelyn, iii. 421, n. 2; *CSPD 1655*, p. 567

Country 1 ib., p. 510; Sandwich, pp. 99, 146; *Cat.*, i. 339; ii. 109; iii. 311–12; iv. 327; Longleat, Coventry MSS 101, ff. 104+

Covent Gdn 1 S. Sorbière, *Relation* (Cologne, 1667), p. 24

2 ix. 151

Coventry, H. 1 Feiling (*see* Bennet, H, n. 1), p. 189

2 *DNB*; HP

Coventry, W. 1 Mapperton, Sandwich MSS, Journal, ix. 248–50; *D*, iv. 156, n. 4; viii. 505; Vale in *Camb. Hist. Journ.*, 12/107+

2 *Life*, ii. 201–2

3 Burnet, i. 478; North (ed. Jessop), i. 119

Cowes 1 *CSPD 1655–6*, p. 408; *Cat.*, i

Cowley 1 PRO, Adm 2/1725, f. 2; Adm 42/379; *Letters*, pp. 35–6; will in A. H. Nethercot, *A. Cowley* (1931), pp. 298–301

Cox, J. 1 Longleat, Coventry MSS 99, f. 91r; *CSPD 1654*, p. 87 etc.; *1660–1*, p. 324; PRO, Adm 42/379; *Cat.*, i. 15–16, 340

Cox, T. 1 Firth and Rait, ii. 1062, 1320, 1455; GL, MS. 186/1, pp. i, ii

Cragg 1 *Harl. Soc. Reg.*, 64/e.g. 42, 67

Craven 1 *DNB*; GEC; J. C. R. Childs, *Army of Charles II* (1976), pp. 233, 240; Sainty. Engraved portrait in PL 2576 (2)/10

Creed 1 *CSPD 1655–6*, p. 249; *1659–60*, p. 438; BL, Add. MSS 9304, f. 154

2 *CSPD 1659–60*, p. 551; *1663–4*, p. 8; *1664–5*, p. 250; *Add. 1660–85*, p. 87; PRO, Adm 2/1725, ff. 30*v*–31*r*; Adm 2/1745; Adm 20/1 nos 592, 900; 20/4, p. 254 etc.

3 Carte 73, f. 323

4 ii. 98–9; v. 107–8; vi. 15; ix.542–3

5 HMC, *Hodgkin*, e.g. pp. 154, 158; *D*, v. 51

6 W. Smalley Law, *Oundle's Story* (1922), pp. 91, 98, 103, 108

7 Aylmer, p. 70; B. Worden, *Rump Parl.* (Camb. 1974), p. 115; PRO, E 403/1756, p. 128; PRO, AO1/1710/101, f. 5*v*

Creighton 1 iii. 42, n. 5; Venn; *DNB*; *Bull. IHR*, 19/17; M. Nedham, *The case of the Commonwealth* (ed. Knackel, Charlottesville 1969), pp. 66–7

Cresset 1 PRO, LC 3/73, pp. 39, 42, 43

Crew 1 N. Crew, *Mem.* (Camden Soc. Misc. 9, 1893), p. 2

2 HP; GEC; PRO, PCC King 158; Carte 73, f. 51

3 PRO, PCC Coker 23

4 HP; PRO, PCC Pyne 279; Morant (*see* Bendish, n. 1), i (Tendring) 437

5 *DNB*; N. Crew, op. cit. Engraved portrait in PL 2980/101b

6 George Baker, *Hist. Northants.* (1822–41), i. 684

7 Foster

8 Morant, loc. cit.

Crisp 1 GLRO, MR/TH/7, m.1d; *CSPD 1663–4*, p. 165; PRO, LC 5/40, p. 105

Crisp, E. 1 *CTB*, i. 324, 327; W. R. Chaplin, *Trin. House* (1952); PL 2867, p. 335

Crisp, N. 1 *DNB*; *Merc. Pub.*, 6 Dec. 1660, pp. 781+; Rawl. A 478, f. 78; Carlisle (*see* Baber, n. 1), p. 174; PRO, PCC Mico 42

Crispin 1 PRO, LC 3/73, p. 173

Crofts, T. 1 *CSPD 1667*, p. 449

Crofts, W. 1 GEC; *DNB* (*Supp.*)

Cromleholme 1 *DNB*; Mercers' Co. MSS, St Paul's School Accts 1638–60; McDonnell (*see* Baines, n. 1)

Croone 1 *DNB*; Munk

Crow, Capt. 1 *Cat.*, i

Crow, W. 1 iv. 404, n. 1; Woodhead; PRO, E 179/252/27, f. 26*v* (R)

Crowther 1 Foster

Croxton 1 PRO, E 179/147/627, p. 195 (R)

Crutched Friars 1 Hatton, vol. i, sect. i

Cuckold's Pt 1 Wheatley and Cunningham

Cumberland, H. 1 GL, MS. 6540/1, burials, 2 Feb. 1663; inf. from Miss L. Kirk

Cumberland, R. 1 GL, MS. 6554/1, f. 244

2 Inf. from Miss L. Kirk

3 qu. G. V. Bennet, *White Kennet* (1957), p. 208

4 PL 1808, 988 ~ Venn; Magd. Coll., Reg., ii, ff. 64b, 66a, 99b; *Pepysiana*, p. 101; *DNB*; life by Squier Payne (1720)

5 GL, MS. 6536

Curle 1 *CSPD 1655–6*, p. 486; *1659–60*, p. 461; *Cat.*, i

Curtis 1 *CSPD 1655–6*, p. 486; *1660–1*, p. 199

Custis 1 Boyd 8483; *CSPD 1665–6*, p. 513; PL 2882, pp. 843, 850, 852

Custom Ho. 1 *London Topog. Rec.*, 21/1+

Cutler, J. 1 Woodhead; HP

Cutler, W. 1 Boyd 35102; PRO, E 179/147/617, p. 153 (R); *CSPD 1661–2*, p. 151; PRO, PCC Eure 85; ib. King 30

Cuttance 1 *DNB*; *Cat.*, i and ii; Longleat, Coventry MSS 99, f. 91*r*

Cuttle 1 *CSPD 1655–6*, p. 424; *1659–60*, p. 555; *Cat.*, i

Daking 1 *CSPD 1653–4*, pp. 536, 553 ∼ ib. *1661–2*, p. 9; *1665–6*, p. 82; Harris, i. 175–6; Sandwich, p. 109

Dalmahoy 1 i. 134, n. 6; Burnet, i. 363, n.; HP; VCH, *Surrey*, iii. 374

Dalton 1 PRO, LS 13/35, p. 42

Dalziel 1 vii. 390, n. 6; *Reg. P.C. Scot. 1665–9*, pp. 211, 241; Dalton, i. 121; Robert Chambers (ed.), *Biog. dict. eminent Scotsmen* (1875)

Daniel, R. 1 Rawl. A 216, f. 203

Daniel, S. 1 *Cat.*, i, iii ('Danerell')

Darcy, M. 1 *Bull. IHR*, 19/15; Carlisle (*see* Baber, n. 1), p. 163

Darcy, W. 1 iii. 269 ∼ *CSPD* esp. *1660–1*, p. 78; *1661–2*, p. 239

Darling 1 *See* Taverns, named, n. 112

Darnell 1 Lafontaine

Dashwood 1 Beaven; PRO, PCC Drax 54

Da Silva 1 T. H. Lister, *Life of Clarendon* (1838, 1837), iii. 193, n.

Davenant 1 *DNB*; ed. of *The siege of Rhodes* by A-M. Hedbäck (Uppsala 1973). Engraved portrait PL 2980/203g

Davenport, F. 1 Highfill; Wilson, p. 137

Davenport, H. 1 Highfill; Wilson, pp. 137–8

Davenport, ——. 1 Hunts. Rec. Off., dd M 43a/9

Davies, J. 1 *CSPD 1649*, p. 330; *1663–4*, p. 39; Duke of York, *Mem. (naval)*, p. 86; Carte 74, f. 225*v*

Davies, T. 1 iii. 264, n. 2; Plomer, i; Woodhead

Davis, J. 1 ii. 55; iv. 408; *CSPD 1660–1*, p. 308; GEC; *Harl. Soc. Reg.*, 46/194; Collinge

2 *CSPD 1669*, p. 162

Davis, M. 1 Highfill; Wilson, pp. 139–41

Davis, T. 1 *CSPD 1659–60*, p. 559

Day, J. ('**uncle**') 1 iv. 300, n. 2; Whitear, pp. 16–17, 137–9; Chappell, pp. 29, 102

Day, J. 1 Whitear, pp. 17–18

Deane 1 See also Pepys, *Mem.*, p. 28

2 PL 2979/127b. He also possessed a copy of Kneller's portrait of Deane: Harvard, Houghton Lib., b MS Eng 991

3 PL 2910; also e.g. 2241, 2501 ∼ Collinge; *DNB*; HP; *Priv. Corr.*, ii. 317

Debusty 1 *CSPD 1664–5*, p. 339; *CTB*, iii. 1244, 1282

Delaune 1 iii. 296, n. 4; Wren and Hackett (*see* Aleyn, n. 1), pp. 19–20

Denham 1 Evelyn, iii. 301

2 H. M. Colvin, *Biog. dict. Brit. Architects 1600–1840* (1978); *DNB*

Deptford 1 In Camden's *Britania* (ed. Gibson, 1698), pp. 229–30

2 VCH, *Kent*, ii. 337+; Ehrman, pp. 83–4; D. C. Coleman in *Ec. Hist. Rev.*, n.s. 6/134+

Dering 1 HP; *CSPD 1660–1*, p. 212; *Parl. diary Sir E. Dering 1670–3* (ed. B. D. Henning, New Haven 1940); *Diaries . . . of Sir E. Dering* (ed. M. F. Bond 1976). There is an engraved portrait of the 1st Baronet in PL 2979/109a.

De Vic 1 GEC; HMC, *Rep.*, 8/1/2/278a

Devonshire Ho. 1 PRO, E 179/147/624

Diamond 1 *CSPD 1651–2*, pp. 247, 332; *1652–3*, p. 19; *1657–8*, p. 61; *Cat.*, i

Diary and MSS 1 iv. 346; viii. 95 & n. 2; iii. 48

2 PL 2265–6, 2867, 2869–80

3 PL 2581; *D*, v. 116, n. 1

4 PL 2237

5 *Letters . . . of S. Pepys; Letters of S. Pepys and his family circle*. Others were published by Braybrooke in his editions of the diary and by

John Smith in his *Life, journals and correspondence of S. Pepys* (2 vols, 1841).

6 Rawl. C 859A

7 Rawl. A 190, C 859A and B

8 Rawl. D 916, f. 64r; Bodl., Ballard MSS, ii. 188v

9 PL (unoff.), Jackson MSS, 20 (3) (4)

10 Rawl. D 916, loc. cit. Rawlinson wrote in some of the volumes 'Mr Carte has seen'.

11 They are now principally Rawl. A 170–95; the whole set is listed and briefly calendared in W. D. Macray, *Catalogi codicum manuscriptum Biblioth. Bodl.*, pt 5, fasc. 1–4 (Oxf. 1862–98). Accounts in Macray, *Annals of Bodl. Lib.* (Oxf. 1890), pp. 231, 235, 236; and by C. H. Firth in *MM*, 3/226+

12 NMM, LBK/8; cf. *D*, vii. 266 & n. 1

13 Sotheby's *Cat.*, 1 Apr. 1931, lot 18. They were resold in 1980 to a private and anonymous purchaser: Christie's *Cat.*, 11 June 1980, lot 363

14 *Further Corr. of S. Pepys 1662–1679; Shorthand letters of S. Pepys*

15 Ehrman in *MM*, 34/269–70

16 Nine volumes (ed. M. A. E. Green, 1860–94) cover 1660–9. Two volumes of addenda were published in 1895 and 1939.

Dickons 1 GL, MS. 10, 116, file 1

2 Reg. All Hallows, Barking, 14 and 22 Oct.; GL, MS. 872

Digby, F. 1 *Cat.*, i; Clowes, ii. 430

Digby, G. 1 *DNB*; Burnet, i. 183

Dillon 1 GEC

Dobbins 1 Chaplin (*see* Crisp, E., n. 1); *CSPD 1665–6*, pp. 415, 486, 500; PL 2867, p. 335

Dockyards 1 See esp. D. C. Coleman in *Ec. Hist. Rev.* (ser. 2), 6/134+

2 BL, Add. MSS 9302, ff. 183–91

3 PRO, PC 2/54, f. 59r

4 PRO, Adm 7/633

5 PRO, Adm 2/1745, f. 66r

6 iii. 80 & n. 4

7 BL, Add. MSS 9311, f. 83r

8 iii. 234 & n. 2

9 BL, Add. MSS 9311, f. 32r; PL 2874, p. 444

10 Further reading: VCH, *Kent*, ii. 336+; M. Oppenheim, *Admin. royal navy 1509–1660* (1896); J. P. W. Ehrman, *The navy in the war of William III* (Camb. 1953)

Doling 1 i. 14, n. 4; PRO, SP 25 I 108/75

Douglas 1 Dalton, i. 63, 215; GEC

Doves 1 *CSPD 1664–5*, pp. 222, 481; *1665–6*, p. 348; *Add. 1660–85*, pp. 165, 231

Downes 1 iv. 247, n. 1; Venn

Downing, G. 1 J. L. Sibley, *Biog. sketches graduates of Harvard* (Camb. Mass.), i (1873), p. 37, n. 1

2 *DNB*; HP; life by J. Beresford (1925)

Downing, J. 1 vii. 119, 138; *CSPD 1667*, pp. 62, 432

Downing, Capt. 1 viii. 538, n. 2; Dalton, i. 7, 98, 160

Doyly 1 HP

Draghi 1 Grove (6th ed.); PRO, SP 44/23, p. 29; *Pub. Cath. Rec. Soc.*, 38/xxxi

Drawwater 1 Reg., St Peter-le-Poer

Dress 1 In *Le mercure galant*: see J. L. Nevinson in *Connoisseur*, 136/87+

2 cf. i. 121

3 i. 95; ii. 296 & n. 2

4 iii. 241 & n. 2

5 iii. 77

6 *Apollo*, 20/319

7 vii. 324 & n. 3

8 ii. 29

9 ix. 551

10 viii. 437

11 ii. 132

12 iii. 97; v. 22–3

13 viii. 247

14 *Journal to Stella* (ed. Williams, Oxf.

1974), p. 47; J. Spence, *Anecdotes* (ed. Singer, 1820), p. 329

15 viii. 63

16 iii. 298

17 vii. 162

18 e.g. Ashton (*see* Coffee-Houses, n. 3), p. 277

19 Nevill Williams, *Powder and paint* (1957), p. 43

20 J. Bulwer, *Anthropometamorphosis* (1653), p. 261

21 i. 269, 283

22 ix. 186

23 viii. 463; ib. 439, 454, 503

24 For this last, *see* Large Glossary

25 vi. 238 & n. 3; vii. 329

26 vii. 178

27 ii. 203

28 vi. 40

Drink 1 Bryant, ii. 410

2 Aubrey, i. 109

3 cf. P. Earle, *World of Defoe* (1976), pp. 154+

4 B. K. Mitchell and P. Deane, *Abstract Brit. hist. statistics* (1962), pp. 251+

5 D. W. R. Bahlmann, *Moral revolution of 1688* (New Haven 1957)

6 Bryant, ii. 412

7 Sir Hugh Platt, *Jewel house of art and nature* (1605), sig. C27; cf. T. Tryon, *The way to health, long life and happiness* (1691)

8 Recipe in *Diana Astry's recipe book c. 1700* (ed. Stitt, Beds. Hist. Soc, 1957), p. 128

9 iv. 100; cf. Evelyn, iv. 329

10 Tanner, p. 240

11 *L. & T.*, iii. 199

12 Recipe in *The ladies cabinet enlarged and opened* (1667), p. 241; cf. Sir W. Dugdale, *Origines Juridiciales* (1680), p.204

13 *Commons Debates 1621* (ed. W. Notestein et al., New Haven 1935), iv. 108; vii. 77+

14 Rum had not yet displaced brandy as the seamen's grog except on the W. Indies station: *Priv. Corr.*, i. 122[1696]

15 ix. 477 & n. 3

16 *Britannia Languens* (1680), qu. J. R. McCulloch (ed.), *Early Engl. tracts on commerce* (Camb. 1954), p. 420

17 *Kingdomes Intelligencer*, 29 Dec., p. 847

18 *Merc. Polit.*, 23–30 Sept. 1658, p. 887; see also Boyne, i. 593; Rugge's 'Mercurius' (BL, Add. MSS 10116–17), i, f. 33; David Macpherson, *Eur. commerce with India* (1812), pp. 128–32; H. B. Morse, *Chronicles of E. India Co.* (Oxf. 1926), i. 9+

19 *Pub. Advertiser*, 16 June; see also F. P. and M. M. Verney, *Mem. Verney family* (1925), i. 9 [?1650]; *L. & T.*, i. 189 [1654]; Rugge, op. cit., i, f. 33 [1659]; H. Stubbes, *The Indian nectar* (1662), pp. 101+; *Harl. Misc.* (1808–12), i. 532–4 [1682]

20 Mapperton, Sandwich MSS, Letters from Ministers, f. 31*v*; Journal, ii. 321; ix. 50–60, 66–78; Bryant, iii. 44

21 *Advice to a son* (repr. Washington D.C. 1962), p. 53; cf. also T. Muffet, *Healths improvement* (1655), ch. xiv; R. Burton, *Anat. of melancholy* (ed. Shilleto, 1893), i. 250; Hooke (*see* Carkesse, n. 2), p. 4 etc.; Sir Jack Drummond and Anne Wilbraham, *Englishman's Food* (rev. Hollingsworth, 1958), pp. 123–5. For hot milk, see Hooke, loc. cit.; *Tangier Papers*, pp. 20, 28

22 Further reading: Drummond and Wilbraham (*see above*, n. 21); J. Bickerdyke, *Curiosities of ale and beer* (1886); P. Mathias, *Brewing ind. in Engl.* (Camb. 1959); A. L. Simon, *Hist. wine trade in Engl.* (3 vols, 1906–9); ib., *Bottlescrew Days*

(1926); R. Lennard (ed.), *English-men at rest and play 1558–1714* (1931)

Drumbleby 1 E. Halfpenny in *Galpin Soc. Journal*, 12 (1959)/48–9; Boyd 16724, 17253

Dryden 1 *Trans. Camb. Bibliog. Soc.*, viii, pt i, pp. 130+
2 Venn; *Letters*, pp. 280–1; PL 2442. Engraved portraits in PL 2947; 2980/210b

Dudley 1 HP; Carte 223, f. 246r

Duell 1 GL, MS. 10116/1

Duke 1 C. M. Andrews, *Brit. councils of trade* (Baltimore 1908), p. 75; PRO, SP For. 84/168, f. 32; *CSPD 1663–4*, p. 438; *Letters*, p. 38

Duncombe 1 Venn; HP; H. Rose-veare, *Treasury* (1969), pp. 62+; PRO, E 179/252/32, St Martin's, f. 2v (R); WRO, F 388

Dunn 1 PRO, SP 46/136/395; BL, Add. MSS 9313, f. 1r

Dunster 1 HP; *CSPD 1668–9*, p. 213; *1671*, p. 510

Dupuy 1 v. 279, n. 2; HMC, *Rep.*, 8/1/2/278; *CSPD 1664–5*, p. 122

Durham Yd 1 BL, Add. MSS 5098 (55–7)

Dury 1 WRO, E 172, 176

Dutch Ch. 1 Wheatley and Cun-ningham; Moens (*see* Benson, n. 1)

Dutch Wars 1 v. 35
2 v. 353
3 qu. C. R. Boxer, *Second Dutch War* (1967), p. 6
4 See ii. 223 & n. 1
5 J. R. Powell, *Robert Blake* (1972), pp. 139+
6 R. Ollard, *Man of War: Sir R. Holmes* (1969), p. 172
7 Ralph Davis, *Rise of Engl. shipping ind.* (1972), pp. 303–7
8 In his *Profit and power* (1957)
9 qu. Boxer, *Anglo-Dutch wars of 17th cent.* (1974), p. 4
10 Davis, op. cit. p. 51
11 v. 352

12 viii. 491
13 Sandwich, pp. 239+. Dr Ander-son's introduction to this volume gives perhaps the best account of the naval operations of 1665.
14 *Rupert and Monck letter book 1666* (ed. J. R. Powell and E. K. Timings, NRS, 1969), pp. 79, 87. This has much valuable day-to-day detail.
15 ib., p. 104
16 vii. 158, 160
17 *Rupert and Monck letter book*, p. 104
18 ib., pp. 182–3. For Pearse's author-ship, see my note in *MM*, 57/215
19 vii. 226
20 See P. G. Rogers, *Dutch in Medway* (1970): the fullest and best modern account
21 For this, see Ollard, *Pepys* (1974), pp. 159+
22 See Ollard, *Man of War*, pp. 172+
23 R. C. Anderson (ed.), *Journals etc. of Third Dutch War* (NRS, 1946). His introduction is the authorita-tive account of the war at sea.
24 viii. 267
25 *See* Navy pp. 290–1 & n. 16 ∼ Further reading (apart from books already cited): K. G. Feiling, *Brit. for. po . 1660–72* (1930); D. Ogg, *Engl. in age of Charles II* (2nd ed., 2 vols, Oxf. 1955)

Dyke 1 Chappell, p. 49

Dymoke 1 *DNB*

E. India Ho. 1 Sir W. Foster, *E. India House* (1924), illust. facing p. 126; Defoe, *Tour* (ed. Cole 1927), i. 342

Edisbury 1 ii. 68, n. 3; Oppenheim p. 281; Aylmer (*see* Barcroft, n. 1), p. 78; J. Hollond, *Discourses* (ed. Tanner, NRS 1896), p. xi; Hasted (*see* Boreman, W., n. 1), i. 20n.; BL, Add. MSS 5439, f. 106r

Edlin 1 Venn; Magd. Coll., Reg., ii. 28; GLRO/TH/7, m. 28; MJS/SBB/191, p. 6; WRO, E 172 (1658), F 388 (1660)

Edwards 1 ii. 162
2 Collinge; Chester-Foster 443; Bryant, ii. 390; Wheatley, 27 Aug. 1664, n.
3 Bryant, ii. 390; iii. 229, n. 3; PL (unoff.), Jackson MSS 22 (Receipts 1686–1701), p. 7; *Priv. Corr.*, ii. 315; *Pepysiana*, pp. 52, 253
4 *Letters*, p. 128; *Priv. Corr.*, loc. cit.

Elborough 1 Venn

Elliott 1 *Further Corr.*, pp. 244, 260, 337; Bryant, ii. 35–6
2 Longleat, Coventry MSS 99, f. 91*v*; *Cat.*, i, ii

Ellis 1 *DNB*

Ensum 1 PL (unoff.), Jackson MSS 1 (cf. Whitear, pp. 77–8); *Family Letters*, p. 47

Ent 1 Munk; *DNB*. Engraved portrait in PL 2980/187c

Erwin 1 *Cat.*, i, iii; *CSPD 1664–5*, p. 83 etc.; *1665–6*, p. 123 etc.

Esquier 1 PRO, LC 3/73, p. 68; LC 5/62, pp. 5, 48, 81

Ethell 1 Hunts. Rec. Off., MS. dd M 43a/9

Evans 1 Lafontaine

Evelyn 1 vii. 26; Evelyn, *Diary and corr.* (ed. Wheatley, 1879), iii.329 +
2 C. Marburg, *Mr Pepys and Mr Evelyn* (Phila. 1935), pp. 117–80
3 *Diary and corr.*, iii. 435 +; *Priv. Corr.*, i. 97, 100–1; ii. 247–8
4 PL 2237
5 *Diary and corr.*, iv. 644. There are engraved portraits in PL 2979/126d, 127a.
6 *Diary and corr.* iii. 406; Marburg, op. cit., pp. 115 +; *Priv. Corr.*, i. 14–18; *Letters*, p. 266
7 The best account of Evelyn is in the introduction to vol. i of E. S. de Beer's edition of the diary (6 vols, Oxf. 1955).

Evett 1 *Cat.*, i; *CSPD 1664–5*, p. 277; *Add. 1680–85*, p. 175

Ewens 1 *Cat.*, i; Chaplin (*see* Crisp, E., n. 1)

Exch. Alley 1 Hatton, vol. i, sect. i

Exchequer 1 Colvin, v. 412
2 List of officials in Aylmer (*see* Barcroft, n. 1), pp. 477–8
3 Firth and Rait, ii. 918–21
4 L. Squibb, *A book of all the several officers of the . . . Exchequer* (ed. Bryson, Camden Soc., ser. 4, vol. xiv, *Miscell.* 26, 1975), p. 133
5 viii. 180; ix. 535
6 vi. 100, 157; vii. 125, 168, 398
7 The maximum of 10% established in Henry VIII's reign had been reduced by acts of 1651 and 1660 to 6%.
8 iii. 297; vi. 133, n. 4; vii. 407
9 viii. 16; C. Clay, *Public finance and private wealth* (Oxf. 1978)
10 viii. 131–2, 238, 425
11 ib. 132
12 ib. 572, 576, 590
13 ib. 591; ix. 386–7, 402, 447–8
14 Further reading: S. B. Baxter, *Devel. of Treasury 1660–1702* (1957); H. Roseveare, *Treasury* (1969); C. D. Chandaman, *Engl. pub. revenue 1660–88* (Oxf. 1975)

Excise Off. 1 Wheatley and Cunningham; PRO, E 179/147/617, p. 137; E. Freshfield, *Vestry min. St Barth. Exchange* (1890), pp. 1, 75, 82; GL, MS 84/3, f. 142*v*; PRO, op. cit., f. 51

Exeter Ho. 1 Evelyn, iii. 203–4; *Survey of London*, 18/125; Haley (*see* Aldersgate St, n. 2), p. 206

Exton 1 Venn; PRO, Adm 2/1725, ff. 11*v*–12; (Anon.), *List of civilians* (1811), n.p.

Eyres 1 Firth and Davies, esp. pp. 528–9

Fage 1 Woodhead

Fairbrother 1 Venn; Lib. Soc. Geneal., P. Boyd, Index to Marriages 1538–1837 (Cambs.)

Fairfax 1 *DNB*

Faithorne 1 *DNB*; WRO, B 5 passim; Boyd 22444

Falconer 1 *CSPD 1660–1*, p. 359
2 ib. *1665*, p. 67; *1659–60*, p. 418; *1663–4*, p. 646

Fanshawe 1 *Memoirs* (ed. H. C. Fanshawe) ~ *DNB*; GEC; E. Prestage, *Diplom. relations of Portugal* (Watford 1925)
2 HMC, *Heathcote*, p. vii; *CSPD 1666–7*, p. 345

Farriner 1 vii. 268, n. 1; PRO, E 179/252/32, London 4 (R)

Fauconberg 1 Aylmer, p. 100; PRO, E 403/1756 passim; *CSPD 1660–1*, p. 283; *CTB*, v. 323

Fauntleroy 1 WRO, E 170, 173 (refs from Miss M. Swarbrick). The accounts for 1660 are missing.

Fazeby 1 *Cat.*, i

Fenchurch St 1 Hatton, vol. i, sect. i

Fenn 1 PRO, Adm 106/2886, pt i; *Cat.*, i

Fenner 1 Whitear, pp. 18–19; PRO, PCC Bruce 53; ib. Bunce 72; BL, Add. MSS 5069 (28)

Ferrabosco 1 Pulver; Lafontaine; G. E. P. Arkwright in *Musical Antiquity* 3/220+, 4/42+; G. Livi in ib. 4/121+

Ferrer 1 Mapperton, Sandwich MSS, App., ff. 83, 105; Carte 233, f. 1r; PRO, LC 3/73, p. 111; ib. 37, f. 7v
2 Rawl. A 174, ff. 425, 427; Carte 74, f. 365v
3 Mapperton, op. cit., ff. 83, 84v; Journal, vi. 256; Letters from Ministers, ii. 168; *Pepysiana*, p. 286

Fetters 1 GL, Ref. Lib., typescript list

Finances 1 J. Thirsk and J. P. Cooper, *17th-cent. econ. documents* (Oxf. 1972), pp. 780–1
2 ib., p. 779
3 *Herefordshire militia assessments 1663* (ed. M. A. Faraday, Camden Soc., ser. 4, vol. x), p. 17
4 i. 2; ii. 1
5 Rawl. A 185, ff. 17–18, 19, 21, 23 (1667, 1668, 1669)

6 i. 56, 57–8
7 i. 216
8 i. 223
9 iii. 40
10 ii. 127; v. 196
11 v. 269
12 Backwell's Ledger 'M' (Glyn Mills and Co., London); for the statutory maximum, *see* Exchequer, n. 7
13 Inf. from Prof. F. T. Melton
14 vii. 90 & n. 1
15 vii. 367
16 viii. 474
17 vii. 252–3
18 ix. 90, 99
19 viii. 106
20 ix. 86, 529
21 B. S. Yamey in *Econ. Hist. Rev.* (ser. 2), 1/99+
22 Aubrey, ii. 246
23 vi. 207; viii. 580
24 ix. 551
25 ix. 89; cf. vii. 112–13; ix. 20
26 ix. 406
27 v. 267
28 Tanner, pp. 226–7
29 *Naval Minutes*, p. 272, n. 1.; *Pepysiana*, p. 259

Finch, F. 1 HP

Finch, H. (Nottingham) 1 *DNB*

Finch, H. (Winchilsea) 1 qu. *N. & Q.* (ser. 2), 1/325 ~ GEC; HMC, *Finch*, vol. i

Finch, ——. 1 Boyd 4294; PRO, PCC Eure 87

Fire 1 For a summary, *see* vii. 267, n. 2
2 Inf. from T. F. Reddaway; parish reg., St Peter-le-Poer
3 See T. F. Reddaway, *Rebuilding of London* (1940); *Fire Court* (ed. Philip E. Jones), i (1966), esp. Intro.
4 VCH, *Northants.*, iii. 31+; David Johnson, *Southwark* (1969), p. 296; VCH, *Warwicks.*, viii. 429+
5 vi. 49
6 Davis (*see* Books, n. 8), p. 110

7 Pepys reports the wind but not the fires: iii. 31–2.

8 Colvin, v. 263 n., 268, 277; *Survey of London*, 13/37, 39–40

9 *See* Navy Office p. 299

10 Bryant, iii. 93–4

11 PL 2972/76 (in the same volume are other views of the Fire and its effects) ∼ Further reading: Walter G. Bell, *Great Fire* (1923); Keith Thomas, *Religion and decline of magic* (Penguin 1973), pp. 17+; Reddaway (*see above*, n. 3); Jones (*see above*, n. 3); G. V. Blackstone, *Hist. Brit. fire service* (1957)

Fisher, Capt. 1 PRO, SP 29/149, no. 89, f. 169r; GL, MS. 186/1, p. xxviii

Fisher, Mrs 1 Rawl. A 186, f. 233v; Bryant, iii. 222; PRO, PCC Admon. 1660, f. 27; *Pepysiana*, p. 25; *A list of officers claiming to the sixty thousand pounds* (1663), p. 18

Fishmongers' Hall 1 PL 2972/246a–247a

Fist 1 PL 2874, p. 405; Collinge; *Tangier Papers*, p. 95

Fitch 1 Firth and Davies, pp. 342–4, 518–19

Fitzgerald 1 J. Treglown (ed.), *Letters of Rochester* (Oxf. 1980), p. 192 ∼ Dalton, i. 33, 34, 38, 39; Routh, pp. 27, 91; *CSPD 1671–2*, p. 236

Fleet Prison 1 Wheatley and Cunningham

Fleet St Conduit 1 William Maitland, *Hist. London* (1756), p. 992

Fletcher 1 *Cat.*, i; *CSPD 1672*, pp. 624–5

Fogarty 1 R. Hayes, *Biog. dict. Irishmen in France* (Dublin 1949), pp. 99–100

Foley 1 *Trans. Worcs. Arch. Soc.* (1944)/6+; VCH, *Worcs.*, ii. 269, 280; iii. 440; R. Baxter, *Reliquiae* (ed. Sylvester, 1696), iii. 93; PRO, Adm 2/1725, f. 18r

Food 1 This paragraph is based largely on Davis (*see* Books, n. 8).

2 PL 2973/426–39

3 Drummond and Wilbraham (*see* Drink, n. 21), p. 125; (cf. *D*, iv. 285); M. Misson, *Mémoires* (qu. Drummond etc., p. iii)

4 repr. *How they lived*, ii (*1485–1700*, ed. M. Harrison and O. M. Royston, Oxf. 1963), p. 61

5 Bryant, ii. 411; cf. *Tangier Papers*, p. 56

6 Bryant, ii. 345

7 iv. 354

8 ib., loc. cit., n. 2

9 iii. 264–5

10 Constance A. Wilson, *Food and drink in Britain* (1973), p. 316

11 Further reading: Wilson, op. cit.; Davis (*see above*, n. 1); Drummond and Wilbraham (*see above*, n. 3); R. Lennard (*see* Drink, n. 22); W. C. Hazlitt, *Old cookery books* (1886)

12 *The compleat cook* [c. 1685], sig. A 7; PL 362, p. 847

13 (1685 ed.), pp. 121–2

14 i. 203; viii. 371

15 May, op. cit., p. 230

16 *The closet of Sir Kenelm Digby Kt opened* (ed. A. Macdonnell, 1910), pp. 112–13

17 *The gentlewomans cabinet unlocked* [c. 1680], sig. A 3v; PL 363, p. 81

18 iii. 21–2

19 op. cit., p. 234

Ford 1 *CSP Clar.*, v. 457

2 Boyd 15732; HP; Woodhead; BL, Add. MSS 9317, f. 1

3 PRO, E 179/147/617, p. 10 (R)

4 PRO, PCC Cottle 117

Fossan 1 Venn; Bodl., Clar. dep. c. 399/42

Foster 1 Rochester, *Letters* (*see* Fitzgerald, n. 1), p. 70n.

Foulkes 1 *CSPD 1663–4*, p. 669; *1667–8*, p. 597

Fountaine 1 *DNB*; Whitear, pp. 78–9

Fowke 1 Woodhead; G. Yule, *Independents in Civil War* (Camb. 1958), p. 98
Fowler, J. 1 *CSPD 1653-4*, p. 186; *1667*, p. 11; BL, Add. MSS 9304, f. 200r; 9317, f. 2v, 13; Sainty
Fowler, R. 1 *CSPD 1661-2*, p. 370; Frederick F. Smith, *Hist. Rochester* (Rochester 1928), p. 497
Fowler, ——. 1 *Vorträge Int. Pharm. Kongresses* (1965), p. 277 (ref. from T. D. Whittet)
Fownes 1 vii. 407, n. 3; PRO, Adm 106/3520, f. 27v; Adm 42/379; NWB, p. 51
Fox 1 viii. 16
  2 Evelyn, iv. 218-19; *DNB*; HP; life by C. Clay (Oxf. 1978)
Foxe 1 *DNB*; *Visit. Essex 1664-8* (ed. J.J. Howard, 1888), p. 102
Fraiser 1 Munk; Venn; *DNB* (rev.)
Franke, E. 1 Rawl. A 182, f. 339; PRO, PCC May 110; Boyd 52860
Franke, F. 1 *CSPD 1661-2*, p. 166
Franklin 1 Munk; Foster; Smyth, p. 96
Frederick 1 Woodhead; HP
Freeman 1 *CSPD 1660-1*, p. 138; Sir John Craig, *Royal Mint* (Camb. 1953), pp. 146, 154; *Bull. IHR*, 19/46
Freemantle 1 PRO, PCC Pyne 279
French Ch. 1 viii. 137
  2 PL (unoff.), Jackson MSS 22 (Receipts 1688-1701), p. 67; printed *Priv. Corr.*, i. 239-40
  3 R. D. Gwynn, *Eccles. organisation of French Protestants in Engl. in late 17th cent.* (1976); id., (ed.) *Cal. Letter bks French ch. in London 1643-59* (Hug. Soc. London, 1979); also *CSPD 1660-1*, p. 277; Evelyn, iii. 545 & nn.; F. de Schichter, *Les églises du refuge en Angleterre* (Paris 1892), ii. 218+; Somerville (*see* Cary Ho., n. 1), pp. 77+
Frost 1 Aylmer, pp. 254-6

Frowde 1 Andrews (*see* Duke, n. 1), p. 75; HMC, *Rep.*, 8/1/2/279; Duke of York, *Mem. (naval)*, p. 96; *CTB*, ii. 159; Marvell, ii. 263
Fuller, R. 1 PRO, E 179/252/32 (18), f. 22 (R); Boyd 12935
Fuller, T. 1 Aubrey, i. 257 ~ *DNB*; W. Addison, *Worthy Dr Fuller* (Berkeley 1951); Dewi Morgan, *Phoenix of Fleet St* (1973), p. 118. Engraved portrait in PL 2980/113f
Fuller, W. 1 Foster; *DNB*
Fulwood 1 Bodl., Tanner 43, ff. 22-4 ~Venn; Harris, ii. 173; Reg. All Saints, Huntingdon
Funerals 1 vi. 114 & n. 1
  2 North (ed. Jessop), iii. 229; *Occ. Papers*, ii. 63
  3 *Priv. Corr.*, ii. 314+
  4 v. 90
  5 Bodl., Ballard MSS, 12, f. 149
  6 Lady Fanshawe, *Memoirs* (1829), p. 26; Harris, ii. 206. cf. also Barnard (*see* Angier, n. 2), pp. 79+
Furzer 1 *CSPD 1664-5*, pp. 36, 67; *1667-8*, p. 250; Pepys, *Mem.*, p. 73; Collinge; *Priv. Corr.*, ii. 316
Gale 1 Venn
Gallop 1 *CSPD 1659-60*, p. 504
Garraway 1 HP; Bryant, ii. 110-12, 150, 195, 199, 264, 266, 315
Gatehouse 1 Wheatley and Cunningham; Evelyn, v. 27; *Priv. Corr.*, i. 32; Tanner, p. 270
Gauden 1 GLRO, MJS/SBB/219, p. 37
  2 Tanner, p. 245
  3 Luke (*see* Cholmley, n. 3), p. 83 ~ Woodhead
  4 Boyd 15763; Hollond (*see* Edisbury, n. 1), p. 297n.; *Cat.*, i–iv passim; VCH, *Kent*, ii. 362; inf. from E. E. F. Smith
  5 *DNB*; F. F. Madan, *New bibliog. of Eikon Basilike* (1950), pp. 126, 130-1

Gaultier 1 *Burwell lute tutor* (facsimile, Leeds 1974), f. 5*v*; Ernst Pohlmann, *Laute, Theorbe, Chitarrone* (Bremen 1971), pp. 62–3; Lafontaine

Geere 1 GL, MS. 84, ii (Mills), f. 137*v*; PRO, PCC Eure 112 (R)

Gens 1 PRO, Adm 20/1, pp. 135, 841

Gentleman 1 Mapperton, Sandwich MSS, Journal vi. 252; viii. 183

Gery 1 Sandwich, p. 75; *Pepysiana*, p. 286; Carte 73, f. 467*r*

Gibbons 1 Aubrey, i. 196
2 Ed. E. J. Dent, *Musica Britannica*, ii (1965)
3 Wood, *L. & T.*, ii. 5 ~ Pulver; Lafontaine; Rimbault

Gibbs 1 Mapperton, Sandwich MSS, App., f. 83

Gibson 1 *Further Corr.*, p. 69; *Priv. Corr.*, i. 54–5
2 Copy in *Priv. Corr.*, i. 118–26
3 *Naval Minutes*, passim
4 BL, Add. MSS 11602 (1650–1702)
5 *Priv. Corr.*, ii. 315 ~ Collinge; Sainty; Gibson's own account of his career in BL, Sloane MSS 2572, ff. 79–87

Gifford, G. 1 Foster; *Naval Minutes*, p. 122; John Ward, *Lives of Gresham professors* (1740)

Gifford, H. 1 *CSPD 1655*, p. 127; *CTB*, i. 13

Gifford, T. 1 Boyd 54195; *CTB*, i. 951

Giles 1 Whitear, p. 20; PRO, PCC Penn 120

Gilsthorpe 1 NWB, p. 185

Glanville 1 Evelyn, ii. 539 & n. 2; v. 236, n. 2, 496–7, 497–8; E. S. de Beer (ed.), *Corr. J. Locke* (Oxf. 1976–), i. 293n.

Glascock 1 Whitear, p. 19
2 PRO, PCC Hyde 48; E 179/252/32: St Bride's, p. 31 (R)
3 Venn

Glemham 1 Wood, *Ath. Oxon.*, iv. 837–8

Goddard 1 Munk; *DNB*; Sherwood, pp. 110–12

Godfrey 1 iv. 384–5, n. 1; Whitear, pp. 19, 20, 151, 154 etc.; PL (unoff.), Freshfield MSS 8, 9

Godolphin 1 PRO, SP 29/253, f. 68*r*
2 HP

Goffe 1 *DNB*; Clarendon, *Hist.*, iv. 338; v. 233; A. Wood, *Fasti Oxon.* (ed. Bliss, 1815–20), i. 494

Gold, N. 1 GEC; D. Brunton and D. H. Pennington, *Members of Long Parl.* (1954), pp. 59, 60, 135; Wheatley, 20 June 1664, n.

Gold, ——. 1 NMM, 35 MS. 0328; *CSPD Add. 1660–85*, p. 335; LRO, Repert. 73, f. 11*v*; *CTB*, iii. 1079

Golding 1 *Cat.*, i

Goldsmiths' Hall 1 Strype, iii. 99; W. Maitland, *Hist. London* (1756), ii. 763

Gomme 1 *DNB*; Tomlinson, pp. 100, 224, 239

Goodenough 1 PRO, Adm 20/4, pp. 224, 227; Boyd 48233

Goodgroome 1 Pulver; Rimbault, p. 228
2 Braybrooke (1858), i. 198; cf. *D*, ii. 126, n. 2

Goods 1 Mapperton, Sandwich MSS, Journal, vi. 252; App. f. 83*v*

Goodson 1 *DNB*

Goodyear 1 *Harl. Soc. Reg.*, 46/57, 60; Boyd 38432

Gordon 1 GEC

Gorham 1 Hunts. Rec. Off., Wills (Lincoln; Brampton Peculiar)
2 P. Clarke in D. H. Pennington and K. Thomas (eds), *Puritans and revolutionaries* (Oxf. 1978), p. 53

Goring Ho., 1 Evelyn iii. 404; H. Clifford Smith, *Buckingham Palace* (1931), pp. 14 +, 271.

Gosnell 1 G. deF. Lord (ed.), *Poems on affairs of state*, vol. i, *1660–78* (New Haven 1963, p. 369) ~ Highfill; S. Rosenfeld in *Theatre Notebook*, 2/no. 3

Gouge 1 Venn; *Calamy Rev.*; C. Hill in H. E. Bell and R. L. Ollard (eds), *Hist. Essays 1660–1750* (1963), pp. 57–9

Grabu 1 PL 2684, 2588 ∼ Pulver; Lafontaine; M. Benoît, *Versailles et les musiciens du roi* (Paris 1971), pp. 103–7, 340

Gracechurch St 1 Strype, i. 25; ii. 106

Gramont 1 Life by Warren H. Lewis (1958)

Graunt 1 Goldsmiths' Co., MS. 1924, ff. 21–6; MS. 1917, ff. 67, 109 (R) 2 *DNB*; Aubrey, i. 271 +

Gray's Inn 1 Wheatley and Cunningham

Greatorex 1 *DNB*; Taylor, p. 229; *Notes and Rec. Roy. Soc.*, 7/172, 191

Greene, J. 1 Whitear, pp. 79–80, 146; PRO, C 7/280/89

Greene, Maj. J. 1 Woodhead; Boyd 16710

Greene, L. 1 ix. 6, n. 1; *Cat.*, i. 356; iii. 5; *Rupert and Monck letter book* (*see* Batts, n. 1), p. 180; *CSPD 1672*, p. 278; Longleat, Coventry MSS 91, f. 91*v*

Greene, W. 1 *CSPD Add. 1660–85*, pp. 35, 71; PRO, Adm 20/3, no. 1083 etc.

Greenleaf 1 Burke (*see* Beale, F., n. 1), p. 655; *see also* Adams

Greeting 1 PRO, LC 3/25 ∼ C. Welch, *Six lectures on the recorder* (1911), pp. 60–9; S. Godman in *Monthly Musical Record*, 86/20–6; Pulver

Gregory, E. 1 PRO, Adm 2/1732, f. 142*v*; *CSPD 1663–4*, p. 470; *1664–5*, p. 245; R. Rawlinson, *Hist. cath. Rochester* (1717), pt iv. 19–20

Gregory, Sir E. 1 PL 2874, p. 502 ∼ Ehrman, p. 645; Rawl. C 199

Gregory, J. 1 *CTB*, vol. ii, p. liv

Gregory (musicians) 1 Pulver; Lafontaine

Grenville 1 Burnet, i. 178 ∼ *DNB*

Gresham Coll. 1 Strype, i. 125 + ; J. Ward, *Lives of Gresham Professors* (1740)

Grey 1 HP

Griffin 1 GEC; Wheatley, 18 Oct. 1664, n.; Dalton, i. 24, 42, 50, 92, 97; *CTB*, i. 271 2 *CSPD 1661–2*, pp. 30, 508; *CTB*, i. 6, 271, 360

Griffith, J. 1 Dalton, i. 24, 42, 50; Rawl. A 477, f. 117

Griffith, W. 1 PRO, Adm 2/1725, f. 11*v*; PRO, AO1/1724/145; *Priv. Corr.*, ii. 316

Griffith(s), W. 1 PRO, PCC Carr 144

Griffith, ——. 1 HMC, *Rep.*, 8/1/2/278b; *Bull. IHR*, 19/15, 19

Grove 1 vi. 130, n. 2; *CSPD 1656–7*, p. 536; *1659–60*, p. 528; *Cat.*, i

Guildhall 1 S. Sorbière, *Voyage to England* (trans. 1704), p. 16 2 Engraving in PL 2972/83b

Gunning 1 Evelyn, iii. 203–4 2 *DNB*. Engraved portrait in PL 2980/106d

Gunpowder Plot 1 In 1660, 1661 and 1664 2 Haley (*see* Aldersgate St, n. 2), p. 339 3 R. Josselin, *Diary* (ed. Macfarlane, 1976), p. 571 4 Furley in *History*, 44/16 + 5 Steele, nos 3711, 3734, 3754 6 ib., no. 3824 7 See esp. Luttrell, *Brief Relation* (Oxf. 1857), i. 236, 362, 388, 419, 600 8 *CSPD 1611–18*, p. 151

Guy, Capt. T. 1 *CSPD 1659–60*, pp. 116, 226, 245; Dalton, i. 194, 302

Guy, Capt. 1 *Cat.*, i; Sir T. Allin, *Journals 1660–78* (ed. R. C. Anderson, NRS, 1939–40), i. 298; *CSPD 1666–7*, p. 221

Guyat 1 *Harl. Soc. Reg.*, 46/69, 200 etc.; GL, MS. 872/7; PRO, E

179/252/32 (18), f. 24*v* (R); cf. also *CSPD Add. 1660–85*, p. 363

Gwyn 1 viii. 503
2 Burnet, i. 483–4
3 LCC, *Survey*, 29/377–8 ∼ *DNB*; life by John H. Wilson (1952). Engraved portraits in PL 2979/186b, c

Hackney 1 GLRO, MR/TH/4, mm. 1–4d

Hadley 1 *Harl. Soc. Reg.*, 46/198, 243; GL, MS. 10942/1

Hailes 1 WRO, E 174; BL, Egerton MSS 2542, f. 379*r*

Haines 1 Anthony Ashton qu. McAfee, p. 217 ∼ Foster

Hall, B. 1 Highfill

Hall, J. 1 Van Lennep, p. 288; *CSPD Add. 1660–85*, p. 344; Gramont, pp. 112–13

Hall, Capt. 1 *Cat.*, i; Sandwich, p. 99 etc.

Halsall 1 *CSP Clar.*, iv. passim; *Bull. IHR*, 19/16; Dalton, i. 52, 315; Firth and Davies, pp. 615–16; *CSPD 1685*, p. 44

Hamilton 1 *DNB*; *Memoirs of Gramont* (ed. C. H. Hartmann, 1930)

Hammersmith 1 GLRO, MR/TH/3, mm. 7d–10d

Hammond 1 *Harl. Soc. Reg.*, 46/68, 206; PRO, PCC Duke 38; ib. Hene 47

Hampstead 1 GLRO, MR/TH/2, mm. 29–31

Hampton Ct 1 Colvin, v. 153 +

Hanbury 1 PRO, E 179/249/122/226; *Trans. Cambs. and Hunts. Antiq. Soc.*, 2/14

Hannam 1 Longleat, Coventry MSS 99, f. 91*v*; Clowes, ii. 205; *CSPD 1668–9*, p. 63; *Cat.*, i

Hanson 1 Evelyn, iii. 147 ∼ BL, Harl. MSS 4898, pp. 28, 423, 666; HMC, *Rep.*, 7/App., pp. 88–93

Harbord 1 Carte 75, ff. 19–20, 26–7, 67

2 Mapperton, Sandwich MSS, Journal, esp. ii. 6 ∼ R. W. Ketton-Cremer, *Norf. Assembly* (1957), pp. 41 +
3 Bryant, ii. 165, 218

Harding 1 Lafontaine; Rimbault

Hardy 1 *DNB*; Venn

Hargrave 1 WRO, F388; PRO, PCC Carr 54, Hene 82, Juxon 3

Harley, E. 1 HP

Harley, R. 1 HP; Firth and Davies, pp. 692–3

Harman, J. 1 *DNB*; WRO, E 172, 174

Harman, P. 1 Boyd 32342
2 ib. 2654; Chester-Foster 627; *Harl. Soc. Reg.*, 7/254; PRO, E 179/252/27, f. 54 (R); BL, Add. MSS 5069 (28) (R)

Harper 1 *CSPD 1663–4*, p. 322; Duke of York, *Mem. (naval)*, pp. 86–7

Harrington 1 Boyd 25061; *CTB* e.g. i. 425; PRO, E 179/252/32 (18), f. 22*r* (R); *Harl. Soc. Reg.*, 46/211

Harris, H. 1 McAfee, p. 218

Harris, J. 1 PRO, Adm 2/1725, f. 4*r*

Harrison, B. 1 Chaplin (*see* Crisp, E., n. 1), p. 13

Harrison, J. 1 *Bull. IHR*, 19/21

Hart, C. 1 McAfee, p. 224

Hart, J. 1 *Cat.*, i; Longleat, Coventry MSS 99, f. 91*v*

Hart, T. 1 Firth and Davies, pp. 166, 192, 197; Dalton, i. 76

Hartlib 1 H. R. Trevor-Roper, *Religion, Reformation and social change* (1972), p. 250 ∼ ib., pp. 249 +; G. H. Turnbull, *S. Hartlib* (1920); R. Boyle, *Works* (1744), v. 267, 285; WRO, E 174
2 PRO, SP 25 I 208, p. 74; *CSPD 1666–7*, p. 65; *1671–2*, p. 252

Harvey 1 O. Manning and W. Bray, *Hist. Surrey* (1804–14), i. 401, 402, 416; *CTB*, i. 612; Alfred C. Wood, *Levant Co.* (1935), p. 250

Harwich 1 Ehrman, pp. 84, 434;

VCH, *Essex*, ii. 284–6, 292, 306; Ranft in *Journ. Mod. Hist.*, 24/368+; Bryant, ii and iii passim

Hatton, C. 1 *DNB*; Carte 74, ff. 302+; *CSPClar.*, v. 828 (Index)
2 Underdown (*see* Baron, H., n. 1), pp. 310–11
3 *Naval Minutes*, p. 315; *Priv. Corr.*, esp. vol. i, pp. xii, xlii

Hatton, T. 1 HP: *CSPClar.*, loc. cit.

Hatton Gdn 1 Hatton, vol. i, sect. i; GLRO, MR/TH/2, m. 21

Hawkyns 1 Foster

Hawles 1 ib.; S. L. Ollard, *Fasti Wyndesonienses* (Windsor 1950), p. 121; R. S. Bosher (*see* Cade, T., n. 1), p. 287

Hawley 1 J. Thurloe, *State Papers* (ed. Birch, 1742), vii. 9, 360

Hayes, J. 1 *CSPD 1660–85*, p. 260; *Add. 1660–70*, p. 186

Hayes, W. 1 Taylor, p. 239

Hayls 1 Inf. from Sir O. Millar
2 GLRO, MR/TH/2, m. 8d; WRO, F398
3 GLRO, Reg. St Martin's
4 PRO, PCC Prob 6/55, f. 12v

Hayter 1 NWB, p. 122
2 *CSPD 1659–60*, p. 302; Collinge; Sainty

Hayward, C. 1 D. H. Boalch, *Makers of the harpsichord etc. 1440–1840* (Oxf. 1974), pp. 65–7

Hayward, E. 1 *CSPD 1651–2*, p. 511; *1655*, p. 349; *1658–9*, p. 228; *1660–1*, pp. 318, 404

Hayward, J. 1 S. R. Gardiner and C. T. Atkinson (eds), *First Dutch War* (NRS 1898–1912), i. 65; Sandwich, p. xviii; *Cat.*, i

Haywood 1 viii. 92; HMC, *Rep.*, 8/1/280a; *CSPD* e.g. *1662–3*, p. 396

Hazard 1 *Harl. Soc. Reg.* vol. 10 passim; GL, MS. 4374/1; GLRO, WJS/SBB/170, p. 45; WRO, E 292

Health 1 I acknowledge with gratitude the advice and information given to me by Dr C. E. Newman in the composition of this article. He is not however to be held responsible for any errors, either of commission or omission, in it.
2 Rawl. A 184, ff. 206–13; printed Bryant, ii. 405–13
3 Bryant, ii. 410–11
4 See BL, Sloane MSS 1536, ff. 60r, 63v: a copy of the prescription given for treatment after the operation. The date of the operation is there given as 28 March, but Pepys always celebrated the anniversary of the event on the 26th. cf. i. 97
5 cf. Lord Taylor in *St James's Hosp. Gazette*, 33/248
6 Josselin (*see* Gunpowder Plot, n. 3) pp. 516, 567
7 Evelyn, iii. 529; *D*, v. 247, 255
8 iii. 247; vi. 5
9 viii. 187
10 See esp. Bryant, ii. 409–10
11 ii. 154
12 Sir D'Arcy Power in *Occ. Papers*, i. 64
13 F. H. Garrison and L. T. Morton, *Medical Bibliog.* (1970), p. 681
14 ix. 565, n. 1
15 *Priv. Corr.*, i. 227 ~ For these illnesses from 1686, see *Family Letters*, p. 205; *Priv. Corr.*, ii. 382 (Index)
16 *Priv. Corr.*, i. 306–7
17 ib., ii. 312–14
18 Bodl., Ballard MSS, i. 122; printed *Priv. Corr.*, ii. 311–12. The doctors who performed the post-mortem were Hans Sloane, John Shadwell and Charles Bernard.

Heath 1 HP; BL, Add. MSS 9317, f. 1r; *Harl. Soc. Reg.*, 46/277

Hebdon 1 Boyd 15749; Thurloe (*see* Hawley, n. 1), vii. 328; *CSPClar.*, v. 52; *CSPD 1661–2*, p. 271; *1667*,

p. 65; PRO, Adm 20/5, p. 439; Rawl. A 178, ff. 193–5

Heemskerck 1 ix. 171, n. 2; *Cat.*, i; PRO, Adm 20/7/1, no. 2886; R. Ollard, *Man of war* (1969), pp. 148–9

Hely 1 cf. GL, Mormon Index of Christenings etc. [London; Westminster]; *Surrey Wills* (Surrey Rec. Soc., vol. iv, 1920), p. 187 [Southwark]

Hempson 1 *CSPD 1661–2*, p. 446; *1670*, p. 107

Henrietta 1 Feiling (*see* Bennet, H., n. 1), p. 55

2 *DNB*; C. H. Hartmann (ed.), *The King my brother* (1954)

Herbert, P. 1 ix. 150–1 ∼ GEC; *DNB*

Herbert, Capt. 1 *Cat.*, i; *DNB*

Hermitage 1 R. Davis (*see* Dutch Wars, n. 7), p. 206

Herring, J. 1 *Calamy Rev.*

Herring, M. 1 Heal (*see* Atkinson, n. 1), p. 173; Firth and Rait, i. 315, 701, 914

Herringman 1 Arber qu. Plomer, i ∼ Donald F. McKenzie, *Masters etc. of Stationers' Co. 1605–1800* (Wellington, N.Z. 1974)

Hervey 1 HP; Collinge; Sir J. Gage, *Hist. Suff.* (Thingor Hundred) (1838), pp. 286+

Hesilrige 1 *DNB*

2 HP; *DNB*

Hetley 1 Carte 73, f. 469

2 VCH, *Hunts.*, ii. 27, 93, 94, 160; iii. 16; *Letters*, p. 2

Hewer, T. 1 PRO, Adm 20/1, no. 879 etc.

2 Boyd 22085; GL, MS. 72/10; PRO, Adm 20/9, nos 45, 197; *Priv. Corr.*, i. 31; *Occ. Papers*, ii. 72; PL (unoff.), Misc. MSS 26

Hewer, W. 1 Ehrman, p. 206

2 Harvard, Houghton Lib., MS.Eng 991.1

3 BL, Harl. MSS 7170, ff. 42–8, 72–84

4 HP; inf. from Prof. R. Walcott; Pool (*see* Bagwell, n. 3), pp. 14–16

5 *Occ. Papers*, ii. 58+; LCC, *Survey*, 18 pt ii/69–74; PL (unoff.), Freshfield MSS, Misc. Receipts 1686–1703; Bryant, iii. 225–6, 228–9

6 Plan in Bodl., MS. Aubrey 4, f. 32*v*

7 Evelyn, 23 Sept. 1700

8 *Occ. Papers*, ii. 68+; Manning and Bray (*see* Harvey, n. 1), iii. 363; PL (unoff.), Jackson MSS 20 (3); inf. from E. E. F. Smith

9 PL (unoff.), Misc. MSS 26

10 BL, SC 378 (2), 557 (3)

11 Whitear, pp. 139+

12 Jackson MSS 20 (3) (4) ∼ HP; Collinge. Drawing of Kneller portrait in PL 2979/127f

12 Jackson MSS 20 (3) (4) ∼ HP; Collinge. Drawing of Kneller portrait in PL 2979/127f

Hewet 1 Collinge. In the official records his name is spelt Howet.

Hewitt 1 *CSPD Add. 1660–85*, pp. 103–4

Hickes, B. 1 GEC; GLRO, MR/TH/3, m. 4

Hickes, W. 1 *DNB*; GEC

Hickman, H. 1 i. 227, n. 1

2 Wood, *Ath. Oxon.*, iv. 369 ∼ *DNB*; Foster

Hickman, W. 1 HP

Highgate 1 GLRO, MR/TH/2, mm. 29–31

Hill, G. 1 GLRO, MR/TH/7; Grove (6th ed.)

Hill, J. (mcht) 1 Rawl. A 174, f. 44r

Hill, J. (agent) 1 ib., f. 171r

Hill, Jos. 1 Magd. Coll., Reg., 21 Oct. 1653 (ptd HMC, *Rep.*, 5/482)

2 P. Fraser, *Intelligence of Secretaries of State* (Camb. 1956), p. 164

3 *DNB*; Venn; Magd. Coll., Reg., i. 108b; ii. 26, 60a, 63b, 70; William Steven, *Hist. Scottish church Rotterdam* (1832), pp. 319, 325

4 *Priv. Corr.*, i. 142, 145; Rawl. A
178, f. 88r; A 183, f. 245r; A 185,
f. 398r; A 189, f. 23r; *Naval
Minutes*, p. 424; cf. PL 2643, pp.
i, 85+

Hill, R. 1 Lafontaine; Rimbault, p. 13

Hill, T. 1 Rawl. A 193, f. 214r

2 *Letters*, pp. 41–2, 49 (also *Home
Counties Mag.*, 6/121+); Houblon
(*see* Barr, n. 1), passim; PRO, PCC
Bence 50

Hill, W. 1 *CSPD 1652–3*, p. 191;
Sandwich, p. 111; *Cat.*, i; Longleat, Coventry MSS 99, f. 91v

Hill, ——. (i) 1 WRO, E 176; inf.
from H. M. Nixon

Hill, ——. (ii) 1 *Bull. IHR*, 19/18;
Westminster Abbey Muniments,
Reg. St Margaret's (ref. from
H. M. Nixon); WRO, E 1613

Hinchingbrooke 1 qu. N. Pevsner,
Buildings of Engl.; Beds., Hunts. etc.,
(1968), p. 264 ~ VCH, *Hunts.*,
ii. 135+ (views facing p. 138);
Harris, ch. i; Earl of Sandwich,
Hinchingbrooke (priv. ptd 1910)

Hingston 1 PRO, LC 134, p. 364.
Pulver conflates him with an
earlier John Hingston.

2 Pulver; Lafontaine

Hinton 1 Heal (*see* Atkinson, n. 1), p.
175; Sir Henry Ellis (ed.), *Orig.
Letters* (1846), ser. 3, iv. 297, 310;
BL, Add. MSS 5099 (15); Munk

Hoare, J. 1 Craig (*see* Freeman, n. 1),
pp. 154–5; [H. P. R. Hoare],
Hoare's Bank (priv. ptd 1932), p. 4;
Priv. Corr., i. 167

Hoare, R. 1 Evelyn, ii. 559 & n. 2;
PL 2983, p. 250

Hoare, W. 1 Venn; Munk; WRO,
E 172; PRO, PCC Mico 23

Hodges, T. 1 v. 178, n. 5; Foster;
PRO, PCC Eure 121

Hodges, ——. 1 PRO, E 179/252/32,
St Giles p. 14 (R)

Hogg 1 BL, Add. MSS 9311, f. 109r;
Rawl. A 174, f. 3r

Holborn 1 Hatton, vol. i, sect. i

Holborn Conduit 1 Strype, i. 25;
iii. 283; H. A. Harben, *Dict.
London* (1918); S. Sorbière, *Voyage
to Engl.* (trans. 1709), p. 15

Holcroft 1 Whitear, pp. 21, 146,
148; *Priv. Corr.*, ii. 315

Holden 1 PRO, E 179/252/32, St
Bride's, p. 8 (R); Boyd 23400; inf.
from Lord Hylton

Holder 1 PRO, A 03/1; Mapperton,
Sandwich MSS, Letters from
Ministers, ii, f. 146; Duke of York,
Mem. (naval), p. 96; HMC, *Rep.*,
8/1/2/281

Holinshed 1 *Family Letters*, pp. 170,
194

Holland, G. 1 *Cat.*, i; C. Welch,
Hist. Cutlers' Co. (1906–23), ii. 40

Holland, P. 1 *Cat.*, i; *CSPD 1652–3*,
p. 316; Sandwich, p. xviii; PRO,
Adm 20/7, pt ii. 690; *Naval
Minutes*, pp. 20, 26–7, 342, 345;
CSPD 1671–2, p. 390; *1672*, p.
390

Holles, D. 1 *DNB*; life by P. Craw-
ford (1979)

Holles, F. 1 HP; *Cat.*, i; Longleat,
Coventry MSS 99, f. 91v; HMC,
Buccleuch, i. 540+. Engraved
portrait in PL 2979/238

Hollier 1 *Family Letters*, p. 54

2 G. C. R. Morris in *Annals R. Coll.
Surgeons*, 61/224+; Boyd 14177;
CSPD 1652–3, p. 259; F. G.
Parsons, *Hist. St Thomas's* (1932–
6), ii. 53 etc.

Hollins 1 Venn; Magd. Coll., Reg.,
ii. 66a, 67a, 70a, 73a, 107a

Hollond 1 iii. 145, n. 1; *Two Discourses* (ed. Tanner, NRS 1896).
Tanner's statement (p. xxix) that
he was Carteret's clerk in 1660 is
perhaps based on a misreading of
the reference at i. 306.

Hollworthy 1 PRO, E 179/252/32
(18), f. 23v (R); Boyd 10684

Holmes, J. 1 HP

Holmes, R. 1 *Letters*, pp. 75, 215
2 PL 2698 ~ HP; life by R. Ollard (*Man of war*, 1969)
Holt 1 PL 2873, p. 487; *CSPD 1659–60*, p. 532 etc.
Homewood 1 BL, Add. 9308, f. 124r; *CSPD Add. 1660–85*, p. 235; *Further Corr.*, pp. 285, 291; Bryant, iii. 228
Honywood 1 Josselin (*see* Gunpowder Plot, n. 3), esp. pp. 151, 181
2 PL 1434 (7) ~ *DNB*; GEC; PRO, PCC Mico 129; ib. North 163
3 Everitt (*see* Blount, n. 1), p. 147
4 *DNB*; Venn; J. H. Srawley, *M. Honywood* (Linc. Minster Pamph. no. 5, 1950); PRO, PCC North 130
5 *CSPD 1662–3*, p. 344; *1664–5*, p. 520; R. East, *Extracts from records of Portsmouth* (Portsmouth 1891), p. 66; PRO, PCC Cann 6; Underdown (*see* Baron, H., n. 1), e.g. pp. 186–8
6 Venn; PRO, PCC Cann 151
7 Venn; PRO, PCC Juxon 131
Hooke, R. 1 *Diary* (*see* Carkesse, n. 2), p. 105
2 PL 2116
3 *See above*, n. 1. ~ *DNB*; Andrade in *Notes and records Roy. Soc.* (1960), pp. 137+; Colvin (*see* Denham, n. 2); life by M.P. 'Espinasse (1956)
Hooke, T. 1 Venn
Hooker 1 Woodhead; PRO, E 179/252/32, London 2 (R)
Hooper 1 Pulver; Jocelyn Perkins, *Organ and bells of Westminster Abbey* (1937), pp. 12–14
Horneck 1 viii. 580, n. 1; Evelyn, iv. 306 & n. 4; *DNB*
Horse Guards 1 Wheatley and Cunningham; Colvin, v. 433
Hosier 1 Duke of York, *Mem.* (naval), pp. 121–2; *Further Corr.*, p. 69; Collinge
Houblon 1 Lady A. Archer Houblon, *Houblon Family* (1907), i. 95–6, 166

2 Evelyn, iv. 162
3 PL 2979/127c ~ HP; Woodhead; Lady Houblon, op. cit., ch. xiv; *Priv. Corr.*, esp. i. 36, ii. 105
4 *Letters*, p. 112; Bryant, ii. 314, 327, 346, 360
5 Houblon, op. cit., passim
Household etc. 1 Pepys's clerks living in the household and occasionally running errands etc. are not included here.
2 viii. 82
3 Grey, vii. 310; *Letters*, p. 91
4 Tanner, p. 245
5 *Letters*, p. 272–3; Bryant, iii. 226n.; PL (unoff.), Jackson MSS 22, pp. 40, 45
6 *Priv. Corr.*, ii. 313
7 G. King, *Natural and political observations upon the state and condition of Engl.* (1696); G. S. Holmes in *TRHS*, (ser. 5), 27/41+
8 iii. 53; iv. 86; v. 158
9 Tanner, p. 272
10 ix. 236, 224
11 *Pepysiana*, p. 253. cf. above, Edwards, n. 3
12 *Pepysiana*, p. 52
13 vi. 238, n. 3
14 vii. 24
15 A testimonial given by Pepys to his coachman survives in Rawl. A 183, f. 173.
16 iv. 282
17 ii. 196
18 J. J. Hecht, *Dom. servant class in 18th-cent. Engl.* (1956), pp. 29–30
19 i. 233
20 ii. 196
21 iv. 438
22 cf. P. Earle, *World of Defoe* (1976), p. 175
23 F. O. Skyllon, *Black people in Britain 1555–1833* (1974), esp. pp. 10, 13, 15
24 Tanner, p. 245; Bryant, iii. 270 (cf. PL 2861, pp. 408–9)
25 PRO, PCC Carr 144

26 Further reading: Hecht, op. cit.; D. Marshall in *Economica*, ix; D. M. Stuart, *Engl. Abigail* (1946)

Howard, B. 1 GEC; Gerald Brenan and E. P. Statham, *House of Howards* (1907), p. 612

Howard, C. 1 GEC; HP; Burnet, ii. 277. Engraved portrait in PL 2576: [J. Guillim], *Display of heraldry: Analogia Honorum*, 1679, facing p. 10

Howard, D. 1 Evelyn, iii. 345, n. 4, 529, n. 6

Howard, Eliz. 1 ib., iii. 345, n. 4; iv. 88, n. 6

Howard, Lady Essex 1 GEC

Howard, H. 1 GEC; Bryant, ii. 87, 105-7

Howard, J. 1 GEC; W. Addison, *Audley End* (1953)

Howard, P. 1 HP; HMC, *Rutland*, ii. 51; Bryant, ii. 227, 229

Howard, Card. P. 1 *DNB*; Brenan, op. cit., pp. 592+. Engraved portrait in PL 2980/25c

Howard, R. 1 *Further Corr.*, p. 341

2 PL 2070, 1604 (11), 877 ∼ *DNB*; HP; life by H. J. Oliver (Durham N.C. 1963). Engraved portrait in PL 2980/206a

Howard, T. (Berkshire) 1 qu. GEC

Howard, T. 1 ib.

Howe 1 *Letters*, pp. 96-7

2 Sandwich, p. 4; *CSPD 1664-5*, p. 443; Mapperton, Sandwich MSS, Letters from Ministers, ii, f. 56*v*; Bryant, iii. 232; *CSP Am. and W. Indies 1681-5*, p. 778; R. Ollard, *Pepys* (1974), p. 263; *Letters*, pp. 114-15

Howell, R. 1 PRO, Adm 2/1732, f. 16*v*; NWB, p. 50; Chester-Foster 678

Howell, W. 1 Magd. Coll., Reg., ii. 64a, 65b. There is no evidence there of his being in residence after 1656.

2 *DNB*; Venn; Gibbon, *Autobiog.*

(Everyman ed., 1923), p. 35; PL 2727-9

Howlett, L. 1 Whitear, pp. 14, 35, 143

Howlett, ——. 1 WRO, E 1621, p. 21

Hoxton 1 GLRO, MR/TH/4, mm. 5-11d

Hubbard 1 *CSPD 1668-9*, p. 603 ∼ *Cat.*, i; Longleat, Coventry MSS 99, f. 91*v*

Hudson, J. 1 PRO, E 179/252/32, St Olave's, f. 27*r* (R)

Hudson, M. 1 PRO, Adm 2/1725, f. 19*r*; Venn

Hudson, N. 1 PRO, PCC Hyde 27; GL, MS. 872/7

Hudson, ——. 1 GLRO, MR/TH/7, m.2

Hughes, P. 1 Van Lennep, pp. 238, 256; Wilson, pp. 149-51

Hughes, W. 1 PRO, Adm 2/1725, f. 11*r*

Hughes, ——. 1 Orlo C. Williams, *Clerical organization of H. of Commons* (Oxf. 1954), p. 32

Humfrey 1 The note at iv. 394 conflates two separate settings of the same text. What Pepys heard was *Musica Britannica*, 34/item 4a.

2 PRO, LC 9/258 ∼ P. Dennison (ed.), *P. Humfrey: complete church music* (*Musica Britannica*, 34/item 35)

Hunt, J. and E. 1 GLRO, MR/TH/7, m. 1d; *CTB*, i. 175

Hunt, ——. 1 PRO, E 179/252/32, Mr Izod's acct (R)

Hutchinson 1 *Naval Minutes*, p. 252 ∼ Aylmer, pp. 247-50; *CSPD 1668-9*, pp. 351, 605

Hyde, E. 1 *DNB*. cf. *Naval Minutes*, p. 116. Lives by T. H. Lister (1837-8) and H. Craik (1911). Engraved portraits in PL 2980/162, 163b

Hyde, H. 1 *DNB*; *Priv. Corr.*, ii. 317 etc.

Hyde, L. 1 *DNB*

Hyde, R. 1 *DNB*

Hyde Pk 1 i. 121, n. 1; iv. 95, n. 3; Evelyn, iii. 82, n. 6; Z. C. von Uffenbach, *London in 1710* (ed. Quarrell and Mare, 1934), p. 15; John Ashton, *Hyde Park* (1896)

Ibbot 1 Venn; *CSPD 1656–7*, pp. 512, 514; PRO, Adm 2/1745, f. 44v; Mapperton, Sandwich MSS, Journal, vi. 252

Impington 1 BL, Add. MSS 5805: printed Walter C. Pepys, *Genealogy of Pepys family* (1952 ed.), pp. 37–8 ∼ N. Pevsner, *Buildings of Engl.: Cambs.* (1950); PRO, E 179/244/22, p. 136; *Country Life*, 7 Feb. 1963 (illust.)

Ingoldsby 1 *DNB*; HP

Ingram, A. 1 Woodhead; *Merc. Pub.*, 6 Dec. 1660; Kenneth G. Davies, *R. African Company* (1957), p. 159 n.; PRO, PCC North 130

Ingram, T. 1 Carlisle (*see* Baber, n. 1), p. 170; *Merc. Pub.*, loc. cit.; PRO, LC 3/73, p. 12; *CSPD 1663–4*, p. 644; *Acts P.C. Col.*, v. 631; PRO, PCC Eure 16

Ingram, Mrs 1 *Harl. Soc. Reg.*, 46/68, 76, 208; PRO, PCC North 130

Ireton 1 *Gray's Inn Reg.*

Ironmongers' Hall 1 Wheatley and Cunningham; Evelyn, 21 Sept. 1671

Isham 1 *CSPD 1660–1*, p. 31
2 ib. *1657–8*, p. 139
3 ib. *1660–1*, p. 449; *1663–4*, p. 475; *1665–6*, p. 470 ∼ *Geneal. Mag.*, 13/70+; BL, Add. MSS 34015; Harris, i. 18; *CTB*, ii. 411, 421; inf. from the late Sir G. Isham

Islington 1 GLRO, MR/TH/1, mm. 29d–32d

Ivy Lane 1 LCC, *Survey*, 18/84, 120–4; Somerville (*see* Cary Ho., n. 1) p. 222

Jackson 1 Chappell, p. 57. There was a Jackson who was one of Robert Pepys's tenants: ii. 148

2 PL (unoff.), Jackson MSS 1
3 *Family Letters*, p. 160
4 ib., pp. 36–7, 41–7, 159, 161, 163, 170, 171, 182, 192, 202; Chappell, pp. 56, 57
5 qu. Bryant, iii. 101
6 *Family Letters*, esp. p. 196; *Priv. Corr.*, ii. 200; Bryant, iii. 101; *Pepysiana*, pp. 259–60
7 Hunts. Rec. Off., Hunts. Archdeaconry marriage bonds etc. (inf. from Miss Bowie)
8 Venn; Foster; *Family Letters*, esp. p. 196; *Priv. Corr.*, passim; *Occ. Papers*, ii. 65; inf. from E. E. F. Smith
9 PRO, PCC Prob. 6/99, f. 42v

Jackson, ——. 1 Woodhead

Jacombe 1 qu. *DNB*; *Calamy Rev.*

Jaggard 1 qu. Woodhead ∼ Boyd 38382; *Cat.*, i. 165; ii. 138; PRO, PCC Box 42; Whitear, pp. 82–3

James, D. of York 1 Frontis. to his Catalogue, vol. 1. In the library itself there are 13 engraved portraits of James.
2 Tanner, p. 234
3 Bryant, ii. 380
4 ib., iii. 222
5 ib., iii. 311–13 & nn; *Naval Minutes*, p. 272 n.
6 PL 2862, pp. 435–6
7 PL (unoff.), Jackson MSS 22, no. 13 (poll-tax 1692)
8 *Naval Minutes*, pp. 217, 321
9 PL 2295/95
10 Sotheby, *Cat.* 11 Apr. 1919, lots 941, 935
11 HMC, *Bath*, iii. 256, 261 ∼ Further reading: lives by F. C. Turner (1948); J. Miller (1978)

James, ——. 1 vii. 36
2 iv. 163–4; v. 266

Jefferies 1 Chappell, pp. 38, 51; Whitear, p. 131

Jefferys 1 *CSPD 1653–4*, p. 546; Gardiner (*see* Hayward, J., n. 1) v. 17; vi. 236; *Cat.*, i

Jegon 1 *Surrey Q. Sessions Rec. 1663–6* (ed. H. Jenkinson and D. L. Powell, Surrey Rec. Soc., 1934–8), pp. 28, 155; BL, Add. MSS 14286, f. 26*v*

Jenifer 1 *Cat.*, i; *Further Corr.*, p. 298; PL 2894

Jenkins 1 GLRO, WJS/SBB/173a, pp. 57–8; WRO, E 172

Jennens 1 *DNB*; *Further Corr.*, p. 37; *Naval Minutes*, p. 35

Jermyn (St Albans) 1 Gramont, p. 99; GEC; Bittner u. Gross (*see* Barckmann, n. 1)

Jermyn (Dover) 1 Gramont, pp. 100, 111 etc.; GEC; HMC, *Rep.*, 8/1/2/278

Jervas 1 WRO, E 176; E 1608, p. 46; E 1609; Burke (*see* Beale, F., n. 1), p. 370; PRO, KB 9/890
  2 WRO, E 1608

Jessop 1 Aylmer, pp. 234–8; inf. from Sir R. Somerville

Johnson 1 Coleman in *Econ. Hist. Rev.* (ser. 2), 6/137n
  2 p. 163
  3 *Further Corr.*, p. 337

Jolliffe, G. 1 *Brit. Journ. Surgery*, 18/544+ (repr. *Occ. Papers*, i. 60+); BL, Sloane MSS 1536, f. 63*r*

Jolliffe, J. 1 Woodhead; *Merc. Pub.*, 6 Dec. 1660; Mapperton, Sandwich MSS, Letters from Ministers, ii. 108; Journal, iii. 875

Jones, A. 1 *Harl. Soc. Reg.*, 46/217

Jones, P. 1 *DNB*

Jordan 1 *Cat.*, i; *DNB*. Engraved portrait in PL 2979/233

Jowles, H. 1 Chester-Foster 779

Jowles, V. 1 *CSPD 1659–60*, p. 481, 542 ~ ib., *1657–8*, p. 457; *Cat.*, i

Joyce 1 Boyd 27867; Whitear, pp. 119–20
  2 BL, Add. MSS 5065 (11); PRO, E 179/147/627, p. 69 (R); ib. 252/32, St Martin's, f. 30*v* (R); WRO, E 1621, p. 64; Jones (*see* Fire, n. 3), i. 98

Jegon 3 vii. 286; Boyne, i. 633; PRO, PCC Herne 14 (ptd Whitear, p. 23)

Keene 1 *Harl. Soc. Reg.*, 46/181

Kelsey 1 *Cat.*, i

Kelyng 1 Clarendon qu. E. Foss, *Judges of Engl.* (1848–64), vii. 138
  2 qu. HMC, *Rep.*, 6/App. p. 370 ~ *DNB*

Kembe 1 WRO, E 172

Kempthorne 1 *DNB*; *Cat*, i; *Further Corr.*, pp. 344–5 etc.

Kensington 1 Lillywhite 14411; GLRO, MR/TH/3, mm. 3–5

Kent St 1 Meekings (*see* Arthur, n. 1), p. xc

Killigrew, H. 1 *DNB*; HMC, *Rep.*, 8/1/2/278b

Killigrew, H. ('Young') 1 John H. Wilson, *Court Wits* (Durham, N.C. 1963), esp. pp. 211–12; Charles II to Madame, 17 Oct. 1667 in C. H. Hartmann, *The King my brother* (1954), p. 202

Killigrew, P. 1 GEC; *Bull. IHR*, 19/15

Killigrew, T. 1 *DNB*; Wilson, op. cit.; PL 2157

Killigrew, W. 1 *DNB*; HP

Kinaston 1 *CSPD 1667–8*, pp. 570, 582; Boyd 29237

King E. 1 PRO, Adm 106/2, f. 31; Firth and Davies, pp. 262–3, 276, 543

King, T. 1 v. 294, n. 1; HP

King, W. (clerk) 1 *CSPD* e.g. *1654*, p. 513

King, W. 1 *DNB*

King, W. (vicar) 1 *Calamy Rev.*; Meekings (*see* Arthur, n. 1), p. 91

Kingdon 1 *CTB*, i. 728; *CSPD 1651–2*, p. 267; *1655–6*, pp. 220, 224; *1659–60*, p. 251; *1662* and *1663*, passim; *1665–6*, pp. 55, 83; *Merc. Pub.*, 4 Oct. 1660; F. B. Kingdon, *The Kingdon family* (priv. ptd, n.d.)

Kinnersley 1 PRO, E 403/1756, Aug. 1656; ib. 1760, f. 29*v*

Kinward 1 Colvin, v, esp. p. 472

Kipps 1 *CTB*, i. 183; *CSPD 1666–7*, p. 598

Kirby 1 *CSPD 1653–4*, p. 551; *Cat.*, i. 374–5

Kirton 1 Plomer, i; PRO, E 179/252/ 32 (5) (R)
2 Donald F. McKenzie, *Stationers' Co. apprentices 1641–1700* (Oxf. 1974), p. 94

Kite 1 Whitear, esp. pp. 33+

Knapp 1 Bodl., Tanner 306, f. 431 (qu. Venn)

Knepp 1 Van Lennep, p. 238; Lib. Soc. Geneal., P. Boyd, Index to Marriages 1538–1837 (Mdx); Wilson, pp. 154–6

Knight, J. 1 *Merc. Pub.*, 5 July 1660; *Bull. IHR*, 19/20; Sidney M. Young, Hist. Barber-Surgeons (1890), p. 9; *Pepysiana*, p. 286

Knight, Sir J. 1 ix. 235, n. 2; *Trans. Bristol and Glouc. Arch. Soc.*, 68/ 129; *N. & Q.*, 29 Apr. 1899

Knightley, Rich. 1 Foster

Knightley, Rob. 1 Woodhead; *Naval Minutes*, p. 117

Kynaston 1 Van Lennep, pp. 5, 440, 502; McAfee, p. 225

Lacy 1 Van Lennep, pp. cxliv–cxlv, 299; McAfee, p. 226

Lamb 1 *DNB*

Lambert, D. 1 *Cat.*, i; *CSPD Add. 1660–85*, pp. 113–14

Lambert, James 1 *Cat.*, i; *CSPD 1653–4*, p. 565

Lambert, John 1 *Tangier Papers*, p. 7
2 *DNB*; life by W. H. Dawson (1942). Engraved portrait in PL 2979/269a

Lambeth 1 Engraved views in PL 2972/224 a, b, and c, 225

Langford 1 PRO, E 179/147/627, p. 195 (R); ib. 179/252/32, p. 8 (R); Rawl. A 182, f. 325r; GL, MS. 14819, f. 22v

Langley 1 *Bull. IHR*, 19/18

Language 1 Because of their number, notes giving references to the diary text are omitted.
2 *Leviathan* (ed. Oakeshott, Oxf., n.d.), pp. 18, 22
3 PL 2356
4 *Timber, or Discoveries* (ed. Gollancz, 1898), p. 100
5 *Prose Observations* (ed. de Quentin, Oxf. 1979), pp. 257–8
6 John Byng, *Torrington Diaries* (ed. Andrews, 1954), p. 156
7 *The diary of Ralph Thoresby* (ed. Hunter, 1830), ii. 9
8 Verney (*see* Drink, n. 19), i. 548
9 In 1614. Fourteen editions of the original (first pub. 1587) had appeared by 1644.
10 Anthony Powell, *John Aubrey and his friends* (1963), p. 179
11 'Epistle Dedicatory' to *Troilus and Cressida*, in Dryden, *Comedies, tragedies and operas* (1701), ii. 200
12 C. Bastide, *Anglo-French entente in 17th cent.* (1914), e.g. pp. 24, 149, 166
13 'Monumenta Britannica' (Bodl., MS. Topog. Gen. c. 24, 25), ii, f. 238v
14 *Essays* (ed. Ker, Oxf. 1900), i. 5
15 ib., i. 170
16 E. H. W. Meyerstein (ed.), *Adventures by sea of Edward Coxere* (Oxf. 1945), p. 23
17 Further reading: Margaret Williamson, *Colloquial language of the Commonwealth and Restoration* (Engl. Assoc., pamph. 73, 1929)

Lanier 1 Pulver; Lafontaine; John Wilson (ed.), *Roger North on music* (1959), pp. 265, 295; Mrs R. L. Poole in *Musical Antiquary*, 4 (1913), p. 148 and pl. Engraved portrait in PL 2980/213a

Lanyon 1 PRO, Adm 106/3520, f. 3v; Rawl. A 193, ff. 204–18

Lashmore 1 PRO, Adm 20/4, no. 1728; *CSPD 1664–5*, p. 20

Lawes 1 W. McC. Evans, *H. Lawes*

(N.Y. 1941); P. J. Willets, *The H. Lawes Manuscript* (1969). Engraved portrait in PL 2980/216a

Lawrence 1 Woodhead

Lawson 1 PRO, PCC Hyde 98 ~ *DNB*; *Cat.*, i; *CSPD 1664–5*, pp. 488–9, 502; *CTB*, i. 694. Engraved portrait in PL 2979/231b

Laxton 1 Barrett (*see* Chase, n. 1), pp. 71, 76

Lea 1 PRO, SP 25 I 108, no. 45; HMC, *Ormonde* (n.s.), iii. 393

Le Brun 1 *Harl. Soc. Reg.*, 46/62, 270 etc.

Lee 1 HP; Sainty; Burnet, ii. 92

Leeson 1 Young (*see* Conny, n. 1), p. 10

Legge 1 Tomlinson, pp. 16–17, 100, 223, 226n.; *Tangier Papers*, esp. xliv–xlv; *DNB*; GEC

Leighton 1 *Examen* (1740), p. 488
2 *DNB*; Bryant, ii. 206, 272

Lely 1 BL, Add. MSS 34014, f. 23*v*; PRO, E 179/252/32, f. 42*r*; WRO, F 398
2 Harvard, Houghton Lib., b MS. Eng 991 (MS. list, 1824)
3 Listed in R. Latham (ed.), *Cat. of Pepys Library*, vol. iii, pt i (comp. A. W. Aspital, Woodbridge 1978) ~ R. B. Beckett, *Lely* (1951). Engravings of self-portrait in PL 2980/259 a, b

Le Neve 1 *Cat.*, i. 378; Wheatley, 23 Nov. 1666, n.

Lenthall 1 *DNB*
2 ib.; *Surrey Q. Sessions, Order Book 1661–3* (ed. H. Jenkinson and D. L. Powell, Surrey Rec. Soc., 1935), passim
3 HP; Wood, *Ath. Oxon.*, iii. 902

Leonard 1 PRO, SP 25 I 108, p. 74

Le Squire 1 HMC, *Rep.*, 7/41; J. L. Chester, *Reg. Westminster Abbey* (1876), p. 151

L'Estrange 1 PL 2450–1, 2249 (17) ~ *DNB*; *CSPD 1663–4*, pp. 240, 260; life by G. Kitchin (1913)

Lethieullier 1 Woodhead

Lever 1 NWB, pp. 55, 56; PRO, Adm 20/6, p. 158

Levitt 1 PRO, E 179/147/617, p. 138 (R); Frank T. Phillips, *Hist. Co. Cooks* (1932), p. 89; W. J. Harrison, *Life in Clare Hall 1658–1713* (Camb. 1958), p. 27

Lewin 1 Dalton, i. 121, 244

Lewis, J. 1 Woodhead; *Merc. Pub.*, 6 Dec. 1660; Rawl. A 478, f. 78*r*

Lewis, T. (mcht) 1 Woodhead; PRO, PCC Bath 97

Lewis, T. (clerk) 1 *CSPD 1659–60*, p. 13; PL 2873, p. 486; Collinge; *Cat.*, ii. 175

Lewis, ——. 1 (Anon.), 'Records of the Cooks' Company 1678–1705', p. 23 (typescript in Inst. Hist. Research, Univ. London)

Ley 1 GEC; *Merc. Pub.*, 6 Dec. 1660, pp. 781–3; Rawl. A 478, f. 78*r*

Lidcott 1 i. 45, n. 3; Thurloe (*see* Hawley, n. 1), vol. i, p. xix; *CJ*, vii. 742

Liddell 1 GEC; *CSPD 1661–2*, p. 509; *1663–4*, pp. 129, 227, 495

Lilly 1 *DNB*; *Life* (autobiog., first pub. 1715; ed. K. M. Briggs 1974). Engraved portrait in PL 2980/288a

Limehouse 1 GLRO, MR/TH/4, mm. 101d–111d

Lincoln's Inn Flds 1 v. 43

Lisle 1 Young (*see* Conny, n. 1), pp. 9, 19

Littleton, J. 1 *CSPD 1668–9*, p. 642; *1671*, p. 63; *CTB*, iii. 285, 1224

Littleton, T. 1 *Naval Minutes*, p. 257
2 GEC; Sainty; *Cat.*, i; *Priv. Corr.*, ii. 316

Llewellyn 1 PRO, PCC Carr 94 ~ iv. 295, n. 2; *CSPD 1659–60*, p. 350; *1660–1*, p. 21; *CSP Ireland 1660–5*, p. 627; Wheatley, 20 Nov. 1665, n.

Lloyd, G. 1 *DNB*; *Naval Minutes*, p. 29

Lloyd, P. 1 Baxter, pp. 220–5

Lloyd, R. 1 HP

Lloyd, T. 1 *CSPD 1665–6*, p. 437; *1666–7*, p. 583 etc.

Lock 1 Aylmer, pp. 262–3; BL, Add. MSS 38848, f. 18r

Locke, M. (musician) 1 Rosamund E. M. Harding, *Thematic cat. of works* (Oxf. 1971); *Musica Britannica*, 31, 32, 38 (1971–6)

London Br. 1 PL 2972/246b–247b. cf. *D*, v, illust. facing p. 307. See also Wheatley and Cunningham; Charles Singer et al. (eds), *Hist. Technology* (Oxf. 1954–8), iii. 420–1

Long, R. 1 Baxter, pp. 126–7, 135–6, 168; PRO, E 179/143/404 (R)

Long, ——. 1 Venn

Long Acre 1 Hatton, vol. i, sect. i

Long Lane 1 ib.

Longrack 1 PRO, Adm 20/7, pt ii, p. 699, no. 391

Loud 1 Mapperton, Sandwich MSS, App. f. 83; Harris, ii. 286; *Naval Minutes*, p. 39

Love 1 HP; Woodhead

Lovelace 1 iii. 285, n. 1; *DNB*

Lovell 1 Venn

Lower 1 North (ed. Jessop), ii. 331
2 *Priv. Corr.*, i. 32, 123 ~ *DNB*; Wood, *Ath. Oxon.*, iv. 297

Lowther 1 HP; Sainty

Loxton 1 Lafontaine, p. 383

Lucy (mcht) 1 Woodhead; PRO, E 179/252/32 (2) (R); *CTB*, iii. 774

Lucy (soldier) 1 A. Fairfax-Lucy, *Charlecote* (1958), p. 163; Dalton, i. 262

Ludgate 1 Wheatley and Cunningham

Luffe 1 Hunts. Rec. Off., Wills (Lincoln, Buckden Peculiar); *Trans. Cambs. and Hunts. Antiq. Soc.*, 5/316

Luke 1 *DNB*

Lurkin 1 WRO, F 4535

Lynes 1 Rawl. A 67, f. 361r

Mabbot 1 J. Frank, *Beginnings of Engl.*

newspapers 1620–60 (Camb. Mass. 1961), pp. 135+, 152+; J. B. Williams, *Hist. Engl. journalism* (1908), pp. 66+; *CSPD 1650*, p. 236

Mackworth 1 *CSPD 1656–7*, p. 313; Harris, i. 83

Madden 1 *CSPD 1664–5*, p. 87

Maddox 1 Collinge; Adm 20/1, no. 593; NWB, p. 185

Madge 1 Lafontaine; Hookes, *Amanda*, p. 58

Magdalene 1 N. Pevsner, *Buildings of Engl.: Cambs.* (1970), pp. 115+; R. Comm. Hist. Mon., *City of Camb.*, pt ii (1959), p. 139
2 W. T. Costello, *Curriculum at early 17th-cent. Cambridge* (Camb. Mass. 1958), S. E. Morison, *Harvard Coll. in 17th cent.* (Camb. Mass. 1936), esp. i. 74+; (D. Waterland), *Advice to a young student* (1730)
3 Magd. Coll., Reg., e.g. i. 108
4 T. Fuller, *Hist. Camb.*, (1840 ed.), p. 171. Numbers were then high: 35 matriculated in 1623: VCH, *Cambs.*, iii. 454
5 J. B. Mullinger, *Hist. Univ. Camb.* (Camb. 1873–1911), iii. 307–8; E. K. Purnell, *Magd. Coll.* (Camb. 1904), p. 109; Camb. Univ. Lib., Univ. Archives: graph by J. and J. A. Venn; Magd. Coll., Reg., i. 108
6 Calamy, qu. *DNB*
7 Magd. Coll., Reg., ii. 12b, 64b, 92b
8 Purnell, op. cit., pp. 117, 124; Magd. Coll., Reg., ii. 26
9 viii. 199
10 J. and J. A. Venn, op. cit.; VCH, *Cambs.*, iii. 454
11 *Letters*, pp. 115–16; Bryant, ii. 359
12 Hooke (*see* Carkesse, n. 2), p. 281; *Letters*, pp. 89–90, 110; HMC, *Rep.*, 5/483–4; R. Willis and J. W. Clark, *Archit. hist. Camb.* (Camb.

1886), ii. 366+; R. Comm. Hist. Mon., op. cit., ii. 139; Pevsner, op. cit.

Maitland 1 *DNB*; GEC. For *D*, v. 57, n. 1 see *Lauderdale Papers* (ed. O. Airy, Camden Soc., 1884–5), i. 191; Burnet, i. 263+; Clarendon, *Life*, i. 434+; HMC, *Ormonde* (n.s.) iii. 134; Thomas Brown, *Misc. Aulica* (1702), pp. 206+. Engraved portrait in PL 2979/52c

Mallard 1 Sherwood, pp. 136, 170; *Bull. IHR*, 19/16; PRO, LS 13/31, p. 37; Adm 20/7, pt i. 125

Man 1 LRO, Journal 41, f. 219; HMC, *Rep.*, 8/1/2/280b

Manley 1 HP; Howard Robinson, *Brit. Post Office* (Princeton 1948), pp. 40–1, 42; PL 2911, p. 17

Manning 1 W. H. and H. C. Overall, *Analytical index to Remembrancia 1579–1664* (1878), p. xii

Mansell 1 R. Ollard, *Escape of Charles II* (1966), pp. 112–14, 146–7; *CSPD 1659–60*, p. 206; *1661–2*, pp. 21, 286; *CTB*, i. 3; Carte 75, ff. 92, 94

2 Harris, i. 285

Marescoe 1 Boyd 14280; Beaven; NWB, p. 50; PRO, Adm 20/8, nos 3328, 3348; inf. from H. Roseveare

Margetts 1 *CSPD*, e.g. *Add. 1660–85*, p. 431

Markham 1 PRO, PCC Penn 130; *CSP Col. Am. and W. Indies 1681–5*, p. 207

Marlowe 1 Collinge

Marriott 1 Sherwood, pp. 131, 170; PRO, LC 3/73, p. 115

Marsh, A. 1 Pulver; Lafontaine; Rimbault

Marsh, G. 1 *CSPD 1666–7*, p. 565; Tomlinson, pp. 225+

Marsh, J. 1 *CSPD 1659–60*, pp. 47, 223, 360

Marsh, R. 1 Rawl. A 182, f. 302 ∼ Tomlinson, loc. cit.; G. W. Hill

and W. H. Frere, *Mem. Stepney parish* (Guildford 1890–1), esp. p. 238; *Journ. Friends' Hist. Soc.*, 3/147, 155; *CSPD 1663–4*, p. 101

Marsh, T. 1 Williams (*see* Hughes, —, n. 1), pp. 29, 281; *CSPD 1668–9*, p. 124; *Add. 1670*, p. 622; *CTB*, v. 1353

Marshall 1 Van Lennep, pp. 15, 247; Wilson, pp. 168–70

Marshall, ——. 1 *CSPD 1660–1*, p. 593; *1663–4*, p. 38

Martin, B. 1 WRO, E 1613

2 *N. & Q.*, Feb. 1960, pp. 68–9 and authorities cited. ('East Herford', Notts., at p. 68, must be a slip for East Retford.)

3 *Cat.*, ii. 363

4 vii. 394, n. 1; *Harl. Soc. Reg.*, 64/43

Martin, J. 1 Plomer, i, ii

Martin, W. 1 *Cat.*, i

Marylebone 1 GLRO, MR/TH/2, m. 31 (R)

Mason 1 *CSPD Add. 1660–85*, e.g. p. 151; *Econ. Hist. Rev.* (ser. 2) 6/148–50

Matthews, J. 1 *CSPD 1661–2*, p. 409

Matthews, R. 1 Sandwich, pp. 45, 148

Mauleverer 1 HP; GEC

May, A. 1 *Bull. IHR*, 19/16

May, B. 1 *DNB*; HP; Burnet, i. 472

May, H. 1 Colvin (*see* Denham, n. 2); Reddaway (*see* Fire, n. 3) passim

Mayers 1 PRO, Adm 20/1, no. 1300; *CSPD Add. 1670*, p. 550

Maynard 1 North (ed. Jessop), i. 149–50; *DNB*

Mayne 1 *DNB*; Wood, *Ath. Oxon.*, iii. 971, 972

Maypole 1 Aubrey, ii. 77; Strype, iv. 104, 106, 112; B. Lillywhite, *London Signs* (1972), no. 10399

Meggot 1 v. 356, n. 2; Venn; McDonnell (*see* Baines, n. 1), p. 196; Evelyn, iii. 443. Engraved portrait in PL 2980/117b

Meggs 1 Van Lennep, p. 94; John H. Wilson, *Nell Gwyn* (1952), p. 21

Mennes 1 PL 2874, pp. 394–5
2 *DNB*; Collinge; also (for his appointments) Rawl. A 478, f. 78r; PRO, SP 29/96, no. 66
3 PRO, PCC Duke 38
Mercer 1 *Harl. Soc. Reg.*, 46/passim (summarised Whitear, pp. 86–7); PRO, E 179/252/32 (18), f. 23v (R)
Mercers' Hall 1 PL 2972/83a
Meres 1 HP; Sainty
Meriton 1 Venn
Merrett 1 *DNB*; Munk
Mervin 1 PRO, AO 1/310/1220
Meynell 1 Woodhead
Middleton 1 viii. 462; *CSPD 1665*, p. 76 ~ Collinge; *Cat*, i; *CSP Col. Am.* etc. *1661–8*, pp. 1–2, 18
2 NWB, pp. 149, 185
3 *CSPD 1664–5*, p. 192; *1665–6*, pp. 32, 53
4 *Harl. Soc. Reg.*, 46/207; PRO, PCC Eure 152
Mile End 1 GLRO, MR/TH/4, mm. 99–101 (R)
Miller 1 Firth and Davies, pp. 541–2; Dalton, i. 8, 54
Milles 1 Venn; PRO, Adm 82/4; BL, Add. MSS 9303, f. 3r; PL 2867, p. 335
2 A large house rated on 10 hearths: PRO, E 179/252/32 (18), f. 27v (R)
3 iii. 54, n. 1
4 Bryant, ii. 372; iii. 205
5 Her Christian name is given in *Harl. Soc. Reg.*, 46/, e.g. 68; his will is in PRO, PCC Ent 161 and mentions his second wife Leah. The first marriage has not been traced: the Brampton registers have no record of marriages 1626–75.
6 Rawl. A 183, f. 264r; Collinge
7 *Harl. Soc. Reg.*, 46/68, 282
Millet 1 *Cat.*, i; *CSPD 1667–8*, p. 71
Minors 1 *Cat.*, i
Mitchell 1 Plomer, i; *Merc. Pub.*, 18 Dec. 1662, p. 815; WRO, E 172

2 GL, MS. 3461 II f. 45v (R); PRO, E 179/252/23 (R); Whitear, p. 127
Mohun, M. 1 Van Lennep, pp. 15, 304, 314; McAfee, p. 229
Mohun, R. 1 *Cat.*, i; *CJ*, ix. 628
Molins 1 Sherwood, p. 110
2 F. G. Parsons, *Hist. St Thomas's* (1932), ii. 95+; *CSPD 1663–4*, p. 311; inf. from Dr G. C. R. Morris
Monck 1 *DNB*; life by M. P. Ashley (1977). There are four engraved portraits in the PL.
2 Aubrey, ii. 73; L. Magalotti, *Travels of Cosmo the Third* (1821), pp. 468, 470
3 *See* Clarendon House. Engraved portrait in PL 2979/16b
Montouth 1 *CSPD 1665–6*, p. 499
Moore, F. 1 ib., *1660–1*, p. 57
Moore, H. 1 Wheatley, 2 Jan. 1660 n.; *Letters*, p. 8
2 Mapperton, Sandwich MSS, Letters from Ministers, ii. 127v
3 ib., Journal, iii. 64 etc.
Moore, J. 1 *DNB*; Tomlinson, p. 84 etc.; J. Seller, *Engl. Pilot* (1671), bk i, App.; *Naval Minutes*, p. 135. Engraved portrait in PL 2979/118b
Moorfields 1 Wheatley and Cunningham
Moray 1 *DNB*; Burnet, i. 105
Mordaunt, E. 1 *Letters*, e.g. p. 140
2 *Pepys* (1974), p. 264
3 *Letters*, p. 47
4 (corresp.); *Letters*, esp. pp. 41–2, 50; GEC, *Baronetage*, i. 62; Evelyn, iv. 206, n. 1; v. 84; Bryant, ii, esp. pp. 327, 383–6
Mordaunt, H. 1 GEC; HMC, *Rep.*, 8/1/2/280; Ailesbury, *Memoirs* (Roxb. Club, 1890), i. 153; LCC, *Survey, St Martin's*, iii. 126; C. H. Josten (ed.), *Ashmole* (Oxf. 1950–1), i. 150 etc.
Mordaunt, J. 1 vii. 386 etc.; *Letter book of Mordaunt 1658–60* (ed. M. Coate, Camden Soc. 1945);

Underdown (*see* Baron, H., n. 1), passim

Morden 1 Plomer, i; R. Bowes, *Hist. Cambridge books* (Camb. 1894); Cambs. Rec. Off., Churchwardens' Accts, St Mary-the-Great; George J. Gray and W. M. Palmer, *Abstracts from wills of printers of Cambridge 1504–1699*, (1915), p. 118

Morice 1 *DNB*; HP

Morland 1 Bryant, iii. 184

2 LCC, *Survey*, 30/547; *D*, v. 330, n. 3; Taylor, p. 230; *Letters*, p. 184

3 *DNB*; *Priv. Corr.*, vol. i. p. iii; *Letters*, esp. pp. 175–6, 187–8; *Cat.*, iii. 329; North (ed. Jessop), i. 384–6; P. Fraser, *Intelligence of Secretaries of State* (Camb. 1956), pp. 24–5. Engraved portrait in PL 2979/118f

Morrice 1 GL, St Bride's Reg.

2 Baxter, p. 140

3 Lib. St Paul's Cath., J. Pridden's MSS, 51. D. 8 (ref. from D. Scott)

Morris, J. 1 *See* Taverns etc., named, n. 97

Morris, Rob. 1 Boyd 22127; PRO, LC 3/73, f. 178r; LRO, Misc. MS. 86.4

Morris, Rog. 1 Woodhead; *CTB*, ii. 431

Mossom 1 *DNB*; *Walker Rev.*

Motham 1 *CSPD 1651–2*, p. 527 etc.; *Cat.*, i; Clowes, pp. 187, 210

Mount 1 i. 26; ii. 51; PRO, PCC Pett 10

Mountagu, E. (Manchester) 1 Mordaunt (*see* Mordaunt, J., n. 1), pp. 12, 73, 163, 178; *CSPClar.*, iv. 190

2 *DNB*

Mountagu, E. (Sandwich) 1 Mapperton, Sandwich MSS, Journal, vols ii–viii. His admirals' logs 1659–65 were edited for the Navy Records Society in 1929 by Dr R. C. Anderson.

2 *Priv. Corr.*, ii. 110

3 v. 257

4 For her will, see PRO, PCC Bunce 24 (where her name is mistakenly given as Elizabeth)

5 Harris, ii. 235

6 qu. ib., ii. 289

7 This account is based on the life of Sandwich by F. R. Harris (2 vols, 1912). Sandwich's will is in PRO, PCC Eure 113. Portraits in PL 2979/35a, 36a

Mountagu, E. (Ned) 1 Harris, i. 139 etc.; ii. 141

Mountagu, G. 1 PRO, E 179/143/404 (R)

2 HP; VCH, *Hunts.*, ii. 30; PRO, LC 3/73, p. 8; Mapperton, Sandwich MSS, Letters from Ministers, ii. 85; Sandwich, *Journal*, pp. 16, 45

Mountagu, R. 1 iii. 43

2 *DNB*

Mountagu, Walter 1 *DNB*

Mountagu, Wm. 1 ib.; *Harl. Soc. Vis.*, 87/138; letters to Sandwich (from Dec. 1657) in Carte 73, ff. 181, 223, 264, 341

Mountney 1 *CTB*, iii. 247

Moxon 1 NWB, p. 58

2 Moxon, *Mechanick Exercises* (ed. Davis and Carter, Oxf. 1958), Intro., esp. p. xxxiii; *DNB*; Taylor, pp. 233–4. Engraved portrait in PL 2980/288c

Moyer 1 Firth and Rait, i. 914; ii. 365, 382; *CSPD 1660–1*, pp. 484–5; PRO, PCC Cann 96, 106

Moyses 1 i. 57, n. 3; *CSPD 1656–7*, pp. 315, 361

Muddiman 1 J. G. Muddiman, *King's Journalist* (1923); Fraser (*see* Morland, n. 3), passim

Mumford 1 WRO, E 1609, E 1621

Murford, W. 1 PRO, Adm 20/9, nos 289, 1679; Rawl A. 185, f. 23r

Murford, Capt. 1 PRO, PCC Mico 101; PRO, SP 29/58, no. 48

Murford, Mrs 1 WRO, E 1609

Music 1 vii. 69

2 ib. 228

3 i. 313. The range of Pepys's voice is clear from the MS. volume PL 2591, where the songs 'for a Single Voice' are adjusted to his 'particular Compass'.

4 *Diary and will of Ashmole* (ed. R. T. Gunther, Oxf. 1927), p. 10

5 *Priv. Corr.*, ii. 109

6 For the virginals, see *Family Letters*, p. 14

7 cf. P. A. Scholes, *Puritans and music* (1934), esp. pp. 282–3; PRO, 12/2 (for Whitelocke's embassy to Sweden, 1655)

8 Wood, *L. & T.*, i. 298; Wilson (*see* Lanier, n. 1), p. 294

9 Scholes, op. cit., pp. 282–3

10 Wood, *L. & T.*, i. 257

11 *Parl. Intell.*, 1660, no. 21, p. 334

12 cf. John Harley, *Music in Purcell's London* (1968), pp. 13–21

13 Hartmann (*see* Corbetta, n. 1), p. 68

14 Wilson, op. cit., p. 299; *D*, iv. 394

15 A. Bryant (ed.), *Letters etc. of Charles II* (1968), p. 30

16 For the date, see HMC, *Rep.*, 5/App. p. 154

17 iii. 190 & n. 3, 197. The violins were playing in the theatres by 20 March 1664: PRO, LC e.g. 5/119

18 PRO, SP 44/7, p. 36

19 BL, Harl. MSS 7338, f. 3*r*

20 Wilson, op. cit., p. 4

21 For Banister's French expedition, see PRO, SP 5, p. 62 (2 Dec. 1661); both this and Humfrey's French leave were funded from secret service monies.

22 cf. PRO, SP 29/113/117; ib. 175/99

23 cf. W. McC. Evans, *H. Lawes* (N.Y. 1941)

24 PL 2803, ff. 97*v*–108*r*

25 Wilson, op. cit., p. 294

26 *See* Davenant, Sir W.

27 Zenti probably came to England in 1662 and left in 1664: PRO, SP

29/233/132 and SP 44/16, p. 12. For his invention of the spinet, see D. H. Boalch, *Makers of the harpsichord etc. 1440–1800* (Oxf. 1974), pp. 192–3

28 cf. A. Baines, *Woodwind instruments and their history* (1967), pp. 275–80

29 viii. 40; cf. also Large Glossary: Treble

30 Keyboard tablature was, of course, a theoretical possibility. It was employed on the Continent – notably in Germany – but not in England.

31 i. 302

32 [—Park], *A new and easier method to learn to sing by book* (1686), sigs A4*v*, A5*r*.

33 Evelyn, iii. 377

34 PL 1712; it seems from his catalogue that Pepys believed it to be by Dr John Wallis.

35 Thomas Warton, *The life of Ralph Bathurst* (1761), p. 201

36 Further reading: John Harley, *Music in Purcell's London: the social background* (1968); Sir F. Bridge, *S. Pepys, lover of musique* (1903)

Myddelton 1 W. M. Myddelton (ed.), *Chirk Castle accounts 1605–66* (St Albans 1908), vol. i, facing p. 26

Myngs 1 *DNB*; *Cat.*, i

Navy 1 Evelyn, v. 538

2 *Navy of Britain* (1948), p. 241

3 p. 59

4 Sandwich, p. xlvi

5 qu. G. J. Marcus, *Naval hist. Engl.*, i (1961), p. 334

6 C. H. Wilson, *Profit and power* (1957), passim

7 See M. A. Lewis, *England's Sea officers* (1939), p. 86; and the same author's *Navy of Britain*

8 Duke of York, *Mem. (naval)*, pp. 85–6

9 Davis (*see* Dutch Wars, n. 7), p. 12

10 ib., p. 391

11 A. W. Tedder, *The navy of the Restoration* (Camb. 1916) pp. 12–14, 35; *Cat.*, i. 221, 256+

12 *Cat.*, i. 306

13 Sandwich, p. xlvi

14 vi. 306

15 *Naval Minutes*, p. 260

16 *British Seaman* (1968), p. 76 ∼ Further reading: M. Oppenheim, *Administration of Royal Navy 1509–1660* (1896); Ehrman; R. Ollard, *Pepys* (1974), and *Man of war: Sir R. Holmes* (1969); F. Fox, *Great Ships: the battle fleet of Charles II* (Greenwich, 1980)

Navy Board 1 *CSPD Add. 1660–85*, p. 223

2 Duke of York, *Mem. (naval)*, pp. 58–60

3 iii. 24 & n. 1

4 *Ec. Hist. Rev.* (ser. 2), 6/136

5 PRO, Adm 2/1745, ff. 163–6

6 ix. 289 & n. 1

7 For the rates, see *Cat.*, i. 140–51

8 Further reading: *Pepys's Memoires of the Royal Navy 1679–88* (repr., ed. Tanner, Oxf. 1906); J. R. Tanner, *S. Pepys and the Royal Navy* (Camb. 1920); J. P. W. Ehrman, *The navy in the war of William III* (Camb. 1953); G. F. James and J. J. Sutherland Shaw in *Bull. IHR*, 14/10+, 166+; B. Pool, *Navy Board contracts 1660–1832* (1966)

Navy Off. 1 iv. 27, n. 2

2 PRO, E 179/152/32 (18), f. 27r (R)

3 This figure is the total of the sums given in the Navy Treasurer's ledgers: PRO, Adm 20/1–12

4 Pepys describes the fire in PRO, Adm 106/2887. cf. also Hooke (*see* Carkesse, n. 2), p. 25

5 HMC, *Lindsey (Supp.)*, p. 116; *Further Corr.*, p. 280; Bryant, ii. 91 & n.

6 Engraving (1714) repro. Wheatley (1893–9), vol. i, facing p. 192

7 For the history of the office from the early 17th century, see Reddaway in *Bull. IHR*, 30/175+, on which this account is based.

Navy Tr. 1 ib.

Naylor, O. 1 Venn; Chappell, p. 50

Naylor, W. 1 Whitear, pp. 24–5

Neale 1 HMC, *Rep.*, 7/105

2 HP; Craig (*see* Freeman, n. 1), pp. 179–80

Neile 1 *DNB*; PRO, LS 1/4; *Notes and records Roy. Soc.* (1960), pp. 159+

Nevill 1 PRO, E 179/252/32, Mr Izod's acct (R)

Newbery 1 *CSPD 1644–5*, p. 325; *1649–50*, p. 201; *1659–60*, p. 593; Gardiner (*see* Hayward, J., n. 1), v. 250

Newell 1 Foster

New Exchange 1 Wheatley and Cunningham

Newman 1 Firth and Rait, i. 674, 692; Everitt (*see* Blount, n. 1), pp. 216, 284, 312

Newport 1 HP; *DNB*; *Bull. IHR*, 19/16; PRO, SP 29/96 no. 66

2 ix. 218 & n. 4; Lord (*see* Gosnell, n. 1), p. 354

Nicholas, E. 1 *DNB*; HP; life (1955) by Donald Nicholas

Nicholas, J. 1 *See* preceding n.

Nicholson 1 Venn; Roger Howell, *Newcastle* (Oxf. 1967), p. 187 etc.; *CSPD 1661–2*, p. 170

Nixon 1 vi. 104, n. 4; *CSPD* e.g. *1665–6*, p. 539; *Cat.*, i

Noble 1 Rawl. A 182, f. 301r

Noell 1 Andrews (*see* Duke, n. 1), pp. 49+; Edward Hughes, *Studies in administration etc.* (Manchester 1934), pp. 132+; M. P. Ashley, *Fin. and commercial policy under the Protectorate* (Oxf. 1934), esp. p. 102; PRO, PCC Hyde 120, 129

Nokes 1 PRO, E 179/252/32, London 16 (R)

Nonsuch 1 Manning and Bray, (*see* Harvey, n. 1), ii. 602+ (details from survey, 1650). Views in A. W. Clapham and W. H. Godfrey, *Some famous buildings* (1913), pp. 1–12; PL 2972/219

Norbury 1 Whitear, pp. 67–9, 161–5; Hunts. Rec. Off., Manchester MSS 19/5; *Gray's Inn Reg.*
2 *See* Woolley

Norman 1 PRO, Adm 20/1, nos 1301, 1341; *CSPD 1663–4*, p. 145; *Further Corr.*, p. 195; *CSPD 1670*, p. 463

Norris 1 PRO, E 179/252/32, St Martin's, f. 39r (R)
2 BL, Add. MSS 32476, f. 26r; *Bull. IHR*, 19/21; Edward Chamberlayne, *Angliae Notitia* (1684); inf. from Sir O. Millar

North 1 *Hist. Engl.* (Everyman 1927), i. 397 ~ HP; GEC; *DNB*

Norton, D. 1 HP (s.n. Chicheley, Sir J.)

Norton, J. 1 Chappell, pp. 36, 48

Norton, M. 1 Wilson, pp. 175–6; Van Lennep, p. 53

Norton, R. 1 HP; G. N. Godwin, *Civil War in Hants.* (1904)

Norwood 1 HP; Mordaunt (*see* Mordaunt, J., n. 1), p. 32n.; *Bull. IHR*, 19/16; Dalton, i. 18, 24, 34; *Letters*, p. 84; Bryant, ii. 270, 271, 353, 360

Nott 1 BL, *Sale Catalogues*, 923; Plomer, ii; Howe; *Naval Minutes*, pp. 104, 105

Nun 1 PRO, LC 5/62, pp. 43, 92 etc.; *Pub. Cath. Rec. Soc.*, 38/p. xxxi; *DNB*

Oakeshott 1 *CSPD 1659–60*, p. 239; *CJ*, vii. 809; *Pepysiana*, p. 133; Longleat, Coventry MSS 13, f. 156r

O'Brien, C. 1 *Cat.*, i; *CSPD 1667–8*, pp. 31, 35, 46; NWB, pp. 221, 228

O'Brien, M. 1 i. 321 & n. 2; Rugge (*see* Drink, n. 18), i. 84; GEC

Offley 1 Venn; Bryant, ii. 106, 108, 146

Ogle 1 HMC, *Rep.*, 8/1/2/279; Evelyn, iv. 70–1 & n.

Ogilby 1 *DNB*; Sir H. G. Fordham, *Ogilby, his Britannia* (1925); Aubrey, ii. 99+; *The Library* (ser. 4), 6/157+. Engraved portraits in PL 2980/205 c, b

Okey 1 *DNB*

Old Bailey 1 Hatton, vol. i, sect. i
2 LRO, MS. G 6. View in PL 2973/315a

Oldenburg 1 *DNB*; A. R. and M. B. Hall (eds), *Corresp. Oldenburg* (Madison 1965–), vol. i, pp. xxix+; LCC, *Survey*, 30/547

Ordnance 1 H. C. Tomlinson, *Guns and government* (1979)

Osborne, H. 1 19 and 20 Car. II, c. 1; *CTB*, ii. 611; iii. 1051; *CSPD 1660–1*, p. 144; *1667–8*, p. 478; PRO, Adm 2/1745, f. 30r

Osborne, N. 1 v. 216; Boyd 34084; HMC, *Rep.*, 8/1/1/132

Osborne, T. 1 *Naval Minutes*, p. 257
2 NWB, pp. 136–7
3 *DNB*; A. Browning, *Danby* (Glasgow 1944–51), esp. i. 87, 558–9. Engraved portrait in PL 2979/17a

Oviatt 1 iii. 264 & n. 1; *CSPD Add. 1660–85*, p. 422; *Harl. Soc. Reg.*, 46/passim

Owen, G. 1 *DNB*; Smyth, p. 63

Owen, J. 1 *CSPD 1663–4*, p. 373

Packer 1 Colvin, v. 11; Evelyn, ii. 548, n. 1; iii. 72; *CSPD 1667–8*, p. 507; *1668–9*, p. 163; Carte 73, f. 540r

Page, D. 1 NWB, p. 207
2 ib., loc. cit.

Page, ——. 1 Meekings (*see* Arthur, n. 1), p. 115

Page, T. 1 *Cat.*, i; *CSPD 1666–7*, p. 469; Longleat, Coventry MSS 99, f. 92r

Pall Mall 1 LCC, *Survey*, 29/24–5, 322–3, and fig. 58

Palmer, Barbara 1 Howard Robinson, *Brit. Post Office* (Princeton 1948), p. 79
2 Colvin v. 267–8 ~ *DNB*; lives by G. S. Steinman (Oxf. 1874, 1878); E. Hamilton (1980). Engraved portrait in PL 2979/184a
Palmer, Ben 1 *Harl. Soc. Reg.*, 66/47
Palmer, J. 1 *DNB*
Palmer, R. 1 GEC
Papillon 1 Woodhead
Pargiter 1 Inf. from Miss S. Hare
2 *CSPD*, e.g. *1661–2*, p. 543
Parham 1 Boyd 33572; Rawl. A 478, f. 78
P. Clerks' Hall 1 R. H. Adams, *Parish clerks of London* (1971), ch. ix
Parker, J. 1 *Cat.*, i; *CSPD*, e.g. *1653–4*, p. 145
Parker, —— 1 *Harl. Soc. Reg.*, 46/67; *Merc. Pub.*, 6 Dec. 1660
Parkhurst 1 HP; Evelyn, iv. 255; Manning and Bray (*see* Harvey, n. 1), i. 157
Parl. Stairs 1 Hatton, vol. ii, sect. vii
Parry 1 *CSPD*, e.g. *1659–60*, p. 594
Parson's Gn 1 Bryant, ii. 183, 270, 360
Pat. Row 1 Hatton, vol. i, sect. i
Payler 1 *CSPD*, e.g. *1654*, p. 76
Peachell 1 *DNB*; Purnell (*see* Magdalene, n. 5), pp. 141+; Bryant, iii. 273
Pearse, A. 1 Carte 73, ff. 64, 104; *CSPD 1656–7*, p. 517; PRO, Adm 20/3, p. 323; Adm 20/9, p. 408
Pearse, J. 1 *CJ*, vii. 828; *CSPD 1658–9*, p. 402; Duke of York, *Mem. (naval)*, p. 112; Rawl. A 170, f. 79
2 Harris, ii. 182. Lady Sandwich wrote that he was 'the famostes Docr. in lingland' for that malady; ib., loc. cit.
3 PL 2879, pp. 103+
4 PRO, Adm 2/1732, f. 1r; PRO, LC 3/24; *D*, iv. 255
5 Young (*see* Conny, n. 1), p. 9;

Parsons (*see* Molins, n. 2), ii. 116–17
6 WRO, E 174; PRO, E 179/252/32, St Paul's, Cov. Gdn, p. 3 (R); *Priv. Corr.*, i. 112
7 PRO, PCC Coker 162; *Priv. Corr.*, loc. cit.
8 Yonge (*see* Addis, n. 1), p. 156; *Priv. Corr.*, loc. cit.
9 Bryant, iii. 385–6
10 A. H. Nethercot, *A. Cowley* (1931), pp. 5, 294 ~ see Keevil (*see* Cocke, Capt., n. 2); R. Ollard, *Pepys* (1974), esp. pp. 235–7
Pedley 1 HP: *Family Letters*, pp. 158, 163, 170, 171–2
[Pelling, J.] 1 Foster
Pelling, —— 1 Woodhead; *CSPD Add. 1660–85*, p. 157; *Vorträge . . . Int. Pharm. Kongresses* (1965), p. 279 (ref. from T. D. Wittet)
Penington 1 qu. Maria Webb, *Penns and Penningtons* (1891), p. 311
Penn, G. 1 Granville Penn, *William Penn* (1833), i. 550+
Penn, Sir W. 1 vii. 194 & n. 3
2 D. Hannay, *Short hist. royal navy 1217–1688* (1898), pp. 225, 235
3 Firth and Rait, ii. 812
4 Granville Penn, op. cit., ii. 589+. Thomas Turner of the Navy Office claimed to be its author: viii. 227
5 vii. 211
6 vii. 189
7 *Journ. Friends' Hist. Soc.*, 5/118; Lysons (*see* Chelsea, n. 1), iv. 224
8 Granville Penn, op. cit., ii. 559, 560; Howard M. Jenkins, *Family of Penn* (1899), p. 25
9 Inf. from A. D. Law ~ life by Granville Penn, op. cit.; *DNB*
Penn, W. 1 PRO, PCC Penn 130
2 *Priv. Corr.*, ii. 317 ~ *DNB*; lives by J. Stoughton (1882), B. Dobrée (1932)
Penny 1 Rawl. A 182, ff. 154, 353; *Family Letters*, p. 231

Penrose 1 *CSPD*, e.g. *1652–3*, p. 590; *Cat.*, i; Longleat, Coventry MSS 99, f. 92r

Pepper 1 Venn; J. Peile, *Biog. reg. Christ's Coll.* (Camb. 1910)

Pepys family 1 As early as 1567–8 he was the largest landowner in Cottenham: PRO, E 179/82/248.

2 See Chappell; W. C. Pepys, *Geneal. of Pepys family 1273–1887* (1952 ed.); F. M. Page, *Estates of Crowland Abbey* (Camb. 1934). Also iii. 27, n. 1; viii. 261, n. 4

3 v. 134

4 W. C. Pepys, op. cit., p. 45

5 PRO, E 179/244/22

6 viii. 274

Pepys, A. 1 iii. 107; *Pepysiana*, p. 25; Bryant, iii. 222

Pepys, B. 1 Chappell, p. 58; *Priv. Corr.*, ii. 368–9 (Index); *Naval Minutes*, p. 470 (Index); Venn

Pepys, C. 1 Chester-Foster 1044

2 PRO, E 179/252/32, Mr Izod's acct (R)

3 See e.g. *Priv. Corr.*, i. 138–9; *Letters*, pp. 212–13; Rawl. A 170, ff. 22, 24, 26, 28, 36, 44

4 Chappell, p. 54; Whitear, pp. 29, 143–4

5 *Pepysiana*, p. 252

Pepys, Ed. 1 Chappell, pp. 48–9

Pepys, Eliz. 1 *Family Letters*, p. 26

2 ix. 94; cf. v. 218

3 Westminster Abbey Muniments, St Margaret's reg.; *D*, vii. 237

4 See ii. 194, n. 3; and corresp. in *TLS* 7, 21 Apr., 19 May 1932; *N. & Q.*, 1 July 1933

5 i. 33 & n. 2; ix. 499

6 ii. 153; iv. 277

7 iv. 158

8 Carte 73, f. 187r

9 vii. 289

10 *Letters*, p. 37; *Harl. Soc. Reg.*, 46/208

11 NWB, p. 244

12 Wheatley, vol. i, p. xxxvi

13 *Atlantic Monthly*, 67/574

14 *Journ. R. Soc. Antiq. Ireland*, 38/119; *Harl. Soc. Vis.*, 74/39–40; W. K. Cook Kingsmill, 'The Kingsmill records' (typescript; Lib. Soc. Geneal.)

15 vii. 44, n. 2

Pepys, J. and M. (parents) 1 See Kite

2 Whitear in *Athenaeum*, 6 June 1914, p. 795

3 Carte 73, f. 619; *D*, vii. 22 & n. 4

4 *Family Letters*, pp. 13–14

5 i. 76

6 PL 2141a (title-page)

7 PRO, PCC Admon. Bks (19 Oct. 1680); cf. *Family Letters*, pp. 18–19 ~ Whitear, pp. 39–42; *Pepysiana*, p. 15; *Family Letters*, passim

Pepys, J. (Ashtead) 1 Chappell, pp. 22, 28, 36, 37; Charles W. James, *Chief Justice Coke* (1929), pp. 46, 49, 81, 91, 114; Meekings (*see* Arthur, n. 1), pp. 128, 175

Pepys, Dr J. 1 Venn; *Pepysiana*, opp. p. 8; Chappell, p. 43; [C. Coote], *Engl. Civilians* (1804), p. 83

Pepys, John (brother) 1 Venn; Christ's Coll., Admission Bk 1622–75, f. 136v

2 *Letters*, p. 39

3 *Family Letters*, e.g. pp. xx–xxi

4 ib., pp. 60–1

5 Chappell, p. 57

Pepys, Rich. (Ashen) 1 i. 252 & n.3; Chappell, p. 50

Pepys, Rich. (upholder) 1 Chappell, pp. 26, 35, 94; Jones (*see* Fire, n. 3), ii. 355–6; PRO, PCC King 62; ib. Bence 22

Pepys, Rob. (uncle) 1 Whitear, p. 166

2 Chappell, p. 30

3 Firth and Rait, ii. 1071, 1433; *CSPD 1659–60*, pp. 24, 51

4 PRO, PCC May 128 (ptd Whitear, pp. 145+)

5 Chappell, p. 39

6 iv. 352

7 PL (unoff.), Freshfield MSS 8
8 ii. 138; Freshfield MSS 8
9 ii. 182
10 *Family Letters*, pp. 4–5
11 iii. 222, 240, 256, 261, 265–6; Freshfield MSS 6
12 Freshfield MSS 4
13 Francis Edwards, bookseller, *Cat.*, Nov. 1929, no. 261
14 *Family Letters*, pp. 171–3; PL (unoff.), Jackson MSS 2
15 Jackson MSS 2(b), 4, 17

Pepys, Roger 1 A. Browning, *Danby* (Glasgow 1951), iii. 37, 38, 99
2 Chappell, pp. 42–3, 57; Whitear, p. 45; Venn; HP; *Priv. Corr.*, ii. 314

Pepys, Talbot 1 Whitear, pp. 51+; Chappell, p. 30; Firth and Rait, passim

Pepys, Thomas (uncle) 1 PRO, PCC Bence 104
2 Mercers' Co. Archives; inf. from Miss S. Hare
3 Whitear, pp. 53–5, 148; Chappell, p. 39; *Proc. Hug. Soc. London*, 15 no. 2/3, 319–20

Pepys, Thomas ('Executor') 1 Chappell, p. 50; Manning and Bray (*see* Harvey, n. 1), i. 255
2 Chappell, p. 41; Whitear, p. 11
3 vii. 112 & n. 3; viii. 305; ix. 182; Firth and Rait, ii. 1074, 1373, 1437; *CSPD 1658–9*, p. 222; GLRO, WJS/SBB/173, pp. 240, 304
4 Bodl., Clar. dep c 406, p. 33
5 Carte 73, f. 325r
6 WRO, F 387, 388; PRO, PCC, Admon. Bk, f. 123
7 Chappell, pp. 50, 63; *Letters*, pp. 97–8, 157–8; *Priv. Corr.*, i. 126–7; *Family Letters*, p. 239

Pepys, Thomas (tailor) 1 *Family Letters*, p. 6
2 PRO, E 179/252/32, St Bride's, p. 8; cf. ib. 179/147/627, p. 195 (R). cf. Mrs Butler's complaint about

the smallness of the house: iii. 231
3 *Family Letters*, pp. xx–xxi, 231; Chappell, p. 56

Pepys, Dr Thomas 1 *Family Letters*, pp. 8–9; *D*, vi. 16
2 Venn; Chappell, p. 43; Munk; Horatio R. F. Brown, *Inglesi all'universita di Padova* (Venice 1921), p. 158; PRO, PCC Hyde 18

Pepys, Thomas ('turner') 1 PRO, E 179/252/27, m. 19 (R)
2 *Priv. Corr.*, i. 139; ii. 318
3 iii. 266; PL (unoff.), Freshfield MSS 5, 6
4 Lib. Soc. Geneal., P. Boyd, Index to Marriages 1538–1837 (Mdx)

Perkin 1 PRO, E 179/244/22, p. 159
2 Chappell, pp. 40, 55; Whitear, pp. 145, 161

Perkins 1 *Cat.*, i

Perriman 1 PRO, Adm 20/9, pp. 20, 189, 490; Rawl. A 190, f. 45r

Petit 1 *Harl. Soc. Reg.*, 46/313; Bodl. Clar. dep. c. 400, p. 14

Petre 1 GEC; *DNB*

Pett, C. 1 vii. 106
2 *CSPD 1645–7*, p. 608; *1651–2*, p. 353; *1667*, p. 464; *The Ancestor*, 10/158–9; PRO, PCC Hene 51

Pett, Comm. Peter 1 PRO, PCC Eure 153
2 HP; Aylmer, pp. 156+; *DNB*; *The Ancestor*, 10/168–72

Pett, Peter 1 *The Ancestor*, 10/159; *DNB*; *Middle Temple Reg.*

Pett, Comm. Phineas 1 PL 2869 (pub. NRS 1917, ed. W. G. Perrin) ∼ *DNB*

Pett, Phineas 1 *MM*, 12/431–2

Pett, Capt. Phineas 1 ib., 433

Petty 1 Rawl. A 171, ff. 274–5 ∼ *DNB*; *Notes and records Roy. Soc.*, (1960)/79+; C. H. Hull (ed.), *Econ. writings of Sir W. Petty* (Camb. 1899); R. Latham (ed.), *Cat. of Pepys Library* (Woodbridge, 1978–), vols i, iii pt ii. Engraved portrait in PL 2979/125d

Phelps 1 PRO, E 403/1758, f. 72v; Baxter, p. 140

Philips, J. 1 Phillips (*see* Levitt, n. 1), pp. 85–6

Phillips, H. 1 PRO, SP 25 I 108, p. 74

Phillips, L. 1 Brampton par. reg. 1665, 1670; VCH, *Hunts.*, ii. 16, 152

**Phillips, —— ** 1 *CSPD 1663–4*, p. 531

Phipps 1 *CSPD 1667*, pp. 78, 117

Pickering 1 *A list of [those] that sat in the Other House* (1657), p. 4

2 GEC; *DNB*; Sherwood, pp. 65, 138–9; PRO, PCC Eure 153

3 PRO, E 403/1757; *CSPD 1659–60*, p. 415

4 *Cat.*, i. 393; ii. 391

5 PRO, PCC Cann 7; HMC, *Buccleuch*, i. 331–2; *Harl. Soc. Vis.*, vol. 87

6 iv. 239 & n. 2

7 North (ed. Jessop), i. 76–8

8 Wren and Haskett (*see* Aleyn, n. 1), p. 17; John Bridges, *Hist. Northants.* (1791), ii. 387

Piggot 1 Fly-leaf, bass part, John Playford, 'Collection of songs and gleas': MS. Ewing Coll., Glasgow Univ. Lib. ∼ Grove (6th ed.)

Pigott 1 Hunts. Rec. Off., Wills (Lincoln; Brampton Peculiar)

Pinchbeck 1 *CSPD 1640–1*, p. 492; *CTB*, iii. 827; Dalton, i. 137

Pinkney 1 *N. & Q.*, Jan. 1958, pp. 2+, 336+; *CSPD 1660–1*, p. 558; *1663–4*, p. 358; Heal (*see* Atkinson, n. 1), p. 223; Hilton Price, *Handbook London bankers* (1890–1), p. 63

Pitts 1 *CSPD 1658–60*, p. 469; Collinge

Plague 1 J. F. D. Shrewsbury, *Hist. of bubonic plague in British Isles* (Camb. 1970), pp. 189–92, 487

2 J. Sutherland, *Defoe* (1937), pp. 6–10; cf. J. Landa (ed.) *Defoe's Journal of the Plague Year* (Oxf. 1972), p. ix

3 W. Boghurst, *Loimographia* (ed. Payne, 1894); cf. W. Nicholson, *Hist. sources of Defoe's Journal of the Plague Year* (Boston 1967) passim

4 R. Pollitzer, *Plague* (Geneva, 1954), pp. 340–3, 350–1

5 C. Morris in *Hist. Journ.*, 14/206–7; cf. J-N. Biraben, tr. L. Bradley and R. Schofield, in *The Plague reconsidered* (Matlock, 1977), pp. 25–36

6 L. F. Hirst, *Conquest of plague* (Oxf. 1953) pp. 33–5; cf. Wu Lien Teh, *Treatise on pneumonic plague* (Geneva 1926) passim, and Morris, op. cit., pp. 207–10

7 A. Hirsch, *Handbook of geog. and hist. pathology* (tr. Creighton, 1883) i. 494–502; C. Creighton, *Hist. of epidemics in Britain* (Camb. 1891), i. 177–206, 282–373, 471–566; W. J. Simpson, *Treatise on plague* (Camb. 1905), pp. 5–36; J. Saltmarsh in *Camb. Hist. Journ.*, 7/23–41; R. S. Gottfried, *Epidemic disease in 15th-cent. Engl.* (Leicester 1978), pp. 35–52

8 Gottfried, op. cit., pp. 126–38; Walter G. Bell, *The Great Plague in London 1665* (1951), pp. 250–2

9 Creighton, op. cit., i. 533; Morris, op. cit., pp. 210–11; Simpson, op. cit., pp. 27–30

10 Boghurst, op. cit., p. 26; cf. Nathaniel Hodges, *Loimologia* (1667) tr. J. Quincy (1720), p. 5; Bell, op. cit., p. 18

11 Creighton, op. cit., i. 533

12 *Reliquiae Hearnianae* (1720), 21 Jan.; cf. Bell, op. cit., pp. 47, 155–6

13 Bell, op. cit., pp. 92, 148, 242; cf. *CSP Ven. 1664–6*, p. 182

14 Bell, op. cit., pp. 312, 325, 330

15 Hodges, op. cit., p. 15

16 Wood, *L. & T.*, ii. 46

17 Dryden, *Annus Mirabilis*, ll. 1065–1070

18 Bell, op. cit., pp. 224–5

19 Thomas Vincent, *God's terrible voice in the City* (1667), 1722 ed., p. 37; cf. letter of Arlington to the King in July, *CSPD 1664–5*, p. 497, and Bell, op. cit., pp. 225–9

20 Bell, op. cit., pp. 37–9, 47, 88–9, 316–19; cf. *CSPD 1665–6*, p. xiii

21 For plague water see Hodges, op. cit., pp. 173–174. For Venice Treacle, *see* Large Glossary.

22 G. Thomson, *Loimotomia, or The pest anatomised* (1666); cf. Bell, op. cit., pp. 203–6, 335–8

23 Bell, op. cit., p. 203

24 *CSPVen. 1664–6* p. 182; cf. Bell, op. cit., pp. 82–4, 278

25 Bell, op. cit., pp. 236–8. For a contrary medical opinion, see Hodges, op. cit., p. 20

26 *Letters*, pp. 24–5

27 Bell, op. cit., pp. 268–74

28 Hirsch, op. cit., i. pp. 500–1; Simpson, op. cit., p. 33; Hirst, op. cit., pp. 15–16; H. H. Scott, *Hist. tropical medicine* (1942), ii. 708–9

29 Bell, op. cit., p. 329; cf. Shrewsbury, op. cit., pp. 428, 531

30 Sir William Petty, 'Of the Growth of the City of London' in *Essays* (ed. H. Morley 1888), p. 51; cf. *The Petty Papers* (ed. Marquis of Lansdowne, 1927), i. 274; ii. 233

31 Bell, op. cit., pp. 252–3

32 Wu Lien Teh, J. W. H. Chun, R. Pollitzer and C. Y. Wu, *Plague, a manual for medical public health workers* (Shanghai 1936), pp. 92–6; Hirst, op. cit., pp. 266–7; Pollitzer, *Plague* (Geneva 1954), pp. 115–16

33 Biraben, op. cit., pp. 31–2; Pollitzer, op. cit., pp. 298–9

34 Biraben, op. cit., p. 35; Pollitzer, op. cit., p. 14; Wu Lien Teh et al., op. cit., p. 9; Hirst, op. cit., pp. 123–4

35 Pollitzer, op. cit., pp. 133–4; Hirst, op. cit., pp. 258–9; Wu Lien Teh et al., op. cit., pp. 227–8, 398;

G. S. Wilson and A. A. Miles, *Topley's principles of immunity and bacteriology* (1975), ii. 2136

36 G. Melvyn Howe, *Man, environment and disease in Britain* (Pelican, 1976), pp. 29–35

37 I owe this information to an unpublished lecture given by the late Dr G. S. Graham-Smith, formerly of the Indian Plague Commission.

38 Further reading: the works cited in nn. 1, 5, 6, 7, and 32 above. Pepys preserved in his library a drawing entitled 'Miseries of the Plague': 2973/447d

Playford 1 Plomer, i, ii; *Playford's English Dancing Master 1651* (ed. M. Dean-Smith, 1957). Engraved portrait in PL 2980/216d

Plays 1 ix. 395

2 viii. 7, 101

3 ix. 183; viii. 121

4 v. 232; ix. 419, 395

5 J. E. Spingarn (ed.), *Critical essays of 17th cent.* (Oxf. 1908), ii. 164

6 v. 78–9; viii. 44, 421, 551–2; vii. 176

7 v. 33

8 vii. 255

9 *Diary*, iii. 350

10 Further reading: H. McAfee, *Pepys on the Restoration stage* (1916); Montague Summers, *The playhouse of Pepys* (1935); T. W. Craik (ed.), *The Revels hist. of drama in English*, vol. v, *1660–1750* (1976)

Pointer 1 vi. 315; Collinge

Poole 1 Granville Penn (*see* Penn, G., n. 1), ii. 17, 559–60; *Cat.*, i; Clowes, ii. 445–6; PL 2813

Poole's tav. 1 *CSPD Add. 1660–85*, p. 3

Pooley 1 HP; Bittner u. Gross (*see* Barckmann, n. 1); *Cal. Comm. Comp. 1643–6*, p. 1475; *CTB*, ii. 3, 26, 76 etc.; *CSPD 1667*, p. 122

Poortmans 1 *CSPD 1651–2*, p. 540;

Porter 1 *DNB*; North (ed. Jessop), i. 382

Portsmouth 1 VCH, *Hants.*, v. 380+; *Kent*, ii. 336; Ehrman, esp. pp. 84, 629

Postal services 1 e.g. *Merc. Pub.*, 2 May 1661, p. 264
2 12 Car. II, c. 35
3 Howard Robinson, *Brit. Post Office* (Princeton 1948); Fraser (*see* Morland, n. 3), esp. pp. 20, 33, 128–9; Sir W. Dugdale, *Life*, diary etc. (ed. Hamper 1827), pp. 447–8, 468; Defoe, *Tour* (ed. Cole 1927), i. 343–4

Post Office 1 PRO, E 179/147/617, p. 133 (R)
2 Robinson, op. cit.; *London Gazette*, 4 Sept. 1666; PRO, SP/29/214/109 (ref. from R. M. Willcocks)

Poundy 1 *Priv. Corr.*, ii. 236–7

Povey 1 Bryant, iii. 167–8
2 Evelyn, iv. 84; J. Treglown, *Letters of Rochester* (Oxf. 1980), p. 188
3 GLRO, MR/TH/7, m. 13
4 Evelyn, iii. 447, n. 3
5 R. W. Symonds in *Connoisseur*, 85, no. 345/275 +; ib. no. 346, pp. 353+
6 *DNB*; Andrews (*see* Duke, n. 1), pp. 51+, 64

Powell, J. (messenger) 1 PL 2873, p. 483; PRO, Adm 20/1, no. 587

Powell, J. (steward) 1 *CSPD 1659–60*, p. 576

Powell, J. (curate) 1 Venn

Powell, R. (clerk to B) 1 Collinge

Powell, R. (clerk to C) 1 *CSPD 1667*, p. 187; Rawl. A 185, f. 283; *CSPD 1670*, p. 481

Powell, R. and D. 1 WRO, E 1609

Poynton 1 GEC, *Baronetage*; Dalton, i. 134; Braybrooke (1858), iv. 96, n.

Poyntz, F. 1 *CSPD 1660–1*, p. 25;
1666–7, p. 390; *CTB*, ii. 47; iii. 1313
2 *CSPD 1667–8*, p. 143; PRO, LC 3/61, f. 26r

Poyntz, J. 1 BL, Add. MSS 19256, esp. f. 78

Prat 1 Carte 223 e.g. ff. 47, 77; Mapperton, Sandwich MSS, Letters from Ministers, i. 112; Journal, iii. 230

Price, G. 1 Lafontaine; A. F. Hill in *Musical Antiquary*, 3 (1912)/178–9; Duke of York, *Mem. (naval)*, pp. 106–7

Price, J. 1 PRO, SP 25 I 108, p. 74

Primate 1 iv. 425–6 & n.; PRO, E 179/252/32, St Bride's, p. 6 (R)

Prin 1 L. Vallas in *Bull. français de la soc. internationale de musique*, 4 (1908); Grove (6th ed.). The note at viii. 500 follows Galpin (*Old Engl. instruments*, rev. Dart 1965, pp. 72–4) in conflating father and son.

Pritchard 1 *CSPD 1663–4*, p. 350; 1671, p. 211

Privy Seal 1 Aylmer, esp. pp. 47–8
2 Harris, i. 11; *CSPD 1636–7*, p. 534
3 No. 72 on plan in Colvin, v, pl. 36. In 1677 an office was constructed for the Privy Seal over the lobby of the House of Lords: ib., p. 399

Proctor 1 PRO, PCC Hyde 84

Proger 1 *Bull. IHR*, 19/11, 15; J. A. Bradney, *Hist. of Monmouthshire* (1904), ii. 199–200; Gramont, p. 359

Prowd 1 Chaplin (*see* Crisp, E., n. 1); *CSPD*, e.g. 1664–5, p. 402

Prujean 1 Munk; Venn; PRO, PCC Mico 122

Pulford 1 *CSPD 1651–2*, p. 38; GEC

Pumpfield 1 *CSPD Add. 1660–85*, p. 110

Punnett 1 ib., p. 407; 1667–8, p. 485

Punt 1 Firth and Rait, e.g. ii. 1326, 1370, 1433; Carte 73, f. 284r

Purcell 1 PRO, LC 3/25, p. 38
  2 F. B. Zimmerman, *H. Purcell* (1967), pp. 6–9 and App. III
Putney 1 Meekings (*see* Arthur, n. 1), p. xcii
  2 VCH, *Surrey*, iv. 79
Pym 1 HMC, *Portland*, iii. 249; GLRO, MR/TH/7, m. 28
  2 Mapperton, Sandwich MSS, App., f. 83*v*; Lister (*see* Da Silva, n. 1), iii. 537; PRO, PCC Eure 64
Pye 1 i. 47 & n. 2; HP; PRO, PCC Nabbs 191
Pyne 1 *CSPD 1665–6*, pp. 101–2; *1667–8*, pp. 103, 158, 200, 485; Tomlinson, p. 238
Quartermain 1 HP; Munk; *Bull. IHR*, 19/19
Radcliffe 1 Venn
Rainbowe 1 ib.; Wood, *Ath. Oxon.*, iv. 865; White Kennet, *Register* (1728), p. 353; life (1688) by Jonathan Banks
Ratcliff 1 GLRO, MR/TH/4, mm. 112–130*r* (R)
Raven 1 Carte 73, ff. 234, 362
Rawlins 1 HMC, *Rep.*, 8/1/2/278
Rawlinson 1 Wheatley, 28 June 1660, n.
  2 *CSPD 1663–4*, p. 638
  3 *See above* Diary p. 90 ~ *DNB*; Boyd 11526; PRO, PCC North 31
Raworth 1 *Gray's Inn Reg.*
Rayner 1 PRO, Adm 2/1732, f. 11*v*
Reade 1 Foster; Wood, *Ath. Oxon.*, iii. 831
Reeves, R. 1 Taylor, pp. 223–4, 276
Reeves, S. 1 Beaven
Reggio 1 PL 2803 ~ G. Rose in *Music and Letters*, 43 (1965)/207+; Shadwell, *Works* (ed. Summers, 1927), v. 239+
Religion 1 A. Grey, *Debates of H. of Commons 1667–94* (1796), ii. 246 (where Thurscrosse is mistakenly given as 'Twiscrosse')
  2 i. 289, 206
  3 i. 76; cf. also iv. 164

  4 Grey, loc. cit.
  5 iv. 127–8; Ollard (*see* Howe, n. 2), p. 279
  6 vii. 123; viii. 91 ~ iii. 72; iv. 259
  7 i. 238; ii. 107, 171
  8 ix. 164
  9 iii. 178
 10 ix. 379
 11 i. 257, 141
 12 v. 125, 227
 13 W. P. Baker in Lennard (*see* Drink, n. 22), pp. 130–1
 14 vii. 164
 15 iii. 54, n. 1
 16 iv. 419; viii. 439; vii. 325
 17 iv. 164–5
 18 ix. 371
 19 ix. 286
 20 i. 190
 21 ii. 12
 22 v. 87
 23 *Tangier Papers*, p. 13
 24 ib., p. 49
 25 Sotheby's *Catalogue*, 11 Apr. 1919, lot 944 (1¼ pp.); PL 1325, 1401
 26 *Priv. Corr.*, ii. 36, 38–9, 238–9, 241–2
 27 Braybrooke (1854), iv. 323–4
 28 *The sick man visited* (first pub. 1712)
 29 PL 2858, p. 154
 30 *Priv. Corr.*, ii. 312–13
 31 Further reading: G. Bradford, *The soul of Pepys* (Boston 1924)
Reymes 1 HP; life by H. A. Kaufman (1962)
Reynolds 1 *CSPD* e.g. *1649–50*, p. 111; *Cat.*, i
Riccard 1 PRO, E 179/252/32, London 18, f. 22*r* (R)
  2 Beaven; PRO, PCC Eure 112
Richardson 1 Howe
Rider 1 George W. Hill and W. H. Frere, *Mem. of Stepney* (Guildford 1890–1), p. 244 & n. 1
  2 Routh, p. 31; BL, Add. MSS 9317, f. 1; PRO, SP 29/96/66; *Further Corr.*, p. 30

Robartes 1 PRO, E 179/252/32, Chelsea (R) ~ GEC; *DNB*; Clarendon *Life*, i. 463–4; Burnet, i. 76; North (ed. Jessop), i. 300, 301. Engraved portrait in PL 2979/37a

2 GEC

Robert 1 Lafontaine, p. 321

2 *CTB*, iii. 780

3 M. Benoît, *Versailles et les musiciens du roi* (Paris 1971), p. 342; *Musiques de cour* (Paris 1971), p. 28 ~ Y. de Brossard, *Les musiciens de Paris 1535–1792* (1965)

Robins, A. 1 *CSPD 1659–60*, pp. 47, 583, 591; WRO, E 172, E 174

Robins, Mrs 1 Bryant, iii. 228

Robinson, H. 1 W. K. Jordan, *Men of substance* (Chicago 1942), pp. 51+, 86+, 178+, 215+

Robinson, Sir J. 1 Woodhead

Robinson, L. 1 HP

Robinson, Sir R. 1 NWB, p. 229 ~ *CSPD* e.g. *1652–3*, p. 591; *Cat.*, i; Longleat, Coventry MSS 99, f. 92r; PL 2351, pp. 21+, 67+, 177+

Robson 1 Collinge; *CSPD 1668–9*, p. 155; Longleat, Coventry MSS 101, f. 116v

Roche 1 PRO, LC/73, p. 159; John Ward, *Diary* (ed. Severn, 1839), p. 168; inf. from R. D. Gwynn

Roettier 1 L. Forrer, *Biog. dict. medallists* (1904–16)

Rogers 1 *Harl. Soc. Reg.*, 88/88

Rolt 1 Sotheby's *Catalogue*, 11 Apr. 1919, lot 943; BL, Add. MSS 40708, f. 33v

2 Whitear, p. 91

3 W. C. Abbott, *Writings etc. of Oliver Cromwell* (Camb. Mass. 1937), iii. 712, 797; M. Noble, *House of Cromwell* (1787), i. 287; *CSPD 1655–6*, p. 585; *1656–7*, p. 121; Rawl. A 36, pp. 397–424; Sherwood, pp. 71, 77, 169

4 Dalton, i. 76; Whitear, p. 92

Rooth 1 Longleat, Coventry MSS

99, f. 92r; *CSPD*, e.g. *1655–6*, p. 530; *Cat.*, i

Rothe 1 K. H. D. Haley in D. H. Pennington and K. Thomas (eds), *Puritans and revolutionaries* (Oxf. 1978), pp. 310+

Rotherhithe 1 Meekings (*see* Arthur, n. 1), p. lxxxix

2 Hatton, vol. ii, sect. vii

Rouse 1 Meekings, op. cit., pp. 128, 175; Bodl., Clar. dep. c. 401, p. 37; *Pub. Cath. Rec. Soc.* 38, p. xxx

Rowley 1 Venn

R. Exchange 1 BL, Add. MSS 5101 (10)

2 Views (pre- and post-fire) in PL 2972/62–71a; see also view by Hollar in *D*, iv, facing p. 151 ~ Davis (*see* Books, n. 8), pp. 162–3; Wheatley and Cunningham

3 vi. 155, 318

4 iv. 264

R. Fishery 1 Based on T. W. Fulton, *Sovereignty of the sea* (1911); Charles H. Wilson, *Profit and power* (1957); William R. Scott, *Joint-Stock Companies* (Camb. 1910–12), ii. 361+

R. Mews 1 Colvin, v. 209

2 ib., 208–9; Wheatley and Cunningham

R. Society 1 See *Record of the Royal Soc.* (1940), and articles in *Notes and records of Roy. Soc.*, vol. 23 (1968)

2 In 1663 naval vessels under Capt. Robert Holmes – well known to Pepys – made trials of Christiaan Huygens's marine chronometers. The connection of Greenwich Observatory (1675) with navigation is well known.

3 vi. 7, 8

4 Kepler said that comets move in straight lines, and Descartes that they follow irregular paths round vortices. At this time several astronomers thought they moved

in circular orbits around other stars than the sun, and so might be seen more than once.

5 vi. 48
6 *Voyage into Engl.* (1709), pp. 36–7
7 viii. 543, 554
8 Further reading: Marjorie H. Nicolson, *Pepys' diary and the new science* (Charlottesville 1965)

Ruddiard 1 *CTB*, e.g. i. 242
Rumbold 1 BL, Egerton MSS 2551, f. 17r; *TRHS* (n.s.) 6/163; Carte 75, f. 393r; *CSPD 1660–1*, p. 74; *CTB*, i. 414; Routh, p. 85, n. 3
Rundell 1 PRO, Adm 2/1732, f. 9; BL, Add. MSS 9307, f. 175r
Rupert 1 *DNB*; life by Maurice P. Ashley (1976); *Rupert and Monck letter bk* (*see* Batts, n. 1). Engraved portrait in PL 2978/78a
Rushworth 1 HP; Aylmer; *CTB*, i. 215–16; Aubrey, ii. 209. Engraved portrait in PL 2979/117c
Russell, H. 1 PRO, Adm 20 e.g. 7/1, no. 987; Bryant, iii. 270
Russell, J. 1 p. 152 ∼ GEC; Dalton, i. 7, 37, 146
Russell, R. 1 Woodhead; PRO, Adm 2/1725, f. 15r; *CSPD Add.* 1660–85, pp. 420, 430; PRO, PCC Juxon 8
Russell, Maj. 1 PRO, E 179/252/32, p. 8 (R)
Russell, Sir W. 1 iv. 244, n. 4; *DNB*
Russell, —— 1 *CSPD*, e.g. *1663–4*, p. 636; *CTB*, iii. 667
Rutherford 1 GEC; Routh; Sir J. B. Paul (ed.), *Scots Peerage* (Edinburgh 1904–11)
Sabbath 1 1 Car. I, c. 1
2 3 Car. I, c. 1
3 Firth and Rait, i. 599
4 ib., ii. 1163
5 Steele, no. 3383
6 *A volume of posthumous discourses* (1726), p. 341
7 29 Car. II, c. 7 ∼ Further reading: W. P. Baker in R. Lennard (ed.)

Englishmen at rest and play (1931), pp. 81+; W. B. Whitaker, *Sunday in Tudor and Stuart times* (1933), pp. 128+; id., *The 18th-cent. Engl. Sunday* (1940); J. H. Overton, *Life in Engl. church 1660–1714* (1885), pp. 318+
St James's Flds 1 LCC, *Survey*, vols 29 and 30, passim
St James's Pal. 1 Colvin, v. 233+; views in PL 2972/103b, 104–5, 186
2 *CSPD 1650*, pp. 418, 436
3 Colvin, v. 244+; view (interior, 1688) in PL 2972/186
4 Colvin, loc. cit.
St James's Pk 1 i. 246 & n. 2; v. 127 & n. 1; Evelyn, iii. 573, n. 3; *CTB*, i. 719
St James's Sq. 1 LCC, *Survey*, 29/ 58+
St John 1 *DNB*; B. Worden, *Rump Parl.* (Camb. 1974), pp. 178–9, 278
St Katharine's 1 C. Jamison, *Hist. Royal Hosp. St Katharine* (Oxf. 1952)
St Martin's La. 1 Hatton, vol. i. sect. i
St Martin's le G. 1 ib., loc. cit.
St Michel, A. and D. 1 cf. iv. 277, 429: 'friends' may, in both entries, mean family.
2 *Family Letters*, p. 27
3 *CSPD 1664–5*, pp. 405, 467
4 This account is largely based on Balty St Michel's letter to Pepys, 8 Feb. 1674, in *Family Letters* pp. 25+ Much remains uncertain.
St Michel, B. and E. 1 Pepys (1974), p. 255
2 *Family Letters*, p. 164
3 Chester-Foster 929
4 *Family Letters*, p. 183
5 vi. 140
6 *Family Letters*, pp. 224–6; *Priv. Corr.*, ii. 307–9; *TRHS* (ser. 5) 7/153
7 op. cit., p. 63 ∼ *Family Letters*, pp. xxiv–xxviii and passim

St Olave's 1 A. Povah, *Annals St Olave, Hart St* (1894)

St Paul's Cath. 1 iv. 261, n. 1; ix. 288 & n. 1; H. H. Milman, *Annals St Paul's* (1869); Colvin (*see* Denham, n. 2). Pepys collected a number of views of both the old and the new cathedral: see list in R. Latham (ed.), *Catalogue of Pepys Library*, vol. iii, pt i (*Prints: General*, comp. A. W. Aspital, Woodbridge, 1980)

St Paul's Sch. 1 PRO, E 179/252/32, Mr Izod's acct (R)

2 Strype, i. 164. Drawing in PL 2972/146a

3 PL 2972/146b

4 Strype, i. 168

5 Sir Michael McDonnell, *Hist. St Paul's School* (1909); and *Annals St Paul's School* (1959). He gives an account (*Hist.*, pp. 212+) of the 11 contemporaries of Pepys mentioned in the diary.

St Valentine 1 *Letters* (ed. Parry, Wayfarers' Lib., n.d.), pp. 214–15

2 iii. 29

3 viii. 184

4 L. Whistler, *Engl. Festivals* (1947), p. 90+; *Times*, 11 Feb. 1961

5 Further reading: Whistler, op. cit.; Arthur R. Wright, *Brit. calendar customs* (ed. Lones, 1936), ii. 136+

Salisbury Ct Th. 1 BL, Add. MSS 5064 (154) (R)

Saltonstall 1 *DNB* s.n. Sir Richard; BL, Add. MSS 10117, f. 12r

Samford 1 *CSPD 1655–6*, pp. 500, 546; Aylmer, p. 253

Sanderson 1 *DNB*; Chappell, pp. 26, 35; Whitear, p. 92; Evelyn, iv. 94, n. 4; *Family Letters*, e.g. p. 118; *Bull. IHR*, 19/15

Sandys 1 HP

2 viii. 583; HP

Sankey 1 Venn; Magd. Coll., Reg., ii, ff. 64a, 69a, 72b; PRO E 179/244/22; PRO, PCC Poley 285

Sansum 1 *CSPD 1649–50*, p. 600 etc.; *Cat.*, i

Santhune 1 Chappell, p. 54; Whitear, pp. 42–3; *Proc. Hug. Soc. London* 15/319–20; inf. from R. D. Gwynn

Saunders, F. 1 *Cat.*, i

Saunders, J. 1 ib.

Saunders, ——. 1 *CSPD* e.g. *1650, 1651–2*; *Cat.*, i

Savage 1 Carlisle (*see* Baber, n. 1), p. 165; *CSPD 1665–6*, p. 21; *1667*, p. 462; *1668–9*, p. 308; *CTB*, ii. 594

Savile 1 Life by H. C. Foxcroft (2 vols, 1898); *Works*, ed. Raleigh (Oxf. 1912)

2 *Naval Minutes*, p. 257; Bryant, ii. 272

Savoy 1 Sir R. Somerville, *The Savoy* (1960); Colvin, v. 359+. View by Hollar in PL 2972/137 d, e

Sawyer 1 Magd. Coll., Reg., ii, ff. 64a, 65b; HP; *DNB*; Burnet, ii. 344; North (ed. Jessop), i. 376

Sayers 1 PRO, E 101/441, nos 3, 4 [1662, 1663]; LS 13/34, p. 43 [1664]

Scarburgh 1 Bryant, ii. 378 ~ Munk; *DNB*; Evelyn, v. 206

Scawen 1 HP; D. H. Pennington in *Essays in econ. and hist. Tudor and Stuart Engl.* (ed. F. J. Fisher, Camb. 1961), pp. 185–6, 191

Science 1 i. 97; cf. also ii. 12

2 v. 30

3 iv. 59

4 iv. 143–8

5 iv. 343–4, 406

6 v. 27

7 v. 28

8 iii. 164; iv. 257

9 ii. 68

10 iv. 185–6 & n.; vii. 382 & n. 2

11 ix. 208

12 v. 359 & n. 1; iv. 338 & n. 2

Scient. Instrs 1 iv. 266

2 viii. 450–1

3 ix. 116–17

4 vii. 226

5 vii. 254

6 Further reading: Michael Hunter, *Science and society in Restoration Engl.* (Camb. 1981); Charles Webster, *The Great Instauration* (1975); Sir W. Abell, *The shipwright's trade* (Camb. 1948)

Scobell 1 i. 12–13 & n.; Williams (*see* Hughes, ——, n. 1), pp. 7–8; Firth and Rait, ii. 88–9; PRO, PCC Nabbs 256

Scot 1 GL, MS. 10116/1; P. J. Anderson, *Alumni of Aberdeen Univ. 1596–1860* (Aberdeen 1900), p. 22

Scott, B. 1 Chappell, p. 51; PRO, PCC Hyde 27

Scott, E. 1 Dalton, i. 120; *CSPD 1667–8*, pp. 82, 594; Luke (*see* Cholmley, n. 3), p. 130

Scott, —— 1 Evelyn, iii. 317; PRO, PCC Carr 11

Scott, Mrs 1 WRO, E 1609

Seabrook 1 R. Newcourt, *Repertorium* (1708–10), i. 272; Foster

Seale 1 *Cat.*, i

Seddon 1 BL, Add. MSS 11602, f. 317r; Collinge

Sedgwick 1 *Gray's Inn Reg.*

Sedley 1 PL 1604 (10) ~ *DNB*; John H. Wilson, *Court wits of Restoration* (Princeton 1948), esp. pp. 215–16; life by V. de Sola Pinto (1927)

Seeley 1 *Cat.*, i

Seething La. 1 Hatton, vol. i, sect. i

Seymour, E. 1 BL, Harl. MSS 1509, f. 28r; 1510, f. 147r

2 *Letters*, p. 214 ~ North (ed. Jessop), i. 299–300; HP; *DNB*; Collinge; Sainty

Seymour, H. 1 *Cat.*, i; *CSPD 1665–6*, pp. 1, 579

Seymour, J. (i) 1 *CSPD 1663–4*, pp. 80, 232; also ib., *Add. 1660–85*, p. 217; *1665–6*, pp. 237, 293; *1667–8*, p. 129

Seymour, J. (ii) 1 Mapperton, Sandwich MSS, Letters from

Ministers, ii, ff. 85r, 120v, 124r, 126r; *Middle Temple Reg.*

Shadwell, T. (i) 1 PRO, E 403/1758, f. 56v; *CTB*, iii. 378; Chester-Foster, p. 23, n. 2

Shadwell, T. (ii) 1 qu. *DNB*

Shafto 1 Venn

Shalcross 1 Boyd 17545. Possibly son of Thomas (q.v. Arthur H. Johnson, *Hist. Drapers' Co.*, Oxf., 1914–22, iii. 176, 186, 342)

Shales 1 Marvell, ii. 342–3

2 *Further Corr.*, p. 69 ~ PL 2287, pp. 477–8; 2266, pp. 194, 195, 207; *CSPD 1668–9*, p. 264; *1670*, p. 561; *Cat.*, i. 73, 74, 79; Baxter, pp. 73–4, 232–3

Shatterell 1 Van Lennep, p. 314; Braybrooke (1858), ii. 363, n.

Shaw, J. 1 PRO, E 179/147/617, p. 164 (R)

2 HP

Shaw, R. 1 *CSPD 1661–2*, pp. 336, 340. For his two marriages, see Burke (*see* Beale, F., n. 1), p. 661; Chester-Foster 1213; LRO, Mayor's Court Depositions 1663–4

Sheeres 1 *Letters*, pp. 144–5

2 *Priv. Corr.*, esp. ii. 317 ~ *DNB*; Luke (*see* Cholmley, n. 3), pp. 44, 108, 121, 177, 211; *Naval Minutes*, esp. p. 104; PL 558, 1139, 1476

Sheldon, J. 1 viii. 320, n. 1; PRO, E 179/252/32, Mr Izod's acct, St Botolph's, Aldersgate, London I post-Fire, p. 15 (R)

Sheldon, W. 1 PRO, Adm 2/1732, f. 5r

Shelston 1 Boyd 41939

Sheppard 1 *Cat.*, i

Shergoll 1 PRO, Adm 20/1, no. 1348

Sherwyn 1 *See above* Pepys, E., p. 316

2 Aylmer, pp. 99, 253–4; Baxter, pp. 146–9; *Rep. Deputy Keeper Public Rec.*, 30/360

Shipley 1 Carte 73, esp. f. 336r; HMC, *Hodgkin*, p. 159; PL 2049

Shipman, A. 1 Sir William Foster,

Southwell 1 ix. 59; *Letters*, p. 125
2 ib., p. 170 ~ *DNB*; Bittner u. Gross (*see* Barckman, n. 1); *Letters*, pp. 125–6, 173; *Naval Minutes*, pp. 111, 156 etc.

Spark 1 *DNB*; Venn

Sparling 1 *CSPD*, e.g. *1649–50*, p. 193; *Cat.*, i; *CSPClar.*, iv. 673

Spicer 1 *CTB*, i. 274; iii. 220; PRO, E 407/1

Spong 1 Taylor, p. 228; GL, St Bride's Reg.

Spragge 1 *DNB*; *Cat.*, i; HP; VCH, *Kent*, iii. 354. Engraved portraits in PL 2979/235, 236a

Spry 1 HP; *CJ*, viii. 225

Squibb 1 G. E. Aylmer, *King's Servants* (1961), pp. 90, 388; and *State's Servants* (1973), pp. 216–18; *CSPD 1661–2*, p. 369; *1663–4*, pp. 121, 582; *1666–7*, pp. 182–3, 535; *1671*, p. 357; inf. from G. D. Squibb
2 *CTB*, i. 1, 3, 182, 392

Stacey 1 *CSPD*, e.g. *1664–5*, p. 132; Woodhead

Staines 1 *CSPD 1663–4*, p. 395; *1664–5*, p. 55

Stankes 1 ix. 309 & n. 2; *Family Letters*, pp. 1, 4; Hunts. Rec. Off., Wills, Brampton Peculiar

Stanley 1 Venn

Stapely 1 *CSPD*, e.g. *1665–6*, p. 132

Starkey, J. 1 PRO, E 179/252/27, m. 35d
2 BL, Add. MSS 36916
3 Plomer, i; PL 2372; E. Arber, *Term Cat.* (1903–6), vol. i, p. viii; T. J. Crist, 'Francis Smith and the opposition press 1660–88' (unpub. thesis, Camb. 1977), esp. pp. 48, 159, 238, 334, 358

Starkey, P. 1 Sherwood, p. 36 ~ PRO, E 179/147/617, p. 164 (R); Phillips (*see* Levitt, n. 1), p. 130; *CSPD 1678*, p. 318

**Starkey, —— ** 1 *Gray's Inn Reg.*

Starling 1 vii. 282, n. 1; PRO, E 179/

252/32, London 18, f. 11 (R); PCC Bunce 28

Stat. Hall 1 Wheatley and Cunningham

Stayner 1 *DNB*; *Cat.*, i

Stefkins 1 Grove (6th ed.); J. A. Westrup in *Musical Quart.* 27/81; Wilson (*see* Lanier, n. 1), p. 298; Huyghens, *De Briefwisseling* (ed. J. A. Worp, The Hague, 1911–17), no. 4725

Stephens, R. 1 Goldsmiths' Co., MSS 1916, f. 33*v*; 1917, f. 32*r*; 1918, f. 75*r* (R)

Sterry 1 *CSPD 1657–8*, p. 89; *1659–60*, p. 595; Masson (*see* Agar, n. 1), v. 71

Stevens 1 BL, Add. MSS 28040, f. 12*r*; Baxter, p. 73

Steventon 1 PRO, Adm 2/1725, f. 5*v*; R. East, *Extracts from records of Portsmouth* (Portsmouth 1891), pp. 21, 22, 355
2 *Further Corr.*, pp. 38–9
3 PRO, SP 46/121, no. 314; NWB, p. 14; *Cat.*, iii. 298

Steward 1 *CSPD* e.g. *1649–50*; *Cat.*, i; Longleat, Coventry MSS 99, f. 92*r*

Stoakes 1 Clowes, ii. 215–17; *Cat.*, i; *CSPD 1664–5*, p. 201

Stockdale 1 *CSPD 1665–6*, p. 71; Duke of York, *Mem.* (*naval*), pp. 116–17; *CTB*, ii. 92 etc.

Stokes 1 PRO, E 179/252/32, London, 2 (R); Jones (*see* Fire, n. 3), ii. 219; PRO, Adm 20/7/1, p. 237 etc.; Heal (*see* Atkinson, n. 1), p. 250

Stone 1 Aylmer, p. 241

Story 1 *CTB*, e.g. i. 641; ii. 105; iii. 386

Stowell 1 ib., ii. 45; Hasted (*see* Boreman, W., n. 1), iii. 54
2 *CSPD*, e.g. *1659–60*, p. 459; PRO, Adm 42/1

Strachan 1 *CSPD Add. 1660–85*, p. 164; Duke of York, *Mem.* (*naval*), pp. 129–30

2 i. 301 & n. 1; Adm 20/1, no. 1529; Adm 20/6, no. 1851; *CTB*, iii. 148

Strange 1 *CTB*, e.g. i. 216

Strangeways 1 HP

Streeter 1 *DNB*; *Burlington Mag.*, 84/1–12; WRO, F 398

Strode 1 Dalton, i. 9n.; *Naval Minutes*, pp. 155, 249

Strudwick 1 Chappell, p. 51; PRO, E 179/147/627, p. 80 (R)

2 PRO, E 179/252/23 (R); letter, 30 Sept. 1678, in possession of C. D. L. Pepys

3 John Brown, *Bunyan* (1885), pp. 371, 377, 382

Strutt 1 iii. 284, n. 1; *CSPD*, e.g. *1661–2*, p. 618

Stuart 1 Gramont, p. 111; life by C. H. Hartmann (1924). Engraved portrait in PL 2979/187a

Stuckey 1 *CTB*, ii. 344; Mapperton, Sandwich MSS, Letters from Ministers, i, f. 95*v*

Sutton 1 Whitear, p. 57

Swaddell 1 *CSPD 1663–4*, p. 251; *Add. 1660–85*, p. 403; Tomlinson, pp. 59–60, 224 & n.

Swan, H. 1 *CSPD*, e.g. *1664–5*, p. 132

Swan, W. 1 PRO, E 403/1756; PRO, Index, Pipe Off. Decl. Accts

Swynfen 1 HP; J. C. Wedgwood, *Staffs. parl. hist.* (W. Salt Arch. Coll., 1919–33), ii. 76+

2 Foster; *CSPD 1663–4*, p. 623

Symons, T. 1 ib., *1659–60*, pp. 202, 243; Young (*see* Conny n. 1), p. 10

Symons, W. 1 PRO, SP 25 I 108, 74; Westminster Abbey Archives, St Margaret's reg.; PL 2874, p. 387; PRO, PCC Nabbs 256

Symons, —— 1 Barnard (*see* Angier, n. 2), p. 23

Taaffe 1 GEC; John D'Alton, *Illust. of King James's Irish army list* (Dublin 1855); T. Crist (ed.), *Charles II to Lord Taaffe: Letters in exile* (priv. ptd, Camb., 1974), esp. pp. 11–12

Talbot, C. 1 *Cat.*, i; *Shorthand Letters*, p. 31

Talbot, P. 1 Clarendon, *Life*, iii. 117–18; J. J. Delaney and J. E. Tobin, *Dict. Cath. biog.* (1962)

Talbot, R. 1 *DNB*; HMC, *Rep.*, 8/1/2/279a

Tallents 1 Venn; Magd. Coll., Reg., ii. 9b, 64a, 65a

2 *Calamy Rev.*

Tangier 1 J. R. Powell (ed.), *Letters of R. Blake* (1937), p. 163

2 qu. Routh, p. 6

3 *Journal* (ed. Lubbock, 1934), i. 70

4 iv. 319

5 iii. 171

6 v. 280

7 iv. 326–7

8 ib., 269

9 Routh, p. 163

10 viii. 167

11 Routh, p. 201

12 ib., p. 203

13 ib., p. 232

14 ib., p. 234

15 iv. 27

16 qu. Routh, p. 248, n.

17 The best edition is that by E. Chappell (with W. Matthews), pub. as Pepys's *Tangier Papers* (NRS, 1935).

18 *Tangier Papers*, p. 4

19 ib., p. 16

20 ib., p. 89

21 ib., p. 224

22 Routh, pp. 254, 255

23 *Tangier Papers*, p. 25

24 ib., p. 30

25 *Hist.* (1838 ed.), p. 757

26 Routh, p. 344, n. 3

27 qu. ib., pp. 354–5

28 PL 2985, pt ii/294–307; also 2062[3] (Hollar) ∼ Further reading: E. M. G. Routh, *Tangier* (1912; on the mole, ch. xvii and App. IV); P. Earle, *Corsairs of Malta and Barbary* (1970); John Luke, *Journal* (ed. Kaufman,

Geneva 1958); W. B. T. Abbey, *Tangier under British rule* (1940); C. Lloyd, *Engl. corsairs on the Barbary coast* (1981)

Tasborough I *CSPD 1670*, p. 585

Tatnell I ib. *1653–4*, p. 71; *Cat.*, i

Taverns etc. I Overall (*see* Manning, n. 1) p. 159; H. A. Monckton, *Hist. Engl. ale and beer* (1966), p. 113

2 ix. 86

3 e.g. vii. 424

4 cf. Defoe qu. S. and B. Webb, *Hist. liquor licensing* (1903), p. 24 n.

5 cf. inventory (1644) in *Trans. London and Mdx Arch. Soc.*, 20/194+

6 i. 88, 212

7 i. 52, 61; v. 128; vii. 414; viii. 133

8 vii. 237; ix. 179

9 ii. 30; iii. 165

10 ix. 42

11 vi. 44; viii. 553–4

12 i. 263; iii. 269; iv. 189

13 Further reading: R. F. Bretherton in R. V. Lennard (ed.), *Englishmen at work and play* (1931), pp. 147+; S. and B. Webb, *Hist. liquor licensing 1700–1830* (1903); Dorothy Davis, *Hist. of shopping* (1966)

Taverns (named) I Lillywhite 2184

2 WRO, E 174; GLRO, MR/TH/7, m. 5; *Harl. Soc. Reg.*, 33/42; Boyne, p. 647

3 Kenneth Rogers, *Signs and taverns* (1937), p. 62

4 WRO, E 174; E 1608, p. 33; PRO, SP 29/448

5 GL, MS. 3461 II f. 26r; Boyne, p. 1017

6 Strype, iv. 118

7 PRO, E 179/252/27, m. 29d

8 WRO, E 172, 174; E 1608, p. 1; GLRO, MR/TH/7, m. 2d

9 Strype, iv. 112; GLRO, MR/TH/7, m. 53; PRO, PCC, Alchin 21

10 John Taylor, *Carriers' Cosmography* (1637), in E. Arber, ed., *Engl. Garner* (1903–4), i. 234 etc.; Boyne, p. 631

11 von Uffenbach (*see* Hyde Pk, n. 1)), pp. 179–81; qu. Boyne, p. 534

12 Lillywhite 3847

13 qu. Boyne, p. 534

14 Strype, ii. 107, 109 (map); J. Taylor, op. cit., i. 232; PRO, E 179/252/32 (19), p. 1 (R); Wheatley and Cunningham

15 Lillywhite 4053; Boyne, p. 542

16 WRO, E 172, 174; E 1608, p. 46; E 1621, pp. 15, 56; GLRO, MR/TH/7, m. 7d

17 *Reg. St Mary Woolnoth* (ed. J. M. S. Brooke and A. W. C. Hallen, 1886), p. 245; PRO, E 179/252/32 (3), p. 1 (R)

18 e.g., Shadwell's *The Humorist* (pub. 1670), act V; Wycherley's *Country Wife* (written 1670–1), act I, Sc. i. PRO, LS 8/3, p. 183; ib. 8/5, n.p; North (ed. Jessop), i. 66; Lillywhite 1919

19 GLRO, MR/TH/7, m. 25; WRO, E 172, 174; J. Taylor (above, n. 10), i. 229

20 ib., i. 239, 242; BL, Add. MSS 34014, f. 39r

21 Boyne, p. 520; Lillywhite 4754 (1672); K. Rogers, *Mermaid etc. Taverns* (1928), pp. 148, 149

22 J. Boys's diary (*N. & Q.*, 27 Dec. 1930, p. 455 etc.); Wheatley and Cunningham; Lillywhite 4884

23 Strype, iv. 17; GL, MS. 2969 I, f. 125; *N. & Q.*, 7 July 1928

24 J. Taylor, op. cit., i. 235

25 GL, MS. 2969 II, p. 402; MS. 3018, passim; Boyne, p. 603; PRO, E 179/252/27, f. 35v; ib., (8) (R)

26 WRO, E 172, 174, 176; WRO, Wills (William's proved 18 Apr.

1667; Alice's, 26 Jan. 1670); GLRO, MR/TH/7, m. 1d

27 BL, Add. MSS 5063 (84), 5065 (22); PRO, E 179/147/617, p. 134; ib. 252/23, n.f. (R); Sir H. Lyons, *Roy. Soc.* (Camb. 1944), p. 170

28 Wheatley and Cunningham; LRO, Control Room 101, f. 26; Assessment Box 10, MS. 7; PRO, E 179/252/27, f. 35v (R)

29 WRO, E 172, 174, 176; GLRO, WR/TH/7, m. 7; *Daily Post*, 15 July 1727

30 J. Taylor (above, n. 10), i. 231, 242; Strype, ii. 109

31 LRO, Hustings Roll 250 (27), 263, (43); PRO, E 179/252/32 (18), f. 28 (R)

32 Lillywhite 6401, 6402

33 Lillywhite 6498, 6493, 6494

34 BL, Add. MSS 5063 (20); Boyne, p. 574; K. Rogers, *Mermaid and Mitre taverns*, p. 24; Strype, ii. 149; PRO, E 179/252/27, f. 54 (R)

35 i. 307 & n. 2; Lillywhite 6520; Boyne, pp. 574-5; PRO, PCC Eure 119; Wheatley and Cunningham; GLRO, MR/TH/7, m. 51

36 *Tijdschrift voor tael en letteren*, May 1939, pp. 286-7; Magalotti (*see* Annesley, n. 1), p. 127; von Uffenbach (*see* Hyde Pk, n. 1), p. 130; PL 2972/238-9

37 PRO, E 179/252/27, f. 36r; ib. 179/147/627, p. 68 (R)

38 BL, Add. MSS 5063 (79), 5064 (150); Strype, iv. 108 (no. 14 on map); Boyne, p. 757

39 WRO, E 172, 174, 176; GLRO, MR/TH/7, m. 1d

40 Taylor (above, n. 10), i. 230-1, 241; Strype, iii. 283; iv. 75; Boyne, p. 630

41 Lillywhite 7135; Boyne, p. 658 (n.d.)

42 PRO, E 179/252/27, f. 32v (R)

43 WRO, F 388, 1092

44 PRO, E 179/251/22, f. 8v (R)

45 Boyne, p. 650

46 Lillywhite 7954

47 BL, Add. MSS 5063 (34); LRO, Hustings Roll 338, m. 55; PRO, E 179/147/627, f. 99v (R)

48 WRO, F 388, 1092; WRO 4533; GLRO, MR/TH/7, m. 32

49 Lillywhite 8322

50 WRO, F 388, 1092; PRO, PCC Duke 27; PRO, E 179/252/32 (R)

51 WRO, E 172, 174, 176; GLRO, Wills 845; GLRO MR/TH/7, m. 1

52 PRO, E 179/252/32, St Bride, p. 35 (R)

53 WRO, E 172, 174; ib. 176 (Mr S. Baker's ward); Wheatley and Cunningham

54 Fuller, *Worthies* (1662), p. 236; GLRO, MR/TH/7, m. 7d; WRO, E 172, 174, 176; E 1621, p. 16; E 1608, p. 48 etc; J. Rushworth *Hist. Coll.* (1703-8), vii. 1355; Wheatley and Cunningham

55 GL, MS 2969/1, f. 124; ib. 2/402; MS. 3018, f. 140r+; Boyne, p. 603-4; A. L. Simon, *Hist. wine trade* (1906-9), iii. 229; Lord King, *Locke* (1858), p. 35; PRO E 179/252/27, f. 32v; ib. 32 (8) (R)

56 WRO, E 172, 174

57 BL, Add. MSS 5074 (7); Boyne, p. 771; PRO, E 179/252/32 (4) (R)

58 GL, MS. 2969; Boyne, p. 603

59 Lillywhite 9010; Boyne, p. 581 (n.d.); Bryant, ii. 381-2

60 Boyne, p. 558; GLRO, MR/TH/7, m. 2d; *N. & Q.*, 27 Dec. 1930, p. 454

61 Lillywhite 621, 9164; Wheatley and Cunningham

62 Boyne, p. 813

63 Boyne, pp. 554, 555; Wheatley

and Cunningham; PRO, E 179/
252/32 (8) (R)

64 PRO, PCC Cottle 4; GLRO,
MR/TH/7, m. 30; PRO, E 179/
252/32, St Martin, f. 25r (R)

65 BL, Add. MSS 5075 (36); LRO,
Hustings Roll 340, m. 245; PRO, E
179/252/32 (4) (R); Boyne, p. 681

66 v. 101

67 K. Rogers, *Mermaid and Mitre
taverns*, p. 74

68 Lillywhite 9755; Boyne, pp. 777,
778; PRO, E 179/252/32 (18) (R)

69 WRO, E 174

70 WRO, E 172, 174; E 1608, p. 6;
Boyne, pp. 647, 648

71 GLRO, MR/TH/7, m. 7d; Boyne,
p. 684; PRO, E 179/143/335 (R)

72 LCC, *Survey*, 16/89; Lillywhite
10087

73 PRO, E 179/252/27, f. 61 (R)

74 BL, Add. MSS 5064 (124), 5075
(38), 5076 (6) (R); PRO, E
179/252/32 (19), p. 4 (R); *Trans.
Lond. and Mdx Arch. Soc.* (1925)/
1 +

75 BL, Add. MSS 5080 (25); PRO,
E 179/252/27, f. 35v (R); Boyne,
p. 604; K. Rogers, *Mermaid and
Mitre taverns*, pp. 131 +; Bell,
Fire, p. 155

76 opera cit.

77 LRO, Control Room 101, f. 19v;
PRO, E 179/252/32 (R)

78 Ogilby and Morden's map
(1677); Boyne, p. 561; PRO, E
179/252/27, f. 24 (R)

79 *CJ*, vii. 600; GL, Alchin Coll.,
H/103/451; K. Rogers, *Old
London* (1935), p. 19

80 PRO, PCC Hale 97; E 179/
252/32 (19) (R)

81 BL, Add. MSS 5063 (65); PRO,
E 179/252/32 (4), p. 1 (R)

82 PRO, E 179/252/32, St Bride's
p. 5 (R)

83 GL, MS. 2969/1, f. 126r; PRO,
E 179/252/32 (8) (R)

84 LRO, Hustings Roll 340 (116);
MS. 4069, ii. f. 287v; Lillywhite
1870; PRO, E 179/252/32 (3),
p. 1 (R); E 179/252/32 (R)

85 BL, Add. MSS 34014, f. 54r;
PRO, E 179/252/32, London I
post-Fire, p. 12 (R)

86 WRO, E 172; GLRO, MR/TH/7,
m. 3d

87 Lillywhite 12342

88 WRO, E 168; E 1608, p. 41; E
1621, f. 14v; E 172; E 176; E 292;
GLRO, MR/TH/7, m. 2

89 WRO, E 172, 174, 176; WRO,
Wills; GLRO, MR/TH/7, m. 7;
Strype, vi. 67 (map)

90 Boyne, p. 715; GLRO, MR/
TH/7, m. 50d; PRO, E 179/
251/22, f. 10v (R)

91 WRO, E 172, 174; PRO, PCC
Penn 147

92 Boyne, p. 778

93 Boyne, p. 660; PRO, E 179/
252/32 (2) (R)

94 PRO, E 179/252/32 (18), f. 36v (R)

95 ib., (5) (R)

96 BL, Add. MSS 5099 (16); PRO,
E 179/147/617, p. 137 (R);
Lillywhite 1924

97 LRO, MS. Box 56.22, p. 5;
Boyne, p. 595; PRO, E 179/
252/32 (R)

98 Lillywhite, p. 493

99 ib., 13354

100 Ogilby and Morgan's map
(1677); Goldsmiths' Co., MS.
1737, ff. 26–8 (R); LRO, 84/3,
f. 10 (R); PRO, E 179/252/27,
f. 24 (R)

101 Boyne, p. 778

102 GL, MS. 2969, i. 125; PRO, E
179/147/617, p. 35 (R); E 179/
252/32 (8) (R); PRO, PCC
North 9

103 GL, MS. 2969/1, f. 128r; PRO,
E 179/252/32 (8) (R)

104 PRO, PCC Hene 119; E 179/
252/32 (4) (R)

105 WRO, E 172, 174, 176; GLRO, MR/TH/7, m. 2d

106 vi. 44 & n. 1; Lillywhite 14064; GLRO, RB (St Bartholomew Exchange); Boyd 30496; Meekings (*see* Arthur, n. 1), p. 37; PRO, E 179/252/23 (R); K. Rogers, *Mermaid and Mitre taverns*, pp. 67+

107 BL, Add. MSS 5090 (46), 5093 (27) (R); PRO, E 179/252/32 (3) (R)

108 GLRO, MR/TH/7, m. 7; WRO, E 1621, p. 15; E 1608, p. 47

109 *N. & Q.*, 27 Dec. 1930, p. 454; PRO, E 179/252/22, f. 12*v* (R); LRO, Alchin Coll., 451/H/103/11

110 Boyne, p. 687

111 ib., p. 704

112 Wheatley and Cunningham; WRO, F 388, 1092; PRO, PCC Bence 37; GLRO, MR/TH/7, m. 25d

113 BL, Add. MSS 5079 (79); LRO, Alchin Coll., H/103/11; PRO, PCC Ent 179; E 179/252/23, m. 6d (R)

114 BL, Add. MSS 5073 (85); Boyne, p. 622

115 Lillywhite 11164; Boyne, p. 559 (n.d.)

116 WRO, E 172, 174, 176; GLRO, Wills; MR/TH/7, m. 5d

117 J. Taylor (above, n. 10), i. 235

118 K. Rogers, *Mermaid and Mitre taverns*, pp. 91–3; BL, Add. MSS 5066 (76), 5070 (27); Boyd 1795; *Reg. St Mary Woolnoth* (*see above*, n. 17), pp. 51, 56, 59; PRO, E 179/252/32 (3), p. 3 (R)

119 Lillywhite 16401

120 WRO, E 174, 176; *Lond. Gazette*, 22 Oct. 1691

121 WRO, F 388; F 4541

122 Simon (*see above*, n. 55), iii. 245 ~ I regret that G. Berry, *Taverns and tokens of Pepys' London* (1978) came to my notice too late to be used in this section.

Taylor, G. 1 PRO, Adm 20/1, nos 599, 1376; Longleat, Coventry MSS 98, f. 195r

Taylor, J. 1 NWB, pp. 3–4

2 *Further Corr.*, pp. 171–3 ~ *CSPD 1659–60*, p. 41; *1663–4*, pp. 68, 145; *1664–5*, p. 75; *1670*, p. 629; *Cat.*, i; PRO, Adm 2/1732, f. 19*v*

Taylor, S. 1 BL, Add. MSS 4910 ~ *DNB*; *Further Corr.*, pp. 80, 82, 85; Aubrey, ii. 254

Taylor. T. 1 Venn

Taylour 1 PRO, E 403/1760, f. 32*v*; E 407/1; Baxter, p. 143

Teddeman 1 *DNB*; *CSPD*, e.g. *1652–3*, p. 601; *1653–4*, p. 221; *Cat.*, i; John B. Jones, *Annals of Dover* (Dover 1916), p. 305

2 *CSPD*, e.g. *1652*, p. 506; *Cat.*, i; Longleat, Coventry MSS 99, f. 92*v*; inf. from J. E. Hobbs

Teil 1 *CSPD 1670*, pp. 690–1; Bodl., Clar. MSS 28, f. 249*v*

2 viii. 147; *CSPD 1670*, p. 178 etc.; *Cat.*, i. 346

3 *Cat.*, loc. cit.

Tempest 1 Sainty, *Sec. of State*; Crist (*see* Starkey, J., n. 3), p. 161

Temple, J. 1 PRO, PCC Coke 90; Heal (*see* Atkinson, n. 1)

Temple, R. 1 HP

Temple, Mrs 1 GEC; Gramont, pp. 224–5, 229, 323

The Temple 1 View in PL 2972/240c

Temple Bar 1 Views in PL 2972/88b, 89

Templer 1 iii. 22, n. 2; Venn

Terne, C. 1 Munk

Terne, H. 1 *CSPD*, e.g. *1655*, p. 526; *Cat.*, i

Thatcher 1 Lafontaine

Theatre 1 See J. Orrell in *Theatre Notebook*, 34/6

2 L. Hotson, *Commonwealth and Restoration stage* (Camb. Mass. 1928), p. 252

3 viii. 487

4 Hotson, p. 245

5 J. Dryden 'Prologue spoken at the opening of the New House, 26 Mar. 1674' (*Works*, Univ. Calif. edition, *Poems 1649–80*, ed. Hooke and Swedenberg, 1956, i. 148)

6 ix. 425

7 J. Downes, *Roscius Anglicanus* (ed. Summers, 1928), p. 20

8 For instance, at *The Bondman*: D, v. 224

9 viii. 421, 422. See Lacey's troubles after the performance of *The Change of Crowns* on 15 Apr. 1667: viii. 167–8, 172

10 C. Cibber, *Apology* (ed. R. W. Lowe, 1889), i. 132–3

11 ib., i. 142

12 Sir John Hill, *The Actor* (1750), p. 187

13 Downes, op. cit., p. 21

14 A. Nicoll, *Hist. of Restoration drama* (Camb. 1923), p. 8

15 vii. 267, 399 & n. 3

16 J. Dennis, *Critical Works* (ed. Hooker, Baltimore 1939–43), i. 293

17 Further reading: in addition to Hotson's and Nicoll's studies referred to above, see W. Van Lennep (ed.), *The London stage 1660–1800*, vol. i, *1660–1700* (Carbondale, 1965) and P. D. Holland, *The ornament of action: Text and performance in Restoration comedy* (Camb. 1979)

Thompson, A. 1 Taylor, pp. 220–1

Thomson, G. 1 Oppenheim, passim; *DNB*; Firth and Rait, passim

2 Oppenheim; Firth and Rait; PL 2873, p. 483

3 HP

4 *CSPD 1665–6*, pp. 457–8

Thornborough 1 PRO, SP 29/60, nos 64, 65; PRO LS 13/35, p. 42; GLRO, MR/TH/7, m. 1d; *Harl. Soc. Reg.*, 46/68; GL, MS 10116, file 1

Thornton 1 i. 112, n. 2; HP

Three Cranes 1 Hatton, vol. ii, sect. vii

Throgmorton 1 *CSPD 1659–60*, p. 136; *CTB*, i. 155

Ticket Off. 1 PRO, Adm 20/6, no. 1833; ib. 7/1, nos 1520, 2803; LRO, Assessments Box 16.1, p. 33; LRO, MS. 872; BL, King's MSS 43, ff. 147–51 (plan and elevation c. 1683)

Tinker 1 *Cat.*, i; *CSPD 1664–5*, pp. 189, 257

Tippetts 1 *Further Corr.*, p. 270

2 PRO, Adm 2/1725, ff. 15–16; *Cat.*, i; Collinge

3 Collinge

Tite 1 *Harl. Soc. Reg.*, 46/52, 54; PRO, E 179/252/32, f. 24*v* (R)

Titus 1 HP

Tolhurst 1 HP; *CTB*, i. 344; Firth and Davies, p. 459; Roger Howell, *Newcastle* (Oxf. 1967), pp. 215, 313; *CSPD 1663–4*, p. 649; *1667–8*, p. 247

Tomkins 1 *Continuation* (Oxf. 1759), pp. 840–1

2 HP

Tompson, J. 1 viii. 389, n. 4; Venn

Tompson, R. 1 Plomer, i, ii. Engraved portrait in PL 2980/290b

Tooker 1 *CSPD 1656–7*, p. 134; *1659–60*, p. 551; *1664–5*, p. 398; *Add. 1660–85*, p. 202

Topham 1 Overall (*see* Manning, n. 1), p. xii

Toriano 1 Woodhead

Tower 1 Tomlinson, p. 150

2 L. G. Wickham Legg, *Engl. coronation records* (1901), p. xxi. cf. ii. 81, n. 2

3 von Uffenbach (*see* Hyde Pk, n. 1), p. 38. Views of building in PL 2972/249, 250

Townshend 1 PRO, LC 3/61, p. 10; PRO SP 29/253, f. 28*v*; PRO PCC North 36

2 E. Chamberlayne, *Angl. Notitia* (1671), p. 406; Mapperton, Sandwich MSS, Letters from Ministers, i, f. 117

Travel 1 ix. 224

2 iii. 246

3 *Hist. Engl.* (Everyman ed., 1927), i. 289

4 8 and 9 William and Mary, c. 16

5 ix. 240

6 Joan Parkes, *Travel in Engl. in 17th cent.* (Oxf. 1925), pp. 155–6

7 viii. 286

8 viii. 475

9 Tanner, p. 271; *Pepysiana*, p. 46

10 See discussion in *Ec. Hist. Rev.* (ser. 2), 30/73+ ; 33/92+

11 Parkes, op. cit., p. 80

12 ib., p. 65; see also Ralph Straus, *Carriages and coaches* (1912), pp. 116+

13 T. Delaune, *Angl. Metropolis* (1690), pp. 401+

14 A. Everitt (ed.) *Perspectives in Engl. urban hist.* (1973), p. 101

15 Wood, *L. & T.*, ii. 221. Cambridge could be reached within a day but only by changing coach and horses at Bishop's Stortford: ix. 209

16 12 Car. II, c. 35

17 iv. 183

18 Everitt, op. cit., pp. 91+

19 ix. 231

20 ii. 149

21 v. 273

22 vi. 221

23 14 Car. II, c. 2

24 *Journal des voyages* (Lyon 1665–6), ii. 12

25 ix. 166

26 ix. 470

27 iii. 39–40

28 *A hue & cry after P and H* (1679), p. 3

29 v. 307

30 ix. 474

31 v. 307

32 Lord Mahon (ed.), *Spain under Charles II* (1844), p. 61

33 M. P. Ashley, *Life in Stuart Engl.* (1964), p. 85

34 v. 357

35 Further reading: Parkes, op. cit., (*see above*, n. 6)

Tresham 1 Carte 73, ff. 527, 536; Mapperton, Sandwich MSS, App. f. 76

Treswell 1 *CSPD 1660–1*, pp. 206, 259; *1664–5*, p. 87; *1670*, p. 696

Trevanion 1 *Cat.*, i

Trice 1 Chappell, p. 52; Whitear, p. 151; Rawl. A 182, ff. 325, 343

Trinity Ho. 1 *Further Corr.*, pp. 80–1

2 Listed in R. Latham (ed.), *Catalogue of Pepys Lib.*, vol. v, pt 1 (*Modern Manuscripts*, comp. C. S. Knighton, Woodbridge 1981)

3 Based on G. G. Harris, *The Trinity House 1514–1660* (1970). See also Tanner in *EHR*, 44/573+. Views of almshouses in PL 2972/114–15, 254–5

Troutbeck 1 Dalton, i. 3, 253; PRO, PCC Hare 139

Trulocke 1 J. N. George, *Engl. guns and rifles* (Plantersville S. C. 1947), p. 69; WRO, F 4541

Trumbull 1 *DNB*; Sainty, *Sec. of State*; *Tangier Papers*, esp. p. xlix; Tomlinson, pp. 61, 66

Turberville 1 Foster; Verney (*see* Drink, n. 18), ii. 228; Yonge (*see* Addis, n. 1), p. 154

Turlington 1 Smyth, p. 82; PRO, PCC Coke 90

Turner, F. 1 *Cat.*, i; *CSPD 1666–7*, p. 17; *1667–8*, p. 31; Sainsbury, *1664–7*, p. 420; ib. *1668–70*, p. 3

Turner, J. 1 Venn; Magd. Coll., Reg., ii. 63b, iii. 276

2 Carte 74, ff. 31, 35; PRO, PCC Eure 113

3 *Family Letters*, pp. 157–64, 202; *Priv. Corr.*, i. 137–8

Turner, J. and J. 1 PRO, E 179/
149/627, f. 100v; ib. 252/23 (R)
2 Chappell, pp. 49, 62–3; Whitear,
pp. 59+; CSPD 1661–2, p. 234;
F. Drake, Ebor. (1736), p. 368;
GEC; parish reg. Kirkleatham;
PRO, PCC Fane 94

Turner, T. 1 Aylmer, p. 266; CSPD
1655, p. 414; PRO, Adm 2/1725,
f. 14r; Adm 20/1, nos 1293–4
2 Ch. Ch. Oxford, Evelyn MS. 397
3 PRO, PCC Cottle 10
4 Hasted (see Boreman, W., n. 1),
p. 31

Turner, T. jr. 1 Venn; Harl. Soc.
Reg., 46/53; PRO, Adm 82/3, n.p.

Turner, W. 1 Foster; [C. Coote],
Engl. Civilians (1804), p. 81

Turner, Ald. Sir W. 1 Country Life,
20 Jan. 1977, p. 134
2 ib., loc. cit. and 6 Jan. 1977 ∼
Woodhead; GL, MS. 5107/1, f.
163v; Rawl. A 182, f. 301r; W.
Westergaard (ed.), First Triple
Alliance (New Haven 1947), p. 70

Turner, Mrs 1 Harl. Soc. Reg., 46/272

Turnham Gn 1 GLRO, MR/TH/3,
m. 6d

Tweedy 1 Firth and Rait, i. 27;
Oppenheim, p. 347; PRO, PCC
Aylett 380

Twysden 1 Munk; DNB; Sir J. R.
Twisden, Family of Twysden and
Twisden (1939), Geneal. Table

Tyler 1 CSPD 1666, pp. 257, 298;
1663–4, p. 112

Udall 1 vii. 355, n. 2; Harl. Soc. Reg.,
64/177

Unthank 1 GLRO, MR/TH/7, m. 25d

Utber 1 Cat., i; Allin (see Guy, Capt.,
n. 1), vol. ii, p. lii

Uthwayt 1 PRO, Adm 42/379;
Hasted (see Boreman, W., n. 1), p.
31; CSPD 1670, p. 484; CTB, iii.
792; PRO, PCC Bunce 110

Vallière 1 Jules Lair, La Vallière
(trans., 1908), pp. 129, 132. Engraved portraits in PL 2979/218a, c

Vandeput 1 CTB, i. 117; CSPD, e.g.
1668–9, p. 134; PRO, E 179/252/
32, f. 41v (R); PRO, PCC Coke 27

Vaughan, E. 1 HP: Burnet, ii. 92–3

Vaughan, Sir J. 1 DNB; HP. Portraits in PL 2552 (2)/116; 2980/
163a, 165b

Vaughan, J. 1 HP

Vauxhall 1 von Uffenbach (see Hyde
Pk, n. 1), p. 131

Venner 1 Foster; PL 1425

Vere, A. de 1 GEC; PRO, E 179/
252/32, St Paul's Covent Gdn, p.
11 (R)

Vere, Lady 1 GEC; Samuel Clarke,
Lives of sundry eminent persons
(1685), pp. 145, 146

Vernatty 1 vii. 264, n. 2; PRO, CO
279/1, 3 passim; ib. 4, f. 138r;
Carte 75, ff. 27, 103; BL, Sloane
MSS 1956, f. 16r
2 Rawl. A 10, f. 391r

Vernon, E. 1 HMC, Ormonde (n.s.)
iii. 305 etc.; Bull. IHR, 19/15;
VCH, Kent, iii. 354

Vernon, J. 1 CSPD 1659–60, p. 13

Vict. Off. 1 Ehrman, pp. 153+

Villiers, E. 1 HMC, Rep., 8/1/2/
279a; GEC

Villiers, G. 1 Bryant, iii. 206+
2 DNB; lives by H. W. Chapman
(1949), and John H. Wilson (1954).
Engraved portraits in PL 2976
(2)/32; 2979/13

Vincent 1 WRO, E 174, 176; PRO,
LS 1/3; LS 8/3, p. 15

Vines 1 Bodl., Tanner, 318, f. 87r;
PRO, E 12/19, Hilary 1659, p. 3;
PCC Juxon 54
2 PRO, E 403/1760, f. 33v; WRO,
E 1610; PRO, PCC Eure 1672
3 Rep. Deputy Keeper Pub. Rec.,
5/258; PRO, E 12/19, Hilary 1659,
p. 3; CSPD 1670, p. 622
4 Burke (see Beale, F., n. 1), pp. 12,
259, 658

Vyner 1 Woodhead; Heal (see
Atkinson, n. 1); R. R. Sharpe,

London and the kingdom (1894–5), i.
390; Chester-Foster 1392

Wade 1 *CSPD 1652–3*, pp. 151, 537;
1658–9, p. 472; WRO, E 172;
CTB, i. 6

Wadlow 1 *CTB*, iii. 812 ~ Rogers
(*see* Taverns etc., named, n. 18),
pp. 146–7

Wager 1 *Cat.*, i; *DNB* s.n. Sir Charles
Wager

Waith 1 PRO, Adm 20/1, no. 1288;
CSPClar., iv. 134; Chester-Foster
1395; PRO, PCC Cann 99

Waldegrave 1 Munk; Evelyn, iv.
48 & n. 2

Walden 1 Grey (*see* Religion, n. 1),
i. 87, 323 ~ HP

Waldron 1 Munk

Wale 1 Woodhead; PRO, E 179/
147/617, p. 153 (R)

Walker, E. 1 *DNB*

Walker, W. 1 [C. Coote], *Engl.
Civilians* (1804), p. 84 ~ Venn;
HMC, *Rep.*, 8/1/2/280

Wallace 1 *Lauderdale Papers* (ed. O.
Airy, Camden Soc., 1884–5), i.
254 n.

Waller, E. 1 HP; Burnet, ii. 91.
Engraved portraits in PL 1155/1;
2980/204b

Waller, H. 1 *DNB*

Wallington 1 Possibly the Benoni
Wallington of St Dionis Backchurch listed as Boyd 12244

Wallis 1 *DNB*; *Notes and Records
Roy. Soc.* (1960), pp. 47+

2 *Priv. Corr.*, ii. 257, 268, 269, 276,
279–80

3 *DNB*

4 *Priv. Corr.*, ii. 316

Walter 1 *DNB*; Aubrey, ii. 283

2 Lord George Scott, *Lucy Walter*
(1947), p. 200; *Bull. IHR*, 19/15

Walton 1 *DNB*

Wandsworth 1 Meekings (*see*
Arthur, n. 1), p. xcii

Wanley 1 WRO, E 172; *CSPD
1661–2*, p. 209; *1665–6*, pp. 290,

346, 494; *Proc. Hug. Soc. London*,
18/52, 73

2 PRO, PCC Mico 183; ib. Coke 45

3 6 and 7 William and Mary, c. 20

Warcupp 1 Feiling in *EHR*, 40/235+

Ward 1 *CSPD 1665–6*, pp. 136, 402

2 ib. *1663–4*, pp. 85, 394

3 *Cat.*, i; Mapperton, Sandwich
MSS, Letters from Ministers, ii.
56, 164; Journal, x. 21

Wardour 1 Baxter, p. 124

Wardrobe 1 E. Chamberlayne, *Angl.
Notitia* (1669), pp. 264–5; Harris,
i. 242

2 Chamberlayne, op. cit., p. 263; *D*,
viii. 597, n. 1; *CTB*, ii. 227

3 *CTB*, iii. 131; BL, Egerton MSS
2543, f. 132r

4 *CSPD 1671*, p. 418 ~ Harris, i.
241+; ii. 187

Ware 1 WRO, E 174; GLRO,
MR/TH/7, m. 5

Warren, T. 1 *Harl. Soc. Reg.*, 46/66,
70; Sir Godfrey Fisher, *Barbary
Legend* (Oxf. 1957), p. 309; PRO,
PC 2/59, f. 256v; AO 1/310/1220

2 Hinton (*see* Barker, n. 1), p. 221;
CSPD 1665–6, p. 130; *1667–8*, pp.
41, 245, 274, 288

Warren, W. 1 vi. 32

2 PL 2874, pp. 377, 400+, 515+,
559+

3 HMC, *Lindsey (Supp.)*, pp. 116+

4 *CTB*, v. 1299–1300

5 Rawl. A 179, f. 68r; Ehrman, p. 60

6 Woodhead

7 GLRO, MR/TH/4, m. 55 (R);
GL, MS. 2745 (R); PRO, E 179/
252/32, St Mary Matfellon, p. 67
(R); PL 2997, p. 17; Woodhead

8 Jones (*see* Fire, n. 3), vol. i, p. xx

Warwick 1 HP; Burnet, i. 171;
Baxter, pp. 176+; PRO, E 179/
252/32 St Martin's, f. 2r (R); LCC,
Survey, 29/427+

Washington, H. (excise) 1 *CTB*, i.
732

2 ix. 187

Washington, H. (soldier) 1 Firth and Davies; Dalton, i. 7; *Northants. Past and Present*, 3/263–4

Washington, R. 1 *CSPD* 1664–5, p. 42

Washington, ——. 1 *CSPD 1665–6*, pp. 596–7

Waterhouse, E. 1 ix. 432, n. 4; Venn; *Past and Present*, no. 62/27+; *CSPD 1667–8*, p. 185

2 A. Wood, *Fasti Oxon.* (ed. Bliss, 1813–20), ii. 163. Engraved portrait in PL 2979/117b

Waterhouse, N. 1 *CSPD*, e.g. *1654*, p. 92; *1655*, p. 220; *1659–60*, p. 146; Sherwood, p. 172 etc.

Watkins 1 E. Chamberlayne, *Angl. Notitia* (1671), p. 25; E. S. de Beer (ed.), *Corr. John Locke* (Oxf. 1976–   ), vi. 436, n.

Weather 1 p. 132

2 T. Sprat, *Hist. Roy. Soc.* (1667), pp. 173–9; *Notes and records Roy. Soc.* (1960), p. 142

3 *Diary* (*see* Carkesse, n. 2), passim

4 *Philos. Trans.* 15/932+; 20/45+; 21/45; 22/527+; 23/1443

5 MS. 9374, 8 A 1

6 BL, Add. MSS 10116–17; ptd incompletely by W. L. Sachse, *The diurnal of Thomas Rugg* (Camden Soc., ser. 3, vol. 91, 1961)

7 ed. A. Macfarlane (1976)

Weaver, E. 1 Van Lennep, pp. 1, 262; Wilson, pp. 142–4

Weaver, R. 1 Parish reg.

Weddings 1 J. Brand, *Pop. Antiquities* (ed. Hazlitt, 1905), ii. 499, 626+; H. Misson, *Mémoires* (The Hague, 1698), pp. 316+

2 iii. 22; i. 27; iv. 37–8. cf. *DNB* s.n. Dorothy Spencer, Countess of Sunderland

Weld 1 Wren and Hackett (*see* Aleyn, n. 1), p. 17; *CTB*, iii. 693–4

Wells, J. 1 Inf. from R. A. Barker ∼

CSPD 1625–6, p. 517; *1663–4*, p. 322; Oppenheim, pp. 266–7

Wells, Wm 1 Venn

Wells, W. 1 Gramont, esp. p. 218

Wendy 1 HP

Werden 1 HP; HMC, *Rep.*, 8/2/278; E. Chamberlayne, *Angl. Notitia* (1669), p. 308

Westminster Pal. 1 For the building at this period, see Colvin, v. 385+

2 WRO, E 1613

3 PRO, E 351/3274, f. 6r (R)

4 i. 140. Views in PL 2972/100a, b, 101a, b, 102 (exterior); ib., 326b, 328c, 363 (interior)

5 Views in PL, esp. 2972/101a, b

6 PRO, E 351/3274, f. 7r (R)

Wheatley 1 Rawl. A 182, f. 304r

Wheler 1 GLRO, MR/TH/7, m. 6 ∼ M. F. Keeler, *Members Long Parl.* (Phila. 1954), pp. 386–7; *Letters*, p. 3; Carte 73, ff. 52, 73, 78, 100, 331, 376; Mapperton, Sandwich MSS, Journal, iii, f. 94; *CSPD 1639–40*, p. 423; *1651–2*, p. 160; *1655–6*, p. 54; Firth and Rait, passim

Whetstone Pk 1 Wheatley and Cunningham

Whistler 1 Munk; *DNB*; Wood, *Ath. Oxon.*, iv. 134; Evelyn, iv. 307

White 1 Rawl. A 56, p. 272; PL 2873, p. 485; Duke of York, *Mem.* (naval), pp. 122–3

Whitehall Pal. 1 For the building at this period, see Colvin, v. 263+ and LCC, *Survey*, vol. 13 pt 2, on which much of the following account is based.

2 *Lettres sur les Anglois* (ed. C. Gould, Paris 1933), p. 155

3 Household Ordinances, c. 1660–c. 70: BL, Stowe MSS 562, ff. 11–12

4 PL 2972/227b, c; 228, a, b (general); Banqueting House, ib./96–7, 98 a, b; Chapel, ib./185c; King's Gate, ib./99a, b

5 PRO, LC 5/12, p. 275

6 BL, Stowe MSS, loc. cit.

Whitfield 1 *Harl. Soc. Reg.*, 46/241; Collinge; Bodl., Tanner 38, f. 151r

Whittington 1 *CSPClar.*, iv. 302; HMC, *Ormonde* (n.s.), i. 49, 50, 100; *CTB*, i. 13

Whitton 1 ii. 155; BL, Add. MSS 9317, f. 13r; PRO, Adm 20/1, no. 1338

Whitty 1 *Cat.*, i

Wiborow 1 Venn; BL, Add. MSS 5805, f. 95r

Widdrington 1 Venn; Peile (*see* Pepper, n. 1); GLRO, WJS/SBB/172 (1658), p. 38; *DNB*

Wight 1 PRO, E 179/252/32 (19) and London, p. 10 (R)

2 v. 145–6

3 Chappell, p. 29; Whitear, pp. 64+, 161+; *Harl. Soc. Vis.* 60/121 (*Surrey 1662-8*); VCH, *Surrey*, iii. 4–5

Wildman 1 *Hist. Engl.* (Everyman ed., 1929), i. 402

2 Bryant, iii. 297

3 *DNB*; life by M. P. Ashley (1947)

Wilford 1 Venn

Wilgress 1 *CSPD 1657-8*, p. 497; *Cat.*, i; Longleat, Coventry MSS 99, f. 92v

Wilkes 1 Mapperton, Sandwich MSS, App., f. 80r; *Bull. IHR*, 19/19; *CSPD 1673-5*, p. 119

Wilkins 1 *Naval Minutes*, p. 177 ~ *DNB*; *Notes and records Roy. Soc.* (1960), pp. 47+. Engraved portrait in PL 2980/106c

Wilkinson, R. 1 Gardiner (*see* Hayward, J., n. 1), v. 34, 51; *Cat.*, i

Wilkinson, —— 1 *CTB*, ii. 579, 626; T. D. Hardy, *Cat. of Lord Chancellors* (1843), p. 110

Willet 1 Parish reg., St Stephen's; inf. from Miss E. Ralph

Williams, A. 1 Wilson, p. 191 ~ PRO, PCC Hare 39

Williams, —— 1 *Bull. IHR*, 19/19

Williamson, J. 1 PRO, SP 29/231, 253 ~ *DNB*

Williamson, R. 1 *CSPD 1657-8*, p. 409; *Cat.*, i

Willoughby 1 Oppenheim, pp. 326, 347, 349

Willys 1 For Morland's account, see J. Willcock, *Life of Sir H. Vane the Younger* (1913), pp. 372+; for Willys's, see *N. & Q.*, 11, 18 Feb. 1922. cf. also Mordaunt (*see* Mordaunt, J., n. 1), esp. pp. 183–4; *EHR*, 169/33+; Underdown (*see* Baron, H., n. 1), *passim*

2 i. 112, n. 2; HP

Wilmot 1 Robert Parsons, *Sermon at funeral of Rochester* (1680)

2 *Letters*, p. 105

3 PL 810 ~ *DNB*; lives by V. de Sola Pinto (1962); John H. Wilson, *Court wits of the Restoration* (New York 1948); J. Treglown (ed.), *Letters of John Wilmot, Earl of Rochester* (Oxf. 1980). Engraved portrait in PL 2980/209

Wilson 1 PL 2873, p. 483; PRO, Adm 20/1, no. 580; ib. 2, p. 28; ib. 9, p. 431; Longleat, Coventry MSS 99, f. 195r; Collinge; *Further Corr.*, pp. 69, 194; *Cat.*, iii. 185; PRO, PCC Bence 58; Chester-Foster 1485

Wine 1 PRO, LS 8/3, p. 17; ib. 13/35, p. 53; E 179/252/32 (4)

Wingate 1 Sir H. Chauncy, *Hist. Herts.* (1826), ii. 30, 31; *Herts. County Records: Sessions Rolls*, vol. i. (ed. W. J. Hardy, Hertford 1905), p. 251

Winter 1 *CSPD 1639-40*, p. 567; *CTB*, i. 308; C. E. Hart, *Free Miners* (Gloucester 1953), pp. 204+; inf. from G. Hammersley

Wintershall 1 Van Lennep, p. 6; McAfee, p. 231

Wise 1 HMC, *Rep.*, 8/1/2/279; *CSPD* 1670, pp. 685–6

Wiseman 1 Venn; PL 2873, p. 483

Witherley 1 Venn; Munk

Withers 1 *CSPD 1664–5*, p. 364; *1661*, pp. 558–9; VCH, *Lancs.*, viii. 148 & n.

Wivell 1 *CSPD 1659–60*, p. 554; *1664–5*, p. 201; *1670*, p. 47

Wolfe 1 Boyd 48940; PRO, E 179/252/32 (R)

Wolstenholme 1 LRO, Assessments Box 56.22, p. 4 (R); *CTB*, i. 226; ii. 48

Wood, H. 1 GEC; HP; PRO, LS 13/32, p. 17

Wood, T. 1 S. L. Ollard et al., *Dict. Engl. church hist.* (1948); North (ed. Jessop), i. 186

Wood, Wr. 1 *CSPD* e.g. *1650*; *Cat.*, i

Wood, Wm 1 *Shorthand Letters*, pp. 32–3
2 PRO, PCC Reeve 35; *CSPD*, e.g. *1664–5*, p. 133
3 PRO, Prob 11/358, f. 135
4 i. 102; NWB, p. 33

Woodall 1 PRO, LC 3/24; *Bull. IHR*, 19/20

Woodcock 1 Venn; *Calamy Rev.*

Woodeson 1 Sainty, *Sec. of State*

Woodfine 1 *CSPD 1660–1*, p. 273

Woodroffe 1 PRO, E 407/1; Baxter, p. 87; *The Ancestor*, 10/172

Woolley, J. 1 *CTB*, ii. 639; iii. 177

Woolley, R. 1 Woodhead; Whitear, pp. 67–9, 164

Woolwich 1 VCH, *Kent*, ii. 355+; D. C. Coleman, 'Economy of Kent under later Stuarts' (unpub. thesis, London Univ. 1951), p. 248; Ehrman, p. 84

Worc. Ho. 1 PRO, E 179/147/627, p. 196 (R); T. H. Lister, *Life of Clarendon* (1838, 1837), iii. 109; Clarendon, *Life*, iii. 456. View in PL 2972/237c

Wotton 1 GL, MS. 2969, i, f. 122*v*; ii, p. 418; PRO, E 179/252/32 (8)

2 *Priv. Corr.*, i. 205

Wren, C. 1 Listed in R. Latham (ed.), *Cat. of Pepys Library*, vol. iii, pt 1 (comp. A. W. Aspital, Woodbridge, 1980)

Wren, M. 1 DNB; HP; PRO, PCC Pye 1 (R)

Wren, —— 1 *CSPD 1666–7*, p. 243; *Cat.*, i; PRO, Adm 2/1734, f. 122*r*; *Tangier Papers*, p. 241

Wright, H. 1 ii. 217 & n. 1
2 HP; PRO, Adm 2/1745, f. 29*v*; PRO, PCC Bruce 74; Morant (*see* Bendish, n. 1), ii. 568

Wright, Dr 1 Venn

Wriothesley 1 DNB

Wyld 1 PRO, PCC North 130; GEC, *Baronetage*, s.n. Willys

Wyndham 1 J. Collinson, *Hist. Somerset* (Bath 1791), iii. 492; Clarendon, *Hist.*, iv. 17, 22, 23; v. 205; H. A. Wyndham, *Family hist. of Wyndhams 1410–1688* (1939), pp. 177, 262, 278
2 Sandwich, p. 263; Wyndham, op. cit., pp. 264–5

Wynn 1 Sainsbury, *1664–7*, e.g. p. 141

Yeabsley 1 *CSPD*, e.g. *1664–5*, p. 417; *1668–9*, p. 138; Yonge (*see* Addis, n. 1), p. 143

Yelverton 1 *Letters* (ed. Parry, Wayfarers' Lib. ed., n.d.), p. 154; HP

Yorke 1 *Family Letters*, p. 29

York Ho. 1 *Occ. Papers*, ii. 58+. Views in PL 2972/237b; P. H. Hulton, *Drawings of Engl. in 17th cent.* (Walpole Soc., vol. 35), vol. ii, pls 28a, b

Young, J. (i) 1 PRO, Adm 2/1725, f. 14*v*

Young, J. (ii) 1 PRO, LC 5/39, p. 23 etc.

Young, J. (actor) 1 Van Lennep, pp. 53, 238, 246

LARGE GLOSSARY

This Glossary lists:

(1) words and phrases now obsolete or employed in senses not obvious from their modern use (American usage being taken into account) – the modern meaning has not necessarily been noted;
(2) words which have not changed their sense, but for which Pepys is an early or the earliest witness;
(3) technical words not explained in the footnotes;
(4) proverbs and proverbial phrases.

It does not include place names. These appear in the Select Glossary (in vols i–ix) in cases where Pepys's spelling or mode of reference might give difficulty to the modern reader.

The entry word represents the spelling most common in the diary; less common but noteworthy spellings follow, but no attempt has been made to include all variants. References by volume and page have been provided so that form and meaning may be examined in context, but are restricted to one per sense or form of a word, the reference given being chosen as typical. No attempt has been made to record common spelling variants of words in modern use, nor to translate foreign words and phrases unless they are proverbial.

Extensive use has been made of the *Oxford English Dictionary* and, in the case of proverbs, of the *Oxford Dictionary of Proverbs*, from which virtually all the dates of first record derive. These dates have been noted where:

(1) they fail to take account of Pepys's use;
(2) the diary is cited as the earliest record;
(3) they closely antedate the diary;
(4) Pepys's use might reasonably be presumed to be early, but in fact is not;
(5) a proverb or proverbial phrase is in question.

Where no date is given the premise is that the word in question was standard English when Pepys wrote, and had been current for a substantial period. In the case of dates in category 3 (and very occasionally 1) the source has been cited if there is a Pepysian connection, whether through reading (e.g. Bacon), or acquaintance (e.g. Evelyn), or both (e.g. Fuller). When Pepys uses two synonymous words indifferently, one of which has become archaic and the other not, this is indicated in the entry (e.g. Volary/Aviary). Nonce words explained in footnotes have only been glossed when they are of linguistic interest. Foreign words appear in forms of the period.

Conventions

OED   *Oxford English Dictionary*
ODP   *Oxford Dictionary of English Proverbs* (3rd ed. 1970)
P   Pepys
Blount   Thomas Blount, *Glossographia* (1656; unless a later ed. is cited)
Florio   John Florio, *Queen Anna's new world of words, or Dictionarie of the Italian and English tongues* (1611)
Phillips Edward Phillips, *New world of words* (1658; unless a later ed. is cited)
Dyche   Thomas Dyche and William Pardon, *A new general dictionary* (1735) (the major part of this dictionary was compiled some years before its date of publication; though it nevertheless postdates Pepys by a considerable margin, it has often shed light where other works have not)

In the body of each entry a colon separates definition from commentary, but where definition has seemed otiose commentary follows the reference immediately. Different senses of the same entry-word are separated by semi-colons.

A date without additional comment signifies: 'the earliest recorded instance in *OED* is . . .'. *OED* P signifies: 'the earliest instance in *OED* is from Pepys'; where Pepys uses the word or phrase before *OED*'s particular example from the diary the earlier reference has been silently supplied. *OED* followed by a date signifies: 'the earliest example recorded in *OED* is . . . but this overlooks Pepys's use, here instanced'.

I am grateful to Professor A. Rupert Hall, Mr J. L. Nevinson and Dr C. E. Newman for help with certain technical terms. I am particularly indebted to Robert Latham, who placed all his materials at my disposal and offered most valuable criticisms of the final drafts.

(Richard Luckett)

A'BACKWAY: viii. 430 indirectly, by means of a secondary entrance

ABATEMENT: iii. 261 alleviation, compensatory concession: a Common Law term, but used by P in its general sense

ABLE: vi. 296 wealthy: 1578, and cf. *Ecclesiasticus* 'Rich men furnished with ability'. vii. 311 competent

ABRIDGE: iii. 193 to deprive

ABROAD: ii. 79 away, out of doors

ABUSE (v.): ii. 164 to mislead, take (bad) advantage of

ACCENT (of speech): viii. 65 the accentuation and the rising and falling of speech in pronunciation: 1581 Sidney

ACCIDENTAL: vii. 234 incidental

ACCOUNTANT: viii. 194 official responsible for expenditure etc.

ACHIEVEMENT: iv. 424 funerary hatchment, panel or canvas bearing the 'achievement' (properly the full coat of arms including, where applicable, supporters, helmet, wreath and crest) of the deceased, hung on the house until the funeral, in church thereafter

ACTING: v. 335 performance, simulation: *OED* P in this sense. vii. 254 practical

ACTION: viii. 116 gesture, acting, performance: *Hamlet* III ii 19 'Sute the Action to the Word, the Word to the Action'

ACTOR: viii. 14 male or female theatrical performer: 1581 Sidney

ADMIRAL SHIP: iv. 110 flagship carrying admiral

ADMIRATION: iii. 209 a condition of (or inducing) wonder

ADMIRE: ix. 347 to wonder at

ADMITTABLE: iv. 8 admissible, decent

ADVENTURE: v. 204 premium

ADVENTURER: v. 221 investor, speculator, shareholder in a merchant adventure

ADVICE: ii. 110 consideration. viii. 298 counsel (here medical)

ADVISE WITH: viii. 601 seek advice from

AFFECT (v.): v. 203 to be fond of, concerned

AFFECTION: iv. 96 attention

AGAIN: i. 81 against

AGUE: vii. 255 a violent fever. vi. 212 feverish fit

AIR; AYRE: vi. 64 general term for all gases: 1641. ix. 507 attitude, expression: 1650

AKINNED: i. 301 related

ALL THE WORLD RIDES US: v. 239 everyone tyrannises over us: 1583

ALONELY: vi. 149 solitarily, lonelily: standard, but the context suggests an intensification not found in *OED*

ALPHABET: iii. 105 index

AMAZE (s.): ii. 103 state of amazement, wonder: cf. Maze

AMBAGE: iv. 273 equivocation, circumlocution

AMMUNICION: ii. 114 ? modern sense; *OED* gives as earliest record Bacon, 1626, and insists that it signifies military stores generally; the quotations sustain the case but P's use implies the more specialised later meaning of 'powder and shot'

AMUSED, AMUZED: iv. 269 bemused, astonished: 'put into a muse'

ANABAPTIST: ii. 57 in England used very loosely both for Baptists and other dissenters: Swift in 1708 equated 'Anabaptist' and 'Presbyterian'

ANCHORSMITH: iii. 72 smith who forges anchors: *OED* P only

ANDIRONS: v. 271 fire-dogs

ANGEL: vi. 220 gold coin worth c. 10*s*.: abbreviation of angel-noble, a coin bearing the archangel Michael killing the dragon

ANGELIQUE: i. 183 type of archlute (Fr. *angélique*, It. *angelica*) having 16 or 17 strings, in single courses, tuned diatonically throughout: a simplified instrument designed for ease of playing

ANNOY: viii. 256 molest, hurt

ANOTHER-GATE'S BUSINESS: ix. 300 different altogether: more commonly 'another-gate's matter': 'another-gates' (i.e. of another gait, fashion) 1594

ANTIC, ANTIQUE: viii. 243, viii. 163 fantastic (It. *antico* used as a synonym for *grottesco*): the 16th-17th-cent. English form does not, despite the possible spelling, derive from 'antique' or denote 'old-fashioned'

ANTIPATHY: vii. 204 allergy: 1626 Bacon

ANUS: iv.252 as English rather than Latin 1658

APERN: ix. 557 apron: follows the traditional but disappearing pronunciation

APOTHECARY, POTHECARY, POTTICARY: viii. 490 preparer and seller of medicinal drugs: member of the London Society of Apothecaries (est. 1617)

APPOSITION, OPPOSICION: i. 42, iv.33 public examination of scholars; Apposition Day was held at St Paul's School at Candlemas

APPRENSION: iii. 115 apprehension, anticipation

APPROVE OF: viii. 310 criticise

APT: i.27 inclined, prone. i. 232 quick-witted

AQUA FORTIS (FARTIS): iv. 145 nitric acid

ARRAND: iii. 66 errand

ARREST (Fr. *arrêt*): vi. 156 law, proclamation, order

ARROGATE: iv. 115 to claim that to which one is not entitled

ARTICLE: iv. 375 to indict, bring charges (articles) against

ARTIST: iv. 84 craftsman, technician, practitioner. iv. 234 astrologer, fortune-teller

ASSE, like an: iv. 395 common in English from c. 1500: *OED* observes that prior to 1500 the phrase is more commonly scriptural and neutral

ATTORNEY, ATTURNY: ii. 178 attorney-at-law, legal agent in the courts of Common Law doing most of the work of the modern solicitor

AURICULAR CONFESSION: iii. 178 confession made aloud to a priest, as in the church of Rome

AWRY: v. 119 crooked

AYERY: iv. 239 airy, sprightly, stylish: 1644

BACK . . . BROAD ENOUGH TO BEAR IT: vi. 263 common in various forms from 1471

BACK-BLOW: viii. 496 reversal: 1642

BACKWARDNESS: viii. 296 reluctance, slowness

BAGGAGE: vii. 53 impudent woman (apparently used by P affectionately, cf. ix. 480): *OED* (in affectionate sense) 1672

BAGNARD: ii. 34 bagnio, prison or lock-up in oriental town

BAGPIPE: ii. 101 either the mouth-blown bagpipe (now most familiar in its Highland form) or the bellows-blown *musette*: for a near contemporary account of the types current in England, cf. William A. Cocks (ed.), 'James Talbot's . . . Bagpipes' in *Galpin Soc. Journ.*, vol. v (1952)

BAILEY, BAYLY: ix. 561 bailiff

BAIT, BAYTE (s.): iii. 225 refreshment on journey for horses and travellers (implying a rest as well as food). Also, i. 66 (as v.)

BALCON(E): vi. 114 balcony: 1618

BALK(E): iii. 119 (technical) roughly-squared beam of Baltic timber; any substantial beam of wood

BALLERS: ix. 218 an association of rakish young courtiers, comparable to the Hell-fire Club in the next century (cf. Henry Savile in John Wilmot, Earl of Rochester, *Letters* ed. J. Treglown, 1980, p. 63, and for 'Ballock Hall', the presumably mythical base of their activities, J. H. Wilson (ed.), *Court satires of the Restoration*, Columbus 1976, pp. 32, 58): *OED* ?P

BALLET, BALLAT: ix. 200, i. 41 ballad, broadside

BALSAM: iv. 64 a preparation made from the resin of *Balsamodendron* used for healing wounds: prescription in N. Culpeper, *Pharmacopoeia Londinensis* (ed. Cole, 1661), p. 314

BAND: i. 85 neckband

BANDOLEERE (Sp. *bandolera*): viii. 307 belt worn over shoulder with cases for musket charges: 1596

BANDORE: iii. 224 pandora, plucked bass instrument with a scalloped body, 6 or 7 double courses of wire strings and frets (the orpharion was a smaller equivalent): used for the bass part in theatre bands and by waits; obsolescent in 1662

BAND-STRINGS: ii. 80 strings for fastening neck-bands: often elaborate and ornamented with tassels

BANDY: vii. 228 to argue strenuously: 1642, the sense becoming progressively weakened thereafter

BANQUET: ii. 8 course of fruits, sweets and wine, slight repast

BANQUET-, BANQUETING-HOUSE: iv. 117, iii. 175 summer-house

BARBE (s.): i. 275 Arab (Barbary) horse: 1636

BARB(E) (v.): vi. 311 to shave

BARE: viii. 275 bareheaded

BARGE: i. 253 large rowing vessel, attached to the Navy Office, for use on the Thames. i. 158 ship's tender for use of flag-officer (cf. ii. 96). ii. 216 royal barge. viii. 254 flat-bottomed trading vessel, working largely under sail

BARR, behind the: i. 301 in the private quarters of a public house: 'bar' 1592

BARRECADOS (naval): vii. 206 fenders

BARREL: 36 gallons (beer). 32 gallons (ale). c. 4 doz. (oysters)

BASE, BASS: iii. 121 bass viol. viii. 167 thorough-bass. iii. 3, low, unworthy

BASKET-HILT: i. 62 (of swords) having a protective hilt of narrow steel plates in basket shape: synecdoche for the unfashionable, stiff and antiquated throughout the Restoration period

BASS VIALLIN: ix. 12 violoncello: as the 'bass violin' in use in England from the beginning of the century, particularly for dance music, but tuned a tone lower than the modern 'cello (cf. Playford, *Introduction to the skill of musick*, 1687, p. 108)

BASTE, BASTE HIS COAT: i. 307, vi. 77 beat, chastise

BATTELL: iv. 428 contest of fighting cocks

BAULKE (v.): iii. 243 to avoid

BAVIN: viii. 82 bundle of kindling wood, brushwood

BAYLY: *see* Bailey

BAYT(E): *see* Bait

BEARD: vii. 26 facial hair, moustache ('mustacho' iii. 198)

BEAST (Fr. *beste*): ii. 3 card game for 3, 4, 5 or more players, originally French and similar to nap (cf. [Charles Cotton], *The Compleat Gamester*, 1674, p. 153): OED 1668

BEAT ONE'S BRAINS: ix. 37 think hard

BEAUTIFULLEST: ix. 399 most beautiful: 1642 Fuller

BEAVER: ii. 203 hat made of beaver's fur or of an imitation of it: 1528

BECOME: iii. 3 to be congruous, grace

BEDAGGLED: i. 193 bedraggled, muddied: particularly of the 'bottoms or skirts of a garment' (Dyche), common in 17th–18th cent.

BEFOREHAND, to be/get: i. 240 to have money in hand

BEGIN THE WORLD: vii. 98 start in (adult) life: OED 1833

BEHINDHAND, to be: vii. 414 to be entitled to money which is in arrears: OED P only.
v. 82 ('to run behindhand') to be in arrears

BELL: v. 362 to throb. v. 362 to swell up like a boil

BELL-MAN: i. 19 crier with a bell who called the hours, announced deaths, etc.

BELLY FULL, give a: vii. 158 as 'to have a' 1475; cf. also viii. 399

BELOW: iv. 204 downstream from London Bridge

BEND (naut.) (s.): iv. 236 'the outmost timbers on the ship sides' (*Seaman's Grammar*, 1627), but here probably the sheer

BEND (v.): v. 106 to apply oneself

BENEVOLENCE, the: ii. 167 'a Collection of free gifts to the King through the Kingdom' (cf. ii. 111, n. 4)

BESIDES: ii. 41 incidentally, as well

BESPATTER: vi. 291 smear, vilify

BESPEAK: i. 39 to order

BETIMES: ix. 199 early, promptly

BETWITT: ii. 65 to speak slightingly or challengingly: emphatic of 'twit', OED P only

BEVER: ii. 127 beaver, fur hat

BEWPERS: v. 289 bunting, fabric used for flags: origin unknown (? Beaupreau, Fr. town) (elsewhere 'blufers' and other variants) 1592

BEZAN, BIZAN (Du. *bezaan*): iii. 188 small yacht: OED P only

BICHERING: vii. 297 Evelyn's word is apparently nonce, but OED has 'bitching' with this sense from Cotton 1675, 'Jove, thou now art going a Bitching'

BILL: ii. 215 legal warrant, writ. vi. 166 bill of exchange. vi. 173 Bill of Mortality, weekly list of burials

BILL OF FARE: iv. 354 menu: at feasts by late 16th cent., though hailed as 'new and admirable contrivance' in 1748 (*see* OED), this presumably referring to use in private households

BILLANDER (Du. *bijlander*): viii. 349 bilander, small two-masted merchant-man: 1656

BIRDING-PIECE: iv. 138 fowling-piece (which is recorded 1596)

BIRD'S EYE: vi. 102 spotted fabric: named after the small, bright, round flowers. OED P

BIT INTO MOUTH, get the: ix. 294 more commonly 'take the bit in his teeth': 1546

BITE AT THE STONE AND NOT AT THE HAND THAT FLINGS IT: ix. 62 apparently unrecorded

BITTMAKER: vi. 140 earlier known as 'lorimer': P antedates OED

BIZAN: *see* Bezan

BLACK (s.): ii. 61 negro

BLACK (adj.): i. 25 brunette, dark in hair or complexion

BLACK AND WHITE, in: viii. 426 unequivocally: 1656 in phr. as 'in', 1599 'under black and white'

BLACK(E)MORE: vi. 244 negro, negress: *also* 'black'

BLADE: ix. 172 gallant, free-and-easy fellow: 1592. vii. 144 ('high blade') court roisterer

BLANCH (of coins): iv. 146 to silver

BLAND: ii. 178 smooth and suave, emollient. OED P

BLATHER: ii. 233 bladder: cf. 'lather' = 'ladder'

BLIND (s.): ii. 195 out of the way, private, obscure: cf. 'blind alley'

BLIND (v.): iii. 193 to obscure, darken

BLINDE (s.): iv. 270 a ruse. OED 1664

BLINDED: viii. 145 blindfold

BLOAT-HERRING: ii. 192 bloater, smoked half-dried herring

BLOT(T): vii. 306 a mistake: cf. vi. 92 'blotts and blurrs'

BLOWN OVER: viii. 326 passed away, come to an end: common in 17th cent.

BLOWN UP, to be: v. 244 exploded, unmasked. 1660

BLUR(R): viii. 501 innuendo, aspersion on character

BOATE, BOOT: viii. 396 boot, open compartment (sometimes used for luggage or with boxes for luggage under) on side of coach: an extensive footboard where attendants sat in a sideways position

BODY (s.): iii. 149 structure and form. iv. 227 sectional drawing (of ship): OED 1691

BOEUF-A-LA-MODE: viii. 211 beefsteak larded with bacon and spiced, fried, then simmered in a closed pot: *à-la-mode* is widely used in English, in many different collocations, from 1649

BOGGLE (v.): v. 275 to demur, hesitate. viii. 375 ('make a boggle') 1638

BOLTHEAD: v. 123 globular glass vessel with long straight neck

BOMBAZIN: vii. 182 bombasine, twilled or corded mixture of silk and worsted for dresses

BOOT, to: i. 54 in addition

BORDER: iv. 130 toupée

BOSSED: v. 199 with bosses

BOTARGO (It. *botargo*): ii. 115 dried mullet-roe: 1598

BOTTOMARYNE, BOTTUMARY, BUM-MARY: iv. 401 mortgage on ship: 1622

BOUND: iv. 333 constipated

BOUT: i. 43 a quarrel. vii. 79 a 'go'

BOWPOTT: vi. 222 bough-pot, flower vase: P has 'flower-pott' (1583) ix. 515

BOX: iv. 426 Christmas box, tip: apprentices would collect with boxes at Christmastide

BOY-ROPE: iii. 149 cable from anchor mooring buoy

BRACE: iii. 53 pair

BRANSLE (Fr. *bransle*): iii. 300 branle, brawl, round dance originally in duple or triple measure, by 1660 in duple measure: a dance of ceremony, used to open a ball

BRAVADO: ix. 96 a hector, a bravo. 1653

BRAVE: i. 10 fine, enjoyable

BRAVE (v.): iv. 47 to threaten, challenge

BRAWN: ii. 225 soused, pickled or potted boar's flesh: a Christmastide speciality

BREAK (v.): iv. 197 to fail, go bankrupt

BREAK MY BRAINS: ii. 135 rack my brains: recorded as idiomatic 1690

BREAK BULK: vi. 274 to remove part of cargo

BREAK IN PIECES: viii. 477 to fall out, be at odds

BREAK MY THOUGHTS: i. 16 disclose: 'to break one's mind/heart' is a common 17th-cent. phr.

BREAK UP, to: i. 22 to end a party or social gathering. ii. 72 to end a school term: marked by celebrations at which pupils treated masters, cf. J. R. Macgrath (ed.), *Flemings in Oxford*, i. 200, n. 3

BREECH: vii. 303 buttocks

BREED ILL-BLOOD: viii. 84, 164 stir up strife: *OED* 1704

BREEDLING: iv. 311 native: dialect use recorded by P

BREW AS SHE HATH BAKED, let her: v. 242, ix. 195 (slightly altered) prov. as 'as they brew so let them drink' c. 1300, 'suche bread as they baye, suche must they eate' 1548, 'as they brew so let them bake' 1599, 'but as bake may times, so they brue' 1579: a triumph of sound over sense

BREW SOMETHING FOR: ix. 542 contrive, prepare

BRIDEMAN: ix. 19 young man performing duties at wedding, incl. leading bride to bridegroom: 1663

BRIDEWELL BIRD: vii. 191 jailbird

BRIDGE: iii. 175 jetty, landing stairs

BRIDLE: iv. 64

BRIEF: ii. 128 church collection, authorised by Lord Chancellor and requested in the King's name, for a charitable purpose

BRIG, BRIGANTINE: i. 158 small vessel equipped both for sailing and rowing: *OED* 1720

BRING NIGHT HOME: iii. 289, viii. 500 return home at nightfall: apparently idiomatic

BRISTOL MILK: ix. 236 sweet sherry (cf. fn. 1)

BROKE: v. 155 broken down in health. viii. 263 bankrupt

BROKER: ii. 163 a legal agent

BROOK (v.): i. 105 to tolerate

BROTHER: vi. 257 brother-in-law. ii. 4 colleague

BRUSH: i. 254 graze: *OED* 1692

BRYERS, get out of the: viii. 518 get out of troubles, difficulties: *OED* 1674, but in rel. phr. from 1563

BUBO: vi. 165 tumour, especially in groin or arm-pits

BUCKLE: ii. 161 defer to. v. 348 give way, collapse

BUCKSOME: iv. 263 buxom: probably still in its early sense of 'unresisting', 'pliant', rather than modern 'plump and comely'

BUFFLEHEAD: iv. 77 fool, blockhead: 1659

BULLET: viii. 308 cannon ball. i. 209 small round ball

BUMMARY: *see* Bottomaryne

BURGES(s): i. 102 M.P. for borough, corporate town or university

BURN MY FINGERS: vii. 334 proverbial by 1551

BURNT WINE, BURNED WINE: ii. 14 mulled red wine: in the 17th cent. and early 18th cent. 'burnt' applied to red wine, 'mulled' to white wine (cf. Dyche's *Dictionary* for an express statement); the rule is not invariable (cf. *Twelfth Night* II iii. 206 'Ile go burne some Sacke') but P's usage conforms. viii. 124 ('to burn') to mull wine

BURY (of money): v. 283 pour in, salt away, invest: not in *OED*

BUSHELL: v. 188 measure of dry goods by volume, equivalent to 4 pecks or 8 gallons; a container of that volume

BUSSE: iii. 274 two- or three-masted vessel chiefly for the North Sea fishery, heavily built and of about 60 tons

BUTT: iii. 14 cask of 26 gallons (wine). 108 gallons (ale). 1 butt = 2 hogsheads

BUTTERED ALE: iii. 275 made of sugar, cinnamon, butter and beer brewed without hops

BUTTERY: i. 29 room, in large private house or college, for the storage and service of beer, wine, bread, butter and cheese; the preserve of the butler

BY-BOOK: v. 25 notebook, book used for rough drafts

BY-DISCOURSE: viii. 236 incidental treatise, learned parenthesis

CABAL(L): vi. 266 inner group of ministers, the 'Committee for Foreign Affairs' which was the precursor of the modern cabinet: *OED* P the acronymic application to Clifford, Arlington, Buckingham, Ashley, Lauderdale is a witticism of 1673. viii. 93 knot, faction engaged in intrigue; fig. use from the preceding

CABARETT (Fr. *cabaret*): iii. 204 tavern: 1655

CABINETT: iv. 138 the King's cabinet council: 1644 in this shortened form

CAJOLE (Fr. *cajoler*): iv. 78 to persuade a person into an action by false means: 1645

CAKE WILL BE DOE, all my: vi. 90 all my plans will miscarry: 1559

CALKERS: vi. 131 caulkers, workmen who caulked seams of ships

CALL (v.): ix. 398 to call on/for. ix. 17 to drive (i.e. 'to call for and drive to', understood)

CALL COUSIN, to: i. 259 to establish intimacy on the basis of a discovered kinship: a common phrase

CAMELOT, CAMLET(T), CAMLOTT: iii. 42 robust ribbed cloth made of wool or, more rarely, goat hair

CAN: i. 96 drinking vessel, usually wooden

CANAILLE, CANNELL, CHANNEL, KENNEL: v. 83 sewer. vii. 207 ornamental canal (in St James's Park): *OED* P (Fr. *canal*)

CANARY: ii. 211 light sweet wine from Canary Islands

CALM AS A LAMB: *see* Lamb

CANCEL: vi. 217 obliterate, destroy by tearing up

CANCRE, CANKER: i. 48 canker, ulcer, sore

CANDLE-LIGHT(ING): iv. 290, ix. 288 the time at which candles are lit, dusk: *OED* P

CANONS: i. 156 canions, boot hose tops: 'old-fashioned ornament for the legs' (Phillips, 1706)

CANTON (heraldic): iv. 152 small division of shield

CAPABLE OF, to be: i. 257 to be eligible, qualified for: 1605

CAPER (ship, Du. *kaper*): viii. 162 privateer: 1657

CAPITALL: iii. 106 standing at head of page or beginning of line or paragraph

CAPON: i. 78 castrated cock

CARBONADO: ii. 3 to grill, broil, and hence meat so treated: *Coriolanus* IV 5 'He scotched him and notcht him like a Caribonado'; distinct from Flemish and N. French *carbonade*, meat braised in beer

CAREENING: vii. 345 action of 'to careen', heeling of a stationary ship to make possible work on her bottom: *OED* 1667

CARESSE: iii. 123 to make much of: 1658

CARPENTER: *see* Joyner

CARPET: i. 232 thick patterned fabric: can refer to covering for tables, beds etc. or (ix. 469) the floor

CARRIAGE: vii. 260 conduct. viii. 408 bearing, deportment

CARRMAN: iv. 77 carter, carrier

CARRY (a person): i. 70 to conduct, escort. (a matter) iii. 185 to succeed in

CASE: i. 220 condition, state

CAST (v.): iii. 120 to defeat in an action at law. vii. 301 to calculate, reckon up. (around, about) v. 134, viii. 280

CASTING: vi. 271 calculation

CAST OF OFFICE: viii. 166 taste of quality

CATALOGUE: ix. 72 list arranged on methodical principle: *OED* P

CATAPLASM(E): iii. 24 poultice

CATCH, KATCH: i. 205 round song. (ship) i. 242 ketch

CATT WILL BE A CATT STILL: vii. 180 evidently proverbial but not apparently recorded elsewhere

CATT-CALL: i. 80 whistle. OED P

CAUDLE: i. 104 thin gruel, served warm and spiced, mixed with wine or ale

CAUSE: iv. 170 law case

CAVEAT: ii. 153 'when a person is dead, and a competition ariseth for the Executorship, or Administratorship, the party concerned enters a Caveat, to prevent or admonish others from intermedling' (Blount, 1656)

CAZZO DRITTO NON VUOLT CONSIGLIO: iv. 137 there are versions in several languages, e.g. Scots 'a standing cock has nae conscience': Burns, *The merry muses of Caledonia* (ed. Barke and Goodsir Smith, 1965), p. 35; Rochester's poem on this theme was written before 20 Jan. 1674, cf. Vieth (ed.), *Complete Poems* (1960), p. 60

CELLAR: ix. 145 for bottles: 1632

CERE CLOTH: viii. 340 cloth impregnated with wax and medicaments, used as a plaster (cf. N. Culpeper, *Pharmacopoeia Londinensis*, ed. Cole, 1661, p. 195)

CERTIFICATE: i. 265 testimonial

CESTORNE, SESTORNE: viii. 424 cistern, vessel used for washing plates during meal: OED P

CHAFE: ii. 59 heat, anger

CHAFING-DISH: vii. 10 dish to hold burning charcoal, used to keep plates and food warm, and for cooking operations requiring a low heat

CHAGRIN (Fr. *chagrin*): vi. 12 disquieted, troubled: 'often referred to, c. 1700, as an affected and frenchified term' (OED)

CHALD(E)RON: viii. 296 1⅓ tons (London measure)

CHAMBER: ii. 88 small piece of ordnance for firing salutes

CHANGELING: v. 71 idiot, half-wit: 1642

CHANNEL: see Canaille

CHAPEL, the: usually the Chapel Royal as constituted at Whitehall Palace (the Chapel Royal was a limb of the Court, not a place, and if the Court moved the 'Chapel Royal' moved with it)

CHAPTER (L. *capitulum*, Fr. *chapitre*): i. 206 usually of Bible

CHARACTER: i. 22 code, cipher

CHARGE (s.): i. 32 a duty, something one is charged with. iv. 42 expense, cost. iii. 101 quantity

CHARGE (v.): ii. 9 to load

CHARGEABLE: v. 298 costly

CHARIOT(T): viii. 289 a light four-wheeled carriage usually drawn by two horses, distinguished from a coach by having only back seats, but from a post-chaise by having a coach-box. OED P

CHARM: viii. 85 'to charm the country people's mouths': an ambiguous expression, perhaps implying both 'to delight their sense of taste' and 'to entice them into goodwill'; there are precedents for either sense

CHASED-WORK: i. 192 engraved work

CHAW: ii. 128 chew

CHEAP (s.): v. 75 bargain. (a. & adv.) ix. 415 contemptible

CHEAPEN: ix. 207 to ask the price of, bargain

CHECK: i. 255 reproof, warning, 'telling-off'

CHEEK BY JOWL: viii. 481 side by side: 1577

CHEST: the Chatham Chest, the pension fund for seamen

CHEST OF DRAWERS: ii. 130 'this class of furniture only came into its own at the end of the century' (P. Thornton, *17th-century interior decoration in England, France and*

Holland, 1978, p. 295); as late as 1683 there were very few examples amongst the extensive furnishings of Ham House (cf. P. Thornton and M. Tomlin, *The furnishing and decoration of Ham House*, 1980, p. 117)

CHILD, to be with: i. 138 eager, anxious to: 1548

CHILLISH: iii. 26 on the verge of a cold: not recorded in this sense by OED

CHIMNEY/CHIMNEY-PIECE: ix. 266, 1.69 structure over and around fireplace: OED 1680 but Inigo Jones so labelled an appropriate design (*A Chymnye peece at Arundelle House*, coll. R.I.B.A.) 1619

CHIMNEY-PIECE: iii. 25 picture over fireplace

CHINA-ALE: iv. 16 ale flavoured with china-root: 1659

CHINA ORANGE: i. 57 *citrus aurantium*, the sweet orange: OED P

CHINE: i. 242 rib (beef), saddle (mutton)

CHOQUE: vii. 43 a choke, an obstruction: not in OED, which has 'choke' 1674

CHOUSE: iv. 139 to swindle, trick: 1659

CHURCHED, to be: iii. 259 to be purified after childbirth according to the rite of churching of women in the *Book of Common Prayer*

CHYMISTRY: iv. 362 the practice of medicine by the Paracelsian method: OED 1674

CHYRURGEON: ii. 103 surgeon

CINQUE PORTS: ancient ports on S.E. coast, originally five in number, providing men and ships for the navy and receiving certain privileges in return

CIVILIAN: iv. 102 civil lawyer

CIVITT CATT: iii. 25 civet-cat: popular as courtly gift from early 16th cent.

CLAP: vi. 60 gonorrhoea

CLAP-UP: i. 48 imprison. viii. 427 knock together, finalise

CLERK OF THE CHEQUE: iv. 228 principal clerical officer of a dockyard

CLOATH (of meat): vii. 352 skin, coating: a rare transferred use

CLOCKWORK, CLOCKE-WORK: iv. 265 automaton: not in OED

CLOSE (s.): vii. 254 shutter: not in OED. (of music) viii. 59 cadence. vi. 212 enclosed field

CLOSE (adj.): i. 113 secret, confidential. viii. 287 in private. viii. 45 hard at it

CLOSE-KNEED: iv. 105 close-fitting at the knees: as opposed to the bagginess fashionable earlier

CLOSET(T): i. 19 any small or private room

CLOUD, under a: vii. 317 in disfavour: 1500

CLOUTERLY: ix. 337 clumsily

CLOWN(E): vii. 405 countryman, clodhopper

CLOWNISH: v. 260 rustic, uncouth

CLOYED: iii. 190 surfeited

CLUB (s.): i. 190 share of expenses: OED P. vi. 148 meeting at which expenses are shared: 1648. *Also* v.

CLYSTER, GLISTER, GLYSTER: iv. 332 enema

COACH: i. 113 captain's state-room in large ship, over the steerage: OED P

COATE: iii. 213 profession, cloth: 'very common in 17th cent.' (OED). iv. 107 coat of arms

COCK(E) ALE: iv. 32 ale mixed with jelly or meat of a boiled cock: 1648

COCKPIT(T): usually the theatre in the Cockpit buildings, Whitehall Palace; the buildings themselves

COD(D): ii. 197 testicle

COD OF MUSKE: vii. 22 odoriferous reddish brown secretion from the abdominal gland of a male musk-deer: an object much misunderstood in the 17th cent., when it was popularly believed to be the testicle of a beaver, sacrified by that animal to placate hunters; P was probably unable to smell it as the chief function of the secretion, in perfumery, is to act as a reagent for other scents; he was also fortunate – the smell is unpleasant, and causes headache

CODLIN TART: iv. 251 apple (codling) tart: a codling was a cooking apple

CODPIECE: viii. 421 bagged appendage in the front of breeches

COFFEE: v. 14 coffee-house

COG: iv. 197 to cheat. v. 349 to wheedle: originally to cheat at throwing dice

COLEWORTS: ii. 52 cabbage

COLLACION: iv. 200 'a repast: a treat less than a feast': Dr Johnson's definition, though anachronistic, is valid

COLLAR DAY: iii. 207 day on which knights of chivalric orders wore insignia at court

COLLECT: iv. 273 to deduce

COLLEGUE: i. 321 college friend, 'fellow collegian': not in *OED*, which does however cite 'colleagen' as comb. of 'colleague' and 'collegian'

COLLIER: iii. 25 coal-heaver. vi. 3 coal ship

COLLOPS: v. 95 as 'collops and eggs', ham or bacon and eggs: *OED* observes 'derivation obscure' and distinguishes two senses, one pertaining to eggs, the other to slices of meat, a distinction which is manifestly confused by the customary liaison of the two comestibles in this familiar English dish; the explanation is probably a common derivation from Ger. *geklopten* (beaten), which could be used of either eggs or slices of meat (as in U.S. 'tenderised'), the latter application giving Fr. *escalope*

and hence Eng. and Scots (still current) 'collop', the prevailing sense of which, in Pepys's lifetime and for many years before and after, was 'a large slice or cut of flesh' (Dyche), the alternative application to eggs having long been obsolete; a further complexity is illustrated by James Jenks, *The Complete Cook* (1768) when, at the end of his recipe for Scotch-collops (scotched – i.e. beaten – sliced veal dished up with 'crisp bacon') he notes that 'This is called by some cooks *a fillet of veal with collops*', which suggests that by the mid-18th cent. 'collops' had come to have a particular association with fried bacon, though its use in a more general sense continued

COLLY-FEAST: i. 24 feast of collies (cullies, good companions) at which each pays his share

COMEDIAN: iv. 207 actor

COMEDY: v. 230 play

COMFIT: iii. 114 sweet

COMMEND: v. 7 presumably 'commend *her*' understood

COMMON TUNE: v. 18 generic name for the tunes used in church to which metrical psalms were sung

COMPASS (v.): viii. 273 achieve, contrive

COMPASS TIMBER: iv. 326, n. 1 curved timber: used in ship-building for 'grown' knees (the strongest variety); much in demand (cf. *London Gazette*, 2122/4, 1686, a plea for 'compass or knee Tymber' for naval use)

COMPLACENCY, COMPLAISANCE: ii. 36, viii. 403 civility, wish to fall in with the wishes of others: 1651

COMPLEXED: vi. 335 complicated: 1646

COMPLEXION: vii. 315 aspect

COMPOSE: iii. 27 to put music to words. iv. 78 to make up a quarrel

COMPOSITION: viii. 55 setting of words to music *OED* P. iii. 218 settlement, compromise agreement

CON: iii. 10 study, look over

CONCEIT: v. 51 idea, notion

CONCERNMENT: v. 205 interest, involvement

CONCLUDE: ix. 116 to agree. vi. 337 to include

CONDITION (s.): vii. 314 social position. v. 35 state of wealth

CONDITION (v.): viii. 100 to make conditions

CONDITIONED: i. 202 having a (specified) disposition or social position

CONEY: v. 298 rabbit

CONFESS AND BE HANGED: iii. 191 proverbial from 1589

CONGEE (Fr. *congé*): i. 160 bow at parting

CONGRATULATE (v.): ix. 108 used (twice) without the customary modern reflexive reference (i.e. in modern usage 'to congratulate my sister upon her marriage;' 'to congratulate me upon my speech')

CONJUROR: ix. 373 fortune-teller

CONSIDERABLE: viii. 310 worthy of consideration: 1619: cf. Observable

CONSTER: iv. 236 to construe, translate

CONSTRUE: i. 44 to decipher

CONSULT MY PILLOW: vi. 106 take a night for reflection: 1530

CONSUMPTION: viii. 337 (any) wasting disease. *Also* i. 202 'consumptive'

CONTEMPTIBLY: vii. 204 contemptuously

CONTENT, by/in: i. 290 without examination: 1646. vi. 100 at a rough guess

CONTINGENCY: i. 301 money against extraordinary expenses: 1626 Bacon

CONVENIENCE: vi. 292 advantage

CONVENTICLE: iv. 159 a meeting of Dissenters for religious worship: application formalised by the Conventicle Act of 1664

CONVERSATION: iii. 254 acquaintance, society; elsewhere, demeanour, behaviour

COOLE: iii. 202 cowle

COPPER: iii. 261 utensil for boiling washing in

COPULO (It. *cupola*): ix. 182 cupola: 1549

COPY, COP(P)YHOLD: ii. 227, ii. 135 tenure of manorial lands by copy of the customs of the manor

COQUIN (Fr.): v. 264 rogue, knave

CORANT(O): iv. 122 dance in 3/2 or 6/4 time, involving a running or gliding step: despite the possible Italian spelling of its name, it was the French *courante* that was danced in Restoration England

CORE: viii. 507 the hard knob of dead tissue in the centre of a boil

CORNET: ix. 554 the cavalry equivalent of an ensign, who customarily carried the colours

CORRESPONDENCE: i. 243 familiarity, interchange of visits

COSEN, COUSIN: i. 259 almost any collateral relative

COUNT: v. 217 reckon, estimate, value

COUNTENANCE: iii. 6 recognition, acknowledgement. viii. 96 'bear the countenance of', have the appearance of

COUNTRY (s.): ix. 15 county, district. (adj.) iv. 242 rustic. ix. 17 native

COUNTRY DANCE: iv. 126 dance for groups of 4, 6, 8 or more, in squares, 'longways' and rounds: very popular in England from the 1550s; steps and tunes collected in Playford's *English Dancing Master* (cf. iii. 263 & n.)

COURSE (s.): vii. 310 career. ix. 565 way of proceeding

COURSE, in: iv. 75 in sequence

COURSE, of: iv. 75 as usual

COURSE, take a: viii. 336 have a tilt at (as in the lists)

COURT BARON: iv. 308 manorial court (civil)

COURT DISH: i. 245 dish with a cut from every meat

COURT LEET(E): iv. 308 local criminal court

COXON: i. 114 coxswain (of ship)

COY: ix. 521 disdainful

CRACK A NUT, as easily as: iv. 61 unrecorded, though 'crack me that n.' common from 1545

CRADLE: iv. 409 fire-basket

CRAMBO: i. 149 rhyming game: *OED* P, a player gives a word or verse, to which each of the others must find a rhyme

CRANE-HOUSE: viii. 309 shed containing a windlass: *OED* 1705

CRAVETT (Fr. *cravate*): ii. 229 'that Linnen which is worn about Mens (especially Souldiers and Travellers) Necks, in stead of a Band' (Blount, 1674): 1656

CRAZY: viii. 181 infirm

CREATURE (of persons): vii. 312 puppet, instrument

CRIBBIGE: i. 5 cribbage: card game for 2 players employing board with pegs for scoring (cf. [Charles Cotton], *The Compleat Gamester*, 1674, pp. 106–10); according to Aubrey, ii. 245, invented by Sir John Suckling: 1630

CROOKED (of a person): i. 53 crookbacked, hunch-backed

CROP: iv. 120 a crop-eared animal: *OED* 1689

CROSS (s.): iii. 244 a vexation, that which thwarts or crosses: 1573

CROSS (v.): iv. 182 to thwart

CROSS-GRAINED: ii. 233 refractory, perverse: 1647

CROSS PURPOSES: vii. 422 a question-and-answer game with forfeits

CROUCH (v.): viii. 549 to cringe

CROWNE EARTHEN-POT: v. 47 earthenware pot of superior finish: modern 'crownware'

CRUCING: vi. 39 cruising

CRUMB, I have got up my: iv. 401 improved my condition: usually to 'get' or 'gather' one's crumbs, proverbial from 1474

CRUSADO: iii. 100 Portuguese coin worth 3s.

CRUSH: iv. 391 conflict, clash: apparently unrecorded by any authority on standard or dialect English, but clear in context

CRY UP, to: i. 19 to praise

CUDDY (Du. *kajuit*): i. 137 cabin in large ship in which officers took their meals: *OED* P

CUDS ZOOKES: vii. 164 gads zookes, God's zookes: 'origin disputed' (*OED*)

CULLY, COLLY: ix. 219 dupe. i. 24 friend: *OED* 1664

CUNNING: i. 241 knowledgeable. also as s., 'knowledge'

CUP, get a: iv. 386 get drunk

CURIOUS: vii. 97 painstaking, careful. vi. 48 discriminating. viii. 522 fine, delicate

CURRANT: iv. 108 out and about

CURRENT: vii. 312 fluent

CUSTOMER: vii. 31 customs officer

CUSTOS ROTULORUM (L.): i. 79 principal Justice of the Peace (usually Lord Lieutenant) in a county, having custody of the rolls and records of the sessions of the peace

CUT (v.): v. 274 to carve meat. ii. 7 allocate by lot: *see* Draw cuts

CUT . . . ME OUT FOR: viii. 419 to fix upon me for: *OED* P

CUT OUT WORK FOR: v. 262 to prepare work for: 1619

CUT(T) (s.): v. 38 an engraving: 1646; at vii. 102 P has 'printed picture'

CUTTING-HOUSE: i. 84 tailor's cutting room: *OED* P

CYPHER: viii. 544 monogram: 1631

DAGGER-DRAWING, be at: vi. 317 the original form of 'at daggers drawn', which first occurs 1680: 1540

DAMASKE: vii. 31 silk or linen woven in pattern of flowers etc.

DAMP: i. 81 dump, state of dejection

DARK, in the: viii. 263 in a state of ignorance: *OED* 1677

DASH, at first: viii. 120 at once, immediately

DAUB: iv. 162 to dirty

DAUGHTER-IN-LAW: ii. 12 step-daughter

DEAD COLOUR: ii. 233 preparatory layer of colour in a painting: 1658

DEADLY: i. 280 excessive, 'terrible': *OED* P. iv. 197 dangerously

DEAD PAYS: iv. 334 sailors or soldiers kept on pay roll after death

DEAL OF DO: vii. 86, ix. 245 to-do, trouble: 'common in 17th cent.' (*OED*)

DEALS: iv. 426 sawn timber used for decks etc.: customs regulations applied the term to boards of 7 to 11 inches in width, 18 to 20 feet in length, and not more than $3\frac{1}{4}$ inches in thickness; narrower boards were 'battens', wider 'planks'. i. 324 for use in house building

DEDIMUS (L.): i. 240 writ empowering Justice of the Peace: from L. *dedimus potestatem*, 'we have given the power'

DEFALK: vii. 173 to subtract

DEFEND: iv. 358 to prevent

DEFLUXION: viii. 302 a discharge of 'humorous' liquid to any part of the body, any rheum or issue

DEFYANCE (Fr.): iii. 4 mistrust

DELICATE: iv. 247 pleasant

DELIRIUM: vii. 28 uncontrollable excitement: 1599 colloquial c. 1650

DEMORAGE: iv. 368 demurrage, compensation from the freighter due to a ship-owner for delaying vessel beyond time specified in charter-party: 1641

DENIZEN: vi. 248 formally naturalised immigrant

DEPORT: v. 174 to conduct oneself, comport

DESCANT UPON: iv. 135 to subject to particular comment

DESERT: ii. 230 deservingness, value

DESPERATE: vi. 207 'risky' rather than 'despaired of': cf. Selden, *Table Talk* (1654) 'marriage is a desperate thing'

DEVIL'S ARSE A-PEAK: iv. 19 The 'Devil's Arse' is the famous cave above Castleton, Derbyshire, a by-word long before Chesterfield sent his wife there, as the allusions to 'Devil's-arse-a-Pekian' in Jonson's *Gypsies Metamorphos'd* (1621) demonstrate (cuckoldry is a topic in the masque): cf. also Pepys Ballads, v. 307 (PL 2509) 'An Answer to the Poor Whore's Complaint', 'Yet here they come up ev'ry week/From the very *Devil's Arse-a-peak*,/Both *East*, West, North and *South*'

DEVISE: vii. 113 to decide, discern

DIALECT: iv. 394 jargon

DIALL, double horizontal: iv. 173 ordinary sundial and analemmatic dial mounted together on one plate, thus making compass orientation unnecessary: cf. [William Oughtred], *The description and use of a double horizontall dyall* (1652) and, for a modern account, Frank W. Cousins, *Sundials* (1969), pp. 56–9

DIAPER: i. 290 linen fabric with small flower pattern

DIARY: ii. 81 a day's entry in a journal: but compare modern sense at ii. 73; usually, however, the book is termed a 'journal', as at viii. 264

DIET (v.): vii. 296 feed, provide food for: 1635

DIFFERENCE: ii. 32 dispute, falling out.

viii. 378 distinction of class or quality

DIRECTING: iii. 234 supervision of making

DIRT, all in the: viii. 72 thrown out: *OED* P

DISCOMPLIANCE: v. 219 refusal to comply: *OED* P

DISCONTENT (s.): ix. 523 malcontent

DISCOVER: v. 293 to disclose, reveal

DISCREET: ix. 127 discerning, judicious

DISGUST: ix. 336 to dislike

DISH OF COFFEE: v. 76 cupful of coffee: *OED* 1679

DISMAYING (vbl s.): vii. 195 dismay: common 15th–17th cents.

DISPENSE: v. 265 outgoings

DISTASTE: vii. 284 difference, quarrel, offence: 1622.

DISTEMPER (s.): vii. 104 illness. ix. 434 tempera: 1632

DISTEMPER (v.): iv. 237 to put out of sorts

DISTINCT: vii. 121 discerning, discriminating

DISTRINGAS: ix. 535 writ of distraint

DIVERTISEMENT (Fr. *divertissement*): viii. 7 an entertainment, a ballet or entr'acte: *OED* P. iii. 225 recreation, amusement: 1651 Hobbes

DIVERTIZE, DIVERTISING: viii. 380, viii. 240 entertain: 1651 entertaining 1652

DOASE: i. 311 dose of medicine

DOATE: i. 305 to nod off to sleep. ii. 207 to enthuse over, admire

DOCKET(T): i. 198 abstract of a letter-patent. ix. 480 register of legal judgements: *OED* P

DOCTOR: i. 11 clergyman, don

DOE: dough: *see* Cake

DOG (v.): v. 292 to follow

DOG CART: ix. 234 sledge drawn by dog

DOGGED: viii. 333 determined, with a fixed intent

DOGGS: iv. 301 firedogs

DOLLER: *see* Rix Doller

DORTOIRE (Fr.): viii. 26 dorter, monastic dormitory

DOTE: ii. 240 to be inordinately affectionate

DOTY: iv. 161 darling: not in *OED*

DOUBT (v.): ii. 137 to fear. v. 180 to wonder, be perplexed as to

DOUBTFUL: v. 277 fearful, careful

DOWDY (s.): ii. 116 a woman shabbily dressed

DOXY: vi. 213 whore, mistress

DRAM: iii. 118 timber from Drammen, Norway. viii. 497 measure of spirits

DRAUGHT: iii. 174 drawing. i. 70 a drink (viii. 4 'Christmas draught')

DRAW: i. 36 to draw up, parade. vii. 375 to draft

DRAW CUTS, to: ix. 409 to draw lots

DRAWER: i. 250 tapster, barman

DRESS: iv. 342 to cook, prepare food. viii. 129 to be formally dressed. iii. 213 to dress hair

DRESSER: iii. 74 tirewoman

DRESSING BOX: ix. 91 case of toilet utensils: 1663

DRESSING-ROOM: ix. 491 room for dressing: *OED* 1675 but found in a Dublin inventory of 1656 and as a 'Tiring Chamber', 1610 (cf. P. Thornton, *17th-century interior decoration in England, France and Holland*, 1978, p. 301)

DROLENESSE: ii. 196 comical simplicity

DROLL(E): viii. 5 comic song. vi. 119 a wag

DROLLING, DROLLY: i. 255, iii. 250 comical, comically

DROP (v.): viii. 589 to leave, 'drop off'

DRUDGER: vii. 34 dredger: possibly a container for sweetmeats (Fr. *drageoir*) or, in the modern sense, a container for sugar with a perforated lid

DRUDGING: viii. 126 laborious: apparently not opprobrious

DRUGGERMAN: vii. 251 dragoman, interpreter

DRUM: i. 42 a drummer playing his instrument

DRUNK AS A DOG: vi. 290 not recorded, but 'dry as a dog' from c. 1591 and 'a drunken man is always dry' 1560: proverbial logic is relentless

DRY BEATEN: ix. 435 beaten without drawing blood

DRY MONEY: v. 284 hard cash

DUANA: iv. 369 divan, council

DUCCATON: i. 166 ducatoon, large silver coin of the Netherlands worth 5s. 9d.

DUCKET(T): i. 160 ducat, foreign gold coin (here probably Dutch) worth 9s.

DUDGEON: iii. 14 anger

DULCIMORE: iii. 90 dulcimer, musical instrument, rectangular or triangular and akin to a psaltery in shape, having 10 or more wire strings running parallel over shaped bridges on a flat soundboard. The strings are struck with two hammers, one in each hand of the player. Known in England since the 12th cent. and still surviving as a folk instrument in East Anglia

DULL: i. 87 limp, spiritless

DUMP, DUMPISH: vi. 60, ix. 364 fit of sorrow, melancholy

DUMP, to be in a: vi. 60 to be depressed: common from 1555

DUN: v. 82 'a word lately taken up by fancy, and signifies to demand earnestly, or press a man to pay for commodities taken up on trust, or other debt' (Blount, 1656)

DYALL: vii. 276 sundial

EARES, together by the: ix. 489 at odds, variance: 'to set' or 'fall together by the ears' proverbial by 1530

EARNEST: iv. 183 deposit, instalment

EARTH: viii. 26 earthenware

EASILY AND EASILY: vi. 131 more and more slowly

EFFECTUAL: i. 108 'powerful enough to do what is wanting' (Dyche)

EFFEMINACY: viii. 288 love of women: *OED* records 'effeminately' in the 'pseudo-etymological' sense of 'devoted to women', but does not note 'effeminacy' in the same sense

EGREGIOUS: ix. 149 flagrant

ELABORATORY: ix. 416 laboratory: 1652 Evelyn

ELECTUARY: iv. 329 paste of honey or syrup with powdered drugs; taken by licking (from a stick) as the name implies (cf. N. Culpeper, *Pharmacopoeia Londinensis*, ed. Cole, 1661, pp. 142+)

ELL: iv. 425 a measure of 45 inches

EMBARRAS (Fr.): v. 208 embarrassment: *OED* P

EMBERS, lie under the: v. 208 liable to be raked up: 1650

EMBLEME: v. 241 type, example

EMERODS: ii. 132 haemorrhoids

EMPTION: ix. 330 purchase

ENDICT: iii. 205 to write

ENGINE: i. 263 hydraulic machine. viii. 320 fire-engine: 1645

ENGLISH BACON: iii. 51 sweet-cured: cf. French Bacon

ENGROSS, INGROSS: i. 205 to record. ii. 202 to take over

ENTENDIMIENTO (Sp.): i. 129 understanding

ENTER (of horse): ix. 398 to break in. (of person) iv. 343 to introduce to a subject

ENTERTAIN: i. 232 to retain, employ

ENTRY-MONEY: iv. 122 fee payable to a master on commencing a course of instruction: *OED* 1864

EPICURE-LIKE: ii. 93 taking conscious pleasure in the choiceness of food and drink: 1586 ('epicure')

EPICURISME: ii. 183 conscious delight in the sensation of

ESPINETTE (s.): ix. 149 *see* Spinet: *OED* P

ESPY: v. 22 spy: OED suggests obsolescent by this date

ESSAY: iv. 145 to assay

ESTABLISHMENT (Fr. *établissement*): i. 98 memorandum setting out the organisation and strength of a fleet, etc.

ESTEEM: ii. 140 value, estimate: a common 17th-cent. use in the form 'put an esteem on'

EUPHROE (Du. *jonkvrouw*): iii. 119 uphroe, 'a long piece of wood with a number of holes in it' (R.C. Anderson, *17th-cent. rigging*, Watford, 1955, p.69): in later usage a cylindrical block with a hole in it

EVEN (adv.): ii. 51 surely

EVEN, to (of accounts): iii. 82 to balance, settle. 'to make even' i. 62

EVENT: vii. 315 outcome

EXAMPLE: iv. 35 paradigm

EXCEPT: v. 300 to accept

EXPECT: ix. 34 to await (vii. 84, with sense 'will receive')

EXPEDIENT (s.): viii. 40 contrivance, device: 1653

EXPENSEFUL: viii. 287 expensive

EXPRESS: i. 60 to effect, achieve. i. 146 to represent

EXTRAORDINARIES: vii. 314 extraordinary charges

EYES . . . FALL OUT OF MY HEAD: viii. 537 an early and perhaps the earliest use of this phrase

FACTION: viii. 412 the government's parliamentary critics. ix. 146 a spirit of dissent. iii. 15 a group with a common aim

FACTIOUS: ix. 280 able to command a following. ix. 264 inclined to faction

FACTOR: ii. 197 mercantile agent

FACTORY: v. 49 trading station

FACULTY: i. 318 a power, capacity: much used in scholastic philosophy to explain the actions of natural bodies

FAGOTT: ii. 87 bundle of sticks or twigs for fuel

FAIN, to be: i. 254 to be obliged

FAIR: i. 174 clean: a common use 14th-18th cents.

FAIR-CONDITIONED: i. 202 in good circumstances

FAIRING: ii. 166 small present (as from fair)

FAIRLY: v. 72 gently, quietly

FALCHON: viii. 209 falchion, curved sword

FALL (v.): v. 1 to go bankrupt

FALL FOUL, to: ix. 20 to quarrel

FALL (FOUL) ON: viii. 110 to attack, make a hostile descent on

FALL OUT: iii. 252 occur, happen

FALL TO: i. 33 to set to

FALLACY: v. 240 a sophistical argument: OED 1777, but, as a 'sophism', 1562

FALSE-SPELT: iv. 29 mis-spelled: 'false writer' for 'one who writes incorrectly' occurs from 1440 (OED)

FAMILY: i. 1 household (including servants)

FANATIC, PHANATIQUE: ii. 67 extreme nonconformist, both politically and religiously: 'a new word coined, within few months . . . which . . . seemeth well . . . proportioned to signify . . . the sectaries of the age' (Fuller, *Mixt contemplations on these times*, 1660), but in fact in use from 1525; ii. 67 shows how it gradually became a hostile epithet for all Nonconformists

FANCY (music): iv. 160 fantasia, contrapuntal piece for instruments, particularly viols

FANFARROON (Fr. *fanfaron*): vi. 190 fanfaron, braggart: 1622

FANTASKE (Fr. *fantasque*): iii. 299 fanciful, affected: OED 1701

FARANDINE, FARRINDIN: *see* Ferrandin

FARCE: ii. 166 comical afterpiece. ix. 420 comical interlude. viii. 387, ix. 270 in modern sense: P's remark at viii. 387 would not have been appreciated by Dryden: 'I detest those *Farces*, which are now the most frequent Entertainments of the Stage ... *Farce* entertains us with what is monstrous and Chimerical' (Preface to *An Evening's Love*, 1668)

FART, worth a: viii. 289 current from 1440

FASHION (of metal, furniture): ix. 89 design. v. 301 fashioning, manufacture. (of persons, v.) vii. 46 to shape, train

FAST (s.): i. 58 fast-day (ordinarily Friday) service. iv. 29 a fast-day

FASTEN DISCOURSE: i. 147 impose conversation on, 'chat up': as in 'fasten a quarrel', 1663 Dryden

FASTEN ON ME, to: viii. 392 to fix an imputation upon

FAT: i. 119 vat

FATHER: i. 29 father-in-law (similarly with 'mother' etc.). ii. 199 mentor

FAVOUR (s.): viii. 73 small bunch of ribbons given to those attending marriages, burials etc.

FEATHER ONE'S NEST: iii. 104 enrich oneself: 1553

FEATHERS: ii. 172 worn as ornaments in hat bands

FELLET (of trees): iv. 413 a cutting, felling: not in *OED* but current in 19th cent.

FELLMONGER: ii. 146 dealer in skins and furs

FELLOW COMMONER: v. 277 undergraduate paying high fees and enjoying some of a fellow's privileges

FERKIN: i. 222 firkin, c. 56 lbs; a cask holding that weight of a commodity (e.g. butter-firkin)

FERRANDIN, FARRINDIN, FARANDINE (Fr. *ferrandine*): iv. 28 cloth of silk mixed with wool or hair: *OED* P. allegedly invented by one Ferrand, c. 1630

FETCH UP (naut.): viii. 257 make a course towards

FICKLY: vii. 85 in a fickle fashion, changeably

FIDDLE (s.): i. 285 violin: and possibly on occasion jocular for treble viol. ii. 71 player of bowed string instrument (inc. viol): a common musician rather than a master

FIG, care a: viii. 584 not to value at all: 'a fig', as something worthless, from c. 1400

FIGARY: viii. 463 fegary, vagary: a common corruption

FILE, FYLE (v.): ii. 171 to place on a file: 1601, originally to string upon a thread, but ii. 171 makes it clear P used a spike or some other device

FIND IT OUT WHO CAN: iv. 257 apparently a prov. phrase

FINE (s.): i. 213 payment for lease

FINE, in: ii. 165 in short

FINE FOR OFFICE (v.): iv. 404 to avoid office by payment of fine

FIREMEN: iv. 217 gunners, musketeers

FIRESHIP: vii. 165 ship filled with combustibles used to ram and set fire to enemy

FIRING: i. 58 firewood

FISH FROM HIM, to: iv. 301 ascertain, elicit

FIT (v.): ii. 68 to make fit, prepare

FITTING (a ship or fleet): ii. 62 fitting out, preparing for sea

FLAG, FLAGGMAN: vi. 262, vii. 102 flag officer: *OED* P

FLAGEOLET, FLAGELETTE (Fr. *flageolet*): i. 33 whistle-flute with four holes in front and two thumb holes at the back: 1659, very popular in France in the 1640s and '50s, and in England in the 1660s

FLAGON: i. 322 table vessel for wine or beer, customarily holding 2 quarts

FLAME (s.): viii. 204 rage

FLEECE OUT OF HIS COAT, have a good: v. 22 have a good share: a number of common 17th-cent. expressions draw on the metaphor, though not exactly in this form

FLEER: viii. 102 to look contemptuously at, sneer

FLESHED: ix. 466 grown relentless, proud, fleshed upon

FLING, FLING UP, OFF: iii. 133, viii. 293, iv. 160 to resign, abandon. 'have a fling at' vii. 319 make a (speculative) attack on

FLOCK-BED: i. 40 bed having mattress stuffed with wool or cotton tufts

FLOOD: ix. 300 rising tide, flowing in of the tide; converse of ebb

FLORENCE WINE: ii. 8 a ladies' tipple: OED 1707, but cf. *Francis Mortoft: His Book* (Hakluyt Society, 1925, p. 51) 19 Dec. 1658, 'the wyne which is called Florence wyne, and is so much esteemed by the women in England in regard of the pleasantnesse of the Taste'

FLOUNCE (v.): v. 84 to express displeasure by exaggerated movements: OED 1702

FLOURISHING: vi. 339 calligraphic ornamentation

FLOWER: vi. 114 a beautiful girl: OED as common in M.E., but cf. fn. and also OED's additional sense of 'the pick of the bunch': Pepys Ballads, v. 418 (PL 2509) has 'The next is Mistriss Joan that famous Flower'

FLOWER IN THE CROWNE: vii. 408 apparently a derivative of 'flower in my garland' (cf. 'flowers in my garden'), which perhaps involves a fusion or confusion with 'jewel in the crown', current by 16th cent.

FLOWER-POTT: ix. 515 here a painting of a flower-pot, on the analogy of 'landskip' etc.

FLOWERS IN MY GARDEN, one of the best: v. 280 originally 'flower in my garland': 1546

FLUTTER, make a: viii. 408 make an ostentatious fuss: OED P but to 'flutter the dovecote' from 1608

FLUX (s.): viii. 572 issue, discharge

FLUXED (of the pox): vi. 12 salivated: OED 1679

FLYING ARMY/FLEET: v. 56, viii. 88 small mobile force: OED 1665

FOIBLE: ii. 174 weakness of character: OED 1673

FOMENTACION: iv. 385 fomentation, the application of warm herbs, in dry or liquid form, to a diseased part

FOND; FONDNESS: ix. 417; ii. 213 foolish; folly

FOND (Fr. *fond*): viii. 143 fund: OED 1673

FOOT IT, to: ii. 22 to go by foot: cf. Horse it, to

FOOT, upon the: vii. 19 on the basis of

FORAIGNER: ii. 81 not native to, or enfranchised of, a place (cf. fn.)

FORENOON: i. 255 morning

FORETOPP: iii. 123 strictly, the top (planked platform) at the foremast head; as a place for flying flags, the foretopmast head

FORM(E): iv. 8 bench. viii. 529 formality. v. 209 style of dress: OED P. ix. 144 essential determinant principle (philosophical and scientific)

FORMALITY: vi. 65 requirement made for the sake of form: 1647 vii. 96 ceremony: OED P

FORMOSA: vi. 103 formose, beautiful

FORSOOTH: ii. 15 to speak ceremoniously: 1604

FORTY: v. 300 many, scores of (biblical)

FORWARDNESS: ii. 112 preparedness

FOULE COPY: i. 288 rough copy

FOX, to: i. 274 to intoxicate

FOXED: i. 85 intoxicated: 1611

FOY, FOY-FEAST, FOY-DINNER: i. 92, iv. 171 departure feast (or gift)

FOYLE: viii. 103 a repulse, a baffling check

FRAME (v.): i. 29 make, contrive, prepare

FRANTIC: viii. 543 mad

FRENCH BACON: viii. 254 not apparently elsewhere recorded, but bacon was extensively exported from Bordeaux in the 1660s; cf. Francisque-Michel, *Histoire du commerce et de la navigation à Bordeaux* (Bordeaux 1869–70), ii. 264; L.-E. Audot, *La Charcuterie* (Paris 1818) makes a basic distinction between French hams and *jambon à l'anglaise*, the former being cured with brine and saltpetre, the latter with brine and sugar; the distinction apparently holds good for the 17th cent.

FRENCH DINNER: vi. 112 with soup, and each course served separately (cf. viii. 211, n. 1)

FRENCH LUTE: viii. 558 lute tuned in the French manner (*nouveau ton* or *new tuning*) first publicised in a collection edited by Pierre Ballard, 1638, and introduced into England by French players and teachers

FREQUENT: v. 288 to busy oneself

FRETTED: viii. 198 having a moulded plasterwork ('fretwork') ceiling: cf. R.T. Gunther (ed.), *The architecture of Sir Roger Pratt* (Oxf. 1928), p.227

FRICASSE (Fr. *friquassée*): iv. 95 originally meat broken and fried (*frire* to fry, *casser* to break), then stewed and served with a sharp sauce based on verjuice: P's use (not in *OED*) shows shift to later sense of a *ragoût*, a mixture of meats or poultry; cf. G. Markham, *The English Hus-wife* (1615) 'dishes of manie compositions . . . all beeing prepared and made ready in a frying panne'

FRIENDS: i. 20, ix. 32 parents, relatives

FRIEZE MANTLE: i. 60 cloak of coarse woollen cloth

FRIGATE: viii. 357 fast sailing ship with low decks and guns near the water: 1630, but as a fighting ship reputedly an invention of Phineas Pett, 1646 (cf. Evelyn, i. 22 and references there cited); P's meaning seems clear, but as Frank Fox points out (*Great Ships: the battlefleet of King Charles II*, Greenwich, 1980, p. 204) there are four distinct mid-17th cent. senses of the word, some of them contradictory

FRITTERS: ii. 43 pancakes: some 17th-cent. recipe books distinguish fritters as filled pancakes, but Pepys appears to use the term indiscriminately, as the Shrove Tuesday context implies

FRIZE (v., Fr. *friser*): i. 299 to closely curl or crisp the hair: *OED* P

FROST (v.): vi. 309 protect horses against slipping by shoeing with frost nails or roughening hooves: 1572, despite the novelty of the term to P

FROST-BITE: viii. 1 to invigorate by exposure to cold

FROWARD: ii. 64 peevish, petty, hard to please

FUDDLED: ix. 512 drunk: *OED* 1656 'to fuddle' as 'to tipple' (1588)

FULL: ix. 426 concerned, anxious

FULL MOUTH, with: vii. 250 eagerly, openly, loudly

FULL (OF) TERME: ii. 31 period in which legal business was transacted at Westminster Hall

FUMBLER: iii. 50 'an unperforming husband' (*OED*): 1640

FUNERALS: vi. 114 funeral rites, obsequies: a direct anglicization of L. *Funeralia*, 'Funeral rites or ceremonies', (Thomas Thomas's *Dictionarium*, ed. Philemon Holland, 1614)

FURBISH: ii. 28 clean, polish, put in order: particularly used of weapons

FURNITURE: i. 236 furnishings generally, and in particular hangings and drapery

FUSTY: ix. 244 peevish: OED P

GAD ABROAD: viii. 375 wander about, play truant: 1460

GALL: viii. 317 harass

GALLANT[E]: iii. 188 one (of either sex) who wears fine apparel: 1550

GALLANTRY: i. 139 elegant appearance and demeanour, stylishness

GALLEY, GALLY: ii. 101 large open rowing boat plying on Thames

GALLING: v. 298 friction creating sores

GALLIOTT, GALLYOT (Du. *galjoot*): vii. 202 small lightly built single-masted gaff-rigged vessel, but sometimes carrying a lateen mizen, designed for both sailing and rowing, shipping 16 or 20 oars: much used when speed was necessary

GALLOSH: vi. 299 overshoe

GAMMER: i. 36 old woman

GAMUT: *see* Scale

GANG: ix. 26 company of workmen, crew: 1627, originally nautical

GARB(E): i. 299 clothing

GAVELKINDE: i. 63 equal division of property amongst sons of the deceased (primarily a Kentish custom)

GAYETE DE COEUR, en (Fr.): viii. 112 lightness of heart: the phr. occurs in Molière, *Amphitryon* (1668), II vi

GENERALL-AT-SEA: i. 71 naval commander: 1589, a post, not a rank

GENIUS: v. 178 inborn character, natural aptitude: 1649, Milton

GENT: vii. 406 graceful, polite

GENTEEL(E), GENTILE: i. 40 fashionable, elegant. iv. 67 of gentle birth

GENTILELY: ix. 11 obligingly: 1637

GEORGE: i. 160 jewel forming part of insignia of order of Garter

GET A CUP: *see* Cup

GET UP, to: ii. 209 to recover one's former (good) condition: OED 1788

GIBB-CAT: viii. 553 tom-cat

GILDER, GUILDER: i. 164 Dutch money of account worth 2s.

GET UP ONE'S CRUMB: *see* Crumb

GET WITHOUT BOOK: vi. 284 to memorise

GETTINGS: iv. 202 gains

GILL: vi. 224 a quarter of a pint: 'a measure . . . much used by wine drinkers in a morning' (Dyche)

GIMP (Du. *gimp*): ii. 117 twisted thread of material with wire or cord running through it: OED 1664, but Randle Holm has 'gimp fring', 1649

GIRDLE, at his: ix. 71 'in his pocket'

GIRKIN, DANTZICKE GIRKIN (Du. *gurkijn*): ii. 225 small pickled cucumber: OED P. The word is Slavonic in origin.

GITTAR, GUITTAR: i. 172 guitar: the Spanish guitar, which reached England via Italy and France, having five (rather than the modern six) double courses of gut strings

GITTERNE: i. 169 small member of the guitar family, pear-shaped in outline but with flat back, having four double courses of gut strings

GIVE: v. 222 to answer

GIVE THE DEVIL HIS DUE: ix. 350 proverbial by 1589

GIZZARD, something in her: ix. 243 topic of reproach not yet broached: OED P

GLASS: i. 110 telescope. vi. 168 window of coach. ix. 533 lens

GLASS BUBBLE: *see* Hydrometer

GLASS-HOUSE: ix. 457 factory for the manufacture of glass

GLEEK: iii. 14 glecko, three-handed card game: 'most frequently they play at Farthing, Half-penny, or Penny Gleek, which in play will amount considerably' [Charles Cotton], *The Compleat Gamester*, 1674, pp. 90–6

GLISTER, GLYSTER: *see* Clyster

GLORY (Fr. *gloire*): i. 63 halo: 1646

GLOSSE, by a fine: vi. 337 by a plausible pretext

GO FOR COMPANY: ix. 295 out of loyalty rather than necessity

GOARE-BLOODE, all of a: ii. 228 all be-smeared with

GO(O)D BWYE, GOD-BWY: iii. 163 God be with ye, good-bye

GOODFELLOW: ix. 477 convivial person, good-timer

GOOD-FELLOWSHIP: ix. 475 roistering habits

GOOD RIDDANCE: iii. 179 OED 1782, but a 'fair riddance' from c. 1613

GOOD-SPEAKER: v. 88 one who speaks well of others

GOOD WORD: vii. 132 good news

GORGET: iv. 279 neckerchief for women,? a wimple

GOSSIP (v.): ii. 146 to act as godparent, to attend a new mother. *Also* (s.) v. 222. viii. 118 chatterbox

GOUTY: iii. 219 swollen, tumid

GOVERNMENT: viii. 50 office or function of governor

GOVERNOR: i. 180 tutor, guardian

GRACE: viii. 598 good fortune: from sense of 'divine favour'

GRAIN: iii. 75 sum of money: perhaps from a 'grain' of gold

GRAND TOUR (Fr.): vii. 126 OED 1670 (R. Lassels, *Voyage of Italy*) where used as Fr.

GRAPPLING: viii. 357 grappling-iron, grapnel

GRAVE: v. 237 to engrave

GRAZE: viii. 266 to ricochet: 1632

GRÉ, against the (Fr. *contre son gré*): vii. 384 against the will or pleasure of: OED P

GREAT, to be . . . with: i. 44–5 to be in favour with, intimate with

GREATEN: viii. 348 to increase

GREEN GOOSE: v. 195 a young or midsummer goose, so called till four months old

GREENS: viii. 469 plants (creepers): OED 1697 Dryden

GRIEF: viii. 13 bodily pain

GRILLED (Fr. *griller*): ix. 317 broiled on a gridiron: OED P

GRIZZLY: ix. 398 grizzled: 1594

GROAT: i. 287 silver coin worth 4*d.*: minting ceased 1662

GROUND: ix. 505 foundation, origin

GRUDGEING/GRUTCHING: vi. 67 a 'touch' of an ailment

GUESSE: iv. 173 guests

GUEST: v. 235 nominee

GUILDER: *see* Gilder

GUINEA: vii. 346 gold coin first minted 1663, when worth 20*s.*, worth 30*s.* 1695, legal tender at 21*s.* from 1717, not coined since 1813: from Guinea (Africa)

GULL (v.): vii. 411 to deceive

GUN: i. 152 flagon of ale: 1645, Evelyn. iii. 50 cannon, salute

GUNDALOW, GUNDILOW: viii. 56 gondola

HABITT: i. 259 dress of office, robe worn by cleric, ii. 80 peer. ii. 233 settled tendency: 1581

HACKNEY, HACKNY, HACQUENEE: i. 286 (of coach) vehicle plying for hire. vi. 180 workhorse. ix. 62 (fig.) drudge, hack

HAIR, against the: viii. 281 against the lie of an animal's hair, 'against the grain'

HALF-A-PIECE: i. 86 gold coin worth c. 10*s.*

HALF-DECK: i. 112 intermediate deck between the quarter-deck and the full deck: the after half-deck cabin was the province of lesser officers on a ship

HALF-NOTE: viii. 142 quaver

HALF-SHIRT: ii. 195 sham shirt front or shirt without tails: OED P.

HAMACCO (Sp. *hamacca*): vi. 40 hammock: Carib in origin

HAMPER, HAMPIRE: i. 46 any large basket, or wickerwork receptacle

HAND: vii. 374 signature

HAND, at the best: i. 201 to best advantage: 'to make a hand', make a profit, from 1538, 'make a better hand' 1669

HAND TO, to have: *see* Have a hand to

HAND-TO-FIST: v. 45 going with a will, with determination: 1653 'to set hand to fist', set to resolutely

HANDKERCHER, HANKERCHER: iv. 37 neck- or head-scarf

HANDSEL, HANSEL: iv. 101 to try out, use for the first time

HANDSOME: i. 9 generous

HANDSPIKE (naut.): ii. 13 wooden crowbar used for turning capstan for weighing anchor, tautening hawsers etc.: 1615

HANDYCAPP: i. 248 handicap, a card game

HANG IN THE HEDGE: vii. 343 to be delayed

HANG OFF: ix. 146 hesitate: 1641

HANGER: iv. 307 small sword, of curved or cutlas shape: cf. Florio 'Coltellaccio, *a cutleax, a hanger*'

HANGING JACK: i. 41 turnspit for roasting meat: *OED* P

HANGING SLEEVES: ix. 507 sleeves longer than arms, slit in sides for hands: worn by children, once fashionable in adult dress, by 1668 an archaism

HANK: iv. 378 hold, grip

HAPPILY: ix. 135 perchance. viii. 519 fortuitously

HARE: v. 177 to harry, rebuke

HARP AND CROSS: iv. 148 & n. 2, coins issued under the Commonwealth

HARP UPON: viii. 277 dwell wearisomely on: 1562

HARPSIC(H)ON, HARPSICHORD: i. 90 keyboard instrument (resembling in shape a grand piano, with the strings running directly away from the keys) in which the strings are plucked by quill plectra; several types of harpsichord, deriving from different national schools of manufacture, were known in England in the 17th cent., though only two or three native specimens survive; it seems likely that most examples would have been single manual instruments of the simplest kind

HARSLET: v. 79 haslet, roasted or fried pork offal: cf. James Jenks, *The Complete Cook* (1767): 'The Entrails are called a haslet, which consists of the liver, crow, kidney and skirts'

HASH (Fr. *haché*): iv. 14 braised sliced meat, a *ragoût*: *OED* P but cf. iv. 249 for a usage that anticipates the modern pejorative sense of a minced *réchauffage*

HATCH: iii. 194 half-door; wicket, kitchen or back-door

HAVE A HAND: v. 84 to have leisure, freedom: the converse is 'to have one's hands full'

HAWSE, thwart their: viii. 357 across their bows: 1630

HEAD-PIECE: viii. 473 helmet

HEAFTED: i. 298 hafted, with a handle of

HEART: viii. 241 courage

HEART-BURNING: viii. 49 resentment: (vii. 207 'heartburne' used to describe ailment)

HEART . . . INTO MY MOUTH: viii. 90 prov. phrase by 1537

HEARTS, to their: viii. 97 heartily

HEAVE AT: vii. 41 to oppose, to aim at with hostile intent

HECTOR (s.): viii. 255 street-bully, swashbuckler: 1655

HECTOR (v.): v. 60 to play the hector, to bully or intimidate: *OED* P

HEELS, behind their: iii. 184 heedlessly behind one: not in *OED*

HEINOUSLY, to take: ii. 228 to take grievously: as phr. from 1632

HERBAL(L): vi. 289 botanical encyclopaedia. viii. 421 ('natural Herball') *hortus siccus*, book of dried and pressed plants

HERE (Du. *heer*): viii. 347 lord

HIERARCHY: ix. 73 the bench of bishops: 1563

HIGH: ii. 57 arrogant, proud, highhanded

HIGH FLYER: viii. 85 high churchman (in sense of 'church-and-state' man). iv. 159 a highly ambitious person: *OED* P

HOG-HIGH: i. 76 obstinately, pigheadedly

HOGS TO A FAIR MARKET, to bring: viii. 148 in prov. use by 1600

HOGSHEAD: iii. 14 2 hogsheads = 1 butt

HOLD WATER: viii. 546 bear examination: 1535

HOLLAND: iii. 61 a linen fabric

HOMAGE: iii. 222 jury of presentment at a manorial court

HOMILY: i. 271 set passage, from *The Book of Homilies*, for reading in lieu of a sermon at divine service

HONE (s.): vii. 368 a whetstone

HONEST (of a woman): ii. 152 virtuous

HONEY AND THEN ALL TURD, sometimes all: iv. 417 apparently proverbial but not otherwise recorded

HOOKS, off the: iii. 73 out of condition, out of humour: 1612

HOPEFUL: vi. 13 promising

HORNE CROOKE: viii. 339 shepherd's crook with a head made from a ram's horn

HORSE (v.): ii. 181 to go by horse

HORSE-REDISH ALE: v. 272 ale flavoured with horse-radish: *OED* P. J. Gerard, *The Herball* (1597) observes of horseradish 'used in Germany'; its English popularity came later

HOSTELLER: vii. 398 keeper of an

hostelry: distinct from 'hostler', 'ostler', a stableman

HOT-HOUSE: vi. 40 bath-house

HOT FOR, to be: viii. 332 to be ardent for

HOT THAT, it was: viii. 16 it was hot news that

HOUSE OF OFFICE: iv. 233 latrine

HOUSE-WARME: vii. 351 to take part in a house-warming: *OED* P, 'house-warming' 1577

HOY: ii. 123 small passenger and cargo vessel, usually single masted and fore-and-aft rigged; 'Everybody knows, or ought to know, what a hoy is – it is a large sailing boat, sometimes with one deck, sometimes with none' (R. S. Surtees, *Jorrocks's Jaunts* etc. 1843)

HOYSE: iii. 123 to hoist

HUBBUB: vii. 151 noisy commotion, excitement: 1619 Gaelic

HUDDLE (v.): iii. 85 to bustle, act hastily or in disorder: 1646

HUDDLE UP, to: ix. 102 to assemble in haste, gather hastily

HUFFE: iv. 279 fit of petulance caused by an affront. *OED* 1684, in first part of century a gust of anger, from 'huff', a squall of wind

HUG BUSINESS: viii. 101 concentrate on business: 'hug' in the general sense of this and the following entry common from the 1590s, but neither of these instances recorded

HUG THE OCCASION: viii. 100 make the most of

HUMOUR (s.): i. 257 mood, good or ill temper. viii. 100 character, characteristic. viii. 584 any fluid that is generated by, or affects the health of, the body

HUMOUR (v.): viii. 59 to set words suitably to music: 1648, Milton

HUSBAND: iii. 194, v. 82 one who gets good/bad value for money. vi. 74 supervisor, steward

HUSBANDLY: ix. 484 economical
HUSBANDRY: viii. 565 ('good h.') economy. ix. 496 agriculture
HUSH: vii. 213 silent: cf. *Hamlet*, II ii 508 'the Orbe below/As hush as death'
HUSH UP: iv. 325 to suppress, damp down: 1632
[**HYDROMETER**]: ix. 390 & n. 2 glass vessel weighted with mercury, the stem graduated so as to show the density of the fluid by the depth of its immersion
HYPOCRAS: iv. 354 hippocras, sweet, spiced wine, red or white but commonly a mixture of both: supposed to have been devised by Hippocrates for medicinal purposes

ICHING: iv. 286 etching
I LOVE MY LOVE WITH AN A: ix. 469 & n. 2, round game
ILL-TEMPERED: v. 191 out of sorts, ill-adjusted, having one's 'humours badly tempered'
IMBROIDERY: ii. 82 cloth richly embroidered with gold and silver: as '*opus anglicanum*' formerly regarded as an English speciality
IMMORTAL: ix. 430 lasting, perpetual: as mod. 'undying enmity'
IMPERTINENCE: ix. 474 irrelevance, garrulity, folly.
IMPERTINENT: iii. 214 irrelevant: cf. i. 45 'Monsieur L'impertinent'
IMPOSSIBLE WOULD BE FOUND IMPOSSIBLE AT LAST: ix. 448 apparently unrecorded
IMPOST(H)UME: vii. 94 abscess
IMPRESSION (of book): vi. 53 edition, printing; P used 'edicion' iv. 33
IMPREST: ii. 112 money paid in advance by government to public servant
INCOGNIT, INCOGNITO, INCOGNITA: viii. 193, i. 157 unknown, with identity concealed: 'incognit' (l.h.) is probably 'incognite' (1609), whilst

'incognito' = fashionable Italian usage (1649, Evelyn)
INCOHERENCY: viii. 514 inconsistence: *OED* 1684, (P uses 'inconsistent' viii. 518)
INCONGRUITY: v. 240 infelicity, inaptness: 1626
INCONTINENT: iii. 43 unchaste
INDENTURE: i. 240 article of agreement for an apprenticeship, period in service, etc.
INDIAN BLUE: v. 8 indigo
INDIAN GOWN: ii. 130 loose gown of glazed cotton: *OED* 1673
INDIAN INK: viii. 181 a crimson pigment, prepared from stik-lac: 1616
INDIAN VARNISH: ii. 79 clear lacquer
INDIFFERENT: iii. 83 moderate in quality or extent. v. 119 inferior (sentence also illustrates previous sense of 'moderate in extent'). vii. 284 apathetic
INDIFFERENTLY: viii. 103 without coming down on one side or the other
INGENIOUS, INGENUOUS: ii. 26, v. 46 clever, intelligent: *OED* notes 'ingenuous' as a customary 17th-cent. misuse for 'ingenious'
INGENUITY: v. 207 wit, intelligence. v. 226 freedom
INGENUOUS: *see* Ingenious
INSIPID: iii. 208 stupid, dull: 1649, Evelyn
INSTITUTIONS: iii. 24 instructions
INSTRUMENT: viii. 219 agent. ix. 151 clerk
INSULT: vii. 169 to exult over
INTELLIGENCE: vii. 180 information. ix. 70 the obtaining of information
INTEREST: ii. 44 personal influence
INTERSTICE: v. 46 interval, interregnum: 1639
INTRATUR: vi. 70 warrant authorising payment by Exchequer
INWARD (adj.) viii. 106 intimate, confidential

INWARDNESS: ix. 286 intimacy

IRONMONGER: viii. 226 often a large-scale merchant, not necessarily a retailer

ISLE: v. 90 aisle

ISSUE: ii. 170 outcome, result

JACK(E): viii. 283 flag used as signal or mark of distinction: 1633 i. 273 spit. *See also* Hanging jack; Play the jack

JACKANAPES COAT: i. 193 monkey jacket, sailor's short close-fitting jacket; a 'jackanape' = ape or monkey: 'monkey-jacket' first recorded 1840

JACOB(US): iii. 265 gold sovereign coined under James I

JADE: iv. 120 horse of inferior breed. v. 110 term of reprobation fig. applied to a woman. iv. 79 baggage, used of a woman affectionately: *OED* P

JAMAICA BRAWN: iv. 79 brawn from the celebrated wild boars of Jamaica: the West Indies abounded in wild pig which was hunted and salted or preserved by the buccaneers

JANGLE: iv. 177 quarrel: 1641

JAPAN: viii. 84 a black lacquer, something so lacquered: *OED* 1678

JARR, JARRING: vii. 163 quarrel

JEALOUS: vii. 178 fearful, suspicious, mistrustful. *Also* vii. 65 'jealousy'

JEALOUSYS: iii. 237 fears

JEERE: ii. 48 mock, burlesque: 1625 in a close but not identical sense

JERK(E): vii. 172 captious remark: fig. from a lash, stroke with a whip

JESIMY GLOVES: vii. 344 gloves perfumed with jasmine

JES(S)IMY: vii. 344 jasmine

JEW'S TRUMP: viii. 240 Jew's harp

JIG(G): vii. 246 'a brisk and airy dance' (Dyche). viii. 101 a staged afterpiece consisting of verses, often satirical or scurrilous, sung to

popular tunes and interspersed with dances: for a discussion of the involved inter-relation of the two significations, and a still more involved etymology, cf. C. R. Baskerville, *The Elizabethan jig* (Chicago 1929)

JOBB: i. 167 piece of work or transaction done with an eye to hire or profit: *OED* P. viii. 160 a public service or trust turned to private gain: *OED* P

JOCK(E)Y: ix. 384 horsedealer: 1638

JOCO (It. *gioco*): v. 20 a joke: 1663, 'joque' first reported 1670

JOLE (of fish): i. 24 jowl, a cut consisting of the head and shoulders. *See also* Pole

JOY (v.): iv. 277 to wish someone joy. viii. 525 to congratulate. vii. 404 'joy . . . at' to rejoice at

JOYNER: vii. 252 joiners undertook finer work than carpenters and belonged to a different Company, the two often being in conflict during the diary period; 'Cabinets or Boxes . . . Cupboards . . . All sorts of presses . . . with dovetailed joints, pinned or glued' were joiners' work: GL, MS. 8332

JOYNT-STOOL(E): ii. 133 stool with turned legs joined by stretchers: common from 1600; the simpler stool without stretchers was known as a 'staked' or 'country' stool

JOYNTURE: v. 40 jointure, sum settled by husband on his wife in return for the dowry brought by her at marriage

JULIPP: i. 181 julep, sweet drink made from syrup

JUMBLE: viii. 499 to take for an airing: *OED* P

JUMP WITH: viii. 154 to synchronise with, move together with

JUNIPER WATER: iv. 329 juniper-flavoured cordial

JUNK (naval): vii. 206 old rope

JURATE (of Cinque Ports): i. 130 jurat, alderman

JUSTE-AU-CORPS: viii. 187 close-fitting long coat, knee-length, worn by both men and women: 1656

KATCH (ship): i. 105 ketch, a two-masted vessel, square-rigged on the fore (= main) mast

KEEP (v.): iii. 126 to housekeep, to live or stay: 1513

KEEP IN WITH: ii. 14 remain in favour with: 1598

KENNEL: *see* Canaille

KERSEY: ix. 388 piece of kersey, flannel-like narrow cloth, often ribbed

KETCH (s.): viii. 168 catch, song in canon

KETCH (v.): viii. 232 to catch

KETTLE: v. 49 broad open vessel used to boil food and liquids in

KEY: vi. 183 quay

KICK, give a: vii. 215 get back into the game: not in *OED*

KINDNESS: vi. 214 affection, amorousness

KINGDOM, I used to call it her: v. 103 possibly quasi-proverbial, cf. fn.

KITCHIN KNIFE: iv. 345 *OED* P

KITLIN: vi. 64 kitling, kitten

KNACK: viii. 222 personal habit of speaking in a particular way: *OED* 1674, 'knack' in other applications common from 14th cent.

KNEES: iv. 326 timbers of angular shape used in ship-building: such timbers were either naturally shaped ('grown', *see* Compass-Timber) or, an inferior variety, 'sawn'. iii. 106 part of garment covering knees: *OED* P

KNOT (s.): i. 147 flower bed. iv. 308 difficulty. iii. 284 clique, band

KNOT (v.): iii. 178 to join, band together

KNOWING: i. 134 knowledgeable, informed: 1651

KNOWN: viii. 90 famous

KNOWNLY: ix. 347 notoriously: 1643 as 'in a known manner'

LABARINTH (Fr.): vii. 182 a maze of paths enclosed by high hedges: 1611

LACE: vii. 341 usually braid made with gold – or silver – thread

LAISSER ALLER LES FEMMES (Fr.): vi. 20 let women alone: according to *OED* laisser-aller, in various conjunctions, was common in 19th-cent. adopted phrases, but this suggests that it was common much earlier

LAMB, calm as a: ix. 394 apparently unrecorded: 'chast as a lamb' 1526, 'innocent as' 1589

LAMB'S-WOOL: vii. 364 hot ale with apples, sugar and spice: 1592 'The Wassail Bowl, or Lamb's Wool, is another joyous accompaniment of [Christmas] eve, a composition of ale, nutmeg, sugar, toast, and roasted crabs or apples, still preserved in many parts. According to Vallancey (*Collectanea*, iii. 444), the term Lamb's Wool is a corruption from *La Mas Ubhal*, the day of the apple fruit, pronounced Lamasool': William Sandys, *Christmas Carols* (1833), p. liii

LAMP-GLASS: i. 273 magnifying lens used to concentrate lamp-light

LAMPOONE (Fr. *lampon*): vii. 207 virulent satire on an individual: 1645, Evelyn

LANDS (shipbuilding): iv. 134 framing members running fore and aft and scarfed into ribs; in a set of lines the equivalents of these members

LANSKIP(P) (Du. *landschap*): vii. 81 landscape: 1598. ix. 423 'lanskip painter'. ix. 514 'lanskip-drawer'

LARD (v.): i. 29 to place strips of fat bacon in, around or upon meat before cooking: O. Fr. *lard*, unsmoked bacon

LARGE AND BY: vii. 215 by and large

LARUM: iv. 228 alarm

LARUM-WATCH: vi. 158: *OED* 1683 for combined form, but 'larum' for alarm clock, 1586

LAST: iii. 137 waggon or boat load, measure of tar

LATE: vii. 103 recent

LATHER: ii. 61 ladder: cf. Blather

LATITUDINARIAN: ix. 485 broad-churchman; in narrowest sense Anglican who, whilst attached to Episcopalianism, was prepared to tolerate the coexistence of other churches, in widest sense Anglican who believed the basis of the settlement of 1662 should be broadened to include moderate nonconformists: 1662

LAVER: v. 179 basin of a fountain: 1605

LAY (v.): vi. 267 levy (of tax)

LAY BY THE HEELS: vi. 301 arrest, confine: 1585, 1510 as 'set fast by the heels', i.e. to fetter, put in gyves

LAY OUT, to: ii. 208 to spend money

LAY WEIGHT UPON, to: vii. 192 to attach importance to: *OED* P

LAYINGS-OUT: i. 213 expenditure

LEADS: i. 277 flat space on roof top, sometimes boarded over

LEAN: vi. 247 to lie down

LEASE: vi. 220 a leash, a set of three: a term of venery

LEAVE: vi. 267 to end

LEAVE BEHIND THE HEELS, to: iii. 184 to forget: not in *OED*

LECTURE: iii. 70 religious service, often on a weekday, consisting mostly of a sermon. v. 6 a lesson

LEGERDEMAINE (Fr.): viii. 234 sleight of hand: common from 15th cent.

LESSON: i. 29 piece of music, a composition for a single instrument: 1593

LETHARGY: ix. 334 enervating disease

LETTERS OF MART: v. 115 letters of marque, royal licence to fit out a vessel to attack shipping of hostile states

LET THE WORLD GO HANG: vii. 97: cf. World

LEVETT (It. *levata*): iii. 224 reveille, reveille music: 1625

LIBEL(L): ix. 65 leaflet, broadside. iv. 33 (in legal proceedings) written charge

LIE A'BLEEDING: vi. 20 to suffer: a common 16th-17th cent. phrase, as in the flower name 'Love lies a 'bleeding'

LIE ADMIRAL: iv. 171 to serve as commander of the senior guardship: Allin's own description of his job (*Journal*, 1939, i. 113) is to 'Ride Commander' and he had a static rather than a roving warrant, his duty being to protect shipping in the Downs, therefore lying or riding at anchor for much of the commission

LIE UP (naut.): ii. 198 to lay up, to spend period out of commission and refurbishing

LIE UPON: i. 203 to press, insist

LIFE: iii. 223 life interest

LIGHT (s.): iii. 193 window

LIGHT (v.): i. 71 to alight, dismount

LIGHT UPON: ii. 136 to make a choice of (with implication 'having discovered by chance')

LIGNUM VITAE: i. 298 hard W. Indian wood with medicinal qualities, often used for drinking vessels: 1594

LIKE (v.): viii. 372 please, suit: this reflexive use was common throughout the late 16th cent. and the 17th cent.

LIKE, to have . . . to: i. 24 to come close to, be near to doing something

LIKELY: iv. 80 promising (? possibly with sexual connotation)

LIMB: vi. 98 to limn, paint, draw

LIME (of dogs): vi. 2 to mate

LIMNER: ii. 145 painter: P also uses 'painter' ii. 218 and 'picture-drawer' vii. 81, as well as 'lanskip painter' ix. 423 and 'history-painter' ix. 434; but 'limner', though shortly to become archaic, was still in regular use

LIMNER IN LITTLE: iii. 2 miniature painter

LINE-MAKER: viii. 344 manufacturer of rope, sashcords, etc.: OED P

LINK(E): i. 209 torch, boy carrying torch

LINNING: i. 156 linen

LIQUIDATE: vii. 86 make clear, set out clearly: 1622 (late L. *liquidare*)

LIST: ii. 84 desire, need

LITTERA SCRIPTA MANET (L.): viii. 15 the written word abides (i.e. be chary of putting it in writing)

LOAD (of timber): iv. 326 50 cu. feet

LOADEN (adj.): viii. 270

LOCK: ii. 101 waterway between arches of bridge: the waterways of London Bridge were particularly so called. vii. 346 tress of artificial hair: 1600

LOGGERHEAD: v. 307 'an opprobrious name for a dull, stupid, heavy fellow' (Dyche)

LOMBRE: *see* Ombre

LOOK (v.): vii. 161 to look at/for. vi. 325 'to look to', to expect, anticipate

LOOK AFTER: v. 184 to have eyes on

LOOK ASKEWE: ii. 161 to look with contempt or disdain

LOOK LIKE DEATH: vii. 389 apparently more literal than the modern colloquialism

LOP (s.): iii. 35 branch lopped off a tree

LOP (v.): iii. 35 to cut or trim

LORDSHIP: iii. 222 manor

LOSE THE BALL: vii. 215 lose the initiative

LOVE THE TREASON I HATE THE TRAITOR, though I: viii. 100–01 recorded as

an alliterative phrase from 1586; the sentiment occurs in Tacitus

LUTE: i. 29 plucked instrument in shape of halved pear having six courses (five double, the highest single) of gut strings and a peg-box at right-angles to the neck; various tunings were employed (*see* French lute) and additional strings were sometimes added (*see* Theorbo)

LUTESTRING: ii. 38 lustring, a glossy silk: OED P

LYNCETT OYLE: iv. 346 linseed oil

LYON'S SKIN TO THE FOXES TAIL, joyne the: iii. 295 the saying is confused (cf. fn.) and apparently unrecorded even in a coherent form; however 'Fox's wiles never enter lion's head' 1580, and other prov. conjunctions of lion and fox occur

LYRA-VIALL: i. 295 small bass (or 'division') viol used with a 'lyra' or 'harp-way' tuning: the 'lyra' tunings (there are several possibilities) were an English innovation of the end of the 16th cent., designed to facilitate chordal playing, which was also furthered by the use of a small instrument; nevertheless any viol could be tuned harp-ways and used as a lyra-viol (cf. ii. 71)

MACH: ii. 65 match, marriage. ii. 235 pair. ii. 206 slowmatch

MACHINE: vii. 76 mechanical device for creating spectacular stage effect

MAD: viii. 594 whimsical, wild, extravagant

MAD (v.): viii. 436 to anger

MAD, LIKE: iv. 182 recorded as phrase from 1653

MADAM(E): iv. 272 prefix used mainly of widows, elderly/foreign ladies: 'a Title of Honour . . . but grown a little too common of late' (Phillips, 1696)

MAIN (adj.): viii. 283 strong. vii. 292

bulky: a sense indirectly preserved in 'main force'

MAIN (s.): viii. 276 chief purpose or object: 'I doubt it is no other, but the maine/His Fathers death, and our o'er-hasty marriage' (*Hamlet* II ii 56)

MAIN CHANCE, the: iv. 138 the most important point at stake: 1579, originally a term in the game of hazard

MAIN SEA: viii. 359 the high sea, open sea

MAIN TIMBER: vii. 292 timbers in a bulk, from the trunk: not in *OED*, but 'small timber' is recorded from 1612

MAIN-TOP: iii. 123 a loose but common use for the main-top-gallant masthead: *see* Foretopp

MA(I)STER: v. 194 expert, professional. iv. 403 sailing master

MAKE (s.): iv. 428 (of fighting cocks) match, pair of opponents

MAKE A STAND: vi. 106 pause, hesitate (be at a stand)

MAKE LEGS: vii. 11 to bow, curtsey

MAKE LIGHT OF IT: v. 43 phrase recorded from 1526

MAKE NO BONES OF: vi. 270 have no hesitation about: 1548

MAKE SURE TO: vi. 16 plight troth

MALAGO SACK, MALAGO WINE: iv. 235, iii. 14 wine from Malaga is recorded from 1608

MANAGE: v. 303 to arrange, negotiate

MANAGED-HORSE (cf. Fr. *manège*): iv. 120 horse trained in riding school: 1644 Evelyn

MANDAMUS: v. 135 royal mandate under seal

MAN OF BUSINESS: iv. 297 executive agent, administrator

MAN THAT CANNOT SIT STILL IN HIS CHAMBER . . . AND HE THAT CANNOT SAY NO . . . NOT FIT FOR BUSINESS: iii. 160 not apparently elsewhere recorded

MANY HANDS . . . MAKES GOOD RIDDANCE: iii. 179 not apparently elsewhere recorded: 'many hands make light work' c. 1350

MARGENTING: iv. 23 putting margin-lines on paper: 1610

MARK: ii. 7 token; elsewhere, as money: 13s. 4d., ⅔ of a £ sterling

MARMALETT (Port. *marmelado*): iv. 361 marmalade, preserve made by boiling fruit, originally the quince (Port. *marmelo* is a variety) which was being replaced by the orange at latest by 1615 when G. Markham, *The English Hus-wife*, gives a recipe for 'Marmalade of Oranges'

MARMOTTE (Fr., term of affection): iii. 270 young girl: not recorded in *OED* but 'marmoset' in this sense 1526

MARY ANDREY: ix. 293 Merry Andrew, clown: *OED* (which notes this use but, for no apparent reason, denies that it can in fact mean 'Merry Andrew') 1673 Dryden

MASS BOOK: i. 281 missal

MASSY: i. 116 solid, weighty

MASTY: i. 138 burly: 1384 Chaucer (orig. a pig fattened on mast): cf. mastiff

MATCH: viii. 82 tinderbox and wick. ii. 152 'the making of an agreement to . . . play at any exercise, is called a *match*' (Dyche)

MATHEMATICIAN: iv. 84 mathematical instrument maker

MATRIX: viii. 8 womb; acc. to Blount, however, 'matrice, the place in the womb where the child is conceived'

MATTED: iii. 47 spread with matting or mats: 1607

MAUDLIN: viii. 447 tearfully sentimental: 1631 from maudlin drunk, 'Some *maudlin* drunken were, and wept full sore/Others fell fast asleep, began to snore . . .' G[eorge] M[eriton], *The praise of Yorkshire ale* (York 1685), p. 8

MAZE: iv. 131 confusion: 1430

MEAT: ix. 511 food. i. 77 meal: the derivation is from O.Fr. *mets* (L. *missum*), that which is prepared for, sent to, table, as opposed to A. S. *meat*, flesh

MEAT WILL BE PICKED, a great deal of good: viii. 515 proverbial from 1585

MECHANIQUE: vii. 116 one having a manual occupation (as opposed to a gentleman)

MEDIUM: vii. 301 mean, average: 1612

MEDDLE NOR MAKE, neither: ii. 209 have nothing to do with: as phr. from 1564

MELIORATION: viii. 562 improvement: 1626

MENSES: ii. 24 menstrual periods: 1597

MERMIDON: vii. 204 myrmidon, unscrupulously faithful follower or henchman: after Achilles's followers in *The Iliad*

MESCHANT (Fr.): v. 264 miscreant, villain

MESS: v. 269 dish of: cf. Meat

MESS OF POTAGE: viii. 211 prov. from c. 1456 when 'pottage' signified the English dish of pot-cooked meat and vegetables; P's use however obviously refers to Fr. *potage* – ? a humorous locution

MESSE: iv. 355 group dining together: usually, as in the Inns of Court today, of four people: cf. Meat

METHEGLIN: i. 72 strong mead flavoured with herbs: often known as the wine of Wales

MICROSCOPE: v. 48 first made in England by Cornelius Drebbel 1621; by the 1660s regularly made by expert optical instrument makers; with these lenses magnification might reach about 60x, but

the quality of the image was poor: cf. *also* Perspective

MIDDLE-MAID: ix. 510 servant who assisted both cook and housemaid, 'tweeny: not otherwise recorded

MILKE-MEAT: viii. 435 dairy produce

MILL (v.): iv. 147 to serrate the edges of coins: 1659

MILLON: ii. 186 water-melon: the muske or common melon (i. 230) was known in England from the 16th cent.; acc. to Olivier de Serres the cultivation of the watermelon commenced in France 1629, but it does not appear to have reached England at that time, though it is described in Gerard's *Herbal*; at ii. 191 P calls the unfamiliar variety a 'portugall millon'

MINCE THE MATTER: v. 187 to make light of the matter: 1535

MIND: iii. 239 inclination

MINE: vii. 191 mien, carriage

MINIKIN: viii. 119 the highest string of a lute or viol

MIND, to my: v. 327 expressing my opinion, 'speaking my mind'

MIRTH BUT NO GREAT MATTER, much: ii. 162 the prov. nature of this phrase is implied by *Winter's Tale* I ii 166 'He's all my Exercise, my mirth, my Matter'

MIS: viii. 101 *OED* P, as title. Evelyn (ii. 448, June 1645) refers to the 'Common *Misses* or Whores' of Venice, and (9 Jan. 1662) uses 'Misse' and observes 'as at this time they began to call lew'd women'; it is not clear, therefore, whether P is employing the modern or a pejorative sense

MISCARRIAGES: iv. 108 mistakes, blunders: 1614

MISLING, MISLY: vi. 226, viii. 29 mizzling, the falling of fine rain or drizzle

MISTRESS (prefix): used of unmarried

girls and women as well as of young married women

MISTRESS: viii. 498 sweetheart

MITHRYDATE: v. 118 opiate drug: named after Mithridates VI of Pontus, who 'rendered himself proof against poisons by the constant use of antidotes' (*OED*); 'formerly supposed to be a great antidote against poison, but it is now out of date for that purpose; it is still used as an opiate' (Dyche)

MITTIN: viii. 22 mitten, glove without separate stalls for fingers

MODERN(E) (Fr. *moderne*): iii. 220 fashionable in appearance, up to date: 1650

MODEST (of woman): ix. 189 virtuous

MODISH: v. 255 fashionable, following the mode: 1660

MOHER (Sp. *mujer*): vi. 318 woman, wife

MOIS, MOYS: iii. 3 menstrual periods

MOLD, MOLDE, MOLLE (archit.): iv. 45 mole, breakwater

MOLEST: vii. 245 to annoy

MOND: ii. 84 mound, orb (royal jewel in form of globe)

MONEY . . . SWEETENS ALL THINGS: iv. 6 apparently not recorded, but 'm. answers all things' 1630, 'provideth all things' 1584

MONKEY DOTH USE THE CAT'S FOOT, as the: vii. 150 use as a cat's paw: 'cat's paw' *ODP* 1785: cf. La Fontaine IX, xvii

MONTEERE, MOUNTEERE (Sp. *montero*): i. 92 riding cap with spherical crown and ear-flaps: 1622

MONTH'S MIND, have a: i. 150 to have a great desire: from the pre-Reformation commemoration of a deceased person by a mass a month after date of death, prov. by 1575

MOPED: viii. 179 bemused

MOPISH: viii. 81 dejected, melancholy: 1621

MORENA (Sp.): iii. 19 brunette

MORNING DRAUGHT: i. 43 drink (sometimes with snack) taken mid-morning

MORNING GOWN: viii. 468; 1620

MORTAR-PIECE: viii. 188 short piece of artillery with large bore, for throwing shells at high angles

MORTIFYED: vi. 267 humbled, reduced: *OED* P as jocular use

MOTHER: i. 29 mother-in-law

MOTHER, fits of the: viii. 368 hysterics: the 'mother' was the womb, its 'rising' supposedly the cause of hysteria

MOTHER-IN-LAW: ii. 171 stepmother (similarly with 'father-in-law' etc.)

MOTION (s.): iii. 95 impulse. i. 48 (in Court of Exchequer) application. iii. 254 puppet play

MOTION (v.): iii. 159 to propose

MOULDING: ix. 538 ornamental contour: *OED* 1679 as applied to woodwork, but 1643 Evelyn in archit. context, and cf. R. T. Gunther, (ed.) *The architecture of Sir Roger Pratt* (Oxford 1928), p. 273, 1 Nov. 1665

MOUSETRAPP: ii. 19 the 17th-cent. mousetrap was a cage or deadfall rather than spring-loaded; 'there are many kinds of mice-traps where mice do perish by the waight thereof' (E. Topsell, *The historie of four-footed beasts*, 1607, p. 510): 1475

MOUNTEERE: see Monteere

MOUTH WATER, made my: i. 216 as phrase from 1555

MOYRE (Fr. *moire*): i. 298 watered silk: *OED* P, but 'Blak silk moyhair' occurs in an account book of 1649, cf. P. Thornton, *17th-century interior decoration in England, France and Holland* (1978), p. 357

MUCHNESS: ix. 500 greatness, extent of

MUFF(E): iii. 271 fur cylinder to protect and warm the hands: 1599

MULCT (s.): iv. 367 a penalty, fine

MUM (Ger. *mumme*): v. 142 strong spiced ale, made from wheat-malt, imported from Brunswick and elsewhere in Germany

MUMBLE: iv. 236 to mutter, grumble

MUSCADINE, MUSCATT: i. 296, iii. 89 muscatel wine: the use 'muscatt', which puzzled P, *OED* 1747, though 'musticat' 1578 (Scotland) and 'muscat' for 'muscat grape' 1655; muscatel is strong and sweet, and the description was accorded to strong sweet wines even when not products of the muscat grape

MUSIC, MUSIQUE: vii. 414 band, choir, performers

MUSTER (s.): i. 242 a parade

MUSTY: iv. 161 peevish, sullen: 1620

NAKED BED, go to one's: i. 151 to go to bed without night-clothes

NAPIERS BONES: viii. 451 *see* fn. 1

NATIVITY: i. 274 horoscope, astrological prediction based on date of birth

NAUGHT, NOUGHT: ii. 203 worthless, bad in condition or quality. v. 82 sexually wicked

NAUGHT, matters are all: iv. 66 things are all awry: as phrase from 1542

NAVY: iv. 170 Navy Office

NAVY OFFICERS: Principal Officers of the Navy – i.e. the Treasurer, Comptroller, Surveyor, Clerk of the Acts, together with a variable number of Commissioners; members of the Navy Board: cf. Sea-officers

NEAR-HAND: viii. 433 near at hand, close to

NEARLY: v. 203 deeply, closely

NEAT (adj.): viii. 197 handsome, elegant

NEAT (s.): i. 29 ox/oxen, cattle

NEGLIGENCE, à la (Fr.): iv. 230 inform-ally, with a 'natural look': effectively anglicised by 1680, cf. 'T' affect the purest Negligences/In Gestures, Gaits and Miens' (Butler)

NEIGHBOURHOOD: vi. 298 proximity, being a neighbour

NEST: vi. 153 litter: used in 16th and 17th cents. for broods of animals as well as birds and insects

NETTLE-PORRIDGE: ii. 43 a thick nettle soup, rather than modern porridge: *OED* P. Gerard commends nettles for diseases of the lungs and as an aphrodisiac (cf. ii. 44)

NEWS TO ME: viii. 301 apparently an early use, though 'news' in the singular occurs from 1565

NEWSBOOK: i. 219 newspaper (weekly, octavo): in common use c. 1650–1700

NEW-VAMP: ix. 458 to make good, refurbish: 1640

NIBBLE AT: i. 282 to bite at little by little: 1630

NICK-WORD: iv. 285 nick-name: not in *OED*

NICOTIQUES: viii. 213 narcotics, medicines: not in *OED*

NIGHT-BAG: viii. 263 travelling-bag holding necessities for night: *OED* P

NIGHT-CLOTHES: viii. 589 evening clothes: *OED* P; 'night-clothes' was concurrently in use in modern sense

NIGHT-DRESSINGS: iv. 6 night-clothes: 1622

NIGHT GEERE: iii. 255 night-clothes: 1560

NIGHTGOWN(E): i. 137 dressing gown

NIGHT-LINEN: viii. 20 night-clothes

NOISE: ii. 61 band, group of musical instruments playing together

NO PURCHASE, NO PAY: viii. 226 no booty, no pay: *ODP* 1700 a buccaneering and piratical maxim which P's ref. shows to have been current in the 1660s; cf. J. Esquemeling, *Bucaniers of America* (1684), p. 86: 'no prey, no pay'

NORTHDOWNE ALE: i. 244 Margate ale

NOSE (v.): v. 203 to insult, affront: 1629

NOSE, lead one by: ix. 342 to manipulate, bearlead: prov. in Eng. from 1540; there is a L. equivalent

NOSE OUT OF JOYNT, to put one's: iii. 97 to offend by supplanting: 1581

NOTE (s.): viii. 155 observation, thing deserving of note. i. 32 note of credit

NOTORIOUS: ix. 392 famous, well known

NOUGHT: *see* Naught

NULLA PUELLA NEGAT (L.): i. 239 no girl ever says no

OARES: ii. 226: *see* Pair of oares

OBLIGATION: v. 171 compulsion, moral forcefulness: *OED* P (only) glosses implausibly as 'obligingness, civility'. v. 48 vow

OBNOXIOUS: v. 162 liable to, exposed to

OBSERVABLE (adj.): vi. 236 noteworthy. viii. 352 notorious

OBSERVABLE (s.): iv. 59 thing or matter worthy of observation

OBSERVATION: vii. 119 criticism

OBVIATE: iv. 197 circumvent, clear away a difficulty

OCCUPY (v.): v. 323 to have sexual relations with

ODIUM: viii. 204 reproach: *OED* 1678

OFFICE: ix. 355 a meeting of the Navy Board

OFFICE DAY: ii. 11 day on which a meeting of the Navy Board was held

OFFICERS OF THE NAVY: *see* Navy Officers

OLD SPECTACLES: viii. 519 spectacles suited to the old, i.e. long-sighted

OLEO (Sp. *olla*): ix. 509 olio, Spanish stew with a variety of ingredients:

1643, but G. Markham, *The English Hus-wife* (1615) has a recipe for *olepotrige*

OMBRE (Sp. *hombre*): vi. 218 card game for three persons: 1661 as 'a new game at cards now in fashion at court'

ONLY (adj.): viii. 468 main, principal, best

OPEN: vii. 230 unsettled

OPERA: viii. 56 spectacular entertainment (involving use of painted scenery and stage machinery), often with music: 1644 Evelyn

OPINIASTRE, OPINIASTREMENT (Fr.): v. 169 stubborn, stubbornly: Eng. forms close to the Fr. were current by the 1680s, e.g. 'opiniater', 'opinionativeness'

OPPONE: viii. 192 to oppose, hinder

OPPOSICION-DAY: *see* Apposition

ORA (L.): v. 298 'the brim of a pot or any other measure' (T. Thomas, *Dictionarium linguae latinae*, ed. P. Holland, 1630): this definition, from the standard Cambridge dictionary, suggests a fountain of the type in which water falls from a bowl or basin

ORDER (v.): ix. 7 to put in order. viii. 574 to punish

ORDERS: ii. 117 holy orders

ORDINARY (s.): i. 23 eating place serving fixed-price meals. iii. 195 peacetime establishment (of navy, dockyard, etc.)

OTACOUSTICON: ix. 146 ear trumpet: 'See in the clouds the *Cherubs* listen yon,/Each Angel with an Otocousticon' (N. Hookes, *Amanda*, 1653, p. 19)

OUT: i. 260 out of fashion: *OED* P. ii. 51 made public: 1625

OUTPORTS: viii. 88 ports other than London: 1642

OVERBALANCE: i. 17 preponderance: 1659 Harrington

OVERCHARGE: iv. 49 a charge in

excess of the correct (or estimated) amount: OED P

OVER-EXPECT: iv. 233 to expect too much

OVER(-)REACH: iv. 254 to outdo, outwit

OVERSEEN: iv. 396 guilty of oversight: from to have 'overseen oneself', failed to see the proper course to take

OVERSHOES: ix. 429 committed, irreversibly involved: 'to run overshoes' 1579 and in prov. forms from 1603

OVERSIGHT: viii. 38 omission, neglectfulness

OWE: v. 202 to own

OWN TO: vii. 343 admit, acknowledge: 1655

OYER AND TERMINER (Law Fr.): iv. 76 a commission to 'hear and determine', permitting the recipient to exercise a given judicial function

PACKED: viii. 194 manipulated to serve a particular end: 1643

PADRON (?Sp. ?It. *padrone*): ii. 34 master

PAGEANT: iii. 175 decorated symbolic float in procession

PAINFUL: ii. 55 painstaking

PAIR OF OARES: viii. 351 large riverboat rowed by two watermen, each using two oars: commonly abbreviated by P and his contemporaries to 'Oares', cf. Scull, and for the contrast between sculls and oars vii. 181; for 'pair' cf. Pair of Organs

PAIR OF ORGANS, VIRGINALS: viii. 150, vii. 271 a single instrument: in such phrases 'pair' signifies a set of parts forming a collective whole; P often uses 'organs' for 'organ' as a consequence of this locution

PALE: iv. 51 fence

PALER: iv. 109 parlour: but iv. 18 'parler'

PALLIATE: vi. 342 to mitigate: OED Ṗ in this sense, rather than earlier 'to cloak or hide'

PALPABLE: i. 9 manifest, plainly observable

PALTERLY: viii. 77 paltry, mean, shabby: OED P

PAN(N)YARD: ii. 149 pannier, basket

PARAGON: i. 82 heavy rich cloth, partly of mohair; a heavier version of 'Camelott' (q. v.)

PARALLELOGRAM: *see* Parrallogram

PARBOIL: ix. 233 boil thoroughly: 1566, from O.Fr. *parboiller* though subsequently confounded with 'part boil', the modern sense; ? jocular at ref.

PARCEL: v. 179 share, lot, part, isolated group

PARE: iii. 247 cut, trim

PARMAZAN CHEESE: vii. 274 1519 especially commended by Dr Thomas Muffet (*Health's Improvement*, 1655) who implies that it was on such a cheese that 'Zoroaster lived in the Wilderness twenty years together without any other meat' (cf. Pliny *Lib.* 36 *cap.* 1)

PARRALLOGRAM, PARRALLELOGRAM, PARALELLOGRAMM: ix. 340 pantograph: c. 1656 Sir W. Petty; a pencil in the corner duplicates, on a larger scale, the movement of a pointer on a linked smaller scale, or vice versa; used for enlarging or reducing plans, etc.

PARTS: viii. 11 accomplishments

PASQUIL(L): iv. 26 a lampoon: 1533 from the satirical verses customarily placed on the statue of *Pasquino* or *Pasquillo* near the Piazza Navona, Rome

PASSION: viii. 36 feeling, mood. vii. 353 the Crucifixion of our Lord

PASSIONATE: vi. 175 irascible, vehement. vi. 212 provocative of compassion

PASSIONATELY: vi. 246 in a passion, in a temper

PASSIONATENESS: vii. 355 ill-temper, irascibility

PASTY (O.Fr. *pasté*): i. 9 pasties differ from pies in being baked without a dish; 17th-cent. form would have more often resembled modern meat (or fish) *en croûte* than the modern Cornish pasty

PATENT: i. 128 conferred by letters patent

PATTEN: i. 27 overshoe: an oval iron ring fixed beneath a wooden sole raised the wearer an inch or two off the ground

PAY, the: iii. 193 paying-off day (of a ship). iii. 193 quarterly pay-day (of a dockyard). vi. 318 employment

PAY (v.): viii. 176 to berate, beat

PAY HIS COAT: viii. 348 to beat, chastise

PAYSAN (Fr.): viii. 375 country style

PEASE PORRIDGE: i. 36 a thick pea soup, often tawny in colour and much eaten in Lent (cf. v. 117)

PECK: i. 291 a snack: as a measure a peck = two gallons, but 'a peck of oysters' is presumably to be understood as a lesser quantity

PEEVISH: ix. 520 perverse, refractory

PENDANCES, PENDENTS, PENDANTS: iv. 100 ear-rings

PENNORTH, PENNYWORTH: v. 244 pennyworth, value for money

PERCH (of a coach): ix. 438 the centre pole connecting hinder-carriage to fore-carriage: OED P

PERPLEX: viii. 53 to vex

PERPLEXED: v. 43 complicated

PERSPECTIVE: ix. 534 the art of drawing in perspective. iv. 18 (piece of) illusionistic painting: 1644 Evelyn

PERSPECTIVE, PERSPECTIVE GLASS(E): ix. 261, i. 95 probably binoculars: though 'perspective' is good 17th-cent. Eng. for a telescope (cf. Blount) when P is describing an undoubtedly monocular instrument he terms it (vii. 240) a 'glass'; it is worth noting, however, that 'perspective glass' could mean microscope (cf. the anonymous 1653 trans. of William Harvey, *De motu cordis*, ed. Geoffrey Keynes, London 1938, p. 103)

PERUQUES: iii. 51 artificial curls mounted on wires

PESLEMESLE (Fr. *pallemaille*): ii. 64 pall-mall, game the object of which was to drive a boxwood ball through a hoop suspended in an alley: P's spelling suggests a confusion with 'pell-mell' (Fr. *pêle-mêle*), a common exp., unconnected with the game, for a disordered mingling

PESTILENT: viii. 406 destructive of religion and morals

PET(T): iii. 37 state of pettishness, short-temper: 1629

PETTY BAG: iv. 350 petty cash

PHANATIQUES: i. 109 religious and political extremists: Fifth Monarchy men, etc.: cf. Fanatic

PHILOSOPHY: vi. 48 natural science

PHYSIC, PHISIQUE: i. 164 laxative, purge

PHYSICALLY: iii. 282 without sheets, uncovered

PICHER: ii. 72 pitcher, earthenware jug, usually large

PICK: viii. 536 pique

PICK A HOLE IN HIS COAT: i. 31 pick a quarrel, complain: 1533

PICKAROON (Sp. *picarón*): viii. 595 pirate, privateer: 1624

PICKLE, to be in a: i. 254 to be in a state, a mess: 1573, a prov. phrase that P usually intensifies (with e.g. ii. 133 'ugly', iv. 167 'sad', vii. 218 'dirty', viii. 447 'maudlin', i. 297 'washing')

PICQUANT: iv. 9 stinging

PIECE (PEECE): vi. 244 gold coin worth c. 20s.: originally the unite, issued

1604 as worth 20s., raised to 22s. 1612. 'Half-a-piece': ii. 66

PIECE (PEECE) OF EIGHT: iv. 132 Spanish silver coin worth 4s. 6d.

PIGEON, show the: vii. 322 act like a coward, show the white feather

PIGEONS A L'ESTEUVE (Fr. *étuvée*): viii. 211 stewed pigeons

PINCH: viii. 177 emergency, shortage of money; 'at this pinch' viii. 257

PINK(E): iii. 47 small broad-beamed, narrow-sterned ship. iii. 95 sweet-smelling garden flower. iii. 116 poniard, pointed weapon

PINKED: vii. 324 ornamented with punched holes or scallops revealing an undergarment

PINNER: v. 126 fill-in above low décolletage. ix. 557 coif with two long flaps

PINTLE: iii. 124 penis: the O.E. word

PIPE (musical): iv. 189 flageolet: P's references to playing the recorder (after 16 Apr. 1668) specify that instrument

PIPESTAVES: vii. 76 planks for cooperage of a size suitable for a pipe cask (cf. Tierce): 1599

PIPKIN: ii. 197 'a small earthen pot with a handle to it, made on purpose to boil or heat things in over the fire' (Dyche)

PISTOLE, PISTOLL: i. 121 French gold coin worth 16s.

PITCH UPON: ix. 333 make a choice of, settle, resolve: 1628

PI(T)CHER: iv. 355 a jug, rather than a drinking vessel

PLACKET: viii. 283 petticoat

PLAGUY: vi. 217 pestilent, confounded: 1615

PLAIN: viii. 443 unaffected

PLANK(E): vi. 185 sawn wood 2–8 inches thick but at least 11 inches in width (cf. Deals), used for outer skin and decks of ships, mostly Baltic or English oak, sometimes elm, beech or fir

PLASTERER, PLAISTERER, PLAYSTERER: i. 254 modern sense. ix. 442 modeller in plaster, maker of life and death masks

PLAT(T): v. 303 plate, plan, chart, map. v. 222 level: this use, common in M.E., last rec. *OED* 1584. vii. 213 flower-plot

PLATERER: v. 117 one who works silver plate

PLATERY: v. 118 craft of silver plating: *OED* P

PLAY (s.): vii. 369 gambling

PLAY (v.): ix. 3 to play for stakes. vi. 196 to come into action, open fire

PLAY, in good: vii. 386 actively engaged: 1548 'to kepe hym playe'; 'play' here and in next entry retains primal sense of action; not a sporting metaphor

PLAY, out of: ii. 170 out of office: *OED* P

PLAY PRIZES: iv. 167 to fight for money

PLAY SMALL GAMES: vii. 223 to play for small stakes: 1641

PLAY THE GOODFELLOW: viii. 481 live it up, roister: 1606

PLAY THE JACKE: v. 41 play the knave, do a mean trick: 1610

PLEDGE (v.): ii. 16 to offer a toast to, drink to

PLIGHT: v. 359 condition (good or bad)

PLUM-PORRIDGE: iii. 293 an exceptionally dense soup of prunes, currants, raisins and spices in thickened and sweetened beef-stock: a Christmas dish

PLUNGE: viii. 540 depress, cast down. Dyche defines the more common s. as 'any sort of trouble, difficulty, grief or affliction'

PLUSH: v. 309 imitation velvet: from Fr. *peluche*

POALE: ix. 404 pole, central shaft by which horses are harnessed to coach or waggon

POINT, POYNT: iv. 337 point lace, thread lace made wholly with the needle: 1662 Evelyn

POINT DE GESNE (Fr.): viii. 413 Genoa lace

POLE: i. 28 head-and-shoulder (of fish, and particularly the ling). viii. 152 poll-tax

POLICY: viii. 262 (modern sense). v. 7 cunning. viii. 110 self-interest

POLLARD: v. 300 closely-trimmed tree: cut so as to produce head ('poll') of young branches

POOR JACK: iii. 28 dried salt cod: OED 1682 but cf. Sir Thomas Allin, *Journals* (ed. Anderson, 1939), 28 Dec. 1660

POORLY: v. 355 abjectly, mean spiritedly

POOR WRETCH: iv. 310 poor dear (term of affection), used of both sexes

PORRINGER: ii. 109 small basin for soup, porridge, children's food

PORTION: ii. 159 dowry

PORTMANTEAU (Fr.): i. 140 bag suitable for carrying on horseback

POSE (v.): iv. 33 to question, examine: aphetic form of 'appose'

POSER: v. 38 apposer, examiner

POSSET: i. 11 drink (sometimes jelly) made of hot milk curdled with spices and wine (or beer)

POSSIBLY: i. 321 P uses in modern sense: cf. Addison, *Tatler* 243 'He cannot possibly live till Five'

POST (s.): iii. 51 stand for the display of playbills etc. iv. 74 the official organisation for the transmission of letters: OED P

POST (v.): v. 128 to expose, pillory: 1642

POSTHOUSE: ii. 15 inn where changes of post-horses were stabled: 1645 Evelyn

POST-NIGHT: vii. 79 night on which letters are dispatched: 1657

POST, take: vii. 146 ride post, i.e.

ride hired posthorses: OED reports 'ride post' but not this form

POSTURE: i. 173 condition, state

POSY: i. 39 verse or phrase engraved on inside of ring: from 'poesy'

POT BOYLE, make the: viii. 229 as 'make his pot seeth' 1577

POT, go to the: viii. 293 to be cut in pieces like meat for the pot, be ruined; 1530

POTAGE: viii. 211 presumably 'French Pottage', a soup containing bread sops, rather than the long naturalised 'Standing Pottage', a soup heavily thickened with barley or other grains: cf. Mess of Potage

POTHECARY, POTTICARY: see Apothecary

POTTLE: viii. 248 half a gallon (liquid measure), a vessel of that capacity

POT VENISON: i. 26 venison baked with butter, pounded to a paste with spices, and stored in a pot with clarified butter poured over the paste: 17th-cent. recipes make it clear that it was the equivalent of a modern pâté

POUND: vii. 390 an enclosed place offering no escape-route

POWDERED (of meat or poultry): iv. 3 salted

PRACTICE: vi. 202 trick

PRAEJUDICE: viii. 384 modern sense: 1643 Browne

PRAGMATIC, PRAGMATICAL: ix. 238, ix. 134 interfering, conceited, dogmatic: 1611

PRATE: vi. 331 to talk idly

PRATIQUE: iv. 418 ship's licence for port facilities given on presentation of clean bill of health: 1611

PREBEND: i. 261 prebendary canon of a cathedral, member of cathedral chapter with obligation to officiate according to a rota

PRECISENESS: i. 67 manner of speech particularly attentive to moral decorum; affected by Puritans

PRESBITERY: i. 152 the elders of the church, ministers who attempted to work a presbyterian polity

PRESBYTERIAN: i. 126 adherents of the system of church government (incompatible with episcopacy) by presbyters, or sessions of elders: 1641

PRESBYTER JOHN: v. 96 puritan parson: humorous adaptation of 'Prester (or Presbyter) John', the legendary Emperor/Patriarch of Ethiopia

PRESENT, PRESENTLY: vii. 159 immediate, immediately

PRESENT MONEY: ii. 50 ready money

PRESENT (s.): vi. 196 shot, volley: *OED* 1833

PRESS (s.): iv. 353 cupboard. vii. 214 bookcase

PRESS (v.): viii. 256 to impress, forcibly enlist in the state's service

PRESS BED: i. 139 bed folding into or built inside cupboard: *OED* P

PREST MONEY (milit., naval): vii. 187 earnest money paid in advance: no connection with pressed men

PRETENCE: ix. 443 right, claim

PRETEND TO: v. 175 to allege: 1647. v. 96 to claim: thus the 'pretended freight' at v. 340 may not primarily mean 'falsified'

PRETTY: vi. 242 (of men) fine, elegant. iii. 186 (of a thing) neat, ingenious. ix. 208 (of food) delectable. viii. 204 (adv.) fairly, tolerably

PREVENT (v.): viii. 473 to anticipate

PRICK (s.): vii. 400 penis

PRICK (v.): i. 324 to write out music

PRICK-LOUSE: iv. 121 tailor (opprobrious): 'to prick a louse', as cant for 'to be a tailor' 1630; a barbed insult in the light of Pepys's father's trade

PRICK OUT: iii. 147 to strike out, delete

PRINCE: vi. 325 ruler

PRINCIPLES (of music): iv. 93 natural aptitude for, grasp of basic elements

PRINT: ix. 130 impression, trace

PRISE, PRIZE: v. 14 price, worth, value. *Also* (v.) ii. 190 apprise, value

PRIVATE: iii. 17 small. vi. 149 secret. viii. 421 quiet

PRIVATE BOXES: v. 152 secret drawers

PRIVITIES: viii. 360 private parts: cf. Secrets

PRIVITY: ix. 341 cognisance

PRIZE, PRIZE FIGHT: iv. 167, v. 133 fencing match fought for money. *See also* Prise

PROCEEDINGS: v. 74 progress

PRONOUNCE: v. 245 to judge, criticise

PRONUNCIATION: vii. 327 elocution, delivery

PROPER: ix. 18 distinctive, formally constituted

PROPRIETY: i. 17 property, ownership. viii. 51 appropriateness: 1615

PROTEST (a bill of exchange): viii. 579 to record non-payment, to re-present bill after payment has been refused to establish fact of refusal for purposes of any subsequent legal action by holder

PROUD (of animals): v. 94 on heat

PROVISIONS: ii. 93 stores generally (not restricted to victuals)

PUBLISH: v. 130 publicise, make known

PUFFE: viii. 44 artificial roll of hair: 1601 so P's 'as my wife calls them' probably expresses contempt of the objects rather than ignorance of the designation

PULL A CROW: iii. 261 to quarrel: 1460

PULL, try a: viii. 441 have a go: a 'pull' is a bout, trial of strength; in phrase as 'stand/wrestle a pull' from c. 1381

PULL-BACKE (s.): iii. 302 set-back: not in *OED* as s., though common as v.

PULLING OF CHERRIES: vi. 132 playing at bob-cherry

PUMICE STONE: iii. 91 stone of lava; used for smoothing parchment and removing stains from material as well as removing facial hair

PUNCH: ix. 538 (cf. n.) *OED* P

PUPPY-DOG WATER: v. 78 a distillation made from a mixture of wine and other ingredients including roast pig or puppy-dog (Evelyn, *Mundus Muliebris*, 1690, pp. 22–3)

PURCHASE: viii. 226 booty: originally 'the action of hunting; the chase; the catching or seizing of prey'

PURELY: v. 105 excellently, without the admixture of impurities

PURL(E): i. 59 hot beer with bitter herbs: *OED* P

PUSS: iv. 264 ill-favoured woman: 1608

PUT HARD: viii. 117 suffer

PUT IN: ix. 72 come in, drop in

PUT OFF: ix. 110 to sell, dispose of: 1639. v. 183 to dispose of in marriage

PUT (a person or group) ON: i. 51 employ upon (a particular task): *OED* 1867

PUT OUT: i. 316 to invest

PUT OUT OF COUNTENANCE: ix. 289 disconcert, abash

PUT UP: iv. 20 to send up, present to: 1641

PYONEER: v. 97 pioneer, ditch digger, labourer

QU: viii. 463 cue

QUAKER: ii. 149 member of Society of Friends: George Fox, the founder, recounts that the name was coined by Justice Bennet, Derby, 1650 'because I [Fox] bid them, Tremble at the Word of the Lord'; but in fact it had already been applied to a foreign extremist sect, 1647

QUALITIED: v. 250 furnished with ability

QUANTUM: vi. 227 percentage, share, portion: 1649

QUARREFOUR (Fr. *carrefour*): iii. 268 crossroads: 'formerly quite naturalised but now treated only as Fr.' (*OED*)

QUARTER, keep a: ix. 42 to make a disturbance: 1632

QUARTER (s.): iii. 87 (of lamb) the shoulder and scoven (i.e breast and ribs)

QUARTERAGE: vi. 49 'any salary, pension, or sum paid quarterly' (Dyche)

QUARTER-DECK: i. 104 deck over the half-deck, extending between the mizen-mast and the stern, from which the captain commanded his vessel

QUARTERS: ii. 94 lodging place

QUEST-HOUSE: ix. 36 house used for inquests, parish meetings

QUICK: vii. 290 living, alive

QUICKEN (of woman): iv. 1 reach stage of pregnancy at which child shows signs of life

QUICKER PLEASURES AND SHARPER AGONYES: iv. 31 'sharpe or quick' in phr. from 1578

QUIRISTER: ii. 215 chorister

QUITLY: v. 100 quickly

RACE: iv. 41 to rase, destroy

RAINY DAY, lay by against a: vii. 350 as phrase from c. 1566

RAKE-SHAMED: iv. 52 disreputable, disgraceful: 'perhaps suggested by "rakehell" (*OED*), common in 17th cent.'

RANCONTRE (Fr. *rencontre*): ii. 91 adventure met by chance: P uses the word in its fashionable and *gallant* Fr. sense, rather than in the predominantly serious anglicised senses recorded by *OED*

RANGE: i. 204 kitchen-range, oven

RAPIER: i. 94 a sword convenient for thrusting, adorned with a more or less elaborate guard: 1530, when

it is defined as a 'Spanishe sworde';
'The etymology of the word
Rapier is obscure. Some derive it
from the German *rappen*, or *raffen*,
to tear out. Others connect it,
through *raspière*, to the Spanish
raspar, to scrape or scratch': Egerton
Castle, *Schools and masters of fence*
(1910), p. 329, n.

RARE: ix. 22 fine, splendid

RASPBURY SACK: ii. 212 raspberry wine
and raspberry vinegar are recorded
from the beginning of the 18th
cent., raspberry juice from 1661;
raspberry sack and raspberry wine
were identical. (cf. *A Butler's
Recipe Book*, ed. P. James, Cambridge 1935, p. 21); the 'respyce
[wine], the whiche is made of a
bery' described by Andrew Boorde,
A Compendyous Regyment (1542) is
presumed by *OED* to be 'raspis
wine' (It. *raspato*)

RATE (v.): v. 176 to berate, scold

RATE (s.): i. 29 manner

RATEING: viii. 417 scolding

RATHER (adv.): iii. 295 slightly, somewhat: *OED* P (in coll. with
'better' etc.)

RATHER, the: ix. 60 the more likely:
1657

RATTLE: viii. 378 to scold. ix. 498
to shake, discompose

RATTOON: i. 244 rattan cane

RAYLES: ii. 81 railings

READER: ii. 237 lay-reader, allowed to
read prayers and common services
in church: it is exceptional to find
one preaching. vi. 49 Bencher of
the Inns of Court appointed to
lecture on law

READING-GLASS: viii. 519 large magnifying glass used for reading:
OED 1670 Wood

READING-PEW: iii. 235 pew from
which lessons are read in church:
OED P

READY: iv. 189 quick, accomplished

REAKES: ix. 79 tricks: *OED* records
plural only; 'to play reaks' 'very
common in 17th cent.'

REBUS: ix. 227 punning emblem
representing word or name in
pictures or figures: 1605

RECEIPT: v. 64 reception. vii. 148
recipe, formula

RECEPI: i. 198 writ of receipt issued by
Chancery

RECITATIVO (It. *stilo recitativo*): viii. 55
declamatory style of singing,
intended to represent the natural
inflexions of speech, developed in
Florence in the 1590s for the purposes of opera, used by Nicholas
Lanier in England 1617 and subs.
a great influence on English vocal
style; distinct from the fast *parlando*
recitative of 18th-cent. opera

RECKONING: ii. 125 bill

RECLUSE (adj.): iii. 90 secluded, shut up

RECONCILE: iv. 133 to determine the
truth. iv. 190 to bring into accord
with

RECORDER: ix. 157 end-blown eight-
holed whistle or fipple flute:
recorders were built in several
different sizes, but the treble in F
(as played by P) was the most
common; the instrument, originally built in one piece, was redesigned with three joints and a
much increased range in France in
the 1650s and in this new form
came to enjoy its great vogue in
England c. 1668–1740

RECOVERY (legal): iii. 223 process for
re-establishment of ownership

RECRIMINATE: viii. 76 to excuse an
accusation by charging accuser
with a commensurate or greater
crime: 1611

REDUCEMENT: ix. 132 to bring back
to a previous and better state: the
primary sense, though the word is
recorded synonymously with
'reduction' from 1619

REFERRING: iii. 108 indebted, beholden to

REFORM (mil.): v. 310 to disband: orig. to break up unit to form a new one, but soon acquiring this sense

REFORMADO: i. 256 naval/military officer serving without commission

REFORMATION AND REDUCEMENT: ix. 132 not a new slogan, but current with the 'root and branchers' of 1641/2; cf. Sir E. Dering, *A collection of speeches* (1642), p. 83: 'Reforme, reduce, replant our Bishop President . . .'

REFRESH (of a sword): ii. 24 to sharpen

REGIO FLORET PATROCINIO COMMERCIUM, COMMERCIOQUE REGNUM: iv. 153 under kings trade flourishes; by trade kingdoms prosper

REIMBURSE: iv. 424 to repay or make up to one: 1611

RELENT: ix. 345 to repent: 'obs. and rare' (*OED*); but commonplace in 17th cent. (e.g. def. in Dyche)

RELIGIOUS (s.): viii. 182 monk, nun

RELISH TO THE HEART: vi. 267 ? poss. prov. phrase; cf. 'take to heart' and related locutions

REMAIN: vi. 79 remainder

REMEMBER: iv. 92 to remind

REMISSNESS: viii. 219 carelessness, negligence

RENDEZVOUS (v.): vi. 222 to assemble: 1662 Stillingfleet

RENT: viii. 599 a tear

REPAIR TO: ii. 13 gather to, rally to, 'to go to a certain place . . . as of soldiers going to the parade' (Dyche)

REPAYRE (v.): ii. 29 to put in order, restore to a just state

REPINING: iv. 135 grumbling: particularly, in 17th-cent. use, envious grumbling

REPLICACION (legal): iii. 85 replication, plaintiff's answer to defendant's plea

REPREHENSION: iii. 164 admonition

REPRIMENDE (Fr. *réprimende*): viii. 482 a reprimand: 1652 Evelyn 'repriment'

RESEMBLE: vi. 191 to represent, figure

RESENT: viii. 490 to receive with a particular reaction. ix. 61 to be indignant at

RESHIFT: vi. 153 to change back again: *OED* P

RESPECT (s.): ii. 3 courtesy. viii. 163 curtsey

RESPECTFUL: ii. 2 respectable

REST (s.): iv. 90 wrest, tuning hammer (i.e. key)

RESTING: iv. 148 remaining

RESTITUTION: i. 21 restoration

RETAIN (a writ, bill): iv. 347 to maintain a court action or process from term to term

REVIVE (s.): iv. 239 a revival: *OED* P only

REVOLUTION: vii. 55 sudden change: not necessarily violent

RHODOMONTADO (Sp.): ix. 25 boast, brag: 1612 Donne

RIDES US, all the world: v. 239 to be oppressed or harassed: in phr. from 1583

RIDING (s.): viii. 257 a skimmington ride, satirical procession in which a woman considered a scold or shrew would be paraded through the streets on a horse or donkey, and mocked by the clashing of kitchen utensils, etc. (cf. Thomas Hardy, *The Mayor of Casterbridge*, ch. xxxix for the survival of the custom): *OED* P

RIG (v.): iii. 61 to dress: 1534, generally sardonic

RIGHT-HAND: vi. 165 trusted assistant

RIGHT-HAND MAN: vi. 318 soldier on whom drill manoeuvres turn: *OED* P

RIGHTS, to: iv. 177 immediately, directly: not recorded by *OED*

RING OF IT: ix. 108 to echo with, universally talk of: 1608

RINGO-ALE: ii. 203 ale flavoured with eryngo (sea holly)

RIP UP: iv. 46 to reveal, expose, rake up: 1570 orig. probably 'to reap'

RIS (v.): i. 313 rose, risen

RISE: vii. 156 origin: 1630

RIX DOLLER: i. 140 Dutch or N. German silver coin (*Rijksdaalder, Reichsthaler*) worth c. 4s. 9d.

ROATE, by: iv. 231 by rote, automatically

ROB THE DEVIL AND THE ALTER: vi. 218 apparently unrecorded

ROCKE (Du. *rok*): iv. 20 distaff

ROLL-TOBACCO: vi. 120 tobacco leaves rolled into a cylinder and cured: 1633

ROMANCE: v. 31 tale: 1638

ROMANTIQUE: viii. 454 having the characteristics of a tale ('Romance'): 1659, but used on title-page of Thomas Bayley's *Herba Parietis, or The Wall Flower* (1651). vii. 59 appearing as it might in a tale: an alternative 17th-cent. form is 'romancy'

ROOM OF, in the: viii. 482 in the place of

ROPE-GROUND, ROPEYARD: v. 181, v. 265 ropewalk, place where ropes are manufactured: 'ropewalk' is not recorded until 1692

ROPE-HOUSE: viii. 308 store for ropes in dockyard

ROUNDHOUSE: i. 153 uppermost cabin in stern of ship, forming the top deck of the aftercastle and generally used by the captain or master

ROUNDLY: viii. 247 promptly, briskly

ROUT: v. 158 crowd. viii. 412 defeat, disaster

ROWE: iv. 413 roe deer

ROWL OUT: ix. 76 dismiss: converse of enroll, not otherwise recorded

RUB(B): v. 308 check, stop, obstacle

RUDENESS: viii. 56 backwardness, lack of culture

RUFFIAN: iii. 105 pimp: 'a common sense in the Romance languages' (*OED*)

RULE OF ART: i. 274 principle, governing practice of science or trade

RUMP: i. 45 remnant of the Long Parliament: 1659

RUMPER: i. 81 member or supporter of the Rump: OED P

RUNLETT: iv. 405 cask: by 1660 most commonly of small capacity

RUNNING: ix. 149 temporary: 1632

RUSSES: viii. 428 Russians

SAC: ix. 464 French gown: OED observes that Fr. lexicographers do not recognise Fr. *sac* as denoting this; 'the finest loose Sackes the Ladies use to be put in' (Jonson, *The Poetaster*, 1601, IV i)

SACK(E): i. 230 white wine from Spain or Canaries: the origin of the word is contentious; some authorities favour Fr. *vin sec*

SACK-POSSET: i. 9 eggs beaten with sugar and curdled milk in white wine

SAD: i. 92 sombre-coloured

SADDLE, get into the: i. 75 gain control, get into office: OED P

SAFT: iii. 81 soft

SAGE, juyce of: v. 222 more often commended for hoarseness than impotence

SAINTLY: vii. 17 pious: OED P 'befitting a saint', but the 'saint' is likely to imply a puritan of the Interregnum

SALAT, SALET: iii. 87 salad

SALT: v. 266 salt-cellar

SALT-EELE: iv. 109 rope or belt used for punishment: 1622

SALVE UP THE MATTER: v. 134 smooth over: common in first half of the 17th cent.

SALVO: vii. 396 excuse, explanation:

from L. phrases beginning *salvo*, abl. neut. sing. of *salvus*, 'intact', 'uninjured'

SAMPHIRE: i. 250 a seaside plant much used in pickles

SARCENET: iii. 65 thin taffeta, fine silk cloth

SASSE (Du. *sas*): iii. 18 lock: 1642, Sir C. Vermuyden, *Discourse on the draining of the fens*

SAVE: vi. 327 to preserve, not to lose, to catch, hence to be in time for: *OED* 1732, the application to tides a naut. commonplace today and probably in P's day also

SAY: ii. 124 fine woollen cloth, a light-weight serge

SCALE (of music): vi. 227 Guidonian scale, gamut, the hexachordal system used before the emergence of the modern major/minor key system: 1597 Morley; it was based on the six-tone pattern c d e f g a, which might be repeated on g or (utilising b-flat) on f. Seven such overlapping hexachords made up the scale from G to e″

SCALLOP: iii. 216 scalloped lace collar. i. 57 scollop

SCALLOP-WHISK: iii. 285 *see* Whiske

SCANDALIZE: iv. 161 to speak scandal of

SCAPE (s.): viii. 123 adventure

SCAPE (v.): vii. 229 to escape

SCARE-FIRE: iv. 6 sudden conflagration

SCENES: ii. 161 scenery: 1605 (cf. ii. 131, n. 2)

SCEPTICALL: i. 141 'that contemplates, or always seekes and never finds' (Blount): 1639 Fuller. iv. 185 doubtful: close to modern sense

SCEPTICKE, SCEPTIQUE (Fr. *sceptique*): i. 201 'a kinde of Philosophers called Scepticks . . . (that is to say Doubters) which did rather suspend their Judgements concerning the Godhead then call it in question' (Golding's *De Mornay*, 1592)

SCHOOL: iii. 250 to scold, rebuke

SCHOOL-LEARNING: vii. 327 knowledge of scholastic philosophy

SCHUIT (Du.): i. 145 Dutch canal boat, barge

SCONCE: iii. 3 bracket-candlestick, candlestick

SCO(A)RE (s.): viii. 153 account

SCORE (v.): v. 57 to rate, scold: *OED* U.S. 1891 only

SCOTCH CAKE: viii. 559 oatcake

SCOTOSCOPE: v. 240 portable *camera obscura* (i.e. spyglass for seeing objects in a dark room): *OED* P

SCOWRE: iii. 23 to beat, punish

SCREW: iii. 50 key, screw-bolt. iv. 146 a part of a press

SCRIVENER: iv. 344 a professional copyist, also fulfilling some of the functions of modern notary/solicitor

SCRUPLE (v.): vii. 40 to hesitate, dispute

SCUCHEON: iv. 424 escutcheon, shield of arms

SCULL: ii. 226 small river-boat rowed by a single waterman using one pair of oars: 1611: cf. Pair of oars

SCULLER: ii. 118 waterman rowing scull

SCURVY: iii. 43 worthless, contemptible

SCUTTLE: i. 98 any opening in deck or topsides of ship smaller than hatchway

SEA-CARD: vii. 292 chart: 1571

SEA-HORSE TEETH: iii. 297 walrus tusks

SEALED-PAPER: vii. 332 paper bearing a stamp indicating that it had paid duty

SEA-OFFICERS: commissioned officers of the Navy: cf. Navy Officers

SEARCH: iii. 117 to examine medically

SECLUDED MEMBER: i. 62 M.P. excluded from the House in 1648 in Pride's Purge: 1649 Prynne

SECOND MOURNING· ii. 203 half-mourning

SECRESY: ii. 219 uncommon knowledge of an art or trade

SECRET: i. 285 secretive

SECRETS: iv. 383 private parts

SEDAN: viii. 114 enclosed chair, borne on two poles by bearers: 1635

SEEK, to be to: ii. 8 to be at a loss for: in phr. from c. 1386

SEEL (of a ship): i. 142 to lurch

SEEM: ii. 196 to pretend. viii. 298 to appear to be

SELFE-MURDER: ix. 33 suicide: a common 17th- and 18th-cent. usage

SELLING OF A HORSE FOR A DISH OF EGGS AND HERRINGS: i. 38 game: untraced

SENNIT: i. 14 sevennight, a week (cf. fo[u]rt[een]night)

SENSE: i. 1 sensation, awareness. vii. 74 concentration

SENSIBLE: vi. 8 aware

SENSIBLE PLANT: i. 80 *mimosa pudica* or other plant that closes when touched

SERAPHIC: ix. 211 ecstatic: 1659 Boyle, who offers it as a neologism expressing a 'flaming Nature'

SERPENT: vii. 152 firework burning with serpentine motion: 1634

SERVANT: iv. 10 suitor, lover

SET (of fiddlers): i. 130 band, consort: OED 1684, but 'a set of viols' 1611, referring to instruments rather than players; the transference is conventional: cf. Drum

SET (v.): i. 21 to sit. ii. 136 to reside. ix. 24 to set in order, arrange

SET FIELD: vi. 38 duel

SET ON: ix. 297 to accost

SET UP/OFF ONE'S REST: iv. 8 to be content, settle upon, make one's whole aim: originally a gaming expression from *primero*, where the 'rest' was a reserved stake, ventured in a last resort, upon the loss of which the game ended, says OED, recording it from 1561; however the use 'to set up one's rest at an inn', to establish oneself, with rest in its literal sense, has an alternative claim; P uses it, of horses, i. 69

SEVEN TIMES MORE: iv. 422 seven was traditional and biblical for a large number or quantity: cf. Forty

SHAG(G): iv. 357 worsted or silk cloth with a velvet nap on one side

SHAPE: ii. 7 guise, costume indicating character: 1603

SHARP: viii. 379 pointed, tart

SHASH: viii. 462 sash

SHEATH (of a ship): ii. 45 to encase the hull as a protection against worm, either with copper or, more commonly at this time, with tar and hair or broom covered by a thin second skin of plank

SHELFE: vii. 4 shoal

SHERRY: iii. 180 still white wine from Xeres, not necessarily fortified: 1608

SHIFT (s.): ii. 71 trial, attempt, arrangement. viii. 463 dressing room

SHIFT (v.): vi. 152 to change clothes. i. 223 to dodge a round in paying for drinks

SHIFT FOR MYSELF: viii. 323 to provide for one's safety, livelihood: 1513

SHIRKE (s.): ix. 109 a slow payer, tardy debtor: 1639

SHIT IN HIS HAT AND THEN CLAP IT ON HIS HEAD, as if a man should: i. 261 prov. though not recorded; compare ' "The trumpeter shit in his hat", said the Epicurean – "and clapt it on his head", said the Pythagorean': Blake, *An Island in the Moon* c. 1787 (*Poetry and Prose*, ed. G. Keynes, 1961, p. 674)

SHITTEN-COME-SHITS: ii. 78 prov. phr. by 1659

SHITTLE-COCK: i. 15 shuttle-cock

SHOE-STRINGS: ix. 188 shoe laces

SHOEMAKER'S STOCKS: vii. 107 new shoes, ready-made: OED 1700

SHOT, pay: viii. 555 pay share in the cost of a feast or entertainment

SHOVE AT: viii. 180 to apply one's energies to

SHREVALTY: iv. 319 shrievalty, period of office as sheriff

SHROWD (shrewd): viii. 204 pointed, damaging

SHROWD: viii. 131 shrewd, astute

SHUFFLEBOARD: iii. 150 shovelboard, shoveha'penny

SHUFFLING: iv. 151 deceitful

SHUT THE DOOR AFTER THE HORSE IS STOLE, which is to: ix. 57 Fr. 1190, Eng. c. 1350

SICE, pay: iii. 187 to pay dearly (sixfold): 'sice', six as marked on dice, 'to throw a six' when it is disadvantageous

SICK DRESS: vi. 181 invalid dress

SIDE-SADDLE: ii. 180 saddle constructed so that a woman rider could sit with both feet to near side of horse

SIGHTS: viii. 486 spectacles: 1619

SILLABUB, SULLYBUB, SYLLABUB: iii. 154 milk mixed with wine or cider, usually sweetened

SILLILY: viii. 311 poorly, badly

SILLY: viii. 312 simple, foolish

SIMPLE: ii. 175 foolish. viii. 492 straightforward. ii. 74 humble

SIMPLY: v. 347 foolishly

SINGLE (dance, Fr. *simple*): iv. 161 the single is most commonly a step in dancing, forming a section of a basse dance, but it was also the basis of the single branle, which is probably intended here: cf. Thoinot Arbeau, *Orchesography* (trans. Evans, ed. Sutton, N.Y. 1967), p. 132

SIT: ix. 29 to hold a meeting. vii. 74 to pose for a portrait

SIT CLOSE: *see* Close

SITHE: iv. 375 sigh

SCKEATES, SCATES (Du. *schaetse*): iii. 272 skates: OED P

SKELLUM (Du. *schelm*): iv. 93 rascal, thief: 1611

SKIMMER: i. 24 flat pan with perforated bottom for skimming liquids

SKIRT-SUIT: i. 38 'suit with great skirts', i.e. lower portions of coat: fashionable from 1655 well into 18th cent.

SLABBER: v. 139 to slubber, to dirty in a disagreeable way

SLEEVE-HANDS: vi. 125 cuffs

SLICE: vi. 57 flat plate

SLIGHT (v.): viii. 265 to dismantle a fortress or (vi. 194) dockyard: 'common 1640-80' (OED). ix. 64 to disregard, ignore

SLIGHT; SLIGHTLY: vi. 94, vii. 11 contemptuous; slightingly, without ceremony

SLIP CALF/FILLY: v. 275, vi. 71 abort: OED P but 'slip' as 'abortion' 1657 W. Harvey

SLOOP (Du. *sloepe*): viii. 358 small vessel (c. 42 feet in length) which might be variously rigged and was often employed as an auxiliary to larger vessel. cf. E. Keble Chatterton, *Fore and aft craft* (1927), pp. 66-9

SLOP(P)S: iv. 74 seamen's ready-made clothes: OED P but in general sense of loose outer garments, particularly seamen's broad trousers, in use much earlier

SLUBBER: iv. 270 to perform something in a slovenly fashion: 1596 Shakespeare: cf. *also* Slabber

SLUG(G): vii. 328 slow heavy boat, 'sluggard': orig. a slow heavy person. vi. 30 rough metal projectile: 1622

SLUT: v. 55 drudge, wench (not always opprobrious); ii. 166 (opprobrious)

SLYME, SLIME: iv. 345 mucus

SMACK: i. 232 single-masted sailing vessel used as coaster or tender: 1611

SMALL (of drink): iii. 220 light, of low alcoholic content

SMART (adj.): viii. 531 sharp, reproving

SMELL (v.): iii. 106 to guess, suspect

SMOCK: i. 88 a woman's undergarment, a chemise

SMOOTH (v.): iv. 354 to iron (linen etc.): 1617

SMOTHERING: viii. 358 smouldering

SMUTTY: ix. 247 indecent: *OED* P

SNAP(P) (s.): viii. 5 bite, snack, small meal: 1642 Fuller. iv. 249 snatch (of music)

SNAP (v.): vi. 184 to ambush, cut down/out/off

SNAPS AT, have: v. 21 take snacks from (fig.), have amorous passages with: *OED* records the plur. 1631 and glosses 'have a sudden snatch or catch at' but the sense here differs, whilst being close to the common Restoration 'let me snack' (let me share)

SNEAKE: ix. 113 a despicable person: 1643

SNUFF (v.): vii. 80 to speak scornfully, to sniff at

SNUFF, go in: vi. 233 to go in dudgeon, anger: 1560

SNUFF, take in: viii. 50 to take offence: from the unpleasant smell left by the 'snuff' (smoking wickend) of a candle

SNUFFE-DISH: viii. 40 dish to hold the snuff (stubs) of candles

SNUFFER: i. 15 candle snuffer

SOKER: vi. 36 old hand, pal, ?toper: *OED* P but the usage need not imply excessive drinker since non-bibulous 'old soakers' occurs 1593

SOLEMNISE: i. 3 to celebrate, observe

SOL(L)ICITOR: ix. 223 agent. viii. 537 one who solicits business

SOLICITOUS IN: vii. 359 anxious about, concerned in

SON: i. 29 son-in-law (similarly with 'daughter' etc.)

SON-IN-LAW: vii. 12 stepson

SORT: iv. 317 set, crew

SOT: ii. 217 sat: part-participle of to sit

SOUND: ii. 196 fish-bladder

SOW GELDER: viii. 313 Sow gelders signalled their presence with a horn (cf. Marcellus Laroon, *The cryes of . . . London*, 1711, pl.2) and were a byword for raucousness; the horn was probably a horn-pipe sounded with a double reed

SPANIEL, as supple as a: vii. 83 the fawning of spaniels prov. from 1574, but this felicitous alliteration not otherwise recorded. i. 159 P has 'officious as a'

SPARAGUS, SPARROWGRASS: iii. 69, viii. 173 asparagus: the correct form and the aphetic 'sparagus' antedate by 200 years the corruption, assimilated to 'sparrow' and 'grass' (1658)

SPEAK BROAD: viii. 542 to speak fully, frankly

SPEAK FOR: ii. 114 to request

SPEAK VERY HIGH: i. 1 to speak out, speak forcefully

SPECIES (optical) iv. 160 image: 1598 'common in 17th cent.' (*OED*). ii. 160 a clearly distinct class of animals: 1608 Topsell

SPEED: v. 83 to succeed

SPEND: iii. 191 to ejaculate sexually. ii. 42 to cost: viz. 'expend'. ii. 47 to exercise

SPHERE OF WIRE: i. 14 armillary sphere, skeletal celestial globe in which the wire bands of which it is made represent the lines of the equator, the tropics, etc.

SPIKET: i. 120 spigot, tap, faucet

SPILT: *see* Spoilt

SPINET, SPINETTE: ix. 265 plectral keyboard instrument in shape of harp laid horizontally, with the strings running at 45° to the keyboard, having one manual and one set of strings only (though exceptions exist): the standard domestic keyboard instrument gradually superseding the oblong virginals from c. 1665 onwards; for all practical purposes a small harpsichord

SPIRITS: iv. 221 alcoholic liquor distilled for drinking: OED 1664

SPIT (v.): i. 321 to roast on turnspit

SPITTAL: i. 48 hospital, almshouse

SPITTING-SHEET: iii. 262 sheet for spitting on in sickness: OED P but in general use

SPLEEN: vii. 325 malice: in humour-theory the spleen was regarded as the source of melancholy and morosity

SPLIT HIMSELF . . . WITH LAUGHING: vii. 77 OED 1677

SPOIL: ix. 19 to deflower: OED 1678. vii. 423 to injure

SPOILT, SPILT: iii. 212 ruined

SPOON (v.): vii. 234 to run before the wind

SPOTS: vi. 9 patches (cosmetic)

SPRANKLE: v. 124 sparkling remark, *bon mot*: fig. from 'spranke' (s. & v.) Du. *sprankelen*, sparkle: OED does not record in this sense, though in others from 1387

SPRING-LOCK: iv. 282 self-locking, but commonly with a catch, comp. modern Yale

SPRUCE: ix. 217 neat, fashionable: 1599

SPUDD: viii. 473 a fork or spade for digging: OED P

SPURT, all of a: vi. 332 all of a sudden, in a short space of time: 1591

SQUEAMISH: i. 104 slightly affected with nausea: OED P though in stronger sense from c. 1450

STACIONER: iii. 1 bookseller (often also publisher): P also uses bookseller (e.g. ix. 22). iv. 410 modern sense

STAGGER (v.): viii. 131 to create worry and uncertainty

STAIRS: ix. 92 landing stage

STAMP: ii. 38 die-stamp

STAND, put to a: i. 68 bring to a stop: 1649

STAND A TUG FOR: vi. 105 endure pressure on behalf of a particular cause

STAND AND FALL AS THEY PLEASE: viii. 136 OED 1683 (as 'stand or fall')

STAND IN: iii. 14 to cost

STAND IN SLIPPERY PLACES: iii. 283 (cf. fn.)

STAND TO IT: viii. 8 to stick to it

STAND UPON: i. 177 to hold out for

STAND UPON MY OWN LEGS: v. 22 OED P, though in variants from 1624

STANDING OFFICERS: vii. 334 permanent officers of ship, dockyard

STANDING WATER: viii. 202 between tides

STANDISH: iii. 139 stand for ink, pens, etc.

STANDS, pair of: iii. 34 small pedestals or frames on which candlesticks could be set: 1664

STARK: ii. 87 utterly, completely

STARTED: viii. 287 startled

STATE: i. 133 Commonwealth

STATE-CUP: v. 47 cup for ceremonial and formal occasions

STATE-DISH: i. 192 richly decorated dish, often with a round lid or canopy

STATE-ROOM (naut.): i. 114 captain's cabin: OED P

STATESMAN: ii. 225 Commonwealth's-man: not in OED

STATIONER: see Stacioner

STAY (v.): iv. 251 to wait for. iv. 7 to sustain, comfort

STAY, at a: iv. 62 level with

STEEPLE: ix. 288 tower

STEMPEECE: iv. 91 main vertical timber of ship's bow

STICK: ix. 23 blockhead

STICK AT NOTHING: ix. 504 to be unscrupulous: 1615

STICK-RAPIER: i. 95 sword-stick

STICK TO: i. 7 adhere to (a person or faction)

STINGY: i. 186 mean: 1659

STINK, to be in a: viii. 259 evidently prov. phrase, but unrecorded

STIR(R): ii. 7 commotion

STOCKING: i. 94 legging, 'boot-stocking': *OED* 1676 Wood

STOICKE: i. 201 'Sect of Philosophers of Athens . . . they held, a wise man ought to be free from all passions, never to be moved either with joy or grief, and esteeming all things to be ordered by an inevitable necessity of Fate' (Blount)

STOMACH: v. 84 courage, pride. vi. 319 appetite

STOMACH, to have no: iv. 130 to have no wish to

STOMACHFULLY: vi. 46 proudly

STONE, incite a . . . to revenge: vii. 379 not recorded, but 'heart of stone' common from 1385

STONE-HORSE: iv. 120 a stallion, uncastrated horse

STOOP FOR A PIN, WILL NEVER BE WORTH A POUND, he that will not: ix. 7 as prov. from 1609

STOP: ix. 95 hesitation

STORY: viii. 517 history

STOUND: viii. 144 astonishment

STOUT: viii. 593 brave, courageous

STOVE (v.): vi. 35 to dry hawsers in a stove, preparatory to tarring: 1625

STOWAGE: ii. 122 storage, payment for storage

STRAIGHT-LACED: v. 222 wearing stays or bodice tightly laced: 1626

STRANG: ix. 500 strong

STRANGENESS: v. 36 distance, coolness

STRANGER: vi. 12 foreigner

STRIKE: ii. 223 (naut.) to lower topsail or (iii. 6) flag in salute. vi. 157 (of Exchequer tallies) to make, cut: 1626

STRINGS (on a book): iv. 133 cords, ribbons or leather straps attached to edges of covers to keep them closed

STRONG WATER: i. 76 distilled spirits: 1613

STROWED: i. 129 strewed

STRUCK WITH: vii. 161 to be attracted by one of the opposite sex: *OED* 1796

STUDY OF, to: i. 39 to contrive

STUFF: ii. 60 woollen fabric: but also (viii. 525) any fabric

STUMBLED AT, to be: vii. 301 to be nonplussed: 1548

STUPENDOUS: vii. 129 *OED* P as correct Eng. form of L. *stupendus*, superseding 'stupendious', common from 1547

SUBTILITY: i. 233 cunning

SUCCESS(E): ii. 185 occurrence, eventuality (good or bad), outcome

SUDDENLY: i. 221 in a short while

SUFFER (v.): iii. 163 permit, allow

SUGAR SOPPS: iv. 104 slices of bread steeped, sweetened and cut into fingers

SULLEN: ix. 555 gloomy

SULLYBUB, SULLABUB: ix. 541: *see* Sillabub

SUMMER HOUSE: viii. 469 garden building designed to give shelter and shade: 1440

SUMPTER-CLOTH: ix. 281 richly embroidered cloths covering pack mules

SUPERNUMERARIES: vii. 215 seamen extra to ship's complement: *OED* P

SUPPLE: ix. 412 pliant, adaptable

SURLY: ii. 100 imperious, lordly

SURPRIZE: ix. 518 alarm, access of emotion

SURRENDER (legal): ii. 135 deed yielding up tenancy in a copyhold estate to the lord of the manor (necessary if the ownership of land was to be transferred)

SWINE-POX: i. 17 chicken-pox

SWOUNE: i. 250 to swoon, faint

SYLLABUB: *see* Sillabub

SYMPHONY: iii. 197 instrumental introduction, interlude etc., in a vocal
composition. i. 10 It. *sinfonia*, piece
for instruments

TAB(B)Y: iv. 197 ribbed silk, plain or
watered: 1638 Fr. *tabis*, Sp. *tabi*,
orig. Arabic

TABLE: iv. 29 tablet, legend or key
attached to print etc. viii. 41 bony
layer of skull

TABLE BOOK: viii. 208 memorandum
book: 1596

TABLES: vi. 221 backgammon (and
similar games played on 'tables',
boards)

TAG, RAG AND BOBTAIL: i. 78 all and
sundry, mixture of people, particularly of lower orders; 'Tom,
Dick and Harry': 1645

TAILLE (Fr.): iv. 230 figure, shape (of
person): OED P

TAKE (v.): i. 1 to catch. ii. 47 to work,
prove effective, 'take on'

TAKE A CRAP: i. 197 defecate

TAKE A SHORT LEAVE: viii. 461 to leave
abruptly

TAKE EGGS FOR MONEY: vii. 184 cut
one's losses, accept something

TAKE IN TAX: viii. 220 take to task:
OED P

TAKE IT VERY WELL: v. 184 OED gives
early examples of 'to take ill' (1300)
rather than 'well', but the phrase
appears to have been current in M.E.

TAKE MAIDENHEAD OF: ix. 379 to use
for the first time: in this transferred
sense 1550

TAKE OUT: iv. 93 to learn, or having
learnt, to perform: 1591. vi. 79 to
be led out to dance: 1613

TAKE POST: *see* Post

TAKE UP: vii. 340 to patch up,
temporarily make up: sense clear
from context but earlier uses in
OED signify 'settle amicably'.
ii. 213 reform, check one's self:
1613

TAKING, in a: ii. 88 in a condition,
plight (in unfavourable sense): 1522

TALE: vi. 259 tally, reckoning, number

TALK BASELY, to: i. 12 to talk meanly,
debasingly

TALKING: ix. 193 talkative

TALLE: v. 179: *see* Taille

TALLY: vi. 106 wooden stick used by
the Exchequer in accounting, in
two matching parts for security,
and notched according to value

TAMPKIN: viii. 351 tompion, wooden
block used to plug muzzle of gun
when not cleared for action: 1625

TANSY, TANZY: vi. 117 sweetened egg
pudding or omelette, originally
flavoured with tansy, but by
Pepys's time generally having
spinach as its predominant flavour-
ing

TARGETT: ii. 85 shield

TARPAULIN: viii. 304 'tar', a sea-bred
captain as opposed to a gentleman-
captain: OED 1690, from the
waterproof tarred canvas of which
common sailors' clothes were made

TASTE: ix. 148 appetite, relish for

TATTLE(s.): ii. 141 gossip

TAWDRY: vii. 311 showy, gaudy,
without real value: OED in
proximate sense 1671; from
'tawdry lace' (or St Audrey's lace),
a silk lace often, in 17th cent.,
showy but shoddy

TAXOR: iii. 218 financial official of
university: at Cambridge regulat-
ing rent of students' lodgings,
price of commodities, and accuracy
of weights and measures within
town

TEAR LIKE A PRINCE, to: vii. 398 to
rant, to ride a high horse: 'to tear'
1601, phrase apparently not recorded

TELESCOPE: vii. 240–1 the tubes in the
larger models were of wood, in
the smaller of pasteboard covered
with vellum, with an outer tube

covered in leather; the Galilean (concave) eyepiece was used only in the smaller types; the larger ones had three or four convex lenses producing an erect image

TELL, TELL OVER: ix. 459 to count, reckon up

TELL TO HIS TEETH: iv. 344 to assert openly, to a person's face: 1542

TEMPER (s.): iv. 46 moderation. v. 1 temperament, mood. v. 191 physical condition

TEMPER (v.): iv. 361 to moderate, control

TENDER: ix. 83 cautious, chary

TENT: ii. 98 absorbent material rolled to a pointed (tent-like) shape used for probing wounds or keeping them open. iv. 405 (Sp. *tinto*) red wine

TERCE, TIERCE: iv. 171 measure of wine (42 galls. one-third of a pipe)

TERELLA: iv. 323 terrella, spherical magnet, terrestrial globe containing magnet: 1613

TERM(ES): i. 1 menstrual periods

THEORBO: ii. 193 large lute having two heads, the additional head carrying diapason strings, the number of courses variable, but typically 7–8 main, 6–7 bass: 1605, but from 1544 in Italy (*tiorba*); much used as accompanying instrument and gaining in popularity over ordinary lute throughout 17th cent.; early examples strung in single courses, later mainly double (cf. ii. 201)

THREAD: ii. 138 linen, or fine woollen material

THREE GREAT TRADES OF THE WORLD ARE, THE LAWYER[S], WHO GOVERN THE WORLD – THE CHURCHMEN WHO ENJOY THE WORLD – AND A SORT OF FOOL THEY CALL SOULDIERS, WHO MAKE IT THEIR WORK TO DEFEND THE WORLD: ix. 396–7 cf. n.: unrecorded, but compare inn-

sign of *The Four Alls*, a King saying 'I rule all', a priest 'I pray for all', a soldier 'I fight for all', and John Bull or a farmer, 'I pay for all' (J. C. Hotten, *Hist. Signboards*, 1866, p. 451)

THRIVE ONE WITH ANOTHER BY CHEATING ONE ANOTHER, let them: viii. 101 not apparently recorded as prov.

THRUSH: vi. 131 inflammation of throat and mouth: *OED* P

TICKELED: vi. 312 annoyed, irritated: not in *OED*

TICKET(T): i. 306 seaman's pay-ticket. ii. 73 invitation (to funeral) (cf. R. Latham (ed.), *The Illustrated Pepys* (1978), p. 72)

TICKET-MONGER: ix. 103 dealer or tout working the market in seamen's tickets

TIERCE: *see* Terce

TIGHT: i. 226 watertight

TILL: v. 9 closed compartment in part of larger box or chest

TILT: v. 156 awning over river-boat: 1611

TIMBER: iv. 259 wood for the frame of a ship (as distinct from planks or deals used for the decks, cabins, gun platforms etc.)

TIRE: vii. 194 tier, gun-deck

TISSUE: iii. 297 rich fabric, often interwoven with gold and silver

TITTLE-TATTLE (s.): viii. 303 chatter, gossip

TO: v. 89 against: common 17th-cent. use in phrases such as 'make faction to'

TOILETTE CAPP: i. 239 cap worn whilst dressing: *OED* P

TOKEN: iii. 75 keepsake. iv. 169 coin of little value: from coin privately issued to make up small change. iv. 391 a gift: virtually synonymous with bribe (cf. iv. 409)

TOKEN, by the same: i. 70 so, then, and, the proof of this being that:

OED observes the progressive weakening of this phrase

TONE: i. 311 accent: *OED* 1680

TONGUE: vii. 165 reputation, fame

TOOK ONE STONE FROM THE CHURCH DID TAKE TWO FROM HIS CROWN, he that: ix. 502 both sentiment and metaphor are close to recurrent passages in the *Eikon Basilike*, but this formulation does not occur

TOP TO BOTTOM: vii. 160 as phrase 1621

TOPS: iv. 357 turnovers of stockings

TORTOY'S SHELL: vii. 185 tortoise-shell: true tortoise-shell first used for decorative purposes in England during second quarter of 17th cent.

TORY: ii. 220 Irishman: orig. (1646) outlaw, then applied to Irish royalists; not narrowly political until c. 1675

TOSS (v.): viii. 571 to confuse

TOSSE (s.): viii. 472 fright, confusion: *OED* P

TOUCHED: vi. 322 annoyed, vexed

TOUCH-WOOD: vii. 368 a fungus found growing on trees, *touchwood boletus*: 1598

TOUR, the: iv. 95 coach parade of *beau monde* in Hyde Park

TOW: v. 182 flax fibre for ropemaking

TOWN(E): ii. 182 manor

TOWSE: iv. 203 to tousle/tumble a woman

TOWZER: v. 51 a large dog: as designation *OED* 1678

TOYLE (Fr. *toile*): iv. 413 snare, net into which game is driven: 1529

TRADE: iv. 22 manufacture, industry. ii. 127 business

TRAINEBAND, TRAYNE BAND, TRAIN-BAND: ii. 9 trained-band, troop of city militia: ordinarily of London, but existing elsewhere (iv. 420)

TRANSIRE: vi. 256 warrant allowing goods through customs: 1599, L. *transire*, to go across

TRAPAN (s.): iv. 55 a trick, trap: 1665

TRAPAN, TREPAN (v.): viii. 35 to perform brain surgery. ii. 177 to cheat, trick, trap, inveigle: 1656

TRAPBALL: ix. 191 cat and trap-ball, tip cat: the player strikes the trap with his bat, thus pitching the ball into the air to be hit away

TREASURY, the: the Navy Treasury or the national Treasury

TREAT (s.): ix. 459 entertainment of food and drink: 1651 Evelyn

TREAT (v.): iv. 417 to handle (literally). iii. 70 to entertain

TREATER: viii. 285 envoy, emissary

TREATY: iv. 212 negotiation

TREBLE: vii. 338 treble viol: 1634. iv. 310 violin: P's phrase 'as he calls it' would fit a fiddler's application to his instrument of a term proper to the more serious viol; for confirmation that it was in fact a violin, ii. 96

TRENCHED IN: ix. 240 entrenched, (dry)moated

TRENCHERFULL: i. 57 as much as a trencher will hold: *OED* P, a trencher (Fr. *trancher*) being originally a flat piece of wood on which meat was cut and served and then by extension a wooden, metal or earthenware plate

TRENCHER-SALT: ix. 406 a small salt cellar placed near a guest's trencher at a meal: 1614

TREPAN: *see* Trapan

TRIANGLE, TRYANGLE: ii. 121 triangular virginals: probably an *ottavino* (i.e. at 4ft pitch)

TRILL(O): ii. 128 vocal ornament consisting of the repetition of the same note: 'the Trill . . . is upon one Note only' (Playford. *Introduction to the skill of music*, 1674, p. 47), a vital feature of the Italian declamatory vocal style; 'trill' was simultaneously used in its modern sense of an ornament on two notes, and with the waning of the declamatory style P's sense vanished; later eds. of Playford omit the passage cited

TRIM: iii. 91 to shave: P uses 'shave' ix. 398

TROY: iv. 144 troy weight: for precious metals, 12 oz to 1 lb

TRUCKLE/TRUNDLE BED: ix. 231, viii. 470 low bed on castors which could be put under main bed

TRUCKLE UNDER: viii. 415 to be subservient to: OED P

TRUMPET: i. 319 trumpeter: cf. Drum etc.

TRUMP MARINE: viii. 500 *tromba marina*, tall single-stringed bowed instrument, triangular in section, having sympathetic strings within the sound-box and a bridge of which only one end was fixed, the other vibrating freely on the soundboard: admired by M. Jourdain as well as P; 'La trompette marine est un instrument qui me plaît et qui est harmonieux', *Le bourgeois gentilhomme* II i; for a history cf. P. Garnault, *La trompette marine* (Nice 1926)

TRUSS(E): viii. 232 a supporting appliance for rupture: 1543

TRYANGLE: *see* Triangle

TUBB: viii. 217 tub, steam bath

TUBE-SPECTACLE: ix. 277 arrangement of tube or tubes in spectacle frame intended to shade and help focus eyes

TUITION: iii. 176 guardianship: L. *tuitio*, tuition, safe keeping

TUMBLER: v. 302 a drinking cup, originally with a rounded or pointed bottom so that it could not be set down until empty: OED P

TUNE: viii. 53 pitch: OED 1694

TUNE, out of: v. 49 out of sorts, distempered

TUNEABLE: ix. 232 tuneful: much used of bells from 1510

TUNIQUE: viii. 489 a man or woman's

(cf. viii. 576) close fitting body coat: 1666 Evelyn

TURK, the: used of all denizens of the Turkish Empire, but usually here of the Berbers of the N. African coast, especially Algiers

TURKEYWORK: iv. 329 tapestry, rug or similar material used for upholstery, usually red and yellow, loosely derivative of the Anatolian style: 1537, by the end of the 16th cent. extensively manufactured at Norwich

TURKY-STONE: ix. 78 turquoise: 1607

TURN: ii. 7 opportunity, occasion. vii. 188 reversal

TURNE, take a: viii. 305 take a trip: 1400. ii. 4 a walk around

TURRET-GARDEN: ii. 123 apparently a roof-garden (cf. ii. 116)

TWAT(T)LING: vii. 219 chattering, gossiping: 1573, apparently from 'tattling' as in 'tittle-tattle'

TWEEZERS (Fr. *étuis*): iii. 115 a set ('pair') or case of small instruments, which would include tweezers in modern sense: 1654 but Florio, 1611, has 'estui . . . a pocket case or little sheath with cizers, bodkin, penknife . . . in it,' cf. G. Bernard Hughes, 'Elegance of the étui', *Country Life*, 19 July 1973; 'to pack up knowledge in a Small case (like a Paire of Twises) . . . S. Butler, *Prose Observations*, ed. H. de Quehen (Oxford 1979), p.135

TWIST: iv. 357 strong thread of twisted fibre

UDDER: i. 263 an udder was eaten roast, having been preboiled, stuck with cloves, and basted with butter

UGLY: ii. 74 unpleasant, offensive

UMBLES (O. Fr. *nombles*): viii. 526 edible entrails, giblets, of deer: as 'umble-pie' (iv. 221) OED P but common in the corrupt form 'humble pie'

UNBESEEMING: v. 278 undignified: 'very common in 17th cent.' (*OED*)

UNBESPEAK: ii. 204 rescind invitation. ix. 518 countermand: *OED* P: cf. Uninvite

UNBIDD: ii. 29 uninvited

UNCOUTH: i. 159 out of sorts or order, uneasy, at a loss: *OED* P. vii. 116 unfamiliar

UNDERRATE: viii. 601 to classify a ship at an unduly low rate (cf. fn.)

UNDERSTAND: ii. 64 to conduct oneself properly: 1602

UNDERTAKER: iv. 36 contractor: 1602. ix. 71 parliamentary manager: 1620

UNHAPPY, UNHAPPILY: v. 258 unlucky, unluckily

UNHUNG (of a room): ix. 468 bare, without having its hangings in place: 1648

UNINVITE: vi. 310 *OED* P

UNKNOWN: vii. 221 unheard of, unprecedented

UNORDINARY: viii. 243 extraordinary: 1547

UNREADY: v. 95 undressed: iii. 220 'to make unready', get undressed

UNTILE: iv. 52 strip a roof of tiles: 1400, a trad. act of vengeance against a popularly disliked figure

UNTRUSS: vi. 87 to undo one's breeches, defecate

UPHOLST(ER)ER: i. 263 dealer in upholstery, furniture and fabrics: 1613 (as 'uphoulster'); originally 'upholder' (1459), at which date it signified a dealer in second-hand household goods; by the 17th cent. the upholsterer dealt exclusively in new materials; in 1747 described as 'a Connoisseur in every article that belongs to a House', cf. P. Thornton, *17th-century interior decoration in England, France and Holland* (1978), p. 99

UPPER BENCH: name given in Interregnum to King's Bench

USE: i. 285 usury, interest; also 'use upon use' as compound interest

USE (v.): vii. 284 to be accustomed

VAPOURING: ii. 17 pretentious, foolish: 1647 P's use is distinct from that of the 18th cent., implying liability, characteristically feminine, to depressive fits

VARIETY: iv. 17 of many sorts, plenitude

VAUNT: v. 35 to vent, vend, sell: 'very common from c. 1600 to c. 1700' (*OED*)

VENETIAN CAP: i. 324 peaked cap as worn by Venetian Doge

VENICE TREACLE: iv. 39 commonly used though costly cure-all: also known as 'treacle of Andromachus' as it was reputedly invented by Nero's physician; prescriptions usually had 60 or more ingredients (e.g. J. Quincey, *Pharmacopoeia*, 1720, pp. 406-7)

VENTURE (s.): i. 258 speculative enterprise of a business nature

VERIEST: ix. 204 most typical, quintessential: a common 17th-cent. superlative

VERSE: ix. 11 verset, short piece for organ in fugal style: orig. liturgical, used for organ piece replacing verse of plainsong psalm, canticle or hymn; later a general term, with exemplars from Byrd to Purcell. iii. 197 section of an anthem

VESPERS: i. 257 evensong: *OED* P noting rarity as applied to service in the Church of England

VEST: vii. 315 'a long Cassocke close to the body' (vii. 324): *OED* P in this sense; as a loose outer garment, 1613

VESTS: iv. 44 robes, vestments: *OED* P 'rare'

VEXED ... TO THE BLOOD: iii. 217 possibly prov. phrase as recurs iv. 342

VIALL, VIOL: i. 59 flat-backed fretted bowed instrument with six gut strings, held between the knees and bowed with an underhand grip, existing in three sizes, treble, tenor and bass: extensively used in England from early 16th cent. to 1670s when surpassed in popularity by violin family, though the bass survived as the 'viola da gamba'

VICIOUSNESS: vii. 323 prevalence of vice

VIRGINALS: ix. 149 generic name for all plectral keyboard instruments (hence 'Virginall-maister' ii. 44) but at this time also used to differentiate the small oblong instrument (in which the strings, a single set, run at right angles to the keyboard), from the harpsichord and the spinet. In the oblong virginals both bridge and nut are on the sound-board, giving a distinctive tone; the last recorded English specimen of the oblong shape is dated 1679 (cf. Luckett, 'The English virginals', *Engl. Harpsichord Magazine*, 1974, pp. 69–72)

VIRTUOSO (It.): iv. 297 man of wide learning, 'a learned or ingenious person, or one that is well qualified' (Blount)

VISIONAIRE (Fr. *visionnaire*): ix. 386 one who sees visions: the King appears to have treated the word as French, where it comes into prominence in these years, customarily in a derisory sense; but 'visionary' was used as an English word, with similar intent, by Hobbes in *Leviathan* (1651)

VISITANT (Fr.): v. 328 visitor: 'very common in 16th and 17th cents.' (OED)

VIZARD: viii. 423 vizard mask: 'very common from c. 1560–c. 1700' (OED). ix. 463 a mask to protect the eyes

VOCALITY: viii. 599 consonance of words and music: OED P

VOLARY: iv. 272 aviary: 1630, from Fr. *volière*; P makes no distinction of meaning and the French-based word, though later, proved the less durable

WACHMAKER: vi. 100 watchmaker: 1630: cf. Watch

WAFER: ii. 110 a light, thin, crisp cake, baked in wafer-irons, eaten with wine

WAGER-BOAT: ii. 101 light racing sculling boat: OED 1844

WAGGONERS: iv. 240 book of charts (cf. fn.)

WAINSCOTE: i. 243 panelling, generally of oak

WAISTCOAT, WASTECOATE, WASTCOATE: i. 298 male undergarment designed to be partly exposed through the doublet

WAIT, WAYT (at court etc.): ii. 64 to serve a turn of duty (usually a month) as an official

WAKENING: v. 152 rousing, stimulating

WALL, take the: i. 46 to walk on the inside of the road or pavement

WARDROBE: iv. 336 a cloakroom

WARM: iii. 302 comfortable, well-off: 1571

WASHEALL-BOWLE: ii. 239 wassail bowl, for making wassail (spiced ale drunk on Christmas Eve and Twelfth-night), carried on their rounds by wassailers, who sang carols from house to house: 1606

WASSELL, WASSAIL: iv. 45 entertainment (e.g. a play acted by children): presumably derived from the Christmastide ritual; not in OED

WASTECLOATH: i. 130 waistcloth; cloth hung on ship as decoration between quarter-deck and forecastle (and camouflage for those on deck in action): 1615

WAST(E)COATE: *see* Waistcoat

WATCH: i. 120 clock

WATER: viii. 504 strong water, spirits. i. 54 medicament

WATER GRUELL: iv. 40 invalid food of oatmeal or groats boiled in water, sometimes seasoned with salt and butter

WAY, in the: iv. 17 in a suitable condition

WAY, out of the: iv. 199 inaccessible: 1598

WAYTES: iv. 249 waits, municipal musicians

WEAR AND TEAR: vii. 301 deterioration through use: OED P

WEATHER-GLASS: iii. 203 thermometer (or, less likely, barometer): 1626 Bacon; OED does not accept as clear designation for true barometer ('Toricellian glass') until 1695

WEIGH, WEIGH UP (of ships): vi. 54 to raise a sunken ship: 'to weigh', carry, lift, as in 'weigh anchor'

WEIGHT ON MY MIND: vii. 425 apparently coll. phr. by this date

WELCH HARP: i. 15 harp with straight pillar and flat soundboard: probably triple strung to achieve chromatic tuning, but the precise date at which the term became associated with this feature is in doubt

WELL-LOOKED: viii. 472 good-looking: 'well' in this sense, 1600

WELL OPINIONED: i. 300 having a good opinion of: 'rare' (OED)

WENCHER: viii. 364 one who pursues wenches: 1593

WESTPHALIA HAM: ii. 160 strongly salted and smoked bacon, originally imported from Westphalia c. 1650, subsequently imitated in England

WHEEDLE: ix. 167 'a late word of fancy, and signifies to draw one in, by fair words or subtile imagination, to act anything of disadvantage or reproof' (Blount)

WHEELS A'GOING, keep our: ix. 402 keep us going as we are: OED P

WHERRY: ii. 121 small river boat for passengers

WHISKE: i. 299 woman's stiffened neckerchief or collar: 1654

WHIP A CAT: vi. 190 ? to do the most trivial business: OED admits bafflement at the phrase, but records it, 18th and 19th cents., as meaning 'to do itinerant labour', which suggests a connection

WHITING: ii. 119 whitewashing

WHITSTER: viii. 385 bleacher, launderer

WHOLESAYLE MAN: iii. 163 one who sells a commodity by wholesale: 1645

WIGG: ii. 50 wig, cake, bun made of fine flour

WILDE: viii. 145 wile, trick, device: 'wile' iv. 309

WILDERNESS: ix. 207 a piece of ground in a large garden or park planted with trees and laid out in ornamental or fantastic manner: 1644, but cf. *The Diary of Lady Anne Clifford* (ed. V. Sackville-West, 1923), 25 Oct. 1617, 'I walked ... all the Wildernesse over'; the Knowle Wilderness survives

WIND (s.): vii. 274 wine: 'in old registers the word "wine" is frequently written "wind"': *The Torrington Diaries* (ed. C. Bruyn Andrews, 1954), p. 338n.

WIND, go down the: iii. 157 to decline: 1600

WIND LIKE A CHICKEN: vi. 7 to manipulate, to wind round one's little finger: origin obscure, possibly from the common trick of hypnotising a chicken and compelling it to follow movements of a particular object

WINDFUCKER: viii. 275 talkative braggart: 1602

WIND UP, to: iii. 240 to conclude: *OED* 1740

WIPE (s.): iv. 216 sarcasm, insult

WISTELY: iv. 226 wistly, with close attention

WIT: v. 51 (of men) cleverness, intelligence. viii. 522 (of a play) liveliness and quickness of fancy: in its literary sense the word was extensively debated throughout the 17th cent.; P's 'independent sentence of wit' (ix. 206) demonstrates the distinction between his use of the word and the modern sense (which he effectively adumbrates)

WITHDRAWING-ROOM: iii. 262 a room to withdraw to for private discussion (rather than for ladies to withdraw to after dinner): 1591, but as 'chamber' from late 14th cent.

WITNESS: iii. 146 godparent: 1597

WITTILY: iv. 398 intelligently

WITTY: v. 51 clever, intelligent

WOODMONGER: viii. 520 fuel merchant

WOOLGATHERING, my mind is run a': vi. 253 daydreaming: 1553

WORD: ix. 132 utterance, phrase, slogan. i. 144 motto, inscription

WORD, a good: vii. 132 good news

WOREMOODE: iii. 49 wormwood

WORK (s.): iv. 14 needlework

WORK LIKE A HORSE: vii. 14 *ODP* 1710

WORLD GO HANG, let the: viii. 97 more commonly 'let the world wag/slide' (from 1425)

WORMWOOD WINE, WORMEWOOD, WOREMOODE (G. *wermut*, O.E. *wermod*): i. 301 wine infused with *artemisia absinthium*, the distinguishing ingredient in modern vermouth

WRACK, go to: viii. 131 as phr. from 1412

WRACKE (s.): iii. 237 rack, instrument of torture

WRAP UP: ix. 94 to enwrap, enfold, soothe

WRETCH: ix. 89: *see* Poor Wretch

WROUGHT: vii. 115 as past-participle of 'to work'

YAGHT (Du. *jaghte*): i. 286 yacht: 1557 the guttural *gh* of the Dutch, with no Eng. equivalent, accounts for the extraordinary variation in 17th-cent. spellings; P also uses (iii. 63) 'pleasure-boat'

YARD: iv. 329 penis

YARE: vii. 418 ready, skilful

YOUTHSOME: ii. 205 youthful in disposition: *OED* P

ZOUNDS: iv. 334 'by God's wounds'

CHRONOLOGY

1633   23 February: Born in Salisbury Court, Fleet Street

3 March: Baptised in St Bride's, Fleet Street

c. 1644   At the grammar school, Huntingdon

c. 1646–50   At St Paul's School, London

1649   Saw Charles I beheaded

1650   Awarded leaving exhibition

1651–4   At Magdalene College, Cambridge

1651, 1653   Awarded scholarships

1654   Takes his B.A.

?1654   Appointed secretary or domestic steward to Edward Mountagu in Whitehall Palace

?1654   Appointed clerk to George Downing, Teller of the Receipt in the Exchequer

1655   1 December: Married to Elizabeth St Michel in St Margaret's, Westminster

1658   26 March: Operated on for the stone
c. August: Moves to Axe Yard

1659   May: Carries letters to Mountagu in the Baltic

1660   1 January: Begins diary
April–May: Accompanies Mountagu's fleet to Holland to bring over Charles II
28 June: Resigns clerkship in Exchequer
29 June: Appointed Clerk of the Acts to the Navy Board
23 July: Sworn in as Mountagu's deputy as clerk in Privy Seal Office

1661   *23 April: Coronation of Charles II*
5 July: Uncle Robert Pepys dies

1662   15 February: Admitted as Younger Brother of Trinity House
17 August: Resigns deputy-clerkship in Privy Seal
20 November: Appointed to Tangier Committee

1664   15 March: His brother Tom dies
8 April: Appointed to Corporation for the Royal Fishery

1665   15 February: Elected Fellow of the Royal Society
22 February: Second Dutch War begins
20 March: Appointed Treasurer of Tangier Committee
Spring: Great Plague begins in London

3 June: *Battle of Lowestoft*
5 July: Moves family to Woolwich
21 August: The Navy Office moves to Greenwich
October: Takes lodgings at Greenwich
4 December: Appointed Surveyor-General of the Victualling

1666   January: Navy Office and Pepys household move back to London
March: Sandwich arrives in Spain as Ambassador
1–4 June: Four Days Fight
25 July: St James's Day Fight
2–5 September: The Great Fire of London

1667   25 March: His mother dies at Brampton
10–13 June: Dutch raid on Thames and Medway
13 June: Sends his gold to Brampton
28 July: Resigns Surveyorship of Victualling
31 July: End of Second Dutch War
7–12 October: Visits Brampton to recover his gold
22 October: Defends Navy Board before parliamentary Committee on Miscarriages

1668   27 February: His sister Paulina marries John Jackson
5 March: Defends Navy Board before House of Commons
5–17 June: His holiday tour to West Country
September: Sandwich returns
25 October: Elizabeth discovers him *in flagrante* with Deb

1669   31 May: Discontinues his diary
June–October: Travels to France and Low Countries
10 November: Elizabeth dies; he erects a monument to her in St Olave's, Hart Street

1670   30 March: His brother John appointed Clerk to Trinity House

1672   24 January: Admitted as Elder Brother of Trinity House
17 March: Third Dutch War begins
28 May: Death of Sandwich in Battle of Sole Bay

1673   29 January: Navy Office destroyed by fire; he moves to Winchester Street
15 June: Duke of York resigns as Lord High Admiral under terms of Test Act (March) excluding Roman Catholics; office put in commission
18 June: Appointed Secretary to Admiralty Commission; is succeeded at Navy Board by his brother John and Thomas Hayter as joint Clerks
4 November: Elected M.P. for Castle Rising, Norfolk

1674   January: Moves to Derby House, new headquarters of Admiralty
19 February: End of Third Dutch War

1676   1 February: Appointed Governor of Christ's Hospital
22 May: Elected Master of Trinity House

1677   15 March: His brother John buried
8 August: Elected Master of Clothworkers' Company

1679   5 February: Elected M.P. for Harwich
         21 May: Resigns as Secretary to Admiralty and Treasurer for Tangier
         22 May–9 July: In Tower on suspicion of treasonable correspondence
         with France
         July: Moves to W. Hewer's house in York Buildings, now no. 12
         Buckingham Street

1680   30 June: Proceedings against him abandoned
         c. September: His brother-in-law John Jackson dies
         3, 5 October: Takes down at King's dictation story of his escape after
         Battle of Worcester
         4 October: His father buried at Brampton

1682   May: Accompanies Duke of York to Edinburgh

1683   30 July: Sets out for Tangier as secretary to expedition under Lord
         Dartmouth to evacuate colony

1683–4 December–February: Visits Spain

1684   30 March: Returns to England
         10 June: Appointed King's Secretary for the affairs of the Admiralty
         1 December: Elected President of Royal Society

1685   *6 February: Death of Charles II; accession of Duke of York as James II*
         19 May: Takes seat as M.P. for Harwich, having been elected for both
         Harwich and Sandwich
         20 July: Nominated Master of Trinity House by King under new charter

1686   March: Special Commission 'for the Recovery of the Navy' begins to sit
         30 November: Resigns Presidency of Royal Society

1688   Spring: Moves to house now no. 14 Buckingham Street
         29 June: Called as witness in Trial of Seven Bishops
         October: Special Commission dissolved
         5 November: William of Orange lands
         23 December: James II takes flight to France

1689   16 January: Defeated in parliamentary election at Harwich
         13 February: William and Mary become joint sovereigns
         20 February: Resigns his Secretaryship
         May–July: Detained on suspicion of Jacobitism
         26 August: Resigns Mastership of Trinity House

1690   25–30 June: Imprisoned on suspicion of Jacobitism
         Publishes his *Memoires relating to the state of the Royal Navy* [1679–88]

1699   27 April: Made freeman of city of London for services to Christ's
         Hospital

1701   c. June: Retires to Hewer's house at Clapham

1703   26 May: Dies at Clapham
         4 June: Buried at St Olave's, Hart Street

1723   His nephew and heir, John Jackson, dies

1724 July: His library moved from Clapham to Magdalene College, Cambridge

1766 His account of the King's escape after the Battle of Worcester first published by Sir David Dalrymple

1825 His diary first published by Lord Braybrooke from the transcription by John Smith

1841 His Tangier Journal first published by John Smith

1884 His monument erected in St Olave's

1903 The Samuel Pepys Club founded in his honour

GENEALOGICAL TABLES
AND MAPS

THE PEPYS FAMILY c.1519–1723

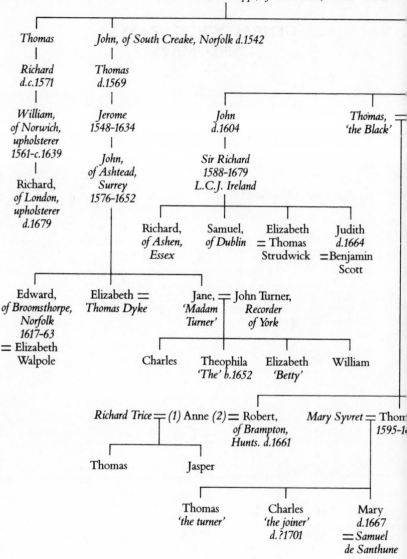

William Pepys, of Cottenham, Cambs. d.1519

Thomas
|
Richard
d.c.1571
|
William,
of Norwich,
upholsterer
1561–c.1639
|
Richard,
of London,
upholsterer
d.1679

John, of South Creake, Norfolk d.1542
|
Thomas
d.1569
|
Jerome
1548–1634
|
John,
of Ashtead,
Surrey
1576–1652

John
d.1604
|
Sir Richard
1588–1679
L.C.J. Ireland

Richard,
of Ashen,
Essex

Samuel,
of Dublin

Elizabeth
= Thomas
Strudwick

Judith
d.1664
= Benjamin
Scott

Thomas,
'the Black'

Edward,
of Broomsthorpe,
Norfolk
1617–63
= Elizabeth
Walpole

Elizabeth =
Thomas Dyke

Jane, = John Turner,
'Madam   Recorder
Turner'   of York

Charles

Theophila
'The' b.1652

Elizabeth
'Betty'

William

Richard Trice = (1) Anne (2) = Robert,
of Brampton,
Hunts. d.1661

Mary Syvret = Thom
1595–1

Thomas   Jasper

Thomas
'the turner'

Charles
'the joiner'
d.?1701

Mary
d.1667
= Samuel
de Santhune

Based on E. Chappell, *Eight generations of the Pepys family 1500-1800* (Blackheath, London, 1936). All names except those in italic are those of living persons mentioned in the diary. Some members of the family, of minor importance in the diary, are omitted, either from lack of information or lack of space.

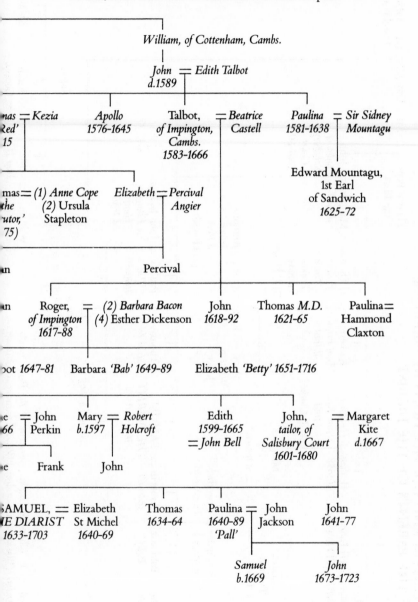

RELATIVES AND CONNECTIONS BY MARRIAGE OF THE PARENTS OF THE DIARIST

Based on E. Chappell, *Eight generations of the Pepys family 1500–1800* (Blackheath, London, 1936). All names except those

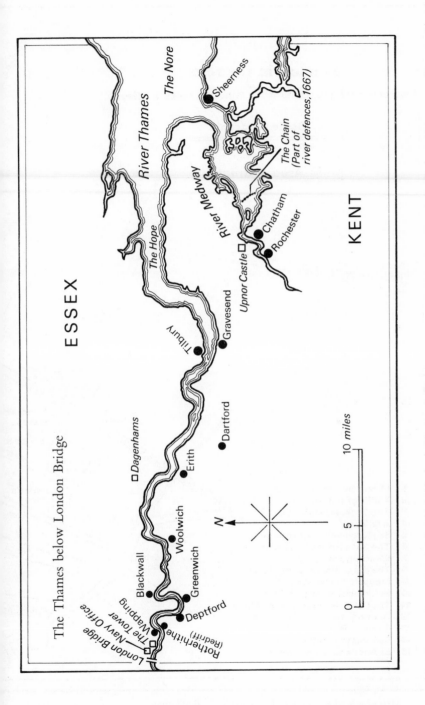

The Thames below London Bridge

ESSEX

KENT

River Thames

The Nore

Sheerness

River Medway

The Chain
(Part of
river defences, 1667)

The Hope

Upnor Castle

Chatham

Rochester

Gravesend

Tilbury

Dartford

□ Dagenhams

Erith

Woolwich

Blackwall

Greenwich

Deptford

Rotherhithe
(Redriff)

Wapping

London Bridge

Navy Office

The Tower

N

0   5   10 miles

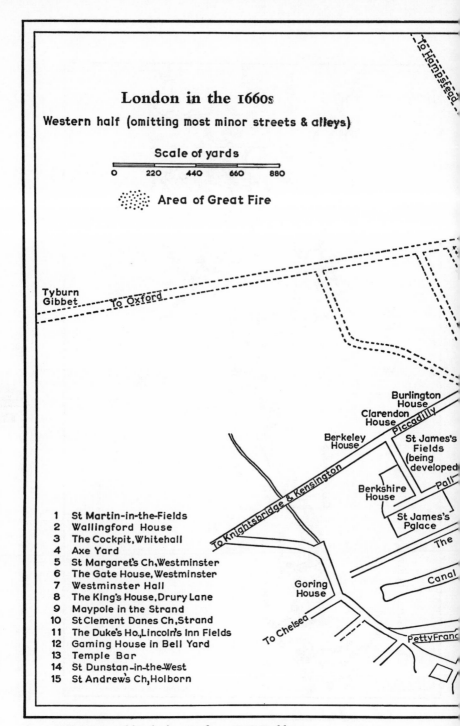

London in the 1660s

Western half (omitting most minor streets & alleys)

Scale of yards

0   220   440   660   880

Area of Great Fire

To Hampstead Rd

Tyburn Gibbet

To Oxford

Burlington House
Clarendon House
Piccadilly
Berkeley House
St James's Fields (being developed)
Berkshire House
Pall
St James's Palace
The
Canal
To Knightsbridge & Kensington
Goring House
To Chelsea
PettyFranc

1   St Martin-in-the-Fields
2   Wallingford House
3   The Cockpit, Whitehall
4   Axe Yard
5   St Margaret's Ch, Westminster
6   The Gate House, Westminster
7   Westminster Hall
8   The King's House, Drury Lane
9   Maypole in the Strand
10   St Clement Danes Ch, Strand
11   The Duke's Ho., Lincoln's Inn Fields
12   Gaming House in Bell Yard
13   Temple Bar
14   St Dunstan-in-the-West
15   St Andrew's Ch, Holborn

Map prepared by the late Professor T. F. Reddaway